International
Encyclopedia of the
SOCIAL
SCIENCES

International Encyclopedia of the SOCIAL SCIENCES

DAVID L. SILLS EDITOR

VOLUME 5

The Macmillan Company & The Free Press

International Encyclopedia of the

SOCIAL

SCIENCES

E

[C O N T I N U E D]

ELECTIONS

I
THE FUNCTIONS OF ELECTIONS

Elections may be regarded as one procedure for aggregating preferences of a particular kind.

Liberal democratic theories attribute special authority to the amalgamation of the expressed preferences of individuals through recognized procedures. They reject the idea that social choice can be made by some sort of group mind or interpersonal entity built out of individuals but different from them in kind. They also reject the idea that social choice is a mere illusion, that is, the notion that what appears to be a choice between alternatives is really no more than the consequence of the interplay of various forces.

But it has been argued, in the attack on welfare economics (Arrow 1951; Little 1950), that the preference schedules of individuals cannot be amalgamated without paradox except on one of two conditions: either through the operation of a market or through the compliance of individual participants with decisions by a recognized authority.

Liberal theories would certainly accept the idea that in certain cases to be defined social choice is made and should be made through the market or by relying on authority. But they postulate also that there are and should be public decisions in which citizens make an explicit choice between alternative courses of public action. This can be done in practice only through forms of procedure generally accepted as binding within the political society.

Voting is one of these procedures but not the only one. It is relevant to quote an authority on the practice of the Dominican order in the Middle Ages (Galbraith 1925, p. 33) to the effect that choice might be made by vote, by explicit agreement after negotiation, or "as if by the inspiration of God." Certainly one finds everywhere, even in the most developed societies, choice by bargaining between factions and choice by acclamation, and there may be other procedures as well. It appears, however, that in "liberal" societies voting is held in reserve as a procedure possessing special authority within the group, organization, or state. Conversely, elections are by no means the only occasion for procedure by vote. Voting on propositions is of great practical importance in many different social and political situations, and it raises similar problems of formal analysis (Black 1958).

Voting in nationwide elections has a position of special importance in Western democracies. Its authority is strengthened because similar procedures are used for social choice in many institutions, large and small, public and private, throughout the society. (It is not greatly weakened by the existence of formal paradoxes of voting, even though these anomalies are of some tactical importance to groups seeking victory for their own interests.) This predominance has led to the export of voting in elections to countries where voting procedure has not historically possessed the same social authority as in the West: countries of the Soviet bloc on the one hand and developing countries on the other. This may give rise to situations in which the procedure exists but the element of choice does not.

Definition of elections

Thus, it is not always easy to answer the question, What is a *real* election?—and it may be useful to attempt a formal definition. What follows is based on English usage of political terms and may not have general validity, but it will serve to indicate important points for discussion.

One requires, first, the concept of recognized positions or roles ("offices") which confer certain powers and duties within an organization. Individuals may be assigned to office either by choice or by a method independent of choice, such as a rule of inheritance, or seniority, or regulated trial by competition. Next, a general concept is needed, such as "to choose a man for a job" or perhaps "to decide between candidates for a job." Within this concept, one must distinguish among "electing," "appointing," and "co-opting" a man. In English each word has overtones of political evaluation. "Election" (provided it is "free") would be deemed "democratic" and therefore good, but for certain positions only. "Appointment" would be regarded as "patronage" that tends to increase the power of the patron, except insofar as it is hedged by rules specifying the field of "qualified" candidates. "Co-option" smacks of oligarchy, the self-perpetuation of a ruling group, unless similarly regulated.

On this basis election might be defined as *a form of procedure, recognized by the rules of an organization, whereby all or some of the members of the organization choose a smaller number of persons or one person to hold office of authority in the organization.*

This definition raises a number of points. (1) It attempts to embrace both formal procedure and social significance—both "rules" and "choice." Ideally, both elements should be present in an election. To mark a ballot paper and drop it in a ballot box is not "electing" unless the actor "chooses" in some socially significant sense. But equally a choice is not a "vote in an election" unless the chooser conforms to the specified legal procedure. J. L. Austin made the same point (1961; 1962) when he said that "I vote for Mr. A" is not a statement but a verbal act or performative utterance and that the same act can be achieved without words where this is the proper procedure. Nevertheless, it may be convenient to use the word "election" for something that falls short of such completeness; for instance, where procedure is followed but no choice is present, or where there is a significant element of choice without close conformity to a socially recognized procedure (Akzin 1960).

(2) The rather loose word "organization" is chosen here deliberately. The word "election" is not used only for "state" elections to a hierarchy of public bodies. Indeed, it could be maintained that state elections are effective only where electoral procedure is regarded as a usual procedure throughout the society and is therefore written into the rules of all sorts of nonpublic bodies, such as business companies, trade unions, free churches, sports clubs, and so on. Nor would it do to replace "an organization" by "a society." This might imply that a voter can choose only within his society, whereas multiple membership of overlapping organizations is characteristic of complex societies, and one man may be a voter in many different capacities and under different rule systems.

(3) Two phrases in the definition—"the rules of an organization" and "the members of an organization choose"—refer to fundamental conceptual problems in social science. All that need be said here is that ordinary language about elections deals with persons acting within systems of ethical norms and legal procedures. It is possible to reject this language, as would happen if either economic determinism or behaviorism were strictly applied in social science. Such studies might have substantial predictive value in relation to electoral behavior, but they would leave unanswered some fundamental questions about what men think they are doing when they participate in elections.

(4) The word "office" implies a position designated by the same system of rules that determines the electoral procedure. The general problem is that in all social systems persons must somehow be linked to offices; election is one of many different procedures used to ensure legal succession to office in different organizations and societies.

(5) It remains to distinguish election from appointment or co-option. There are ambiguities in usage here. For instance, fellows of a college would use the word "elect" both for choosing a master and for choosing a junior colleague; critics of the college system might accept the former usage but would describe the latter as "co-option." Political advantage may be drawn from these ambiguities at various levels of political debate; in England, at least, "election" is a good word, "patronage" is a bad word, and "co-option" lies in between. This usage suggests the following distinctions:

(*a*) In an election the choosers are a relatively numerous body. Choice by one voter would, of course, be an appointment. But how many choosers are needed to make an election?

(*b*) There is a question of proportion as well as of absolute number. If ten choosers voted to fill one office, one might call it election; if they filled 100 offices, one would tend to call it appointment (or even patronage). But once again there is no sharp point of division.

(*c*) There is a question of the relationship between the choosers and the office to be filled. A person co-opted would be a colleague; a person appointed would be a subordinate, even though he might exercise great discretionary power; a person elected would hold an office of authority, which might include authority over those who elected him.

(*d*) It may be said that when electing, the voters act independently of one another and more or less at the same time, whereas an appointing body acts in consultation, with each member sharing in the deliberation and expressing his point of view in turn until a conclusion is reached (Akzin 1960). This is a very important problem in the study of political development, but it seems to be a distinction between voters and councilors, rather than between election and appointment. Deliberative procedure in council is very widespread in human societies at all stages; under some circumstances (which have nowhere been seriously studied) the device of voting is used to bring issues to a conclusion. But election does not inevitably entail voting; in certain societies the proper procedure for election is by council, in others by acclamation, and in yet others by voting.

Historical development

Elections first took a central place in politics in the Greek city-states of the eastern Mediterranean in the fifth and sixth centuries B.C. There has been no systematic study of elections in societies independent of this Western tradition; certainly, traces are to be found elsewhere, but it does not seem that elections have played a central part in other societies. In the following discussion it has been assumed that electoral procedures can usefully be studied historically in terms of the diffusion of a social pattern from a single source and its modification in a great variety of situations. Further, it is assumed that these procedures correspond functionally to certain general social needs, which are particularly marked in literate, technological, and mobile societies; hence they have periodically reappeared, after setbacks, in new forms in new corners of Western society. Finally, it is assumed that where these procedures meet no social needs they may be retained as forms but are filled with a new content.

The heroic age.   The poems of Homer reflect a state of society in which rule was by kings whose position was conspicuously unlike that of the "Oriental despots" of the river valley civilizations with which they came in contact. The evidence of the mythological and epic narratives is difficult to use, but it suggests a situation roughly parallel to cases found in mobile African societies where the king, although drawn from a royal lineage, emerges as leader by a process which may include competition, conciliar election, and acclamation by the people. Clearly the leader of the war coalition, Agamemnon, had attained his precarious eminence among other kings by a process of this kind. Analogies can be drawn from Tacitus' account of the Germans and from the world of Teutonic, Scandinavian, and Icelandic epics.

The Greek democracies.   The epic period of tribal mobility was succeeded by one of peasant agriculture tempered by growing commercial activity and emigration to colonies overseas. From this situation emerged the strife between the well-born and the people, which affected Greek ideas and practice about political institutions almost everywhere. Where this strife was intense, Greek elections assumed new forms, either through a complete popular victory or through attempts at compromise.

We are primarily concerned not with voting on measures in popular assemblies but with the choice of persons to fill offices of authority. Two points are of general importance. First, in voting on propositions in the assembly of the citizens the rule was apparently that of individual voting by show of hands ($\chi\epsilon\iota\rho\rho\tau\sigma\nu\epsilon\hat{\iota}\nu$). Use was also made of written votes (in the procedure of ostracism) and of ballots in the form of pebbles ($\psi\hat{\eta}\phi\sigma\iota$)—hence, psephology. There was at times a leader of the assembly who held his informal position (for example, Pericles, Cleon, Demosthenes) because of fairly stable majority support. But holders of certain legally recognized offices (in particular, archons and generals) were elected by nonlocal constituencies known as tribes ($\phi\nu\lambda\hat{\alpha}\iota$), which were held to have been instituted deliberately so as to cut across local divisions of interest within Attica. The number of voters in each tribe must have differed a good deal.

Second, the principle of election was accepted somewhat grudgingly in Athenian democratic theory; it infringed the principle of equality among citizens, and it was dangerous because it opened the way to power for ambitious, attractive, and well-trained young men of the old families (for example, Alcibiades) and equally for ambitious men of the people who were prepared to perpetuate their electoral victory by force (the common pattern of Greek "tyranny"). The orthodox principle was that citizens should hold offices of authority in rotation, the order to be determined by lot; this was the practice for the Council of 500 and its monthly committees, which maintained continuity in the control of public business, and also for the selection of juries (methods of "balloting" for juries are described in great detail by Aristotle, *Politeia athenaiōn*, chapters 63–66). Similar institutions were common in early English and American practice, and rotation in office is still quite usual in small voluntary societies. But there has been no modern discussion of the relation between the principles of rotation in office and that of election by vote. It is notable, however, that in general the Athenians used voting for elections to offices requiring special skills, such as military leadership, whereas in Western countries voting is now used to fill offices of a representative character, for which the Athenians used the lot; offices requiring special skills are now generally filled by appointment from a field determined by specified professional qualifications.

The Roman republic. Even under the republic the Romans never accepted the principle of "one man, one vote." Decision in legislation and in the choice of the principal officials was by a plurality of "centuries" or by a plurality of "tribes": within each of these constituencies one man, one vote prevailed, but the units varied in size. It was tactically important that each of them had some local basis, but locality was not decisive in their composition.

The medieval church. The tradition of ancient elections was preserved in the church rather than in the state. It continued unbroken in the Roman Catholic church, but many national and nonconformist churches also developed the use of elections as the basis of a legitimate claim to hold office. (It is an interesting coincidence that "election" has in Protestant theology a different meaning: that of the granting of spiritual grace to God's elect.)

The most ancient and continuous tradition has been that of the election of superiors (popes, bishops, deans, priors, and so on) by a relatively small electorate consisting of those next in rank. Up to a point the procedure is deliberative, tending toward a conclusion by "sense of the meeting." But there are also ancient and complex rules about voting procedures. These rights of election were defended, strongly but not always with success, against hierarchical and secular attempts to substitute appointment.

There is an undercurrent (almost Athenian in tone) emphasizing the electoral rights of the many against the few. In Presbyterian terms, the congregation will defend the position of the elders in appointing a minister insofar as that position is endangered by the lay patron, but it claims the right to confirm or to upset the verdict of the elders. Dissent sometimes accepts the authority of a charismatic leader; but it often tends toward the equal sovereignty of all true believers, which may be shown either by election or by rotation in office.

Feudalism. The position of the feudal emperor, king, or overlord was deemed to be limited by law and custom and to some extent by the consent of his vassals.

The relation between king and lord and between lord and man was in principle one of consent leading to binding mutual obligation. The vassal chose to do homage, the lord chose whether or not to accept it. It was not a long step from this to an elected emperor and (in a few instances) an elected king. The social situation greatly limited the application of the principles of consent and election in practice; but the idea of a binding legal right of succession to office emerged slowly, along with the growth of other notions of private and heritable property.

In principle, the king was independent insofar as he could "live of his own." But this was a limited independence in a period of quite rapid change, and in many cases its boundaries were obscure. Hence the need for consultation, first with a feudal council, then with assemblies "representing" others besides immediate vassals. These assemblies were the basis of the parliamentary tradition in Europe. They embodied two principles not yet wholly obsolete:

(*a*) The separate representation of "estates," which might be more or less numerous; for instance, great lords, great clergy, lesser lords, lesser clergy, burghers, peasants.

(*b*) The representation of local communities but not of individuals. The classic case is that of the English House of Commons, based on two knights from every shire and two burgesses from every burgh. Apart from the great men of the realm, the "units of account" in government were shires and burghs, not individuals. The choice of representatives by communities was a matter for each community, within the general law of the land. Elections thus established themselves in national government but without any national enactment about electoral procedure.

The seventeenth and eighteenth centuries. In most of Europe the assemblies of estates were displaced by autocratic, modernizing monarchies. For the diffusion of elections the only important survival was in England (the parliaments of Scotland and Sweden survived but had little or no influence outside their own countries) and in colonial assemblies based on the English model. During the struggle for survival certain basic principles of consent, franchise, and representation were hammered out; although these principles were never fully applied in practice, they were recognized as the ideological basis of a system of democratic elections. The classic statements are those of English popular leaders in the 1640s and 1650s: their language recalls both that of nonconformist congregations and that of Athenian democracy. The principle, in brief, is that all governments owe their just powers to the consent of the governed and that in numerous societies this consent may be expressed by representatives freely elected on a basis of universal adult suffrage.

This principle can readily be elaborated in institutional form, for example, by the extension of the suffrage, the equalization of constituencies, proportional representation, the elimination of intimidation and corruption, and so on. These elaborations in turn lead to political situations which illustrate ambiguities in the principle; for instance, as regards the relation between elected and electors, is there a difference between a "representative" and a "delegate"? [See REPRESENTATION.]

Parties in elections. By far the most important of these new problems is that of parties as intermediaries between voter and assembly. Clear recognition of this situation came first in American presidential elections, but it spread rapidly with the extension of the franchise in large states in the nineteenth century. By the last quarter of that century, parties and elections had become interdependent. Electoral parties were no longer limited to national politics; trade unions and large cooperative societies are obvious examples. But national elections are henceforth intelligible *only* in terms of parties; the traditional principles demand the scrutiny of procedure within parties, since they control the first stage of national elections. [See PARTIES, POLITICAL.]

Plebiscitary democracy and "unfree" elections. The predominance of parties has led to a change in the character of national elections, even in countries where electoral procedure is in constant use at subnational levels. The choice of a man to hold office as a member of an assembly has given place to a national vote between different "packages" consisting of leadership, party, and program. The election is a choice of government or even of regime,

and voting procedure is called on to bear new strains. In stable democracies the strains are mitigated because there is an understood difference between governmental structure ("government") and government in power ("regime"), and the former is not questioned by electors. But where this distinction is not drawn the strain may prove too great for the electoral system to bear, and the element of choice is removed (or greatly reduced) by various devices. The oldest of these are plebiscitary democracy, which dates from the time of Napoleon I, and the exercise of influence on elections by officials of the government in power, without blatant breach of legality. The *reductio ad absurdum* of these trends appears in "elections" such as those of East Germany, where a vote of 99.9 per cent was recorded in favor of the government in 1964. Such a result could only be due to fraud, or pressure, or both. However, the fact that the regime deems elections necessary seems to pay tribute to the immense strength of the tradition that elections confer legitimacy. [See DEMOCRACY.]

The functions of elections

This brief historical summary illustrates the persistence and adaptability of the use of electoral procedure as a means of legitimating the assignment of a person to an office of authority. It may be said that electoral procedure is functionally analogous to procedure in a marriage ceremony: "Do you take this man (or woman) to be your lawfully wedded husband (or wife)?" "I do" (Austin 1962). The point in time at which "I do" is said is not psychologically a moment of choice or decision—that came earlier; it is the point at which an individual preference becomes a social commitment. The words and acts are "performative"; if correctly said and done in the right context, they establish new social relationships of a binding character.

Such acts are generally associated with ritual which underlies the multiple relationships linking them to a complex system of behavior and belief. To continue the analogy with marriage ceremonies, there is a possible range of ritual complexity from ostentation to extreme simplicity—but even in marriage by registration in an advanced secular society, some elements of ritual are present. There is the same wide range in electoral ritual—for example the election of a pope and that of the directors of a manufacturing company; but in both cases there is a procedure which has binding effect if properly followed.

Thus, it is possible to speak of elections in general as a "ritual of choice"; the binding character of elections derives from the participation of an individual as chooser in a social act, and legitimate authority is thus conferred on the person chosen. But such a generalization tells one little about the position of elections in any given society.

Men are called by different kinds of elections to different offices in different societies. The historical sketch given above notes only a limited range of cases, but it may be sufficient to indicate that it is rash to talk of *the* function of elections. This may be illustrated by the British case. A British general election serves to choose a governing party and thus a government. But (on the one hand) that government, though powerful, has not a monopoly of legitimate authority in the political system. This authority is shared by many others—those professionally qualified by education and experience, the leaders of organized interests, property owners of various kinds, and so on. On the other hand, the electoral system serves many other functions besides choice of a government; the party organization based on it serves as a market place and reconciler of interests, a ladder for the political careers of national and local officials, a forum of national discussion, and so on. It would be quite amiss to assume at once that the same functions were filled by elections in Athens, or in the medieval church, or even in other industrial societies today.

Argument about the merits of different electoral systems is generally based on assessments of their efficiency in relation to one or more of their many possible functions. The political literature of England in the nineteenth and twentieth centuries contains a rich store of such arguments; and this has been added to in the process of "decolonization," since "free elections" were assumed to be a necessary step toward independence in most of Britain's dependent territories. This is, therefore, a convenient testing ground for theories about the nature of political argument, and in particular about the relation of ideology to rationality on one flank and to self-interest on the other.

A. H. Birch (1964) has shown how contemporary debate about elections in Britain draws in arguments from various historical stages, a mixture which can be logically justified only if one assumes that elections in England serve many functions that are not necessarily compatible with one another. If one had to ground the defense of elections on a single maxim it would doubtless be that of the Puritan revolution: "There are no laws that in their strictness and vigour of justice any man is bound to that are not made by those whom he doth consent to." Parallels for this maxim could be found in many other political cultures. The doctrine or ideology is one of great and continuing power: but it remains empty until expressed in terms of institutions and interests, and its simplicity is then obscured and complicated by arguments drawn from other streams of political doctrine.

There has been no general study of choice as an element in the legitimation of authority. Such a study would present great difficulties. It is safe to guess that where choice is an element in determining authority in simpler societies it is entangled with other factors such as seniority, lineage, and personal ascendancy. Isolating one factor would distort the situation. In complex societies elections appear in many different contexts, private and public, and electoral procedure often survives as a ritual although the element of choice is absent; so that it would be difficult, perhaps unwise, to take the forms of electoral procedure as a guide in unraveling the complexities of modern political structure.

It would be of value, nevertheless, if pilot studies could be made of the place of elections in one or two cases of simple and complex societies. Very little work has been done on the legitimation of authority in contemporary societies; it seems probable that the part played by elections is relatively small even in established democracies, if elections are considered separately as a single factor. An attempt to isolate this factor might therefore break down; but it could hardly fail to sharpen our perception of the problem, which is of central importance in political science and is now within the grasp of empirical inquiry.

W. J. M. MACKENZIE

[*See also* AUTHORITY; CONSTITUTIONS AND CONSTITUTIONALISM; DEMOCRACY; GOVERNMENT; LEGITIMACY; MAJORITY RULE; REPRESENTATION.]

BIBLIOGRAPHY

The bibliography for this article is combined with the bibliography of the article that follows.

II
ELECTORAL SYSTEMS

Elections are institutionalized procedures for the choosing of officeholders by some or all of the recognized members of an organization. Whether the organization is a club, a company, a party, or a territorial polity, an electoral institution can be described in a series of dimensions: the scope and structure of the organizational unit; the tasks and the authority of the offices to be filled; the types and levels of membership in the organization and the qualifications for participation in the choice of officers; the criteria, if any, used in differentiating the numerical weight of the choice of each qualified member; the extent and character of the subdivisions instituted within the organizations for purposes of such choice; the procedures for the setting of the alternatives of choice; the procedures used in eliciting and registering choices among these alternatives; and the methods used in translating the aggregated choices of members into authoritative collective decisions on the attribution of the given offices.

A club might recognize as qualified electors only a few senior members and require these to vote by a show of hands or by acclamation. This practice would contrast on a number of dimensions with the elaborate procedures of some joint-stock companies: all shareholders have the right to participate, but the weight of their votes is a function of the number of shares they hold; their preferences are expressed under elaborate provisions of secrecy, and their votes are aggregated through strict rules of accountability. A systematic discussion of all such dimensions of variation, even for just the major types of organizations, would take us far afield. In this article the discussion will center on one distinct type of organization: the territorially defined units of the nation-state—the self-governing local community and the overarching unitary, or federal body politic.

The histories of the known political systems present a bewildering variety of electoral arrangements (Braunias 1932; Meyer 1901). Any attempt to account for these variations through the construction of a basic model of strategic options and structural restraints must start out from an analysis of the histories of changes in each of six dimensions of the local and the national electoral system.

(1) The qualifications for franchise: how does a subject of the territory acquire political citizenship rights?

(2) The weighting of influence: how many votes are formally attributed to each elector and on what grounds? what is done to ensure differentiation or equality in the actual influence of each vote?

(3) The standardization of the voting procedures and the protection of the freedom to choose: what is done to ensure uniform and accountable practices of electoral administration, and what provisions are made to equalize the immediate cost of all alternatives for the elector?

(4) The territorial levels of choice: how is the territory divided for purposes of election, and how many levels of electoral aggregation are distinguished?

(5) The stages of electoral choice: how are the alternatives set for the electors? to what extent are the alternatives set in advance, and to what extent is the range still open for the electors?

(6) The procedures of calculation: how are the votes aggregated, and how are the aggregated distributions translated into authoritative collective decisions on territorial representation?

One man, one vote, one value

The Western developments toward equalitarian electoral democracy may conveniently be analyzed against an "ideal-type" model of five successive phases.

(1) An early, prerevolutionary phase was characterized by marked provincial and local variations in franchise practices but implicit or explicit recognition of membership in some corporate estate (the nobility, the clergy, the city corporations of merchants and artisans, or, in some cases, the freehold peasantry) as a condition of political citizenship (Hintze [1941] 1962; Lousse 1943; Palmer 1959).

(2) In the wake of the American and French revolutions, there was a period of increasing standardization of franchise rules; the strict regulation of access to the political arena under a *régime censitaire* was accompanied by formal equality of influence among the citizens allowed to vote under the given property or income criteria (Meyer 1901; Williamson 1960).

(3) In the first phase of mass mobilization the suffrage was greatly extended, but formal inequalities of influence persisted, under arrangements for multiple votes or for differential ratios of votes to representatives.

(4) In the next phase, manhood suffrage, all significant social and economic criteria of qualification for men over a given age were abolished. Although there were now no formal inequalities of voting rights within constituency electorates, marked differences in the weight of votes across the constituencies still existed (Zwager 1958).

(5) Finally, in the current phase, one of continued democratization, steps were taken toward the maximization of universal and equal citizenship rights by (*a*) extension of the suffrage to women, to younger age groups (down to 21 or even 18), and to short-term residents (reductions in "quarantine" periods) and (*b*) further equalization of voter–representative ratios throughout the national or federal territory.

Only three of the nation-states of the West passed through these five stages in anything like a regular sequence: England, Belgium, and Sweden. The step-by-step evolution characteristic of these countries contrasts violently with the abrupt and revolutionary changes in France (Bendix 1964; Rokkan 1961).

In England (Seymour 1915) the process took more than one hundred years, from the Reform Act of 1832 to the abolition of multiple votes in 1948. In Sweden (Verney 1957) the system of estate representation was abolished in 1866, but the extreme inequalities of electoral influence were maintained until 1921. The Belgians (Gilissen 1958) passed from the phase of estate representation into a *régime censitaire* as soon as they had achieved independence in 1831 and went through an intriguing phase of multiple voting from 1893 to 1917: all men over 25 were enfranchised, but additional votes were granted not only on *censitaire* criteria but also in recognition of educational achievement (*principe capacitaire*) and of responsibility for the maintenance of a family.

By contrast, in France (Bastid 1948; Charnay 1965) the transition from the first to the fourth stage took a mere four years: the Law of January 1789 maintained a system of indirect elections within the recognized corporations of nobles, clergy, and the *tiers état*; the constitution of 1791 stipulated a tax-paying criterion and introduced the concept of the *citoyen actif*; and the constitution of 1793 went straight to the stage of manhood suffrage, the only remaining qualification being a six-month minimum residence in the canton. This sudden thrust toward maximal mass democracy proved very short-lived: the Terror intervened, and for decades France was torn between traditionalist attempts to restrict the suffrage to a narrow stratum of owners and high officials and radical–plebiscitarian pressures for universal and equal elections. The period from 1815 to 1848 was one of classic *régime censitaire*: the property qualifications limited the franchise to less than 100,000 out of 7 million adult males before 1830 and to roughly 240,000 in 1848. The Revolution of 1848 brought on the next sudden thrust toward maximal democracy: the first modern mass election took place on Easter day that year, and 84 per cent of the 9,360,000 electors went to the polling stations.

The electoral histories of the rest of Europe fall at various points between these two models. In northwest Europe the Dutch went through the same sequence as the British and the Swedes, while Denmark and Norway came closer to the French model. The Dutch passed from estate representation to *régime censitaire* in 1848 but did not go through any phase of plural voting before they opted for manhood suffrage during World War I (Geismann 1964). Denmark, the most absolutist

of the Nordic polities, went through a brief period of estate representation after 1831 and then moved straight into a system of nationwide elections under a very extensive manhood suffrage in 1849: the result, again as in France, was a half century of constitutional struggle between an oligarchic elite and a coalition of urban radicals and the mobilizing peasantry. Under the impact of the struggle for independence, the dependent "colonial" territories of the north all proceeded rapidly to maximal suffrage. Norway gave the vote to close to half her adult males on establishing her own parliament in 1814 and proceeded to full manhood suffrage during the conflict over union with Sweden in the 1890s. Finland stuck to the inherited Swedish system of four estates until 1906 and then all of a sudden passed from the first to the fifth phase of the model: not only all men but also all women were given the vote, and the process of mass mobilization had gone so far under the restrictive estate system that the turnout at the first election under universal suffrage reached the record height of 70.7 per cent. Developments in the third of the Nordic "colonies" were less spectacular: Iceland saw the re-establishment of its parliament in 1874 and then passed through two successive phases of *régime censitaire* before the stage of near-universal suffrage for men and women was reached in 1915 (as in most other countries of the north, paupers receiving public assistance were kept out in the first round; the Icelanders did not admit them until 1934).

The German territories were torn among several competing models of the representative polity: the traditional notions of election through established estates; the *altliberale* ideology of unified national representation under a property or income suffrage; the Napoleonic ideas of plebiscitarian mass democracy; and the Roman Catholic models of functional representation within the corporate state, the *Ständestaat*. This electoral schizophrenia found a number of intriguing expressions. In Prussia and the Bismarckian Reich, two sharply contrasted systems of elections coexisted for half a century. In Prussia the "lower orders" had been given the right to vote in the wake of the Revolution of 1848, but the weight of their votes was infinitesimal in the three-class system introduced to protect the interests of the landowners and the officials. By contrast, the Reichstag was elected on strict criteria of equal suffrage for all men: this principle had been laid down, after much debate, by the German National Assembly in Frankfurt in 1848 but was not enforced until 1867, when Bismarck saw the importance of general elections as a source of legitimacy for the new Reich. The Hapsburg empire went through a much longer and more tortuous process of democratization: first, estate representation; from 1861, corporate-interest representation under a system of four *curiae*; in 1896, an extraordinary attempt to stave off equalitarian democracy, by adding a fifth *curia*, for the citizens so far without representation; and finally, in 1907, a unified system of national representation and enforcement of "one man, one vote, one value."

By the end of World War I the great majority of European and European-settled polities had opted for manhood suffrage, many of them even for universal suffrage for women as well. Suffrage for women (Kraditor 1965) came first in the settler nations (Wyoming, 1890, all of the United States, 1920; New Zealand, 1893; South Australia, 1895) and in Scandinavia (Finland, 1906; Norway, 1910 to 1913; Denmark, 1915; Sweden, 1918 to 1921). The British proceeded by steps: restricted suffrage for women in 1918; full suffrage, on a par with men, in 1928. The "Roman" countries took longer to recognize the rights of women: France, Belgium, and Italy waited until the end of World War II before they admitted all women to political citizenship, and Switzerland has still, after 120 years of smoothly functioning manhood democracy, to reach agreement on the enfranchisement of her women.

With the victory over the Axis powers in World War II and the subsequent dismantling of colonial empires, the principle of "one man, one vote" gained ground throughout the world, even in countries at the lowest level of literacy and without a trace of the traditions of pluralist competition, which had been essential for the growth of effective party oppositions in the West. In an increasing number of newly independent states the enforcement of equal and universal rights of political citizenship was no longer seen as a means for the channeling of legitimate claims against the power holders but was regarded simply as an element in a strategy of national unification and the control of dissidence. Really serious struggles over the old cry of "one man, one vote, one value" only occurred in the ethnically most divided polities, e.g., South Africa, Rhodesia, and the United States.

Resistance to electoral equalitarianism has generally tended to be stronger at the level of local government than at the national or federal level. Payment of local property taxes remained in many cases a criterion of local franchise long after the abolition of *régime censitaire* at the national level. Residence requirements, too, were retained much longer for local than for national elections. In fact, in recent years the increased flow of labor from the backward to the economically advanced countries is bringing about extensive disfranchisement even at the national level. In the earlier phase the migrant workers within the one national territory were kept locally disfranchised; today vast numbers of immigrants are denied political rights in their host countries because of the high barriers against citizenship. "One man, one vote, one value" may be upheld as a principle within a population of settled territorial citizens, but it breaks down at the cross-national level.

Standardization of electoral practices

The extension of the franchise to the economically and culturally dependent strata of each national society increased the pressures for a standardization of electoral practices. Before elections could be established as essential instruments of legitimation, local variations in the arrangements for the elicitation and recording of choices had to be minimized. The electoral returns constituted claims to legitimate representation that had to be established through procedures acceptable to all, or at least to the dominant, competitors for office and power. The history of the democratization of the suffrage was paralleled in country after country by a history of increasing standardization of administrative procedures in all phases of the electoral process: the establishment of registers; the determination of voting rights; the maintenance of order at the polling stations; the casting of the vote; the recording of the act in the register; the counting of choices; the calculation of outcomes.

Of all the issues facing the national administrations in the early phases of suffrage extension, one was of particular importance for the functioning of the electoral system: the measures taken to insure the independence of the individual electoral decision (Rokkan 1961).

The defenders of the estate traditions and the *régime censitaire* had argued that economically and culturally dependent subjects could not be expected to form independent political judgments and therefore the vote should be given only to citizens likely to withstand social or economic pressures and able to take public responsibility for their choices on election day.

Liberal advocates of an extended suffrage, such as John Stuart Mill, were placed in a dilemma. They knew that the new voters could easily be swayed by their social superiors or their economic masters, yet they were convinced that the vote ought to be open, that each voter ought to be prepared to defend his decision in his day-to-day environments. This moralist argument for the old tradition of open voting soon had to yield to another imperative: the safeguarding of the integrative and legitimizing functions of the electoral ritual. To generate legitimacy, elections had to be dignified and without any tinge of violence. The maintenance of the system of open voting under the conditions of mass elections could lead only to alienation, corruption, and disrespect for the institutions of the nation.

The result was a widespread movement to ensure the secrecy of the act of voting. To qualify as "democratic," elections had to be not only universal and equal but also secret. The French were the first to introduce this principle. The electoral law establishing the States General in 1789 retained open oral voting at the level of the general electorate but called for secret ballots in the colleges of delegates. The electoral law establishing the first legislative assembly in 1791 introduced secrecy at all levels of the electorate, but very little was done to ensure regular enforcement. There was a great deal of opposition to the principle; the Jacobins, in particular, wanted open voting to control dissidence. The constitution of 1793 left it to the voters themselves to decide whether to vote openly or in secret. Subsequent laws reintroduced the principle of secrecy for all voters, but electoral administration remained at a low level of standardization throughout the nineteenth century. The *isoloir* and the standard envelope for the ballot were introduced by law in 1913, but even these highly detailed provisions left leeway for a variety of abuses and manipulations, particularly in the south, in Corsica, and in the overseas *départements* (Charnay 1965).

The extension of the suffrage to vast numbers of illiterates made it impossible to stick to a strict rule of secrecy. In the economically and culturally backward areas of the national hinterland particularly, it proved easy to control the votes of the lower classes even under strict rules of secrecy. The secret ballot expressed an essential feature of literate urban society: it introduced an element of anonymity, specificity, and abstraction in the system of political interchange.

Significantly, the countries that retained the old tradition of open and oral voting longest were all heavily dominated by landed interests: Denmark did not abolish it until 1901; Iceland, until 1906; Prussia, until the collapse of the Reich in 1918; and Hungary retained it even into the 1930s. By contrast, Belgium, Switzerland, and Sweden had opted for secrecy even under the *régime censitaire*, and the English had only waited five years after the Reform Act of 1867 to introduce the Ballot Act,

which ensured the freedom of the voters from intimidation and bribery. In the settler nations overseas, the principle of secrecy was recognized quite early but there were marked local variations in enforcement. One of the Australian states developed an effective procedure of secret voting as early as 1856, and this innovation, the "Australian ballot," (Wigmore 1889) spread very rapidly through the United States during the 1880s and 1890s. The open recognition of legitimate partisanship made secrecy less important in the United States than in Europe. Most states allow primary elections within each party, and participation in these cannot easily be hidden from the public.

In all these countries the underlying purpose of the introduction of the ballot system was to take the act of voting out of the regular give and take of day-to-day life and enhance its dignity and ritual significance by isolating it from the sordid pressures and temptations of an unequal and divided society. Most histories of electoral arrangements emphasize the importance of secrecy, as a device to protect the economically dependent from the sanctions of their superiors. This was the essence of the Chartists' early demands in England, and it has traditionally been a basic concern of working-class movements. What has often been overlooked is that the provisions for secrecy could as easily cut the voter off from his peers as from his superiors. In fact, the secrecy provisions fulfill two distinct functions: first, they make it possible for the voter to keep his decision private and avoid sanctions from those he does not want to know; second, they make it impossible for the voter to prove how he voted to those he does want to know. The very rigorous rules set up in country after country for the invalidation of all irregularly marked ballots was directed to this second point. They were devised to ensure that the citizen could no longer treat his vote as a commodity for sale. He might well be bribed, but the price per vote clearly would decrease as soon as it proved impossible to check whether it was actually delivered. The salient point here is that by ensuring the complete anonymity of the ballots it became possible not only to reduce bribery of the economically dependent by their superiors but also to reduce the pressures toward conformity and solidarity within the working class.

With the secret ballot, a personal choice was placed before the worker that made him, at least temporarily, independent of his immediate environment: was he primarily a worker or primarily a citizen of the broader local or national community? Secret voting made it possible for the inarticulate rank and file to escape the pressures of their organizations, and at the same time it put the onus of political visibility on the activists within the working-class movement. The established national "system" opened up channels for the expression of secret loyalties, while forcing "deviants" to declare themselves openly. Some socialist parties tried to turn the tables by establishing intimate organizational ties with the trade unions and imposing political levies on their members, irrespective of their actual preferences. The controversy over "contracting in" versus "contracting out" in the British labor movement can be interpreted as the counterpart of the controversy over open versus secret voting in the total system. The Labour party wanted to put the onus of visibility on its own "deviants," the trade union members who did not want to vote for the party (contracting out), while the Conservatives and Liberals wanted the inarticulate masses to stay out of political commitments and to put the onus of visibility on the socialist militants (contracting in).

The introduction of mass elections in the developing countries of Africa and Asia during the final phases of decolonization raised a number of technical issues (MacKenzie & Robinson 1965; Maquet 1959; Smith 1960). In some British territories a system of separate ballot boxes for each candidate or party was introduced. These were marked by distinguishing symbols (a lion, an elephant, etc.) and the illiterate voters were asked to drop their ballot paper into the box of their choice. There were elaborate rules for the stamping of official identification marks on the ballot papers and for the screening of the ballot boxes from the eyes of the officials, but this procedure still left a wide margin for interference with the choice of individual voters. In other British colonies with high rates of illiteracy the voters had to mark off on the ballot the candidates of their choice. This often made it essential to allow election officials to accept "whispering votes" from voters who could not read the names on the ballot. The French colonies and their successor states adopted the system of separate party ballots and the *isoloir* for the placing of the chosen list in the official envelope. This simplified procedures (although it wasted a lot of paper) but still left a great deal of leeway for the exertion of social pressure. Even if the village chieftains or the political agents could not see what the voter did inside the *isoloir*, they could either observe him when he chose his party ballot from the separate piles placed at the polling station or, what was more common, prevail upon him to show them afterward the ballots he had not used, as proof

that he had voted as instructed. There was nothing new about this, of course. The experiences in the developing countries simply confirmed what had been known about voting in the backward rural areas of Europe for decades. Any attempt to uphold strict rules of secrecy in societies at low levels of economic differentiation is bound to run into difficulties. Relationships are too diffuse and the possibilities of observation too many to allow individuals to escape from control through the isolation of particular acts from their daily contexts.

From votes to seats

The emergence of mass electorates produced a great literature of political engineering, not just on the organization of party work and the waging of campaigns but also on the territorial structuring of constituencies and on the strategic pros and cons of alternative procedures of translating the registered distributions of votes into legitimate decisions on representation. Of the extraordinary tangle of issues debated in this literature, only two interconnected issues will be discussed here: the delimitation of units of aggregation, and the procedures for the allocation of seats within each unit. Basically, the bitter debates over the two issues reflect fears and resentments generated through changes in the equilibrium of political power under the impact of mass democracy: the influx of new voters altered the character of the system and a great variety of stratagems were tried out to bring it back into equilibrium.

Varieties of majority systems. The early systems of electoral representation all rested on some kind of majority principle. The will of a part of the electorate was taken to express the will of the whole, and all the participants were taken to be bound in law and conscience by the decision reached through this procedure.

Three distinct varieties of majoritarian decision-making procedure established themselves during the early phases of electoral development. The first of these stipulated *one* round of election, with decisions by simple plurality. The second and the third both stipulated *several* rounds and required absolute majorities in the first round. They differed, however, in their requirements for the final and decisive round. The second allowed an open field of candidacies and simple plurality; the third restricted the competition to the two foremost candidates and retained the absolute-majority requirement to the very end.

The first of the three procedures had been established in England since the Middle Ages and had been used to ensure the election of "two knights from every shire and two burgesses from every borough" to the House of Commons. It also became the standard method in the United States and soon spread to the other English-settled nations overseas. The method was originally used in two-member constituencies, but it met with general acceptance even when applied in single-member units.

The method of repeated ballots had a long tradition in the Roman Catholic church (Moulin 1953) and was formally instituted in the French *ordonnance* calling for elections to the States General in 1789. This stipulated three successive ballots —the first two open, the final one restricted to just twice as many candidates as there were seats left to fill. Three-ballot systems of this type prevailed throughout the *régime censitaire*. This method was clearly best suited to elections restricted to the economically independent classes, with leisure enough to travel to electoral sessions and spend the day or more required to get through all the balloting. The Revolution of 1848 swept away this system and introduced single-ballot mass elections. The old habit of repeated ballots persisted, however. Only four years after the revolution, Napoleon III devised a system of two-ballot elections suited to the new situation of manhood suffrage. He broke with the old tradition on a point of fundamental importance: he allowed an open field of candidacies even at the second ballot and required simple plurality only. This was an astute strategic move; in the half-free elections of the Empire, it allowed the officials maximal freedom of maneuver against the opposition. Interestingly, there was no return to the principle of second-ballot absolute majority in the Third, Fourth, or Fifth Republic: none of the parties or *groupements* wanted to be faced with the cruel yes-or-no alternatives of the two-way fight.

Other polities on the European continent stuck to the old rule of absolute majority and restricted last-ballot candidacies. This was the system upheld in the German Reich down to its defeat in 1918; it was, also, used in Switzerland until 1900 and in Austria, Italy, and the Netherlands until the end of World War I.

These majoritarian electoral methods came under heavy attacks in the later phases of democratization. The extension of the suffrage made possible the organization of strong lower-class parties but the electoral systems, inherited from the ages of estate representation and *régime censitaire*, set high barriers against the entry of such parties into national politics. The German rule of absolute majority set the highest barrier. A lower-class party had to reach the 50 per cent mark or go without

representation. The French and the Anglo–American systems also set high barriers against rising movements of the hitherto disfranchised, but the initial levels were not frozen at 50 per cent; the height of the barriers varied with the strategies of established, *censitaire*, parties. The essential difference between the French and the Anglo–American systems was that the one made for much greater local variations in such counterstrategies than the other: the first-ballot results offered a basis for bargaining among the established parties, and the coalition strategies would of necessity vary from constituency to constituency. The height of the barrier against new entrants depended essentially on the willingness of the established parties to enter into alliances. This was not always exclusively a matter of immediate payoffs but of trust and the openness of communication channels.

Origins of proportional representation. Karl Braunias (1932) distinguished two phases in the spread of proportional representation: the "minority protection" phase, before World War I; and the "antisocialist" phase, in the years immediately after the armistice. It was no accident that the earliest moves toward proportional representation (PR) came in the most ethnically heterogeneous European countries: Denmark in 1855; the Swiss cantons in 1891; Belgium in 1899; Moravia in 1905; Finland in 1906. In linguistically and religiously divided societies majority elections could clearly threaten the continued existence of the political system. The introduction of some element of minority representation came to be seen as an essential step in a strategy of territorial consolidation.

As the pressures mounted for extensions of the suffrage, demands for proportionality were also heard in the culturally more homogeneous nation-states. In most cases the victory of the new principle of representation came about through a convergence of pressures from below and from above. The rising working class wanted to lower the thresholds of representation in order to gain access to the legislatures, and the most threatened of the old established parties demanded PR to protect their position against the new waves of mobilized voters created by universal suffrage. In Belgium the introduction of graduated manhood suffrage in 1893 brought about an increasing polarization between the Labor party and the Catholics and threatened the continued existence of the Liberals. The introduction of PR restored some equilibrium to the system (Gilissen 1958).

The history of the struggles over electoral procedures in Sweden and Norway tells us a great deal about the consequences of the lowering of one threshold for the bargaining over the level of the next. In Sweden, Liberals and Social Democrats fought a long fight for universal and equal suffrage and at first also advocated PR, to ensure easier access to the legislature. The remarkable success of their mobilization efforts made them change their strategy, however, and from 1904 onward they advocated majority elections in single-member constituencies (Verney 1957). This aroused fears among the farmers and the urban conservatives, who, to protect their own interests, made the introduction of PR a condition for acceptance of manhood suffrage. Accordingly, the two barriers fell together. It became easier to enter the electorate and easier to gain representation. In Norway (Rokkan & Hjellum 1966) there was a longer lag between waves of mobilization. The franchise was much wider from the outset, and the first wave of peasant mobilization brought down the old regime as early as 1884. As a result, the suffrage had been extended well before the final mobilization of the rural proletariat and the industrial workers, under the impact of rapid economic change. The victorious radical–agrarian "left" felt no need to lower the threshold of representation and, in fact, helped to raise it through the introduction of a two-ballot system of the French type in 1906. There is little doubt that this contributed greatly to the radicalization and alienation of the Norwegian Labor party, which in 1915 gained 32 per cent of all the votes cast but which was given barely 15 per cent of the seats. The "left" did not agree to lower the threshold until 1921; the decisive motive was clearly not just a sense of equalitarian justice but the fear of rapid decline, with further Labor advances across the majority threshold.

In all these cases the high threshold might have been maintained if the parties of the property-owning classes had been able to make common cause against the rising working-class movements. But the inheritance of hostility and distrust was too strong. The Belgian Liberals could not face the possibility of a merger with the Catholics, and the cleavages between the rural and the urban interests went too deep in the Nordic countries to make it possible to build up any joint antisocialist front. By contrast, the higher level of industrialization and the progressive merger of rural and urban interests in Britain made it possible to withstand the demand for a change in the system of representation: the Labour party was seriously underrepresented only during a brief initial period, and the Conservatives were able to establish broad enough alliances in the counties and the suburbs to keep their votes well above the critical point.

Threshold strategies under PR. PR systems differ markedly in their threshold levels, however, and the struggles over these details of electoral engineering tell us a great deal about the dynamics of multiparty systems.

The variant most frequently introduced in continental Europe was the one invented by the Belgian professor Victor d'Hondt (1878; 1882): the method of the "largest average." This method favors the largest party and, in fact, lowers the threshold very little in constituencies electing few members and choosing among few competing party lists. If the total number of votes cast is designated as V, the total number of mandates as M, and the total number of parties as P, the threshold formula for the d'Hondt procedure will read

$$T = \frac{V - 1}{M + P - 1}.$$

This means that the smallest number of votes (T) required for representation will be a function not only of the size of the constituency and its share of seats but also of the number of parties. A fragmented party system lowers the threshold but, by implication, also increases the overrepresentation of the largest of the parties (particularly if $P > M$, since the votes for a number of the small parties must of necessity go unrepresented).

Thus, the debates and bargains over electoral arrangements in a great number of PR countries have centered on the questions, Should there be some gentle overrepresentation of the largest party? and Should the threshold for the first seat be set high enough to discourage new parties and splinter movements? These concerns have been particularly prominent in the Scandinavian countries: the typical constellation there has been one party, Labor, in the range just below the 50 per cent mark; three or four parties, all nonsocialist, in the 5–20 per cent range; and one or two very small parties, with only minimal chances of representation. In such constellations the d'Hondt procedure would give the largest party more seats than its votes justified. In fact it often gave the Labor parties clear majorities in parliament without majorities among the voters. This overrepresentation was essentially achieved at the expense of the very smallest of the parties, such as the Communist, but often hurt the efforts of the one-seat parties to gain additional representation. A variety of remedies were suggested. The Danes retained the high d'Hondt threshold but ensured greater proportionality among the already represented parties through a two-level procedure: any underrepresentation produced at the constituency level was corrected through the allocation of additional seats at the regional level. In Sweden and in Norway the nonsocialist parties opted for another strategy: they found it impossible to join forces under one single list, but they were anxious to increase their representation through provisions for electoral cartels. In Sweden such cartels were allowed after 1921 and cost the Social Democrats a substantial number of seats. The system placed the Agrarians in a very difficult position. To avoid underrepresentation, they were tempted to join in cartels with the other nonsocialist parties; but to advance the interests of the farmers they found it best to support the Social Democratic government. In the end the provisions for cartels were abolished and the Sainte-Laguë method (1910) of calculation was introduced.

By a curious coincidence this alternative was adopted in all the three Scandinavian countries during 1952 and 1953. The Norwegian Labor party had gained a majority in parliament in 1945 and by 1947 had abolished the cartels. As a result, the party received 45.7 per cent of the votes but 56.7 per cent of the seats in the 1949 election. This caused a great deal of recrimination, and the party finally accepted the new method of allocation in 1952. A similar lowering of threshold was also brought about in Denmark, through provisions in the constitution of 1953.

The Sainte-Laguë method was once described as a "miracle formula" by the leader of the Swedish Agrarian party. In the typical Scandinavian situation it had a threefold effect: it strengthened the middle-sized nonsocialist parties by reducing the overrepresentation of the Social Democrats; it was nevertheless of strategic advantage to the governing parties because it reduced the pay-offs of mergers within the opposition; and finally, it helped all the established parties by discouraging splinters and new parties. How could all this be achieved in one formula? To explain this, we have to go into some technicalities of electoral mathematics (Janson 1961; Rokkan & Hjellum 1966).

Two procedures were frequently suggested as alternatives to d'Hondt in the discussions in the Scandinavian countries: the method of the "greatest remainder" and the Sainte-Laguë system of successive division by odd integers.

The method of the "greatest remainder" lowers the threshold of representation to a minimum: the threshold formula is $T = V/(MP)$. This is a direct invitation to party fragmentation, since the threshold decreases rapidly with increases in the number of parties. The simple Sainte-Laguë formula does not go quite that far. The threshold formula is $(V - 1)/(2M + P - 2)$. Its crucial contribution is the progressive increase in the cost of new seats. The greater the number of seats already won by a party in a given constituency, the more votes it will take to add yet another. The d'Hondt formula makes no distinction between first and later seats. The total votes cast for each party are divided successively by $1, 2, 3, \cdots$. The Sainte-Laguë method is to divide by $1, 3, 5, \cdots$. Thus, if the first seat costs each party 1,000 votes, the second seat will cost the party $(1,000 \cdot 3)/2 = 1,500$ votes and the third seat $(1,000 \cdot 5)/3 = 1,667$ votes, and so on. This is definitely the optimal formula for small parties: it is easy to gain representation but hard to reach a majority in parliament. At the same time, it discourages mergers and cartels. Two parties polling just beyond the threshold for their first seats will, in fact, lose out if they merge.

This procedure appealed both to the nonsocialist parties, typically at the one-seat level in most constituencies, and to the governing Social Democrats. The nonsocialists were anxious to reduce the "government bonus" built into the d'Hondt procedure, and the Social Democrats wanted to make sure that their opponents did not find it profitable to merge into one broad competitive party.

But this was not all. The electoral strategists went even further to ensure the perpetuation of the established party constellations. They wanted lower thresholds, but they wanted them set just below the typical voting levels of the smallest of the established parties. If the threshold were to be set much lower, it would increase the chances of even smaller, "antisystem" parties and encourage splinter movements. The solution proved very simple: the first divisor was set, not at 1, but at 1.4. In the example already used, this would mean that the first seat would cost 1,400 votes as against 1,500 for the second and 1,667 for the third. It cost more to gain entry, but once a party was in, the steps toward further representation were no longer so steep.

This formula fitted the established power constellations as closely as any procedure at this level of simplicity could ever be expected to. It had all the appearance of a universal rule, but in fact it was essentially designed to stabilize the party system at the point of equilibrium reached by the early 1950s.

Developments in the late 1950s and the early 1960s showed that even this formula would not protect the system against change. The Social

Democrats began to regret that they had given up so much of their "government bonus." Their parliamentary majorities had become very small and highly vulnerable, and they were reluctant to contemplate long-term alliances with one of the opposition parties. In Sweden the Royal Commission on Constitutional Reform proposed in 1963 a two-tier system of representation. They wanted to use the Sainte-Laguë procedure at the level of the old constituencies and the d'Hondt procedure to elect regional members at large. This was a deliberate attempt to bring back into a system some measure of overrepresentation for the largest party. The motive was explicitly stated to be the need for some stabilization of the majority basis for the cabinet. This proposal is still under debate, and there is no basis for any final prediction of the outcome of the complex bargaining currently under way. Similar discussions got under way in Norway in the wake of the defeat of the Labor party in the election of 1961. Some Labor strategists have guardedly suggested a return to d'Hondt or even a switch to simple majority elections of the British type, while their rivals in the nonsocialist camp have put forth a diametrically opposed solution: the lowering of the Sainte-Laguë threshold to 1.3 or even 1.2. Paradoxically, the old Labor party, once the champion of PR, now wants to increase the threshold of representation, while their opponents, once the defenders of the old majority threshold, now advocate a radical lowering. Their aim is clearly to encourage the Left Socialist splinters from Labor, but this gain can be bought only at the cost of all future mergers of the nonsocialist parties (Rokkan & Hjellum 1966).

PR without party lists. By 1920 PR systems of one sort or another had won out throughout Europe. Even the French gave up their two-ballot, single-member procedure from 1917 to 1927 and introduced a curious mixture of d'Hondt proportionality and majoritarianism. These systems all required the voter to elect several representatives at the same time and to choose among a number of lists of candidates. These lists were normally set up by competing political parties. The voters might have some influence on the fate of individual candidates on such lists, but it was nearly impossible to elect anyone not appearing on the initial lists. The Continental PR was a product of party bargaining. The parties wanted to survive and saw that they rated the best chances under a system that would allow them not only to control nominations but also to gain representation even when in minority.

In the Anglo-Saxon countries this type of PR never caught on. There were strong party organizations, but there was also a strong tradition of direct territorial representation through individual representatives. The early English advocates of proportionality were profoundly indifferent to the survival of organized parties; they wanted to equalize the influence of individual voters. The great innovation of these electoral reformers was the introduction of a procedure for the aggregation of individual rank-order choices. The election was not to be decided through the counting of so many choices for X and so many for Y but through the comparison of schedules of preference. The possibilities of such aggregations of rank orders had been analyzed with great ingenuity by Charles de Borda and the Marquis de Condorcet in the eighteenth century (Black 1958; Ross 1955), but these theoretical discussions had been confined to decision making in committees and assemblies. The French method of repeated ballots, in fact, developed out of decision-making situations in assemblies and entailed a rank ordering of preferences; the voters for the candidates at the bottom had to decide on their next-order preferences. The Australian system of the "alternative vote" is another approximation; the voter indicates his second and third choices, as well as his first, and knows that these lower preferences will be brought into the count if his first preference should not receive enough support. These methods, however, aim at the maximizing of support behind each candidate. First preferences count to the end, even when there are many more than needed to elect the given candidate. The great strength of the movement for the "single transferable vote" lay precisely in the insistence on the effective use of all the preference schedules, not only the ones given to the candidates with the smallest followings but also of those "wasted" through overconcentration on a single candidate.

This required the setting of a quota—the smallest number of preferences required for election. The inventors of the system, a Dane, Andrae (1855), and an Englishman, Hare (1857), set it at Votes ÷ Seats, but this was quickly shown to be too high. H. R. Droop (1868) had no difficulty in demonstrating that the correct quota would be [Votes ÷ (Seats + 1)] + 1. This would be just enough to beat competitors for the last of the seats.

Once the quota had been set, the procedure was in itself straightforward, if time consuming. The wasted first preferences at the top of the poll were treated just like the wasted ones at the bottom—the lower preferences were entered when the first ones could no longer help. There was one difference. At the bottom all the first preferences were wasted and had to be examined for lower preferences, while at the top it was impossible to say which ones were wasted—which ones were in the quota and which ones were beyond. The solution was to work out proportional shares of lower preferences. If an elected candidate had received 10,000 first preferences but needed only 9,000, the below-quota candidates would get $(10,000 - 9,000) \div 10,000 = \frac{1}{10}$ of the second preferences given each of them by those 10,000 voters (Lakeman & Lambert 1955).

The Andrae variant of this system was used in the election of some of the members of the Danish Rigsraad from 1855 to 1866 and in the electoral colleges for the Upper House from 1866 to 1915, but the method has otherwise found acceptance only in Britain and the British-settled areas: Tasmania since 1907, the two Irelands since 1920 (quickly abolished in Northern Ireland), Malta since 1921, New South Wales since 1932, and the Australian Senate since 1949. The "single transferable vote" was ardently advocated by British Liberals but never gained much of a foothold in England. Most Conservatives were against it, and the Labour party found it less and less interesting as they grew in strength. There was a strong move toward proportionalism in 1931. Labour promoted an "alternative-vote" bill and was supported by the Liberals in the House of Commons, but the government fell and the law was never enacted (Butler 1953).

On the European continent there has always been a great deal of resistance to the dominance of the organized parties in the determination of the lists of candidates, and a variety of devices has been invented to ensure some measure of voter influence on the fate of individual candidates. Denmark was the only country on the Continent to go as far as to opt for PR without party lists. Under the current system they provide three levels of electoral aggregation. At the level of the nomination district the voters choose among individual candidates; at the level of the constituency their votes are aggregated by party to determine the allocation of direct seats; while at the level of the region there is a further round of aggregation to decide the attribution of additional seats designed to maximize proportionality (Pedersen 1966). Another multilevel solution has been devised in the German Federal Republic. There the voters are allowed two votes, one for a simple plurality election in single-member constituencies, the other for a PR election among party lists. A high degree of candidate orientation can also be achieved in a single-level PR system. The Finnish system provides the most interesting example. The parties do not present multicandidate lists or indicate a preferred order among them but submit a number of separate candidacies. The voters then choose individual candidates only, but the votes are aggregated by party within each constituency to determine the allocation of seats.

Single-member versus multimember constituencies. On the Continent the conflict between the majority principle and the proportionality principle was, at the same time, a conflict over conceptions of the territoriality of elections. Majority elections were typically tied to single-member constituencies and posited close interaction between the elected representative and the entire local electorate. Proportional elections were held in larger constituencies and posited interaction between organized parties and functionally defined core sectors of the population. The Single Transferable Vote made little sense in single-member constituencies but offered an alternative to party dominance in multimember units. The voter was free to establish his own list of candidates and did not have to abide by any party nominations. Thomas Hare (1857) and John Stuart Mill went so far as to propose that all of Britain be turned into one single constituency, but this clearly would make for enormously laborious computations of transfers. The Government of Ireland Act of 1920 stipulated constituencies of three to eight members each, and most advocates of the Hare system now give five seats as the ideal (O'Leary 1961; Ross 1959).

PR-list systems have allowed wide variations in the size of constituencies. Several countries have, in fact, made the entire national territory one constituency. This was the system of the Weimar Republic, and it is still the system in use in the Netherlands; it has also been used in Israel since 1949. This does not necessarily mean that the same set of candidates is presented throughout the national territory. There may be primary constituencies for the presentation of local party lists, but the fate of these lists is not determined within that constituency alone but by the success of the party in the total national territory. The electoral arrangements in Denmark and in the German Federal Republic are of this type. Some of the seats are allocated directly by constituency (in Denmark by the Sainte-Laguë formula, in Germany by plurality); others are allocated on the basis of the nationwide result, to ensure proportionality.

Such large constituencies obviously favor the formation of splinter parties: direct PR thresholds are functions of both the number of seats and the number of parties. To guard against party fragmentation, many systems have introduced higher barriers, either on the basis of the percentage share of the total national vote or on the basis of the number of direct seats already won. Danish law requires as a condition for the allocation of "proportionalized seats" that the party has (*a*) gained one direct seat or (*b*) received 2 per cent or more of the vote across the nation or (*c*) received in two of the three regions a total number of votes higher than the average regional cost of direct seats. The German threshold is 5 per cent of the federal vote or three direct seats.

Cross-constituency equality. The demand for equality of representation was at first met at the constituency level only. "One man, one vote, one value" was enforced within the local unit of aggregation but not throughout the national territory. There were everywhere highly vocal movements for the equalization of electoral districts, but these demands met with greater resistance than the claims for equality of influence within each unit. Under the inherited systems of estate representation, elections were taken to express the will, not of individual citizens, but of the corporate units of the nation. A shire or borough might have declined in population or in number of enfranchised citizens, but it still constituted a unit of government worthy of representation on a par with larger units. Even after the Reform Act of 1832 in England, differences between the lowest and the highest numbers of constituents per representative were of the order of 1 to 60. The radical redistribution carried out in 1885 brought the ratio down to 1 to 7, but further progress was slow. Even after the reorganization of 1948 there are still constituencies with electorates only one-third the size of the largest in the country.

Great variations in the ratios of representatives to electorates was the rule throughout Europe and the West until well into the twentieth century. On the European continent the early systems of representation generally gave great advantages to the cities; the centers of commerce and industry were still small in population but had major stakes in the building of the nations. The continuing growth of the national economies brought about changes in this urban–rural balance. As the populations of the cities grew and the franchise was widened, the rural areas gradually gained in their electorate–representative ratios and became heavily overrepresented. This inequality of representation proved highly resistant to protest movements. The more conservative voters in the cities had found important allies in the countryside and preferred to stay underrepresented at home as long as their allies could help them in their fight against urban

radicals (Cotteret et al. 1960; David & Eisenberg 1961–1962; De Grazia 1963).

In some countries this urban–rural conflict was reinforced through conflicts between the central districts and the peripheries. The constituencies farthest away from the capital and the economically most advanced areas of the nation claimed a right to numerical overrepresentation to offset the difficulties of communication with the decision makers and the officials at the center. In Denmark the constitution of 1953 even goes so far as to stipulate that constituencies be allotted seats based not only on their population but also on the size of their territories. A representative speaks not just for a given number of citizens but also for a unit of physical territory. Even in the most "proportionalized" of democracies, the electoral arrangements still reflect tensions between three conceptions of representation: the numerical, the functional, and the territorial.

Priorities for comparative research

The development in so many countries of standardized arrangements for the conduct of elections at several levels of the polity sets a wide variety of challenging tasks for comparative social research. The comparative studies carried out thus far leave great gaps in our knowledge. It is, in fact, much easier to pinpoint lacunae and lost opportunities than to describe positive achievements.

Given the crucial importance of the organization of legitimate elections in the development of the mass democracies of the twentieth century, it is indeed astounding to discover how little serious effort has been invested in the comparative study of the wealth of information available. There is no dearth of literature, but exceedingly little of it stands up to scrutiny in the light of current standards of social science methodology. The great bulk of the items bear on technicalities and controversies within a single national or regional tradition, and the few wider-ranging ones tend to take the form of vehement polemics against competing systems, even when couched in the terms of academic discourse.

The polemical writers tend to fall into two categories: the violent majoritarians or the impassioned single-vote proportionalists. It is hard to trace any distinctive school of list-system proportionalists. The party lists have certainly had their defenders, but these have tended to be pragmatic and contextual in their argumentation and have not been inclined to advertise their solutions as panaceas for all countries of the world.

The majoritarians have been particularly articulate in the three European countries with the unhappiest records of mass politics: Germany, Italy, and France. In all these deeply divided countries there has been widespread nostalgia for the simplicity of the Anglo-Saxon system of plurality elections. A great number of publicists had hoped for the development of unified national political cultures that would foster the kind of trust in territorial representatives they could observe in England and had somehow come to the conclusion that this could be brought about through straightforward electoral engineering.

In its academic guise this argument was developed into a scheme of purportedly universal propositions about the consequences of electoral systems for the health of the body politic (Hermens 1941; 1951). This proved a very difficult enterprise. A great deal of information for a wide range of countries was processed, but the results were meager. The universal propositions gave way to complex statements about concrete sequences of change, and a bewildering multiplicity of conditioning variables had to be brought into the analysis. It turned out to be simply impossible to formulate any single-variable statements about the political consequences of plurality as opposed to those of PR. A variety of contextual conditions had to be brought into the analysis: the character of the national cleavage system; the cultural conditions for the legitimation of representatives; the burdens of government and the leeway for legislative versus executive action (Duverger 1950; 1951; Epstein 1964; Grumm 1958).

This did not reduce appreciably the ardor of the majoritarians. They stuck to their guns in discussing the three major countries of the western European continent, but they admitted that PR might not hurt the functioning of democracy in the smaller nations (Unkelbach 1956). A good case could be made for plurality elections in Germany, within a reasoned analysis of the strategic options for the one country (Sternberger 1964; Scheuch & Wildenmann 1965), but the academic enterprise broke down as soon as attempts were made to argue this move for all full-suffrage democracies, whatever their structure and whatever their experiences in consensus building.

In Anglo-Saxon circles the polemics *against* plurality elections have not been quite as vehement. Advocates of PR could not blame the inherited electoral system for major national disasters, such as Fascism in Italy, National Socialism in Germany, the 1940 debacle in France. The single-vote proportionalists (Lakeman & Lambert 1955; Ross 1955) do have something in common with the majoritarians. They tend to express the same naive belief in the possibilities of electoral engineering, and they show little awareness of the cultural and the organizational conditions for the acceptance of different systems of representation.

The majoritarian–proportionalist polemic has recently been given a new dimension through the discussion of the consequences of electoral arrangements for the achievement and/or survival of democracy in the developing countries. A leading analyst of the conditions of economic growth, W. Arthur Lewis, has formulated a strong indictment of the Anglo–French majority systems which the new African states inherited from their colonial masters. He argues that the Anglo–French systems had been developed and had found widespread acceptance in "class societies" and cannot work in the same way in the African "plural" societies—territorial polities seeking to integrate within their boundaries populations historically hostile to each other.

The surest way to kill the idea of democracy in a plural society is to adopt the Anglo-American electoral system of first-past-the-post. . . . First-past-the-post does not even require 51 per cent of the votes in each constituency to give one party all the votes. If there are three parties it can be done theoretically, with only 34 per cent; or if there are four parties, with only 26 per cent. Governments can get away with this in secure democracies without destroying faith. But if you belong to a minority in a new state, and are being asked to accept parliamentary democracy, you can hardly build much faith in the system if you win 30 per cent of those votes and get only 20 per cent of the seats, or even no seats at all. If minorities are to accept Parliament, they must be adequately represented in Parliament.   (Lewis 1965, pp. 71–72)

These, of course, are exactly the arguments used in the "plural societies" of Europe for the introduction of PR. The entrenched linguistic, religious, or ethnic minorities had no faith in the majority representatives and threatened to disrupt the system. The introduction of PR was essentially part of a strategy of national integration—an alternative to monopolization of influence or civil war. But the extent of minority entrenchment varied greatly from country to country, and the pressures for proportionalization were nowhere exactly the same. This is a high-priority area for comparative research. To bring about some understanding of the great variations in electoral arrangements both in the West and in the postcolonial polities, it will be essential to study the crucial decisions on the suffrage, on privacy versus secrecy, on plurality versus PR, in the context of the process of nation building (Bendix 1964; Rokkan 1961; 1966*b*).

Electoral systems have not changed *in vacuo*. They function within culturally given contexts of legitimacy, and they are changed under the strains of critical "growing pains" in the development of the over-all constellations of national institutions. The comparative study of electoral developments can contribute a great deal to the understanding of processes and strategies of national integration, but the contributions will be meager and unreliable as long as the principal motivation for new research is a concern with the pros and cons of different schemes of electoral engineering.

The conditions for a real advance in comparative electoral research are present. An increasing number of dispassionate analyses of national electoral histories have been forthcoming in recent years, and steps are being taken to facilitate the conduct of statistical investigations through the development of "data archives" for computer analyses of time-series records (Rokkan 1966a; Rokkan & Meyriat 1967). What has been lacking so far has been an international forum for the advancement of detailed comparative studies. A beginning has been made, however, and it is hoped that the next decades will see a breakthrough in the comparative study of electoral systems.

STEIN ROKKAN

[*See also* LEGISLATION; PARTIES, POLITICAL; REPRESENTATION, *article on* REPRESENTATIONAL SYSTEMS; VOTING.]

BIBLIOGRAPHY

THEORIES AND CONCEPTS

AKZIN, B. 1960 Election and Appointment. *American Political Science Review* 54:705–713.

ARROW, KENNETH J. (1951) 1963 *Social Choice and Individual Values.* 2d ed. New York: Wiley.

AUSTIN, JOHN L. 1961 Performative Utterances. Pages 220–239 in John L. Austin, *Philosophical Papers.* Oxford Univ. Press.

AUSTIN, JOHN L. 1962 *How to Do Things With Words.* Oxford: Clarendon.

BIRCH, ANTHONY H. 1964 *Representative and Responsible Government.* London: Allen & Unwin.

BLACK, DUNCAN 1958 *The Theory of Committees and Elections.* Cambridge Univ. Press.

BUCHANAN, JAMES M.; and TULLOCK, GORDON 1962 *The Calculus of Consent: Logical Foundations of Constitutional Democracy.* Ann Arbor: Univ. of Michigan Press.

DAHL, ROBERT A. 1956 *A Preface to Democratic Theory.* Univ. of Chicago Press.

LEIBHOLZ, GERHARD (1929) 1960 *Das Wesen der Repräsentation und der Gestaltswandel der Demokratie im 20. Jahrhundert.* 2d ed. Berlin: Gruyter.

LITTLE, IAN M. D. (1950) 1957 *A Critique of Welfare Economics.* 2d ed. Oxford: Clarendon.

RIKER, WILLIAM H. 1961 Voting and the Summation of Preferences: An Interpretive–Bibliographical Review of Selected Developments During the Last Decade. *American Political Science Review* 55:900–911.

ROSS, JAMES F. S. 1955 *Elections and Electors: Studies in Democratic Representation.* London: Eyre & Spottiswoode.

HISTORICAL DEVELOPMENTS

ARISTOTLE *Aristotle's Politics* and *Athenian Constitution.* Edited and translated by John Warrington. New York: Dutton, 1959.

BARKER, ERNEST 1913 *Dominican Order and Convocation: A Study of the Growth of Representation in the Church During the Thirteenth Century.* Oxford: Clarendon.

CLARKE, MAUDE V. (1936) 1964 *Medieval Representation and Consent: A Study of Early Parliaments in England and Ireland, With Special Reference to the Modus tenendi parliamentum.* New York: Russell.

EHRENBERG, VICTOR (1932) 1964 *The Greek State.* Rev. ed. New York: Barnes & Noble. → First published as *Der griechische und der hellenische Staat.*

GALBRAITH, GEORGINA R. (COLE-BAKER) 1925 *The Constitution of the Dominican Order: 1216–1360.* Manchester Univ. Press.

GLOTZ, GUSTAVE (1928) 1950 *The Greek City and Its Institutions.* London: Routledge. → First published as *La cité grecque.*

GREENIDGE, ABEL H. (1896) 1920 *A Handbook of Greek Constitutional History.* London and New York: Macmillan.

GREENIDGE, ABEL H. (1901) 1930 *Roman Public Life.* New York: Macmillan.

HINTZE, OTTO (1902–1932)1962 *Staat und Verfassung: Gesammelte Abhandlungen zur allgemeinen Verfassungsgeschichte.* 2d enl. ed. Göttingen (Germany): Vandenhoeck & Ruprecht.

LOUSSE, ÉMILE 1943 *La société d'ancien régime: Organisation et représentation corporatives.* Louvain (Belgium): Bibliothèque de l'Université.

MOULIN, LÉO 1953 Les origines religieuses des techniques électorales et délibératives modernes. *Revue internationale d'histoire politique et constitutionnelle* New Series 3:106–148.

PALMER, ROBERT R. 1959 *The Age of the Democratic Revolution: A Political History of Europe and America, 1760–1800.* Volume 1: The Challenge. Princeton Univ. Press.

RYFFEL, HEINRICH 1903 *Die schweizerischen Landsgemeinden.* Zurich: Schulthess.

ULLMANN, WALTER 1961 *Principles of Government and Politics in the Middle Ages.* New York: Barnes & Noble.

MODERN SYSTEMS: GENERAL PROBLEMS

BASTID, PAUL 1948 *L'avènement du suffrage universel.* Paris: Presses Universitaires de France.

BENDIX, REINHARD 1964 *Nation-building and Citizenship: Studies of Our Changing Social Order.* New York: Wiley.

BRAUNIAS, KARL 1932 *Das parlamentarische Wahlrecht: Ein Handbuch über die Bildung der gesetzgebenden Körperschaften in Europa.* 2 vols. Berlin: Gruyter.

DIEDRICH, N. 1965 *Empirische Wahlforschung.* Cologne (Germany): Westdeutscher Verlag.

DUVERGER, MAURICE 1950 *L'influence des systèmes électoraux sur la vie politique.* Paris: Colin.

DUVERGER, MAURICE (1951) 1962 *Political Parties: Their Organization and Activity in the Modern State.* 2d English ed., rev. New York: Wiley; London: Methuen. → First published in French.

EPSTEIN, LEON D. 1964 A Comparative Study of Canadian Parties. *American Political Science Review* 58: 46–59.

GOSNELL, HAROLD F. 1930 *Why Europe Votes.* Univ. of Chicago Press.

GRUMM, JOHN G. 1958 Theories of Electoral Systems. *Midwest Journal of Political Science* 2:357–376.

HOGAN, JAMES 1945 *Election and Representation.* Cork Univ. Press.

INSTITUTE OF ELECTORAL RESEARCH, LONDON 1962 *Parliaments and Electoral Systems: A World Handbook.* Lowestoft (England): Scorpion.

INSTITUTE OF ELECTORAL RESEARCH, LONDON *A Review of Elections.* Published annually. See especially the 1960 and the 1961–1962 volumes.

KEY, V. O. JR. (1942) 1964 *Politics, Parties and Pressure Groups.* 5th ed. New York: Crowell.

KRADITOR, AILEEN S. 1965 *The Ideas of the Woman Suffrage Movement, 1890–1920.* New York: Columbia Univ. Press.

MACKENZIE, W. J. M. 1958 *Free Elections: An Elementary Textbook.* London: Allen & Unwin.

MEYER, GEORG 1901 *Das parlamentarische Wahlrecht.* Berlin: Haering.

PORTER, KIRK H. 1918 *A History of Suffrage in the United States.* Univ. of Chicago Press.

ROKKAN, STEIN 1961 Mass Suffrage, Secret Voting and Political Participation. *Archives européennes de sociologie* 2, no. 1:132–154.

ROKKAN, STEIN 1966a The Comparative Study of Electoral Statistics. International Social Science Council, *Social Sciences Information* 5, no. 2:9–19.

ROKKAN, STEIN 1966b Electoral Mobilization, Party Competition and National Integration. Pages 241–265 in Joseph LaPalombara and Myron Weiner (editors), *Political Parties and Political Development.* Princeton Univ. Press.

ROKKAN, STEIN; and MEYRIAT, JEAN (editors) 1967 *International Guide to Electoral Statistics.* Volume 1: National Elections in Western Europe. Paris: Mouton.

SCHEPIS, GIOVANNI 1955 *I sistemi elettorali: Teoria, tecnica, legislazioni positive.* Empoli (Italy): Caparrini.

SEYMOUR, CHARLES 1915 *Electoral Reform in England and Wales: The Development and Operation of the Parliamentary Franchise, 1832–1885.* New Haven: Yale Univ. Press.

SEYMOUR, CHARLES; and FRARY, DONALD P. 1918 *How the World Votes: The Story of Democratic Development in Elections.* 2 vols. Springfield, Mass.: Nichols.

VALEN, HENRY; and KATZ, DANIEL 1964 *Political Parties in Norway: A Community Study.* Oslo: Universitetsforlaget.

VERNEY, DOUGLAS V. 1957 *Parliamentary Reform in Sweden, 1866–1921.* Oxford: Clarendon.

WESTERATH, HERIBERT 1955 *Die Wahlverfahren und ihre Vereinbarkeit mit den demokratischen Anforderungen an das Wahlrecht.* Berlin: Gruyter.

WIGMORE, JOHN H. 1889 *The Australian Ballot System as Embodied in the Legislation of Various Countries.* Boston: Boston Book Co.

WILLIAMSON, CHILTON 1960 *American Suffrage: From Property to Democracy, 1760–1860.* Princeton Univ. Press.

ZWAGER, HAJO H. 1958 *De motivering van het algemeen kiesrecht en Europa: Een historische studie.* Groningen (Netherlands): Wolters.

MODERN SYSTEMS: TECHNICAL PROBLEMS

ANDRAE, POUL G. (1855) 1926 *Andrae and His Invention: The Proportional Representation Method.* Copenhagen: Privately published. → Chapters 3, 4, and 5 and part of Chapter 9 of the Danish original have been omitted in translation.

COTTERET, JEAN MARIE; ÉMERI, CLAUDE; and LALUMIÈRE, PIERRE 1960 *Lois électorales et inégalités de représentation en France, 1936–1960.* Paris: Colin.

DAVID, PAUL T.; and EISENBERG, RALPH 1961–1962 *Devaluation of the Urban and Suburban Vote: A Statistical Investigation of Long-term Trends in State Legislative Representation.* 2 vols. Charlottesville: Univ. of Virginia, Bureau of Public Administration.

DE GRAZIA, ALFRED 1963 *Essay on Apportionment and Representative Government.* Washington: American Enterprise Institute for Public Policy Research.

DROOP, HENRY R. 1868 *On Methods of Electing Representatives.* London: Macmillan.

HARE, THOMAS 1857 *The Machinery of Representation.* London: Maxwell.

HERMENS, FERDINAND A. 1941 *Democracy or Anarchy? A Study of Proportional Representation.* Univ. of Notre Dame Press.

HERMENS, FERDINAND A. 1951 *Europe Between Democracy and Anarchy.* Univ. of Notre Dame Press.

HOAG, CLARENCE G.; and HALLETT, GEORGE H. 1926 *Proportional Representation.* New York: Macmillan.

HONDT, VICTOR D' 1878 *La représentation proportionelle des partis.* Ghent.

HONDT, VICTOR D' 1882 *Système pratique et raisonné de représentation proportionelle.* Brussels: Muquardt.

JANSON, CARL GUNNAR 1961 *Mandatilldelning och regional röstfördelning.* Stockholm: Idun.

LAKEMAN, ENID; and LAMBERT, JAMES D. 1955 *Voting in Democracies: A Study of Majority and Proportional Electoral Systems.* London: Faber.

MÜLLER, PETER F. 1959 *Das Wahlsystem: Neue Wege der Grundlegung und Gestaltung.* Zurich: Polygraphischer Verlag.

O'LEARY, CORNELIUS 1961 *The Irish Republic, and Its Experiment With Proportional Representation.* Univ. of Notre Dame Press.

ROSS, JAMES F. S. 1959 *The Irish Election System: What It Is and How It Works.* London: Pall Mall.

SAINTE-LAGUË, A. 1910 La représentation proportionelle et la méthode des moindres carrées. Académie des Sciences, Paris, *Comptes rendus hebdomadaires* 151: 377–378.

STERNBERGER, ADOLF 1964 *Die grosse Wahlreform: Zeugnisse einer Bemühung.* Cologne (Germany): Westdeutscher Verlag.

UNKELBACH, HELMUT 1965 *Grundlagen der Wahlsystematik: Stabilitätsbedingungen der parlamentarischen Demokratie.* Göttingen (Germany): Vandenhoeck & Ruprecht.

UNKELBACH, HELMUT; and WILDENMANN, RUDOLF 1961 *Grundfragen des Wählens.* Frankfurt am Main (Germany): Athenäum.

MODERN SYSTEMS: REGIONAL AND NATIONAL

BUTLER, DAVID E. (1953) 1963 *The Electoral System in Britain Since 1918.* Enl. ed. Oxford: Clarendon. → First published as *The Electoral System in Britain: 1918–1953.*

CAMPBELL, PETER 1958 *French Electoral Systems and Elections: 1789–1957.* New York: Praeger.

CARSON, GEORGE BARR JR. 1955 *Electoral Practices in the U.S.S.R.* New York: Praeger.

CHARNAY, JEAN PAUL 1965 *Le suffrage politique en France: Élections parlementaires, élection présidentielle, référendums.* Paris: Mouton.

CRUTTI, MARIO; PIZZARI, M.; and SCHEPIS, G. 1951 *Profilo storico degli ordinamenti elettorali.* Empoli (Italy): Caparrini.

GEISMANN, GEORG 1964 *Politische Struktur und Regierungssystem in den Niederlanden.* Kölner Schriften zur politischen Wissenschaft, vol. 4. Frankfurt am Main (Germany): Athenäum.

GERMANY (FEDERAL REPUBLIC), WAHLRECHTSKOMMISSION 1955 *Grundlagen eines deutschen Wahlrechts: Bericht.* Bonn (Germany): Bonner Universitäts-Buchdruckerei.

GILISSEN, JOHN 1958 *Le régime représentatif en Belgique depuis 1790.* Brussels: Renaissance du Livre.

LACHAPELLE, GEORGES 1934 *Les régimes électoraux.* Paris: Colin.

LEWIS, W. ARTHUR 1965 *Politics in West Africa.* London: Allen & Unwin.

MACKENZIE, W. J. M.; and ROBINSON, KENNETH (editors) 1960 *Five Elections in Africa: A Group of Electoral Studies.* Oxford: Clarendon.

MAQUET, JACQUES J.; and HERTEFELT, MARCEL D' 1959 *Élections en société féodale: Une étude sur l'introduction du vote populaire au Ruanda-Urundi.* Académie Royale des Sciences Coloniales, Classe des Sciences Morales et Politiques, Mémoires in 8°, New Series, Vol. 21, part 2. Brussels: Académie Royale.

PEDERSEN, MOGENS N. 1966 Preferential Voting in Denmark. *Scandinavian Political Studies* 1:167–187.

ROKKAN, S.; and HJELLUM, T. 1966 Norway: The Storting Election of September 1965. *Scandinavian Political Studies* 1:237–246.

SCHEPIS, GIOVANNI 1958 *Le consultazioni popolari in Italia dal 1848 al 1957: Profilo storico-statistico.* Empoli (Italy): Caparrini.

SCHEUCH, E.; and WILDENMANN, R. 1965 *Zur Soziologie der Wahl.* Cologne (Germany): Westdeutscher Verlag.

SMITH, T. E. 1960 *Elections in Developing Countries: A Study of Electoral Procedures Used in Tropical Africa, South-east Asia, and the British Caribbean.* New York: St. Martins.

ELECTROCONVULSIVE SHOCK

It has been known for many years that electric current applied to an animal's head can elicit a convulsion. The procedure of eliciting seizures by electrical stimulation is termed "electroconvulsive shock" (ECS). The term "electroshock therapy" (EST) is used in medical references. In the early 1930s drug-induced convulsions (using insulin or Metrazol, for example) were adopted as a treatment for patients with severe mental disorders. In 1938 Cerletti and Bini demonstrated that ECS provided a more highly controlled and reliable means of eliciting convulsions. ECS gradually replaced drugs in convulsive therapy treatments and is still used to some extent as a treatment for mental disorders. It is considered to be particularly effective in the treatment of severely depressed patients (Ulett et al. 1962). Since Cerletti and Bini introduced ECS there have been numerous extensive clinical and experimental studies of the nature and bases of its behavioral effects.

The ECS convulsion. Rats or other rodents have been used as subjects in the majority of experimental studies of ECS. In general, the pattern of the convulsion obtained with rats is similar to that obtained with larger mammals, including humans. Convulsions are usually elicited by stimulating the rats with 25 to 100 milliamperes of current (AC) for approximately 0.2 to 1 second. The current is delivered through electrodes that are either attached to the animal's ear or applied directly to the rat's corneas. The maximal seizure (*grand mal*) consists of a highly stereotyped sequence of movements. The animal's hind legs are first drawn up and then extended. This tonic extension lasts for several seconds and is followed by a brief phase of whole-body clonus. The animal then remains in an immobile state for several minutes. A maximal convulsion can again be elicited in approximately ten minutes. For about 15 minutes following the convulsion the animals are usually hyperirritable. Current below that necessary to elicit a maximal seizure may produce violent running, temporary immobilization, or clonic convulsions. Maximal seizures can be prevented by administering to the animals such depressant drugs as ether, phenobarbital, or diphenylhydantoin prior to the ECS stimulation (Toman et al. 1946). Maximal seizure thresholds increase with the age of the animals and, in different laboratory species, vary directly with the weight of the animals.

Behavioral effects of multiple ECS

In the clinical use of ECS, patients are usually given a series of treatments. Most experimental studies with laboratory animals have adopted this procedure. This procedure is, of course, appropriate for research viewed as an experimental analogue of the clinical treatments. However, recent evidence indicates that ECS has numerous behavioral effects and that the effects of a single ECS treatment are quite different from those produced by a series of treatments.

Activity, sexual and maternal behavior. When rats are given a series of ECS treatments (one or more per day for 7 to 25 days) their behavior is markedly affected. Spontaneous activity is depressed, male sexual arousal is impaired, and maternal behavior (for example, nest building and care of the young) is disrupted (Munn 1950; Beach et al. 1955). The animals' behavior usually returns to normal within a few weeks after the treatments are discontinued.

Learning and retention. Multiple ECS treatments have also been found to impair rats' maze learning and retention. The degree of impairment is directly related to the complexity of the maze task. However, the impairment appears to be temporary. Little impairment is found if a month elapses between the last ECS treatment and the maze learning or retention tests. There is no impairment of performance if convulsions are prevented by the delivering of the ECS stimulation while the animals are anesthetized with ether (Munn 1950; Russell 1948).

Studies of memory in human patients given a series of ECS treatments yield findings similar to those of the rat studies. Patients typically experience impaired memory for several weeks following the termination of the treatments. This deficiency is fairly general and typically involves difficulty remembering well-learned life-history data as well as recently experienced events. Although the deficits generally disappear within a few weeks, deficits have been observed over a period of months in some patients. Some investigators have suggested that temporary memory impairment may contribute in some way to the therapeutic effectiveness of ECS treatments (Janis & Astrachan 1951).

Conditioned emotional response. A number of studies have shown that a series of ECS treatments is particularly effective in attenuating a learned emotional response (Hunt 1965). In these studies rats were first trained to press a lever for a water reward. They then were presented with a series of trials in which a clicking noise was followed by a painful shock delivered to their feet. Within a few trials the clicking noise elicited a conditioned emotional response (CER) consisting of crouching, urination, defecation, and depressed rate of lever pressing. The rats were then given a series of 21 ECS treatments—three per day for seven days. On subsequent tests the clicking noise failed to elicit the CER. Less of an attenuating effect was found if fewer ECS treatments were given or if several weeks elapsed between the CER training and the ECS treatments. The differential effect of ECS on the lever-pressing response and the CER is not due to the fact that the CER was the last response learned. Similar results are obtained when the CER training is given prior to the learning of the lever-pressing response. The effects of multiple ECS on the CER, like those found with

maze learning and retention as well as sexual and maternal behavior, are transient. The CER typically reappears within a month following the treatments. The convulsions appear to play a critical role in attenuating the CER. Multiple ECS treatments do not attenuate the CER if the convulsions are prevented by etherizing the rats prior to each ECS treatment.

It is clear from these studies that a series of ECS treatments markedly affects rats' behavior. The findings indicate, however, that the effects are for the most part temporary. Effects on sexual arousal and learning and retention generally last for only a few weeks following the treatments. Further, it seems clear that the convulsions are essential for the effects observed. There is little evidence of behavioral effects of multiple ECS treatments when convulsions are prevented by anesthetization of the animals prior to the treatments.

Behavioral effects of a single ECS

Shortly after the introduction of ECS clinical observations indicated memory loss as a common consequence of such treatments. In addition to a general loss of ability to remember names, events, and personal life history, patients seemed to have amnesia for events that had occurred shortly before each treatment. This phenomenon has been termed "retrograde amnesia." Systematic studies of memory in patients treated with ECS have confirmed this clinical observation. In an early study, for example, patients were shown a series of pictures prior to receiving an ECS treatment. In tests given the next day they showed poorest retention of the last pictures seen before convulsion (Mayer-Gross 1943).

Evidence that ECS produces retrograde amnesia has been obtained in a large number of experiments with rats. In the first two of such studies (Duncan 1949; Gerard 1955) rats and hamsters, respectively, were given a single ECS treatment after each trial in a learning task. The animals were arranged in different groups and each group was given the ECS treatment at a different time interval after each trial. With the intervals shorter than one hour, the rate of learning increased directly with increases in the length of the interval between the trial and the ECS treatment. Learning was not affected by the treatments given one hour or longer after each trial. Inasmuch as all of the experimental animals were given a series of ECS treatments, it is not possible to discount the possibility that at least some of the effects observed in these studies were due to the cumulative effects of repeated

ECS treatments. It is important to note, however, that treatments did not affect behavior unless they were administered shortly after each training trial. Thus, these findings contrast with findings of a general learning and retention impairment in rats given a series of ECS treatments prior to learning or retention tests.

Evidence of the retrograde amnesic effect of ECS has also been obtained in a large number of studies in which the animals were given only a single ECS treatment. In a series of experiments Thompson and his associates (for example, Thompson & Dean 1955) administered an ECS to different groups of rats at different intervals following massed training trials on a visual discrimination problem. The findings were similar to those obtained by Duncan and Gerard. On retraining trials, 48 hours later, animals given an ECS treatment four hours after the training did not react differently from the controls. In animals treated within one hour after the training, efficiency of relearning varied directly with the interval between the training and the ECS treatments.

In other research Thompson and other investigators have shown that the degree of the retrograde amnesia found with ECS depends upon numerous conditions, including the age and strain of the subjects, degree or strength of original learning, and complexity or difficulty of the learning task. The greatest effects are found when the rats are young or brain damaged and when the learning task is difficult. The duration of the retrograde amnesic effect of ECS is typically limited to a few minutes when a relatively simple learning task is used (Glickman 1961).

Basis of retrograde amnesic effect

During recent years most of the interest in ECS has centered on the problem of the basis of the retrograde amnesic effect. Various hypotheses have been proposed.

Brain damage.   A number of investigators have suggested that the amnesic effect of the ECS may be due to brain damage produced by the current. Studies of the brains of experimental animals subjected to ECS treatments indicate that there is some evidence that ECS produces some changes in the brains—particularly small hemorrhages. However, the changes are generally minor and reversible (Madow 1956). It could be that the confusion and general impairment of learning and retention found with a series of ECS treatments is due in part to reversible vascular damage. Such effects could not, however, account for the retrograde amnesic effects of ECS. A single ECS treatment has little or no

amnesic effect if the treatment is given several hours after training has been terminated. Further, a single ECS does not impair rats' subsequent ability to learn a new task or perform previously well-learned tasks. Thus, although ECS may produce brain damage, it would be difficult to explain the differential effects of ECS on recent and older memories in terms of brain damage.

Interference with memory consolidation.   The most generally accepted interpretation of the retrograde amnesic effect of ECS is that the ECS interferes with the neurophysiological processes involved in storage or consolidation of memory traces (Glickman 1961). Evidence from a variety of clinical and experimental studies has provided strong support for the hypothesis that memory trace consolidation is based upon the perseveration of neurophysiological processes initiated by an experience. In humans retrograde amnesia is a common consequence of head injuries. In experimental studies with laboratory animals retrograde amnesia comparable to that found with ECS treatments has been produced by such treatments as hypoxia, drugs, and audiogenic seizures. The treatments seem to prevent the storage of information acquired during the training trials just prior to the treatment. According to this interpretation the memory loss should be permanent. Available evidence is consistent with this hypothesis. In a study by Chevalier (1965) rats were trained for a task and then given a single ECS. Clear evidence of retrograde amnesia as long as 60 days later was obtained.

Some investigators have assumed that the time required for consolidation to occur after training is indicated by the minimum interval between training and ECS treatment within which no memory impairment is found. However, since different kinds of post-training treatments produce varying degrees of retrograde amnesia, it is more likely that memory storage involves a sequence of processes and that the different treatments are capable of interfering with different processes. For example, with ECS treatments retrograde amnesia is usually obtained only when a few minutes or at most an hour elapses between training trials and treatments. With drugs (for example, Metrazol and puromycin) retrograde amnesia has been found with training-treatment intervals as long as several days (McGaugh & Petrinovich 1965). As indicated above, the deficits in learning and memory observed following a series of ECS treatments tend to disappear within a few weeks.

Most of the experimental studies of ECS effects on memory have used learning tasks employing aversive motivation—usually punishing shock. Consequently, it has been suggested that the ECS treatments may produce only a selective amnesia for the aversive stimulation. This intriguing hypothesis, however, is not supported by the data. Clear evidence of retrograde amnesia has been obtained in studies using food and water rewards. Further, in studies using shock motivation in discrimination learning tasks, the ECS seems to have its primary effects on the memory of the correct cue rather than on the motivation for responding.

Punishing effects of ECS. The findings of several studies suggest that impairment of performance found following repeated ECS treatments may be due in part to aversive effects of the treatments. For example, Friedman (1953) found that rats' performance of a lever-pressing response for food reward was depressed after the animals were given a series of ECS treatments in the apparatus. Behavior of the animals suggested that they had learned to fear the apparatus. The animals urinated, defecated, trembled, approached the lever hesitantly, and then ran away from it. The depression of responses and emotional behavior was considerably less marked in animals given the ECS treatments in a dissimilar apparatus. No effects were observed, however, in subjects treated while under ether anesthesia. The behavioral effects appeared to be due to the convulsions rather than to the ECS current.

Other studies have shown that rats tend to stop performing responses that are repeatedly followed by ECS treatments. These findings have lead some investigators to suggest that the learned fear rather than amnesia may be the cause of the impaired performance of subjects given ECS shortly after training. Recent evidence indicates that, paradoxically, ECS treatments have both amnesic and aversive effects; the amnesic effects, however, cannot be explained in terms of the aversive effects. In one study rats were given a single foot shock as they stepped from a small platform to the floor of a table; half of the rats were given an ECS within a few seconds. The next day the rats were placed on a platform again; those that had received the foot shock but no ECS tended to remain on the platform; those that had been given the ECS treatment displayed little evidence of remembering the previous foot shock and most of them readily stepped off the platform. In a subsequent study using a similar procedure rats were given an ECS in the apparatus each day for eight days immediately after they had stepped from the platform. Latencies of stepping from the platform increased gradually over the eight days. Other rats were given only a foot shock, and most of these animals learned to stay on the platform within two trials. The performance of rats given foot shocks followed by ECS was similar to that of rats given only ECS treatments. Neither amnesic nor punitive effects were found when the ECS treatments were given one hour after each trial (McGaugh 1965). The results of these studies indicate that the aversive effects of ECS are found with repeated treatments, whereas retrograde amnesia can be obtained with a single ECS treatment. Thus, the amnesic effects of a single ECS cannot be explained in terms of the punishing effects of the treatment.

The paradox remains, however. What is the basis of the punishment if the treatment produces amnesia for events just prior to the ECS stimulation? One possibility is that the subjects learn gradually to associate the apparatus cues with the aftereffects of the convulsion. Patients given a series of ECS treatments tend to develop a fear of the treatments (Gallinek 1956). The patients readily admit that they do not experience any discomfort during the treatment. The fear seems to be based on the severe disorientation experienced while recovering from each treatment. The finding that the aversive effects in rats are eliminated by administering the ECS while the animals are anesthetized lends support to the interpretation that the aversion is based on the aftereffects of the convulsions. A more complete understanding of the basis of the aversive effects of ECS treatments requires additional research [see LEARNING, *articles on* REINFORCEMENT *and* AVOIDANCE LEARNING].

Competing response hypothesis. Lewis and Maher (1965) have proposed still another interpretation of the amnesic effects of ECS. These investigators suggested that through conditioning, the cues in the apparatus elicit behavioral inhibition, that is, a general muscular relaxation and lowered level of activity that competes with and thus interferes with the performance of the previously learned response. Most of the findings of ECS studies, however, are clearly inconsistent with this hypothesis. First, as indicated above, amnesia is found with a single treatment while other behavioral effects, including changes in response latency and freezing and crouching, appear only after a series of ECS treatments. Second, retrograde amnesia is obtained with a single treatment even when the treatment is administered outside of the training apparatus (this, in fact, is the typical procedure). Third, rats given a series of ECS treatments in an apparatus do not appear to be relaxed. They typically urinate, defecate, and tremble. Further, rats will actively avoid a place in an apparatus where they are given repeated ECS treatments (McGaugh 1965). These findings are clearly inconsistent with the conditioned inhibition interpretation of ECS effects.

Contribution of the convulsions. There is clear evidence that the effects of repeated ECS treatments are different from those produced by a single ECS. The effects of repeated ECS treatments seem to be due to the convulsions rather than to the current. Impaired maternal behavior, learning and retention deficits, suppression of a CER, and punishing effects are not found if the convulsions are prevented by the administration of the ECS while the subjects are anesthetized. Recent work indicates, however, that the convulsions are not essential for the production of retrograde amnesia with a single ECS treatment. In unpublished research McGaugh and Alpern obtained clear evidence of retrograde amnesia in animals anesthetized with ether just prior to receiving a single ECS treatment. These findings suggest that the retrograde amnesic effect of ECS is produced by the current rather than the convulsion and are consistent with other recent evidence that retrograde amnesia can be produced by restricted subcortical (and subconvulsive) electrical stimulation of the brain (Williston et al. 1964).

Although many of the effects of ECS remain to be explained, it is clear that ECS has a variety of behavioral effects and that the varied effects are not readily explained in terms of any single hypothesis. In particular, the retrograde amnesic effects of ECS must be considered separately from the diverse and complex effects found when ECS is repeatedly administered. The results of experimental studies of ECS have, as yet, shed little light on the basis of the therapeutic effectiveness of ECS in human patients. The findings have, however, had considerable influence on theories and research concerned with learning and memory. It may be that the therapeutic effectiveness is due to the learning and memory effects; an evaluation of this hypothesis must await further research.

JAMES L. McGAUGH

[*Other relevant material may be found in* DEPRESSIVE DISORDERS; MENTAL DISORDERS, TREATMENT OF, *article on* SOMATIC TREATMENT; NERVOUS SYSTEM, *article on* BRAIN STIMULATION.]

BIBLIOGRAPHY

BEACH, FRANK A.; GOLDSTEIN, A. C.; and JACOBY, G. A. JR. 1955 Effects of Electroconvulsive Shock on Sexual Behavior in Male Rats. *Journal of Comparative and Physiological Psychology* 48:173–179.

CERLETTI, U.; and BINI, L. 1938 L'elettroshock. *Archivio generale di neurologia, psichiatria, e psicoanalisi* 19: 266–268.

CHEVALIER, JACQUES 1965 Permanence of Amnesia After a Single Posttrial Electroconvulsive Seizure. *Journal of Comparative and Physiological Psychology* 59:125–127.

DUNCAN, CARL P. 1949 The Retroactive Effect of Electroshock on Learning. *Journal of Comparative and Physiological Psychology* 42:32–44.

FRIEDMAN, MERTON H. 1953 Electroconvulsive Shock as a Traumatic (Fear Producing) Experience in the Albino Rat. *Journal of Abnormal and Social Psychology* 48:555–562.

GALLINEK, ALFRED 1956 Fear and Anxiety in the Course of Electroshock Therapy. *American Journal of Psychiatry* 113:428–434.

GERARD, R. W. 1955 Biological Roots of Psychiatry. *Science* New Series 122:225–230.

GLICKMAN, STEPHEN E. 1961 Perseverative Neural Processes and the Consolidation of the Memory Trace. *Psychological Bulletin* 58:218–233.

HUNT, HOWARD F. 1965 Electro-convulsive Shock and Learning. New York Academy of Sciences, *Transactions* Series 2 27:923–945.

JANIS, IRVING L.; and ASTRACHAN, MYRTLE 1951 The Effects of Electroconvulsive Treatments on Memory Efficiency. *Journal of Abnormal and Social Psychology* 46:501–511.

LEWIS, DONALD J.; and MAHER, BRENDAN A. 1965 Neural Consolidation and Electroconvulsive Shock. *Psychological Review* 72:225–239.

McGAUGH, JAMES L. 1965 Facilitation and Impairment of Memory Storage Processes. Pages 240–291 in Daniel P. Kimble (editor), *The Anatomy of Memory.* Palo Alto, Calif.: Science and Behavior Press.

McGAUGH, JAMES L.; and PETRINOVICH, LEWIS F. 1965 Effects of Drugs on Learning and Memory. *International Review of Neurobiology* 8:139–196.

MADOW, LEO 1956 Brain Changes in Electroshock Therapy. *American Journal of Psychiatry* 113:337–347.

MAYER-GROSS, W. 1943 Retrograde Amnesia. *Lancet* [1943], no. 2:603–605.

MUNN, NORMAN L. 1950 *Handbook of Psychological Research on the Rat.* Boston: Houghton Mifflin.

RUSSELL, ROGER W. 1948 Contributions of Research on Infrahuman Animals to the Understanding of Electric Convulsive Shock Phenomena. *Journal of Personality* 17:16–28.

THOMPSON, ROBERT; and DEAN, WAID 1955 A Further Study of the Retroactive Effect of ECS. *Journal of Comparative and Physiological Psychology* 48:488–491.

TOMAN, JAMES E. P.; SWINYARD, E. A.; and GOODMAN, L. S. 1946 Properties of Maximal Seizures, and Their Alteration by Anticonvulsant Drugs and Other Agents. *Journal of Neurophysiology* 9:231–239.

ULETT, GEORGE A.; SMITH, K.; and BIDDY, R. 1962 Shock Treatment. *Progress in Neurology and Psychiatry* 17: 559–571.

WILLISTON, JOHN S. et al. 1964 Disruption of Short-term Memory by Caudate Stimulation. *American Psychologist* 19:502 only.

ELECTROENCEPHALOGRAPHY
See under NERVOUS SYSTEM.

ELITES

The concept of elites is used to describe certain fundamental features of organized social life. All societies—simple and complex, agricultural and industrial—need authorities within and spokesmen and agents without who are also symbols of the common life and embodiments of the values that maintain it. Inequalities in performance and reward support this arrangement, and the inequality in the distribution of deference acknowledges the differences in authority, achievement, and reward. Elites are those minorities which are set apart from the rest of society by their pre-eminence in one or more of these various distributions. We shall concentrate here on the elites of industrial society.

In modern societies of the West, there is no single comprehensive elite but rather a complex system of specialized elites linked to the social order and to each other in a variety of ways. Indeed, so numerous and varied are they that they seldom possess enough common features and affinities to avoid marked differences and tensions. Leading artists, business magnates, politicians, screen stars, and scientists are all influential, but in separate spheres and with quite different responsibilities, sources of power, and patterns of selections and reward. This plurality of elites reflects and promotes the pluralism characteristic of modern societies in general.

For virtually every activity and every corresponding sphere of social life, there is an elite: there are elites of soldiers and of artists, as well as of bankers and of gamblers. This is the sense in which Pareto (1902–1903) used the term. There is, however, an important factor that differentiates these various elites, apart from their different skills and talents: some of them have more social weight than others because their activities have greater social significance. It is these elites—variously referred to as the ruling elite, the top influentials, or the power elite—which arouse particular interest, because they are the prime movers and models for the entire society. We shall use the term *strategic elites* to refer to those elites which claim or are assigned responsibilities for and influence over their society as a whole, in contrast with segmental elites, which have major responsibilities in subdomains of the society.

Strategic elites are those which have the largest, most comprehensive scope and impact. The boundaries that separate strategic and segmental elites are not sharply defined because of the gradations of authority and the vagueness of the perceptions that assign positions to individuals. The more highly organized elites are, the easier it is to estimate their boundaries and membership. Thus, the more readily identifiable elites in Western societies are those of business, politics, diplomacy, and the higher civil and armed services. Elites in the arts, in religion, and in moral and intellectual life are more vaguely delimited and hence also more controversial.

The differentiation of elites. Even the earliest-known human societies had leading minorities of elders, priests, or warrior kings, who performed elite social functions. A chief in a primitive society, for example, enacted one complex social role in which were fused several major social functions, expressed through the following activities: organization of productive work; propitiation of, and communication with, supernatural powers; judgment and punishment of lawbreakers; coordination of communal activities; defense of the community from enemy attack; discovery of new resources and of new solutions to the problems of collective survival; and encouragement or inspiration of artistic expression. As societies expand in size and in the diversity of their activities, such activities also expand, and more elaborate, specialized leadership roles emerge. Following are some of the major forms of societal leadership.

(1) *Ruling caste.* One stratum performs the most important social tasks, obtains its personnel through biological reproduction, and is set apart by religion, kinship, language, residence, economic standing, occupational activities, and prestige. Religious ritual is the main force that supports the position of this ruling stratum [see CASTE].

(2) *Aristocracy.* A single stratum monopolizes the exercise of the key social functions. The stratum consists of families bound by blood, wealth, and a special style of life and supported by income from landed property.

(3) *Ruling class.* A single social stratum is associated with various key social functions, and its members are recruited into its various segments on the basis of wealth and property rather than of blood or religion. Historically, ruling classes have held economic rather than political power, but their influence tends to extend to all important segments and activities of society. Although various differentiated and specialized sectors may be distinguished, they are bound together by a common culture and by interaction across segmental boundaries.

(4) *Strategic elites.* No single social stratum exercises all key social functions; instead, these functions and the elites associated with them are specialized and differentiated. The predominant

justification for holding elite status is not blood or wealth as such but, rather, merit and particular skills. Accordingly, these elites are recruited in various ways adapted to their differentiated tasks and are marked by diversity as well as by impermanence.

In general it appears that where the society as a whole is relatively undifferentiated, elites are few in number and comprehensive in their powers; where social differentiation is extensive, elites are many and specialized. The principal social forces underlying the change from societal leadership based on aristocracy or ruling class to that based on strategic elites are population growth, occupational differentiation, moral heterogeneity, and increased bureaucratization. In a large, industrialized mass society, marked by innumerable ethnic, regional, and occupational differences and stratified as to work, wealth, prestige, style of life, and power, leadership cannot be entrusted to a single ruler, be he chief, warrior, or priest, or to a single stratum marked by hereditary exclusiveness and traditionalism. Instead, the elites of this society will tend to be varied, specialized, and differentiated as to skill, style, background, and rewards. In this way the characteristic attributes of the larger society are mirrored in the strategic elites through whom that society tries to realize its main goals and projects. The division of a society into many groups and strata is therefore paralleled by its reunification around a symbolic center, or core, that signifies the common and enduring characteristics of the differentiated whole. The shape of this center is determined by the complexity and variety of the whole. In this way a society, consisting of a multitude of individuals and groups, can act in concert despite its moral, occupational, and technological diversity and can maintain the sense of unity necessary for collective achievements.

The functions of strategic elites. In every differentiated society, there are patterns of beliefs and values, shared means of communication, major social institutions, and leading individuals or groups concerned with the maintenance and development of the society and its culture. These leading elements, by focusing attention and coordinating action, help keep the society in working order, so that it is able to manage recurrent collective crises.

The best efforts at classifying elites are still those of Saint-Simon (1807) and Mannheim (1935), whose approaches, although separated by a century, have much in common. Saint-Simon divided elites into scientists, economic organizers, and cultural–religious leaders. This classification parallels Mannheim's distinction between the organizing and directing elites, which deal with concrete goals and programs, and the more diffuse and informally organized elites, which deal with spiritual and moral problems.

Elites may also be classified according to the four functional problems which every society must resolve: goal attainment, adaptation, integration, and pattern maintenance and tension management. Goal attainment refers to the setting and realization of collective goals; adaptation refers to the use and development of effective means of achieving these goals; integration involves the maintenance of appropriate moral consensus and social cohesion within the system; and pattern maintenance and tension management involve the morale of the system's units—individuals, groups, and organizations.

Accordingly, four *types* of strategic elites, which may include a far larger *number* of elites, may be identified: (1) the current political elite (elites of goal attainment); (2) the economic, military, diplomatic, and scientific elites (elites of adaptation); (3) elites exercising moral authority—priests, philosophers, educators, and first families (elites of integration); and (4) elites that keep the society knit together emotionally and psychologically, consisting of such celebrities as outstanding artists, writers, theater and film stars, and top figures in sports and recreation (pattern-maintenance elites).

Thus, the general functions of elites appear to be similar everywhere: to symbolize the moral unity of a collectivity by emphasizing common purposes and interests; to coordinate and harmonize diversified activities, combat factionalism, and resolve group conflicts; and to protect the collectivity from external danger.

Societies differ, however, in the way they incorporate these functions into living institutions. In some societies, usually at simpler stages of development, one agent assumes responsibility for all four system functions; in others, several specialized agents emerge. In advanced industrial societies the tendency is clearly toward several elites whose functional specialization is accompanied by a growing moral and organizational autonomy among them. At the same time, however, the overriding goals of these elites are, as they have always been, the preservation of the ideals and practices of the societies at whose apex they stand.

Recruitment of strategic elites. Elite replacement, which occurs in all societies, involves both the attraction of suitable candidates and their actual selection. What is considered suitable depends on the structure of the elite groups and on whether these elites assume comprehensive or specialized functional responsibilities. Recruitment mechanisms, however varied in practice, reflect only two fundamental principles: recruitment on the basis of biological (and, implicitly, social) inheritance and recruitment on the basis of personal talents and achievements. Although these two systems are not mutually exclusive, one or the other tends to prevail, depending on the system of social stratification, on the values placed on ascription and achievement, and on the magnitude of demand for elite candidates in relation to the supply. Broadly stated, these principles reflect the general tendencies within a social system toward expansion or toward consolidation. Under conditions of expansion, recruitment on the basis of personal achievement is likely to be the rule; under con- solidation, recruitment based on inheritance of status. Each principle, moreover, has profound social repercussions on social mobility, on the stimulation of individual ambitions and talents, and on levels of discontent among different social strata. Each, furthermore, affects not only the composition of the elites but also their spiritual and moral outlook.

In modern industrial societies recruitment and selection patterns reflect the changes toward differentiation and autonomy among the elites. According to available evidence from a number of such societies, recruitment based on social inheritance is giving way to recruitment based on individual achievement. This is true for England (Cole 1955; Guttsman 1963; Thomas 1959), Germany (Deutsch & Edinger 1959; Stammer 1951; Dreitzel 1962), France (Aron 1950), the United States (Warner & Abegglen 1955; Mills 1956; Matthews 1960; Keller 1963), and the Soviet Union (Fainsod 1953; Crankshaw 1959), among others. Nonetheless, taking the elite groups as a whole, we note the simultaneous operation of several recruitment and selection principles. Some elites stress ancestry; others, educational attainments; still others, long experience and training. Some elites are elected by the public, others are appointed by their predecessors, and still others are born to their positions. The members of some elites have relatively short tenure, while that of others is lifelong. This is a dramatic contrast to other types of societies with relatively small leadership groups that have diffuse and comprehensive functional responsibilities and comprise individuals trained for their status from birth on.

Of course, looking at modern developments at a single point in time, we note that the hold of the past, with its emphasis on property or birth,

is still very strong among some elites. Conspicuous achievements are still often facilitated, if not determined, by high social and economic position, since wealth and high social standing open many doors to aspiring candidates and instill in them great expectations for worldly success. From a long-range perspective, however, it is clear that the link between high social class and strategic elite status has, in many modern societies, become indirect and informal. Ascribed attributes, such as birth, sex, and race, although they play a greater role in some elites than in others, have decreased in importance in comparison with achieved attributes. This is in line with the general modern trend toward technological and scientific specialization, in which individual skill and knowledge count more than does a gentlemanly upbringing in the traditions and standards of illustrious forebears.

Rewards of strategic elites. The process of selection or allocation is facilitated by the system of rewards offered to individuals assuming leadership positions in society. Some rewards are tangible material benefits, such as land, money, cattle, or slaves, and others are intangible, such as social honor and influence. The specific rewards used to attract potential recruits to elite positions depend on the social definition of scarce and desirable values and the distribution of these values.

Rewards play a twofold role in the recruitment of elites: they motivate individuals to assume the responsibilities of elite positions, and they maintain the high value placed on these positions. They thus serve as inducements to individuals, as well as indicators of rank.

Rewards, too, have become specialized in modern industrial societies. Some elites enjoy large earnings; others, popularity or fame; and still others, authority and power. Not all elites are equally wealthy, not all have equal prestige; only some have much more power than others, and none have influence in all spheres. The assumption of elite positions thus also involves the acceptance of specific rewards associated with them. Responsibilities and rewards form parts of a whole and may be discussed jointly. And each is linked to recruitment, for rewards are the spur to the expenditure of effort that the duties of strategic positions demand.

The process of recruiting elites and the manner of rewarding them must not be confused with their purposes and status. For although recruitment and rewards affect the composition and performance of elites, they do not alter their functions. As Mosca (1896) clearly demonstrated, democratically and hereditarily recruited elites differ in many important ways, but they nonetheless function as elites.

The tendency toward a pluralization of elites is likely to conflict with the older tendency toward the monolithic exercise of power and leadership. This is a problem in totalitarian as well as in liberal societies. In totalitarian societies, the problem is how to permit the desired flexibility and variety without corroding social stability. Conversely, in liberal pluralist systems, the problem is how to achieve the necessary degree of social cohesion and moral consensus among partly autonomous, highly specialized, yet functionally interdependent elites. The cohesion and consensus are necessary if the society is to pursue common goals and is to be unified in more than name only.

These recent tendencies and trends are neither absolute nor inevitable. They are clearly manifested today in a wide variety of contexts and reflect the tempo of social change in a technologically expanding world. Should this tempo slow down markedly or cease altogether, the impulses toward rigidity and ascription may well come to the fore once again, albeit within a social structure shaped by centuries of industrialism. Some security and stability will be gained, but at the price of adventure and novelty—a familiar exchange in the annals of history and one bound to be reflected in the character and stamp of the strategic elites.

SUZANNE KELLER

[*See also* BUREAUCRACY; COMMUNITY, *article on* THE STUDY OF COMMUNITY POWER; POLITICAL SOCIOLOGY; *and the biographies of* ARISTOTLE; MANNHEIM; MICHELS; MILLS; MOSCA; PARETO; PLATO; SAINT-SIMON.]

BIBLIOGRAPHY

ARON, RAYMOND 1950 Social Structure and the Ruling Class. *British Journal of Sociology* 1:1–16, 126–143.

BOTTOMORE, THOMAS B. 1964 *Elites and Society.* London: Watts.

COLE, G. D. H. 1955 *Studies in Class Structure.* London: Routledge. → See especially pages 101–146 on "Elites in British Society."

CRANKSHAW, EDWARD 1959 *Khrushchev's Russia.* Harmondsworth (England): Penguin.

DEUTSCH, KARL W.; and EDINGER, LOUIS J. 1959 *Germany Rejoins the Powers: Mass Opinion, Interest Groups, and Elites in Contemporary German Foreign Policy.* Stanford (Calif.) Univ. Press.

DREITZEL, HANS P. 1962 *Elitebegriff und Sozialstruktur: Eine soziologische Begriffsanalyse.* Stuttgart (Germany): Enke.

FAINSOD, MERLE (1953) 1963 *How Russia Is Ruled.* Rev. ed. Russian Research Center Studies No. 11. Cambridge, Mass.: Harvard Univ. Press.

GUTTSMAN, WILHELM L. 1963 *The British Political Élite.* London: MacGibbon & Kee.

HUNTER, FLOYD 1959 *Top Leadership, U.S.A.* Chapel Hill: Univ. of North Carolina Press.

JAEGGI, URS 1960 *Die gesellschaftliche Elite: Eine Studie zum Problem der sozialen Macht.* Bern (Switzerland) and Stuttgart (Germany): Haupt.

KELLER, SUZANNE 1963 *Beyond the Ruling Class: Strategic Elites in Modern Society.* New York: Random House.

LASSWELL, HAROLD D. 1936 *Politics: Who Gets What, When, How?* New York: McGraw-Hill.

MANNHEIM, KARL (1935) 1940 *Man and Society in an Age of Reconstruction: Studies in Modern Social Structure.* New York: Harcourt. → First published as *Mensch und Gesellschaft im Zeitalter des Umbaus.*

MATTHEWS, DONALD R. 1960 *U.S. Senators and Their World.* Chapel Hill: Univ. of North Carolina Press.

MILLS, C. WRIGHT 1956 *The Power Elite.* New York: Oxford Univ. Press.

MOSCA, GAETANO (1896) 1939 *The Ruling Class.* New York: McGraw-Hill. → First published as *Elementi di scienza politica.*

PARETO, VILFREDO 1902–1903 *Les systèmes socialistes.* 2 vols. Paris: Giard.

PARSONS, TALCOTT; BALES, R. F.; and SHILS, E. A. 1953 *Working Papers in the Theory of Action.* Glencoe, Ill.: Free Press.

SAINT-SIMON, CLAUDE HENRI DE (1807) 1859 *Oeuvres choisis.* Volume 1. Brussels: Meenen & Cⁱᵉ.

SERENO, RENZO 1962 *The Rulers.* New York: Praeger; Leiden (Netherlands): Brill.

STAMMER, OTTO 1951 Das Elitenproblem in der Demokratie. *Schmollers Jahrbuch für Gesetzgebung, Verwaltung und Volkswirtschaft* 71, no. 5:1–28.

THOMAS, HUGH (editor) 1959 *The Establishment: A Symposium.* London: Blond.

WARNER, W. LLOYD; and ABEGGLEN, JAMES C. 1955 *Occupational Mobility in American Business and Industry: 1928–1952.* Minneapolis: Univ. of Minnesota Press.

ELLIS, HAVELOCK

Havelock Ellis was born on February 2, 1859, in Croydon, England, the son of an English sea captain, Edward Peppen Ellis. His mother, Susannah Wheatley Ellis, was a highly energetic and vivacious woman. Ellis felt, however, that he owed much to the mediocrity of his father's family, most of whose males, "whatever their occupation, have all the qualities of trustworthy bank clerks"; and their temperate and cheerful acceptance of the world, according to Ellis, helped to modify his own literary–aesthetic temperament and prevent him from adopting a one-sided, excessive, or eccentric view of life.

Ellis went to a boarding school, the Poplars, at Tooting, where he was well grounded in French, German, and Italian. It was here that one of his masters, Angus Mackay, revealed to him the delights of nineteenth-century English literature and helped arouse his vital interest in philosophic and politico–economic questions of the day. At 16 he began an undistinguished career as a teacher and later headmaster in Australia. At the age of 19, however, he came under the influence of and was in effect converted by the writings of the philosopher–surgeon James Hinton. Hinton's book *Life in Nature* made such a profound impression on young Ellis that he decided to undertake the study of medicine in order to do research and writing in the field of sex. Ellis received his medical training at St. Thomas' Hospital in London, and as a medical assistant he attended a number of patients, many of them women in labor. He obtained his M.D. in 1889 but did not practice medicine; instead, he devoted the rest of his life to editing—for many years his main source of income—and writing.

During the 1880s Ellis wrote on literary and social subjects for first-rate English journals and edited the Mermaid Series of Elizabethan dramatists (a series of scholarly reprints), the Contemporary Science Series, and other works. He made a name for himself in the field of belles-lettres with such books as *The Soul of Spain*, 1908, and *Impressions and Comments*, 1914–1924, and in the field of science and its social implications with such writings as *A Study of British Genius* (1904), *The World of Dreams* (1911), and *The Dance of Life* (1923).

Havelock Ellis is known best as a researcher and philosopher in the field of sex and love. Beginning his studies of human sexuality with a fact-packed book, *Man and Woman* (1894), he went on to write his monumental seven-volume *Studies in the Psychology of Sex* (1897–1928). Although originally banned in his native England, the *Studies* became widely read and cited in all other parts of the world and were without question the most influential and precedent-shattering volumes on human sexuality ever written, up to the time of the publication of the Kinsey reports. They were followed by several other important books on sex–love relations from Ellis' pen, including *The Task of Social Hygiene* (1912), *Little Essays of Love and Virtue* (1922–1931), *Psychology of Sex* (1933), *My Life* (1939), and *Sex and Marriage* (1951).

It is difficult to spotlight the most important and influential of Ellis' contributions to the subject of sex. He produced the first notable scientific book on homosexuality; he pioneered in the presentation of full case histories, diaries, and letters on sexual subjects; he was the first important popularizer of the subject of sex–love relations; he was an outstanding crusader against sex censorship; he convincingly showed the interrelationships between human sexuality and the love emotions; he did some original research on masturbation, using himself as a subject; and he presented many original and well-formulated ideas on sexual modesty, the biology and psychology of the sexual impulse, sexual periodicity, erotic symbolism, transvestitism, and several other sexual–amative aspects of life. He and Sigmund Freud did more to make sex a respectable word than any other writers of their day. Although Ellis was largely a devotee of the library rather than a clinician or a laboratory scientist, his careful sex research has inspired much clinical and laboratory investigation.

The remarkable thing about Havelock Ellis' sex writings is that while they are factual, objective, and coolly analytical, they are often pervaded with a thoroughly humane, love-centered (rather than sex-centered), and at times aesthetic–mystic quality that makes his views acutely personal as well as dispassionately scientific. He himself was a mild undinist, suffering from sexual shyness and inadequacy during his youth. Ellis was married for 25 years to a basically lesbian woman, Edith Lees Ellis, with whom he nonetheless had a remarkably intense love relationship. He achieved real sexual fulfillment, however, during the last twenty years of his life in his extramarital relationship with Françoise Delisle (he died in 1939 in Suffolk). It seems clear that Ellis' own sex experiences, as well as his personal naturist–humanist philosophy of life (which he carried to almost religious extremes), combined to enable him to view human sexuality in a uniquely realistic yet essentially poetic way and to make him the best and most effective antipuritan of the late nineteenth and early twentieth centuries.

ALBERT ELLIS

[*For discussion of the subsequent development of Ellis' work, see* SEXUAL BEHAVIOR.]

WORKS BY ELLIS

Works of purely literary interest have not been included.

(1894) 1929 *Man and Woman: A Study of Secondary and Tertiary Sexual Characters.* Rev. & enl. ed. Boston: Houghton Mifflin.

(1897–1928) 1936 *Studies in the Psychology of Sex.* 4 vols. Reissued in a new form. New York: Random House. → First published in seven volumes.

(1904) 1926 *A Study of British Genius.* New rev. & enl. ed. Boston: Houghton Mifflin.

(1911) 1926 *The World of Dreams.* New ed. Boston: Houghton Mifflin.

1912 *The Task of Social Hygiene.* Boston: Houghton Mifflin.

(1922–1931) 1937 *On Life and Sex: Essays of Love and Virtue.* 2 vols. in 1. New York: Garden City Pub. → The two volumes were originally published as *Little Essays of Love and Virtue,* 1922, and *More Essays of Love and Virtue,* 1931.

(1923) 1929 *The Dance of Life.* Boston: Houghton Mifflin.

1933 *Psychology of Sex: A Manual for Students.* New York: Emerson; London: Heinemann.

1939 *My Life: Autobiography.* Boston: Houghton Mifflin.

(1951) 1952 *Sex and Marriage: Eros in Contemporary Life.* Edited by John Gawsworth. New York: Random House; London: Williams & Norgate.

WORKS ABOUT ELLIS

COLLIS, JOHN STEWART 1959 *Havelock Ellis; Artist of Life: A Study of His Life and Work.* New York: Sloane. → Published in England as *An Artist of Life: A Study of the Life and Work of Havelock Ellis.*

DELISLE, FRANÇOISE 1946 *Friendship's Odyssey.* London: Heinemann. → An autobiography, with an account of the author's relations with Havelock Ellis from 1916 to 1939.

PETERSON, HOUSTON 1928 *Havelock Ellis: Philosopher of Love.* Boston: Houghton Mifflin.

ELLWOOD, CHARLES A.

Charles Abram Ellwood (1873–1946), known for his efforts to establish a scientific psychological sociology in the United States, was born near Ogdensburg, New York. He entered Cornell University in 1892, initially intending to study law. However, at Cornell he met Edward A. Ross, later a famous sociologist and then, early in his career, teaching economics. Ross induced Ellwood to abandon his plans for a legal career and to turn to the social sciences. Ellwood specialized in sociology and economics. His studies in statistics and demography were mainly directed by Walter F. Willcox; those in political science and economic research by Jeremiah W. Jenks. His instructors were oriented toward social reform, and by the time he was graduated, in 1896, he had become convinced that the main objective of social science should be to improve public well-being. This became the leitmotiv of his sociological writings throughout his life.

Ellwood went to the University of Chicago to pursue graduate work in sociology, being guided by W. I. Thomas and George H. Mead in social psychology, John Dewey in psychology and pragmatic philosophy, and Albion W. Small in systematic sociology and social-reform doctrine. Small advised him to spend a year at the University of Berlin, which he did in 1897/1898, studying historical and reformist economics, mainly under Gustav Schmoller, and philosophy and ethics, under Friedrich Paulsen.

He returned to Chicago in 1898 to complete his doctorate, producing as his dissertation, in 1899, *Some Prolegomena to Social Psychology.* This was the first presentation of social psychology to be firmly based on the principles of academic psychology. The concepts laid down here were amplified and revised in his later systematic works in this field, chiefly under the influence of Charles H. Cooley. Some fifteen years later, in 1914 and 1915, Ellwood studied in England under Leonard T. Hobhouse and Robert R. Marett, leaders in cultural sociology and anthropology, and was led thereby to place psychological sociology within the larger framework of a cultural interpretation of the social process.

Ellwood traveled extensively in Europe in 1927 and 1928 and in Latin America in 1937, thereby developing a deep interest in international relations, which he interpreted from the standpoint of practical pacifism, holding that world peace is essential to any successful program of social amelioration. Ellwood's travels, especially in Europe, led him to form many contacts with foreign sociologists. He developed considerable prestige among them and served as president of the International Institute of Sociology in 1935/1936.

In 1900 Ellwood accepted the newly established chair in sociology at the University of Missouri, and he remained there for three decades, turning out students who became distinguished sociologists, such as E. B. Reuter, Luther L. Bernard, and Herbert Blumer. In 1930 he was called to Duke University to establish a new department of sociology, and he remained there until his death. Among his better-known students at Duke were Paul E. Root, Guy V. Price, Austin L. Porterfield, and Leonard Broom.

Ellwood's most important work in the field of psychological sociology, and the one for which he will also be best remembered as a sociologist, is his *Sociology in Its Psychological Aspects* (1912), which, as a comprehensive psychological interpretation of human behavior, was far ahead of any other work in the field at this time. This synthesis combined contributions from the evolutionary perspective of Darwin; the biological approach of Lloyd Morgan and E. L. Thorndike; the neurology and comparative psychology of Jacques Loeb, as passed on to Ellwood by W. I. Thomas; Thomas' own views of folk psychology; William James's pragmatic and dynamic instrumentalism, especially his emphasis on the importance of habit; the functional psychology of J. R. Angell and John Dewey; the social psychology of G. H. Mead and

C. H. Cooley; and Lester Ward's contention that psychic factors exert dominant control over human and social behavior. Later on, Ellwood's work was far surpassed by that of specialists like L. L. Bernard. Ellwood's *Introduction to Social Psychology* (1917) and *Psychology of Human Society* (1925a), while broader in perspective than his previous works, were less successful as psychological sociology because he tried to weave into them the cultural concepts that had begun to influence him deeply soon after he finished his masterpiece in 1912.

The cultural approach to the social process dominated Ellwood's work in formal sociology during the two decades before his death. He had received some suggestions here from W. I. Thomas during his student days at Chicago, but the main impetus to this shift in emphasis came from his work with Hobhouse and Marett. The cultural interpretation was set forth in his *Cultural Evolution: A Study of Social Origin and Development* (1927a). Primarily because of his contact with Marett, Ellwood was one of the first Americans to cut loose from the unilateral evolutionism of Herbert Spencer, Lewis Henry Morgan, Charles Letourneau, and their associates, which had dominated the historical sociology of the Ward–Giddings–Howard era. Ellwood had a drastically revised and expanded version of his work ready for publication at the time of his death, and it is a serious loss to sociological literature that it was never published.

Ellwood's comprehensive knowledge of the fields and methods of sociology was best and most constructively exhibited in his *Methods in Sociology: A Critical Study* (1933). Ellwood cautioned in a reasonable manner against what he deemed to be danger signs in the sociological trends of the mid-1930s: the attempt to recast sociology in the terms and techniques of natural science; increasing fragmentation; excessive emphasis on quantitative methods; and the repudiation of value judgments and of proper recognition of the ultimate role of social amelioration.

Ellwood's interest in practical sociology was reflected in his 1910 textbook, the first textbook in sociology that appealed to college students. Over 300,000 copies were marketed before it came to be supplanted in the mid-1930s by more substantial and sophisticated textbooks on social problems. Ellwood produced a number of books (see, for example, his 1915 book) that presented his general solutions to social problems, with increasing emphasis on the responsibility of religion. He had planned to expand his introductory treatment of social ethics as a guide to social reconstruction into

a comprehensive and systematic work on social ethics, but the strong impulses from the deep-seated religious experience of his younger days eventually led him to regard a modernized Christianity as the best stimulus and guide to needed social reform. Hence, he revamped his presentation and published *The Reconstruction of Religion* (1922), which became his most widely read book outside college classrooms. This was supplemented by *Christianity and Social Science* (1923). These books gained for Ellwood a large and powerful following among liberally inclined and social-reformist clergymen. Although Ellwood constantly stressed the fact that social change must be guided by scientific and rational principles, he attributed more significance and potency to religious views and values than any other leading American sociologist of his generation. He especially evaded any attempt to apply rational interpretations to sexual problems.

In seeking to summarize Ellwood's place in the development of American sociology, one may safely say that he will be remembered first and foremost for the fact that he executed far and away the most successful of the early attempts to link up scientific psychology with systematic sociology. Other sociologists, such as Tarde, Le Bon, Durkheim, Sighele, Giddings, Ross, and Cooley, had produced more striking interpretations of social behavior from the psychological point of view, but most of them selected some special psychological factor, such as invention, imitation, impression, suggestion, crowd psychological impulses, creativeness, sympathy, and the like, rather than having a comprehensive psychological approach to the subject. Moreover, most of them, save for Durkheim and Cooley, had little technical knowledge of formal psychology and based their analysis and generalization on common-sense and rule-of-thumb psychological concepts.

Influenced by Comte, Ward, and Hobhouse, Ellwood shared with Small the mantle of Ward in presenting social *telesis*, expertly planned social guidance, as the main role and justification of social science in general and of sociology in particular. Ellwood assigned to modern religion a more important role in social telesis than any other leading sociologist of his time.

In our era, which may have settled down to accepting a pattern of "perpetual war for perpetual peace," Ellwood's views on international relations are especially wholesome and pertinent. While primarily concerned with social amelioration, Ellwood, inspired by his reading of Kant, was convinced that there is no likelihood of establishing a social utopia or of perpetuating democratic society unless world peace can be attained, and he believed that this was possible only in connection with a strong world organization.

HARRY ELMER BARNES

[*For the historical context of Ellwood's work, see* SO-CIAL PROBLEMS *and the biographies of* DEWEY; HOBHOUSE; MARETT; MEAD; MORGAN, C. LLOYD; SCHMOLLER; SMALL; THOMAS; WILLCOX; *for discussion of the subsequent development of Ellwood's ideas, see* EVOLUTION; PACIFISM; *and the biography of* BERNARD.]

WORKS BY ELLWOOD

(1899) 1901 *Some Prolegomena to Social Psychology.* Univ. of Chicago Press.
(1910) 1943 *Sociology: Principles and Problems.* New ed., rev. & enl. New York: American Book. → First published as *Sociology and Modern Social Problems.*
(1912) 1921 *Sociology in Its Psychological Aspects.* 2d ed. New York and London: Appleton.
(1915) 1919 *The Social Problem: A Reconstructive Analysis.* Rev. ed. New York: Macmillan.
1917 *An Introduction to Social Psychology.* New York and London: Appleton.
1922 *The Reconstruction of Religion: A Sociological View.* New York: Macmillan.
1923 *Christianity and Social Science.* New York: Macmillan.
1925a *The Psychology of Human Society.* New York: Appleton.
1925b The Group and Society. *Journal of Applied Sociology* 9:401–403.
1925c The Cultural or Psychological Theory of Society. *Journal of Applied Sociology* 10:10–16.
1925d Intolerance [Presidential Address]. American Sociological Society, *Papers and Proceedings* 19:1–14.
1925e *Unsere Kulturkrise: Ihre Ursache und Heilmittel.* Stuttgart (Germany): Kohlhammer.
1927a *Cultural Evolution: A Study of Social Origin and Development.* New York: Century.
1927b Recent Developments in Sociology. Pages 1–49 in *Recent Developments in the Social Sciences.* Philadelphia: Lippincott.
1927c The Social Development of Morality. *Sociology and Social Research* 12:18–25.
1927d The Development of Sociology in the United States Since 1910. *Sociological Review* (London) 19:25–34.
1927e Primitive Concepts and the Origin of Cultural Patterns. *American Journal of Sociology* 33:1–13.
1927f Social Evolution and Cultural Evolution. *Journal of Applied Sociology* 11:303–314.
1929a *Man's Social Destiny in the Light of Science.* Nashville, Tenn.: Cokesbury.
1929b The Background of Good-will. Pages 29–37 in *Pacificism in the Modern World.* Edited by Devere Allen. Garden City, N.Y.: Doubleday.
1929c Sociology in Europe. *Sociology and Social Research* 13:203–210.
1929d Charles Horton Cooley: 1864–1929. *Sociology and Social Research* 14:3–9.
1930a Social Education in the United States. Pages 253–270 in Paul D. Schilpp (editor), *Higher Education Faces the Future: A Symposium.* New York: Liveright.
1930b Recent American Sociology. *Scientia* 47:335–343.
1930c The Uses and Limitations of Behaviorism in the Social Sciences. Pages 187–211 in William P. King (editor), *Behaviorism: A Battle Line.* Nashville, Tenn.: Cokesbury.
1930d Uses and Limitations of Behaviorism in Sociology. American Sociological Society, *Publications* 24:74–82.
1931a The Implications for Religion of Current Trends in the Social Sciences. Pages 74–83 in Milton C. Towner (editor), *Religion in Higher Education.* Univ. of Chicago Press.
1931b Scientific Method in Sociology. *Social Forces* 10:15–21.
1931c The Philosophy of Protestantism in Its Relation to Industry. *Religious Education* 26:420–426.
1933 *Methods in Sociology: A Critical Study.* Durham, N.C.: Duke Univ. Press.

SUPPLEMENTARY BIBLIOGRAPHY
CRAMBLITT, MARY V. 1944 *A Bibliography of the Writings of Charles Abram Ellwood.* Durham, N.C.: Duke Univ. Press.

ELY, RICHARD T.

Richard Theodore Ely (1854–1943), American economist, probably exerted a greater influence upon American economics during its vital formative period than any other individual. Although Ely's writings were prolific, timely, and vigorous, he made a more lasting impact on his discipline through his achievements as a founder and organizer of scholarly associations, institutes, and research projects.

Ely's career began when the influence of German scholarship upon the United States was at its height. Born in Ripley, New York, of pious Congregationalist stock, he graduated from Columbia College in 1876 and spent the next four years in Germany, primarily at Heidelberg, where he was strongly influenced by Karl Knies, one of the leading historical economists. From 1881 to 1892 Ely taught economics at the then new Johns Hopkins University and produced several books and innumerable articles for scholarly journals, magazines, and newspapers, including pioneer studies of socialism, organized labor, and state taxation. He was an impulsive, outspoken, and contentious man, whose academic friends and foes alike complained of his emotionalism and carelessness. His eager participation in contemporary reform movements brought him both lavish praise and severe condemnation. For example, his sympathetic study *The Labor Movement in America* (1886) provoked his Johns Hopkins colleague Simon Newcomb to declare him unfit to hold a university chair; and in 1894, when he was at the University of Wisconsin, Ely was publicly denounced for preaching socialism and encouraging strikes. In fact, however, he was a moderate reformer, an optimist, and a progressive who favored a mean between individualism and socialism. After a widely publicized "trial," the regents of the university exonerated him and issued a classic declaration in favor of academic freedom.

Ely figured prominently in the controversy between the "old" and "new" schools of American economics during the 1880s. His main contribution to the debate was a polemical monograph entitled *The Past and the Present of Political Economy* (1884), in which he attacked the old school orthodoxy based on Ricardo and Mill and advocated a closer link between economics and ethics and an increased use of a crudely inductive "look and see" method. However, he never rejected Ricardo *in toto* and specifically exempted Ricardian rent doctrine from his general criticism of Ricardian economics. The following year he and several other new school rebels founded the American Economic Association to propagate their ideas and promote the scientific study of economic problems. Ely became the association's first secretary and its most active proponent, but his sentimentalism and reforming zeal at first discouraged more conservative economists from participating. However, even before 1892, when Ely resigned his secretaryship and moved to the Middle West, the organization was turning from social reform to a more neutral scholarly approach. Ely was president of the association from 1900 to 1902. During the 1880s and 1890s, he was prominent in such religious reform organizations as the Christian Social Union and the American Institute for Christian Sociology and was sometimes regarded rather as a preacher than an economist. *An Introduction to Political Economy* (1889a), which Ely prepared for use in connection with his teaching at the Chautauqua Methodist summer school, sold 30,000 copies in a decade, and he subsequently published an even more successful academic textbook, *Outlines of Economics* (1893), which eventually sold more than 350,000 copies.

On his move to Wisconsin in 1892, Ely inaugurated a school of economics, political science, and history. The school, staffed by such scholars as Frederick J. Turner, Edward A. Ross, and John R. Commons, all of whom had been Ely's pupils at Johns Hopkins, became internationally famous because of its collaboration with the Wisconsin government, led by the Progressive politician Robert La Follette. Ely's new school teaching constituted a direct link between German historical economics and twentieth-century institutional economics. His major contribution to this economic tradition was *Property and Contract in Their Re-*

lations to the Distribution of Wealth (1914), and his interest in this field eventually led him to establish in 1920 the Institute for Research in Land Economics and Public Utilities and the associated *Journal of Land and Public Utility Economics* (later called *Land Economics*). Also at Wisconsin Ely helped to launch the American Association for Labor Legislation (of which he became president) and obtained private resources to finance Commons' massive 11-volume *Documentary History of American Industrial Society*, 1910–1911.

Ely was neither an original theorist nor a seminal thinker; he was, however, a stimulating teacher who exerted a profoundly liberating influence on his students, many of whom became distinguished scholars or public figures. Until his death at the age of 89, he remained remarkably active, writing on a variety of topical issues and eventually editing more than a hundred volumes. During his later years he abandoned his earlier defense of the Ricardian rent doctrine and emphasized the parallels between land and capital; one indication of his increasing conservatism is the fact that his Institute for Research was attacked in 1926 as a tool of the public utilities. In a sense, this was a sign of the change in the tone of American economics since Ely's "trial" in 1894.

A. W. COATS

[*For the historical context of Ely's work, see* ECONOMIC THOUGHT, *articles on* THE HISTORICAL SCHOOL *and* THE INSTITUTIONAL SCHOOL; *and the biographies of* KNIES; MILL; RICARDO.]

WORKS BY ELY

1883 *French and German Socialism in Modern Times.* New York: Harper.

1884 *The Past and the Present of Political Economy.* Baltimore: Johns Hopkins Press.

1885 *Recent American Socialism.* Baltimore: Johns Hopkins Press.

1886 *The Labor Movement in America.* New York: Crowell.

(1888) 1890 *Problems of To-day: A Discussion of Protective Tariffs, Taxation and Monopolies.* New ed., rev. & enl. New York: Crowell.

1888 ELY, RICHARD T.; and FINLEY, JOHN H. *Taxation in American States and Cities.* New York: Crowell.

1889a *An Introduction to Political Economy.* New York: Chautauqua.

(1889b) 1895 *Social Aspects of Christianity, and Other Essays.* New York: Crowell.

(1893) 1937 ELY, RICHARD T.; and HESS, RALPH H. *Outlines of Economics.* 6th ed. New York: Macmillan.

1894 *Socialism: An Examination of Its Nature, Its Strength, Its Weakness, With Suggestions for Social Reform.* New York: Crowell.

(1900) 1906 *Monopolies and Trusts.* New York: Grosset & Dunlap.

1903 *Studies in the Evolution of Industrial Society.* New York: Macmillan.

(1914) 1922 *Property and Contract in Their Relations to the Distribution of Wealth.* 2 vols. New York: Macmillan.

1924 ELY, RICHARD T.; and MOREHOUSE, EDWARD W. *Elements of Land Economics.* New York: Macmillan.

1938 *Ground Under Our Feet: An Autobiography.* New York: Macmillan.

(1940) 1964 ELY, RICHARD T.; and WEHRWEIN, GEORGE S. *Land Economics.* Madison: Univ. of Wisconsin Press.

SUPPLEMENTARY BIBLIOGRAPHY

COATS, A. W. 1960 The First Two Decades of the American Economic Association. *American Economic Review* 50:555–574.

DORFMAN, JOSEPH 1946–1959 *The Economic Mind in American Civilization.* 5 vols. New York: Viking. → See especially Volumes 3 and 4.

EVERETT, JOHN R. 1946 *Religion in Economics: A Study of John Bates Clark, Richard T. Ely and Simon N. Patten.* New York: King's Crown Press.

FINE, SIDNEY 1951 Richard T. Ely: Forerunner of Progressivism, 1880–1901. *Mississippi Valley Historical Review* 37:599–624.

NOBLE, DAVID W. 1958 *The Paradox of Progressive Thought.* Minneapolis: Univ. of Minnesota Press. → See especially "Richard T. Ely: The Economist as Christian and Prophet," pages 157–173.

EMIGRATION

See MIGRATION *and* REFUGEES.

EMOTION

It is virtually impossible to give a definition of emotion that all psychologists will accept, although there is fair agreement that such phenomena as fear, anger, joy, disgust, and affection should be classified as emotions. Nearly all theorists relate emotion in some way to motivation, and all assign important roles in emotion to the functioning of the autonomic nervous system. All, except the most rigidly behavioristic, classify emotions as *affective* phenomena.

One difficulty in defining emotion is that emotional phenomena are exceedingly complex and must be observed and analyzed from different points of view. An emotional episode can be observed and studied as a conscious experience from the point of view of the experiencing individual. It can be analyzed from the point of view of a behavioral scientist, a physiologist, a social scientist, or a psychiatrist.

Emotion as a conscious experience

Emotions and other affective processes. The term "emotion" is sometimes used to include the whole gamut of affective experiences, but this usage is too broad. Traditionally, the term applies to a single variety of the affective process. The term "affect," in psychiatry, designates a class of experiences including, among others, emotions, moods, and guilt feelings.

The main varieties of affective processes can be classified as follows: (1) A simple feeling of *pleasantness* is associated with such sensory stimulations as the odor of a perfume, a sweet taste, or a musical harmony, and a feeling of *unpleasantness* with a painful burn, a bitter taste, or a bad odor. (2) Pleasant *organic feelings* are associated with good health, buoyancy, or sexual satisfaction, and unpleasant feelings with hunger, thirst, fatigue, cramps, or headaches. (3) *Interests* are mild feelings of pleasantness associated with games, sports, plays, and other activities. *Aversions* are unpleasant affects associated with the rejection of foods, persons, and activities. (4) *Sentiments* are feelings associated with something valued or held sacred; they are based upon past experience and training. There are patriotic, moral, religious, aesthetic, and intellectual sentiments. The term "sentiment" also refers to a stable disposition to react with feeling to a class of objects or situations. (5) *Emotions* are acute affective disturbances arising from the psychological situation and expressing themselves in conscious experience, behavior, and physiological processes. (6) *Moods* are typically less intense and more chronic than emotions but are similar in affective tone and underlying dynamic mechanisms. (7) *Temperament* designates the affective aspect of personality as a whole. Temperaments are said to be apathetic, moody, phlegmatic, cheerful, vivacious, depressed, sanguine, etc. Although temperaments are stable, they are known to change with age, health, and environmental conditions.

In this classification, it will be noted that emotions and moods are distinguished, but they are closely related. An emotion may calm down into a mood or a mood build up into an emotion. Thus a fright may taper off into a mood of anxiety; anger may subside into a mood of hostility or resentment; laughter may become a mood of cheerfulness; weeping, a mood of sorrow or grief. Depression is a mood characterized by the decrease of an individual's vitality, hopes, aspirations, and self-esteem. The mood may be a mild feeling of tiredness or sadness. In psychopathic states a depression may become a profound apathy with psychotic disregard for reality and with suicidal tendencies. Moods and emotions cannot be sharply distinguished; any line of distinction is arbitrary.

"Emotion" is a substantive term; the adjective "emotional" would better characterize the process. Emotional activities are commonly contrasted with rational, intellectual, or even mental processes, as well as with motivational processes.

Emotions and cognition. Emotions are elicited by the awareness of a situation in which an individual finds himself. Magda B. Arnold (1960) argued that emotional behavior follows the intuitive appraisal of a situation. She defined emotion as a felt tendency to move toward anything intuitively appraised as good (beneficial) or away from anything intuitively appraised as bad (harmful). Thus, the feelings of a male enticing a female are emotional; the feelings of a man running a race for his life are emotional.

The cognitive basis of emotion becomes clear when we consider conditions that elicit emotions in different societies. For example, among the Negroes of the Niger delta, it is a rule that if a woman gives birth to twins, she and the twins are put to death. If the mother is allowed to live, her life is little better than a living death, for she becomes an outcast and must live the rest of her days in the forest. But among the Bankundo of the Congo valley, the mother of twins becomes an object of veneration. She is entitled to wear a special badge and her name is changed to "Mother-of-Twins." Obviously, the type of affective arousal by such an event as the birth of twins depends upon the beliefs, attitudes, and practices of a group.

Emotion and motivation. Although it is generally agreed that emotions bear an important relation to motivation, there is disagreement concerning the exact nature of the relationship. In general, there are two main views: First, it is claimed that emotion is a conscious experience associated with purposive, organized activity. Second, it is claimed that emotion is a disorganized experience due to conflict, frustration, thwarted expectation, tension, or the release of tension.

Emotion as organized experience. The first view of emotion is illustrated in the writings of William McDougall (1908), who defined emotion as the consciously felt aspect of instinctive activity. He paired instincts with emotions: the instinct to flee from danger was paired with the emotion of fear; the instinct of pugnacity was paired with the emotion of anger; parental instinct, with tender emotion; sexual instinct, with lust; self-abasement, with the emotion of subjection; self-assertion, with the emotion of elation. McDougall regarded instinctive behavior as always purposive, goal-directed, and integrated, and emotion as the felt equivalent of instinctive behavior.

Other psychologists, e.g., Carl R. Rogers, have emphasized that "emotion" facilitates goal-directed behavior. Feelings of success, self-confidence, and cheerfulness do, in fact, facilitate performance. A question can be raised, however, whether these feelings are properly classified as emotions.

Emotion as disorganized experience. The second view—that emotion is a disorganized experience dependent upon a dynamic disturbance—is widely held by psychiatrists, clinical psychologists, and others who are concerned with health, counseling, and human adjustment. Thus, the psychologist Édouard Claparède argued that emotion occurs precisely when adaptation is hindered for any reason whatever: the man who can run away does not have the emotion of fear; fear occurs only when flight is impossible. Anger is experienced only when one cannot strike his enemy. The uselessness, or even the harmfulness, of emotion is known to everyone, said Claparède.

There has been considerable controversy over these basic concepts. Robert W. Leeper (1948) regards disorganization as a concept inadequate to define emotion and prefers a "motivational" definition. Paul T. Young (1949), in a reply to Leeper, pointed out that the problem is one of definition and emphasis. Some affective reactions are organized and organizing; some facilitate performance. But the term "emotion" has been used traditionally to define a special class of affective processes characterized by disturbance, upset, and disorganization. Affective disturbances, both pleasant and unpleasant, assuredly exist. If there were no disturbances, the term "emotion" could be dropped from the psychological vocabulary, because existing motivational and affective terms and concepts are fully adequate for the descriptive analysis of organized, adaptive activity.

Emotional behavior

The radical behaviorist does not recognize conscious feelings as such but restricts the science of psychology to the phenomena of behavior and associated bodily processes that can be objectively observed. It was John B. Watson, the founder of American behaviorism, who defined emotion as "an hereditary pattern-reaction involving profound changes of the bodily mechanism as a whole, but particularly of the visceral and glandular systems" (1919, p. 165). He described the stimulating situations and the pattern-reactions for three basic emotions in the infant: fear, rage, and love.

The pattern-reaction theory of emotion has been popular with physiologists and physiological psychologists for obvious reasons: The patterns of reaction appear reflectively under specified conditions of stimulation. They resemble simple reflexes but are more complex. They are well integrated. The emotional patterns can be conditioned and extinguished. The neural mechanisms that regulate many of the emotional patterns have been described and localized within subcortical regions of the brain.

Among the patterns of reaction that have been described and analyzed are the following: There is the rage pattern in cats, dogs, and other animals, as well as a similar pattern called "sham rage" in decorticate animals. There are patterns of escape, including impulses to run or fly or dart away when startled and patterns of defense that differ from species to species. There are male and female patterns of sexual response, the startle pattern in man and other animals, and the disgust pattern. There are internal patterns of visceral and glandular response that differ in hostility and fear. There are human patterns of facial expression—smiling, laughing, crying, and weeping. There is no doubt about the objective existence and functional importance of these patterns of reaction.

Critique of the pattern-reaction theory.   Despite the obvious advantages of a pattern-reaction theory of emotion, there are certain difficulties. The theory does not distinguish between emotional and nonemotional patterns. Coughing, sneezing, hiccoughing, sucking, swallowing, and blinking are well-integrated reflexive patterns that are frequently accompanied by changes regulated through the autonomic nervous system. No one regards these reflexes as emotions. Again, the startle pattern, described in detail by Carney Landis and William A. Hunt, was regarded by them as a general skeletal reflex rather than as a true emotional pattern, because startle is completed in the fraction of a second before visceral responses can get under way.

Further, it is difficult to specify the grouping of elements that constitute an emotional pattern. For example, Watson claimed that "fear" is an innate emotional pattern in infants; but his description of "fear" included patterns known to be more elementary: crying, catching the breath, the startle response, possibly the Moro reflex, and an impulse to crawl away. Watson's "fear" is thus a complex of more elementary patterns.

The pattern-reaction concept disregards the acute affective disorganization that is characteristic of emotion. And, further, the observed patterns do not correspond to the "emotions" of everyday life. What patterns, for example, correspond to mother love, pride, embarrassment? It would be wiser, we believe, to describe the patterns of reaction that occur *in* or *during* emotion for their own sake than to define emotion as a pattern of reaction.

The expressions of emotion.   The objective expressions of emotion have been observed and studied since the earliest times. Charles Darwin (1872) made detailed observations on emotional behavior in man and other animals. After studying the data, he formulated three principles of emotional expression.

First, Darwin believed that many expressions of emotion are reduced segments of biologically serviceable acts or acts that once were serviceable in an earlier stage of evolution. Thus an angry man raises the lips involuntarily and shows the canine teeth although he does not intend to bite. The complete expression would be biting and hostile attack.

When a dog is about to attack, it approaches its enemy with a stiff gait and tail erect; the head is slightly raised; the hair, especially along the neck and back, bristles; the ears are pricked up and directed forward; the eyes are wide open and have a fixed stare; the animal shows its teeth and growls. No one is likely to misinterpret the significance of this emotional behavior. Even a small part of the total reaction, e.g., showing the teeth and growling, expresses hostility.

Second, Darwin pointed out that some emotional expressions are directly antithetical to biologically serviceable behavior. To illustrate, suppose the hostile dog suddenly perceives that a man it is approaching is not an enemy but its beloved master. The bearing of the animal instantly changes. Instead of walking upright with a stiff gait, the body sinks downward or even crouches; the animal's movements are flexuous and supple; its tail, instead of being stiff and upright, is lowered and wagging from side to side; the hair is smooth; the ears are depressed and relaxed backwards; its lips hang loosely, and it salivates; the eyelids become elongated, and the eyes no longer appear round and staring. The behavior of the friendly dog is directly antithetical to that of the hostile animal.

Third, Darwin recognized that the above two principles do not explain all expressions of emotion. He formulated a third principle: Some emotional expressions can be explained only in terms of the constitution of the nervous system and associated bodily mechanisms. For example, the writhing of an animal during the birth of young can be explained only in terms of bodily constitution. The excessive activity is neither biologically serviceable nor antithetical to a serviceable act.

Emotional and social expressions.   In an experiment on the facial expressions of emotion, Carney Landis (1924) drew an important distinction between *emotional* and *social* expressions. The emotional expressions, he said, are involuntary and reflexive. They involve changes in the skeletal musculature, glands, and smooth muscles. They are regulated by neural mechanisms that include processes within the autonomic nervous system. The social expressions are voluntary and learned.

Otto Klineberg (1938) studied expressive behavior as recorded in the Chinese novel and drama. He found that many phrases in the Chinese language describe involuntary changes that anyone will recognize as emotional. For example, fear is indicated by such expressions as "every one of his hairs stood on end, and the pimples came out on the skin all over his body" and "they were so frightened that their waters and wastes burst out of them." The meaning of other expressions, however, would not be recognized by persons in Western society. For example, the phrase "they stretched out their tongues" indicates surprise; "he made his two eyes round and stared at him" means anger; "he scratched his ears and cheeks" (in the novel *Dream of the Red Chamber*) means happiness; "he clapped his hands" is likely to mean worry or disappointment.

These conventional expressions are culture-bound. They serve to communicate feelings within a group as spoken words convey meanings. We have all learned, of course, to express joy, sorrow, concern, amusement, and other feelings sympathetically, as actors do on the stage. The voluntary and conventional expressions are not true reflexive patterns of emotion. [*See* EXPRESSIVE BEHAVIOR.]

The physiology of emotion

Walter B. Cannon (1915) supplemented and extended the Darwinian doctrine of biological utility by carrying the principle of adaptation to the interior of the body. In a series of experiments, he showed how the bodily changes in pain, fear, and rage are serviceable and adaptive in a struggle for existence. During a biological crisis, widespread organic changes mobilize the energy reserves of the body for a prolonged fight or flight.

During an emergency there is a diffuse discharge across the sympathetic nervous network and increased secretion of the adrenal glands. This neural and glandular discharge produces widespread bodily changes: (1) cessation of processes in the alimentary canal, thus freeing the energy supply for muscles and brain; (2) shifting of blood from abdominal organs to the organs immediately essential to muscular exertion; (3) increased vigor of contraction of the heart; (4) discharge of extra blood corpuscles from the spleen, thus facilitating the process of oxygenation; (5) dilation of the bronchioles, along with deeper respiration; (6)

quick abolition of the effects of muscular fatigue through adrenal discharge; and (7) mobilization of sugar in the circulation. All of these changes, Cannon claimed, are directly serviceable in making the organism more effective in the violent display of energy that fear, rage, or pain may involve.

Critique of the emergency theory. Physiological studies (for example, Arnold 1960) have pointed to weaknesses in Cannon's emergency theory of emotion. Critics agree on the following points: (1) Emotional processes are a function of the entire autonomic nervous system, not of the sympathetic division alone. The sympathetic and parasympathetic divisions of the autonomic system function simultaneously and reciprocally in fear, rage, "sham rage," pain, general excitement, and sexual and other emotions, producing patterns of visceral response that differ from one emotional state to another. (2) Whereas Cannon thought that the secretion of epinephrine was the main hormone in the defensive fight–flight reactions, it is now known that there are two chemical factors —norepinephrine and epinephrine—involved in this reaction. These two hormones are secreted independently and have different physiological effects: norepinephrine appears to be concerned with hostile states, and epinephrine with fear and anxiety. Hormones from the pancreas and pituitary body also are involved in emotional reactions. (3) The autonomic nervous system is on continuous duty 24 hours a day, and the bodily changes produced during a biological crisis correspond to departures from normal conditions. The autonomic system has two main functions: first, it prepares the body to respond defensively to danger; second, it plays its major role in maintaining homeostasis. (4) Cannon emphasized the utility of bodily changes in emotion, but many changes are disruptive, disturbing, and disintegrating rather than an aid in adaptive behavior.

Cannon's work should be brought into relation with that of Hans Selye (1956) upon the general adaptation syndrome and the adjustments of the organism to stress [*see* STRESS].

The neural basis of emotion. The phylogenetically older structures, collectively, and the limbic system and hypothalamus, in particular, are actively involved in pleasurable and painful experiences, in emotional behavior associated with fight, flight, food, and sex. We are just beginning to understand the central dynamics of the emotional reactions.

The hypothalamus is of critical importance in the regulation of emotional behavior. It has long been recognized as a center of endocrine and autonomic-nervous-system control. It forms a critical juncture in the circular feedback system that regulates neural impulses concerned with emotions and neuroendocrine activity. The hypothalamus influences and is influenced by the reticular activating system, the limbic system, secretions of the pituitary, and other endocrine glands, as well as by the neocortex.

The explorations of the reticular activating system by Magoun and associates (Magoun 1958) have altered neurophysiological thinking about motivation and emotion. It is now known that every sensory stimulation has two kinds of effects upon the cerebral cortex: (1) impulses discharged through thalamic nuclei are relayed to the cortex, where they provide sensory information; (2) sensory stimulation also sends impulses through collaterals into the reticular activating system. These impulses are conducted over multisynaptic pathways to the cortex, where they have a non-specific activating influence. The degree of activation varies with intensity of stimulation. In emotional excitement there is a high level of cortical activation, as Donald B. Lindsley has shown in studies with the electroencephalograph.

The limbic system has been called the "visceral brain" by McLean (1949), who considers that it mediates visceral needs rather than ideational processes; it is concerned with feelings rather than with symbolic activities. The frontotemporal limbic activities may be concerned with self-preservative behavior; the more posterior regions, with sexual behavior and sexual hormones.

The limbic system is involved in positive and negative affective arousals. James Olds (1955) implanted bipolar needle electrodes within the limbic system of rats' brains and demonstrated that electrical stimulation of subcortical points could be either rewarding or punishing. When stimulated within the septal area, the rats acted as if they were pleased; but when stimulated within the *medial lemniscus*, the animals acted as if the stimulation had hurt them and had been unpleasant. Clearly the neural locus of affective arousals, physiological drives, and emotions is being penetrated. [See NERVOUS SYSTEM, *article on* BRAIN STIMULATION.]

The dynamics of emotion

A dispositional approach. According to David Rapaport (1942), a good deal of confusion concerning the definition of emotion has been the result of a failure of investigators to distinguish between the phenomena of emotion and the underlying dynamic mechanisms. The phenomena of emotion are complex but can be analyzed from several points of view. The phenomena include (1) the consciously experienced affect, (2) the emotional behavior, and (3) the physiological processes occurring during emotional upheavals. The dynamic mechanisms, in contrast, are always inferred or assumed.

Psychologists assume persistent dispositions that were originally formed by emotional experiences. For example, an intense fright may produce a phobia for high places, enclosures, blood, or some other thing. The grounds of a phobia may seem unreasonable to the subject, but nevertheless the fear persists. Children normally develop fears of thunder, darkness, death, insects, ghosts, and other things on the basis of some fright. The emotion clearly leaves a disposition to fear [see PHOBIAS].

Attitudes and motives are formed on the basis of emotional experiences. The story is told that when Abraham Lincoln saw slaves being sold on the New Orleans market, he was so disturbed emotionally that he resolved: "If ever I have the chance, I will hit that thing hard." The emotional disturbance left upon him an indelible imprint that later may have influenced his decisions and actions.

A dispositional approach to the study of emotion implies a *temporal* dimension. Whenever we speak of emotional development, emotional maturity, or emotional stability, we imply a persisting individual with persisting dispositions.

Dispositions include memory traces, attitudes, beliefs, specific motives, expectancies, hopes, and desires, as well as conflicts and unsolved problems. All of these are residues from the past. Among the dynamic conditions that produce emotional upsets, moods of anxiety, depression, and the like are conflicts, frustrations, thwarted expectations, successes, failures, tensions and the release of tensions, painful stimulations, and other factors of stress. A dispositional approach to the complex phenomena of emotion can bring unity out of the diverse data.

Emotion and mental health. In an address to the American Neurological Association in New York City in 1876, George M. Beard maintained that disease might appear and disappear without the influence of any other agent than some form of emotion. Fear, terror, anxiety, grief, anger, wonder, and a definite expectation he regarded as mental conditions likely to produce disease [see Lewis 1959, p. 8]. Beard argued that certain emotional states could neutralize therapeutics and increase the effects of drugs. At the time, his ideas were new and startling; later the ideas were recognized in a movement known as psychosomatic medicine.

Today, it is widely accepted that persistent emotional disturbances constitute an important factor in certain disorders, such as peptic ulcer, essential hypertension, rheumatoid arthritis, ulcerative colitis, bronchial asthma, hyperthyroidism, and neurodermatitis. The health of a patient is strongly influenced by stressful conditions of living that produce emotional traumata, such as financial failure, bereavement, insult, injury, unrequited love, threatened divorce, and loss of self-esteem. These several factors are well recognized by clinical psychologists and psychiatrists.

Emotion plays an important role in psychotherapy. The psychiatric examination is concerned with the whole personality but places special emphasis upon emotions as related to thought processes. During an interview the psychiatrist observes emotional reactions as the patient talks and seeks to elicit thoughts that accompany the emotional reactions. A dominant emotion is associated with something important to the patient, something that affects him deeply. Why it is important can be learned only by getting the patient to tell his thoughts.

Psychoanalysts have long recognized the importance of affects, especially repressed emotional experiences, in the etiology and treatment of neuroses. Some repressed hostility or an unsolved emotional conflict, possibly unknown to the patient, may underlie neurotic symptoms. Free association, aided recall, and the interpretation of dreams, along with free emotional expression, may reveal unconscious motivations and alleviate the mental disorder.

According to Robert W. White (1948), psychotherapy is not an intellectual process. It has wrongly been said that the way to bring about readjustment is to help an individual understand his problems. Awareness of motivations and frustrations on the cognitive level is helpful but not enough to effect a cure. Psychotherapy operates in the sphere of emotion. The main aim of psychotherapy is to provide corrective emotional experience by relaxing the subject's defenses and permitting him to reappraise his anxieties. In the major methods of psychotherapy, the subject is encouraged to *feel*, to express his emotions.

It should be pointed out that emotional upsets are only one manifestation of neurosis. There are other aspects, such as dissociation, delusion, amnesia, tics, and functional paralyses. Emotional upsets appear also in psychoses and disorders that have a definite organic basis as well as in normal everyday living.

In the light of the above discussion, an emotion may be defined as an acute affective disturbance originating within the psychological situation and expressing itself in conscious experience (affect), emotional behavior, and physiological processes. The dynamic determinants of emotion include conflict, frustration, thwarted (or satisfied) expectation, tension or its release, painful stimulation, threat, insult, and similar conditions of stress and relief. Clinically viewed, an emotion is a persisting dynamic disturbance within the individual that may influence his health, happiness, and well-being.

PAUL THOMAS YOUNG

[*Other relevant material may be found in* AFFECTION; AGGRESSION; CONFLICT; DRIVES; MOTIVATION; SYMPATHY AND EMPATHY.]

BIBLIOGRAPHY

ARNOLD, MAGDA B. 1960 *Emotion and Personality.* 2 vols. New York: Columbia Univ. Press. → Volume 1: *Psychological Aspects.* Volume 2: *Neurological and Physiological Aspects.*

CANNON, WALTER B. (1915) 1953 *Bodily Changes in Pain, Hunger, Fear and Rage: An Account of Recent Researches Into the Function of Emotional Excitement.* 2d ed. Boston: Branford.

DARWIN, CHARLES (1872) 1965 *The Expression of the Emotions in Man and Animals.* Edited by Francis Darwin. Univ. of Chicago Press.

ENGLISH, HORACE B.; and ENGLISH, AVA C. (1958) 1962 *A Comprehensive Dictionary of Psychological and Psychoanalytical Terms: A Guide to Usage.* New York: McKay.

KLINEBERG, OTTO 1938 Emotional Expression in Chinese Literature. *Journal of Abnormal and Social Psychology* 38:517–520.

LANDIS, CARNEY 1924 Studies of Emotional Reactions. 2: General Behavior and Facial Expression. *Journal of Comparative Psychology* 4:447–501.

LEEPER, ROBERT W. 1948 A Motivational Theory of Emotion to Replace "Emotion as Disorganized Response." *Psychological Review* 55:5–21.

LEWIS, NOLAN D. C. 1959 American Psychiatry From Its Beginnings to World War II. Volume 1, pages 3–17 in *American Handbook of Psychiatry.* Edited by Silvano Arieti. New York: Basic Books.

MCDOUGALL, WILLIAM (1908) 1950 The Principal Instincts and the Primary Emotions of Man. Chapter 3 in William McDougall, *An Introduction to Social Psychology.* London: Methuen. → A paperback edition was published in 1960 by Barnes and Noble.

MCLEAN, PAUL D. 1949 Psychosomatic Disease and the "Visceral Brain": Recent Developments Bearing on the Papez Theory of Emotion. *Psychosomatic Medicine* 11:338–353.

MAGOUN, HORACE W. (1958) 1963 *The Waking Brain.* 2d ed. Springfield, Ill.: Thomas.

OLDS, JAMES 1955 Physiological Mechanisms of Reward. Volume 3, pages 73–139 in Marshall R. Jones (editor), *Nebraska Symposium on Motivation.* Lincoln: Univ. of Nebraska Press.

RAPAPORT, DAVID (1942) 1950 *Emotions and Memory.* 2d ed. New York: International Universities Press.

SELYE, HANS 1956 *The Stress of Life.* New York: McGraw-Hill.

WATSON, JOHN B. 1919 A Schematic Outline of the Emotions. *Psychological Review* 26:165–196.

WHITE, ROBERT W. (1948) 1956 *The Abnormal Personality: A Textbook.* 2d ed. New York: Ronald.

YOUNG, PAUL T. 1949 Emotion as Disorganized Response: A Reply to Professor Leeper. *Psychological Review* 56:184–191.

YOUNG, PAUL T. 1961 *Motivation and Emotions: A Survey of the Determinants of Human and Animal Activity.* New York: Wiley.

EMPATHY

See SYMPATHY AND EMPATHY. *Also relevant is* MODERNIZATION, *article on* SOCIAL ASPECTS.

EMPIRES

The term "empire" has normally been used to designate a political system encompassing wide, relatively highly centralized territories, in which the center, as embodied both in the person of the emperor and in the central political institutions, constituted an autonomous entity. Further, although empires have usually been based on traditional legitimation, they have often embraced some wider, potentially universal political and cultural orientation that went beyond that of any of their component parts. Such "imperial" designation has been attached to a great variety of sociopolitical systems, from relatively ephemeral frameworks like that of the Mongol empires of Genghis Khan and Kublai Khan to the various more modern "colonial" empires, which did not usually evince territorial continuity.

However, the fullest and most succinct development of the major characteristics of empires as distinct political systems can be found in what may be called the "historical bureaucratic empires." In order to explain the meaning of this term, a number of further distinctions need to be made (for a fuller treatment, see Eisenstadt 1963).

Types of imperial systems. The connotation of the term "imperial," as it evolved within political and social consciousness in the history of mankind, evinced throughout its development some common characteristics. At the same time, it also changed greatly between historical, premodern, and modern times. Its basic connotation, as manifest in the Latin *imperium*, is the existence of relatively concentrated authority and rule, focused in a relatively strong center and diffusing its authority over broad territorial contours. In premodern times this designation commonly referred to an authority that extended over territorially contiguous units so that the latter attained some symbols of common political identity. This authority and the concomitant political identity certainly did not connote national sovereignty, but rather the existence of a center of authority that was accepted and hallowed beyond the confines of narrow territorial, kinship, or city limits.

The authority that was enacted in these systems consisted of a special mixture of Weber's three types: the charismatic, the traditional, and the legal–rational. Such authority was usually rooted in a charismatic personality or group whose major orientations were traditional in the sense of upholding a "given" order hallowed by tradition, but not, as we shall see, in the sense of accepting the traditional organizational confines of this order. At the same time, it often contained important elements of a more legal–rational type of authority.

The connotation of imperial has greatly changed in modern times, when it has come to denote rather a type of political system through which one political community or nation has extended its rule over other political units, mostly territorially noncontiguous ones, without fully incorporating them into a framework of common political symbols and identity.

In this article we shall deal only with the first type of imperial system, focusing our analysis on those historical systems within which the basic characteristics of this type of system became most fully developed and institutionalized. Thus we shall not deal with those "conquest" empires, such as those of the Mongols, where the conquering rulers attempted to establish such authority but in which, for a variety of reasons, no such common symbols of identity became accepted and in which the conquerors retained their separate ethnic and political identities. Nor shall we deal with the colonial empires of the nineteenth and twentieth centuries, although this does not preclude examination of their origins.

Formation of bureaucratic empires

Examples of centralized bureaucratic empires are to be found throughout history; the principal ones, which comprise the major historical societies, are as follows:

(*a*) The ancient empires, especially the Egyptian, Babylonian, and, possibly, the Inca and Aztec.

(*b*) The Chinese Empire from the Han period to the Ch'ing.

(*c*) The various Iranian empires, especially the Sassanid and, to a smaller extent, the Parthian and Achaemenid.

(*d*) The Roman Empire and the various Hellenistic empires.

(*e*) The Byzantine Empire.

(*f*) Several ancient Hindu states (especially the Maurya and Gupta) and the Mogul empires.

(g) The Arab Caliphate (especially from the reign of the Abbassides and Fatimides), the Arab Muslim states in the Mediterranean and Iran, and the Ottoman Empire.

(h) European states during the age of absolutism, and to some extent their initial colonial empires, especially insofar as they were built with the idea of the direct extension of the patrimony and its central authority and not as merchant colonies or purely colonial settlements of small groups. Of these, the Spanish American Empire is probably the nearest to the ideal type of a historical bureaucratic empire.

The majority of these empires developed from one of the following types of political systems: (a) from *patrimonial empires* such as the Egyptian and the Sassanid empires; (b) from *dualistic nomad–sedentary empires*, necessarily sharing many characteristics in common with the patrimonial type; (c) from *feudal systems*, as did the European absolutist states; and (d) from *city-states*, as did the Roman and Hellenistic empires.

Despite the great variety of historical and cultural settings, some common features in the first stages of the establishment of such polities may be found. The initiative for the establishment of these polities came, in all cases, from the rulers—emperors, kings, or some members of a patrician ruling elite (like the more active and dynamic element of the patrician ruling elite in republican Rome). In most cases these rulers either came from established patrician, patrimonial, tribal, or feudal families, or they were usurpers, coming from lower-class families, who attempted to establish new dynasties or to conquer new territories. In some cases they were conquerors who attempted to establish their rule over various territories.

In most cases such rulers arose in periods of unrest, turmoil, acute strife, or dismemberment of the existing political system. Usually their aim was the re-establishment of peace and order. They did not, however, attempt to restore the old order in its entirety, although for propagandist and opportunistic reasons they sometimes upheld such restoration as a political ideology or slogan. They always had some vision of the distinctly political goals of a unified polity. They aimed to establish a more centralized, unified polity in which they could monopolize political decision making and the setting of political goals, without being bound by various traditional aristocratic, tribal, or patrician groups. Even when they were conquerors, as in the case of the Roman, Islamic, and Spanish American empires, they also had some such vision and at-

tempted to transmit it to at least part of the conquered population.

Of crucial importance in shaping the activities of these rulers was the geopolitical situation of the polity that they tried to organize—as, for instance, the specific geopolitical situation of Byzantium at the crossroads of Europe and Asia or the vast hydraulic arrangement of China and its special relation with the steppe frontiers. These geopolitical factors indicated, in a sense, the nature of the specific international system to which these empires had to respond, as well as the range of problems to which the rulers were willing and able to address themselves.

The aims of the rulers were very often oriented against, and encountered the opposition of, various social and political groups. However great the turmoil, unrest, and internal strife may have been, there were always some groups that either benefited from this state of affairs—or hoped to do so—or aimed to re-establish the old order, in which they held positions of power and influence. These hostile elements, usually consisting of some aristocratic groups or some of the more traditional urban and cultural elites, usually felt themselves menaced by the new aims and activities of the rulers. They felt that their position was threatened by the trend toward political centralization, and they were therefore unwilling to help in the implementation of this trend. Accordingly, they often attempted to deny resources and support to the rulers, plotting and working against them either in open political warfare or by infiltration and intrigue.

The rulers had to find allies, whether passive or active, in order to be able to implement their aims in the face of these various aristocratic forces. Thus they had to forge various instruments of power and policy with which to mobilize the various resources needed by them—whether economic resources, manpower, or political support. Naturally, the rulers tried to find such allies among the groups and strata whose interests were opposed to those of the more traditional and aristocratic elements and who thus could benefit by the weakening of the latter and by the establishment of a more unified polity. The rulers' allies were therefore of two principal kinds: the more active (mostly urban) economic, cultural, and professional groups who, whether by origin or by their social interests and orientations, were opposed to the aristocratic–traditional groups; and the wider and politically and socially more passive strata, especially the peasants and (to a smaller extent) the urban lower classes.

It was from these various groups and strata that

the rulers hoped to mobilize the various resources they needed. But in order to do this they also had to forge some instruments of political and administrative action on which they could rely and through which they could provide various services to their potential allies. Most rulers were able to form an entourage by recruiting from established administrative and political bodies; however, even when such organs of administration were available, they had to be adapted to the rulers' particular purpose. Insofar as the existing personnel were related to the aristocratic forces, the rulers had in many cases to find replacements. Nor was this enough; loyalty to the ruler had to be secured against bids from opposing forces. Moreover, the rulers had to make sure that these administrative bodies would be effectively organized for their tasks. To this end, the rulers attempted to concentrate the nominations to these positions in their own hands. They tried, as far as possible, to appoint persons who were loyal and who had the necessary administrative qualifications. The rulers also attempted to control the administrative budget, making sure that it was adequate for official salaries as well as other running expenses. This enabled them to lay emphasis on the dependent position of the officials: they were to be "servants," either of the individual ruler or of the polity that he wanted to establish. Accordingly, representation by officials of group or class interests was henceforth to be eliminated.

Thus, in general, the rulers attempted to make these administrative bodies, as far as possible, independent of the more traditional and aristocratic strata and groups and to give them some power and prestige vis-à-vis these strata. Here the rulers had, necessarily, to allow these bodies some measure of autonomy and independence and had to enable them to perform some services to the population. True, the rulers very often wanted to use these administrative bodies only, or mainly, for exploitative purposes. But if the rulers wanted to perpetuate their rule, they had to allow these services to take into account at least some of the needs of some of the social groups, if only to provide them with peace, security, and certain minimal services.

Thus, the development of an imperial system (in the sense of a historical bureaucratic empire) was dependent on two conditions. One condition was the existence, within the preceding social structure, of a relatively high level of societal differentiation, which limited the place of basic ascriptive units—such as family, kinship, or traditional status groups—in the social division of labor and created many forces cutting across them. On the one hand, this differentiation created problems of integration that called for new solutions, while on the other hand it provided the resources needed for new organizations that could attempt to deal with some of these problems. The second condition was the development of a new type of political leader and elite with wider aims and perceptions of political authority and the ability to serve as a focus of the new imperial authority and symbols and to articulate new, more differentiated, and broader political goals.

The existence of only one of these conditions was not sufficient for the institutionalization of an imperial system. Thus, for instance, in the city-states of Greece, as compared with republican Rome (within which there was a similar level of differentiation), there did not develop such an internally new leadership. Contrariwise, in the Carolingian and Mongol states (or empires), while there did develop rulers with such new styles of leadership, there did not exist an appropriate level of differentiation; thus the imperial system could not become institutionalized, and these polities remained at the level of loosely integrated "conquest" empires, in which the different regions or groups (conquerors and conquered) were not integrated into a polity bound by common symbols of identity.

Although the general existence of a certain level of differentiation was a necessary precondition of the institutionalization of the political systems of such empires, their concrete structures could range from that of the city-state or feudal system to that of the patrimonial empire. Similarly, the social origins, composition, and internal cohesion of the new ruling groups could vary greatly, and the combination of these variations could greatly influence the concrete contours of the developing imperial systems. This tendency was manifest, first, in the tendency toward political centralization; second, in the development by the rulers of autonomous political goals; and third, in the relatively high extent of organizational autonomy of executive and administrative activities.

But the extent of differentiation of political activities, organization, and goals was, in these political systems, still limited by several important factors. First, the legitimation of the rulers was, in these regimes, usually couched in basically traditional–religious terms, even if the rulers tended to stress their own ultimate monopoly of such traditional values and tried to deny that other (traditional) groups could also share in this monopoly. Second, the basic political role of the subject was not fully distinguished from other basic societal roles, such as, for instance, membership in local communities; it was often embedded in such groups, and the citizen or subject did not exercise any direct political rights through a system of voting or franchise. Third, many traditional ascriptive units, such as aristocratic lineages or territorial communities, still performed many crucial political functions and continued to serve as units of political representation. As a consequence, the scope of political activity and participation was far narrower than in most modern and contemporary political systems.

The existence of both traditional and differentiated political orientations, activities, and organizations created within these empires a complex interrelation between the political institutions and other parts of the social structure. The rulers were in need of both traditional and more complex, differentiated political support and were dependent on both. The rulers' traditional dependence on other parts of the social structure was manifest in their need to uphold their traditional legitimation and the traditional, unconditional political attitudes and identifications of many groups. On the other hand, however, the rulers' tendency to political independence and autonomy made them dependent on types of resources that were not available through various traditional ascriptive commitments and relations. In order to implement their various political goals as they pleased, the rulers were in need of more flexible support and resources, which would not be embedded in traditional ascriptive groups or committed for more or less fixed goals (Eisenstadt 1963, chapter 6; Altheim 1955).

Among these flexible resources, the most important were economic and political ones. In the economic field, the rulers needed manpower and goods that could be available not through the fixed commitments of ascriptive kinship and status groups but that could be allocated directly. Among such economic resources, the most important were manpower (military and administrative) for services and for relatively free and flexible occupational choices and various goods and commodities for direct spending or for payment of services.

In principle, such resources could have been the same as those used *within* the various ascriptive groups and in their fixed interrelations. But the very emphasis on their flexibility entailed the possibility of their greater mobility and hence of their necessary translatability into media of exchange such as money, credits, and their equivalents. Once some such media of exchange were established, it was highly necessary to maintain markets and organizational frameworks within which they could flow continuously. Similarly, it was very important to maintain conditions and frameworks in which possibilities of relatively free occupational choices and avenues of mobility could be realized.

A similar situation developed in the field of political support and organization. The rulers were in need of commitments and loyalties that could be made available without the restrictions of such ascriptive groups, and this necessarily entailed the organization of new types of political organizations and leadership that could mobilize such support. Parallel needs could also be found in the cultural, social, and religious fields.

The political demands made on the rulers by the various groups in the society were of both the traditional and the more complex, differentiated types. On the one hand, the rulers were expected to uphold traditional ascriptive rights and benefits; on the other, they were faced with demands for participation in the formulation of the political balance of power—or even in the process of legitimating their own authority. Thus the authority of the rulers, "traditional" though it may have been, was no longer automatic; merely to raise the question of the rulers' accountability was to deny them fixed support.

These different types of political activities and orientations did not coexist in these political systems in separate "compartments," bound together only in some loose and unstable way. They were bound together within the same institutions, and the continuity of each type of political activity was dependent on the existence of both types of political orientation. Because of this, the activities of the rulers were, paradoxically, oriented to maintaining basic *traditional* legitimation through manipulation not only of traditional but also of nontraditional support and to the mobilization also of traditional resources for politically autonomous goals and through nontraditional channels.

Hence, the political system of these empires could subsist only insofar as it was possible to maintain simultaneously and continuously, within the framework of the same political institutions, both the traditional and the more differentiated levels of legitimation, support, and political organization. The continuity of these systems hinged on the continuous existence of a certain balance between political activity and involvement on the part of some segments of the population and of political noninvolvement or apathy toward central political issues by most segments of the population. The limited political involvement could assure some of the more flexible political support, while the apathy, in its turn, was necessary for maintenance of the traditional legitimation of the rulers.

Contradiction and conflict

It was the interplay between these varied orientations of the rulers—their dependence on both traditional and differentiated resources—that greatly influenced their concrete policies and gave rise to some of the basic contradictions that developed within those policies. The rulers of these empires tended to develop three major types of basic political orientations. First, they were interested in the limited promotion of free resources and in freeing them from commitments to traditional aristocratic groups. Second, the rulers were interested in controlling these resources and committing them to their own use. Third, the rulers tended also to engage in various goals—military expansions, for example—which alone could exhaust many of the available free resources. Between these various tendencies of the rulers, serious contradictions easily developed. These contradictions, although not always consciously grasped by the rulers, were nevertheless implicit in their structural position, in the problems and exigencies with which they dealt, and in the concrete policies they employed in order to solve their problems.

These contradictions were exhibited mainly in the sphere of legitimation and stratification. As we have seen, the rulers often attempted to limit the aristocracy's power and to create new status groups. But these attempts faced several obstacles. Regardless of the extent of the monarchs' independent activities in this field, the number of new titles created, and the degree of encouragement of new strata, the symbols of status used by the rulers were usually very similar to those borne by the landed hereditary aristocracy or by some religious elites. The creation of an entirely new secular and rational type of legitimation, in which the social groups or universalistic principles would be the foci of legitimation, was either beyond their horizon or against their basic interest. It would necessarily involve extending the sphere of political participation and consequently increasing the influence of various strata in the political institutions.

Therefore, the rulers were usually unable to transcend the symbols of stratification and legitimation borne by the very strata whose influence they wanted to limit. Consequently, the ability of the rulers to appeal to the lower strata of the population was obviously limited. Even more important, because of this emphasis on the superiority

and worth of aristocratic symbols and values, many middle or new strata and groups tended to identify with them and consequently to "aristocratize" themselves.

The contradiction in the rulers' policies and goals could develop also in a different direction. However tradition-bound the ruling elites may have been, their policies required the creation and propagation of more flexible "free" resources in various institutional fields. Here again, the major types of free resources were, in the economic field, money and easily exchangeable goods, free manpower in general, and free professional manpower in particular; and, in the political and social fields, relatively free commitments and possibilities of support. The propagation of such free resources either gave rise to many religious, intellectual, and legal groups whose value orientations were much more flexible than the traditional ones, or else it promoted such groups. Moreover, the orientations and values of the broader middle strata of the society sometimes were similar to those propagated by these more active elite groups. Although in many cases all these elements were very weak and succumbed to the influence of the more conservative groups and policies of the ruling elite, in other cases—as in Europe—they developed into relatively independent centers of power, whose opposition to the rulers was stimulated only by the rulers' more conservative policies.

The rulers' activities in the economic field were similarly inconsistent. Their main economic aims posed a series of dilemmas that could be extremely acute in relatively undifferentiated economic systems and that could give rise to intensive contradictions between long-term and short-term economic policies. Thus, the continuous necessity to mobilize extensive resources at any given moment could often exhaust the available free resources on which the rulers' economic independence rested. The big landowners and merchants, who constituted important centers of economic power, quite often tried to intensify this contradiction by providing the government with short-term loans or allocations of manpower for very limited periods and purposes; this increased the dependency of the rulers at the same time that it buttressed their own position. Although these allocations were usually insufficient to take care of their long-term needs, the rulers had to pay dearly in terms of the various free resources at their disposal. The rulers had to avail themselves of the various services and other resources of these more tradition-minded groups, giving them in return various concessions that often tended to undermine the long-run availability of free resources. In this way, the position of the rulers gradually became weaker (Eisenstadt 1963, chapter 12).

A similar contradiction existed between the long-range and short-range policies dealing with problems of administrative manpower. In many cases there was not enough manpower available for the execution of various administrative and political tasks, or because of inadequate communication and technical facilities it was very difficult to supervise such personnel effectively. It then became necessary to farm out various functions and positions either to local gentry and landowners or to officials who gradually became "aristocratized."

The best example of how the social groups created by the ruling elite became partially opposed to its aims and basic political premises is the development of the system of sale of offices, which was closely connected, in these empires, with the entire process of recruitment into the bureaucracy (Swart 1949). At first this system was usually introduced by the rulers as a means of solving their financial problems and admitting new (nonaristocratic) elements into their service. But in time, in most of these societies, the bureaucracy came to regard its offices as possessions and either transmitted them in the family or sold them in the market; in this way the rulers, despite many efforts to the contrary, slowly lost control over these offices.

This trend was connected, in general, with the tendency by the bureaucracy itself—the very instrument of power of the rulers—to aristocratize itself, to acquire symbols of aristocratic status, and to ally itself with aristocratic forces. In such cases the bureaucracy very often displaced its goals of service to the rulers for those of self-aggrandizement. Its members used their positions for enriching themselves and their families, thus becoming a growing burden on the economy and losing their efficiency.

This development necessarily affected the nature and extent of political activity and the scope of mobilization of political leadership. Insofar as these processes of aristocratization became intensified, they usually depleted the supply of political leaders to the central political institutions. The more active elements became alienated from the regime, whether their alienation took the form of succumbing to the aristocratic forces, falling into complete political apathy, or becoming centers of social and political upheaval and change.

Politics and social class. Similar contradictions tended also to develop in the political attitudes and activities of the major strata in these societies.

Several basic attitudes of various strata and groups toward the basic premises of the political systems of these empires and toward the basic aims of their rulers can be distinguished. The first attitude, evinced chiefly by the aristocracy, was one of opposition to these premises—an opposition that was often shared by the peasantry and sometimes also by other groups that were interested only in maintaining their own limited local autonomy and their immediate economic interests.

The second attitude consisted of basic identification with the political premises of the imperial system, combined with a willingness to fight for one's own interests within the framework of existing political institutions. This attitude was to be found mostly among the bureaucracy and among various elements of the urbanized professional and cultural elites.

The third attitude, developed mainly by the more differentiated urban groups and professional and intellectual elites, favored changes in the extension of the scope of political systems. This attitude, which was most clearly evinced by the European middle class and intellectual groups at the end of the eighteenth century (Beloff 1954), was manifested in various attempts to change the basic value premises of the political system, to widen the patterns of political participation within it, and to find referents of political orientation that transcended the given political system.

These attitudes often overlapped in concrete instances and varied by group and stratum in different societies and periods. Moreover, the attitudes of any one group were never homogeneous and stable, and they could change greatly according to political conditions. The various political attitudes of the major social groups greatly influenced the extent of their political participation and the scope and the nature of the political leadership that tended to develop from within them. Here again the most significant factor, from the point of view of the continuity of the imperial system, was the bureaucracy's tendency to aristocratize itself and thus to undermine the very conditions of such continuity. No less important was the possibility that the very administrative organs created for the implementation of the rulers' policies could develop autonomous orientations and activities that might become opposed to the basic premises of the imperial system.

Imperial decline

It was the interplay between the policies of the rulers and the political orientations and activities of the major social groups that constituted the crux of the processes of change within the empires and also brought about the development of conditions that could facilitate their downfall. These processes were rooted in the basic characteristics of the social and political structures of all the historical bureaucratic empires. However, the exact ways in which these conditions for change developed, as well as the exact processes that caused them, varied in different empires according to the specific constellation of their structural characteristics, the various external processes that impinged on them, and their unique historical circumstances.

Among the *internal* aspects of the social structure of these empires which influenced the processes of change was, first, the nature of the goals of the rulers. Whether chiefly military and expansionist, or more oriented to the maintenance of a cultural order, or concerned mainly with economic advancement, each kind of goal made different kinds of demands on the various types of resources available in the society. The processes of change and disintegration were also set in motion by (*a*) the policies that the rulers developed for the implementation of their goals and the repercussions of these policies on the relative strength of different social strata; (*b*) changes in the relative strength of such strata as a result of internal economic, religious, or political developments; and (*c*) the development of various internal and external crises and the ways in which the policies developed to deal with them influenced the strength of different groups.

The direction taken by an empire's decline and the rate at which it declined were also greatly influenced by two residual factors: the initial level of social and economic differentiation in the society and the initial strength of its various social groups in relation to one another. Within this context, of special importance was the extent to which there existed common cultural and political bonds encompassing these major social groups and the rulers, as for instance in the case of the Confucian order in China (see Eisenstadt 1963, chapter 11; Balázs 1964, chapters 1–2).

Among the more "accidental" or *external* factors that influenced the processes of change, we should mention different extents of external pressure, major movements of population, conquests of nomads, international economic fluctuations, and the degree to which there existed from the beginning ethnic heterogeneity in a given society. Of equally crucial importance was the specific geopolitical situation of any polity: for instance, the special geopolitical situation of Byzantium at the crossroads of Europe and Asia. In general, it was some combination of external and internal pressures and exigencies that precipitated change in the political systems of these empires. The greater the intensity of these internal contradictions, and the more intractable the external crises by which the empires were faced, the quicker and more intensive was the onslaught of change.

Thus, to give only some very preliminary examples (for a fuller exposition, see Eisenstadt 1963, chapter 12), the fact that in China various invasions, rebellions, and the famous "dynastic cycles" did not undermine for a very long period of time the basic institutional structure of the Chinese Empire (from the Han to the Ch'ing) can be understood if one remembers its geopolitical position, which made it relatively immune to the heavy impact of external forces. Furthermore, in China the relative weakness of the aristocracy and the predominance of the gentry tended to enhance the position of the centralized rulers; and the Confucian literati and bureaucracy, who constituted the backbone of the social and political structure, intervened between the central government and the major social strata and provided an indispensable framework of continuity and unity for the empire. By contrast, the geopolitical exposure of the Byzantine Empire, with its strong sensitivity to invasions and continuous internal struggle between the aristocracy and the free peasantry, led to its complete downfall. Similarly, the Roman and Arabic empires, with their extended boundaries that embraced a great variety of autonomous religions and cultural groups, were unable to contain internal dissension at the same time that they were forced to deal with external pressures.

The foci of change

The policies of the rulers and the political orientations and activities of the major social groups within the empires were greatly influenced by two major sources (both external and internal) of pressure and change. As we have seen above, the external, geopolitical factors, in the broadest sense, provided not only the general setting for these polities but also constituted sources of many concrete pressures, such as external pressures of population and problems of military security or of adjustment to international trade. These geopolitical settings indicated, as we have seen, the nature of the international system within which the rulers of the empires worked and the types of problems to which they were especially sensitive. It has been rightly claimed that in many of these empires there existed, because of their basic structural characteristics, what has been called *Primat der Aussenpolitik* (Altheim 1955), or the priority of foreign policy; this implied a much greater sensitivity to a variety of such external pressures than in many other types of political systems. These external pressures were very often connected with internal problems. For instance, close relations obviously developed between problems of international trade and the situations and activities of merchant groups or between military problems and problems of manpower recruitment. Thus it was the *combination* of external and internal pressures that constituted the major foci of change in the empires.

In more concrete terms, the main factors generating processes of change in these empires were (*a*) the continuous needs of the rulers for different types of resources and especially their great dependence on various flexible resources; (*b*) the rulers' attempts to maintain their own positions of control, in terms of both traditional legitimation and of effective political control over the more flexible forces in the society; (*c*) the great and continuous sensitivity of the internal structure of these societies to various external pressures and to political and economic developments in the international field; (*d*) the consequent needs of the rulers to intensify the mobilization of various resources in order to deal with problems arising out of changes in military, diplomatic, and economic international situations; and (*e*) the development of various autonomous orientations and goals among the major strata and their respective demands on the rulers.

Insofar as there developed strong contradictions between these different factors and especially insofar as the rulers emphasized very expensive goals, which exhausted the available economic and manpower resources, the rulers found themselves in various dilemmas. In such situations, the special sensitivities of these political systems were brought out, and forces were generated that could undermine the delicate balance between political participation and apathy on which the continuity of these systems depended. This meant that the rulers' tendency toward maintenance of active control over different strata could become predominant, thus increasing the power of traditional forces, sharpening the conflicts between them and the more flexible, differentiated strata, and either depleting or alienating the more "free" groups and strata from the rulers. This depletion may have taken varying forms: outright reluctance to have children (or "demographic apathy," as it is sometimes called), weakening of the more independent economic elements and their subordination to more conservative, aristocratic–patrimonial (or feudal) elements, and depletion or flight of mobile capital (Eisenstadt 1963, chapter 12).

These processes were usually closely connected with the aristocratization or ossification of the bureaucracy, with its growing parasitic exploitation of the economy, and with the depletion of active political leadership identified with the regime. Such parasitic exploitation of the economy by the rulers was in a way an intensification of the usual economic activities of the rulers of the empires. The special parasitic nature of their activities in periods of decline—or of the setting in of decline—was evident not so much in the mere extension of the demands for taxes or for manpower as in the fact that the resources mobilized by the rulers were used for the creation of new ascriptive positions and groups. Instead of promoting conditions that could have encouraged the extension of greater resources, through trade or the facilities for training professional manpower, the rulers depleted their resources by adding to their already overdeveloped bureaucracies.

Thus there often developed a continuous flux of foreign elements into the centers of the realms. Initially mere merchants, hirelings, and personal helpers of the rulers, these foreign military groups gradually succeeded in infiltrating some of the most important political posts and finally in totally usurping the supreme political power. This was made possible by the depletion of native strata, together with the mounting internal and external crises. Similar developments could take place with regard to foreign merchants who sometimes, as in Byzantium or the Ottoman Empire, finally managed to monopolize all the trading posts abandoned by the indigenous merchants (Ostrogorski 1940). In those cases, as in Europe, in which these economically and socially more active strata were depleted, they became alienated from the rulers and their policies, as well as from the political institutions of the society, and turned to fomenting change and revolt.

SHMUEL N. EISENSTADT

[*See also* BUREAUCRACY; CIVIL SERVICE; COLONIALISM.]

BIBLIOGRAPHY

ALTHEIM, FRANZ 1955 *Gesicht von Abend und Morgen.* Frankfurt (Germany): Fischer.

BALÁZS, ÉTIENNE 1964 *Chinese Civilization and Bureaucracy: Variations on a Theme.* New Haven: Yale Univ. Press.

BAYNES, N. H. 1943 The Decline of the Roman Power in Western Europe: Some Modern Explanations. *Journal of Roman Studies* 33:29–35.

BELOFF, MAX (1954) 1962 *The Age of Absolutism: 1660–1815.* New York: Harper. → See especially pages 170–180, "Absolutism in Transformation."

BOAK, ARTHUR E. R. (1923) 1955 *History of Rome to 565 A.D.* 4th ed. New York: Macmillan.

CAHEN, C. 1955 L'histoire économique et sociale de l'Orient musulman médiéval. *Studia islamica* 3:93–116.

EBERHARD, WOLFRAM (1948) 1960 *A History of China.* 2d ed. Berkeley: Univ. of California Press. → First published in German.

EDGERTON, WILLIAM F. 1947 The Government and the Governed in the Egyptian Empire. *Journal of Near Eastern Studies* 6:152–160.

EISENSTADT, SHMUEL N. 1963 *The Political Systems of Empires.* New York: Free Press.

GRIFFIN, C. C. 1949 Economic and Social Aspects of the Era of Spanish-American Independence. *Hispanic American Historical Review* 29:170–187.

HAMILTON, E. M. 1954 The Decline of Spain. Pages 215–226 in Eleanora Carus-Wilson (editor), *Essays in Economic History.* London: Arnold.

HARING, CLARENCE H. 1947 *The Spanish Empire in America.* New York: Oxford Univ. Press.

JONES, A. H. M. 1955 The Decline and Fall of the Roman Empire. *History* 40:209–226.

LEWIS, BERNARD (1950) 1958 *The Arabs in History.* Rev. ed. London: Hutchinson.

LEWIS, BERNARD 1958 Some Reflections on the Decline of the Ottoman Empire. *Studia islamica* 9:111–127.

MOSCA, GAETANO (1896) 1939 *The Ruling Class.* New York: McGraw-Hill. → First published as *Elementi di scienza politica.* See especially paragraphs 6, 7, and 8 in Chapter 2, "The Ruling Class."

OSTROGORSKI, GEORGIJE (1940) 1957 *History of the Byzantine State.* New Brunswick, N.J.: Rutgers Univ. Press. → First published in German.

ROSTOVTSEV, MIKHAIL I. (1926) 1963 *The Social and Economic History of the Roman Empire.* New ed., 2 vols. Oxford: Clarendon.

STANGE, O. H. 1950 Geschichte Chinas vom Urbeginn bis zur Gegenwart. Pages 363–542 in *Geschichte Asiens,* by Ernst Waldschmidt et al. Munich: Bruckmann.

SWART, KOENRAAD W. 1949 *Sale of Offices in the Seventeenth Century.* The Hague: Nijhoff.

WEBER, MAX (1906–1924) 1946 *From Max Weber: Essays in Sociology.* Translated and edited by Hans H. Gerth and C. Wright Mills. New York: Oxford Univ. Press. → See especially pages 162–171, "The Economic Foundations of 'Imperialism.'" First published in German.

WEBER, MAX (1922) 1957 *The Theory of Social and Economic Organization.* Edited by Talcott Parsons. Glencoe, Ill.: Free Press. → First published as Part 1 of *Wirtschaft und Gesellschaft.*

WITTFOGEL, KARL A. 1957 *Oriental Despotism: A Comparative Study of Total Power.* New Haven: Yale Univ. Press. → A paperback edition was published in 1963.

EMPLOYMENT AND UNEMPLOYMENT

The commercialization and industrialization of a large part of the world during the past several centuries have involved a radical change in the way in which human labor is directed toward productive ends. Two centuries ago, or more, most of the world's work force tilled the soil, as is still largely true except in North America and Europe. This work was performed in good part under conditions of status, in which a man was tied to a particular place and particular job by institutional arrangements which offered an individual and his family a sense of stability and security.

Today, in the more developed countries and in the commercial–industrial sectors of the less developed economies, command over labor is acquired in the market place. The interaction of demand and supply in the labor market determines, within limits, the level of wages and wage differentials, the volume of employment—and the volume of unemployment. As the relative importance of agriculture and other forms of self-employment has declined, the interplay of demand and supply, in the economy as a whole and in labor markets in particular, has come to be crucial in determining both long-term trends and short-run fluctuations in the volume of employment and unemployment.

The personal insecurity and widespread hardship that frequently resulted from the impersonal market determination of the level of employment began to influence government policies in the most industrialized countries in the latter part of the nineteenth century and became increasingly influential in the twentieth (Beveridge 1909). But intense world-wide concern with the welfare implications of widespread unemployment did not come until the great depression of the 1930s. Out of the shock of that experience and the economic planning that followed came the modern concern with maintaining the level of employment. This development was greatly stimulated by the "Keynesian revolution" in economic thinking, which dates from the mid-1930s.

Today "full employment" is an almost universally espoused goal. Virtually every advanced country that depends to a significant degree on private markets consciously formulates and tries to implement an employment policy. This was not true before the 1930s. The Beveridge Report of 1944, *Full Employment in a Free Society*, represents a landmark in this development. For the United States a comparable landmark is the Employment Act of 1946. The international concern at the end of World War II with the need to maintain a high and stable level of employment is suggested by the pledge, made by the governments subscribing to the United Nations Charter, to take action to promote "higher standards of living, full employment, and conditions of economic and social progress and development" (United Nations . . . 1949, p. 5).

The goal of full employment may conflict with other economic goals. Thus, full employment may not be compatible with the desired degree of stability in the price level, and at times governments have felt compelled to sacrifice some employment in order to correct a disequilibrium in the balance of payments. The question of how to reconcile these goals was being debated vigorously in the Western world in the mid-1960s.

Table 1 offers some historical background on the changing pattern of employment in broad industrial sectors. In the nineteenth century the shift away from agriculture had been most marked in the United Kingdom, and in the first decade of the twentieth century agriculture already accounted for less than 15 per cent of the British labor force. In the other leading industrial countries the agricultural sector of the labor force had already fallen below 50 per cent by the beginning of the twentieth century.

The shift of labor out of farming continued steadily during the first half of the twentieth century and has, indeed, accelerated since the end of World War II (Twentieth Century Fund 1961, pp. 72–74). The movement has been not only toward what is loosely called "industry" (manufacturing, mining, construction, and electric power and gas) but also into the trade and service sectors. This latter movement has been particularly marked in the United States. It is also noteworthy that the relative contribution of industry to total employment actually declined in the United States from 1950 to 1962. Involved here is not only the changing pattern of demand but also a more rapid rise

Table 1 — Percentage distribution of labor force by industrial sector in selected countries, 1910–1962

	1962	About 1950	About 1930	About 1910
France				
Agriculture[a]	21	34	36	43
Industry[b]	40	33	36	32
Service[c]	39	33	27	25
Germany				
Agriculture	14	23	29	34
Industry	49	44	41	40
Service	38	33	30	26
United Kingdom				
Agriculture	4	5	6	12
Industry	48	47	43	43
Service	48	48	51	45
United States				
Agriculture	9	12	22	31
Industry	33	35	31	31
Service	59	53	47	38

a. Agriculture includes forestry and fishing.

b. Industry includes manufacturing, mining, construction, gas, electricity, and water.

c. Service includes trade, banking and finance, transport and communication, and all other services (including government).

Sources: 1910–1950 data from Kuznets 1957, appendix, table 4; 1962 data from Organization for Economic Cooperation and Development 1963.

Table 2 — Percentage distribution of total employment by occupational classification in the United States, 1900–1963

Occupational group	1963	1950	1940	1930	1920	1910	1900
White-collar workers	43.9	36.6	31.1	29.4	24.9	21.4	17.6
Manual workers	36.3	41.1	39.9	39.6	40.2	38.2	35.8
Service workers	13.1	10.5	11.7	9.8	7.8	9.1	9.1
Farm workers*	6.7	11.8	17.4	21.2	27.0	31.1	37.5

* Includes farmers and farm laborers.

Sources: For 1900–1950, U.S. Bureau of the Census 1960; for 1963, U.S. President 1964.

in labor productivity in manufacturing than in the trade and service sectors.

Another change in the pattern of employment involves a gradual shift to white-collar occupations. This change has been particularly notable in the United States, as indicated in Table 2.

Other changes in the composition of employment can be mentioned only in passing; for example, the decline in the importance of self-employment, the rise in the participation of women in the non-agricultural labor force, an upward trend in the age at which children leave school and enter the labor force, and earlier retirement for older workers [see LABOR FORCE]. These trends are expected to continue into the future.

Unemployment

The historical record. During the decade from the mid-1950s to the mid-1960s, unemployment in western Europe was at a lower level than in any earlier peacetime decade in this century. Data on unemployment for selected countries since 1913 are presented in Table 3. By the standards of recent experience, unemployment was high even in the 1920s in a number of countries, notably Germany and the United Kingdom. The catastrophe of the great depression is suggested by the soaring unemployment rates during the 1930s. In the worst year of the depression, a sixth of the German labor force was unemployed, an eighth of the British, virtually a fifth of the Canadian, and as much as a quarter of the American.

The record of the 1950s and 1960s provides a highly encouraging contrast. Since the mid-1950s unemployment rates in western Europe have generally been below 4 per cent, and since 1960 they have typically been below 3 per cent. In contrast, unemployment in the United States, which in the first postwar decade tended to run at a rate of 4 per cent or less except during brief cyclical recessions, failed to fall below 5 per cent in any year after 1957 (through 1964).

This is not to say that European countries have

Table 3 — Unemployment rates in selected countries, 1913–1962[a]
(per cent of the labor force)

Year	France	Germany (later F.R.G.)	Italy	Sweden	United Kingdom	Canada	United States
1913	1.0	1.9	1.7	1.1	1.2	3.0	4.3
1920	b	1.7	b	1.3	1.8	b	5.2
1921	2.5	1.2	b	6.4	9.6	5.8	11.7
1922	b	0.7	b	5.5	8.1	4.4	6.7
1923	b	4.5	b	2.9	6.6	3.2	2.4
1924	b	5.8	b	2.4	5.8	4.5	5.0
1925	b	3.0	b	2.6	6.4	4.4	3.2
1926	1.1	8.0	b	2.9	7.1	3.0	1.8
1927	b	3.9	b	2.9	5.5	1.8	3.3
1928	b	3.8	b	2.4	6.1	1.7	4.2
1929	b	5.9	1.7	2.4	5.9	2.9	3.2
1930	b	9.5	2.5	3.3	9.3	9.1	8.9
1931	2.1	13.9	4.3	4.8	12.6	11.6	16.3
1932	b	17.2	5.8	6.8	13.1	17.6	24.1
1933	b	14.8	5.9	7.3	11.7	19.3	25.2
1934	b	8.3	5.6	6.4	9.9	14.5	22.0
1935	b	6.5	b	6.2	9.2	14.2	20.3
1936	4.2	4.8	b	5.3	7.9	12.8	17.0
1937	b	2.7	5.0	5.1	6.7	9.1	14.3
1938	3.6	1.3	4.6	5.1	8.1	11.4	19.1
1950	1.4	7.2	8.7	1.7	2.5	3.6	5.3
1951	1.3	6.4	9.2	1.6	2.2	2.4	3.3
1952	1.3	6.1	9.8	1.7	2.9	2.9	3.1
1953	1.6	5.5	10.2	1.9	2.6	2.9	2.9
1954	1.6	5.2	8.7	1.8	2.3	4.5	5.6
1955	1.5	3.8	7.5	1.8	2.1	4.3	4.4
1956	1.2	3.1	9.3	1.6	2.2	3.3	4.2
1957	1.0	2.7	8.1	1.7	2.4	4.5	4.3
1958	1.1	2.7	6.4	2.0	3.0	6.9	6.8
1959	1.3	1.9	5.4	1.8	3.1	5.9	5.5
1960	1.3	0.9	4.0	1.6	2.5	6.9	5.6
1961	1.2	0.6	3.4	1.5	2.4	7.1	6.7
1962	1.3	0.5	2.9	1.3	2.9	5.8	5.6

a. The unemployment rates shown for the various countries do not all reflect precisely the same coverage and definitions, although some limited standardization has been applied to the figures. Thus, the figures shown here do not agree completely with those in Table 4, where, for a more limited period, complete comparability with American definitions and coverage has been attempted.

b. Not available.

Sources: For all countries except United States, 1913–1960 from Maddison 1964, table E-1; 1961–1962 adapted from Organization for Economic Cooperation and Development 1963; for United States, 1913–1960 from Lebergott 1964, p. 512; for 1961–1962, from U.S. President 1964, p. 195.

not had pockets of serious unemployment with which to deal. Various countries continue to have their depressed regions—the Italian Mezzogiorno and Northern Ireland, for example—and differentially high unemployment rates may exist in particular countries for teen-agers, the older age groups, or the least skilled.

The relatively high unemployment that persisted in the United States after the mid-1950s gave rise to a vigorous debate as to its causes and appropriate cures (Ross 1964). On the one hand have been those who argued that the high level of unemployment reflected primarily a deficiency of aggregate demand. The argument has run that a higher and more rapidly rising level of total demand, sup-

ported by appropriate monetary–fiscal policies, could increase employment to the point where unemployment would again be brought down to a rate of 4 per cent or less.

Opposing this view has been the structuralist argument that the main problem has been not a lack of jobs in the aggregate but a failure of the labor supply to adjust sufficiently to the rapidly changing pattern of employment opportunities (U.S. Congress, Senate . . . 1963, part 5, pp. 1461–1499). The changing pattern of the demand for labor—resulting from automation and other technological change and from the shift in the composition of output toward services—has greatly increased the demand for highly educated and white-collar workers and reduced the demand for blue-collar, unskilled, and poorly educated workers. And, the argument runs, it has not been possible to make the necessary adjustments in labor supply. As a result, the structuralist position has maintained, merely expanding aggregate demand would lead to labor shortages in occupations in which unemployment rates were already relatively low without materially reducing the rates among the groups that had the highest unemployment.

In the early 1960s the consensus among those who had studied the problem was that the high level of unemployment in the United States was primarily the result of the failure of aggregate demand to expand rapidly enough. There was general agreement also, however, that the heterogeneous character of the American labor force created a persistent structural problem of poor employment opportunities for the underprivileged parts of the labor force (Ross 1964; Gordon 1964). There was increasing recognition on all sides that there was need for a vigorous and comprehensive manpower policy to expedite the absorption into gainful employment of the least qualified groups in the labor force (U.S. Senate . . . 1964).

When is a person unemployed? There is no single unambiguous definition of unemployment. Different purposes call for different definitions. Further, the definitions that are implicit in the official figures published in different countries may vary because of the way in which unemployment statistics are compiled.

The difficulties involved in arriving at a generally accepted definition of unemployment can be illustrated by the household survey utilized in the United States. Information is secured for each person in the household aged 14 and over. For those for whom it is reported that they did not work for pay outside the home at least one hour during the reference week, the question is then asked: "Was . . . looking for work?" An affirmative reply settles the matter; the person is listed as unemployed. A change in this procedure was under consideration in 1966.

This procedure raises the following definitional questions, among others:

(1) Should unemployment be measured in hours or persons? If a person wanting to work full-time can find only a half-time job, should he be counted as half unemployed? Similarly, if an unemployed person seeks only a part-time job, should he be counted as wholly unemployed? In all countries, the official figures refer to persons wholly unemployed, that is, persons who are not working at all

and are seeking full-time or part-time work. But some data on part-time unemployment are available, and the American government now publishes a monthly figure on "percent of labor force time lost" through unemployment.

(2) What should a person have done to look for work, and on what terms should he be willing to accept a job, if he is to be counted as unemployed? What sorts of overt action—such as registering at an employment office or applying personally at a factory or office—should he have taken? And how recently should he have taken such action? Further, if he is willing to work only at his former wage while a job is available to him at a lower wage, should he be counted as unemployed? These are questions that have no single and obvious answer.

(3) A question frequently asked is whether one should include among the unemployed those who are only marginally in the labor force—for example, boys and girls in school seeking part-time jobs or housewives who wish to work to supplement the family income or enjoy a more varied life. Those who would exclude such persons are in effect suggesting that hardship be the primary criterion in defining who is unemployed. Quite clearly, unemployment does not imply the same degree of hardship to all persons seeking jobs at a particular time. The answer here seems fairly clear-cut. An inclusive definition of unemployment should be used by those who compile the data, but the latter should be published in sufficient detail—for example, by age, sex, and marital status—so that the user can combine the subtotals in whatever way best fits the particular definition he wants to use.

(4) The question of marginal attachment to the labor force can cut two ways. The official count of the unemployed may include some persons who are only marginally attached to the labor force. But it also excludes an unknown number who would like to work and would look for work under more favorable conditions. This is not a serious issue if jobs are plentiful, but it does assume importance when unemployment is at a high level. Such a situation of more or less forced withdrawal from the labor force is frequently characterized as one of disguised unemployment.

Disguised unemployment was certainly of some importance in the United States after 1957, when the national unemployment rate remained above 5 per cent. This is an area in which it is difficult to obtain reliable figures. But there has been a growing body of evidence that the lack of jobs created disguised unemployment among women, older persons, the unskilled, those with the least education, and nonwhites (U.S. President 1964, pp. 30–31). Or to put the matter in other terms, labor-force participation rates among these groups were depressed by relatively high unemployment rates.

(5) Some other questions that arise in defining and measuring unemployment can only be mentioned. What should be done about those who are presumably unemployable because of physical or psychological handicaps? Should any attempt be made to measure "underemployment," that is, the extent to which persons are employed at jobs that call for less than their highest current level of skill? While it would certainly be desirable to have even partial measures of such underemployment, the obstacles in the way of developing such data are virtually insuperable.

The problem of underemployment is most frequently discussed in another connection—the very low average productivity and virtually zero marginal productivity of the agricultural populations in some of the least developed parts of the world. Here the pressure of population on natural resources is such that, given the state of production techniques, a moderate decline in the agricultural work force would lead to little if any reduction in total output. This condition is sometimes said to create "disguised unemployment," a term that we have used to mean withdrawal from the labor force because of the scarcity of jobs.

Methods and problems of measurement.   It has already been noted that unemployment is measured in different ways in different countries. Systems of compiling unemployment data can be grouped under five headings: (1) sample surveys of the labor force; (2) compulsory unemployment-insurance statistics; (3) unemployment-relief data; (4) trade union records of unemployment; and (5) registrations at government employment offices.

Of these, the first and the last are the most common (U.S. President's Committee . . . 1962, appendix A). In 1964 sample surveys were the source of the official data on unemployment in Canada, Japan, and the United States; and such surveys have been used as a supplementary source of information in a number of other countries—for example, France, Germany, Italy, and Sweden. Employment-office registrations were the primary official source in France, Germany, Great Britain, Italy, Sweden, and elsewhere.

Section A of Table 4 presents the official unemployment rates for a number of countries for the years 1960–1962. Differences in definition and method of measurement, however, mean that a number of adjustments are necessary to make these

Table 4 — Unemployment rates in selected countries, as published and after adjustment to United States definitions, 1960–1962 (per cent of the labor force)

	A. OFFICIAL FIGURES AS PUBLISHED			B. ADJUSTED TO U.S. DEFINITIONS		
	1960	1961	1962[a]	1960	1961[a]	1962[a]
United States	5.6	6.7	5.6	5.6	6.7	5.6
Canada	7.0	7.2	6.0	7.0	7.2	6.0
France	1.0	0.9	0.9	1.9	1.7	1.8
Germany (F.R.G.)	1.2	0.8	0.7	1.0	0.5	b
Great Britain	1.6	1.4	1.9	2.4	2.2	2.8
Italy	8.2	7.6	6.3	4.3	3.7	3.2
Japan	1.0	0.9	0.9	1.1	1.0	1.0
Sweden	1.4	1.2	1.3	b	1.5	1.5

a. Some figures for these years are preliminary.
b. Not available.

Source: Myers 1964, p. 174.

figures fully comparable. Among the points of difference are the following:

(1) Treatment of unpaid family workers. Japan, for example, includes in the labor force unpaid family workers who worked as much as one hour during the survey week. The United States includes them only if they worked 15 hours.

(2) The treatment of persons on temporary layoff and of those waiting to start a new job. Before 1957 these groups were counted as employed in the United States; they are now treated as unemployed. In Japan, they are considered to be employed.

(3) The age at which children are included in the labor force.

(4) The period to which the data apply. In the United States, for example, the period is a week, and anyone working even one hour during the week is counted as employed. In Germany and Great Britain, on the other hand, the reference period is a day. A person not working on that day is counted as unemployed, although he may have worked on one or more other days during that week.

(5) The various unemployed groups that may be excluded from the unemployed. It is fairly common to exclude the self-employed, who are included in the United States. If the data come from unemployment-insurance records, those ineligible for coverage would be excluded. If the figures are based on registrations at employment offices, persons who are seeking jobs but do not register will be excluded.

(6) The computation of the unemployment rate. To compute an unemployment rate it is necessary to divide the number unemployed by some figure that includes the employed. In the United States, the denominator is taken to be the total civilian labor force. The self-employed are included. In a

number of countries, the unemployment rate represents only the percentage of wage-and-salary workers who are unemployed.

In 1962 the U.S. Bureau of Labor Statistics made the first intensive attempt to standardize the unemployment figures in a number of countries, the basis of comparison being the definitions in use in the United States. The results are shown in Section B of Table 4. Of the countries listed, the largest relative adjustments were in the British, French, and Italian figures—the first two upward and the last downward. Even after these adjustments the unemployment rates of all the other countries except Canada were below that of the United States for each of the years 1960–1962.

The kinds of unemployment. For both analytical and policy reasons, it would be extremely useful to be able to distinguish among various kinds of unemployment. In the classifications that have been attempted, the categories that one most frequently encounters bear the titles "frictional," "seasonal," "cyclical" (or "deficiency-of-demand"), and "structural" unemployment (U.S. Congress, Joint Economic Committee 1961).

Virtually all attempts at classification seek to take account of three sets of factors that tend to create a varying gap between the size of the labor force and total employment. These factors may be summarized as follows:

1. *Frictional and seasonal unemployment.* Even with a satisfactory level of aggregate demand and a homogeneous labor force, movement to a new job takes time. Hence, under the best of circumstances, there will be a minimum "float" of workers in the process of moving to new jobs. This can be called "minimum frictional unemployment." Such frictional unemployment is assumed to be balanced by an equal or larger number of job vacancies. If the labor force is not perfectly homogeneous, this frictional minimum may be different for different segments of the working population.

Seasonal unemployment is frequently included in this notion of frictional unemployment. Even if seasonal workers withdraw from the labor force or find other work in the off season, the frictions and time involved in such movements create a seasonal pattern in total unemployment. The seasonal pattern of unemployment does not remain constant over the years, and it is related, in ways which are still not well understood, to changes in the level of aggregate demand.

Seasonal unemployment creates a variety of problems, not the least of which is the problem of measurement. Considerable research has been aimed at improving existing methods of adjusting unemployment figures for seasonal variation (U.S. President's Committee . . . 1962, chapter 6). And various measures by both government and private employers have had some effect in dampening the amplitude of seasonal movements in unemployment in particular industries. An interesting example was the effect of *Schlechtwettergeld* (bad-weather compensation) in reducing recorded seasonal unemployment in the German construction industry (Germany [Federal Republic] . . . 1962, pp. 56–57).

In Sweden in the early 1960s unemployment in midwinter tended to run three to four times as high as in midsummer. It is not surprising that such countries as Sweden and Norway have devoted considerable effort to reducing these wide seasonal swings. In the United States in 1964 the official seasonal index of the unemployment rate for experienced wage and salaried workers ranged from 84.1 in October to 122.9 in February (see "Rates of Unemployment" 1964). The seasonal amplitude in Canada was still wider.

2. *Cyclical unemployment.* Next is the set of factors implied by what formerly was called "cyclical" and is now frequently termed "deficiency-of-demand" unemployment. What is implied here is that the *total* demand for goods and services, given existent wage rates and labor productivity, is not sufficient to generate jobs for all those who want to work (after appropriate adjustment for minimum frictional unemployment). The number of job vacancies open in the economy as a whole is significantly less than the total number of people seeking work. This is the kind of unemployment that was so predominant during the great depression, and it is to the prevention of this kind of unemployment in particular that so-called full-employment policies are addressed.

3. *Structural unemployment.* The term "structural" unemployment is most frequently associated with the third set of factors. While this term has been used in different ways, structural unemployment almost always implies the following:

(*a*) There are particular sectors of the labor force from which workers cannot easily and quickly move into other sectors in search of jobs.

(*b*) In some or all of these sectors with impaired mobility, unemployment significantly exceeds available vacancies. And because of inadequate mobility, labor supply does not easily adjust to the inadequate level of demand. Hence, unemployment rates are higher in these sectors than in the economy as a whole, and such differentially high unemployment rates tend to persist for relatively long periods.

(c) There may be insufficient demand for particular types of labor for a number of reasons. Three in particular might be cited. First, the demand for particular skills may be reduced because of technological change or a shift in the pattern of demand. Discussions of structural unemployment in the United States in the early 1960s emphasized this factor particularly. Second, there may be a shift of economic activity out of a geographical region not matched by a comparable exodus of workers. This leads to the problem of "depressed areas." And third, there may be an influx of workers—of a particular type or into a particular region—at such a rate that they cannot be quickly absorbed into jobs. The influx of refugees into West Germany after World War II led to considerable debate regarding the size of the structural unemployment problem in that country (Germany [Federal Republic] . . . 1952).

The three kinds of causes of structural unemployment cited in the preceding paragraph all have to do with identifiable shifts in the pattern of demand for or supply of labor, to which the economy finds it difficult to adjust because of some degree of labor immobility. It is also possible that demand and supply for a particular kind of labor may have been out of balance as far back as our records go. Immobility, however it came to exist, may perpetuate such sectoral imbalances and create differentially high unemployment rates that continue indefinitely. Such more or less permanent immobility may be associated with a variety of institutional factors. Thus, we expect to find that unemployment rates are higher among the least skilled and least educated. We should also expect that unemployment rates would be higher at the extremes of the age distribution than in the prime working ages. In the United States unemployment rates have been higher among Negroes than among whites since unemployment data were first recorded [see Discrimination, economic].

These structural differentials will be the more marked the more heterogeneous is the labor force—and the measure of heterogeneity in this context is intersectoral immobility. These unemployment differentials are particularly marked, and the labor force is particularly heterogeneous, in the United States.

These differentially high unemployment rates may contain a frictional as well as a deficient-demand element. Among construction workers, for example, there may be ample vacancies, but the element of weather plus the need to move from job to job will cause frictional unemployment to be higher than in most other industries. Over and above such differentially high frictional unemployment, there may also be a shortage of jobs in relation to supply of this particular kind of labor.

It might be added that it is not easy in fact to differentiate between unemployment due to an economy-wide deficiency of demand and that due to structural factors in the sense defined above. For one thing, variations in aggregate demand affect different groups differently. For another, even the most persistent structural reasons for differential-employment opportunities tend to weaken in very tight labor markets; the extreme labor tightness during World War II illustrates this. Or, to cite

Table 5 — Unemployment rates for different sectors of the labor force, United States, 1948–1963
(per cent of sectoral labor force)

Sector	1965	1963	1959	1956	1953	1948
All civilian workers[a]	4.6	5.7	5.5	4.2	2.9	3.8
By age and sex[a]						
Men 20 years and over	3.2	4.5	4.7	3.4	2.5	c
Women 20 years and over	4.5	5.4	5.2	4.2	2.9	c
Both sexes, 14–19 years	13.6	15.6	13.2	10.4	7.1	c
Married men[a]	2.4	3.4	3.6	2.3	c	c
By occupation[b]						
White collar	2.3	2.8	2.6	1.7	1.4	2.1
Professional, technical only	1.5	1.8	1.7	1.0	0.9	1.7
Blue collar	5.3	7.2	7.5	5.1	3.5	4.3
Unskilled laborers only	8.4	12.1	12.4	8.2	6.1	7.5
By color[b]						
White	4.1	5.1	4.9	3.3	2.3	3.2
Nonwhite	8.3	10.9	10.7	7.5	4.1	5.2

a. The figures for 1948–1956 in these categories have been adjusted to account for a moderate change in definitions beginning in 1957.
b. The figures for 1948–1956 in these categories have not been so adjusted.
c. Not available.

Sources: "Rates of Unemployment" 1964, pp. 34–35; "Unemployment Rate" 1966; U.S. President 1964, p. 201; 1966, pp. 166–170.

another example, the structural unemployment resulting from the influx of refugees into West Germany largely disappeared in the very tight labor market of the late 1950s and early 1960s.

Table 5 gives some notion of the heterogeneity of the American labor force and of the resulting wide spread in unemployment rates for different parts of the working population. Thus, the unemployment rate for teen-agers has tended to run about 2.5 times the national rate. The rate for white-collar workers has tended to be about half the national rate, while the incidence of unemployment among unskilled laborers is more than twice as heavy as for the labor force as a whole. Similarly, the unemployment rate for nonwhites is about twice the national average. It is hardly necessary to elaborate upon the social and political, as well as economic, consequences of these high unemployment rates. This is particularly so with respect to what is referred to as "the Negro problem" in the United States.

In European countries the labor force is more homogeneous. Also, far fewer data are available on differential unemployment rates by age, occupation, etc., than is the case for the United States. As noted previously, however, every country has some relatively depressed areas, and a regional breakdown of the unemployed is available for a number of countries. Thus, in the United Kingdom in 1962 regional unemployment rates varied from 1.3 per cent in London and southeastern England to 3.7 per cent in Scotland and to no less than 7.5 per cent in Northern Ireland.

The goal of full employment

A high level of employment—or "full employment"—is now an accepted goal of national policy in virtually all of the economically advanced countries of the world. The acceptance of this goal immediately raises two questions. How is the goal of full employment to be defined? And how is this goal related to other economic objectives with which it may sometimes conflict—for example, stability of the price level and equilibrium in a country's balance of payments?

A variety of definitions of full employment has been offered. One made famous by Sir William Beveridge (1944) involves "having always more vacant jobs than unemployed men." The criterion that vacancies should exceed unemployment has frequently been criticized as inflationary, and a common alternative definition runs in terms of approximate equality between vacancies and unemployment.

In recent years, with growing sensitivity to the potential conflict between the goals of full employment and price stability, there has been a tendency to define the employment objective in an alternative way: as the lowest level to which unemployment can be pushed by an expansion of aggregate demand without bringing about an unacceptable rise in the price level. Here, the definition makes it explicit that the employment target depends on the nature of the trade-off between a fall in unemployment and the associated rise (if any) in the price level.

Most definitions of full employment have sought to describe "a situation in which unemployment does not exceed the minimum allowances that must be made for the effects of frictional and seasonal factors" (United Nations . . . 1949, p. 13). The continued high level of unemployment in the United States between 1957 and 1965, however, raised the question as to how full employment should be defined if a significant amount of structural unemployment exists.

The problem here can be illustrated by Figures 1 and 2. In Figure 1 the job-vacancy rate is measured on the vertical axis and the unemployment rate on the horizontal. The 45° line portrays all possible situations that correspond to an equality of vacancies and unemployed. Curve *AA'* represents one "structural situation." Vacancies rise as unemployment falls (assuming general expansion with structural rigidities) and vice versa; point *C* represents a situation of "full" employment, in which vacancies and unemployment are equal—at an over-all unemployment rate of 3 per cent in the diagram.

Assume now that, because of structural changes, the curve shifts to *BB'*. Vacancies now equal un-

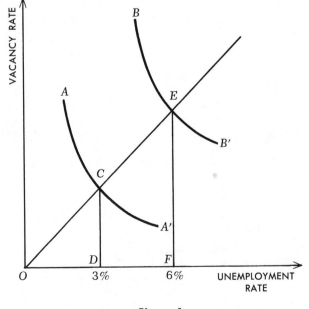

Figure 1

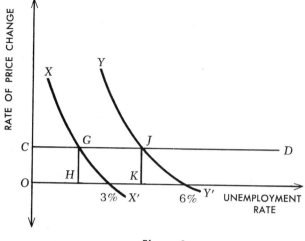

Figure 2

employment at an unemployment rate of 6 per cent. If the attempt were made to force unemployment much below this by expansionary measures, labor shortages would mount while unemployment would decline only slowly and painfully, with substantial upward pressure on wages and prices. Is 6 per cent to be considered the full-employment target, including not only frictional but also structural unemployment?

The second definition cited suggests the relationships illustrated in Figure 2. Here, again, unemployment is measured along the horizontal axis, but now the rate of change in the price level is represented on the vertical axis. This is a variant of what has come to be called the "Phillips curve," which relates wage changes rather than price changes to the level of unemployment (see Phillips 1958). The curves *XX′* and *YY′* describe two possible relationships between price-level changes and unemployment. The curve *XX′* implies that prices can be kept stable at an unemployment rate of 3 per cent. Lower unemployment leads to price increases at an accelerating rate.

Let the situation change to that portrayed by *YY′*. This upward shift is most commonly associated with labor's increased bargaining strength; but the curve might also shift because of the sort of structural change previously described, with the result that labor shortages in some sectors of the economy are associated with unemployment in excess of vacancies in other sectors. (Not only immobility between sectors but also downward wage rigidity is assumed.) As a result, in the second situation, price stability can be maintained only at an unemployment rate of 6 per cent. Is this full employment?

Since World War II it has been clear that all countries have been willing to settle for something less than absolute price stability. Probably no gov-

ernment would be prepared to pay a significant price in terms of higher unemployment in order to keep the rise in the price level below the rate of, say, 2 per cent per year. This upper limit on the rate of inflation that would be tolerated can be represented by the horizontal line *CD* in Figure 2. Then *OH* and *OK* represent the minimum levels to which unemployment could be reduced in the two cases.

This discussion suggests that the definition of full employment should be approached in two stages. First, we may define "aggregative full employment" as corresponding to that unemployment rate that meets the over-all criterion: total vacancies equal to total unemployment or the smallest amount of unemployment consistent with the desired degree of price stability.

Given the goal of aggregative full employment, which can best be implemented through the use of monetary–fiscal policy, we then need to ask the following question. By means of the various instruments of manpower policy (training and retraining programs, relocation of workers and industry, reduction of discrimination in hiring, and so on), how far is a government prepared to go in reducing the amount of structural unemployment that exists at aggregative full employment? Or, in terms of the diagrams, how far is it prepared to go in seeking to shift the *BB′* and *YY′* curves to the left? The answer to this question, when costs and benefits are weighed on the scales of the policy makers' value system, yields what we may call aggregative *and* structural full employment. In the United States, aggregative full employment in the early 1960s was assumed to correspond to an unemployment rate of about 4 per cent, and it was believed by many that unemployment might, by means of an intensive manpower policy, be brought down to 3 per cent—at a cost that was worth incurring in terms of the benefits to be achieved (U.S. Senate . . . 1964).

It is one thing to conceptualize the goal of full employment; it is another thing to quantify it. Most governments have been reluctant to announce the precise unemployment rate they consider to be equivalent to full employment. One can, however, draw some inferences from recent policy actions and statements. Thus, in 1964–1965 it was reasonable to assume that the full-employment targets in the leading European countries ranged between about 1.5 and 3 per cent unemployment, using American definitions (Gordon 1965). For the United States the corresponding target figure would be about 4 per cent.

The targets cited here correspond to what has been called "aggregative full employment." In addition, governments have various kinds of manpower policies aimed at reducing structural and frictional unemployment.

Other aggregative goals. The potential conflict between full employment and price stability has already been mentioned. There are also at least three other "aggregative" goals that need to be taken into account when a government seeks to pursue a full-employment policy. They are balance-of-payments equilibrium, growth of total output, and what has come to be called "incomes policy" (chiefly keeping the rise in wages in line with the increase in productivity).

There is normally no conflict between the goals of full employment and rapid economic growth. But there is some conflict between full employment and the other goals. Involved here is a set of interrelationships that can conveniently be discussed in two parts.

First, relative price stability is a goal that is desired to some extent for its own sake. The more rapidly prices rise or fall—apart from balance-of-payments considerations—the greater is the damage to economic welfare as seen by those who frame economic policy. In recent years Germany and the United States have been the two large countries that have shown the greatest sensitivity to inflationary pressures. In most European countries, however, the trade-off between unemployment and price stability seems to be such that the governments concerned would not be willing to sacrifice much, if any, employment in order to reduce the rate of price increase—*provided* that (1) prices in other countries rose also, so that serious balance-of-payments problems did not arise, and (2) the rise in prices did not degenerate into runaway inflation.

This brings us to the second aspect of the potential conflict between full employment and the other aggregative goals. The strongest threat to pursuit of a vigorous full-employment policy comes from the possibility of balance-of-payments disequilibrium. If expansionary policies cause spending and prices to rise faster at home than abroad, a country may incur a deficit in its balance of payments which, if continued long enough, will force it to devalue its currency. This is an especially serious problem for countries for which international trade is particularly important. Such countries will, from time to time, be forced to pursue restrictive monetary and fiscal policies, sacrificing some employment in order to protect international monetary reserves. In the early 1960s the United States was apparently prepared to put up with unemployment considerably in excess of what was widely considered to be the full-employment target, in part because of the need to reduce the persistent deficit in its balance of payments. In 1966, the British government felt compelled to impose strong deflationary measures to protect the balance of payments.

It is in this connection that price stability plays its most important role. Price stability is a means of achieving balance-of-payments equilibrium. It is primarily a means, rather than an end in itself. It might be noted that what is important here for the balance of payments is not the behavior of the domestic price level by itself but the behavior of domestic prices relative to that of foreign prices.

As the 1960s began, there was increasing recognition on both sides of the Atlantic of the need for an incomes policy that would hold the rise in wages roughly in line with the rise in labor productivity (Organization for Economic Cooperation and Development . . . 1962; U.S. President 1962, pp. 185–190). The Netherlands has had an official, but only partially successful, incomes policy since the end of the war. Here again there is a potential conflict with a vigorous full-employment policy. An incomes policy is extremely difficult to apply unless a government is prepared either to exercise compulsion or to accept a higher level of unemployment than would otherwise be necessary. It is not surprising, therefore, that efforts to implement an incomes policy have not so far been very successful.

The events of the decade from the mid-1950s to the mid-1960s suggest a strong contrast between the ways in which western Europe and the United States reconciled the full-employment and other aggregative goals during this period. The United States was prepared to sacrifice a significant amount of employment in order to keep a relatively stable price level, partly for its own sake but chiefly for the sake of its balance-of-payments position. The relative emphasis put on a fairly strict interpretation of the full-employment goal was considerably stronger in Europe. (For further discussion of the issues in this section see Gordon 1965; Ross 1964, pp. 155–171; Gordon & Gordon 1966.)

Development of manpower programs. The increasing recognition of the need to formulate the goal of full employment in structural as well as aggregative terms calls for not only the appropriate use of monetary–fiscal measures but also the development of a comprehensive manpower program.

Manpower policy is concerned with the structural aspects of employment and unemployment—with facilitating the adjustment of the composition of labor supply to the changing composition of labor demand. A well-developed manpower program would include measures of the following types: (1) an active and comprehensive employment service to assist in placement, to provide vocational guidance, and possibly to collect data on vacancies; (2) an adequate system of unemployment insurance, integrated with a system of subsistence allowances for retraining and aid in the relocation of workers; (3) programs to facilitate the geographical mobility of workers; (4) heavy emphasis on training and retraining to assist workers in acquiring new skills; (5) special programs for the physically and mentally handicapped and for older workers; (6) a well-developed program of projecting the future demand for labor and prospective shortages and surpluses of particular kinds of labor, and wide dissemination of such information; (7) cooperation with the schools in the improvement of vocational education; and (8) special employment projects to assist particular regions or groups of workers in making difficult adjustments to new patterns of demand.

Sweden has a particularly well-developed manpower program that aims to be "so varied, so individualised as—in time—to fit every single person on the employment market" (Olsson 1963, p. 411). Most of the other western European countries have significant manpower programs, which vary in the aspects that have been particularly emphasized. Thus, training and retraining have been stressed in France and Italy; Sweden has emphasized regional labor mobility as well as retraining; regional industrial development has played a key role in manpower policy in the United Kingdom. All of these countries—as well as the other countries of western Europe—have also developed, to different degrees, various of the other dimensions of manpower policy previously listed. It is interesting to note also that elements of an international manpower policy have been developed within the European Common Market.

Spurred by high over-all unemployment and concerned with the especially high unemployment rates in particular segments of the labor force, the United States began to move toward a comprehensive manpower policy at the beginning of the 1960s. A decentralized employment service had existed since the 1930s, as had a system of unemployment insurance. In 1961 the Area Redevelopment Act was passed, followed in 1962 by the much more comprehensive Manpower Development and Training Act. The emphasis in the latter was almost entirely on retraining. Other measures have involved acceleration of public works, federal support of education, special provisions for the training and rehabilitation of underprivileged youth, and special measures to counter discrimination against Negroes (U.S. President 1963; 1964).

By 1965 no country had yet developed a manpower program "so varied, so individualised as to fit every single person on the employment market." But movement toward this goal, more rapid and systematic in some countries than in others, was the trend. Avowed full-employment goals and systematic manpower policies did not exist in the Western world when the great depression struck. Considerable progress toward the formulation of such goals and the implementation of such policies has been made since then.

R. A. GORDON

[See also MONETARY POLICY; FISCAL POLICY; INFLATION AND DEFLATION; and the biography of BEVERIDGE.]

BIBLIOGRAPHY

BEVERIDGE, WILLIAM H. (1909) 1930 *Unemployment: A Problem of Industry.* London: Longmans.

BEVERIDGE, WILLIAM H. (1944) 1945 *Full Employment in a Free Society.* New York: Norton.

Employment and Unemployment: Government Policies Since 1950: I. 1956 *International Labour Review* 74:1–22.

GERMANY (FEDERAL REPUBLIC), BUNDESMINISTERIUM FÜR ARBEIT UND SOZIALORDNUNG 1952 *Analyse der westdeutschen Arbeitslosigkeit, Statistik.* Bonn: The Ministerium.

GERMANY (FEDERAL REPUBLIC), BUNDESANSTALT FÜR ARBEITSVERMITTLUNG UND ARBEITSLOSENVERSICHERUNG 1962 *Ein Jahrzehnt Bundesanstalt für Arbeitsvermittlung und Arbeitslosenversicherung: 1952–1962.* Nuremberg: The Institute.

GORDON, R. A. 1964 Has Structural Unemployment Worsened? *Industrial Relations* 3:53–77.

GORDON, R. A. 1965 Full Employment as a Policy Goal. Pages 25–55 in Arthur M. Ross (editor), *Employment Policy and the Labor Market.* Berkeley: Univ. of California Press. → From the second Conference on Unemployment and the American Economy, held in 1964 at Boulder, Colorado.

GORDON, R. A.; and GORDON, MARGARET (editors) 1966 *Prosperity and Unemployment.* New York: Wiley.

KUZNETS, SIMON 1957 Quantitative Aspects of the Economic Growth of Nations: 2. Industrial Distribution of National Product and Labor Force. *Economic Development and Cultural Change* 5, no. 4, part 2.

LEBERGOTT, STANLEY 1964 *Manpower in Economic Growth: The American Record Since 1800.* New York: McGraw-Hill.

MADDISON, ANGUS 1964 *Economic Growth in the West: Comparative Experience in Europe and North America.* New York: Twentieth Century Fund.

MYERS, ROBERT J. 1964 Unemployment in Western Europe and the United States. Pages 172–198 in Arthur M. Ross (editor), *Unemployment and the American Economy.* New York: Wiley. → From the first Conference on Unemployment and the American Economy, held in 1963 at Berkeley, California.

OLSSON, B. 1963 Employment Policy in Sweden. *International Labour Review* 87:409–434.

ORGANIZATION FOR ECONOMIC COOPERATION AND DEVELOPMENT 1963 *Manpower Statistics: 1950–1962.* Paris: The Organization.

ORGANIZATION FOR ECONOMIC COOPERATION AND DEVELOPMENT, ECONOMIC POLICY COMMITTEE 1962 *Policies for Price Stability: A Report to the Economic Policy Committee by Its Working Party on Costs of Production and Prices.* Paris: The Organization.

PHILLIPS, A. W. 1958 The Relation Between Unemployment and the Rate of Change of Money Wage Rates in the United Kingdom: 1861–1957. *Economica* New Series 25:283–299.

Rates of Unemployment. 1964 U.S. Bureau of Labor Statistics, *Monthly Report on Labor Force, Employment, Unemployment, Hours and Earnings* [1964] January:34–35.

ROSS, ARTHUR M. (editor) 1964 *Unemployment and the American Economy.* New York: Wiley. → From the first Conference on Unemployment and the American Economy, held in 1963 at Berkeley, California.

TWENTIETH CENTURY FUND 1961 *Europe's Needs and Resources: Trends and Prospects in Eighteen Countries.* New York: The Fund.

Unemployment and Structural Change. 1962 International Labour Office, *Studies and Reports* New Series [1962] No. 65.

Unemployment Rate. 1966 U.S. Bureau of Labor Statistics, *Employment and Earnings and Monthly Report of the Labor Force* [1966] February:20–24.

UNITED NATIONS, DEPARTMENT OF ECONOMIC AFFAIRS 1949 *National and International Measures for Full Employment.* Lake Success, N.Y.: United Nations.

U.S. BUREAU OF THE CENSUS 1960 *Historical Statistics of the United States; Colonial Times to 1957: A Statistical Abstract Supplement.* Washington: Government Printing Office.

U.S. CONGRESS, JOINT ECONOMIC COMMITTEE 1961 *Unemployment: Terminology, Measurement and Analysis.* Washington: Government Printing Office.

U.S. CONGRESS, SENATE, COMMITTEE ON LABOR AND PUBLIC WELFARE 1963 *Nation's Manpower Revolution: Hearings Before the Subcommittee on Employment and Manpower of the Committee on Labor and Public Welfare.* Washington: Government Printing Office.

U.S. PRESIDENT 1962 *Economic Report of the President.* Washington: Government Printing Office. → Published annually since 1947.

U.S. PRESIDENT 1963 *Manpower Report of the President.* Washington: Government Printing Office.

U.S. PRESIDENT 1964 *Manpower Report of the President.* Washington: Government Printing Office.

U.S. PRESIDENT 1966 *Manpower Report of the President.* Washington: Government Printing Office.

U.S. PRESIDENT'S COMMITTEE TO APPRAISE EMPLOYMENT AND UNEMPLOYMENT STATISTICS 1962 *Measuring Employment and Unemployment.* Washington: Government Printing Office.

U.S. SENATE, LABOR AND PUBLIC WELFARE COMMITTEE 1964 *Toward Full Employment: Proposals for Comprehensive Employment and Manpower Policy in the United States.* Washington: Government Printing Office.

ENCLAVES AND EXCLAVES

Enclaves and exclaves are discontiguous territories of states which are located within the territory of other states. Seen from the state within which the outlier is located, it is an *enclave;* seen from the state to which the outlier belongs, it is an *exclave.* A typical example is the Spanish town of Llivia in the eastern Pyrenees of France: this is an exclave of Spain, entirely surrounded by French territory and located about four miles from the main Spanish territory; it is also a Spanish enclave within French territory.

Enclaves (exclaves) may be accessible to the main territory of the state to which they belong by land, through the territory of other states, as well as by sea. A typical example is the former German exclave of East Prussia, which from 1919 to 1939, as well as in previous centuries, was separated from the main German territory by Polish territory and the Baltic Sea. However, if discontiguous territories are accessible only by sea, they are usually described as islands; if they are located on other continents, as colonies or associated territories. Thus Hong Kong is regarded as a colony of Great Britain in eastern Asia, although, from the Chinese point of view, it is sometimes described as a British enclave surrounded, on the landward side, by Chinese territory. Gibraltar can similarly be regarded as a British colony on the continent of Europe and as an enclave within Spain. In these cases the nomenclature is necessarily vague; however, this does not detract from the political, economic, and historical significance of enclaves and exclaves.

Territorial waters have the same sovereign attributes as land, and enclaves may therefore exist within territorial waters. A typical example is the islands of Chisamula and Likoma in Lake Nyasa; they are located within the territorial waters of Portuguese Mozambique but are exclaves of Malawi.

States entirely surrounded by territory of one other state, for example, the Vatican, share the characteristics of enclaves and are sometimes referred to as *virtual exclaves.* Contiguous territories of states which for all regular commercial and administrative purposes can be reached only through the territory of other states are called *pene-enclaves* (*pene-exclaves*). These have virtually the same characteristics as complete enclaves (exclaves). A typical example is the Drumully area of the Republic of Ireland, which can be reached by road and rail only through territory of Great Britain (Northern Ireland).

Enclaves (exclaves) should be distinguished

from *neutral territories* that sometimes separate states, for example, those on the northeastern border of Saudi Arabia. Sovereignty in neutral territories is shared between two or more states, and territorial discontiguity is not an essential characteristic. However, for convenience of administration some governmental functions, for example, customs and excise, may be relinquished by the sovereign of the enclave (exclave) to the sovereign of the surrounding territory, and thus an impression of shared sovereignty can result.

Except for the unique cases of East Pakistan and West Berlin, enclaves are today relatively unimportant economically and cover only small areas, usually less than 20 square kilometers. Their political and military value is probably also very limited. Some enclaves (exclaves), for example, West Berlin (including Steinstücken, Papenberger Wiesen, etc.) consist of several parcels of territory, which makes accurate statistical accounting virtually impossible.

Origin of the terms.   Use of the terms originated during the late Middle Ages. The first diplomatic document to contain the word "enclave" was the Treaty of Madrid, signed in 1526. Since then the terms have also been used outside political geography; parks, for example, have been described as rural enclaves within cities. Similarly, areas of low prices located within higher price regions, for example, areas along major highways within a high price region where low gasoline prices are posted, are described as low-price enclaves.

Geographical distribution.   Most enclaves today are relics of the feudal era, and western Europe contains the largest number, about fifteen. Formerly there were many more; for example, prior to 1866 Prussia alone consisted of more than 270 discontiguous pieces of territory. India also contained large numbers of enclaves prior to independence. During and after the crusades, enclaves were a fairly widespread phenomenon in the eastern Mediterranean region, and presumably they also existed elsewhere during periods of feudal rule. Through accidents of discovery and difficulties of inland penetration, enclaves were also frequently established during the colonial era in or near the coasts of Africa and Asia. Today only a few survive, for example, the Portuguese Cabinda enclave north of the mouth of the Congo. When considered as enclaves, British Hong Kong and Gibraltar fall into this category. Similar Portuguese (Goa, for instance, but also complete exclaves entirely surrounded by non-Portuguese territory, such as Nagar Aveli) and French enclaves (such as Pondicherry, but also complete exclaves, such as Chandernagore) in India have disappeared from the map since India gained independence.

Throughout history, enclaves were sometimes deliberately established to assure control of neighboring areas, for example, by the settlement of Roman veterans in classical times; a modern example is that of the British enclaves on Cyprus created in 1960 to control the eastern Mediterranean and the Middle East. Errors of definition with respect to straight-line boundaries have caused the establishment of two enclaves in North America near the 49th parallel (Point Roberts, Washington, and Lake of the Woods County, Minnesota, both of which are in Canada). Where rivers form boundaries between states, changes of river courses have frequently created enclaves on opposite shores, as on the Mississippi River; where such changes resulted in international boundary problems, these enclaves were usually eliminated by exchange of territory and other compensation, as occurred between the United States and Mexico on the Rio Grande.

The enclaves of West Berlin and of the Hebrew University campus (part of Israel within Jordanian territory) were the result of recent armistice agreements. Similar temporary arrangements have been recorded frequently, particularly in feudal times. The enclaves of East Prussia and of East Pakistan were created in this century to accommodate national or religious aspirations. For the same national reasons the internal spatial organization of the Soviet Union exhibits several enclaves. Parts of former German East Prussia now constitute an enclave of the Russian Soviet Federated Socialist Republic. To what extent the enclaves shown on maps of the Soviet Union are economically or politically significant is not known. Although several enclaves have survived since the early Middle Ages, most have disappeared with the growth of centralized states, and many appear to be only temporary features of modern political geography.

Theories of origin.   Most settlements were virtually self-sufficient before the advent of modern transportation, and generally only goods of high value and little bulk were exchanged over distances of more than a few miles. Because of high costs of transportation, most settlements and their environs were surrounded by undeveloped lands separating them from neighboring settlements (Thünen 1826–1863). In the feudal era each of these settlements became dominated by a local ruler who, by war, marriage, or purchase, tried to enlarge his territories. Messengers and the small armies of the era could move through the undeveloped lands between the settlements, and since there was also little trade, there was no need for feudal territories to be contiguous. Thus the pattern of enclaves which is so characteristic of this period gradually evolved. Territorial discontiguity was found not only at the lowest but also at the highest level of the feudal hierarchy. Even self-governing cities contained both enclaves and exclaves. Territorial discontiguity was most marked in Germany but also existed in much more centralized Great Britain, where a few enclaves survive to this day among county areas, for example, in Flintshire.

The modern era. As a result of the growth of the modern state, enclaves were gradually absorbed into the new national territories. Ratzel (1896) and other German geographers, particularly the later German school of "geopolitics," regarded this absorption as an "organic" phenomenon in the evolution of so-called natural boundaries of states. These are frequently related to physical features of geography, such as seacoasts, watersheds, or mountain crests, but usually are poorly definable except in the context of nationalistic ambition. Arguments of this nature were, for example, used by India to defend its action in occupying the Portuguese enclaves and exclaves on the Indian subcontinent. At the time of the French Revolution the process of absorption was already virtually complete in the Iberian Peninsula, Great Britain, and Scandinavia. As a result of the French Revolution the many vestiges of enclaves (particularly with respect to internal tariffs) disappeared from France, and the number of enclaves was considerably reduced in central Europe and Italy. Because of the lesser significance of feudalism in eastern Europe, enclaves were far less important, and they completely disappeared during the nineteenth century.

The final reduction in the number of enclaves to the present low and insignificant figure took place during the period of railway construction. Enclaves came to be regarded as economically and politically absurd, as revealed in the discussion of the problem of German East Prussia during the period between the two world wars. The introduction of motorcars also increased the possibility of smuggling from enclaves (always a serious matter) and assisted public demand for the abolition of enclaves, as in India and Switzerland. Within sovereign states, administrative enclaves, usually relics of the process of state amalgamation following the feudal era, were also greatly reduced in number by the redefinition of local boundaries, as in India and Germany. However, many enclaves have survived in the cantonal system of the Swiss Confederation.

Since World War II the development of air transportation and the building of limited-access highways and railways with systems of overpasses and underpasses have presented new opportunities for connecting enclaves to other territory of the same state. The air lanes, highways, and railways connecting West Berlin to West Germany are an example, although these connections have not worked very satisfactorily. The United Nations partition scheme in 1947 for the former British mandate of Palestine called for a series of discontiguous Arab and Jewish territories, each consisting of a main territory and two exclaves. These exclaves were to touch the main territories at two junction points, where short overpasses and underpasses of limited-access transportation avenues were to connect them with the main territories. While the violent rejection of this partition scheme was the result of other more serious national considerations, there appears to be little doubt that these connecting links between exclaves and main territories were also regarded as highly unsatisfactory. For all these reasons it is unlikely that the new means of transportation will bring about an increase in the number of enclaves.

ALEXANDER MELAMID

BIBLIOGRAPHY

LÖSCH, AUGUST (1940) 1954 *The Economics of Location.* New Haven: Yale Univ. Press. → First published as *Die räumliche Ordnung der Wirtschaft.*

MELAMID, ALEXANDER 1955 The Economic Geography of Neutral Territories. *Geographical Review* 45:359–374.

MELAMID, ALEXANDER 1966 Municipal Quasi-exclaves: Examples From Yonkers, New York. *Professional Geographer* 18, no. 2:94–96.

MINGHI, JULIAN V. 1963 Boundary Studies in Political Geography. Association of American Geographers, *Annals* 53:407–428.

RATZEL, FRIEDRICH 1896 Die Gesetze des räumlichen Wachstums der Staaten. *Petermann's Mitteilungen* 42:97–107.

ROBINSON, G. W. S. 1959 Exclaves. Association of American Geographers, *Annals* 49:283–295. → Contains the best listing of the exclaves existing in 1958.

THÜNEN, JOHANN H. VON (1826–1863) 1930 *Der isolierte Staat in Beziehung auf Landwirtschaft und Nationalökonomie.* 3 vols. Jena (Germany): Fischer.

ENCULTURATION
See SOCIALIZATION.

ENDOGAMY
See INCEST *and* MARRIAGE.

ENGAGEMENT
See MARRIAGE *and* NUPTIALITY.

ENGEL, ERNST

Ernst Engel (1821–1896) was a German statistician. After his early training at a mining academy in Germany, Engel went to the École des Mines in Paris, where he came under the influence of Frédéric Le Play, a pioneer in the study of family budgets, who was a professor there. During a subsequent stay in Belgium he became acquainted with Adolphe Quetelet, well-known for his faith in the possibility of discovering quantitative social laws. Upon his return to Germany Engel took up statistics as a profession and became director of the statistical bureaus of Saxony, 1850–1858, and Prussia, 1861–1882. As a vigorous administrator and inspiring teacher he did much to establish the modern tradition of official statistics; in particular, he insisted on making statistical data accessible and intelligible to the general public. He was also active in the social reform movement, which he supplied not only with figures but also with various practical proposals. In 1881 he published a pseudonymous attack on Bismarck's agricultural protectionism and was promptly relieved of his position on grounds of ill-health. Of the great work on "demology" that he then set out to write only a fragment was completed.

His greatest contribution to the social sciences soon became known as "Engel's law." It states that the proportion of a consumer's budget spent on food tends to decline as the consumer's income goes up, or, in more technical terms, that the income elasticity of demand for food is less than one. Engel derived this generalization from the budgets collected in different countries by his teacher Le Play and from Belgian data compiled by Édouard Ducpétiaux; it has since been invariably confirmed in hundreds of more elaborate surveys in all parts of the world.

Engel published his discovery in the context of a study of the economic development of Saxony (1857), in which he demonstrated that a general rise in productivity requires a shift of population from agriculture to manufacturing because of the effect of an increase in income on the pattern of demand. He also advanced his observations as an argument against Malthus' fears of overpopulation.

From a methodological point of view Engel's law is important as the first significant quantitative law ever established by empirical economic data.

Formulated when economic theory proceeded largely by deduction from a priori assumptions, the law pointed the way to a more reliable approach. It also drew attention to the study of demand, which had been neglected by the classical economists, and suggested that economic development is not merely a matter of capital accumulation. Engel, however, was not much interested in economic theory and considered himself primarily a statistician, as did his numerous followers in the empirical study of family budgets, at least until recently.

Attempts were soon made to find similar generalizations for other categories of expenditure, such as housing and clothing. But here the pattern of demand was not so simple, at least when analyzed in terms of increasing or decreasing budget shares. Thus the "laws" of Schwabe for housing and Schiff for clothing, which state that the share of these categories respectively falls and rises as income increases, are not as universally valid as Engel's law, although they probably hold in a majority of budget surveys. For these two categories the income elasticity is normally so close to one that in a particular survey it may be on either side of unity. From a review of the evidence accumulated during the century following the enunciation of Engel's law, Houthakker (1957) concluded that the typical elasticity with respect to total expenditure is 0.6 for food, 0.8 for housing, 1.2 for clothing, and 1.6 for all other expenditures combined.

The relation between the expenditure on a particular item or group of items on the one hand and income or total expenditure on the other is now generally known as an "Engel curve." Such curves have been extensively studied, especially after the development of regression analysis around the turn of the century. Engel could not avail himself of this technique and had to fit his food–total expenditure relationship by graphical methods. Perhaps the most important instance of an Engel curve is Keynes's consumption function (1936), which relates total expenditure to income and has become the cornerstone of macroeconomic analysis. There is a clear line of descent from Engel's law to Keynes's "fundamental psychological law," according to which the proportion of total consumption to income falls as income goes up.

Engel refined his analysis of family budgets by taking household composition into account. In his little book *Der Kostenwerth des Menschen* ("The Cost of Man"), published in 1883, he proposed what has since become known as an equivalent adult scale to give appropriate weights to persons of different ages and sexes; Engel's unit, however, was not the consumption of an adult male, as in most later scales, but the consumption of an infant under one year. He called this unit "quet" in honor of Quetelet. In this book there are also interesting calculations on some economic aspects of education.

With a little more perseverance Engel could have established another claim to fame, namely, to have initiated not only the cross-section analysis but also the time-series analysis of demand. In a paper of 1861 on the Prussian grain market he derived an empirical demand curve for rye with a price elasticity of about one-half, but he did not consider the results sufficiently trustworthy to pursue the subject, although he did claim to have refuted Gregory King's "law" on the demand for grain. The lack of suitable curve-fitting techniques may have held back his work in this area, and the estimation of empirical demand curves had to wait until the twentieth century.

Engel wrote on many other subjects, including labor and industry, taxation, insurance, banking, and war. His influence extended into many other countries; in the United States, Carroll Wright, founder of the Bureau of Labor Statistics, was his principal follower. Engel was also active in the International Statistical Congresses, the forerunners of the International Statistical Institute of which he was a founder in 1886.

H. S. HOUTHAKKER

[For the historical context of Engel's work, see the biographies of KING; LE PLAY; MALTHUS; QUETELET. For discussion of the subsequent development of his ideas, see CONSUMERS, article on CONSUMPTION LEVELS AND STANDARDS; CONSUMPTION FUNCTION; DEMAND AND SUPPLY, article on ECONOMETRIC STUDIES.]

WORKS BY ENGEL

(1857) 1895 Die Productions- und Consumtionsverhält-nisse des Königreichs Sachsen. International Statistical Institute, *Bulletin* 9, no. 1, supplement 1. → First published in Volume 3 of Saxony, Statistisches Landes-amt, *Zeitschrift des statistischen Bureaus des Königlich Sächsischen Ministeriums des Innern.*

1861 Die Getreidepreise, die Ernteerträge und der Getreidehandel im preussischen Staate. Prussia, Statistisches Landesamt, *Zeitschrift des Königlich Preussischen Statistischen Bureaus* 1:249–289.

(1866) 1872 *Der Preis der Arbeit: Zwei Vorlesungen.* 2d ed. Berlin: Habel.

1872a Beiträge zur Statistik des Krieges von 1870–1871. Prussia, Statistisches Landesamt, *Zeitschrift des Königlich Preussischen Statistischen Bureaus* 12:1–318.

1872b Die Wohnungsnoth: Ein Vortrag auf der Eisenacher Conferenz. Prussia, Statistisches Landesamt,

Zeitschrift des Königlich Preussischen Statistischen Bureaus 12:379–402.

1875 Die Klassen- und klassificirte Einkommensteuer und die Einkommensvertheilung im preussischen Staat in den Jahren 1852 bis 1875. Prussia, Statistisches Landesamt, *Zeitschrift des Königlich Preussischen Statistischen Bureaus* 15:105–148.

1881 *Deutschlands Getreideproduktion, Brodbedarf und Brodbeschaffung.* By C. Lorenz [pseud.]. Volkswirthschaftliche Zeitfragen, Vol. 3, Part 6. Berlin: Simion.

1883 *Der Kostenwerth des Menschen.* Berlin: Simion. → Published as Part 1 of Engel's *Der Werth des Menschen*, a projected multivolume edition.

1895 Die Lebenskosten belgischer Arbeiter-familien früher und jetzt. International Statistical Institute, *Bulletin* 9, no. 1:i–vi, 1–124.

SUPPLEMENTARY BIBLIOGRAPHY

ALLEN, ROY G. D.; and BOWLEY, ARTHUR L. 1935 *Family Expenditure: A Study of Its Variation.* London School of Economics and Political Science, Studies in Statistics and Scientific Method, No. 2. London: King.

BLENCK, E. 1896 Zum Gedächtniss an Ernst Engel: Ein Lebensbild. Prussia, Statistisches Landesamt, *Zeitschrift des Königlich Preussischen Statistischen Bureaus* 36:231–238. → Contains a partial bibliography.

FEIG, J. 1907 Ernst Engel. *Allgemeines statistisches Archiv* 7, no. 1:349–359.

FÖLDES, BÉLA 1918/1919 Ernst Engel. *Allgemeines statistisches Archiv* 11:229–245.

HOUTHAKKER, H. S. 1957 An International Comparison of Household Expenditure Patterns, Commemorating the Centenary of Engel's Law. *Econometrica* 25:532–551.

KEYNES, JOHN MAYNARD 1936 *The General Theory of Employment, Interest and Money.* London: Macmillan. → A paperback edition was published in 1965 by Harcourt.

KNAPP, G. F. 1897 *Grundherrschaft und Rittergut.* Leipzig: Duncker & Humblot.

PRAIS, S. J.; and HOUTHAKKER, H. S. 1955 *The Analysis of Family Budgets With an Application to Two British Surveys Conducted in 1937–1939 and Their Detailed Results.* Cambridge Univ. Press.

STIGLER, GEORGE J. 1954 The Early History of Empirical Studies of Consumer Behavior. *Journal of Political Economy* 62:95–113.

ZIMMERMAN, CARLE C. 1936 *Consumption and Standards of Living.* New York: Van Nostrand.

ENGELS, FRIEDRICH

Friedrich Engels was born in Barmen, Germany, in 1820 and died in London in 1895. He was the closest friend of Karl Marx and cofounder of so-called scientific socialism.

Engels was the oldest son in a family of eight children. His father owned a cotton-spinning mill in Barmen and was a partner in another spinning mill, Ermen and Engels, of Manchester and Engelskirchen. Engels attended the *Realschule* in Barmen and the Gymnasium in Elberfeld. To prepare himself for the study of jurisprudence, he studied mercantile problems, first in his father's firm, and then, from 1838 to 1841, in Bremen. Engels then did a year's military service.

He was greatly impressed in his youth with the contrast between the pietistic Calvinism of the middle class in his native city and the misery of the working class, demoralized by drink. Using the pseudonym of Oswald he wrote about this situation in his "Briefe aus dem Wuppertal" (1839), a vivid description of these conditions that shows how early his literary and journalistic ability developed. Little by little he turned away from pietism and religion, strongly influenced by David Friedrich Strauss's critique of the Gospels in *Das Leben Jesu* and, above all, by Ludwig Feuerbach's *Wesen des Christentums*. He affirmed his radical break with religion in his *Schelling und die Offenbarung* (1842a) and in his spirited, witty satire, *Schelling, der Philosoph in Christo* (1842b). These were writings in part aimed at the king of Prussia, who had appointed Schelling to the University of Berlin as Hegel's successor, hoping that he would become the intellectual exponent of his "Christian state." Engels read political criticisms by the members of the "Junge Deutschland," particularly those of Ludwig Börne, and he began to write as a Young Hegelian, one of that group of left-wing intellectuals in Berlin that included the brothers Edgar and Bruno Bauer and the anarchist Max Stirner. Karl Marx also belonged to this group while he was a student in Berlin. Engels' satirical Christian epic, "Die frech bedräute, jedoch wunderbar befreite Bibel: Oder Triumph des Glaubens" (1842c), which was published anonymously, reflected the views of this group. Engels wrote this work when the king of Prussia withdrew Bruno Bauer's *venia legendi* at the University of Bonn because of his criticism of the Gospels. It was Moses Hess who guided Engels to the work of the early French socialists such as Saint-Simon and Charles Fourier and boasted that he had transformed this "revolutionary of the year 1" (i.e., 1793) into a communist.

Engels moved to Manchester in October 1842 to complete his commercial training. He criticized English political and social conditions in the *Rheinische Zeitung*, to which he had contributed since March 1842. At the same time he also wrote for the periodicals of the Chartists and Owenites, describing the development of socialism on the Continent. He supplemented his empirical observations by studying the English economists. In his brilliant "Umrisse zu einer Kritik der Nationalökonomie" (1844), which appeared in the *Deutsch–Französische Jahrbücher*, edited by Marx and the Young Hegelian Arnold Ruge, there is, according to Marx,

an early formulation of the general principles of scientific socialism. Engels here demonstrated the contradictions in liberal economic doctrine and showed that all economic phenomena are, in the end, based on private property. He demanded that private property be abolished. After the publication of this essay, Marx and Engels began to correspond. When they met in Paris in the autumn of 1844, they found, according to Engels, that they were in "complete agreement in all theoretical areas."

There are similarities in the early development of Marx and Engels that seem, on the surface, astonishing: a common literary and poetic bent, a common concern with religious problems, and a similar involvement in juridical–political discussion that led both of them from left-wing Hegelianism to communism. But it was, of course, the situation in Germany during that time that largely determined their common concerns, especially the authoritarianism of Friedrich Wilhelm IV and the political radicalization of the German intellectuals that was a reaction to it. Marx and Engels went beyond bourgeois–liberal criticism, however, thus parting from their former friends, whom they subjected to merciless criticism in *The Holy Family* (1845a), mainly written by Marx, and *The German Ideology* (1845–1846), published posthumously. Their reasons for becoming communists were not identical, to be sure. Engels was brought to the point of revolutionary outrage by his observation of the workers' misery, while Marx, the rationalist, identified the proletariat as the only class that might be fitted by its extreme misery to effect a revolutionary transformation. More subject as Engels was to intense personal and emotional impressions, he always remained second in achievement to Marx. He phrased this aptly himself: "I could never have achieved what Marx did. Marx stood higher, saw farther, and had a broader and quicker grasp of a situation than all the rest of us. Marx was a genius; we others were at best talented" ([1886] 1941, p. 292).

This estimate, however, should not let us overlook the fact that at the beginning of their collaboration it was Engels who was the leading partner, precisely because he assimilated knowledge readily and because his occupation brought him much closer to economics. This is illustrated by *The Condition of the Working Class in England* (1845b), which was planned as a chapter of a comprehensive social history of England. This work by the "doubtless most talented and well-informed of all German writers on sociology," as Hildebrand called him ([1848] 1922, p. 170), is according to Lorenz von Stein, "a picture of the deepest poverty, taken from the dirtiest district of the dirtiest factory town in England, full of incontrovertible facts from this most miserable sphere of the industrial world, beyond any question the best invective ever written in Germany against industrial society and its conditions, a partisan book like no other. That is why the book had so powerful an effect, much more convincing by its exaggerations and errors than by its truths, as is the fate of all such works" (1852, p. 538).

After he and Marx began to work together, Engels seems intentionally to have left to Marx theoretical work, thus acknowledging (and later expressly emphasizing) that the elaboration of the materialist conception of history was essentially Marx's work. He himself took credit for only a "very small part" thereof, asserting that most of the basic ideas, especially in the economic and historical fields, and more particularly their final acute formulations, were due to Marx. While Marx was writing the important theory sections of *The German Ideology* and was criticizing Proudhon in *The Poverty of Philosophy* (1847a), Engels was engaged as an agitator. As early as 1843 he had established contact in London with the leaders of a German secret society, the League of the Just. At the end of 1844 he and Moses Hess held communist meetings in the Rhineland, until such meetings were suppressed. In Brussels, where he moved in April 1845 in order to be close to Marx, he was mainly active in the International Communist Committee of Correspondence, founded by Marx and himself. In August 1846 he went to Paris, where after prolonged discussions he succeeded in weaning the local group of the League of the Just from the influence of Wilhelm Weitling, the early German socialist, and P. J. Proudhon, the French anarchist. At the first congress of the League in London in June 1847, he succeeded in transforming it into the Communist League. The second congress, in the fall of 1847, commissioned him and Marx to draw up a party program. Engels prepared a draft of such a program, *Principles of Communism* (1847b), written in the form of a catechism. It is significant as a draft of the famous *Communist Manifesto* (1848), but the *Manifesto* itself clearly bears the intellectual and stylistic stamp of Marx.

After the outbreak of the Revolution of 1848, Engels and Marx went to Cologne. There Engels worked as editor of the *Neue Rheinische Zeitung* (published by Marx), since journalism was easier for him than for Marx. At various times there was a warrant out for his arrest because of his journal-istic activity. He also participated in the Elberfeld civil insurrection, but its leaders repudiated him as a "Red." After the suspension of the *Neue Rheinische Zeitung* in May 1849, he vainly endeavored, together with Marx, to expand the armed uprising in Baden and the Palatinate into a general German revolution. After the uprising collapsed he left for Switzerland and, in October 1849, for London. He portrayed these events in series of articles published in 1849 and 1850.

In London Engels wrote *The Peasant War in Germany* (1850). He hoped that the revolutionary traditions of the peasants might pave the way for a new German revolution, and he was convinced that the success of such a revolution depended on supporting the proletarian revolution by some second edition of the peasants' war of the sixteenth century. Engels' characterization of Thomas Münzer, one of the leaders of that revolt, reveals his insight into his own position. He believed that Münzer had been in a hopeless position: he was the leader of an extremist party, forced to take over a government prematurely, before the dominance of the class he represented could be accepted, and before the measures that the rule of his party implied could successfully be carried out ([[1850] 1956, pp. 138–139).

Engels, nevertheless, made a very intensive study of the wars of the French Revolution after 1792 to prepare himself for the military leadership of the future revolution. He expounded principles of revolutionary action in a series of articles, *Germany: Revolution and Counter-revolution* (1851–1852), the authorship of which was wrongly attributed to Marx. Engels' maxims were never to play with insurrection and always to act with the greatest resoluteness and to seize the offensive.

The defensive is the death of every armed rising; surprise your antagonists while their forces are scattering, prepare new successes, however small, but daily; keep up the moral ascendancy which the first successful rising has given you; rally those vacillating elements to your side which always follow the strongest impulse, and which always look out for the safer side; force your enemies to retreat before they can collect their strength against you; in the words of Danton, the greatest master of revolutionary policy yet known: *"de l'audace, de l'audace, encore de l'audace."* (Engels [1851–1852] 1933, p. 100)

From 1854 until 1870, when Engels was an employee and then a partner in his father's firm in Manchester, his writings dealt primarily with military science and earned him the sobriquet "General" among his friends. In the future proletarian revolution he was presumably cast for a role comparable to that of Carnot, the organizer of the *levée en masse* and the army of the French Revolution. He contributed articles to the *New American Encyclopedia* on the army, cavalry, fortifications, infantry, the navy, and so on. As a journalist he repeatedly described the armies of the various countries and evaluated their combat effectiveness. However, his writings went beyond topical journalism. He also concerned himself, in detail, with armaments, with the radical changes in warfare produced by the new industrial technology, and with the political implications of these developments (1859–1861). Thus he advocated expansion of the war of France and Italy against Austria into a German war against Napoleon III, whom he saw as the main adversary of the revolution. His *Die preussische Militärfrage und die deutsche Arbeiterpartei* (1865) was also primarily political: in the Prussian constitutional conflict over expansion of the army, he opposed Ferdinand Lassalle's complete dissociation of the interests of the workers from those of the middle class.

The most important evidence for Engels' activities in this period is his correspondence with Marx, which shows Engels' continuing financial assistance to Marx as well as his encouragement of Marx's writings. Engels' loyal friendship even led him to assume the paternity of Marx's illegitimate son, although this was also an expression of his unconventional conception of relations between the sexes. He himself lived for nearly twenty years with Mary Burns, an Irish working girl, and after her death in 1863 he lived with her sister Lizzy, marrying her only on her deathbed in 1878.

After he moved from Manchester to London in the autumn of 1870, Engels became a member of the General Council of the First International (founded in 1864) and its corresponding secretary for Spain, Portugal, Italy, Ireland, and for a time, Belgium. He played a prominent part in the dispute with Bakunin. He wrote *L'alliance de la démocratie socialiste et l'association internationale des travailleurs* (1873*b*) together with Marx and "Die Bakunisten an der Arbeit" (see 1873*a*) by himself. *Anti-Dühring: Herr Eugen Dühring's Revolution in Science* (1878) was aimed at Dühring's strong influence on German social democracy. Notwithstanding its polemics, it was the first popular exposition widely to promote the teachings of Marx. His *Socialism: Utopian and Scientific* (1880), a summary of the first three chapters of the *Anti-Dühring*, was even more popular.

Up to the death of Marx on March 14, 1883, Engels' major effort was devoted to the incomplete *Dialectics of Nature* (1873–1883). Conceived initially as an argument with Ludwig Büchner, it became an attack on the kind of metaphysics in the natural sciences that regarded natural phenomena as immutable, instead of considering them as ever-flowing, changing facts. By including the natural sciences, Engels made dialectics a "science of all interrelationships" and went beyond Marx's materialist conception of history to the *Weltanschauung* of "dialectical materialism." Engels extended the original concept yet further to include prehistory in *The Origin of the Family, Private Property, and the State* (1884*a*). This work, written after Marx's death, was based on L. H. Morgan's *Ancient Society* of 1877 and on Marx's synopsis of Morgan's book—in fulfillment of a legacy, so to speak.

After Marx's death Engels edited Volume 2 of *Capital* and prepared Volume 3 for the press, using the outlines left by Marx and making some studies of his own. No critical analysis of the extent of Engels' contributions to *Capital* has yet been made.

Engels took care of Marx's works in general, arranging new editions, providing them with his own prefaces, and defending Marx against learned attacks. This greatly overshadowed his own literary activity. Yet he did make important contributions to the history of Marxism: "Marx und die *Neue Rheinische Zeitung*" (1884*b*); "History of the Communist League" (1885); and *Ludwig Feuerbach and the Outcome of Classical German Philosophy* (1886). In the last years of his life, Engels wrote an important series of letters to Conrad, Schmidt, Bloch, Mehring, and Borgius in which he admitted the possibility that the superstructure could affect the economic infrastructure and thus opposed an overemphasis upon the regularity of historical events. This significant theoretical clarification had a considerable influence upon developments in the Soviet Union.

Engels was Marx's political as well as his literary heir. He played a very important part in the genesis of the Second International in 1889. He continued to act as an adviser to the various socialist parties, through Marx's son-in-law Lafarge in France and through Liebknecht, Bebel, and Bernstein in Germany. His forcing the party to publish Marx's *Critique of the Gotha Programme* (1875–1891), which condemned the theoretical concessions of the Lassalleans, led to violent intraparty disputes. In his "Introduction" to Marx's *The Class Struggles in France* (1895), Engels still defended revolutionary tactics despite the great successes achieved by social democracy after the establishment of universal suffrage. To be sure, he did stress that they must be different from earlier tactics: "The time is past for a revolutionary surprise attack carried out by small conscious minorities at the head of the uncomprehending masses." He attributed special importance to the problem of disarmament (1893) and foresaw the possibility of a future world war. He was stricken with cancer of the esophagus in the midst of his work.

In the influence exerted by Marxism, Engels' work continues to play its part. The extent of the effect of his military–scientific writings on, say, the Russian or the Chinese revolutions cannot yet be assessed, nor has scholarly work distinguishing between his specific views and those of Marx proceeded very far; in view of the decisive influence of Marx and the way in which these thinkers stimulated each other, this distinction is extremely difficult to draw. However, in the intellectual history of Marxism one might say that Engels represented its descent from early socialism, especially early French socialism, while Marx gave it the imprint of classical German philosophy.

THILO RAMM

[*For the historical context of Engels' work, see* MARX-ISM; REVOLUTION; SOCIALISM; *and the biographies of* BAKUNIN; FOURIER; MARX; MORGAN, LEWIS HENRY; PROUDHON; SAINT-SIMON. *For discussion of the subsequent development of his ideas, see the biographies of* BERNSTEIN; KAUTSKY; LENIN; TROTSKY.]

WORKS BY ENGELS

(1839) 1930   Briefe aus dem Wuppertal. By F. Oswald [pseud.]. Section 1, volume 2, pages 23–118 in Karl Marx and Friedrich Engels, *Historisch-kritische Gesamtausgabe: Werke, Schriften, Briefe.* Berlin: Marx-Engels Verlag. → First published in *Telegraph für Deutschland.*

(1839–1895a) 1927–1935   MARX, KARL; and ENGELS, FRIEDRICH *Historisch-kritische Gesamtausgabe: Werke, Schriften, Briefe.* 12 vols. Edited by David Riazanov; commissioned by the Marx–Engels Institute, Moscow. Frankfurt am Main, Berlin, and Moscow: Marx–Engels Verlag. → Includes manuscripts published posthumously.

(1839–1895b) 1956   MARX, KARL; and ENGELS, FRIEDRICH *Karl Marx, Friedrich Engels: Werke.* Volume 1. Berlin: Dietz. → The first volumes of a projected 36-volume edition.

1842a   *Schelling und die Offenbarung.* Leipzig: Bamberg. → Published anonymously.

1842b   *Schelling, der Philosoph in Christo: Oder die Verklärung der Weltweisheit zur Gottesweisheit.* Berlin: Eyssenhardt. → Published anonymously.

(1842c) 1930   Die frech bedräute, jedoch wunderbar befreite Bibel: Oder Triumph des Glaubens. Section 1, volume 2, pages 173–281 in Karl Marx and Friedrich Engels, *Historisch-kritische Gesamtausgabe: Werke, Schriften, Briefe.* Berlin: Marx-Engels Verlag. → Published anonymously.

(1843–1895) 1956   MARX, KARL; and ENGELS, FRIEDRICH *Karl Marx and Frederick Engels: Selected Correspondence.* Moscow: Foreign Languages Publishing House.

(1844) 1930   Umrisse zu einer Kritik der Nationalökonomie. Section 1, volume 2, pages 379–404 in *Historisch-kritische Gesamtausgabe: Werke, Schriften, Briefe.* Berlin: Marx–Engels Verlag. → First published in the *Deutsch–Französische Jahrbücher.*

(1845a) 1956   MARX, KARL; and ENGELS, FRIEDRICH *The Holy Family.* Moscow: Foreign Languages Publishing House. → First published as *Die heilige Familie.*

(1845b) 1958   *The Condition of the Working Class in England.* Oxford: Blackwell. → First published as *Die Lage der arbeitenden Klasse in England.*

(1845–1846) 1939   MARX, KARL; and ENGELS, FRIEDRICH *The German Ideology.* Parts 1 and 3. With an introduction by R. Pascal. New York: International Publishers. → Written in 1845–1846, the full text was first published in 1932 as *Die deutsche Ideologie* and republished by Dietz Verlag in 1953.

(1847a) 1963   Introduction. In Karl Marx, *The Poverty of Philosophy.* New York: International Publishers. → First published in French. A paperback edition was published in 1964.

(1847b) 1952   *Principles of Communism.* New York: Monthly Review. → Written in 1847; first published posthumously in 1914 as *Grundsätze des Kommunismus,* edited by Eduard Bernstein.

(1848) 1963   MARX, KARL; and ENGELS, FRIEDRICH *The Communist Manifesto.* New York: Russell. → A paperback edition was published in 1964 by Washington Square Press.

(1848–1898) 1962   MARX, KARL; and ENGELS, FRIEDRICH *Selected Works.* 2 vols. Moscow: Foreign Languages Publishing House. → Includes works published posthumously.

(1850) 1956   *The Peasant War in Germany.* Moscow: Foreign Languages Publishing House. → First published as "Der deutsche Bauernkrieg" in the *Neue Rheinische Zeitung: Revue.*

(1851–1852) 1933   *Germany: Revolution and Counterrevolution.* New York: International Publishers. → First published as a series of articles in the *New York Daily Tribune.*

(1852) 1960   MARX, KARL; and ENGELS, FRIEDRICH Die grossen Männer des Exils. Volume 8, pages 233–335 in *Karl Marx, Friedrich Engels: Werke.* Berlin: Dietz. → First published in 1930, in Russian. Written in 1852.

(1859–1861) 1915   *Po und Rhein; Savoyen, Nizza und der Rhein.* Edited by Eduard Bernstein. Stuttgart (Germany): Dietz. → Published anonymously.

(1865) 1963   *Die preussische Militärfrage und die deutsche Arbeiterpartei.* Berlin: Dietz.

(1870–1871) 1923   *Notes on the War.* Vienna: Wiener Volksbuchhandlung. → Contains sixty articles reprinted from the *Pall Mall Gazette.*

(1873a) 1957   *Internationales aus dem Volksstaat (1871–1875).* Berlin: Dietz. → See especially Chapter 2 on "Die Bakunisten an der Arbeit."

1873b   *L'alliance de la démocratie socialiste et l'association internationale des travailleurs.* London and Hamburg. → A leaflet.

(1873–1883) 1960   *Dialectics of Nature.* New York: International Publishers. → First published in German.

(1875–1891) 1959   MARX, KARL; and ENGELS, FRIEDRICH *Critique of the Gotha Programme.* Moscow: Foreign

Languages Publishing House. → Written by Marx in 1875 as "Randglossen zum Programm der deutschen Arbeiterpartei." First published with notes by Engels in 1891.

(1878) 1959 *Anti-Dühring: Herr Eugen Dühring's Revolution in Science.* Moscow: Foreign Languages Publishing House. → First published as "Herrn Eugen Dührings Umwälzung der Wissenschaft" in *Vorwärts* (Leipzig).

(1880) 1935 *Socialism: Utopian and Scientific.* New York: International Publishers. → First published in French.

(1884a) 1942 *The Origin of the Family, Private Property and the State.* New York: International Publishers. → First published as *Der Ursprung der Familie, des Privateigentums und des Staats.*

(1884b) 1934 Marx und die *Neue Rheinische Zeitung.* Volume 2, pages 27–37 in Karl Marx, *Ausgewählte Schriften.* Edited by V. Adoratskij. Zürich (Switzerland): Ring. → First published in *Der Sozialdemokrat.*

(1885) 1933 History of the Communist League. Pages 120–131 in Friedrich Engels, *Germany: Revolution and Counter-revolution.* New York: International Publishers. → First published as "Zur Geschichte des Bundes der Kommunisten" in *Der Sozialdemokrat* and added to the 1933 edition of Engels 1851–1852.

(1886) 1941 *Ludwig Feuerbach and the Outcome of Classical German Philosophy.* New York: International Publishers. → First published in German.

(1891) 1963 Introduction. In Karl Marx, *The Civil War in France.* Moscow: Foreign Languages Publishing House. → First published in German. A paperback edition was published in 1964 by International Publishers.

1893 *Kann Europa abrüsten?* Nürnberg (Germany): Wörlein.

(1895) 1964 Introduction. In Karl Marx, *The Class Struggles in France: 1848–1850.* New York: International Publishers.

SUPPLEMENTARY BIBLIOGRAPHY

ADLER, MAX (1920) 1925 *Engels als Denker.* 2d ed. Berlin: Dietz.

BERLIN, ISAIAH (1939) 1963 *Karl Marx: His Life and Environment.* 3d ed. New York: Oxford Univ. Press.

BOLLNOW, HERMANN 1954 Engels' Auffassung von Revolution und Entwicklung in seinen *Grundsätzen des Kommunismus (1847).* Volume 1, pages 77–144 in *Marxismusstudien.* Schriften der Evangelischen Studiengemeinschaft, No. 3. Tübingen (Germany): Mohr.

BÜNGER, SIEGFRIED 1962 *Friedrich Engels und die britische sozialistische Bewegung, 1881–1895.* Berlin: Rütten & Loening.

COATES, ZELDA (KAHAN) (1920) 1945 *The Life and Teachings of Friedrich Engels.* London: Lawrence & Wishart. → First published as *The Life and Work of Friedrich Engels.*

CORNU, AUGUSTE 1955–1962 *Karl Marx et Friedrich Engels: Leur vie et leur oeuvre.* Paris: Presses Universitaires de France.

FETSCHER, IRING 1957 Von der Philosophie des Proletariats zur proletarischen Weltanschauung. Volume 2, pages 26–60 in *Marxismusstudien.* Schriften der Evangelischen Studiengemeinschaft, No. 5. Tübingen (Germany): Mohr.

Friedrich Engels: Der Denker. (1935) 1945 Basel: Mundus. → First published in *Bol'shaia sovetskaia entsiklopediia.*

[GOLDENDACH, DAVID B.] 1927 *Karl Marx and Friedrich Engels,* by D. Riazanov [pseud.]. London: Lawrence & Wishart.

HILDEBRAND, BRUNO (1848) 1922 *Die Nationalökonomie der Gegenwart und Zukunft, und andere gesammelte Schriften.* Jena: Fischer.

KAUTSKY, KARL (1895) 1899 *Friedrich Engels: His Life, His Work and His Writings.* Chicago: Kerr. → First published in German.

LUCAS, ERHARD 1964 Die Rezeption Lewis H. Morgans durch Marx und Engels. *Saeculum* 15:153–176.

LUCAS, ERHARD 1964 Marx' und Engels' Auseinandersetzung mit Darwin: Zur Differenz zwischen Marx und Engels. *International Review of Social History* (Amsterdam) [1964]:433–469.

MAREK, FRANZ (1950) 1953 *Friedrich Engels: Denker und Kämpfer.* Leipzig: Fachbuch Verlag.

MAYER, GUSTAV (1920–1934) 1936 *Friedrich Engels: A Biography.* Introduction by G. D. H. Cole. London: Chapman. → First published in German. The best biography of Engels.

RAMM, THILO 1957 Die künftige Gesellschaftsordnung nach der Theorie von Marx und Engels. Volume 2, pages 26–60 in *Marxismusstudien.* Schriften der Evangelischen Studiengemeinschaft, No. 5. Tübingen (Germany): Mohr.

RUBEL, MAXIMILIEN 1956 *Bibliographie des oeuvres de Karl Marx: Avec en appendice un répertoire des oeuvres de Friedrich Engels.* Paris: Rivière. → A 74-page supplement was published in 1960.

SEEGER, REINHARD 1935 *Friedrich Engels als "junger Deutscher"* . . . . Halle (Germany): Klinz.

STEIN, LORENZ VON 1852 Der Sozialismus in Deutschland. *Gegenwart: Eine encyklopädische Darstellung der neuesten Zeitgeschichte für alle Stände* 7:517–563. → Translation of the extract in the text was provided by Thilo Ramm.

THIER, ERICH 1954 Etappen der Marxinterpretation. Volume 1, pages 1–38 in *Marxismusstudien.* Schriften der Evangelischen Studiengemeinschaft, No. 3. Tübingen (Germany): Mohr.

ENGINEERING

Engineering is a relatively new profession compared with the professions of law, medicine, and the ministry. Like other professions, engineering struggles with such problems as redesigning the curricula of its professional schools and raising standards for entry to the field. In addition, engineering has some distinctive occupational problems. Can it increase the commitment of its members to the profession in the face of mounting pressures not to pursue it as a lifelong career? Can it assume the responsibility for the social effects of technological change? As the progenitors of new technologies that are transforming modern society, engineers are among the most important agents of social change. This article will consider some of the problems and potentialities of the profession, that is, some of the factors favoring or inhibiting the further professionalization of engineering as an occupation.

Professionalism and professionalization. In identifying various attributes of a profession, sociologists have often taken as their model the older professions of law, medicine, and the ministry. Although there is no consensus as to the definition of a profession, there is a growing awareness that professionalism is a multidimensional phenomenon and that occupations differ in their degree of professionalism.

An index of professionalism may be based on ratings of such attributes as (*a*) the possession of a body of technical and systematic knowledge that guides professional practice; (*b*) an orientation of service to society rather than self-interest; (*c*) autonomy in rendering professional service; and (*d*) societal sanction of professional authority. To develop and transmit the body of technical and systematic knowledge, professional schools and training programs are established. To contribute to the fund of professional knowledge, to promote a service orientation, and to increase autonomy in professional practice, professional associations are formed and codes of ethics are developed. To protect professional authority and enhance occupational prestige, societal sanction is sought in various forms, such as the licensing of graduates and the exercising of control over the curricula of professional schools.

The process of professionalization involves the transformation of an occupation in accordance with the ideal–typical components of professionalism. Although the dynamics of professionalization may differ for different occupations, and possibly for the same occupation in different countries, one study suggests that it entails the following sequence of stages: (1) full-time performance of the occupational function; (2) establishment of a school that is not connected with a university; (3) establishment of a university school; (4) formation of a local professional association; (5) formation of a national professional association; (6) enactment of a licensing law; and (7) development of a formal code of ethics (Wilensky 1964). Even if this sequence of stages is neither invariant nor exhaustive, it may provide a useful description and prediction of the process of professionalization.

Whatever stages of professionalization are postulated or demonstrated, it does not follow that a particular profession has reached the same level of professionalization in all countries. Nor does it follow that professionalization of a given occupa-

tion is irreversible. It is frequently assumed, however, that newer professions will follow the pattern of development established by the older professions and that this pattern is irreversible. The question of the conditions under which an occupation may be deprofessionalized has hardly been raised.

Before examining some current problems of the professionalization of engineering, we shall briefly review the factors that led to the emergence of this profession.

Emergence of the engineering profession. Engineering as art long antedates engineering as a profession. The invention of the stone ax in the Paleolithic age was among man's first engineering achievements. In the civilizations of antiquity considerable technological progress was made, as evidenced by such accomplishments as pyramids, aqueducts, canals, bridges, and lighthouses. Directing these engineering feats were highly gifted individuals, some of whom we would today consider engineers. But despite the outstanding work of individual engineers, no professional group came into being for many centuries. Several factors delayed the formation of a profession of engineering. The economies of ancient civilizations did not require the organized development and application of technology, for which an engineering profession was necessary. The prevailing technology was a product of trial and error, intuition, artistry, and the gross synthesis of experience, unsupported by science. In fact, there was pronounced contempt for technology in ancient times. Finally, the tradition of "craft mystery" interfered with the codification and public transmission of technical knowledge. This pattern persisted through the Middle Ages.

During the Renaissance the demand for engineering skills increased. The urgent and recurrent demands of war stimulated the development of many engines of battle, whence came the term "engineer." With the advent of modern science, in the sixteenth and seventeenth centuries, there was a gradual transition from "craft mystery" to science as a basis for technology. The founding of learned societies such as the Royal Society of London, in 1662, the Académie des Sciences, in 1666, and several decades later, the Berlin Academy of Sciences and the Academy of St. Petersburg, reflected and promoted the growing influence of science on technology. During the eighteenth century the services of engineers were enlisted to perform a variety of functions in civilian, as well as in military, life. In France the Corps des Ingénieurs des Ponts et Chaussées, established by the government in 1716, was considered as necessary as the Corps des Ingénieurs de Génie Militaire. In Great Britain engineers were commissioned to drain mines, build roads and canals, and perfect navigational techniques. Thus, the initial stage of the development of engineering as a profession—the need for trained, full-time engineers—comes into view.

Engineering schools were gradually established in place of traditional methods of apprenticeship and pupilage. Among the earliest engineering schools to be founded were the École de Ponts et Chaussées in 1747 and the École Polytechnique in 1795. During the American Revolution, George Washington, deploring the shortage of engineers, asked the Continental Congress to provide facilities for the training of a corps of engineers; in 1802 his proposal was implemented with the establishment of the military academy at West Point, modeled after the École Polytechnique. Efforts were made to provide professional training, not only through special technical schools but also at institutions of higher learning. In England a first chair in civil engineering was established in 1841.

Local professional associations had been established in various parts of England and Scotland during the latter part of the eighteenth century. One was the Society of Civil Engineers, founded in 1771 by John Smeaton, a member of the Royal Society, who is alleged to have been the first Englishman to describe himself as a "civil engineer." In 1818 the first national professional association for engineers was established in England. Similar organizations came into existence in the United States in 1852 and in Canada in 1887.

Thus, the sequence of early developments leading to the emergence of the engineering profession conforms approximately to the first five stages of professionalization mentioned earlier. As engineering became a full-time occupation, in the seventeenth and eighteenth centuries, schools not connected with a university were established, local professional societies were formed, followed by national associations, and engineering was gradually introduced into the curriculum of universities.

Social structure and engineering. The emergence of the engineering profession in western Europe and in North America points up the impact of industrialization on this occupation. Economic development requires and generates technological development, for which engineers and other professionals are essential. Since societies differ markedly in their level of economic development, we would also expect them to differ in their technological capabilities and in the nature and role of their engineering professions. In effect, we are hypothesizing that the relationship between the economic

development and technological development of a society is partly mediated by its engineering profession. Some data bearing on the economic and technological development of various countries and the size of their engineering professions are presented in Table 1.

For present purposes, economic development is indexed by per capita share of gross national product (GNP), and technological development is indexed by the number of patents issued in a year and the percentage of GNP expended for research and development (R & D) in any given year. In Table 1, countries for which data are available are ranked according to the GNP per capita variable. The higher the ranking of a country on GNP per capita, the more likely it is that it ranks higher on the size of its engineering profession and the number of patents issued, and on the percentage of GNP expended for research and development. These data suggest one possible systemic pattern of relationships between these variables. A highly industrialized society has the resources to educate a sizable number of engineers, some of whom, together with scientists, engage in research and development, for which a substantial proportion of such a society's resources is expended; this organized approach to scientific discovery and invention results in increasing numbers of patents; and in turn, the process of invention—in which engineers play a prominent role (Gilfillan 1935, pp. 52, 82–91)—stimulates economic development, which then confronts the engineering profession with new technical problems.

Another feature of the social structure (apart from the economy and technology) that influences the engineering profession is the political system. In highly centralized and relatively unindustrialized societies, such as some under communist regimes, the engineering profession may be disproportionately large because of the government's concern with accelerating the process of industrialization. Under such conditions, the autonomy of the profession may be circumscribed and it may be called upon to perform functions other than those of a technological nature.

The level of industrialization of a society has another effect on the engineering profession, which is not reflected in the statistics in Table 1. As industrialization increases, there is a concomitant increase in the number of specialties in the occupation. From the relatively undifferentiated field of engineering existing in the seventeenth and eighteenth centuries, civil engineering emerged and itself gave rise to mechanical engineering, mining and metallurgical engineering, and electrical and

Table 1 — Gross national product (GNP) per capita, number of engineers, number of patents issued, and percentage of GNP expended for research and development (R & D) in selected countries

	GNP PER CAPITA IN 1957	NUMBER OF ENGINEERS			PATENTS ISSUED IN 1964[a]	PER CENT OF GNP FOR R & D	
	U.S. dollars	Number	Per 10,000 population	Year of information	Number	Percentage	Year of information
United States	2,577	783,000[b]	4.4	1959	47,378	2.8	1960/1961
Canada	1,947	60,400[c]	3.2	1963	24,589	1.2	1960
Switzerland	1,428	14,440[b]	2.9	1955	10,350		
Sweden	1,380	52,400[b]	6.8	1965	6,125	1.8	1959
Belgium	1,196	30,492[b]	3.3	1964			
United Kingdom	1,189	156,000[b]	2.9	1963	34,060	2.5	1958/1959
Norway	1,130	32,020[b]	8.6	1965	1,985	0.7	1960
Denmark	1,057	20,900[b]	4.5	1963	2,833		
France	943	112,000[c]	2.3	1963	33,850	1.3	1961
West Germany	927	226,200[b, d]	4.5	1956	20,150	1.4	1959
Netherlands	836	36,139[b]	2.9	1959; 1965[e]	13,900		
Austria	670	36,559[b]	5.2	1961	6,850		
Soviet Union	600	1,325,000[b]	6.0	1962	6,850	2.3	1960
Ireland	550	2,800[c]	1.0	1962	434		
Italy	516	190,000[b]	3.9	1957			
Argentina	490	15,400[c]	.8	1960			
Greece	340	5,756[c]	.7	1959			
Spain	293	13,035[c]	.4	1960			
Yugoslavia	265	27,429[c]	1.4	1965		0.7	1960
Turkey	220	9,106[c]	.3	1960			
Iran	108	7,510[c]	.4	1960			
Communist China	73	175,000[f]	.3	1957			

a. Calculated by subtracting the number of patents on hand in January 1964 from the number on hand in January 1965 and adjusting the difference to put it on an annual basis.
b. Combined total of engineers with university training and those with formal training just below the university level.
c. University-trained engineers.
d. Includes chemists.
e. Count of university-trained engineers in 1965, other count in 1959; number per 10,000 population is based on 1965 population data and probably is an underestimate.
f. Engineering and technical personnel.

Sources: GNP from Russett et al. 1964, pp. 155–157. Number of engineers from Organization for Economic Cooperation and Development 1963, pp. 225–229, tables 13 and 14; Korol 1965, p. 244, table A-I; Emerson 1965, p. 138, table 7; Horowitz 1965, p. 7, table 1.4; Baldwin 1965, p. 155, table 5.2; Demographic Yearbook 1963. Patents from U.S. Patent Office, Official Gazette . . . 1964, p. 777, and 1965, p. 2. Per cent of GNP for R & D from Dedijer 1962.

chemical engineering, which were followed by automotive and aeronautical engineering. In the decades since World War II various economic, scientific, and political developments have stimulated the rise of new specialties, such as nuclear engineering, computer technology, astronautical engineering, and systems engineering.

As the engineering profession becomes increasingly differentiated and heterogeneous, a recurrent question arises regarding the identity of engineers. Periodically, engineering educators, officials of professional societies, and census officials discuss the question, Who is an engineer? In the United States the census definition relies, in effect, on the respondent's decision as to whether he is an engineer. Professional engineering societies emphasize formal training in an engineering school and/or a minimum number of years of engineering experience. This concern with clarifying the definition of an engineer reflects a changing social and technical environment of the occupation, which is due to the accelerating rate of growth of scientific knowledge and increasing levels of industrialization. The

changing environment confronts the occupation with dilemmas as to the meaning of professionalism and the direction of further professionalization. These dilemmas arise in connection with the process of recruitment to the profession, the education of engineers, the career decisions of engineers, the functions of professional societies, the problem of responsibility for the social impact of technological change, and the prestige of the profession.

The recruitment process. In highly industrialized societies engineering is one of the fastest-growing occupations. The average annual rate of growth of the profession in some countries tends to exceed the rates of growth of the economy and of the population. In Communist China the engineering profession had an average annual growth rate of 67.1 per cent during the years 1955 through 1962 (computed on the basis of data in Chêng 1964, pp. 111–113); and in the Soviet Union the comparable rate for these years was 32.2 per cent (based on data in Korol 1965, pp. 242–244, table A-1). In comparison, the annual rate of growth for the engineering profession in Great Britain during the years 1959 through 1963 was 5.5 per cent; in France it was 3.2 per cent for the same period; and in Sweden it was only 2 per cent for the period 1955 through 1960 (Organization for Economic Cooperation and Development 1963, pp. 136–175). Maintaining a balance between the demand for and the supply of engineers has been a problem in the post-World War II period and will probably continue to be a problem in the future (e.g., U.S. Department of Commerce 1963).

The engineering profession, probably more than the older, established professions, tends to recruit its members—at least in highly industrialized societies—from heterogeneous social origins. According to one study, a substantial proportion of graduate engineers in Great Britain have middle-class or working-class backgrounds: 36 per cent of their father's occupations are white-collar and 22 per cent are blue-collar (Gerstl 1963, p. 19; see also Jahoda 1963, p. 54). Several studies of engineering students in the United States also indicate a substantial degree of recruitment from middle-class and working-class backgrounds: 44 per cent of the fathers of engineering students at Northwestern University pursue manual or white-collar occupations (Krulee 1963, p. 20); and 50 per cent of engineering students at the University of California at Berkeley come from working-class or middle-class backgrounds (Trow 1959, p. 68). In the Netherlands, on the other hand, opportunities for entry into the engineering profession appear to be more limited than in the United States and Great Britain: approximately 28 per cent are recruited from working-class and middle-class backgrounds (Kuiper 1956, p. 233, table 2).

The more heterogeneous the social origins of engineers, the more diverse, in all likelihood, are the motivations and values involved in their choice of occupation. In a study of students at 11 American universities who chose engineering as a career, 38 per cent stressed the "chance to earn a great deal of money"; 52 per cent, the opportunity to be creative and original; and 28 per cent, the opportunity to be helpful to others (Goldsen et al. 1960, pp. 43–44). A study of American students from 135 colleges and universities who chose engineering as a career in the freshman year found that 25 per cent mentioned money as a factor, 26 per cent mentioned opportunity to be original, and 7 per cent gave "people" as a reason (Davis 1965, p. 188). In Great Britain a study of sixth-form boys found that, of those interested in engineering, 32 per cent gave "money" or "good prospects" as their reason; 19 per cent mentioned that it affords an opportunity to be creative; and 13 per cent said that they were interested because it combines theory

and practice (Oxford University 1963, pp. 37–38). At two London polytechnics a survey of evening students which inquired into their motivations for attendance found that 36 per cent hoped for a better-paid job, 10 per cent for more job security, 16 per cent for a more interesting job, and 9 per cent for a job with a higher social standing (Cotgrove 1958, pp. 102–103). In short, the values of money, prestige, security, creativity, integration of theory and practice, and helping people are but a few of the values affecting the choice of engineering as a career. The old hypothesis of a relationship between social-class heterogeneity and occupational attrition has recently found some support in a study of the occupational structure of the United States: "The more heterogeneous in social origins the young men entering an occupation are, . . . the greater is their tendency to leave it later for a variety of other occupations. This finding suggests that homogeneity in background fosters social solidarity, which lessens the inclination of its members to leave an occupational group" (Blau 1965, p. 490). Thus, we may infer that social-class heterogeneity among engineers very likely contributes to occupational attrition, because of reduced social solidarity.

The diversity of motives prompting students to enter the field of engineering also creates various difficulties for the profession. First, the very existence of a diversity of values regarding engineering acts to lower the feeling of solidarity among engineers as an occupational group. Second, the prevalent "extrinsic" values, such as money, prestige, and security, contrast with such "intrinsic" work values as the opportunity to be creative or to link theory with practice. Intrinsic values are probably more associated with commitment to a profession than are extrinsic values. Finally, the socially heterogeneous recruits to engineering impose an even greater demand for professional socialization during and after the period of formal education than would socially homogeneous recruits.

Educational patterns. The educational resources of a society, which vary with the level of industrialization, greatly affect not only the number of engineers recruited but also their quality and, in turn, their capability to contribute to technological development. The feedback effects of an adequate supply of well-trained engineers and scientists on economic growth has stimulated widespread interest in developing educational institutions and enlarging enrollments, as an investment in "human capital." That facilities for educating engineers vary in large measure with the level of industrialization of a society can be shown by examining the relationship between the number of enrolled engineering students in various countries and the GNP per capita for these same countries. The higher the degree of industrialization, as measured by GNP per capita, the greater is the number of engineers enrolled (unpublished research by the author, based on data in Russett et al. 1964, pp. 155–157; UNESCO, *Statistical Yearbook 1963*, pp. 226–249, table 16; DeWitt 1961, p. 318). It is noteworthy that, in their effort to accelerate economic growth, communist countries have greatly expanded their facilities for the education of engineers. In China engineering enrollment increased from 30,300 in 1949, when the new regime was established, to 177,600 in 1957 (Orleans 1961, pp. 68–69); in the same year, 40 per cent of all students enrolled in Chinese institutions of higher learning were majoring in engineering (*ibid.*). In the Soviet Union the comparable percentage was 39 per cent in 1958 (DeWitt 1961, p. 318), and in the United States it was 5 per cent in 1962 (computed from statistics in U.S. Office of Education 1965, p. 81, table 58, and in U.S. Bureau of the Census 1963, p. 136, table 177).

Critical as is the *quantity* of engineers educated for the economic and technological development of a society, the principal problems of professionalism and professionalization revolve around the *quality* of their education. Engineering curricula are periodically reviewed by engineering educators and professional societies. This, to be sure, is necessary because the rapid rate of growth of science and technology requires that engineering schools continually revise their curricula to insure that they are transmitting the new state of the art. The task of reducing the time lag between the development of new knowledge and its incorporation into the curriculum is often fraught with difficulty. A case in point is the time lag involved in introducing courses on computers in engineering schools.

Designing and redesigning engineering curricula in response to technological change is beset by many problems other than recruiting a competent and adaptable faculty. One of the problems is that the practice of engineering is generally based on an undergraduate level of education. The fact that relatively high proportions of engineers in some countries have not received even this minimal level of training highlights the unsolved problems of professionalizing this occupation. For example, in China only 35 per cent of engineers had undergraduate engineering degrees in 1955 (Chêng 1964, p. 35), and in the United States only 56 per cent had such degrees in 1960 (Organization for Economic Cooperation and Development 1966). The length of full-time training in engineering

schools ranges from three to five and one-half years, with many European countries and the Soviet Union at the high end of this scale (Conference of Representatives 1960, vol. 2, p. 42).

Associated with the time limitation of an undergraduate level of engineering education is the problem of determining how much of the curriculum should be devoted to fundamental sciences, to engineering sciences, to engineering applications, to specialization in the various fields of engineering, and to nonengineering subjects (American Society for Engineering Education 1955, pp. 11–23; Wood 1961). This problem is closely related to another, which is bound to receive more attention in the future, namely, whether engineers should be trained in a specific branch of engineering or in the fundamentals of engineering. The fact that the main branches of engineering—civil, mechanical, electrical, chemical, and aeronautical—are becoming increasingly interrelated in new technologies makes this problem increasingly significant.

As might be expected, countries differ in the degree to which engineering education is oriented to the acquisition of knowledge in a particular specialty. In the United Kingdom, where about one-half the engineers are trained in part-time, "sandwich," or cooperative programs in technical colleges, and in the United States, where the variation in quality in the more than 250 engineering schools is considerable, there is probably a greater degree of specialization than in some countries in continental Europe. In the Soviet Union and Communist China the degree of specialization appears to be greater still (Korol 1957, pp. 252–253; Chêng 1964, p. 98). In underdeveloped countries, which tend to emulate the educational systems of developed countries, an argument has been advanced for training *general* engineers, rather than specialists, in order to help initiate the process of industrialization (Hunt 1960).

The role of nonengineering subjects in the curriculum—what types and how many courses should be offered in the humanities, in problems of management, or in social sciences—is also an open question. There is notable variation between countries in this respect, as shown by a recent study of some systems of engineering education (Conference of Representatives 1960, vol. 2, p. 44). In part the variation is due to differences in the quality of secondary school education; in part it reflects variation in the assessment of the kinds of knowledge and skills required of a practicing engineer.

Rarely considered in the recurrent reappraisals of engineering education is the question of the inculcation of basic values of professionalism in the training of engineers (see National Society of Professional Engineers 1963). Among the basic professional values to which engineering students might be socialized are: (a) the importance of contributing to technological innovation, rather than accepting the technological *status quo*; (b) the awareness of and concern for the social impact of technological innovations; and (c) the conception of professional education as a lifelong activity that is not confined to the years of formal training in engineering schools. Whether and how to inculcate these and other professional values are still frontier problems in professionalizing engineering. For example, the novel and presumably controversial practice, at a French institution of higher learning at Sacley, of awarding a degree in reactor engineering for a limited period—subject to revalidation after five years by means of attendance at refresher courses and success at future examinations—is based on a conception of engineering education as a lifelong process (King 1965).

Problems of redesigning engineering curricula in a quickly changing technological and social environment defy easy and durable solutions. They are even more resistant to solution without full cognizance of the types of careers pursued by engineers following graduation from an engineering school.

Career patterns. The process of professional socialization obviously does not end upon graduation from an engineering school. The organizational context in which an engineer works and the type of function he performs affect not only the course of his career in engineering but also his career orientation and his degree of commitment to the profession.

Unlike the members of some of the older professions, engineers are predominantly salaried employees, with the exception in some countries of a small subgroup of engineers who are self-employed and engage in consulting work (see, for example, Engineers Joint Council 1965, p. 17). Typically,

engineers are employed in manufacturing organizations and in various construction operations of a governmental nature. Within the past several decades, as the number of research-and-development laboratories has rapidly increased, new work contexts have opened up for engineers. In the less industrialized countries most engineers still perform various production functions, whereas in the more industrially developed countries a rising proportion are engaged in research-and-development activities. This variation in function is suggested by the data in Table 2. In the United States and the Soviet Union, two of the more highly industrialized countries, approximately one-third and one-fifth, respectively, of the engineers work in research and development.

As several studies of occupations other than engineering have shown, the first job after graduation usually has more effect on career opportunities than do subsequent jobs. Engineering is no exception to this. Among the factors affecting the engineer's first career decision is the quality of the engineering school he attended. A graduate of an elite school often has the opportunity to begin his career in an organization which is in the main stream of technological development. He also has the opportunity—as is true, for example, of the graduate of the École Polytechnique—to orient his career toward top management (Granick 1962, pp. 26–30).

If the engineer begins his career in a production setting, he is unlikely to subsequently enter a research-and-development organization or engage in teaching and research in an academic environment. The only two probable career lines open to him are management of a technical or a nontechnical function and the pursuit of an occupation other than engineering. The career path of an engineer in a research-and-development organization or in a university is probably quite different from that of an engineer employed in a production organization. In either case, the probability is

Table 2 — Distribution of engineers by type of work, for selected countries: per cent

	Year	Production	Management and administration	Research and development	Teaching	Other
Austria	1961	51	33.5	3	3.5	9
Canada	1959	30	28	23	3	15
Greece[a]	1959	80	7	3	8	1
Soviet Union	1964	33	10	22	7	28
United States	1959	40	8	30		21[b]

a. Includes scientists.
b. Includes engineers engaged in teaching.

Source: Organization for Economic Cooperation and Development 1963, pp. 134 ff. Data for the Soviet Union are estimates computed for the author by Alexander G. Korol.

higher that he will not leave engineering for another occupation; on the other hand, the likelihood is that, after some years in research-and-development work, the engineer may transfer to a production or a management function, especially management of a technical operation. The relatively small percentage of engineers who enter teaching and research in an academic environment, as shown in Table 2, in all likelihood continue in this function; if they leave the academic environment, their career paths are likely to be in research rather than in production (LeBold et al. 1960; Gerstl & Hutton 1966).

As a salaried employee, the engineer experiences organizational constraints that he finds difficult to reconcile with his expectations as a professional (Kornhauser 1962). The type of function he performs as an engineer affects his role conception, as well as the length of his career in engineering. In a production function his role relationships involve interaction with production workers and engineering technicians, on the one hand, and with managers, on the other. As a staff engineer, he lacks the authority of the manager, and he tends to be treated, in some organizational contexts, in the same manner that an engineering technician or a production worker is treated. The norm of obedience is more characteristic of the relationship he has with his superiors and subordinates than the norm of service, which is typical of a professional, or the norm of autonomy, which is typical of a scientist (Evan 1962, p. 352).

In a research-and-development organization the engineer's role tends to subject him to the typical dilemmas of a marginal man (Shepard 1957). The scientist regards him as a "nuts-and-bolts" engineer; the manager, as someone who is insufficiently sensitive to cost factors in engineering. In a research-and-development setting, however, there is less likelihood for his role to be confused with the role of an engineering technician or a production worker. (For an analysis of the occupational marginality of engineering technicians, see Evan 1964.) Probably only the small proportion of engineers engaged in basic or applied research escape some of the problems of marginality: their work is governed, not by a norm of service, but rather by a norm of autonomy.

As a consequence of the rapid rate of technological change, there is a growing tendency for the careers of engineers to be abbreviated. The knowledge and skills of engineers obsolesce so quickly that engineers, especially in highly industrialized countries, find it necessary to shift into management work or nonengineering occupations in the middle of their careers (see, for example, Evan 1963). No longer can the new graduate engineer assume, as some of his predecessors did years ago, that he will spend his entire working career in engineering.

To cope with the growing problem of technical obsolescence, programs of continuing education are being established in the United States, France, Germany, and some other countries. The theory and methodology required for the retraining of engineers in the middle of their careers remain to be developed. As yet there is scant evidence as to the effectiveness of continuing-education programs in helping engineers to cope with their technical-updating problems. Another career problem is the flattening of the salary curve with age, which may be related to the declining market value of older engineers undergoing technical obsolescence (see, for example, Kornhauser 1962, pp. 128–130). These and other career problems of engineers are solved in some countries, not by changing employers, labor markets, or occupations, but by means of emigration. The limited statistics on the migration of engineers makes it difficult to ascertain the countries of origin and destination of engineers who emigrate. However, we do know that this mode of adaptation to career problems has created concern in the countries of emigration. In the face of a shortage of technically trained manpower in most countries of the world, emigration of engineers is looked upon as a "brain drain." This is particularly true in the case of a relatively underdeveloped country, such as Argentina, where engineers have emigrated in substantial numbers to the United States (Oteiza 1965).

In short, the organizational contexts in which engineers are employed, the types of functions they perform, and the types of role relationships in which they are involved have not been conducive to an effective process of professional socialization. After his graduation from engineering school, his work experiences often do not tend to imbue the engineer with a dedication to the occupation (Wilensky 1964, pp. 150–155) or an increasing awareness of the social consequences of technological change. Professional associations have a significant function to perform in making up for the deficiencies of the work context as an agent of professional socialization.

Professional associations. Only some of the career problems encountered by engineers have thus far received attention by professional associations of engineers. Economic problems have largely been ignored, although licensing regulations may have had an indirect beneficial effect on the earnings of some engineers. Sporadic efforts in some countries to organize trade unions of engineers to promote their economic interests have not been successful (see, for example, Goldstein 1954; Walton 1961). Unlike the medical profession, engineering has not acted in unison to enhance the economic position of its members. One factor that has hindered the professional societies in performing an economic function has been the lack of organizational unity within the profession. Instead of there being a single professional association of all engineers in a country, there has been a tendency toward the "Balkanization" of the occupation. As new specialties in engineering arise, new professional associations come into being, and the proliferation of such societies makes for ever greater difficulties in unifying the profession. This tendency has occurred both in the United States and in the United Kingdom, as well as in western Europe. In the more industrialized societies, where the profession is further developed, there are a greater number of professional associations and correspondingly more difficulty in unifying them.

The principal function that professional societies appear to perform is that of a learned society. In other words, they see themselves principally as an instrument for advancing and disseminating engineering knowledge, thus supplementing the functions performed by universities and research institutes. It follows, therefore, that they can contribute significantly to the engineer's need for continuing education. In the future, even more than in the present, they are likely to help engineers continue their professional development by means of seminars, abstracting services, and special conferences. Thus, participation by engineers in the activities of professional associations may increasingly reflect the degree of their professional commitment. In the more industrialized countries, where the educational services of professional societies are apt to be in greater demand, memberships of engineering societies are likely to be larger than in the less industrialized societies.

Another noteworthy feature about professional associations of engineers is the relatively modest progress they have made to date in organizing international professional associations. Since World War II several regional associations of engineering societies have come into being, notably the Conference of Engineering Societies of Western Europe and the United States of America, the European Federation of National Associations of Engineers, and the Pan-American Federation of Engineering Societies. Another significant development was the founding of the Union of International Engineering Organizations, under the aegis of UNESCO, in 1950. These are in the nature of nongovernmental organizations, whose unit of membership is the national society of engineers, not the individual engineer. The strength of such international bodies depends very much upon the strength of the constituent societies. In their relatively brief history these organizations have not yet contributed noticeably to new modes of international cooperation between engineers, to new media for dissemination of technological knowledge, or to an awareness of membership in a world-wide profession.

In addition to performing economic, educational, and knowledge-advancing functions, professional associations seek to regulate their members' conduct by establishing codes of ethics. To the extent that professional engineering associations have concerned themselves with ethical issues, they have attended mostly to the relations of the engineer with his fellow engineer and his employer. Ethical codes have set forth very general guidelines regulating conduct in these spheres. Only in most general terms do canons of ethics touch upon the relations of the engineer to the public or to society as a whole (National Society of Professional Engineers 1962). Thus far, ethical codes have scarcely concerned themselves with the complex and diffuse ethical question of the responsibility of the engineering profession for the social consequences of technological change.

Dilemmas of social responsibility. One reason for the widespread neglect on the part of engineers of the problem of social responsibility for technological change is the difficulty of accepting responsibility for events over which they exercise virtually no control. As salaried employees, performing in the main a staff function, engineers are rarely in a position to make policy decisions concerning the wisdom of developing or not developing a new engineering product or concerning what, if any, action might be taken to counteract its potential or actual negative social effects. This is particularly true for the overwhelming proportion of engineers engaged in production or in development research, where the norms governing their conduct emphasize obedience to directives from management (Evan 1962). Since management makes the decision to produce or not to produce a particular engineering product or service, the salaried engineer probably feels that he scarcely has an occasion for any ethical decision concerning the possible adverse effects of a technological innovation.

In the past the staff function of the engineer has in fact absolved him from actively concerning himself with the question of responsibility for adverse social consequences of technological innovations (Merton [1949] 1957, p. 568). However, it is unlikely that this absolution of responsibility will be acceptable to engineers in the future, as technological advances generate problems of unemployment, environmental pollution, invasion of privacy, and an increasing threat of accidental or deliberate nuclear war. Pressures from within and without the profession will probably stimulate engineers to come to grips with the social ramifications of the technological changes they help develop.

Some of these ethical dilemmas may be solved by new innovative technology; others may require innovative social changes. Although it is unlikely that the individual engineer will succeed in coping with the many complex ethical dilemmas that arise in the process of technological innovation, collective action by professional associations might prove effective. In other words, if the engineering profession assumes a social responsibility for the problems of negative effects of technological change, it may contribute significantly to their solution.

Prestige of the profession. The prestige of the engineering profession may be affected by, among other things, the attitudes of the public toward the engineer's role in generating positive or negative social consequences of technological innovations. The increasing prominence of the role of technology in society has probably elevated the prestige of engineering in recent years. On the other hand, the fact that engineering does not require a formal education as prolonged as some other professions and the fact that the members are recruited from heterogeneous social origins may contribute to a lowering of its prestige, relative to other professions, in some countries.

The prestige of engineering has received some attention from sociologists in several countries. As a result of the interest among sociologists in studying systems of social stratification in different societies, several parallel studies of the prestige of various occupations, including engineering, have been undertaken. The methodological differences between these studies make a comparison of the findings hazardous. Nevertheless, on the basis of these studies, it is clear that engineering does not have the same prestige in all countries. For example, in the Soviet Union engineers ranked second in prestige as compared with other occupations (Inkeles & Rossi 1956, pp. 336–337); in the Philippines engineers ranked fourth (Tiryakian 1958, p. 394); in Great Britain they were in eighth place (Hutton & Gerstl 1964, p. 13); in West Germany they were in tenth place (Inkeles & Rossi 1956,

pp. 336–337); and in the United States their prestige rank was 21.5 (Hodge et al. 1964, p. 290). Moreover, the data suggest that the prestige of the engineering profession varies inversely with the degree of industrialization as indicated by GNP per capita. Presumably, as the division of labor becomes more specialized in more industrialized societies and as the proportion of professionals in the labor force increases, engineering faces more competition from other occupations for rewards, monetary and other. In addition, as a society becomes more industrialized, the engineering profession tends to increase in size, which may also become a factor in lowering its prestige. Changes in the internal structure of the engineering profession and in its social role are likely to affect its prestige in the future.

Potential social roles. What types of roles engineers will play in the future depends in part on the course of professionalization of the occupation and in part on the course of political and economic development. If the occupation becomes increasingly professionalized, we may observe a threefold division.

The appreciable segment of the occupation that has received limited or low-quality training in engineering schools and whose knowledge is based largely on practical experience will tend to coalesce with engineering technicians (Evan 1964, p. 108). This tendency will be encouraged by the progressive application of automation to some of the production and design functions performed by engineers, thus, in effect, de-professionalizing some members of the occupation. At the opposite end of the expertise continuum within the profession, there is a relatively small but probably increasing proportion of engineers working at the frontiers of engineering knowledge, who will tend to merge with applied scientists. The intermediate and by far the largest segment of the occupation will continue to perform a high caliber of technical engineering work. This group may be impelled in one of two directions in the future: toward the acquisition of power at organizational levels or at the national level or toward a new conception of professional service.

In his manifesto to engineers in the 1920s, Veblen ([1919] 1921, pp. 138–169) urged them to replace "absentee owners" and to run industry rationally, in accordance with the "instinct of workmanship" rather than the principles of the "price system." Unlike Marx and Engels in their manifesto to the proletariat, Veblen expressed no hope that his technocratic vision would be realized. In the decades since Veblen's essay was published, the rise of highly centralized political systems has increased the need for engineers to assist in the planning and decision-making process. In communist countries the political and economic exigencies in domestic and foreign affairs may require, in the decades ahead, an even greater reliance on engineers to perform a technocratic role. In France, as we have seen, the recruitment of engineering graduates from the École Polytechnique and several other *grandes écoles* to commanding positions in industry and in the civil service is another example of a trend for engineers to perform a technocratic role (Granick 1962, pp. 60–72). The engineer imbued with the technocratic vision believes, on the one hand, in the capacity of technology to solve all social problems without recourse to value considerations and, on the other hand, in the importance of integrating engineers into the political power structure of society.

An alternative role for engineers is that of a professionally self-conscious agent of the technological and economic development of a society. Although performing principally a staff function, engineers would explicitly concern themselves with developing technology for human welfare and, more specifically, with the predictable social ramifications of any new engineering design, product, or service (see, for example, Boguslaw 1965, pp. 23–29, 181–204). To distinguish this type of social role from both the technocratic role and the prevailing amoral professional role, we might designate it a "professional-technologist" role. In accordance with this role model, an engineer would be guided by an explicit orientation of professional service in his relations with the technological system of a society.

If the new role of professional technologist is to become institutionalized, at least two developments would have to occur. First, if the tempo of development in science and technology stimulates a large proportion of practicing engineers to acquire a postgraduate degree, say at the master's level, such a trend would increase the exposure of engineers to professional socialization in the context of engineering schools. Second, if a "technological community" transcending national boundaries (and parallel to the prevailing "scientific community") comes into being, it would provide the normative foundations for the professional-technologist role. Such a community would be guided by a set of norms and values concerning technical as well as social facets of engineering, not unlike some of the norms current in the scientific community (Merton

[1949] 1957, pp. 550–561). The implementation of past proposals for an international institute of science and technology (Killian 1962) and the emergence of *transnational* professional societies of engineers—whose unit of membership is the individual engineer—in addition to the present international societies, would probably contribute to the emergence of a technological community.

Which of these two new potential social roles—that of the technocrat or that of the professional technologist—will predominate in the years ahead or whether both roles will become institutionalized, albeit in different societies, is obviously difficult to predict. A conditional prediction, however, may be ventured: the professional-technologist role is likely to become institutionalized in societies where a democratic and antielitist ethos predominates; conversely, in societies with a nondemocratic and elitist ethos, the technocratic role of the engineer is likely to become institutionalized. A political–ecological factor that may affect this prediction is the relationship between international conflict and the course of technological development. If international conflict in the next decades comes under effective international regulation—thus reducing the chances of nuclear war—technology, and in turn the engineering profession, will be able to continue its development largely independent of international political and military conflicts. Such an international political environment would be conducive to the institutionalization of the role of the professional technologist, particularly in industrialized societies, and to the growth of a technological community, both of which would usher in a new level of professionalization of engineering.

WILLIAM M. EVAN

[*See also* AUTOMATION; LICENSING, OCCUPATIONAL; OCCUPATIONS AND CAREERS; PROFESSIONS; TECHNOLOGY.]

BIBLIOGRAPHY

AMERICAN SOCIETY FOR ENGINEERING EDUCATION, COMMITTEE ON EVALUATION OF ENGINEERING EDUCATION 1955 *Report on Evaluation of Engineering Education, 1952–1955.* Urbana, Ill.: The Society.
ARMYTAGE, W. H. G. 1961 *A Social History of Engineering.* London: Faber.
BALDWIN, GEORGE B. 1965 Iran's Experience With Manpower Planning: Concepts, Techniques and Lessons. Pages 140–172 in Frederick H. Harbison and Charles A. Myers (editors), *Manpower and Education: Country Studies in Economic Development.* New York: McGraw-Hill.
BLAU, PETER M. 1965 The Flow of Occupational Supply and Recruitment. *American Sociological Review* 30: 475–490.

BOGUSLAW, ROBERT 1965 *The New Utopians: A Study of System Design and Social Change.* Englewood Cliffs, N.J.: Prentice-Hall.

CHÊNG, CHU-YÜAN 1964 *Scientific and Engineering Manpower in Communist China, 1949–1963.* Washington: Government Printing Office.

CONFERENCE OF REPRESENTATIVES FROM THE ENGINEERING SOCIETIES OF WESTERN EUROPE AND THE UNITED STATES OF AMERICA 1960 *Report on Education and Training of Professional Engineers.* 3 vols. Brussells: EUSEC.

COTGROVE, STEPHEN F. 1958 *Technical Education and Social Change.* London: Ruskin House.

DAVIS, JAMES A. 1965 *Undergraduate Career Decisions: Correlates of Occupational Choice.* National Opinion Research Center, Monographs in Social Research, No. 2. Chicago: Aldine.

DEDIJER, STEVAN 1962 Measuring the Growth of Science. *Science* 138:781–788. → Data in Table 1, copyright 1962 by the American Association for the Advancement of Science.

Demographic Yearbook 1965. 1965 New York: United Nations. → Data in Table 1, copyright United Nations 1965. Reproduced by permission.

DEWITT, NICHOLAS 1961 *Education and Professional Employment in the U.S.S.R.* Washington: National Science Foundation.

EMERSON, JOHN P. 1965 *Nonagricultural Employment in Mainland China, 1948–1958.* U.S. Bureau of the Census, International Population Reports, Series P-90, No. 21. Washington: Government Printing Office.

ENGINEERS JOINT COUNCIL 1965 *Engineering Manpower in Profile.* New York: The Council.

EVAN, WILLIAM M. 1962 Role Strain in the Norm of Reciprocity in Research Organizations. *American Journal of Sociology* 68:346–354.

EVAN, WILLIAM M. 1963 The Problem of Obsolescence of Knowledge. Institute of Electrical and Electronics Engineers, Engineering Management Group, *IEEE Transactions on Engineering Management* EM 10:29–31.

EVAN, WILLIAM M. 1964 On the Margin: The Engineering Technician. Pages 83–112 in Peter L. Berger (editor), *The Human Shape of Work: Studies in the Sociology of Occupations.* New York: Macmillan.

GERSTL, JOEL E. 1963 Social Origins of Engineers. *New Society* 36:19–20.

GERSTL, JOEL E.; and HUTTON, S. P. 1966 *Engineers: The Anatomy of a Profession.* London: Tavistock.

GILFILLAN, S. COLUM 1935 *The Sociology of Invention: An Essay in the Social Causes of Technic Invention and Some of Its Social Results.* Chicago: Follett.

GOLDSEN, ROSE K. et al. 1960 *What College Students Think.* Princeton, N.J.: Van Nostrand.

GOLDSTEIN, BERNARD 1954 Unions and the Professional Employee. *Journal of Business* 27:276–284.

GRANICK, DAVID 1962 *The European Executive.* Garden City, N.Y.: Doubleday.

HODGE, ROBERT W. et al. 1964 Occupational Prestige in the United States, 1925–1963. *American Journal of Sociology* 70:286–302.

HOROWITZ, MORRIS A. 1965 High-level Manpower in the Economic Development of Argentina. Pages 1–36 in Frederick H. Harbison and Charles A. Myers (editors), *Manpower and Education: Country Studies in Economic Development.* New York: McGraw-Hill.

HUNT, J. B. 1960 Engineer Training in the New Nations. *Engineering* 189:287 only.

HUTTON, S. P.; and GERSTL, JOEL E. 1964 Engineering Education and Careers. Part 3F, pages 1–17 in Institution of Mechanical Engineers, Conference on Engineering Education and Career Patterns, London, *Proceedings.* London: The Institution.

INKELES, ALEX; and ROSSI, PETER H. 1956 National Comparisons of Occupational Prestige. *American Journal of Sociology* 61:329–339.

JAHODA, MARIE 1963 *The Education of Technologists.* London: Tavistock.

KILLIAN, J. R. 1962 An International Institute of Science and Technology. *NATO Letter* 10:7–11.

KING, ALEXANDER 1965 *Education and Change.* London: Junior Club Publications.

KORNHAUSER, WILLIAM 1962 *Scientists in Industry: Conflict and Accommodation.* Berkeley: Univ. of California Press.

KOROL, ALEXANDER G. 1957 *Soviet Education for Science and Technology.* Cambridge, Mass.: M.I.T. Press.

KOROL, ALEXANDER G. 1965 *Soviet Research and Development: Its Organization, Personnel and Funds.* Cambridge, Mass.: M.I.T. Press.

KRULEE, GILBERT 1963 Engineers at Northwestern. *Northwestern Engineer* 22:20–36.

KUIPER, G. 1956 The Recruitment of the Learned Professions in the Netherlands. Volume 3, pages 230–238 in World Congress of Sociology, Third, *Transactions.* London: International Sociological Association.

LEBOLD, WILLIAM K. et al. 1960 *A Study of the Purdue University Engineering Graduate.* Purdue University Engineering Extension Series, No. 99. Lafayette, Ind.: Purdue Univ.

MERTON, ROBERT K. (1949) 1957 *Social Theory and Social Structure.* Rev. & enl. ed. Glencoe, Ill.: Free Press. → See Chapter 16 on "Science and Democratic Social Structure" and Chapter 17 on "The Machine, the Worker and the Engineer."

NATIONAL SOCIETY OF PROFESSIONAL ENGINEERS 1962 *Ethics for Engineers: Canons of Ethics, Creed and Rules of Professional Conduct.* Washington: The Society.

NATIONAL SOCIETY OF PROFESSIONAL ENGINEERS 1963 *Engineering College Instruction in Professionalism: A Survey of Faculty Attitudes.* Washington: The Society.

ORGANIZATION FOR ECONOMIC COOPERATION AND DEVELOPMENT 1963 *Resources of Scientific and Technical Personnel in the OECD Area: Statistical Report.* Paris: The Organization.

ORGANIZATION FOR ECONOMIC COOPERATION AND DEVELOPMENT 1966 Deployment and Utilization of Highly Qualified Personnel, Statistical Index. Unpublished manuscript.

ORLEANS, LEO A. 1961 *Professional Manpower and Education in Communist China.* Washington: Government Printing Office.

OTEIZA, ENRIQUE 1965 Emigration of Engineers From Argentina: A Case of Latin American "Brain Drain." *International Labour Review* 92:445–461.

OXFORD UNIVERSITY, DEPARTMENT OF EDUCATION 1963 *Technology and the Sixth Form Boy.* Oxford and Cambridge Schools Examination Board.

RUSSETT, BRUCE M. et al. 1964 *World Handbook of Political and Social Indicators.* New Haven: Yale Univ. Press.

SHEPARD, HERBERT A. 1957 Engineers as Marginal Men. *Journal of Engineering Education* 47:536–542.

TIRYAKIAN, EDWARD A. 1958 The Prestige Evaluation of Occupations in an Underdeveloped Country: The

Philippines. *American Journal of Sociology* 63:390–399.

TROW, MARTIN 1959 Some Implications of the Social Origins of Engineers. *Scientific Manpower* [1958]: 67–74.

UNESCO *Statistical Yearbook, 1963.*

U.S. BUREAU OF THE CENSUS 1963 *Statistical Abstract of the United States.* Washington: Government Printing Office.

U.S. CONGRESS, JOINT COMMISSION ON ATOMIC ENERGY 1956 *Engineering and Scientific Manpower in the United States, Western Europe, and Soviet Russia.* Washington: Government Printing Office.

U.S. DEPARTMENT OF COMMERCE 1963 *Studies in Scientific and Engineering Manpower.* Washington: Government Printing Office.

U.S. OFFICE OF EDUCATION, DIVISION OF EDUCATIONAL STATISTICS 1965 *Digest of Educational Statistics,* by Kenneth V. Simon and W. Vance Grant. Bulletin, 1965, No. 4. Washington: Government Printing Office.

U.S. PATENT OFFICE *Official Gazette of the U.S. Patent Office.* → See especially January 28, 1964, 798:777 only and January 5, 1965, 810:2 only.

VEBLEN, THORSTEIN (1919) 1921 *The Engineers and the Price System.* New York: Huebsch. → A series of papers reprinted from the *Dial.* A paperback edition was published in 1963 by Harcourt.

WALTON, RICHARD E. 1961 *The Impact of the Professional Engineering Union: A Study of Collective Bargaining Among Engineers and Scientists and Its Significance for Management.* Boston: Harvard Univ., Graduate School of Business Administration, Division of Research.

WILENSKY, HAROLD L. 1964 The Professionalization of Everyone? *American Journal of Sociology* 70:137–158.

WOOD, J. F. D. 1961 Development in Engineering Education Overseas. *Journal of the Institution of Engineers* (Australia) 33:75–83.

ENGINEERING PSYCHOLOGY

Engineering psychology is a branch of applied psychology specifically concerned with the discovery and application of information about human behavior and its relation to machines, tools, and jobs so that their design may best match the abilities and limitations of their human users. The field is also referred to, from time to time, as psychotechnology or applied experimental psychology, but these two names appear to be gradually dropping out of use.

Engineering psychology can be properly viewed as part of *industrial psychology.* The latter includes such additional topics as personnel procurement, selection, training, classification, and promotion; labor relations; morale and human relations; organizational management; and consumer behavior. The field of engineering psychology can also be identified as a subarea of *human factors engineering,* or *human engineering,* as it is generally known in the United States, or of *ergonomics,* as it is usually called in the United Kingdom and Europe. The broader field of human factors engineering includes, in addition to engineering psychology, portions of such human sciences as anatomy, anthropometry, applied physiology, environmental medicine, and toxicology.

These distinctions between engineering psychology, industrial psychology, and human factors engineering are more academic than real. In his practical work, the engineering psychologist needs to know enough about all of these disciplines so that he can make use of them in arriving at sensible and informed design decisions. Rather than calling engineering psychology a distinct entity, it would be more correct to say that this name is more a convenient focus around which training is offered in many universities.

Historical development

In a certain sense it is correct to say that people have been concerned with engineering psychology of a sort ever since man began fashioning implements for his own use. Nonetheless, engineering psychology has emerged as a separate discipline only within the past few decades. It was not until the end of the nineteenth century that the first systematic investigations were conducted on man's capacity to work as it is influenced by his job and his tools. Frederick W. Taylor (1898) made empirical studies of the best design of shovels and of the optimum weight of material per shovelful for handling different products, such as sand, slag, rice coal, and iron ore. Taylor's interests, however, were primarily in rates of doing work and in the effects of incentives and worker motivation on rates of working. It remained for Frank B. Gilbreth to set a firm foundation for this field with his classic study of bricklaying (1909). Among other things, Gilbreth invented a scaffolding which could be quickly adjusted so that the bricklayer could work at the most convenient level at all times. A shelf held the bricks and mortar at their most convenient positions. By further changes of a similar nature Gilbreth was able to increase the number of bricks laid from 120 to 350 per man per hour. This pioneering work of Taylor and Gilbreth was the beginning of that branch of industrial engineering now known as time and motion study.

In the years that followed, time and motion engineers developed a number of principles of motion economy, of the arrangement of work, and of work design that have been widely applied throughout modern industry. Insofar as they have focused on human capacities and limitations and have used this information to redesign the machine, the task, or the work environment, it is correct to say that time and motion engineers are predecessors of the modern engineering psychologist.

Still, the primary emphasis in time and motion engineering has been on man as a worker, that is, as a source of mechanical power. During the two world wars there appeared a new class of machines —machines that made demands upon the operator not in terms of his muscular power but rather in terms of his sensory, perceptual, judgmental, and decision-making abilities. The job of a sonar operator, for example, requires virtually no muscular effort, but it makes severe demands on his sensory capacity, his attentiveness, and his decision-making ability. Problems of this type could no longer be dealt with by common sense or by the time and motion engineer's principles of motion economy.

World War I. When the United States entered World War I in 1917, a group of psychologists under Robert M. Yerkes was organized as the Psychology Committee of the National Research Council. In volunteering their services to the military establishment, they were met at first with considerable skepticism about what they could do of any value in the hard business of war. Gradually these psychologists were able to make some substantial contributions and eventually win the enthusiastic endorsement of the military services.

By and large the psychologists in World War I were concerned with such things as the selection, classification, and training of recruits, and with morale, military discipline, recreation, and problems of emotional stability in soldiers and sailors. A few of them, however, notably Raymond Dodge, Knight Dunlap, and Carl E. Seashore, encountered problems of a different sort—those in which the design of machines and equipment had to be related to the user. These early problems were found in gas masks, in binoculars and monoculars for spotters, in listening devices for locating submarines, and in aircraft. Questions were more numerous than answers, and the war ended before many solid accomplishments had been made.

World War II. After the armistice in 1918 this pioneering work in engineering psychology was almost entirely abandoned. A few scattered studies appeared between the two world wars under the auspices of the Industrial Health Board and the Industrial Fatigue Research Board of the Medical Research Council (Great Britain), but the field was largely neglected until World War II. At that time the machines and problems foreshadowed by World War I reappeared in profusion. Radar, sonar, high altitude and high speed aircraft, naval combat information centers, and air traffic control centers placed demands upon their human operators that were often far beyond the capabilities of human senses, brains, and muscles. Operators sometimes had to look for targets which were all but invisible, understand speech against backgrounds of deafening noise, track targets simultaneously in the three dimensions of space with both hands, and absorb large amounts of information to reach life-and-death decisions within seconds. As a result, bombs and bullets often missed their mark, planes crashed, friendly ships were sunk, and whales were depth-charged. The response to the need was so vigorous and dramatic that only a few highlights can be mentioned here.

Having entered the war before the United States, Great Britain faced these problems first and established a pattern that, in broad outlines, was followed later in the United States. The Medical Research Council was responsible for sponsoring much research on man–machine problems in several large universities and in the military services through the Flying Personnel Research Committee, the Royal Naval Personnel Research Committee, and the Military Personnel Research Committee. In the military services, important work was done at such laboratories as the Royal Aircraft Establishment, Farnborough; the Admiralty Naval Motion Study Unit, London; and the Admiralty Research Laboratory, Teddington, Middlesex.

Although entering the conflict later, the United States met problems equally urgent and dealt with them in substantially the same way. The National Defense Research Committee through the Office of Scientific Research and Development set up numerous research contracts in universities and industries to study these problems. All three military services incorporated civilian and military scientist-psychologists into their research and development laboratories in order that research findings would be put to immediate use. Some of the pioneering work in this area was carried out by the Aero Medical Laboratory of the (then) Army Air Forces Air Materiel Command, Wright Field, Dayton, Ohio; the Army Air Forces School of Aviation Medicine, Randolph Field, Texas; the U.S. Navy Electronics Laboratory, San Diego, California; the Naval Research Laboratory, Washington, D.C.; and the Armored Medical Research Laboratory, Fort Knox, Kentucky.

Present status of the field. Since World War II the growth of engineering psychology has been very rapid. The Society of Engineering Psychologists, Division 21 of the American Psychological Association, had 360 members in 1965. About 770 psychologists are members of the Human Factors Society and, indeed, make up over 60 per cent of the membership of that organization. Psychologists also figure prominently in the Ergonomics Research Society (centered in Great Britain), the Société d'Ergonomie de Langue Française (centered in France), the Nederlandse Vereniging voor Ergonomie, and the Japanese Ergonomics Research Society. Engineering psychologists are employed in every branch of the military service, in many independent research and consulting organizations, and in the aviation, automotive, electronics, communications, and home appliance industries.

At the present time, engineering psychology is most fully developed and exploited as a specialty in the United States. Other countries which give training in this area or make use of it in practical affairs to some degree or other are Australia, Belgium, France, Germany, Great Britain, Israel, Japan, the Netherlands, Sweden, Switzerland, and the U.S.S.R.

Methodology

Engineering psychologists aim to discover principles that can be cast into the form of recommendations for machine design. Unfortunately, they can usually find specific answers for only a small proportion of the questions they face. Part of the difficulty is that man–machine interactions occur in an almost infinite variety. Moreover, the range of these problems is diverging rather than converging. Engineers are busy designing new and complex machines, destined to operate not only in the prosaic world of our everyday lives but in hostile and exotic environments where man has never lived—from the crushing Stygian abysses of our oceans to the infinite voids of deep space. Literally millions of people are actively engaged in the business of designing and constructing machines and machine systems, but there are scarcely a thousand people who make it their primary business to study man in his intimate relations with these machines. For reasons such as these, man–machine problems appear to be multiplying faster than we can do research on them.

The practicing engineering psychologist finds that he spends a considerable portion of his time "trying things out." In some industries and in some laboratories, experimentation of one kind or another may well take up the major part of the engineering psychologist's working time. As one might suppose from the historical development of the field and the nature of the work, methodologies in engineering psychology are diverse and adapted from several disciplines (see Chapanis 1959). The

discovery of new methodologies is also a topic of continuing and active interest in the literature of engineering psychology. For this reason the techniques mentioned below should be regarded as a sample of the ways in which problems have been answered in the past rather than as an exhaustive list of the tools available to the practitioner in this field.

Whenever he can, the engineering psychologist uses full-scale experimentation with the same rigor and sophistication that one expects of the best tradition of experimentation. Because of the complexity of his problems and the many variables that normally influence human behavior in machine situations, the engineering psychologist typically employs experimental designs using several variables, deriving, for example, from methods of analysis of variance. In addition, the psychophysical methods are widely used for obtaining useful data on sensory capacities, as are articulation test methods for measuring the effectiveness of speech communication devices and systems. In preliminary exploratory work on complex systems, the study of critical incidents, accidents, and near accidents has proven widely useful in locating potential sources of man–machine conflict.

From the industrial engineer, the engineering psychologist has borrowed and adapted a number of techniques for directly observing systems in operation. Some of these are activity sampling procedures, process analysis, and micromotion methods. Finally, from more conventional techniques of industrial psychology the engineering psychologist has adapted to his own needs methods of job analysis, task analysis, personnel requirement inventories, questionnaires, tests, and rating scales.

Subject matter

Almost everything that is known about man as a living, feeling, behaving organism is relevant to the engineering psychologist. Current thinking even extends to man as a social organism: a number of recent research findings show clearly that the effectiveness of complex man–machine systems is determined to a considerable extent by the compatibility of the team of men who work in the system. Examples are nuclear submarines and advanced space vehicles, where men are forced to live and work together for extended periods of time in cramped quarters while under unusual stress.

For all that, the amount of information about human behavior that may be required for particular applications varies enormously. In the design of a space vehicle, the engineering psychologist may be faced with problems that cover the full range of human psychology. He needs to consider the sensory capacities of operators as they relate to instrument displays and the sensing of information from inside and outside the vehicle. Knowledge about man's ability to make rapid and correct decisions is vital. Working hours and work–rest cycles are certain to be different from those on earth, and it is important to know how well man can perform under these altered working conditions. The engineering psychologist also needs to consider the human ability to make correct control actions of a great variety. Human reactions to exotic environments, the ability to learn new and complex skills, emotional reactions and personality problems that might arise from the stresses of space flight, social behavior—all of these are relevant for the engineering psychologist. [*See* SPACE, OUTER.]

By contrast with the complexity of a space vehicle, there are many problems in engineering psychology that are much simpler and more circumscribed. The engineering psychologist who works with common consumer items may be faced with questions like: How should the controls be placed on a stove so that housewives correctly turn the correct control to activate a burner? What size and spacing of letters, numbers, and symbols should be used on the labels of household appliances so that they will be easily legible? How should the numbers and letters be arranged on push-button telephones? All of these are examples of relatively restricted but genuine problems encountered in the practical business of engineering psychology.

The man–machine model.   In their work engineering psychologists regard man as an element in a man–machine system. Basically, a person who uses or operates a piece of equipment has to do three things. He has first to sense something and to perceive what this something means. The thing the human operator senses is termed a machine *display*. It may be any of a thousand different things—the position of a pointer on a dial, the print-out of a digital computer, a voice coming over a loudspeaker, a red light flashing on a control panel, a highway sign along a speedway, or the resistance felt in a certain kind of control.

Having sensed a machine output, the man next has to interpret what the display means, understand it, perhaps do some mental computation, and reach a decision of some sort. In so doing, the human operator often uses other important human functions—the ability to remember and recall, to compare what he now perceives against past experiences, to recall operating rules he may have learned during training, or to put what he now

experiences into the context of strategies he may have formed for handling events such as this. A man is not necessarily aware that he is doing any or all of these things, of course. His behavior may be so well practiced and routine that the decision to do one thing or another may be made almost by reflex, just as the experienced driver may decide almost unconsciously whether or not he should stop when he sees a green traffic light change to yellow. All of the functions discussed in this paragraph are ordinarily subsumed under the heading of *higher mental processes* in textbooks of psychology. Engineering psychologists often use machine terminology instead of more familiar psychological terms and, in keeping with this trend, refer to all these higher mental processes collectively as *data processing.*

Having reached a decision about the information he has received through his sense organs and dealt with in his nervous system, the human operator then normally takes some action. The action is normally exercised on some sort of a control—a push button, lever, crank, pedal, switch, or handle. Man's action upon one or more of these controls exerts in turn an influence on the behavior of the machine, its output and displays. Many times, of course, a machine operator monitoring a process may decide to do nothing. This is still regarded as an important human output.

A man–machine system does not exist in isolation but in an environment. The character of this environment influences man's efficiency and performance, and the engineering psychologist is often vitally concerned with these factors. Among the more important environmental influences are such commonplace ones as temperature, humidity, ventilation, lighting, noise, and movement. Some less common but still important ones are vibration and a whole host of noxious gases and contaminants. In more exotic systems the engineering psychologist may also have to be concerned with the effects of increased acceleration, weightlessness (zero gravity conditions), anoxia caused by reduced oxygen at high altitudes, radiation, and the effects of reduced barometric pressures on the body.

The display of information.   The man–machine model described above provides a convenient framework for summarizing the main content areas of engineering psychology. Machine displays, in a manner of speaking, represent the starting point of the man–machine cycle, for it is through such displays that the machine communicates to its human operator. For this reason, a considerable amount of work has been devoted to studies of displays and the ways in which they should be selected and designed. Although man has available a dozen or so sense channels that could conceivably be used to receive information from machine systems, only three—vision, hearing, and the sense of touch or vibration—have been exploited to any great extent.

In the area of visual displays, research has been done on such problems as the design of mechanical indicators; scales; cathode-ray tubes (radar scopes); charts, tables, and graphs; warning lights and signals; abstract visual dimensions (symbols varying in color, shape, brightness, or size) for coding information; and general and specialized lighting systems (for ready rooms and radar rooms).

Problems of auditory displays can be grouped into two broad classes: those dealing with tonal or noise signals (sirens, diaphones, horns, buzzers, bells, gongs, and so on), and those dealing with speech communication systems. Research on the former class of problems has been generally concerned with signal processing and control: the selection of signals and signal characteristics, the filtering of signals to eliminate unwanted or interfering noise, and the use of signals for coding information. Research on speech communication systems has been aimed at the design of special or efficient languages, the design of the components of speech communication systems (microphones, amplifiers, and so on), and the design of speech communication systems as a whole. [*See* HEARING; PERCEPTION, *article on* SPEECH PERCEPTION; VISION.]

Machine displays for senses other than vision and hearing have not been used very much, and perhaps for this reason, research on such displays is relatively meager. Within recent years, however, it has been shown that the vibratory sense can be used for an efficient communication system. Using a special kind of vibratory code applied to a man's chest, Geldard (1957) trained one subject to receive up to 38 words per minute. However, because of the awkwardness of the equipment and the possibility of interference from other sources of vibration, it is doubtful whether that particular system will be put into any operational situation. This research shows, however, that there may be unexplored possibilities for communication through these other senses.

Data processing. One important function which man serves in many man–machine systems is that of data processing. He may be required to perceive things, assimilate large masses of data, evaluate or assess a situation, do computations, and make decisions. Despite much research on these higher mental processes our understanding of the mechanisms by which people do these things is still im-

perfect. As a result, it is in this area of engineering psychology that one finds the fewest principles and concrete recommendations about the ways in which man can be best integrated into man–machine systems. As more and more systems become automated, however, man's role in the system becomes more and more that of a monitor and decision maker. One may expect therefore that some of the greatest research gains are yet to be realized in this area.

Machine controls. Research on the design of machine controls has yielded a substantial number of useful and practical principles. These are concerned with such things as the factors involved in selecting the correct control for a job, control–display ratios, direction-of-movement relationships, control resistance, ways of preventing accidental activation, and control coding. Among the more complex kinds of controls are those involved in what are called closed-loop tracking systems. (Driving a car along a winding road is a simple example of a closed-loop tracking task.) Research on the last kind of problem involves considerations of the mathematical relationships between the movements of the control and the dynamics of the system.

Environmental problems. Although the study of environmental problems might seem to fall exclusively within the province of the applied physiologist, the fact is that psychologists have studied the effects of a wide range of environmental factors on gross behavior. These studies have been concerned with problems of illumination, noise, anoxia (lack of oxygen at high altitudes), certain kinds of noxious gases and contaminants, heat and cold, vibration, and most recently, weightlessness.

The aim of research. In common with research in most other areas of science, research in engineering psychology has as its first aim *understanding*. Beyond this, however, the engineering psychologist hopes that his researches will yield principles which can be put into the form of definite recommendations for machine design. A large number of these are now available, and they can be found in textbooks and guides on this subject (see, for example, Chapanis 1965; McCormick 1957; Morgan et al. 1963). The following example from research on control design will illustrate one of the concepts that originated in engineering psychology and some of the design recommendations that followed from it.

The results of control movements are often shown on a display. The tuning knob on a radio is a familiar example. As you turn the tuning knob, you change a variable condenser inside the radio. At the same time, a pointer moves along a linear or circular scale to show you what frequency or wave length the radio has been tuned to. Examples of linked controls and displays are common in the world of machines. The controls may be knobs, cranks, levers, or translatory controls. Sometimes a control may be in one plane (for example, on the horizontal working surface in front of an operator) and the display in another plane (for example, directly in front of the operator's eyes and at right angles to the surface on which the control is mounted). The number of permutations of controls, displays, and orientations is, of course, very great.

In the case of many control–display combinations it turns out that most people have consistent expectations about the way in which a control should move in order to produce a change in the display. When these expectations are strong and found universally, they are called *population stereotypes*. Controls that conform to these population stereotypes are responded to much more quickly and with far fewer errors than are controls that do not. Human beings are remarkably adaptable and, given sufficient training, can learn to use controls and displays that do not agree with population stereotypes. The interesting thing, however, is that if such an operator is subjected to great stress or to an emergency situation, he frequently regresses or reverts to his natural expectancies. Many accidents in aircraft have been traced to this single factor alone. The design recommendation which follows from this research is clear: Whenever strong population stereotypes exist, control and display movements should agree with them.

Man–machine system design

Although, as was remarked earlier, the scope of engineering psychology covers a range from relatively simple devices to enormously complex machine systems, it is the latter which are the most challenging, most complex, and most difficult to deal with. The design of an air traffic control system, an automated mail handling system, a new guided missile system, or a deep space vehicle system is a problem of gigantic proportions. Thousands of technical and professional experts of a hundred or more different varieties may work for years to bring such a large system into being. Engineering psychologists are generally recognized as important members of such design teams.

In the preceding section the subject matter of engineering psychology has been presented from the standpoint of the way it is organized by the psychologist himself. When we look at the field from the standpoint of what the engineering psy-

chologist contributes to the design of man–machine systems, a somewhat different order of topics results.

Design and planning.   The first step in the creation of any large system is generally called a study phase. It is at this time that engineers study in detail the specifications and requirements of the system. Alternative ways of designing the system to meet the requirements are thought up, tested, tried out, and discarded, modified, or accepted. Contrary to what many lay people think, there is much trial and error involved in this stage of the process, and the final conceptualization of the system may be quite different from initial ideas. During this study phase, engineering psychologists are called upon to study and decide about man's role in the system. They usually assist in making decisions about precisely which functions of the system should be allocated to humans and which to machine components. They prepare estimates of the number and types of people that will be required to man the system when it is completed, the so-called QQPRI (Qualitative and Quantitative Personnel Requirements Information). If personnel with specialized training will be needed, engineering psychologists plan and design training programs and curricula to ensure that qualified people are available to operate the system when it is completed. Finally, they may try to anticipate the social consequences of the system on its human operators or society in general.

Project engineering.   After preliminary designs and plans have been completed, the system goes into actual construction. The first model of any large system is seldom built as originally planned. Difficulties appear at this point which had not been anticipated in the largely paper-and-pencil study phase, and the changes and modifications that must be made often number in the thousands. During the production phase of system design the engineering psychologist usually makes substantial contributions to the man–machine combination, although ultimate responsibility for design usually rests with an engineer. The engineering psychologist studies, tests, and makes recommendations about specific workplace arrangements, solves specific problems of display and control, and makes design recommendations about the solution of environmental problems.

Another important task of the engineering psychologist is that of studying the system from the standpoint of its reliability and maintenance and of anticipating special problems of maintenance. With the increase in the number of highly automated systems, problems of faultfinding and maintenance are becoming increasingly important. For one thing, the cost of a highly automatic system is so great that the user cannot afford to have it idle for long periods of time. At the same time, such systems are so complex that it is becoming increasingly difficult for repairmen to diagnose what is wrong with them and decide how they can be most quickly repaired. As one illustration of the magnitude of the problem, the U.S. Air Force estimates that to repair and maintain a typical system (for example, an aircraft) during its normal lifetime may cost up to ten times the original purchase price of the system. Further, of the total time spent in actively repairing most large systems, as much as 80 per cent of a maintenance man's time is spent in merely discovering what is wrong with it. The engineering psychologist's contributions here are in planning effective faultfinding strategies and in seeing to it that the equipment is so designed (with sufficient test points, accesses, and so on) that it can be easily maintained, that it is installed where it can be readily reached, that appropriate, well-written maintenance manuals are ready as soon as the equipment is completed, that special tools and test equipment are properly designed and constructed, that maintenance men are trained, that adequate work and storage facilities are provided, and that an adequate supply of spare parts and replacements is provided.

The end result of this part of system development is what is usually termed a *prototype*, a first full-scale working model of the system.

Test and evaluation and operational use. Once a protoype of a system is constructed, it usually goes through a series of tests, often termed operational suitability tests or evaluations, to discover if the system really does what it is supposed to do. It is generally recognized that a man–machine system has to be tested as a complete entity and that the human components in a system may make or break it. The problems of testing systems that contain people are far more difficult than conducting simple engineering or physical tests. Because of their special training in experimental methodology and in the problems of conducting studies on people, engineering psychologists are often given major responsibility for the design and conduct of such tests.

When a large system has been tested, accepted, and put into operational use, it may undergo still further modifications as experience with it accumulates. These are usually far fewer in number and less sweeping than those which occur earlier in the design. Although the engineering psychologist may still play some role in this stage of the lifetime of the system, it is usually a much less important one than in earlier design phases. It is at this time that the training and personnel specialist replaces the engineering psychologist in terms of importance.

ALPHONSE CHAPANIS

[*See also* INDUSTRIAL RELATIONS, *article on* INDUSTRIAL AND BUSINESS PSYCHOLOGY. *Other relevant material may be found in* MILITARY PSYCHOLOGY; PSYCHOPHYSICS.]

BIBLIOGRAPHY
CHAPANIS, ALPHONSE 1959 *Research Techniques in Human Engineering.* Baltimore: Johns Hopkins Press.
CHAPANIS, ALPHONSE 1965 *Man–Machine Engineering.* Belmont, Calif.: Wadsworth.
GELDARD, FRANK A. 1957 Adventures in Tactile Literacy. *American Psychologist* 12:115–124.
GILBRETH, FRANK B. 1909 *Bricklaying System.* New York: Clark.
McCORMICK, ERNEST J. (1957) 1964 *Human Factors Engineering.* 2d ed. New York: McGraw-Hill. → First published as *Human Engineering.*
MORGAN, CLIFFORD T. et al. (editors) 1963 *Human Engineering Guide to Equipment Design.* New York: McGraw-Hill.
TAYLOR, FREDERICK W. (1898) 1911 *Scientific Shoveling.* Wyoming, Pa.: The Wyoming Shovel Works.

ENTERTAINMENT

See COMMUNICATION, MASS; DRAMA; FILM; LEISURE; LITERATURE.

ENTREPRENEURSHIP

There are some unresolved differences in the definitions of entrepreneurship, but there is agreement that the term includes at least a part of the administrative function of making decisions for the conduct of some type of organization. One group of scholars would restrict the term to strategic or innovating decisions, and an overlapping group would apply it only to business organizations. The basis for these differences can be understood from the history of the concept.

The word *entrepreneur* appeared in the French language long before there was any general concept of an entrepreneurial function. By the early sixteenth century, men engaged in leading military expeditions were referred to as entrepreneurs. From this usage, it was easy to move to applying entrepreneur to other types of adventurers. After about 1700, entrepreneur was frequently applied by the French to government road, bridge, harbor, and fortification contractors and, somewhat later, to architects (Hoselitz 1951, p. 195). Seeing such activities as the entrepreneurial function, the mid-eighteenth-century French writer Bernard F. de

Belidor further defined it as buying labor and materials at uncertain prices and selling the resultant product at a contracted price (Hoselitz 1951, pp. 198–199).

Richard Cantillon's *Essai sur la nature du commerce en général* (1755), probably written a generation before its publication date, drew attention to *entrepreneur* as a technical term. The essence of the function of the entrepreneur was to bear uncertainty. Conversely to the Belidor emphasis, Cantillon saw the entrepreneur as anyone who bought and sold at uncertain prices. Obviously, there is no contradiction between Belidor and Cantillon in theory, but merely in the type of examples chosen. Except for princes, landowners, and salaried workers, Cantillon regarded everyone engaged in economic activity as an entrepreneur.

The physiocratic economists of the later eighteenth century, such as François Quesnay and Nicolas Baudeau, called the agricultural cultivator an entrepreneur. Since the physiocrats also thought that only the land was a source of social product, this put the entrepreneur in a key position. In the sphere of agriculture, Baudeau credited the entrepreneur with all the essential characteristics of risk taking and innovation that were to be elaborated in later definitions (in his *Première introduction à la philosophie économique*). At about the same time A. R. J. Turgot, in his *Réflexions sur la formation et la distribution des richesses*, spoke of the entrepreneur in manufacturing as one who risked capital (Hoselitz 1951, pp. 205–212).

Thus, by 1800, many French economists had given special meanings to entrepreneur and entrepreneurship, with differences arising largely from the characteristics of the sector of the economy that chiefly attracted their attention. Those economists interested in government saw the entrepreneur as a contractor, the specialists on agriculture as a farmer, and the proponents of industry as a risk-taking capitalist. The "classic" definition, which was to survive until the twentieth century, was written by an aristocratic industrialist who had had unpleasant practical experience, Jean Baptiste Say.

In the *Catechism of Political Economy*, Say wrote of the entrepreneur as the agent who "unites all means of production and who finds in the value of the products . . . the re-establishment of the entire capital he employs, and the value of the wages, the interest, and the rent which he pays, as well as the profits belonging to himself" ([1815] 1816), pp. 28–29). This idea appeared earlier in *A Treatise on Political Economy* (1803), which was not translated into English until 1827. Say's entrepreneur commonly, but not necessarily, supplies either his own or borrowed capital. To succeed, he must have "judgment, perseverance, and a knowledge of the world as well as of business. He must possess the art of superintendence and administration" (1803, p. 295 in the 1827 edition). Say does not, however, discuss the entrepreneur in relation to innovation or capital creation. As in the case of the British classicists, he was unable to make entrepreneurship a ponderable factor in his general economic theory.

In contrast to the tolerably consistent and expanding French definitions of entrepreneur, the English appear to have made rather less use of three terms: *adventurer*, *undertaker*, and *projector*. While the Merchant Adventurers of the sixteenth century were the equivalent of French entrepreneurs, *adventurer* did not come into general use. The seventeenth-century French use of entrepreneur for government contractor had its English counterpart in the term *undertaker*. Near the close of the century, the third term, *projector*, came into use. Daniel Defoe, in *An Essay Upon Projects*, equates the term *projector* with *inventor*, but also with *fraud* or *swindler*. In Malachy Postlethwayt's *Universal Dictionary of Trade and Commerce* the words *adventurer* and *undertaker* are referred to but these terms are not given precise definitions (Redlich 1949, p. 9). Bert F. Hoselitz (1951) finds that by the time of Postlethwayt, *undertaker* could be applied to businessmen in general but that the term was, in fact, becoming obsolete. [*See the biographies of* CANTILLON; QUESNAY; SAY; TURGOT.]

Early treatment in economic theory. As economic theory became more carefully formulated in all the western European nations, no operative place was found for the entrepreneur. This was particularly evident in English classic theory from Smith to Marshall, where many writers made no effort either to define or include entrepreneurship.

The difficulty was that English theory was based upon a normal state of equilibrium, established by the multiple reactions of businessmen, consumers, investors, and workers to the prices of goods and services. Individual variations in behavior were seen either as canceled out in the aggregate or suppressed by competition. In this highly aggregative system, any unknown element was to be derived from the relations of theoretically measurable quantities. Such a system could obviously not utilize unmeasurable social or cultural factors such as entrepreneurship. To say that the entrepreneur was rewarded for risk taking, that is, for uncertainty, was the negation of a proper theoretical explanation.

In addition to the inhospitability of classic theory, the mid-nineteenth-century business structure of small-sized to medium-sized family firms, or closely held firms, obscured the distinctive character of the entrepreneurial function. With few exceptions, the men performing this function were also capitalist owners. Their rewards could be seen as a return on capital rather than as special compensations for entrepreneurial ability per se. In his *Principles of Economics*, Alfred Marshall perceived the changed situation inherent in big, managerially run business: "Those general faculties, which are characteristic of the modern businessman," he wrote, "increase in importance as the scale of business increases" (1891, p. 644). Yet Marshall did not elaborate upon the theoretical significance of this increasing factor, and in discussing the growth of English manufacturing he used capitalist and undertaker interchangeably (1891, pp. 40–43).

Perhaps the relatively early development of big corporations in the United States led American economists to think of entrepreneurship as a function separate from either ownership or the supply of capital. In the late 1870s, Francis A. Walker emphasized the distinction between capitalists and entrepreneurs and called the latter the engineers of industrial progress and the chief agents of production (Dorfman 1946–1959, vol. 3, p. 109). Frederick B. Hawley, writing in 1882, saw risk taking as the distinguishing attribute of the entrepreneur, and ranked this as a factor in production on a par with land, labor, and capital (*ibid.*, p. 132). At the end of the century, the unorthodox John R. Commons gave an explanation of risk-taking entrepreneurship and profit that anticipated some of the more fully elaborated ideas of Joseph A. Schumpeter (*ibid.*, p. 283). According to Commons, one type of profits arose from the ability and risk taking of the entrepreneur and was temporary and contingent on changes in the economic situation. But Schumpeter himself, in 1912, gave John Bates Clark credit for being the first to connect "entrepreneurial profits considered as a surplus over interest (and rent), with successful introduction into the economic process of technological, commercial, or organizational improvements" (*ibid.*, vol. 4, p. 166n). The basic problem of finding an operative role for entrepreneurship in economic theory, however, remained unsolved; and economic theorists, in general, well aware of the incongruity of a nonmeasurable human element in a theoretical structure based on quantifiable assumptions,

moved in other directions, such as the study of business cycles, income, saving, and investment. [*See the biographies of* CLARK, JOHN BATES; COMMONS; MARSHALL; WALKER.]

Schumpeter–Cole views. Schumpeter's acceptance of a chair at Harvard, the translation of *The Theory of Economic Development* into English in 1934, and the great depression all called new attention to his position regarding the essential role of the entrepreneur in creating profits. According to Schumpeter, both interest and profit arose from progressive change, and would not exist in a static society, as he defined it. Change, in turn, was the work of innovating businessmen or entrepreneurs. Since one change was likely to stimulate others, there was a tendency for innovations to cluster and produce long upswings in profits and business activity.

Much additional interest in entrepreneurship arose from the work of two of Schumpeter's colleagues at Harvard, economic historians Edwin F. Gay and Arthur H. Cole. In 1944, in his presidential address to the Economic History Association, Cole offered a historical analysis of the changing character of entrepreneurship. Four years later, he and Schumpeter cooperated in establishing at Harvard the Research Center in Entrepreneurial History. From the work of the center, influenced greatly by Cole and Leland H. Jenks, there emerged an approach to entrepreneurship differing from Schumpeter's.

In the Schumpeterian view, innovation was the criterion of entrepreneurship: ". . . the defining characteristic is simply the doing of new things or the doing of things that are already being done in a new way (innovation)" (Schumpeter 1947, p. 151). The "new way" was a "creative response" to a situation that had, at least, three essential characteristics.

First . . . it can practically never be understood *ex ante*. . . . Secondly, creative response shapes the whole course of subsequent events and their "long-run" outcome. . . . Thirdly, creative response . . . has . . . something to do (*a*) with the quality of personnel available in the society, (*b*) . . . with quality available to a particular field of activity, and (*c*) with individual decisions, actions and patterns of behavior. Accordingly a study of creative response in business becomes coterminous with a study of entrepreneurship. (Schumpeter 1947, p. 150)

Thus, to Schumpeter, a manager was an entrepreneur only while he was making a creative or innovative response.

The Cole view of entrepreneurship, however,

equates it with the continuing general activities of managers. It is "the purposeful activity (including an integrated sequence of decisions) of an individual or group of associated individuals, undertaken to initiate, maintain or aggrandize a profit oriented business unit for the production or distribution of economic goods and services" (Cole 1959, p. 7). "Novelty is successful in the business world only if the institution introducing it is being effectively maintained" (p. 15).

Since the difference in the two definitions involves only the scope within which the term may be applied, the followers of Cole and Schumpeter have worked together with a minimum of friction. Both definitions implied broad social approaches, close to the Germanic tradition of Gustav Schmoller, who had seen the need for "a deeper insight into the social context of the enterprise" (Lane & Riemersma 1953, p. 6), or Alfred Weber, who had regarded entrepreneurship as a socioeconomic function separate from profit making. Both definitions also suggest time spans longer than those of dynamic economic theory. [*See the biography of* SCHUMPETER.]

Recent thought. In spite of the difficulties inherent in long-run analysis and in unmeasurable human factors, the increasing interest of economists in economic development has directed their attention to entrepreneurship. While economists in this field include the entrepreneurial function in empirical studies of situations and in recommending appropriate economic policies, the theoretical problem of finding a place for unmeasurable and socially influenced forces in a mathematically oriented theory has not been solved. More specifically, the difficulty is that entrepreneurial earnings would have to be accounted for in a theory of profit, but no theoretical cost of entrepreneurship can be set.

Entrepreneurial study continues, however, in the unoccupied territory bordered by economics, history, and sociology. Two publications—*Explorations in Entrepreneurial History* (started by R. Richard Wohl and Hugh G. J. Aitken at the research center at Harvard and continued in the 1960s under the editorship of Ralph L. Andreano at Earlham College) and *Economic Development and Cultural Change* (initiated by Bert F. Hoselitz at the University of Chicago)—emphasized, during the 1950s and 1960s, the importance of entrepreneurship. In addition to scores of articles in these two publications, the Harvard center inspired a number of larger empirical studies. Of these, Fritz Redlich's volumes on the military entrepreneur in Europe cover the longest historical time span. In all, a new field of specialization, not firmly

attached to any single discipline, appears to have been established.

Students of entrepreneurship generally have come to agree that while it is a definable function, entrepreneur is a term denoting an ideal type rather than a term continuously applicable to a real person. Any businessman or other official may exercise entrepreneurship, but a classification cannot be devised that would empirically separate entrepreneurs and nonentrepreneurs.

One group of scholars has expanded the Cole point of view that entrepreneurship is a continuous function in business organization.

To the extent that behavior in a business firm is organized (formally or informally), to that extent we have entrepreneurship; to the extent that it is disorganized, random, or self-defeating, to that extent entrepreneurship is lacking. . . . The characteristics conventionally associated with entrepreneurship—leadership, innovation, risk-bearing, and so on—are so associated precisely because, in a highly commercialized culture such as ours, they are essential features of effective business organization. By the same logic, in a differently oriented culture, the typical characteristics of entrepreneurship differ. (Aitken 1963, p. 6).

Another school of thought prefers to keep the Schumpeterian distinction between the entrepreneurial function of making strategically important or innovating decisions and the managerial function of maintaining the more routine operations of a business organization. Nonspecialists, also, tend to emphasize strategic decision making in distinguishing entrepreneurship from management.

THOMAS C. COCHRAN

[*See also* HISTORY, *article on* BUSINESS HISTORY.]

BIBLIOGRAPHY

AITKEN, HUGH G. J. 1963 The Future of Entrepreneurial Research. *Explorations in Entrepreneurial History* Second Series 1:3–9.

CANTILLON, RICHARD (1755) 1952 *Essai sur la nature du commerce en général.* Paris: Institut National d'Études Démographiques.

COLE, ARTHUR H. 1946 An Approach to the Study of Entrepreneurship: A Tribute to Edwin F. Gay. *Journal of Economic History* 6 (Supplement):1–15.

COLE, ARTHUR H. 1959 *Business Enterprise in Its Social Setting.* Cambridge, Mass.: Harvard Univ. Press.

DORFMAN, JOSEPH 1946–1959 *The Economic Mind in American Civilization.* 5 vols. New York: Viking. → See especially volumes 3 and 4.

HOSELITZ, BERT F. 1951 The Early History of Entrepreneurial Theory. *Explorations in Entrepreneurial History* 3:193–220.

LANE, FREDERIC C.; and RIEMERSMA, JELLE C. (editors) 1953 *Enterprise and Secular Change: Readings in Economic History.* Homewood, Ill.: Irwin.

MARSHALL, ALFRED 1891 *Principles of Economics.* 2d ed. New York and London: Macmillan. → The first edition was published in 1890. A ninth, variorum edition was published in 1961.

REDLICH, FRITZ 1949 The Origins of the Concepts of "Entrepreneur" and "Creative Entrepreneur." *Explorations in Entrepreneurial History* 1:1–7.

SAY, JEAN BAPTISTE (1803) 1964 *A Treatise on Political Economy: Or, the Production, Distribution and Consumption of Wealth.* New York: Kelley. → First published as *Traité d'économie politique: Ou, simple exposition de la manière dont se forment, se distribuent, et se consomment les richesses.*

SAY, JEAN BAPTISTE (1815) 1816 *Catechism of Political Economy: Or, Familiar Conversations on the Manner in Which Wealth Is Produced, Distributed, and Consumed by Society.* London: Sherwood. → First published as *Catéchisme d'économie politique.*

SCHUMPETER, JOSEPH A. (1912) 1934 *The Theory of Economic Development.* Cambridge, Mass.: Harvard Univ. Press. → First published in German.

SCHUMPETER, JOSEPH A. 1947 The Creative Response in Economic History. *Journal of Economic History* 7:149–159.

ENVIRONMENT

Environment has been defined as "the aggregate of all the external conditions and influences affecting the life and development of an organism" (Webster's *New Collegiate Dictionary*). The aim, then, with either individual organisms or communities, is to distinguish between factors arising from outside the system and factors inherent in the system itself. This sounds simple enough, but in practice the distinction between organism and environment is not always easy to make.

In the first place, there is a problem of *limits.* This is essentially a matter of definition; to illustrate with an absurd example, when does an apple that a person eats cease to be a part of the environment and start to be a part of the man? Perhaps as soon as it enters the mouth; perhaps not until digestion has been completed. Most people, in any case, would consider indigestion caused by eating a green apple to be an environmental effect. Similarly, internal parasites would be considered part of the environment of the individual in which they live, even though they are entirely inside the system: the question is one of origin rather than present position.

The limit problem is not very serious. More confusing is the problem of *interaction* between organism and environment. The earth's atmosphere, for instance, with oxygen and carbon dioxide as component gases, is an essential part of the environment for life as we know it. Yet we now believe that these gases were not part of the early atmosphere of the planet; their existence is a consequence of the action of living organisms, as well as a necessary condition for life. The relation between vegetation and soil provides another type of example. The kind of forest growing in a particular region is at least partly the consequence of the type of soil in that region; yet the nature of the soil is partly determined by the sort of vegetation that has grown on it.

The interaction problem is particularly confusing in the case of man and the human environment. In orienting and judging our surroundings, we depend on our sensory systems; yet, as psychologists can so easily show, what we perceive is in part a consequence of conditioning and learning. We have thus really *created* many aspects of the shapes, colors, sounds, and smells in the world about us, at least as they influence our behavior.

The concept of *culture* is responsible for many difficulties in this connection. Should culture be looked at as a part of the individual or of the community? Is it a part of the environment? The answer surely varies, depending on the nature of the study.

For instance, if we are concerned with the ways in which peoples (or individuals) cope with their natural environment, we almost necessarily look at the physical man with the cultural equipment at his disposal for this purpose. Thus the same physical surroundings, the same environment, may have quite different meanings for, say, a food-gathering pygmy, an agricultural Bantu, or a western European. We are here concerned primarily with cultural adaptations or maladaptations. This is the case with many sorts of geographical and anthropological studies; in extreme cases, human nature may be taken as a constant to be ignored and study concentrated on the interaction between culture and environment in this sense of the term.

In many kinds of psychological studies, on the other hand, cultural traits are dealt with as parts of the environment: we become interested in the ways in which individuals are taught to accept their culture, or the ways in which they are frustrated by it and the forms that rebellion takes. In physiological studies, by contrast, culture may or may not be considered as environmental at all. Work on heat stress, for instance, may involve a naked man on a treadmill under controlled climatic conditions, in an attempt to eliminate cultural effects; alternatively, it may involve clothed men under natural conditions. Investigations of such concepts as "comfort zones" assume that people will be wearing culturally acceptable clothing.

Clothing illustrates nicely many aspects of the man–culture–environment relationship. Clothing is definitely external, stemming from outside the system of the individual organism. Yet in many kinds of practical studies, we must assume that people are wearing clothes and observe environmental effects on clothed individuals. Furthermore, the kind of clothing worn may influence individual personality—witness the effect of uniforms, of formal dress, or of work clothes.

Organism and environment, then, are not contrasting or mutually exclusive terms; rather, they represent interacting systems, and the distinction is useful in analysis only when this is kept in mind. Environment is often contrasted with heredity, as in the long controversy over "nature versus nurture" in shaping human personality. There is no "versus." Every individual is the product of a certain genetic potentiality finding expression in a particular environment or series of environments.

In studies of biological communities, the concept of *ecosystem* has proved useful: this term covers both the living organisms and the abiotic factors of the environment in which they occur. Biologists thus avoid the dangers of looking at the living members of the community as separate from their surroundings. The extension of this idea to man, to human ecosystems, will surely be rewarding.

Ecologists have tried various ways of analyzing environments to study and compare their different components, but no single system is completely satisfactory. One way involves the separation of the biological and physical environments: the living and the nonliving elements in the surroundings of an individual organism or a species. Thus, one can isolate climate as an aspect of the physical environment. In the case of man, some geographers have thought climate to be a controlling factor in cultural development, considering civilization, for instance, to be a response to a particularly stimulating climatic situation. On the other hand, they see climates that are too warm, too humid, or too cold as having a retarding effect on cultural development.

Climate illustrates another aspect of environment, that of *scale*. Climate is ordinarily measured in standard meteorological stations that reflect conditions under which few organisms live. Conditions in a forest or meadow, within the soil, or in a pond may be quite different from those where the standard measurements are made. It is, in fact, useful to distinguish among three levels of climate: the *microclimate* in which an individual lives, perhaps conditions in a cranny in bark or on the underside of a leaf; the *ecological climate* of some particular habitat, like a forest; and the *geographical climate* measured by the standard station. The

same kind of difference, depending on the focus of interest, applies to many other aspects of the environment.

In the case of man, we have to consider the cultural as well as the biological and physical environments, bringing up the whole series of problems mentioned earlier.

Another way of analyzing environmental factors is in terms of whether or not they affect the particular organism under consideration, and whether or not they are perceived. The sum of the forces and materials in any situation can be looked at as the total environment, but this includes many elements that have no influence on behavior. We live, for instance, in the magnetic field of the earth, but this does not affect our physiology in any known way; and we cannot perceive it without the aid of some instrument like a compass. Similarly, we cannot perceive viruses without instruments, but many of them do affect us by causing disease. Viruses would, then, form part of our operational environment, although not a part of our perceptual environment.

We tend to confuse our own perceptual environment with total reality: to think, for instance, that the forest we see is the "real" forest—for squirrels, birds, and insects as well as for ourselves. Yet it is obvious enough, when we stop to think about it, that each kind of animal lives in a particular sort of perceptual world of its own. The forest that a dog sees, hears, and smells is quite different from the forest that we perceive. This is something that must be clearly kept in mind in studying animal behavior as well as animal ecology.

When we turn to man, the concepts of operational and perceptual environments are inadequate by themselves, just as are those of biological and physical environments. For primitive man, the world is full of spirits which form a very real and important part of his surroundings—form what has sometimes been called the supernatural environment.

This sounds a little condescending; we can see that the people themselves created the spirits that so dominate their lives—that the spirits are merely ideas. Yet our own actions are equally governed by ideas. We may not call them spirits or propitiate them with elaborate rituals, but ideas play roles in our lives that often are at least comparable. We might call this world of ideas the *conceptual environment*. This differs somewhat from the cultural environment: the latter would include all human artifacts, such as clothing, housing, and tools; the former is concerned with the ideas that govern the form and use of the constructs.

When we look at the human environment, the continuing interaction between organism and surroundings is very evident. It is often said that man, far more than any other animal, has developed the ability to modify environment and thus to live under a wide range of physical and biological conditions. He has, in fact, created a new "biome" or ecological formation—the man-altered landscape, which is rapidly replacing other terrestrial landscapes as forests are cleared, grasslands plowed, and deserts irrigated. Man, assuming ecological dominance within this biome, has affected directly or indirectly all other organisms living there; he has become a new geological force.

Most members of the human species now live within this man-altered landscape. But this environment is not only a consequence of human activity; it is also a determinant of that activity. For instance, man has created the city; but the nature of the city, of the urban environment, governs his behavior much as the nature of the forest governs the behavior of tree squirrels. We could perhaps most profitably look at this new kind of biome as forming the human ecosystem.

It is, of course, not a single system; it includes a varied collection of differing environments: cities, towns, rice paddies, orchards, pastures, highway rights of way, abandoned fields, rubber plantations, and areas devastated by industrial wastes. Curiously, both social and biological scientists tend to neglect the study of this human ecosystem, perhaps because its study requires a blending of both social and biological knowledge.

MARSTON BATES

[See also CONSERVATION; CULTURE; ECOLOGY; GEOGRAPHY; PLANNING, SOCIAL, *article on* RESOURCE PLANNING; REGION; REGIONAL SCIENCE.]

BIBLIOGRAPHY

The biological concept of environment is developed in ecological textbooks such as Odum & Odum 1953; *the sociological, in books like* Hawley 1950. *The various textbooks of human geography discuss environmental relationships; the point of view of geographical determinism is expressed in* Huntington & Cushing 1921. *International Symposium 1956 contains much environmental material, with good bibliographies. The point of view of an architect is expressed in* Glikson 1963. Bates 1962 *develops the idea of the conceptual environment.* Dubos 1964 *expresses well the need for intensive study of man's environmental relationships.*

BATES, MARSTON 1962 *The Human Environment.* Berkeley: Univ. of California Press.

DUBOS, RENÉ 1964 Environmental Biology. *BioScience* 14:11–14.

GLIKSON, ARTUR 1963 Man's Relationship to His Environment. Pages 132–152 in Gordon Wolstenholme (editor), *Man and His Future.* Papers and discussion of a conference sponsored by the Ciba Foundation. Boston: Little.

HAWLEY, AMOS H. 1950 *Human Ecology: A Theory of Community Structure.* New York: Ronald Press.

HUNTINGTON, ELLSWORTH; and CUSHING, S. W. (1921) 1951 *Principles of Human Geography.* 6th ed. Revised by E. B. Shaw. New York: Wiley.

INTERNATIONAL SYMPOSIUM ON MAN'S ROLE IN CHANGING THE FACE OF THE EARTH, PRINCETON, N.J., *1955* 1956 *Man's Role in Changing the Face of the Earth.* Edited by William L. Thomas et al. Univ. of Chicago Press.

ODUM, EUGENE P.; and ODUM, HOWARD T. (1953) 1959 *Fundamentals of Ecology.* 2d ed. Philadelphia: Saunders.

ENVIRONMENTALISM

The question of the relations between man in society and the geographical environment in which he lives is a very old one. Hippocrates (fifth century B.C.) wrote a treatise, "On Airs, Waters, and Places," which is generally regarded as the first formed expression of an environmentalist doctrine, although in view of the limited data available to him it is not appropriate to regard this as a statement sufficiently definitive for a serious critique of environmentalism, as Toynbee does (1934). Environmental considerations, especially climatic ones, play a considerable role in Montesquieu (1748) and perhaps reached their peak in the mid-nineteenth century, with Victor Cousin's "give me the [physical] map of a country . . . and I pledge myself to tell you, a priori, . . . what part that country will play in history, not by accident, but of necessity; not at one epoch, but in all epochs" (quoted in Febvre [1922] 1925, p. 10). Such extreme necessitarianism could hardly go unchallenged, and the first serious attack on geographical determinism is associated with the name of Paul Vidal de la Blache, who about the turn of the century became in effect the founder of an opposed doctrine known as "possibilism."

Possibilist doctrine is perhaps best, or at least most characteristically, summed up in a dictum of Lucien Febvre ([1922] 1925, p. 235): "There are nowhere necessities, but everywhere possibilities; and man, as master of the possibilities, is the judge of their use." A protest against crude predestinarianism was certainly in order; but Vidal's own qualifications are perhaps not always faithfully mirrored by his disciples, and Febvre's epigrammatic statements distracted attention from the real task of assessing the probabilities posed by the indisputable fact that the possibilities are distributed over the face of the earth with great inequality. This has recently been elegantly demonstrated by Lukermann (1965). It is also, perhaps, insufficiently noted that French possibilism was itself to some extent determined by a reaction to what we would now call an expansionist *Geopolitik*, expressed in Friedrich Ratzel's *Politische Geographie* of 1897 (Febvre 1922; cf. Spate 1957).

Be that as it may, the French school of geography, particularly noted for its meticulous and luminous style of regional description, was by that very technique often able, quite plausibly, to evade the issue, while more general works, such as those of Brunhes (1910) and Vallaux (1911), tempered possibilism by some allowance for the "influences," although not the "controls," exercised by the physical environment. In Germany, also, the broad strokes of Ratzelian anthropogeography were gradually succeeded by the more subtle chorographic analyses of *Landschaft*, and already in 1907 Alfred Hettner had arrived at a formulation not dissimilar from Febvre's (cf. Hartshorne 1939, p. 123).

In English-speaking countries the evolution was different. With the popularization, or (in both senses) vulgarization, of Ratzel's basically determinist outlook by Semple's *Influences of Geographic Environment* (1911), a somewhat naïve view of environmental "controls" became paramount among geographers in the United States and Britain, and this is what is generally known as "environmentalism." Another powerful influence was that of Ellsworth Huntington, whose numerous works attached a preponderating role to broad climatic factors. But the antienvironmentalist reaction, if much later than in France and Germany, was all the more complete. To some extent both the acceptance and the reaction stemmed from a rather uncritical empiricism, and this was especially notable in Britain. While in Britain possibilism in its purest form held undisputed sway in the 1930s, in the United States environmentalism was not so much negated as simply sidetracked. There were indeed plenty of overt rejections (Sauer 1925; Platt 1948—an extremist case), but on the whole the emphasis was on geography as simply the study of areal differentiation. This, of course, has clear analogues with the German development, and Hettner in particular was a strong influence, especially through the comprehensive methodologic study of Richard Hartshorne (1939). In Britain there was no comparable searching out of fundamentals, and indeed possibilism fitted well into a rather superficial and characteristically "English" empirical distrust of theory. The qualifications, subtle and unstressed but nonetheless significant, of the French school were ignored, and geography became in effect an entirely idiographic study in which it would be indecent to draw conclusions.

There were, of course, heretics: in the United States, Peattie (1940); in Britain, Markham (1942); but they had no effect.

The old view of geography as primarily a study of man–environment relations is now outmoded, and it is probable that a reasonable consensus would be found in favor of Hartshorne's formulation (1959, p. 21): "*accurate, orderly, and rational description and interpretation of the variable character of the earth surface.*" However, relationships vary with the distribution of the phenomena that are in relation, and provided that we do not prejudge the issue by insisting that they are confined to those between man and natural environment or are one-way only, there is still ample scope for the examination of environmental problems. It is not, as Toynbee says (1961, p. 635), modern arrogance, but humility in face of data still inadequate, which refuses to take his refutation of Hippocrates as a final judgment. Moreover, while it may be true that external demands (as from history and sociology) for environmental assessments may represent a hangover from days when geographers were all too ready with crude causal explanations (and they got the habit from historians), it yet remains true that very often historical, sociological, economic, anthropological, political, and even religious and aesthetic phenomena cannot be properly comprehended without careful attention to environmental considerations.

Thus, the question is by no means so decisively closed, in an antienvironmentalist sense, as it seemed two or three decades ago; and as we shall see, it has taken on an entirely new aspect with the application of new techniques to geographical inquiry. While there have always been individual divergences from the general trend and, not infrequently, internal inconsistencies in the work of individuals, whether styling themselves environmentalists or possibilists, the question (as in many controversies) has been bedeviled by the assumption by both sides of a too rigid dichotomy. Whether tenable in strict logic or not, a more balanced probabilistic hypothesis seems warranted. This seems avoidable only if, as Hartshorne hints (1959, p. 55), we altogether abandon any distinction between man and nature; and this repudiation, dubiously metaphysical as it is, in practice seems impossible to maintain (Spate 1963a, pp. 255–259). In practice, except on an absurdly mechanistic plane, it is impossible to hold that all man's activities are absolutely conditioned or determined by his natural environment, even if we resort to intricate rationalizations as to its expression through social institutions. But it is absurd, also, to take

Febvre's dictum at face value and so slide into the position of ignoring the fact that possibilities vary greatly from milieu to milieu and, hence, in any given milieu are in fact limited. One may in a sense overcome this by saying that anything is possible anywhere if only one is willing to pay the price; but then, paying the price is itself a compelled adjustment to the environment. The flight from "controls" into a denial of "influences" takes us nowhere; or, if anywhere, into solipsism.

A reaction against possibilism became apparent around 1950. It avoided the crudity of the earlier concept of environmental control, as well as the dead end of possibilism, by stressing in any given situation the balance of probability, as, of course, both environmentalists and possibilists had often done in practice without admitting it. Some signs of *rapprochement* are found even in contributions avowedly committed to one side or the other (Tatham 1951; Taylor 1951). Perhaps the first really vigorous reassertion of geographic determinism was that of Martin (1952).

This newer and more cautious environmentalism gives more play to social factors than did the old. It recognizes that the geographical environment is only a part of the total environment and allows for the modifications of environment introduced by human activity; geographical influences act through society, and cultural tradition has a certain autonomous and reciprocal effect. Strands of causation may therefore be extremely subtle, and dogmatism is avoided. At the same time, it is firmly held that there is a larger irreducible minimum of influence by the physical environment than possibilism allows for. Although the impact of this will vary with the converse impact of human technological levels, nevertheless there will always be at least the adjustment by price and very often a much more direct adjustment.

The mandates of the geographical milieu are, however, often more negative and permissive than positively imperative. Thus, a total of 200 frost-free nights does not enforce the growing of cotton but does permit it, and fewer frost-free nights inhibit it. Further, while in a given situation the general cast of development may be very strongly influenced or conditioned by geographical factors, the detail may be dependent on quite other factors. This introduces a margin-of-error concept and may be illustrated by the difference between the general location of a frontier zone or a communications node (given the existence of a society with these features), which may be fully conditioned by geography, and the precise siting of a boundary within the frontier zone or of a city near the node, which

may depend on historical accident and which may, perhaps, in turn become a geographical factor in a new chain of relationships (Spate 1957).

This revival of methodological debate in geography owes much to the general increase in sophistication in the social sciences. This is perhaps more particularly true of the newer, quantitative approaches, but is by no means confined to them. It may fairly be said that the net result of the debate has been a material change in the general temper of geographical writing. If there has been no return to the compulsions of the older environmentalist school, as exemplified perhaps not so much in Ratzel himself as in Semple's rendition of him in the *Influences of Geographic Environment* (1911), it is equally true that pure possibilism, in the Febvre version, seems also to be dead. Stimulating as a protest, it was in the long run stultifying. Perhaps its most valuable residuum is that, indirectly at least, it helped to break away from the static concept of environment as a once-and-for-all given thing in itself, and it raised the question, Environment for what? This, however, seems to have no necessary connection with a possibilist view, and it may indeed have gone too far in the direction of a metaphysical identification of man with nature. The newer, probabilistic approach in regional writing is more likely to draw conclusions of general import than possibilism did, or at any rate to draw them more consciously and responsibly.

The debate has not been entirely internal to geography. One factor was the interest aroused by Toynbee's somewhat cavalier direct treatment of environmentalism and by the large if sometimes erratic importance he attached to it in such concepts as "the stimulus of New Ground" and the effects of a *Völkerwanderung* by sea (1934). Toynbee's analyses are of great interest, although vitiated by unfamiliarity with the main current of geographical writing and lack of a sense of scale; but both negatively and positively he contributed to putting environmentalism on the map again. The environmental component in such studies as Wittfogel's *Oriental Despotism* (1957) or, on a different scale, Sahlins' *Moala* (1962) is obvious.

The new trend has not, of course, gone unchallenged. As has been noted, it places some stress on probability, and the almost accidental introduction of the rather clumsy term "probabilism" (for which this writer must regretfully accept responsibility) has naturally attracted some dialectical criticism. Important contributions to the debate are those of Montefiore and Williams (1955) and the Sprouts (1956; 1957; 1965).

The former appear to approach the problem from

the standpoint of logical positivism. Their criticism of a too naïve acceptance of cause and effect as the only way of looking at scientific explanation is acute and vigorous, and they end with calling a plague on both houses: ". . . there can be no further point in their continuing a dispute which has virtually no bearing on their activities as working geographers." However, it may be suggested that this does not dispose of the issue. Belief does normally have some bearing on activity, and the dichotomy has been resurrected in a new (and, to some, alarming) fashion by quantifiers of the type of Warntz and Isard. The fundamentally important papers by the Sprouts include a very careful semantic analysis of hypotheses under the categories "environmental determinism," "mild environmentalism," "environmental possibilism," "environmental probabilism," and "cognitive behaviorism." They point out the logical residuum of environmentalist thinking implied in the possibilist approach and give at least a qualified blessing to probabilism; but it may be said that to a geographer their possibilism looks more like probabilism, and their probabilism seems in turn to hold a more predictive element than those who would not call themselves environmentalists *tout court* would allow.

The rise of applied and quantitative geography has in some respects given a new emphasis to environmental studies. One may instance Soviet geography, in which there is theoretically no problem: the laws of nature govern physical geography but are entirely separate from the social laws which govern man, and therefore there can be no unified geography (which is the essence of environmentalism) but only physical and economic geographies. Practice, and large-scale planning do, however, compel very meticulous attention to environmental factors, and even "influences" are not altogether banned, as they are in pure possibilism (Spate 1963*b*). In practically all fields involving the physical application of technology, whether under Soviet or Western auspices, very careful attention to problems of the physical environment is essential, if only as part of estimating costs.

It is often stated that the impact of modern technology has minimized, even annihilated, the significance of the environmental factor. However, on analysis it will frequently appear that the role of the physical milieu, if less "brutal" than it may be for a primitive-subsistence society, is pervasive in a more subtle way. It may be theoretically possible to grow anything almost anywhere, at a price; but the effect of price itself, in alliance with modern communications, may well be not to widen the range of a given crop but to narrow it to the area physically best suited for it: witness the formerly wide and presently restricted extent of flax growing in Europe and cotton growing in India. Large-scale technical installations may often depend for their economic efficiency on a nice balance of environmental considerations.

The basic assumptions of the new, quantifying schools have strong determinist, if not mechanistic, overtones, as suggested by the very title "social physics" (Stewart & Warntz 1958). At the least, they are strongly probabilistic, as is well demonstrated by Burton (1963). They aim at being nomothetic rather than idiographic, as were possibilism and much of the work of the chorographic approach standard in the Hartshorne era. They avowedly seek out laws with a capital *L*, as did Semple (Dodd & Pitts 1959). They work largely in models, and a high degree of prediction is regarded as the ideal. A culmination of this attitude is that of Isard (1956) in his desire for a "true" set of regions suitable for all purposes. There is often a tendency, as in the concept of population potential (Stewart & Warntz 1958), to abstract all but one or two factors, considered determinative; but these, also, are considered as some sort of summing up of the essence of the total environment.

It cannot, therefore, be assumed, as it was only a few years ago, that the ancient debate regarding the role of environmental factors is played out. That role changes with every change in technology, but it also must enforce technological changes, if the full and effective deployment of technical potential is to be made possible. Nor would the conquest of space necessarily mean the supersession of environment; there may be other than terrestrial environments for man, and these will compel special adjustments, social and technical. Meanwhile, the study of environment on this earth is far from complete; and while claims that it would provide an all-embracing rationale of society are justly dead, its significance must always be reckoned with in such studies as anthropology, archeology, sociology, and political science, to say nothing of history, and it forms an essential bridge between these social studies and the natural sciences.

O. H. K. SPATE

[*See the entries listed under* GEOGRAPHY. *See also* REGIONAL SCIENCE *and the biographies of* FEBVRE; HETTNER; HUNTINGTON; RATZEL; VIDAL DE LA BLACHE.]

BIBLIOGRAPHY

BRUNHES, JEAN (1910) 1924 *Human Geography.* London: Harrap. → First published in French. A fourth French edition was published in 1934 by Alcan.

BURTON, IAN 1963 The Quantitative Revolution and Theoretical Geography. *Canadian Geographer* 7, no. 4:151–162.

DODD, STUART C.; and PITTS, FORREST R. 1959 Proposals to Develop Statistical Laws of Human Geography. Pages 302–309 in International Geographical Union, Regional Conference in Japan, Tokyo and Nara, 1957, *Proceedings of IGU Regional Conference in Japan, 1957*. Tokyo: Science Council of Japan.

FEBVRE, LUCIEN (1922) 1925 *A Geographical Introduction to History*. New York: Knopf. → First published as *La terre et l'évolution humaine*.

HARTSHORNE, RICHARD (1939) 1964 *The Nature of Geography: A Critical Survey of Current Thought in the Light of the Past*. Lancaster, Pa.: Association of American Geographers.

HARTSHORNE, RICHARD 1959 *Perspective on the Nature of Geography*. Association of American Geographers, Monograph Series, No. 1. Chicago: Rand McNally. → A restatement and, in part, an extensive revision of Hartshorne 1939.

HIPPOCRATES On Airs, Waters, and Places. Pages 54–59 in Eric H. Warmington (editor), *Greek Geography*. London: Dent, 1934.

HUNTINGTON, ELLSWORTH (1915) 1924 *Civilization and Climate*. 3d ed., rev. New Haven: Yale Univ. Press.

HUNTINGTON, ELLSWORTH 1945 *Mainsprings of Civilization*. New York: Wiley; London: Chapman.

ISARD, WALTER 1956 *Location and Space-economy: A General Theory Relating to Industrial Location, Market Areas, Trade and Urban Structure*. Cambridge, Mass.: M.I.T. Press; New York: Wiley.

LUKERMANN, F. 1965 The "Calcul des Probabilités" and the École Française de Géographie. *Canadian Geographer* 9:128–137.

MARKHAM, SYDNEY F. (1942) 1947 *Climate and the Energy of Nations*. 2d American ed., rev. & enl. New York: Oxford Univ. Press.

MARTIN, A. F. 1952 The Necessity for Determinism. Institute of British Geographers, *Publications* 17:1–11.

MONTEFIORE, A. C.; and WILLIAMS, W. M. 1955 Determinism and Possibilism. *Geographical Studies* 2:1–11.

MONTESQUIEU, CHARLES (1748) 1962 *The Spirit of the Laws*. 2 vols. New York: Hafner. → First published in French. See especially Book 14, Chapters 12 and 13.

PEATTIE, RODERICK 1940 *Geography in Human Destiny*. New York: Stewart.

PLATT, ROBERT S. 1948 Environmentalism Versus Geography. *American Journal of Sociology* 53:351–358.

RATZEL, FRIEDRICH (1882–1891) 1921–1922 *Anthropogeographie*. 2 vols. Stuttgart (Germany): Engelhorn. → Volume 1: *Grundzüge der Anwendung der Erdkunde auf die Geschichte*, 4th ed. Volume 2: *Die geographische Verbreitung des Menschen*, 3d ed.

RATZEL, FRIEDRICH (1897) 1923 *Politische Geographie*. 3d ed. Edited by Eugen Oberhummer. Munich and Berlin: Oldenbourg.

SAHLINS, MARSHALL D. 1962 *Moala: Culture and Nature on a Fijian Island*. Ann Arbor: Univ. of Michigan Press.

SAUER, CARL O. (1925) 1963 The Morphology of Landscape. Pages 315–350 in Carl O. Sauer, *Land and Life: A Selection From the Writings of Carl Ortwin Sauer*. Berkeley: Univ. of California Press.

SEMPLE, ELLEN C. 1911 *Influences of Geographic Environment, on the Basis of Ratzel's System of Anthropo-geography*. New York: Holt.

SPATE, O. H. K. 1952 Toynbee and Huntington: A Study in Determinism. *Geographical Journal* 118:406–428. → Contains four pages of discussion.

SPATE, O. H. K. 1957 How Determined Is Possibilism? *Geographical Studies* 4:3–12.

SPATE, O. H. K. 1963a Islands and Men. Pages 253–264 in Francis R. Fosberg (editor), *Man's Place in the Island Ecosystem: A Symposium*. Honolulu: Bishop Museum Press.

SPATE, O. H. K. 1963b Theory and Practice in Soviet Geography. *Australian Geographical Studies* 1:18–30.

SPROUT, HAROLD H.; and SPROUT, MARGARET 1956 *Man–Milieu Relationship Hypotheses in the Context of International Politics*. Princeton Univ., Center of International Studies.

SPROUT, HAROLD H.; and SPROUT, MARGARET (1957) 1964 Environmental Factors in the Study of International Politics. Pages 61–80 in William A. D. Jackson (editor), *Politics and Geographic Relationships: Readings on the Nature of Political Geography*. Englewood Cliffs, N.J.: Prentice-Hall. → First published in Volume 1 of the *Journal of Conflict Resolution*.

SPROUT, HAROLD H.; and SPROUT, MARGARET 1965 *The Ecological Perspective on Human Affairs, With Special Reference to International Politics*. Princeton Univ. Press.

STEWART, JOHN Q.; and WARNTZ, WILLIAM 1958 Macrogeography and Social Science. *Geographical Review* 48:167–184.

TATHAM, GEORGE (1951) 1957 Environmentalism and Possibilism. Pages 128–162 in Thomas G. Taylor (editor), *Geography in the Twentieth Century: A Study of Growth, Fields, Techniques, Aims and Trends*. 3d ed., enl. New York: Philosophical Library.

TAYLOR, THOMAS GRIFFITH (1951) 1957 Introduction: The Scope of the Volume. Pages 3–27 in Thomas G. Taylor (editor), *Geography in the Twentieth Century: A Study of Growth, Fields, Techniques, Aims and Trends*. 3d ed., enl. New York: Philosophical Library.

TOYNBEE, ARNOLD J. 1934 *A Study of History*. Volume 2: The Geneses of Civilization. Oxford Univ. Press.

TOYNBEE, ARNOLD J. 1961 *A Study of History*. Volume 12: Reconsiderations. Oxford Univ. Press.

VALLAUX, CAMILLE 1911 *Géographie sociale: Le sol et l'état*. Paris: Doin.

VIDAL DE LA BLACHE, PAUL 1902 Les conditions géographiques des faits sociaux. *Annales de géographie* 11:13–23.

WITTFOGEL, KARL A. 1957 *Oriental Despotism: A Comparative Study of Total Power*. New Haven: Yale Univ. Press. → A paperback edition was published in 1963.

EPIDEMIOLOGY

Epidemiology is a branch of ecology that includes both the sum of what is known concerning the differential distribution of disease throughout a population and the techniques for collecting and analyzing data dealing with the prevalence and incidence of disease among different social groups. While originally limited to the study of epidemics or the spread of contagious disease, epidemiology today covers all types of disease, degenerative as well as communicable, and all population characteristics—social and psychological as well as biological and physical—that may help to describe or explain the prevalence of disease.

Methods of epidemiology. In the broad sense of the term, epidemiology deals with the occurrence and distribution of disease among different population groups, whether human, animal, or plant. The discovery or description of these differences has been called *descriptive*, or comparative, epidemiology, whereas the analysis of the causal factors and conditions producing these differences is usually referred to as *explanatory*, or analytic, epidemiology. As epidemiology becomes increasingly concerned with the study of the origin and course of disease, rather than solely with its distribution, this distinction is gradually disappearing.

Because of its emphasis upon the relationship between environmental factors and disease, epidemiology is properly regarded as a major branch of human ecology, or "the study of the relations between man and his environment, both as it affects him and as he affects it" (Rogers 1960, p. vii). In general, three main sets of interacting factors form the focus of epidemiological interest: the *host*, or human individual varying in genetic resistance, susceptibility, and degree of immunity to the disease; the *agent*, or carrier of the disease, including any adverse process, whether it be an excess, deficiency, or interference of a microbial, toxic, or metabolic factor, and varying according to infectivity, virulence, and pathogenesis; and the *environment*, or surrounding medium, social as well as physical, which affects both the susceptibility of the host, the virulence of the agent or disease process, and the quantity and quality of contact between host and agent (Paul 1950, pp. 53–54). These three sets of factors do not exist in any simple one-to-one relationship but maintain a complex, ever-changing balance. The occurrence of disease, especially mass disease, is the result of a multiplicity of causal factors, each of which contributes to, rather than accounts for, the appearance of the disease.

Epidemiological knowledge consists of the available facts and theories concerning the relationships between these three factors and the various disease entities and health conditions. *Social* epidemiology, as a subdivision of epidemiology, concentrates on the social, as opposed to the physical or biological, factors in the incidence and prevalence of disease. In the case of the chronic, degenerative diseases and the mental and behavioral disorders, both of which constitute primary targets of modern epidemiology, distinctions between host, agent, and environmental factors and between social and biological or physical factors are becoming increasingly difficult to maintain.

As a research method, epidemiology refers to "the application of scientific principles to investigations of conditions affecting groups in the population [*constructive* epidemiology]" (Clark [1953] 1958, p. 65). Predominantly, this involves the observation of the occurrence of disease under natural conditions in whole populations, as opposed to clinical or laboratory investigations. Epidemiological method, for the most part, uses the research techniques of the population survey to discover the relationship between the occurrence of disease and the presence of various biological, physical, and social factors. The kind of "proof" that it tries, for the most part, to obtain is statistical association between the presumed "causal" factor and the occurrence of the disease. Dawber and Kannel (1963, pp. 433–434) have spoken of "macroscopic" studies, which correlate rates of a disease with other statistical measures for an area or population group (ecological correlations), as contrasted with "microscopic" studies, which correlate personal characteristics with the presence or absence of disease within the individual (individual correlations). *Experimental* epidemiology, involving the controlled introduction of epidemic conditions into populations of experimental animals in the laboratory (Greenwood 1932), field experiments to test the efficacy of various immunizing agents, or various types of preventive measures (MacMahon et al. 1960, pp. 268–279), represents an attempt to apply the experimental method to epidemiological problems.

Historical background. The scope of epidemiology, which was "originally concerned only with epidemics, . . . was extended first to include infectious diseases which do not ordinarily occur in epidemic form, such as leprosy, syphilis, and tuberculosis, and later to noninfectious diseases" (Doull 1952, p. 76). The birth of epidemiology as we know it may be traced back to England in the late seventeenth century, when John Graunt in 1662 developed the first mortality tables. However, it was not until the mid-nineteenth century that men like Johann Süssmilch and Adolphe Quetelet utilized these statistics to help identify etiological factors in disease. The major emphasis of epidemiology under such eminent pioneers as John Snow (cholera), Peter Panum (measles), William Budd (typhoid), and Kenneth Maxcy (endemic typhus) was upon the discovery of host, agent, and environmental factors associated with the spread of these highly contagious diseases, or what has been called "the mass-phenomena of infectious diseases" (see Frost 1910–1939).

The dramatic conquest of the infectious diseases in the present century, together with the growing importance of the chronic, degenerative diseases, soon made it apparent that epidemiology could no longer be restricted to epidemics. As a matter of fact, epidemiological studies of nutritional (James Lind on scurvy) and occupational (Henry B. Baker on lead colic) diseases had already demonstrated the applicability of epidemiological method to noninfectious diseases. The use of statistical associations based upon population surveys became one of the foremost methods for studying the occurrence of cancer, cardiovascular disease, and mental illness and for the difficult task of identifying specific etiological agents. Today, the value of epidemiological research for the study of all diseases is well established (James & Greenberg 1957).

Uses of epidemiology. As a standard tool of medical investigation, epidemiology has been brought to bear upon almost all aspects of the prevention and treatment of disease. Morris (1957) has listed seven fundamental applications: the determination of individual risks on the basis of morbidity tables and cohort analysis—for example, the chances of a forty-year-old male getting cancer; the securing of data on subclinical and undetected cases; the identification of syndromes or clusters of symptoms; the determination of historical trends of disease; the diagnosis of community health needs and resources; program planning, operation, and evaluation; and the search for causes of disease. Similar uses are described by Breslow (1957) for a large-scale epidemiological survey of chronic diseases in California. These include a demographic description of the changing population composition, a broad picture of the state of health and illness in the community, more extensive knowledge about disease prevalence, data on the utilization of health services, case rosters for follow-up investigations, and data on etiological factors. Thus, epidemiology provides a large portion of the scientific base for public health practice.

The diversity of these applications would suggest that epidemiological surveys are often combined, or confused, with general community health surveys. A survey that asks questions about health conditions and medical care of a population sample does not automatically become an epidemiological study. From a more rigorous point of view, the major contribution of epidemiological research should be in the development and testing of hypotheses concerning specific factors that may influence the distribution of some particular disease in a defined population. On the basis of existing knowledge, theory, or observation, the epidemiologist identifies subgroups of the population believed to have varying incidence rates of the disease being investigated. He then hypothesizes certain etiological factors related to the disease and also believed to differ among the subgroups being studied. By means of a field survey or the analysis of existing data, he then tests the direction and degree of association between the occurrence of the disease and the presence or absence of the group characteristic hypothesized as the etiological factor.

Epidemiology and social science. Epidemiology has theoretical and methodological ties to the social sciences. Both the epidemiologist and the social scientist are concerned with demography and ecology—the relationship of man to his environment (Fleck & Ianni 1958). When the environment includes sociocultural factors as possible "causes" of disease, either indirectly (as in the case of poverty leading to malnutrition or unsanitary living conditions) or directly (as in the case of emotional disturbance leading to mental disease or addictive disorders, such as drinking and alcoholism or drug addiction), then all three basic components of epidemiology—host, agent, and environment—take on important social dimensions (King 1963). Epidemiology is becoming increasingly concerned with "the social component of environment . . . that part which results from the association of man with his fellow man . . . the attainments, beliefs, customs, traditions, and like features of a people" (Gordon 1952, pp. 124–125). In the current era of chronic, degenerative diseases, in which an individual's whole way of life may become more important than any single infectious agent in the disease process, social factors become a primary target for epidemiological investigation.

Methodologically, both the epidemiologist and the social scientist rely heavily upon the population survey and field experiment. Similar problems of research design confront both groups, while technical considerations such as sampling, questionnaire construction, interviewing, and multivariate analysis are objects of mutual methodological interest (Wardwell & Bahnson 1964).

Recent research. All major diseases today are the subject of epidemiological research, and almost all of these include, at the minimum, such social groupings as sex, age, marital status and family composition, occupation, socioeconomic status, religion, and race. In addition, many studies are specifically aimed at the investigation of social factors, such as social stress, as possible etiological agents in the occurrence of the disease. Comprehensive reviews have been prepared by Glock and Lennard (1956) on hypertension, Graham (1960) on cancer, Mishler and Scotch (1963) on schizophrenia, Dawber and others (1959) on heart disease, Jaco (1960) and Hoch and Zubin (1961) on mental disease, Suchman and Scherzer (1960) on childhood accidents, King and Cobb (1958) on rheumatoid arthritis, among others. The state of knowledge in this field is advancing rapidly, and the findings of epidemiological surveys appear regularly in such periodicals as the *American Journal of Public Health* and the *Journal of Chronic Diseases*.

In general, these studies reveal a large number of significant differences in the occurrence of disease among different subgroups of the population (Pemberton 1963). For example, coronary artery disease is found to vary according to such sociocultural variables as occupation, economic status, race, and rural–urban residence. Cancer of the uterine cervix occurs much less frequently among Jewish women; men are more likely to incur cardiovascular disease; and mental illness is found more often among the lower socioeconomic groups. On a more psychological level, insecurity and stress tend to be associated with a higher incidence of mental illness, alcoholism, narcotics addiction, heart disease, arthritis, and a host of psychosomatic conditions (Leighton 1959). Perhaps the most famous of these epidemiological correlations deals with the association between smoking behavior and lung cancer (Dorn & Cutler 1958).

Some problems of research design. The major conceptual and methodological problems in epidemiological research stem from its dependence, by and large, upon associational evidence. The basic research design of epidemiological method consists in the comparison of two groups, each with varying rates of a disease, with respect to other characteristics hypothesized as explanatory of these varying disease rates. This is essentially an ex post facto form of survey research and one that may undertake *demographic* studies of existing vital statistics or several other types of study using data specially gathered for the purpose. These can be classified as being either *retrospective* studies, which secure data on different group characteristics hypothesized as etiological factors from at least two groups with varying rates of the disease being investigated, or *prospective* studies, which follow up groups of individuals with and

without the hypothesized etiological characteristics in order to determine the differential development of the disease.

In all three study designs, the objective is the determination of a series of statistical associations from which etiological inferences may be drawn. These three types of design offer progressively more rigorous and plausible evidence of causality. The demographic method, relying as it does on ecological correlations, is the weakest, since variations in rates of occurrence between phenomena do not necessarily mean that these phenomena are related (Clausen & Kohn 1954); it is possible to have high ecological associations with little or no individual correlation. Retrospective studies do provide individual correlations, but there is often no way of knowing which of the two factors in an observed correlation came first. Prospective studies using a longitudinal study of cohorts are strongest, since these enable one to define the population at risk *in advance* of the development of disease and then to check one's predictions over time [*see* COHORT ANALYSIS].

Smoking and lung cancer. The association between smoking and lung cancer provides an excellent example of the progression from demographic to retrospective and finally to prospective studies. The initial association was suggested by demographic comparisons showing a much higher incidence of lung cancer among men than women. Retrospective studies revealed a correlation between smoking histories and the occurrence of lung cancer. Finally, intensive prospective studies following up smokers and nonsmokers showed a higher development of lung cancer among the former. The continuing controversy today, however, demonstrates the further need and demand to prove, through experimental rather than epidemiological studies, that smoking can "cause" cancer.

Validity of epidemiological method. The inability of the epidemiologist to "randomize" his experimental and control groups and to alter deliberately the characteristics of his experimental group constitutes an intrinsic conceptual and methodological shortcoming that requires a continuing close working relationship between epidemiological and experimental research. Certain basic prerequisites must be satisfied if epidemiological method is to produce reliable and valid associations. First, the representativeness and generalizability of the sample from whom data are obtained must be ascertainable. This sample should include not only persons who are known to have the disease but also who are free of the disease.

The definition of what is a "normal," or disease-free, control group presents a particularly difficult problem for epidemiological study of the chronic diseases, since these may not become apparent until a fairly late stage. Second, the disease being studied must be defined in such a way that it can be reliably and validly diagnosed using field techniques. Errors due to *false positives* (the proportion of individuals classified as diseased among those truly not diseased) and *false negatives* (the proportion classified as not diseased among those truly diseased) can often lead to spurious associations (Rubin et al. 1956). Third, the hypothesized etiological factors must be similarly capable of objective definition and measurement. These are difficult conditions to meet, especially in relation to the chronic diseases, which often lack both clear-cut diagnostic criteria and well-developed theories of etiology and process (Pollack & Krueger 1960).

Future developments. Epidemiological method is bound to increase in importance as the search for etiological factors in the chronic diseases forces the medical researcher to supplement his laboratory experiments with field studies, both as source and proof of his hypotheses. The multiple nature of etiological factors (many, if not most, of which cannot be reproduced or controlled in the laboratory) will require greater reliance upon population surveys and field trials. Probabilities of disease will replace certainties, and associated conditions rather than specific causes will dominate the picture. Prominent among these conditions will be the cultural, social, and psychological forces that determine how man lives and which in later years influence the degenerative processes. Today we deal with these social factors on the most elementary level, that of descriptive group memberships. Tomorrow we may hope to be able to determine the dynamic factors underlying these group memberships and to develop and test specific hypotheses of how and why social factors relate to the origin and course of disease.

EDWARD A. SUCHMAN

[*See also* DRINKING AND ALCOHOLISM; DRUGS, *article on* DRUG ADDICTION: SOCIAL ASPECTS; ECOLOGY, *article on* HUMAN ECOLOGY; PUBLIC HEALTH; VITAL STATISTICS; *and the biographies of* GRAUNT *and* QUETELET.]

BIBLIOGRAPHY

BRESLOW, LESTER 1957 Uses and Limitations of the California Health Survey for Studying the Epidemiology of Chronic Disease. *American Journal of Public Health* 47:168–172.

CLARK, E. GURNEY (1953) 1958 An Epidemiological Approach to Preventive Medicine. Chapter 3 in Hugh R. Leavell et al., *Preventive Medicine for the Doctor in His Community: An Epidemiologic Approach.* 2d ed. New York: McGraw-Hill.

CLAUSEN, JOHN A.; and KOHN, MELVIN L. 1954 The Ecological Approach in Social Psychiatry. *American Journal of Sociology* 60:140–151.

DAWBER, THOMAS R.; and KANNEL, WILLIAM B. 1963 Coronary Heart Disease as an Epidemiology Entity. *American Journal of Public Health* 53:433–437.

DAWBER, THOMAS R. et al. 1959 Some Factors Associated With the Development of Coronary Heart Disease. *American Journal of Public Health* 49:1349–1356.

DORN, HAROLD F.; and CUTLER, SIDNEY J. 1958 *Morbidity From Cancer in the United States.* U.S. Public Health Service Publication No. 590; Public Health Monograph No. 56. Washington: Public Health Service.

DOULL, JAMES A. 1952 The Bacteriological Era (1876–1920). Pages 74–113 in Franklin H. Top (editor), *The History of American Epidemiology.* St. Louis, Mo.: Mosby.

FLECK, ANDREW C.; and IANNI, FRANCIS A. J. 1958 Epidemiology and Anthropology: Some Suggested Affinities in Theory and Method. *Human Organization* 16, no. 4:38–40.

FROST, WADE HAMPTON (1910–1939) 1941 *Papers of Wade Hampton Frost, M.D.: A Contribution to Epidemiological Method.* Edited by Kenneth F. Maxcy. New York: Commonwealth Fund; Oxford Univ. Press. → These essays provide a brilliant description of the transition to modern epidemiology.

GLOCK, CHARLES Y.; and LENNARD, HENRY L. 1956 Studies in Hypertension. *Journal of Chronic Diseases* 5:178–196.

GORDON, JOHN E. 1952 The Twentieth Century—Yesterday, Today, and Tomorrow (1920–   ). Pages 114–167 in Franklin H. Top (editor), *The History of American Epidemiology.* St. Louis, Mo.: Mosby. → Contains a comprehensive bibliography and discussion of modern developments.

GRAHAM, SAXON 1960 Social Factors in the Epidemiology of Cancer at Various Sites. New York Academy of Sciences, *Annals* 84:807–815.

GREENWOOD, MAJOR 1932 *Epidemiology, Historical and Experimental.* Baltimore: Johns Hopkins Press; Oxford Univ. Press.

HOCH, PAUL H.; and ZUBIN, JOSEPH (editors) 1961 *Comparative Epidemiology of the Mental Disorders.* Proceedings of the 49th annual meeting of the American Psychopathological Association, February 1959. New York: Grune & Stratton.

JACO, E. GARTLY 1960 *The Social Epidemiology of Mental Disorders: A Psychiatric Survey of Texas.* New York: Russell Sage Foundation.

JAMES, GEORGE; and GREENBERG, MORRIS 1957 The Medical Officer's Bookshelf on Epidemiology and Evaluation. Part 1: Epidemiology. *American Journal of Public Health* 47:401–408. → Contains a brief review and bibliography on the epidemiology of various diseases.

KING, STANLEY H. 1963 Social Psychological Factors in Illness. Pages 99–121 in Howard E. Freeman et al. (editors), *Handbook of Medical Sociology.* Englewood Cliffs, N.J.: Prentice-Hall.

KING, STANLEY H.; and COBB, SIDNEY 1958 Psychosocial Factors in the Epidemiology of Rheumatoid Arthritis. *Journal of Chronic Diseases* 7:466–475.

LEIGHTON, ALEXANDER H. 1959 *My Name Is Legion: Foundations for a Theory of Man in Relation to Culture.* The Stirling County Study of Psychiatric Disorder and Sociocultural Environment, Vol. 1. New York: Basic Books. → Contains a theoretical discussion of social stress as a factor in mental illness.

MACMAHON, BRIAN; PUGH, THOMAS F.; and IPSEN, JOHANNES 1960 *Epidemiologic Methods.* Boston: Little. → Contains a critical review of current concepts and methods.

MISHLER, ELLIOT G.; and SCOTCH, NORMAN A. 1963 Sociocultural Factors in the Epidemiology of Schizophrenia. *Psychiatry* 26:315–351.

MORRIS, JEREMY N. 1957 *Uses of Epidemiology.* Baltimore: Williams & Wilkins; Edinburgh: Livingstone.

PAUL, JOHN R. 1950 Epidemiology. Pages 52–62 in David E. Green and W. Eugene Knox (editors), *Research in Medical Science.* New York: Macmillan.

PEMBERTON, JOHN (editor) 1963 *Epidemiology: Reports on Research and Teaching, 1962.* Oxford Univ. Press.

POLLACK, HERBERT; and KRUEGER, DEAN E. (editors) 1960 Epidemiology of Cardiovascular Diseases: Methodology. *American Journal of Public Health* 50 (Supplement): 1–124.

ROGERS, EDWARD S. 1960 *Human Ecology and Health: An Introduction for Administrators.* New York: Macmillan.

RUBIN, THEODORE; ROSENBAUM, JOSEPH; and COBB, SIDNEY 1956 The Use of Interview Data for the Detection of Associations in Field Studies. *Journal of Chronic Diseases* 4:253–266.

SUCHMAN, EDWARD A.; and SCHERZER, ALFRED L. 1960 *Current Research in Childhood Accidents.* Part 1 in Association for the Aid of Crippled Children, *Two Reviews of Accident Research.* New York: The Association.

U.S. SURGEON GENERAL'S ADVISORY COMMITTEE ON SMOKING AND HEALTH 1964 *Smoking and Health.* U.S. Department of Health, Education and Welfare, Public Health Service Publication No. 1103. Washington: Government Printing Office. → Contains a thorough analysis of the epidemiological evidence on smoking as a cause of cancer and other diseases.

WARDWELL, WALTER I.; and BAHNSON, CLAUS B. 1964 Problems Encountered in Behavioral Science Research in Epidemiological Studies. *American Journal of Public Health* 54:972–981.

EQUALITY

I. THE CONCEPT OF EQUALITY   *Felix E. Oppenheim*
II. EQUALITY AS AN IDEAL   *Irving Kristol*

I
THE CONCEPT OF EQUALITY

In the context of the social sciences, the concept of equality refers sometimes to certain *properties* which men are held to have in common but more often to certain *treatments* which men either receive or ought to receive. Traditional characterizations of kinds of treatment as either egalitarian or inegalitarian often turn out to be disguised value judgments or empty statements. It is possible, however, to find descriptive criteria apt to capture the egalitarian and inegalitarian features of principles which have been advocated at different times.

Equality of characteristics. Equality must be construed here in the sense of similarity, that is, of agreement in certain properties. That men are equal means that men share some qualities; these must be specified. Men are evidently unequal in many characteristics. There are natural differences (sex, color, character traits, natural endowments, etc.) and institutional variations (citizenship, religion, social rank, etc.). Other properties are common to all but in varying amounts (age, strength, intelligence, possessions, power, etc.). To claim that all men are equal in such respects can only mean that the resemblances are in some way more significant than the differences, as when Hobbes states that "nature hath made men so equal, in the faculties of the body and mind" that the weakest can kill the strongest and no one can outwit the other.

Men are sometimes held to be equal in the sense of having a common "human nature"—a tautological assertion, unless it is specified that all are naturally good or sinful or that they have the same basic motives (say, self-interest), or common basic needs, or similar capacities to feel pleasure and pain, or the same ability to act deliberately and to choose rationally.

Equality of treatment. Moralists ever since the Stoics have claimed that men, in spite of differences of character or intelligence, are of equal dignity, worth, or desert. Statements of this kind are to be interpreted in a normative sense, to the effect that all men are *entitled* to be *treated* equally. The same applies to the allegation that all men have the same moral or natural rights. To say that I have a moral right implies that others should let me exercise it (whereas to have a legal right means that it is conferred by positive law). Thus, Locke interprets his own statement "that men by nature are equal" as referring, not to "all sorts of equality," since men differ as to "age or virtue," but to "the equal right that every man hath to his natural freedom"; this means that men "should also be equal amongst another," that is, that they *should* be given the corresponding legal rights. Analogously, to claim that those of one nation or race or class are "superior" to all others is to hold that they *ought* to receive preferential treatment.

Whether individuals or groups are, in fact, treated equally or unequally by others depends on the way in which benefits or burdens are allotted to them. These may be legal rights (e.g., to own property, to vote) and legal duties (e.g., to respect the rights of others); material benefits (e.g., wages, unemployment benefits, social services) and liabilities (e.g., punishment, taxation, military service); and opportunities (e.g., to hold certain positions or offices).

Factual statements about equality may be about equality of either characteristics or treatment. Normative statements about equality are always concerned with treatment but may contain references to characteristics as well, as when it is being argued that men *should* be treated equally because they *are* equal in certain characteristics. References to both characteristics and treatment are also contained in general rules of the type: all persons having a certain characteristic are to be allotted a certain benefit or burden (in such and such an amount). This leads to the question of how to determine whether an actual or proposed kind of treatment is egalitarian.

Traditional criteria of egalitarianism

(1) *Impartiality.*   Equal treatment means, first of all, the impartial allocation of some benefit or burden by one actor to another, say, by a judge to a claimant. Equality before the law thus means impartial application of the law. Allocations are impartial or partial only by reference to a rule of allocation. With respect to a specified legal or moral rule, a person is treated impartially by another provided his allotment is determined exclusively by the rule itself and not by other factors, such as the latter person's like or dislike of the former. Partiality (allotments made in violation of some given rule) would be the only kind of inegalitarian treatment in this sense. Since any rule—for example, one restricting suffrage to adult citizens or to white citizens—can be applied impartially or partially, we must determine the conditions under which rules themselves are to be considered egalitarian.

(2) *Equal shares to all.*   According to the utilitarians, "everybody [is] to count for one, nobody for more than one" in the allocation of benefits and burdens—not of every conceivable kind, of course, but of certain specified types. Similarly, "equality" to the French revolutionaries meant that the same basic legal rights should be granted by every government to all its citizens. Rules which allocate a benefit or burden in equal amounts to everyone are undoubtedly egalitarian.

(3) *Equal shares to equals.*   Most rules of allocation grant equal shares of some kind, not to all generally but to all who are equal with respect to some property; for example, all adult citizens have the right to vote; whoever commits a certain

crime shall suffer a certain punishment; persons within the same income bracket are liable to the same income tax. According to the previous criterion, such rules would not be egalitarian. The concept of egalitarianism has therefore been enlarged to cover rules which allot "equal shares to equals"; and a rule is considered inegalitarian by Aristotle "when either equals are awarded unequal shares or unequals equal shares."

Now, every rule may be considered egalitarian in this sense; for a rule stipulates that all, or else that only those who are equal in a specified respect, receive the same specified treatment. Universal suffrage means that the right to vote is given to all adult citizens but not to minors and aliens. A graduated income tax treats any two taxpayers within the same bracket equally and any two within different brackets unequally. To treat all whites alike and all Negroes alike but persons of different color differently is to practice racial discrimination. Every conceivable rule treats equals (in some specified respect) equally and unequals unequally.

(4) *Proportional equality.*   To narrow down the criterion again, unequal allotments have been held, ever since Aristotle, to be egalitarian if and only if they satisfy the requirement of "proportional equality." A rule is generally considered to satisfy this requirement if it provides that the amount of benefit or burden is a monotonically increasing function of the specified characteristic; that is, the more of the characteristic, the more benefit or burden. And any two persons are treated "in proportion to their inequality," provided the difference in the amount allotted to each is similarly correlated to the degree in which they differ in the characteristic specified by the rule. But again, any rule which allots "equal shares to equals" implicitly not only allots "unequal shares to unequals" but also allots them "in proportion to their inequality." Both rules—"to each according to his need" and "to each according to his height"—assign different shares to different persons in the proportion in which they differ as to need or as to height. A flat rate and a graduated income tax both fulfill the requirement of proportional equality.

(5) *Unequal shares corresponding to relevant differences.*   Inequality in allotment has been held to be egalitarian provided it is based on *relevant* differences in personal characteristics. Thus, age and citizenship are relevant to voting rights but not so sex or race or wealth; it is therefore held egalitarian to limit the franchise to adult citizens but inegalitarian to restrict it to men or whites or poll-tax payers. Wealth *is* relevant to taxation; hence, a graduated income tax is viewed as egali-

tarian but not a sales tax, which disregards this relevant criterion by taxing poor and wealthy buyers at the same rate.

Judgments to the effect that characteristic *x* is relevant to treatment *y* are valuational, not factual. That color is not relevant to voting but age is means that it is unjust to base the franchise on color and just to require a minimum age. Equality becomes tantamount to distributive justice: "The unjust is unequal, the just is equal" (Aristotle); that is, it is unjust to make unequal awards to those who share a relevant characteristic. Or, in a recent formulation: to be egalitarian, "a difference of treatment requires *justification* in terms of *relevant* and sufficient differences between the claimants" (Ginsberg 1965, p. 79; italics added). The same purely normative criterion underlies the idea of "equality of consideration," that is, "that none shall be held to have a claim to better treatment than another, in advance of good grounds being produced" (Benn & Peters 1959, p. 110; italics removed). This principle is not only purely valuational but also purely procedural—compatible with whatever substantive discriminatory rule may be established on "good grounds."

(6) *To each according to his desert.* According to Aristotle, a person's desert is the only characteristic relevant to allocations. To be both egalitarian and just, these must therefore be based on proportionate equality on the basis of desert. The problem is here merely pushed a step further back, since judgments of someone's relative desert are again valuational. Unless there are objective criteria for relevant or just or good grounds for differential treatment or for a person's desert or worth, it is impossible to refute the racist's counterclaim that color *is* relevant to franchise or that whites are of superior worth. (His claim that color is relevant to intelligence would be an empirical one and could be refuted on empirical grounds, but it is intelligence rather than color or desert which he proposes in this case as a relevant criterion for granting franchise.) According to criteria 3 and 4, *every* rule of allocation is egalitarian, and *any* rule may be considered just and hence egalitarian according to criteria 5 and 6.

Operational criteria of egalitarianism

(1) *Egalitarian rules of allocation and distribution.* Even advocates of racial discrimination are likely to consider it egalitarian to give preferential treatment to the needy regardless of race but inegalitarian to give it to whites regardless of need. The reason seems to be that the first policy aims at the equal satisfaction of everybody's basic needs, while the second is incompatible with that principle. This points to a distinction which must be made between (1) rules which determine how some benefit or burden is to be *allocated* among persons, that is, how much of it is to be *given* to each or to be *taken* from each, and (2) rules concerning the *distribution* of a benefit or burden which is to result from some allocation, that is, how much each person is to *have* at the end.

Rules of allocation and rules of distribution may be (*a*) egalitarian or (*b*) inegalitarian. Rules of allocation are egalitarian if they allocate the same kind or amount of benefit or burden to all. Similarly, rules of distribution are egalitarian if they stipulate that all are to have equal shares. Here are some examples: (*1a*) universal suffrage, universal head tax; (*1b*) suffrage only for whites, graduated income tax; (*2a*) political equality, equality of possessions; (*2b*) political inequality, inequality of possessions.

(2) *Inegalitarian allocations compatible with egalitarian distributions.* Egalitarian allocations often lead to egalitarian distributions and inegalitarian allocations to inegalitarian distributions. Universal suffrage promotes political equality, not so suffrage for whites only. But an egalitarian distribution does not necessarily require an egalitarian allocation. For example, to bring about an equal *distribution* of the holdings of A, who has 8 units, and of B, who has 2, it is necessary to take, say, 3 from A and to give 3 to B. But taking 1 from A and 1 from B would leave the previous inequality of their distribution unaffected. Egalitarian allocations may thus result in inegalitarian distributions. With respect to an egalitarian rule of distribution, a rule of allocation may be said to be egalitarian if its application is a means to, or a consequence of, the former's implementation and inegalitarian if it is incompatible with the former. A rule of allocation which is intrinsically inegalitarian may thus be egalitarian with respect to some egalitarian rule of distribution, while an intrinsically egalitarian rule of allocation may be inegalitarian in this respect. With respect to equality (or rather, to reducing inequality) of wealth, a graduated income tax is egalitarian and a head tax is inegalitarian.

(3) *Degrees of egalitarianism.* A rule of allocation or of distribution may be considered more egalitarian (or less inegalitarian) than another if it insures "that a larger number of persons (or classes of persons) shall receive similar treatment in specified circumstances" (Berlin [1955–1956] 1961, p. 135)—or rather, similar preferential treat-

ment. Universal suffrage which excludes only minors and aliens is more egalitarian than suffrage which excludes also Negroes and may therefore be considered fully egalitarian for practical purposes. Disenfranchising women is more inegalitarian than disenfranchising Negroes if the latter constitute a small segment of the population but less inegalitarian if Negroes form a large percentage.

On the basis of these purely descriptive criteria, persons with divergent value commitments can agree (or disagree) on an empirical level whether a given rule of allocation or of distribution is egalitarian and to what degree, and whether a rule of allocation is egalitarian with respect to some egalitarian rule of distribution. The resulting classification corresponds in a satisfactory way to our everyday distinctions between egalitarian and inegalitarian treatment.

Instances of egalitarianism

Equality of opportunity.   Equal treatment of all in every respect was advocated by some nineteenth-century anarchists: equality of occupation (for example, intellectuals would participate in manual work), of consumption (all would eat and even dress alike), and especially of education would ultimately wipe out existing inequalities of talent and capacity. Most egalitarians, however, consider such an ultimate goal neither desirable nor possible. They realize that in every society individuals are bound to have varying degrees of ability and to hold positions that yield varying degrees of status if not of remuneration. How to match unequal individuals with unequal positions has been their central concern and equality of opportunity their principal answer. This rule deals with the distribution of access to positions in society, not with the allocation of the positions themselves. Opportunities to occupy all positions, including the most attractive ones, are to be distributed in an egalitarian way to all on a competitive basis, regardless of such differences as social status or economic resources and regardless even of differences of ability, since "the least able and the most able are given an equal start in the race for success" (Pennock 1950, p. 81). If everyone has an equal start, then the position he will occupy at the end will, in theory at least, depend exclusively on how far and how fast he runs, that is, on his own resourcefulness (but also on his luck). As the French Declaration of the Rights of Man proclaimed: all citizens "are equally eligible to all honors, places and employments, according to their different abilities, without any other distinction than that of their virtues and talents."

Legal equality. "Equality of opportunity, in the broad sense of the career open to personality, is and has been the inclusive goal within which the partial goals of the special equalities have their significance" (Hofstadter 1956, p. 137). Equality of legal rights has been, historically, the first of these special equalities. Classical liberalism held that the equal distribution of opportunities required merely the equal allocation of the basic rights of "life, liberty, and property." If legal privileges are abolished and legal rights protected, no obstacle will stand in the way of anyone's pursuit of happiness.

Equal satisfaction of basic needs.   Increasing industrialization brought about an increasing awareness that equality of opportunity cannot be achieved by the "majestic equality of the law which forbids rich and poor alike to steal bread and to sleep under bridges" (Anatole France). Equality of opportunity does presuppose the equal allotment of certain rights, but it also requires the application of another egalitarian rule of distribution, namely, equality of the satisfaction of certain basic needs, which in turn calls for an inegalitarian rule of allotment: privileges for the economically underprivileged. Indeed, those who lack the basic physical or educational necessities do not have the same opportunities to reach the higher positions as do the better endowed. To bring the former up to the general starting line, government must compensate them for these initial disadvantages by means of social legislation and social services such as minimum wages, tax exemptions, unemployment benefits, free public schools, and scholarships.

Equality of opportunity is not simply a matter of legal equality. Its existence depends, not merely on the absence of disabilities, but on the presence of abilities. It obtains in so far as, and only in so far as, each member of a community, whatever his birth, or occupation, or social position, possesses in fact, and not merely in form, equal chances of using to the full his natural endowments of physique, of character, and of intelligence.   (Tawney [1931] 1965, pp. 103–104)

To condemn such inegalitarian allotment is to oppose equality of opportunity. Herbert Spencer agreed with his neoliberal opponents that "insuring to each the right to pursue within the specified limits the objects of his desires without let or hindrance is quite a separate thing from insuring him satisfaction" but insisted that the state should "confine itself to guaranteeing the rights of its members" and not "assume the role of Relievergeneral to the poor." Such advocacy of mere equality of rights had by that time become an inegalitarian policy which deprived the poor of equality of opportunity and promoted the "survival" of the wealthy at their expense.

Privileges for nobles or property owners and disabilities imposed on a particular sex, religion, or race are inegalitarian, not only in themselves but probably also with respect to any conceivable egalitarian rule of distribution. But privileges for religious, racial, or ethnic minorities may constitute an egalitarian policy when these are considered as constituting economically or socially disadvantaged groups.

Economic equality. Equality of the right of property is compatible with extreme inequality in the distribution of property. Equality of opportunity does not imply equalization of wealth either, certainly not at the end of the "race for success." Nevertheless, to give all an equal start, some must be lifted up and others moved down. The equal satisfaction of basic needs as a precondition for equality of opportunity does require economic equality, that is, a reduction of extreme inequalities in the distribution of commodities. "By equality, we should understand, not that the degree of power and riches be absolutely identical for everybody, but that . . . no citizen be wealthy enough to buy another, and none poor enough to be forced to sell himself" (Rousseau). "The socialist seeks a distribution of rewards, status, and privileges egalitarian enough to . . . equalize opportunities" (Crosland [1956] 1957, p. 113). With respect to this goal, unequal taxation of unequal incomes is egalitarian.

Common ownership of the means of production. Marx, too, realized that "one man is superior to another physically and mentally" and interpreted equality—at least in the first phase of communism—as the opportunity for each to occupy the position which corresponds to his ability. Contrary to the neoliberals and socialists, Marx believed that this goal could not be reached through a redistribution of the means of consumption (the demand for fair distribution as well as for equal rights was to him "obsolete verbal rubbish") but only through the abolition of private control of the means of production. Their "common ownership" would eliminate the possibility of exploitation and class struggle; and "with the abolition of class distinctions, all social and political inequality arising from them would automatically disappear by itself."

To each according to his merit. If there is equality of opportunity and if higher positions bring higher salaries, both will go to those of greater merit or ability. The result would ideally be, "not an aristocracy of birth, not a plutocracy of wealth, but a true meritocracy of talent" (Young [1958] 1959, p. 19). Unequal allocation of rewards, correlated with inequality of ability, is a consequence of equal distribution of opportunities. With respect to equality of opportunity, rewards according to merit in the sense of ability is therefore an egalitarian principle.

This is not so with rewards according to merit in the sense of desert. Plato and Aristotle held not only that people's relative desert or moral worth can be objectively ascertained but also that "there are *innate* differences which fit them for different occupations" (Plato), that "a distinction is already marked, immediately *at birth* between those who are intended for being ruled and those who are intended to rule" (Aristotle), and between those who are "by nature" either slaves or free. Each is to be assigned the function corresponding to his pre-established desert. Aristotle's principle of "proportional equality according to desert" is really inegalitarian, not only intrinsically but also with respect to equality of opportunity and probably every other egalitarian rule of distribution. For the same reason, all rigidly stratified societies are inegalitarian, from feudalism to the Indian caste system.

To each according to his need. Equality of opportunity does not, however, necessarily entail that rewards (as well as positions) go to each according to his ability. Marxists believe that the first stage of communism, in which means of consumption are distributed according to the work performed, will inevitably evolve, in Lenin's words, "from formal equality to real equality, i.e., to realizing the rule: 'From each according to his ability, to each according to his need.'" Positions would still be correlated to ability, but everyone (so Marxists believe) will work spontaneously to the best of his ability even without incentives, and compensations will differ according to need, regardless of the type of work. With respect to equality of opportunity to occupy various positions, this would be another egalitarian rule of allocation.

Political equality. While some political thinkers have advocated the equalization of political power through direct democracy or predicted the abolition of political power through the withering away of the state, it is generally assumed that political power is ubiquitous and always unevenly distributed and that political equality can only mean equality of opportunity to participate in the political process. Political equality has therefore been associated with the democratic institutions of suffrage, representation, and majority rule. Early liberals did not include political rights among the basic rights to be given to all; they demanded merely that wealth should replace birth as a criterion for franchise. Extending suffrage to all property owners was originally an egalitarian demand directed against hereditary privileges of the nobility. Property qualifications for voting rights became an inegalitarian rule when it was invoked in defense of vested property interests against proponents of universal suffrage (which was not instituted in most countries until the decline of laissez-faire liberalism).

Egalitarianism and other social goals

Egalitarian rules may conflict not only with one another (for example, equality of rights and of opportunities, equality of opportunities and of welfare) but also with other social goals. The equal distribution of welfare does not necessarily lead to its maximization. The latter goal might be most effectively realized by slavery or by wage incentives to higher production far greater than would be compatible with equality of welfare and even of opportunity. Equal welfare and equal freedom, too, are competing goals, since the former goal requires government to impose greater restrictions on the freedom of economically dominant groups. Freedom of all citizens with respect to government may result in suppression of freedom of the minority of individualists by the majority of conformists. Equalization of wealth does away with the leisure class, which some consider essential to cultural development. Egalitarianism may thus lead to downward leveling and stifle individuality, diversity, and cultural excellence. Greater equality of opportunity may also generate more frustration and greater unhappiness. Political equality entails majority rule, but the majority may decide on inegalitarian policies. Both Edmund Burke and J. S. Mill were in substantial agreement as to these causal ramifications; yet, the former drew the balance in favor of inegalitarianism, while the latter espoused egalitarianism.

Inegalitarian rules are usually advocated as means to other goals, such as order, efficiency, diversity, and cultural excellence. Egalitarianism, on the other hand, is more often considered intrinsically desirable and morally right. Both egalitarian and inegalitarian principles have been held demonstrably valid on the ground that they are "in agreement with nature." That men should receive equal treatment has been taken as a normative conclusion from the factual premise that "men are equal"—unless this statement itself is interpreted in a normative sense (see above). But it has also been argued that men ought to be treated unequally because they are of unequal rank or ability or race.

Yet, normative principles cannot be derived from factual generalizations; neither equality nor inequality of characteristics entails the desirability of either egalitarian or inegalitarian treatment. There is surely no inconsistency in maintaining that men should be treated equally (e.g., as to rights) in spite of the fact that they are unequal (e.g., as to natural endowments) or that they should be treated unequally (e.g., as to salary) regardless of their common features (e.g., as to basic needs). Once the causal connections between egalitarianism or inegalitarianism and other social goals have been clarified, the adoption of one or the other of these two normative doctrines remains a matter of subjective commitment.

FELIX E. OPPENHEIM

[*See also* DEMOCRACY; JUSTICE; POLITICAL THEORY.]

BIBLIOGRAPHY

BENN, STANLEY I.; and PETERS, RICHARD S. 1959 *Social Principles and the Democratic State.* London: Allen & Unwin. → See especially Chapters 5 and 6.

BERLIN, ISAIAH (1955–1956) 1961 Equality as an Ideal. Pages 128–150 in Frederick A. Olafson (editor), *Justice and Social Policy: A Collection of Essays.* Englewood Cliffs, N.J.: Prentice-Hall. → First published in Volume 56 of Aristotelian Society, *Proceedings.*

CROSLAND, CHARLES A. R. (1956) 1957 *The Future of Socialism.* New York: Macmillan.

GINSBERG, MORRIS 1965 *On Justice in Society.* Ithaca, N.Y.: Cornell Univ. Press. → A paperback edition was published in 1965 by Penguin.

HOFSTADTER, ALBERT 1956 The Career Open to Personality. Pages 111–142 in Conference on Science, Philosophy and Religion in Their Relation to the Democratic Way of Life, *Aspects of Human Equality: Fifteenth Symposium of the Conference on Science, Philosophy, and Religion.* Edited by Lyman Bryson et al. New York: The Conference; Harper.

LAKOFF, SANFORD A. 1964 *Equality in Political Philosophy.* Cambridge, Mass.: Harvard Univ. Press.

PENNOCK, J. ROLAND 1950 *Liberal Democracy: Its Merits and Prospects.* New York: Rinehart.

PENNOCK, J. ROLAND (editor) 1967 *Equality.* Nomos No. 9. New York: Atherton.

SARTORI, GIOVANNI 1962 *Democratic Theory.* Detroit, Mich.: Wayne State Univ. Press. → A paperback edition was published in 1965 by Praeger.

TAWNEY, R. H. (1931) 1965 *Equality.* 4th ed., rev. New York: Barnes & Noble.

WILLIAMS, BERNARD (1962) 1963 The Idea of Equality. Pages 110–131 in Peter Laslett and W. G. Runciman (editors), *Philosophy, Politics and Society (Second Series): A Collection*. New York: Barnes & Noble.

Wollheim, Richard (1955–1956) 1961 Equality and Equal Rights. Pages 111–127 in Frederick A. Olafson (editor), *Justice and Social Policy: A Collection of Essays*. Englewood Cliffs, N.J.: Prentice-Hall. → First published in Volume 56 of Aristotelian Society, *Proceedings*.

Young, Michael D. (1958) 1959 *The Rise of the Meritocracy, 1870–2033: The New Elite of Our Social Revolution*. New York: Random House.

II
EQUALITY AS AN IDEAL

Among the definitions of "equality" provided by the *Oxford English Dictionary* are the following three: (1) "the condition of having equal dignity, rank, or privileges with others"; (2) "the condition of being equal in power, ability, achievement, or excellence"; (3) "fairness, impartiality, equity, due proportion, proportionateness."

A moment's contemplation will reveal that these three definitions of "equality," although all of them are consistent with common usage, are not entirely or necessarily consistent with one another. If, for example, men are unequal in power, ability, achievement, or excellence, then an adherence to definition (3) will lead to a violation of definition (1), while an adherence to definition (1) will lead to a violation of definition (3). It is only if men *are* in fact equal in power, ability, and excellence that equity preserves a condition of equal rank.

But, in fact, men are not equal in power, ability, and excellence. From this it would seem to follow that justice requires a certain measure of inequality. And, indeed, in all social orders, no matter how vehement their passion for equality, we observe that some inequalities are regarded as inevitable and natural. At the same time, no egalitarian society can have an easy conscience about the inequalities within it. There is a sentiment, inchoate yet profound, that no matter how unequal men may be in their abilities, in some deeper sense all men are equal merely by virtue of being men.

The issue of legitimacy. It is certainly true that, in Western civilization at least, men have always believed that equality is in some sense the norm from which inequality represents a deviation. As Wollheim and Berlin have pointed out (1955–1956, pp. 281 ff.), the "naturalness" of the idea of equality seems to derive from the dual assumption that (*a*) men are all members of one species, of a simple class of objects (i.e., human beings) and (*b*) all members of a class should be treated uniformly, unless there is good and sufficient reason not to do so. This assumption, Berlin emphasizes, is so pervasive that it has almost the

status of a category (in the Kantian sense) of human rationality:

If I have a cake, and there are ten persons among whom I wish to divide it, then if I give exactly one tenth to each, this will not, at any rate automatically, call for justification; whereas if I depart from this principle of equal division I am expected to produce a special reason. It is some sense of this, however latent, that makes equality an ideal which has never seemed intrinsically eccentric . . . . (*ibid.*, p. 305)

This being the case, it is not surprising that all the golden ages, all the utopias, and all the paradises created by the human imagination are egalitarian (although not necessarily democratic—there may be an infinitely benevolent, if scrupulously egalitarian, despot). However, whereas in classical antiquity, utopia is located in word, not in deed, and in the succeeding Christian centuries it is located in transcendent hope rather than in actuality, in the modern era utopia has become an "ideal" to be realized (if never fully realized) by human effort.

For Plato, as later for Augustine and Aquinas, utopia is conceived as prehistorical, as existing prior to some primordial Fall—a catastrophe that implicates the entire human race and that sets the conditions of its destiny and its progress. The outstanding consequence of this Fall is the abolition of original equality and the establishment of the principle of hierarchy as the "natural" principle of cosmic and social order. The original, harmonious prehistorical unity is shattered, and the universe becomes subject to differentiation—soul and matter, spirit and flesh, idea and reality are now opposite poles, between which the tension of existence tries to maintain an equilibrium. The most perfect equilibrium (indeed, the only enduring one) is, obviously, that which recognizes the superiority of the noble over the base—of soul over matter, spirit over flesh, idea over actuality. The articulation of this order results in a metaphysics of hierarchy, in which both the cosmos and human society are envisaged as part of a "great chain of being," with precedence and consequence clearly defined and with *noblesse oblige* and humble obedience the only two reasonable political perspectives available to the human imagination.

It requires more empathy than most twentieth-century men possess to realize how utterly "natural" the idea of hierarchy came to seem to classical and medieval thinkers—and even to most modern thinkers prior to the American and French revolutions. We are inclined to view this as an antiegalitarian mode of thought, but the idea of hierarchy saw itself as containing the only feasible idea of political equality, rather than as in any way opposing equality. For equality was defined in terms of justice—of giving each man his due, so that equal men received equal rewards. That all men were not equal—and certainly not equal in all respects—was a platitude confirmed daily by the most casual observation. The hierarchical idea was accepted in good faith and good conscience by almost everyone; if we now deem it an ideology, then it was the ideology not of a class but of an entire historical epoch.

It is Shakespeare, through the sublimity of his language, who makes the older idea of hierarchy available to us better than any political philosopher. Ulysses' speech on "degree," in *Troilus and Cressida,* is the *locus classicus*:

The heavens themselves, the planets, and this centre
Observe degree, priority, and place, . . .
But when the planets
In evil mixture to disorder wander,
What plagues and what portents! what mutiny!
What raging of the sea! shaking of earth!
Commotion in the winds! Frights, changes, horrors,
Divert, and crack, rend and deracinate
The unity and married calm of states
Quite from their fixture! O, when degree is shak'd,
Which is the ladder to all high designs,
Then enterprise is sick! How could communities,
Degrees in schools, and brotherhoods in cities,
Peaceful commerce from dividable shores,
The primogenitive and due of birth,
Prerogative of age, crowns, sceptres, laurels,
But by degree, stand in authentic place?
Take but degree away, untune that string,
And, hark, what discord follows! Each thing meets
In mere oppugnancy. . . .   (Act I, scene 3)

Yet even as Shakespeare wrote these lines, the planets were on their way "in evil mixture to disorder wander." As Sanford A. Lakoff pointed out in his historical survey *Equality in Political Philosophy* (1964), the new astronomy replaced the cosmos with a neutral universe in which "the laws of nature" applied without distinction to heavenly and earthly bodies. Simultaneously, the rise of experimental science and the overthrow of Aristotelian teleology nullified previous distinctions between "base" and "noble" in nature—and, most especially, in human nature. Just as the new physical science declared all the parts of nature to be equal, so the new scientific (i.e., materialistic) psychology declared all the parts of man to be equal—none was intrinsically base or intrinsically noble. The denial of the superiority of spirit over matter, and of mind over body, inevitably suggested that there was no good reason for those who worked with their hands to have an inferior status compared with those whose work was nonmanual and nonmenial. In this way the philosophical foundations of modern bourgeois society were established.

Christianity itself, in the course of its several "reformations," buttressed these new foundations (without, however, necessarily intending this result). Luther's denial of the distinction between "spiritual" and "carnal" authorities and vocations was destructive of churchly hierarchy. The keys of St. Peter were distributed among the congregation of believers, as the monopoly of the Catholic clergy over the apostolic succession was denied and as its exclusive authority to interpret Scripture faithfully was transferred to the entire body of Christendom. Successive generations of reformers carried this antiauthoritarian impulse forward, so that Christendom itself experienced the multiplication of new self-governing and (in the literal sense of the term) self-righteous sects and denominations.

The response to inequality. But while these secular and religious trends were to create the bourgeois world, energies were being released that were to point beyond this world. Even during the Middle Ages, Christian Messianism was only with difficulty kept within the confines of the church; and as the authority of the church crumbled, this messianism became an independent spiritual and political force. The kingdom of God was transferred from a transcendental hereafter to this world, this time, this place.

It was during the English revolution of 1640–1660 that Christian Messianism first revealed its full political ambitions. There had been previous incidents, to be sure (e.g., the Anabaptist revolts in Germany), but these had as their primary aim the creation of local utopias. In contrast, the left-wing Commonwealth's-men sought not only to transform their own national society but also to prescribe principles for all truly Christian and truly just societies. Overton, the Leveller, spoke in the recognizable accents of modernity when he said: "Every man by nature being a king, priest, prophet in his own natural circuit and compass, whereof no second may partake but by deputation, commission, and free consent from him whose right and freedom it is" (Lakoff 1964, p. 65). In declarations such as these, the metaphysical foundations of egalitarian, representative self-government were firmly outlined. It required only the slightest amendment for these metaphysical foundations to be entirely secularized, with "rights" and "freedoms" the prerogatives of men qua men, rather than merely men qua Christians. The political philosophers of the seventeenth and eighteenth centuries moved steadily in this direction, and the political ideologists of the American and French revolutions acted violently upon these new principles of civic organization.

As has been noted, however, even as modern, liberal society was being formed, there was an egalitarian perspective that looked beyond it. This perspective delineated not merely an equality of rights and freedoms but a fraternal equality of condition. Thus, Winstanley, the Digger, prefigured the socialist idea of equality with his declaration that "the earth was made by Almighty God to be a common treasury of livelihood for whole mankind in all his branches . . ." (Lakoff 1964, p. 79). This is socialism, but of a premodern kind. The "common treasury" is a static conception of wealth, and all premodern socialist thinkers envisaged a good society as one of economic modesty rather than of economic abundance—goods were to be distributed equally, and everyone was to be content with what he had. It was not until the nineteenth century that modern socialism, alert to the possibilities of the industrial and technological revolutions it was witnessing, put forward the prospect of equality conjoined to increasing wealth for all. Since premodern socialism demanded a certain measure of asceticism from its adherents, while modern socialism could appeal simultaneously to human idealism and to human appetites, it is not surprising that modern socialism has a far more powerful popular appeal.

It is a distinguishing characteristic of the modern age that "equality" should be not merely an abstract ideal but also a politically aggressive idea. It is generally accepted—it is, indeed, one of the most deeply rooted conventions of contemporary political thought—that the existence of inequality is a legitimate provocation to social criticism. Every inequality is on the defensive, must prove itself against the imputation of injustice and unnaturalness. And where such proof is established, it never asserts itself beyond the point where inequality is to be tolerated because it is, under particular conditions, inescapable. That inequality may be per se desirable is a thought utterly repugnant to the modern sensibility.

The modern egalitarian impulse has had its objective social correlatives. Modern society tends to have a more equal distribution of income and wealth than previous social orders in Western history. Statistics are fragmentary and are open to dispute as to their significance. But, for France, Jean Fourastié ([1951] 1960, p. 30) has made the following estimate: "The salary of a councilor of state increased by a factor of at least 40 from 1800 to 1948; the salary of a professor at the Collège de France by 100; the average salary of an office boy in a government agency by 220; the hourly wages of labourers in provincial cities by more than 400." The general tendency would seem to be unmistakable.

The limits and potential of equality. Nevertheless, there is considerable controversy over the issue of whether equality has been adequately realized in our modern social arrangements. This controversy derives in large part from the ambiguities inherent in the idea of equality. Thus, a comparative percentile increase for lower-income groups represents a step toward equality only from a limited, statistical point of view. In another perspective, it can be regarded as a movement toward further inequality. For when a man's income is increased from a million dollars a year to two million (i.e., doubled), while another's income is increased from one thousand to five thousand (i.e., quintupled), it can fairly be said that the rich man has benefited more notably—in absolute magnitudes—than the poor. Whether one wishes to make such an assertion will depend entirely upon one's conception of equality—whether, that is, one is measuring equality by absolute or relative standards. The progressive income tax represents an effort by the modern state to mediate between these two notions of equality.

A similar ambiguity—between equality of condition and equality of opportunity—plays a most significant role in American social and political thought. Equality of opportunity will inevitably result in inequality of condition, since some men are more able, more energetic, and more fortunate than others. The American creed sanctions such inequality—but only halfheartedly. For there has always been an implicit corollary—derived from the premise that all men are created equal—that equality of opportunity ought to lead to approximate equality of condition, and that failure to realize this goal reflects a deficiency (if not a positive error) in the existing social and economic arrangements. The tides of American politics flow between these two polar conceptions of equality.

In recent years, some of the leading thinkers of American sociology have attempted to transcend this debate over equality by declaring inequality to be a necessary condition of all social organization. To some extent, this effort originates in the experience of just how little effect popular or political ideas about equality have on comparable social structures. The distribution of income in all modern industrialized nations is astonishingly similar, no matter whether the governing ideology of this nation be socialist (e.g., Sweden) or capitalist (e.g., the United States). Instead of wondering about the origins of inequality and of social classes —as did the sociologists of the eighteenth and nineteenth centuries—such thinkers as Talcott Parsons, Kingsley Davis, and Wilbert E. Moore have attempted to demonstrate that social differentiation and social stratification are indispensable to the very existence of a social structure—that each society has functional "norms," both inwardly and outwardly coercive, which prescribe the acceptable degrees and kinds of inequality to be tolerated.

This sociological thesis represents a covert return to the hierarchical principles of distributive justice and proportional equality elaborated by Aristotle in Book v of the *Ethica nicomachea* and Book iii of the *Politics*. And since the history of the idea of equality in the Western world is to a considerable extent a record of intermittent, and sometimes violent, dissatisfaction with these principles, it is understandable that the debate over equality should be an unending one, with every new resolution the occasion for a new beginning.

IRVING KRISTOL

[*See also* DEMOCRACY; HUMAN RIGHTS; JUSTICE.]

BIBLIOGRAPHY

ARISTOTLE *Ethica nicomachea.* Translated by W. D. Ross. Oxford: Clarendon Press, 1925.
ARISTOTLE *Politics.* With an English translation. London: Heinemann; Cambridge, Mass.: Harvard Univ. Press, 1959.
DAHRENDORF, RALF 1962 On the Origin of Social Inequality. Pages 88–109 in Peter Laslett and W. G. Runciman (editors), *Philosophy, Politics and Society (Second Series): A Collection.* New York: Barnes & Noble.
EMERSON, RALPH WALDO (1844) 1920 Politics. Pages 310–323 in Ralph Waldo Emerson, *Essays: First and Second Series.* New York: Dutton.
FOURASTIÉ, JEAN (1951) 1960 *The Causes of Wealth.* Glencoe, Ill.: Free Press. → First published in French.
LAKOFF, SANFORD A. 1964 *Equality in Political Philosophy.* Cambridge, Mass.: Harvard Univ. Press.
WOLLHEIM, RICHARD; and BERLIN, ISAIAH 1955–1956 Equality. Parts 1–2. Aristotelian Society for the Systematic Study of Philosophy, London, *Proceedings* 56: 281–326.

EQUILIBRIUM
See ECONOMIC EQUILIBRIUM *and* HOMEOSTASIS.

ERASMUS

Desiderius Erasmus (1466?–1536) (he was baptized Erasmus Rogerii, or Gerards—Desiderius was his own addition), a Dutch humanist, spent his early youth in Gouda and later attended the Latin schools at Deventer and 's Hertogenbosch. There he had contact with the *devotio moderna* and joined the canons regular of the Augustinian monastery of Steyn near Gouda, taking his monastic vows in 1488. Between 1493 and 1516 he lived a wandering life: in service with the bishop of Cambrai, studying at the University of Paris with Robert Gaguin, Jean Vitrier, and Lefèvre d'Étaples, making three visits to England, where he met John Colet and Thomas More and studied theology and Greek, and visiting Italy and Basel. From 1517 to 1521 he taught at Louvain, then lived in Basel until the Reformation was instituted there, and in Freiburg from 1529 to 1535; he died in Basel.

Erasmus was above all a remarkable classical scholar. He fiercely deplored the corrupt state of the Latin of his time and advocated the use of Cicero's language, which he used in all his writings and for which he wrote manuals. Following the example of the Italians, he sought out what, in his opinion, were the most authentic texts of the classics, of which he drew up annotated editions, the Greek with Latin translations. In addition to many classical works he edited the New Testament and the writings of the church fathers.

Erasmus also had great influence on his contemporaries through his hortatory works: humorous and satirical sketches of the life of his contemporaries (*Colloquia* 1518; Eng. trans. *The Colloquies of Erasmus*), paraphrases of the Gospels and Epistles, and his most famous essays: *Enchiridion militis christiani* (1503) and *Moriae encomium* (1511; Eng. trans. *In Praise of Folly*). In them he bitterly mocked stupidity, selfishness, and vanity and pointed out that man can find the true happiness that lies in harmony and peace only through leading a truly Christian life and increasing one's knowledge. Rulers, including the pope, were sharply criticized by Erasmus for their destructive and useless wars. Education to rationality can and must be the key to a better public life; to this end he wrote, among other things, *Institutio principis christiani* (1515–1516; Eng. trans. *The Education of a Christian Prince*), dedicated to Charles v.

Erasmus took up arms early in his career against the idle disputations of the Scholastics, the formalism of the church of his time, the wealth and temporal power of the priesthood, and later, above all, against the monks, whom he regarded as his archenemies and whose monastic life he saw as useless. He hoped for a reconstruction of the church in line with what he saw as primitive Christianity: not a doctrine of redemption from sin and death, but a *philosophia Christi* that teaches man to live in conformity with the commandments of love of neighbor, mercy, self-control, and reason, as the best of the classics also taught. He did not regard the sacraments as means of grace. He condemned the church's doctrine of absolution by penance and good works, the worship of saints and their relics, and the practice of pilgrimages. Edification by word and example, he held, is the only task of the priest. At the same time, he wanted to retain the principal dogmas (including papal power, provided it was confined to matters of faith). However, his interpretation of these dogmas differed so far from that professed by the church that the authorities, even after the Council of Trent, condemned his writings. But his ideas found much support and are still alive, both among Catholics and liberal Protestants.

Erasmus greeted Luther's public stand against the church's doctrine of penance with sympathy. But he soon realized that Luther had in mind an entirely different reformation of the church than he himself desired. At the same time, he continued to advocate a conciliatory attitude toward Luther and opposed his condemnation. It was only after much pressure had been exerted that Erasmus wrote the *Diatribe de libero arbitrio* (1524; Eng. trans. *Discourse on Free Will*) against Luther. In it he set forth his own conception of human dignity and free will, which was related to the ideas of the Italian humanists and the classics, as opposed to the total depravity of man that Luther preached. However, he did this in such a way that his book pleased the Catholics no more than the Protestants. Until his death he pleaded for reconstruction of the church and a *rapprochement* between the Roman and Lutheran factions.

H. A. ENNO VAN GELDER

WORKS BY ERASMUS

(1484–1521) 1962 *The Epistles of Erasmus: From His Earliest Letters to His Fifty-fifth Year.* 3 vols. New York: Russell & Russell.

(1484–1536) 1906–1958 *Opus epistolarum Des. Erasmi Roterodami.* Edited by P. S. Allen. 12 vols. Oxford: Clarendon Press.

(1503) 1963 *The Enchiridion.* Translated and edited by Raymond Himelick. Bloomington: Indiana Univ. Press.

(1511) 1942 *In Praise of Folly.* With a short biography of Erasmus by Hendrik Willem van Loon. New York: Black.

(1515–1516) 1936 *The Education of a Christian Prince.* New York: Columbia Univ. Press.

(1518) 1965 *The Colloquies of Erasmus.* A new translation by Craig R. Thompson. Univ. of Chicago Press.

(1524) 1961 *Discourse on Free Will.* Translated and edited by Ernest F. Winter. New York: Ungar.

Ausgewählte Werke. Edited by Hajo Holborn. Munich: Beck, 1933.

Desiderii Erasmi Roterodami opera omnia. 10 vols. Leiden (The Netherlands): Vander, 1703–1706. → Volume 1: *Qvae ad institvtionem literarvm spectant.* Volume 2: *Adagia.* Volume 3: *Epistolae.* Volume 4: *Qvae ad morvm institvtionem pertinent.* Volume 5: *Qvae ad pretatem institvvnt.* Volume 6: *Novvm Testamentvm.* Volume 7: *Paraphrases in N. Testamentvm.* Volume 8: *Versa e patribvs graecis.* Volume 9: *Apologia I.* Volume 10: *Apologia II.*

Erasmi opuscula. A supplement to the *Opera omnia*, edited with introduction and notes by Wallace K. Ferguson. The Hague: Nijhoff, 1933.

Poems. With introductions and notes by Cornelis Reedijk. Leiden (The Netherlands): Brill, 1956.

SUPPLEMENTARY BIBLIOGRAPHY

BATAILLON, MARCEL 1937 *Érasme et l'Espagne: Recherches sur l'histoire spirituelle du XVIᵉ siècle.* Paris: Droz.

Bibliotheca Erasmiana. (1897–1915) 1964 Pages 271–1048 in *Bibliotheca Belgica.* Volume 2: *Bibliographie générale des Pays-Bas.* Brussels: Culture et Civilisation.

EIJL, E. J. M. VAN 1963 Erasmus en de hervorning van de theologie. *Archief voor de geschiedenis van de katholieke kerk in Nederland* 5:129–219.

FLITNER, ANDREAS 1952 *Erasmus im Urteil seiner Nachwelt: Das literarische Erasmus-Bild von Beatus Rhenanus bis zu Jean Le Clerc.* Tübingen (Germany): Niemeyer.

GELDER, H. A. ENNO VAN (1961) 1964 *The Two Reformations in the Sixteenth Century: A Study of the Religious Aspects and Consequences of Renaissance and Humanism.* The Hague: Nijhoff.

HUIZINGA, JOHAN (1924) 1952 *Erasmus of Rotterdam.* 3d ed. London: Phaidon. → First published in Dutch.

MESTWERDT, PAUL 1917 *Die Anfänge des Erasmus: Humanismus und "Devotio Moderna."* Leipzig: Haupt.

RENAUDET, AUGUSTIN (1916) 1954 *Préréforme et humanisme à Paris pendant les premières guerres d'Italie 1494–1517.* 2d ed., rev. Paris: Librairie d'Argences.

RENAUDET, AUGUSTIN 1926 *Érasme, sa pensée religieuse et son action d'après sa correspondance (1518–1521).* Paris: Alcan.

RENAUDET, AUGUSTIN 1939 *Études érasmiennes (1521–1529).* Paris: Droz.

RENAUDET, AUGUSTIN 1954 *Érasme et l'Italie.* Travaux d'humanisme et renaissance, No. 15. Geneva: Droz.

RHENANUS, BEATUS 1536 *Desiderii Erasmi Roterodami viri incomparabilis vita, et epitaphia quaedam.* Antwerp (Belgium): Vorstermann. → The first biography of Erasmus.

ROTTERDAM, BIBLIOTHEEK EN LEESZALEN DER GEMEENTE 1937 *Catalogus van geschriften over leven en werken van Desiderius Erasmus aanwezig in de Bibliotheek der gemeente Rotterdam.* Rotterdam (The Netherlands): The Library.

SMITH, PRESERVED 1923 *Erasmus: A Study of His Life, Ideals and Place in History.* New York and London: Harper.

SMITH, PRESERVED 1927 *A Key to the Colloquies of Erasmus.* Oxford Univ. Press.

ERGONOMICS

See ENGINEERING PSYCHOLOGY.

ERRORS

I. Nonsampling Errors   *Frederick Mosteller*

II. Effects of Errors in
     Statistical Assumptions   *Robert M. Elashoff*

I
NONSAMPLING ERRORS

The view has sometimes been expressed that statisticians have laid such great emphasis on the study of sampling errors (the differences between the observed values of a variable and the long-run average of the observed values in repetitions of the measurement) that they have neglected or encouraged the neglect of other, frequently more important, kinds of error, called nonsampling errors.

Errors in conception, logic, statistics, and arithmetic, or failures in execution and reporting, can reduce a study's value below zero. The roster of possible troubles seems only to grow with increasing knowledge. By participating in the work of a specific field, one can, in a few years, work up considerable methodological expertise, much of which has not been and is not likely to be written down. To attempt to discuss every way a study can go wrong would be a hopeless venture. The selection of a kind of error for inclusion in this article was guided by its importance, by the extent of research available, by the ability to make positive recommendations, and by my own preferences.

Although the theory of sampling is generally well developed, both the theory and practice of the control of nonsampling errors are in a less satisfactory state, partly because each subject matter, indeed each study, is likely to face yet uncatalogued difficulties. Empirical results of methodological investigations intended to help research workers control nonsampling errors have accumulated slowly, not only because of myriad variables but also because the variables produce results that lack stability from one study to another.

This article deals mainly with techniques for reducing bias. The portions on variability are not exceptions, for they offer ways to avoid underestimating the amount of variability. The presentation deals, first, with the meaning of bias and with conceptual errors; second, with problems of nonsampling errors especially as they arise in the sample survey field through questionnaires, panel studies, nonresponse, and response errors; and, third, with errors occurring in the analysis of nearly any kind of quantitative investigation, errors arising from variability, from technical problems in analysis, in calculations, and in reporting. Some discussions of nonsampling errors restrict themselves to the field of sample surveys, where problems of bias and blunder have been especially studied, but this article also treats some nonsampling errors in experimental and observational studies.

Bias and conceptual errors

Bias and true values. What is bias? Most definitions of bias, or systematic error, assume that for each characteristic to be measured there exists a true value that the investigation ideally would produce. Imagine repeatedly carrying out the actual proposed, rather than the ideal, investigation, getting a value each time for the characteristic under study, and obtaining an average value from these many repetitions. The difference between that average value and the true value of the characteristic is called the bias. The difference between the outcome of *one* investigation and the true value is the sum of bias and sampling error. The point of averaging over many repetitions is to reduce the sampling error in the average value to a negligible amount. (It is assumed that for the process under study and for the type of average chosen, this reduction is possible.)

Is there a true value? The concept "true value" is most touchy, for it assumes that one can describe an ideal investigation for making the measurement. Ease in doing this depends upon the degree of generality of the question. For example, the measurement of "interventionist attitude" in the United States during World War II is discussed below. For such a broad notion, the concept of a true value seems vague, even admitting the possible use of several numbers in the description. It is easier to believe in a true value for the percentage of adults who would respond "Yes" to "Should we go to war now?" Even here the training of the interviewers, the rapidly changing fraction of the population holding given opinions, and the effect of the social class and opinions of the interviewer upon the responses of those interviewed must raise questions about the existence of a true value. At the very least, we wonder whether a true value could represent a time span and how its conditions of measurement could be specified. In designing an ideal sample survey, what kind of interviewer should be used?

Today some scientists believe that true values do not exist separately from the measuring process to be used, and in much of social science this view can be amply supported. The issue is not limited to social science; in physics, complications arise from the different methods of measuring microscopic and macroscopic quantities such as lengths. On the other hand, because it suggests ways of improving measurement methods, the concept of "true value" is useful; since some methods come much nearer to being ideal than others, the better ones can provide substitutes for true values. (See the discussion on describing response error in the section on "Response error," below.)

To illustrate further the difficulty of the notion of a true value, consider an example from one of the most quantitative social sciences. When the economist assesses the change in value of domestic product, different choices of weights and of base years yield different results. He has no natural or unique choice for these weights and years. He can only try to avoid extremes and unusual situations. While, as noted above, the belief in a true value independent of the measuring instrument must be especially weak in the area of opinion, similar weaknesses beset measures of unemployment, health, housing, or anything else related to the human condition. [*See* INDEX NUMBERS.]

Conceptual errors.   Since the variety of sources of biases is practically unlimited, this article discusses only a few frequently encountered sources.

Target population–sampled population.   Often an investigation is carried out on a sample drawn from a population—the sampled population—quite different from that to which the investigator wants to generalize—the target population. This mismatch makes the inference from sample to target population shaky. To match target and sampled population perfectly is usually impossible, but often the expenditure of time and money or the use of special skills or cooperation can patch what cannot be made whole.

Some examples of this process follow: (1) The psychologist wants to establish general laws of learning for all organisms, and especially for man, but he may choose to study only the college sophomore, usually in his own college and rarely outside his own country. His principal alternatives are the rat and the pigeon. Reallocation of time and money may extend the sampled population and bring him closer to the target he has in mind.

(2) The sociologist may want to study the actual organization of trade unions and yet be hard pressed to study in depth more than a single union. This limitation is impossible for an individual to overcome, but cooperative research may help. (For a remarkable cooperative anthropological study of child rearing, see *Six Cultures: Studies of Child Rearing* [Whiting 1963].)

(3) The historian or political scientist may want to exposit the whole climate of opinion within which an important decision is made, yet he must pick some facts and omit others, emphasize some and not others. The sampling of historical records offers a compromise between scanning everything, which may be impossible or unsatisfactorily superficial, and the case study of a single document or of a small collection.

(4) The man who generalizes on educational methods on the basis of his studies in one class, or one school subject, or one grade, or one school, or one school system, or even one country, needs to consider whether the bases of his investigations should be broadened.

(5) The investigator, especially in studies where he does not regard his investigation as based on a sample, but on a population or census, would be wise to consider what population he hopes his investigation applies to, whether the full breadth of it has had an appropriate chance to contribute cases to his study and, if not, how he might get at the rest. He may be satisfied with describing the population under study, but often he is not.

(6) More narrowly, in sampling the membership of a professional society, the investigator may find his published membership list out of date by some years. For a fee the society may be willing to provide its current mailing list, which is probably as close as one can get to the target population. Obviously, the target population changes even while the study is being performed.

Incompatibility of meaning.   While arguing for statistical thinking in the attempt to generalize one's results, one must not fall into the pit of statistical nonsense. Both anthropologists and historians call attention to mistakes that can come from regarding seemingly like objects, rituals, or behavior in different cultures as exchangeable commodities for statistical purposes. The notion of "father" without distinction between "pater" and "genitor" offers an example. In the Trobriands, a boy lives with his benign, biological father until he is nine or ten years old, then moves to his mother's brothers' village for training and discipline, and there he inherits property. In the United States the biological father theoretically plays the role of disciplinarian, and the uncles frequently play benign, indulgent roles.

Pilot studies.   Toward the completion of a study, investigators usually feel that it would have been better done in some other way. But a study can be petted and patted so long that, before completion, its value is past. The huge, never-completed study usually damages the investigator's reputation, however wise the termination. Much can and must be learned by trying, and therefore nearly any investigation requires pilot work. Pilot work is little written about, perhaps because it is hard to summarize and perhaps because the results usually sound so obvious and often would be were they not hidden among thousands of other possible obvious results that did not occur. The whole spectrum from the tightest laboratory experiment to the loosest observational study requires careful pilot work. Pilot studies pinpoint the special difficulties of an investigation and, by encouraging initial action, overcome doctrines of omniscience that require a complete plan before starting. While it is true that the statistician can often give more valuable aid at the planning stage by preventing errors than by salvaging poor work through analysis, firm plans made in the absence of pilot studies are plans for disaster.

Hawthorne effects.   Psychologists sadly say that even under the most carefully controlled conditions, laboratory animals do as they please. Humans do even worse. When Roethlisberger and Dickson (1939) carried out their experiments to find conditions that would maximize productivity of factory teams at the Hawthorne Works of Western Electric, they found that every change—increasing the lighting or reducing it, increasing the wage scale or reducing it—seemed to increase the group productivity. Paying attention to people, which occurs in placing them in an experiment, changes their behavior. This rather unpredictable change is called the Hawthorne effect. Instead of trying to eliminate this effect, it has been suggested that all educational efforts should be carried out as portions of experiments, so as to capitalize on the Hawthorne effect. No doubt boredom, even with experimentation, would eventually set in.

The existence of Hawthorne effects seriously restricts the researcher's ability to isolate variables that change performance in a consistent manner. Although experimenters, by adjusting conditions, may create substantial changes in behavior, what causes the changes may still be a mystery. Reliable repetition of results by different experimenters using different groups can establish results more firmly.

What treatment was applied?   In experimental work with humans, it is especially difficult to know whether the treatment administered is the one that the experimenter had in mind. For example, in an unsuccessful learning experiment on the production of words by individuals, subjects in one group were instructed that every word in the class of words that they were seeking contained the same letters of the alphabet. When no differences in learning rates emerged between these subjects and those told nothing about the class of words being sought, further investigations were made. It turned out that few subjects listened to this particular instruction, and among those who did, several forgot it during the early part of the experiment. If a particular instruction is important, special efforts have to be made to ensure that the subject has received and appreciated it.

One approach to the problem of Hawthorne effects uses, in addition to experimental groups, two kinds of control groups: groups who are informed that they are part of an experiment and other groups who are not so informed. As always, the investigator has to be alert about the actual treatment of control and experimental groups. L. L. Thurstone told me about experimenting for the U.S. Army to measure the value of instruction during sleep for training in telegraphy. Thurstone had control squads who were not informed that they were in the study. The sergeants instructing these control squads felt that the "sleep learning" squads were getting favored treatment, and to keep their squads "even," they secretly instituted additional hours of wide-awake training for their own squads, thereby ruining the whole investigation.

Randomization.   Generally speaking, randomization is a way to protect the study from bias in selecting subjects or in assigning treatments. It aids in getting a broad representation from the population into the sample. Randomization helps to communicate the objectivity of the study. It provides a basis for mathematical distribution theory that has uses in statistical appraisals and in simulations. [*See* EXPERIMENTAL DESIGN; RANDOM NUMBERS.]

Bad breaks in random sampling.   Valuable as randomization is, chance can strike an investigator stunning blows. For example, suppose that a psychological learning experiment is intended to reinforce 5 randomly chosen responses in each burst of 20. If the randomization accidentally gives reinforcement to the first 5 responses in each burst of 20, the psychologist should notice this and realize that he has selected a special kind of periodic reinforcement. The objectivity of the random assignment cannot cure its qualitative failure.

Similarly, suppose that in preparing to study fantasy productions under two carefully controlled conditions the clinical psychologist observes that his randomizing device has put all his scientist subjects into one group and all his humanist subjects into another. In that case, he should reconsider the grouping.

In principle, one should write down, in advance, sets of assignments that one would not accept. Unfortunately, there are usually too many of these, and nobody is yet adept at characterizing them in enough detail to get a computer to list them, even if it could face the size of the task. One solution is to describe a restricted, but acceptable, set of assignments and to choose randomly from these. Omitting some acceptable assignments may help to make the description feasible while keeping the list satisfactorily broad.

If this solution is not possible, then one probably has either to trust oneself (admittedly risky) or else get a more impartial judge to decide whether a particular random assignment should be borne.

If there are many variables, an investigator cannot defend against all the bad assignments. By leaning upon subject matter knowledge and accepting the principle that the variables usually thought to be important are the ones to be especially concerned about, stratification, together with randomization, can still be of some assistance. For example, the stratification might enforce equal numbers of each sex, with individuals still randomly chosen from the potential pools of men and women. In studying bad breaks from randomization, the investigator can afford to consider rejecting only the assignments too closely related to proved first-order or main effects and not second-order effects or boomerang possibilities conceived in, but never observed from, armchairs.

Random permutations. Although arranging objects in a random order can easily be done by using an ordinary random number table, few people know how to do it. In any case, making these permutations is tedious, and it is worth noting the existence of tables of random permutations in some books on the design of experiments and in the book by Moses and Oakford (1963) that offers many permutations of sets numbering 9, 16, 20, 30, 50, 100, 200, 500, 1,000 elements. A set of any other size less than 1,000 can be ordered by using the permutations for the next larger size. With larger sets, some stratification is almost sure to be valuable.

Example. One (nonstratified) permutation for a set of 30 elements is shown in Table 1 (read left

to right). To arrange at random the letters of the alphabet, we might assign the integers, starting with 1 for *a* and ending with 26 for *z*, to the positions of the letters in the alphabet. Then, according to the permutation of Table 1, 11 and 5 correspond to *k* and *e*, 29 is omitted, 26 corresponds to *z*. Continuing gives the permutation:

kezcasndtxyfiomrlvghqbupjw.

For a random sample of 5 letters from the alphabet, drawn without replacement, we could just take the first 5 listed.

Simulations for new statistical methods. Large-scale simulation of economic, political, and social processes is growing in popularity; social scientists who invent new statistics would often find it profitable to try these out on idealized populations, constructed with the aid of random number tables, to see how well they perform their intended functions under perfectly understood conditions. This sort of exploration should be encouraged as part of the pilot work. To illustrate the lack, many books and hundreds of papers have been written about factor analytic methods, yet in 1966 it is hard to point to more than a single published simulation (Lawley & Swanson 1954; Tucker 1964) of the methods proposed on artificially constructed populations with random error.

Nonsampling errors in sample surveys

Questionnaires. Questionnaires themselves present many sources of bias, of which the wording of questions and the options offered as answers are especially important. Some topics discussed below ("Panel studies," "Nonresponse," and "Response error") also treat questionnaire matters. [*See especially* SAMPLE SURVEYS; SURVEY ANALYSIS; *see also* INTERVIEWING.]

Wording. The wording and position of questions on questionnaires used in public opinion polls and other investigations illustrate the difficulties surrounding the notion of true value mentioned earlier. Rugg and Cantril's survey article (1944) analyzes and illustrates the effects of the manner of questioning on responses. For example, prior to the U.S. entry into World War II, variations on a question about American aid to Great Britain, asked of American citizens within a period of about six weeks, produced the following percentages in favor of the "interventionist" position: 76, 73, 58, 78, 74, 56. Here the interventionist position meant approval of "giving aid even at the risk of war." At much the same time, unqualified questions about "entering the war immediately" produced the following percentages in favor, 22, 17, 8, numbers

Table 1

11	5	29	26	3
1	19	14	4	20
24	25	27	6	9
30	15	13	18	12
28	22	7	8	17
2	21	16	10	23

substantially different from those in the previous set. Although one would be hard put to choose a number to represent degree of support for intervention, the interval 55 to 80 per cent gives a range; this range was clearly higher than that in support of entering the war immediately.

Pilot studies of the wordings of questions test their meaning and clarity for the intended population. Phillip Rulon recalls interviews with very bright second graders from a geography class to discuss a test item that they had "missed": "Wind-eroded rocks are most commonly found in the (*a*) deserts, (*b*) mountains, (*c*) valleys." They chose "valleys" because few people would *find* wind-eroded rocks in the mountains or the deserts, however many such rocks might be in those places. After a question previously found to be unsatisfactory is reworded, bitter experience advises the testing of the new version.

In single surveys, one needs to employ a variety of questions to get at the stability and meaning of the response. The use of "split ballots" (similar but modified questionnaires administered to equivalent samples of individuals) offers a way to experiment and to control for position and wording.

Changing opinions.   To ignore the results of the polls because of the considerable variation in responses would be as big a mistake as to adopt their numbers without healthy skepticism. Since opinion in time of crisis may move rapidly, it is easy to misappraise the tenor of the times without a systematic measuring device. For example, between July 1940 and September 1941, the per cent of U.S. citizens saying that they were willing to risk war with Japan rather than to let it continue its aggression rose from 12 to 65 per cent. Again, although in June 1940 only 35 per cent thought it more important to help England than to keep out of war, by September 1940 the percentage had risen to the 50s (Cantril 1944, p. 222). In September 1940, President Roosevelt made a deal that gave Great Britain 50 destroyers in return for leases of bases (Leuchtenburg 1963, pp. 303–304); in the face of the fluctuations of public opinion a historian considering the destroyer deal might easily believe that Roosevelt acted against, rather than with, the majority. (As I recall from experience at the Office of Public Opinion Research, Roosevelt had his own personal polls taken regularly, with reports submitted directly to him, usually on a single question.)

Seemingly minor variations in questions may change the responses a good deal, and so to study changes over time, one needs to use one well-chosen question (or sequence) again and again.

Naturally, such a question may come under attack as not getting at the "true value." If the question is to be changed, then, to get some parallel figures, it and the new question should be used simultaneously for a while.

Intercultural investigations.   Considering the difficulty of getting at opinions and the dependence of responses upon the wording of the questions asked, even within a country, the problem of obtaining comparable cross-cultural or cross-national views looks horrendous. Scholars planning such studies will want to see three novel works. Kluckhohn and Strodtbeck's (1961) sociological and anthropological *Variations in Value Orientations* especially exploits ranking methods in the comparison of value orientations in Spanish-American, Mormon, Texas, Zuñi, and Navajo communities. Subjects describe the many values of their culture by ordering their preferences, for example, for ways of bringing up children: past (the old ways), present (today's ways), or future (how to find new ways to replace the old). Cantril's (1966) social-psychological and internationally oriented *Pattern of Human Concerns* uses rating methods and sample surveys to compare values and satisfactions in the populations of 15 nations. For example, the respondent's rating, on a scale of 0 to 10, expresses his view of how nearly he or his society has achieved the goal inquired about, and another rating evaluates how much either might expect to advance in five years. In international economics, measurements may be more easily compared, although the economist may be forced to settle for measuring the measurable as an index of what he would like to evaluate. Harbison and Myers' study, *Education, Manpower, and Economic Growth* (1964), illustrates this approach.

Panel studies.   Although the single sample survey can be of great value, in some problems it is desirable to study the changes in the same people through time. The set of people chosen for repeated investigation is called a panel. One advantage of the panel study over the single survey is the deeper analysis available. For instance, when a net 5 per cent change takes place, does this mean that only 5 per cent of the people changed, or perhaps that 15 per cent changed one way and 10 per cent another? Second, additional measurement precision comes from matching responses from one interview to another. Third, panel studies offer flexibility that allows later inquiries to help explain earlier findings. [*See* PANEL STUDIES.]

Dropouts.   Panel studies, even when they start out on an unbiased sample, have the bias that the less informed, the lower-income groups, and those not interested in the subject of the panel tend to drop out. Sobol (1959) suggested sampling these people more heavily to begin with, and she tried to follow movers. According to Seymour Sudman of the National Opinion Research Center, in national consumer panels and television rating panels where a fee is paid to the participant, the lower-income groups do not drop out.

Beginning effects. When new individuals or households first join a panel, their early responses may differ from their later ones. The "first-month" effect has unknown origins. For example, after the first month on the panel, the fraction of unemployed reported in private households decreases about 6 per cent. Over the course of several panel interviews, more houses become vacant and consumer buying decreases (Neter & Waksberg 1964a; Waksberg & Pearl 1964). Household repairs decreased by 9 per cent between the second and third interview. In consumer panels, the reports made during the first six or eight weeks of membership are usually not included in the analysis. The start-up differences are not clear-cut and emphatic but unsettling enough that the data are set aside, expensive as that is.

Sample surveys are not alone in these "first-time" effects. Doctors report that patients' blood pressures are higher when taken by a strange doctor. In the Peirce reaction-time data, presented in Table 4, the first day's average reaction time was about twice those of the other 23 days.

Long-run effects. A most encouraging finding in consumer panel studies has been the stability of the behavior of the panelists. By taking advantage of the process of enlarging two panels, Ehrenberg (1960) studied the effects of length of panel membership in Great Britain and in Holland. When he compared reports of newly recruited households (after their first few weeks) with those of "old" panel members, he found close agreement for purchasing rates, brand shares of market, and diary entries per week.

Panels do have to be adjusted to reflect changes in the universe, and panel families dissolve and multiply.

Nonresponse. The general problem of nonresponse arises because the properties of the nonrespondents usually differ to some degree from those of respondents. Unfortunately, nonresponse is not confined to studies of human populations. Physical objects can be inaccessible for various reasons: records may be lost, manholes may be paved over, a chosen area may be in dense jungle, or the object may be too small to be detected. One tries to reduce nonresponse, adjust estimates for it, and allow for it in measures of variability.

Mail questionnaires. The following advice, largely drawn from Levine and Gordon (1958–1959) and Scott (1961), is intended to increase response from mail questionnaires:

(1) Respondent should be convinced that the project is important.

(2) Preparatory letter should be on the letterhead of a well-known organization or, where appropriate, should be signed by a well-known person. In the United States and in Great Britain, governmental agencies are more likely to obtain responses than most organizations. Indeed, Scott (1961) reports 90 per cent response! Special populations respond to appeals from their organizations.

In pilot studies preparatory to using mailed census questionnaires in the initial stage of enumeration for the 1970 census (enumerator to follow up nonrespondents), the U.S. Bureau of the Census got the percentages of responses to the mailing shown in Table 2.

Table 2

| | PERCENTAGE OF RESPONSE | |
	Long form	Short form
Cleveland, Ohio	78	80
Louisville, Kentucky	85	88

(3) Rewards may be used (gifts, trading stamps, sweepstakes). Do not offer a copy of the final report unless you are prepared to give it.

(4) Make questionnaire attractive (printing on good paper is preferred), easy to read, and easy to fill in, remembering that many people have trouble reading fine print. Longer questionnaires usually lower the response rate.

(5) Keep questions simple, clear, as short as possible, and where multiple-choice answers appear, make sure that they do not force respondent to choose answers that do not represent his position.

(6) Try to keep early questions interesting and easy; do not leave important questions to the end; keep related questions together, unless there are strong reasons to act otherwise.

(7) Use a high class of mail, first-class, airmail, and even special delivery, both for sending the questionnaire and on the return envelope. Do not expect respondent to provide postage. In Great Britain, Scott (1961) found that compared with a postcard a card to be returned in an envelope raised response.

(8) Follow hard-core resistance with repeat questionnaire (the sixth mailing may still be rewarding), telegram, long-distance phone call, or even personal interview, as discussed below. Small response from early mailings may be badly biased;

for example, successful hunters respond more readily than unsuccessful ones to questions about their bag (Kish 1965, p. 547).

(9) Do not promise or imply anonymity and then retain the respondent's identity by subterfuge, however worthy the cause. Views on the effects of anonymity are mixed. If respondent's identity is needed, get it openly.

The principles set out above for mail questionnaires and those below for personal interviews may well be culture-bound for they are largely gathered from Western, English-speaking experience. For example, where paper is expensive, questionnaires on better paper may be less likely to be returned than those on poorer paper.

Sample surveys using personal interviews. In personal interviews, 80 to 90 per cent response has been attained even on intimate topics. In 1966, 85 per cent was regarded as rather good for pre-designated respondents in household surveys. In addition to the relevant maxims given above for mail surveys, to reduce nonresponse in personal interview surveys Sharp and Feldt (1959), among others, suggest some of the following:

(1) Send preview letter; use press to announce survey. In three lengthy surveys on different topics, according to Reuben Cohen of the Opinion Research Corporation, a letter sent in advance led to an average gain of 9 per cent in reaching, after four calls, urban adult respondents randomly drawn from the household list. Cohen also suggests that follow-up letters, after unsuccessful interviewing attempts, can reduce urban nonresponse by about one-third. Some students of polling believe that the actual impact of the preview letter is largely on the interviewer, who thinks that obtaining cooperation will be easier because of it—and so it is.

(2) Use trained interviewers, that is, interviewers trained especially to handle opening remarks, to explain the need for full coverage, and to get information about profitable times to make later calls ("callbacks") to reach respondents who are initially not at home. Experienced interviewers have had 3 per cent to 13 per cent fewer nonrespondents than inexperienced ones.

(3) Be flexible about calling at convenience of respondent, even at his place of work or recreation, on evenings and on week ends.

(4) Allow interviewer to call back many times to locate assigned respondent.

(5) Employ interpreter when appropriate.

(6) In more esoteric situations, know the culture. Do not plan to interview farmers in the peak periods of farm activity. An anthropologist scheduled a survey of current sexual behavior among

South Sea islanders during the season when women were taboo to fishermen—the natives, finding it a great joke, were slow to explain.

Extra effort. When a survey carried out in the usual way produces a surprisingly large nonresponse, an all-out effort may be mounted using many of the devices mentioned earlier. A rule of thumb is that the nonresponse can be reduced by about half.

Oversampling nonrespondents. Repeated callbacks are the traditional method for reducing nonresponse in personal interviews, and careful cost analysis has shown that their cost per completed interview is lower than was at first supposed when quota sampling was popular. Kish and Hess (1959) report a procedure for including in the current sample nonrespondents from similar previous surveys, so as to have in advance an oversupply of persons likely not to respond. Then the sample survey, although getting responses from these people at a lower rate than from others, more nearly fills out its quotas.

Subsampling nonrespondents. To reduce nonresponse in mail surveys, subsampling the nonrespondents and pursuing them with personal interviews has been used frequently (formulas for optimum design are given in Hansen & Hurwitz 1946). In methods thus far developed the assumption is made that nonrespondents can surely be interviewed. When this assumption is unjustified, the method is less valid.

Adjusting for respondents not at home. The next method adjusts for those not at home but does not handle refusals, which often come to about half the nonresponse. Bartholomew (1961) has got accurate results by assuming that most of the bias arises from the composition of the population available at the first call. By finding out when to call back, the interviewer reduces later biases from this source. The interviewer gets information either from others in the house or from neighbors. To illustrate, in empirical investigations of populations of known composition, Bartholomew studied the percentage of men in political wards of a city. In four wards, differences between first-call and second-call samples in percentage of men were 17 per cent, 29 per cent, 36 per cent, and 38 per cent, substantial differences. But the differences between the second-call percentage of men and the actual percentage of men not reached by the first call were only 6 per cent, 2 per cent, 2 per cent, and 2 per cent, supporting Bartholomew's point.

Suppose that proportion p of the population has the characteristic of interest. It is convenient to regard p as the weighted average $\rho p_1 + (1 - \rho)p_2$, where ρ is the proportion of first-call responders in the population, p_1 is the proportion of first-call responders having the characteristic, and p_2 is the proportion of others in the population having the characteristic. (It is assumed that p_2 is independent of response status after the first call.) Now if N, the total sample size, is expressed as $N = N_1 + N_2 + N_3$, where N_1 is the number of first-call responders in the sample, N_2 is the number of second-call (but not first-call) responders in the sample, and N_3 is the number of others, then p is naturally estimated by N_1/N (the proportion of first-call responders in the sample), and p_1 by n_1/N_1 (the proportion of first-call responders in the sample who have the characteristic) and p_2 by n_2/N_2 (the proportion of second-call responders in the sample having the characteristic). Putting these estimators in the weighted average gives, as estimator of p,

$$\frac{1}{N}\left[n_1 + \frac{n_2(N - N_1)}{N_2} \right].$$

For example, if the number of men in the first call is $n_1 = 40$ out of $N_1 = 200$ interviewed, the second-call data are $n_2 = 200$, $N_2 = 400$, and the original sample size is $N = 1{,}000$, then the estimate of the proportion of men is 0.44. Even if the theory were exactly true, some increase in variance would arise from using such weights instead of obtaining the whole sample (Kish 1965, secs. 11.7B, 11.7C).

Extrapolation. Hendricks (1956) suggests plotting the variable being measured against the percentage of the sample that has responded on successive waves and extrapolating to 100 per cent. This simple, sensible idea could profit from more research, empirical and theoretical.

Effect on confidence interval. In sample surveys, nonresponse increases the lengths of the confidence intervals for final estimates by unknown amounts. For dichotomous types of questions, the suggestion is often made that all the nonresponses be counted first as having the attribute, then as not having it. The effect on the 95 per cent confidence interval is shown in Table 3. When such extreme allowances are required, the result of, say, 20 per cent nonresponse is frequently disastrous. For large random samples, this treatment of nonresponse, as may be seen from Table 3, adds approximately the per cent of nonresponse to the total length of the confidence interval that would have been appropriate with 100 per cent response. For example, with a sample of 2,500 from a large population, a 95 per cent confidence interval from 58 per cent to 62 per cent would be lengthened by 20 per cent nonresponse to 48.5 per cent to 71.5 per cent. This additional length gives motivation enough for wanting to keep nonresponse low.

Table 3 — Allowance to be added to and subtracted from the observed percentage to give at least 95 per cent confidence of covering the true value*

PER CENT NONRESPONSE	SAMPLE SIZE		
	100	2,500	Infinite
0	9.8	2.0	0.0
5	10.7	4.1	2.5
10	12.9	6.6	5.0
15	15.1	9.0	7.5
20	17.4	11.5	10.0

* These numbers are approximately correct for percentages near 0.50; they are likely to be conservative otherwise.

Source: Cochran, Mosteller, and Tukey 1954, p. 280.

No one believes that these "worst possible" limits represent the true state of affairs, nor should anyone believe the optimist who supposes that the nonrespondents are just like the respondents. In large samples, differences as large as 28 per cent in the fraction possessing a characteristic between the first 60 per cent interviewed and the next 25 per cent have been reported. To develop a more sensible set of limits in the spirit of Bayesian inference would be a useful research job for sample survey workers and theoretical statisticians. [See BAYESIAN INFERENCE.] This urgently needed work would require both empirical information (possibly newly gathered) and theoretical development.

The laboratory worker who studies human behavior rarely has a defined target population and he frequently works with a sample of volunteers. Under such circumstances we cannot even guess the extent of nonresponse. Again the hope is that the property being studied is independent of willingness or opportunity to serve as a subject—the position of the optimist mentioned above.

Since a few experimenters do sample defined populations, the argument that such sampling is impossible has lost some of its strength. The argument that such sampling is too expensive has to be appraised along with the value of inferences drawn from the behavior of undefined sampled populations.

Studying differences between groups offers more grounds for hope that bias from nonresponse works in the same direction and in nearly the same amount in both groups and that the difference may still be nearly right. This idea comes partly from physical measurements where sometimes knowledge can make such arguments about compensating errors rigorous. But, as Joseph Berkson warns, no general theorem states "Given any two wrong numbers, their difference is right."

Response error. When incorrect information about the respondent enters the data, a response error occurs. Among the many causes are misunderstandings, failures of memory, clerical errors, or deliberate falsehoods. The magnitudes of some of these errors and some ways to reduce them are discussed below.

Telescoping events. In reporting such things as amount of broken crockery or expenditures for household repairs, some respondents telescope the events of a considerable period into the shorter one under study. As a possible cure, Neter and Waksberg (1964*b*) have introduced a device called "bounded recall." In a study of household repairs, the respondent was interviewed twice, first under unbounded recall, during which the full story of the last month, including the telescoping from previous months, was recorded by the interviewer. Second, in an interview using bounded recall a month later, the respondent was deliberately aided by the record of repairs from the first interview. The magnitudes of the effects of telescoping are considerable, because the "unbounded" interview for household repairs gave 40 per cent more jobs and 55 per cent higher expenditure than did the "bounded" interview. Data from a "bounded" interview produce less bias.

Forgetting. Although telescoping occurs for some activities, chronic illness (Feldman 1960), which had already been clinically diagnosed, was reported only at a 25 per cent rate in household interviews. Others report rates in the 40 per cent to 50 per cent range. Feldman despairs of the household interview for this purpose; but if improvement in reports is to be attempted, he recommends more frequent interviews by competent, trained interviewers and, in a panel study, the use of a morbidity diary to improve self-reporting. One limitation, not attributable to forgetting, is set because physicians choose not to inform their patients of every illness they diagnose.

Sudman (1964) compared consumer panel reports based upon diary records with reports based upon unaided recall. First, he shows that for 72 grocery products (55 being food), the purchases recorded in the diary underestimate the amount shipped by the manufacturer (after adjustment for nonhousehold use) by a median of about 15 per cent. The underreporting was highly predictable, depending on both the properties of the product (frequency of purchase, where most often purchased) and its treatment in the diary (type size, page number, position on page). Second, when recall was compared with diary, the median ratio of purchases (purchases recalled divided by purchases in diary) was 1.05 for nonfood products, 1.83 for perishable food, 1.54 for staple foods. Leading nationally advertised brands have their

market shares overstated under recall by 50 per cent compared to diary records, and chain brands are understated.

Use of experts. After respondents had valued their own homes, Kish and Lansing (1954) obtained expert appraisals for a sample of the homes. The comparison of the experts' appraisal with the homeowners' appraisal can be used to adjust the total valuation or to adjust valuations for groups of houses. For example, the homeowners may average a few per cent too high.

Editing records. Whenever a comparison of related records can be made, the accuracy of records can probably be improved. For example, Census Bureau editors, experienced in the lumber business, check annual sawmill production reports against those of the previous year, and large changes are rechecked with the sawmill.

Describing response errors. One common measure in the analysis of nonsampling errors puts bias and sampling variability into one index, called the mean square error. The larger the mean square error, the worse the estimate. The mean square error is the expected squared deviation of the observed value from the true value. This quantity can be separated into the sum of two parts, the variance of the observation around its own mean and the square of the bias. Although true values are not available, in the United States, the Bureau of the Census, for instance, tries to find standards more accurate than the census to get an estimate of the response bias to particular questions. For example, using the Current Population Survey as a standard, the Bureau of the Census not only finds out that the census underestimates the percentage in the labor force, but the bureau also gets data on the portions of the population not being satisfactorily measured, either because of variability or bias. Using such information, the bureau can profitably redesign its inquiries because it knows where and how to spend its resources.

Response uncertainty. In attitudinal studies (Katz 1946), the investigator must be especially wary of reports obtained by polling the public on a matter where opinion is not crystallized. The No Opinion category offers one symptom of trouble: for example, Katz reports that in 1945 only 4 per cent had No Opinion about universal military training in the United States, 13 per cent had No Opinion about giving the atom bomb secret to the United Nations, and 32 per cent had No Opinion about U.S. Senate approval of the United Nations charter. Even though the vote was 66 per cent to 3 per cent in favor of approving the charter, the 32 per cent No Opinion must suggest that the 69 per cent who offered an opinion contained a large subgroup who also did not hold a well-formed opinion.

Errors in analysis

Troubles with variability. In analyzing data, the presence of variability leads to many unsuspected difficulties and effects. In addition to treating some of the common traps, this section gives two ways to analyze variability in complicated problems where theoretical formulas for variance are either unavailable or should be distrusted.

Inflated sample size. The investigator must frequently decide what unit shall be regarded as independent of what other unit. For example, in analyzing a set of responses made by 10 individuals, each providing 100 responses, it is a common error to use as the sample size $10 \times 100 = 1,000$ responses and to make calculations, based perhaps on the binomial distribution, as if all these responses were independent. Unless investigation has shown that the situation is one in which independence does hold from response to response both within and between individuals, distrust this procedure. The analysis of variance offers some ways to appraise both the variability of an individual through time and the variation between individuals.

Use of matched individuals. Some investigators fail to take advantage of the matching in their data. Billewicz (1965, p. 623) reports that in 9 of 20 investigations that he examined for which the data were gathered from matched members in experimental and control groups, the analysis was done as if the data were from independent groups. Usually the investigator will have sacrificed considerable precision by not taking advantage in his analysis of the correlation in the data. Usually, but not always, the statistical significance of the results will be conservative. When matched data are analyzed as if independent, the investigator owes the reader an explanation for the decision.

Pooling significance tests. In the same vein, investigators with several small effects naturally wish that they could pool these effects to get more extreme levels of significance than those given by the single effects. Most methods of pooling significance tests depend upon independence between the several measures going into the pool. And that assumption implies, for example, that data from several items on the same sample survey cannot ordinarily be combined into a significance test by the usual pooling methods because independence cannot be assured. Correlation is almost certainly present because the same individuals respond to each item. Sometimes a remedy is to form a battery or scale that includes the several items of interest and to make a new test based upon the battery (Mosteller & Bush 1954, pp. 328–331). Naturally, the items would be chosen in advance for the purpose, not based *post hoc* upon their results. In the latter case, the investigator faces problems of multiplicity, discussed below.

Outlying observations. Frequently data contain suspicious observations that may be outliers, observations that cannot be rechecked, and yet that may considerably alter the interpretation of the data when taken at their face value. An outlier is an observation that deviates much more from the average of its mates or has a larger residual from a predicted value than seems reasonable on the basis of the pattern of the rest of the measurements. The classic example is given by the income distribution for members of a small college freshman class, exactly one member of which happens to be a multimillionaire. The arithmetic mean is not typical of the average member's income; but the median almost ignores an amount of income that exceeds the total for all the others in the class. Sometimes the outliers can be set aside for special study.

One current approach tailors the analysis to the type of outlier that is common in the particular kind of investigation by choosing statistics that are both appropriate and not especially sensitive to outliers. For example, as a measure of location, one might systematically use the median rather than the mean, or for more efficiency, the trimmed mean, which is the average of the measurements left after the largest and smallest 5 per cent (or 100α per cent) of the measurements have been removed (Mosteller & Tukey 1966, secs. $A5$, $B5$). In normal populations, the median has an efficiency of about 64 per cent, but the trimmed mean has most of the robustness of the median and an efficiency of about $1 - \frac{2}{3}\alpha$, where α is the proportion trimmed off each end. For $\alpha = 0.10$, the efficiency is 93 per cent. [*See* ERRORS, *article on the* EFFECTS OF ERRORS IN STATISTICAL ASSUMPTIONS; NONPARAMETRIC STATISTICS, *article on* ORDER STATISTICS; STATISTICAL ANALYSIS, SPECIAL PROBLEMS OF, *article on* OUTLIERS.]

Shifting regression coefficients. When one fits a regression equation to data, this regression equation may not forecast well for a new set of data. Among the reasons are the following:

(1) The fitted regression coefficients are not true values but estimates (sampling error).

(2) If one has selected the best from among many predictive variables, the selected ones may not be as good as they appeared to be on the basis of the sample (regression effect).

(3) Worse, perhaps none of the predictive variables were any good to start with (bad luck or poor planning).

(4) The procedure used to choose the form of the regression curve (linear, quadratic, exponential, . . .) has leaned too hard on the previously available data, and represents them too well as compared with the total population (wrong form).

(5) The new sample may be drawn from a population different from the old one (shifting population).

What are the effects of (2) and (5)? Consider the regression of height (Y) on weight (X) for a population of boys. Suppose that the true regression equation for this population is

$$E(Y) = a + b(X - \mu_x),$$

where a and b are unknown constants, $E(Y)$ is the expected value of Y for a given value of X, and μ_x is the mean of X. Suppose that an individual's height has a predictive error e that has mean 0, variance σ^2, and is unrelated to X, Y, and the true values of a and b.

Suppose that the experimenter chooses fixed values of X, x_i, such as 70, 80, 90, 100, 110, 120, 130, 140 pounds, obtaining boys having each of these weights and measuring their heights y_i. Then the data are paired observations (x_i, y_i), $i = 1, 2, \cdots, n$.

Estimating a and b from the sample by the usual least squares formulas one gets $\hat{a}$ and $\hat{b}$. Given a new sample with the same values of X from the same population, one can estimate the Y's for the new sample by

$$\hat{Y}_i = \hat{a} + \hat{b}(x_i - \bar{x}),$$

(where $\bar{x}$ is the average of the X_i) and then the expected mean square error of the estimates for the new sample is

expected value of $\sum(Y'_i - \hat{Y}_i)^2/n = \sigma^2(1 + 2/n)$,

where Y'_i is the height for an individual in the new sample. Note that σ^2 is the expected mean square error that would obtain were a and b known exactly instead of having been estimated.

Suppose that in addition to this population, there is a new population with different values of a and b, say a' and b'. Both populations come from a group of several populations with a and b varying from population to population and having $\bar{a}$ and $\bar{b}$ as the mean values of a and b, respectively, and σ_a^2 and σ_b^2 as the variances of these sets of regression coefficients. For the example of the boys' weights, consider the distribution of values of a and b from one city to another.

The regression line fitted on the basis of the sample from one population and then used on another population yields expected mean square error

$$\left(1 + \frac{2}{n}\right)\sigma^2 + 2(\sigma_a^2 + \sigma_x^2\sigma_b^2),$$

where σ_x^2 is the variance of the chosen set of x's. The first term comes as before from ordinary sampling variation of the Y's around the fitted regression line (the 2 of $2/n$ being the dimension of the parameter space), but the $2(\sigma_a^2 + \sigma_x^2\sigma_b^2)$ comes from drawing two sets of regression coefficients from the population of regression coefficients. This term may be substantial compared to $2\sigma^2/n$ or even σ^2.

We need extensive empirical results for such experiments to get a notion of the size of $2(\sigma_a^2 + \sigma_x^2\sigma_b^2)$ in various settings of interest to social and natural scientists. These investigations have not yet been carried out. The formulas for mean square error in this realistic situation must cause concern until more empirical studies are done. The existence of the added term should be recognized and an attempt made to assess its contribution numerically.

Uncontrolled sources of variation.   Although the important formula $\sigma_{\bar{x}} = \sigma/\sqrt{n}$ for the standard deviation of a mean $\bar{X}$, a random variable, is correct when n uncorrelated measurements are drawn from a distribution with standard deviation σ, two difficulties arise. The measurements may not be uncorrelated, and the distribution may change from one set of measurements to another.

Peirce's data illustrate these difficulties. In an empirical study intended to test the appropriateness of the normal distribution, C. S. Peirce (1873) analyzed the time elapsed between a sharp tone stimulus and the response by an observer, who made about 500 responses each day for 24 days. Wilson and Hilferty (1929) reanalyzed Peirce's data. Table 4 shows sample means, $\bar{x}$, estimated standard deviations of the mean $s_{\bar{x}}$, and the ratio of the observed to the estimated interquartile range, $Q_3 - Q_1$. The observed interquartile range is based on percentage points of the observed distribution; the estimated interquartile range is based on the assumption of a normal distribution and has the value $2(0.6745s)$, where s is the sample standard deviation. In passing, note that the ratio is systematically much less than unity, defying the normality assumption. More salient for this discussion is the relation of day-to-day variation to the values of $s_{\bar{x}}$ based on within-day variation. The latter varies from 1.1 to 2.2 (after the first day's data, whose mean and standard deviation are obviously outliers, are set aside). These limits imply naive standard

Table 4 — Daily statistics from Wilson and Hilferty's analysis of C. S. Peirce's data

Day	$\bar{x} \pm s_{\bar{x}}$ (milliseconds)	$\dfrac{Q_3 - Q_1}{2(0.6745s)}$
1	475.6 ± 4.2	0.932
2	241.5 ± 2.1	0.842
3	203.1 ± 2.0	0.905
4	205.6 ± 1.8	0.730
5	148.5 ± 1.6	0.912
6	175.6 ± 1.8	0.744
7	186.9 ± 2.2	0.753
8	194.1 ± 1.4	0.840
9	195.8 ± 1.6	0.756
10	215.5 ± 1.3	0.850
11	216.6 ± 1.7	0.782
12	235.6 ± 1.7	0.759
13	244.5 ± 1.2	0.922
14	236.7 ± 1.8	0.529
15	236.0 ± 1.4	0.662
16	233.2 ± 1.7	0.612
17	265.5 ± 1.7	0.792
18	253.0 ± 1.1	0.959
19	258.7 ± 1.8	0.502
20	255.4 ± 2.0	0.521
21	245.0 ± 1.2	0.790
22	255.6 ± 1.4	0.688
23	251.4 ± 1.6	0.610
24	243.4 ± 1 1	0.730

Source: Wilson & Hilferty 1929.

deviations of the difference between means for pairs of days ranging from 1.6 to 3.1. If these applied, most differences would have to be less than twice these, 3.2 to 6.2, and practically all less than 4.8 to 9.3. Table 4 shows that the actual differences −38, +2, −57, +27, ⋯, +11, −4, −8 impolitely pay little attention to such limitations.

In the language of analysis of variance, Peirce's data show considerable day-to-day variation. In the language of Walter Shewhart, such data are "out of control"—the within-day variation does not properly predict the between-days variation [see QUALITY CONTROL, *article on* PROCESS CONTROL]. Nor is it just a matter of the observer "settling down" in the beginning. Even after the twentieth day he still wobbles.

Need for a plurality of samples. The wavering in these data exemplifies the history of the "personal equation" problem of astronomy. The hope had been that each observer's systematic errors could be first stabilized and then adjusted for, thus improving accuracy. Unfortunately, attempts in this direction have failed repeatedly, as these data suggest they might. The observer's daily idiosyncrasies need to be recognized, at least by assigning additional day-to-day variation.

Wilson and Hilferty (1929, p. 125) emphasize that Peirce's data illustrate "the principle that we must have a plurality of samples if we wish to

estimate the variability of some statistical quantity, and that reliance on such formula as $\sigma / \sqrt{n}$ is not scientifically satisfactory in practice, even for estimating unreliability of means" (see Table 4).

Direct assessment of variability. One way to get a more honest estimate of variability breaks the data into rational subgroups, usually of equal or nearly equal sizes. For each subgroup, compute the statistic (mean, median, correlation coefficient, spectral density, regression equation, or whatever), base the estimate for the whole group on the average of the statistic for the subgroups, and base the estimate of variability on Student's t with one degree of freedom less than the number of subgroups. That is, treat the k group statistics like a sample of k independent measurements from a normal distribution. [*This method, sometimes called the method of interpenetrating samples, generalizes the method for calculating the sampling error for non-probability samples described in* SAMPLE SURVEYS, *article on* NONPROBABILITY SAMPLING.]

At least five groups (preferably at least ten) are advisable in order to get past the worst part of the t-table. This suggestion encourages using more, not fewer, groups. For two-sided 5 per cent levels, see Table 5.

Two major difficulties with this direct assessment are (a) that it may not be feasible to calculate meaningful results for such small amounts of data as properly chosen groups would provide, or (b) even if the calculations yield sensible results, they may be so severely biased as to make their use unwise.

A method with wide application, intended to ameliorate these problems, is the *jackknife*, which offers ways to reduce bias in the estimate and to set realistic approximate confidence limits in complex situations.

Assessment by the jackknife. Again the data are divided into groups, but the statistic to be jackknifed is computed repeatedly on all the data except an omitted group. With ten groups, the statistic is

Table 5 — Two-sided 5 per cent levels for Student's t for selected degrees of freedom

Degrees of freedom	5 per cent critical point
1	12.7
2	4.3
3	3.2
5	2.6
10	2.23
20	2.09
60	2.00
500	1.96
∞	1.96

computed each time for about 90 per cent of the data.

More generally, for the jackknife, the desired calculation is made for all the data, and then, after the data are divided into groups, the calculation is made for each of the slightly reduced bodies of data obtained by leaving out just one of the groups.

Let $y_{(j)}$ be the result of making the complex calculation on the portion of the sample that omits the jth subgroup, that is, on a pool of $k-1$ subgroups. Let y_{all} be the corresponding result for the entire sample, and define *pseudo values* by

$$(1) \qquad y_{*j} = k y_{all} - (k-1) y_{(j)}, \qquad j = 1, 2, \cdots, k.$$

These pseudo values now play the role played by the values of the subgroup statistics in the method of interpenetrating samples. For simple means, the jackknife reduces to that method.

As in the method of interpenetrating samples, in a wide variety of problems, the pseudo values can be used to set approximate confidence limits through Student's t, as if they were the results of applying some complex calculation to each of k independent pieces of data.

The jackknifed value y_*, which is the best single result, and an estimate, s_*^2, of its variance are given by

$$y_* = \frac{1}{k}(y_{*1} + \cdots + y_{*k}),$$

$$s^2 = \left[\sum y_{*i}^2 - k y_*^2 \right] \Big/ (k-1),$$

$$s_*^2 = s^2/k.$$

If the statistic being computed has a bias that can be expressed as a series in the reciprocal of the sample size, N, the jackknife removes the leading term (that in $1/N$) in the bias. Specifically, suppose that $\hat{\mu}$, the biased estimate of μ, has expected value

$$E(\hat{\mu}) = \mu + \frac{a}{N} + \frac{b}{N^2} + \cdots,$$

where a, b, and so on are constants. If $\hat{\mu}_*$ is the jackknifed estimate, its expected value is

$$E(\hat{\mu}_*) = \mu + \frac{\alpha}{N^2} + \frac{\beta}{N^3} + \cdots,$$

where α, β, and so on are constants. To give a trivial example, $\sum (X_i - \bar{X})^2/N$ is a biased estimate of σ^2. Its expected value is $\sigma^2 - (\sigma^2/N)$, and so it has the sort of bias that would be removed by jackknifing.

To understand how the first-order bias terms are removed by jackknifing, one might compute the expected value of y_* for the special case where

$$E(\hat{\mu}) = \mu + a/N.$$

Then with the use of k groups of equal size, n, so that $kn = N$,

$$E(y_{(j)}) = \mu + a/(k-1)n$$
$$E(y_{all}) = \mu + a/kn$$
$$E(y_{*j}) = E[k y_{all} - (k-1) y_{(j)}]$$
$$\qquad = k\mu + a/n - [(k-1)\mu + a/n]$$
$$\qquad = \mu.$$

Finally,

$$E(y_*) = k\mu/k = \mu.$$

The leading term in the bias was removed in the construction of the y_{*j}'s. Even if the sample sizes are not equal, the leading term in the bias is likely to have its coefficient reduced considerably.

Example of the jackknife: ratio estimate. In expounding the use of ratio estimates, Cochran ([1953] 1963, p. 156) gives 1920 and 1930 sizes (number of inhabitants) for each city in a random sample of 49 drawn from a population of 196 large U.S. cities. He wishes to estimate the total 1930 population for these 196 cities on the basis of the results of the sample of 49, whose 1920 and 1930 populations are both known, and from the total 1920 population. The example randomly groups his 49 cities into 7 sets of 7 each. Table 6 shows their subtotals.

The formula for the ratio estimate of the 1930 population total is

$$\frac{(1930 \text{ sample total})}{(1920 \text{ sample total})} \times (1920 \text{ population total}),$$

so that the logarithm of the estimated 1930 population total is given by $\log(1930 \text{ sample total}) - \log(1920 \text{ sample total}) + \log(1920 \text{ population total})$. Consequently the jackknife is applied to $z = \log(1930 \text{ sample total}) - \log(1920 \text{ sample total})$, since this choice minimizes the number of multiplications and divisions.

Further computation is shown in Table 7 where in the "all" column the numbers 5,054 and 6,262 come directly from the totals of the previous table, and in the "$i = 1$" column the numbers $4,303 = 5,054 - 751$ and $5,347 = 6,262 - 915$ are the re-

Table 6 — Subtotals in thousands for sets of 7 cities

	1920	1930
First 7	751	915
Second 7	977	1,122
Third 7	965	1,243
Fourth 7	385	553
Fifth 7	696	881
Sixth 7	830	937
Seventh 7	450	611
Total	5,054	6,262

Source: Cochran [1953] 1963, p. 156.

Table 7 — Details of jackknifing the ratio estimate

	all	$i=1$	$i=2$	$i=3$	$i=4$	$i=5$	$i=6$	$i=7$
$x_{(i)}$ (1920 sample)	5,054	4,303	4,077	4,089	4,669	4,358	4,224	4,604
$\log x_{(i)}$	3.70364	3.63377	3.61034	3.61162	3.66922	3.63929	3.62572	3.66314
$y_{(i)}$ (1930 sample)	6,262	5,347	5,140	5,019	5,709	5,381	5,325	5,651
$\log y_{(i)}$	3.79671	3.72811	3.71096	3.70062	3.75656	3.73086	3.72632	3.75213
$z_{(i)} = \log [y_{(i)}/x_{(i)}]$	.09307	.09434	.10062	.08900	.08734	.09157	.10060	.08899
$z_{*i} = 7z_{all} - 6z_{(i)}$	—	.08545	.04777	.11749	.12745	.10207	.04789	.11755
rounded z_{*i}	—	.085	.048	.117	.127	.102	.048	.118

Sum $= .645$; $.645/7 \cong .092 =$ mean $= z_*$

Sum Sq. $= .065979$; $.065979 - (.645)^2/7 = .006547 =$ sum sq. deviations

$$\frac{.006547}{6 \times 7} \cong .00015588 = s_*^2$$

$$\sqrt{.00015588} \cong .0125 = s_*$$

$$|t_6|_{.95} = 2.447; \quad (.0125)\ (2.447) = .0306 = \text{allowance}$$

sults of omitting the first 7 cities, and so on for the other columns. Five-place logarithms have obviously given more than sufficient precision, so that the pseudo values of z are conveniently rounded to three decimals. From these are computed the mean z_* and the 95 per cent limits = mean ± allowance. Table 8 gives all the remaining details. The resulting point estimate is 28,300, about 100 lower than the unjackknifed estimate. (Since the correct 1930 total is 29,351, the automatic bias adjustment did not help in this instance. This is a reminder that bias is an "on the average" concept.) The limits on this estimate are ordinarily somewhat wider than would apply if each city had been used as a separate group, since the two-sided 95 per cent level for Student's t with 6 degrees of freedom is $|t_6|_{.95} = 2.447$, while with 47 degrees of freedom it is $|t_{47}|_{.95} = 2.012$. The standard error found here was .0125 in logarithmic units, which converts to about 840 in the final total ($4.360 + z_* + s_* = 4.464$; antilog $4.464 \cong 29,140$; $29,140 - 28,300 = 840$). The conversion from logarithmic units to original units for the confidence interval represent an approximation that may not always be appropriate [*see* STATISTICAL ANALYSIS, SPECIAL PROBLEMS OF, *article on* TRANSFORMATIONS OF DATA]. (Further material on the jackknife can be found in Mosteller and Tukey 1966, sec. *E*).

Table 8 — Final computations for the ratio estimate*

	VALUE OF ESTIMATE	95 PER CENT CONFIDENCE INTERVALS
log ratio	$z_* = 0.092$	0.062 to 0.123
log total	$4.360 + z_* = 4.452$	4.422 to 4.483
total	antilog $4.452 = 28,300$	26,000 to 30,400

* Base data: 1920 total = 22,919, log (1920 total) = 4.360
log total = log (1920 total) + log ratio

Analytical difficulties. In analyzing data or planning for its analysis, the choice of a base for rates is not always obvious; comparing many things leads to biases that need adjustment, selection reduces correlation, and selection for excellence leads to disappointments. This section treats these matters.

Bases for rates. The investigator should think about more than one possible base for a percentage or a rate and consider the value of reporting results using different bases. Examples from accident statistics may suffice. Are young women safer drivers than young men? Yes: in the United States in 1966 insurance rates for young women were ordinarily lower because they caused less expensive damage. On the other hand, these rates were based on total disbursements in a fixed period of time. Young women may well drive much less than young men, and if so, their accident rate per mile may be the higher.

Coppin, Ferdun, and Peck (1965) sent a questionnaire on driving in 1963 to a sample of 10,250 California drivers who were aged 16 to $19\frac{1}{2}$ at the beginning of the period. Based on the information from the 65 per cent of questionnaires returned, where respondents estimated mileage driven per week, and on accidents reported in the respondents' Motor Vehicle Department files, the accident rates per 100,000 miles shown in Table 9 were found. On accidents, nonrespondents were very similar to respondents, but nonrespondents had considerably more violations. Since the mileage is estimated, the evidence is weak; but it seems to be the best available. Boys had more accidents per mile at 16, girls at 17, and after that their rates were nearly equal.

How should airplane safety (or danger) be as-

Table 9 — Accidents and violations per 100,000 miles

	ACCIDENTS		VIOLATIONS	
Age	Males	Females	Males	Females
16	2.9	2.1	7.1	4.9
17	1.9	2.3	6.1	4.2
18	1.4	1.4	5.6	3.7
19	1.4	1.5	5.4	3.5

Source: Coppin et al. 1965, pp. 27–28.

sessed? Deaths per million passenger miles, deaths per trip, and casualties per hour flown suggest themselves, and each can be supported.

In general, different answers may be appropriate for different questions, as was the case in the insurance companies' view versus the accident-per-mile view of the safety of young drivers given above. Ease and economy may recommend giving several answers as well as the investigator's judgment about their merits. In some problems, no resolution may be possible, and then the investigator would do well to admit it.

Problems of multiplicity. When methods of appraisal designed for single comparisons are used to compare many things, the multiplicity may mislead. When means of two samples drawn from the same normal population are compared, they differ by more than twice the standard deviation of their difference in less than 5 per cent of the sample pairs. Among ten sample means from the same population, some pair is more likely than not to differ this much (Table 11). Although statistics has come a long way in providing honest methods of making comparisons when there are many to be made, it has largely done this in the framework of a closed system, where the particular items to be compared have already been specified. For example, many workers have offered suitable ways to measure the significance not only of all possible differences but also of all possible linear contrasts (weighted sums, the weights adding to zero) on the same data. [*See* LINEAR HYPOTHESES, *articles on* MULTIPLE COMPARISONS.]

Statistics has not yet provided a way to test the significance of results obtained by peeking at large bodies of data and developing hypotheses as one goes along. The facility of the human brain for rationalizing almost any observed fact immediately after its realization is something that cannot yet be allowed for. This means that it is rarely possible to validate a hypothesis on the same body of data that suggested it and usually new studies are necessary to test hypotheses developed on completely different data (Mosteller & Tukey 1966, sec. *B6*).

Selection effects. Users of tests for purposes of selection (admission to college, personnel selection) often complain that the scores used to make the selection do not correlate well with the in-service performance of the individuals after selection. Possibly the chosen test does not give scores that correlate well with the performance being measured, but one must remember that when a population is truncated on one of its variables, the correlation of that dimension with the others is likely to be reduced toward zero. To illustrate, suppose that freshman calculus grades Y and pre-course examination grades X are bivariately normally distributed with correlation coefficient ρ. Suppose that only individuals whose pretest scores exceed a certain value $X = x$ are admitted to the calculus course. This means that selection is based on the variable X with the criterion x. The new correlation ρ' between the grades of those taking the course and their pretest scores would be given (see Cochran 1951, p. 453) as

$$\rho' = \rho \sqrt{\frac{1 - A}{1 - A\rho^2}},$$

where

$$A = \frac{z}{p}\left(\frac{z}{p} - t\right),$$

$p =$ proportion that the selected group is of the whole population,

$t =$ standard normal deviate having proportion p to the right,

$z =$ height of the standard univariate normal at the position t.

If the proportion selected $p = 0.05$, then $t = 1.645$, $z = 0.1031$. Values of ρ' for selected values of ρ and p are shown in Table 10. To return to the example, if pretest scores and calculus grades had originally been correlated $\rho = 0.8$, in the 5 per cent selected the correlation would drop to 0.44.

Table 10 shows that as the percentage truncated increases the correlation in the remaining population slowly decreases from its initial value. For initial correlations between .1 and .8 the reduction is between a half and a third of the original correlation when 75 per cent of the population has been removed. A very rough approximation for ρ' is $(.7p + .3)\rho$ for $p > .25$ and $0 \leqslant \rho \leqslant .7$. The new correlation decreases sharply for the higher initial correlation coefficients when more than 90 per cent of the population is deleted. Unfortunately, these results may be rather sensitive to the detailed shape of the bivariate population studied and so this bivariate normal example can only illustrate the possibilities.

Table 10 — Values of ρ' for various values of 100(1−p), ρ pairs

100(1−p) PER CENT TRUNCATED	VALUES OF ρ							100p PER CENT SELECTED
	.100	.300	.500	.700	.800	.900	.950	
5	.090	.272	.461	.661	.768	.881	.939	95
10	.085	.256	.438	.637	.747	.867	.932	90
25	.073	.224	.389	.583	.698	.834	.912	75
50	.060	.186	.329	.509	.626	.780	.878	50
75	.049	.153	.273	.434	.548	.712	.831	25
90	.041	.128	.231	.374	.481	.647	.781	10
95	.037	.116	.210	.342	.444	.609	.749	5
99	.031	.098	.178	.293	.385	.542	.689	1

Regression effect.   Suppose that a fallible measure selects from many individuals a few that appear to be best. On a reassessment based on fresh performance data, the selected ones will ordinarily not do as well as they originally appeared to do on the selection test. The reason is that performance varies and on the occasion of the test some individuals accidentally perform much better than their average and are selected. Happily, individuals selected to be worst do not do as badly on reassessment. This phenomenon is known as regression toward the mean; instances are sometimes called regression effects or shrinkage effects. To illustrate, Mosteller and Wallace (1964, p. 209) selected words and obtained weights for their rates of use with intent to discriminate between the writings of Alexander Hamilton and James Madison. Writers differ in their rate of use of such words as *of, and, the, to,* and *upon.* On the basis of the writings used for the selection and weighting of the word counts, the two statesmen's writings were separated by 6.9 standard deviations. When the same words and weights were applied to fresh writings not used in selecting or weighting, the new writings were separated by 4.5 standard deviations—still good discrimination, but a loss of 2.4 standard deviations is substantial and illustrates well the effect. Losses are usually greatest among the poorer discriminants. Usages of the word *upon* originally separated the writings by 3.3 standard deviations, and did even better, 3.8, in the fresh validating materials; but a less effective set of words giving originally a separation of 1.3 standard deviations dropped to 0.3 on retesting. The lesson is that optimization methods (such as least squares and maximum likelihood) do especially well on just the data used to optimize. Plan for validation, and, where hopes are high for much gain from many small effects, prepare for disappointment.

Weights.   If individuals are sampled to find out about their families, as in investigations carried out in schools, unless some account is taken of weights, a peculiar distribution may arise. For example, if a sample of girls is asked to report the numbers of sons and of daughters (including themselves) in their families, it turns out that the average number of daughters observed in the sample is approximately one more than the average number of sons. (More precisely, mathematics not given here shows the difference to be: [*variance of number of daughters* minus *covariance of number of sons and daughters*] divided by [*average number of daughters*]. When the distribution of the number of daughters is approximately Poisson and the numbers of sons and of daughters are independent, the ratio is approximately unity.) Essentially, families of three girls report three times as often as families with one girl, and families with no girls do not report at all. If account is taken of the dependence of frequency of reporting upon the number of daughters, this matter can be adjusted, provided information about families with no daughters is available or is not needed.

Similarly, in studying the composition of special groups, unless the analysis is done separately for each family size, one needs to remember that more children are first-born than second, and so on.

Errors in calculation.   A well-planned format for laying out calculations and careful checking aid in getting correct answers. To give a base line, a sample survey by the Internal Revenue Service (Farioletti 1952, pp. 65–78) found arithmetical errors in only 6 per cent of 160,000 personal income tax returns. Considering that the task is sometimes troublesome and often resented, this record appears good.

In scientific work, misreadings of numbers, misplaced decimals, errors in the application of formulas all take their toll. As a first step in the control of error, regard any unchecked calculation as probably wrong.

Overmechanization.   Overmechanization of computing puts great pressure on the analyst to make one enormous run of the data and thereby economically get all the analyses he wished. Alas, one great sweep is never the way of good data analysis. Instead, we learn a little from each analysis and return again and again. To illustrate, in deciding whether to transform the data to square roots, logarithms, inverse sines, or reciprocals before launching on the major analysis, tests may be run for each function separately, leading to the choice of one or two transformations for use in the next stage. Otherwise the whole large calculation must be run too many times because there are many branch points in a large calculation with several choices available at each. Furthermore, data analysis requires extensive printout, little of which will be looked at; therefore the data analyst must resist the notion that the good computer user makes the machine do all the work internally and obtains very little printout. He must also resist the idea of having ever speedier programs at the cost of more and more time for programming and less and less for analysis. Fine programs are needed, but the cost of additional machine time from slow programs may be less than the cost of improvements in programming and of the waiting time before analysis can begin.

Possibly with the increase of time-sharing in high-speed computation and the handy packaging of general purpose programs for the analysis of data, the opportunities for making studied choices at each point in the analysis will become easier and less time-consuming.

Preserving data from erasure. After processing, data should usually be preserved in some form other than a single magnetic tape. Contrary to theory and rumor, magnetic tapes containing basic data are occasionally erased or made unusable in the high-speed computing process, and all the explanations in the world about how this could or could not have happened cannot restore a bit of information. One remedy is to have a spare tape with your data or program copied upon it. When disaster strikes, remember that few things seem more likely to recur than a rare event that has just happened, and so copy your spare tape before you submit it to the destroyer.

Hand copying. Since human copying is a major source of error, keep hand copying to a minimum and take advantage where possible of the high-speed computer's ability to produce tables in immediately publishable form and of mechanical reproduction processes. Editing can be done by cutting, pasting, and painting out. When copying is necessary, checks of both column totals and row totals are believed superior to direct visual comparisons of individual entries with the manuscript.

Checks. Checking the programming and calculations of a high-speed computer presents a major unsolved problem. One might suppose that once a machine began producing correct answers, it always would thereafter. Not at all. It may respond to stimuli not dreamed of by the uninitiated. To find, for example, that it throws a small error into the fifth entry in the fourth column of every panel is disconcerting and scary, partly because small errors are hard to find and partly because one wonders whether undetected errors may still be present. Thorough and systematic checking is advised. Some ways are through sample problems; through fuller printout of the details of a problem already worked by hand; by comparing corresponding parts of several problems, including special cases whose answers are known by outside means; and by solving the problem in more than one way.

In addition to the checks on the final calculations, check the input data. For input punched on cards, for example, some process of verifying the punching is required. Methods of checking will vary with the problem. Partly redundant checking may not be wasteful. Look for impossible codes in columns, look for interchanges of columns. Try to set up checks for inconsistency in cards. (In Western cultures, nursery school children are not married, wives don't have wives, and families with 42 children need verification.) Consider ways to handle blanks based on internal consistency.

In working with computers, be wary of the way symbols translate from keyboard to card or tape—dashes and minus signs or zeros, letter O's, and blanks are a few sources of confusion. In dealing with numbers using, say, a two-digit field, a number such as 6, unless written 06, may wind up as 60 or as a meaningless character. The possibilities here are endless, but in a given problem it is usually worth organizing systematic procedures to combat these difficulties.

Order-of-magnitude checking. When calculations are complete, order-of-magnitude checks are always valuable. Are there more people in the state of New York than in the United States? Does leisure plus work plus sleep take much more than 24 hours per day? Exercises in calculations of comparative orders of magnitude can be rewarding in themselves because new connections are sometimes made between the research and the rest of the subject matter.

Significant figures. Both hand and high-speed calculations require numbers to be carried to more places than seem meaningful and to more places than simple rules learned in childhood would suggest. These rules seem dedicated to rounding early so as not to exaggerate the accuracy of one's result. But they may erase the signal with the noise. About the only reassuring rule for complex calculations is that if the important digits are the same when the calculation is carried to twice as many places, enough accuracy has likely been carried.

The old rules for handling significant figures come from a simplified idea that a number can report both its value and its accuracy at the same time. Under such rules the numbers 3.26 and 0.0326 were thought of as correct to within half a unit in the last place. Sometimes in mathematical tables this approach is satisfactory. For data-based numbers, the uncertainty in a number has to be reported separately.

One-of-a-kind calculations. One-of-a-kind calculations, frequent in scientific reports, are especially error prone, both because the investigator may not set up a standard method of calculation, complete with checks, and because he does not have the aid of comparisons with other members of a long sequence. For example, some pollsters believed that their wrong forecast about a vote would have been close had proper weighting for household size been applied, a claim worth checking. Their ultimate error was in thinking that this claim was right. How did they make it? Pages of weightings carefully checked down to, but not including, the final estimate showed no error in their reanalysis. But their one-of-a-kind calculation leading to the final estimate was a ratio composed of an inappropriate numerator and an inappropriate denominator grabbed from the many column totals. By accident this meaningless quotient gave a number nearly identical with that produced by the voters. And who checks further an answer believed to be correct? Actually, the weighting for household size scarcely changed their original forecast. The moral is that the one-of-a-kind calculation offers grave danger.

Consequently, each new calculation can well be preceded by a few applications of the method to simple made-up examples until the user gets the feel of the calculation, of the magnitudes to be expected, and of a convenient way to lay out the procedure. Having someone else check the calculation independently requires that the investigator not teach the verifier the original mistakes. Yates has suggested that, in a large hand calculation, independence could nearly be preserved when different individuals calculate on separate machines in parallel in two different numerical units; for ex-

ample, one computes in dollars, the other in pounds. At the end, the final answers are converted for comparison.

Gross errors in standard deviations. Since the sample range w (largest measurement minus smallest measurement) is easy to compute, it is often used to check the more complicated calculation of a sample standard deviation s. In the same sample, the ratio w/s must lie between the lower and upper bounds given in Table 11 or else the range, sample standard deviation, or quotient is in error. The table shows the 2.5 per cent and 97.5 per cent point of the distribution of w/s for a normal distribution. When calculations lead to ratios falling outside these limits but inside the bounds, they are not necessarily wrong; but further examination may pay.

Table 11 also shows the median of the distribution of the range of a sample of size n drawn from a standard normal distribution. It gives one an idea of the spread measured in standard deviations to be expected of the sample means of n equal-sized groups whose population means are identical. Note that through $n = 20$ a rough rule is that the

Table 11 — Bounds on the ratio: range/standard deviation[a]

n	Lower bound	w/s 2.5%	w/s 97.5%	Upper bound	Median of w/σ
2	1.41	1.41	1.41	1.41	.95[b]
3	1.73	1.74	2.00	2.00	1.59[b]
4	1.73	1.93	2.44	2.45	1.98
5	1.83	2.09	2.78	2.83	2.26
6	1.83	2.22	3.06	3.16	2.47
7	1.87	2.33	3.28	3.46	2.65
8	1.87	2.43	3.47	3.74	2.79
9	1.90	2.51	3.63	4.00	2.92
10	1.90	2.59	3.78	4.24	3.02
15	1.94	2.88	4.29	5.29	3.42
20	1.95	3.09	4.63	6.16	3.69
30	1.97	3.37	5.06	7.62	4.04
50	1.98	3.73	5.54	9.90	4.45
100	1.99	4.21	6.11	14.07	4.97
200	1.99	4.68	6.60	19.95	5.49[c]
500	2.00	5.25	7.15	31.59	6.07[c]
1,000	2.00	5.68	7.54	44.70	6.48[c]

a. Lower bound, 2.5% point, 97.5% point, and upper bound for the ratio: range/sample standard deviation (w/s); median of the distribution of the ratio: range/population standard deviation (w/σ); the sample size is n. The upper and lower bounds apply to any distribution and sampling method; the percentage points and median are computed for random sampling from a normal distribution, but they should be useful for other distributions.

b. This is not an error. The median is expressed as the multiplier of the *population* standard deviation, whereas the bounds relate range and *sample* standard deviation.

c. The mean of the distribution is given as an approximation to the median because the latter is not available.

Sources: Pearson & Stephens 1964, p. 486, for lower and upper bounds and for 2.5% and 97.5% points; Harter 1963, pp. 162–164, for medians; Pearson & Hartley 1954, p. 174, for means.

median distance between the largest and smallest sample mean is $\sqrt{n}\sigma_{\bar{x}}$.

Reporting. When writing the final report, remember that making clear the frame of reference of a study helps the reader understand the discussion.

Need for full reporting. In reporting on the investigation, be sure to give detailed information about the populations studied, the operational definitions used, and the exceptions to the general rules. Unless the details are carefully reported, they are quickly forgotten and are soon replaced by cloudy fancies. Discussions of accuracy, checks, and controls are needed in the final report.

Full and careful reporting can lead to ample prefaces, numerous appendixes, some jargon, and lengthy discussions. Shrink not from these paraphernalia, so amusing to the layman, for without them the study loses value; it is less interpretable, for it cannot be properly compared with other studies. Jargon may be the price of brevity.

The reader may object that editors will not allow such full reporting. Certainly the amount of detail required does vary with the sort of report to be made. Many studies that are published in short reports turn out to present a long sequence of short articles, and these, in one place or another, can give the relevant details.

Try to go beyond bare-bones reporting by giving readers your views of the sorts of populations, circumstances, or processes to which the findings of the study might apply. Warn the reader about generalizations that you are wary of but that he, on the basis of your findings, might reasonably expect to hold. While such discussions can be criticized as speculation, you owe it to the reader to do your best with them and to be as specific as you can be.

Beyond all this, where appropriate, do write as nontechnical a summary as you can for the interested public.

Suppression of data. In pursuit of a thesis, even the most careful may find it easy to argue themselves into the position that the exceptions to the desired proposition are based upon poorer data, somehow do not apply, would be too few to be worth reporting if one took the trouble to look them up, would mislead the simpleminded if reported, and therefore had best be omitted. Whether or not these views are correct, and some of them may well be, it is preferable to present the whole picture and then to present one's best appraisal of all the data. The more complete record puts readers in a much better position to consider both the judgments and the proposition.

FREDERICK MOSTELLER

[*Directly related are the entries* EXPERIMENTAL DESIGN; FALLACIES, STATISTICAL; SAMPLE SURVEYS.]

BIBLIOGRAPHY

BARTHOLOMEW, D. J. 1961 A Method of Allowing for "Not-at-home" Bias in Sample Surveys. *Applied Statistics* 10:52–59.

BILLEWICZ, W. Z. 1965 The Efficiency of Matched Samples: An Empirical Investigation. *Biometrics* 21:623–644.

CANTRIL, HADLEY (1944) 1947 The Use of Trends. Pages 220–230 in Hadley Cantril, *Gauging Public Opinion.* Princeton Univ. Press.

CANTRIL, HADLEY 1966 *The Pattern of Human Concerns.* New Brunswick, N.J.: Rutgers Univ. Press.

COCHRAN, WILLIAM G. 1951 Improvement by Means of Selection. Pages 449–470 in Berkeley Symposium on Mathematical Statistics and Probability, Second, *Proceedings.* Edited by Jerzy Neyman. Berkeley: Univ. of California Press.

COCHRAN, WILLIAM G. (1953) 1963 *Sampling Techniques.* 2d ed. New York: Wiley.

COCHRAN, WILLIAM G.; MOSTELLER, FREDERICK; and TUKEY, JOHN W. 1954 *Statistical Problems of the Kinsey Report on Sexual Behavior in the Human Male.* Washington: American Statistical Association.

COPPIN, R. S.; FERDUN, G. S.; and PECK, R. C. 1965 The Teen-aged Driver. California, Department of Motor Vehicles, Division of Administration, Research and Statistics Section, *Report* 21.

EHRENBERG, A. S. C. 1960 A Study of Some Potential Biases in the Operation of a Consumer Panel. *Applied Statistics* 9:20–27.

FARIOLETTI, MARIUS 1952 Some Results From the First Year's Audit Control Program of the Bureau of Internal Revenue. *National Tax Journal* 5, no. 1:65–78.

FELDMAN, JACOB J. 1960 The Household Interview Survey as a Technique for the Collection of Morbidity Data. *Journal of Chronic Diseases* 11:535–557.

HANSEN, MORRIS H.; and HURWITZ, WILLIAM N. 1946 The Problem of Non-response in Sample Surveys. *Journal of the American Statistical Association* 41:517–529.

HARBISON, FREDERICK; and MYERS, CHARLES A. 1964 *Education, Manpower, and Economic Growth: Strategies of Human Resource Development.* New York: McGraw-Hill.

HARTER, H. LEON 1963 The Use of Sample Ranges and Quasi-ranges in Setting Exact Confidence Bounds for the Population Standard Deviation. II. Quasi-ranges of Samples From a Normal Population—Probability Integral and Percentage Points; Exact Confidence Bounds for σ. → ARL 21, Part 2. Wright-Patterson Air Force Base, Ohio: U.S. Air Force, Office of Aerospace Research, Aeronautical Research Laboratories.

HENDRICKS, WALTER A. 1956 *The Mathematical Theory of Sampling.* New Brunswick, N.J.: Scarecrow Press.

KATZ, DANIEL 1946 The Interpretation of Survey Findings. *Journal of Social Issues* 2, no. 2:33–44.

KISH, LESLIE 1965 *Survey Sampling.* New York: Wiley.

KISH, LESLIE; and HESS, IRENE 1959 A "Replacement" Procedure for Reducing the Bias of Nonresponse. *American Statistician* 13, no. 4:17–19.

KISH, LESLIE; and LANSING, JOHN B. 1954 Response Errors in Estimating the Value of Homes. *Journal of the American Statistical Association* 49:520–538.

KLUCKHOHN, FLORENCE R.; and STRODTBECK, FRED L. 1961 *Variations in Value Orientations.* Evanston, Ill.: Row, Peterson.

LAWLEY, D. N.; and SWANSON, Z. 1954 Tests of Significance in a Factor Analysis of Artificial Data. *British Journal of Statistical Psychology* 7:75–79.

LEUCHTENBURG, WILLIAM E. 1963 *Franklin D. Roosevelt and the New Deal: 1932–1940.* New York: Harper. → A paperback edition was published in the same year.

LEVINE, SOL; and GORDON, GERALD 1958–1959 Maximizing Returns on Mail Questionnaires. *Public Opinion Quarterly* 22:568–575.

MOSES, LINCOLN E.; and OAKFORD, ROBERT V. 1963 *Tables of Random Permutations.* Stanford Univ. Press.

MOSTELLER, FREDERICK; and BUSH, ROBERT R. (1954) 1959 Selected Quantitative Techniques. Volume 1, pages 289–334 in Gardner Lindzey (editor), *Handbook of Social Psychology.* Cambridge, Mass.: Addison-Wesley.

MOSTELLER, FREDERICK; and TUKEY, JOHN W. 1966 Data Analysis, Including Statistics. Unpublished manuscript. → To be published in the revised edition of the *Handbook of Social Psychology,* edited by Gardner Lindzey and Elliot Anderson.

MOSTELLER, FREDERICK; and WALLACE, DAVID L. 1964 *Inference and Disputed Authorship: The Federalist.* Reading, Mass.: Addison-Wesley.

NETER, JOHN; and WAKSBERG, JOSEPH 1964a Conditioning Effects From Repeated Household Interviews. *Journal of Marketing* 28, no. 2:51–56.

NETER, JOHN; and WAKSBERG, JOSEPH 1964b A Study of Response Errors in Expenditures Data From Household Interviews. *Journal of the American Statistical Association* 59:18–55.

PEARSON, E. S.; and HARTLEY, H. O. (editors) (1954) 1958 *Biometrika Tables for Statisticians.* Volume 1, 2d ed. Cambridge Univ. Press.

PEARSON, E. S.; and STEPHENS, M. A. 1964 The Ratio of Range to Standard Deviation in the Same Normal Sample. *Biometrika* 51:484–487.

PEIRCE, CHARLES S. 1873 On the Theory of Errors of Observations. U.S. Coast and Geodetic Survey, *Report of the Superintendent* [1870]:200–224.

ROETHLISBERGER, FRITZ J.; and DICKSON, WILLIAM J. (1939) 1961 *Management and the Worker: An Account of a Research Program Conducted by the Western Electric Company, Hawthorne Works, Chicago.* Cambridge, Mass.: Harvard Univ. Press. → A paperback edition was published in 1964 by Wiley.

RUGG, DONALD; and CANTRIL, HADLEY (1944) 1947 The Wording of Questions. Pages 23–50 in Hadley Cantril, *Gauging Public Opinion.* Princeton Univ. Press.

SCOTT, CHRISTOPHER 1961 Research on Mail Surveys. *Journal of the Royal Statistical Society* Series A 124:143–205.

SHARP, HARRY; and FELDT, ALLAN 1959 Some Factors in a Probability Sample Survey of a Metropolitan Community. *American Sociological Review* 24:650–661.

SOBOL, MARION G. 1959 Panel Mortality and Panel Bias. *Journal of the American Statistical Association* 54:52–68.

SUDMAN, SEYMOUR 1964 On the Accuracy of Recording Consumer Panels: I and II. *Journal of Marketing Research* 1, no. 2:14–20; 1, no. 3:69–83.

TUCKER, LEDYARD R. 1964 Recovery of Factors From Simulated Data. Unpublished manuscript.

WAKSBERG, JOSEPH; and PEARL, ROBERT B. 1964 The Effects of Repeated Household Interviews in the Current Population Survey. Unpublished manuscript.

WHITING, BEATRICE B. (editor) 1963 *Six Cultures: Studies of Child Rearing.* New York: Wiley.

WILSON, EDWIN B.; and HILFERTY, MARGARET M. 1929 Note on C. S. Peirce's Experimental Discussion of the Law of Errors. National Academy of Sciences, Washington, D.C., *Proceedings* 15:120–125.

II
EFFECTS OF ERRORS IN STATISTICAL ASSUMPTIONS

All physical and social laws or models rest ultimately upon assumptions. These laws do not yield exact numerical statements. Even the much admired exactness of the physicists' laws means only very close approximation—how close depends upon the circumstances. So, too, techniques for statistical analysis require assumptions about the data to justify the use of the techniques in particular situations. When these assumptions are not correct for the data under study, the results of the statistical analysis may be very misleading. This article discusses the effects on statistical analysis of incorrect assumptions and considers some ways of mitigating the problem. The discussion is set in the frameworks of the matched-pairs design, a time-series design, the one-way analysis of variance, and a repeated-measurements design.

The matched-pairs design

In the matched-pairs design two treatments or conditions are studied by assigning one treatment to each member of a pair of matched individuals. For example, a department of Slavic languages is interested in finding out whether one of two different teaching methods for a first-year language course is better than the other. A language aptitude and proficiency examination is given on the first day of class, and the scores on these tests are used to pair students who have approximately the same aptitude and proficiency. Then, for each pair of students, one student is randomly assigned to one teaching method and the other student is assigned to the other method. An examination is given at the end of the term to determine whether differences exist between the teaching methods.

Comparisons between the treatments are based on the difference between the responses to the treatments within each pair. Thus the data consist of the n differences $X_1, X_2, \cdots, X_n$, where X_j denotes the difference between the response scores in the jth pair. It is assumed that $X_1, X_2, \cdots, X_n$ constitute a simple random sample from some population; possible further assumptions will be discussed in the next section.

A social scientist may want to make inferences about several features of the probability distribution underlying his matched-pairs experiment. He may ask which estimators or formulas should be used to estimate the unknown mean or median μ. In addition, he may want to know which significance test to use to find out whether the treatments differ. The following sections indicate how answers to these questions may be obtained.

Criteria for point estimation. An investigator is frequently faced with a dilemma in his choice of an estimator. Suppose in the matched-pairs design he wants to estimate μ, the mean difference between treatments. If he is willing to assume that the observations are randomly drawn from a normal distribution, then the sample mean $\bar{X} = (1/n)\sum X_j$ is the unique "best" unbiased estimator for μ.

Evidence may exist, however, that although the underlying distribution is symmetrical, there are too many extreme values for the normality assumption to be correct. For distributions of this long-tailed kind, the sample mean may have a very large variance. The sample median is generally a reasonable estimator to use for such distributions but has a higher variance than the sample mean for more nearly normal distributions. How can one achieve a reasonable compromise—an estimator that is good under reasonable assumptions?

Here, consideration is restricted to long-tailed symmetrical distributions and, in particular, to compound normal distributions that arise in the following way: (1) An observation is randomly drawn from one of two normal populations. (2) With probability $1 - \tau$, this observation is randomly drawn from a normal population that has mean μ and variance σ^2. (3) With probability τ, this observation is randomly drawn from another normal population having mean μ and variance $K^2\sigma^2$. The values of K and τ that are considered are $K \geqslant 2$ and $0 \leqslant \tau \leqslant .10$. In short, the compound normal distributions considered are *mixtures* of two normal distributions with a common mean. [*See* DISTRIBUTIONS, STATISTICAL, *article on* MIXTURES OF DISTRIBUTIONS.]

A useful way to compare any two unbiased estimators of the same parameter is to compute their efficiency. The *efficiency* of estimator 1 relative to estimator 2 is defined as

$$e(1, 2) = \frac{\text{variance of estimator 2}}{\text{variance of estimator 1}} \times 100.$$

An estimator is chosen that compares favorably in terms of efficiency with its competitors over the range of plausible distributions. An estimator has robustness of efficiency relative to another if the above ratio does not dip far below 100 per cent for plausible alternatives.

Estimators of the mean (or median). One possible compromise between the sample mean and the sample median is

$$\frac{X_{(2)} + X_{(3)} + \cdots + X_{(n-1)}}{n - 2},$$

where $X_{(j)}$ is the jth smallest observation; that is, the largest and smallest observations are discarded and the mean of the remaining observations computed. [*See* NONPARAMETRIC STATISTICS, *article on* ORDER STATISTICS.]

In general, an arbitrary percentage of the observations may be discarded. Define the α per cent *trimmed mean*, $\bar{X}_\alpha$, as the mean of the observations remaining after the smallest $(\alpha/100)n$ observations and the largest $(\alpha/100)n$ observations are excluded. The 0 per cent and 50 per cent trimmed means are the sample mean and the sample median, respectively; thus, in particular, $\bar{X}_0 = \bar{X}$.

Efficiency comparisons of the 0 and 6 per cent trimmed means for the compound normal distribution in large samples with $K = 3$ and $0 \leqslant \tau \leqslant .10$ are given by Tukey (1960). He shows, for example, that the 0 per cent trimmed mean $\bar{X}$ is the best possible estimator if $\tau = 0$ (that is, if all observations are from one population), but that, even in this extreme case, $\bar{X}_6$ has efficiency 97 per cent relative to $\bar{X}$. On the other hand, if $\tau = .05$, $\bar{X}_6$ has approximately 143 per cent efficiency with respect to $\bar{X}$. These computations (and many more) indicate that there is more to gain than to lose by discarding some extreme observations. It is important to add that in many problems the study of extreme observations may give important clues to the improvement of the experimental or observational technique. [*See* STATISTICAL ANALYSIS, SPECIAL PROBLEMS OF, *article on* OUTLIERS.]

Test and confidence interval criteria. A test is to be chosen to compare the null and alternative hypotheses

$$H_0: \mu = 0$$
$$H_1: \mu \neq 0 \quad (\text{or } H_1': \mu > 0),$$

respectively. From the test, confidence intervals for μ are to be obtained. The one-sided and two-sided t tests are the "best" tests of H_0 against H_1 or H_1' if the underlying distribution is normal, but the goal is to choose a good test under less stringent assumptions.

Two requirements for a good test are that it must possess robustness of validity and robustness of

Table 1 — Values of γ_1 and γ_2 for some familiar distributions

	CHI-SQUARE (χ^2_{df}) DISTRIBUTION*			COMPOUND NORMAL DISTRIBUTION		
				$\tau = 0$ $K = 3$	$\tau = .05$ $K = 3$	$\tau = .10$ $K = 3$
	$df = 1$	$df = 5$	$df = 10$			
γ_1	2.83	1.26	0.89	0.00	0.00	0.00
γ_2	12	2.40	1.20	0.00	4.65	5.33

* Degrees of freedom denoted by *df*.

efficiency over the range of plausible underlying distributions (Box & Tiao 1964; Tukey 1962).

A statistical test or confidence interval has validity if the basic probability statements asserted for the procedure are correct or nearly so. Thus, from *t* tables, the one-sided *t* test with 9 degrees of freedom has probability .05 of exceeding 1.833 under the null hypothesis $\mu = 0$. This statement is valid if the normal assumption holds. But suppose the normality assumption is in error. Can *t* tables still be used to find the probability that *t* will be greater than an arbitrary value t_0 for plausible underlying distributions? If the answer to this question is "yes," then the one-sided *t* test and associated confidence intervals are said to have robustness of validity. Robustness of validity has not been defined rigorously. A quantitatively precise definition of robustness of validity is difficult to give, since it must depend upon the interpretation of the outcome of a significance test in the given experiment.

In addition to possessing robustness of validity, the test should be a good discriminator between the hypotheses. The discriminating ability of a test is measured by its power, which is the probability of rejecting H_0 given that H_1 (or H_1') is true [see HYPOTHESIS TESTING]. Both the one-sided and two-sided *t* tests have the strong property that their power is higher than the power of any other reasonable test if the normality assumption obtains. This is no longer true for nonnormal distributions, however, and competitors must be sought.

Thus a way to compare two tests is necessary. It is natural to make such comparisons by defining a concept of relative efficiency for two tests, 1 and 2, representable by a numerical index $e(1, 2)$. Efficiency of tests and estimators are related concepts [see NONPARAMETRIC STATISTICS for a discussion of efficiency]. If $e(1, 2)$ is greater than one, test 1 is more powerful than test 2. A test is said to have robustness of efficiency if its efficiency relative to its competitors is not appreciably below one for credible alternative distributions.

Tests and confidence intervals. The information available on the validity and efficiency properties of the *t* test, the Wilcoxon signed-rank test,

and the sign test under nonnormality is now summarized [see NONPARAMETRIC STATISTICS for these tests]. The trimmed *t* promises to be a strong competitor to the preceding tests (Tukey & McLaughlin 1963).

The one-sided and two-sided *t* tests are valid in large samples, although this validity does not extend to very high significance levels, such as .001, and .0001 (see Hotelling 1961).

The validity of the *t* test will be considered for two different nonnormal distributions. First, assume that the nonnormal distribution has the compound normal form considered above. Second, the nonnormal distribution is assumed to be an Edgeworth distribution with skewness parameter γ_1 and kurtosis (or peakedness) parameter γ_2.

Langley and Elashoff (1966) have conducted a Monte Carlo investigation of the performance of the one-sided *t* test. One thousand samples of *n* ($n = 6, 9, 16$) observations each were taken from compound normal distributions with $K = 3$ and $\tau = 0.0, 0.20, 0.40$. In all these situations, the empirical probability of *t* being greater than the normal theory .05 point was between .04 and .06.

The effects on the one-sided *t* test when sampling is from an Edgeworth population with parameters γ_1, γ_2 will be studied next. For symmetrical distributions $\gamma_1 = 0$, while $\gamma_1 > 0$ for distributions with a long right tail; for normal distributions $\gamma_2 = 0$, but $\gamma_2 > 0$ for bell-shaped symmetrical distributions with long tails and $\gamma_2 < 0$ for similar distributions with short tails (see Scheffé 1959, pp. 331–333). In order to provide some feel for the decriptive meaning of the γ_1, γ_2 parameters, Table 1 gives values of γ_1 and γ_2 for several nonnormal distributions. For normal distributions $\gamma_1 = \gamma_2 = 0$.

Table 2 indicates the performance of the one-sided *t* test on a sample of 10. Each entry denotes the probability that $t \geq 1.833$ if the null hypothesis that $\mu = 0$ is true (under normal theory this probability is .05). The performance of the one-tailed *t* test as shown in Table 2 may be summarized as follows: (1) The true significance level α is always slightly less than .05 for long-tailed symmetrical distributions and slightly greater than .05 in short-

Table 2 — Probability that t ⩾ 1.833

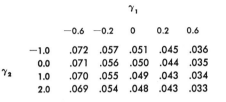

		γ_1			
	−0.6	−0.2	0	0.2	0.6
−1.0	.072	.057	.051	.045	.036
0.0	.071	.056	.050	.044	.035
γ_2 1.0	.070	.055	.049	.043	.034
2.0	.069	.054	.048	.043	.033

Source: Srivastava 1958, p. 427.

tailed symmetrical distributions. (2) Skewness (γ_1) is more important than kurtosis (γ_2). In fact, the true significance level is almost constant in each column. A long right tail means that the true significance level is much less than .05; a long left tail leads to a true significance level much greater than .05. The skewness values covered in Table 2 represent very moderate skewness. The two-sided *t* test is less affected by skewness and kurtosis (see Srivastava 1958).

The Wilcoxon signed-rank test is the most frequently used competitor to the *t* test. It was designed to have perfect robustness of validity with respect to significance level for symmetrical distributions; its validity in asymmetrical distributions is unknown. The sign test has perfect robustness of validity with respect to significance level for both symmetrical and asymmetrical distributions.

Some efficiency computations are reported here [*they use the definition of large sample efficiency given in the article* NONPARAMETRIC STATISTICS, *which also discusses the properties of these tests*]. Table 3 presents some efficiency computations of the Wilcoxon and sign tests relative to the *t* test when the underlying distribution is a compound normal type. If the underlying distribution is normal, the corresponding efficiencies are $e(w, t) = .955$ and $e(s, t) = .636$.

The preceding validity analysis and suggestive efficiency study permits these recommendations: (1) The Wilcoxon signed-rank test should be used for symmetrical distributions with moderately long tails. If confidence intervals are desired, the Walsh

Table 3 — Efficiency of the Wilcoxon and sign tests relative to the t test

	K					
	2		3		5	
	τ		τ		τ	
	.05	.10	.05	.10	.05	.10
$e(w,t)$[a]	1.23	1.53	1.45	2.07	2.20	3.52
$e(s,t)$[b]	0.69	0.74	.83	.99	1.29	1.83

a. The efficiency of the Wilcoxon signed-rank test relative to the *t* test.

b. The efficiency of the sign test relative to the *t* test.

procedure should be employed. (2) If samples are large and the underlying symmetrical distribution has long tails, the routine use of the Wilcoxon test and Walsh confidence procedure may require a large computing cost. In these instances, if the distribution has only moderately long tails, the *t* test and its confidence procedure should be a reasonable compromise. If the distribution has very long tails, the sign test and its associated confidence interval procedure provide a reasonable compromise.

A simple time-series design

Nonrandomness among observations can occur in two ways: (1) the observations may not be independent or (2) the observations may not have a common distribution. Each type of nonrandomness will be considered below to show the important effects such nonrandomness may have on statistical methods based upon the assumption of randomness.

Dependence among the observations. A psychologist observes an individual's response at n points in time. Suppose that X_t, $t = 1, 2, \cdots, n$, denotes the individual's response at time t. The psychologist assumes that the response has a linear regression over time; that is,

$$(1) \qquad X_t = \alpha + \beta\left(\frac{t}{n} - \frac{n+1}{2n}\right) + e_t.$$

(The use of $(t/n) - [(n+1)/(2n)]$ instead of just t represents merely a convenient coding of the t values. In particular, $(n+1)/(2n)$ is just the average of the (t/n)'s: $(n+1)/(2n) = (1/n) \cdot \sum_{t=1}^{n} (t/n)$.) The e_t may represent errors of measurement or errors in the assumption of linear regression and are assumed to be random. The psychologist suspects that the e_t, and hence the X_t, may be correlated; that the e_t all have the same distribution is not questioned here. The goal of the experiment is to estimate and test hypotheses about the intercept, α, and the slope, β.

In the estimation problem only two estimators for α and two estimators for β will be studied here. Furthermore, each estimator is a linear combination of the X's ($a_1X_1 + a_2X_2 + \cdots + a_nX_n$). The reasons for this restriction are that such estimators have been studied most thoroughly and that under normality they have optimal properties. Johnston (1963) studies the estimation problem in some detail.

Suppose, at first, the psychologist believes that there is no dependence among the observations. Then reasonable estimators for α and β are found by the method of unweighted least squares, which gives

$$\hat{\alpha} = \sum_{t=1}^{n} X_t / n,$$

$$\beta = \sum_{t=1}^{n} (X_t - \bar{X}) \frac{t}{n} \Bigg/ \sum_{t=1}^{n} \left(\frac{t}{n} - \frac{n+1}{2n} \right)^2.$$

If no dependence exists, then these estimators have minimum variance among all linear estimators that are unbiased. The standard errors of $\hat{\alpha}$ and $\hat{\beta}$ are

$$(2) \quad \begin{aligned} \text{s.e. } \hat{\alpha} &= \sqrt{\sigma^2/n}, \\ \text{s.e. } \hat{\beta} &= \sqrt{ \sigma^2 \Bigg/ \sum_{t=1}^{n} \left(\frac{t}{n} - \frac{n+1}{2n} \right)^2 }, \end{aligned}$$

where σ^2 is the variance of X_t.

Now, suppose that dependence exists among the observations and assume that the correlation between X_t and X_s, denoted by ρ_{st}, is given by the relation

$$(3) \qquad \rho_{st} = \rho^{|s-t|},$$

where $|s - t|$ denotes the absolute value of the difference $s - t$. What are the effects of nonzero values of ρ on the estimators $\hat{\alpha}$ and $\hat{\beta}$? First, while these estimators are still unbiased, they are in this case no longer the minimum variance linear unbiased estimators (see Johnston 1963 for the way to construct the latter estimators). Efficiency computations comparing $\hat{\beta}$ and the minimum variance linear unbiased estimator, β^*, are given in Table 4, where cell entries are the ratio of the variance of β^* to the variance of $\hat{\beta}$ for a sample of size 5.

Table 4 — Efficiency comparison of $\hat{\beta}$ and β^*

ρ	−.40	−.20	0	.20	.40
var β^*/var $\hat{\beta}$	.921	.982	1	.990	.972

The estimator β^* used in Table 4 is computed under the assumption that ρ is known. When the sample size is large, $\hat{\beta}$ has efficiency one compared with β^* for the particular pattern of correlation considered.

A second effect of nonzero ρ is that the standard errors $\hat{\alpha}$ and $\hat{\beta}$ given in (2) are incorrect. The correct standard errors in large samples for the example are

$$(4) \quad \begin{aligned} \text{s.e. } \hat{\alpha} &= \sqrt{ \frac{\sigma^2}{n} \left(1 + \frac{2\rho}{1-\rho} \right) }, \\ \text{s.e. } \hat{\beta} &= \sqrt{ \frac{\sigma^2}{\sum_t \left(\frac{t}{n} - \frac{n+1}{2n} \right)^2} \left(1 + \frac{2\rho}{1-\rho} \right) }. \end{aligned}$$

These standard errors may depart quite radically from (2) as Table 5 shows. The ratios obtained in Table 5 are identical to the corresponding ratios of s.e. $\hat{\alpha}$. Since the standard errors in (2) may be in serious error, it is clear that the standard error of prediction, that is, the standard error of $\hat{\alpha} + \hat{\beta}[(t/n) - (n+1)/(2n)]$, may also be very wrong. The third effect of ignoring correlation between the observations concerns s^2, the conventional estimator of σ^2, the underlying variance;

$$s^2 = \sum_{i=1}^{n} \left[X_t - \hat{\alpha} - \hat{\beta} \left(\frac{t}{n} - \frac{n+1}{2n} \right) \right]^2 \Bigg/ (n-2).$$

If $\rho \neq 0$, then s^2 is a biased estimator of σ^2. Some sampling experiments by Cochrane and Orcutt (1949) suggest that the expected value of s^2 is less than σ^2; when there are a large number of observations, the bias is negligible.

Table 5 — Ratio of incorrect to correct s.e. $\hat{\beta}$

ρ	−.50	−.20	−.10	0	.10	.20	.50
s.e. $\hat{\beta}$ from (2) / s.e. $\hat{\beta}$ from (4)	1.73	1.22	1.10	1	.90	.82	.57

In testing hypotheses about α and β a primary concern is with the behavior of the standard t test,

$$t = \sqrt{ \sum \left(\frac{t}{n} - \frac{n+1}{2n} \right)^2 } \cdot \hat{\beta} / \sqrt{s^2},$$

to examine $H_0: \beta = 0$ against the alternative $H_1: \beta \neq 0$ in the presence of the correlation model (3). Table 6 gives the probability that $|t_f| \geqslant 1.96$ if $H_0: \beta = 0$ is true when the sample size is large (if $\rho = 0$ this probability is .05). Table 6, and additional tables when H_1 is true, vividly demonstrates the sensitivity of the standard t test to nonzero correlation between the observations when (1) and (3) hold. The nonrobustness of t comes primarily from the use of an incorrect standard error of $\hat{\beta}$ in the denominator of t. The probability computations in Table 6 also hold when $H_0': \alpha = 0$ is tested against $H_1': \alpha \neq 0$ using the statistic $t = \sqrt{n}\,\hat{\alpha}/\sqrt{s^2}$. In many social science problems $\rho > 0$; as seen from Table 5 the null hypothesis would be rejected more often than the nominal 5 per cent level in such situations, assuming that the null hypothesis is true.

Hoel (1964) has reported on a sampling experiment to assess the effects of correlation in small sample sizes on an F test for a polynomial trend. His results support the conclusions reached in the preceding paragraph. Readers interested in robust tests, assuming the correlational structure (3), should consult Hannan (1955).

Table 6 — Large sample probability that $|t| \geq 1.96$ when correlation exists

ρ	−.50	−.40	−.30	−.20	−.10	0	.10	.20	.30	.40	.50
Probability	.00068	.0026	.0076	.0164	.0302	.0500	.0762	.1096	.1498	.1994	.2576

It is important to remember that the magnitude of effects on a statistical technique from dependence among the observations is a function of the technique, the model of dependence, and the values of correlational parameters.

Nonidentically distributed observations. Suppose that the psychologist is principally interested in testing the hypothesis H_0: $\alpha = 0$ against H_1: $\alpha \neq 0$. Now, however, assume that strong evidence exists that $\rho = 0$. The psychologist believes $\beta = 0$ in (1), but he is not certain about this belief. Thus he asks the question, "What is the effect on the t test of examining H_0: $\alpha = 0$ against H_1: $\alpha \neq 0$, assuming $\beta = 0$, if in fact $\beta \neq 0$?" The t statistic the psychologist wants to employ (assuming $\beta = 0$) is $t = \sqrt{n}\,\bar{X}/\sqrt{s^2}$, where now s^2 is given by $\sum(X_t - \bar{X})^2/(n-1)$.

Table 7 gives the probability that $|t| \geq 1.96$ if H_0: $\alpha = 0$ is correct for various values of $|\beta|$ and σ^2 when n is large (the nominal significance level is .05).

Table 7 — Probability that $|t| \geq 1.96$ when a slope, assumed zero, is not zero

		$|\beta|$		
	0	.25	.50	1.0
.25	.05	.0414	.0238	.0028
.50	.05	.0477	.0414	.0238
σ 1.00	.05	.0488	.0477	.0414
2.00	.05	.0500	.0488	.0477

Two important effects of incorrectly assuming that $\beta = 0$ are apparent from Table 7: (1) the behavior of the t statistic depends upon the unknown σ^2 as well as $|\beta|$, and (2) the stated significance level .05 is always at least as large as the true significance level.

It must be remembered that the effects of nonidentically distributed observations depend on the model underlying the observations and the statistical method being used.

The one-way analysis of variance

The one-way analysis of variance may arise when n individuals are randomly assigned to k treatments. The data consist of the n_i response scores x_{ij} ($i = 1, \cdots, k$; $j = 1, \cdots, n_i$) with $\sum_{i=1}^{k} n_i = n$. The observations are assumed to be independent, and the probability distributions of the response variable are assumed identical for individuals receiving the same treatment.

The one-way layout is frequently employed to estimate the means or medians, μ_i, and the variances, σ_i^2, of the treatments, to establish confidence intervals on the differences, $\mu_i - \mu_j$, and to test hypotheses about the μ_i and σ_i^2. The point estimation problems present no essentially new questions.

Tests and confidence intervals for the median or mean. To discriminate between the null and alternative hypotheses

(5) $\qquad H_0$: $\mu_1 = \mu_2 = \cdots = \mu_k$

(6) $\qquad H_1$: $\mu_i \neq \mu_j$ for some i, j,

one ordinarily employs the F test, the Kruskal–Wallis H test, or the k sample median test [*see* NONPARAMETRIC STATISTICS, *article on* RANKING METHODS; LINEAR HYPOTHESES, *article on* ANALYSIS OF VARIANCE]. The F test is usually a very good way to make this discrimination if (1) the observations are drawn from a population in which each treatment has the same underlying normal distribution except for possible differences among the μ_i, and (2) the alternative hypothesis is not further specified.

The following sections discuss the validity of these tests. Note that the discussion is germane to the validity of Scheffé's method of multiple comparisons [*see* Scheffé 1959, chapter 3; *see also* LINEAR HYPOTHESES, *article on* MULTIPLE COMPARISONS], since that method is equivalent to the confidence set based on the F test.

Validity assuming $\sigma_i^2 = \sigma^2$ for all i. The F test has perfect validity for all sample sizes if the populations are normal with equal variances and the observations are independent; that is, if the k samples are drawn from the same normal distribution. In large samples the standard F statistic

$$F_{k-1,\,n-k} = \frac{\sum n_i(\bar{X}_i - \bar{X})^2/(k-1)}{\sum\sum(X_{ij} - \bar{X}_i)^2/(n-k)}$$

provides a valid test for the hypothesis (5) except at high significance levels. For small samples it will be assumed that departures from normality can be represented by an Edgeworth distribution with skewness and kurtosis parameters γ_{1i} and γ_{2i} in each population. Table 8 gives the probability that $F \geq 2.87$ if (5) is true (under normal theory this probability is .05) for $\gamma_{1i} = \gamma_1$ and $\gamma_{2i} = \gamma_2$ for all i, $k = 5$, all n_i's = 5.

Table 8 — Probability that $F \geqslant 2.87$ for $k = 5$ and all $n_i = 5$

		\multicolumn{5}{c}{γ_2}
		-1	-0.5	0	0.5	1
γ_1^2	0	0.053	0.051	0.050	0.049	0.048
	0.5	0.053	0.051	0.050	0.049	0.048
	1	0.053	0.052	0.050	0.050	0.049

Source: Box & Andersen 1955, p. 14.

Table 8 and other work indicate that the F test for (5) possesses robustness of validity relative to significance levels (type 1 error) and power when $\gamma_{1i} = \gamma_1$, all i (Gayen 1949; Pearson 1931). The kurtosis parameter γ_2 has practically no effect on the F test for (5). However, when $\gamma_{11} \neq \gamma_{12}$, it is known that for $k = 2$ the one-sided t test does not have robustness of validity.

The Kruskal–Wallis test and the median test are valid under the null hypothesis that the k samples come from the same population. When $k = 2$, the Kruskal–Wallis test is equivalent to the two-tailed Wilcoxon rank-sum test. In this case of $k = 2$, if $\gamma_{11} \neq \gamma_{12}$ and $\gamma_{21} \neq \gamma_{22}$, the one-sided Wilcoxon test appears to be less robust than the one-sided t test relative to significance levels when the null hypothesis is (5) and μ is a median or mean (Wetherhill 1960).

Inequality of variance. The validity of the preceding tests and some further tests when the assumption of equal variances is dropped will be studied; the normality assumption is retained unless otherwise indicated.

It is necessary at this point to examine the rationale for carrying out a test. Suppose a random sample of n mental patients is drawn and n_1 are assigned to treatment 1 and n_2 ($= n - n_1$) are assigned to treatment 2. After a period of treatment, each patient is tested and given a score that is assumed to be normally distributed in each population. The null hypothesis tested is that $\mu_1 = \mu_2$ (μ_i is the mean for treatment i); suppose the conclusion is that $\mu_1 < \mu_2$. If high scores are indicative of improvement, a decision is made to use the second treatment. Why?

When the variances are equal, the treatment with the higher mean is more likely to give rise to scores greater than or equal to any given score w_0. Thus the significance test gives the psychiatrist usable results, especially if a score at w_0 or above means release from the psychiatric hospital.

Suppose now that each treatment has a different variance and that $\mu_1 < \mu_2$. Then it is by no means uniformly true that the treatment with the higher mean is more likely to give rise to scores greater

than or equal to a release score of w_0. For example, suppose that the scores for treatment 1 and treatment 2 follow normal distributions with $\mu_1 = 0$, $\sigma_1^2 = 9$ and $\mu_2 = 1$, $\sigma_2^2 = 1$, respectively ($\sigma_i^2 = $ variance of treatment i scores). In this case Table 9 gives the probability that a randomly chosen score on treatment i exceeds w_0, $i = 1, 2$.

Nonetheless, it is often appropriate to test equality of means even when the variances may be different, and the remainder of this section deals with that case. This problem is often called the Behrens–Fisher problem. Consider, first, the large sample validity of the two-tailed, two-sample t test (equivalent to F when $k = 2$) based on

$$t = \frac{\bar{X}_1 - \bar{X}_2}{\sqrt{\left(\dfrac{1}{n_1} + \dfrac{1}{n_2}\right) s^2}},$$

where

$$s^2 = \frac{(n_1 - 1) s_1^2 + (n_2 - 1) s_2^2}{n_1 + n_2 - 2}.$$

The denominator of t is not a consistent estimator of the standard error of $\bar{X}_1 - \bar{X}_2$ unless either $\sigma_1^2 = \sigma_2^2$ or $n_1 = n_2$. This fact partly explains the nonrobustness of t clearly shown in Table 10.

Table 10 gives the probability that $|t| \geqslant 1.96$ for different values of $\theta = \sigma_1^2 / \sigma_2^2$ and $R = n_1 / n_2$ when the null hypothesis of equal means holds. Table 10 indicates the importance of equal sample sizes in controlling the effects of unequal variances: the significance level remains at .05 irrespective of the value of θ if $R = 1$. Moreover, if $\theta < 1$ and $R > 1$ so that the most variable population has the smallest sample, the true significance level is always larger than .05 and may be seriously so. On the other hand, if $\theta > 1$ and $R > 1$, the true significance level is always less than .05. These results are essentially independent of γ_1 and γ_2 because of the large sample sizes. This lack of robustness of significance-level validity extends to power. The small sample validity of t follows along the lines of the large sample theory (see Scheffé 1959, p. 340).

Since equal sample sizes are sometimes difficult to obtain, even approximately, considerable research has been focused upon alternative ways to

Table 9 — Probability that a randomly chosen score on treatment i exceeds w_0

Release score w_0	\multicolumn{2}{c}{Treatment}
	1	2
1.0	.3707	.5000
1.5	.3085	.3085
2.0	.2514	.1587
2.5	.2033	.0668

Table 10 — Large sample probability that $|t| \geqslant 1.96$ when sample sizes and variances differ

		θ				
		.20	.50	1.0	2.0	5.0
R	1	0.050	0.050	0.050	0.050	0.050
	2	0.120	0.080	0.050	0.029	0.014
	5	0.220	0.120	0.050	0.014	0.002

Source: Scheffé 1959, p. 340.

test (5) versus (6). Transformation of the response variable may achieve equality of variance for the transformed variable, so that t may be used. But the user must note that a hypothesis on the means of the *transformed* variates is being tested. [*See* STATISTICAL ANALYSIS, SPECIAL PROBLEMS OF, *article on* TRANSFORMATIONS OF DATA.]

Welch (1938; 1947) investigates the alternative test statistic,

$$v = \frac{\bar{X}_1 - \bar{X}_2}{\sqrt{\dfrac{s_1^2}{n_1} + \dfrac{s_2^2}{n_2}}},$$

and indicates how to obtain significance levels (see also Dixon & Massey [1951] 1957, p. 123). Note that the statistics v and t are the same if $n_1 = n_2$. Furthermore, Welch (1938) shows that the approximate significance level of v may be obtained from tables of the t distribution with f degrees of freedom, where

$$f = \frac{\left(\dfrac{s_1^2}{n_1} + \dfrac{s_2^2}{n_2}\right)^2}{\dfrac{s_1^4}{n_1^2(n_1-1)} + \dfrac{s_2^4}{n_2^2(n_2-1)}}.$$

The v test is valid for both significance level and power in large samples and is much less sensitive to θ than the usual t in small samples. For example, if $\theta = 1$ and $n_1 = 5$, $n_2 = 15$, the exact probability that $|v| \geqslant 5.2$ is .05, where 5.2 is the 5 per cent point of the exact distribution of v. The probability that $|v| \geqslant 5.2$ for any other θ value is always between .035 and .085. In addition, even if $\theta = 1$, so that the t test is valid, the v test is nearly as efficient as t. When both n_1 and n_2 are small, s_1^2 and s_2^2 will have low precision. In these situations, compute f from the following formula:

$$f = \frac{\left(\dfrac{1}{n_1} + \dfrac{1}{n_2}\right)^2}{\dfrac{1}{n_1^2(n_1-1)} + \dfrac{1}{n_2^2(n_2-1)}}.$$

Alternative testing methods for $k = 2$ exist (see Behrens 1963; Cochran 1964).

Inequality of variance also affects the signifi-

cance levels of the Wilcoxon rank-sum test w and the median test. H. R. van der Vaart (1961) gives significance levels of the Wilcoxon test for various θ values, assuming normal distributions and large samples. Pratt (1964) extends van der Vaart's investigation in several ways. Surprisingly, w is sensitive to θ in the case of equal samples, while t remains unaffected. The median test appears to have greater robustness of significance-level validity than t or w near $\theta = 1$ when the three tests are comparable.

The conclusions concerning the effects of inequality of variance on the usual F test for $k = 2$ generally hold for arbitrary k. Robust tests along the lines of Welch's v test have been developed for general k (see James 1951).

Efficiency considerations. When the shapes (including variances) of the k distributions are different, it is important to be precise about which null hypothesis is being tested. The null hypothesis of equality of means is tested by F; the null hypothesis that $p = \frac{1}{2}$ is tested by the Kruskal–Wallis method (when $k = 2$, p is the probability that a random observation under treatment 1 is greater than a random observation under treatment 2). The null hypothesis of equality of medians is tested by the median test. The means may be equal but the medians different, or conversely. Either the means or the medians may be equal, but $p \neq \frac{1}{2}$, or conversely. These facts imply the noncomparability of the three tests if shape differences exist. They also imply that a satisfactory analysis of the data may require an investigator to assemble evidence from all three significance tests—and possibly additional tests.

If the k distributions have the same shape, the following conclusions are justified: the F test does not have robustness of efficiency for bell-shaped symmetrical distributions with moderately long tails. No adequate study has been made of the robustness of efficiency of the Kruskal–Wallis test, but for distributions such as that described above, no competitor is in sight. The median test should have high efficiency for very long tailed symmetrical distributions.

Tests for equality of variances. In many data analyses an investigator is interested in comparing variability among the k treatments; thus he may carry out a test of

$$H_0: \sigma_1^2 = \sigma_2^2 = \cdots = \sigma_k^2$$

against

$$H_1: \sigma_i^2 \neq \sigma_j^2 \text{ for some } i, j.$$

and find confidence intervals for all ratios σ_j^2/σ_i^2, $i \neq j$ [see *the article on* VARIANCES, STATISTICAL

STUDY OF]. The robustness of validity of Bartlett's test for homogeneity of variance, and hence the validity of confidence intervals derived from Bartlett's test, will next be investigated. Bartlett's test is based upon the statistic M:

$$M = (\sum n_i - k) \ln s_w^2 - \sum (n_i - 1) \ln s_i^2,$$

where

$$s_w^2 = \sum (n_i - 1) s_i^2 / (\sum n_i - k),$$
$$s_i^2 = \sum (X_{ij} - \bar{X})^2 / (n_i - 1).$$

The significance level of M may be approximated from a χ^2 table with $k - 1$ degrees of freedom. The M test requires normality and has almost no robustness of validity, as may be seen from Table 11 where the nonnormality is characterized by the γ_2 parameter ($\gamma_1 = 0$).

The disastrous behavior of M for long-tailed symmetrical distributions may be explained by the following suggestive argument by Box (1953). Let T denote a statistic; for example, $\bar{X}$, s_1^2/s_2^2, M are statistics. Then, in large samples, T divided by its estimated standard error is usually normally distributed by the central limit theorem and associated mathematical facts. Thus, even though sampling may be from a nonnormal distribution, $\bar{X}/(s/\sqrt{n})$ is normally distributed. This result explains the robustness to nonnormality of the t test in the matched-pairs design and the F test in the one-way analysis of variance when the populations have the same shape. But Bartlett's M test does not have this structure of T divided by its standard error; hence, it does not find protection under the central limit theorem.

The nonrobustness of the M test requires the use of an alternative test. Scheffé (1959) has developed a robust test and a robust multiple comparison method for this problem from a suggestion by Box (1953).

The extreme sensitivity of the M test for equality of variances to the value of γ_2 indicates that one may expect trouble with the normal theory analysis of the random effects model, sometimes called model II [see LINEAR HYPOTHESES, *article on* ANAL-YSIS OF VARIANCE; *see also* Dixon & Massey (1951) 1957, p. 174]. Real difficulties do exist with such analyses, even in large samples.

A repeated-measurements design

An investigator records the response of each individual to a stimulus repeated at each of p different points in time. The data consist of response scores, X_{it}, where X_{it} denotes the score of the ith individual at time t, $i = 1, 2, \cdots, n$ and $t = 1, 2, \cdots, p$. Each individual has p response scores. The investigator assumes that

$$(7) \qquad X_{it} = \mu + \alpha_i + \tau_t + e_{it}.$$

The α_i and τ_t denote the individual and time effects, respectively. It is assumed that the random errors e_{it} have a common distribution and that the correlation between e_{it} and e_{is} is given by $\rho^{|t-s|}$. It is assumed then that an individual's response at time t is correlated with his response at another time s, but that the responses of different individuals are independent. The investigator's principal interest lies in testing the hypotheses.

$$(8) \qquad H_0^\alpha: \alpha_1 = \alpha_2 = \cdots = \alpha_n;$$
$$\text{against } H_1^\alpha: \alpha_i \neq \alpha_j \text{ for some } i, j$$

$$(9) \qquad H_0^\tau: \tau_1 = \tau_2 = \cdots = \tau_p;$$
$$\text{against } H_1^\tau: \tau_t \neq \tau_s \text{ for some } t, s.$$

Assume that the e_{it} are normal and study the effects of nonzero ρ on the standard F tests in the two-way analysis of variance.

The hypotheses (8) and (9) may be examined, respectively, by the statistics

$$F_{n-1, (n-1)(p-1)}^\alpha = \frac{\sum_{i=1}^{n} (\bar{X}_{i.} - \bar{X})^2 / (n - 1)}{\text{MSE}},$$

$$F_{p-1, (n-1)(p-1)}^\tau = \frac{\sum_{t=1}^{p} (\bar{X}_{.t} - \bar{X})^2 / (p - 1)}{\text{MSE}},$$

where MSE represents the mean square error, that is, $\sum (X_{it} - \bar{X}_{i.} - \bar{X}_{.t} + \bar{X})^2 / (n-1)(p-1)$. Table 12 gives the probability that $F^\alpha \geq 3.01$ for different values of ρ (the exact probability is .05 for $\rho = 0$) and the probability that $F^\tau \geq 3.01$ when $n = p = 5$.

Table 12 shows clearly the considerable effect of correlation on the test for individuals and the slight effect such correlation has for the test on times. In the terminology of the two-way analysis of variance, if individuals denote the rows and times denote the columns, then correlation within a row seriously affects the test on rows and only slightly affects the test on columns—with the given model for the correlation. Two explanations for the

Table 11 — True probability of exceeding the .05 normal theory point of M in large samples

		γ_2			
		−1	0	1	2
	2	.0056	.05	.11	.166
	3	.0025	.05	.136	.224
k	5	.0008	.05	.176	.315
	10	.001	.05	.257	.489

Source: Box 1953, p. 320.

Table 12 — *Probability that $F^\alpha \geqslant 3.01$ and probability that $F^\tau \geqslant 3.01$ in the presence of correlation*

| | Correlation, ρ | | | | |
	−0.40	−0.20	0.0	+0.20	+0.40
Exact probability for the F^α test on individuals	.0003	.0101	.05	.1305	.2470
Exact probability for the F^τ test on different times	.0590	.0527	.05	.0537	.0668

* The cell entries were computed assuming $\rho^{|t-s|} = \rho$ if $|t-s| = 1$ and $\rho^{|t-s|} = 0$ if $|t-s| \geqslant 2$ in order to simplify the computations. This approximation correctly indicates the order of magnitude of the more general model $\rho^{|t-s|}$.

Source: Box 1954, p. 497.

nonrobustness of the F^α test are (1) the numerator and denominator of F^α are correlated, contrary to the ideal condition, and (2) essentially the wrong standard error of the means for individuals is used.

It has been shown that statistical analyses based on assumptions that are incorrect for the data can produce misleading inferences. Furthermore, ways have been indicated to choose good statistical analyses, based on plausible assumptions, so that inferences will not be distorted. The question arises, "How does one decide which assumptions to make?" For example, suppose that there is interest only in making inferences about the mean difference. It then seems preferable to use an inference procedure that is robust against suspected departures from assumptions rather than to make preliminary significance tests of the assumptions of equality on variances, normality and/or symmetry, randomness, and so forth. A procedure that is robust against all failures in assumptions cannot be found, so a procedure must be chosen that is robust against those failures in assumptions that are known to be likely from experience with the problem under study or that would distort the inferences most severely.

ROBERT M. ELASHOFF

[*See also* FALLACIES, STATISTICAL; NONPARAMETRIC STATISTICS.]

BIBLIOGRAPHY

ASPIN, ALICE A. 1949 Tables for Use in Comparisons Whose Accuracy Involves Two Variances, Separately Estimated. *Biometrika* 36:290–293.

BEHRENS, W.-U. (1963) 1964 The Comparison of Means of Independent Normal Distributions With Different Variances. *Biometrics* 20:16–27. → First published in German. Discusses alternative tests to t or v based upon Fisher's fiducial theory of inference and the use of Bayesian methods.

BOX, GEORGE E. P. 1953 Non-normality and Tests on Variance. *Biometrika* 40:318–335. → Readers will find sections 1, 2, 7, 8, 9 accessible in general. The discussion section is particularly important.

BOX, GEORGE E. P. 1954 Some Theorems on Quadratic Forms Applied in the Study of Analysis of Variance Problems. II: Effects of Inequality of Variance and of Correlation Between Errors in the Two-way Classification. *Annals of Mathematical Statistics* 25:484–498.

BOX, GEORGE E. P.; and ANDERSEN, S. L. 1955 Permutation Theory in the Derivation of Robust Criteria and the Study of Departures From Assumptions. *Journal of the Royal Statistical Society* Series B 17:1–34. → The discussion on pages 26–34 presents some of the best thinking on statistical practice and is accessible in general.

BOX, GEORGE E. P.; and TIAO, G. C. 1964 A Note on Criterion vs. Inference Robustness. *Biometrika* 51:168–173. → The authors discuss robustness of validity and efficiency with a concrete example.

COCHRAN, WILLIAM G. 1964 Approximate Significance Levels of the Behrens–Fisher Test. *Biometrics* 20: 191–195.

COCHRANE, DONALD; and ORCUTT, G. H. 1949 Application of Least Squares Regression to Relationships Containing Auto-correlated Error Terms. *Journal of the American Statistical Association* 44:32–61.

DIXON, WILFRID J.; and MASSEY, FRANK J. JR. (1951) 1957 *Introduction to Statistical Analysis*. 2d ed. New York: McGraw-Hill.

GAYEN, A. K. 1949 The Distribution of "Student's" t in Random Samples of Any Size Drawn From Non-normal Universes. *Biometrika* 36:353–369. → The method and tables (like Table 2) and discussion are the important features of this and the next reference.

GAYEN, A. K. 1950 The Distribution of the Variance Ratio in Random Samples of Any Size Drawn From Non-normal Universes. *Biometrika* 37:236–255.

GEARY, R. C. 1966 A Note on Residual Heterovariance and Estimation Efficiency in Regression. *American Statistician* 20, no. 4:30–31.

HANNAN, E. J. 1955 An Exact Test for Correlation Between Time Series. *Biometrika* 42:316–326.

HOEL, PAUL G. 1964 Methods for Comparing Growth Type Curves. *Biometrics* 20:859–872.

HOTELLING, HAROLD 1961 The Behavior of Some Standard Statistical Tests Under Nonstandard Conditions. Volume 1, pages 319–359 in Berkeley Symposium on Mathematical Statistics and Probability, Fourth, University of California, 1960, *Proceedings*. Berkeley and Los Angeles: Univ. of California Press.

JAMES, G. S. 1951 The Comparison of Several Groups of Observations When the Ratios of the Population Variances Are Unknown. *Biometrika* 38:324–329. → The author's method for testing the null hypothesis (eq. 5) is accessible.

JOHNSTON, JOHN 1963 *Econometric Methods*. New York: McGraw-Hill. → An exposition of regression methods.

LANGLEY, P. A.; and ELASHOFF, R. M. 1966 A Study of the Hodges–Lehmann Two Sample Test. Unpublished manuscript.

PEARSON, EGON S. 1931 The Analysis of Variance in Cases of Non-normal Variation. *Biometrika* 23:114–133. → The author investigates the validity of the F test by Monto Carlo sampling.

PRATT, JOHN W. 1964 Robustness of Some Procedures for the Two-sample Location Problem. *Journal of the American Statistical Association* 59:665–680. → Readers with a modest statistical background will find sections 1 and 2 accessible. The author investigates the validity of several tests under inequality of variance.

SCHEFFÉ, HENRY 1959 *The Analysis of Variance*. New York: Wiley. → Chapter 10 is one of the most comprehensive accounts of the effects of departures from statistical assumptions. Readers with a modest statistical background will find pages 360–368 accessible.

SRIVASTAVA, A. B. L. 1958 Effect of Non-normality on the Power Function of *t*-Test. *Biometrika* 45:421–429.

TUKEY, JOHN W. 1960 A Survey of Sampling From Contaminated Distributions. Pages 448–485 in *Contributions to Probability and Statistics: Essays in Honor of Harold Hotelling*. Edited by Ingram Olkin et al. Stanford Univ. Press. → The author reviews his previous research on robust estimators for μ and σ^2 and gives a good bibliography.

TUKEY, JOHN W. 1962 The Future of Data Analysis. *Annals of Mathematical Statistics* 33:1–67, 812. → The author outlines his views on data analysis and makes several specific suggestions for handling spotty data. The first 21 pages are accessible; thereafter, some parts are accessible, others are not.

TUKEY, JOHN W.; and MCLAUGHLIN, DONALD H. 1963 Less Vulnerable Confidence and Significance Procedures for Location Based Upon a Single Sample: Trimming/Winsorization. *Sankhyā: The Indian Journal of Statistics* Series A 25:331–352. → The trimmed *t* is discussed. The beginning sections of the paper are accessible.

VAN DER VAART, H. R. 1961 On the Robustness of Wilcoxon's Two Sample Test. Pages 140–158 in Symposium on Quantitative Methods in Pharmacology, University of Leiden, 1960, *Quantitative Methods in Pharmacology: Proceedings*. Amsterdam: North-Holland Publishing. → The introduction and conclusion, together with the table and graphs, are accessible.

WELCH, B. L. 1938 The Significance of the Difference Between Two Means When the Population Variances Are Unequal. *Biometrika* 29:350–362.

WELCH, B. L. 1947 The Generalization of "Student's" Problem When Several Different Population Variances Are Involved. *Biometrika* 34:28–35.

WETHERHILL, G. B. 1960 The Wilcoxon Test and Non-null Hypotheses. *Journal of the Royal Statistical Society* Series B 22:402–418.

ESPIONAGE

See INTELLIGENCE, POLITICAL AND MILITARY.

ESTATE TAXES

See TAXATION, *article on* DEATH AND GIFT TAXES.

ESTHETICS

See AESTHETICS.

ESTIMATION

I. POINT ESTIMATION   *D. L. Burkholder*
II. CONFIDENCE INTERVALS
AND REGIONS   *J. Pfanzagl*

I
POINT ESTIMATION

How many fish are in this lake? What proportion of the voting population favors candidate A? How much paint is needed for this particular room? What fuel capacity should this airplane have if it is to carry passengers safely between New York and Paris? How many items in this shipment have the desired quality? What is the specific gravity of this metal? Questions like these represent problems of point estimation. In present-day statistical methodology, such problems are usually cast in the following form: A mathematical model describing a particular phenomenon is completely specified except for some unknown quantity or quantities. These quantities must be estimated. Galileo's model for freely falling bodies and many models in learning theory, small group theory, and the like provide examples.

Exact answers are often impossible, difficult, expensive, or merely inconvenient to obtain. However, approximate answers that are quite likely to be close to the exact answer may be fairly easily obtainable. The theory of point estimation provides a guide for obtaining such answers; above all, it makes precise, or provides enough framework so that one could make precise, such phrases as "quite likely to be close" and others such as "this estimator is better than that one."

As an introduction to some of the problems involved, consider estimating the number N of fish in a given lake. Suppose that M fish are taken from the lake, marked, and returned to the lake unharmed. A little later, a random sample of size n of fish from the lake is observed to contain x marked fish. A little thought suggests that probably the ratio x/n is near M/N or that the unknown N and the ratio Mn/x (defined only if $x > 0$) are not too far apart. For example, if $M = 1,000$, $n = 1,000$, and $x = 20$, it might be reasonable to believe that N is close to 50,000. [*A similar example, concerning moving populations of workers, is discussed in* SAMPLE SURVEYS.]

Clearly, this procedure *may* lead one badly astray. For example, it is possible, althoughly highly unlikely, that the same value $x = 20$ could be obtained, and hence, using the above procedure, N be estimated as 50,000, even if N is actually as small as 1,980 or as large as 10,000,000. Clearly, considerations of probability are basic here. If $L(N)$ denotes the probability of obtaining 20 marked fish when N fish are in the lake, it can be shown that $0 = L(1,979) < L(1,980) < \cdots < L(49,999) = L(50,000)$ and $L(50,000) > L(50,001) > \cdots$; that is, $N = 50,000$ maximizes the *likelihood* of obtaining 20 marked fish.

Design of experiments. What values of M and n are most satisfactory in the above experiment? Clearly, the bigger n is, the better it is for estimation purposes, but the more expensive the experiment [*see* EXPERIMENTAL DESIGN]. A balance has to be reached between the conflicting goals of minimizing error and minimizing expense. Also, perhaps another experimental design might give better results. In the above problem, let $M = 1,000$, but instead of pulling a fixed number of fish out of the lake, pull out fish until exactly x marked fish have been obtained, where x is fixed in advance. Then n, the sample size, is the observation of interest [see SEQUENTIAL ANALYSIS]. Which design, of all the possible designs, should be used? This kind of question is basic to any estimation problem.

Testing hypotheses. An altogether different problem would arise if one did not really want the value of N for its own sake but only as a means of deciding whether or not the lake should be restocked with small fish. For example, it might be desirable to restock the lake if N is small, say less than 100,000, and undesirable otherwise. In this case, the problem of whether or not the lake should be restocked is equivalent to testing the hypothesis that N is less than 100,000 [see HYPOTHESIS TESTING]. In general, a good estimator does not necessarily lead to a good test.

Confidence intervals. The value of an estimator, that is, a point estimate, of N for a particular sample is a number, hopefully one close to N; the value of a confidence interval, that is, an interval estimate, of N for a particular sample is an interval, hopefully one that is not only small but that also contains N [see ESTIMATION, article on CONFIDENCE INTERVALS AND REGIONS]. The problem of finding a good interval estimate is more closely related to hypothesis testing than it is to point estimation.

Note that certain problems are clearly point estimation problems rather than problems of interval estimation: when deciding what the fuel capacity of an airplane should be, the designers must settle on one particular number.

Steps in solving an estimation problem

The first step in the solution of an estimation problem, as suggested above, is to design an experiment (or method of taking observations) such that the outcome of the experiment—call it x—is affected by the unknown quantity to be estimated, which in the above discussion was N. Typically, x is related to N probabilistically rather than deterministically. This probability relation must be specified. For example, the probability of obtaining x marked fish in a sample of size n is given by the hypergeometric distribution,

$$\binom{M}{x}\binom{N-M}{n-x} / \binom{N}{n},$$

provided the sample has been drawn randomly without replacement [see DISTRIBUTIONS, STATISTICAL, article on SPECIAL DISCRETE DISTRIBUTIONS]. (The denominator is the number of combinations of N things taken n at a time, and so forth.) If the randomness assumption is not quite satisfied, then the specified probability relation will be only approximately true. Such specification problems and their implications will be discussed later. Next, after the experiment has been designed and the probability model specified, one must choose a function f defined for each possible x such that if x is observed, then $f(x)$, the value of the function f at x, is to be used as a numerical estimate of N. Such a function f is called an *estimator* of N. The problem of the choice of f will be discussed later. Finally, after a particular estimator f has been tentatively settled on, one might want to calculate additional performance characteristics of f, giving further indications of how well f will perform on the average. If the results of these calculations show that f will not be satisfactory, then changes in the design of the experiment, for example, an increase in sample size, might be contemplated. Clearly, there is a good deal of interplay among all the steps in the solution of an estimation problem outlined here.

Terminological note. Some authors distinguish terminologically between the *estimator*, the function f, and its numerical value for a particular sample, the *estimate*. Another distinction is that between a random variable and a generic value of the random variable. (Some authors use X for the former and x for the latter.) Such distinctions are sometimes important, but they are not generally made in this article, although special comments appear in a few places. Otherwise it should be clear from context whether reference is made to a function or its value, or whether reference is made to a random variable or its value.

Choice of estimator

As a means of illustrating the various considerations influencing the choice of an estimator, a few typical examples will be discussed.

Example 1. Let x be the number of successes in n independent trials, the probability of a success on an individual trial being p. (For example, x might be the number of respondents out of n questioned in a political poll who say they are Democrats, and p is the probability that a randomly chosen individual in the population will say he is a Democrat.) Here p is unknown and may be any number between 0 and 1 inclusive. An estimator f of p ideally should be such that $f(x)$ is close to p no matter what the unknown p is and no matter what the observation x is. That is, the error $f(x) - p$ committed by using $f(x)$ as an approximation to p should always be small. This is too much to expect since x can, by chance, be quite misleading about p. However, it is not too much to expect that the error be small in some average sense. For example, the mean squared error,

$$E_p(f - p)^2 = \sum_{x=0}^{n} [f(x) - p]^2 \binom{n}{x} p^x (1-p)^{n-x},$$

should be small no matter what the unknown p is, or the mean absolute error $E_p|f - p|$ should be small no matter what p is, or the like. For the time being, estimators will be compared only on the basis of their mean squared errors. A more general approach, the underlying ideas of which are well illustrated in this special case, will be mentioned later. The first question that arises is, Can one find an estimator f such that, for every p satisfying $0 \leqslant p \leqslant 1$, the mean squared error of f at p is smaller than (or at least not greater than) the mean squared error at p of any other estimator? Obviously, such an estimator would be best in this mean squared error sense. Unfortunately, and this is what makes the problem of choosing an estimator a nontrivial problem, a best estimator does not exist. To see this, consider the estimates f_1 and f_2 defined by $f_1(x) = x/n$ and $f_2(x) = \frac{1}{2}$. It is not hard to show that $E_p(f_1 - p)^2 = p(1 - p)/n$, and clearly, $E_p(f_2 - p)^2 = (\frac{1}{2} - p)^2$. If a best estimator f existed it would have to satisfy $E_p(f - p)^2 \leqslant E_p(f_2 - p)^2$. But the latter quantity is zero for $p = \frac{1}{2}$, implying that $f = f_2$. However, f_2 is not best since $E_p(f_1 - p)^2$ is smaller than $E_p(f_2 - p)^2$ for p near 0 or 1.

Although no best estimator exists, many good estimators exist. For example, there are many estimators f satisfying $E_p(f - p)^2 \leqslant 1/(4n)$ for $0 \leqslant p \leqslant 1$. The estimator f_1, defined above, is such an estimator. The estimator f_3 defined by $f_3(x) = [\sqrt{n}(x/n) + \frac{1}{2}]/(\sqrt{n} + 1)$ with mean squared error $E_p(f_3 - p)^2 = 1/[4(1 + \sqrt{n})^2]$ is another. If n is large, the mean squared error of any such estimator is small for each possible value of p. In this problem, as is typical, any one of many good available estimators would no doubt be reasonable to use in practice. Only by adding further assumptions, for example, assumptions giving some information about the unknown p, can the class of reasonable estimators be narrowed. Note that estimators are still being compared on the basis of their mean squared errors only.

The estimator f_3 is *minimax* in the sense that f_3 minimizes $\max_{0 \leqslant p \leqslant 1} E_p(f - p)^2$ with respect to f. The minimax approach focuses attention on the worst that can happen using f and chooses f accordingly [*see* DECISION THEORY]. Note that the estimator f_1 ($f_1(x) = x/n$) does have slightly larger mean squared error than does f_3 for values of p near $\frac{1}{2}$; for values of p near 0 or 1 the advantage lies

wholly with f_1. Other properties of these estimators will be discussed later.

Example 2. Suppose that $x_1, x_2, \cdots, x_n$ are observations on n independent random variables, each having the Poisson distribution with parameter λ, where λ is unknown and may be any nonnegative number [*see* DISTRIBUTIONS, STATISTICAL, *article on* SPECIAL DISCRETE DISTRIBUTIONS]. For example, x_k could be the number of occurrences during the kth time interval of unit length of any phenomenon occurring "randomly" over time, possibly telephone calls coming into an exchange, customers coming into a store, and so forth [*see* QUEUES]. Knowing that λ is both the mean and variance of the Poisson distribution, it might not be unreasonable to suppose that both the sample mean,

$$m(x) = m(x_1, \cdots, x_n) = \sum_{k=1}^{n} x_k/n = \bar{x},$$

and the sample variance,

$$s^2(x) = \sum_{k=1}^{n} (x_k - \bar{x})^2/(n - 1)$$

(here, one must assume that $n > 1$), provide good estimators of the unknown λ. It is not hard to show that m is *better* than s^2, that is, $E_\lambda(m - \lambda)^2 \leqslant E_\lambda(s^2 - \lambda)^2$ for all $\lambda \geqslant 0$, with strict inequality for some $\lambda \geqslant 0$.

An estimator is *inadmissible* (with respect to a given criterion like mean squared error) if a better one exists; accordingly, the estimator s^2 is here inadmissible. An estimator is admissible if it is not inadmissible. Although it is not obvious, the estimator m is admissible. In fact the class of admissible estimates is very large here, as is typically the case. In example 1, all three estimators discussed, f_1, f_2, and f_3, are admissible.

Example 3. Let $x_1, x_2, \cdots, x_n$ be observations on n independent random variables each having the normal distribution with mean μ and variance σ^2, where both μ and σ^2 are unknown; μ may be any real number and σ^2 may be any positive number. One might be interested in estimating only μ, only σ^2, the pair (μ, σ^2), or perhaps some combination such as μ/σ.

Example 4. Let $x_1, x_2, \cdots, x_n$ be observations on n independent random variables each having the uniform distribution over the set of integers $\{1, 2, \cdots, N\}$, where N may be any positive integer. For example, in a state where automobile license plates are numbered from 1 to N, each x_i would be the number of a randomly chosen license plate. What is a good estimator of N?

Sufficient statistics. A simple and effective way to narrow the class of estimators that one ought to consider when choosing a good estimator is to identify a sufficient statistic for the problem and to consider only those estimators that depend on the sufficient statistic [see SUFFICIENCY]. Roughly speaking, if t is a sufficient statistic, knowing $t(x)$ is as useful as knowing x. The following result is important. If t is a sufficient statistic and f is an estimator with finite mean squared error and f does not depend on t (that is, f is not essentially expressible as $f = h(t)$ for some function h), then there is another estimator f_0 that does depend on t and such that f_0 is better than f (in the technical sense defined above). One f_0 that works is the conditional expectation of f relative to t.

In example 2, m is a sufficient statistic, hence only estimators depending on m need be considered. In particular s^2, which does not depend on m in the sense defined above, need not be considered. In example 3, the ordered pair (m, s^2), where m and s^2 are defined as in example 2, is a sufficient statistic. In example 4, the estimator $2m$ might seem at first to be a plausible estimator of N. However, it does not depend on the sufficient statistic u defined by $u(x) =$ the largest of the x_k. Much better estimators than $2m$ exist. For example, the rather complicated

$$f_4 = \frac{u^{n+1} - (u-1)^{n+1}}{u^n - (u-1)^n}$$

is such an estimator. (Note that f_4 is approximately equal to $(n+1)u/n$.)

Further criteria for choice of estimator. So far estimators have been compared on the basis of their mean squared errors only. Since no best estimator exists, a unique solution to the problem of choosing an estimator is generally not obtainable by this approach. This is not really too regrettable since many good estimators usually exist. Even demanding that an estimator be minimax, not necessarily always a reasonable demand, does not always lead to a unique estimator. In example 2, every estimator of λ has unbounded mean squared error; and in example 3 every estimator of μ has unbounded mean squared error. Hence, in these two examples, all estimators of λ and μ, respectively, are minimax, but the concept loses all interest. In example 1, demanding minimaxity does lead to the unique minimax estimator f_3. A unique minimax estimator is clearly admissible.

The strong intellectual and psychological tendency of human beings to be satisfied only with unique answers has often led to further demands being placed on estimators in addition to the one that their mean squared errors be small.

Unbiasedness. An estimator is *unbiased* if the mean value of the estimator is equal to the quantity being estimated. In example 1, f_1 is unbiased since $E_p f_1 = p$, $0 \leqslant p \leqslant 1$. Both m and s^2 are unbiased estimators of λ in example 2. In example 3, m is an unbiased estimator of μ and s^2 is an unbiased estimator of σ^2. In example 4, both $2m$ and f_4 are unbiased estimators of N. The search for a best unbiased estimator often leads to a unique answer. In example 2, an estimator f would be best unbiased (or minimum variance unbiased) if it is unbiased and satisfies

$$E_\lambda(f-\lambda)^2 \leqslant E_\lambda(f^*-\lambda)^2$$

for every $\lambda \geqslant 0$ and every unbiased estimator f^*. The estimator m is such an estimator for this problem and is the only such estimator. The estimator f_1 is the best unbiased estimator of p in example 1; the estimator m is the best unbiased estimator of μ in example 3; and the estimator f_4 is the best unbiased estimator of N in example 4. The *relative efficiency* of two unbiased estimators is the ratio of their reciprocal variances. Relative efficiency may well depend on the parameter value.

Unbiased estimators fail to exist in some important problems. Using the first design mentioned in the problem of estimating the number of fish in a lake, N, no unbiased estimator of N exists. Although in example 3, s^2 is a best unbiased estimator of σ^2, another estimator of σ^2, $(n-1)s^2/(n+1)$, despite being biased, is actually better than s^2 in the sense of mean squared error. This shows that placing extra demands on estimators can actually come into conflict with the small mean squared error demand. Of course, the relative importance of the various properties an estimator may have will no doubt be judged slightly differently by different reasonable individuals.

Invariance. Notions of invariance can sometimes be invoked so that a best invariant estimator exists. For example, if $x = (x_1, \cdots, x_n)$, b is a real number, and $y = (x_1 + b, \cdots, x_n + b)$, the estimator m is invariant in the sense that it satisfies $m(y) = m(x) + b$. It turns out that among all the estimators of μ in example 3 with this property of scale invariance, the estimator m is best in the usual mean squared error sense. The argument for invariance may be stated rather loosely as follows. Irrelevancies in the data (for example, whether time is measured from 12 noon New York time or from 12 noon Greenwich time) should not make a fundamental difference in the results obtained from the analysis of the data.

A different kind of invariance problem can be troublesome in some circumstances. Suppose in example 1 that interest centers not on p but on some function of p, say $1/p$. If f is a satisfactory estimator of p, it need not follow that $1/f$ is a satisfactory estimator of $1/p$, for properties like unbiasedness, mean squared error functions, etc., can change drastically under nonlinear transformations. Fortunately, in many problems the parameter itself, or a single function of it, is of central interest, so that this kind of noninvariance is not serious.

Specification problems. So far, estimators have been chosen relative to given probability models. If an estimator seems satisfactory for a given probability model, it may be relevant to ask if this estimator is also good for probability models closely related to the given one. For example, it is too much to expect that a model postulating normal distributions describes exactly the practical situation of interest. Fortunately, in many common problems slight changes in the probability model will not materially affect the goodness of an estimator reasonable for the original model [*see* ERRORS, *article on the* EFFECTS OF ERRORS IN STATISTICAL ASSUMPTIONS]. For example, the estimator m of μ in example 3 is actually a fairly reasonable estimator of the population mean μ in a large variety of cases, particularly if the population variance σ^2 is finite and the sample size n is not too small, as can be seen from the formula for its mean squared error, σ^2/n. Circumstances arise, however, in which alternative estimators, for example, the sample median, not so much affected by slight changes in the tails of the distribution, may need to be considered. [*A process for arriving at other such estimators, called Winsorization, is discussed in* NONPARAMETRIC STATISTICS, *article on* ORDER STATISTICS; *the closely related concept of trimming is discussed in* ERRORS, *article on the* EFFECTS OF ERRORS IN STATISTICAL ASSUMPTIONS.]

More than one parameter. Most of the material of this article deals with estimation of a single parameter. The multiparameter case is, of course, also important and multiparameter analogues of all the topics in this article exist. They are treated in the references, for example by Kendall and Stuart (1946), Cramér (1945), and Wilks (1962).

Constructive estimation methods

Maximum likelihood estimators. In example 1, the estimator f_1 is the maximum likelihood estimator of p: For each x, $f_1(x)$ is that value of p maximizing $\binom{n}{x} p^x (1-p)^{n-x}$, the probability of obtaining x. In example 2, m is the maximum likelihood estimator of λ. In example 3, $(m, [n-1]s^2/n)$ is the maximum likelihood estimator of (μ, σ^2). In example 4, u is the maximum likelihood estimator of N. In the problem of estimating the number of fish in a lake, N, using the first design, no maximum likelihood estimator exists since no such

estimate can be defined for $x = 0$, although for $x > 0$ no trouble occurs. In some examples, there is no unique maximum likelihood estimator.

Maximum likelihood estimators are often easy to obtain. A maximum likelihood estimator does not necessarily have small mean squared error nor is it always admissible. So the maximum likelihood principle can sometimes conflict with the small mean squared error principle. Nevertheless, maximum likelihood estimators are often quite good and worth looking at. If the sample size is large, they tend to behave nearly as nicely as the estimator m of μ in example 3.

Maximum likelihood estimation is often constructive, that is, the method provides machinery that often gives a unique estimating function. There are other constructive methods, three of which are described here: the method of moments, least squares, and Bayes estimation. One or another of these constructive methods may provide a simpler or a better behaved estimator in any particular case.

The method of moments. The approach of the method of moments (or of expected values) is to set one or more sample moments equal to the corresponding population moments and to "solve," if possible, for the parameters, thus obtaining estimators of these parameters. The method is particularly appropriate for simple random sampling. In example 1, if the sample is regarded as made up of n observations, the kth being a 1 (success) or 0 (failure), the sample mean is x/n and the population mean is p, so the resulting method of moments estimator is x/n. In example 4, the method of moments, as it would ordinarily be applied, leads to a poor estimator. The method can, nonetheless, be very useful, especially in more complex cases with several parameters.

Least squares. The least squares approach is especially useful when the observations are not obtained by simple random sampling. One considers the formal sum of squares $\sum_k (x_k - EX_k)^2$, where x_k is an observation on the random variable X_k with expectation EX_k (depending on the parameters to be estimated). Then one attempts to minimize the sum of squares over possible values of the parameters. If a unique minimum exists, the minimizing values of the parameters are the values of their *least square estimators*.

The method is particularly appropriate when the X_k are independent and identically distributed except for translational shifts that are given functions of the parameters. If the X_k all have the same expectation, as in examples 1–4, the least squares estimator of that expectation is the sample mean. Least squares estimation, without modification or extension, does not provide estimators of parameters (like σ^2 in example 3) that do not enter into expectations of observations. [*A fuller treatment of this topic appears in* LINEAR HYPOTHESES, *article on* REGRESSION.]

Bayes estimation.   Consider example 1 again, this time supposing that the unknown p is itself the outcome of some experiment and that the probability distribution underlying this experiment is known. For example, x could be the number of heads obtained in n tosses of a particular coin, the probability of a head for the particular coin being p where p is unknown, but where the coin has been picked randomly from a population of coins with a known distribution of p values. Then it would be reasonable to choose an estimator f that minimizes the mean value of the squared error $[f(x) - p]^2$ where the averaging is done with respect to the *known* joint distribution of x and p. Such a minimizing estimator is called a *Bayes estimator*; of course it depends on the distribution assigned to p [*see* BAYESIAN INFERENCE]. A distribution may be assigned to p merely as a technical device for obtaining an estimator and completely apart from the question of whether p actually is the outcome of an experiment. This is the spirit in which Bayes estimators are often introduced, as a way of obtaining an estimator that may or may not have good properties. On the other hand, one may assign a distribution to p in such a way that those values of p that seem more likely to obtain are given greater weight. Of course, different individuals might assign different distributions, for this is a matter of judgment. However, this approach does provide one possible method for using any previously obtained information about p that may be available. It would be rather rare that the *only* information available about p before the experiment is that $0 \leqslant p \leqslant 1$.

Examples of Bayes estimators include the estimator f_3 of example 1, obtained by assigning a certain beta distribution to p, and the estimator f_5 of p, defined by $f_5(x) = (x + 1)/(n + 2)$, obtained by assigning to p the uniform distribution on the interval between 0 and 1. [*See* DISTRIBUTIONS, STATISTICAL, *article on* SPECIAL CONTINUOUS DISTRIBUTIONS, *for discussions of these specific distributions.*] Even f_2 is a Bayes estimator. However, f_1 is not a Bayes estimator but is rather the limit of a sequence of Bayes estimators.

Restricting attention to estimators that are Bayes or the limits (in a certain sense) of sequences of Bayes estimators usually assures one of not overlooking any admissible estimator. Bayes methods frequently prove useful as technical devices in solving for minimax estimators and in many other situations.

Asymptotic estimation theory

Because it is often difficult to compare estimators for small sample sizes, much research on point estimation is in terms of large sample sizes, working with limits as the sample size goes to infinity. In this context, an estimator itself is not considered, but rather a *sequence* of estimators, each member of which corresponds to a single sample size. For example, consider the sequence of sample means $m_1, m_2, \cdots$, where $m_n(x_1, \cdots, x_n) = \sum_{k=1}^{n} x_k / n$. If a sequence of estimators has desirable properties in a limiting large sample sense, it is often presumed that particular members of the sequence will to some extent partake of these desirable properties.

Consistency.   An asymptotic condition that is often regarded as essential is that of *consistency*, in the sense that the sequence of estimators is close to the true value of the parameter, with high probability, for large sample sizes. More precisely if $\{t_n\}$ is the sequence of estimators, and if θ is the parameter being estimated, the sequence $\{t_n\}$ is said to estimate θ consistently if, for every interval I containing θ in its interior, the probability that the value of t_n belongs to I approaches 1 as n approaches infinity, no matter what the value of θ is. (There is also a nonasymptotic concept of consistency, closely related to the above. Both ideas, and their applications, originated with R. A. Fisher.)

Comparison of estimators.   For simplicity, consider now independent identically distributed random variables with common distribution depending on a single parameter, θ. Let ϕ_θ be the density function (or frequency function) corresponding to that common distribution for the parameter value θ. A large number of regularity conditions are traditionally, and often tacitly, imposed on ϕ_θ; for example, distributions like those of example 4 do not come under the standard theory here. In this brief summary, the regularity conditions will not be discussed. With almost no modifications, the discussion applies to qualitative, as well as numerically valued, random quantities.

Two sequences of estimators, competing as estimators of θ, are often compared by considering the ratios of their asymptotic variances, that is, the variances of limit distributions as n approaches infinity. In particular, one or both sequences may have the lowest possible asymptotic variance. In discussing such matters, the following constructs, invented and named by R. A. Fisher, are important.

Score, Fisher information, and efficiency.   The *score* of the single observation x_k is a function of both x_k and θ, defined by

$$s_\theta(x_k) = \frac{\partial}{\partial \theta} \ln \phi_\theta(x_k),$$

and it provides the relative change in ϕ (for each possible value of x_k) when θ is slightly changed. Two basic facts about the score are $E_\theta s_\theta = 0$, $\mathrm{var}_\theta s_\theta = -E_\theta(\partial s_\theta/\partial\theta)$. The quantity, $-E(\partial s_\theta/\partial\theta)$, is often called the *Fisher information* contained in a single observation and is denoted by $I(\theta)$.

For the entire sample, $x = \{x_1, x_2, \cdots, x_n\}$, the *sample score* is just the sum of the single observation scores,

$$s_{\theta n}(x) = \sum_{k=1}^{n} s_\theta(x_k).$$

The Fisher information $I_n(\theta)$ contained in the entire sample is defined as above with $s_{\theta n}$ replacing s_θ; it is just the sum of the Fisher information values for the n single observations. Under the assumptions, each observation contributes the same amount to total information—that is, $I(\theta)$ is the same for each observation—so that $I_n(\theta) = n\, I(\theta)$.

Except for sign, $I_n(\theta)$ is the curvature of the likelihood function near the true value of θ. Roughly speaking, sharp curvature of the likelihood function corresponds to sharper estimation, or lower variance of estimation. The *information inequality* says that, for sequences of estimators $\{t_n\}$ such that $\sqrt{n}\,(t_n - \theta)$ converges in distribution to a distribution with mean zero and variance σ^2,

$$\sigma^2 \geqslant \frac{1}{I(\theta)}.$$

Nonasymptotic variants of this inequality have been explored by Darmois, Dugué, Cramér, Rao, and others. The basic variant, for an unbiased estimator t_n, based on a sample of size n, is

$$\mathrm{var}_\theta t_n \geqslant \frac{1}{I_n(\theta)}.$$

(This is usually called the Cramér–Rao inequality.) Under the tacit regularity conditions, this inequality becomes an equality just when

$$t_n = \theta + \frac{s_{\theta n}}{I_n(\theta)}.$$

This can happen only if the right side is not a function of θ, and this in turn occurs (under regularity) when and only when the distributions given by ϕ_θ form an exponential family [see DISTRIBUTIONS, STATISTICAL, *article on* SPECIAL CONTINUOUS DISTRIBUTIONS].

The maximum likelihood estimator of θ based on $x = (x_1, \cdots, x_n)$, say $\hat{\theta}_n$, is (under regularity) the solution of the *likelihood equation* $s_{\theta n}(x) = 0$. Under these circumstances, $s_{\theta n}/\sqrt{I_n(\theta)}$ and $\sqrt{I_n(\theta)}\,[\hat{\theta}_n - \theta]$ are both asymptotically normal with zero mean and variance unity. Further, the difference between these two quantities converges to zero in probability as n increases.

Thus the maximum likelihood estimator is *asymptotically efficient*, in the sense that its asymptotic variance is as low as possible, for it satisfies the asymptotic information inequality. In general there exist other (sequences of) estimators also satisfying the information inequality; these are called *regular best asymptotically normal* (RBAN) estimators. The RBAN estimators are those that are indistinguishable from the maximum likelihood estimator in terms of asymptotic distribution, as it is traditionally construed. Often some RBAN estimator distinct from the maximum likelihood estimator is easier to compute and work with.

The word "regular," used above, refers in part to regularity conditions on the estimators themselves, considered as functions of the sample. Without that restriction, somewhat strange *superefficient* estimators can be constructed.

The concept of asymptotic treatment has been extended recently in other directions than those summarized above, in particular by the work of R. R. Bahadur and C. R. Rao.

A more general approach to estimation

So far the discussion has been based largely on comparing estimators through their mean squared errors. The mean absolute error could, of course, have been used. More generally, suppose that $W(\theta,d)$ is the *loss* incurred when the numerical estimate d is used as if it were the value $g(\theta)$. Here θ is the unknown parameter of the probability distribution underlying the outcome x of an experiment, and $g(\theta)$ is to be estimated. If f is an estimator, x has been observed, and $f(x)$ is used as if it were the value of $g(\theta)$, then the loss incurred is $W[\theta,f(x)]$. The mean loss, $E_\theta W(\theta,f)$, denoted by $r(\theta,f)$, a function of both θ and f, is of interest. The function r is called the *risk function*. Now such terms as *better, admissible, minimax, Bayes*, and so forth could be defined using the risk function, r, rather than mean squared error. For example, f is better than f^* (relative to the loss W) if $r(\theta,f) \leqslant r(\theta,f^*)$ for all θ with strict inequality for some θ [see DECISION THEORY].

In the earlier discussion, W was taken to be $W(\theta,d) = [d - g(\theta)]^2$ and r was therefore mean squared error.

In the more general multiparameter context mentioned earlier, θ is a vector of more than one ordinary (scalar) parameter, and so may be $g(\theta)$, the quantity to be estimated. For example, in example 3, $\theta = (\mu,\sigma^2)$, $g(\theta)$ could be θ, and $W(\theta,d)$ could be $(d_1 - \mu)^2 + (d_2 - \sigma^2)^2$, where $d = (d_1,d_2)$

is an ordered pair of real numbers. Or consider the following example in which an infinite number of quantities are simultaneously estimated.

Example 5. Let $x_1, x_2, \cdots, x_n$ be observations on n independent random variables each having the same distribution function F, where F may be any distribution function on the real line. The problem is to estimate the whole function F, that is, to estimate $F(a)$ for each real number a. Here $\theta = F$, $g(\theta) = F$, d may be any distribution function, and $W(\theta, d)$ may be given, for example, by sup $|d(a) - F(a)|$, where the supremum (least upper bound) is taken over all real a. A quite satisfactory estimator, the sample distribution function, exists here. For large n, its risk function is near 0. For $x = (x_1, x_2, \cdots, x_n)$, the value of the sample distribution function is that distribution that places probability $1/n$ on each of $x_1, x_2, \cdots, x_n$ if these values are distinct, with the obvious differential weighting otherwise.

One difficulty with the more general approach to estimation outlined here is that the loss function W is often hard to define realistically, that is, in such a way that $W(\theta, d)$ approximates the actual loss incurred when d is used as if it were the value of $g(\theta)$. Fortunately, an estimator that is good relative to one loss function, say squared error, is often good relative to a wide class of loss functions.

Perhaps the key concept in estimation theory is *better*. Once it has been decided what "this estimator is better than that one" should mean, a large part of the theory follows naturally. Many definitions of *better* are possible. Several others besides the one mentioned here appear in the literature, but none has been so deeply investigated.

History

The theory of point estimation has a long history and a huge literature. The Bernoullis, Moivre, Bayes, Laplace, and Gauss contributed many important ideas and techniques to the subject during the eighteenth century and the early part of the nineteenth century. Karl Pearson stressed the method of moments and the importance of computing approximate variances of estimators. During the early twentieth century, no one pursued the subject with more vigor than R. A. Fisher. His contributions include the development of the maximum likelihood principle and the introduction of the important notion of sufficiency. Neyman's systematic study of interval estimation appeared in 1937. Although the possibility of a loss function approach to statistical problems had been mentioned by Neyman and E. S. Pearson in 1933, its extensive development was not initiated until the work of Abraham

Wald in 1939 [*see the biographies of* BAYES; BERNOULLI FAMILY; FISHER, R. A.; GAUSS; LAPLACE; MOIVRE; PEARSON; WALD].

New and nonstandard estimation problems requiring new and nonstandard techniques of solution will no doubt continue to arise. Remarkable solutions to two such problems have recently been proposed under the general name of *stochastic approximation* [*see* SEQUENTIAL ANALYSIS].

Ideally, scientific constructs should possess not only great explanatory power but simplicity as well. The search for both will, no doubt, encourage more and more mathematical model building in the social sciences. Moreover, it is quite likely that these models will have to become more and more probabilistic if they are to achieve these aims. As a consequence, the statistical problems involved, checking the goodness of fit of the model, estimating the unknown parameters, and so forth, will have to be handled with ever-increasing care and knowledge.

D. L. BURKHOLDER

[*See also* STATISTICS, DESCRIPTIVE.]

BIBLIOGRAPHY

Many elementary textbooks on statistical theory discuss the rudiments of point estimation, for example, Hodges & Lehmann 1964. *Fuller treatments will be found in* Cramér 1945, Wilks 1962, *and* Kendall & Stuart 1946. *Large sample theory is treated at length in* LeCam 1953. *Further discussion of estimation from the loss function point of view will be found in Chapter 5 of Wald 1950. Lehmann 1959 treats sufficiency and invariance in some detail. Chapter 15 of Savage 1954 contains many illuminating comments on the problem of choosing a good estimator.*

CRAMÉR, HARALD (1945) 1951 *Mathematical Methods of Statistics.* Princeton Mathematical Series, No. 9. Princeton Univ. Press.

FISHER, R. A. (1922) 1950 On the Mathematical Foundations of Theoretical Statistics. Pages 10.308a–10.368 in R. A. Fisher, *Contributions to Mathematical Statistics.* New York: Wiley. → First published in Volume 222 of the *Philosophical Transactions,* Series A, of the Royal Society of London.

FISHER, R. A. (1925) 1950 Theory of Statistical Estimation. Pages 11.699a–11.725 in R. A. Fisher, *Contributions to Mathematical Statistics.* New York: Wiley. → First published in Volume 22 of the *Proceedings* of the Cambridge Philosophical Society.

HODGES, JOSEPH L. JR.; and LEHMANN, E. L. 1964 *Basic Concepts of Probability and Statistics.* San Francisco: Holden-Day.

KENDALL, MAURICE G.; and STUART, ALAN (1946) 1961 *The Advanced Theory of Statistics.* Volume 2: Inference and Relationship. New York: Hafner; London: Griffin. → Kendall was the sole author of the 1946 edition.

KIEFER, J.; and WOLFOWITZ, J. 1952 Stochastic Estimation of the Maximum of Regression Function. *Annals of Mathematical Statistics* 23:462–466.

LeCam, Lucien 1953 On Some Asymptotic Properties of Maximum Likelihood Estimates and Related Bayes' Estimates. California, University of, *Publications in Statistics* 1:277–329.

Lehmann, Erich L. 1959 *Testing Statistical Hypotheses.* New York: Wiley.

Neyman, Jerzy 1937 Outline of a Theory of Statistical Estimation Based on the Classical Theory of Probability. Royal Society of London, *Philosophical Transactions* Series A 236:333–380.

Pitman, E. J. G. 1939 The Estimation of the Location and Scale of Parameters of a Continuous Population of Any Given Form. *Biometrika* 30:391–421.

Robbins, Herbert; and Monro, Sutton 1951 A Stochastic Approximation Method. *Annals of Mathematical Statistics* 22:400–407.

Savage, Leonard J. 1954 *The Foundations of Statistics.* New York: Wiley.

Wald, Abraham 1939 Contributions to the Theory of Statistical Estimation and Testing Hypotheses. *Annals of Mathematical Statistics* 10:299–326.

Wald, Abraham (1950) 1964 *Statistical Decision Functions.* New York: Wiley.

Wilks, Samuel S. 1962 *Mathematical Statistics.* New York: Wiley.

II

CONFIDENCE INTERVALS AND REGIONS

Confidence interval procedures—more generally, *confidence region procedures*—form an important class of statistical methods. In these methods, the outcome of the statistical analysis is a subset of the set of possible values of unknown parameters. Confidence procedures are related to other kinds of standard statistical methods, in particular to point estimation and to hypothesis testing. In this article such relationships will be described and contrasts will be drawn between confidence methods and superficially similar methods of other kinds, for example, Bayesian estimation intervals [*see* Bayesian inference; Estimation, *article on* point estimation; Hypothesis testing].

As an example of this sort of procedure, suppose the proportion of voters favoring a candidate is to be estimated on the basis of a sample. The simplest possible answer is to give a single figure, say 47 per cent; this is the type of procedure called *point estimation*. Since this estimate of the proportion is derived from a sample, it will usually be different from the true proportion. How far off the true value is this estimate likely to be? This question can be answered by supplementing the estimate with error bounds, say ±.5 per cent. Thus, one might say that the true proportion lies between 46.5 per cent and 47.5 per cent. This statement might be false. One task of the statistician is to develop a procedure for the computation of such intervals, a procedure that guarantees that the statements are true in, say, 99 per cent of all appli-

cations of this procedure. Such procedures are called confidence procedures.

Estimation by confidence intervals. It is perhaps easiest to begin with a simple example from normal sampling theory.

Example 1. Let $X_1, \cdots, X_n$ be a random sample of size n from a normal distribution with unknown mean μ and known variance σ^2. Then the sample mean $\bar{X} = \sum_i X_i / n$ is a reasonable point estimator of μ. Hence $\pm 2.58 \sigma / \sqrt{n}$ are reasonable error bounds in the following sense: the estimator $\bar{X}$ lies between $\mu - 2.58 \sigma / \sqrt{n}$ and $\mu + 2.58 \sigma / \sqrt{n}$ with probability .99. In other words, the interval $(\mu - 2.58 \sigma / \sqrt{n}, \ \mu + 2.58 \sigma / \sqrt{n})$ contains the estimator $\bar{X}$ with probability .99; that is, whatever the value of μ really is,

$$P_\mu \{ \mu - 2.58 \sigma / \sqrt{n} < \bar{X} < \mu + 2.58 \sigma / \sqrt{n} \} = .99.$$

This probability statement follows directly from the facts that $(\bar{X} - \mu)/(\sigma / \sqrt{n})$ has a unit normal distribution and that a unit normal random variable lies in the interval $(-2.58, +2.58)$ with probability .99.

This statement can be given a slightly different but equivalent form: the interval $(\bar{X} - 2.58 \sigma / \sqrt{n}, \ \bar{X} + 2.58 \sigma / \sqrt{n})$ covers μ with probability .99, or whatever μ really is,

$$P_\mu \{ \bar{X} - 2.58 \sigma / \sqrt{n} < \mu < \bar{X} + 2.58 \sigma / \sqrt{n} \} = .99.$$

The interval $(\bar{X} - 2.58 \sigma / \sqrt{n}, \ \bar{X} + 2.58 \sigma / \sqrt{n})$ is called a confidence interval for μ with confidence coefficient (or confidence level) .99. The confidence interval is a random interval containing the true value with probability .99. Note that it would be incorrect to say, after computing the confidence interval for a particular sample, that μ will fall in this interval with probability .99; for μ is an unknown constant rather than a random variable. It is the confidence interval itself that is subject to random variations.

Generally speaking, there is an unknown parameter, say θ, to be estimated and an estimator $f(X)$ depending on the sample $X = (X_1, \cdots, X_n)$. In example 1, θ is called μ and $f(X)$ is $\bar{X}$. As this estimator f is based on a random sample, it is itself subject to random variations. If f is a good estimator, its probability distribution will be concentrated closely around the true value, θ. From this probability distribution of f, one can often derive an interval, with lower bound $\underline{c}(\theta)$ and upper bound $\bar{c}(\theta)$, containing the estimator $f(X)$ with high probability β (for example, $\beta = .99$). That is, whatever the actual value of θ,

$$(1) \qquad P_\theta \{ \underline{c}(\theta) < f(X) < \bar{c}(\theta) \} = \beta.$$

Often these inequalities can be inverted, that is, two functions $\underline{\theta}(X)$ and $\bar{\theta}(X)$ can be specified such that $\underline{\theta}(X) < \theta < \bar{\theta}(X)$ if and only if $\underline{c}(\theta) < f(X) < \bar{c}(\theta)$. Then, whatever θ really is,

$$(2) \qquad P_\theta\{\underline{\theta}(X) < \theta < \bar{\theta}(X)\} = \beta.$$

This means that the interval $(\underline{\theta}(X), \bar{\theta}(X))$ contains the true value θ with probability β. Quantities like $\underline{\theta}(X)$ and $\bar{\theta}(X)$ are often called confidence limits. In example 1, the bounds $\underline{c}(\theta), \bar{c}(\theta)$ and $\underline{\theta}(X), \bar{\theta}(X)$ are given by $\mu \pm 2.58\sigma/\sqrt{n}$ and $\bar{X} \pm 2.58\sigma/\sqrt{n}$, respectively.

It is also possible to develop the concept of a confidence region procedure in general, without reference to point estimation. Denote by P_θ the assumed probability distribution depending on a parameter θ (which may actually be a vector of several univariate, that is, real valued, parameters). Let Θ be the set of all possible parameter values θ. By a confidence procedure is meant a rule for assigning to each sample X a subset of the parameter space, say $\Theta(X)$. If $\Theta(X)$ contains the true value θ with probability β, regardless of the true value of θ (that is, if for all $\theta \in \Theta$, $P_\theta\{\theta \in \Theta(X)\} = \beta$), then $\Theta(X)$ is called a confidence region for θ. The probability β that the true parameter value is covered by $\Theta(X)$ is called the confidence coefficient.

In example 1, the interval $(\bar{X} - 2.58\sigma/\sqrt{n}, \bar{X} + 2.58\sigma/\sqrt{n})$ is the confidence region for the sample $X = (X_1, \cdots, X_n)$ with confidence coefficient .99.

The probability specified by the confidence coefficient has the following frequency interpretation: If a large number of confidence regions are computed on different, independent occasions, each with a confidence coefficient β, then, in the long run, a proportion β of these confidence regions will contain the true parameter value. There is some danger of misinterpretation. This occurs if θ itself is erroneously considered as a random variable and the confidence statement is given the following form: the probability is β that θ falls into the computed confidence set $\Theta(X)$. It should be clear that $\Theta(X)$ is the random quantity and not θ.

In the simplest applications, θ is a real parameter and the confidence region $\Theta(X)$ is either a proper interval $(\underline{\theta}(X), \bar{\theta}(X))$ or a semi-infinite interval: $(-\infty, \bar{\theta}(X))$ or $(\underline{\theta}(X), +\infty)$. If for all θ, $P_\theta(\theta < \bar{\theta}(X)) = \beta$, then $\bar{\theta}(X)$ is called an upper confidence bound for θ with confidence coefficient β. Similarly, $\underline{\theta}(X)$ is a lower confidence bound.

Let $\underline{\theta}(X)$ and $\bar{\theta}(X)$ be lower and upper confidence bounds with confidence coefficients β_1 and β_2,

and suppose that $\underline{\theta}(X) < \bar{\theta}(X)$ for all samples X. Then the interval $(\underline{\theta}(X), \bar{\theta}(X))$ is a confidence interval with confidence coefficient $\beta_1 + \beta_2 - 1$. If $\beta_1 = \beta_2$, that is, if $P_\theta\{\bar{\theta}(X) < \theta\} = P_\theta\{\theta < \underline{\theta}(X)\}$, the confidence interval $(\underline{\theta}(X), \bar{\theta}(X))$ is called central.

Example 2. As in example 1, let $X = (X_1, \cdots, X_n)$ be a sample of n independent normally distributed random variables with unknown mean μ and known variance σ^2. Then $\bar{\theta}(X) = \bar{X} + 2.33\sigma/\sqrt{n}$ is an upper confidence bound for μ at confidence level .99. Thus $(-\infty, \bar{X} + 2.33\sigma/\sqrt{n})$ is a semi-infinite confidence interval for μ with confidence coefficient .99, as is $(\bar{X} - 2.33\sigma/\sqrt{n}, +\infty)$. Hence $(\bar{X} - 2.33\sigma/\sqrt{n}, \bar{X} + 2.33\sigma/\sqrt{n})$ is a central confidence interval for μ with confidence coefficient $.98 = .99 + .99 - 1$. This central confidence interval differs from that in example 1 in that the latter has confidence coefficient .99 and is correspondingly wider.

Example 3. Let $X = (X_1, \cdots, X_n)$ be a random sample from a normal distribution with known mean $\mu = 0$ and unknown variance σ^2. In this case $S_1^2 = \sum_i X_i^2/n$ is a reasonable estimator of σ^2. (A subscript is used in "S_1^2" because "S^2" will later denote a more common, related, but different quantity.) Suppose $n = 10$. Then the central confidence interval for σ^2 with confidence coefficient .98 is given by $(10S_1^2/23.21, 10S_1^2/2.56)$. The constants 23.21 and 2.56 are readily obtained from a table of quantiles for the chi-square distribution, for nS_1^2/σ^2 has a chi-square distribution with 10 degrees of freedom. This example shows that the endpoints of a confidence interval are generally not symmetric around the usual point estimator.

Relation to point estimation. The computation of confidence intervals is often referred to as *interval estimation*, in contrast to *point estimation*. As outlined above, in many practical cases, interval estimation renders information about the accuracy of point estimates. The general definition of confidence intervals is, however, independent of the problem of point estimation.

In many cases, a particular point estimator is related to the set of central confidence intervals. One forms the estimator for a given sample by thinking of the progressively narrowing intervals as the confidence level decreases toward zero. Except in pathological cases, the interval will squeeze down to a point, whose numerical value furnishes the estimator. Such an estimator is, for continuous distributions, median unbiased; that is, it is equally likely to be above and below the parameter under estimation.

Relation to hypothesis testing. The theory of confidence intervals is closely related in a formal way to the theory of hypothesis testing [*see* HYPOTHESIS TESTING].

Example 4. In example 1, the confidence interval for μ with confidence coefficient .99 was given by $\bar{X} - 2.58\sigma/\sqrt{n} < \mu < \bar{X} + 2.58\sigma/\sqrt{n}$. To test the hypothesis $\mu = \mu_0$ against the alternative $\mu \neq \mu_0$ at significance level .01, accept the hypothesis if

$$(3) \quad \mu_0 - 2.58\sigma/\sqrt{n} < \bar{X} < \mu_0 + 2.58\sigma/\sqrt{n};$$

reject it otherwise. This is the customary two-sided test.

Observe that, given $\bar{X}$, the confidence interval consists of all those values μ_0 for which the hypothesis $\mu = \mu_0$ would be accepted. In other words, the confidence interval consists of all μ_0 whose acceptance region contains the given $\bar{X}$.

On the other hand, given the confidence interval with confidence coefficient .99, it is easy to perform a test of a hypothesis $\mu = \mu_0$: Accept the hypothesis if the hypothetical value μ_0 belongs to the confidence interval; otherwise reject the hypothesis. Proceeding in this way, the pattern is precisely that of testing the hypothesis $\mu = \mu_0$, since μ_0 belongs to the confidence interval if and only if (3) is fulfilled, that is, if the hypothesis $\mu = \mu_0$ would be accepted according to the test procedure.

This duality is illustrated generally in Figure 1. The figure is directly meaningful when there is a single (real) parameter θ and when the sample can be reduced to a single (real) random variable. The latter reduction can frequently be accomplished via a sufficient statistic [*see* SUFFICIENCY]. When the problem is more complex, the figure is still of schematic use.

The figure shows that for each value of θ there is an acceptance region, $A(\theta)$, illustrated as an interval. The two curves determine the lower and upper bounds of this interval respectively. The set of all those θ for which $A(\theta)$ contains a given X, $\Theta(X)$, is the interval on the vertical through X between the two curves.

If the graphic representation is considered in a horizontal way (in terms of the X axis), the lower curve represents the lower confidence bound $\underline{\theta}(X)$ as a function of X, and similarly the upper curve represents the upper confidence bound $\bar{\theta}(X)$. If it is considered from the left (in terms of the θ axis), the functions $\underline{\theta}(X)$ and $\bar{\theta}(X)$ depending on X are inverted into the functions $\bar{c}(\theta)$ and $\underline{c}(\theta)$ respectively, depending on θ. (For this reason the letters are turned.)

The general duality between the testing of simple hypotheses and confidence procedures may be described as follows: Let Θ be the set of unknown parameter values and assume that to each sample X a confidence set $\Theta(X)$ is assigned, such that $P_\theta\{\theta \in \Theta(X)\} = \beta$ for all $\theta \in \Theta$. On the basis of such a confidence procedure, a test for any hypothesis $\theta = \theta_0$ can easily be defined as follows: Let $A(\theta)$ be the set of all X, such that $\theta \in \Theta(X)$. Then the events $X \in A(\theta)$ and $\theta \in \Theta(X)$ are equivalent, whence $P_\theta\{X \in A(\theta)\} = P_\theta\{\theta \in \Theta(X)\} = \beta$. Therefore, if $A(\theta_0)$ is taken as the acceptance region for testing the hypothesis $\theta = \theta_0$, a test with acceptance probability β (or significance level $\alpha = 1 - \beta$) is obtained. On the other hand, given a family of acceptance regions (that is, for each hypothesis $\theta \in \Theta$ an acceptance region $A(\theta)$ contains the sample X with probability β when θ is the case), it is possible to define a confidence procedure by assigning to the sample X the set $\Theta(X)$ of all θ for which $A(\theta)$ contains X (that is, the set of all parameter values θ for which the hypothesis θ would be accepted on the evidence X). Then, again $\theta \in \Theta(X)$ if and only if $X \in A(\theta)$, whence $P_\theta\{\theta \in \Theta(X)\} = P_\theta\{X \in A(\theta)\} = \beta$. These remarks refer only to the case of simple hypotheses. In practice the more important case of composite hypotheses arises if several real parameters are present and the hypothesis consists in specifying the value of one of these. (This case is dealt with in "Nuisance parameters," below.)

Under exceptional circumstances the confidence set $\Theta(X)$ may show an unpleasant property: For some X, $\Theta(X)$ might be empty, or it might be identical with the whole parameter space, Θ. Those cases are usually of little practical relevance.

Thus a confidence statement contains much more information than the conclusion of a hypothesis test: The latter tells only whether a specified

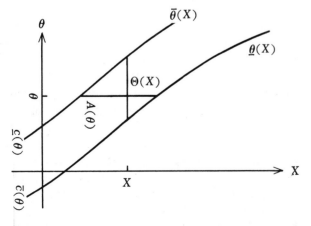

Figure 1 — A confidence region for the parameter θ

hypothesis is compatible with the evidence or not, whereas the confidence statement gives compatibility information about *all* relevant hypotheses.

Optimality. The duality between confidence procedures and families of tests implies a natural correspondence between the optimum properties of confidence procedures and optimum properties of tests.

A confidence procedure with confidence region $\Theta'(X)$ is called *most accurate* if $\Theta'(X)$ covers any value different from the true value with lower probability than any other confidence region $\Theta(X)$ with the same confidence coefficient:

$$P_{\theta_0}\{\theta \in \Theta'(X)\} \leqslant P_{\theta_0}\{\theta \in \Theta(X)\} \quad \text{for any } \theta \neq \theta_0.$$

Another expression occasionally used instead of "most accurate" is "most selective." The term "shortest," originally introduced by Neyman, is now unusual because of the danger of confusing shortest confidence intervals and confidence intervals of minimum length.

The family of tests corresponding to most accurate confidence procedures consists of uniformly most powerful tests: Let $A'(\theta)$ and $A(\theta)$ be the acceptance regions corresponding to the confidence regions $\Theta'(X)$ and $\Theta(X)$ respectively; then

$$P_{\theta_0}\{X \in A'(\theta)\} = P_{\theta_0}\{\theta \in \Theta'(X)\}$$
$$\leqslant P_{\theta_0}\{\theta \in \Theta(X)\} = P_{\theta_0}\{X \in A(\theta)\}$$
$$\text{for any } \theta \neq \theta_0.$$

Therefore, by using the acceptance region A' the false hypothesis θ is accepted with lower probability than by using A.

Uniformly most powerful tests exist only in exceptional cases. Therefore, the same holds true for most accurate confidence procedures. If, however, the class of tests is restricted (to unbiased tests or invariant tests, for example), the restricted class often contains a uniformly most powerful test within that class. Similarly, tests most powerful against a restricted class of alternatives can often be obtained. In the case of a real parameter a test for the hypothesis θ_0 that is most powerful against all $\theta > \theta_0$ may typically be found. All these restricted optimum properties of tests lead to corresponding restricted optimum properties of confidence procedures.

A confidence procedure is called unbiased if the confidence region covers no parameter value different from the true value with probability higher than its probability of covering the true value. The corresponding property of tests is also called unbiasedness. Therefore, families of uniformly most powerful unbiased tests lead to most accurate un-

biased confidence procedures, that is, confidence procedures that are most accurate among the unbiased confidence procedures: No other unbiased confidence procedures exist leading to confidence regions that contain any value different from the true value with lower probability. The confidence interval given in example 1 is unbiased and most accurate among all unbiased confidence procedures with confidence coefficient .99. On the other hand, the confidence interval given in example 3 is not unbiased.

The optimum properties discussed above are related to concepts of optimality derived from the duality to the testing of hypotheses. A completely different concept is that of minimum length. For instance, the confidence interval given in example 1 is of minimum length. In general the length of the confidence interval is itself a random variable, as in example 3. It is therefore natural to consider a confidence procedure as optimal if the expected length of the confidence intervals is minimal. This concept is appropriate for two-sided confidence intervals. For one-sided confidence intervals the concept is not applicable immediately, as in this case the length is infinite. However, the expected value of the boundary value of the one-sided confidence interval can be substituted for expected length.

In general, confidence intervals with minimum expected length are different from, for example, most accurate unbiased confidence intervals (where such intervals exist). Under special circumstances, however (including the assumption that the distributions of the family have the same shape and differ only in location), invariant confidence procedures are of minimum expected length. The confidence procedure given in example 3 is not of minimum expected length.

Two objections that may be raised against the use of expected length as a criterion are (1) when a confidence interval fails to cover the true parameter value, a short interval is undesirable in that it pretends great accuracy when there is none, and (2) expected length depends strongly on the mode of parameterization, for example, there is no sharp relation between the expected length of a confidence interval for θ and that of the induced interval for θ^3.

Discrete distributions. In the general consideration above it was assumed that there exists a confidence procedure with confidence coefficient β in the sense that, for all θ in Θ, the probability of covering the parameter θ is exactly β when θ is the true parameter. This means that for each θ there exists an acceptance region $A(\theta)$ such that

$P_\theta\{A(\theta)\} = \beta$. This is, however, in general true only for distributions of the continuous type, not for discrete distributions such as the binomial and Poisson distributions [*see* DISTRIBUTIONS, STATISTICAL]. Thus acceptance regions $A(\theta)$ of probability approximately β must be chosen, with the degree of approximation depending on θ. In practice the acceptance region is selected such that $P_\theta\{A(\theta)\}$ approximates β as closely as possible, either with or without the restriction $P_\theta\{A(\theta)\} \geqslant \beta$. These acceptance regions $A(\theta)$ define the confidence regions $\Theta(X)$ with (approximate) confidence coefficient β. When the restriction $P_\theta\{A(\theta)\} \geqslant \beta$ is made, the term "bounded confidence region" is often used, and the region is said to have bounded confidence level β.

Example 5. Let X be the number of successes in n independent dichotomous trials with constant probability p of success. Then X is binomially distributed, that is, $P_p\{X = k\} = \binom{n}{k}p^k(1-p)^{n-k}$. Choose the confidence coefficient $\beta = .99$. Choose for each p, $0 \leqslant p \leqslant 1$, the smallest integer $c(p)$ such that

$$\sum_{k=0}^{c(p)} \binom{n}{k} p^k (1-p)^{n-k} \geqslant 0.99.$$

Inverting the bound $c(p)$ one obtains one-sided confidence intervals of confidence coefficient .99 for p.

As an illustration, let $n = 20$ and $p = .3$. Since $P\{X \leqslant 11\} = .995$ and $P\{X \leqslant 10\} = .983$, the smallest integer such that $P\{X \leqslant c(p)\} \geqslant 0.99$ is $c(p) = 11$. Troublesome computations of $c(p)$ can be avoided by use of one of the tables or figures provided for this purpose. For references see Kendall and Stuart ([1943–1946] 1961, p. 118).

Nuisance parameters. In many practical problems, more than one parameter is involved. Often the interest is concentrated on one of these parameters, say θ, while the others are regarded as nuisance parameters. The aim is to make a confidence statement about θ that is true with high probability regardless of the values of the nuisance parameters. The corresponding test problem is that of testing a composite hypothesis that specifies the value of θ without making any assertion about the nuisance parameters. The test is required to have significance level less than or equal to a prescribed α regardless of the nuisance parameters. The corresponding confidence procedure will yield confidence intervals that cover the true value at least with probability $1 - \alpha$ regardless of the nuisance parameters, that is, confidence intervals with bounded confidence level $1 - \alpha$. A special role is played by the so-called similar tests, having exactly

significance level α for all values of the nuisance parameters. They lead to confidence intervals covering the true value with probability exactly $1 - \alpha$ regardless of the nuisance parameters.

Example 6. Let $X_1, \cdots, X_n$ be a random sample from a normal distribution with unknown mean μ and unknown variance σ^2. The variance σ^2 is to be considered a nuisance parameter. Let $\bar{X} = \sum_i X_i / n$ and $S^2 = \sum_i (X_i - \bar{X})^2 / (n - 1)$. For $n = 10$ a (similar) confidence interval for μ with confidence coefficient .99 is given by $\bar{X} - 3.17\, S/\sqrt{10} < \mu < \bar{X} + 3.17\, S/\sqrt{10}$. For general n, the confidence interval with confidence coefficient .99 is given by $\bar{X} - t_{.005,n-1}\, S/\sqrt{n} < \mu < \bar{X} + t_{.005,n-1}\, S/\sqrt{n}$, where $t_{.005,n-1}$ is the upper .005 point of the tabled t-distribution with $n - 1$ degrees of freedom, for example $t_{.005,9} = 3.17$. Hence the above confidence procedure corresponds to the usual t-test. As for large n, because $t_{.005,n-1}$ is close to 2.58, the confidence interval given here corresponds for large n to the confidence interval given in example 1. The confidence procedure given here is most accurate among unbiased confidence procedures.

Example 7. Consider μ in example 6 as the nuisance parameter. Define S^2 as in example 6 and again take $n = 10$. Then a one-sided confidence interval for σ^2 of confidence coefficient .99 is given by $\sigma^2 \leqslant 9\, S^2/2.09$. In general, the one-sided confidence interval for σ^2 with confidence coefficient .99 is given by $\sigma^2 \leqslant (n-1)S^2/\chi^2_{.01,n-1}$, where $\chi^2_{.01,n-1}$ is the lower .01 point of the chi-square distribution with $n - 1$ degrees of freedom. Observe that here the number of degrees of freedom is $n - 1$ while in example 3 it is n.

Confidence coefficient. The expected length of the confidence interval depends, of course, on the confidence coefficient. If a higher confidence coefficient is chosen, that is, if a statement that is true with higher probability is desired, this statement has to be less precise; the confidence interval has to be wider.

It is difficult to give general rules for the selection of confidence coefficients. Traditional values are .90, .95, and .99 (corresponding to significance levels of .10, .05, and .01, respectively). The considerations to be made in this connection are the same as the considerations for choosing the size of a test [*see* HYPOTHESIS TESTING].

Nested confidence procedures. One would expect the wider confidence interval (belonging to the higher confidence level) to enclose the narrower confidence interval (belonging to the lower confidence level). A confidence procedure with this property is called "nested." All the usual confidence procedures are nested, but this is not a fully general property of confidence procedures.

Sample size.   Given the confidence coefficient, the expected length of the confidence interval depends, of course, on the sample size. Larger samples contain more information and therefore lead to more precise statements, that is, to narrower confidence intervals.

Given a specific problem, the accuracy that it is reasonable to require can be determined. In order to estimate the number of housewives knowing of the existence of the superactive detergent X, a confidence interval of ±5 per cent will probably be sufficiently accurate. If, on the other hand, the aim is to forecast the outcome of elections and the percentage of voters favoring a specific party was 48 per cent in the last elections, an accuracy of ±5 per cent would be quite insufficient. In this case, a confidence interval of length less than ±1 per cent would probably be required.

Given the accuracy necessary for the problem at hand, the sample size that is necessary to achieve this accuracy can be determined. In general, however, the confidence interval (and therefore the necessary sample size as well) depends on nuisance parameters. Assume that a confidence interval for the unknown mean μ of a normal distribution with unknown variance σ^2 is needed. Although in example 6 a confidence interval is given for which no information about σ^2 is needed, such information is needed to compute the expected length of the confidence interval: The length of the confidence interval is $2t_{.005,n-1} S/\sqrt{n}$, the expected value for large n is therefore nearly equal to $2t_{.005,n-1} \sigma/\sqrt{n}$. Therefore, in order to determine the necessary sample size n, some information about σ^2 is needed. Often everyday experience or information obtained from related studies will be sufficient for this purpose. If no information whatsoever is at hand, a relatively small pilot study will yield a sufficiently accurate estimate for σ^2. This idea is treated rigorously in papers on sequential procedures for obtaining confidence intervals of given length (Stein 1945). In the case of the binomial distribution, no prior information at all is needed, for $\sigma^2 = p(1-p) \leqslant \frac{1}{4}$, whatever p might be. Using $\frac{1}{4}$ instead of σ^2 can, however, lead to wastefully large samples if p is near 0 or 1.

Robustness—nonparametric procedures.   Any statistical procedure starts from a basic model on the underlying family of distributions. In example 1, for instance, the basic model is that of a number of independent normally distributed random variables. Since it is never certain how closely these basic assumptions are fulfilled in practice, desirable statistical procedures are those that are only slightly influenced if the assumptions are violated. Statistical procedures with this property are called *robust* [see HYPOTHESIS TESTING]. Another approach is to abandon, as far as possible, assumptions about the type of distribution leading to nonparametric procedures.

As the duality between families of tests and confidence procedures holds true in general, robust or nonparametric tests lead to robust or nonparametric confidence procedures, respectively. [*Examples showing the construction of confidence intervals for the median of a distribution from the sign test and from Wilcoxon's signed rank test are given in* NONPARAMETRIC STATISTICS.]

Relationship to Bayesian inference.   If the parameter is not considered as an unknown constant but as the realization of a random variable with given prior distribution, Bayesian inference can be used to obtain estimating intervals containing the true parameter with prescribed probability [see BAYESIAN INFERENCE].

Confidence statements can be made, however, without assuming the existence of a prior distribution, and hence confidence statements are preferred by statisticians who do not like to use "subjective" prior distributions for Bayesian inference. A somewhat different, and perhaps less controversial, application of subjective prior distributions is their use to define so-called subjective accuracy. Subjectively most accurate confidence procedures are defined in analogy to the most accurate ones by averaging the probability of covering the fixed parameter with respect to the subjective prior distribution. It can be shown that a most accurate confidence procedure is subjectively most accurate under any prior distribution with a positive density function (Borges 1962).

Relation to fiducial inference.   Fiducial inference was introduced by R. A. Fisher (1930). This paper and succeeding publications of Fisher contain a rule for determining the fiducial distribution of the parameter on the basis of the sample X [see FIDUCIAL INFERENCE].

As in Bayesian inference, this distribution can be used to compute "fiducial intervals," giving information about the parameter θ. The fiducial interval is connected with a probability statement, which admits, however, no frequency interpretation (although some advocates of fiducial methods might disagree).

For many elementary problems, fiducial intervals and confidence intervals are identical. But this is not true in general. One of the attractive properties of fiducial inference is that it leads to solutions even in cases where the classical approach failed until now, as in the case of the Behrens–Fisher problem.

Many scholars, however, find it difficult to see a convincing justification for Fisher's rule of computing fiducial distributions and to find an intuitive interpretation of probability statements connected with fiducial intervals.

A reasonable interpretation of fiducial distributions would be as some sort of posterior distributions for the unknown parameter. It can be shown, however, that fiducial distributions cannot be used as posterior distributions in general; a Bayesian inference, starting from two independent samples and using the fiducial distribution of the first sample as prior distribution to compute a posterior distribution from the second sample, would in general lead to a result different from the fiducial distribution obtained from both samples taken together. For the comparison of fiducial and Bayesian method, see Richter (1954) and Lindley (1958).

Prediction intervals, tolerance intervals. Whereas confidence intervals give information about an unknown parameter, prediction intervals give information about future independent observations. Hence prediction intervals are subsets of the sample space whereas confidence intervals are subsets of the parameter space.

Example 8. If $X_1, \cdots, X_n$ is a random sample from a normal distribution with unknown mean μ and unknown variance σ^2, the interval given by $(\bar{X} - t_{\alpha,n-1} S \sqrt{(n+1)/n}, \bar{X} + t_{\alpha,n-1} S \sqrt{(n+1)/n})$ is a prediction interval containing a future independent observation X_{n+1} with probability $1 - 2\alpha$, if $t_{\alpha,n-1}$ is the upper α point of the t-distribution with $n - 1$ degrees of freedom. Note that the probability of the event

$$\bar{X} - t_{\alpha,n-1} S \sqrt{(n+1)/n}$$
$$< X_{n+1} < \bar{X} + t_{\alpha,n-1} S \sqrt{(n+1)/n}$$

is $1 - 2\alpha$ before the random variables $X_1, \cdots, X_n$ are observed. For further discussion of this example see Proschan (1953); for discussion of a similar example, see Mood and Graybill (1950, pp. 220–244, 297–299).

The prediction interval, computed in example 8 above, must not be interpreted in the sense that it covers a proportion α of the population. In a special instance, the interval computed according to this formula might cover more or less than the proportion α. Only on the average will the proportion be α.

In many cases, there is a need for intervals covering a proportion γ with high probability, say β. This is, however, not possible. In general, it is possible only to give rules for computing intervals covering *at least* a proportion γ with high probability β. Intervals with this property are called γ-proportion tolerance regions with confidence coefficient β. In the normal case, one might, for example, seek a constant c, for given γ and β, such that, whatever the values of μ and σ,

$$P\left\{ \int_{\bar{X}-cS}^{\bar{X}+cS} f(u; \mu, \sigma)\, du \geqslant \gamma \right\} = \beta,$$

where $f(u; \mu, \sigma)$ is the normal density with mean μ and variance σ^2.

The constants c, leading to a γ-proportion tolerance interval $(\bar{X} - cS, \bar{X} + cS)$ with confidence coefficient β, cannot be expressed by one of the standard distributions (as was the case in the example of the prediction interval dealt with above). Tables of c can be found in Owen (1962, p. 127 ff.). For further discussion see Proschan (1953), and for nonparametric tolerance intervals see Wilks (1942). [*See also* NONPARAMETRIC STATISTICS.]

Confidence regions. In multivariate problems, confidence procedures yielding intervals are generalized to those yielding confidence regions.

Example 9. Let X and Y be two normally distributed random variables with unknown means μ and ν, known variances 2 and 1, and covariance -1. A confidence region for (μ, ν) with confidence coefficient .99 is given by $(X - \mu)^2 + 2(X - \mu)(Y - \nu) + 2(Y - \nu)^2 \leqslant 9.21$. The figure 9.21 is obtained from a chi-square table, since the quadratic form on the left is distributed as chi-square with two degrees of freedom. The confidence region is an ellipse with center (X, Y). When such a region is described in terms, say, of pairs of parallel tangent lines, the result may usefully be considered in the framework of multiple comparisons. [*See* LINEAR HYPOTHESES, *article on* MULTIPLE COMPARISONS.]

J. PFANZAGL

BIBLIOGRAPHY

The theory of confidence intervals is systematically developed in Neyman 1937; 1938b. *Prior to Neyman, this concept had been used occasionally in a rather vague manner by a number of authors, for example, by Laplace 1812, section 16, although in a few cases the now current meaning was clearly stated, perhaps first by Cournot 1843, pp. 185–186. A precise formulation without systematic theory is given in* Hotelling 1931. *A more detailed account of the history is given in* Neyman 1938a.

BORGES, RUDOLPH 1962 Subjektivtrennscharfe Konfidenzbereiche. *Zeitschrift für Wahrscheinlichkeitstheorie* 1:47–69.

COURNOT, ANTOINE AUGUSTIN 1843 *Exposition de la théorie des chances et des probabilités*. Paris: Hachette.

FISHER, R. A. (1930) 1950 Inverse Probability. Pages 22.527a–22.535 in R. A. Fisher, *Contributions to Mathematical Statistics*. New York: Wiley. → First published in Volume 26 of the *Proceedings* of the Cambridge Philosophical Society.

FISHER, R. A. 1933 The Concepts of Inverse Probability and Fiducial Probability Referring to Unknown Parameters. Royal Society of London, *Proceedings* Series A 139:343–348.

HOTELLING, HAROLD 1931 The Generalization of Student's Ratio. *Annals of Mathematical Statistics* 2:360–378.

KENDALL, MAURICE G.; and STUART, ALAN (1943–1946) 1961 *The Advanced Theory of Statistics*. Volume 2: Inference and Relationship. New York: Hafner; London: Griffin. → See especially pages 98–133 on "Interval Estimation: Confidence Levels" and pages 518–521 on "Distribution-free Tolerance Intervals." (Kendall was the sole author of the first edition.)

LAPLACE, PIERRE SIMON DE (1812) 1820 *Théorie analytique des probabilités*. 3d ed., rev. Paris: Courcier. → Laplace's mention of confidence intervals first appeared in the 2d (1814) edition.

LEHMANN, ERICH L. 1959 *Testing Statistical Hypotheses*. New York: Wiley. → See especially pages 78–83, 173–180, and 243–245.

LINDLEY, D. V. 1958 Fiducial Distributions and Bayes' Theorem. *Journal of the Royal Statistical Society* Series B 20:102–107.

MOOD, ALEXANDER M.; and GRAYBILL, FRANKLIN A. (1950) 1963 *Introduction to the Theory of Statistics*. 2d ed. New York: McGraw-Hill. → See especially pages 220–244 on "Interval Estimation." (Mood was the sole author of the 1950 edition.)

NEYMAN, JERZY 1937 Outline of a Theory of Statistical Estimation Based on the Classical Theory of Probability. Royal Society of London, *Philosophical Transactions* Series A 236:333–380.

NEYMAN, JERZY (1938a) 1952 *Lectures and Conferences on Mathematical Statistics and Probability*. 2d ed. Washington: U.S. Dept. of Agriculture. → See especially Chapter 4, "Statistical Estimation."

NEYMAN, JERZY 1938b L'estimation statistique traitée comme un problème classique de probabilité. *Actualités scientifiques et industrielles* 739:26–57.

OWEN, DONALD B. 1962 *Handbook of Statistical Tables*. Reading, Mass.: Addison-Wesley. → A list of addenda and errata is available from the author.

PROSCHAN, FRANK 1953 Confidence and Tolerance Intervals for the Normal Distribution. *Journal of the American Statistical Association* 48:550–564.

RICHTER, HANS 1954 Zur Grundlegung der Wahrscheinlichkeitstheorie. *Mathematische Annalen* 128:305–339. → See especially pages 336–339 on "Konfidenzschluss and Fiduzialschluss."

SCHMETTERER, LEOPOLD 1956 *Einführung in die Mathematische Statistik*. Berlin: Springer. → See especially Chapter 3 on "Konfidenzbereiche."

STEIN, CHARLES 1945 A Two Sample Test for a Linear Hypothesis Whose Power Is Independent of the Variance. *Annals of Mathematical Statistics* 16:243–258.

WILKS, S. S. 1942 Statistical Prediction With Special Reference to the Problem of Tolerance Limits. *Annals of Mathematical Statistics* 13:400–409.

ETHICS

I

ETHICAL SYSTEMS AND SOCIAL STRUCTURES

In a consideration of the relationship of ethical systems to social structure, it is important to show how these terms are being used; different meanings can represent different degrees of abstraction, and the kinds of relationship possible will vary accordingly.

"Social structure" has been taken by Radcliffe-Brown (1952, p. 11; compare pp. 188–204) to mean "an arrangement of persons in institutionally controlled or defined relationships"; in this case, the term stands for a social organization with actual individuals as its constituents. It may be taken, as by Evans-Pritchard ([1940] 1963, p. 262), to exclude relations between persons, but to describe such relations between *groups* as have a high degree of constancy and consistency. Or it may be taken in a still more abstract sense—as a network of relationships between sets of institutionalized social roles (Firth 1954; Nadel 1957; Emmet 1960; 1966).

The view here adopted is that although observation must start from the first of these senses (interactions between persons) and may proceed through the second (regularities in group interactions), the systematic notion of a "social structure" will need to be couched in the abstract terminology of relationships between *roles*.

The notion of an ethical system is even less clearly determined. It may be taken to mean (*a*) the mores of a given society as a sociologist observes them; (*b*) a systematic code of moral principles, such as that of the Roman Catholic church; and (*c*) a philosophical theory about the rationale of moral action, such as utilitarianism.

Ethics and social structure. In considering relationship to a social structure, we would be tempted to say that we need be concerned only with (*a*). This, however, would be unsatisfactory, since to talk of an ethical system is to imply far more than a pattern of observed forms of behavior; rules of conduct, as derived from ethical notions, may be honored in the breach as well as in the observance. In order to discover a people's ethical system even in sense (*a*), it will therefore be necessary to take into account their statements about what is considered right and wrong and why, as well as to describe conformities in their behavior and the working of sanctions against deviation.

For this reason, it might be logically preferable to consider an ethical system simply in sense (*b*), as a body of beliefs about right and wrong, although these are unlikely in many cases to be as systematic as those connected with a formulated theological position, such as that of the Roman Catholic church. Sense (*b*), however, can be related to social structure only by showing how the ethical beliefs in question affect the ways members of the society behave in their social roles.

Social structure in theory and practice. We also need to distinguish here between an *idealized* view of the social structure, seen as a network of roles played according to the rules (or, where rules are broken, corrected by sanctions) and the social structure as a generalized *description* of typical role behavior that may fall short of official ethical prescriptions. In the latter case, however, ethical prescriptions must be taken into account in seeking to understand the behavior, if only to show ways in which the prescriptions are being evaded; the notion of "role expectations," often used in speaking of social structures, can thus be ambiguous. It may stand for predictions of how a person is likely to behave in a given role. It may also stand for "what is expected of him" (normatively) in that role; and notoriously people do not always live up to these "expectations." An ethical system as a set of norms for action needs to be distinguished, therefore, from a descriptive account of the mores as customary ways of behavior (cf. Sumner [1906] 1959, chapter 2).

Distinctiveness of ethical judgments. It is also important to try to distinguish those aspects of the mores that should properly be called ethical from those more properly called religious, legal, political, or matters of etiquette. This is a matter in which the anthropologists of the late nineteenth and early twentieth centuries, such as Westermarck, were interested, but to which less direct attention has been paid more recently, perhaps because moral values pervade these other aspects of social life and are difficult to isolate from them (Edel 1962). Some recent work has been done by moral philosophers on what may be the distinctive criteria of moral as distinct from other kinds of judgment (Ladd 1957; Brandt 1954; cf. Macbeath 1952). But the question of whether these criteria are logically necessary to anything that can be called an ethical system, or whether they are culture bound, is a matter calling for cooperative work between philosophers and anthropologists. Until there is a larger body of material for comparative study directed to such questions as whether primitive peoples have specifically *ethical* notions that are independent of their religious or political notions, the field of study will remain largely speculative.

Two kinds of ethical relativism. The distinction between the logical criteria of what makes a system an ethical system and the substantive principles it contains has not always been drawn by writers on the cultural conditioning of ethical beliefs. While generally holding that ethical beliefs are "relative" to a culture, they do not always distinguish the "reductionist" form of ethical relativism, which presents the ethical beliefs of a people as functionally dependent on their other beliefs and practices, and the kind of "content" relativism which, while allowing that substantive ethical beliefs and practices may be affected by other factors within the society, nevertheless recognizes that there may be distinctive *moral* interests not exhaustively explicable in terms of other interests. The difference between these two approaches can be summarized by saying that the reductionist maintains that the ethical beliefs of a people can be exhaustively rendered in terms of their nonethical interests, such as the familial or economic, whereas the "content" relativist is prepared to admit that the belief that "X is right" can provide a bona fide reason for acting accordingly, although the content of X may be culturally variable (Emmet 1966, chapter 5).

The latter approach would be concerned with seeing how these different interests may affect each other in producing a particular "way of life"; an instance is Max Weber's well-known thesis on the relation between the Puritan ethic and capitalism in the seventeenth century (Weber 1904–1905). This need not be taken (as by some Marxists) to mean that the ethical ideas of the Puritans were simply a superstructure rationalizing their economic behavior. On the contrary, it can mean that the kinds of behavior, such as hard work and thrifty living, prescribed by their ethical beliefs fitted the kinds of behavior needed for successful entrepreneurial activity in the early stages of a capitalist economy. Thus, a mutual reinforcement of two strong human interests—the ethical and the economic—would be produced and a way of life with survival value established. This type of analysis aims at finding functional interrelations between ethical and other practices within a society without prejudging the question of whether, nevertheless, there may not be *distinctively* ethical motives and interests; for instance, the belief that hard work is morally commendable need not only be a disguised way of saying hard work is economically profitable, nor is it *necessarily* caused by the fact that hard work is profitable.

Ethical systems—form and content.   The question of the distinctive criteria of ethical as distinct from other kinds of judgment has not been overlooked, however, by all writers on the social relativism of morals. Westermarck, in particular, held that there was a universal form of ethical judgments inasmuch as they expressed *disinterested* retributive emotions (1906–1908; 1932). This question of the distinction between the general logical character and the particular substantive content of an ethical system is a point where the third meaning of the term that we distinguished earlier—philosophical theories about the nature of ethical systems—becomes relevant. Edel and Edel (1959) have suggested that an ethical system may be distinguished by certain broad notions that any such system may be supposed to provide for; for example, it will contain some kind of sanction, reasons justifying some kinds of conduct and not others, and, more specifically, some means of controlling aggression and some notion of distributive justice. This may be compared with what Hart (1961, p. 189) has called the minimum content of natural law. This is not a notion of natural law as a universal rational code of ethical principles but a listing of certain basic requirements that any code must somehow meet if people are to live together sufficiently permanently to satisfy the logical and empirical requirements of constituting a "society" (see also Levy 1952, chapter 4 on "The Functional Requisites of Any Society"). Comparative work on these requirements, and on what differences of emphasis may be given them, would be one of the ways in which the study of ethical systems and social structures could be brought together.

Some alternatives to functionalism.   The structural–functionalist approach reflected in the terms "ethical system" and "social structure" has sometimes been interpreted as assuming a more highly integrated and normatively controlled unity within a society than need in fact obtain. The work of Parsons, especially *The Social System*, 1951, has been criticized on these grounds (Lockwood 1956; see also Emmet 1958 for a more extended discussion of the issues). An approach of perhaps more immediate empirical applicability has been outlined by Merton (1957, chapters 8 and 9), who uses the term "reference group" to denote the group or groups from which an individual may take his ethical cues. Modern societies in particular may contain many persons who, although they are conformists from the point of view of their own reference group, are deviants by the values of the larger society of which their group is a part. Study of deviance and conformity in terms of reference groups may have the effect of reviving interest in the *formal* means, such as political and legal systems, of preserving social cohesion within pluralistic societies. Structural–functional studies, on the other hand, have been mainly concerned with the less formal sanctions of custom and unplanned institutional practices [*see* REFERENCE GROUPS].

Students of organizations have also drawn attention to the importance of informal as well as formal structures. The workings of a large industry cannot be understood simply by looking at the organization chart or by consulting official statements of aims; it is also necessary to discover the unofficial networks of communication, interaction, and leadership. In some cases, elements within these unofficial structures may have their own ethical systems (for example, views on the amount of work that ought to be done), and these can frustrate the official system unless they are taken into account [*see* ORGANIZATIONS, *article on* EFFECTIVENESS AND PLANNING OF CHANGE].

Role, status, and the individual.   If we recognize the looseness of the texture of actual social life, in contrast with any simplified model of the social structure, we see the individual not only as carrying specified role obligations but also as having to meet the demands of a number of different and perhaps conflicting roles. A variety of social structures can be abstracted from the whole field of human relationships: professional, political, family, and friendship roles may all be played by the same individual and are likely to produce competing pressures. Barnard (1938) has called attention to this in the case of high executives, showing how positions of responsibility produce conflicting claims that make heavy demands on an individual's intellectual and moral resources. It is unlikely that any ethical system can be so structured as always to show the priorities among these claims, or any social structure be so simple as not to produce these conflicts.

In relating ethical systems to social structure, therefore, it may be asked whether the former can thereby be *explained* in terms of the latter. A "sociological explanation," following Durkheim (1895), may here be taken to mean an account of behavior not in terms of historical or psychological causation, but in terms of the ways groups are related to one another within the society. Role behavior in social groups is defined partly with reference to ethical norms of expected conduct (cf. Durkheim 1893 on how this is so even in the economic field);

we may therefore say that the ethical system of defining role obligations can be considered as an *aspect* of the social structure, insofar as ethical notions enter into the ways roles are seen and performed. Here a mutual conditioning between ethical beliefs and social arrangements, as we have said, seems more plausible than a one-way causation of the one by the other.

Role performance and social change. It may, of course, be asked whether an *individual* may not be conditioned by the training he receives through the institutions of his society in order to see his role obligations in only one particular way. However, individuals can have their own styles in role performance; they may deviate in various ways; they will have to decide between conflicting role obligations; and in some cases they may create a new role for themselves. There may thus be much individual behavior that will not enter into the description of a social structure except insofar as it may produce innovations that alter the image of an existing role or create a new one. Indeed, it may be said that individual innovation becomes sociologically important only when it modifies role behavior to such an extent that social structure is affected (Emmet 1966, chapters 7 and 8). Individual conduct, therefore, is not being considered as such and is more properly left to psychologists and philosophers.

Nevertheless, the study of social structure can show how certain kinds of behavior will be expected and certain possibilities will be foreclosed because of features in the social situation; and to study the nature of ethical systems in relation to the social structures in which they are embedded may help us to understand why certain actions are thought of as right or wrong in particular societies. These two kinds of understanding can thus fructify one another without being thought of as mutually reducible.

DOROTHY EMMET

[See also ROLE; SOCIAL STRUCTURE; STATUS, SOCIAL; UTILITARIANISM; *and the biographies of* BARNARD; DURKHEIM; WESTERMARCK.]

BIBLIOGRAPHY

BARNARD, CHESTER I. (1938) 1962 *The Functions of the Executive.* Cambridge, Mass.: Harvard Univ. Press.

BRANDT, RICHARD B. 1954 *Hopi Ethics: A Theoretical Analysis.* Univ. of Chicago Press.

DURKHEIM, ÉMILE (1893) 1960 *The Division of Labor in Society.* 2d ed. Glencoe, Ill.: Free Press. → First published in French.

DURKHEIM, ÉMILE (1895) 1958 *The Rules of Sociological Method.* 8th ed. Edited by George E. G. Catlin. Glencoe, Ill.: Free Press. → First published in French.

EDEL, ABRAHAM 1962 Anthropology and Ethics in Common Focus. *Journal of the Royal Anthropological Institute of Great Britain and Ireland* 92:55–72.

EDEL, MAY; and EDEL, ABRAHAM 1959 *Anthropology and Ethics.* Springfield, Ill.: Thomas.

EMMET, DOROTHY M. 1958 *Function, Purpose and Powers.* London: Macmillan; New York: St. Martins.

EMMET, DOROTHY M. 1960 How Far Can Structural Studies Take Account of Individuals? *Journal of the Royal Anthropological Institute of Great Britain and Ireland* 90:191–200.

EMMET, DOROTHY M. 1966 *Rules, Roles and Relations.* London: Macmillan; New York: St. Martins.

EVANS-PRITCHARD, E. E. (1940) 1963 *The Nuer: A Description of the Modes of Livelihood and Political Institutions of a Nilotic People.* Oxford: Clarendon.

FIRTH, RAYMOND 1954 Social Organization and Social Change. *Journal of the Royal Anthropological Institute of Great Britain and Ireland* 84:1–20.

HART, HERBERT L. A. 1961 *The Concept of Law.* Oxford: Clarendon.

LADD, JOHN 1957 *The Structure of a Moral Code: A Philosophical Analysis of Ethical Discourse Applied to the Ethics of the Navaho Indians.* Cambridge, Mass.: Harvard Univ. Press.

LEVY, MARION J. 1952 *The Structure of Society.* Princeton Univ. Press. → See especially Chapter 4.

LOCKWOOD, DAVID 1956 Some Remarks on *The Social System. British Journal of Sociology* 7:134–146.

MACBEATH, ALEXANDER 1952 *Experiments in Living: A Study of the Nature and Foundations of Ethics or Morals in the Light of Recent Work in Social Anthropology.* London: Macmillan; New York: St. Martins.

MERTON, ROBERT K. 1957 *Social Theory and Social Structure.* Rev. & enl. ed. Glencoe, Ill.: Free Press. → The first edition was published in 1949.

NADEL, SIEGFRIED F. 1957 *The Theory of Social Structure.* London: Cohen & West; Glencoe, Ill.: Free Press.

RADCLIFFE-BROWN, A. R. 1952 *Structure and Function in Primitive Society.* London: Cohen & West.

SUMNER, WILLIAM GRAHAM (1906) 1959 *Folkways: A Study of the Sociological Importance of Usages, Manners, Customs, Mores, and Morals.* New York: Dover.

WEBER, MAX (1904–1905) 1930 *The Protestant Ethic and the Spirit of Capitalism.* Translated by Talcott Parsons, with a foreword by R. H. Tawney. London: Allen & Unwin; New York: Scribner. → First published in German. The 1930 edition has been reprinted frequently.

WESTERMARCK, EDWARD A. (1906–1908) 1924–1926 *The Origin and Development of the Moral Ideas.* 2 vols., 2d ed. London: Macmillan.

WESTERMARCK, EDWARD A. 1932 *Ethical Relativity.* New York: Harcourt. → A paperback edition was published in 1960 by Littlefield.

II

ETHICAL ISSUES IN THE SOCIAL SCIENCES

Ethics is concerned with standards of conduct among people in social groups; for this reason, research in social science is inextricably bound up in ethical problems. The initial choice of a problem for investigation by the social scientist is often value-laden. The process of inquiry in the social sciences, engaging as it frequently does the lives of people, must meet moral as well as scientific standards. And the product of inquiry constantly adds new data and new theories requiring the revision of established ethical systems. Ethics and social science thus move in contrapuntal relationship, each adding to the character of the other (Shils 1959).

Old issues and new. There are a number of principles of ethics in social science research that are so widely recognized and honored that they do not need detailed discussion. Among these are maintaining highest standards of work, reporting procedures and results faithfully, protecting information given in confidence, giving appropriate credit to co-workers, making appropriate acknowledgment of other writers' materials, representing accurately one's own qualifications, and acknowledging, when appropriate, sources of financial support. The central issue in all of these is integrity, as indeed it is in every step of a true research endeavor. For this reason some social scientists have objected to proposals to define ethical standards for research, arguing that the canons of science are an exacting and sufficient guide to conduct. However, new problems arise as scientists move into new areas under new auspices; old problems appear in new contexts and require new solutions. Ethical standards must be redefined continually to keep them relevant to contemporary situations. Below are several issues that are subjects of concern and of lively debate as this article is written. If these issues are soon dated and no longer lively, it is probably a healthy sign that consensus is being reached on them and that new issues are capturing concern.

Deception in social science research. In many experiments or inquiries in the social sciences, it is necessary, or has been widely considered necessary, to disguise the nature of the task assigned to the subject. The procedure arises usually from the need to control the "set" or "expectancy" with which the subject approaches the task, since set is known to be an important determinant of responses. While in most instances the consequences are trivial, in some instances they may not be trivial at all. In all instances the issue is raised, Is deception ever justified?

Clearly, scientists think that deception is sometimes required to achieve a good that would not otherwise be achievable. For example, it is common practice in medical research to administer a pla-

cebo to a control group in order to assess the effects of a drug. No harm is done; the control subjects might still be given the drug if it proves effective. But the outcome of deception is not always benign. In one of the classical experiments on deceit, the investigators tempted children to steal and deceived them into believing that their action could not be detected. Some children did indeed steal. The investigators concluded that honesty is often influenced by the situation, a point demonstrated as much in their own behavior as in that of the children (Hartshorne & May 1928). In a second well-known investigation, social psychologists infiltrated a religious group, posing as converts (Festinger et al. 1956); their conduct has been questioned (Smith 1957). In an experiment on the effects of group pressure on judgment, five co-workers of the experimenter were represented as uninstructed subjects, just like the person whose resistance to social pressure was to be tested (Asch 1948). Both the deception and the stress generated thereby may be questioned, from an ethical viewpoint. Russian psychologists investigating the same problem have avoided the need for deception by using all naive subjects and analyzing the data for trends that occur naturally, accepting the loss in experimental efficiency.

A reasonable ethical standard for such a situation would be that the investigator has an obligation to inform his prospective subject of any aspect of the experiment that might be considered an important factor in the subject's decision to serve. While such an ethical policy obviously has much to commend it, the losses would be great; many experiments concerned with the dynamics of human behavior would be made impossible. Ethics aside, there are pragmatic arguments in favor of a policy of full disclosure of intent. With growing sophistication, the public may come to regard all social science experiments as situations in which deception is to be expected. At this point even truth is suspect. The problem is not simple, nor is it unimportant. Perhaps a minimum obligation of the social scientist is to make the public aware of the problem.

Stress in social science research. While many experimenters have subjected participants in research to stress, one investigator has been taken to task for his seeming insensitivity to the excruciating ordeal his subjects were going through and for his failure to see the larger implications of his methodology. The critic (Baumrind 1964) very reasonably questioned the ethics of subjecting people to extreme stress and pointed out the moral parallels to historical situations in which innocent people have been tortured in the interest of science. The experimenter's rejoinder (Milgram 1964) provides further instruction in the complexity of the problem and demonstrates the value of a continuing debate of ethical issues in research.

The customary routine is to talk with the subject after an experiment involving stress, to explain the procedure, and to try to relieve any residual discomfort. This procedure may suffice in many investigations, but there are others reported in the literature in which the stress is so severe that one could not realistically hope to repair the damage by such a postsession conference. A suitable topic for cross-disciplinary research would be an investigation of possible lingering or delayed effects of experiments involving stress or deception.

It has been proposed that there is already enough stress in life arising from natural causes and that social scientists should not add to it. An alternative is to study stress reactions in natural settings. Many of these are unpredictable and are amenable only to observational study after the event, but some excellent research has been done following disasters, such as tornadoes and earthquakes, by sociologists who were prepared to take advantage of an unpredictable event. There are also predictable and necessary stressful situations that are a normal part of living and could be used in research. A first-grade classroom on the first day of school and the father's waiting room at a maternity hospital are settings where stress can be studied without the investigator's causing it. Webb and his co-workers (1966) have provided an imaginative and useful examination of methodological options in "nonreactive research in the social sciences," including attention to ethical problems.

Protection of research data. The right of the clinician to keep data confidential is widely (though not universally) recognized by custom and in some states and countries by law. But the scientific investigator does not as clearly enjoy such protection. For example, the social scientist engaged in survey research may encounter a serious ethical problem, and lack clear guidelines for conduct, when his evidence is introduced in a court as legal testimony. The court or either contending party may have a legitimate interest in the reliability of the survey and may demand that respondents be identified in order to call them as witnesses. But survey data are generally obtained with assurances of anonymity; a violation of this pledge would not only involve a betrayal of confidence but would also impair the survey method as a research technique by diminishing public confidence in agencies

that use the procedure. In at least one ruling, a court has sustained the right of a survey agency to keep confidential the names of persons interviewed, but other judges may rule differently. Obviously, the social scientist engaged in survey research has a minimum obligation to inform himself on the issues involved so that he can behave responsibly toward people who supply him with information (King & Spector 1963). He might also be expected to anticipate such problems in the planning stages of a study and to take protective measures against a number of contingencies. The issue of proper protection of data, here discussed with reference to surveys, may be equally relevant in other kinds of research. The problem is complicated by the investigator's obligation to keep his work open for scrutiny by competent scientists.

The invasion of privacy. Privacy is a most cherished right of the individual in a free society, and it may well be an important condition for the integration of experience and the achievement of autonomous selfhood. Social scientists are engaged in a number of enterprises that can lead to a reduction of individual privacy. The ethical issue that seems most frequently involved is that information about a person or his family may be collected, and perhaps used officially, without the individual's being aware of what is happening. The use of personality tests for appraising prospective employees, screening school children, and so on has recently attracted public attention. In some instances, restrictive regulations have been imposed to prevent what is seen as an undue invasion of privacy.

Privacy is not always an individual matter but may involve social institutions which depend for their effectiveness on assurances against intrusion; such is true of the jury system in the United States. In 1955, some sociological investigators, with the permission of the trial judge and the contending lawyers, concealed microphones in a jury room and recorded the jury's deliberation. Although the information obtained was treated with scrupulous care by the investigators, the incident created a national furor. The jurors had clearly been deceived and were appropriately indignant. An issue of broader concern involved in this instance was the appropriateness of scientific inquiry into an established social institution; the social scientist who undertakes such studies must be uncommonly concerned with ethical issues, since damage may be done both to social science and to the institutions studied by social scientists.

As computers become increasingly available and efficient in both storage and processing capacities, we face the prospect of an invasion of privacy of quite a different sort. With various agencies collecting diverse data about an individual over a sufficient period of time, and with the data centrally stored and processed, the possibility is imminent that extensive and reliable inferences can be made about an individual that far exceed his intentions of disclosure. The protection of privacy that has come from fragmentation of information or from the sheer tedium and expense of analysis may indeed be lost.

One example may suffice to indicate the further significance of technological developments: it is now possible to obtain, by mail order, a detailed analysis of an individual's responses to the Minnesota Multiphasic Personality Inventory; the evaluation that once required the services of a highly skilled clinician can be provided now, in much shorter time, by a computer. The ethical implications of advances in computer technology are yet to be explored.

The invasion of privacy issue arises at the point of intersection of two highly valued social goods: the need for knowledge about problems, opinions, motivations, and expectancies of people and the need for preservation of personal rights. While the conflict of social values involved is an ancient one (the rack and screw were information-obtaining devices), the problem is of notable contemporary importance because of the steady increase in amount of, and reliance on, social science research, on the one hand, and the advances in the technology of inquiry, including electronic listening devices, recorders, cameras, computers, personal inventories, projective techniques, and planted informers or confederates, on the other hand.

Among the issues that must be considered in achieving a proper balance of conflicting social and individual interest are the importance of the investigation, the informed consent of subjects, the preservation of confidentiality, and the judicious use of records of research. The individual scientist's decisions about these moral issues must be harmonious with the opinion of his peers or with a community consensus. As the social scientist comes to have more of value to offer the community, he can expect more community understanding and support of the unavoidable violation of privacy attendant upon much social science research. (For an informed and sophisticated analysis of the problem of privacy, see Ruebhausen & Brim 1965.)

The issue of informed consent. In medical research it has generally been the practice to obtain the informed consent of a patient as a condition for his participation in an investigation; however, loose definitions of what is meant by *informed* have permitted great latitude in practice. In a decision that will have implications for all research involving human subjects, the Board of Regents of the University of the State of New York in 1966 stringently defined expectations for medical investigators:

No consent is valid unless it is made by a person with legal and mental capacity to make it, and is based on a disclosure of all material facts. Any fact which might influence the giving or withholding of consent is material. A patient has the right to know he is being asked to volunteer and to refuse to participate in an experiment for any reason, intelligent or otherwise, well-informed or prejudiced. A physician has no right to withhold from a prospective volunteer any fact which he knows may influence the decision. It is the volunteer's decision to make, and the physician may not take it away from him by the manner in which he asks the question or explains or fails to explain the circumstances. (Langer 1966, p. 664)

In this statement the words *social scientist* might be substituted for *physician* and *subject* for *patient* to arrive at an important guideline for research in the social sciences.

But again the issue is not simple. Is a patient in a control group in a medical experiment to be told that the treatment he will receive is known to have no physiological effect but will be administered to control for psychological effects? If such candor were required, much medical research would be impossible. And so it is with social science research, where possible gains in socially valuable knowledge must be weighed against possible losses of individual prerogatives. For a clear joining of the issue, in regard to psychological research, see the correspondence of Miller and Rokeach (1966). Rokeach wrote, to define the complexity of the problem: "What is typically involved in making a decision about moral values, whether in or out of science, is not a choice between good and evil but a choice between two or more positive values, or a choice between greater and lesser evils" (1966, p. 15). All-or-none solutions are seldom satisfactory.

Cross-cultural studies. The many ethical issues involved in cross-cultural and transnational investigations, long a concern of the professional anthropologist (see, for example, Redfield 1953 and also the "Statement on Ethics of the Society for Applied Anthropology" 1963–1964), were thrust into public prominence, in 1965, by the debacle of Project Camelot, an inquiry sponsored by the U.S. Department of Defense into "the causes of revolutions and insurgency in underdeveloped areas of the world." Exposure of the project in a South American country led to protests from the U.S. ambassador, a Congressional investigation, the cancellation of the project, and a policy requiring that all government-sponsored, foreign-area research be approved by the U.S. Department of State. The fact that Camelot became a national and international *cause célèbre* involving ambassadors, senators, cabinet members, newspapermen, university officials, social scientists, and the president himself, and that it was interpreted as a cloak-and-dagger operation in spite of the sincerity and good will of the participating scientists, has served to obscure the ethical issues involved, issues that demand serious and sophisticated consideration by the social scientist, whether involved in cross-cultural studies or not.

Among the ethical issues are these: Should the intentions of a sponsoring agency be the concern of a social scientist even when he is personally allowed full freedom of inquiry? Should the social scientist be concerned with the uses to which the results of his studies will be put? What is the responsibility of the social scientist for ensuring that the very process of inquiry does not have a deleterious effect on the people being studied? Does the social scientist have an obligation to preserve access to people for subsequent investigators? Is there a point at which inadequacies of design or procedure, or lack of scientific merit in a study, become intrinsically ethical issues by virtue of their imposition on others? These and similar questions may appear to have easy answers, but a sympathetic study of Project Camelot will show their complexity and emphasize the need for social scientists to consider them anew in the context of every proposed investigation (Horowitz 1965).

Social science and social issues. Social science may often have relevance to crucial matters of public policy. With increasing frequency advocates of diverse political and social policies turn to the social scientist for support of their position. Or the social scientist himself, exercising the prerogative of a citizen to make public statements on social and political issues, may find his statements given credence beyond what could be supported by data, by virtue of his being recognized as a scientist, regardless of his competence on the particular topic. Drawn into such an unaccustomed arena, the social scientist must be especially mindful of how he presents his qualifications and of the ethical implications of his statements. Issues related to racial characteristics, for example, have so conjoined science and public policy that they

have been made the subject of study by the Committee on Science in the Promotion of Human Welfare of the American Association for the Advancement of Science ("Science and the Race Problem" 1963).

Care of animals in research. The psychologist has relied heavily on animals—rats, dogs, birds, primates—as subjects in research. To protect laboratory animals from neglect or abuse, formal regulations governing the management of animal laboratories have been developed. These require the provision of adequate food, water, and medical care, the maintenance of sanitary living quarters, the use of anesthetics to prevent pain in operations and other procedures, the provision of postoperative care, and the destruction of animals by humane means. Committees on care of laboratory animals review problems periodically. The U.S. Public Health Service publishes a booklet entitled "Guide for Laboratory Animal Facilities and Care" (Animal Care Panel 1963) and requires recipients of grant support to observe the requirements to assure proper and humane treatment of research animals. The American Psychological Association requires posting in "all rooms where animals are housed and where animal experimentation is conducted" of regulations titled "Guiding Principles for the Humane Care and Use of Animals." In spite of these efforts to assure highest ethical standards in the care of laboratory animals, there is a perennial demand for federal legislation to control practices, especially with respect to dogs and cats. In 1964 there were eight bills introduced in the 88th Congress of the United States, two of which would have been severely restrictive. Although there are occasional cases of negligence or of needless infliction of pain, animals are generally well cared for, and the Congress has shied away from enacting legislation on the matter (Brayfield 1963).

Communication in social science research. Marin Mersenne promoted science in seventeenth-century France by copious letter writing; the problem of communication in science has since become exceedingly complex, with many attendant ethical issues. Ethical problems have involved such issues as plagiarism, misrepresentation of data, the betrayal of confidence, claiming undue credit, and other clearly unacceptable behavior. With the development of what has been called "big science" with extensive government support, problems of a new and more subtle character have emerged. For example, the assignment of credit for research accomplished by a large organization seems to be solved neither by crediting the director alone, as has been done and protested, nor by crediting

30 contributors, as was done in a recent listing of authors. Although promotions may depend on publications, there is a growing need to limit publication to significant findings likely to be of value to others. The sheer volume of reports threatens to overwhelm our most efficient systems for coding, storing, and finding information. Thus, for an investigator to impose the same findings twice on about the same audience constitutes an offense to the development and dissemination of knowledge. The following statement has been proposed to control the volume of publication: "... *scientific publication [should] be considered a privilege consequent upon the finding of something which people may need to read, rather than as a duty consequent upon the spending of time and money. . . . Furthermore . . . no paper [should] be committed more than once to the published literature without very special pleading*" (Price 1964).

Research on moral development.   Thus far certain theoretical and practical problems relating to ethics and social science research have been considered. It should be noted now that social science research itself is a potential major source of understanding of ethical conduct, of the origins and development of moral standards. Pioneer work was done by Hartshorne and May (1928). Piaget (1932) provided a theoretical matrix for illuminating stages in the moral development of the child. Anthropologists and social psychologists (Whiting 1963) have studied the influence of the family on character formation in different cultures. Russian pedagogical specialists are working explicitly to provide educational experiences to instill communist values in children (Bronfenbrenner 1962). In the United States, the establishment of the National Institute of Child Health and Human Development, to promote research on normal development, can be expected to encourage basic research on the problem.

Social control of scientific inquiry.   Various professional, trade, labor, and fraternal groups exert a major influence on the behavior of individuals in contemporary society. Perhaps because of their very diversity they escape attention as instruments of social control, yet it has been contended that they speak with more authority today than do organized religious groups and, further, that they influence day-by-day conduct even more than do local, state, and national governments.

Many of these associations have formal codes of ethics. For the most part these codes have been found to have little effect on the behavior of members of the group (American Academy of Political and Social Science 1955). They are one of the appurtenances of associations and are designed with an eye to building public confidence. However, the traditions, mores, and expectancies that are generated in professional groups do affect behavior, often holding members to extraordinarily high standards of conduct. When codes of ethics are in harmony with long-established tradition (as in *The Principles of Medical Ethics*) or when they are backed up by effective machinery for enforcement, they can be powerful instruments of social control.

The American Psychological Association has applied social science theory and methodology to the task of developing a code of ethics (Hobbs 1948). The critical incidents technique was used to obtain the basic data for the construction of the code. Members of the association were asked to supply descriptions of situations in which a psychologist took some action that either upheld or violated ethical standards. From over a thousand such incidents a committee extracted the principles that appeared to be involved in the behavior reported. The result is two documents: a succinct code (American Psychological Association 1963) and a book-length statement (American Psychological Association 1953) of ethical standards that includes principles, discussions of issues, and illustrations drawn from the collection of critical incidents. Now underway is a new inquiry directed specifically at ethical issues in psychological research; the critical incident technique is again being used to develop basic data from which ethical principles will be derived.

The psychologists' statement of ethical standards is being augmented by a collection of case studies drawn from the files of ethics committees responsible for the enforcement of the code. The assumption is made that the definition of ethical standards is an ongoing, never-finished process and that participation in the process by members of the association may be more important than the written code itself in nurturing high ethical standards in the profession. The Committee on Cooperation Among Scientists of the American Association for the Advancement of Science is collecting similar descriptions, not necessarily to prepare a code of ethics but to illuminate the ethical problems encountered by scientists in all fields.

When scientists fail to regulate their own behavior to the satisfaction of informed members of the community, one can confidently predict that controls will be imposed by legislation or by administrative regulations. In 1965–1966, two major federal agencies adopted procedures governing ethical issues in research supported by their grants.

One agency requires that tests, questionnaires, and other data-gathering devices be approved in Washington by a special review group composed of staff members, with the assistance of consultants. The other agency has established a requirement that grant requests involving possible ethical issues must be reviewed by a recognized local committee of peers of the investigator. The second solution appears to offer protection to research subjects on the basis of competent review without the danger of overcentralized control of scientific inquiry. However, there are responsible investigators who contend that a prescribed review by local peers is an invidious requirement implying incompetence and guilt when competence and rectitude should be assumed, with intervention indicated only when there is some evidence to the contrary. Here again a social process to define appropriate procedures is underway, with the proper resolution still unclear.

It can be expected that society will develop, in time, a productive balance between its need for knowledge and the individual's need for protection against intrusion, inconvenience, or discomfort. A dialectic tension involving values fundamental to a democracy must be resolved, both in terms of general principles and in terms of particular instances. For example, freedom of inquiry must be balanced against rights of privacy, both cherished values in our society. While the issues are complex, resolution is possible. The accommodation, both in substance and in process, will probably be comparable in character to rules governing the right of eminent domain and the right of the individual to own property.

The individual investigator is not without common-sense guidelines. While the answers may not always be clear, some of the questions are: Is the knowledge to be gained worth the imposition involved in obtaining it? Would another design be equally productive but less intrusive? Has fullest advantage been taken of the subject's informed willingness to cooperate? Has the proposed inquiry been designed to minimize effects on the subject population so that subsequent investigators will not be handicapped? To what extent are the proposed procedures consonant with emerging standards, or a calculated departure from them?

Nor is the investigator without criteria to assess and perhaps discover the adequacy of his answers to such questions: first, his own standards as an investigator, concerned quite as much with ethical as with statistical elegance of design; then the approbation of other competent scientists; and,

finally, the appreciation of the larger community, or of significant sections of it, whose support is essential to the continued development of the social sciences.

It is of greatest importance to keep ethical problems under continuing scrutiny and debate, in journals, in training programs, in public forums, with social scientists themselves taking the initiative in the process, in order to provide increasingly instructive principles for clarifying ethical issues in social science research.

NICHOLAS HOBBS

[*See also* MORAL DEVELOPMENT; PRIVACY; SCIENCE.]

BIBLIOGRAPHY

AMERICAN ACADEMY OF POLITICAL AND SOCIAL SCIENCE 1922 *The Ethics of the Professions and of Business.* Edited by Clyde L. King. Annals, Vol. 101, no. 190. Philadelphia: The Academy.

AMERICAN ACADEMY OF POLITICAL AND SOCIAL SCIENCE 1955 *Ethical Standards and Professional Conduct.* Edited by Benson Y. Landis. Annals, Vol. 297. Philadelphia: The Academy.

AMERICAN PSYCHOLOGICAL ASSOCIATION 1953 *Ethical Standards of Psychologists.* Washington: The Association.

AMERICAN PSYCHOLOGICAL ASSOCIATION 1963 Ethical Standards of Psychologists. *American Psychologist* 18:56–60.

AMERICAN STATISTICAL ASSOCIATION, BOSTON, DECEMBER, *1951* 1952 Standards of Statistical Conduct in Business and Government. *American Statistician* 6, no. 1:6–20.

ANIMAL CARE PANEL, ANIMAL FACILITIES STANDARDS COMMITTEE 1963 *Guide for Laboratory Animal Facilities and Care.* U.S. Public Health Service, Publication No. 1024. Washington: Government Printing Office.

ASCH, SOLOMON E. 1948 The Doctrine of Suggestion, Prestige and Imitation in Social Psychology. *Psychological Review* 55:250–276.

BARNES, JAMES A. 1963 Some Ethical Problems in Modern Fieldwork. *British Journal of Sociology* 14:118–134.

BAUMRIND, DIANA 1964 Some Thoughts on Ethics of Research: After Reading Milgram's *Behavioral Study of Obedience. American Psychologist* 19:421–423.

BRAYFIELD, ARTHUR H. 1963 Humane Treatment of Laboratory Animals. *American Psychologist* 18:113–114.

BRONFENBRENNER, URIE 1962 Soviet Methods of Character Education: Some Implications for Research. *American Psychologist* 17:550–564.

BURGESS, ROBERT W. 1947 Do We Need a "Bureau of Standards" for Statistics? *Journal of Marketing* 11:281–282.

COMMISSION DE DÉONTOLOGIE DE LA SOCIÉTÉ FRANÇAISE DE PSYCHOLOGIE 1960 Projet de code déontologie à l'usage des psychologues. *Psychologie française* 5:1–27.

FESTINGER, LEON; RIECKEN, H. W.; and SCHACHTER, STANLEY 1956 *When Prophecy Fails.* Minneapolis: Univ. of Minnesota Press.

FREEMAN, WILLIAM W. K. 1963 Training of Statisticians in Diplomacy to Maintain Their Integrity. *American Statistician* 17, no. 5:16–20.

HARTSHORNE, HUGH; and MAY, MARK A. 1928 *Studies in Deceit.* 2 parts. New York: Macmillan.

HOBBS, NICHOLAS 1948 The Development of a Code of Ethical Standards for Psychology. *American Psychologist* 3:80–84.

HOBBS, NICHOLAS 1959 Science and Ethical Behavior. *American Psychologist* 14:217–225.

HOROWITZ, I. L. 1965 The Life and Death of Project Camelot. *Trans-action,* 3, no. 1:3–7, 44–47.

KELMAN, HERBERT C. 1965 Manipulation of Human Behavior: An Ethical Dilemma for the Social Scientist. *Journal of Social Issues* 21:31–46.

KIMBALL, A. W. 1957 Errors of the Third Kind in Statistical Consulting. *Journal of the American Statistical Association* 52:133–142.

KING, ARNOLD J.; and SPECTOR, AARON J. 1963 Ethical and Legal Aspects of Survey Research. *American Psychologist* 18:204–208.

LANGER, ELINOR 1966 Human Experimentation: New York Verdict Affirms Patient's Rights. *Science* 151:663–666.

MILGRAM, STANLEY 1964 Issues in the Study of Obedience: A Reply to Baumrind. *American Psychologist* 19:848–852.

MILLER, SAMUEL E.; and ROKEACH, MILTON 1966 [Letters] Psychology Experiments Without Subjects' Consent. *Science* 152:15 only.

PIAGET, JEAN (1932) 1948 *The Moral Judgment of the Child.* Glencoe, Ill.: Free Press. → First published in French.

PRICE, DEREK J. DE SOLLA 1964 Ethics of Scientific Publication. *Science* 144:655–657.

REDFIELD, ROBERT 1953 *The Primitive World and Its Transformations.* Ithaca, N.Y.: Cornell Univ. Press.

RUEBHAUSEN, OSCAR M.; and BRIM, ORVILLE G. JR. 1965 Privacy and Behavioral Research. *Columbia Law Review* 65:1184–1211.

SAUVY, ALFRED 1961 La responsabilité du statisticien devant l'opinion et les pouvoirs publics. International Statistical Institute, *Bulletin* 38, no. 2:573–578.

Science and the Race Problem: Report of the AAAS Committee on Science in the Promotion of Human Welfare. 1963 *Science* 142:558–561.

SHAKOW, DAVID 1965 Ethics for a Scientific Age: Some Moral Aspects of Psychoanalysis. *Psychoanalytic Review* 52:335–348.

SHILS, EDWARD 1959 Social Inquiry and the Autonomy of the Individual. Pages 114–157 in Daniel Lerner (editor), *The Human Meaning of the Social Sciences.* New York: Meridian.

SILVERT, K. H. 1965 American Academic Ethics and Social Research Abroad: The Lesson of Project Camelot. American Universities Field Staff [*Reports From Foreign Countries*]: *West Coast South America Series* 12, no. 3.

SMITH, M. BREWSTER 1957 Of Prophecy and Privacy: [A Book Review of] *When Prophecy Fails,* by L. Festinger, H. W. Riecken, and S. Schachter. *Contemporary Psychology* 2, no. 4:89–92.

SNOW, CHARLES P. 1961 The Moral Un-neutrality of Science. *Science* 133:255–262. → With comments by Warren Weaver, Theodore M. Hesburgh, and William O. Baker.

Statement on Ethics of the Society for Applied Anthropology. 1963–1964 *Human Organization* 22:237 only.

U.S. OFFICE OF SCIENCE AND TECHNOLOGY 1967 *Privacy and Behavioral Research.* Washington: Government Printing Office.

WEBB, EUGENE et al. 1966 *Unobtrusive Measures: Nonreactive Research in the Social Sciences.* Chicago: Rand McNally.

WHITING, BEATRICE B. (editor) 1963 *Six Cultures: Studies of Child Rearing.* New York: Wiley.

ZIRKLE, CONWAY 1954 Citation of Fraudulent Data. *Science* 120:189–190.

ETHNIC GROUPS

An ethnic group is a distinct category of the population in a larger society whose culture is usually different from its own. The members of such a group are, or feel themselves, or are thought to be, bound together by common ties of race or nationality or culture. The nature of an ethnic group's relationships with the society as a whole, and with other groups in it, constitutes one of the main problems in describing and analyzing such societies. As Ruth Benedict said of race conflict, it is not *race* that we need to understand, but *conflict;* so, for an understanding of ethnic groups in a social system, it is not on racial or cultural differences that we need to focus our attention, but on group relations.

Historical outline

The existence of distinct ethnic and cultural groups within societies is widespread and ancient and occurs at most levels of culture, ranging from the Bushmen of the Kalahari, who live within the framework of Tswana society, to modern Europe and America. Ethnic groups in the Near East were recorded by Herodotus almost 2,500 years ago and remained a persistent feature of the Byzantine, the Ottoman, and other Near Eastern empires. Similar situations also occurred in ancient India and in Chinese civilization at all stages of its expansion.

Although scholars in the past have often noted the existence of multiracial and multicultural societies, systematic examination of the sociological consequences of the phenomenon did not begin before the eighteenth century. And then it was principally in connection with the concepts of race and race relations as developed in the next century by writers such as Gobineau (1853–1855) and Chamberlain (1899). Linguistic scholars like Sir William Jones, the Grimm brothers, and Max Müller not only examined the construction and development of Indo-European languages but also inadvertently encouraged the growth and elevation of the idea of race as an ideology and as the most significant index distinguishing culturally different groups from one another.

Earlier historians, including the writers of the

Old Testament, had noted that ethnic groups might be found in a society as a result of the gradual migration of either whole populations or of segments, such as religious refugees, traders, craftsmen, or manual laborers. They also observed that military conquest might bring in its train soldiers and civilians, who either settled permanently in the area or administered their conquests for a period of years before retiring and being replaced from the homeland. Or, again, ethnic groups might be incorporated into a society by altered political boundaries. Sometimes a combination of processes was at work; but however a multiracial or multicultural system came into existence, the types of society in which ethnic groups could be found varied as widely as the processes that brought them into being.

Most investigations of ethnic groups have been made in connection with studies of race relations and stratified societies such as are found in Africa (MacCrone 1937; Patterson 1953), the southern states of the United States (Dollard 1937), parts of the Caribbean (Smith 1955; 1956), Central and South America (Freyre 1933), and in the plural societies of former colonial areas of Asia (Furnivall 1942). Ethnic groups that are not an integral part of a system of over-all social stratification are also found in countries like Switzerland and Nigeria, where they form units in the political system which, although perhaps internally stratified, are not ranked in relation to one another. Other types of multiracial and multicultural situations, as, for example, in northern Laos, Thailand, Burma, and India, have as yet hardly been examined. Frequently in these countries adjacent villages, or even sections of one village, may be linguistically and culturally different and yet be held together in a traditional system of social relations that is not part of the apparatus of a central government (Leach 1954). Similar conditions have been observed, although seldom analyzed, in the Indonesian archipelago, New Guinea, and parts of Africa.

Definitions. At this point it would be wise, for the sake of clarity, to make the distinction between a social group and a social category. By a group, sociologists usually mean an aggregation of people recruited on clear principles, who are bound to one another by formal, institutionalized rules and characteristic, informal behavior. Unless a group is to be no more than a temporary aggregation, it must in addition be organized for cohesion and persistence; that is to say, the rights and duties of membership must regulate internal order and relations with other groups. Members usually identify themselves with a group and give it a name. In practice social groups vary in the degree to which they are corporate; and in certain situations one of the principal difficulties of analysis may be to decide whether a particular social entity is in fact a social group or a mere category of the population, such as red-haired people, selected by a criterion that in the context is socially neutral and that does not prescribe uniform behavior. For any study of group relations this distinction is essential.

In east Africa, the African, the Arab, the European, and the Indian elements of society are closer to being categories of the population than social groups. Although, for example, a fully institutionalized Indian group, recruited from the general category of Indians, is likely to act in the Indian sphere of life, there is no certainty that it will; relations between the ethnic categories may therefore become blurred. The sections of an ethnically and culturally divided population may, according to circumstances, be institutionalized groups related to one another in a system of stratification, or they may be groups living side by side and related in other ways. Ethnic divisions may simply be categories of the population, as are Welshmen and Scotsmen living in England, or Indians, Chinese, and Creoles in Mauritius, who are beginning to lose a sense of ethnic separateness. It is, therefore, always important to be sure what is the exact sociological status of an ethnic or cultural division. Clarity in analysis depends upon it.

Ethnic groups in stratified societies

The division of society into broad *strata*, which form a hierarchy of prestige, wealth, and power, is a feature common to most societies and is one that has been used for classification. A few societies, mostly primitive or small in size, may not be stratified; social positions may not be sufficiently numerous or diverse to be easily grouped into strata or aggregates of individuals sharing an equivalent status that would differentiate them from members of other similar aggregates. This is not to say, of course, that statuses in such small societies may not be ranked but is merely to point out that they do not constitute groups. Sociologists traditionally classify the types of stratification as caste, estate, or class systems. As ethnic and subcultural groups may form the basis of a system of stratification, a closer examination of the matter is needed.

In any system of social stratification the following apply: (1) Individuals belong to strata that are *groups* in the sense that everybody in them shares some obligatory ways of acting that are typically and intentionally different from those in other strata. (2) Strata must be *exclusive*, so that nobody may belong to more than one at the same time. (3) Strata must be *exhaustive*, so that everybody in the society belongs to one. (4) Strata must be *ranked*. In using this criterion, differential access to political and economic resources is taken to be the most significant aspect of the ranking. These criteria do not distinguish different types of stratification, any one of which may be exemplified in a society where ethnic groups are a component element of the system.

Caste groups. One sociological definition of a caste system is that it is a hierarchy of endogamous groups in which status is rigidly ascribed by birth and in which mobility from one group to another is not possible. Correct relations between groups are maintained and validated by religious rules, especially the rule that improper contact between castes produces a state of impurity that entails ritual, legal, and other penalties.

In this definition no careful distinction is usually made between the four-fold division of Indian society into castes (*varna*) and subcastes (*jati*). In early literature the *varna* (priests, soldiers, businessmen, and laborers) are sometimes described in terms of what appear to be ethnic differences; but in historical times they have not constituted more than categories of value against which individuals and members of subcastes could measure their own and other people's prestige. They were not groups, in the sense of imposing duties that were uniform throughout India. In short, the *varna* were ranked categories, not stratified groups. Not dissimilar arrangements are also found in some of the multiracial societies of Africa and the Caribbean.

Empirically, Indian society was made up of many small self-contained caste systems, each of which was a hierarchy of subcaste groups. Subcastes in turn were organized so that social labor was divided among them. Each subcaste traditionally held a monopoly of a particular service, so that all washermen, for example, although not bound to that occupation, could prevent others from practicing it. The essence of this division of labor was that it was cooperative and complementary, not competitive. In these small, closed caste systems relationships between individuals tended to be multiple in that two individuals could fill a number of roles in relation to each other. This "summation" or "involution" of roles is an attribute of small-scale and not large-scale social systems (Nadel 1957, pp. 64–72). The argument may be summarized

thus: (1) Caste groups must be recruited by birth, that is to say, they must be *closed*. (2) Relationships between groups must be *cooperative*, not *competitive*.

In India subcastes are not usually separate ethnic or cultural groups, but an understanding of caste systems is essential in the analysis of society in Iran and parts of the Near East where a multiplicity of ethnic and cultural groups appears to be organized in small-scale caste systems (Barth 1960). It is possible, too, that society in certain parts of the southern states of the United States is similarly arranged (Dollard 1937).

If we are content to say, as are many students, that South Africa and India both exhibit a caste system, then no further distinctions need be sought. But writers on India do not usually agree that "color-bar" societies are *ipso facto* caste systems. Although the population of India was always very large, society there was characteristically composed of separate small-scale involute caste systems. South Africa, although less populous, is typical of large-scale Western society where relationships between roles are usually single-stranded and not the multiple ties of a small-scale society.

In certain ways the system of closed groups in South Africa is nearer the model of an estate system than that of a caste or social-class system, but the sociological status of "color-bar" societies needs to be carefully re-examined. Studies of them have for the most part either used the concepts of stratification without careful consideration or have directed attention to economic functions (Boeke 1953) or to attitudes and other psychological concomitants of the existence of ethnic groups. [*See* CASTE.]

Social class groups. In some places, such as parts of the West Indies, ethnic groups are regarded as, and may in fact be, *social classes*. Sociologists generally consider a class to be an aggregate of people occupying roughly the same status, which is different from that of people in other classes and which, unlike status in a caste or estate system, allows movement from one stratum to another. It is never easy to decide to what degree a social class is an institutionalized group or exactly how it is related to economic and political status and prestige. When some of the qualifications for membership are also those for belonging to an ethnic category or group, the difficulties of analysis may become very great indeed. An aggregate of people is not a social class just because they think of themselves as one; it is a social class because some activities are obligatory to all or most members and act as a sign that the people form a group and are eligible for access (appropriately graded according to their class) to resources that are valued by the society. When these activities are also qualifications for membership of ethnic or cultural groups, then ethnic and class groups coincide.

The types of stratification that have been mentioned are, of course, models; and a particular system, whether its constituent elements are ethnic groups or not, may not correspond with the model. Racial differences used as insignia or badges to mark off groups from one another are not different in kind from clothing, speech, manners, property, or other cultural emblems that may serve the same ends. But since physical differences are permanent and may be strikingly visible and may also carry much emotion, the understanding of societies such as are found in Mexico, Nigeria, or Kenya has been made difficult by treating them as if they were altogether different from those more familiar to sociologists. The fact that signs of a special kind are used for distinguishing groups in multiracial societies does not mean that such societies are radically different from others.

In a study of early twentieth-century Burma and Netherlands Indonesia, Furnivall argued that countries in which "there is a plural society, with different sections of the community living side by side, but separately, within the same political unit" ([1948] 1956, p. 304) were "a distinctive form of society with a characteristic political and economic constitution" (1942, p. 195). In such a situation, he believed, members of society are unable to develop the common values and demands generated by sharing common institutions. Another writer, M. G. Smith, regards Furnivall's concepts as essential to comparative sociology, arguing that a plural society is composed of readily identifiable sections held together only by the fact that they are part of one central political system. Such sections, it should be noted, are not necessarily *ethnic* groups. Each is distinguished by having its own "core" of "basic" or "compulsory" institutions. Social systems may therefore be placed on a scale ranging from those that are fully plural with distinct sections fulfilling particular economic, political, religious, or other functions, to homogeneous systems in which one set of basic institutions is shared by all members (Smith 1960). Models of this kind have attracted anthropologists, historians, and economists, especially those working in multiracial or multicultural areas; but most sociologists have found the concept of a basic core of differentiating institutions even harder to define and handle than the concepts with which they were more familiar,

and they have preferred to rely on older and better tested theories of social differentiation. [See STRATIFICATION, SOCIAL.]

Ethnic groups in nonstratified societies

Not all societies having ethnic groups within their boundaries incorporate them into a unified system of social stratification, and relations among ethnic groups may (to use a political metaphor) be more of a "federal" nature than one of ranked access to social resources.

Societies with a single administrative system. In Switzerland or Canada, for instance, cultural groupings are clearly differentiated and maintained, and each may be separately stratified; but access to power in the wider society is not limited by either ethnic or cultural origins, nor is it conditioned by a ranked evaluation of ethnic groupings within the society. In Malaya, too, although there are distinct ethnic groups, they are not stratified in relation to one another. The population is divided between Malays and immigrant Chinese and Indians. Constitutionally the machinery of government is in the hands of people selected by voting. The workings of electoral procedures and the staffing of the civil service and the armed forces have, in fact, placed most of the political machinery in the hands of Malays, leaving economic power largely with the Chinese. This distribution of the different kinds of power, with its open possibilities of real loss or gain, has tended to consolidate ethnic categories into political parties (Freedman 1960).

In Mexico, on the other hand, ethnic criteria have, on the whole, been abandoned in the formation of social groups because they no longer mark off differences considered significant. The people who control political, legal, and economic matters attain their positions without reference to race, although not without acquiring the dominant Spanish culture. In Thailand, too, the balance struck between demographic, political, economic, and cultural factors is such that the dominant Buddhist, Thai-speaking group is able to pursue a policy of assimilating ethnic minorities. The policy has had a measure of success with Chinese immigrants, but no attempt has been made to absorb the Muslim, Malay-speaking inhabitants of the southern provinces.

Where ethnic or cultural differences coincide with groups that tenaciously hold different religious opinions, the relationships of one group to another and to the central government may become very complex indeed and lead to serious conflict. But the problem is not one peculiar to ethnically diverse societies. In the sixteenth century, the division of

France into Roman Catholic and Protestant Christians did not make it a plural society, even though some Protestants, especially in the south, were culturally and linguistically separate. Nor did it mean that groups that held these different opinions were different in kind from other groups that had been competing for political power before the religious differences arose.

The point here is an essentially simple one. In any society the immediately effective determinants of most social action lie in the political, legal, and economic spheres; and whether or not the main component groups of the society are stratified in relation to one another, an examination of the social system must be primarily concerned not only with relations between groups but also more specifically with those between rulers and ruled. The latter problem is an aspect of the former, but in a society with groups that differ ethnically, whose interests are in fact opposed to one another, the ensuing conflict may be phrased in racial terms and thus provoke more bitter hostility than in other struggles of the ruled against their rulers.

Societies without a single administrative system. In the examples considered so far, ethnic or cultural groups have formed part of an organized administrative and political system. Understanding the significance and range of such groups and their economic, political, religious, and cultural importance has revolved around the problem of ascertaining the exact position that they occupy in the system. In northern Thailand, Burma, and New Guinea, where small ethnic and cultural groups are dispersed and mingled over a wide area without traditionally being under the direct control of a single administrative system, it is also necessary to determine their exact relationship to one another.

A number of such "tribal" groups have been studied, but because anthropological fieldwork tends toward village studies and because the linguistic difficulties of examining such a heterogeneous system are very great, students have seldom made the study of the wider system the main focus of their attention. Groups of this kind appear to be linked to one another in a network of political, economic, ritual, and marriage alliances about which little information is available. But here, as in more politically unified systems, the balance struck in one place is seldom exactly the same as that in another, where the weighting of economic, political, cultural, and ideological forces may be different. The use of models of the kind that have been discussed in this article is essential in the analysis of any society; and where useful models do not exist, as is probable in the study of such

tribally mixed areas as those just noticed, then they must be constructed. But their usefulness must not be misunderstood. It is highly unlikely that any model will correspond in detail with the complexity and variety of real life, especially that of multiracial and multicultural societies.

Specialization of ethnic groups

This article is concerned mainly with the theoretical problems of describing and analyzing the place of ethnic and cultural groups within social systems of different types. Most studies of societies of this kind have dealt less with theoretical problems than with the consequences of economic, political, or religious specialization of such groups within the wider society. Often these consequences are the result of the structural position of the group, but this in turn may be the result of the specialized tasks that it performs.

When Europeans first began to govern east Africa the difficulties of setting up an administration and of stimulating the trade needed to produce a revenue gave an opening to Indian immigrants, who were ethnically and culturally very different from the African and Arab inhabitants of the region. Even where common beliefs in Islam were held, this fact did not submerge ethnic or cultural differences or the hostility to, and suspicion and fear of, the immigrants, whose interests as middlemen and skilled workers brought them into conflict with all other ethnic categories of the population. Such a conflict tends to make a structural alignment even more rigid and to confirm and perpetuate associated attitudes.

The point can be illustrated in many parts of the world. Studies of Jewish ethnic groups have long been concerned with the political and other social results of economic specialization and the ways in which specialized minority groups, once established, are modified and maintained. Similarly, in all parts of southeast Asia, economic and political developments have produced ethnic specialization with a wide range of conflict.

The political consequences of the specialization of ethnic groups by occupation, and therefore of the kinds of power that they hold in society, is a problem of which all historians of colonial empires, from that of the Romans and the imperial Chinese to the sixteenth-century Spanish and the modern Europeans, are well aware. But it is also a problem that needs even closer attention in postcolonial societies, where, although the structural alignment of groups within them may have altered, the problems of cultural and ethnic diversity remain.

With the growth of good communications and

the spread of travel, ethnically and culturally diverse societies are likely, in the short term, to increase in number rather than diminish. As the sociological study of society ceases to be solely a Western discipline, the need to find appropriate conceptual tools for analyzing ethnic and cultural variation will undoubtedly become a major preoccupation of the discipline.

H. S. MORRIS

[*See also* MINORITIES; PEASANTRY; RACE RELATIONS; SOCIAL STRUCTURE; TRIBAL SOCIETY. *Other relevant material may be found in* ASIAN SOCIETY, *article on* SOUTH ASIA; CARIBBEAN SOCIETY; LINGUISTICS, *article on* THE SPEECH COMMUNITY.]

BIBLIOGRAPHY

BARTH, FREDRIK 1960 The System of Social Stratification in Swat, North Pakistan. Pages 113–146 in Edmund R. Leach (editor), *Aspects of Caste in South India, Ceylon and North-west Pakistan.* Cambridge Papers in Social Anthropology, No. 2. Cambridge Univ. Press.

BENEDICT, BURTON 1962 Stratification in Plural Societies. *American Anthropologist* New Series 64:1235–1246.

BOEKE, JULIUS H. 1953 *Economics and Economic Policy of Dual Societies as Exemplified by Indonesia.* New York: Institute of Pacific Relations.

CHAMBERLAIN, HOUSTON STEWART (1899) 1910 *Foundations of the Nineteenth Century.* New York and London: John Lane. → First published in German.

COX, OLIVER C. 1948 *Caste, Class and Race: A Study in Social Dynamics.* Garden City, N.Y.: Doubleday.

DOLLARD, JOHN (1937) 1957 *Caste and Class in a Southern Town.* 3d ed. Garden City, N.Y.: Doubleday.

FREEDMAN, MAURICE 1960 Growth of a Plural Society in Malaya. *Pacific Affairs* 33:158–168.

FREYRE, GILBERTO (1933) 1956 *The Masters and the Slaves: A Study in the Development of Brazilian Civilization.* 2d ed., rev. New York: Knopf. → First published in Portuguese.

FURNIVALL, JOHN S. 1942 The Political Economy of the Tropical Far East. *Journal of the Royal Central Asian Society* 29:195–210.

FURNIVALL, JOHN S. (1948) 1956 *Colonial Policy and Practice: A Comparative Study of Burma and Netherlands India.* Issued in cooperation with the International Secretariat, Institute of Pacific Relations. Cambridge Univ. Press; New York Univ. Press.

GOBINEAU, JOSEPH ARTHUR DE (1853–1855) 1933 *Essai sur l'inégalité des races humaines.* 6th ed., 2 vols. Paris: Firmin-Didot. → Partially translated into English in 1915 as *The Inequality of Human Races.*

JAYAWARDENA, CHANDRA 1963 *Conflict and Solidarity in a Guianese Plantation.* London School of Economics and Political Science, Monograph on Social Anthropology, No. 25. London: Athlone.

LEACH, EDMUND R. 1954 *Political Systems of Highland Burma: A Study of Kachin Social Structure.* London School of Economics and Political Science; Cambridge, Mass.: Harvard Univ. Press.

MacCRONE, IAN D. 1937 *Race Attitudes in South Africa: Historical, Experimental and Psychological Studies.* Oxford Univ. Press.

MORRIS, H. S. 1957 The Plural Society. *Man* 57:124–125.

NADEL, SIEGFRIED F. 1957 *The Theory of Social Structure.* London: Cohen & West; Glencoe, Ill.: Free Press.

PATTERSON, SHEILA 1953 *Colour and Culture in South Africa.* London: Routledge; New York: Humanities.

REX, JOHN A. 1959 The Plural Society in Sociological Theory. *British Journal of Sociology* 10:114–124.

SMITH, M. G. 1955 *Framework for Caribbean Studies.* Mona (Jamaica): University College of the West Indies.

SMITH, M. G. 1956 Community Organization in Rural Jamaica. *Social Economic Studies* 5:295–312.

SMITH, M. G. 1960 Social and Cultural Pluralism. New York Academy of Sciences, *Annals* 83, no. 5:763–785.

ETHNOCENTRISM

See CULTURE, *article on* CULTURAL RELATIVISM.

ETHNOGRAPHY

The data of cultural anthropology derive ultimately from the direct observation of customary behavior in particular societies. Making, reporting, and evaluating such observations are the tasks of ethnography. Although the successful carrying out of these tasks is intimately related to the validity of cultural and social anthropological interpretations, ethnography itself has received little serious attention. However, as the social sciences have become more critical of their source materials, more concerned with how data are recorded, verified, and analyzed, interest has developed in ethnographic method and theory and in the more technical and personal aspects of conducting ethnographic research.

While the scope and definition of ethnography have varied considerably and opinions differ on many details, contemporary usage does permit a few general terminological distinctions and implications. An ethnographer is an anthropologist who attempts—at least in part of his professional work—to record and describe the culturally significant behaviors of a particular society. Ideally, this description, an ethnography, requires a long period of intimate study and residence in a small, well-defined community, knowledge of the spoken language, and the employment of a wide range of observational techniques including prolonged face-to-face contacts with members of the local group, direct participation in some of that group's activities, and a greater emphasis on intensive work with informants than on the use of documentary or survey data. Used nonspecifically, ethnography refers to the discipline concerned with producing such cultural descriptions. With a regional reference (e.g., "Polynesian ethnography"), the term designates either the way in which ethnography is conceived and practiced in the area or the collective or comparative treatment of the ethnographies written about the peoples living in the region. This last usage is frequently referred to as comparative ethnology, or simply ethnology [see ETHNOLOGY].

History of ethnography

Although the roots of ethnographic description are lost in antiquity and most observations and interpretations (or misinterpretations) of human societies have continued to be transmitted orally, some early written accounts have been preserved. Permanent documentation of such observations increased markedly with European voyages of discovery and exploration. Despite organizational and stylistic differences, it is possible to discern in the literature the transition from the curious recountings of strange, exotic, or bizarre practices to the present attempts at producing valid cultural descriptions. In comparing the successive steps in this transition, one should note changes not only in the content and purpose of ethnography but also in the preparation and background of the investigators and in the circumstances under which field work is conducted. (It is impossible to treat in detail many individual and institutional differences, such as the varying views of ethnographic work among American, British, and European anthropologists; see, for example, Eggan 1961; Firth 1957; Gluckman 1961; Griaule 1957; Kroeber 1957; Lowie 1953; Richards 1939.)

Early ethnography. Beginning in the late fifteenth century and continuing for several hundred years, descriptions of unfamiliar cultural practices were written largely as a result of explorations, missionizing, and the establishment of colonial governments and outposts (see Howell 1642; Rowe 1964). Although there were some exceptional reports such as Pigafetta's observations on Cebu, included in his chronicle of the Magellan voyage (1525), and the extensive Mexican texts recorded in the sixteenth century by Sahagún (see Sahagún, *General History of the Things of New Spain*), the dominant form of early ecclesiastic and governmental records was ethnographically unimpressive. In the nineteenth century, as territorial exploration intensified and the writings of natural historians, travelers, and museum collectors began to augment missionary and official documents, ethnographic inquiry became a somewhat more organized procedure. Many questionnaires, lists, instructions,

and regional guides were written (see Lewis 1814; British Association . . . 1852; Neumayer 1875). In Europe and the United States, professional anthropological societies were supported at first by travelers, government employees, and other amateurs and later encouraged by museums. Institutionalization stimulated the publication of monograph series devoted largely to cultural descriptions (notably, for example, the publications of the Bureau of American Ethnology, the American Ethnological Society, and the larger natural history museums). Landmarks include Morgan's account of Seneca culture (1851), such turn-of-the-century reports of field research as Rivers' study of the Toda (1906), and a few refreshingly innovating works like Barton's study of Ifugao law (1919), in which the value of the case-method approach is demonstrated. Up to the end of World War I vast quantities of published ethnographic material had accumulated from many regions, but although some scholars (such as Boas) had begun to work in depth with informants on particular linguistic and other cultural problems (see Jakobson 1959; Smith 1959), most of this literature had been produced by nonanthropologists (e.g., Morgan was a lawyer, Barton a schoolteacher and dentist), who for a variety of reasons had become attracted to the subject matter, and in the course of short visits, surveys, or by accidental association, had acquired sufficient field experience to write interesting accounts of their observations. Toward the end of this period, museums provided most of the support for field research. In general, ethnographic inquiry was correspondingly dominated by object-centered interests, a standardized topical format for observation and recording, and extensive use of interpreters. [See BOAS; MORGAN, LEWIS HENRY; RIVERS.]

Ethnography before World War II. By 1925 ethnographic field work had become an established professional activity. There was a distinct shift away from mere acceptance of field work toward a more critical and craftsmanlike attention to its execution, a shift from a dominant concern with data accumulation to the deeper analysis of particular cultural patterns. Many of these changes resulted directly from the influence of Malinowski's reports (especially 1922; 1935) based on his lengthy and detailed observations in the Trobriand Islands. His insistence on using the local language, residing for a long time with the group being studied, and delineating functionally related cultural phenomena in specifiable contexts spurred serious rethinking of many aspects of ethnographic research [see MALINOWSKI]. Increased interest in cultural contexts led to a concern with the ethnographer's role in the field situation and a more careful assessment of the way in which field data are recorded (Mauss 1947; Mead 1947; Osgood 1940). Partly as a result of developments in linguistics, sociology, and psychology, ethnographers began to show greater interest in general theory and descriptive methods, as well as to take advantage of an expanded range of research techniques such as the recording of life histories, the administering of projective tests, and the extensive use of film. Field inquiry was increasingly guided by an interest in general problems of cultural variability and of the nature of cultural universals. In the 1930s, attempts to provide needed ethnographic information for trait analysts and hypothesis testers led to various forms of standardization, such as the *Outline of Cultural Materials* (Yale University 1938), to help organize the recording and cross-indexing of field observations. This development aided quantitative and comparative studies and expanded significantly the existing inventories of cultural detail.

The detail, however, often lacked contextual specification, and these efforts thus drew attention to the inherent weakness of relying on prepared formats to guide functionally oriented field research. Similar criticism and experimentation with many field methods and techniques helped to meet the new demands of higher research standards. During this phase the influence of museum sponsorship and amateur ethnography declined. Field workers were mostly trained as anthropologists in graduate university departments and were supported by private foundation and government grants.

Ethnography after 1950. Following World War II, ethnography began to attract more theoretical and methodological attention. Of particular note was the renewed and expanded interest in classification, which is crucially important (Needham 1963, pp. vii–ix). There was also an increased emphasis on communications systems and structural models (e.g., Lévi-Strauss 1958); on the extension of principles developed in structural linguistics to ethnographic descriptions (e.g., Goodenough 1951); on the detailed study of cultural subsystems (e.g., Conklin 1957; Frake 1964b; Pospisil 1958); on contrasts between qualitative and quantitative aspects of field observations (Leach 1961); and on the development of more effective means of accounting for both cultural and personal variables in actual field situations (Condominas 1966). At the beginning of this phase there was a marked increase in the numbers of professional ethnographers, in sources of support, and in opportunities for field work.

Theory and method

The cumulative efforts of ethnographers to go beyond the uncritical narrative and rambling presentation of assumed cultural detail have focused on determining what constitutes a valid cultural description, on developing a theory that permits evaluation of alternative descriptions, and on formulating methods that may be most effective in deriving general statements from recorded observations. For example, it has been suggested that ideally an ethnography constitutes a cultural grammar, an abstract theory which provides the rules for producing, anticipating, and interpreting appropriate cultural behaviors in given settings (Conklin 1964; Frake 1964a; Goodenough 1957). Ethnographic theory, in this view, is concerned with evaluative criteria such as completeness (in both depth and breadth), conciseness, and accuracy. New approaches for providing reliable, valid, and more revealing field analyses have included (1) the formal treatment of cultural subsystems in which the relevant cultural phenomena are discretely organized or relationally describable in terms of a small number of dimensional contrasts or processes—componential definitions and formulaic reduction and rearrangement of terms by specified rules have been applied most frequently to kinship analysis (see Lounsbury 1964); and (2) the intracultural analysis of folk classifications, especially those of natural phenomena. The study of folk science (see Colby 1964) has led to a number of developments such as the more specific analysis of folk taxonomies (Berlin et al. 1966; Conklin 1962). Together with other types of contrast-set, subsegregate, and network linkage analysis, these efforts have sometimes been referred to as *ethnoscience* (Sturtevant 1964). Problems of alternative methodological procedures (Burling 1963) and of multiple contexts and code channels (Hymes 1962) are also being examined. The principles guiding many recent efforts reflect influences from linguistics, logic, mathematics, and systematic biology. Early results of their application in ethnography are, in turn, stimulating developments in such fields as sociology (Cicourel 1964) and archeology (Chang 1967). Furthermore, it is generally agreed, even where opinions on the nature of valid evidence differ widely (e.g., Metzger 1965), that theory and method as well as technique must be constantly tested in the field. [*See* Cognitive theory; Communication; Componential analysis.]

Techniques

Instruments for gathering, storing, retrieving, rearranging, expressing, and using field data while still in the field have multiplied with technical developments (Kano & Segawa 1945; Rowe 1953). Tape recording, cinematography, photogrammetry, aerial mapping, and the use of computers in text and demographic analysis are only a few of the frequently employed technical developments in the treatment of ethnographic data. Selecting from among these many devices and varied interactional techniques those most appropriate for keeping ethnographic records is a complex task. The ethnographer tries not to rely upon published outlines and questionnaires; he shuns interviews with informants carried out in artificial settings; and he avoids premature quantification or overdifferentiated measurement. Initially, at least, flexibility, curiosity, patience, and experimentation with many alternative devices and procedures are desirable. In everyday conversations between field worker and informant, for example, attention to and use of such verbal techniques as the following have been used profitably, although not always with equal success: recording and using natural question and comment frames (i.e., the ways in which information is normally solicited and transmitted in the local language); noting and using question–response sequences and implications; testing by intentional substitution of acceptable and incongruent references; testing by paraphrase; testing by reference to hypothetical situations; testing by experimental extensions of reference; and testing by switching styles, channels, code signals, message content, and roles (by reference or impersonation). Similarly, in the making of visual and nonverbal observations initial experimentation and flexibility help to determine focuses and boundaries of scenes, scheduled events, key roles, etc. Graphic and plastic modeling media have provided additional dimensions for the exploration of actual or hypothetical situations otherwise not easily investigated. Furthermore, ethnomodels, often ignored or treated only anecdotally, may clarify and facilitate field observation. When local systems have been qualitatively established, other procedures such as scaling techniques may be applied to increase the range of observations and provide some basis for quantification by various kinds of discrete, direct, or indirect measures. As available technology makes more elaborate manipulation of field data possible, greater attention can be given to informant–ethnographer interaction, not only in terms of eliciting routines but also with reference to critical and probabilistic changes in the microsociological environment. [*See* INTERVIEWING.]

Personnel. Because ethnographers interact personally and socially with informants, they find themselves carrying on a unique type of natural history, in which the observer becomes a part of (and an active participant in) the observed universe. The extent of this involvement and its importance for ethnographic recording depend on many situational considerations, including the personalities of the ethnographer and his informants. In some types of field inquiry the ethnographer's practical success or failure may depend as much on those impressions he makes locally (Goffman 1956) as on the cultural events being observed. Informal recognition of these variables is frequently reflected in the nontechnical literature and in humorous anecdotes circulated among colleagues. More systematic accounts of these personal background factors and their consequences have appeared with increasing frequency (e.g., Berreman 1962; Casagrande 1960). Especially where long-term investigation of intimate personal relationships is concerned, most anthropologists would agree with Condominas (1965, p. 35) in stressing the "nécessité d'ethnographier les ethnographes." Methods of assessing such contextual information are not yet well developed, but more careful and sensitive reporting of the kinds of transactions involved in ethnographic inquiry (Oliver 1958) and of the total spectrum of social involvements affecting these transactions (Junker 1960; Mintz 1960) may lead to the desired awareness, and thus to appropriate adjustments in continued research. The possibility of combining such sensitivity with technical mastery of ethnographic analysis has been dramatically illustrated in recent contributions by Paul Friedrich (see Tagari 1964) and Laura Bohannan (1966). [*See* OBSERVATION.]

Translation. The problems of ethnography are in the largest sense those of translation. Eventually, all observations must be "translated" into the ethnographer's descriptive code. Thus, linguistic theory, and translation theory in particular, has special relevance for ethnography (Gumperz & Hymes 1964; Nida 1964). And although ethnography and linguistics are not identical, they are to some extent mutually dependent (Hockett 1954). Furthermore, in spite of the fact that much ethnographic research concerns nonverbal behaviors, observations of even the most inarticulate cultural process are often identified, tallied, and even quantified by means of informant-expressed judgments. General linguistic and anthropological interest in semantic theory has been very responsive to discussions of ethnographic problems (e.g., Colby 1966; Conklin 1962; Lamb 1966; Romney & D'Andrade 1964; cf. Malinowski 1935). In particular, attention has been drawn to the diversity of semiotic relations, the multiplicity of contexts and related communication systems, and the importance of contrastive analysis of complete terminological sets [*see* SEMANTICS AND SEMIOTICS].

Since 1950 the critical re-evaluation of theory and practice has led to greater appreciation of the technical and human problems that are inherent in ethnographic research. Intellectual excitement and controversy have intensified efforts to refine methods for reducing apparent cultural complexity and indeterminacy to clear, systematic, and effective statements.

HAROLD C. CONKLIN

[*Directly related are the entries* ANTHROPOLOGY; COMPONENTIAL ANALYSIS; FIELD WORK; LANGUAGE, *article on* LANGUAGE AND CULTURE; LINGUISTICS; SEMANTICS AND SEMIOTICS.]

BIBLIOGRAPHY

Significant sources other than those listed below may be found in the bibliographies of Colby 1966; Conklin 1962; 1964; Nida 1964; Sturtevant 1964. The articles and appended references in the following collections should also be consulted: Adams & Preiss 1960; Casagrande 1960; Firth 1957; Gumperz & Hymes 1964; Romney & D'Andrade 1964. Most of the early references in this bibliography consist of guides, questionnaires, or sets of instructions to explorers, travelers, and collectors. Other items are listed only if cited in the text.

ADAMS, RICHARD N.; and PREISS, JACK J. (editors) 1960 *Human Organization Research: Field Relations and Techniques.* Homewood, Ill.: Dorsey.

BARTON, ROY F. 1919 *Ifugao Law.* University of California Publications in American Archaeology and Ethnology, Vol. 15, No. 1. Berkeley: Univ. of California Press.

BERLIN, BRENT; BREEDLOVE, DENNIS E.; and RAVEN, PETER H. 1966 Folk Taxonomies and Biological Classifications. *Science* 154, no. 3746:273–275.

BERLIN, K. MUSEEN, MUSEUM FÜR VÖLKERKUNDE 1896 *Instruction für ethnographische Beobachtungen und Sammlungen in Central Ostafrika.* Berlin: The Museum.

BERREMAN, GERALD D. 1962 *Behind Many Masks: Ethnography and Impression Management in a Himalayan Village.* Society for Applied Anthropology, Monograph No. 4. Ithaca, N.Y.: The Society.

BOHANNAN, LAURA 1966 Shakespeare in the Bush. *Natural History* 75, no. 7:28–33.

BRITISH ASSOCIATION FOR THE ADVANCEMENT OF SCIENCE 1852 *A Manual of Ethnological Inquiry: Being a Series of Questions Concerning the Human Race, for the Use of Travellers and Others, in Studying the Varieties of Man.* London: Taylor & Francis.

BRITISH ASSOCIATION FOR THE ADVANCEMENT OF SCIENCE (1874) 1951 *Notes and Queries on Anthropology.* 6th ed., rev. London: Routledge.

BRITISH MUSEUM, DEPARTMENT OF THE BRITISH AND MEDIAEVAL ANTIQUITIES AND ETHNOGRAPHY, BUREAU OF ETHNOGRAPHY 1905 *Anthropological Queries for Central Africa.* Compiled by C. H. Read. London: The Museum.

BURLING, R. 1963 Garo Kinship Terms and the Analysis of Meaning. *Ethnology* 2:70–85.

CASAGRANDE, JOSEPH B. (editor) 1960 *In the Company of Man: Twenty Portraits by Anthropologists.* New York: Harper.

[CASS, LEWIS] 1823 *Inquiries Respecting the History, Traditions, Languages, Manners, Customs, Religion, etc., of the Indians Living in the United States.* Detroit, Mich.: Sheldon & Reed.

CHANG, KWANG-CHIH 1967 *Rethinking Archaeology.* New York: Random House.

CICOUREL, AARON V. 1964 *Method and Measurement in Sociology.* New York: Free Press.

COLBY, B. N. 1964 Folk Science Studies. *Palacio* 70, no. 4:5–14.

COLBY, B. N. 1966 Ethnographic Semantics: A Preliminary Survey. *Current Anthropology* 7:3–32.

CONDOMINAS, GEORGES 1965 *L'exotique est quotidien: Sar Luk, Viet-nam Central.* Paris: Plon.

CONKLIN, HAROLD C. 1957 *Hanunóo Agriculture: A Report on an Integral System of Shifting Cultivation in the Philippines.* FAO Forestry Development Paper No. 12. Rome: Food and Agriculture Organization.

CONKLIN, HAROLD C. 1962 Lexicographical Treatment of Folk Taxonomies. Pages 119–141 in Conference on Lexicography, Indiana University, 1960, *Problems in Lexicography.* Edited by Fred W. Householder and Sol Saporta. Bloomington: Indiana Univ., Research Center in Anthropology, Folklore, and Linguistics. → Also published as Volume 28, no. 2, part 4 of the *International Journal of American Linguistics,* and as Publication No. 21 of Indiana University, Research Center in Anthropology, Folklore, and Linguistics.

CONKLIN, HAROLD C. 1964 Ethnogenealogical Method. Pages 25–55 in Ward H. Goodenough (editor), *Explorations in Cultural Anthropology: Essays in Honor of George Peter Murdock.* New York: McGraw-Hill.

EGGAN, FRED 1961 Ethnographic Data in Social Anthropology in the United States. *Sociological Review* 9:19–26.

FIRTH, RAYMOND (editor) (1957) 1964 *Man and Culture: An Evaluation of the Work of Bronislaw Malinowski.* New York: Harper.

FOUCART, GEORGE 1919 *Introductory Questions on African Ethnology.* Cairo: Printing Office of the French Institute of Oriental Archaeology.

FRAKE, CHARLES O. 1964a Notes on Queries in Ethnography. *American Anthropologist* New Series 66, no. 3, part 2:132–145.

FRAKE, CHARLES O. 1964b A Structural Account of Subanun "Religious Behavior." Pages 111–129 in Ward H. Goodenough (editor), *Explorations in Cultural Anthropology: Essays in Honor of George Peter Murdock.* New York: McGraw-Hill.

FRAZER, JAMES G. (1907) 1916 *Questions on the Customs, Beliefs and Languages of Savages.* Cambridge Univ. Press.

GLUCKMAN, MAX 1961 Ethnographic Data in British Social Anthropology. *Sociological Review* 9:5–17.

GOFFMAN, ERVING (1956) 1959 *The Presentation of Self in Everyday Life.* Garden City, N.Y.: Doubleday.

GOODENOUGH, WARD H. 1951 *Property, Kin, and Com-*

munity on Truk. Yale University Publications in Anthropology, No. 46. New Haven: Yale Univ. Press.

GOODENOUGH, WARD H. (1957) 1964 Cultural Anthropology and Linguistics. Georgetown University, Washington, D.C., Institute of Languages and Linguistics, *Monograph Series on Languages and Linguistics* No. 9:167–173.

GRIAULE, MARCEL 1957 *Méthode de l'ethnographie.* Paris: Presses Universitaires de France.

GUMPERZ, JOHN J.; and HYMES, DELL H. (editors) 1964 The Ethnography of Communication. *American Anthropologist* New Series, Special Issue 66, no. 6, part 2.

HOCKETT, CHARLES (1954) 1958 Chinese Versus English: An Exploration of the Whorfian Theses. Pages 106–123 in Harry Hoijer (editor), *Language and Culture: Conference on the Interrelations of Language and Other Aspects of Culture.* Univ. of Chicago Press. → See also Hockett's comments in the discussion.

HOCKETT, CHARLES 1964 Scheduling. Pages 125–144 in F. S. C. Northrop and Helen H. Livingston (editors), *Cross-cultural Understanding: Epistemology in Anthropology.* New York: Harper.

HOWELL, JAMES (1642) 1895 *Instructions for Forreine Travell.* London: Moseley.

HYMES, DELL H. 1962 The Ethnography of Speaking. Pages 13–53 in Anthropological Society of Washington, *Anthropology and Human Behavior.* Washington: The Society.

JACKSON, JOHN R. 1834 *Aide-mémoire du voyageur: Ou questions relatives à la géographie physique et politique, etc.* Paris: Bellizard.

JAKOBSON, ROMAN 1959 Boas' View of Grammatical Meaning. Pages 139–145 in Walter Goldschmidt (editor), *The Anthropology of Franz Boas.* American Anthropological Association, Memoir No. 89. Menasha, Wisc.: The Association.

JUNKER, BUFORD H. (1960) 1962 *Field Work: An Introduction to the Social Sciences.* Univ. of Chicago Press.

KANO, TADAO; and SEGAWA, KOKICHI (1945) 1956 *An Illustrated Ethnography of Formosan Aborigines.* Volume 1: The Yami. Rev. ed. Tokyo: Maruzen.

KELLER, ALBERT G. 1903 *Queries in Ethnography.* New York and London: Longmans.

KIRSCHBAUM, FRANZ J.; and FÜRER-HAIMENDORF, CHRISTOPH VON 1934 *Anleitung zu ethnographischen und linguistischen Forschungen mit besonderer Berücksichtigung der Verhältnisse auf Neuguinea und den umliegenden Inseln.* St. Gabriel-Mödling (Austria): Verlag "Anthropos."

KROEBER, ALFRED L. 1957 *Ethnographic Interpretations: 1–6.* University of California Publications in American Archaeology and Ethnology, Vol. 47, No. 2. Berkeley: Univ. of California Press. → See especially Chapter 1, "What Ethnography Is."

LAMB, SYDNEY M. 1966 Epilegomena to a Theory of Language. *Romance Philology* 19:531–573.

LEACH, EDMUND R. 1961 *Pul Eliya, a Village in Ceylon: A Study of Land Tenure and Kinship.* Cambridge Univ. Press.

LÉVI-STRAUSS, CLAUDE (1958) 1963 *Structural Anthropology.* New York: Basic Books. → First published in French.

LÉVI-STRAUSS, CLAUDE 1966 Anthropology: Its Achievements and Future. *Current Anthropology* 7:124–127.

LEWIS, MERIWETHER (1814) 1922 *History of the Expedition Under the Command of Captains Lewis and Clark to the Sources of the Missouri, . . .* 3 vols.

New York: Allerton. → A questionnaire for Lewis and Clark's ethnographic observations is included in Volume 1, pages xxvii–xxviii. A paperback edition was published in 1965 by Dover.

LOUNSBURY, FLOYD G. 1964 A Formal Account of the Crow- and Omaha-type Kinship Terminologies. Pages 351–393 in Ward H. Goodenough (editor), *Explorations in Cultural Anthropology: Essays in Honor of George Peter Murdock.* New York: McGraw-Hill.

LOWIE, ROBERT H. 1953 Ethnography, Cultural and Social Anthropology. *American Anthropologist* New Series 55:527–534.

LUSCHAN, FELIX VON (1904) 1909 *Anleitung für ethnographische Beobachtungen und Sammlungen in Afrika und Oceanien.* 3d ed. Berlin: Unger.

LUSCHAN, FELIX VON 1906 Anthropologie, Ethnographie und Urgeschichte. Volume 2, pages 1–123 in Georg von Neumayer (editor), *Anleitung zu wissenschaftlichen Beobachtungen auf Reisen.* 3d ed. Hanover (Germany): Jänecke.

MALINOWSKI, BRONISLAW (1922) 1960 *Argonauts of the Western Pacific: An Account of Native Enterprise and Adventure in the Archipelagoes of Melanesian New Guinea.* London School of Economics and Political Science, Studies, No. 65. London: Routledge; New York: Dutton. → A paperback edition was published in 1961 by Dutton.

MALINOWSKI, BRONISLAW (1935) 1965 *Coral Gardens and Their Magic.* 2 vols., with a new introduction by E. R. Leach. Bloomington: Indiana Univ. Press. → Volume 1: *Soil-tilling and Agricultural Rites in the Trobriand Islands.* Volume 2: *The Language of Magic and Gardening.*

MARIN, LOUIS (1924) 1925 *Questionnaire d'ethnographie: Tables d'analyse en ethnographie.* Alençon (France): Laverdure. → First published in the *Bulletin* of the Société d'Ethnographie de Paris.

MAUSS, MARCEL 1947 *Manuel d'ethnographie.* Paris: Payot.

MEAD, MARGARET 1947 *The Mountain Arapesh:* III. Socio-economic Life. IV. Diary of Events in Alitoa. American Museum of Natural History, *Anthropological Papers* 40, part 3.

METZGER, DUANE 1965 [A Review of] *The Nature of Cultural Things,* by Marvin Harris. *American Anthropologist* New Series 67:1293–1296.

MINTZ, SIDNEY W. 1960 *Worker in the Cane: A Puerto Rican Life History.* Caribbean Series, II. New Haven: Yale Univ. Press.

MORGAN, LEWIS HENRY (1851) 1962 *The League of the Iroquois.* New York: Citadel. → First published as *The League of the Ho-dé-no-sau-nee, or Iroquois.* A 1901 edition was edited with many notes by Herbert M. Lloyd. A two-volume paperback edition, a reprint of the 1901 edition, was published by the Human Relations Area Files in 1954.

NEEDHAM, RODNEY 1963 Introduction. Pages vii–xlvii in Émile Durkheim and Marcel Mauss, *Primitive Classification.* Translated and edited by Rodney Needham. Univ. of Chicago Press.

NEUMAYER, GEORG VON (editor) 1875 *Anleitung zu wissenschaftlichen Beobachtungen auf Reisen.* 2 vols. Berlin: Oppenheim.

NIDA, EUGENE A. 1964 *Toward a Science of Translating.* Leiden (Netherlands): Brill.

OLIVER, DOUGLAS 1958 An Ethnographer's Method for Formulating Descriptions of "Social Structure." *American Anthropologist* New Series 60:801–826.

OSGOOD, CORNELIUS 1940 *Ingalik Material Culture.* Yale University Publications in Anthropology, No. 22. New Haven: Yale Univ. Press.

PIGAFETTA, ANTONIO (1525) 1906 *Magellan's Voyage Around the World.* Edited by James A. Robertson. 2 vols. Cleveland: Clark.

POSPISIL, LEOPOLD 1958 *Kapauku Papuans and Their Law.* Yale University Publications in Anthropology, No. 54. New Haven: Yale Univ., Dept. of Anthropology.

RICHARDS, AUDREY I. 1939 The Development of Field Work Methods in Social Anthropology. Pages 272–316 in Frederic C. Bartlett et al. (editors), *The Study of Society.* New York: Macmillan.

RIVERS, WILLIAM H. R. 1906 *The Todas.* New York and London: Macmillan.

ROMNEY, A. KIMBALL; and D'ANDRADE, ROY GOODWIN (editors) 1964 Transcultural Studies in Cognition. *American Anthropologist* New Series 66, no. 3, part 2. → A special issue.

ROWE, JOHN H. 1953 Technical Aids in Anthropology: A Historical Survey. Pages 895–940 in International Symposium on Anthropology, New York, 1952, *Anthropology Today.* Edited by Alfred L. Kroeber. Univ. of Chicago Press.

ROWE, JOHN H. 1964 Ethnography and Ethnology in the Sixteenth Century. Kroeber Anthropological Society, *Papers* No. 30:1–19.

SAHAGÚN, FRAY BERNADINO DE *General History of the Things of New Spain, Florentine Codex.* Books 1–13. Translated by A. J. O. Anderson and C. E. Dibble. Santa Fe, N.M.: School of American Research, 1950–1964.

SMITH, MARIAN W. 1959 Boas' "Natural History" Approach to Field Method. Pages 46–60 in Walter Goldschmidt (editor), *The Anthropology of Franz Boas.* American Anthropological Association, Memoir No. 89. Menasha, Wisc.: The Association.

STURTEVANT, WILLIAM C. 1964 Studies in Ethnoscience. *American Anthropologist* New Series, Special Issue 66, no. 3, part 2:99–131.

TAGARI SHIVASHANKARA PILLAI 1964 Under the Mango Tree. *Texas Quarterly* 7, no. 2:54–63. → Translated and edited by Paul Friedrich and K. N. Parameshwaran Nayar.

YALE UNIVERSITY, INSTITUTE OF HUMAN RELATIONS (1938) 1961 *Outline of Cultural Materials.* 4th ed., revised by George P. Murdock et al. New Haven: Human Relations Area Files.

ETHNOHISTORY
See under HISTORY.

ETHNOLINGUISTICS
See LANGUAGE, *article on* LANGUAGE AND CULTURE; LINGUISTICS.

ETHNOLOGY

Ethnology is generally regarded as one of the major subdivisions of cultural anthropology, the others being anthropological archeology and anthropological linguistics. Anthropology is prefixed to the latter two terms because they refer to the archeology and linguistics largely of preliterate and preindustrial peoples. The archeology of classical Greece and the linguistics of contemporary France would rarely, if ever, be taught in an anthropology department. The claim that anthropology embraces all peoples past and present has been exaggerated by some anthropologists, although the present trend, especially in ethnology, is toward giving attention to a wider range of peoples. In the United States today, but less so in Europe, ethnology is joined to social anthropology. [*See* ANTHROPOLOGY, *articles on* CULTURAL ANTHROPOLOGY *and* SOCIAL ANTHROPOLOGY.]

Interesting insight into the scope of ethnology can be gained by looking at the names of early anthropological societies. In 1843 the Ethnological Society was founded in England, and in that same year it published the first edition of its guide to field work, an inventory of data to be obtained. This guide included some material on all fields of anthropology but gave the most space to social anthropology. In 1863 the Anthropological Society was founded in England; this was a group of former members of the Ethnological Society who wanted to stress political issues, such as slavery, more heavily. In 1871 the two societies joined to form the Anthropological Institute of Great Britain and Ireland, to which name the word "Royal" was prefixed in 1907. In the United States, the American Ethnological Society was founded in 1842, the Anthropological Society of Washington in 1879, and the American Anthropological Association in 1902. In France, the Société Ethnologique de Paris was established in 1838 and the Société d'Anthropologie de Paris in 1858. In Germany, the Gesellschaft für Anthropologie, Ethnologie, und Urgeschichte was founded in 1869.

It is clear from these examples that "ethnology" was used as a blanket term to cover the entire range of the subject we now label "anthropology" and that the latter term came to be used in the wider sense at a later date. Through much of the nineteenth century the concepts of biological race, language, and culture were confused; one was inferred from the other, and reconstructions of human development combined all three aspects. Ethnology was historically oriented from the start and attempted to account for extant races, languages, and cultures in terms of migration, diffusion, and other historical processes [*see* DIFFUSION].

In the twentieth century, "ethnology" has come to mean the comparative study of documented and contemporary cultures and has largely excluded their bioanthropology, archeology, and linguistics. "Ethnography," in contrast, is best used to describe the study of the culture of a single tribe or society; but because almost all ethnographies make comparisons at least with neighboring peoples, the distinction between ethnography and ethnology is not sharp and may be compared to that between geography and geology. This article is limited almost completely to comparative ethnology.

Oscar Lewis (1956) gives an excellent idea of the contemporary scope of comparative ethnology. Comparisons may range from two ethnic units (societies) to hundreds, the largest sample so far being Murdock's "Ethnographic Atlas" (Murdock et al. 1962–1966), which is approaching one thousand ethnic units. They may deal with a few adjacent peoples, or a larger number in a culture area, a continent, a hemisphere, or the entire world. The content to be compared may vary from a single culture element to a long list of elements and assemblages of them covering practically every aspect of culture. Verne Ray's list of 7,633 culture elements for the plateau area of North America (1942) is the longest enumerated list so far, and Murdock's world-wide "Ethnographic Atlas" has reached nearly one thousand culture trait categories. Data for comparison may be based on library research, field research, or a combination of the two. The purpose of comparisons may be limited to uncovering the range and kind of variations for the subject at hand and to locating them in space and time; or it may be aimed at establishing culture area groupings, cross-cultural regularities, evolutionary trends, or other hypotheses. The research design may range all the way from a few illustrations of loose-jointed generalizations to a rigid statistical method.

The subject coverage of ethnology includes that of social anthropology and sociology, but it is much broader. For instance, ethnology also includes technology and crafts, plastic and graphic arts, music, dancing, oral literature, dream analysis, religion, world view, ethics, and ethnomedicine. For a much longer list of the subject content of ethnology, see the *Outline of Cultural Materials* (Yale Univ. 1938).

The dominant trend in nineteenth-century ethnology–social anthropology was an evolutionary explanation of how things came to be as they are. In its most extreme form, unilinear evolution, it was assumed that culture change came about largely from causes operating within single societies and that all peoples would, sooner or later, evolve through a half-dozen or more stages of development in the same sequence if their progress were not interrupted by some catastrophe, such as military invasion by an alien power [*see* EVOLUTION, *article on* CULTURAL EVOLUTION].

Historical ethnology

Toward the end of the nineteenth century two schools of ethnology were founded, one by Boas in the United States and the other by Ratzel and Frobenius in Germany. Both schools emphasized the historical processes of diffusion and migration. Boas' best demonstrations of the process of relay diffusion are to be found in his comparative studies of North American Indian folklore (1895; 1916). By tracing motifs and tale types among groups of contiguous tribes, he showed the overwhelming tendency of these phenomena to cluster into areal types which crosscut language-family boundaries, thus suggesting diffusion. If such material were independently invented over and over again, tribes separated by great distances would exhibit as many resemblances in folklore as neighboring tribes do; but because contiguous tribes shared much more folklore inventory than distant tribes did, diffusion was the obvious explanation.

Boas' diffusion emphasis was most fully developed by A. L. Kroeber and by Clark Wissler, trained as a psychologist but long curator of anthropology in the American Museum of Natural History. Although the earliest American culture area scheme was that of Livingstone Farrand (1904), his work had less impact than that of Kroeber and Wissler. In 1904 Kroeber was the first to classify California Indian cultures, and in 1906 Wissler was the first to mention major North American areas. Wissler (1917) published the first map of culture areas for the hemisphere, and Kroeber (1923) followed Wissler closely in a parallel scheme. In these and later works both authors postulated that the most significant aspects of culture in each area arose at the center and tended to diffuse outward toward the margins. On the assumption that all aspects of culture diffused at about the same rate, the age–area hypothesis, by which the age of a culture trait or complex was determined by the extent of its geographical distribution, was employed by both men.

In addition to the scheme of 15 culture areas for the two American continents endorsed by both men, each also regarded the area from Mexico to Peru as the culture center of a vast Pan-American culture area. Kroeber (1923, fig. 35) presented a large histogram in which the supposedly oldest traits occurred at the bottom, as in archeological stratification, and the youngest at the top. Age was determined largely by the extent of geographical distribution, but typological complexity was also taken into account, as well as a little direct sequential evidence from archeology. Although the horizontal dimension represented dispersal of the culture elements by diffusion and migration, the vertical dimension clearly showed an evolution from the simple to the complex. Thus, in Mexico the sequence included basketry, shamanism, and family groups in the earliest level; then patrilineal clans, simple weaving frame, domesticated plants, pottery, solstitial calendar, stone buildings, town life, cotton growing and loom weaving, matrilineal clans, textile clothing, priesthood, confederacy, sculpture, metallurgy, markets, human sacrifice, temples, empire, mathematics, astronomy, cycle calendar, writing, and books, in that order. Kroeber rejected nineteenth-century unilinear evolution and the theory of many independent origins of cultural resemblances, but he constructed a new kind of evolution with few independent origins and many diffusions and migrations from tribe to tribe and area to area. The age–area hypothesis demands a sequential arrangement of the material, and when this shows a temporal progression in complexity, it becomes evolutionary.

A major weakness of culture area and age–area theory is that culture areas are of varying sizes. Local developments may originate in the "centers" of small areas and tend to spread toward the margins, but at the same time new culture elements and assemblages may arise in the "centers" of larger culture areas and spread by diffusion or migration to the smaller ones, thus mixing elements of internal and external origin; and still more invention may occur in "centers" of each hemisphere and spread widely throughout many culture areas of different sizes in the same hemisphere. The hope of unscrambling this sort of mixture without the help of archeology and historical linguistics is dim. [See ARCHEOLOGY; HISTORY, article on CULTURE HISTORY; LINGUISTICS, article on HISTORICAL LINGUISTICS.]

Wissler's derivation of historical inferences from geographical distributions was so bold an attempt that he was heavily criticized, especially by Dixon (1928). Kroeber, in contrast, modified his views as new evidence came to light, and in 1939 he published his well-received "Cultural and Natural Areas of Native North America." This was fundamentally an intuitive scheme of culture areas without detailed supporting geographical or historical evidence. Between the time this book was finished —1931—and the time it was published—1939— Kroeber supervised the University of California Culture Element Survey, which, with the help of 13 field workers, collected responses to questionnaires from old informants in 254 localities in western North America, from the continental di-

vide to the Pacific and from the Mexican border to Alaska. This was aimed at collecting enough data to produce a definitive taxonomy of the nineteenth-century cultures, which Kroeber hoped would lead to a fuller set of interpretations. After all this effort, interest in areal classification ebbed to the extent that no one has yet used this vast quantity of data to produce a much superior areal scheme based on a wealth of specific detail. The largest comparative study incorporating this culture element material is still that of Driver (1941), who limited his subject coverage to girls' puberty rites [see CULTURE AREA; KROEBER; WISSLER].

In Germany, Friedrich Ratzel (1887) introduced the "criterion of form," which argued that all specific resemblances in the form of two or more museum objects, other than those determined by the material from which they were made or the use to which they were put, must be explained by a single origin and subsequent diffusion to the localities from which the museum specimens were obtained in the field, no matter how widely separated these localities might be. This was a much more extreme diffusionist position than that of Boas, Boas' pupils, or even Wissler. Frobenius (1898) was the first to use the term Kulturkreis, best translated as "culture area" or "culture region"; he also introduced the criterion of quantity, which argued that the larger the number of arbitrary resemblances not due to the nature of the material or the use to which the object was put, the stronger the case for diffusion.

Two early applications of the Kulturkreis rules for determining areal clusters, time sequences, and dispersal, those of Graebner (1905) and Ankermann (1905), were fairly well received and not much less tenable than the works of Wissler. They, too, emphasized material culture and arranged their data in a series of temporal strata, or Schichten. Neither author gave any explicit technique for packaging culture elements into Kreise or Schichten, but Czekanowski (1911) showed clearly that the reality of Ankermann's two African Kreise could be demonstrated with a correlation technique. Using Yule's Q coefficient, Czekanowski intercorrelated Ankermann's 17 traits of material culture among 47 African tribes and arranged the correlations in a single matrix which clearly showed two distinct intertrait clusters. When mapped, these clusters yielded a twofold areal classification, which conformed to Ankermann's intuitive grouping.

Although no one today subscribes to the idea of single origin and subsequent world-wide dispersal by migration and diffusion of any of the Kreise or Schichten of, say, Schmidt and Koppers (1924), some of the correlations and functional associations of the *Kreise* and *Schichten* have been confirmed or repostulated by later researchers of different schools. For example, the correlation between moieties and matrilineal descent, challenged by Lowie (1937, p. 182), has been confirmed by Murdock (1949, p. 49). The functional complex of hoe farming by women, matrilocal residence, matrilineal descent, monogamy, and bride service, and the temporal sequence from division of labor to residence to descent has been confirmed or postulated by Murdock (1949), Driver (1956), and Aberle (1961).

The world-wide inferred temporal strata of the *Kulturkreis* school produce an evolution which differs from that of the nineteenth century in calling for single origins or a very small number of independent origins and subsequent dispersal of the phenomena by migration and diffusion; but since such dispersals are multiple, they overlap each other geographically and produce a "layer cake" of temporal stages. Kroeber and Wissler confined their postulated dispersals to a culture area or a hemisphere for the most part, while Schmidt and Koppers more often included the entire world [*see* GRAEBNER; KOPPERS; RATZEL; SCHMIDT].

Kroeber's interest in culture areas and diffusion stimulated Clements (Clements et al. 1926; Clements 1928; 1931) and Driver (see Driver & Kroeber 1932) to determine areal groupings of ethnic units by intercorrelating their inventories of culture traits. These papers were read by three young men in Europe who were familiar with *Kulturkreis* theory and the intertrait correlations of Czekanowski (1911). Almost simultaneously they published four papers which combined the intertrait correlations of Czekanowski with the intertribe correlations of Kroeber, Clements, and Driver (Fürer-Haimendorf 1934; Klimek 1935; Milke 1935; Klimek & Milke 1935). They computed the coefficient Q_6 for three sets of traits: intertribe, intertrait, and tribal cluster with trait cluster. All three assembled their coefficients in rectangular matrices and converted them to shades of gray (as Czekanowski had done in 1911) for quick comprehension. They also mapped their clusters. Interpretation of the resemblances and the groupings was limited to historical factors, but because all of these studies were confined to small regions of culture area size, this wholesale historical explanation was probably not far from the truth although incomplete. A simplified explanation in English of their technique may be found in Driver (1961).

Knowledge of statistical mechanics was so scant

among ethnologists of both schools that few at the time understood that these studies integrated the approaches of the American culture area and the German *Kulturkreis* schools. They offered an objective method for determining both intertribal (culture area) and intertrait (*Kulturschicht-Kulturkreis*) groupings. If every writer in these schools had empirically demonstrated his intertribal and intertrait groupings in this manner, the differences between the schools would have been less marked and much useless polemic would not have been written. Differences in interpretation of the data grouped in these ways still exist, but the reality of the groupings themselves could have been established objectively.

Driver, in his "Girls' Puberty Rites in Western North America" (1941), used a multiple clustering technique parallel to that of the Europeans, but his interpretation of the results went beyond any of that group. His area was larger and posed more problems of interpretation. He distinguished several kinds of resemblances: universals, cultural heritages spread by migrations, relayed diffusions, and convergences. He pointed out (1) that elements of universal or near universal occurrence should not be used to establish historical connection between ethnic units in limited areas; (2) that elements closely associated with a language family might be regarded as a cultural heritage from the protoculture associated with the protolanguage of the group; (3) that continuously distributed resemblances which crossed over language-family boundaries were best regarded as diffusions; and (4) that the group ceremony for pubescent girls among the Apacheans represented an independent origin and a convergence with that held in southern California. He also wrote a chapter on the psychological aspects of menstrual taboos, described the functional position and significance of the girls' puberty rite in each of the subareas into which the entire area had been divided, and assessed the influence of geographical environment on the data.

Functionalism

In addition to the American and German historical schools just described, there arose in the early part of this century the functional schools, which rebelled against not only the nineteenth-century unilinear evolutionists but also the culture historicalists. Malinowski and Radcliffe-Brown are both identified as functionalists, although some significant divergences exist. Malinowski was generally both antihistorical and anticomparative, while Radcliffe-Brown was antihistorical (except in his later years) but never anticomparative. For this reason the latter figures more prominently in comparative ethnology and will be singled out for brief appraisal here.

Radcliffe-Brown discovered a number of generalizations that would now be called correlations. One of the earliest (1913) was his discovery that preferred marriage to a first cross-cousin was associated with kinship terminology of one type, while preferred marriage to a second cross-cousin was found with kinship terminology of another type. This and other perfect or high correlations are given in his important *The Social Organization of Australian Tribes* (1931), where he used the term "correlation" but did not compute any coefficients. In 1935 he wrote: ". . . we can expect to find, in the majority of human societies, a fairly close correlation between the terminological classification of kindred or relatives and the social classification," as revealed "in the attitudes and behavior of relatives to one another" (Radcliffe-Brown 1935, p. 531). His greatest contribution lies in the emphasis on this relationship.

The principal opponent of Radcliffe-Brown was Kroeber, who said:

Kin-term systems, . . . are subject to modification from within and without. There is always a sufficient number of such "accidents" to disguise the basic patterns more or less. . . . the essential features of the pattern are . . . likely to be the ones which have the greatest historic depth. The search for them therefore implies a willingness and ability to view data historically. Without such willingness, it is as good as impossible to separate the significant from the trivial . . . and the work done becomes merely sociological, an affair of schemes. . . . (Kroeber 1934, pp. 21–22)

This position is echoed by E. W. Gifford, a colleague of Kroeber, who wrote: ". . . kinship systems are first of all linguistic phenomena . . . and only secondarily social phenomena. As such they . . . constitute an archaic and highly refractory nucleus, which yields unevenly and only here and there to influences from . . . social structure" (Gifford 1940, pp. 193–194). Kroeber (1936) modified his view in the direction of that of Radcliffe-Brown in a conciliatory paper, and a year later (1937) made the first reconstruction of a protokinship terminology for a language family.

No historian of ethnological thought has yet pointed out that the opposing views of Radcliffe-Brown and Kroeber stem directly from the areas with which each was most familiar. The kinship terminologies and social organization of native Australia are among the most highly integrated of any in the world. High correlations are the rule rather than the exception. California native cultures, in contrast, are among the least integrated in this respect, and correlations are low or non-existent, as Tax (1937), a pupil of Radcliffe-Brown, showed in an excellent and very thorough study. Australia remained one of the most isolated areas in the world, with little contact with the outside, while California, in contrast, has been exposed to contact on all sides except the Pacific, and the multiplicity of language families and phyla suggests much migration into and out of the area. Australian social organizations and languages had centuries and millennia to simmer down and become integrated, while those of California were constantly being disturbed by intrusions from without. Radcliffe-Brown and Kroeber both failed to understand the limitations of their samples, and it was not until Murdock's *Social Structure* (1949) that an adequate sample and statistical technique were combined to produce more tenable generalizations on this subject [*see* KINSHIP].

Cross-cultural studies

In the United States cross-cultural studies were founded by G. P. Murdock and carried on by his pupils, including J. W. M. Whiting, Whiting's pupils, and others. Murdock has concentrated on kinship and social organization, and his *Social Structure* (1949) is a monumental work in its field. He studied the association between rules of marriage, residence, and descent, as well as kinship terminology, in 250 societies in all the major areas of the world. He used no explicit sampling technique, but his selection was large and widely distributed, and his results have not been seriously challenged to date. Using functional theory, he ran off a list of hypotheses and then confirmed most of them with the Q coefficient of association and chi-square. His general conclusions were that the semantic categories of kinship terms are the result of social organization rather than the cause, and that they are determined principally by forms of marital residence and rules of descent. Marriage prescriptions showed practically no correlation with kinship terminology, while residence and descent yielded many significant correlations.

Murdock further postulated three kinds of developmental cycles, two of which began with the dominance of one sex in the economy, followed by corresponding forms of residence, descent, and kinship terminology. Thus a patri-dominated economy would give rise to patrilocal residence, patrilineal descent, and Iroquoian or Omaha kinship categories. In a similar fashion a matri-dominated economy would produce matrilocal residence, matrilineal descent, and Iroquoian or Crow kinship classification. A sexually balanced economy, in turn, would give rise to bilocal residence, bilateral descent, and Eskimo or Hawaiian kinship terminology. This cyclical theory was confirmed statistically by Driver (1956), who found that the correlations based on about 250 North American peoples could be arranged in a matrix which could be explained in this way. However, Driver failed to measure the potency of genetic factors at this time, although he did so in 1966 in a more methodologically rigorous study (Driver 1966).

Whiting and his followers have centered their interests in the socialization process, the ways and means by which a child acquires the culture in which he is born and reared. The basic work in this field is Whiting and Child (1953). Before their work, good field studies in this subject were so rare that the authors were able to assemble fewer than fifty societies for their comparisons. They used no sampling technique because the total number of tribes was so small, but since every continental area in the world, plus Oceania, was represented, their sample is a rough approximation to a random one. Three "judges" carefully read the same field reports and coded the various societies independently on multistep rating scales. The published ratings are the scores of all three judges combined by summation.

Whiting and Child tested a number of neo-Freudian hypotheses with this method. For instance, they divided severity of socialization into the following five aspects, each of which was rated separately by each of the "judges": anal, oral, sexual, dependence, aggression. The ratings on these five aspects were intercorrelated, and the highest positive correlation turned out to be that between the oral and dependence aspects. These ratings were also correlated with other aspects of culture; for instance, amount of oral socialization anxiety correlated with presence of oral explanations of illness showed a high degree of relationship. On the other hand, they found a zero correlation between anal socialization anxiety and anal explanations of illness. [See SOCIALIZATION.]

A later and more transparent study by Whiting, Kluckhohn, and Anthony (1958) revealed a positive correlation between male initiation ceremonies at puberty, patrilocal residence, exclusive mother–infant sleeping arrangements, and a long *post partum* sex taboo. These variables are also positively correlated with a long lactation period and other kinds of long and close association of the infant with the mother. The authors' explanation was that the resulting strong attachment to the mother had to be broken by an initiation rite which separated the boy from his mother entirely and prepared him for an adult masculine role. Societies which lacked the long and close association of mother and young son did not need an initiation because there was no strong attachment to sever. Although the results achieved so far in this difficult field of psychological ethnology are less impressive than those in the field of social organization, the difference is due to the inherent complexities of the problems and the scarcity of field material rather than to methodology.

These cross-cultural studies of world-wide scope stem from the evolutionary interests of the nineteenth century. When Tylor (1888) read his now famous paper in which he anticipated correlation methods, Francis Galton challenged the historical independence of Tylor's 350 cases (societies). Tylor's use of probabilities and his conclusion that, for instance, mother-in-law–son-in-law avoidance was caused by matrilocal residence implied that this form of residence occurred first in each society and that it gave rise to this form of avoidance independently over and over again in each society where the avoidance was found. This is a functional–causal–evolutionary explanation. When such explanations include the Oedipus complex or the incest taboo, they may be called psychofunctional–causal–evolutionary. The contrasting explanation has been called geographical–historical, historical, or genetic; it holds that once a custom becomes established, it may be relayed from society to society by means of intermarriage and other kinds of contact. It is not necessary to postulate any necessary antecedent because a behavior may spread like a fashion. Continuity of geographical distribution is generally regarded as evidence of such diffusion. Tylor failed to provide an answer to the question Galton raised, and it plagued cross-cultural research until the 1950s.

Stephens in 1959 paired his 56 societies on the basis of membership in the same genetic language family and geographical proximity, and he concluded that geographical–historical factors determined about as much association as did psychofunctional ones. Landauer and Whiting (1964) compared, in a similar way, associations found within culture areas with those found across culture areas and concluded that the latter were relatively free of historical factors. Raoul Naroll (1961) and Naroll and D'Andrade (1963) have developed other specific techniques to show the effect of genetic versus psychofunctional–evolutionary factors on correlations. Their general conclusion is that both kinds of explanations must be used to account for most correlations and that they are of about equal potency. Cultural behaviors with functional or causal relationships, such as unilateral descent, cross-cousin marriage, and corresponding types of kinship terminology, tend to diffuse as a unit; or if part of such an assemblage is already present, the other members will diffuse more readily because they are compatible with it. Thus both internal and external factors determine the cultural inventory of societies.

Driver (1966) employed still another method and found that genetic factors were a little more powerful than psychofunctional–evolutionary ones but that both were at work. He used a sample of 277 peoples from native North America alone and postulated only four or five historically independent origins of the kin avoidances, which formed the subject of his study. This was determined by a combination of areal clustering, culture-area membership, and language-family affiliation. If other areas show a similar number of origins, this would add up to no more than about twenty for the world. With only twenty cases for a test of the significance of correlations involving kin avoidances, it would require a rather high correlation to achieve significance. Many of the cross-cultural correlations so far computed, for which significance is claimed on the assumption of the historical independence of every positive instance, would by this criterion be judged to be not significant at all.

The principal weakness of most cross-cultural studies so far is that their instances hop, skip, and jump across the map in such a manner that continuity of geographical distribution and other clues to genetic explanations are missing. A world-wide study of a well-reported subject, such as kinship behavior, would require data from at least a thousand societies in order to insure sufficient geographical continuity to permit valid inferences about the number of independent origins of the phenomena. This has not yet been achieved.

Although significant positive correlations in cross-cultural research are relatively easy to find, causal relationships are more difficult to establish, and the direction of causation is still more elusive. Nevertheless, progress has been made in this respect. The direction of causation and sequence of stages in evolution have been determined by constructing a Guttman cumulative scale (Carneiro & Tobias 1963), and the direction of cycling by arranging correlations in a temporal matrix (Driver 1956; Ascher & Ascher 1963; Blalock 1960).

Naroll (1964) has drawn attention to the many problems surrounding the nature of the ethnic unit used in cross-cultural research. Because this is the unit counted in all intertrait cross-cultural correlations, its definition is crucial to such studies. Although there were more differences than agreements in the comments on this article, the major

issues are now aboveboard, and refinements of definitions of ethnic units will surely follow. The nature of culture traits or variables also needs to be re-evaluated.

Coult and Habenstein (1965) give over 500 pages of cross tabulations of raw frequencies, phi-coefficients, and tests of significance for the 210 culture categories and 565 ethnic units of Murdock's 1957 sample.

Textor (1966) offers a still more massive package of similar measures computed largely from the data of Murdock's 1962–1966 sample. These two compilations provide important sources of reference to tens of thousands of relationships which can test many hypotheses, but they are so myopic that they may obscure some of the broader relationships within the data.

Sawyer and Levine (1966) have reduced Murdock's 1957 sample to thirty variables, intercorrelated and factor-analyzed these variables, and produced some compact generalizations about the whole sample which run only to article length. They have also run the same correlations separately for each of the six areas into which Murdock divided the world and have found rather marked areal differences. Some correlations are significantly positive in one area and significantly negative in another, or zero in one area and significantly positive or negative in another. Such areal differences can only be explained by ecological and historical factors. They cast doubt on the importance of universal "laws" or regularities but do not demolish such concepts entirely. What is needed next is a series of correlation studies intermediate between the highly particularized computer print-outs and the grosser generalizations.

It is thus apparent that recent studies have made considerable gains in understanding both genetic and evolutionary relationships and in the statistical rigor with which these relationships have been demonstrated. Although few ethnologists claim that their explanations of relationships among the cultures of nonliterate peoples are of timeless infallibility, validation of hypotheses has reached a respectable level which compares favorably with that of other behavioral sciences.

HAROLD E. DRIVER

[See also ANTHROPOLOGY, *article on* THE COMPARATIVE METHOD IN ANTHROPOLOGY.]

BIBLIOGRAPHY

ABERLE, DAVID F. 1961 Matrilineal Descent in Cross-cultural Perspective. Pages 655–727 in David M. Schneider and Kathleen Gough (editors), *Matrilineal Kinship*. Berkeley: Univ. of California Press.

ANKERMANN, B. 1905 Kulturkreise und Kulturschichten in Afrika. *Zeitschrift für Ethnologie* 37:54–84.

ASCHER, MARCIA; and ASCHER, ROBERT 1963 Chronological Ordering by Computer. *American Anthropologist* New Series 65:1045–1052.

BLALOCK, H. M. JR. 1960 Correlation Analysis and Causal Inferences. *American Anthropologist* New Series 62:624–631.

BOAS, FRANZ 1895 *Indianische Sagen von der nord-pacifischen Küste Amerikas.* Berlin: Asher.

BOAS, FRANZ 1916 *Tsimshian Mythology.* Smithsonian Institution, Bureau of American Ethnology, Annual Report No. 31. Washington: Government Printing Office.

CARNEIRO, ROBERT L. 1962 Scale Analysis as an Instrument for the Study of Cultural Evolution. *Southwestern Journal of Anthropology* 18, no. 2:149–169.

CARNEIRO, ROBERT L.; and TOBIAS, STEPHEN F. 1963 The Application of Scale Analysis to the Study of Cultural Evolution. New York Academy of Sciences, *Transactions* Second Series 26:196–207.

CLEMENTS, FORREST E. 1928 Quantitative Method in Ethnography. *American Anthropologist* New Series 30:295–310.

CLEMENTS, FORREST E. 1931 Plains Indian Tribal Correlations With Sun Dance Data. *American Anthropologist* New Series 33:216–227.

CLEMENTS, FORREST E.; SCHENCK, SARA M.; and BROWN, T. K. 1926 A New Objective Method for Showing Special Relationships. *American Anthropologist* New Series 28:585–604.

COULT, ALLAN D.; and HABENSTEIN, ROBERT W. 1965 *Cross Tabulations of Murdock's "World Ethnographic Sample."* Columbia: Univ. of Missouri Press. → See Murdock 1957.

CZEKANOWSKI, JAN 1911 Objektive Kriterien in der Ethnologie. Deutsche Gesellschaft für Anthropologie, Ethnologie, und Urgeschichte, *Korrespondenz-Blatt* 42:1–5.

DIXON, ROLAND B. 1928 *The Building of Cultures.* New York: Scribner.

DRIVER, HAROLD E. 1941 Girls' Puberty Rites in Western North America. California, University of, *Anthropological Records* 6:21–90.

DRIVER, HAROLD E. 1956 An Integration of Functional, Evolutionary, and Historical Theory by Means of Correlations. Indiana University, *Publications in Anthropology and Linguistics* Memoir No. 12.

DRIVER, HAROLD E. 1961 Introduction to Statistics for Comparative Research. Pages 303–331 in Frank W. Moore (editor), *Readings in Cross-cultural Methodology.* New Haven: Human Relations Area Files.

DRIVER, HAROLD E. 1962 The Contribution of A. L. Kroeber to Culture Area Theory and Practice. Indiana University, *Publications in Anthropology and Linguistics* Memoir No. 18.

DRIVER, HAROLD E. 1966 Geographical–Historical *Versus* Psycho–Functional Explanations of Kin Avoidances. *Current Anthropology* 7:131–148.

DRIVER, HAROLD E.; and KROEBER, A. L. 1932 Quantitative Expression of Cultural Relationships. California, University of, *Publications in American Archaeology and Ethnology* 31:211–256.

DRIVER, HAROLD E.; and MASSEY, WILLIAM C. 1957 Comparative Studies of North American Indians. American Philosophical Society, *Transactions* 47:165–456.

FARRAND, LIVINGSTONE (1904) 1964 *The Basis of American History.* New York: Harper.

FROBENIUS, LEO 1898 *Der Ursprung der afrikanischen Kulturen.* Berlin: Gebrüder Borntraeger.

FÜRER-HAIMENDORF, C. VON 1934 Völker- und Kulturgruppen im westlich Hinterindien, dargestellt mit Hilfe des statistischen Verfahrens. *Anthropos* 29:421–440.

GIFFORD, E. W. 1940 A Problem in Kinship Terminology. *American Anthropologist* New Series 42:190–194.

GRAEBNER, FRITZ 1905 Kulturkreise und Kulturschichten in Ozeanien. *Zeitschrift für Ethnologie* 37:28–53.

GRAEBNER, FRITZ 1911 *Methode der Ethnologie.* Heidelberg (Germany): Winter.

HYMES, DELL H. (editor) 1965 *The Use of Computers in Anthropology.* The Hague: Mouton.

KLIMEK, STANISLAW 1935 The Structure of California Indian Culture. California, University of, *Publications in American Archaeology and Ethnology* 37:1–70.

KLIMEK, STANISLAW; and MILKE, WILHELM 1935 An Analysis of the Material Culture of the Tupi Peoples. *American Anthropologist* New Series 37:71–91.

KLUCKHOHN, CLYDE (1953) 1961 Universal Categories of Culture. Pages 89–105 in Frank W. Moore (editor), *Readings in Cross-cultural Methodology.* New Haven: Human Relations Area Files Press. → First published in International Symposium on Anthropology, 1952, *Anthropology Today.* Edited by A. L. Kroeber.

KROEBER, ALFRED L. 1904 Types of Indian Culture in California. California, University of, *Publications in American Archaeology and Ethnology* 2:81–103.

KROEBER, ALFRED L. (1923) 1948 *Anthropology: Race, Language, Culture, Psychology, Prehistory.* New ed., rev. New York: Harcourt. → First published as *Anthropology.*

KROEBER, ALFRED L. 1934 Yurok and Neighboring Kin Term Systems. California, University of, *Publications in American Archaeology and Ethnology* 35:15–22.

KROEBER, ALFRED L. 1936 Kinship and History. *American Anthropologist* New Series 38:338–341.

KROEBER, ALFRED L. 1937 Athabascan Kin Term Systems. *American Anthropologist* New Series 39:602–608.

KROEBER, ALFRED L. 1939 Cultural and Natural Areas of Native North America. California, University of, *Publications in American Archaeology and Ethnology* 38:1–242.

KROEBER, ALFRED L. 1940 Stimulus Diffusion. *American Anthropologist* New Series 42:1–20.

KROEBER, ALFRED L. 1962 *A Roster of Civilizations and Culture.* Viking Fund Publications in Anthropology, No. 33. New York: The Fund.

LANDAUER, THOMAS K.; and WHITING, JOHN W. M. 1964 Infantile Stimulation and Adult Stature of Human Males. *American Anthropologist* New Series 66:1007–1028.

LEWIS, OSCAR 1956 Comparisons in Cultural Anthropology. Pages 259–292 in Yearbook of Anthropology, 1955, *Current Anthropology: A Supplement to* Anthropology Today. Edited by William L. Thomas, Jr. Univ. of Chicago Press.

LOWIE, ROBERT H. 1937 *The History of Ethnological Theory.* New York: Farrar & Rinehart.

MILKE, WILHELM 1935 *Südostmelanesien: Eine ethnostatistische Analyse.* Würzburg (Germany): Triltsch.

MURDOCK, GEORGE P. 1945 The Common Denominator of Cultures. Pages 123–142 in Ralph Linton (editor),

The Science of Man in the World Crisis. New York: Columbia Univ. Press.

MURDOCK, GEORGE P. 1949 *Social Structure.* New York: Macmillan. → A paperback edition was published in 1965 by the Free Press.

MURDOCK, GEORGE P. 1957 World Ethnographic Sample. *American Anthropologist* New Series 59:664–687.

MURDOCK, GEORGE P. et al. 1962–1966 Ethnographic Atlas. *Ethnology* 1–4: last article in every issue.

NAROLL, RAOUL 1961 Two Solutions to Galton's Problem. *Philosophy of Science* 28:15–39.

NAROLL, RAOUL 1964 On Ethnic Unit Classification. *Current Anthropology* 5:283–312.

NAROLL, RAOUL; and D'ANDRADE, ROY G. 1963 Two Further Solutions to Galton's Problem. *American Anthropologist* New Series 65:1053–1067.

RADCLIFFE-BROWN, A. R. 1913 Three Tribes of Western Australia. *Journal of the Royal Anthropological Institute of Great Britain and Ireland* 43:143–194.

RADCLIFFE-BROWN, A. R. (1931) 1948 *The Social Organization of Australian Tribes.* Glencoe, Ill.: Free Press. → First published in Volume 1 of *Oceania*.

RADCLIFFE-BROWN, A. R. 1935 Kinship Terminologies in California. *American Anthropologist* New Series 37:530–535.

RATZEL, FRIEDRICH 1887 Die geographische Verbreitung des Bogens und der Pfeile in Afrika. Akademie der Wissenschaften, Leipzig, *Berichte über die Verhandlungen* Philologisch-historische Klasse 39:233–252.

RAY, VERNE F. 1942 Culture Element Distributions: XXII Plateau. California, University of, *Anthropological Records* 8:99–258.

SAWYER, JACK; and LEVINE, ROBERT A. 1966 Cultural Dimensions: A Factor Analysis of the World Ethnographic Sample. *American Anthropologist* New Series 68:708–731.

SCHMIDT, WILHELM (1937) 1939 *The Culture Historical Method of Ethnology: The Scientific Approach to the Racial Question.* New York: Fortuny. → First published as *Handbuch der Methode der kulturhistorischen Ethnologie.*

SCHMIDT, WILHELM; and KOPPERS, WILHELM 1924 *Völker und Kulturen.* Regensburg (Germany): Habbel.

TAX, SOL (1937) 1955 Some Problems of Social Organization. Pages 3–34 in Fred Eggan (editor), *Social Anthropology of North American Tribes.* 2d ed. Univ. of Chicago Press.

TEXTOR, ROBERT B. 1966 A Cross-cultural Summary. Unpublished manuscript, Human Relations Area Files.

TYLOR, EDWARD B. (1888) 1961 On a Method of Investigating the Development of Institutions: Applied to Laws of Marriage and Descent. Pages 1–28 in Frank W. Moore (editor), *Readings in Cross-cultural Methodology.* New Haven: Human Relations Area Files. → First published in Volume 18 of the *Journal of the Royal Anthropological Institute of Great Britain and Ireland.*

WHITING, JOHN W. M.; and CHILD, IRVIN L. 1953 *Child Training and Personality: A Cross-cultural Study.* New Haven: Yale Univ. Press. → A paperback edition was published in 1962.

WHITING, JOHN W. M.; KLUCKHOHN, RICHARD; and ANTHONY, ALBERT 1958 The Function of Male Initiation Ceremonies at Puberty. Pages 359–371 in Society for the Psychological Study of Social Issues, *Readings in Social Psychology.* 3d ed. New York: Holt.

WISSLER, CLARK 1906 Ethnic Types and Isolation. *Science* 23:147–149.

WISSLER, CLARK (1917) 1957 *The American Indian: An Introduction to the Anthropology of the New World.* 3d ed. Gloucester, Mass.: Smith.

WISSLER, CLARK (1923) 1938 *Man and Culture.* New York: Crowell.

YALE UNIVERSITY, INSTITUTE OF HUMAN RELATIONS (1938) 1961 *Outline of Cultural Materials.* 4th ed., revised by George P. Murdock et al. New Haven: Human Relations Area Files.

ETHNOMEDICINE

See under MEDICAL CARE.

ETHNOMUSICOLOGY

See under MUSIC.

ETHNOSCIENCE

See ETHNOGRAPHY.

ETHOLOGY

Ethology has existed as a concept since 1762 when it was defined in France as the study of animal behavior. In this sense it carries the same meaning as the Greek word "ethos," from which the modern term ethology is derived. However, a separate meaning of the word ethology, related to the term "ethics," has been used in the Anglo-Saxon literature to define the "science of character."

The founder of modern ethology is Konrad Z. Lorenz, physician, zoologist, and comparative anatomist. By systematic application of biological research methods to the analysis of animal behavior, he provided the initial impetus in the 1930s. The first modern ethology textbook, *The Study of Instinct,* was written by Nikolaas Tinbergen in 1951, and E. H. Hess (1962) and Eibl-Eibesfeldt (1966) recently produced summaries of the modern concepts of behavior. The observations of a number of pioneers, including Spalding (1873), Darwin (1872), Whitman (1898), Altum (1868), Heinroth (1911), and Craig (1918), awakened scientific interest in animal behavior, and ethology came to be considered an independent branch of zoology around 1910. As with every young science, ethology inevitably suffers, on the one hand, from the incorporation of concepts whose meaning has oscillated or has already become too specialized (such as "instinct") and, on the other hand, from the application of provisional concepts, which may alter in meaning with advances in knowledge, to contemporary working hypotheses.

The term "ethology" is now attached to the scientific investigation of the behavior of animals and of some aspects of human behavior. Pronouncements about inaccessible psychic phenomena are avoided; the term "animal psychology" is still occasionally used but on purely historical grounds. Ethology is concerned with the investigation of animals, whether these be single cells—either as individual protozoans or as parts of metazoans—or more complex animal structures, that is, individuals, groups, or so-called animal colonies (e.g., ants, bees, and termites).

The behavior of an animal is equated with changes brought about by effectors (e.g., movements, sounds, scent production, color changes). Such effector responses are temporal events. For this reason only effector responses which repeatedly and identifiably occur are open to scientific analysis; they are then termed "fixed action patterns." It is important to note that these temporal events can be recorded by tape and film, except in the case of chemical or tactile signals. The locomotion of an animal can be subdivided into the movement of the extremities, of antagonistic muscle groups, of single muscles, and ultimately of the muscle fibers. The smallest identifiable effector components, occurring either singly or in combination with other components, are chosen as the units of ethological study.

The aim of ethology is to explain both phylogenetically and physiologically the functional relationships of all factors involved in behavior. This is evident in the modern definition of instinct suggested by Tinbergen: " . . . a hierarchically organized nervous mechanism which is susceptible to certain priming, releasing and directing impulses of internal as well as of external origin, and which responds to these impulses by coordinated movements that contribute to the maintenance of the individual and the species" (1951, p. 112). The touchstone for ethological hypotheses is the reliable prediction of the behavior of a living system in any given situation.

Ethologists are zoologists; they are thus interested in the biology of a species, and their prime interest is behavior as it occurs under natural conditions. The ethologist always begins by compiling an "action catalogue," or *ethogram* of the species in question, that is, as complete a description as possible of the behavior throughout the animal's life cycle. This simply describes what the animal does, not why it does it.

The various behavior patterns are then classified and compared with those of other species, especially with closely related species. It is important that the animals should be observed in their natural habitats or in surroundings which closely resemble them. Additional observations in captivity are often necessary. A very useful expedient, first known to have been practiced by Baron Ferdinand Adam von Pernau in 1702, is to rear the animals to be both tame and unconfined.

Learning, maturation, and genetics. Although learning is considered to be very important in animal behavior, the first concern of the ethologist is with behavior patterns typically performed by all animals of a species, because it is necessary for him to know the basic predetermined responses before proceeding to study changes brought about by learning. This is important, since not every change of form or effectiveness of a given behavior pattern occurring during the life of an individual involves learning in the form of acquisition by experience. As early as 1760 a professor in Hamburg, Hermann Samuel Reimarus, discovered the phenomenon of *maturation* of instincts and pointed out the difference between innate and acquired skills. The innate skills, for example, the collection of food or the performance and "understanding" of the dance language in bees, are present from the time of birth or of hatching from the egg or pupa. Without involving a definition of learning, the problem can be formulated as follows: the majority of behavior patterns in most animals are adapted (adjusted) to special situations in their respective environments. Since this fact cannot be explained as a chance phenomenon and since it is not a self-evident phenomenon, an explanation must be provided. In order to behave adaptively, the animal must have at its disposal information about the environment. This information can be stored either in the chromosomes or in memory; that is, it can be either innate or acquired. In complex behavior patterns, there is often an interaction between innate and acquired elements. However, although we know of perceptual and motor skills in which learning plays no part, it is impossible to postulate a completely learned element of behavior that is not based on genetically determined and, therefore, delimited capabilities. Further, no one has so far been able to demonstrate the infinite modifiability of any arbitrarily chosen, innately determined element of behavior or the possibility that learning could be the function of a nonorganized aggregate of neural elements. In learning, the fact that the organism selects "good" and not "bad" behavioral responses or stimuli logically implies a built-in mechanism which is able to direct learning toward survival value.

A particularly good method for distinguishing between the learned and innate elements of behavior is contained in the *deprivation experiment*: the animal, usually isolated from members of its own species, is deprived of certain experiences and later tested in the situation to which the behavior pattern in question is normally adapted. As a control a normal animal must be tested in the same situation. (This is one of several safety precautions which are necessary in the evaluation of the deprivation experiment.) The majority of behavior patterns do not follow the all-or-none law but can occur at varying intensities. The lowest intensities, where it is just possible to recognize which pattern has been activated, are referred to as *intention movements*. The intensity with which a behavior pattern is performed depends upon both internal and external factors.

The appearance of a particular fixed action pattern in animals isolated from their own species is clear evidence of genetic fixity. It is a constant characteristic of the species concerned and is based upon a specific central nervous mechanism that is inherited just as are morphological and physiological characteristics. (This had already been stated by the English naturalist Spalding in 1873.) A particularly good example is provided by many bird songs which develop into the species-specific pattern even in completely isolated animals. Research into the genetic basis of behavior patterns is developing as an important part of ethology. For example, crossing two duck species which differ in their courtship behavior can give rise to hybrids exhibiting courtship motor sequences not evident in any known species of duck or sometimes to hybrids possessing behavior patterns absent in both parent species but present in some presumed ancestral type (Wall 1963). However, it is still not clear what changes in the complex physiological basis of such behavior patterns are responsible for these differences. Dilger investigated the carrying of nest material in F_1 hybrids of *Agapornis roseicollis parrat* (male) × *A. personata fischeri* (female). Both parent species cut strips of paper or leaves and carry them to the nest. Females of the first species carry the strips in their bills, while females of the second species tuck the strips under special feathers on the lower back. The hybrids attempted to perform this latter pattern but failed for various reasons. For example, some were unable to let go of the strip of paper and tried to carry the strips in the bill *and* under the feathers at the same time. Within two years the behavior of the hybrids improved through learning, but they continued to perform ineffective tucking movements (Dilger 1962).

The genetic fixity of elements of behavior and the fact that they are nearly always to be found in more than one species prove their taxonomic value. In fact they are often characteristic of genera, families, or even higher taxonomic categories. For this reason it is possible to employ behavior patterns in the investigation of the relationships between animals. Indeed, Whitman (1898) and Heinroth (1911) investigated the behavior of doves and ducks respectively in the hope of finding characteristics useful for a more systematic analysis of their interrelatedness. In some grasshopper and toad species, species-specific calls or songs are used for species recognition; thus they represent barriers to interspecific reproduction. On the other hand, it is possible to reconstruct the phylogeny of behavior patterns on the basis of variations in the form of the same basic pattern between closely related species, as was pointed out by Darwin in *The Expression of the Emotions in Man and Animals* (1872). Exactly the same method is used in comparative anatomy and morphology. Although no behavioral fossils exist, more transitional forms exist between different behavioral types than is the case with morphological characteristics; behavioral characteristics occur repeatedly and at different intensities, while a leg is formed only once. The individual elements of various behavior patterns are, however, more open to formation of novel combinations (e.g., in contrast to the bones of the skull in vertebrates). For this reason, the phylogeny of behavior patterns must be based on the simplest possible elements.

We know that no behavioral characteristic is dependent upon only one gene, that each hereditary component affects several characteristics, and that there are not two separate sets of hereditary material governing body construction and behavioral features. The interaction of a behavior pattern with its effector organ is thus just as labile as the coadaptation of several functionally correlated organs.

Evolution and selection. Reimarus pointed out that in many instances behavior patterns adapted to the use of certain organs are performed, at times, even before these organs are developed. Apart from differences in speed of development of behavior patterns and their effector organs, it is also possible that one survives when the other is lost; a cerambycid beetle will continue to preen its antennas after they have been removed by dissection, mutant fruit flies (*Drosophila*) with no wings still perform the wing-preening movements typical of the species, stump-tailed monkeys, when they run along a branch, still show the balancing movements once effective in their long-tailed ancestors. Such historical carry-overs can also be observed in behavior patterns originally adapted to certain environmental conditions which have since changed. Ground-breeding birds regularly use the beak to perform specific behavior patterns for rolling the eggs back into the nest if they are found outside. Tree-breeding birds do not show this, since the eggs that fall disappear. However, Poulsen (1953) was able to show that some birds which have recently evolved from ground-living stock to a tree-living habit still exhibit egg-rolling patterns, while some recently evolved ground-breeding birds lack this pattern. There are other examples which show that fixed action patterns can be extremely conservative in the evolution of a species. On the other hand, closely related species occupying the same area exhibit rapid phylogenetic changes in the sexual behavior patterns serving for sexual recognition. In fact, in some such species greater differences in species recognition signals are seen where two species occur together than where either species occurs in isolation. This phenomenon has been called *character displacement*.

Intraspecific signals usually undergo selection for better recognition (to avoid "misunderstandings") and tend to become more and more conspicuous and outlandish. The behaviors involved are performed more conspicuously and are emphasized by morphological characteristics of color, form, or odor. In addition such behaviors are often rhythmically repeated. This fixed patterning often ceases to show different degrees of intensity. The level of motivation is no longer expressed in the intensity of the behavior but in how often it is repeated at one and the same *fixed intensity* (Morris 1957), much as the urgency of a telephone call is indicated by *how often* the bell rings and not *how loud* it rings. Finally such a recently formed fixed action pattern may become motivationally autonomous of the situation in which it was originally aroused by a process that Tinbergen has called *emancipation*. These and other changes in signal behavior patterns, leading to improved communication between signal sender and signal receiver, are referred to as *ritualization*. We still know very little regarding the physiological and neuroanatomical basis of both nonritualized and ritualized behavior patterns. [*See* COMMUNICATION, ANIMAL.]

It is commonplace to say that no animal performs the behavior patterns in its repertoire in random order. An animal responds to signals according to set principles. It is the task of the behavioral physiologist to analyze this phenomenon. This task involves large-scale studies of sensory physiology, since the animal receives the stimuli with its sense organs; of hormone physiology, since hormones can decide whether the sight of the female elicits courtship by the male, and so on; and of the physiology of the central nervous system, which is responsible for the analysis of the stimuli and for the coordination of the requisite behavior patterns.

Releasing mechanisms. The carnivorous water beetle *Dysticus marginalis* does not react to the sight of prey (e.g., a tadpole in a glass tube), although it has perfectly developed eyes, but it does react to the chemical stimuli emanating from the prey. If some prey-extract solution is added to the water, the beetle will clasp even inanimate objects immersed in the water. A male robin will attack a bundle of red feathers but not a perfect dummy of a male lacking the characteristic red breast. Such examples show that animals respond with quite specific reactions to quite specific stimuli among the many perceived from the environment. These relevant stimuli are called *sign stimuli*, or *releasers*.

Sign stimuli act upon specific functional units of the central nervous system, the so-called *releasing mechanisms*. The specific properties of these units may likewise be either genetically determined, in which case they are termed *innate releasing mechanisms* (IRM), or partially determined by learning. The releasing mechanism filters out the sign stimuli and thereby triggers off specific behavior patterns. Some behavior patterns čan be elicited by more than one stimulus (e.g., an odor or a vibration). The vigor of the reaction generally depends upon the strength of the stimulus, and heterogeneous stimuli may summate (the same intensity of a reaction may be shown toward a strong odor or a strong vibration or a weak odor together with a weak vibration). Sometimes it is possible to present the animal with an abnormally strong stimulus and obtain a response stronger than that released by the naturally occurring stimulus; Magnus (1958) has shown that the males of the silver-washed fritillary butterfly react with courtship toward the orange and black color pattern of the female's fluttering wings. By placing orange and dark stripes on a cylinder and rotating it, he proved that more rapid color–dark alternation than the rate characteristic of the female was more effective in eliciting the male's reaction. The greater the speed of rotation of the cylinder, the greater were the courtship responses, right up to the physiologically demonstrated flicker-fusion frequency for the species concerned. [*See* SEXUAL BEHAVIOR, *article on* ANIMAL SEXUAL BEHAVIOR.] This susceptibility of animals to *supernormal releasers* provides us with an insight into the reason for the development of bizarre morphological signal structures such as the feathers of the peacock. Some parasitic birds even capitalize on this phenomenon when their young are larger and more babyish than, and therefore preferred to, the host's own young.

Motivation and drives. It has been observed that one individual will sometimes respond to a weak stimulus with a strong response, while at other times respond only at the same intensity or not at all to a much stronger releasing stimulus. It is therefore necessary to measure independently the specific "readiness" of the animal to react, apart from the strength of the stimulus. The strength of a reaction often decreases sharply with repeated equivalent stimulation, as is the case with escape attempts in aquarium fish in response to tapping on the glass pane or with gaping in young birds when the nest is lightly shaken. The readiness of an animal to perform certain patterns exhibits extensive and independent variation; an animal which is not prepared to eat may nevertheless exhibit readiness to flee. The readiness to perform a certain pattern is referred to as the *motivation*. Motivation (e.g., in hunger) often increases with the time interval from the last elicitation of the type of behavior concerned ("damming effect," an effect which is related to the corresponding stimulus threshold). In the extreme case the action pattern can occur without any evident external elicitation—as *vacuum activity*. However, an animal with high motivation to perform specific behavior patterns (where the "drive" is under restraint) usually performs certain behavior patterns suitable for attainment of a stimulus situation appropriate to the motivated patterns. In simple terms, the animal "searches." Craig (1918) observed the occurrence of restlessness, varied movements, and searching behavior as symptoms of a physiological state of appetite for specific stimuli and labeled such behavior *appetitive* behavior, as distinct from *consummatory* behavior, which lowers the degree of motivation when performed and leads to a *state of satisfaction*. It is important to note that the animal does not attempt to achieve the biological effect associated with the consummatory act but merely the performance of the consummatory behavior itself. The state of satisfaction can also be achieved by abreaction in response to models. In the simplest case, appetitive behavior consists of undirected locomotion, but many animals (especially higher-developed forms) learn from experience and modify the appetitive behavior, so that it more rapidly leads to success. They learn when, where, and how they can attain the releasing situation. Briefly, appetitive behavior is typically variable (plastic), whereas the consummatory act is relatively fixed (stereotyped).

Motivational analysis attempts to demonstrate how many behavior patterns are dependent upon the same motivational source and how many partially or completely independent motivational centers are present in a given animal species. It is taken as axiomatic that there are fewer independent sources of motivation than observably distinct behavior patterns and that behavior patterns which regularly occur within short intervals from one another are thus commonly motivated—the motivational state of the animal oscillates more slowly than the alternation of behavior patterns. Further, it is known that behavior patterns exist which are characteristic for specific conflict situations; in the conflict between attack and flight these are represented by threat behavior. Such patterns are certainly motivated from different sources, which may vary independently from one another. It is not known from the outset how many of the behavior patterns observed have mixed motivation, but for the purposes of analysis it is assumed that it is the minimum possible. Wiepkema, a Dutch ethologist, carried out the following model experiment (1961) with the European bitterling: First he recorded the occurrence of the behavior patterns which he had identified for this species (ramming the flank of a conspecific with the head, scouring of the substrate, tail-beating, swimming before the female, etc.) over a long period of time. In this process typical locomotory sequences are found to occur regularly, while some behavior patterns are seen to be mutually exclusive within a given time interval. Wiepkema computed the minimum number of independent variables (i.e., motives) necessary to account for the observed distribution of action patterns. Mixed motivation was taken into account, but it was assumed that one given motive was predominant in each case. For the reproductive period of the bitterling it was found that three independent motivational sources are necessary and that each source governs a group of motor patterns which are totally or predominantly dependent upon the source concerned. These groups are comprised of (1) behavior patterns directed at the rival, objectively termed "fight," (2) behavior patterns directed away from the rival, termed "flight," and (3) the patterns carried out in combination with the female in association with spawning. Accordingly it is possible to refer to the predominant motivation in each case as (1) fight drive, (2) flight drive, and (3) sex drive. Some behavior patterns lie between these groups, however, and are thus more or less equally dependent upon more than one motive. For example, spreading of the fins combined with an undulating movement of the entire body, which we refer to as "threat," is motivated by both fight and flight drives; a specific courtship pattern is motivated by both fight and sex drives. Using factor analysis it is even possible to rank the action patterns according to a scale of ratios between different drives. [*See* DRIVES; MOTIVATION.]

Various phenomena occur in conflict situations; the animal may combine two behavior patterns (e.g., warding off a rival and eating), it may oscillate between the intention movements of different action patterns (e.g., oscillation between motions toward attack and flight without actually attacking or fleeing), it may exhibit abreaction of an inhibited behavior pattern by transferring the direction to a neutral object (e.g., gulls which do not dare to attack a stronger rival may tear and pluck at tufts of grass), or it may exhibit a behavior pattern which does not belong to either of the motivational sources directly involved in the conflict. This last pattern is referred to as *displacement activity*. For example, domestic cocks will start to eat when they are involved in a conflict between attack and flight, while avocets will assume a sleeping posture. The physiological foundations of displacement activities have been investigated only in a few cases and appear to vary from case to case. Some behavior patterns may be dependent upon the same releasing stimuli as well as upon the same motivational sources. [*See* CONFLICT, *article on* PSYCHOLOGICAL ASPECTS.]

Sequential and hierarchical organization. The fact that some elements of behavior can give rise to conflict at corresponding integrational levels, while others are mutually exclusive, indicates that groups of elements are governed by superior systems which can similarly show mutual interference, promotion, inhibition, or exclusion. In this way, we arrive at the concept of a hierarchical system of dominant and subordinate drives. The same concept emerges from the comparison of releasing situations and appetitive behavior.

A hungry squirrel (1) climbs (2) trees (3) looking for cones; when motivated to build a nest, it (1) climbs (2) trees (3) looking for twigs. Thus different motivations may employ the same "lower" motor and orientation components. The latter are called *taxes*, a taxis being defined as orientation of the whole body or parts of it with respect to the source of stimulation. Further, the distinction between appetitive behavior and consummatory behavior is a relative one. Normally, certain appetitive behavior leads to a stimulus situation which initiates another, more specific, appetitive behavior. This fact has been carefully worked out by Baerends (1941) and Tinbergen (1951). The three-spined stickleback is brought into reproductive motivation by the gradual increase in day length in spring and begins migration inland into shallow fresh-water habitats. This factor, together with the rise in water temperature and the visual stimulation of heavily vegetated sites, is a releasing mechanism for the establishment of a suitable territory by the males. A territory is necessary for the male to acquire its characteristic red belly. Only then does it begin to react to particular stimuli which previously had no effect. The male will build a nest with suitable material, fight against rival males (where the releasing stimulus is the red belly of the male intruding into his territory), and court passing females, which present their silvery, swollen, egg-filled bellies to the male in a characteristic manner. Thus, the stimuli emanating from a territory will activate the fighting, building, and mating drives, which must then be elicited by special releasers. Fighting itself consists of a number of behavior patterns (chasing, threatening, tail-beating, biting), each dependent upon still further, highly specific stimuli emanating from the intruder's behavior. The behavioral sequences of male and female form an alternating chain of reactions, each action of one partner releasing the following appropriate reaction of the other partner until the female spawns and the male fertilizes the eggs. The act of fertilization initiates brood care in the male; he now fans fresh water onto the eggs and continues to drive off rivals but does not exhibit further courtship until the young hatch. It is thus clear that there are chains of behavioral tendencies connected at higher and lower levels of integration and that these different levels are organized into a hierarchical system. The advantage of a hierarchy, as opposed to a stereotyped series of single fixed actions, lies in its adaptability to unpredictable sequences of events.

Neurophysiological aspects. It seems evident that some structural organization must exist within the central nervous system, paralleling the observed organization of behavioral responses—in particular the hierarchical organization. Neurophysiological investigation of fixed action patterns has therefore become an important branch of ethological research. Extending the earlier experiments of W. R. Hess (1949), Holst and Saint Paul (1959) demonstrated the existence of structural hierarchical organization of the mechanisms underlying behavior by electrically stimulating specific areas of the brain in chickens. Well-coordinated, complete sequences of movements identical with those observed in normal behavior were elicited. All these sequences of behavior were composed of single actions, each of which could be obtained in isolation by stimulation of specific brain areas. Holst and Saint Paul combined brain stimulation with the normal releasing stimuli, electrically changed the "mood" (motivational state) of the animal and studied artificial conflict between drives by producing interaction of different behavior patterns with simultaneous elicitation.

Neurological research has substantiated the conclusion, derived from ethological field studies, that the coordination of many locomotive patterns arises from impulses generated in the central nervous system. Potent support has also been provided for Lorenz' hypothesis postulating constant production of *action-specific potentials* in the central nervous system.

Habituation and imprinting. Most of the original schemata postulated for the functional structure of behavior have been shown to be simplifications, though correctly describing special cases. In order to arrive at a generalized schema, it is still necessary to modify repeatedly such hypothetical schemata. Even the hierarchical system must be altered to a multidimensional network. The concept of *habituation* likewise increases in complexity with time. A behavior pattern repeatedly elicited by a particular sign-stimulus will cease to occur after a given time. The sense organ can nevertheless be demonstrated to be fully capable of functioning, and it is not even necessary to presume that the motivation of the animal to perform this pattern is entirely extinguished; it is often possible to elicit the same behavior pattern immediately afterward with another sign-stimulus. In such cases, it is necessary to assume that central cut-off systems are involved. Such systems are capable of very complex functions; mechanisms of this type in turkeys extinguish flight behavior in response to all relatively slow-flying objects which occur frequently, and the adult animal flees only in response to uncommon flying objects. In fact, the most infrequently occurring objects which (relative to their own size) are slow-flying are birds of prey. The adult turkey thus shows a well-adapted flight reaction in response to predatory birds—but also to advertising balloons. It is a question of definition whether or not one refers to this effect as learning; it takes place without marked exogenous reward or punishment. The same is true of *imprinting*, which was described by Spalding as early as 1873. In imprinting, a specific reaction of the animal (which need not be functional at the time of imprinting) becomes attached to an object which later functions as the releasing agent. This occurs within a limited sensitive period, usually at a young age. In contrast to learning by association, there is no reward (as in the previous example), and even punishing stimuli have a reinforcing effect. If ducks or doves are reared by other species they will later show a pairing preference toward a partner belonging to the foster species, even when a conspecific partner is available. [*See* IMPRINTING.]

Phenomena similar to imprinting have been discovered in many fields. Some juvenile birds learn the song entirely from the "father" and will learn the song of a foster-father even in the midst of conspecifics. Since later offspring learn from these birds, the possibility of "speech dialects" arises. In different mammal species there have been cases of *traditions* which largely concern food preferences or forms of food acquisition, although traditions may also arise in the avoidance of enemies.

IRENÄUS EIBL-EIBESFELDT
AND WOLFGANG WICKLER

[*Directly related are the entries* PSYCHOLOGY, *article on* COMPARATIVE PSYCHOLOGY; SOCIAL BEHAVIOR, ANIMAL. *Other relevant material may be found in* COMMUNICATION, ANIMAL; DRIVES; EVOLUTION; GENETICS; IMPRINTING; INSTINCT; LEARNING; MOTIVATION.]

BIBLIOGRAPHY

ALTUM, BERNARD (1868) 1910 *Der Vogel und sein Leben.* 9th ed. Munster (Germany): Schöningh.

BAERENDS, G. P. 1941 Fortpflanzungsverhalten und Orientierung der Grabwespe *Ammophila campestris* Jur. *Tijdschrift voor entomologie* 84:68–275.

CRAIG, WALLACE 1918 Appetites and Aversions as Constituents of Instincts. *Biological Bulletin* 34:91–107.

DARWIN, CHARLES (1872) 1965 *The Expression of the Emotions in Man and Animals.* Edited by Francis Darwin. Univ. of Chicago Press.

DILGER, WILLIAM C. 1962 The Behavior of the Lovebirds. *Scientific American* 206, no. 1:88–98.

EIBL-EIBESFELDT, IRENÄUS 1966 Ethologie: Die Biologie des Verhaltens. Volume 5, pages 341–549 in *Handbuch der Biologie.* Edited by Ludwig von Bertalanffy. Potsdam (Germany): Akademische Verlagsgesellschaft Athenaion.

HEINROTH, OTTO 1911 Beiträge zur Biologie, namentlich Ethologie und Psychologie der Anatiden. Pages 589–702 in International Ornithological Congress, Fifth, Berlin, 1910, *Verhandlungen.* Berlin: Deutsche Ornithologische Gesellschaft.

HESS, ECKHARD H. 1962 Ethology: An Approach Toward the Complete Analysis of Behavior. Pages 157–266 in *New Directions in Psychology,* by Roger Brown et al. New York: Holt.

HESS, WALTER R. (1949) 1954 *Das Zwischenhirn: Syndrome, Lokalisationen, Functionen.* Basel: Schwabe.

Holst, Erich von; and Saint Paul, Ursula von   (1959) 1963   On the Functional Organisation of Drives. *Animal Behaviour* 11:1–20. → First published in German.

Lorenz, Konrad Z.   1965   *Evolution and Modification of Behavior.* Univ. of Chicago Press.

Magnus, Dietrich   1958   Experimentelle Untersuchungen zur Bionomie und Ethologie des Kaisermantels Argynnis paphia (lep. Nymph). *Zeitschrift für Tierpsychologie* 15:397–426.

Morris, Desmond   1957   "Typical Intensity" and Its Relation to the Problem of Ritualization. *Behaviour* 11: 1–12.

Poulsen, Holger   1953   A Study of Incubation Responses and Some Other Behaviour Patterns in Birds. Dansk Naturhistorisk Forening, Copenhagen, *Videnskabelige meddelelser* 115:1–131.

Reimarus, Hermann S.   (1760) 1798   *Allgemeine Betrachtungen über die Triebe der Thiere, hauptsächlich über ihre Kunsttriebe.* Hamburg (Germany): Bohn.

Spalding, Douglas A.   (1873) 1954   Instinct, With Original Observations on Young Animals. *British Journal of Animal Behaviour* 2:2–11.

Thorpe, William H.   (1956) 1963   *Learning and Instinct in Animals.* 2d ed., rev. & enl. Cambridge, Mass.: Harvard Univ. Press.

Tinbergen, Nikolaas   1951   *The Study of Instinct.* Oxford: Clarendon.

Wall, W. von de   1963   Bewegungsstudien an Anatinen. *Journal für Ornithologie* 104:1–15.

Whitman, C. O.   1898   Animal Behavior. Woods Hole, Mass., Marine Biological Laboratory *Biological Lectures* [1898]:285–338.

Wiepkema, P. R.   1961   An Ethological Analysis of the Reproductive Behaviour of the Bitterling (Rhodeus amarus Bloch). *Archives néerlandaises de zoologie* 14:103–199.

ETHOS

See Culture, *article on* cultural relativism; Values, *article on* value systems; World view; *and the biography of* Redfield.

EUGENICS

Eugenics is an applied science that seeks to maintain or to improve the genetic potentialities of the human species. In practice, eugenics is concerned with any qualities that parents confer on their children, because genetic and cultural traits are often correlated or indistinguishable, and because measures that improve one at the expense of the other are to be avoided. Genetics provides the core of eugenic theory, while any implementation must be broadly based on demography, medicine, psychology, and sociology.

Founded by Sir Francis Galton at the end of the nineteenth century, before the rediscovery of Gregor Mendel's laws of heredity, the early eugenics movement had an insecure scientific foundation and soon became contaminated with class and race prejudice. In the first half of the twentieth century,

eugenics was challenged by the growth of equalitarian sentiments and suffered especially from the demonstration of perverted eugenics in Nazi Germany. Since mid-century, the movement has gained respectability by repudiating its early errors and by assimilating scientific advances.

False concepts are still widely propounded in the name of eugenics, and there is disagreement even among geneticists as to the desirability and the urgency of eugenic measures. While some deterioration of hereditary capacities is sure to result from preservation of physically or mentally handicapped persons and from increased irradiation of the population, the rate of this deterioration may be exceedingly slow. Furthermore, medical procedures that ameliorate genetic handicaps do not usually restore complete physical and social normality, so that natural selection still operates against the defects. Although intelligent parents have in the recent past tended to have fewer children than the less intelligent, early predictions of declining general intelligence have not been borne out. Analysis of present trends in reproduction indicates that the increased use and effectiveness of contraception may reverse this fertility difference (Osborn 1963*a*; 1963*b*).

The case for eugenics.   Three lines of reasoning support the case for eugenics. First, individual families can be spared suffering and disruption if severe hereditary defects are identified and the parents given medical advice or assistance in preventing further births.

Second, the high correlation between parents and children in mental characteristics has some of the same implications whether attributed mainly to heredity or mainly to cultural transmission. Mentally handicapped persons, whose children stand the greatest risk of mental handicap, should at least be assisted if they wish to limit their offspring. More intelligent parents who can provide healthy home environments should be encouraged to bear as many children as they can support.

Third, even a very small improvement in the intelligence of a large civilized population may be expected to increase available leadership significantly. The argument for eugenics does not depend on proving that present trends are downward but on evidence that in important respects the population would be better off with eugenic measures than without them (Shapiro 1959). The only assurance against genetic deterioration is demonstrable genetic improvement.

Modern governments and institutions cannot avoid taking action in the sphere of eugenics. Every large-scale social or economic measure alters the distribution of births among segments of the population, and this distribution determines the genetic potentials of the next generation.

Present problems and applications

Radiation effects. In the past two decades public attention has been focused on possible genetic effects of radiation, namely, gene mutations. Children born to survivors of the atomic bombs in Japan have not shown significant genetic effects, and this supports the belief that to date the deleterious effects of atomic bursts on human heredity are small in comparison with natural mutations already accumulated in concealed form. Yet in absolute numbers, the new induced mutations are probably numerous and destined to take a proportionate toll in death and suffering spread over many generations.

In medically advanced countries the population receives radiation from medical X rays that may greatly exceed the present dosage from fall-out of atomic tests. The debt incurred for future generations by use of X rays or atomic testing must be weighed against the supposed immediate gains in health or national security. Some drugs also induce mutations, and these may need to be controlled in the future. Among the consequences of induced mutations, it is likely that physical defects would be less of a threat to man's survival under civilization than innumerable small mental impairments.

Race mixture. There is a broad consensus among geneticists that race mixture in man is no eugenic hazard. In plants and animals, the crossing of races may have unpredictable results. Especially if the parent populations were closely inbred, the new generation may show "hybrid vigor"; some other hybrids may show serious disharmonies. In the case of man there is little evidence for either hybrid vigor or hybrid disharmony, and if they occur they are overshadowed by social and cultural phenomena (Chung & Morton 1961). If some small hybrid populations appear to be genetically and culturally inferior to surrounding peoples, this may be due to isolation, inbreeding, or the quality of people who originate or who join such groups. Gene frequencies are not altered by race crossing but only by mutations and selection.

Population policies. The immediate problem of curbing world population growth overshadows problems of population quality. Nevertheless, population policies adopted now are likely to exert qualitative effects for a long time in the future, and these effects should be weighed.

Birth rate differences between educational classes or between occupations appear in most civilized countries to be unfavorable to social and genetic progress. Eugenically sound population policies would therefore reduce or reverse these differentials at the same time that they accomplish their main purpose. A program to reduce births might, for example, facilitate voluntary family limitation and at the same time extend and advertise the economic benefits of such limitation to the more fertile and less secure economic classes. A program to increase births might best achieve this by assisting with higher education and other goals that deter reproduction by persons of high ability.

Genetic counseling. Genetic factors undoubtedly play some role in nearly all diseases and abnormalities, but avoidance of reproduction is genetically indicated only in conditions for which the risk is known to be high. Even in these instances the advisability of reproduction depends on the nature of the disease, on other genetic variables, on socioeconomic circumstances, and above all on the parents' willingness to sustain the risk. People who avoid childbearing for fear of hereditary defects sometimes have negligible genetic risks and are potentially superior parents. Yet those who seek genetic advice often fail to make use of it. Many universities now have centers for genetic counseling, but hereditary diseases will remain unchecked until family planning becomes general and effective. Whether it will ever be possible to transform harmful genes to the normal form by artificial means is a subject of speculation (Hotchkiss 1965).

Theoretical aspects of eugenics

Heredity and behavior. Galton believed that human behavior could be improved by genetic as well as by cultural progress (1883). Is there today any secure basis for such a belief? On theoretical grounds, the answer to this question is clearly yes. Over the past million years man's forebears made rapid genetic progress with respect to intelligence and social behavior. The only known mechanism of genetic progress is natural or artificial selection of favorable variations, and selection produces permanent gains only if the selected variations are hereditary. Therefore, hereditary variation must have existed as long as mental capacities were evolving, and there is no theoretical reason to suppose that it has now disappeared. Such hereditary variation in behavior provides the necessary basis for further genetic improvement.

Many psychologists and geneticists have adduced what they regard as evidence for hereditary psychological differences. The most important variation seems to be that between individuals, whereas the observed differences between races and social classes are mainly cultural in origin. Even the concept of good and bad "family stock" is erroneous; both good and bad may occur in any family, and psychological traits shared with grandchildren or cousins must be attributed in large part to common environmental factors or to assortative (selective) mating.

Natural selection.   Natural selection is the only known guiding influence in organic evolution and is a necessary correlate of reproduction in a genetically variable organism. Individuals who contribute more progeny than others to the next generation have, by definition, greater *biological fitness*. So far as the differences in fitness may be hereditary and the environment stable, the next generation will have a higher average ability to survive and reproduce. At equilibrium the gain in each generation is offset by new harmful mutations. The first test of fitness is survival; but even among the survivors, natural selection operates through differences in fertility.

Although it acts on whole organisms, natural selection produces evolutionary effects by changing the relative frequencies of single genes. In each generation, sexual reproduction recombines genes so that all are tested in new combinations. The ultimate frequency of a gene depends on its average effect on survival and reproduction; if it is to become frequent, a new gene must be consonant with the major existing adaptations of the species. Natural selection is therefore conservative, tending usually to stabilize established norms.

Natural selection is inefficient for at least three reasons: (1) Many deaths or reproductive failures are due to chance. (2) Individual differences in fitness are often not hereditary. (3) Most hereditary differences in fitness are small. Some of this inefficiency can be overcome under artificial selection, but at a price. When it entails breeding from a few selected individuals, artificial selection may sacrifice both genetic stability and reserve variability. The artificial reproductive success conferred by the breeder on animals with commercially valuable traits may result in feeble or sterile strains. On the other hand, natural selection adapts a species only to its present environment or set of environments, and when the environment changes radically the species may become extinct. Man can foresee some changes in the environment and can, if he will, select for long-term fitness. In the last analysis this is probably a crucial advantage of scientific eugenics over natural selection.

The genetic stability of populations.   Evolution is slow not only because natural selection is inefficient but because natural populations have a great inherent genetic stability. This stability is con-

siderable even in small populations, for example, with a few hundred breeding individuals. Because of large numbers and small individual contributions to the next generation (compared with most species), civilized human populations should be very resistant to change.

Genetic stability resides primarily in the "gene pool" of a population. Each gene has a characteristic frequency, usually determined by a stable equilibrium between opposing forces of selection and mutation. Sudden changes in selective pressures may have more effect on complex traits than on the underlying gene frequencies, but even such traits are not likely to change fast. Thus, if lactation ceases to have survival value, its dependence on several physiological systems may make it vulnerable to mutations in any of a great many genes. Before any single genetic defect reached a frequency of 2.0 per cent, most women might have one or two rarer defects that prevented lactation. But an increase from 0.1 per cent to 2.0 per cent by mutation would take at least a hundred generations. Defects of lactation that were positively selected because of effects on other traits might increase ten times this fast, but they would be few and represent coincidence only.

Probably all human behavioral traits, except some grossly pathological ones, are controlled by multiple genetic factors and by the environment. Most of these traits are graded or continuous. Natural selection tends to eliminate both extremes in such a continuum and produces evolutionary change mainly from slight differences in fitness among the more numerous intermediate individuals. Thus, the gene pool retains a large reserve of variability and accommodates any new variations that do not have extreme effects.

Sources of variation.   It has been suggested that ionizing radiation may speed human evolution by inducing more mutations. While mutations are the raw material of evolution, increased mutation rates now would probably do much more harm than good. First, nearly all mutations are harmful and must be eliminated by impaired fitness of the carriers, often extending over many generations. Second, nearly all of the possibly beneficial mutations have occurred before and are already so frequent that rare additions will not help. Third, the few new useful mutations would increase so slowly under moderate selective pressures that they would remain very rare for centuries.

Variations already present in human populations would suffice to carry human evolution forward a very long distance. New useful mutations that have arisen in the past few millennia are still in the early stages of response to natural selection. The great majority of variable genes, kept at intermediate frequencies by conflicting or inefficient selection, should have an immense potential for improving the species. Some useful genes may be mainly restricted to small populations or to certain races; intermarriage between nationalities and between races will make these generally available. Finally, man's constantly changing environment under civilization changes the survival value of genes, making some useful that were previously neutral or harmful.

The role of an optimum environment. Early Darwinian enthusiasts supposed that natural selection was inevitably cruel and that human evolution could proceed only in a harsh environment. Diverse environments are desirable since they develop diverse potentials and, under natural selection, maintain genetic variability. But present human environments are often restricting and largely beyond control of the individual and even of the family.

Man's future environment will probably be closer to the best than to the worst of present living standards. Eugenic planning for long-term adaptation should seek not only to equalize opportunity but to equalize it at a high economic and educational level. This would have no eugenic effect by itself but would enhance whatever selection was operative, either negative or positive.

Direction and choice in programs. A number of experts have warned that man may become dangerously dependent on medical technology. Such dependence, on a genetic basis, may develop gradually over centuries or millennia, but it is evident that throughout human evolution innate physical capacities have tended to deteriorate as compensatory mental abilities increased. In subhuman evolution, adaptability has repeatedly proved superior to specialized adaptation, and intelligence in its many aspects opens the way to almost unlimited adaptability. In any eugenic program, therefore, intelligence, broadly defined, should take precedence over physical fitness.

The above implied choice is an example of problems that would continually arise in eugenics. It is sometimes contended that the planning of human evolution would require superhuman wisdom. In practice, eugenics need not imply detailed foresight or genetic planning but would select for adaptability and diversity among variations already discernible. If the problems were faced one by one and periodically reviewed, they should be no more grave or insoluble than present political, educational, and social problems.

Dysgenic and eugenic environments. The environment is the instrument of natural selection since it sets the conditions for individual biological fitness, that is, the ability to survive and reproduce. For the continuation of our culture, and perhaps ultimately of the species, some other traits are as important as fertility. A society in which culturally important traits are positively correlated with fertility may be defined as a eugenic environment; the opposite is a dysgenic environment. One society may be eugenic within some social strata and dysgenic in others. Any discussion of a eugenic environment requires specification of the traits considered culturally important. One might assume that the greatest need in our culture is for traits leading to superior achievement in one's chosen occupation. A thorough treatment of the subject would give weight to more specific traits such as intelligence, social maturity, and parental responsibility.

Proposed systems of selection

Promoting optimum expression of each person's genetic capacities would not by itself constitute genetic progress. Eugenic selection, either natural or artificial, is also needed. Any deliberate program to promote eugenic selection would require much research before it could be instituted and careful monitoring of its progress.

Breeding programs. Next to preoccupation with race, the advocacy of artificial breeding programs has probably done most to make eugenics unacceptable. Early proposals were incompatible with concepts of conventional marriage and families as social units. Since the introduction of artificial insemination, the possibility of multiplying the progeny of selected men has become real. If artificial insemination from donors is practiced, all eugenists would agree that the donors should be carefully selected. But proposals for large-scale use of semen from a few great men (Muller 1960) may attach too much importance to fortunate combinations of genes that have little general value in the gene pool or in ordinary environments.

Assistance to selected families. British eugenists, especially, have advocated financial assistance, resembling scholarships, to parents with good eugenic prognosis (Blacker 1952, p. 307). This would enable them to have as many children as they wanted. Economically dependent families, with generally poorer prognosis, would be assisted in limiting their progeny.

With exceptions for grossly pathological heredity, eugenic prognosis in such a program ought to be based upon a couple's social and cultural attainments and on physical and mental health of their earliest progeny. Discrepancies between attainments and genetic potential might be compensated by social transmission of traits, so that this eugenic program would achieve limited cultural improvement if not also genetic improvement. If future environments achieve near equality of opportunities, attainments will more closely reflect genetic capacities.

Automatic selection.   Some eugenists have been dissatisfied with the potential for error or misuse in any arbitrary system of selection. Others see eugenic processes as requiring both broad application across all families and stability beyond that of most political systems. From these concerns have come suggestions for automatic selection: economic measures or social conditions under which natural selection will favor qualities of greatest value to society.

If the newest methods of contraception become widely available, they may eliminate nearly all unwanted pregnancies. This in itself would bring family size more in line with parents' capacities for education and achievement (Osborn 1963a). The rewarding of fertility with uniform family allowances is not eugenically effective, but some countries offer other benefits. Highly effective automatic selection would require a more carefully planned eugenic environment (Osborn 1940). This might include high degrees of (1) social mobility, (2) individual opportunity, and (3) voluntary assortative marriage, that is, between persons with similar abilities. It might also require special educational, economic, and social measures to make child rearing more acceptable to socially competent persons and less so to the socially inadequate.

GORDON ALLEN

[*Other relevant material may be found in* EVOLUTION; GENETICS; RADIATION; *and in the biographies of* DARWIN *and* GALTON.]

BIBLIOGRAPHY

BLACKER, CHARLES P.   1952   *Eugenics: Galton and After.* London: Duckworth.

CHUNG, C. S.; and MORTON, N. E.   1961   Genetics of Interracial Crosses in Hawaii. Volume 1, pages 134–138 in International Congress of Human Genetics, Second, Rome, *Proceedings.* Rome: Istituto G. Mendel.

DOBZHANSKY, THEODOSIUS   1962   *Mankind Evolving.* New Haven: Yale Univ. Press. → An authoritative exposition for the general scientist of genetic principles relevant to human evolution.

Evolution and Man's Progress.   1961   *Dædalus* 90:409–586. → A symposium. See especially pages 416–476, dealing with genetic evolution.

GALTON, FRANCIS   (1883) 1952   *Inquiries Into Human Faculty and Its Development.* London: Cassell.

HALLER, MARK H.   1963   *Eugenics: Hereditarian Attitudes in American Thought.* New Brunswick, N.J.: Rutgers Univ. Press.

HOTCHKISS, ROLLIN D.   1965   Portents for a Genetic Engineering. *Journal of Heredity* 56:197–202.

MEDAWAR, PETER B.   1960   *The Future of Man.* New York: Basic Books; London: Methuen. → A simple discussion of some central questions.

MULLER, HERMAN J.   1960   The Guidance of Human Evolution. Pages 423–462 in Sol Tax (editor), *The Evolution of Man.* Volume 2: Evolution After Darwin. Univ. of Chicago Press.

OSBORN, FREDERICK H.   (1940) 1951   *Preface to Eugenics.* Rev. ed. New York: Harper.

OSBORN, FREDERICK H.   1963a   Excess and Unwanted Fertility. *Eugenics Quarterly* 10:59–72.

OSBORN, FREDERICK H.   1963b   Eugenics and the Races of Man. *Eugenics Quarterly* 10:103–109.

SHAPIRO, HARRY L.   1959   Eugenics and Future Society. *Eugenics Quarterly* 6:3–7.

WORLD HEALTH ORGANIZATION   1957   *Effect of Radiation on Human Heredity.* Geneva: The Organization.

EUROPEAN SOCIETY

See the entries ANGLO–AMERICAN SOCIETY; SOCIETAL ANALYSIS.

EVALUATION RESEARCH

Ours is an age of social-action programs, where large organization and huge expenditures go into the attempted solution of every conceivable social problem. Such programs include both private and public ventures and small-scale and large-scale projects, ranging in scope from local to national and international efforts at social change. Whenever men spend time, money, and effort to help solve social problems, someone usually questions the effectiveness of their actions. Sponsors, critics, the public, even the actors themselves, seek signs that their program is successful. Much of the assessment of action programs is irregular and, often by necessity, based upon personal judgments of supporters or critics, impressions, anecdotes, testimonials, and miscellaneous information available for the evaluation. In recent years, however, there has been a striking change in attitudes toward evaluation activities and the type and quality of evidence that is acceptable for determining the relative success or failure of social-action programs.

Two trends stand out in the modern attitude toward evaluation. First, evaluation has come to be expected as a regular accompaniment to rational social-action programs. Second, there has been a movement toward demanding more systematic, rigorous, and objective evidence of success. The application of social science techniques to the appraisal of social-action programs has come to be called evaluation research.

Examples of the applications of evaluation research are available from a wide variety of fields. One of the earliest attempts at building evaluation research into an action program was in the field of community action to prevent juvenile delinquency. The 1937 Cambridge–Somerville Youth Study provided for an experimental and a control group of boys, with the former to receive special attention and advice from counselors and other community agencies. The plan called for a ten-year period of work with the experimental group followed by an evaluation that would compare the record of their delinquent conduct during that decade with the record of the control group. The results of the evaluation (see Powers & Witmer 1951) showed no significant differences in conduct favorable to the program. A subsequent long-term evaluation of the same program failed to find new evidence of less criminal activity by persons in the experimental group but added a variety of new theoretical analyses to the evaluation (McCord et al. 1959).

Several evaluations of programs in citizenship training for young persons have built upon one another, thus providing continuity in the field. Riecken (1952) conducted an evaluation of summer work camps sponsored by the American Friends Service Committee to determine their impact on the values, attitudes, and opinions of the participants. His work was useful in specifying those areas in which the program was successful or unsuccessful as well as pointing up the importance of measuring unsought by-products of action programs. Subsequently, Hyman, Wright, and Hopkins carried out a series of evaluations of another youth program, the Encampment for Citizenship (1962). Their research design was complex, including a comparison of campers' values, attitudes, opinions, and behavior before and after a six-week program of training; follow-up surveys six weeks and four years after the group left the program; three independent replications of the original study on new groups of campers in later years; and a sample survey of alumni of the program. These various studies demonstrated the effectiveness of the program in influencing campers' social attitudes and conduct; they also examined the dynamics of attitudinal change.

Evaluations have been made in such varied fields as intergroup relations, induced technological change, mass communications, adult education, international exchange of persons for training or good will, mental health, and public health. Additional examples of applications of evaluation research, along with discussions of evaluation techniques, are presented by Klineberg and others in a special issue of the *International Social Science Bulletin* (1955) and in Hyman and Wright (1966).

Defining characteristics

A scientific approach to the assessment of a program's achievements is the hallmark of modern evaluation research. In this respect evaluation research resembles other kinds of social research in its concern for objectivity, reliability, and validity in the collection, analysis, and interpretation of data. But it can be distinguished as a special form of social research by its purpose and the conditions under which the research must be conducted. Both of these factors affect such components of the research process as study design and its translation into practice, allocation of research time and other resources, and the value or worth to be put upon the empirical findings.

The primary purpose of evaluation research is "to provide objective, systematic, and comprehensive evidence on the degree to which the program achieves its intended objectives plus the degree to which it produces other unanticipated consequences, which when recognized would also be regarded as relevant to the agency" (Hyman et al. 1962, pp. 5–6). Evaluation research thus differs in its emphasis from such other major types of social research as exploratory studies, which seek to formulate new problems and hypotheses, or explanatory research, which places emphasis on the testing of theoretically significant hypotheses, or descriptive social research, which documents the existence of certain social conditions at a given moment or over time (Selltiz et al. 1959). Since the burden is on the evaluator to provide firm evidence on the effects of the program under study, he favors a study design that will tend toward maximizing such evidence and his confidence in conclusions drawn from it. Although good evaluation research often seeks explanations of a program's success or failure, the first concern is to obtain basic evidence on effectiveness, and therefore most research resources are allocated to this goal.

The conditions under which evaluation research is conducted also give it a character distinct from other forms of social research. Evaluation research is applied social research, and it differs from other modes of scholarly research in bringing together an outside investigator to guarantee objectivity and a client in need of his services. From the initial formulation of the problem to the final interpretation of findings, the evaluator is duty-bound to keep in mind the very practical problem of assessing the program under study. As a consequence he often has less freedom to select or reject certain independent, dependent, and intervening variables than he would have in studies designed to answer his own theoretically formulated questions, such as might be posed in basic social research. The concepts employed and their translation into measurable variables must be selected imaginatively but within the general framework set by the nature of the program being evaluated and its objectives (a point which will be discussed later). Another feature of evaluation research is that the investigator seldom has freedom to manipulate the program and its components, i.e., the independent variable, as he might in laboratory or field experiments. Usually he wants to evaluate an ongoing or proposed program of social action in its natural setting and is not at liberty, because of practical and theoretical considerations, to change it for research purposes. The nature of the program being evaluated and the time at which his services are called upon also set conditions that affect, among other things, the feasibility of using an experimental design involving before-and-after measurements, the possibility of obtaining control groups, the kinds of research instruments that can be used, and the need to provide for measures of long-term as well as immediate effects.

The recent tendency to call upon social science for the evaluation of action programs that are local, national, and international in scope (a trend which probably will increase in future years) and the fact that the application of scientific research procedures to problems of evaluation is complicated by the purposes and conditions of evaluation research have stimulated an interest in methodological aspects of evaluation among a variety of social scientists, especially sociologists and psychologists. Methodological and technical problems in evaluation research are discussed, to mention but a few examples, in the writings of Riecken (1952), Klineberg (1955), Hyman et al. (1962), and Hayes (1959).

While it is apparent that the specific translation of social-science techniques into forms suitable for a particular evaluation study involves research decisions based upon the special nature of the program under examination, there are nonetheless certain broad methodological questions common to most evaluation research. Furthermore, certain principles of evaluation research can be extracted from the rapidly growing experience of social scientists in applying their perspectives and methods to the evaluation of social-action programs. Such principles have obvious importance in highlighting and clarifying the methodological features of evaluation research and in providing practical, if limited, guidelines for conducting or appraising such research. The balance of this article will discuss certain, but by no means all, of these compelling methodological problems.

Methodological steps and principles

The process of evaluation has been codified into five major phases, each involving particular methodological problems and guiding principles (see Hyman et al. 1962). They are (1) the conceptualization and measurement of the objectives of the program and other unanticipated relevant outcomes; (2) formulation of a research design and the criteria for proof of effectiveness of the program, including consideration of control groups or alternatives to them; (3) the development and application of research procedures, including provisions for the estimation or reduction of errors in measurement; (4) problems of index construction and the proper evaluation of effectiveness; and (5) procedures for understanding and explaining the findings on effectiveness or ineffectiveness. Such a division of the process of evaluation is artificial, of course, in the sense that in practice the phases overlap and it is necessary for the researcher to give more or less constant consideration to all five steps. Nevertheless it provides a useful framework for examining and understanding the essential components of evaluation research.

Conceptualization. Each social-action program must be evaluated in terms of its particular goals. Therefore, evaluation research must begin with their identification and move toward their specification in terms of concepts that, in turn, can be translated into measurable indicators. All this may sound simple, perhaps routine, compared with the less structured situation facing social researchers engaged in formulating research problems for theoretical, explanatory, descriptive, or other kinds of basic research. But the apparent simplicity is deceptive, and in practice this phase of evaluation research repeatedly has proven to be both critical and difficult for social researchers working in such varied areas as mental health (U.S. Dept. of Health, Education & Welfare 1955), juvenile delinquency (Witmer & Tufts 1954), adult education (Evaluation Techniques 1955), and youth programs for citizenship training (Riecken 1952; Hyman et al. 1962), among others. As an example, Witmer and Tufts raise such questions about the meaning of the concept "delinquency prevention" as: What is to be prevented? Who is to be deterred? Are we talking only about "official" delinquency? Does prevention mean stopping misbehavior before it occurs? Does it mean reducing the frequency of misbehavior? Or does it mean reducing its severity?

Basic concepts and goals are often elusive, vague, unequal in importance to the program, and sometimes difficult to translate into operational terms. What is meant, for example, by such a goal as preparing young persons for "responsible citizenship"? In addition, the evaluator needs to consider possible effects of the program which were unanticipated by the action agency, finding clues from the records of past reactions to the program if it has been in operation prior to the evaluation, studies of similar programs, the social-science literature, and other sources. As an example, Carlson (1952) found that a mass-information campaign against venereal disease failed to increase public knowledge about these diseases; nevertheless, the campaign had the unanticipated effect of improving the morale of public health workers in the area, who in turn did a more effective job of combating the diseases. The anticipation of both planned and unplanned effects requires considerable time, effort, and imagination by the researcher prior to collecting evidence for the evaluation itself.

Research design.   The formulation of a research design for evaluation usually involves an attempt to approximate the ideal conditions of a controlled experiment, which measures the changes produced by a program by making comparisons of the dependent variables before and after the program and evaluating them against similar measurements on a control group that is not involved in the program. If the control group is initially similar to the group exposed to the social-action program, a condition achieved through judicious selection, matching, and randomization, then the researcher can use the changes in the control group as a criterion against which to estimate the degree to which changes in the experimental group were probably caused by the program under study. To illustrate, suppose that two equivalent groups of adults are selected for a study on the effects of a training film intended to impart certain information to the audience. The level of relevant information is measured in each group prior to the showing of the film; then one group sees the film while the other does not; finally, after some interval, information is again measured. Changes in the amount of information held by the experimental group cannot simply be attributed to the film; they may also reflect the influence of such factors in the situation

as exposure to other sources of information in the interim period, unreliability of the measuring instruments, maturation, and other factors extraneous to the program itself. But the control group presumably also experienced such nonprogrammatic factors, and therefore the researcher can subtract the amount of change in information demonstrated by it from the changes shown by the experimental group, thereby determining how much of the gross change in the latter group is due to the exclusive influence of the program.

So it is in the ideal case, such as might be achieved under laboratory conditions. In practice, however, evaluation research seldom permits such ideal conditions. A variety of practical problems requires alterations in the ideal design. As examples, suitable control groups cannot always be found, especially for social-action programs involving efforts at large-scale social change but also for smaller programs designed to influence volunteer participants; also ethical, administrative, or other considerations usually prevent the random assignment of certain persons to a control group that will be denied the treatment offered by the action programs.

In the face of such obstacles, certain methodologists have taken the position that a slavish insistence on the ideal control-group experimental research design is unwise and dysfunctional in evaluation research. Rather, they advocate the ingenious use of practical and reasonable alternatives to the classic design (see Hyman et al. 1962; and Campbell & Stanley 1963). Under certain conditions, for example, it is possible to estimate the amount of change that could have been caused by extraneous events, instability of measurements, and natural growth of participants in a program by examining the amount of change that occurred among participants in programs similar to the one being evaluated. Using such comparative studies as "quasi-control" groups permits an estimate of the relative effectiveness of the program under study, i.e., how much effect it has had over and above that achieved by another program and assorted extraneous factors, even though it is impossible to isolate the specific amount of change caused by the extraneous factors. Another procedure for estimating the influence of nonprogrammatic factors is to study the amount of change which occurs among a sample of the population under study during a period of time prior to the introduction of the action program, using certain of the ultimate participants as a kind of control upon themselves, so to speak. Replications of the evaluation study, when possible, also provide safeguards against attributing too much or too little effect to the program under study. Admittedly, all such practical alternatives to the controlled experimental design have serious limitations and must be used with judgment; the classic experimental design remains preferable whenever possible and serves as an ideal even when impractical. Nevertheless, such expedients have proven useful to evaluators and have permitted relatively rigorous evaluations to be conducted under conditions less perfect than those found in the laboratory.

Error control. Evaluation studies, like all social research, involve difficult problems in the selection of specific research procedures and the provision for estimating and reducing various sources of error, such as sampling bias, bias due to nonresponse, measurement errors arising in the questions asked or in recording of answers, deliberate deception, and interviewer bias. The practices employed to control such errors in evaluation research are similar to those used in other forms of social research, and no major innovations have been introduced.

Estimating effectiveness. To consider the fourth stage in evaluation, a distinction needs to be made between demonstrating the effects of an action program and estimating its effectiveness. Effectiveness refers to the extent to which the program achieves its goals, but the question of just how much effectiveness constitutes success and justifies the efforts of the program is unanswerable by scientific research. It remains a matter for judgment on the part of the program's sponsors, administrators, critics, or others, and the benefits, of course, must somehow be balanced against the costs involved. The problem is complicated further by the fact that most action programs have multiple goals, each of which may be achieved with varying degrees of success over time and among different subgroups of participants in the program. To date there is no general calculus for appraising the over-all net worth of a program.

Even if the evaluation limits itself to determining the success of a program in terms of each specific goal, however, it is necessary to introduce some indexes of effectiveness which add together the discrete effects within each of the program's goal areas. Technical problems of index and scale construction have been given considerable attention by methodologists concerned with various types of social research (see Lazarsfeld & Rosenberg 1955). But as yet there is no theory of index construction specifically appropriate to evaluation research. Steps have been taken in this direction, however, and the utility of several types of indexes has been tentatively explored (see Hyman et al. 1962). One type of difficulty, for example, arises

from the fact that the amount of change that an action program produces may vary from subgroup to subgroup and from topic to topic, depending upon how close to perfection each group was before the program began. Thus, an information program can influence relatively fewer persons among a subgroup in which, say, 60 per cent of the people are already informed about the topic than among another target group in which only 30 per cent are initially informed. An "effectiveness index" has been successfully employed to help solve the problem of weighting effectiveness in the light of such restricted ceilings for change (see Hovland et al. 1949; and Hyman et al. 1962). This index, which expresses actual change as a proportion of the maximum change that is possible given the initial position of a group on the variable under study, has proven to be especially useful in evaluating the *relative* effectiveness of different programs and the relative effectiveness of any particular program for different subgroups or on different variables.

Understanding effectiveness. In its final stage, evaluation research goes beyond the demonstration of a program's effects to seek information that will help to account for its successes and failures. The reasons for such additional inquiry may be either practical or theoretical.

Sponsors of successful programs may want to duplicate their action program at another time or under other circumstances, or the successful program may be considered as a model for action by others. Such emulation can be misguided and even dangerous without information about which aspects of the program were most important in bringing about the results, for which participants in the program, and under what conditions. Often it is neither possible nor necessary, however, to detect and measure the impact of each component of a social-action program. In this respect, as in others noted above, evaluation research differs from explanatory survey research, where specific stimuli are isolated, and from experimental designs, where isolated stimuli are introduced into the situation being studied. In evaluation research the independent variable, i.e., the program under study, is usually a complex set of activities no one of which can be separated from the others without changing the nature of the program itself. Hence, explanations of effectiveness are often given in terms of the contributions made by certain gross features of the program, for example, the total impact of didactic components versus social participation in a successful educational institution.

Gross as such comparisons must be, they nevertheless provide opportunities for testing specific hypotheses about social and individual change, thereby contributing to the refinement and growth of social science theories. It is important to remember, however, that such gains are of secondary concern to evaluation research, which has as its primary goal the objective measurement of the effectiveness of the program.

Certain forms of research design promise to yield valuable results both for the primary task of evaluation and its complementary goal of enlarging social knowledge. Among the most promising designs are those that allow for *comparative* evaluations of different social-action programs, *replication* of evaluations of the same program, and *longitudinal* studies of the long-range impact of programs. Comparative studies not only demonstrate the differential effectiveness of various forms of programs having similar aims but also provide a continuity in research which permits testing theories of change under a variety of circumstances. Replicative evaluations add to the confidence in the findings from the initial study and give further opportunity for exploring possible causes of change. Longitudinal evaluations permit the detection of effects that require a relatively long time to occur and allow an examination of the stability or loss of certain programmatic effects over time and under various natural conditions outside of the program's immediate control.

Viewed in this larger perspective, then, evaluation research deserves full recognition as a social science activity which will continue to expand. It provides excellent and ready-made opportunities to examine individuals, groups, and societies in the grip of major and minor forces for change. Its applications contribute not only to a science of social planning and a more rationally planned society but also to the perfection of social and psychological theories of change.

CHARLES R. WRIGHT

[*See also* EXPERIMENTAL DESIGN; SURVEY ANALYSIS.]

BIBLIOGRAPHY

CAMPBELL, DONALD T.; and STANLEY, J. S. 1963 Experimental and Quasi-experimental Designs for Research on Teaching. Pages 171–246 in Nathaniel L. Gage (editor), *Handbook of Research on Teaching*. Chicago: Rand McNally.
CARLSON, ROBERT O. 1952 The Influence of the Community and the Primary Group on the Reactions of Southern Negroes to Syphilis. Ph.D. dissertation, Columbia Univ.
Evaluation Techniques. 1955 *International Social Science Bulletin* 7:343–458.
HAYES, SAMUEL P. 1959 *Measuring the Results of Development Projects: A Manual for the Use of Field Workers*. Paris: UNESCO.
HOVLAND, CARL I.; LUMSDAINE, ARTHUR A.; and SHEFFIELD, FREDERICK D. 1949 *Experiments on Mass Communication*. Studies in Social Psychology in World War II, Vol. 3. Princeton Univ. Press.
HYMAN, HERBERT H.; and WRIGHT, CHARLES R. 1966 Evaluating Social Action Programs. Unpublished manuscript.
HYMAN, HERBERT H.; WRIGHT, CHARLES R.; and HOPKINS, TERENCE K. 1962 *Applications of Methods of Evaluation: Four Studies of the Encampment for Citizenship*. Berkeley: Univ. of California Press.
KLINEBERG, OTTO 1955 Introduction: The Problem of Evaluation. *International Social Science Bulletin* 7: 346–352.
LAZARSFELD, PAUL F.; and ROSENBERG, MORRIS (editors) 1955 *The Language of Social Research: A Reader in the Methodology of Social Research*. Glencoe, Ill.: Free Press.
McCORD, WILLIAM; McCORD, JOAN; and ZOLA, IRVING K. 1959 *Origins of Crime: A New Evaluation of the Cambridge–Somerville Youth Study*. New York: Columbia Univ. Press.
POWERS, EDWIN; and WITMER, HELEN L. 1951 *An Experiment in the Prevention of Delinquency*. New York: Columbia Univ. Press; Oxford Univ. Press.
RIECKEN, HENRY W. 1952 *The Volunteer Work Camp: A Psychological Evaluation*. Reading, Mass.: Addison-Wesley.
SELLTIZ, CLAIRE et al. (1959) 1962 *Research Methods in Social Relations*. New York: Holt.
U.S. DEPT. OF HEALTH, EDUCATION & WELFARE, NATIONAL INSTITUTES OF HEALTH 1955 *Evaluation in Mental Health: Review of Problem of Evaluating Mental Health Activities*. Washington: Government Printing Office.
WITMER, HELEN L.; and TUFTS, EDITH 1954 *The Effectiveness of Delinquency Prevention Programs*. Washington: Government Printing Office.

EVIDENCE, LEGAL

See LEGAL REASONING; PSYCHIATRY, *article on* FORENSIC PSYCHIATRY; STATISTICS AS LEGAL EVIDENCE.

EVOLUTION

I.	THE CONCEPT OF EVOLUTION	*R. C. Lewontin*
II.	PRIMATE EVOLUTION	*Elwyn L. Simons*
III.	HUMAN EVOLUTION	*S. L. Washburn and Jane B. Lancaster*
IV.	CULTURAL EVOLUTION	*Elman R. Service*
V.	SOCIAL EVOLUTION	*Shmuel N. Eisenstadt*
VI.	EVOLUTION AND BEHAVIOR	*Theodosius Dobzhansky*

I
THE CONCEPT OF EVOLUTION

There are few concepts that appear in the history of ideas that are common to many realms of thought in social and natural science and to philosophy in general. Evolution is such a concept, and its origin as a doctrine was deeply embedded in the social and economic conditions of the industrial West. Like all such world views, it embodies many principles, not all of which are admitted in its various uses, so that even those concerned with organic evolution are unable to agree on the essence of the idea of evolution.

Toward a definition

There is a hierarchy of principles in the evolutionary world view: *change, order, direction, progress,* and *perfectibility.* Evolutionary theories are distinguished by how many of these are successively included as essential. Some evolutionists include only change and order, others add direction, and some few, like Teilhard de Chardin, believe in perfectibility as well.

Change. The idea of evolution, in its simplest form, is that the current state of a system is the result of a more or less continual change from its original state. The qualification that the change be continual, or at least frequent or regular, is an essential one and distinguishes evolutionary from static world views. For example, many opponents of organic evolution in the nineteenth century accepted the authenticity of fossils but regarded them as antediluvian, as evidence of one or several floods that caused a total replacement of the world's fauna. Diluvianism, like the closely related vulcanism, which postulated a series of inundations of the earth by lava, was a theory of catastrophic and irregular change. There is no fundamental difference between a theory of special creation that populates the world once with unchanging beings and one that populates it several times. They are both theories of special intervention of unique forces in an otherwise normally static system. The distinction between such a world view and an evolutionary one is important for our understanding of the social and economic origins of evolutionism.

Closely related to the idea that change is a characteristic of a system is the principle of *uniformitarianism,* the principle that the forces causing change are themselves unchangeable general laws that govern the system. Thus, geological evolution is seen as the result of processes of mountain-building, sedimentation, and erosion that have gone on throughout the history of the earth, at least since the time when liquid water was present in appreciable quantities. In like manner the processes of natural selection and mutation that can be seen occurring in the organic world today are assumed to have been the operative forces in all the past history of life. Moreover, since such forces are operating at present, it must be concluded that evolution is still going on. A commitment to an evolutionary viewpoint represents a commitment to the instability of the present order as well as the past. In its simplest and irreducible form, evolutionism is the doctrine that change of state is an unvarying characteristic of natural systems and human institutions and that such change follows immutable laws.

Order. While all evolutionary thought assumes continual change, there is some problem of distinguishing "real" change from a stasis that has only the appearance of change. Let us imagine a deck of cards being shuffled over and over again. In one sense it is obvious that the state of the deck is undergoing continual change, since the cards are being rearranged. But is the deck evolving? For Bergson and Whitehead it is not, because only alternate states of chaos are succeeding each other. *Plus ça change, plus c'est la même chose.* Out of this chaos some organization must appear to be true evolution, and the appearance of new organization, in the view of Whitehead and his followers, is the characteristic of an evolutionary process. In *Science and the Modern World* Whitehead says: "Evolution, on the materialistic theory, is reduced to the rôle of being another word for the description of changes of the external relations between portions of matter. There is nothing to evolve, because one set of external relations is as good as any other set of external relations. There can merely be change, purposeless and unprogressive" ([1925] 1960, p. 157).

But how can we know order as against chaos, except that we have a preconception of order and purpose? To return to the analogy of the deck of cards, if after repeated shuffling, the deck turned out to be grouped by suits, we would certainly say that order had been created. An even higher degree of order would be ascribed to the deck if, in addition, the cards within the suits were arranged in ascending sequence. After all, in poker a royal flush wins and a mixed hand loses. Yet, on any objective criterion a royal flush has exactly the same probability as any given mixed hand, and a completely ordered deck is not less probable than any other given arrangement. The appearance of order is the correspondence between the arrangement of objects and a preconception.

The demand that an evolutionary process create order, or at least that there be a change from one order to a different order, shows clearly that evolution, in this sense, is neither a fact nor a theory, but a way of organizing knowledge.

In contrast to Whitehead, some modern evolutionists are willing to accept any rearrangement of the parts of a structure as evolution. Thus

Dobzhansky (1937) defines organic evolution as "a change in the genetic composition of populations," and he speaks for most students of organic evolution when he says that there are no differences between organisms that cannot be accounted for in this way. But a change in the genetic composition of populations is not different in essence from a reshuffling of cards in that it is for the most part only a change in the relative frequency of elements, all of which are already present. The question of order marks the separation between the completely positivistic evolutionism inherent in Dobzhansky's definition and the creative evolutionism of Bergson and Teilhard. For, once it is proposed that order is the natural outcome of an evolutionary process, ideas of direction, progress, and perfectibility follow swiftly.

Direction. By direction in evolution we mean the concept that there is some natural linear order of states of the system and that an evolutionary process can be described as passing through successive states in this linear order. That is, evolution can be described by a line on a two-dimensional graph with time on one axis and some description of the system on the other. Moreover, this line is supposed to be always ascending or descending. But this description limits evolution to those attributes for which the human mind can make a sensible linear order. It must be possible to describe an evolutionary process as one in which something or other "tends to increase." Thus, it is insufficient to describe the evolution of human culture in terms of a change from hunting and gathering to agriculture, from agriculture to industry. These modes of organization must somehow be placed on a graded scale as, for example, the degree of division of labor (Durkheim) or the degree of complexity (Spencer).

The attempt to find the proper scale on which such a directionality can be measured has been a preoccupation of nonpositivist evolutionists and is the chief point at issue among them. *Complexity* is the scale most appealed to in organic and social evolution. For organic evolution it is supposed that modern organisms have a more complex structure than primitive ones, just as mammals are thought to be more complex than bacteria. Coupled with this idea of increase in structural complexity is the theory that the information content of modern organisms is greater than for past forms. Evolution is, on this theory, a process of accumulation of information about the environment in the complex structure of organisms. Finally, the supposed accumulation of information is thought to be a reversal of the second law of thermodynamics, which prescribes an increase of entropy with time and thus an increase in the randomness of the universe. Evolutionists sometimes talk of the accumulation of "negentropy" in organic evolution, marking off life from the inorganic cosmos.

This view of organic evolution, which is supposed to apply not only to the structure of organisms but to the interrelations between organisms in the total biosphere, suffers from a number of serious difficulties. First, it would be difficult to show exactly in what sense mammals are more complex than bacteria. There is no doubt that there are many more kinds of tissues in mammals, but bacteria are capable of carrying out many synthetic reactions not possible for mammals. At the level of cell physiology and metabolism, bacteria—bringing a greater synthetic repertory—must be regarded as more complex. Moreover, even if we assume that modern organisms are more complex structurally than those of the Cambrian, no criterion of complexity can distinguish between mammals and bony fish, although there are 270 million years between the first appearance of each. Second, the relation between structural complexity and information about the environment is not perfectly clear. No one knows exactly how to measure the information contained in any organism. It might be done, as in the Shannon–Wiener solution, by regarding the genes as a code made up of three-letter words with a four-letter alphabet, corresponding to what is known about the molecular basis of heredity. If this is done, however, many invertebrates turn out to have more information than many vertebrates, and among bacteria there is a very great variation. The real difficulty is that the equation between complexity and information has been chiefly a metaphorical rather than an exact one.

Finally, the equation of information and complexity with a thermodynamic measure of entropy is based on a misunderstanding of the kinetic theory of gases. The second law of thermodynamics, in the early nineteenth century, represented the beginning of modern evolutionary cosmology. The term "entropy," used for a property of the universe that always increases, has the same meaning, etymologically, as "evolution." Originally, the increase in entropy only signified that different parts of a physical system became more and more alike in their energy content, so that less and less useful work could be obtained from an interaction between them. The kinetic theory of gases provided a picture of molecules moving and colliding, and thus explained the gross observation of heat and work. This, in turn, led to a new interpretation of the second law as guaranteeing that a collection of molecules in any region of space would eventually have the same distribution of kinetic energies as in any other region. Two confusions have arisen about the kinetic theory of gases that have had an important effect on evolutionary thinking. First, it is supposed that individual molecules will all have the same kinetic energy rather than that assemblages of molecules will have the same *statistical distribution* of energies. Second, there is a confusion of kinetic energy of molecules with general kinetic and potential energies, especially gravitational and electromagnetic potential. These two confusions give rise to an erroneously derived generalized second law stating that all the molecules in the universe will eventually be equally spaced out from each other. Given such a formless and orderless end, the evolution of life does indeed seem to go in the opposite direction.

The tendency to turn the second law of thermodynamics into a generalized evolutionary world view (with life as an exceptional countercurrent) has been further encouraged by confusion of thermodynamics with yet another evolutionary cosmology, the "expanding universe." According to this cosmogony, the material universe came into being on the order of 10 thousand million years ago in a small region of space, the matter exploded outward, and the material cosmos will continue to expand forever from this original point in space. A consequence of a fixed amount of matter occupying a larger and larger volume is that matter is becoming more thinly spread globally but not necessarily locally. The theory of the expanding universe does not demand, for example, that the earth break up and its pieces spread apart.

In its own way the theory of the expanding universe is another example of the search for directionality in evolutionary systems. More recently, Bondi, Gold, Hoyle, and others have given currency to nondirectional theories of the cosmos. One is a steady-state theory that allows for expansion but holds density everywhere in dynamic equilibrium by continual creation of new matter. The other is an oscillation theory, which postulates a cyclic expansion and contraction of the material cosmos.

Homeostasis, introduced by Cannon as a principle of physiology and evolution, is related to complexity. Homeostasis is the property of a system to hold constant certain of its elements despite external disturbing forces. What is held constant are those qualities of the system that are necessary for its maintenance, such as body temperature in a mammal or ionic strength of the blood. This property of homeostasis is then extended by evolutionists to include communities of organisms occupying different but coordinated positions in the natural economy. Thus, the relation between numbers and efficiency of carnivores that prey on herbivores and herbivores that crop the grass is thought to be stabilized by the process of evolution, so that fluctuation in the abundance of any of these organisms is compensated by changes in the others. The result is a stable community structure. The notion of *stability* is appealing to modern evolutionists, who see evolution as self-fulfilling, as a stabilization of life in a capricious universe. For the nineteenth century it was quite another matter. Is Nature

> "So careful of the type?" But no.
> From scarped cliff and quarried stone
> She cries, "A thousand types are gone:
> I care for nothing, all shall go."
> Tennyson, *In Memoriam*, Part 56, Stanza 1

Perhaps the only evolutionist doctrine that contains no important element of direction is evolutionary geology, which is entirely a cyclic theory. Mountain-building revolutions are followed by erosion, the formation of featureless peneplains, the deposition of sediments in the seas, followed by new uplift and new mountain-building. Of course, it is supposed that the final cooling of the earth's core will at last put an end to the cycle, but this cooling is the only vestige of directionality that is apparent. Geology remains, among the historical sciences, obdurately materialistic and positivist.

Progress. It is not always easy to differentiate evolutionist doctrines of simple direction from those with an element of progress. I distinguish them by the moral or, better, moralistic tone of progressivism, but moralism is sometimes well hidden. For example, the doctrine that homeostasis gives direction to evolution is sometimes arrived at because man is assumed a priori to be the measure of evolution, and it is fairly easy to make the case that man, the rational mammal, is most homeostatic. "L'Homme, seul paramètre absolu de l'Évolution" is even more anthropocentric than it seems at first sight, for Teilhard de Chardin (1956) is referring not simply to the history of life but *cosmic* evolution! But this is simply Whitehead brought up to date, Whitehead who, in *Modes of Thought*, divides occurrences in nature into six types: "The first type is human existence, body and mind. The second type includes all sorts of animal life, insects, the vertebrates, and other genera. . . . The third type includes all vegetable life. . . . The sixth type is composed of the happenings on an infinitesimal scale, disclosed by the minute analysis of modern physics" (1938, p. 214). Man leads all the rest. The shibboleths of progressivism are the superiority of man in the cosmos, industrial man in the world economy, and liberal democratic man in world society.

Spencer makes extensive use of the term "progress," but in a way that seems not to have a normative or moralistic overtone: "From the earliest traceable cosmical changes down to the latest results of civilization, we shall find that the transformation of the homogeneous into the heterogeneous is that in which progress essentially consists" ([1857] 1915, p. 10). In "Progress: Its Law and Cause," Spencer shows that this transformation has occurred in music, poetry, society, government, manufacturing, commerce, language, and so on. He cautions against normative definition of progress. "Leaving out of sight concomitants and beneficial consequences, let us ask what progress is in itself" (*ibid.*, p. 9). But this is a very curious question to ask, what progress is *in itself*, for does not progress, as opposed to simple change, imply a moral direction? What Spencer has done is to equate progress with change, to say that change, whatever its direction may turn out to be, is progressive by its very nature. We come again to that nineteenth-century belief that change is good, in Spencer's words, "a beneficient necessity."

Most modern students of natural evolution, both organic and social, have taken a step toward materialism in omitting the idea of progress from their systems. An exception is B. Rensch (1947), who distinguishes higher and lower forms of life and devotes a special category of evolutionary change, *anagenesis*, to evolution of higher from lower. While he includes under this rubric increases in stability, homeostasis, and complexity that are discussed here simply as directional rather than progressive, Rensch clearly regards man and especially human freedom as the highest and best product of evolution.

Perfectibility. With the exception of the philosopher Teilhard, modern evolutionism does not contain a utopian element. On the contrary, evolution is generally envisaged as an endless process with no particular perfect end or goal. There is some logical difficulty, however, in maintaining that evolution leads to greater homeostasis, greater cerebralization, greater adaptation, while ignoring the possibility of perfect homeostasis, complete cerebralization, or absolute adaptation. It is not at all obvious how homeostasis of individuals or communities can continue to increase forever. Nevertheless, this issue is generally ignored or, as in the case of Spencer, deliberately set aside. The single

important exception is in evolutionary economics, especially various utopian socialisms. Marxism, especially as interpreted by Lenin and Trotsky, is a straightforward progressivist, perfectionist evolutionary theory. A stage of primitive capitalist accumulation through exploitation of the workers and colonies enriches the society. This is accompanied by the bourgeois revolution that leads to liberal bourgeois democracy. In turn comes the proletarian revolution, proletarian democracy, a breakdown of national interests in the face of class interests, and a final total leveling of the class structure. In this utopian scheme there will still be division of labor, but the "entropy" of the social order will be at a maximum. The parallel is with thermodynamic evolution, which is also a leveling theory and is in contrast with those views of organic evolution that depend upon an increase in differentiation, complexity, storage of information, and a decrease in entropy.

Evolution and history

There are close parallels between the methods and statements of evolutionist doctrines in the natural sciences and the methods and statements of historiography. Geology, cosmology, and organic evolution are historical sciences in that they are descriptions of, and attempts to explain, past events in the light of present occurrences. The problems of making laws or lawlike statements about the past and prediction of the future are the same whether the focus of interest is human history or the history of all organic life. Karl Popper, in *The Poverty of Historicism* (1957), asks the question, "Can there be a *law* of evolution?" and answers, " 'No,' the search for the law of the 'unvarying order' in evolution cannot possibly fall within the scope of scientific method, whether in biology or in sociology. . . . The evolution of life on earth, or of human society, is a unique historical process" (pp. 107, 108).

The chief difficulty of the historical sciences is that they fail to meet what is widely accepted as the norm for a science, Popper's criterion of falsifiability. For Popper, scientific laws are universal statements ("All swans are black, all planets move in ellipses," etc.) and therefore are really prohibitions ("A white swan cannot be found, no planet moves in a circle," etc.). Such prohibitions provide a program for testability, for if one wishes to test the universal law about swans, he does not look for black ones but white ones. If a white swan is found, the law is disproved. A white swan is a *potential* falsifier of the law, and any statement that has no potential falsifier (any existentially quantified statement falls in this category) is *metaphysical* and ought to be excluded from a science.

The trouble with historical sciences like organic evolution is that they are almost entirely made up of existential rather than universal statements. We may take modern Darwinism as an example. It asserts that the organisms now living have evolved from ancestral organisms of a different nature and offers the fossil record as direct evidence. Moreover, it asserts that the mechanism of this change is embodied in three principles: (1) different individuals in a species have different morphologies, physiologies, behaviors, that is, there is variation; (2) there is a correlation between the form of the parents and the offspring, that is, the variation is heritable; and (3) different variants have different rates of survival and reproduction in different environments.

Let us now examine these assertions in the light of Popper's criterion. The evidence that evolution has in fact occurred is contained in the succession of fossils found in different geological strata. From the fossil record we can state with confidence that there are many kinds of animals and plants that, having once existed, no longer exist. But that statement of itself, far from being a universal statement, is an existential one; in fact it is a historical statement, exactly corresponding to the assertion that Napoleon once lived or that Martin Luther died on February 18, 1546, at Eisleben.

Can we push this observation further and say that *all* animals and plants in the fossil record are of a kind no longer represented? No, because that does not happen to be true. But can we at least make the much more interesting and important hypothesis that all kinds of animals and plants eventually will be supplanted by other forms? This also is not falsifiable and is really identical to the assertion that every man has his price. It says, in fact, that every species is mortal, that there exists a time in the future at which any given species will no longer exist. If statements about the universality of evolution are historicist rather than scientific, it still might be that the principles underlying the mechanism of evolution are falsifiable in explaining any particular case of evolution. But that is clearly not the case. The statement of natural selection is that there exists an environment—a combination of temperature, humidity, food, soil, competition of other forms—in which different variants will have different relative reproductive rates. But applied to the past or the future, such a statement has such vast explanatory and predictive power that it is empirically empty. To say that the dinosaurs became extinct because *some* change in environment caused their rate of reproduction to be lowered below the replacement point, or to say that certain amphibia gave rise to reptiles because some environment existed which favored heritable variation in that direction, is, by Popper's criterion, to say nothing.

An example of this difficulty is the argument of the selectionist in explaining the observed differences among populations of present-day organisms. Why are the frequencies of blood types different in different human races? The selectionist says these have arisen by natural selection, and even if no differential survival can presently be discovered (as none can), things used to be different and, at one time, the different races lived in such different environments that they were differentially selected. Such an argument bears more than a little similarity to the claim of Hegel that one cannot act on principles deduced from history, because "each period is involved in such peculiar circumstances, exhibits a condition of things so strictly idiosyncratic, that its conduct must be regulated by considerations connected with itself, and itself alone."

Both historical explanation and evolutionary sciences can be concerned only with offering *sufficient* explanations for past events and with prescribing *possible* future events on the basis of the observation of present processes.

Evolutionism—social and economic matrix

While there is no doubt that the publication of Darwin's *On the Origin of Species* (1859) led to an almost immediate explosion of evolutionary thought, it was only the percussion cap for a charge already set. Because a theory of organic evolution touched upon man's origin and presented a materialistic challenge to his preordained primacy in the universe, it was bound to excite great interest. Nevertheless, the *Origin of Species* appeared in the middle of a period of rampant evolutionism and radical political and social change. It served as the issue over which the battle between stasis and change could be fought, a battle for the final supremacy of a world view that had been making steady gains since the beginning of the eighteenth century.

Darwin was the inheritor, not the creator, of the general preoccupation with evolutionism. This is made clear by Spencer in his *Principles of Biology* (1864–1867), when he argues that one of the chief evidences for organic evolution is that, after all, everything else evolves.

It is now universally admitted by philologists, that languages, instead of being artificially or supernaturally formed, have been developed. And the histories of religion, of philosophy, of science, of the fine arts, of the industrial arts show that these have passed through stages. . . . If, then, the recognition of evolution as the law of many diverse orders of phenomena, has been spreading, may we not say that there thence arises the probability that evolution will be recognized as the law of the phenomena we are considering? ([1857] 1915, pp. 432–433)

The theory of organic evolution will be in its proper historical perspective if it is remembered that evolutionary cosmology had been founded in Kant's *Metaphysical Foundations of Natural Science* of 1786 and in Laplace's nebular hypothesis of 1796. At about the same time, Hutton was forming modern geology by his rejection of the catastrophic theories of the origin of geological formations and his introduction of the principle of uniformitarianism. Although the term "entropy" was not introduced until 1865 by Clausius, the second law of thermodynamics was formulated by Sadi Carnot thirty years earlier. By the time of the publication of the *Origin of Species*, the physical sciences were already thoroughly evolutionist in outlook. Moreover, the fact of the evolution of living forms, although not a mechanism for that evolution, was accepted widely in scientific and literary circles. Darwin's grandfather, Erasmus Darwin, in the *Temple of Nature* (1803, p. 3) invokes the Muse to say "How rose from elemental strife, organic forms, and kindled into life." And his Muse reports that even "imperious man, who rules the bestial crowd, . . . arose from rudiments of form and sense" (p. 28). Less romantic students of natural history like Buffon and especially Lamarck, had, by the beginning of the nineteenth century, fully developed theories of the transformation of species. Even Diderot in 1769 in *Le rêve de d'Alembert* asks: "Qui scait les races d'animaux qui nous ont precedes? Qui scait les races d'animaux qui succederont aux notres? *Tout change, tout passe, il n'y a que le tout qui reste*" ([1830] 1951, p. 56, my italics). Seventy years later we hear the echo in Tennyson: "The old order changeth, yielding place to new" ("Morte d'Arthur," l. 408).

It is often thought obvious that scientific discovery influences the direction of social and economic change, or at least its rate. But what must be even more true is that social and economic world views must permeate science. No appeal to a *Zeitgeist* is implied by such a relationship, for the meaning of *Zeitgeist* is that science and other social activities respond equally to some spirit of the age whose source and power are unknown. To appeal to *Zeitgeist* is to reject any legitimate theory of historical causation. On the other hand, there is nothing mystical about the way in which notions of cause and effect, choice and chance, determinacy and freedom, spread from one science to another. Equally, it is entirely within the normal picture of historical causation that general social attitudes and economic relationships between social classes should have a profound effect upon the acceptability and apparent reasonableness of scientific hypotheses. Science is, after all, a social activity.

Prior to the eighteenth century, European social systems were characterized by a determinist world view. A man was born to his estate and occupied it by divine providence. Fixity and static stability were the mark of society, and radical changes in position could occur only as *exceptional* withdrawals or extensions of divine grace. Although Charles I was king of England *Dei gratia*, he could be deposed because, as Cromwell said, divine grace had been removed from him. The fact of his severed head was sufficient proof of that. Occasionally a man might rise from low estate to be the counselor of kings, but again only an extraordinary grace made this possible. Species were fixed as was the position of the earth in the universe. Galileo's heresy was not that the earth was not at the center of the cosmos but that *it moved*. Men reason by analogy from the condition of their lives to the condition of the universe, and a static society could hardly believe in a dynamic cosmos.

In the eighteenth century a change became felt in the condition of society as the influence of the industrial revolution spread. Social mobility became more common, and classes of parvenus acquired political and social power.

"And it is a remarkable example of the confusion into which the present age has fallen" . . . says Sir Leicester, . . . "that Mrs. Rouncewell's son has been invited to go into Parliament."
Miss Volumnia utters a little sharp scream. . . .
"Good gracious, what is the man?"
"He is called, I believe—an—Ironmaster."
Charles Dickens, *Bleak House*, 1853

The phase of bourgeois revolution had begun and from it developed bourgeois revolutionary science. As change became the rule and characteristic of society, catastrophism lost ground in natural science, and a uniformitarian principle of change took its place. It is surely no coincidence that Josiah Wedgwood, who began as a potter's apprentice and ended as one of the great eighteenth-century magnates, was Charles Darwin's maternal grandfather.

Darwin's paternal grandfather, Erasmus, belonged to the circle of new Midland industralists: James Watt, James Keir, Matthew Boulton, and, of course, Wedgwood. Although from the middle class, Erasmus was a self-made man and his son, Robert (Charles's father), emulated him by accepting 40 pounds of his father's money and building it into a respectable fortune with no further aid.

The bourgeois revolution not only established change as the characteristic element of the cosmos but added direction and progress as well. A world in which a man could rise from humble origins must have seemed, to him at least, a good world. Change per se was a moral quality. In this light, Spencer's assertion that change *is* progress is not surprising. Moreover, for those still rising or hopeful of improvement, there is a vested interest in the perpetuity of change, in a uniformitarian principle of replacement of the old by the new.

The bourgeois revolution reached its peak in England in the Reform Bill of 1832 based on Bentham's principle of the "greatest happiness for the greatest number," while on the Continent it took the more violent form of the revolutions of 1848. By the time Darwin published the *Origin of Species*, the ascent of the middle classes was complete and the supremacy of change and progress established in all the natural sciences except biology. The furor against Darwinism was only the last hopeless struggle of an already fatally wounded adversary. It is, of course, true that the principle of natural selection, converted by Spencer to the "survival of the fittest," was used in the last half of the nineteenth century as a justification for laissez-faire practices. But it was only the borrowing of a metaphor to further justify a system already in full operation. It would be quite wrong to propose that Darwinism was an effective agent promoting unlimited economic competition.

Like all revolutions the bourgeois revolution gave way slowly to a period of consolidation, a period in which we still find ourselves. Once the new classes had gained power, it was clearly to their advantage to prevent the revolution from going further. The static hereditary society could hardly be reconstituted, but in its place a system of dynamic stability was erected. Change and social mobility are still accepted as characteristic of society, but it is a running-in-place rather than an overturn of the existing order. Liberal democracy of the twentieth century has a vested interest in maintaining the world social order but allowing individuals, on the basis of relative competitive ability, to find their own place in the social structure.

It is not remarkable, then, that evolutionary theories of the twentieth century are marked by a concern for equilibrium condition and dynamic stability, a playing down of progressivist and perfectionist elements, and a general reliance on the principle that *plus ça change, plus c'est la même chose*. In cosmogony there has been the rise of the steady-state theory of perpetual creation and also of the cyclic expansion–contraction model. Both are characterized by constant movement and change, but neither allows that the universe is going anywhere in particular. In thermodynamics and statistical mechanics there has been emphasis on the local rather than global nature of the law of increase of entropy. It is now admitted that entropy may decrease in other parts of the universe or at other times and that a global statement of the second law of thermodynamics may be too strong. In the realm of organic evolution, progressivism has been entirely abandoned except for a few metaphysical writers. The direction in which evolution is supposed to lead, when a direction is admitted, is that of greater complexity and greater integration leading to greater *stability*. Modern students of evolution are preoccupied with dynamic stability and equilibrium in a global sense. The technical literature of evolutionary genetics is filled with reference to and studies of stable equilibria. This preoccupation would have seemed strange to the evolutionists of the nineteenth century, who saw, reflected in the process of organic evolution, the tendency toward a better world. The evolutionist of the twentieth century presumably sees, in his view of evolution, "the best of all possible worlds."

R. C. Lewontin

BIBLIOGRAPHY

Bergson, Henri (1907) 1944 *Creative Evolution*. New York: Modern Library. → First published in French.

Darwin, Charles (1859) 1964 *On the Origin of Species*. Cambridge, Mass.: Harvard Univ. Press.

Darwin, Erasmus 1803 *Temple of Nature: Or, the Origin of Society; a Poem With Philosophical Notes*. London: Johnson.

Diderot, Denis (1830) 1951 *Le rêve de d'Alembert, Entretien entre d'Alembert et Diderot, et suite de l'entretien*. Edited by Paul Vernière. Paris: Didier. → Written in 1769, but first published in 1830.

Dobzhansky, Theodosius G. (1937) 1951 *Genetics and the Origin of Species*. 3d ed., rev. New York: Columbia Univ. Press.

Mayr, Ernst 1963 *Animal Species and Evolution*. Cambridge, Mass.: Belknap Press.

Popper, Karl R. 1957 *The Poverty of Historicism*. Boston: Beacon. → A paperback edition was published in 1964 by Harper.

Rensch, Bernhard (1947) 1960 *Evolution Above the Species Level*. New York: Columbia Univ. Press. → First published as *Neuere Probleme der Abstammungslehre: Die transspezifische Evolution*.

SPENCER, HERBERT (1857) 1915 Progress: Its Law and Cause. Volume 1, pages 8–62 in Herbert Spencer, *Essays: Scientific, Political, and Speculative.* New York: Appleton. → First published in the *Westminster Review.*

SPENCER, HERBERT (1864–1867) 1914 *The Principles of Biology.* 2 vols. New York: Appleton.

TEILHARD DE CHARDIN, PIERRE (1956) 1963 *La place de l'homme dans la nature: Le groupe zoologique humain.* Paris: Éditions du Seuil. → First published as *Le groupe zoologique humain: Structure et directions évolutives.*

WHITEHEAD, ALFRED NORTH (1925) 1960 *Science and the Modern World.* New York: Macmillan.

WHITEHEAD, ALFRED NORTH 1934 *Nature and Life.* Univ. of Chicago Press.

WHITEHEAD, ALFRED NORTH 1938 *Modes of Thought.* New York: Macmillan. → Lectures delivered between 1934 and 1938. A paperback edition was published in 1958 by Capricorn.

II
PRIMATE EVOLUTION

When Darwin published the *Origin of Species* in 1859, only a handful of fossil primates had been found and recognized as such. But during the last three decades of the nineteenth century a considerable series of fossil primates of Tertiary age were recovered in Europe and the Americas. The earliest scholarly attempts to analyze the course of primate evolution from the evidence of these fossils were made by Schlosser in Munich (1887), by Osborn in New York (1902), and by Wortman at Yale (1903–1904). Among the earliest monographic studies of early Tertiary primates were those of William K. Gregory of the American Museum of Natural History, who best summarized his views on primate evolution in a detailed review of the North American lemurlike primate *Notharctus* (1920). Only a little earlier Stehlin (1912–1916) at Basel had published a complementary review of European Eocene prosimians.

Inadequacies of material and methods. There have been several factors holding back full analysis of the course of primate evolution. A major problem results from their presumed early emergence in the tropical forests of the equatorial zones. Because Tertiary vertebrate fossils from these regions are poorly known, the early history of primates remains relatively obscure. Primates of the past, like those of today, were apparently restricted to relatively warm climates, often to tropical forests, and prosimian remains dating after warm, early Tertiary times are not generally found in the northern continents. Exploration for sites in the tropics where Tertiary land vertebrate fossils do occur is being actively carried out today, and it is from these paleontologically little-known regions that most important future additions to knowledge of primate evolution may be expected.

Most of the primate fossils from the early Tertiary (Paleocene and Eocene epochs) consequently are not found in the equatorial regions, where presumably the mainstream of primate evolution has always been located. Therefore, reconstruction of primate history must, at present, be extrapolated in part from fossil evidence from marginal areas. This gap in knowledge of ancient tropical faunas is somewhat lessened because we know that many extinct primates were wide-ranging species and that the higher Old World primates, particularly apes and pre-men, never diversified into a host of separate lineages, as did some groups of mammals, such as bats and rodents.

Thus, differentiation of the main groups and their interrelationships can be reasonably well understood, even from the occasional sampling typical of our imperfect paleontological finds. This is particularly true for the late Tertiary relatives and ancestors of man. However, two theories, originating outside the realm of paleontological evidence, appear to have been responsible for creating a contrary impression. Although the outlook is seldom specifically articulated, some students seem to believe that in order to produce the brain capacities of modern man there must have been many competing early hominid species. With this goes the assumption that the mental capacities of apes and those presumed for pre-men would have made them near masters of their environment and, therefore, so successful that many species would have arisen. These views, together with an overeagerness to create new species and genera, led some early anthropologists and a few modern students to the false conclusion that a great diversity of fossil apes and prehuman species once existed. A confusing welter of ill-founded names exists in the literature on such extinct primates. Those applied to Tertiary apes and hominids have recently been revised by Simons and Pilbeam (1965). Although over a thousand individual specimens of extinct great apes (pongids) and early hominids are now known from European, Asian, and African Miocene–Pleistocene deposits, only a few genera, *Pliopithecus, Oreopithecus, Dryopithecus, Ramapithecus,* and *Gigantopithecus,* can be shown to be distinct and valid. Thus, the main types of close fossil relatives and forerunners of man (Hominoidea) that can convincingly be demonstrated to have existed in the past are about the same in number as the genera of this group that exist today—*Hylobates* (gibbon), *Symphalangus* (siamang), *Pan* (chimpanzee), *Pongo* (orangutan), *Gorilla* (gorilla), *Homo* (man).

As a consequence of the foregoing problems of approach, the study of primate evolution has been hampered. First, the early history of primates is obscured by inadequate knowledge of equatorial vertebrate faunas; and second, understanding of the later history of the particular group that included man's ancestors has been confounded by the tendency to proliferate invalid genera and species.

Origin of primates

Undoubted primates first appear in the fossil record in North American deposits of early Paleocene age, which are more than sixty million years old. By middle Paleocene, the order had already diversified into three or four different main groups, or families. This would suggest that the initial separation of the order from primitive, insectivore-like stock was considerably earlier, perhaps in the late Cretaceous. Indeed, a species possibly primate, but based only on one tooth, has been reported from late Cretaceous beds in Montana.

The best-known primates of Paleocene times appear to represent specialized side branches, which did not long survive the beginning of the Eocene epoch. Although not directly ancestral, these early species do indicate the starting point of the basic primate arboreal adaptation and give evidence of the gradual transition from nonprimate to primate. It may be that some of the less completely known American Paleocene primates, such as *Palaechthon* and *Plesiolestes,* will eventually prove to be near the ancestry of one or more of the primate families of initial early Eocene appearance.

Origin of major surviving groups

Lemurs. At the beginning of the Eocene, prosimians of lemurlike and tarsierlike aspect appear, nearly simultaneously, in the vertebrate assemblages of Europe and North America but are as yet unknown elsewhere. Three major sorts of primates can be characterized.

The most generalized of these early Eocene prosimians are the loosely defined Adapidae, including such well-known forms as *Pelycodus,* and later *Notharctus* and *Smilodectes* in North America, and *Adapis* in Europe. Species of these genera, together with allied forms, apparently did not advance during the Eocene beyond the "lemuroid" condition represented today by the Malagasy lemurs, whom they resemble both in limb-bone structure and in the structure of the ear region of the skull. However, dental patterns in notharctines and adapines do not show trends evolving toward those of modern lemurs; this appears to indicate

that known Eocene species of Adapidae were not directly ancestral to the living varieties of lemurs. On the other hand, the family Adapidae—now rather broadly defined—could well represent the family from which modern lemurs and possibly the lorises differentiated (Simons 1962*a*).

How and when the true lemurs reached their present limited range of distribution in the island of Madagascar is a most intriguing and nearly insoluble problem on the basis of present evidence. If their introduction to this island was by way of the African continent, it might be expected that some evidence of true lemurs would by now have been recovered from the Egyptian Oligocene or east African Miocene deposits, both of which contain warm-climate forest faunas. Although small, evidently arboreal primates have been found in some abundance in these deposits in Egypt and east Africa, none show any significant similarities to the Malagasy lemurs. On the other hand, similarities between lorises and two European late-Eocene primates, *Pronycticebus* and *Anchomomys,* at present classified as Adapinae, suggest that the introduction of this group into Africa could have been by way of Europe.

Tarsiers. Enough is now known of the craniology and dentition of the so-called "tarsioid" primates to demonstrate the falsehood of the extravagant opinion of Wood-Jones that Hominidae are to be derived directly from *Tarsius*-like forms through an ancestral line not shared by the Old World apes and monkeys. What is perhaps more significant is that the Eocene tarsioids so far discovered could not have given rise to the common stem of monkeys, apes, or men either, for they possess noncatarrhine specializations, and all had apparently lost one pair of lower incisors. All surviving members of Anthropoidea have retained these teeth. Nevertheless, these early tarsioids are of great interest because they presumably represent the general level of organization the unknown forerunners of the living higher primates must have reached as far back as the beginning of the Eocene epoch.

The first Anthropoidea. Another major group of primates appeared in the early Eocene, in Europe, Asia, and North America, and is, with one or two exceptions, restricted in temporal range to this epoch. (Gazin 1958 has reviewed the distribution of middle-Eocene members of this family, together with other contemporary North American primates.) Collectively, members of Omomyidae show greater resemblances to Anthropoidea than do other early prosimians. They could well represent the taxon from which all true Anthropoidea differentiated, a probability that is also sound zoogeographically, in view of their Holarctic distribution. Certainty on this point must wait, however, until better knowledge of cranial and postcranial anatomy is available for members of this family. Partial evidence, derived mainly from remains of a species of the North American middle-Eocene omomyid genus *Hemiacodon gracilis*, shows that this species cannot be regarded as "tarsioid" postcranially (Simpson 1940). This observation, in turn, implies that Anthropoidea in its earliest differentiation may not have passed through a definably tarsioid grade of organization. Rather, the anatomy of both Eocene *Necrolemur* and Holocene *Tarsius* clearly indicates that so-called "tarsioids" and the Anthropoidea probably originated in the same segment of early Prosimii. Although serious gaps in the geologic record of primates prevent any very definite attachment of early Tertiary species successions to those of the later Cenozoic, it is likely that some known Paleocene and Eocene types, at least at the generic level, do pertain to the ancestry of living forms. Because climates were much more equable throughout the early Tertiary, with regions as far north as Montana and England supporting a subtropical flora, we can suppose that many of these Paleocene–Eocene genera contained species having a broad north–south range of distribution. Some of the species we now know from northern areas must have had very close allies in the unknown southern faunas. An example of this sort of distribution is provided by one of the large Eocene herbivores. Skulls and jaws of species of the Wasatch pantodont genus *Coryphodon* found in the Big Bend region of Texas, near the Mexican border, cannot be distinguished from remains of this animal found in northern Wyoming. This represents a north–south separation of about one thousand miles; if paleontological information on Wasatch faunas were available from Canada to Guatemala, this distribution could probably be extended even farther. Nevertheless, as with most attempts to trace phyletic lineages in given groups of fossils, the need to discover a great many more connecting links remains, and the search in the more nearly equatorial regions for early Cenozoic faunas containing primates is one of our major objectives.

For the Oligocene two sets of primate data from equatorial regions have become available through recent research projects.

The first of these projects has provided new evidence on the question of differentiation of cercopithecoid monkeys and hominoids. Discoveries made in Oligocene deposits in Egypt between 1961 and 1966 by Yale expeditions under the writer's direction have added new data on the nature of the initial appearance of these two superfamilies. A jaw fragment of a new small primate, *Oligopithecus savagei* (Simons 1962b), shows the typical lower dental formula of Miocene–Holocene Old World Anthropoidea, in combination with what are the most primitively constituted lower molars known in this suborder. Premolar heteromorphy and slightly bilophodont molars, plus certain other characters, suggest relationships, on the one hand, to Eocene Omomyidae, and on the other, to Miocene–Holocene cercopithecoids. Further finds of this small mammal could strengthen the possibility, which now rests almost entirely on the evidence of this single fragmentary jaw, that cercopithecoids arose from Old World omomyids. Miocene monkeys are known from deposits in Egypt and east Africa. The early history of Old World monkeys remains very poorly understood, and much of the known earliest material has not been described.

The emergence of Hominoidea

To date no significant information whatever on upper tooth structure of earliest (Eocene–Oligocene) African or Eurasian Anthropoidea has been published. This has been a serious gap in our knowledge because upper premolars and molars, being somewhat more complex than lower-cheek teeth, allow for more accurate appraisal of taxonomic affinity. Restudy of the previously poorly known upper molars of *Pondaungia cotteri* from the late Eocene of Burma, together with discovery by the recent Yale expeditions of several partial upper dentitions of *Apidium* and of isolated upper teeth of *Aegyptopithecus* and *Parapithecus*, has greatly added to the data available for consideration of the prosimian sources of the higher primates of the Eastern Hemisphere. Briefly, the dental evidence of these three early species bears on the crucial point of emergence of Hominoidea from Prosimii: the upper molars of *Apidium* and *Pondaungia* show the three primary cusps of the trigon unconnected by ridges. The hypocone is large, and a pitted lingual cingulum is usually present. In both these genera several small accessory cusps occur in the trigon between the three main cusps. In their over-all upper molar morphology, species of these two genera equally resemble prosimians and higher primates. Cheek teeth of *Apidium*, particularly, also show similarities to those of *Oreopithecus*. This may be due to retention of a comparatively primitive molar cusp pattern in the otherwise advanced latter hominoid. Upper molars of *Propliopithecus*, on the other hand, show the typical pattern characteristic of much later apes, near men, and men. However, the cingulum on the inner side of the upper molars is large, which strengthens the view that this is a primitive character of ape dentitions.

Pondaungia cotteri was described by Pilgrim (1927). This specimen was recovered from the Pondaung sandstone of Burma together with a small mammal fauna, which indicates a late Eocene age for this as well as for another primate, *Amphipithecus*. Comparisons based primarily on the anthracotheres of the Pondaung sandstone and those of the Fayum early Oligocene of Egypt suggest that the Burmese fossils may be earlier, but the question is by no means definitely settled. At present it seems best to regard *Amphipithecus* and *Pondaungia* as of late Eocene age, and since both appear to be hominoids, this indicates the upper limit of differentiation for this major group of primates. As Colbert (1937) has already pointed out for *Amphipithecus*, both appear to show close ties with Pongidae. Tentative assignment of *Amphipithecus* and *Pondaungia* to this family does not seem questionable on grounds of their antiquity, inasmuch as a considerable number of presently existing mammalian families have now been traced back to the late Eocene.

Pilgrim's illustrations and comments on *Pondaungia* left much to be desired, and in fact, on the basis of the information he provided, it was hardly possible to accept the species as belonging to the primates. As he mentioned, part of the source of his weak case lay in the fact that a web-like erosion of the enamel of the lower teeth in the type of *Pondaungia* had obscured their crown patterns. He supposed this to be also the case with the upper molars. Microscopic examination of this material indicates that, while the lower molars do appear to have suffered some erosive damage, the crenulations on the upper teeth represent the natural surface except in one or two broken areas. This sort of crenulation is not unusual among primates, being of frequent occurrence in Eocene Omomyidae and in Miocene–Holocene apes. In conclusion, these features of the upper molars, together with some distinguishable details of the lower teeth and mandibles, suggest an assignment to the Pongidae. Indeed *Pondaungia* may not be far from the direct ancestry of such forms as *Propliopithecus* and its less well-known allies from the Oligocene of Egypt. A less likely possibility is that *Pondaungia* is an advanced omomyid primate with teeth paralleling those of early pongids.

All finds of primates from the Old World Oligocene are distributed throughout some six or seven hundred feet of mainly continental sediments of the Qatrani formation, Fayum province, Egypt—generally regarded as being of early Oligocene age. The classic finds of *Parapithecus*, *Propliopithecus*, and *Moeripithecus* are from the lower part of this series, in the "Fossil Wood Zone," while the type of *Apidium* came from about five hundred feet higher. The new species of *Apidium* and one of *Propliopithecus* have been found stratigraphically between the two earlier known levels. There are then three primate-yielding levels, of unknown age separation. Enough time had elapsed between their successive depositions, however, to bring about evolutionary changes among the respective primate lineages represented. In December 1963 the Yale expedition recovered from the upper Fayum deposits two new genera and species of primates. One of these, *Aegyptopithecus*, appears to be a good candidate for the ancestry of *Dryopithecus*, of Miocene–Pliocene age, and was possibly a forerunner of all subsequent apes. The second new find, *Aeolopithecus*, resembles gibbons, living and fossil.

Turning to a consideration of primates of the Miocene epoch, which began perhaps about 25 million years ago, there is more abundant information. From South American deposits, located mainly in Argentina and Colombia, a series of monkey species is known. These have most recently been discussed by Stirton (1951). At least partial skulls and jaws are known for species of three genera, *Homunculus*, *Dolicocebus*, and *Cebupithecia*. These materials show that by Miocene times South American monkeys were structured much as they are today, and therefore they do not provide much evidence as to the origins of this group. Old World monkeys of Miocene age are known only from sites in east Africa and Egypt. The east African Miocene monkey has not yet been named, but that from Egypt was given the rather unfortunate generic name of *Prohylobates* by Fourtau (Egypt 1918).

Broadly contemporary with these monkeys are species of the *Dryopithecus* group of apes (including subgenera *Sivapithecus* and *Proconsul*), which are apparently close to the ancestry of the living African apes. Also represented in Miocene faunas of Europe and Africa are species of *Pliopithecus*, an ancient relative of the present-day gibbons and siamangs of southeast Asia.

Toward the end of the Miocene epoch in Eurasia and Africa, perhaps about fourteen million years ago, species of *Dryopithecus* are contemporary with the oldest undoubtedly manlike primate, *Ramapithecus punjabicus*. Originally discovered in the Siwalik Hills of north India in beds of Miocene–Pliocene age, this species was named by Pilgrim in 1910, but he did not recognize that it belonged to a major new variety of primate and so considered it a species of *Dryopithecus*. Lewis (1934) defined the genus *Ramapithecus*, to which Pilgrim's species has subsequently proved to belong. Lewis initially pointed out that *Ramapithecus* has many manlike features in the upper tooth series. Thus, it can reasonably be placed in Hominidae, the taxonomic family of man (Simons 1963; 1964). To date, however, only parts of upper and lower jaws of this animal have been found. Apparently *Ramapithecus* was a successful and wide-ranging primate. Outside north India, teeth and jaws just like those of the *Ramapithecus punjabicus* have been found at Fort Ternan in Kenya, east Africa; in Yunnan, China; and just possibly in Europe.

Apart from the fact that facial displays and diet in *Ramapithecus* must have been more similar to that of true man than to that of the apes (in view of incisor, canine, and premolar reduction—relative to cheek teeth) little can be inferred about this earliest hominid. It cannot be called man or human, because there is no evidence that *R. punjabicus* manufactured tools. Moreover, nothing is known of its brain size and limb or body skeleton. After this we know little of fossil primates until the earlier Pleistocene.

The Pleistocene and hominid evolution

The Pleistocene was a time of rapid hominid evolution, during which toolmaking first appeared among the ancestors of modern man. In 1925 Dart described an infant skull that he named *Australopithecus africanus*. In spite of the name, which means "African southern ape," Dart recognized *Australopithecus* to be a hominid belonging to the same taxonomic family as modern man, *Homo sapiens*. Nevertheless, his views were not generally accepted until a large number of fossil men or near men of similar age and structural type were recovered by Dart, Broom, and Robinson in south Africa.

More recently, *Australopithecus* has apparently been identified in Java and in north and east African deposits. The proposed name *Homo habilis*, recently coined by Leakey and his associates (1964) on the basis of specimens from Olduvai Gorge in Tanganyika, covers mixed materials, some assignable to the prior south African species *Australopithecus africanus* and some to *Telanthropus capensis* and to *Homo erectus*. In the view of many students (Campbell 1964a), even the first two species are not distinguishable, both belonging to the same small and gracile variety of early man. In addition to the species *A. africanus*, there is

a large and more specialized early hominid form in east and south Africa, which should most correctly be called *Australopithecus robustus*. Both of these species appear to have been habitual bipeds; the postcranial skeletons are similar to that of *Homo sapiens* and little like those of apes. Their jaws and teeth, although relatively large, are strongly reminiscent of teeth of later and better-known fossil men. However, in both species, known brain size was apparently little more than a third that of the average present-day *Homo sapiens*. The small brain size initially caused many students to place *Australopithecus* close to or with the apes. This early and erroneous placement of *Australopithecus* has continued to affect balanced understanding of their relationship to living man. Several poorly known or juvenile *Australopithecus* specimens have been made the "types" of new taxa, said to be more advanced and more like *Homo sapiens*. Both *Telanthropus capensis* and *Homo habilis* fall in this category. As Campbell (1964b) demonstrates, they have not been shown to be different enough from each other or from members of *Australopithecus africanus* to warrant species identification.

Clarification of these taxonomic problems is crucial to discussion of the course of the mainstream of the early evolution of man and is one of the prime areas for future advance in this science. Definition and delineation of species populations is requisite to understanding of the ancestral lineage of modern man. Unfortunately, most anthropologists and anatomists who have been the namers of fossil men and near men were not adequately trained to define taxa in harmony with the concepts of modern systematics and population genetics. That these inadequacies are still leading to confusion in understanding of human evolution was confirmed in the technically incorrect diagnosis of *Homo habilis*. Such neglect of the new taxonomy and systematics has seriously affected understanding of primate and human history. In all discussion of earliest men and pre-men, mammalian taxonomy is an area that needs much more sober scientific attention than it has been given so far.

ELWYN L. SIMONS

BIBLIOGRAPHY

CAMPBELL, BERNARD G. 1964a Just Another "Man-ape"? *Discovery* 25, no. 6:37–38.

CAMPBELL, BERNARD G. 1964b Science and Human Evolution. *Nature* 203:448–451.

CLARK, WILFRID E. LEGROS (1955) 1964 *The Fossil Evidence for Human Evolution*. Rev. ed. Univ. of Chicago Press.

Clark, Wilfrid E. LeGros 1960 *The Antecedents of Man.* Chicago: Quadrangle Books.

Colbert, Edwin H. 1937 A New Primate From the Upper Eocene Pondaung Formation of Burma. *American Museum of Natural History Novitates* 951:1–18.

Egypt, Survey Department (1918) 1920 *Contribution à l'étude des vertébrés miocènes de l'Égypte,* by René Fourtau. Cairo: Government Press.

Gazin, C. Lewis 1958 *A Review of the Middle and Upper Eocene Primates of North America.* Smithsonian Miscellaneous Collections, Vol. 136. Washington: The Institution.

Gregory, William K. 1920 On the Structure and Relations of *Notharctus,* an American Eocene Primate. American Museum of Natural History, *Memoirs* New Series 3:49–243.

Gregory, William K. 1922 *The Origin and Evolution of the Human Dentition.* Baltimore: Williams & Wilkins.

Leakey, L. S. B.; Tobias, P. V.; and Napier, J. R. 1964 A New Species of the Genus *Homo* From Olduvai Gorge. *Nature* 202:7–9.

Lewis, G. Edward 1934 Preliminary Notice of New Man-like Apes From India. *American Journal of Science* Fifth Series 227:161–179.

Osborn, Henry F. 1902 American Eocene Primates and the Supposed Rodent Family Mixodectidae. American Museum of Natural History, *Bulletin* 16:169–214.

Pilgrim, Guy E. 1910 Notices of New Mammalian Genera and Species From the Tertiaries of India. India, Geological Survey, *Records of the Geological Survey of India* 40, no. 1:63–71.

Pilgrim, Guy E. 1927 A *Sivapithecus* Palate and Other Primate Fossils From India. India, Geological Survey, *Palaeontologia indica* New Series 14:1–24.

Schlosser, Max 1887 Die Affen, Lemuren, Chiropteren usw. des europäischen Tertiärs. *Beiträge zur Paläontologie und Geologie Österreich-Ungarns* 6:1–162.

Schlosser, Max 1911 Beiträge zur Kenntnis der Oligozänen Land-Säugetiere aus dem Fayum: Ägypten. *Beiträge zur Paläontologie und Geologie Österreich-Ungarns* 24:51–167.

Simons, Elwyn L. 1962a A New Eocene Primate Genus, *Cantius,* and a Revision of Some Allied European Lemuroids. British Museum of Natural History, *Bulletin* 7, no. 1:1–36.

Simons, Elwyn L. 1962b Two New Primate Species From the African Oligocene. *Postilla* (Yale Peabody Museum) 64:1–12.

Simons, Elwyn L. 1963 Some Fallacies in the Study of Hominid Phylogeny. *Science* 141:879–889.

Simons, Elwyn L. 1964 On the Mandible of *Ramapithecus.* National Academy of Sciences, *Proceedings* 51, no. 3:528–535.

Simons, Elwyn L.; and Pilbeam, David R. 1965 Preliminary Revision of the Dryopithecinae (Pongidae, Anthropoidea). *Folia primatologica* 3:81–152.

Simpson, George G. 1940 Studies on the Earliest Primates. American Museum of Natural History, *Bulletin* 77:185–212.

Stehlin, H. G. 1912–1916 Die Säugetiere des schweizerischen Eocaens. Schweizerische Paläontologische Gesellschaft, *Abhandlungen* 38:1165–1298; 41:1299–1552.

Stirton, R. A. 1951 Ceboid Monkeys From the Miocene of Colombia. California, Univ. of, Publications of the Department of Geological Sciences, *Bulletin* 28, no. 11:315–355.

Wortman, J. L. 1903–1904 Studies of Eocene Mammalia in the Marsh Collection, Peabody Museum, Part 2: Primates. *American Journal of Science* Fourth Series 15:163–176, 399–414, 419–436; 16:345–368; 17:23–33, 133–140, 203–214.

III

HUMAN EVOLUTION

The modern or synthetic theory of evolution considers evolution to be the result of changes in the gene frequencies in populations. Gene frequencies are altered by means of mutation, selection, migration, and certain chance factors such as drift. When mutations are considered relative to their usefulness to the organism and to the population, mutations occur at random. They are not at random relative to the chemical structure of the organism, and mutations are commoner at some locations on the chromosomes than at others. Mutations are mostly disadvantageous, and their frequency is increased by radiation and by certain chemicals. Selection is the primary agent for bringing order to this process. Over the course of time, those genetic combinations that favor reproductive success become more common; and, conversely, those combinations that are less viable decline. It should be stressed that selection is for reproductively successful populations, and, from the viewpoint of evolution or of the species, the individual is only important insofar as he helps or hinders the success of the population. Variability itself is very important, as it permits the species to adapt to changing conditions; and selection is often for variability rather than for homogeneity which demands a single, limited environment. Migration from one population to another may introduce new genes or change gene frequencies, and this means that genes that are favored by selection may spread throughout the species. Partial reproductive isolation permits adaptation to local conditions and the formation of races, but in the long run it is the species that is the evolutionary unit. Especially when the number of individuals in the breeding population is small—as, in fact, was the case throughout most of human history—chance may cause the gene frequencies of one generation to differ from those of the preceding one. This has been called drift, and it can be a source of variability between small populations of a single species. If populations are founded by very few individuals, on the basis of statistical probabilities their gene frequencies are unlikely to be the same as those of the parent population. In summary, evolution is the result of changing gene frequencies. These changes originate by chance and are ordered by selection. They are modified by migration and certain chance factors. The process of natural selection has both directly and indirectly favored highly variable populations, and there has been no tendency for evolution to produce genetically uniform types.

Biological history

The synthetic theory of evolution has many important implications for social science, but it must be remembered that the concepts most frequently borrowed by the social scientists long antedate modern evolutionary theory. The greatest misunderstanding comes from the notion that evolution is directed toward a particular goal, frequently man himself, and that its course is determined by trends (orthogenesis). The reproductive success of populations is determined by the conditions of the moment, not by ultimate desirability or by the remote future. Reptiles succeeded the amphibians because of structural, physiological, and behavioral advantages that led to numerical and adaptive success, not because reptiles were to give rise to mammals, one of which was to become man. The trends seen in evolution are descriptions of what has actually taken place, and if a trend continues it is because selection in each generation has favored a particular course of events. When there are only a few fossils, the course of evolution may appear simple; but when the record is rich, biological history appears as an incredibly complex web of adapting organisms.

These points are made particularly incisively by Simpson (1964). As he emphasizes, evolution is biological history. The mechanism is revealed in the geneticist's laboratory, and the record is discovered in the rocks. But there are no laws in the usual scientific sense determining the course of evolution. In biological history there are no ultimate goals, inevitable trends, or vitalistic explanations.

The contrast between thinking about evolution in terms of inevitable trends and as the result of selection may be illustrated by consideration of the length of the toes of man and his ancestors. Since human toes have become much shorter compared to those of any possible ancestral primate, it is often asked whether this trend will continue; and men of the future are pictured as having still smaller toes. But the length of human toes has not been determined by a trend which is continuing into the future, regardless of the circumstances. When our ancestors became terrestrial animals to a greater extent, selection favored more efficient bipedal locomotion. Selection for shorter toes was a part of this process, but the fact that selection was for different proportions in the foot does not mean

that selection continues to be for even shorter toes. Probably an equilibrium was reached more than a million years ago, and selection for shorter toes has not continued. There is no trend determining the foot proportions of the future; the notion of an inevitable man of the future with a huge brain, tiny face, small limbs, and so forth finds no support in modern evolutionary theory. Future gene frequencies will be determined by selection (i.e., by reproductive success), and man will become more intelligent only if those individuals with the combinations of genes favoring the development of high intelligence leave more offspring. Evolutionary trends are statements of what has actually taken place in the history of forms of life, but there is no biological momentum that carries past trends into the future.

The study of human evolution is particularly beset with the notions of goal and trend and of evolution as a magic process. It might clarify thinking on the subject to omit the word "evolution" for the moment and to consider the history of the forms of life as revealed by the fossil record, the mechanism of change as shown in the laboratory, and the interpretations of these two kinds of data. The study of man's biological history means precisely the same thing as the study of human evolution, and it does not carry the suggestion of inevitable trend or progress toward some desired goal. The statement that we may study human biological history, human cultural history, and the interrelation of the two should mean precisely the same thing as that we may study human biological and cultural evolution. Understanding comes from the study of the data, and no information is added by using the word "evolution" in preference to the word "history."

The importance of using modern concepts is well illustrated by the change in the meaning of the word "origin." In human evolution "origin" has usually meant a relatively restricted time and place in which a new type arose. Thus one theory held that Neanderthal man arose in Europe, another that he evolved in central Asia. But if the populations of the genus *Homo* were not reproductively isolated during the latter half of the Pleistocene period, mutations and gene combinations favored by selection might have spread throughout the whole species. The origin of the Neanderthal populations that inhabited Europe during the last interglacial period was not limited to Europe but depended on the extent to which European populations were in contact with populations in other parts of the Old World. In the traditional typological, local sense there really is no "origin" of Neanderthal but many origins at different times and places which became incorporated in the European gene pool some 50 to 150 thousand years ago. The origins of Neanderthal were going on steadily over large areas for long periods of time, and the populations named Neanderthal were in part the result of events (mutations, drift, selection, migration) taking place in other races of the species.

Stages in human evolution

The characteristics of the main stages of human evolution are based on the fossils and on the structure and behavior of the primates that exist today. Both kinds of evidence are necessary to reconstruct the course of human evolution, and it is important to keep in mind the nature of the understanding that each kind of evidence can give. The fossils are the only direct clue to what the ancestors were like, the only evidence on many forms that have no close living relatives, and the only evidence as to the actual time of appearance of the various groups of primates. But the fossils are limited to those hard parts that do not easily deteriorate, largely jaws and teeth. Study of the contemporary primate forms supplements this record in two ways. The changes that are seen in the fossils may be interpreted more meaningfully if knowledge of the living animals is used. For example, changes in the form of the ethmoid bone may be directly related to changes in the sense of smell; or a particular form of limb bone may be interpreted as showing a special locomotor pattern. In a quite different way the contemporary forms may indirectly suggest characteristics that probably existed in extinct forms. For example, primitive mammals and contemporary prosimians have tactile hairs, scent glands, and a well-developed sense of smell. It is highly probable that these conditions were general for all the primates of the first half of the Age of the Mammals, but there is direct evidence only on the sense of smell. It is probable that this whole complex was reduced at the end of the Eocene or the beginning of the Oligocene, but this may have happened much earlier or later, and different parts of the complex may have changed at different times. If one is interested in general statements about what happened, the evidence is very good. But the more detailed questions one asks, the more the answers are limited to those that may be derived from teeth and bones.

For the first half of the Age of the Mammals the ancestors of man were small, long-snouted prosimians, not distinguished from the other primates of their time in any remarkable way. The prosimians of the Eocene were successful and highly diversified, and the group underwent a major adaptive radiation resulting in the formation of many distinct families. Many of the most successful groups evolved elongated incisor teeth; and if one examined only the Eocene primates, it might be concluded that these were to be the ultimately successful forms. But the majority of these Eocene primates became extinct after the true rodents appeared, and it may be that competition with the rodents was a major factor in their extinction. Unfortunately, the fossil record is particularly scant at the end of the Eocene and at the beginning of the Oligocene, so it is impossible to determine just which of the families of the early primates are ancestral to the later ones. But the main changes, as outlined below, would be similar regardless of just which lineage is eventually proved to be the correct one. While maintaining hands and feet adapted for climbing by grasping and a primitive quadrupedal posture, some primates in both the New World and the Old World independently evolved a new organization of the special senses and the brain. The primitive sense of smell was reduced, and binocular, stereoscopic color vision evolved. The reduction of the sense of smell is directly reflected in the fossil bone. The changes in vision are inferred from the conditions found in contemporary primates and are mirrored, at least to some extent, in the structure of the bony orbit. The brain increased in size at least four or five times and changed in organization from a primitive dependence on the sense of smell to an organization based on vision as the dominant sense. The change from prosimian to monkey is primarily in the brain and special senses, but in addition the face became shorter and deeper. The special senses and the brain determine what aspects of the external world can be perceived and appreciated and how sensations are organized. In a very real sense the world that we think of as normal (a stereoscopic world of color, in which activity is diurnal) began with the monkeys of the end of the Eocene or the beginning of the Oligocene. Judging from contemporary prosimians, the increase in the size of the brain made a great difference in intelligence. But it must be remembered that this reorganization of the structural basis of experience was an adaptation to a particular kind of arboreal life which took place independently in both the New World and the Old World. Although this organization forms the basis for human experience, it initially evolved because it was useful to monkeys, not to prepare the way for man.

Monkeys (Cercopithecidae) have remained quadrupedal, but the apes (Pongidae) evolved a different locomotor pattern. Apes climb by reaching far up above the head and may hang by one arm, swing below a branch, or reach to the side. This manner of locomotion in the trees probably evolved first as a way of feeding out near the ends of small branches. The structures that make this mode of living possible are complex and include a shallow, wide chest, a long clavicle, a special shoulder joint that involves modification of all bones near the joint, and changes in the elbow, wrist joint, and hand. The fossil record is exceedingly scanty, but this whole complex probably evolved during the Miocene, long after the separation between monkeys and apes. At least many monkeylike features persist in the arm bones of such forms of early Miocene ape as *Proconsul* and *Pliopithecus*. Man is similar to the apes in this structure of the trunk and arms (including the form and numbers of vertebrae, the disposition of the viscera, the form of joints and muscles, and the proportions of the trunk and limbs). Again it must be remembered that this complex evolved for a special life in the trees, and it is shared by all the contemporary apes. Man has these features because his ancestors were arboreally adapted apes, not because there was a trend toward man.

By the beginning of the Pleistocene, possibly two million years ago, the family of which man is the sole living representative (Hominidae) was represented by a genus of bipedal, small-brained creatures (*Australopithecus*). The direct fossil evidence shows that the Hominidae must be at least two million years old; but *Australopithecus* already had small canine teeth of human form and a pelvis closely approximating that seen in man (*Homo*), and the foot differed from that of *Homo* only in details. Prior to the Pleistocene, the Hominidae must have been separated from the Pongidae for some substantial period of time during which these characters evolved. Fragments of jaws dating from the end of the Miocene in India (*Ramapithecus*) and Africa (*Kenyapithecus*) suggest that the line leading to the Hominidae may have been distinct at that time; but since the rate of evolution may be very different for different functional complexes, there is no way to tell if these forms were beginning to be bipedal. It has been repeatedly shown that conclusions drawn from such fragmentary remains are likely to be wrong. [See EVOLUTION, *article on* PRIMATE EVOLUTION.]

Stone tools and animal bones have been found with the remains of *Australopithecus;* and it is probable that these creatures made the tools and hunted small animals, just as from their anatomy it appears that the behavior of *Australopithecus* was far more human than apelike. There were at least two species, *A. africanus* and *A. robustus*, a small one and a large one. Judging from the evidence of the teeth and from the associated archeological remains, both probably made tools. The small species may have been directly ancestral to the genus *Homo* of the Middle Pleistocene. The large form lived at the same time as the small one and continued on to be a contemporary of *Homo* before becoming extinct. As man is approached, there is a tendency to label each specimen as distinct and to emphasize differences instead of similarities. The result is a multiplication of species and genera the more the forms resemble man. Actually, the reverse should be the case. The more a primate is bipedal, tool-using, and hunting, the less likely the form is to speciate and the more likely it is to occupy wide areas with only racial differences.

By the Middle Pleistocene men of the genus *Homo* were fully bipedal, and there is every indication that their locomotor system had evolved to virtually its present form. Brains were approximately twice the size of those of *Australopithecus*. Tools were made according to complex traditions of manufacture, which were widely distributed geographically. Large animals were hunted, and fire was used. This fully human way of life appears to have been established by half a million years ago, but it changed very slowly. Approximately fifty thousand years ago men of modern form appeared. Undoubtedly evolution continued, and the populations adapted to local conditions by biological as well as cultural means. But the main events of human evolution had taken place before that time, and culture became increasingly more important in human adaptation. With agriculture and particularly with modern science the whole pattern shifted, numbers increased from a few millions to billions, and recently it is man who has altered the world. Mutation, selection, and migration are changed by the human way of life and at least in part may be brought under human control.

Since the fossil record is so fragmentary, it is important to note that the latest biochemical and cytological evidence supports the classification of the primates and the general stages of human evolution noted above. Immunochemical studies (especially Williams 1964 and Goodman 1963) show that man's closest living relatives are the great apes, especially the chimpanzee and the gorilla. The small apes, the gibbons, are much less similar both in their immune reactions and in chromosome number and types. The Old World monkeys are still further removed, and the prosimians are both very different and highly diversified. For the first half of the Age of the Mammals man's ancestors were prosimians whose primary adaptation was climbing by grasping. At the end of the Eocene a monkey–ape group evolved, characterized by changes in the brain and special senses. This group diversified in the Oligocene, and the special ape locomotor and feeding patterns evolved in the Miocene. A human bipedal group separated later and was fully evolved in locomotor and dental characters by the beginning of the Pleistocene, some two million years ago.

It should be stressed that the Eocene prosimians evolved into many different forms, most of which became extinct. Subsequently, monkeys and apes evolved into dozens of different genera. No general trend dominates the evolution of the primates, and most of primate evolution has no relation to that of man.

Evolution of behavior

The direct evidence for the course of human evolution outlined above is fragmentary and limited primarily to teeth and jaws. Changes in locomotor patterns are directly reflected in the bones, and in a general way the stages outlined above are probably correct; but so few limb bones are preserved that a very wide variety of interpretations is possible. Turning to the evolution of other behaviors, the evidence is even more indirect and is based primarily on the contemporary forms. The general logic in the use of information from the contemporary primates is that if a structure or behavior is common in a group of living primates it was probably present in closely allied fossil forms. Both parallel evolution and convergence may render such conclusions invalid; and since it is highly adaptable, behavior is particularly liable to these sources of error. An example may make the situation clearer. Primitive mammals probably had a litter of several young. In the primates the number of young is usually reduced to one at a time, and that infant is carried by the mother. The general kind of change is clear, but the details cannot be determined from the record. Marmosets do have twins and galagos more than one young. It is probable that the reduction took place several times, and it is possible that the ancestral apes had more than one young. But the most probable interpretation is that in arboreal primates a single infant carried by the mother was more likely to survive, and that this behavioral adaptation had evolved in the prosimians prior to the evolution of the later primate forms.

The human infant is remarkable in being unable to hold onto its mother, and this not only alters the pattern of human mother–child relations but introduces a division of labor and many social problems that are unique to man. George B. Schaller

(1963) observed that the female gorilla also must help her infant for the first six weeks. Thus man is a little less different than had been thought, and perhaps the particular group of apes from which we are descended were more like gorillas in this regard than like all the other apes and monkeys. The matter cannot be proved one way or the other, but it is most likely that the main difference between man and the other primates came with the evolution of large brains in the Pleistocene, long after the human lineage had separated from the other apes.

A problem exists in the examples that follow which is similar to that encountered in our consideration of the number of young in a litter and the degree of dependency of the newborn: that is, comparison of the living forms highlights a situation of importance in the behavior of man, but the time of origin of the behavior can be suggested in only the most general way. However, many important aspects of human evolution can be appreciated only in this way. For example, length of life has increased greatly in man. In small primitive mammals maturity is a matter of months and old age of two or three years. Comparable figures for monkeys are maturity in three or four years and a life span of well over twenty years. In chimpanzees full maturity is in approximately eight to ten years, and the life span is more than forty years. Comparable figures for man are nearly twice as long. Although there is much variation, the time during which the human young enjoy a protected and privileged position has increased, and a human of eight or ten is still learning and playing at an age when most primates would be fully adult. Clearly, selection has favored the long period of development and learning, even at a great biological cost. It might appear that a process based on reproductive success would favor several young and rapid growth, but in the human way of life selection has been for a single infant, growing slowly. Prolonged dependency and the presence of experienced adults have been major factors in the evolution of human society.

In monkeys and apes there is a menstrual cycle of approximately a month in duration. Sexual activity is concentrated in a period of estrus close to the time of ovulation. Females do not come into estrus for a period of some months during the later part of pregnancy and the first part of lactation. These physiological facts have the effect of concentrating sexual activity when conception is most probable and of spacing the infants. The spacing may be further reinforced by a breeding season, or at least a much greater frequency of births in one part of the year. In the human female the basic cycle continues, but estrus behavior has been lost.

Human females experience a period of lowered fertility during early lactation which is probably comparable to that in many monkeys. However, this period is not long enough for the requirements of human infant spacing; the human infant cannot feed itself when it is six months or even a year old. In man the spacing of infants must be extended by taboos and customs which supplement the physiological mechanisms of birth spacing in the nonhuman primate. The loss of the estrus cycle in the human female may be related to the economic division of labor and the interdependency of the sexes, which is unique to man. This loss may be due to the need of the human female to keep the interest of the food-sharing male; but there may well have also been selective pressure against estrus behavior, which would have been disruptive to the stable, interdependent relationships of a family unit.

The monkeys and apes are almost entirely vegetarian, although most will eat birds' eggs and insects. Hunting of small mammals has been observed rarely in chimpanzees and baboons. The range in which monkeys and apes forage is small, varying from much less than a square mile in gibbons to some fifteen square miles in baboons and gorillas. From a human point of view it is remarkable that animals with keen eyesight, who are capable of climbing into trees and surveying the scene and who are well adapted for locomotion on the ground, so restrict their normal activities. It is probable that hunting is the behavioral adaptation that caused the change in man's relation to his physical environment. Intensive hunting would drive game from a small range, and the location of game and the pursuit of wounded animals would lead to the establishment of large territories. In most nonhuman primates ranges are not defended, and the areas occupied by groups of monkeys or apes usually overlap. Human defense of territory may also be the result of hunting.

Tool use is one of man's most distinctive attributes, and the skillful use of objects is unique to man. Manipulative skills depend on the brain as well as on the hand, and the large area in the human brain devoted to the hand is probably the result of the new selection pressures that came into being with the beginnings of tool using. Both the evidence of the teeth and of the associated tools and animal bones suggest that *Australopithecus* was a tool user and had been so for a long time. If this interpretation is correct, then the increase in size of the human brain came long after the use of tools and probably in response to the new ways of life that tools made possible.

Intelligence and learning are not general but are related to specific abilities. For example, human children play with objects as well as with other children. They enjoy practicing using and throwing, and many games are built around objects. In marked contrast, monkeys and apes are tool-dumb, so to speak. Tasks that the human child easily masters are very difficult or impossible for nonhuman primates. Only the chimpanzee uses some minor tools (Goodall 1964). The same principle can be seen in language. In spite of major efforts, it has proved impossible to teach monkeys or apes to speak. This is because the nonhuman primates lack the neural mechanisms necessary for speech. The sounds of the nonhuman primates convey emotion (such as fear) and the location of the calling animal, and they are important especially when combined with gestures in social interaction. The sound systems of primates are not more complex than those of many other mammals; and, like other mammals, primates can be trained to respond to human sounds. The distinctive character of human speech is the naming of objects, and this requires the linking of visual and auditory parts of the cortex of the brain (Geschwind 1964). The necessary connections are not present in the brains of the nonhuman primates. Once naming of objects had commenced in even the most minor way, the success of this revolution changed selection pressures so that the course of evolution of the brain changed, and structures evolved that ultimately made possible language as we now know it. It is likely that the situation which led to object naming was tool use, and it is the uniqueness of this combination of tools and language to man that accounts for why the other primates did not develop even the simplest languages. If language began at the time the brain was doubling in size between *Australopithecus* and *Homo*, this would give a minimum of two million years of stone toolmaking by small-brained bipeds as a time in which the first naming of objects might have occurred. It is tempting to attribute this great increase in brain size to language and all the ways of life that language made possible. But it must be remembered that it is not just increase in size that separates the brain of modern man from that of the contemporary apes. There have been changes of organization in the brain too, and without these changes skills in tool use, language, and social planning would be impossible. Human intelligence is built on specific abilities which are the products of the evolutionary process.

But the world in which man evolved was a very different one from that in which we are living today. Our bodies had evolved to practically their present form some fifty thousand years ago, and since then human adaptations to the environment have been increasingly by technology and custom. This does not mean that evolution has stopped, but it does mean that the direct interrelation that selection had forged between man and his ways of life is no longer functional. As stone tools improved over vast intervals of time, the biology of the users had time to evolve along with their way of life. In the human head we see the product of the interrelations of biology and a succession of ways of life in which selection was for smaller faces and bigger brains. But since the agricultural and scientific revolutions customs have changed so rapidly that there has been no time for corresponding biological evolution to fit the human actors for the modern world. Human biology evolved to be adaptive in a world of small society, great hazards, and personal skill. The human actor in modern society is too aggressive, too dominance seeking, too acquisitive. The kind of planning necessary in the modern world is difficult for an organism built along the lines of *Homo sapiens*. Many acts which now would be judged undesirable (acts of selfishness, cruelty, and war) are easily learned because they are in accord with basic human biology (Hamburg 1963).

Natural selection can bring about adaptation between biology and a way of life only in very long periods of time, and there is no orthogenesis carrying trends of the past into the future. The fit between organism and society must now be determined by science, and for the first time in all of biological evolution both biology and social life can be planned. But planning can be more efficient if planners remember that the actors in modern technical society are products of the past, of times and ways of life long gone.

S. L. WASHBURN AND JANE B. LANCASTER

BIBLIOGRAPHY

BUETTNER-JANUSCH, JOHN (editor) 1963–1964 *Evolutionary and Genetic Biology of Primates.* 2 vols. New York: Academic Press.

DeVORE, IRVEN (editor) 1965 *Primate Behavior: Field Studies of Monkeys and Apes.* New York: Holt.

DOBZHANSKY, THEODOSIUS 1962 *Mankind Evolving: The Evolution of the Human Species.* New Haven: Yale Univ. Press.

GESCHWIND, NORMAN 1964 The Development of the Brain and the Evolution of Language. Georgetown University, Washington, D.C., Institute of Languages and Linguistics, *Monograph Series on Languages and Linguistics* 17:155–169.

GOODALL, JANE 1964 Tool-using and Aimed Throwing in a Community of Free-living Chimpanzees. *Nature* 201: 1264–1266.

GOODMAN, MORRIS 1963 Man's Place in the Phylogeny of the Primates as Reflected in Serum Proteins. Pages 204–234 in Sherwood L. Washburn (editor), *Classification and Human Evolution.* Chicago: Aldine.

HAMBURG, D. A. 1963 Emotions in the Perspective of Human Evolution. Pages 300–317 in Symposium on Expression of the Emotions in Man, New York, 1960, *Expression of the Emotions in Man.* Edited by Peter H. Knapp. New York: International Universities Press.

Index medicus. → Published since 1960. Articles are listed by subject matter and author.

MAYR, ERNST 1963 *Animal Species and Evolution.* Cambridge, Mass.: Belknap Press.

NAPIER, J. R. 1964 The Evolution of Bipedal Walking in the Hominids. *Archives de biologie* (Liège) 75 (Supplement): 673–708.

OAKLEY, KENNETH P. 1964 *Frameworks for Dating Fossil Man.* Chicago: Aldine. → A comprehensive discussion of methods of dating and the dates of fossil man.

PIVETEAU, JEAN (editor) 1957 *Traité de paléontologie.* Volume 7: Vers la forme humaine. . . . Paris: Masson. → The best general source on fossil primates, including man.

SCHALLER, GEORGE B. 1963 *The Mountain Gorilla: Ecology and Behavior.* Univ. of Chicago Press.

SIMONS, ELWYN L. 1963 Some Fallacies in the Study of Hominid Phylogeny. *Science* 141:879–889.

SIMONS, ELWYN L.; and PILBEAM, D. R. 1965 Preliminary Revision of the Dryopithecinae (Pongidae, Anthropoidea). *Folia primatologica* 3:81–152. → Classification of apes and the origin of man.

SIMPSON, GEORGE G. 1964 *This View of Life: The World of an Evolutionist.* New York: Harcourt.

TOBIAS, PHILIP V. 1965 Early Man in East Africa. *Science* 149:22–33. → Most recent review of *Australopithecus* and the problems of the origin of man.

WASHBURN, SHERWOOD L. (editor) 1963 *Classification and Human Evolution.* Chicago: Aldine.

WILLIAMS, C. A. JR. 1964 Immunochemical Analysis of Serum Proteins of the Primates: A Study in Molecular Evolution. Volume 2, pages 25–74 in John Buettner-Janusch (editor), *Evolutionary and Genetic Biology of Primates.* New York: Academic Press.

Zoological Record. → Published since 1865. Covers classification and fossils, topics not in the *Index medicus.*

ZOOLOGICAL SOCIETY OF LONDON 1963 *The Primates.* Proceedings of the Symposium held on April 12–14, 1962, Symposia 10. London: The Society.

IV

CULTURAL EVOLUTION

The grand movement of origin, transformation, and differentiation of our universe, our earth, and life itself is called evolution. Within this total process we are concerned with the transformations that occurred when the biological, or organic, phase arose out of the inorganic and when the later, cultural phase arose from the organic. Despite their interconnections, however, each of these stages has its own characteristic mode and tempo of evolution.

The cultural phase transcended the organic and inorganic when populations of men created new ways of adapting to each other and to the environment. These adaptations occurred after certain gradual changes in the size and complexity of the hominid forebrain made symbolic thought and communication possible. The capacity for, and use of, symbolic manipulation brought forth unprecedented kinds of social behavior. These new ways of behaving were *supra*biological in the sense that such natural primate characteristics as jealousy, fear, sex and food appetites, and so on, were so often channeled, sublimated, or otherwise altered by means of social rules. In a few striking respects, in fact, the new modes of social behavior were *contra*biological inasmuch as they actually repressed such powerful urges as the sexual, for example, and required sharing rather than competing for scarce food.

The sum total of the social and political rules, technological inventions and economic institutions, the arts, shared beliefs and practices—that is, the culture—tends to persist through time because any particular society maintains these parts integrated with each other and with its environment. Evolutionary changes, therefore, do not correspond to a single world-wide pattern, and each society maintains a certain distinctiveness in the course of change. Thus the culture of mankind generally is an evolutionary stage in the universal process, while particular societies differentiate into cultural genera and species, creating heterogeneity. Sometimes this adaptive process brings forth striking advances that permit greater dominance, all-round adaptability, and growth.

All anthropologists would agree that the earliest human societies must have been small and simple in social organization, poor in technological equipment, without formal legal or governmental institutions, and with an ideology based more on the supernatural than on science. Since these characteristics contrast greatly with modern industrial states, we think of evolution as directional: generally from small to large societies, from simple to complex organizations, from informal to formal political institutions, and so on. The idea of directionality is important because it provides the criteria for classifying separate societies into general stages of the evolution of culture as a totality.

A second characteristic of evolution is the relatedness of the sequence of forms. An important aspect of the interpretation of any particular unit is the investigation of the ancestral forms from which it "unfolded"—its phylogeny.

Not many social scientists are evolutionists, and even the anthropologists who agree that there has been general evolutionary growth disagree about whether there has been enough orderliness in the process for the theory to be useful in classifying cultures or in interpreting a purely historical succession of discrete events. But then, of course, even if the orderliness is agreed upon, it is natural to want to know what causes it, and here further disagreement arises. Most of the different conceptions of the nature and causes of cultural evolution arose in the eighteenth and nineteenth centuries, and a brief historical sketch is useful in describing them.

History of the concept

As primitive societies in various parts of the world became known to Europeans during the age of discovery, two different explanations of their primitiveness were offered. The most widespread belief was theological: they had "degenerated" further from an original state of grace than had civilized peoples. The other, the rationalist explanation that became usual among intellectuals in the seventeenth and eighteenth centuries, was that civilization had evolved from earlier primitive types that must have been similar to the culture of contemporary savages and barbarians. There had been, to be sure, evolutionary notions held by philosophers of the classical traditions—by the Greek Epicurus and the Roman Lucretius, for example—but modern ideas about cultural evolution were propounded most influentially by Turgot, Montesquieu, Rousseau, Condorcet, Helvétius, Diderot, and others in France; Kant and Herder in Germany; Vico in Italy; and Hume, Hobbes, and Ferguson in Britain.

As opposed to degenerationism, all of these writers held to a theory of progress. Although modern anthropologists have commonly thought that this theory was merely a happy giddiness induced by the great economic and political advances of the period, most European scholars were actually pessimistic about progress in the future. While all agreed that progress had taken place in the past, and that discernible, orderly stages of its evolution could be demarcated, only Kant, Turgot, and Condorcet thought that progress was inevitable. There were variations in the names and numbers of stages that were proposed, but most accepted either Turgot's stages of hunting, pastoralism, and farming, or Montesquieu's similar typology of savagery, barbarism, and civilization.

Although the modern holistic concept of culture was lacking, the elements that were seen to be evolving were the human institutions of which culture is composed. There was one emphasis in the evolutionary theory that was peculiar to the times —rationalism. Human institutions were viewed as products of the human mind (as indeed in some sense they must be), a mind that was mistaken or irrational in the past, but increasingly less superstitious and more reasonable as time went on. Since civilized man had literally thought himself out of a "state of nature," the degree of orderliness that lay in human history was due to the progressive improvement of mentality.

In the nineteenth century, evolutionary thought became less philosophical and more influenced by empirical aspirations. Tylor in England and Morgan in the United States were prominent in the creation of ethnological evolutionism; Spencer in England, Saint-Simon, Comte, and Durkheim in France were pioneers in sociology; the reworking of Hegel by Marx and Engels was a creative contribution to political–revolutionary theory. They differed from their predecessors and from one another mainly with respect to the following problems: (1) *What* is it that evolves—culture in general or only the institutions of specific societies? (2) *How* does it evolve—by orthogenetic, inevitable progress, by rational thought and intention, survival of the fittest, or an unconscious dialectical struggle? (3) *Where* is the locus of the evolutionary impulse— in the improvements of technology and the material aspect alone, in the division of labor, the political or ideological aspect, or as a force in the cosmos?

The nature of culture. The ethnologists of the late 1800s, convinced of orderliness in evolution, directed themselves to the delineation of stages of *culture*, which E. B. Tylor defined in the anthropological sense in 1871. L. H. Morgan (1877) did not use that word, but in his usage, "society" and "ethnical periods" (for stages) referred essentially to the subject matter of Tylor's concept. Tylor and Morgan, and most ethnologists of their time as well, were concerned with the world-wide manifestation of cultural stages, not with the culture of a particular society. A specific primitive tribe was of interest only as an illustration of aspects of the culture of an entire stage and of a large geographical area.

This concern with culture in its most general sense rather than with particular societies caused a misunderstanding of the ethnological evolutionists by later commentators. Modern anthropologists frequently criticize the nineteenth-century evolutionists as "unilinear," meaning that the latter believed that all societies inevitably progress through the same stages. This would be a powerful blow at nineteenth-century evolutionary theory, if it were true, but it seems doubtful that any of the evolutionists believed such manifest nonsense. In the statement that seems best to serve modern critics, Morgan said:

Since mankind were one in origin, their career has been essentially one, running in different but uniform channels upon all continents, and very similarly in all the tribes and nations of mankind down to the same status of advancement. It follows that the history and experience of the American Indian tribes represent, more or less nearly, the history and experience of our own remote ancestors when in corresponding conditions.   ([1877] 1964, pp. 6–7)

This sounds "unilinear" to a modern ethnologist, whose concern has been restricted to the structure and functioning of unit systems, but inasmuch as ethnologists were not making such studies in the nineteenth century, it seems apparent that Morgan must have meant nothing more than that wherever barbarism (defined by the traits of horticulture or pastoralism) was found, a general stage of hunting–gathering society (savagery) had preceded it and that stages of both had preceded civilization on continents that had achieved civilization. Such a judgment is attested by archeology now as well as by common sense and should evoke no comment, but in Morgan's day it was worth stating because theories of degeneration and catastrophe were still commonly opposed to evolutionism.

The sociologists tended toward the organismic model for society. A society was thought of as a contained unit made up of interdependent parts, each subserving the others. Evolution was seen as the development of more parts and greater differentiation of them. The "parts" are individuals, groups, and specialized persons and groups. Religions, morals, and political, social, and economic institutions function largely to bolster, integrate, and smooth the relations between the social parts. This early model, refined as nonevolutionary structural functionalism, became characteristic of modern American sociology and British social anthropology but had its roots in the eighteenth-century concern with progress.

The third group, the Marxists, was closer to ethnology than to sociology, at least in its beginning phases under Marx and Engels. In fact, Engels' *Origin of the Family, Private Property and the State* (1884) was inspired by Morgan's *Ancient Society* (1877) and borrowed heavily from it. The theory of general developmental stages was the same, and the conception of the evolving unit did not have the organismic particularism of the sociologists. As in Morgan's case, the concept of culture was absent but would have been appropriate, for institutions (especially technological and economic) were not merely subserviently integrative in function but had more of an initiating "prime mover" status than the sociologists believed.

How does culture evolve?   The eighteenth-century evolutionists thought of the progressive improvement of the human condition as a mentalistic evolution and thus took an idealist view of the evolutionary process. Some of the language of nineteenth-century ethnological evolutionism reflects this, so that we find such expressions as Morgan's "growth of the idea of government" and Tylor's frequent use of "mind" and "mental life" as near synonyms of many aspects of culture. But a very important change occurred in the nineteenth-century view of evolution. As it became more scientifically oriented it posited causal and functional connections between different aspects of culture. Tylor, in his greatest book, *Primitive Culture* (1871), devoted much of the introductory chapter ("The Science of Culture") to describing not only cause–effect relations in culture but also the determining of these cultural relations and the thought and will of the individual. The ethnological school of evolution thus made significant moves toward determinism and against assumptions of free will in human affairs.

The "how," the mechanics of the evolutionary process, was not explicitly described, beyond the suggestion that it was unconscious. We are told that new elements tend to replace older ones if they are better, sometimes, but beyond that one has the impression that evolution was taken as a "given," that orthogenetic forces had moved mankind ever upward, however fitfully.

There is a recurrent note reminiscent of the eighteenth-century rationalist ancestry: "Now that we understand evolution we can more consciously control it." Tylor called anthropology a "reformer's science," and Morgan said, "The time will come . . . when human intelligence will rise to the mastery over property. . . ." This was the deterministic paradox: We can scientifically analyze the evolution of culture because it *is* orderly (because it *is* determined); knowing this we can somehow influence the future as we pass, as Tylor put it, "from the age of unconscious to that of conscious progress."

The sociological wing of nineteenth-century evolutionism pursued the implications of the biological analogy. The rationalist optimism of Condorcet was outdated by the obvious attendant evils of industrialization, especially in England, as illustrated by Malthus' pessimistic *Essay on the Principle of Population*. After the great intellectual success of Dar-

win's theory of selection by survival (itself suggested by Malthus' essay), a theory of "social Darwinism" arose, which, whatever its demerits, at least provided a "how" for the evolutionary process: as a result of conflict between societies superior ones replace the inferior. Some added an "internal conflict" aspect: out of the struggle between classes, groups, and even individuals within the society comes the improvement of the society. Walter Bagehot, Auguste Comte, Herbert Spencer, and Ludwig Gumplowicz were the leaders in this mode of thought.

Marx and Engels were even more consistently deterministic and materialistic than the ethnologists and had a much more definite theory of the mechanics of evolution. This theory was orthogenetic in that the impetus for change came from within the society, from the "dialectic" of the class struggle, the resolution of contradictions in terms of either failure or a higher unity. It should be noted that this internal-conflict theory is not like social Darwinism: the ruling or propertied class is not superior. Marx and Engels, like the ethnologists, were insistent on the lawful, determined nature of evolution, and they also believed that evolution could be oriented by the conscious action of man once he understood its processes. Then, by abolishing the capitalist form of production, "Man, at last the master of his own form of social organization, becomes at the same time the lord over nature, his own master—free" (Engels [1882] 1935, p. 75).

Most of the sociologists became less interested in evolution itself than in the more immediate problems of the organismic nature of a society, particularly that of integration. What holds a society together? Following the social contract theories of the eighteenth century, there were psychological theories, mental interaction theories, and imitation theories, all of which took society to be an organismic entity somehow *mentally* constituted. This was the time when sociology became nonevolutionary, as it mostly remains to this day.

The locus of the evolutionary impulse.   Morgan thought that cultural evolution consisted of two distinct aspects—"inventions and discoveries" (the technical order), which evolve in connected, progressive, cumulative relations to one another, and "institutions" (the forms of the family, of government, religion, architecture, property), which stand in "unfolding relations." By this expression he meant that social institutions originate in a few "primary germs of thought" and thereafter independently change form as well as replace previous forms. Tylor also, although not so explicitly, thought that technology, science, and other aspects of material culture undergo evolution rather independent of religion and "intellectual and moral" progress. Nowhere is it demonstrated, however, that one of these aspects is the "prime mover" and the other a dependent variable or superstructure. But again it should be remembered that Morgan and Tylor were not talking about the process of systemic change in any particular society, hence the matter of functional priority of one part over another simply did not concern them.

The sociologists, preoccupied with social integration, psychology, and mentalism, did not see the initiating locus of evolutionary change in any aspect of culture at all. Spencer and his followers saw evolution as a grand cosmic force that generated complexity out of simplicity and heterogeneity out of homogeneity, aided somewhat by Darwinian "conflict and survival." A few Frenchmen, most notably Émile Durkheim (1893), posited that the division of labor in society, like the functional specialization of organs in biological entities (again, the organismic model), is related to population increases, greater social density, and larger, stronger societies. But it is not clear what the causes of these developments are, and Durkheim explicitly denied that the division of labor is increased for utilitarian reasons like "the greatest happiness for the greatest number" or by any other kind of intention or plan.

The Marxians, on the other hand, were firm in the conviction that the locus of evolutionary change lies in the technoeconomic (or material) sector, which then affects the nature of the social classes and their interrelations, and that ideology is mere superstructure. As such, it is the last part of culture to change. This form of the old materialist versus idealist philosophical argument persists strongly to this day.

Twentieth-century evolutionism

Most American ethnologists in the first half of the twentieth century repudiated an evolutionism that they misunderstood in favor of a raw ethnographic, "natural history" approach to the study of primitive culture. In Britain and France, and in sociology nearly everywhere, evolutionism succumbed intellectually to a structural functionalism that had greater utility for the practical solution of social problems through political administration in the colonies and at home.

A. G. Keller, an American sociologist, Leslie A. White and Julian H. Steward, American ethnologists, and V. Gordon Childe, a British archeologist, were virtually alone in opposing the antievolution-

ary temper of the times. It was not until after mid-century that there was any larger shift of opinion toward an evolutionary outlook again, but this took place only in America, only in anthropology, and there only in part.

Twentieth-century evolutionism differs from previous theories in two major respects. The first concerns the cultural adaptations through which evolutionary changes are believed to occur. The concept of cultural adaptation has supplanted the orthogenesis of earlier evolutionists, who had found the only generative impulse in the internal class-struggle dialectic proposed by Marx and Engels and in the social Darwinism of some sociologists. Second, a new theoretical synthesis has been made by the reworking and integration of some of the earlier perspectives that had been thought to be contradictory.

The significance of the adaptation of culture to the natural environment as an important aspect of the evolutionary process was presented as "cultural ecology" by Julian H. Steward. Others have proposed further that in the process of adaptation, the environment includes not only the natural environment but adjustments to other social systems as well. According to this view, inventions and discoveries, borrowings, unconscious historical "accidents," changes from whatever source, are the raw materials for evolutionary change in culture. Some of these "fit" as improvements in the internal functional arrangements, while others solve external environmental problems with respect to nature or competition: thus they are selected simply because they are superior instruments. The advance of this perspective over eighteenth-century and nineteenth-century ideas of the "inevitability of progress" and orthogenesis is manifest: the evolutionary perspective is not mystical and can accommodate and make more intelligible the variety of historical data we now possess.

One of the historical facts of life that has plagued all orthogenetic schemes is that different societies manifest great variation in rates of evolution, from drastic revolution to the other extreme of non-evolution—i.e., stabilization. And in so many instances a society makes a very rapid rise only to reach a long-term plateau. The theory that evolution proceeds by adaptation, however, allows for all of these eventualities, taking stabilization as much for granted as progress. Stabilization, after all, merely bespeaks the success of the adaptive process: when the culture is successfully adapted, it tends to reject subsequent possible changes. This can render explicable what might seem paradoxical: that a culture "high" in one stage might fail to advance to further heights in the next simply because of its earlier success. And, of course, the more specialized its form of adaptation, the more deeply entrenched and committed to its present environment it becomes.

The perspective of cultural adaptation and selection is particularly useful in reconciling opposing viewpoints derived from the nineteenth century.

What is it that evolves? Is it culture in general, through grand stages, or only particular social systems? The reconciliation of these two views is easy: both are correct. The evolution of the totality is the product of the evolution of particular societies. To be sure, there is but a single evolutionary process, the selection of traits and their functional adjustment *via* adaptation in particular systems. This is the way societies become differentiated one from the other, but it is also the way some become superior to others in measurable ways. Thus, two different theoretical perspectives are possible with respect to the same data. These are what Sahlins (Sahlins & Service 1960) calls the *specific* evolutionary perspective as compared with the *general* evolutionary perspective. The former refers merely to the creation of diversity by adaptive modification of related particular societies. The latter is the measurement of progress; some specific evolutionary changes are significant breakthroughs that can be measured by such objective directional criteria of progress as greater all-round adaptability, greater dominance, or greater complexity of organization. In short, specific evolution refers to our concern with descent-with-modification or adaptive variation; general evolution refers to the progressive emergence of superior forms, stage by stage, which can be related to the directional evolution of the total culture of the human species.

How does culture evolve? Is it in some measure intentionally planned, or is it an unconscious and nonrational process, determined by events outside human awareness? Surely an improvement in ideas has something to do with it, and sometimes ideas must be conscious and rational; this is most obvious in science and engineering but also holds true in the institutional realm. Many political institutions, for example, result from attempts to solve social or economic problems purposefully. But, of course, there are often latent and unintended consequences of even the most manifest political expediency.

Again, it would seem that a reconciliation of the opposed views can be made by means of the adaptation–selection perspective. New culture traits or modifications can have any number of sources: inventions, purposeful borrowings, accidents, un-

conscious functional shifts, and so on. The selection or rejection of any of these could also involve conscious intentionality, even if but rarely. The selective process in cultural evolution is only roughly analogous to natural selection in biology; certainly the capacity of a person to analyze his own behavior, predict future events, and rearrange his affairs on that basis is a distinctively human trait. It is more difficult to plan and arrange things on a social or political basis, and the greater the demographic scope the more difficult it is; but it does happen. The adaptation–selection perspective has the great virtue of not prescribing either conscious intention or unconsciousness; it can accommodate either and still lead to greater comprehension of cultural change. And further, determinism in human affairs is not equated with unawareness, indeterminism with awareness. Determinism is a perspective that the analyst takes, not a property of the subject matter under investigation.

Where is the locus of the evolutionary impulse? Does it lie in the mode of production, in technology, in the relations of production, in the class struggle, in the division of labor, in man's view of destiny; or is it a mystical force in the cosmos? It would seem that those who posited mode of production, class struggle, technology, or division of labor were much influenced by the industrial revolution, which has been, of course, a most striking evolutionary prime mover for the past century and a half and promises even more wondrous cultural transformations almost immediately. But has the material, technoeconomic aspect always been the prime mover? The change from primitive chiefdoms to early states and then to empires in Mesoamerica, Peru, and probably elsewhere seems to have been first in the political sector; even the important inventions of writing and mathematics could have originated in the occult mumbo jumbo of priests. The modern evolutionist accordingly wants to know more about particular instances of change and finds no need to insist that the initial loci must be always in the same sector of culture.

Evolutionists of the nineteenth century were more empirical than their predecessors, but their use of ethnographic data was often mere illustration rather than proof of hypotheses. The "comparative method" of some, such as Sir James Frazer, was simply an uncritical, but energetic, "clip and paste." E. B. Tylor (1888) was a notable exception: he originated a method of statistical correlations in his comparative study of marriage and descent rules. Hobhouse, Wheeler, and Ginsberg's work (1915) was another important application of statistics to problems of cultural evolution. Otherwise, both evolutionary theory and the comparative method nearly perished from inattention until mid-twentieth century.

The use of the comparative method began to revive in America during the 1950s, particularly stimulated by George P. Murdock's creation of the Human Relations Area Files and later the "Ethnographic Atlas." Formal graphical means of showing correlations and sequences of culture traits in the course of evolutionary changes have attracted attention recently. (See Naroll 1956; Freeman & Winch 1957; Gouldner & Peterson 1962; and Carneiro & Tobias 1963.) The results of these efforts are meager so far, and several unsolved difficulties attend them. The problems of how to define the significant cultural units to be counted and how to select a random sample of them in the absence of an adequate number of ethnographies of unacculturated societies are serious.

The gravest difficulty of all is caused by the tendency of a culture to become specialized as it adapts to its environment, for to the extent that it is special it is incommensurable. Walter Goldschmidt has aptly called this "the Malinowskian dilemma": Malinowski argued (and successfully demonstrated) that every cultural institution must be understood as a unique product of the cultural whole within which it developed. It would seem to follow, therefore, that the comparative method is wrong, comparing incomparables. Yet, paradoxically, Malinowski often extrapolated from his insights into Trobriand culture to the primitive world in general. Goldschmidt argues that the solution is to compare functions, not institutions: "What is consistent from culture to culture is not the institution; what is consistent are the social problems. What is recurrent from society to society is solutions to these problems" (1966, p. 31).

Julian H. Steward's studies (1955) of "multi-linear evolution" show an awareness of these difficulties. He recommends comparative studies of specific holocultures in evolution, rather than comparisons of isolated traits, in order to find the "regularities" of evolution.

There is a different test of theory that is bound to be used more frequently—the test of fruitfulness. Since one of the main purposes of evolutionary theory is to provide intelligibility to historical data, then the better it fulfills this function, the greater must be its empirical as well as logico-didactic virtues. Guy Swanson's study of religion (1960) is a good example: light is cast on the development of religion, and at the same time evolutionary theory proves to be useful.

Such empirical applications of evolutionary theory can result in its refinement only to the extent that evolutionists maintain an empirical orientation, willing to change the theory in the service of its intellectual functions. Some of the older evolutionary philosophies, particularly those of Marx and Spencer, were too grand in scope and too schematic to be useful. They also became stultified dogmas as they were used by political parties and academic "schools of thought." A better fate may be expected of recent evolutionism, judging from the evidence of new empirical attitudes, particularly if its proponents remain guarded against unnecessary and untested preconceptions that can so easily impede a true evolutionary science of culture.

ELMAN R. SERVICE

[See also ANTHROPOLOGY, articles on THE FIELD and THE COMPARATIVE METHOD IN ANTHROPOLOGY; ARCHEOLOGY, article on THE FIELD; CULTURE; ECOLOGY. Also related are the entries INTEGRATION; SOCIAL DARWINISM; SOCIOLOGY, article on THE DEVELOPMENT OF SOCIOLOGICAL THOUGHT; and the biographies of CHILDE; MORGAN, LEWIS HENRY; SPENCER; TYLOR.]

BIBLIOGRAPHY

CARNEIRO, ROBERT L.; and TOBIAS, STEPHEN F. 1963 The Application of Scale Analysis to the Study of Cultural Evolution. New York Academy of Sciences, *Transactions* Second Series 26, no. 2:196–207.

CHILDE, V. GORDON (1936) 1965 *Man Makes Himself.* 4th ed. London: Watts.

CHILDE, V. GORDON 1951 *Social Evolution.* New York: Schumann.

COTTRELL, WILLIAM F. 1955 *Energy and Society: The Relation Between Energy, Social Change, and Economic Development.* New York: McGraw-Hill.

DOBZHANSKY, THEODOSIUS 1962 *Mankind Evolving: The Evolution of the Human Species.* New Haven: Yale Univ. Press.

DURKHEIM, ÉMILE (1893) 1960 *The Division of Labor in Society.* 2d ed. Glencoe, Ill.: Free Press. → First published in French.

ENGELS, FRIEDRICH (1882) 1935 *Socialism: Utopian and Scientific.* New York: International Publishers. → First published as *Die Entwicklung des Sozialismus von der Utopie zur Wissenschaft.*

ENGELS, FRIEDRICH (1884) 1942 *The Origin of the Family, Private Property and the State.* New York: International Publishers. → First published in German.

FERGUSON, ADAM (1767) 1819 *An Essay on the History of Civil Society.* 8th ed. Philadelphia: Finley.

FREEMAN, LINTON C.; and WINCH, R. F. 1957 Societal Complexity: An Empirical Test of a Typology of Societies. *American Journal of Sociology* 62:461–466; 63:78–79.

GOLDSCHMIDT, WALTER R. 1959 *Man's Way: A Preface to the Understanding of Human Society.* Cleveland: World.

GOLDSCHMIDT, WALTER R. 1966 *Comparative Functionalism: An Essay in Anthropological Theory.* Berkeley and Los Angeles: Univ. of California Press.

GOULDNER, ALVIN W. and PETERSON, R. A.   1962   *Notes on Technology and the Moral Order*. Indianapolis, Ind.: Bobbs-Merrill.

HOBHOUSE, LEONARD T.; WHEELER, GERALD C.; and GINSBERG, MORRIS   (1915) 1965   *The Material Culture and Social Institutions of the Simpler Peoples: An Essay in Correlation*. London School of Economics and Political Science Monographs on Sociology, No. 3. London: Routledge.

HUXLEY, JULIAN S.   1942   *Evolution: The Modern Synthesis*. London and New York: Harper.

HUXLEY, JULIAN S.   1955   Evolution, Cultural and Biological. Pages 3–25 in *Yearbook of Anthropology*. New York: Wenner-Gren Foundation.

KELLER, ALBERT G.   (1915) 1931   *Societal Evolution*. Rev. ed. New York: Macmillan.

MAINE, HENRY J. S.   (1861) 1960   *Ancient Law: Its Connection With the Early History of Society, and Its Relations to Modern Ideas*. Rev. ed. New York: Dutton; London and Toronto: Dent.

MONTAGU, ASHLEY   1962   *Culture and the Evolution of Man*. New York: Oxford Univ. Press.

MORGAN, LEWIS H.   (1877) 1964   *Ancient Society*. Cambridge, Mass.: Harvard Univ. Press.

MUNRO, THOMAS   1963   *Evolution in the Arts and Other Theories of Culture History*. Cleveland (Ohio) Museum of Art.

NAROLL, RAOUL S.   1956   A Preliminary Index of Social Development. *American Anthropologist* New Series 58:687–715.

SAHLINS, MARSHALL D.; and SERVICE, ELMAN R. (editors)   1960   *Evolution and Culture*. Ann Arbor: Univ. of Michigan Press.

SERVICE, ELMAN R.   1962   *Primitive Social Organization: An Evolutionary Perspective*. New York: Random House.

SPENCER, HERBERT   1915   *Works*. 18 vols. New York and London: Appleton.

STEWARD, JULIAN H.   1955   *Theory of Culture Change: The Methodology of Multilinear Evolution*. Urbana: Univ. of Illinois Press.

SUMNER, WILLIAM GRAHAM; and KELLER, ALBERT G.   1927   *The Science of Society*. 4 vols. New Haven: Yale Univ. Press. → Maurice R. Davis was a co-author of Volume 4.

SWANSON, GUY E.   1960   *The Birth of the Gods: The Origin of Primitive Beliefs*. Ann Arbor: Univ. of Michigan Press.

SYMPOSIUM ON THE EVOLUTION OF MAN'S CAPACITY FOR CULTURE, CHICAGO, 1957   1959   *The Evolution of Man's Capacity for Culture*. Detroit: Wayne State Univ. Press.

TYLOR, EDWARD B.   (1871) 1958   *Primitive Culture: Researches Into the Development of Mythology, Philosophy, Religion, Art and Custom*. 2 vols. Gloucester, Mass.: Smith. → Volume 1: *Origins of Culture*. Volume 2: *Religion in Primitive Culture*.

TYLOR, EDWARD B.   (1888) 1961   On a Method of Investigating the Development of Institutions: Applied to Laws of Marriage and Descent. Pages 1–28 in Frank W. Moore (editor), *Readings in Cross-cultural Methodology*. New Haven: Human Relations Area Files Press.

WARD, LESTER F.   (1883) 1926   *Dynamic Sociology: Or, Applied Social Science, as Based Upon Statical Sociology and the Less Complex Sciences*. New York: Appleton.

WHITE, LESLIE A.   1949   *The Science of Culture: A Study of Man and Civilization*. New York: Farrar, Straus. → A paperback edition was published in 1958 by Grove.

WHITE, LESLIE A.   1959   *The Evolution of Culture: The Development of Civilization to the Fall of Rome*. New York: McGraw-Hill.

V

SOCIAL EVOLUTION

Evolutionary theory dominated sociological thought in the nineteenth and early twentieth centuries, but since about 1920 interest in it has, on the whole, given way to preoccupation with systematic analysis of social systems, analysis of broad social and demographic trends, and investigation of the social determinants of behavior (Ginsberg 1932). The recent tentative revival of interest in an evolutionary perspective is closely related to growing interest in historical and comparative studies. It does not, however, denote a mere return to the assumptions of the classical evolutionists, but rather it implies revision and reappraisal of evolutionary theory in the light of recent advances in sociological theory and research.

From the point of view of sociological analysis, the older evolutionary models broke down mainly over two stumbling blocks. The first was the assumption that the development of human societies is relatively cumulative and unilinear and that the major "stages" of development are universal—even if there are many differences in detail and even if not all societies reach every stage of evolution. The second stumbling block was the failure to specify fully the systemic characteristics of evolving societies or institutions or the mechanisms and processes of change through which the transitions from one "stage" to another were effected. Most of the classical evolutionary schools tended, rather, to point out general causes of change (economic, technological, spiritual) or some general trends (for example, the trend to complexity) inherent in the development of societies. Very often they confused such general tendencies with the causes of change or assumed that these general tendencies explained concrete instances of change (Bock 1963).

Attempts to reappraise evolutionary perspectives, therefore, must address themselves to several basic problems inherent in the new analytical developments in sociological theory, on the one hand, and in the general setting of the evolutionary problem, on the other (Wolf 1964; Parsons 1964; Eisenstadt 1963*a*). The first crucial problem concerns the extent to which change from one type of society to another is not accidental or random but, rather, evinces over-all evolutionary or developmental trends. Second is the question of the extent to which such changes are cumulative within any given society and within any given institutional sphere in different societies (Wolf 1964). Third is the problem of the extent to which such changes do indeed enhance the adaptive potential of a society in relation to its cultural and natural environment—however such adaptation and environment are defined (White 1959; Sahlins & Service 1960).

Furthermore, even if some such common characteristics or trends can be found within different and disparate societies, the question remains as to the validity of talking about the evolution of human society or culture as a whole. Here three subproblems exist: the first is the extent to which other societies constitute the "environment" of any society—that is, the environment to which any given single society has to adapt and which can enhance the general reservoir of its techniques of adaptation. The second is a question of the extent to which institutions and forms of organization that have adaptive value can be borrowed and transplanted from one society to another, thus enhancing their adaptive potential. And, finally, we must ask to what extent human society is a "system of points" with some common adaptive and integrative mechanisms. As distinct from the general theory of cultural evolution, which in a way assumes the unity of mankind and hence also the internal transferability of institutions or techniques, the focus of sociological analysis is on the relations between the systemic characteristics of societies in interaction with their natural, social, and cultural environments, on the one hand, and some possible broader trends of changes and transformations in their "transbiological" or superorganic abilities and traditions, on the other (Mead 1964).

The starting point of all these discussions, especially from the point of view of the relation between the transformative capacities of any single society and any possible general trends in the development of human societies and human society in general, is the problem of the extent to which such changes may be envisaged as crystallizing into developmental "stages"—a key concept in classical evolutionary thought (Ginsberg 1932). In the older evolutionary school such stages were construed mostly in terms of "specialization" and "complexity," whereas in recent works these concepts have been to a large extent replaced by that of "differentiation."

Differentiation and institutional growth

Differentiation, like complexity or specialization, is first of all a classificatory concept. It describes the ways through which the main social functions or the major institutional spheres of society become dissociated from one another, attached to specialized collectivities and roles, and organized into relatively specific and autonomous symbolic and organizational frameworks within the confines of the same institutional system. In broad evolutionary terms, such continuous differentiation has usually been conceived as a continuous development starting from the "ideal" type of the primitive society or band, in which all the major roles are allocated on an ascriptive basis and the division of labor is based primarily on family and kinship units. Development then proceeds through various stages of specialization and differentiation.

Specialization is first manifest when each of the major institutional spheres, through the activities of people placed in strategic roles within it, develops its own organizational units and complexes and its specific criteria of action. The latter tend to be congruent with the basic orientations of a given sphere, facilitating the development of its potentialities: technological innovation, cultural and religious creativity, expansion of political power or participation, or development of complex personality structure.

Second, different levels or stages of differentiation denote the degree to which major social and cultural activities as well as certain basic resources —such as manpower and economic resources— have been disembedded or freed from kinship, territorial, and other ascriptive units (Parsons 1964; Bellah 1964; Eisenstadt 1963a). Although these "free-floating" resources pose new problems of integration, they may also become the basis for a more differentiated social order that is, at least potentially, better adapted to deal with a more variegated environment. Thus, a new set of problems—those of integration—emerges as the very crux of the way in which such resources can be utilized for the crystallization of some general transformative potentials within a society.

Problems of integration.   As the more differentiated and specialized institutional spheres become more interdependent and potentially complementary in their functioning within the same over-all institutionalized system, this very complementarity creates more difficult and complex problems of integration. The growing autonomy of each sphere of social activity, and the concomitant growth of interdependence and mutual interpenetration among them, pose for each sphere ever more difficult problems in crystallizing its own tendencies and potentialities and in regulating its normative and organizational relations with other spheres. And at each more "advanced" level or stage of differentiation, the increased autonomy of each sphere creates increasingly more complex problems of integrating these specialized activities into one systemic framework.

The growing autonomy of the different institutional spheres and the extension of their organizational scope not only increase the range and depth of social and human problems but also open up new possibilities for technological development, expansion of political power or rights, and cultural creativity. Growing differentiation also enhances systemic sensitivity to a much wider physical–technical environment and to more comprehensive intersocietal relations. But the growth of systemic sensitivity to new problems and exigencies does not necessarily imply a concomitant development of the ability to deal with these problems, nor does it indicate the ways in which these problems may be solved. At any given level of differentiation an institutional sphere may or may not achieve an adequate degree of integration, and the potentialities unfolded through the process of differentiation may be "wasted"—that is, they may fail to become crystallized into an institutional structure.

Recognition of the integrative problems that are attendant on new levels of differentiation constitutes the main theoretical implication of the concept of differentiation, and it is in the light of the analytical problems raised by this implication that the various questions pertinent to a reappraisal of the evolutionary perspective in social science have to be examined. We are as yet far from any definitive answers to these questions, but at least we can point out some of the most important problems of research in this direction.

Responses to differentiation

The passage of a given society from one stage of differentiation to another is contingent on the development within it of certain processes of change which create a degree of differentiation that cannot be contained within the pre-existing system. Growing differentiation and the consequent structural breakthroughs may take place through a secular trend of differentiation, or through the impact of one or a series of abrupt changes, or both. These tendencies may be activated by the occupants of strategic roles within the major institutional spheres as they attempt to broaden the

scope and develop the potentialities of their spheres. The extent to which these changes are institutionalized and the concrete form they take in any given society necessarily depend on the basic institutional contours and premises of the pre-existing system, on its initial level of differentiation, and on the major conflicts and propensities for change within it (Eisenstadt 1964b).

We need not assume that all changes in all societies necessarily increase differentiation. On the contrary, the available evidence shows that many social changes do not give rise to over-all changes in the scope of differentiation but result, instead, mainly in changes in the relative strength and composition of different collectivities or in the integrative criteria of a particular institutional sphere. Largely because the problem has not yet been fully studied, we do not know exactly what conditions facilitate or precipitate these different types of change in different societies and what makes for variations in innovative or transformative capacities among different societies (Eggan 1963; Sahlins 1964).

Even when social change increases differentiation, the successful, orderly institutionalization of a new, more differentiated social system is not always a necessary outcome. Moreover, at any level of development, response to the problems created by the process of differentiation may take one of several different forms (Weber 1922a; Eisenstadt 1963a). The most extreme outcome is failure to develop any adequate institutional solution to the new problems arising from growing differentiation. Aside from biological extinction, the consequences may be total or partial disintegration of the system, a semiparasitic existence at the margin of another society, or total submersion within another society.

A less extreme type of response tends to lead to "regression," that is, to the institutionalization of less differentiated systems within the more differentiated system that has broken down. Examples include the establishment of small patrimonial or semifeudal chiefdoms on the ruins of the Achaemenid Empire, the development of dispersed tribal–feudal systems at the downfall of the Roman Empire, and similar developments on the ruins of Greek city-states. Many such regressive developments are only partial, in the sense that within some parts of the new institutional structure some nuclei of more differentiated and creative orientations may survive or even develop. Sometimes, but certainly not always, these nuclei "store" entrepreneurial ability for possible—but not inevitable—future developments.

Another possibility, which perhaps overlaps with the last one but is not always identical with it, is the development of a social system in which the processes of differentiation and change go on relatively continuously in one part or sphere of a society without becoming fully integrated into a stable, wider framework. In such situations a continuous process of unbalanced change may develop, resulting either in a breakdown of the existing institutional framework or in stabilization at a relatively low level of integration. Perhaps the best examples of such developments can be found in various "dual conquest" societies (for example, conquest of the sedentary population by nomads in the Mongol Empire) and especially in the pre-independence stages of modern colonial societies.

A fourth, and perhaps the most variegated, type of response to growing differentiation consists of some structural solution that is on the whole congruent with the relevant problems. Within this broad type a wide variety of concrete institutional arrangements is possible. Such different solutions usually have different structural results and repercussions. Each denotes a different structure crystallized according to different integrative criteria and is interpenetrated in a different way by the other major social spheres.

Thus, drawing on examples from the great centralized empires of history, we see that although the initial stages of socioeconomic differentiation were relatively similar in Byzantium, in the later (Abbasside) caliphate, and in post-Han China, each of these societies developed different over-all institutional structures (Eisenstadt 1963a). The Byzantine Empire became a highly militarized and politically oriented system, whereas the caliphate developed a theocratic structure, which was based on continuous attempts to institutionalize a new type of universalistic politicoreligious community. China developed a centralized system based on the power of the emperor and the bureaucracy and, at the local level, on the relative predominance of the gentry; the selective channels of the examination system and the elite formed by the literati were the major mechanisms for integrating the local and central levels.

One very interesting structural solution is the development of a relatively stable system in which the major institutional spheres vary in degree of differentiation. One of the most important examples of such variation occurs in feudal systems, which are characterized by a relatively high degree of differentiation in some of the central cultural roles as against a much smaller degree of differentiation in the economic and political roles.

In cases of such uneven differentiation the more differentiated units of such related societies (for example, the church in feudal or patrimonial systems) often tend to develop a sort of international system of their own, apart from that of their "parent" societies.

The variety of integrative criteria and institutional contours at any level of differentiation is, of course, not limitless. The very notion of interdependence among major institutional spheres negates the assumption that any number of levels of differentiation in different institutional spheres can coalesce into a relatively stable institutional system. The level of differentiation in any one sphere necessarily constitutes, within broad limits, a precondition for the effective institutionalization of certain levels of differentiation in other social spheres. But within these broad limits of mutual preconditioning a great deal of structural variety is possible.

The intersocietal environment. The processes of change and of differentiation, on the one hand, and the development of different integrative responses to them, on the other, do not take place within single, closed societies. They are closely related to the international system that constitutes the broader environment of any society. Each society is related to many others geopolitically, ecologically, and socioculturally. These relations constitute the environment to which each society has to adapt and which may also influence its ability to evolve institutional responses to the processes of change.

Such international geopolitical factors, in the broadest sense, not only provide the general setting for any given society but also give rise to many of the concrete pressures upon it, such as external pressures of population, problems of military security, or adjustment to international trade. Such an intersocietal environment need not always consist of societies of the same type or level of differentiation; it may, indeed, contain many different types of societies. In general, it can be assumed that the more differentiated a society is, the greater is its *systemic* sensitivity—although not necessarily its ability to cope with these problems—to a wider and more variegated international setting.

Thus, at any given level of differentiation, the crystallization of different institutional orders is shaped by the interaction between the broader structural features of the major institutional spheres, on the one hand, and, on the other, the development of elites or entrepreneurs in some of the institutional spheres of that society, in some of its enclaves, or even in other societies with which it is in some way connected.

The variability in the concrete components of such interaction helps to explain the great (but not limitless) variety of structural and integrative forms that may be institutionalized at any given level of differentiation. Although different societies may arrive at broadly similar stages of evolution in terms of the differentiation of their major institutional and symbolic spheres, yet the concrete institutional contours developed at each such step, as well as the possible outcomes of such institutionalization in terms of further development, breakdown, regression, or stagnation, may differ greatly among them.

Reappraising evolutionary theory

The preceding analysis of processes of change and differentiation and of concomitant institutionalization of new structures indicates some of the problems that are posed by any attempt to reappraise the evolutionary perspective in sociological theory.

First is the exploration of the different mechanisms of social change and the distinction between those conditions and processes of change that create potentialities for transformation and those that do not. It is obvious, as indicated above, that not all processes of social change necessarily give rise to changes in over-all institutional systems. Although the potentialities for such systemic changes (as distinct from changes in patterns of behavior, in the composition of subgroups, or in the contents of the major integrative criteria of different spheres) exist in all societies, the very actualization of these potentialities, as well as the tempo and direction of such changes, varies greatly among different societies (Eggan 1963; Eisenstadt 1963a).

Second, and closely connected with the first, is the problem of how cumulative the development is of different types of institutional organization. Here it seems that in some institutions there may indeed be a "scale" or "semiscale" order of development, although the application of scale analysis to this type of phenomenon has so far failed to detect any perfect regularities (Carneiro 1962; Goodenough 1963). Such scale order is probably to be found least in the sphere of kinship or family institutions, whereas it is more pronounced in those institutional spheres, such as economics, politics, and law, that are most closely connected with technology or with organizational problems (Wolf 1964; Schwartz & Miller 1964).

However, even the existence of such scale order does not necessarily imply that developments in any institutional sphere are necessarily cumulative in the sense that they can be transferred easily from one society to another at a similar general level of differentiation; neither does it imply that their development within any single society or their transfer from one to another must necessarily proceed in a certain order or that "jumps" are not possible. Studies of the modernization of traditional societies are especially relevant from the point of view of the possibilities of such jumps, although similar cases can probably be found in other types of societies also (Eisenstadt 1963b). At most, studies of such scale order indicate that a certain trait or organizational type may be a necessary, but certainly not a sufficient, condition for the emergence of another; even here, the findings of "quasi scales" indicate the possibility of many functional equivalents of any such trait in a sequential series—especially in cases of rapid social change (Schwartz & Miller 1964).

Third is the question of the extent to which the problems arising from growing differentiation and the institutional solutions to these problems are indeed the same in different societies, thus creating some common trend of development. This problem is very close to that of the relation, to use Sahlins' and Service's nomenclature (1960), between "specific" and "general" evolution or that of the feasibility of the assumption, as put by Eggan (1963, p. 355), "that these particular developments necessarily add up to 'the succession of culture through stages of overall progress,' which is general evolution." But there appears to be no reason why all societies should reach certain stages of differentiation or why they should necessarily develop the same types of institutional contours once they attain such stages. The most that can be claimed at present is that the processes of differentiation in different societies exhibit similar formal and structural characteristics and that these create somewhat similar integrative problems.

It is in these common characteristics and problems that the fact of the common humanity of all human societies, as well as the possibilities of some common understanding and of intersocietal borrowing and transfer of institutions, is rooted; moreover, these characteristics indicate the existence of some "evolutionary universals" in the development of different human societies (Parsons 1964). However, the variety of possible "functional equivalents" of institutionalized solutions to such problems, as well as the possibilities of "regression," stress the fact that the paths of development of different societies are neither necessarily common nor given. In other words, there is no reason to assume that there is a *necessary* relation and congruity between the mechanisms of genetic (here cultural or social) "transmission and change and the route of development of this or that organism or species" (Gellner 1965, p. 17).

This discussion is closely related to the fourth, very crucial problem involved in the reappraisal of evolutionary perspectives: the explanation of the variability of institutionalized solutions to the problems arising from the development of a given level of structural differentiation. Here it should be recognized that the conditions giving rise to structural differentiation and to "structural sensitivity" to a greater range of problems do not necessarily create the capacity to solve these problems.

Creative entrepreneurial elites. The crucial factor is the presence or absence, in one or several institutional spheres, of an active group of special "entrepreneurs"—that is, an elite that is able to offer solutions to the new range of problems. Among modern sociologists Weber came closest to recognizing this factor when he stressed that the creation of new institutional structures depends heavily on the "push" given by various "charismatic" groups or personalities and that the routinization of charisma is critical for the crystallization and continuation of new institutional structures (Weber [1922b] 1963, chapters 4, 10, and 11). The development of such "charismatic" personalities or groups constitutes perhaps the closest social analogy to genetic mutation. It is the possibility of such mutation that explains why, at any level of differentiation, a given social sphere contains not one but several, often competing, possible orientations and potentialities for development.

As yet, we know little about the specific conditions (as distinct from the more general trend toward structural differentiation) that facilitate the rise of new elites—that is, the conditions which influence the nature of their basic orientations as well as their relations with broader groups, strata, and trends of development, and their ability to forge out and maintain a viable institutional order. There are indications, however, that factors beyond the general trend toward differentiation are important. For example, various special enclaves, such as sects, monasteries, and sectarian intellectual groups or scientific communities, play an important role in the formation of such elites. Furthermore, a number of recent studies (see, for instance, McClelland 1961; Hagen 1962) have indicated the importance of certain familial, ideological, and educational orientations and institutions.

Within this context, it is necessary to re-examine the whole problem of the extent to which institutional patterns are crystallized through diffusion from other societies rather than through independent invention within a society. Cases of diffusion might be partially due to successful importation, by entrepreneurial groups on the margins of a given society, of acceptable solutions to latent problems or needs within that society.

Intersocietal borrowing. The problems of the interaction between processes of change and "mutative" elites are closely related to a set of problems bearing on the intersocietal nature of evolution. We have seen that the international setting not only constitutes the environment to which any single society has to adapt itself but also provides a reservoir of responses that may be available to it; for instance, the setting may provide enclaves from which new elites or adaptive techniques and organizations can be borrowed.

The existence of such interrelationships—in terms of both common problems and the possibility of "borrowing" solutions—necessarily underlies the basic mutual resemblance of human societies, and it is in turn closely related to the problem of the extent to which it is possible to talk about general "social" evolution or the evolution of human society as a total entity. However, the existence of such mutual resemblance certainly does not ensure that the development of "human society" as a unified system with common adaptive mechanisms necessarily increases its ability to deal with over-all problems of adaptation. Paradoxically, the very interrelatedness of societies may create problems with which they may not be able to deal. What may seem to be a positive accumulation of available mechanisms and a repertoire of adaptations from the point of view of human society as a whole may yet, because of the lack of intersocietal integrative and adaptive mechanisms, constitute a very grave problem.

Limitations of evolutionary theory

The considerations presented above constitute the background for a reappraisal of the evolutionary perspective within the framework of recent sociological theory. An evolutionary perspective, from the point of view of human societies, makes sense only so far as at least some of the processes of change that are inherent in any social system create the potentialities for the institutionalization of more differentiated social and symbolic systems. From the point of view of human society or culture as a whole, such a perspective makes sense only insofar as there exist some mechanisms for the transmission of various institutional and adaptive techniques and for creating some common, intersocietal, adaptive and integrative capabilities and frameworks.

With regard to all these areas, several problems for which there exist as yet no adequate solutions have been pointed out above. They have, in a way, all focused on the interaction between processes of social differentiation, on the one hand, and the formation and activities of different elites, on the other. It is this interaction that makes possible the institutionalization of different integrative principles and concrete structures at a given level of societal differentiation. Any search for solutions to these problems must concentrate on the various aspects of these processes. In this endeavor broad evolutionary considerations indicate ranges of possibilities and types of potential breakthroughs but do not in themselves provide answers.

SHMUEL N. EISENSTADT

[*Directly related are the entries on* EMPIRES; FEUDALISM; SOCIAL INSTITUTIONS. *Other relevant material may be found in* ANTHROPOLOGY; DIFFUSION.]

BIBLIOGRAPHY

BELLAH, ROBERT N. 1964 Religious Evolution. *American Sociological Review* 29:358–374.

BOCK, KENNETH E. 1963 Evolution, Function and Change. *American Sociological Review* 28:229–237.

CARNEIRO, ROBERT L. 1962 Scale Analysis as an Instrument for the Study of Cultural Evolution. *Southwestern Journal of Anthropology* 18, no. 2:149–169.

EGGAN, FRED 1963 Cultural Drift and Social Change. *Current Anthropology* 4:347–355.

EISENSTADT, SHMUEL N. 1963a *The Political Systems of Empires.* New York: Free Press. → Contains an extended bibliography.

EISENSTADT, SHMUEL N. 1963b *Modernization: Growth and Diversity.* Bloomington: Indiana Univ., Department of Government.

EISENSTADT, SHMUEL N. 1964a Social Change, Differentiation and Evolution. *American Sociological Review* 29:375–386.

EISENSTADT, SHMUEL N. 1964b Institutionalization and Change. *American Sociological Review* 29:235–247.

GELLNER, ERNEST 1965 *Thought and Change.* London: Weidenfeld & Nicolson.

GINSBERG, MORRIS (1932) 1961 The Concept of Evolution in Sociology. Volume 1, pages 180–199 in Morris Ginsberg, *Essays in Sociology and Social Philosophy.* London: Heinemann.

GOODENOUGH, WARD H. 1963 Some Applications of Guttman Scale Analysis to Ethnography and Culture Theory. *Southwestern Journal of Anthropology* 19: 235–250.

HAGEN, EVERETT E. 1962 *On the Theory of Social Change.* Homewood, Ill.: Dorsey.

MCCLELLAND, DAVID C. 1961 *The Achieving Society.* Princeton, N.J.: Van Nostrand.

MEAD, MARGARET 1964 *Continuities in Cultural Evolution.* New Haven: Yale Univ. Press.

PARSONS, TALCOTT 1964 Evolutionary Universals in Society. *American Sociological Review* 29:339–357.

SAHLINS, MARSHALL D. 1964 Culture and Environment: The Study of Cultural Ecology. Pages 132–147 in Sol Tax (editor), *Horizons of Anthropology.* Chicago: Aldine.

SAHLINS, MARSHALL D.; and SERVICE, ELMAN R. (editors) 1960 *Evolution and Culture.* Ann Arbor: Univ. of Michigan Press.

SCHWARTZ, RICHARD D.; and MILLER, JAMES C. 1964 Legal Evolution and Social Complexity. *American Journal of Sociology* 70:159–169.

WEBER, MAX (1922a) 1957 *The Theory of Social and Economic Organization.* Edited by Talcott Parsons. Glencoe, Ill.: Free Press. → First published as Part 1 of *Wirtschaft und Gesellschaft.*

WEBER, MAX (1922b) 1963 *The Sociology of Religion.* Boston: Beacon. → First published in German.

WHITE, LESLIE A. 1959 *The Evolution of Culture: The Development of Civilization to the Fall of Rome.* New York: McGraw-Hill.

WOLF, ERIC R. 1964 The Study of Evolution. Pages 108–119 in Sol Tax (editor), *Horizons of Anthropology.* Chicago: Aldine.

VI
EVOLUTION AND BEHAVIOR

The fundamental postulate of the modern biological theory of evolution is that the guiding agency of evolutionary changes is adaptation to the environments that a species inhabits. This is equally true of changes in structural features, physiology, and behavior of organisms. Evolutionary developments maintain the adaptedness of the species when the environments change, or they improve the adaptedness if the environments are more or less stationary. The environment does not, however, impose changes on the organism, as was believed by some early evolutionists, particularly by the adherents of the now almost completely abandoned Lamarckian hypothesis. It is more accurate to say that the environment presents challenges, to which a living species may respond by adaptive modification of its genetic endowment (genotype). If a response is elicited, the adaptedness is preserved or improved; if the species fails to respond, its fitness declines and it may become extinct. The genetic raw materials from which evolutionary changes may be constructed are mutations, that is, alterations in the gene or chromosome structures. The effects that mutations produce vary in magnitude all the way from alterations so drastic that the mutant is inviable (lethal, as a fatal hereditary disease causing death before sexual maturity) to changes so slight that the change in fitness, if any, that they produce can be detected only by means of refined statistical study. Mutant genes may be favorable only in heterozygous carriers (hybrid vigor, or heterosis) but unfavorable in double dose (in homozygous condition). Or a genetic change may be favorable in some environments and unfavorable in others. Or, finally, a mutant gene may be favorable in combinations with some genes but unfavorable in combination with others.

The great evolutionary importance of sexual reproduction lies in that it constantly combines and recombines the various genes present in the species population, enabling the favorable gene combinations to arise and to be tested by natural selection. In sexually reproducing and outbreeding species, such as man, no two individuals (except identical twins) have the same genotype. We inherit our genes from our parents and pass them to our children, but the gene constellation, the genotype, of every individual is unique. By and large, the greater the change a mutation produces, the greater the chance it will be harmful to the organism.

The adaptive evolutionary changes are compounded almost exclusively of the slight mutational changes (sometimes termed polygenic changes). Changes of greater magnitudes are important rather as the source of the genetic pathology, incapacitation, or weakness. Such diseases as phenylketonuria, with its associated mental defects, and schizophrenia, to name only two, are examples of deleterious mutants affecting behavior. Apart from their negative importance for public health, mutations that produce strikingly visible alterations are also important as materials for genetic studies. Most of the pioneering work in genetics was done with genetic variants that must be classed as more or less pathological deviants and that play only negative roles in evolution, contributing to the "genetic load" the population carries.

Natural selection.   Mutational changes, those affecting behavior as well as those responsible for structural and physiological alterations, are mostly harmful to the organism. This is the reason why any increase of the frequency of mutations in human populations (for example, through exposure to X rays, other mutagenic radiations, or chemical mutagens) can result only in a reduction of the average fitness of the populations concerned. How, then, can mutations serve as building blocks for adaptive evolutionary changes? The answer is that mutational changes and their combinations are sorted out by natural selection. The majority of mutations that decrease the fitness of their carriers in all environments and in all combinations are cast out of the populations by natural selection; those that are useful in at least some environments and in some combinations are preserved and multiplied.

The action of natural selection is sometimes compared to that of a sieve, separating the useful genetic variants from the harmful ones. This analogy is misleading if it is taken too literally. Human populations, and those of most sexually reproducing and outbreeding species, always carry great stores of genetic variants which arose by mutation in the immediate or remote past. The genetic reassortments, combined with natural selection in changing environments, become a cybernetic process in which the genetic developments that occur at a given time depend upon the changes that have taken place earlier, and, in turn, they condition the developments that may take place in the future.

Mutation, the process that supplies the raw materials from which evolutionary changes can be constructed, is repeatable and reversible; it is a physiological and, in the last analysis, a mechanical process. But the evolution controlled by natural selection becomes a creative process that is unlikely to be reversed or to be repeated. Evolutionary transformations, such as the transformations that have led to the emergence of the human species, are chains of unique, nonrecurrent events.

Importance of environment.   Another consideration, particularly relevant in relation to the evolution of behavior, is that heredity determines not fixed "characters" or "traits" but reactions of the developing organism to the environment. The trait "behavior" obviously cannot be transmitted in inheritance, because it is not present in the sex cells, which are the only material bridge connecting the parents with their progeny. But neither is the skin color inherited in this sense, because no skin pigment is present in the sex cells. What the sex cells do carry are genes, and the genes determine the pattern, or path, that the development of an individual will follow in a given sequence of environments. Another individual with similar genes, an identical twin, may develop differently if his environments are different. A carrier of a different set of genes might also develop differently in similar environments.

We observe that human beings vary with respect to a great many traits—skin color, height, weight, head shape, intelligence, temperament, and special abilities, among countless others. As a broad generalization, it is fair to say that whenever the variation in any trait has been adequately studied genetically, it has been found to be influenced by both genetic and environmental factors. In the past, investigators have often tried to determine which traits are genetic or hereditary and which are environmental; such a dichotomy is now recognized as naive and misleading. All traits, or at any rate a great majority of them, are both genetic and environmental. If everybody had the same genes, as identical twins do, people would look and behave more nearly alike than they actually do. Likewise, if the environments in which people grow and develop were made uniform, this would also result in a reduction of the observed structural and behavioral diversity.

Fixity and conditioned plasticity. No living species inhabits an absolutely uniform and constant environment. Organisms have to face many environments, variable both in space and in time. For example, the inhabitants of the temperate and cold climates must survive in both summer and winter environments. Man achieves more and more effective control over his physical environments, but he must face a great and growing diversity of sociocultural environments. There are two ways to become adapted to a diversity of environments, and both have actually been used in the evolutionary process, including human evolution. One is genetic fixity and genetic specialization; the other is genetically conditioned developmental plasticity. In general, genetic fixity is characteristic of traits whose presence and precise form are indispensable for survival and reproduction. The developmental processes giving rise to such traits are said to be homeostatically buffered, so that they can occur in all environments that the species normally encounters in its habitats. Thus, with very few exceptions, all infants are born with two eyes, a four-chambered heart, physiological systems which digest food and maintain a constant body temperature, ability to learn a symbolic human language, etc. Genetic specialization makes the species polymorphic (consisting of two or more genetically distinct forms living and interbreeding in the same territory) or polytypic (consisting of races that inhabit different territories and are genetically adapted to the environments of their respective territories). For example, the darker and the lighter skin pigmentation of some human races is plausibly supposed to fit them to the climatic conditions of the lands in which they originally lived.

Genetically conditioned developmental plasticity is advantageous when the organism profits by having some traits shaped differently in the different environments that it encounters. The tanning of human skin on exposure to sunlight is an example of such a plasticity. It is important to realize that both fixity and plasticity are genetically deter-mined. Natural selection favored the spread and establishment of mutant genes which in some populations make the skin permanently darkly pigmented and in other races make the pigmentation contingent on sun exposure.

Culture. The most significant product, and the paramount determining factor, of human evolution is culture. The relationships between the biological evolution and culture are frequently misunderstood, and it is important to make them clear. Culture is not transmitted biologically through some special genes; it is acquired anew in every generation by learning and instruction, in large part through the medium of the symbolic language. However, the capacity to learn and to instruct and, most essential of all, the capacity to use the symbolic language, is biologically and genetically vouchsafed to every nonpathological human being. An individual whose genes deprive him of these capacities is an obvious misfit, and his genes are likely to be eliminated by natural selection. Conversely, it is safe to assume that the genetic equipment that made the human species capable of developing and maintaining culture has been compounded by natural selection in the course of the prehuman, subhuman, and human evolution.

Of the many existing forms of human culture, the particular one an individual acquires is determined by the society in which this individual is brought up, rather than by his genes. And yet, not only the ability to acquire any culture at all but also the capacity and inclination to choose this or that occupation, role, or trade within a culture may well be genetically conditioned, facilitated, or hindered. The ability to speak is genetically determined, but what a person will actually say is largely independent of genetics.

Human acquired, extrabiological culture is man's most potent adaptive instrument; it is chiefly by brain, not by brawn, that man controls his environments. Since, however, human environments are preponderantly created by culture, the possession of a genetic endowment that enables members of human populations to adapt themselves to these cultural environments becomes overwhelmingly important. The evolution of the biological basis of human behavior has been controlled by this fact. In all cultures, primitive as well as advanced, the vital ability is, and always was, for every individual to be able to learn whatever is necessary to become a competent member of the culture of which the individual is a part. For this reason, natural selection has favored in human evolution a remarkable plasticity of the behavioral development; man's cardinal adaptive trait is his educability, that is, his capacity to adjust his behavior to circumstances in the light of experience.

Most individuals can be trained, with a greater or lesser facility, for many or most of the occupations and roles that a given culture requires to be filled. Almost everybody could become, if properly brought up, a fairly competent farmer, craftsman, soldier, sailor, teacher, or priest. This is the valid premise of the *tabula rasa* theory, from which this theory draws an erroneous conclusion. First clearly stated by John Locke in 1690, this theory is still popular in many circles. It asserts that a human being at birth is a clean slate on which the environment will inscribe a collection of attributes and qualities. The genetically secured developmental plasticity of human behavior, however, is not at all incompatible with genetic diversity. It is eminently probable that an infant at birth is not a clean slate and that some individuals are, because of their genetic endowments, more easily trainable for some occupations than for others. This is certain for some specialized professions; by no means does everybody have the genetic wherewithal to become a fine singer or a first-class composer or performer of music, or to achieve peak performance in sports or in art.

Biologically, this makes sense; the development of cultures and civilizations has not caused the diversity of vocations to become smaller; on the contrary, this diversity increases by leaps and bounds. The biologically adaptive response to this situation is obviously a combination of an educability or trainability, with an underlying genetic diversity to facilitate the division of labor.

The fallacy of racism.   While the variants of the *tabula rasa* theory would make us believe that all the observed differences, especially all the differences in behavior, between people are the products of upbringing and education, the even more pernicious fallacy of racism would claim that these differences are genetically fixed and largely independent of the environment. One superficially plausible argument often given in favor of racist views is worth discussing here, because it will enable us to bring out clearly an important feature of the evolution of human behavior. It is claimed that the variation in psychic or behavioral traits among human individuals and races must be genetically fixed to about the same extent as it is among breeds of domestic animals. Different breeds of dogs, horses, or cattle are indeed clearly different in behavior, temperament, disposition, intelligence, trainability, etc. These differences are very largely genetically fixed, although by careful training and discipline one can modify them to some

extent. Why then, it is argued, should the differences between humans be supposed to be anything but genetic?

This argument overlooks a profound dissimilarity between the evolutionary histories of the human species and of the animals that man has domesticated. The behavior of a breed of a domestic animal is an essential part of the complex of characteristics that are selected to fit this breed for its intended use. A work horse should not behave like a race horse, because this would make it dangerous and inefficient, and a race horse should not behave like a work horse if it is to win any races. The laboratory mouse and the laboratory rat are sluggish, unaggressive, and apparently dimwitted compared to the wild mouse and the wild rat. They would hardly survive under the conditions in which their wild ancestors thrive; it has been claimed that these species have degenerated when man has furnished their food and shelter. It is, however, obvious that wild mice and wild rats are inconvenient as laboratory animals, and that is why they are seldom used in laboratories.

What would be rated as degenerate in the wild state is a desirable trait in an animal living in a laboratory cage. Man has seen to it that the genes for fixing and stabilizing desirable behavior are established and that the genes for undesirable behavior are bred out of the animals he has domesticated. Although some writers have seen fit to call man a "self-domesticated" animal (a designation accepted by few biologists), his evolutionary pattern is in many ways just the reverse. As previously stated, natural selection may favor mutant genes that confer a developmental fixity on some traits and developmental plasticity on others; the latter is the case with human behavior. A person who is able to learn whatever modes of behavior fit various professions and vocations available in a human society, and to adjust himself to the ways of life that go with these professions and vocations, is likely to have both a social and a biological advantage. An individual set in his ways, always aggressive or always yielding, unable and unwilling to learn or to be trained, is likely to be discriminated against by natural selection. The great developmental plasticity of psychic traits in man is, thus, no biological accident but, on the contrary, a fundamental evolutionary adaptation that distinguishes man from nonhuman animals.

Ethics.   A considerable amount of speculation has been devoted to the problem of whether human ethics could have arisen through the action of natural selection in the evolutionary process. Natural selection is obviously not a benevolent spirit guiding the evolution but a blind and opportunistic process. It is opportunistic in the sense that it promotes the establishment of genes which confer an advantage for survival or reproduction when and where the selection acts, regardless of whether these same genes may be disadvantageous later on. The extinction of countless species of organisms has been due to such a narrow, overspecialized adaptation to the environments that did not endure. Now, it is conceivable that natural selection might encourage genes for altruistic behavior in a species broken up into numerous small colonies or subpopulations. "Altruistic" is in this case to be defined as a behavior benefiting the group (family, clan, tribe) to which the individual so behaving belongs and detrimental to that individual himself. A small population in which genes for such behavior occur may prosper and multiply, despite some of the carriers of these genes sacrificing themselves for the sake of their fellows and thus not transmitting their genes to their own progeny. Conversely, in a large, undivided population, genes for "egotistic" or "criminal" behavior may secure an advantage, if their carriers survive and leave progeny at the expense of other members of the population.

Another possibility is that altruism and egotism are not products of some kind of special genes but, rather, products of cultural developments transmitted not by genes but by learning. C. H. Waddington (1960) has argued that natural selection acts to make man an "ethicizing being" and an "authority acceptor." Particularly in childhood but also during his entire life, a person is able and even eager to acquire, from his parents or from other persons, ideas about what is good and what is evil and to accept instruction or counsel concerning the desirable ways of living in a society with other human beings. According to this view, man is not born virtuous or vicious but with a capacity for both virtue and vice. Biological evolution does not make man ethically better or worse, but it does promote intellectual alacrity and perhaps a sensitivity to ethical issues.

Future developments. Even more speculative and uncertain are the attempts to prognosticate the future evolutionary developments of human behavioral traits and capacities. This is evidently a part of a more general problem of the evolutionary perspectives of the human species. An opinion often expressed is that the biological evolution of man has virtually completed its course, and from now on any further development will be in the cultural realm. This is true to the extent that cultural changes are more rapid than the genetic ones, and this is, in fact, the reason why the development of the capacity for culture has conferred upon the human species an unprecedentedly high biological fitness. It should, however, be kept in mind that the maintenance, not to speak of further expansion, of cultural capacities is possible only on the basis of sound human genetic endowments. Improvement, maintenance, and prevention of deterioration of these genetic endowments is the task of the applied science of eugenics. Many eugenists have been extremely pessimistic about the genetic future of mankind, believing that the genetic processes which go on in human populations trend inexorably toward biological disaster. Others have urged various remedial schemes, such as sterilization of the unfit, or the artificial insemination of women by semen collected from biologically superior donors and preserved in frozen condition for extensive use over the years. During the first third of the twentieth century, eugenics was often used as a support of ultraconservative social philosophies and racist doctrines. All this has made many social scientists, and the public at large, properly skeptical and suspicious of eugenic schemes. Yet eugenics undoubtedly has a sound core; sooner or later man will be forced to take the management of his evolution in his own hands.

THEODOSIUS DOBZHANSKY

[*Other relevant material may be found in* EUGENICS; GENETICS; PSYCHOLOGY, *article on* COMPARATIVE PSYCHOLOGY; *and in the biography of* DARWIN.]

BIBLIOGRAPHY

DOBZHANSKY, THEODOSIUS 1962 *Mankind Evolving: The Evolution of the Human Species.* New Haven: Yale Univ. Press.

DOBZHANSKY, THEODOSIUS 1964 *Heredity and the Nature of Man.* New York: Harcourt.

FULLER, JOHN L.; and THOMPSON, W. ROBERT 1960 *Behavior Genetics.* New York: Wiley.

HALLER, MARK H. 1963 *Eugenics: Hereditarian Attitudes in American Thought.* New Brunswick, N.J.: Rutgers Univ. Press.

HIRSCH, JERRY 1962 Individual Differences in Behavior and Their Genetic Basis. Pages 3–23 in Eugene L. Bliss (editor), *Roots of Behavior: Genetics, Instinct, and Socialization in Animal Behavior.* New York: Harper.

ROE, ANNE; and SIMPSON, GEORGE G. (editors) 1958 *Behavior and Evolution.* New Haven: Yale Univ. Press.

WADDINGTON, CONRAD H. 1960 *The Ethical Animal.* London: Allen & Unwin.

EXCHANGE, ECONOMIC

See EXCHANGE AND DISPLAY; SPECIALIZATION AND EXCHANGE.

EXCHANGE, SOCIAL

See under INTERACTION.

EXCHANGE AND DISPLAY

Exchange refers to the transaction of labor, resources, products, and services within a society. Exchange is not limited to the market economies of industrial societies. Market economies appeared late in world history and until recently were few in number. Even today most of the world's societies do not have fully developed market economies; the range extends from those with no market institutions whatsoever, through those with peripheral markets, to those with important but by no means fully developed market institutions. For such economies as these, it is necessary to consider modes of exchange other than market exchange.

Karl Polanyi (1944; Polanyi et al. 1957) identified and defined three modes of exchange: reciprocal, redistributive, and market. The three modes of exchange are found singly or in combination in the economic organizations of the diverse societies of the world. They seem to be capable of clear and evident definition whatever the complexities required in the analysis of their operation in an economic system. In brief, reciprocity is obligatory gift exchange; redistribution is obligatory payment to an allocative center; and market exchange is purchase and sale with reference to a price system. The three modes subsume all the types of exchange recognized in any society. Transfers or transactions that cannot be included in these categories are considered by a society to be illegitimate or wrong for that very reason.

Most important of all, however, the three modes are the functioning aspects of the integrative structures of various types of economies. A society can be structurally integrated by its social, political, or economic organization, or by some combination of these organizations. When one of these structures predominates or, more rarely, is the sole structure present in the society, a clear model type is discernible. There are three such clear model types. For example, a social economy is one in which the social organization integrates economic life; here reciprocity is the prevailing mode of exchange. In a political economy, the political organization integrates economic life; redistributive exchange prevails. In a market-integrated economy, market exchange prevails. It follows that there will be mixed types of economy ranging through those in which two of the three possible structures of the society seem to be of about equivalent importance, but predominate over the third, to one in which all three have a roughly equivalent importance.

In the comparative study of exchange, the subject of gift giving has a historical and continuing place. It was Marcel Mauss who first investigated the socioeconomic nature of gift giving, and his ideas form part of the present discussion of reciprocal exchange.

The subject of display, which has excited analytical interest since Thorstein Veblen's *The Theory of the Leisure Class* (1899), will be discussed in relation to the three modes of exchange. It will be shown that there are three types of display, each of which is specific to one of the three modes of exchange and its type of economy and social context.

Reciprocity and social economy

Marcel Mauss pointed out the completely obligatory character of gift exchange. He described it as one of the many forms of obligatory reciprocity that expressed and maintained the articulated individual and group relationships of primitive social systems (1925). There existed no "natural," or "pure," market economy in primitive societies. Goods had social or moral value but not some separate economic value. They were exchanged in the same social way as were courtesies and respects or as "entertainments, ritual, military assistance, women, children, dances, and feasts; and fairs in which the market is but one element and the circulation of wealth but one part of a wide and enduring contract." Gift exchange, therefore, was part of a system of "total prestations," as Mauss termed it, in which individuals in a society had both to give and receive in all social exchanges under the "sanction of private or open warfare." If gift giving (or any other sort of social exchange) is often thought of as free and voluntary, it is because the members of a social group far more willingly receive and give than they act in any way that would threaten their membership in the group. The ideas of Mauss continue to be useful but require reworking.

Reciprocity, the receiving and giving of goods and services, is built into the human life cycle and the social order. Without it the nonproducing young could not live and mature to provide the next generation with its livelihood and the social order its continuity. There would be no cushioning of misfortune or infirmity, and the world would be without festivity, hospitality, and benefice. Reciprocity as a mode of exchange is a different matter. It is not universally an important mode of exchange except in those societies that are called primitive by the anthropologist. In nonprimitive folk, peasant, or state-organized societies, reciprocities involve one or both of the other two modes of exchange. For example, for reciprocal gift giving to take place in industrial society, it is necessary for the donors to go into the market for the gifts they will exchange; even the crudest *Kindergarten Handarbeit* will have required for its manufacture some tool or material obtained in the market.

The distinctive character of primitive societies is that they are organized by their social structures. Primitive societies are without independent economic or political structuring. The economic order is "embedded" in the social order as is the political order (Polanyi 1944, p. 57). The rigorous study of such societies is the study of kinship and its extensions and affiliations and of the interrelations of the roles and social groupings formed on a kinship base. Economic aspects can be analyzed out of this social matrix, but such analysis will prove only that in so socialized a situation economic facts are social facts as well, and their ordering follows or is the social organization of the group concerned. It is proposed here that the economic systems of all such groups be called *social economies*. The use of this term sets out the distinguishing features of such systems and prevents the confusions that arise when the economy of such a group is spoken of as if it were a version, albeit a primitive version, of the separable and independent economic systems referred to by the economist.

Reciprocity is the prevailing and characteristic mode of exchange in the world's social economies, which is to say a majority of the world's societies up to the industrial revolution. Nothing other than a social economy existed until the development in the Neolithic of some state organizations or political economies. It is only in the past two centuries that the intrusions of Western market economies or Western political power exerted along economic lines have brought about the extinction of almost all pure social economies save, perhaps, those in Amazonas and the interior of New Guinea. Today, therefore, there are few going social economies in which reciprocity is the sole mode of exchange; but the number in which it is still the dominant mode of exchange is not insignificant, containing as it does a large number of African tribal societies and some Oceanic and American Indian societies.

A full illustration of how reciprocal exchanges follow the lines and groupings of the social structure in a social economy cannot be presented here. The reader is referred to such classic studies as Malinowski's study of the Trobriand Islanders (1922) and Firth's study of the Tikopia (1939). Certain famous institutions of primitive cultures, such as bridewealth, *kula*, and the potlatch have excited interest precisely because each demonstrates the essentially social nature of reciprocal exchange involving valued goods. Anthropologists and other social scientists have examined and re-examined these three institutions as somehow exemplary statements of some key part of the problem of the relation between the economic and the noneconomic in human society.

Bridewealth comprises goods, and sometimes labor services, transferred from the groom's social group to that of the wife. The institution of bridewealth is widespread in Africa, where it is almost always a vitally important institution and quite often highly elaborated. The goods used as bridewealth range from cattle to such items as hoes and pots. Elaborations occur in the amount of the bridewealth; in the number of installments in which it is transferred; in the presence, amount, and number of reciprocal goods (dowry) the wife may bring to the marriage; or in "cattle linking," in which a given marriage and transfer of bridewealth in cattle is determined by past marriages and predetermines future ones. The earlier term used for the institution was "brideprice," but the substitution of the term "bridewealth," suggested by Evans-Pritchard (1931, pp. 36–39), is now widely accepted. "Price" is a term that cannot be lifted out of the context of market economy free of the connotations of purchase and sale. The problem is therefore set: if there is an exchange in which goods of value and a woman are transferred, why is this not a matter of purchase and sale? The anthropologists' answer, although some are not in agreement on this point (Gray 1960), is that this transfer occurs in the context of a rearrangement of the social structure. The marriage creates new reciprocal roles, with new obligations and expectations; the giving of bridewealth is more important symbolically than it is economically. It is thus part of a vast series of social reciprocities and reciprocal exchanges of, as Mauss would say, courtesies, respects, women, dances, and so on, as well as of goods of value. The difference lies precisely in the fact that reciprocal exchange is part of continuing social process and behavior, while market exchange is an isolated, one-time economic act.

Kula is an institution of reciprocal exchange in which permanent partners give and receive recognized treasure items. There are two types of such treasure, which circulate in opposite directions around a *kula* ring made up of a number of island societies of the western Pacific. The institution is best known from the description of the Trobriand Islands by Malinowski (1922). The treasure items are shell armlets and spondylus shell necklaces, which are surrounded by lore and myth and which cannot be exchanged for anything besides one another in the *kula* ring. *Kula* partners engage in reciprocal exchanges of second-grade items (Bohannan 1963, p. 236) as an earnest of the generosity with which they will reciprocate gifts of the treasure items of the greatest possible value in the lore and myth that attaches to them. The whole affair is fraught with the real and magical hazards of long sea voyages by canoe, with elaborate ritual and ceremonial attesting to its importance and assuring its proper conduct and success, and with thrill and wonder about the treasures that have been or might be received. There is no question about the noneconomic nature of the *kula*. It is a reciprocal exchange devoid of economic motive, basis, or gain. This noneconomic interpretation of *kula* itself has been generally accepted, even by those who have claimed that *kula* was a pretext for carrying on a higgling pedestrian trade in very ordinary goods on the side—never with *kula* partners—during *kula* voyages. The problem *kula* sets is the same whatever emphasis is given to the non-*kula* trading on the side. Why is the institution so elaborated, and why are its opportunities so enthusiastically pursued? The only possible answer is that the reciprocal exchange of goods without economic value, no less than economic goods, acknowledges social worth by giving content to the playing of a social role. In *kula*, as is sometimes the case in bridewealth, there is feedback between the recognition of an individual's social prestige within his own society and outside it with his *kula* partners of other societies.

The potlatch of the Indian societies of the northwest coast of North America is an institution of reciprocal exchange in which the frequency, size, and system of exchanges became so great in some cases as to seem not only unique but also bizarre and incredible. It was among the Kwakiutl, in the first quarter of the twentieth century, that the potlatch reached its most extreme development (Codere 1950; 1961). At a potlatch, goods were ceremoniously displayed and then distributed by the potlatcher to a number of individuals of higher and lower social rank. The recipients returned the gift with an increment when they potlatched at some later date. Although the individuals concerned received their potlatch positions through inheritance, it was only by potlatching that the social rank and worth of these positions was maintained or enhanced. Enormous inventories of goods were involved in the over-all system of potlatching and even on the occasion of a single potlatch. The Kwakiutl earned Canadian dollars, particularly in the commercial fishing industry. These earnings were converted into vast quantities of mass-produced Western industrial goods, such as cheap blankets, clothing, housewares, and so on, all of which circulated in the potlatch system in amounts far above consumption needs and possibilities,

along with such traditional non-European goods as wooden canoes. The great season for potlatching was the wintertime, which was largely a time of vacation from economic effort. However, the only vacation from potlatching was just after giving one. The cycle of accumulating property by hard work and by making loans at interest began again as did the accumulation of new indebtedness through receiving goods as new or as returned gifts from other potlatchers. As in the case of *kula*, an immense lore captured the interest of the people. Twenty-five years after the effective end of potlatching, former participants were still recounting the details of past potlatches and the titles, rhetoric, and historical and mythical background associated with them.

The problem set by the potlatch is by now a familiar one with a familiar answer. In a social economy, the ends of all efforts are social; and they are organized along the lines of the social system itself, according to the reciprocal form of all social exchanges.

Redistribution and political economy

Redistribution is the form of exchange that occurs when taxes or other exactions are collected and reallocated by an administrative center. The term is not of the same descriptive accuracy as Polanyi's other two terms, since it does not make clear the nature of the exchange that takes place. Perhaps a better term would be "politically enforced exchange." It is political power that is behind the exaction of goods and services in exchange for membership in good standing in the polity along with whatever reallocations might be received in return. Such reallocations may be in the form of benefit from internal and territorial policing, judicial institutions, and public works or distributions.

Some redistributive exchange exists in many social economies. A rudimentary form of it would be the collection of foodstuffs by a headman for the giving of a feast in which all share. Redistribution also occurs in the relatively few predominantly market economies of the mid-nineteenth-century industrial nations, since some taxation was present in all of them. However, redistribution is the dominant mode of exchange in the political economies that include all those centralized state organizations, archaic and recent, from ancient Egypt, medieval Europe, and pre-Columbian Peru, to precolonial African and Asiatic states. In the political economy, the market is either relatively undeveloped or secondary and subservient to the polity, which, in large part, controls distribution of goods.

The precontact kingdom of Rwanda in east central Africa corresponds to the model of a political economy in which redistribution is the dominant mode of exchange. In Rwanda social life as well as economic life was politicized, although it is the latter that is of concern here (Codere 1962). The masses of the people were peasants who were forced to contribute goods and services to the support of a vast and complex political administration headed by the king, or *mwami* as he was called. Although they are said to have gloried in their poverty and subjugation, which is a matter in doubt, they received little beyond the minimum reallocations in return for almost the entirety of their production over and above what was needed for their own bare subsistence. From their feudal overlords, who were members of the governing caste and often simultaneously their local civil or military administrators, they received the custody and usufruct of a cow. This was probably more important as a symbol of being in good standing with the ruling caste than it was as an economic asset. From their administrators they received military protection, courts, and whatever benefits were inherent in the idea that the entire fertility and welfare of the land and the people depended upon the going order of things with the *mwami* at the head of the centralized state and its administration. The chief redistribution in Rwanda's economy was, in fact, the contribution made by the masses to the support of the few. The ruling caste comprised 15 per cent of the total population and was supported at a level of living that was always higher, and often astronomically higher, than that of the masses. The use or threat of force perpetuated the system.

The use of Rwanda as an example is not to suggest that all political economies have been similarly despotic or similarly one-sided in exacting much and reallocating very little in exchange. Rwanda, however, presents a type case of a political economy in which redistribution is the predominant mode of exchange. Market exchange was virtually nonexistent; and reciprocal exchange was cut back to a minimum, since the masses had neither the kinship organization development nor the economic wherewithal for it. In order to achieve such political ends as improving and maintaining their own power positions within the political hierarchy, the ruling caste engaged in a small number of reciprocal exchanges and in some exchanges of a redistributive character.

Market exchange and market economies

In the comparison of modes of exchange in diverse societies and economies, the salient features of market exchange are purchase and sale at a money price determined by the impersonal forces of supply and demand. It is important to emphasize the abstract and impersonal nature of market exchange as compared to the other two modes. Features that are the essence of reciprocal and redistributive exchange can be, and usually are, eliminated as irrelevancies in market exchange. These include, for example, the social and political roles of the exchangers, the obligatory sociability or ceremoniousness connected with the act of exchange, and social and political restrictions and specifications concerning which goods are exchangeable. To be sure, mutual courtesies and recognition of social worth or political position may accompany any instance of purchase and sale; but they are not necessary. Where they are present, it is either as an irrepressible human element or as part of the amount on the price tag, adjusted to cover such costs as time-consuming courtesy and the elegance of the place of sale.

Although economists have treated most industrial national economies as though they were analogs of the pure market economy model, it is those of the nineteenth century that fit the model best, since they entailed less regulation for any social or political end. Of them, Polanyi wrote (1944, p. 57): "Instead of economy being embedded in social relations, social relations are embedded in the economic system"; and he also stated that "a market economy is an economic system controlled, regulated and directed by markets alone" (p. 68). In a pure market economy, social and political relations are economized. It is not that social and political relations cease to exist; the former are necessary for the continuation of society and the latter for the policing of the market and enforcement of the principle of contract, by means of which it works. Where market exchange prevails, social and political organization give way to economic organization. It was in the dehumanizing and desocializing consequences of market autonomy that such critics of the system as Marx, Engels, Veblen, and Polanyi found their target, just as critics of totalitarian regimes have centered on the human costs of the politicizing of society.

Mixed modes of exchange

Perhaps in no empirical economy in the contemporary world is reciprocity, redistribution, or market exchange the sole mode of exchange, although typically one of the modes may predominate. In primitive societies, the usual situation today is a mixture of the three modes. This has sometimes come about through internal development but more often through the political and economic intrusions of the expanding industrial nations of the West.

In primitive societies where developments, especially of marketlike exchange, have been indigenous and contact influences slight, the three modes of exchange have frequently coexisted as separate spheres that have remained relatively compartmentalized. These have been termed "multicentric" economies by Bohannan and Dalton (1962, p. 3). An example would be Trobriand society (Malinowski 1922; Bohannan 1963, pp. 233–240), in which reciprocity is found in *kula* and kinship relations, redistribution in the exchanges of chiefs and others, and marketlike exchange, or an imperfect and moneyless market exchange, is represented by the ordinary trade accompanying the *kula* and in internal island trade. Another example is provided by Kwakiutl society (Codere 1950; 1961), as it existed from the turn of the century to the depression of the 1930s. Reciprocity characterized many exchanges of subsistence goods between kin and villagers, as well as exchange between individuals in the potlatch system. Market exchange in the Canadian market economy was the source of most of the goods used in potlatching, and some redistribution occurred in the special type of potlatching involved in the purchase of "coppers."

When the three modes of exchange are linked and cross-linked in contemporary economies, they rarely appear as distinct spheres but are relatively integrated by market exchange and the use of money. Thus, many economies today, industrial or nonindustrial, seem to be genuinely mixed economies. Africa furnishes many examples of social or social–political economies that have been permeated by market exchange. Western industrial nations exemplify the process in reverse as their nineteenth-century pure market exchange economies have been transformed into mixed ones. In Africa the European imposition of a money head tax on tribesmen forced the African into market exchange. By the time a man worked for the European to earn money to pay his own tax and that of his kinsmen, and returned with gifts purchased in the market and with money with which to buy a cow or cows for bridewealth, the three modes of exchange were linked and cross-linked. In the Western industrial nations, it was perhaps inevitable that where political power became more widely distributed among the people they would use it to regulate and use the market economy for social ends. For example, the social reciprocity of supporting aged kinfolk is in part taken care of by the payment of taxes and the redistribution to them of money they use in market exchange for purchases to meet their own needs, for gifts to give

reciprocally, and for redistributive payments such as property or sumptuary taxes.

Display

Veblen's *The Theory of the Leisure Class* (1899) is the point of departure for all inquiries into the meaning and uses of display in human society. His terms "conspicuous consumption," "conspicuous waste," and "conspicuous leisure" are still telling, and useful in discussions patterned after his on the universal association of display with social position and prestige. Contemporary social scientists, however, find universals of interest only if they can be fruitfully used in explanations of social behavior. They are not content to conclude, as Veblen did, that display is irrational from an economic point of view, or to leave the discussion of display, irrationality, prestige, and society on a generalized level.

By centering attention on display as it is associated with exchange, it seems possible to discern its essential role in society. This enables us to explain why it takes the forms it does and why it is associated with social prestige, political power, or economic importance.

The most frequent, most important, and most elaborate laying out of goods before the eyes of others will be connected with exchange and specific to the particular mode of exchange. To return to the model systems, in social economies, where reciprocal exchange predominates, the great displays are associated with those exchanges. Similar generalizations can be made for the political and market economies. The great displays are also great events that give visible proof of the productive effort and exchange relations that can be mobilized. They reaffirm and celebrate the system, even while they are part of it.

Displays connected with reciprocal exchange in social economies are frequently modest ones. There is not the production capacity in many cases to achieve anything much more impressive than sufficient food and drink for feasting and sufficient time to prepare for the festivities and participate in them. For example, the Papago Indians of southwestern North America had a saguaro, or cactus-fruit, wine feast, for which everyone produced and set out as many pots of wine as possible and then got publicly, communally, and "beautifully" drunk. In their desert environment and with their specific technology, this was probably the greatest abundance they could have produced; it was witnessed and enjoyed, and it was a great yearly event.

At the other extreme, in the rich natural environment of the northwest coast of North America the displays connected with potlatching were probably the greatest of any ever associated with reciprocal exchange in any primitive society. Wooden statues were often set up a hundred feet or so apart, marking the boundaries of the beachfront display of the goods that had been given away in a potlatch. Of course, these statues then measured the impressiveness of subsequent potlatch displays. The eye of the witness was delighted as well as impressed by various devices of presentation. Gold and silver bracelets, suspended from small stakes planted on the beach, stirred in the breeze and caught the sunlight. Display was part of the actual distribution of goods; every item was publicly and often glowingly mentioned as it was given away, and every lot, of blankets, for example, was publicly counted out. Feasting and entertainment, special carved wooden feast dishes, and special costumes were all part of the show.

Whether modest or pretentious, such displays showed the social worth of the individuals or groups who were responsible for them. Their ability and desire to support social relationships for social as well as private ends were on view.

Display connected with redistributive exchange consists of processions, panoply, public works, and state festivals and entertainments; it is inspiring or intimidating depending upon the nature of the political power concerned and the onlooker's or participant's relation to it.

In the African kingdom of Rwanda, the greatest displays were redistributive. The king's retinue, court, and capital; the review of the royal cattle; the performances of the royal dancers; the magnificence of the royal progress whenever the *mwami* traveled about; and the conspicuous bounty of goods, foodstuffs, milk pots, beer pots, and everything that poured into his household were all part of the pattern. It was repeated on a smaller scale for every lesser political figure in the system.

Other examples of redistributive displays include the Panathenaic festival and the Parthenon; the Roman triumph; and the Coliseum and its circuses. In these societies, which were political economies, however different their polities, the displays connected with redistributive exchange were the most important of any displays that were made in the society. These displays were part of the redistributive exchange itself. The thousands of citizens or subjects whose accumulated tax or tribute payments made such displays possible may have received little in addition to spectacle. The function of such display was the demonstration of political power and its ability to organize all aspects of a society, including the economic aspect.

Display connected with market exchange is so familiar it requires little discussion. Its means are the market place, the fair, the store, the showcase, and so on, not forgetting the ubiquitous extensions of the market place via printing and electronics. While the general purpose of such display is to entice and facilitate purchase, each instance of display has the particular purpose of enabling the particular goods concerned to compete, on as favorable terms as possible, with all the other goods of the market. It is for this reason that its arts and artifices are so highly developed, for they must make up the difference needed for successful sales competition. Display in market economies can be institutional in nature and aim, like some of the great trade fairs. It can also proclaim the ramifications of the system and the general wealth of goods it has made available. However, this is a small part of the total amount of display connected with market exchange; the typical appeal is not "Buy!", but "Buy such-and-such!" It can therefore be said of the display connected with market exchange that its functions and purposes in society are practically the same, that is, to maximize and to integrate the market.

Research on exchange along comparative and behavioral lines will be increasingly developed by anthropologists, if not by economists, since it promises a more profound understanding of the economic aspects of society. There is a need for more detailed and quantified field study of exchange in its full social and cultural context. When such a field as that of kinship and social organization has been developed to the point of rigorous and quasi-mathematical treatment, there seems no good reason why the field of exchange, with its clear factual basis (something being exchanged for something with someone), cannot be reduced to similar clarity, detail, and order.

HELEN CODERE

[*See also* ECONOMIC ANTHROPOLOGY; TRADE AND MARKETS. *Other relevant material may be found in the biographies of* MALINOWSKI; MAUSS; POLANYI; VEBLEN.]

BIBLIOGRAPHY

BOHANNAN, PAUL 1963 *Social Anthropology*. New York: Holt.

BOHANNAN, PAUL; and DALTON, GEORGE (editors) 1962 *Markets in Africa*. Northwestern University Africa Studies, No. 9. Evanston, Ill.: Northwestern Univ. Press.

CODERE, HELEN 1950 *Fighting With Property: A Study of Kwakiutl Potlatching and Warfare, 1792–1930*. American Ethnological Society, Monograph No. 18. New York: Augustin.

CODERE, HELEN 1961 Kwakiutl. Pages 431–516 in Interuniversity Summer Research Seminar, University of New Mexico, 1956, *Perspectives in American Indian Culture Change*. Univ. of Chicago Press.

CODERE, HELEN 1962 Power in Ruanda. *Anthropologica* New Series 4:45–85.

DALTON, GEORGE 1961 Economic Theory and Primitive Society. *American Anthropologist* New Series 63:1–25.

DOUGLAS, MARY 1962 Lele Economy Compared With the Bushong: A Study of Economic Backwardness. Pages 211–233 in Paul Bohannan and George Dalton (editors), *Markets in Africa*. Evanston, Ill.: Northwestern Univ. Press.

EVANS-PRITCHARD, E. E. 1931 An Alternative Term for "Bride-price." *Man* 31:36–39.

FIRTH, RAYMOND W. (1929) 1959 *Economics of the New Zealand Maori*. 2d ed. Wellington: Owen. → First published as *Primitive Economics of the New Zealand Maori*.

FIRTH, RAYMOND W. (1936) 1957 *We, the Tikopia: A Sociological Study of Kinship in Primitive Polynesia*. 2d ed. London: Allen & Unwin. → A paperback edition was published in 1963 by Beacon.

FIRTH, RAYMOND W. (1939) 1965 *Primitive Polynesian Economy*. 2d ed. Hamden, Conn.: Shoe String Press.

FIRTH, RAYMOND W. 1951 *Elements of Social Organization*. London: Watts.

GRAY, ROBERT F. 1960 Sonjo Bride-price and the Question of African "Wife Purchase." *American Anthropologist* New Series 62:34–57.

HERSKOVITS, MELVILLE J. (1940) 1952 *Economic Anthropology: A Study in Comparative Economics*. 2d ed., rev. & enl. New York: Knopf. → First published as *The Economic Life of Primitive Peoples*.

MALINOWSKI, BRONISLAW 1921 The Primitive Economics of the Trobriand Islanders. *Economic Journal* 31:1–16.

MALINOWSKI, BRONISLAW (1922) 1960 *Argonauts of the Western Pacific: An Account of Native Enterprise and Adventure in the Archipelagoes of Melanesian New Guinea*. London School of Economics and Political Science, Studies, No. 65. London: Routledge; New York: Dutton. → A paperback edition was published in 1961 by Dutton.

MANNERS, ROBERT A. 1962 Land Use, Labor, and the Growth of Market Economy in Kipsigis Country. Pages 493–519 in Paul Bohannan and George Dalton (editors), *Markets in Africa*. Evanston, Ill.: Northwestern Univ. Press.

MAUSS, MARCEL (1925) 1954 *The Gift: Forms and Functions of Exchange in Archaic Societies*. Glencoe, Ill.: Free Press. → First published as *Essai sur le don: Forme et raison de l'échange dans les sociétés archaïques*.

MYRDAL, GUNNAR (1956) 1957 *Rich Lands and Poor: The Road to World Prosperity*. Rev. ed. New York: Harper. → First published as *Development and Underdevelopment*.

NASH, MANNING 1964 The Organization of Economic Life. Pages 171–180 in Sol Tax (editor), *Horizons of Anthropology*. Chicago: Aldine.

POLANYI, KARL 1944 *The Great Transformation*. New York: Rinehart. → A paperback edition was published in 1957 by Beacon.

POLANYI, KARL; ARENSBERG, CONRAD; and PEARSON, HARRY W. (editors) 1957 *Trade and Market in the Early Empires*. Glencoe, Ill.: Free Press.

UNDERHILL, RUTH (1937) 1939 *Social Organization of the Papago Indians*. 2d ed. Columbia University Contributions to Anthropology, Vol. 30. New York: Columbia Univ. Press.

VEBLEN, THORSTEIN (1899) 1953 *The Theory of the Leisure Class: An Economic Study of Institutions*. Rev. ed. New York: New American Library. → A paperback edition was published in 1959.

EXCHANGE RATES
See under INTERNATIONAL MONETARY ECONOMICS.

EXCISE TAXES
See under TAXATION.

EXCLAVES
See ENCLAVES AND EXCLAVES.

EXECUTIONS
See CAPITAL PUNISHMENT.

EXECUTIVE, POLITICAL
See POLITICAL EXECUTIVE. *Related material may be found under* ADMINISTRATION *and* LEADERSHIP.

EXISTENTIAL PSYCHOLOGY
See under PSYCHOLOGY.

EXOGAMY
See INCEST *and* MARRIAGE.

EXPECTATIONS, ECONOMIC
See ECONOMIC EXPECTATIONS.

EXPERIMENTAL DESIGN

I
THE DESIGN OF EXPERIMENTS

In scientific research, the word "experiment" often denotes the type of study in which the investigator deliberately introduces certain changes into a process and makes observations or measurements in order to evaluate and compare the effects of different changes. These changes are called the *treatments*. Common examples of treatments are different kinds of stimuli presented to human subjects or animals or different kinds of situations with which the investigator faces them, in order to see how they respond. In exploratory work, the objective may be simply to discover whether the stimuli produce any measurable responses, while at a later stage in research the purpose may be to verify or disprove certain hypotheses that have been put forward about the directions and sizes of the responses to treatments. In applied work, measurement of the size of the response is often important, since this may determine whether a new treatment is practically useful.

A distinction is often made between a controlled experiment and an uncontrolled observational study. In the latter, the investigator does not interfere in the process, except in deciding which phenomena to observe or measure. Suppose that it is desired to assess the effectiveness of a new teaching machine that has been much discussed. An observational study might consist in comparing the achievement of students in those schools that have adopted the new technique with the achievement of students in schools that have not. If the schools that adopt the new technique show higher achievement, the objection may be raised that this increase is not necessarily caused by the machine, as the schools that have tried a new method are likely to be more enterprising and successful and may have students who are more competent and better prepared. Examination of previous records of the schools may support these criticisms. In a proper experiment on the same question, the investigator decides which students are to be taught by the new machine and which by the standard technique. It is his responsibility to ensure that the two techniques are compared on students of equal ability and degree of preparation, so that these criticisms no longer have validity.

The advantage of the proper experiment over the observational study lies in this increased ability to elucidate cause-and-effect relationships. Both types of study can establish associations between a stimulus and a response; but when the investigator is limited to observations, it is hard to find a situation in which there is only one explanation of the association. If the investigator can show by repeated experiments that the same stimulus is always followed by the same response and if he has designed the experiments so that other factors that might produce this response are absent, he is in a much stronger position to claim that the stimulus causes the response. (However, there are many social science fields where true experimentation is not possible and careful observational investigations are the only source of information.) [See, for example, EXPERIMENTAL DESIGN, article on QUASI-EXPERIMENTAL DESIGN; OBSERVATION; SURVEY ANALYSIS.]

Briefly, the principal steps in the planning of a controlled experiment are as follows. The treatments must be selected and defined and must be relevant to the questions originally posed. The *experimental units* to which the treatments are to be applied must be chosen. In the social sciences, the experimental unit is frequently a single animal or human subject. The unit may, however, be a group of subjects, for instance, a class in comparisons of teaching methods. An important point is that the choice of subjects and of the environmental conditions of the experiment determine the range of validity of the results.

The next step is to determine the size of the sample—the number of subjects or of classes. In general, the precision of the experiment increases as the sample size increases, but usually a balance must be struck between the precision desired and the costs involved. The method for allocating treatments to subjects must be specified, as must the detailed conduct of the experiment. Other factors that might influence the outcome must be controlled (by *blocking* or *randomization*, as discussed later) so that they favor each treatment equally. Finally, the responses or criteria by which the treatments will be rated must be defined. These may be simple classifications or measurements on a continuous scale. Like the treatments, the responses must be relevant to the questions originally posed.

History.   The early history of ideas on the planning of experiments appears to have been but little studied (Boring 1954). Modern concepts of experimental design are due primarily to R. A. Fisher, who developed them from 1919 to 1930 in the planning of agricultural field experiments at the Rothamsted Experimental Station in England. The main features of Fisher's approach are as follows (*randomization*, *blocking*, and *factorial experimentation* will be discussed later):

(1) The requirement that an experiment itself furnish a meaningful estimate of the underlying variability to which the measurements of the responses to treatments are subject.

(2) The use of randomization to provide these estimates of variability.

(3) The use of blocking in order to balance out known extraneous sources of variation.

(4) The principle that the statistical analysis of the results is determined by the way in which the experiment was conducted.

(5) The concept of factorial experimentation, which stresses the advantages of investigating the effects of different factors or variables in a single complex experiment, instead of devoting a separate experiment to each factor.

These ideas were stated very concisely by Fisher in 1925 and 1926 but more completely in 1935.

Experimental error

Some sources of experimental error. A major problem in experimentation is that the responses of the experimental units are influenced by many sources of variation other than the treatments. For example, subjects differ in their ability to perform a task under standard conditions: a treatment that is allotted to an unusually capable group of subjects will appear to do well; the instruments by which the responses are measured may be liable to errors of measurement; both the applied treatment and the environment may lack uniformity from one occasion to another.

In some experiments, the effects of subject-to-subject variation are avoided by giving every treatment to each subject in succession, so that comparisons are made within subjects. Even then, however, learning, fatigue, or delayed consequences of previously applied treatments may influence the response actually measured after a particular treatment.

The primary consequence of extraneous sources of variation, called *experimental errors*, is a masking of the effects of the treatments. The observed difference between the effects of two treatments is the sum of the true difference and a contribution due to these errors. If the errors are large, the experimenter obtains a poor estimate of the true difference; then the experiment is said to be of low precision.

Bias. It is useful to distinguish between random error and error due to bias. A bias, or systematic error, affects alike all subjects who receive a specific treatment. Random error varies from subject to subject. In a child growth study in which children were weighed in their clothes, a bias would arise if the final weights of all children receiving one treatment were taken on a cold day, on which heavy clothing was worn, while the children receiving a second treatment were weighed on a mild day, on which lighter clothing was worn. In general, bias cannot be detected in the analysis of the results, so that the conclusions drawn by statistical methods about the true effects of the treatments are misleading.

It follows that constant vigilance against bias is one of the requisites of good experimentation. The devices of randomization and blocking, if used intelligently, do much to guard against bias. Additional precautions are necessary in certain types of experiments. If the measurements are subjective evaluations or clinical judgments, the expectations and prejudices of the judges and subjects may influence the results if it is known which treatment any of the subjects received. Consequently, it is important to ensure, whenever it is feasible, that neither the subject nor the person taking the measurement knows which treatment the subject is receiving; this is called a "double blind" experiment. For example, in experiments that compare different drugs taken as pills all the pills should look alike and be administered in the same way. If there is a no-drug treatment, it is common practice to administer an inert pill, called a *placebo*, in order to achieve this concealment.

Methods for reducing experimental error. Several devices are used to remove or decrease bias and random errors due to extraneous sources of variation that are thought to be substantial. One group of devices may be called refinements of technique. If the response is the skill of the subject in performing an unfamiliar task, a major source of error may be that subjects learn this task at different rates. An obvious precaution is to give each subject enough practice to reach his plateau of skill before starting the experiment. The explanation of the task to the subjects must be clear; otherwise, some subjects may be uncertain what they are supposed to do. Removal from an environment that is noisy and subject to distractions may produce more uniform performance. The tasks assigned to the subjects may be too easy or too hard so that all perform well or poorly under any treatment, making discrimination between the treatments impossible. The reduction of errors in measurement of the response often requires prolonged research. In psychometrics, much of the work on scaling is directed toward finding superior instruments of measurement [*see* SCALING].

Blocking. In many experiments involving comparisons between subjects, the investigator knows that the response will vary widely from subject to subject, even under the same treatment. Often it is possible to obtain beforehand a measurement that is a good predictor of the response of the subject. A child's average score on previous tests in arithmetic may predict well how he will perform on an arithmetic test given at the end of a teaching experiment. Such initial data can be used to increase the precision of the experiment by forming blocks consisting of children of approximately equal ability. If there are three teaching methods, the first block contains the three children with the best initial scores. Each child in this block is assigned to a different teaching method. The second block contains the three next best children, and so on. The purpose of the blocking is to guarantee that each teaching method is tried on an equal number of good, moderate, and poor performers in arithmetic. The resulting gain in precision may be striking.

The term "block" comes from agricultural experimentation in which the block is a compact piece of land. With human subjects, an arrangement of this kind is sometimes called a *matched pairs* design (with two treatments) or a *matched groups* design (with more than two treatments).

A single blocking can help to balance out the effects of several different sources of variation. In a two-treatment experiment on rats, a block comprising littermates of the same sex equalizes the two treatments for age and sex and to some extent for genetic inheritance and weight also. If the conditions of the experiment are subject to uncontrolled time trends, the two rats in a block can be tested at approximately the same time.

Adjustments in the statistical analysis.   Given an initial predictor, x, of the final response, y, an alternative to blocking is to make adjustments in the statistical analysis in the hope of removing the influence of variations in x. If x and y represent initial and final scores in a test of some type of skill, the simplest adjustment is to replace y by $y - x$, the improvement in score, as the measure of response. This change does not always increase precision. The error variance of $y - x$ for a subject may be written $\sigma_y^2 + \sigma_x^2 - 2\rho\sigma_y\sigma_x$, where ρ is the correlation between y and x. This is less than σ_y^2 only if ρ exceeds $\sigma_x/2\sigma_y$.

A more accurate method of adjustment is given by the analysis of covariance. In this approach, the measure of response is $y - bx$. The quantity b, computed from the results of the experiment, is an estimate of the average change in y per unit increase in x. The adjustment accords with common sense. If the average x value is three units higher for treatment A than for treatment B, and if b is found to be $\frac{2}{3}$, the adjustment reduces the difference between the average y values by two units.

If the relation between y and x is linear, the use of a predictor, x, to form blocks gives about the same increase in precision as its use in a covariance analysis. For a more detailed comparison in small experiments, see Cox (1957). Blocking by means of x may be superior if the relation between y and x is not linear. Thus, a covariance adjustment on x is helpful mainly when blocking has been used to balance out some other variable or when blocking by means of x is, for some reason,

not feasible. One disadvantage of the covariance adjustment is that it requires considerable extra computation. A simpler adjustment such as $y - x$ is sometimes preferred even at some loss of precision.

Randomization.   Randomization requires the use of a table of random numbers, or an equivalent device to decide some step in the experiment, most frequently the allotment of treatments to subjects [*see* RANDOM NUMBERS].

Suppose that three treatments—A, B, C—are to be assigned to 90 subjects without blocking. The subjects are numbered from 1 to 90. In a two-digit column of random numbers, the numbers 01 to 09 represent subjects 1 to 9, respectively; the numbers 10 to 19 represent subjects 10 to 19, respectively, and so on. The numbers from 91 to 99 and the number 00 are ignored. The 30 subjects whose numbers are drawn first from the table are assigned to treatment A, the next 30 to B, and the remaining 30 to C.

In the simplest kind of blocking, the subjects or experimental units are arranged in 30 blocks of three subjects each. One in each block is to receive A, one B, and one C. This decision is made by randomization, numbering the subjects in any block from 1 to 3 and using a single column of random digits for the draw.

Unlike blocking, which attempts to eliminate the effects of an extraneous source of variation, randomization merely ensures that each treatment has an equal chance of being favored or handicapped by the extraneous source. In the blocked experiment above, randomization might assign the best subject in every block to treatment A. The probability that this happens is, however, only 1 in 3^{30}. Whenever possible, blocking should be used for all major sources of variation, randomization being confined to the minor sources. The use of randomization is not limited to the allotment of treatments to subjects. For example, if time trends are suspected at some stage in the experiment, the order in which the subjects within a block are processed may be randomized. Of course, if time trends are likely to be large, blocking should be used for them as well as randomization, as illustrated later in this article by the crossover design.

In his *Design of Experiments*, Fisher illustrated how the act of randomization often allows the investigator to carry out valid tests for the treatment means without assuming the form of the frequency distribution of the data (1935). The calculations, although tedious in large experiments, enable the experimenter to free himself from the assumptions required in the standard analysis of variance. Indeed, one method of justifying the standard methods for the statistical analysis of experimental results is to show that these methods usually give serviceable approximations to the results of randomization theory [*see* NONPARAMETRIC STATISTICS; *see also* Kempthorne 1952].

Size of experiment. An important practical decision is that affecting the number of subjects or experimental units to be included in an experiment. For comparing a pair of treatments there are two common approaches to this problem. One approach is to specify that the observed difference between the treatment means be correct to within some amount $\pm d$ chosen by the investigator. The other approach is to specify the power of the test of significance of this difference.

Consider first the case in which the response is measured on a continuous scale. If σ is the standard deviation per unit of the experimental errors and if each treatment is allotted to n units, the standard error of the observed difference between two treatment means is $\sqrt{2}\,\sigma/\sqrt{n}$ for the simpler types of experimental design. Assuming that this difference is approximately normally distributed, the probability that the difference is in error by more than $d = 1.96\,\sqrt{2}\,\sigma/\sqrt{n}$ is about 0.05 (from the normal tables). The probability becomes 0.01 if d is increased to $2.58\,\sqrt{2}\,\sigma/\sqrt{n}$. Thus, although there is no finite n such that the error is certain to be less than d, nevertheless, from the normal tables, a value of n can be computed to reduce the probability that the error exceeds d to some small quantity α such as 0.05. Taking $\alpha = 0.05$ gives $n = 7.7\sigma^2/d^2 \cong 8\sigma^2/d^2$. The value of σ is usually estimated from previous experiments or preliminary work on this experiment.

If the criterion is the proportion of units that fall into some class (for instance, the proportion of subjects who complete a task successfully), the corresponding formula for n, with $\alpha = 0.05$, is

$$n \cong 4[p_1(1 - p_1) + p_2(1 - p_2)]/d^2,$$

where p_1, p_2 are the true proportions of success for the two treatments and d is the maximum tolerable error in the observed difference in proportions. Use of this formula requires advance estimates of p_1 and p_2. Fortunately, if these lie between 0.3 and 0.7 the quantity $p(1 - p)$ varies only between 0.21 and 0.25.

The choice of the value of d should, of course, depend on the use to be made of the results, but an element of judgment often enters into the decision.

The second approach (specifying the power) is appropriate, for instance, when a new treatment is being compared with a standard treatment and when the investigator intends to discard the new treatment unless the test of significance shows that it is superior to the standard. He does not mind discarding the new treatment if its true superiority is slight. But if the true difference (new − standard) exceeds some amount, Δ, he wants the probability of finding a significant difference to have some high value, β (perhaps 0.95, 0.9, or 0.8).

With continuous data, the required value of n is approximately

$$n \cong 2\sigma^2(\xi_\alpha + \xi_{1-\beta})^2/\Delta^2,$$

where

ξ_α = normal deviate corresponding to the significance level, α, used in the test of significance,

and

$\xi_{1-\beta}$ = normal deviate for a *one-tailed* probability $1 - \beta$.

For instance, if the test of significance is a one-tailed test at the 5% level and β is 0.9, so that $\xi_\alpha = 1.64$ and $\xi_{1-\beta} = 1.28$, then $n \cong 17\sigma^2/\Delta^2$. The values of Δ, α, and β are chosen by the investigator.

With proportions, an approximate formula is

$$n \cong 2(\xi_\alpha + \xi_{1-\beta})^2 \bar{p}\bar{q}/(p_2 - p_1)^2,$$

where $\bar{p} = (p_1 + p_2)/2$ and $\bar{q} = 1 - \bar{p}$ and $p_2 - p_1$ is the size of difference to be detected. One lesson that this formula teaches is that large samples are needed to detect small or moderate differences between two proportions. For instance, with $p_1 = 0.3$, $p_2 = 0.4$, $\alpha = 0.05$ (two-tailed), and $\beta = 0.8$, the formula gives $n = 357$ in each sample, or a total of 714 subjects.

More accurate tables for n, with proportions and continuous data, are given in Cochran and Cox (1950) and a fuller discussion of the sample size problem in Cox (1958).

If the investigator is uncertain about the best values to choose for Δ, it is instructive to compute the value of Δ that will be detected, say with probability 80% or 90%, for an experiment of the size that is feasible. Some experiments, especially with proportions, are almost doomed to failure, in the sense that they have little chance of detecting a true difference of the size that a new treatment is likely to produce. It is well to know this before doing the experiment.

Controls. Some experiments require a *control*, or comparison, treatment. For a discussion of the different meanings of the word "control" and an account of the history of this device, see Boring (1954). In a group of families having a prepaid medical care plan, it is proposed to examine the effects of providing, over a period of time, additional free psychiatric consultation. An intensive initial study is made of the mental health and social adjustment of the families who are to receive this extra service, followed by a similar inventory at the end. In order to appraise whether the differences (final − initial) can be attributed to the psychiatric guidance, it is necessary to include a control group of families, measured at the beginning and at the end, who do not receive this service. An argument might also be made for a second control group that does not receive the service and is measured only at the end. The reason is that the initial psychiatric appraisal may cause some families in the first control group to seek psychiatric guidance on their own, thus diluting the treatment effect that is to be studied. Whether such disturbances are important enough to warrant a second control is usually a matter of judgment.

The families in the control groups, like those in the treated group, must be selected by randomization from the total set of families available for the experiment. This type of evaluatory study presents other problems. It is difficult to conceal the treatment group to which a family belongs from the research workers who make the final measurements, so that any preconceptions of these workers may vitiate the results. Second, the exact nature of the extra psychiatric guidance can only be discovered as the experiment proceeds. It is important to keep detailed records of the services rendered and of the persons to whom they were given.

Factorial experimentation

In many programs of research, the investigator intends to examine the effects of several different types of variables on some response (for example, in an experiment on the accuracy of tracking, the effect of speed of the object, the type of motion of the object, and the type of handle used by the human tracker). In factorial designs, these variables are investigated simultaneously in the same experiment. The advantages of this approach are that it makes economical use of resources and provides convenient data for studying the interrelationships of the effects of different variables.

These points may be illustrated by an experiment with three factors or variables, A, B, and C, each at two levels (that is, two speeds of the object, etc.). Denote the two levels of A by a_1 and

a_2, and similarly for B and C. The treatments consist of all possible combinations of the levels of the factors. There are eight combinations:

(1) $a_1b_1c_1$	(3) $a_1b_2c_1$	(5) $a_1b_1c_2$	(7) $a_1b_2c_2$
(2) $a_2b_1c_1$	(4) $a_2b_2c_1$	(6) $a_2b_1c_2$	(8) $a_2b_2c_2$

Suppose that one observation is taken on each of the eight combinations. What information do these give on factor A? The comparison $(2) − (1)$, that is, the difference between the observations for combinations (2) and (1), is clearly an estimate of the difference in response, $a_2 − a_1$, since the factors B and C are held fixed at their lower levels. Similarly, $(4) − (3)$ gives an estimate of $a_2 − a_1$, with B held at its higher level and C at its lower level. The differences $(6) − (5)$ and $(8) − (7)$ supply two further estimates of $a_2 − a_1$. The average of these four differences provides a comparison of a_2 with a_1 based on two samples of size four and is called the *main effect* of A.

Turning to B, it may be verified that $(3) − (1)$, $(4) − (2)$, $(7) − (5)$, and $(8) − (6)$ are four comparisons of b_2 with b_1. Their average is the main effect of B. Similarly, $(5) − (1)$, $(6) − (2)$, $(7) − (3)$, and $(8) − (4)$ provide four comparisons of c_2 with c_1.

Thus the testing of eight treatment combinations in the factorial experiment gives estimates of the effects of each of the factors A, B, and C based on samples of size four. If a separate experiment were devoted to each factor, as in the "one variable at a time" approach, 24 combinations would have to be tested (eight in each experiment) in order to furnish estimates based on samples of size four. The economy in the factorial approach is achieved because every observation contributes information on all factors.

In many areas of research, it is important to study the relations between the effects of different factors. Consider the following question: Is the difference in response between a_2 and a_1 affected by the level of B? The comparison

$$(a_2b_2 − a_1b_2) − (a_2b_1 − a_1b_1),$$

where each quantity has been averaged over the two levels of C, measures the difference between the response to A when B is at its higher level and the response to A when B is at its lower level. This quantity might be called the effect of B on the response to A. The same expression rearranged as follows,

$$(a_2b_2 − a_2b_1) − (a_1b_2 − a_1b_1),$$

also measures the effect of A on the response to B. It is called the *AB two-factor interaction*. (Some writers introduce a multiplier, $\frac{1}{2}$, for conventional reasons.) The AC and BC interactions are computed similarly.

The analysis can be carried further. The AB interaction can be estimated separately for the two levels of C. The difference between these quantities is the effect of C on the AB interaction. The same expression is found to measure the effect of A on the BC interaction and the effect of B on the AC interaction. It is called the ABC three-factor interaction.

The extent to which different factors exhibit interactions depends mostly on the way in which nature behaves. Absence of interaction implies that the effects of the different factors are mutually additive. In some fields of application, main effects are usually large relative to two-factor interactions, and two-factor interactions are large relative to three-factor interactions, which are often negligible. Sometimes a transformation of the scale in which the data are analyzed removes most of the interactions [see STATISTICAL ANALYSIS, SPECIAL PROBLEMS OF, article on TRANSFORMATIONS OF DATA]. There are, however, many experiments in which the nature and the sizes of the interactions are of primary interest.

The factorial experiment is a powerful weapon for investigating responses affected by many stimuli. The number of levels of a factor is not restricted to two and is often three or four. The chief limitation is that the experiment may become too large and unwieldy to be conducted successfully. Fortunately, the supply of rats and university students is large enough so that factorial experiments are widely used in research on learning, motivation, personality, and human engineering [see, for example, TRAITS].

Several developments mitigate this problem of expanding size. If most interactions may safely be assumed to be negligible, good estimates of the main effects and of the interactions considered likely to be important can be obtained from an experiment in which a wisely chosen fraction (say $\frac{1}{2}$ or $\frac{1}{3}$) of the totality of treatment combinations is tested. The device of *confounding* (see Cochran & Cox 1950, chapter 6, esp. pp. 183–186; Cox 1958, sec. 12.3) enables the investigator to use a relatively small sized block in order to increase precision, at the expense of a sacrifice of information on certain interactions that are expected to be negligible. If all the factors represent continuous variables ($x_1, x_2, \cdots$) and the objective is to map the *response surface* that expresses the response, y, as a function of $x_1, x_2, \cdots$, then one of the designs specially adapted for this purpose may

be used. [*For discussion of these topics, see* EXPERIMENTAL DESIGN, *article on* RESPONSE SURFACES; *see also* Cox 1958; Davies 1954.]

In the remainder of this article, some of the commonest types of experimental design are outlined.

Randomized groups. The randomized group arrangement, also called the one-way layout, the simple randomized design, and the completely randomized design, is the simplest type of plan. Treatments are allotted to experimental units at random, as described in the discussion of "Randomization," above. No blocking is used at any stage of the experiment; and, since any number of treatments and any number of units per treatment may be employed, the design has great flexibility. If mishaps cause certain of the responses to be missing, the statistical analysis is only slightly complicated. Since, however, the design takes no advantage of blocking, it is used primarily when no criteria for blocking are available, when criteria previously used for blocking have proved ineffective, or when the response is not highly variable from unit to unit.

Randomized blocks. If there are v treatments and the units can be grouped into blocks of size v, such that units in the same block are expected to give about the same final response under uniform treatment, then a randomized blocks design is appropriate. Each treatment is allotted at random to one of the units in any block. This design is, in general, more precise than randomized groups and is very extensively used.

Sometimes the blocks are formed by assessing or scoring the subjects on an initial variable related to the final response. It may be of interest to examine whether the comparative effects of the treatments are the same for subjects with high scores as for those with low scores. This can be done by an extension of the analysis of variance appropriate to the randomized blocks design. For example, with four treatments, sixty subjects, and fifteen blocks, the blocks might be classified into three levels, *high*, *medium*, or *low*, there being five blocks in each class. A useful partition of the degrees of freedom (df) in the analysis of variance of this "treatments × levels" design is as follows:

	df
Between levels	2
Between blocks at the same level	12
Treatments	3
Treatments × levels interactions	6
Treatments × blocks within levels	36
Total	59

The mean square for interaction is tested, against the mean square for treatments × blocks within levels, by the usual F-test. Methods for constructing the levels and the problem of testing the over-all effects of treatments in different experimental situations are discussed in Lindquist (1953). [*See* LINEAR HYPOTHESES, *article on* ANALYSIS OF VARIANCE.]

The crossover design. The crossover design is suitable for within-subject comparisons in which each subject receives all the treatments in succession. With three treatments, for example, a plan in which every subject receives the treatments in the order *ABC* is liable to bias if there happen to be systematic differences between the first, second, and third positions, due to time trends, learning, or fatigue. One design that mitigates this difficulty is the following: a third of the subjects, selected at random, get the treatments in the order *ABC*, a third get *BCA,* and the remaining third get *CAB.* The analysis of variance resembles that for randomized blocks except that the sum of squares representing the differences between the over-all means for the three positions is subtracted from the error sum of squares.

The Latin square. A square array of letters (treatments) such that each letter appears once in every row and column is called a Latin square. The following are two 4 × 4 squares.

	(1)				(2)		
C	A	B	D	A	B	C	D
A	B	D	C	B	C	D	A
B	D	C	A	D	A	B	C
D	C	A	B	C	D	A	B

This layout permits simultaneous blocking in two directions. The rows and columns often represent extraneous sources of variation to be balanced out. In an experiment that compared the effects of five types of music programs on the output of factory workers doing a monotonous job, a 5 × 5 Latin square was used. The columns denoted days of the week and the rows denoted weeks. When there are numerous subjects, the design used is frequently a group of Latin squares.

For within-subject comparisons, the possibility of a residual or carry-over effect from one period to the next may be suspected. If such effects are present (and if one conventionally lets columns in the above squares correspond to subjects and rows correspond to order of treatment) then square (1) is bad, since each treatment is always preceded by the same treatment (*A* by *C*, etc.). By the use of square (2), in which every treatment is

preceded once by each of the other treatments, the residual effects can be estimated and unbiased estimates obtained of the direct effects (see Cochran & Cox 1950, sec. 4.6a; Edwards 1950, pp. 274–275). If there is strong interest in the residual effects, a more suitable design is the *extra-period Latin square.* This is a design like square (2), in which the treatments *C, D, A, B* in the fourth period are given again in a fifth period.

Balanced incomplete blocks. When the number of treatments, v, exceeds the size of block, k, that appears suitable, a balanced incomplete blocks design is often appropriate. In examining the taste preferences of adults for seven flavors of ice cream in a within-subject test, it is likely that a subject can make an accurate comparison among only three flavors before his discrimination becomes insensitive. Thus $v = 7$, $k = 3$. In a comparison of three methods of teaching high school students, the class may be the experimental unit and the school a suitable block. In a school district, it may be possible to find twelve high schools each having two classes at the appropriate level. Thus $v = 3$, $k = 2$.

Balanced incomplete blocks (BIB) are an extension of randomized blocks that enable differences among blocks to be eliminated from the experimental errors by simple adjustments performed in the statistical analysis. Examples for $v = 7$, $k = 3$ and for $v = 3$, $k = 2$ are as follows (columns are blocks):

		$v = 7, k = 3$							$v = 3, k = 2$	
A	B	C	D	E	F	G		A	B	C
B	C	D	E	F	G	A		B	C	A
D	E	F	G	A	B	C				

The basic property of the design is that each pair of treatments occurs together (in the same block) equally often.

In both plans shown, it happens that each row contains every treatment. This is not generally true of BIB designs, but this extra property can sometimes be used to advantage. With $v = 7$, for instance, if the row specifies the order in which the types of ice cream are tasted, the experiment is also balanced against any consistent order effect. This extension of the BIB is known as an *incomplete Latin square* or a *Youden square.* In the high schools experiment, the plan for $v = 3$ would be repeated four times, since there are twelve schools.

Comparisons between and within subjects. Certain factorial experiments are conducted so that some comparisons are made within subjects and others are made between subjects. Suppose that the criterion is the performance of the subjects on an easy task, T_1, and a difficult task, T_2, each subject attempting both tasks. This part of the experiment is a standard crossover design. Suppose further that these tasks are explained to half the subjects in a discouraging manner, S_1, and to the other half in a supportive manner, S_2. It is of interest to discover whether these preliminary suggestions, S, have an effect on performance and whether this effect differs for easy and hard tasks. The basic plan, requiring four subjects, is shown in the first three lines of Table 1, where O denotes the order in which the tasks are performed.

The comparison $T_2 - T_1$, which gives the main effect of T, is shown under the treatments line. This is clearly a within-subject comparison since each subject carries a + and a −. The main effect of suggestion, $S_2 - S_1$, is a between-subject comparison: subjects 3 and 4 carry + signs while subjects 1 and 2 carry − signs. The TS interaction, measured by $T_2S_2 - T_1S_2 - T_2S_1 + T_1S_1$, is seen to be a within-subject comparison.

Since within-subject comparisons are usually more precise than between-subject comparisons, an important property of this design is that it gives relatively high precision on the T and TS effects at the expense of lower precision on S. The design is particularly effective for studying interactions. Sometimes the between-subject factors involve a classification of the subjects. For instance, the subjects might be classified into three levels of anxiety, A, by a preliminary rating, with equal numbers of males and females of each degree included. In this situation, the factorial effects A, S (for sex), and AS are between-subject comparisons. Their interactions with T are within-subject comparisons.

The example may present another complication. Subjects who tackle the hard task after doing the easy task may perform better than those who tackle the hard task first. This effect is measured by a TO interaction, shown in the last line in Table 1. Note that the TO interaction turns out to be a between-subject comparison. The same is true of the TSO three-factor interaction.

In designs of this type, known in agriculture as

Table 1

Subject	1		2		3		4	
Order	O_1	O_2	O_1	O_2	O_1	O_2	O_1	O_2
Treatment	T_1S_1	T_2S_1	T_2S_1	T_1S_1	T_1S_2	T_2S_2	T_2S_2	T_1S_2
$(T_2 - T_1)$	−	+	+	−	−	+	+	−
$(S_2 - S_1)$	−	−	−	−	+	+	+	+
TS	+	−	−	+	−	+	+	−
TO	+	+	−	−	+	+	−	−

Table 2

Source	df
Between subjects	
S	1
TO	1
TSO	1
Error *b*	$4(n-1)$
Within subjects	
O	1
T	1
TS	1
SO	1
Error *w*	$4(n-1)$

split-plot designs, separate estimates of error are calculated for between-subject and within-subject comparisons. With $4n$ subjects, the partition of degrees of freedom in the example is shown in Table 2 (if it is also desired to examine the TO and TSO interactions).

Plans and computing instructions for all the common types of design are given in Cochran and Cox (1950); and Lindquist (1953), Edwards (1950), and Winer (1962) are good texts on experimentation in psychology and education.

WILLIAM G. COCHRAN

[*Directly related are the articles under* LINEAR HYPOTHESES.]

BIBLIOGRAPHY

BORING, EDWIN G. 1954 The Nature and History of Experimental Control. *American Journal of Psychology* 67:573–589.

CAMPBELL, DONALD T.; and STANLEY, J. S. 1963 Experimental and Quasi-experimental Designs for Research on Teaching. Pages 171–246 in Nathaniel L. Gage (editor), *Handbook of Research on Teaching.* Chicago: Rand McNally.

COCHRAN, WILLIAM G.; and COX, GERTRUDE M. (1950) 1957 *Experimental Designs.* 2d ed. New York: Wiley.

COX, D. R. 1957 The Use of a Concomitant Variable in Selecting an Experimental Design. *Biometrika* 44: 150–158.

COX, D. R. 1958 *Planning of Experiments.* New York: Wiley.

DAVIES, OWEN L. (editor) (1954) 1956 *The Design and Analysis of Industrial Experiments.* 2d ed., rev. Edinburgh: Oliver & Boyd; New York: Hafner.

EDWARDS, ALLEN (1950) 1960 *Experimental Design in Psychological Research.* Rev. ed. New York: Holt.

FISHER, R. A. (1925) 1958 *Statistical Methods for Research Workers.* 13th ed., rev. New York: Hafner. → Previous editions were also published by Oliver & Boyd.

FISHER, R. A. (1926) 1950 The Arrangement of Field Experiments. Pages 17.502a–17.513 in R. A. Fisher, *Contributions to Mathematical Statistics.* New York: Wiley. → First published in Volume 33 of the *Journal of the Ministry of Agriculture.*

FISHER, R. A. (1935) 1960 *The Design of Experiments.* 7th ed. New York: Hafner; Edinburgh: Oliver & Boyd.

KEMPTHORNE, OSCAR 1952 *The Design and Analysis of Experiments.* New York: Wiley.

LINDQUIST, EVERET F. 1953 *Design and Analysis of Experiments in Psychology and Education.* Boston: Houghton Mifflin.

WINER, B. J. 1962 *Statistical Principles in Experimental Design.* New York: McGraw-Hill.

II
RESPONSE SURFACES

Response surface methodology is a statistical technique for the design and analysis of experiments; it seeks to relate an average response to the values of quantitative variables that affect response. For example, response in a chemical investigation might be yield of sulfuric acid, and the quantitative variables affecting yield might be pressure and temperature of the reaction.

In a psychological experiment, an investigator might want to find out how a test *score* achieved by certain subjects depended upon *duration* of the period during which they studied the relevant material and the *delay* between study and test. In mathematical language, the psychologist is interested in the presumed *functional relationship* $\eta = f(\xi_1, \xi_2)$ that expresses the *response score*, η, as a function of the two *variables* duration, ξ_1, and delay, ξ_2. If repeated experiments were made at any fixed set of experimental conditions, the measured response would nevertheless vary because of measurement errors, observational errors, and variability

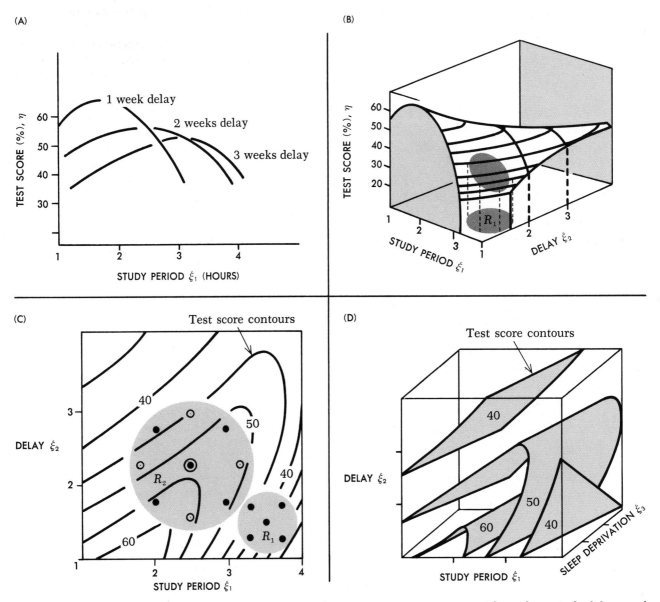

Figure 1 — Geometrical representations of a relationship connecting test scores with study period, delay, and sleep deprivation

in the experimental material. We regard η therefore as the *mean response* at particular conditions; y, the response actually observed in a particular experiment, differs from η because of an (all-inclusive) error e. Thus $y = \eta + e$, and a mathematical model relating the observed response to the levels of k variables can be written in the form

$$(1) \qquad y = f(\xi_1, \cdots, \xi_k) + e.$$

The appropriate investigational strategy depends heavily on the state of ignorance concerning the functional form, f. At one extreme the investigator may not know even which variables, ξ, to include and must make a preliminary screening investigation. At the other extreme the true functional form may actually be known or can be deduced from a mechanistic theory.

Response surface methods are appropriate in the intermediate situation; the important variables are known, but the true functional form is neither known nor easily deducible. The general procedure is to approximate f locally by a suitable function, such as a polynomial, which acts as a "mathematical French curve."

Geometric representation of response relationships. The three curves of Figure 1A, showing a hypothetical relationship associating test score with study period for three different periods of delay, are shown in Figure 1B as sections of a *response surface*. This surface is represented by its response *contours* in Figure 1C. Figure 1D shows how a third variable may be accommodated by the use of three-dimensional *contour surfaces*.

Local graduation. It is usually most convenient to work with coded variables like $x_1 = (\xi_1 - \xi_1^0)/S_1$, $x_2 = (\xi_2 - \xi_2^0)/S_2$ in which ξ_1^0, ξ_2^0 are the coordinates of the center of a region of current interest and S_1 and S_2 are convenient scale factors.

Let $\hat{y}$ represent the calculated value of the response obtained by fitting an approximating function by the method of least squares [*see* LINEAR HYPOTHESES, *article on* REGRESSION]. In a region like R_1 in Figure 1C an adequate approximation can be obtained by fitting the first-degree polynomial

$$(2) \qquad \hat{y} = b_0 + b_1 x_1 + b_2 x_2 .$$

The response contours of such a fitted plane are, of course, equally spaced parallel straight lines. In a region like R_2 a fair approximation might be achieved by fitting a second-degree polynomial

$$(3) \quad \hat{y} = b_0 + b_1 x_1 + b_2 x_2 + b_{11} x_1^2 + b_{22} x_2^2 + b_{12} x_1 x_2.$$

Flexibility of functions like those in (2) and (3) is greatly increased if the possibility is allowed that y, x_1, and x_2 are suitable transformed values of the response and of the variable. For example, it might be appropriate to analyze log score rather than score itself. [*Ways of choosing suitable transformations are described in* STATISTICAL ANALYSIS, SPECIAL PROBLEMS OF, *article on* TRANSFORMATIONS OF DATA; *and in* Box & Cox 1964 *and* Box & Tidwell 1962.]

Uses of response surface methodology

A special pattern of points at which observations are to be made is called an experimental design. In Figure 1C are shown a first-order design in R_1, suitable for fitting and checking a first-degree polynomial, and a second-order design in R_2, suitable for fitting and checking a second-degree polynomial. Response surface methodology has been applied (*a*) to provide a description of how the response is affected by a number of variables over some already chosen region of interest and (*b*) to study and exploit multiple response relationships and constrained extrema. In drug therapy, for example, the true situation might be as depicted in Figure 2. First-degree approximating functions fitted to *each* of the three responses—η_1, therapeutic effect, η_2, nausea, and η_3, toxicity—could approximately locate the point P where maximum therapeutic effect is obtained with nausea and toxicity maintained at the acceptable limits $\eta_2 = 5$, $\eta_3 = 30$. Response surface methodology has also been applied (*c*) to locate and explore the neighborhood of maximal or minimal response. Because problems in (*c*) often subsume those in (*a*) and (*b*), only this application will be considered in more detail.

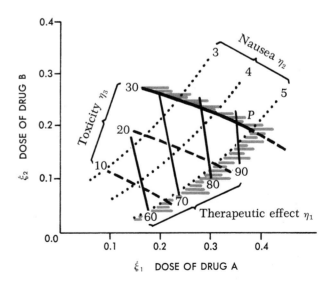

Figure 2 — Dependence of three responses on combined dosages of drugs

Location and exploration of a maximal region. Various tactics have been proposed to deal with the problem of finding where the response surface has its maximum or minimum and of describing its shape nearby. Because the appropriateness of a particular tactic usually depends upon factors that are initially unknown, an adaptive strategy of multiple iteration must be employed, that is, the investigator must put himself in a position to learn more about each of a number of uncertainties as he proceeds and to modify tactics accordingly. It is doubtful whether an adaptive strategy could be found that is appropriate to every conceivable response function. One such procedure, which has worked well in chemical applications and which ought to be applicable in some other areas, is as follows: When the initially known experimental conditions are remote from the maximum (a parallel strategy applies in the location of a minimum) rapid progress is often possible by locally fitting a sloping plane and moving in the indicated direction of greatest slope to a region of higher response. This tactic may be repeated until, when the experimental sequence has moved to conditions near the maximizing ones, additional observations are taken and a quadratic (second-order) fit or analysis is made to indicate the approximate shape of the response surface in the region of the maximum.

An example. In this example iteration occurs in (A) the amount of replication (to achieve sufficient accuracy), (B) the location of the region of interest, (C) the scaling of the variables, (D) the transformation in which the variables are considered, and (E) the necessary degree of complexity of approximating functions and of the corresponding design. The letters A, B, C, etc., are used parenthetically to indicate the particular type of iteration that is being furthered at any stage. Suppose that, unknown to the experimenter, the true dependence of percentage yield on temperature and concentration is as shown in Figure 3A and the experimental error standard deviation is 1.2 per cent.

A first-degree approximation. Suppose that five initial duplicate runs made in random order at points labeled 1, 2, 3, 4, and 5 in Figure 3B yield the results $y_1 = 24$, $y_1' = 27$, $y_2 = 38$, $y_2' = 40$, $y_3 = 42$, $y_3' = 42$, $y_4 = 42$, $y_4' = 41$, $y_5 = 50$, $y_5' = 53$. The average yields at the five points are then $\bar{y}_1 = 25.5$, $\bar{y}_2 = 39$, $\bar{y}_3 = 42$, $\bar{y}_4 = 41.5$, $\bar{y}_5 = 51.5$. At this stage it is convenient to work with the coded variables $x_1 = (\text{temp.} - 70)/10$ and $x_2 = (\text{conc.} - 42.5)/2.5$. Using standard least squares theory the coefficients b_0, b_1, b_2 of equation (2) are then easily estimated

(for example, $b_1 = \frac{1}{4} \{ -\bar{y}_1 + \bar{y}_2 - \bar{y}_4 + \bar{y}_5 \} = 5.9$) and the locally best-fitting plane is

$$(4) \qquad \hat{y} = 39.9 + 5.9\, x_1 + 7.1\, x_2.$$

The differences in the duplicate runs provide an estimate $s = 1.5$, with five degrees of freedom, of σ, the underlying standard deviation. The standard errors of b_0, b_1, and b_2 are then estimated as 0.5, and no further replication (A) appears necessary to obtain adequate estimation of y.

Checking the fit. To check the appropriateness of the first-degree equation it would be sensible to look at the size of second-order effects. For reason of experimental economy a first-order design usually contains points at too few distinct levels to allow separate estimation of all second-order terms. The design may be chosen, however, so as to allow estimates of "specimen" second-order coefficients or combinations thereof. In the present case estimates can be made of $b_{12} = \frac{1}{4}(\bar{y}_1 - \bar{y}_2 - \bar{y}_4 + \bar{y}_5) = -0.9 \pm 0.5$ and $(b_{11} + b_{22}) = \frac{1}{4}(\bar{y}_1 + \bar{y}_2 + \bar{y}_4 + \bar{y}_5) - \bar{y}_3 = -2.6 \pm 1.2$. Some inadequacy of the first-degree equation is indicated, therefore, but this is tentatively ignored because of the dominant magnitude of b_1 and b_2.

Steepest ascent. It is now logical to explore (B) higher temperatures and concentrations. The points 6, 7, and 8 are along a steepest ascent path obtained by changes proportional to $b_1 \times S_1 = 5.9 \times 10° = 59°$ in temperature and $b_2 \times S_2 = 7.1 \times 2.5\% = 17.75\%$ in concentration. Suppose that $y_6 = 59$, $y_7 = 63$, and $y_8 = 50$. Graphical interpolation indicates that the highest yield on this path is between runs 6 and 7, and this is chosen (B) as the center of the new region to be explored.

The path calculated as above is at right angles to contours of the fitted plane when 10-degree units of temperature and 2.5 per cent units of concentration are represented by the same distances. That the experimenter currently regards these units as appropriate is implied by his choice of levels in the design.

Scaling correction. To correct unsuitable scaling (C) the investigator can adopt the rule that if a variable produces an effect that is small compared with that produced by the other variables, the center level for that variable is moved away from the calculated path and a larger change is made for this variable in the next set of runs. No change of relative scaling is indicated here, but progress up the surface would normally be accompanied by reduction in the sizes of b_1 and b_2. Also, the checks have already indicated that second-order effects can scarcely be estimated with adequate accuracy

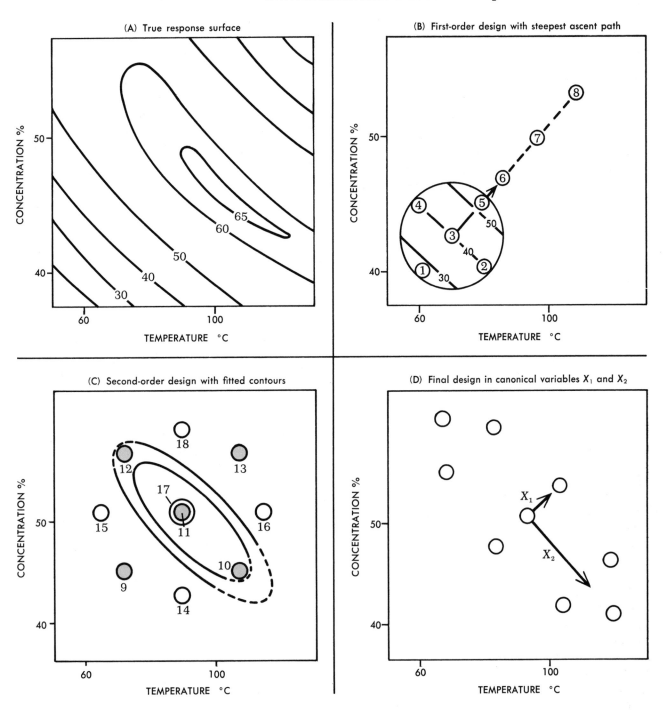

Figure 3 — A true response surface and three successive design patterns

in the present scaling. Thus, wider ranges in both variables should be employed in a second design.

A second-degree approximation. A widened first-order design at the new location might give $y_9 = 50$, $y_{10} = 66$, $y_{11} = 66$, $y_{12} = 63$, and $y_{13} = 52$, as in Figure 3C.

Then $\hat{y} = 59.4 + 1.3\,x_1 - 0.3\,x_2$ is the best-fitting plane, in which x_1 is given by (temp. $- 90)/15$,

x_2 is given by (conc. $- 18.75)/3.75$, and the estimated standard error of the coefficients is about 0.8. In the new scaling the check quantities are now $b_{12} = -6.75 \pm 0.8$ and $b_{11} + b_{22} = 8.25 \pm 1.7$. It is clear, without this time duplicating the design, that first-order terms no longer dominate, and no worthwhile further progress can be made by ascent methods. To make possible the fitting and checking of a second-degree polynomial (E), five additional observations might be taken, say $y_{14} = 54$, $y_{15} = 54$, $y_{16} = 57$, $y_{17} = 65$, $y_{18} = 55$. The last ten observations now form a second-order design. A second-degree equation fitted to these observations gives

$$(5) \qquad \hat{y} = 65.50 + 1.16\,x_1 + 0.05\,x_2$$
$$- 4.31\,x_1^2 - 4.81\,x_2^2 - 6.75\,x_1 x_2.$$

The design allows a check on the adequacy (E) of the second-degree equation by providing estimates of certain "specimen" combinations of third-order terms

$$b_{111} - b_{122} = \tfrac{1}{4}\{y_9 - y_{10} + y_{12} - y_{13} - \sqrt{2}y_{15} + \sqrt{2}y_{16}\}$$
$$= -0.19 \pm 1.03$$

and

$$b_{222} - b_{112} = \tfrac{1}{4}\{y_9 + y_{10} - y_{12} - y_{13} - \sqrt{2}y_{14} + \sqrt{2}y_{18}\}$$
$$= -0.60 \pm 1.03.$$

The estimated standard errors of the linear coefficients b_1 and b_2, of the quadratic coefficients b_{11} and b_{22}, and of the interaction coefficient b_{12} are, respectively, 0.52, 0.62, and 0.73.

Before an attempt is made to interpret equation (5) there must be some assurance (A) that the change in response it predicts is large compared with the standard error of that prediction. For a design requiring N observations and an approximating equation containing p constants, the average variance of the N calculated responses $\hat{y}$ is $(p/N)s^2 = (6/12) \times 2.1 = 1.1$ for this example. The square root (1.0 for this example) gives an "average" standard error for $\hat{y}$. This may be compared with the range of the predicted $\hat{y}$'s, which is 17.08, the highest predicted value being $\hat{y}_{11} = \hat{y}_{17} = 65.50$ and the lowest $\hat{y}_9 = 48.42$.

A more precise indication of adequacy may be obtained by an application of the analysis of variance, but a discussion of this is outside the scope of the present account [see LINEAR HYPOTHESES, article on ANALYSIS OF VARIANCE]. It is to be noted, however, that bare statistical significance of the regression would *not* ensure that the response surface was *estimated* with sufficient accuracy for the interpretation discussed below.

Interpretation. Once adequate fit and precision have been obtained, a contour plot of the equation over the region of the experimental design is helpful in interpretation. Especially where there are more than two variables, interpretation is further facilitated by writing the second-degree equation in canonical form (D). In most cases, this means that the center of the quadratic system is chosen as a new origin, and a rotation of axes is performed to eliminate cross-product terms.

In a final group of experiments the new canon-ical axes and scales could be used to position the design. In Figure 3D the design points are chosen so that they roughly follow a contour and make a rather precise final fitting possible.

It might be asked, Why not simply use the twenty or so experimental points to cover the region shown in Figure 3A with some suitable grid in the first place? The answer is that it is not known initially that the region of interest will be in the area covered by that diagram. The "content" of the space to be explored goes up rapidly as the number of dimensions is increased.

Suitable designs. From the foregoing discussion it will be clear that the arrangements of experimental points suitable for response surface study should satisfy a number of requirements. Ideally, a response surface design should (1) allow $\hat{y}(x)$ to be estimated throughout the region of interest, R; (2) ensure that $\hat{y}(x)$ is as "close" as possible to $\eta(x)$; (3) give good detectability of lack of fit; (4) allow transformations to be fitted; (5) allow experiments to be performed in blocks; (6) allow designs of increasing order to be built up sequentially; (7) provide an internal estimate of error; (8) be insensitive to wild observations; (9) require a minimum number of experimental points; (10) provide patterning of data allowing ready visual appreciation; (11) ensure simplicity of calculation; and (12) behave well when errors occur in settings of the x's.

A variety of designs have been developed, many of which have remarkably good over-all behavior with respect to these requirements. When maximum economy in experimentation is essential, designs that fail to meet certain of these criteria may have to be used at some increased risk of being misled.

G. E. P. Box

BIBLIOGRAPHY

ANDERSEN, S. L. 1959 Statistics in the Strategy of Chemical Experimentation. *Chemical Engineering Progress* 55:61–67.

BOX, GEORGE E. P. 1954 The Exploration and Exploitation of Response Surfaces: Some General Considerations and Examples. *Biometrics* 10:16–60.

BOX, GEORGE E. P. 1957 Integration of Techniques in Process Development. Pages 687–702 in American Society for Quality Control, National Convention, Eleventh, *Transactions*. Detroit, Mich.: The Society.

BOX, GEORGE E. P. 1959 Fitting Empirical Data. New York Academy of Sciences, *Annals* 86:792–816.

BOX, GEORGE E. P.; and COX, D. R. 1964 An Analysis of Transformations. *Journal of the Royal Statistical Society* Series B 26:211–252. → Contains eight pages of discussion.

BOX, GEORGE E. P.; and TIDWELL, PAUL W. 1962 Transformations of the Independent Variables. *Technometrics* 4:531–550.

Box, George E. P.; and Wilson, K. B. 1951 On the Experimental Attainment of Optimum Conditions. *Journal of the Royal Statistical Society* Series B 13:1–45. → Contains seven pages of discussion.

Davies, Owen L. (editor) (1954) 1956 *The Design and Analysis of Industrial Experiments.* 2d ed., rev. New York: Hafner; London: Oliver & Boyd.

Hill, William G.; and Hunter, William G. 1966 A Review of Response Surface Methodology: A Literature Survey. *Technometrics* 8:571–590.

Hotelling, Harold 1941 Experimental Determination of the Maximum of a Function. *Annals of Mathematical Statistics* 12:20–45.

III

QUASI-EXPERIMENTAL DESIGN

The phrase "quasi-experimental design" refers to the application of an experimental mode of analysis and interpretation to bodies of data not meeting the full requirements of experimental control. The circumstances in which it is appropriate are those of experimentation in social settings—including planned interventions such as specific communications, persuasive efforts, changes in conditions and policies, efforts at social remediation, etc.—where complete experimental control may not be possible. Unplanned conditions and events may also be analyzed in this way where an exogenous variable has such discreteness and abruptness as to make appropriate its consideration as an experimental treatment applied at a specific point in time to a specific population. When properly done, when attention is given to the specific implications of the specific weaknesses of the design in question, quasi-experimental analysis can provide a valuable extension of the experimental method.

History of quasi-experimental design. While efforts to interpret field data as if they were actually experiments go back much further, the first prominent methodology of this kind in the social sciences was Chapin's ex post facto experiment (Chapin & Queen 1937; Chapin 1947; Greenwood 1945), although it should be noted that because of the failure to control regression artifacts, this mode of analysis is no longer regarded as acceptable. *The American Soldier* volumes (Stouffer et al. 1949) provide prominent analyses of the effects of specific military experiences, where it is implausible that differences in selection explain the results. Thorndike's efforts to demonstrate the effects of specific coursework upon other intellectual achievements provide an excellent early model (for example, Thorndike & Woodworth 1901; Thorndike & Ruger 1923). Extensive analysis and review of this literature are provided elsewhere (Campbell 1957; 1963; Campbell & Stanley 1963) and serve as the basis for the present abbreviated presentation.

True experimentation. The core requirement of a true experiment lies in the experimenter's ability to apply experimental treatments in complete independence of the prior states of the materials (persons, etc.) under study. This independence makes resulting differences interpretable as effects of the differences in treatment. In the social sciences the independence of experimental treatment from prior status is assured by randomization in assignments to treatments. Experiments meeting these requirements, and thus representing true experiments, are much more possible in the social sciences than is generally realized. Wherever, for example, the treatments can be applied to individuals or small units, such as precincts or classrooms, without the respondents being aware of experimentation or that other units are getting different treatments, very elegant experimental control can be achieved. An increased acceptance by administrators of randomization as the democratic method of allocating scarce resources (be these new housing, therapy, or fellowships) will make possible field experimentation in many settings. Where innovations are to be introduced throughout a social system and where the introduction cannot, in any event, be simultaneous, a use of randomization in the staging can provide an experimental comparison of the new and the old, using the groups receiving the delayed introduction as controls.

Validity of quasi-experimental analyses. Nothing in this article should be interpreted as minimizing the importance of increasing the use of true experimentation. However, where true experimental design with random assignment of persons to treatments is not possible, because of ethical considerations or lack of power, or infeasibility, application of quasi-experimental analysis has much to offer.

The social sciences must do the best they can with the possibilities open to them. Inferences must frequently be made from data obtained under circumstances that do not permit complete control. Too often a scientist trained in experimental method rejects any research in which complete control is lacking. Yet in practice no experiment is perfectly executed, and the practicing scientist overlooks those imperfections that seem to him to offer no plausible rival explanation of the results. In the light of modern philosophies of science, no experiment ever *proves* a theory, it merely *probes* it. Seeming proof results from that condition in which there is no available plausible rival hypothesis to explain the data. The general program of quasi-experimental analysis is to specify and examine those plausible rival explanations of the results that are provided by the uncontrolled variables. A failure to control that does not in fact lend plausibility to a rival interpretation is not regarded as invalidating.

It is well to remember that we do make assured causal inferences in many settings not involving randomization: the earthquake caused the brick building to crumble; the automobile crashing into the telephone pole caused it to break; the language patterns of the older models and mentors caused this child to speak English rather than Kwakiutl; and so forth. While these are all potentially erroneous inferences, they are of the same type as experimental inferences. We are confident that were we to intrude experimentally, we could confirm the causal laws involved. Yet they have been made assuredly by a nonexperimenting observer. This assurance is due to the effective absence of other plausible causes. Consider the inference about the crashing auto and the telephone pole: we rule out combinations of termites and wind because the other implications of these theories do not occur (there are no termite tunnels and debris in the wood, and nearby weather stations have no records of heavy wind). Spontaneous splintering of the pole by happenstance coincident with the auto's onset does not impress us as a rival, nor would it explain the damage to the car, etc. Analogously in quasi-experimental analysis, tentative causal interpretation of data may be made where the interpretation in question is consistent with the data and where other rival interpretations have been rendered implausible.

Dimensions of experimental validity. A set of twelve dimensions, representing frequent threats to validity, have been developed for the evaluation of data as quasi-experiments. These may be regarded as the important classes of frequently plausible rival hypotheses that good research design seeks to rule out. Each will be presented briefly even though not all are employed in the evaluation of the designs used illustratively here.

Fundamental to this listing is a distinction between *internal validity* and *external validity*. Internal validity is the basic minimum without which any experiment is uninterpretable: Did in fact the experimental treatments make a difference in this specific experimental instance? External validity asks the question of *generalizability*: To what populations, settings, treatment variables, and measurement variables can this effect be generalized? Both types of criteria are obviously important, even though they are frequently at odds in that features increasing one may jeopardize the other. While internal validity is the *sine qua non,* and while the question of external validity, like the question of inductive inference, is never completely answerable, the selection of designs strong in both types of validity is obviously our ideal.

Threats to internal validity. Relevant to internal validity are eight different classes of extraneous variables that if not controlled in the experimental design might produce effects mistaken for the effect of the experimental treatment. These are the following. (1) *History:* other specific events in addition to the experimental variable occurring between a first and second measurement. (2) *Maturation:* processes within the respondents that are a function of the passage of time per se (not specific to the particular events), including growing older, growing hungrier, growing tireder, and the like. (3) *Testing:* the effects of taking a test a first time upon subjects' scores in subsequent testing. (4) *Instrumentation:* the effects of changes in the calibration of a measuring instrument or changes in the observers or scorers upon changes in the obtained measurements. (5) *Statistical regression:* operating where groups of subjects have been selected on the basis of their extreme scores. (6) *Selection:* biases resulting in differential recruitment of respondents for the comparison groups. (7) *Experimental mortality:* the differential loss of respondents from the comparison groups. (8) *Selection–maturation interaction:* in certain of the multiple-group quasi-experimental designs, such as the nonequivalent control group design, an interaction of maturation and differential selection is confounded with, that is, might be mistaken for, the effect of the experimental variable [see LINEAR HYPOTHESES, *article on* REGRESSION; SAMPLE SURVEYS].

Threats to external validity. Factors jeopardizing external validity or *representativeness* are: (1) The *reactive or interaction effect of testing,* in which a pretest might increase or decrease the respondent's sensitivity or responsiveness to the experimental variable and thus make the results obtained for a pretested population unrepresentative of the effects of the experimental variable for the unpretested universe from which the experimental respondents were selected. (2) *Interaction* effects between *selection* bias and the *experimental variable.* (3) *Reactive effects of experimental arrangements,* which would preclude generalization about the effect of the experimental variable for persons being exposed to it in nonexperimental settings. (4) *Multiple-treatment interference,* a problem wherever multiple treatments are applied to the same respondents, and a particular problem for one-group designs involving equivalent time samples or equivalent materials samples.

Types of quasi-experimental design.   Some common types of quasi-experimental design will be outlined here.

One-group pretest–posttest design.   Perhaps the simplest quasi-experimental design is the one-group pretest–posttest design, O_1 X O_2 (O represents measurement or observation, X the experimental treatment). This common design patently leaves uncontrolled the threats to internal validity of history, maturation, testing, instrumentation, and, if subjects were selected on the basis of extreme scores on O_1, regression. There may be situations in which the investigator could decide that none of these represented plausible rival hypotheses in his setting: A log of other possible change-agents might provide no plausible ones; the measurement in question might be nonreactive (Campbell 1957), the time span too short for maturation, too spaced for fatigue, etc. However, the sources of invalidity are so numerous that a more powerful quasi-experimental design would be preferred. Several of these can be constructed by adding features to this simple one.

Interrupted time-series design.   The interrupted time-series experiment utilizes a series of measurements providing multiple pretests and posttests, for example:

$$O_1\ O_2\ O_3\ O_4\ X\ O_5\ O_6\ O_7\ O_8 .$$

If in this series, O_4-O_5 shows a rise greater than found elsewhere, then maturation, testing, and regression are no longer plausible, in that they would predict equal or greater rises for O_1-O_2, etc. Instrumentation may well be controlled too, although in institutional settings a change of administration policy is often accompanied by a change in record-keeping standards. Observers and participants may be focused on the occurrence of X and may speciously change rating standards, etc. History remains the major threat, although in many settings it would not offer a plausible rival interpretation.

Multiple time-series design.   If one had available a parallel time series from a group not receiving the experimental treatment, but exposed to the same extraneous sources of influence, and if this control time series failed to show the exceptional jump from O_4 to O_5, then the plausibility of history as a rival interpretation would be greatly reduced. We may call this the multiple time-series design.

Nonequivalent control group.   Another way of improving the one-group pretest–posttest design is to add a "nonequivalent control group." (Were the control group to be randomly assigned from the same population as the experimental group, we would, of course, have a true experimental design not a quasi-experimental design.) Depending on the similarities of setting and attributes, if the nonequivalent control group fails to show the gain manifest in the experimental group, then history, maturation, testing, and instrumentation are controlled. In this popular design, the frequent effort to "correct" for the lack of perfect equivalence by matching on pretest scores is *absolutely wrong* (e.g., Thorndike 1942; Hovland et al. 1949; Campbell & Clayton 1961), because it introduces a regression artifact. Instead, one should accept any initial pretest differences, using analysis of covariance, gain scores, or graphic presentation. (This, of course, is not to reject blocking on pretest scores in true experiments where groups have been assigned to treatments at random.) Remaining uncontrolled is the selection–maturation interaction, that is, the possibility that the experimental group differed from the control group not only in initial level but also in its autonomous maturation rate. In experiments on psychotherapy and on the effects of specific coursework this is a very serious rival. Note that it can be rendered implausible by use of a time series of pretest for both groups thus moving again to the multiple time-series design.

Other quasi-experimental designs.   There is not space here to present adequately even these four quasi-experimental designs, but perhaps the strategy of adding specific observations and analyses to check on specific threats to validity has been illustrated. This is carried to an extreme in the recurrent institutional cycle design (Campbell & McCormack 1957; Campbell & Stanley 1963), in which longitudinal and cross-sectional measurements are combined with still other analyses to assess the impact of indoctrination procedures, etc. through exploiting the fact that essentially similar treatments are being given to new entrants year after year or cycle after cycle. Other quasi-experimental designs are covered in Campbell and Stanley (1963), Campbell and Clayton (1961), Campbell (1963), and Pelz and Andrews (1964).

Correlational analyses.   Related to the program of quasi-experimental analysis are those efforts to achieve causal inference from correlational data. Note that while correlation does not prove causation, most causal hypotheses imply specific correlations, and examination of these thus probes, tests, or edits the causal hypothesis. Furthermore, as Blalock (1964) and Simon (1947–1956) have emphasized, certain causal models specify uneven patterns of correlation. Thus the $A \rightarrow B \rightarrow C$ model implies that r_{AC} be smaller than r_{AB} or r_{BC}. However, their use of partial correlations or the use of Wright's path analysis (1920) are rejected as tests of the model because of the requirement that the "cause" be totally represented in the "effect." In the social sciences it will never be plausible that the cause has been measured without unique error and that it also totally lacks unique systematic variance not shared with the effect. More appropriate would be Lawley's (1940) test of the hypothesis of *single factoredness*. Only if single factoredness can be rejected would the causal model, as represented by its predicted uneven correlation pattern, be the preferred interpretation [*see* Multivariate analysis, *articles on* correlation].

Tests of significance.   A word needs to be said about tests of significance for quasi-experimental designs. It has been argued by several competent social scientists that since randomization has not been used tests of significance assuming randomization are not relevant. On the whole, the writer disagrees. However, some aspects of the protest are endorsed: Good experimental design is needed for any comparison inferring change, whether or not tests of significance are used, even if only photographs, graphs, or essays are being compared. In this sense, experimental design is independent of tests of significance. More importantly, tests of significance have mistakenly come to be taken as thoroughgoing *proof*. In vulgar social science usage, finding a "significant difference" is apt to be taken as *proving* the author's basis for predicting the difference, forgetting the many other plausible rival hypotheses explaining a significant difference that quasi-experimental designs leave uncontrolled. Certainly the valuation of tests of significance in some quarters needs demoting. Further, the use of tests of significance designed for the evaluation of a single comparison becomes much too lenient when dozens, hundreds, or thousands of comparisons have been sifted. And in a similar manner, an experimenter's decision as to which of his studies is publishable and the editor's decision as to which of the manuscripts are acceptable further bias the sampling basis. In all of these ways, reform is needed.

However, when a quasi-experimenter has, for example, compared the results from two intact classrooms employed in a sampling of convenience, a chance difference is certainly *one*, even if only one, of the many plausible rival hypotheses that must be considered. If each class had but 5 students, one would interpret the fact that 20 per cent

more in the experimental class showed increases with less interest than if each class had 100 students. In this case there is available an elaborate formal theory for the plausible rival hypothesis of chance fluctuation. This theory involves the assumption of randomness, which is quite appropriate when the null model of random association is rejected in favor of a hypothesis of systematic difference between the two groups. If a "significant difference" is found, the test of significance will not, of course, reveal whether the two classes differed because one saw the experimental movie or for some selection reason associated with class topic, time of day, etc., that might have interacted with rate of autonomous change, pretest instigated changes, reactions to commonly experienced events, etc. But such a test of significance will help rule out what can be considered as a ninth threat to internal validity; that is, that there is no difference here at all that could not be accounted for as a vagary of sampling in terms of a model of purely chance assignment. Note that the statement of probability level is in this light a statement of the plausibility of this one rival hypothesis, which always has some plausibility, however faint.

Donald T. Campbell

[*Other relevant material may be found in* Hypothesis testing; Personality measurement, *article on* situational tests; Psychometrics; Reasoning and logic; Survey analysis.]

BIBLIOGRAPHY

Blalock, Hubert M. Jr. 1964 *Causal Inferences in Nonexperimental Research.* Chapel Hill: Univ. of North Carolina Press.

Campbell, Donald T. 1957 Factors Relevant to the Validity of Experiments in Social Settings. *Psychological Bulletin* 54:297–312.

Campbell, Donald T. 1963 From Description to Experimentation: Interpreting Trends as Quasi-experiments. Pages 212–242 in Chester W. Harris (editor), *Problems in Measuring Change.* Madison: Univ. of Wisconsin Press.

Campbell, Donald T.; and Clayton, K. N. 1961 Avoiding Regression Effects in Panel Studies of Communication Impact. *Studies in Public Communication* 3: 99–118.

Campbell, Donald T.; and McCormack, Thelma H. 1957 Military Experience and Attitudes Toward Authority. *American Journal of Sociology* 62:482–490.

Campbell, Donald T.; and Stanley, J. S. 1963 Experimental and Quasi-experimental Designs for Research on Teaching. Pages 171–246 in Nathaniel L. Gage (editor), *Handbook of Research on Teaching.* Chicago: Rand McNally.

Chapin, Francis S. (1947) 1955 *Experimental Designs in Sociological Research.* Rev. ed. New York: Harper.

Chapin, Francis S.; and Queen, S. A. 1937 *Research Memorandum on Social Work in the Depression.* New York: Social Science Research Council.

GREENWOOD, ERNEST 1945 *Experimental Sociology: A Study in Method.* New York: Columbia Univ. Press.

HOVLAND, CARL I.; LUMSDAINE, ARTHUR A.; and SHEFFIELD, FREDERICK D. 1949 *Experiments on Mass Communication.* Studies in Social Psychology in World War II, Vol. 3. Princeton Univ. Press.

LAWLEY, D. N. 1940 The Estimation of Factor Loadings by the Method of Maximum Likelihood. Royal Society of Edinburgh, *Proceedings* 60:64–82.

PELZ, DONALD C.; and ANDREWS, F. M. 1964 Detecting Causal Priorities in Panel Study Data. *American Sociological Review* 29:838–848.

SIMON, HERBERT A. (1947–1956) 1957 *Models of Man: Social and Rational; Mathematical Essays on Rational Human Behavior in a Social Setting.* New York: Wiley.

STOUFFER, SAMUEL A. et al. 1949 *The American Soldier.* Studies in Social Psychology in World War II, Vols. 1 and 2. Princeton Univ. Press. → Volume 1: *Adjustment During Army Life.* Volume 2: *Combat and Its Aftermath.*

THORNDIKE, EDWARD L.; and RUGER, G. J. 1923 The Effect of First-year Latin Upon Knowledge of English Words of Latin Derivation. *School and Society* 18: 260–270.

THORNDIKE, EDWARD L.; and WOODWORTH, R. S. 1901 The Influence of Improvement in One Mental Function Upon the Efficiency of Other Functions. *Psychological Review* 8:247–261, 384–395, 553–564.

THORNDIKE, R. L. 1942 Regression Fallacies in the Matched Groups Experiment. *Psychometrika* 7:85–102.

WRIGHT, S. 1920 Correlation and Causation. *Journal of Agricultural Research* 20:557–585.

EXPERIMENTAL PSYCHOLOGY

The subject matter of the field that is traditionally called experimental psychology is included under the entries DRIVES; EXPERIMENTAL DESIGN; FORGETTING; LEARNING; MOTIVATION; PERCEPTION; PSYCHOLOGY, *article on* PHYSIOLOGICAL PSYCHOLOGY.

EXPLANATION

See CAUSATION *and* SCIENTIFIC EXPLANATION.

EXPLORATION OF DATA

See STATISTICS *and* SURVEY ANALYSIS, *article on* METHODS OF SURVEY ANALYSIS.

EXPLORATORY DRIVES

See STIMULATION DRIVES.

EXPORTS

See INTERNATIONAL TRADE.

EXPRESSIVE BEHAVIOR

The term "expressive behavior" refers to those aspects of behavior which manifest motivational states. "Motivational state" is used here to cover emotional attitudes and moods, cognitive attitudes (attention, concentration), activation states (arousal, fatigue), and more-or-less permanent attitudes that are personality attributes.

The study of expressive behavior has a dual origin in psychodiagnostics (falsely attributed to Aristotle) and in rhetoric (Quintilian). Interest in art and, particularly, in the stage (e.g., Engel 1785) stimulated detailed descriptions of expressive movement. More recently, expressive behavior has been discussed in connection with the philosophical problem of knowing other minds (Bain 1859; Lipps 1905; Scheler 1913). At present, the main impetus for the investigation of expressive behavior stems from the study of social perception, emotion, and personality.

"Expressive behavior" is a somewhat misleading term. Many behaviors which are not to be classified as "expressions" still have expressive aspects, e.g., the "deliberate" or "determined" manner of performing actions; the "hesitant" or "emphatic" intonational patterns in speech. The term is misleading, again, since it might suggest an expressive intention or purpose on the part of the subject that in fact is not presupposed. Labeling some behavior as "expressive" does not imply anything about its function or purpose. Expression is not a specific category of behavior, but expressiveness is the result of a perspective on all behavior. Every behavior is expressive when viewed with respect to the motivational state suggested by it. The term "expressive behavior" is misleading, finally, in that it suggests the presence of something, an inner experience, which is expressed but exists distinct from its expression. This, again, is not necessarily the case. Some behavior is expressive without the subject's experiencing the emotions suggested by his behavior, as in a theatrical performance or in an act of deceit. Actually, the investigation of the relationship of expressive behavior to inner states or other dispositions is one of the main tasks in this area.

Phenomena that are functionally quite different are usually classed as expressive behavior; they vary in the manner in which they manifest motivational states:

(*a*) In both expressive movements (movements of limbs, head, facial features, and body) and the manner of performing purposive actions, the movement pattern itself is expressive, that is, it manifests the motivational state. Expressive aspects of vocal behavior and visceral manifestations of emotion can be classed along with expressive movement.

(*b*) In expressive actions, the way in which the environment is treated, rather than the movement pattern itself, is expressive.

(c) Verbal–symbolic behavior is expressive to the extent that it evidences some motivational state of the speaker.

(d) The products of creative behavior, in contrast to the behavior pattern itself, are considered expressive. Professional dancing and singing can, of course, be classified under both (a) and (d).

Expressive movement—descriptive analysis. The study of expressive movement implies (1) carefully describing behavior patterns and (2) ascertaining their meaning, in terms of the subject's introspective report, his earlier or subsequent behavior, or the stimulus situation; or in terms of independently assessed personality traits.

The traditional source for descriptive data on expressive movement is the theater. While posed expressions are still used as stimuli in experiments on recognition of expression, they present obvious and unnecessary difficulties for the analysis of expressive behavior as such. Spontaneous expressions can be collected systematically by exposing the subject to specific stimuli (sudden noises, sweet music, pain); by time sampling during standardized or experimentally varied conditions (stress, task failure); or by electrical brain stimulation (Hess 1962). For recording these movements, refined techniques are sometimes utilized, such as high-speed cinematography (Landis & Hunt 1939) or electromyography (Sainsbury 1955). Sometimes it has been feasible to obtain introspective reports as well (Frijda 1953). Some response patterns have been described in detail, such as the startle pattern (Landis & Hunt 1939) or animal rage patterns (Bard 1950). Correlational studies have been used to identify patterns of individual differences (e.g., Allport & Vernon 1933; for visceral response patterns, see Lacey et al. 1963). Many studies have established the existence of stable individual differences in single expressive traits, such as frequency of nervous movements (Sainsbury 1955) or muscular tension during stress (see Duffy 1962, chapter 11), or size and speed variables, such as size of writing, length, and speed of stride, and rate of speech, as used in the Allport and Vernon study (1933).

A somewhat different approach has been followed in a series of German studies that originated in the work of Piderit (1867). These studies try to describe the variables of expressive movement for various body areas (facial expression, Lersch 1932; general body movement, Strehle 1954; gait, Kietz 1956; gesture, Kiener 1962). They present a large number of hypotheses on personality attributes presumably revealed by the various expressive traits; interpretations are based upon impressions gained during psychodiagnostic sessions. There are no validation studies, however. In general, very little has been established on the relationship between expressive movement and personality, except for some group-comparison studies. For example, patients classified as neurotic or as anxious tend to manifest a higher habitual degree of muscular tension and more frequent nervous movements than normal or nonanxious controls (see Duffy 1962, chapter 11; Sainsbury 1955).

Specificity and meaning. Traditionally it is held that expressive movement expresses emotion; also, that for every linguistically distinguishable emotion there is a corresponding distinct expressive movement pattern. The existence of expressions of other aspects of personality presents difficulties for the first hypothesis. Experimental investigation disproves the second. Landis (1924) elicited spontaneous emotional reactions from a group of subjects. Comparison of these reactions with the subjects' introspective reports revealed that no emotion invariably leads to the same expression in every person and at every moment. Recognition experiments, in which observers are presented with photographs or films showing facial or other expressions, indicate that interpretations of expression are quite often incorrect. Observers attach widely different labels to one and the same expression (see Woodworth & Schlosberg 1955, chapter 5).

The variety of interpretations for a given expression does not mean, however, that expression of emotion is highly ambiguous. Woodworth demonstrated (1938) that there was a high degree of agreement among observers when expressions were judged in terms of emotion groups rather than separate emotions; Schlosberg (1954) showed the same for judgment in terms of three dimensions—pleasantness–unpleasantness, attention–rejection, and level of activation—and demonstrated at the same time the equivalence of these dimension judgments to judgment in terms of emotion groups. These studies suggest that expression does not represent emotions as distinct and discontinuous states; it represents, rather, a set of continuous emotional dimensions. This conclusion is supported by high correlations between dimensional values and measurements of facial features (Frijda & Philipszoon 1963). Every emotion occupies some place in this multidimensional expression space. However, several different motivational states may occupy the same place; hence the confusion in recognition experiments. As yet there is still some uncertainty about the dimensions involved. One of Schlosberg's dimensions, attention–rejection, seems superfluous in view of multidimensional scalings based upon similarity judgments (Abelson & Sermat 1962; Shepard 1962). On the other hand, the importance of additional dimensions is suggested by other studies (Frijda & Philipszoon 1963).

Expressive movement, then, appears to represent the person's state as defined by these dimensions, whose psychological nature can be summarized as the person's attitude, or his readiness to relate to his environment, and his state of activation. Expressive movement, consequently, cannot properly be said to represent emotion. It may manifest some aspect of emotion, emotion being defined by the type of situational determinant in addition to the attitude and the activation state (Frijda 1958; Schachter & Singer 1962). However, the attitude and activation state may instead be part of a cognitive, nonemotional attitude. They may also represent some habitual attitude or activation *modus*, in which case they constitute a personality trait.

Origin. In order to understand the origin and function of expressive movement, a distinction has to be made. Expressive movements which arise spontaneously out of the actual motivational state are called primary; expressions which are made more or less intentionally are called secondary. Secondary expressive behavior overlays and modifies the primary. People frequently exaggerate their spontaneous reactions for reasons of communication or social participation. Sometimes they produce expressive movements when no corresponding emotional attitude is experienced, as to give a social signal, to be polite, or to deceive. They also produce symbolic expressive movements—gestures of doubt, disbelief, denial, or approval—which serve linguistic functions, underlining or replacing verbal behavior.

Primary expressions seem to be unlearned. The evidence comes from different sources: developmental observations; data on generality over species (which in humans means ethnological evidence); and neuropsychological research [*see* INSTINCT].

Within the first few weeks of life a limited but still differentiated repertory of reactions can be observed: crying, generalized excitement, startle, orienting responses, quiet relaxation, and facial contortions typical of disgust (Malrieu 1960). Somewhat later, smiling appears. These expressions can be observed under conditions that make social learning unlikely: absence of social reinforcement (Dennis 1938); blindness; and even a combination of blindness and deafness (Thompson 1941). The blind manifest these expressions in situations that would call forth the same reactions in normal children.

Systematic cross-cultural research on expressive behavior has been rare since 1867, when Darwin sent a questionnaire to informants around the world. Yet, from scattered reports the generalization seems warranted that the same primary expressive patterns are present in every culture, where they indicate the same motivational states; or, rather, that everywhere they appear at least with this common meaning. Laughter is used everywhere to express joy, even if occasionally it may express other things as well and even if joy occasionally is expressed differently.

Some expressive reactions—those considered indicative of rage, fear, or attention—have been evoked in animals by midbrain stimulation (Hess 1962); laughter, smiling, and weeping occur in human subjects who have cerebral lesions or who are subjected to electrical stimulation in the thalamic region (Hassler & Riechert 1961). Still, these data may be interpreted (e.g., by Hess) as the evocation of emotional impulses as such, and these impulses, of course, might also utilize learned behaviors.

Social determinants. The inborn forms of expressive behavior are supplemented by and modified by social learning. To what extent this is the case has been demonstrated by Efron's (1941) comparison of gestural behavior of Jews and Italians in New York City. Jews and Italians who have been minimally acculturated to the general American way of life possess quite different gestural habits, although both gesticulate considerably more than the average American. Among more acculturated groups these differences largely disappear. The findings concerning cultural differences, however, in no way conflict with the notion of universal human expressive patterns with fixed meanings.

The influence of culture on expression can be summarized as follows.

(a) Culture determines to what extent emotional impulses are shown and, consequently, how frequent and pronounced expressive behavior is. The extent to which expressive behavior is encouraged is culturally determined.

(b) Culture may determine under what conditions certain expressions are allowed or prescribed. Weeping by men is, in Western culture, permitted only under special circumstances; in prerevolutionary China the amount of weeping when a relative died was carefully graded by a codex, according to the closeness of the relationship (Granet 1922).

(c) There are cultural differences with regard to the events that elicit given emotional reactions.

In these cases there is not so much difference in expressive behavior as in emotional behavior.

(*d*) Certain more-or-less general motor habits—manner of walking or sitting, gestural accompaniment of speech, intonement of speech—may be culturally determined. Such habits can be quite typical for people of a given culture (Efron 1941; LaBarre 1947). They may reflect some culturally determined mental attitude or they may be the expression of nothing but a cultural-movement norm.

(*e*) Secondary expressive movements, particularly those with linguistic meanings, are based upon cultural conventions: the gestures for "yes" and "no" are well-known examples.

Nature of expressive movement. Why should there be expressive movement, and why does it take a particular form? Several explanatory principles have been adduced, which are all supported by some empirical evidence.

(*a*) Expressive behavior is either adaptive behavior or conditioned but originally adaptive behavior. The addition of "originally adaptive" is obviously needed, since people make "disgusted" faces, possibly useful for getting rid of bad-tasting substances, when they hear morally disgusting stories. It seems certain that much in expressive movement is adaptive not only with regard to our forebears, as Darwin would have it, but here and now. Facial expressions of fear often form part, or the beginning, of general protective responses. Expressive movement, if it is adaptive, is so in a rather special way: not by modifying the environment, but by modifying the organism's relationship to his environment, through approach and withdrawal tendencies and through increase or decrease of sensory readiness of different kinds. To be sure, expression may sometimes be adaptive in only a subjective way—for instance, when a child tries to hide from people's glances by holding its hands before its face. To the extent that expressive movement is adaptive, it is connected to the motivational states in a quite intimate and intrinsic manner, since motives are by definition tendencies for establishing or destroying certain kinds of relationships. Primary expressive movement, according to this view, is the execution of behavior tendencies that define or partly define emotions and other motivational states.

(*b*) Expressive behavior is the direct manifestation of emotional (or other) activation. Drowsiness, energy, joy, and alertness refer to hardly more than quantitative variations of activation; the corresponding expressive movements are indeed mainly different degrees of generalized muscular activity, as correlation studies indicate (Frijda & Philipszoon 1963). In addition, expressive behavior embodies the degree of activity control. When emotions disrupt orientation and planning, behavior becomes disorganized and is, consequently, "expressive" of the disrupted state. In this reformulation of Darwin's "irradiation principle," the expressive components again are connected to the emotional impulses in no fortuitous manner. The expressive components are the consequences of the motivational impulses.

(*c*) Expressive movement might be communicative behavior either instinctively, by means of hereditary patterns, or intentionally, by means of conventional symbols. There is ethological evidence for instinctiveness in animal mating ceremonies or warning calls but little evidence to support or suggest instinctiveness in human expression, except, perhaps, the crying of the infant. Voluntary communicative expression is, of course, evident in verbal behavior and in secondary expressive movement. Primary expressions are rapidly utilized for communication, as is notable in the development of infant crying.

(*d*) Expressive movement might be a release phenomenon, serving to discharge emotional tensions. Introspectively, expressing emotions often gives relief. Freeman and Pathman (1942) found that experimentally induced emotional tension dissipated more rapidly in subjects manifesting much restless behavior than in those manifesting little. The fact that there is tension discharge does not, of course, imply that this is the *raison d'être* for the discharging behavior. The explanation may hold, however, for those nervous movements which arise during emotional stress or conflict ("autistic gestures," Krout 1935), such as scratching, rubbing the nose, nail-biting, etc.

The foregoing principles seem to account for most expressive movement; they seem to apply equally well to extralinguistic vocal expression. There are two important exceptions, however. Laughter and weeping do not seem to allow of any interpretation in terms of past or present adaptive movement, although such an interpretation was tried by Darwin; they cannot be smoothly interpreted as activation *modi* or mere consequences of loss of activity control; and their release function does not explain their form either. As yet, laughter and weeping are riddles of human behavior.

Expressive actions. Every human activity indicates some attitude and is thereby expressive, even if only of unemotional matter-of-factness. This holds particularly for choice behavior—choice of interests, of mates, of possessions, of clothing, etc. Activities which demand special mention, however, are those that are clearly objectively useless and clearly motivated by some sort of emotional excitement—a child's hiding under its mother's skirt, banging on the table, tearing its clothes, etc. In part these are what Lewin (1927) called field actions, which try to change the relationship with the environment. In part they have the distinct function of releasing emotional tensions which cannot find their outlet in a more proper, more adequate way. Little systematic study has been made of these phenomena notwithstanding their social importance, which is shown by the behavior of youthful audiences.

Verbal–symbolic behavior. Verbal–symbolic behavior is expressive, of course, primarily in that the subject desires to communicate his feelings, attitudes, or ideas. There is little relationship between a definition of expressive behavior that covers these phenomena and one that is focused upon expressive movement.

Expressive creative behavior. Creative behavior can justifiably be called expressive: its products stem from some drive to structure and shape. It is primarily this drive, which may get its energy from various sources, which art expresses. Artistic production may also, occasionally, serve the purpose of communication of feelings or ideas. Artistic products are frequently expressive, moreover, in the sense in which this term is primarily used here. Paintings, music, and poetry appear invested with emotional meanings for the spectator; they evidence motivational states. Still, there is an important distinction which separates artistic production from the execution of expressive movements. Functionally, both belong to entirely different classes of phenomena. Expressive movement is a direct manifestation of tendencies inherent in the emotional impulse. Expression in art is, as Langer (1942) emphasized, a representation of some motivational state in the language of the particular artistic mode—pictorial, musical, etc. It is a symbol of a motivational state that need not even be actually experienced at the time of creation. In the fact of its being a representation resides an effect, and possibly a function, of artistic production: in the creative process emotional impulses or experiences become structured, and this may facilitate coming to grips with them. Sometimes artistic products may be pervaded by traces of primary expressive movement: this is clearest in dancing and singing, but it is also true of painting and of some aspects of writing style. Yet the intention to create shape or structure in a conventional symbol system—even if the convention is peculiar to the individual artist—makes this class of phenomena irreducible to other kinds of expressive behavior.

NICO H. FRIJDA

[*Directly related is the entry* EMOTION. *Other relevant material may be found in* ATTENTION; CREATIVITY; SYMPATHY AND EMPATHY; TRAITS.]

BIBLIOGRAPHY

ABELSON, ROBERT P.; and SERMAT, VELLO 1962 Multidimensional Scaling of Facial Expressions. *Journal of Experimental Psychology* 63:546–554.

ALLPORT, GORDON W.; and VERNON, PHILIP E. 1933 *Studies in Expressive Movement.* New York: Macmillan.

ASCH, SOLOMON (1952) 1959 *Social Psychology.* Englewood Cliffs, N.J.: Prentice-Hall. → See especially "The Expression of Emotions," pages 183–204.

BAIN, ALEXANDER (1859) 1899 *The Emotions and the Will.* 4th ed. London: Longmans.

BARD, PHILIP 1950 Central Nervous Mechanisms for the Expression of Anger in Animals. Pages 211–237 in International Symposium on Feelings and Emotions, Second, Mooseheart, Ill., 1948, *Feelings and Emotions.* Edited by Martin L. Reymert. New York: McGraw-Hill.

DARWIN, CHARLES (1872) 1965 *The Expression of the Emotions in Man and Animals.* Edited by Francis Darwin. Univ. of Chicago Press.

DENNIS, WAYNE 1938 Infant Development Under Conditions of Restricted Practice and of Minimum Social Stimulation: A Preliminary Report. *Journal of Genetic Psychology* 53:149–157.

DUFFY, ELIZABETH 1962 *Activation and Behavior.* New York: Wiley. → See especially Chapters 5, 10, and 11.

DUMAS, GEORGES 1948 *La vie affective: Physiologie, psychologie, socialisation.* Paris: Presses Universitaires de France.

EFRON, DAVID 1941 *Gesture and Environment.* New York: King's Crown Press.

ENGEL, JOHANN J. 1785 *Ideen zu einer Mimik.* Berlin: Mylin.

FREEMAN, G. L.; and PATHMAN, J. H. 1942 The Relation of Overt Muscular Discharge to Physiological Recovery From Experimentally Induced Displacement. *Journal of Experimental Psychology* 30:161–174.

FRIJDA, NICO H. 1953 The Understanding of Facial Expression of Emotion. *Acta psychologica* 9:294–362.

FRIJDA, NICO H. 1958 Facial Expression and Situational Cues. *Journal of Abnormal and Social Psychology* 57:149–154.

FRIJDA, NICO H.; and PHILIPSZOON, ELS 1963 Dimensions of Recognition of Expression. *Journal of Abnormal and Social Psychology* 66:45–51.

GRANET, MARCEL 1922 Le langage de la douleur d'après le rituel funéraire de la Chine classique. *Journal de psychologie* 19:97–118.

HASSLER, R.; and RIECHERT, T. 1961 Wirkungen der Reizungen und Koagulationen in den Stammganglien bei stereotaktischen Hirnoperationen. *Nervenarzt* 32:97–109.

HESS, WALTER R. (1962) 1964 *The Biology of Mind.* Univ. of Chicago Press. → First published in German.

See especially "Psychic Functions and Cerebral Organization," pages 38–149.

KIENER, FRANZ 1962 *Hand, Gebärde und Charakter.* Munich: Reinhardt.

KIETZ, GERTRAUD 1956 *Der Ausdrucksgehalt des menschlichen Ganges.* Leipzig: Barth.

KIRCHHOFF, R. (editor) 1965 *Handbuch der Psychologie.* Volume 5: Ausdruckspsychologie. Göttingen (Germany): Hogrefe.

KLAGES, LUDWIG (1943) 1950 *Grundlegung der Wissenschaft vom Ausdruck.* 7th ed., rev. Bonn: Bouvier.

KROUT, MAURICE 1935 Autistic Gestures: An Experimental Study of Symbolic Movement. *Psychological Monographs* 46, no. 4.

LABARRE, WESTON 1947 The Cultural Basis of Emotions and Gestures. *Journal of Personality* 16:49–68.

LACEY, JOHN I. et al. 1963 The Visceral Level: Situational Determinants and Behavioral Correlates of Autonomic Response Patterns. Pages 161–196 in Symposium on Expression of the Emotions in Man, New York, 1960, *Expression of the Emotions in Man.* Edited by Peter H. Knapp. New York: International Universities Press.

LANDIS, CARNEY 1924 Studies of Emotional Reactions. II: General Behavior and Facial Expression. *Journal of Comparative Psychology* 4:447–501.

LANDIS, CARNEY; and HUNT, WILLIAM A. 1939 *The Startle Pattern.* New York: Farrar.

LANGER, SUSANNE (1942) 1957 *Philosophy in a New Key: A Study in the Symbolism of Reason, Rite and Art.* 3d ed. Cambridge, Mass.: Harvard Univ. Press.

LERSCH, PHILIP 1932 *Gesicht und Seele.* Munich: Reinhardt.

LEWIN, K. 1927 Kindlicher Ausdruck. *Zeitschrift für pädagogische Psychologie* 28:510–526.

LIPPS, T. 1905 Die Erkenntnis von fremden Ichen. *Psychologische Untersuchungen* 1:695–719.

MALRIEU, PHILIPPE 1960 Les conditions de l'évolution des émotions dans la première année. *Schweizerische Zeitschrift für Psychologie* 19:207–222.

PIDERIT, THEODOR (1867) 1925 *Mimik und Physiognomik.* 4th ed. Detmold (Germany): Meyer.

SAINSBURY, P. 1955 Gestural Movement During Psychiatric Interview. *Psychosomatic Medicine* 17:458–469.

SCHACHTER, STANLEY; and SINGER, JEROME 1962 Cognitive, Social and Physiological Determinants of Emotional State. *Psychological Review* 69:379–399.

SCHELER, MAX (1913) 1954 *The Nature of Sympathy.* London: Routledge. → First published as *Zur Phänomenologie und Theorie der Sympathiegefühle.* The second revised and enlarged edition, which was later translated into English, was published in 1923 as *Wesen und Formen der Sympathie.*

SCHLOSBERG, HAROLD 1954 Three Dimensions of Emotion. *Psychological Review* 61:81–88.

SHEPARD, ROGER N. 1962 The Analysis of Proximities: Multidimensional Scaling With an Unknown Distance Function. *Psychometrika* 27:125–140, 219–246.

STREHLE, HERMANN 1954 *Mienen, Gesten und Gebärden.* Munich: Reinhardt.

THOMPSON, JANE 1941 Development of Facial Expression of Emotion in Blind and Seeing Children. *Archives of Psychology* No. 264.

WOODWORTH, ROBERT S. 1938 *Experimental Psychology.* New York: Holt.

WOODWORTH, ROBERT S.; and SCHLOSBERG, HAROLD 1955 *Experimental Psychology.* 3d ed., rev. London:

Methuen. → The first edition was published in 1938 with Woodworth as sole author.

YOUNG, PAUL T. 1961 *Motivation and Emotions: A Survey of the Determinants of Human and Animal Activity.* New York: Wiley. → See especially Chapter 9.

EXPROPRIATION
See NATIONALIZATION.

EXTERNAL ECONOMIES AND DISECONOMIES

The concepts of external economies and diseconomies ("externalities") treat the subject of how the costs and benefits that constrain and motivate a decision maker in a particular activity may deviate from the costs or benefits that activity creates for a larger organization. Most of the economic literature on externalities has focused on the operation of an entire economic system, with particular reference to the effectiveness of prices, markets, competition, and profit motivation as regulators of production and consumption.

Economic theory suggests that a system characterized by private ownership of resources and sufficient competition will maximize total income and economic welfare. The system will establish an equilibrium in which product prices equal their costs on their respective margins of production. Costs include an opportunity rate of return on invested capital, which is an element of business accounting profit, and the rewards, or "rent," that especially endowed resources may command. Production costs also reflect technological constraints, and producers employ the least costly method of producing any given output. A further characteristic of the equilibrium is that similar resources, including capital, obtain equal earnings or returns in all activities. If earnings were unequal, resources would enter more profitable activities and leave less lucrative ones until earnings equality comes about. The resulting allocation of resources is also consistent with consumers' preferences. Finally, consumers' demands, through their influence on market prices and hence profits, determine the allocation of resources.

The system works in such a way that the wide diffusion of decision making which is necessary if complex systems are to operate at all is permitted. Each decision maker only needs to have knowledge about the things he consumes, or produces, or his occupation. That individuals can so narrow their focus permits a division of labor and, in turn, the resulting gains of specialization. The vital mechanism (and social institution) that facilitates such specialization is the price system, or market organization. The price system is an "information system" that provides producers and consumers with the signals that guide their behavior. Hence, the economic system is highly interdependent: the combined behavior of individual decision makers spontaneously determines relative prices and quantities of items produced and consumed, while relative prices are the signals, constraints, and opportunities to which individual decision makers respond and adapt.

Such a general equilibrium system has two specific qualities: (1) Production costs of each item, on its respective margin of production, when viewed in a social cost sense, equal the price of each item. (2) The price of each end product accurately reflects the incremental satisfaction that consumers attach to it. These two qualities constitute a "social optimum" in that national income and economic welfare are maximized [*see, however,* WELFARE ECONOMICS]. Note that it is only optimal if the marginal *social costs* of each activity equal the *social benefits* they create. If the social cost of an activity exceeds the costs relevant to the decision makers in the activity, there is an external diseconomy. If the benefits of an activity exceed its marginal cost, there is an external economy.

Due to the extreme interdependence within an economy, the behavior of a given industry can increase the cost of other industries in ways which need not be socially undesirable. Some of these phenomena, too, have been associated with the subject of external economies and diseconomies. One of the difficulties in the evaluation of externalities is the problem of determining which are socially desirable or undesirable and should be promoted or counteracted by public policy measures and which do not warrant government interference with the private sector.

The subject of external economies and diseconomies thus treats possible mechanical shortcomings of an economy that cause individual decision makers to operate in a fashion that thwarts the full attainment of broad social objectives. To some students the possible wide extent of externalities is sufficient basis to justify extensive government intervention in the private sector of the economy. To other students this point is debatable. The resolution of these differences has been, and remains, a major unsettled issue in economics.

External diseconomies

Technical external diseconomies. Technical external diseconomies, sometimes called "nuisance effects," were extensively discussed by A. C. Pigou ([1920] 1960, part 2, chapter 9). They arise from undesirable by-products of a production process. An example used by Pigou is the case of steam locomotives emitting sparks that cause fires. A farmer's livestock that eats his neighbor's crops is another example. Extensive lists of unwanted by-products may be drawn up in modern societies— from air and water pollution to traffic congestion associated with the automobile.

Such unwanted by-products are a natural consequence of many production processes. They impose a cost upon society similar to the cost of productive resources necessary to produce the desired product. They create a social problem insofar as their cost may not be properly allocated between different segments of the economy.

Let us consider further Pigou's example of spark-emitting steam locomotives. Assume that the marginal cost of employing resources to produce a ton-mile of railroad freight service may be 3 cents. The railroad system, however, "causes" 0.5 cents worth of damage per ton-mile because of fires inflicted on farmers' crops adjoining the right-of-way. Whether such behavior creates an unwarranted social cost, and what the appropriate social policy should be to deal with it, pose some subtle and complex issues.

The main force of Pigou's treatment of the subject is that the "social cost" of producing a ton-mile of freight is 3.5 cents (3 cents for the railroad's own costs, plus 0.5 cents for the destroyed crops). The policy prescription is that the railroad should be made to pay farmers for their destroyed crops or that railroads should be taxed or restrained in other ways that will prevent damage.

Coase (1960) has demonstrated, however, that this traditional approach to "nuisance effects" is wrong. The relationship is reciprocal. Crop damage is "caused" just as much by the farmer's growing crops along the railroad's right-of-way as by locomotives emitting sparks (indeed, the doctrine of "causation" is spurious). Moreover, to restrain railroads in arbitrary ways may impose a greater social loss (due to higher-cost railroad services) than the loss of some crops. The proper solution is to design a system that maximizes the economy's total product.

Such a solution might be found by recognizing that in producing the crops associated with the 0.5 cents per ton-mile of damage, farmers must purchase resources worth, say, 0.4 cents. Under these conditions, the railroad could pay farmers 0.1 cent *not* to grow crops along its right-of-way. Farmers would be just as well off as if there were no railroad; freight costs would be 3.1 cents per ton-mile, instead of 3.5 cents if farmers were arbitrarily awarded "full" damages; and 0.4 cents worth of resources would be freed to produce other products. Indeed, this kind of solution is often worked out spontaneously by bargaining between the concerned parties or is brought about through legal adjudication.

The social problems associated with external "nuisance effects" arise when certain scarce resources are treated as if they were "free goods"—because of faulty specification of property rights, or because it is difficult to identify in some quantitative way who causes the nuisance or who suffers from it (or both), or because the administrative costs of "solving" the problem may be more costly than the nuisance itself. Many students suggest that activities imposing unregistered social costs upon society be subjected to special excise taxes; however, the precise design of excise taxes that would not themselves distort resource allocation is difficult. Other students urge extensive state regulation. However, a distressing number of nuisance effects are due to activities that are already either regulated or managed by the state, for example, highway systems and government-owned public utilities, suggesting that effective solutions may not be easily attained from that quarter.

Sweeping solutions to the nuisance effect problem do not appear readily available. Thus far in virtually all social systems they have been coped with on an *ad hoc* basis. Perhaps one of the best ways to achieve better social guidelines for treatment of these problems is for economists to give more attention to the precise content of property rights, in terms of their economic effects, and for lawyers to employ economic analysis to evaluate the social utility of legal principles applied to torts.

Pecuniary external diseconomies. Consider industry A (for illustrative simplicity we assume that it only requires labor as a resource) which expands its output (see Table 1).

Table 1

Output	Workers	Wage	Total cost	Average and marginal cost per unit to firm	"Marginal cost" per unit to industry
100,000	100,000	$10.00	$1,000,000	$10.00	—
101,000	101,000	$10.50	$1,060,500	$10.50	$60.50

This example illustrates an "increasing cost" industry. The wage increase is necessary to induce more workers to enter the industry. The operators responsible for hiring the additional workers, by forcing up the wage, may be said to impose an additional cost upon their colleagues. This kind of cost increase has been termed an "external diseconomy."

It was with reference to cases like this that some students suggested (e.g., Pigou [1920] 1960, pp. 223–225) that the free operation of private business firms resulted in too much output by "increasing cost industries" and that they should be subject to taxation to restrict output. The implication, as illustrated by the arithmetical example, is that the $60.50 is the "social cost" per unit of the additional output; whereas the price that actually emerges in the market is $10.50.

The implication that the increasing cost was a social diseconomy raised some fundamental questions about the nature of costs. The clarification was achieved by D. H. Robertson ([1924] 1952, pp. 143–159) and especially F. H. Knight ([1924] 1952, pp. 160–179) and reiterated by Ellis and Fellner ([1943] 1952, pp. 242–263). The essential points are as follows:

Under competition, with many producers in an industry, each producer will view the cost (or wage) of hiring an additional worker as his marginal cost. In our example, it is $10.50. The $10.50 is also the average cost of production. In a private, competitive equilibrium, the average cost, the marginal cost to each producer, and the market price will be equal. If we take a collective view of the industry (which might be the case if it were operated by a socialist trust or a private monopoly) the "marginal cost" of $60.50 appears, which results from reckoning the possible impact of industry expansion upon the wage level. The question is: Which marginal cost concept is valid from an overall social welfare viewpoint?

The $10.50, rather than the $60.50, is the relevant measure of the marginal social cost. It represents what workers on the margin of production in the given industry could earn producing alternative products in other industries. Increasing the output of industry A requires enticing workers from industry B. If $10.50 is necessary to attract a worker into A, it is because he can earn $10.50 in B. Consumers give up $10.50 worth of B to get an increment of A. The marginal social cost of A is therefore $10.50. It is also the marginal cost upon which private decision makers focus and the signal that the price system generates.

That the shift in consumer demand and the consequential raising of the wage level in industry A operate to create an apparent marginal cost of $60.50 is simply a result of the fact that product prices and wages (and other resource earnings rates) are mutually determined by the operation of the price system. For a central authority to try to prevent the wage increase in industry A would (apart from thwarting consumer preferences) create many problems. First, other means to get additional workers into the industry would have to be found. If, even after getting additional workers into the industry, authorities sought to maintain the $10.00 wage and product price, they would create a rationing problem insofar as consumers would demand more of the commodity at $10.00 than they would at $10.50. Finally, the higher wage of $10.50 for all workers would induce the proper use of the specialized resources: at a $10.00 wage, production managers would not use the workers as efficiently as they would at a $10.50 wage. [*For a further discussion of these points, see* Cost.]

External economies

Technical external economies. Consider the situation where a group of farmers dam a stream in order to obtain a supply of irrigation water. The resulting pond may stimulate the fish population and thus enhance fish output and the earnings of fishermen. Increased irrigated acreage devoted to apples will increase the supply of nectar, improve the productivity of bees, and increase the output of honey; conversely, a larger bee population can increase pollenization and raise apple yields.

Such external economies are creatures of multiproduct activities and are similar to the technical external diseconomies cited above. They are probably not as frequent because private producers are adroit at forming arrangements whereby they can capture their by-products and derive a profit from them. For example, in our irrigation pond–fish example, neither the value of irrigation water nor the extra fish may—separately—justify the expense of the dam that makes both possible. But a merger between a fisherman and a farmer would create the necessary arrangement by which the full gain could be captured privately and thus accrue to society.

Technical external economies may nevertheless exist in important areas—where property arrangements are inadequate to capture privately the full benefits of an activity—and are sufficient to justify state intervention. For example, public education and health are areas where, while it may be of some economic worth to an individual to educate himself (or his child) and to keep his family healthy, greater social benefits are obtained if the state pushes the activity beyond the margins that individual incentive would achieve. Multiple-purpose river development projects are further cases in point. Such projects can provide electric power, flood control, navigable waterways, irrigation, and recreational facilities. In principle, a private group with a charter granting it proprietary rights over an entire river basin could construct and operate an appropriate multipurpose river development project. But such a monopoly would have to be carefully controlled by the state to prevent the private group from exploiting such a powerful ownership right in unsocial ways. Hence, it is simpler for the state to design, create, and operate such multipurpose projects.

It should be recognized, however, that this type of argument is used to justify or rationalize many kinds of subtle and not-too-subtle forms of state intervention in support of various industries or forms of consumption. In prewar Germany agriculture enjoyed state subsidies on the ground that peasant boys made good soldiers; in the United States at present the maritime industry enjoys subsidies and the mineral industries enjoy preferential tax treatment in the cause of national defense. Whether the relationship between the costs and the benefits of each of the many government interventions warrants the government action is moot: very few such programs are actually subjected to rigorous cost–benefit analysis based upon modern quantitative and analytical techniques.

Economies of scale. When an industry expands its output, it will normally procure additional goods and services from other firms or industries. Some of the supplying industries may operate under conditions which would permit them to enjoy "economies of scale." Such a condition means that an industry is not fully utilizing its capacity, perhaps because the market demand is not large enough to take all of the output the plant is efficiently capable of producing. Where economies of scale exist, it is possible to produce additional output at lower average unit costs. Because the industry utilizes its capacity more intensively, it spreads its overhead and fixed capital costs over a larger output and enjoys an "internal economy." Industries that can exploit internal economies are also termed "decreasing cost industries."

When a given industry expands its output in a way that necessitates purchases from decreasing cost industries, the industry that expanded initially may also enjoy lower costs. For example, as coal mines in a given district increase output, the railroad serving the mines may experience lower average unit costs. If the lower unit costs are passed on to the coal mine operators, the latter experience a "pecuniary external economy."

The extent to which such pecuniary external economies occur, and the impact they have on market prices, depends on several factors that can only be determined empirically on a case-by-case basis. First, it is a question of fact as to just how important economies of scale are in the economic system and how important their variation between different industries. Although railroads and electric utilities are often cited as examples of decreasing cost industries, what if the railroad or power plant is already fully utilized? Second, when a firm enjoys economies of scale, the activity is imperfectly competitive, or even monopolistic. As illustrated by the coal mining–railroad example, the railroad enjoys a monopoly subject only to the competitive constraint imposed by, say, motor trucks. Unless there is some institutional arrangement such as a public utility commission that forces a rate reduction, the larger coal traffic and consequent lower unit costs will only increase railroad profits. The "internal economy" will not become an external economy to anyone else.

Finally, whether an external pecuniary economy actually permits lower prices for the expanding industry's end product depends upon two opposing forces: the external pecuniary economy will lower cost; however, the industry's expansion can bid up the prices of hired resources and other inputs. The net balance of these opposite forces can only be determined through examination of the composition of the expanding industry's required inputs.

Division of labor and economic growth. Another set of external economies is dynamic and closely associated with economic growth and development. As an industry expands, the growth can create a number of supplying firms and activities which, through increased specialization, afford lower-cost products and labor services. There can arise specialized banking and financial facilities, firms that specialize in machinery design and repair, warehousing and transportation specialists, and numerous other activities oriented to servicing the industry. A labor force will emerge that is more sophisticated. If an industry is concentrated in a given region, knowledge gained in one segment rapidly spreads and speeds the rate at which cost reductions occur and are "competed away" through lower prices. The phenomenon was well treated by Young (1928).

Thus industry expansion stimulates the division of labor. The keener division of labor lowers costs. The lower costs and resulting lower prices increase output even more, which permits a further division of labor. Such a process helps explain the historical development of great regional industrial areas. The phenomenon, when it cuts across an entire economy, can provide a basis for a "take-off" toward the goal of a high degree of economic development.

The external economies associated with industrial development and growth (as well as those associated with economies of scale) pose special problems in the planning and public policy of undeveloped countries. These countries usually produce raw materials or semifinished goods for export and import finished products. Policy makers thus face interesting but perhaps difficult options. To exploit externalities originating in the division of labor at a minimum cost of scarce capital, the best place to start might be the industries that are already the most developed. However, these industries are likely to be the raw material or semifinished product export industries. If they are developed further, the external economies may accrue mainly to foreigners through lower-priced exports. It may thus appear more attractive to concentrate on the development of industries that will produce products which are extensively imported. The foundation for such a development strategy may be meager, however, and the cost-effectiveness per unit of investment may be low.

But it is in manufacturing industries where great gains—apparently resulting from exploiting both the dynamics of the division of labor and economies of scale—have eventually occurred. In recognition of these historical phenomena in Western developed countries, some students (e.g., Rosenstein-Rodan 1943) have advanced the doctrine of "balanced growth." This doctrine suggests that economic development should be promoted on a wide front so that the external economies of each industry will be mutually reinforcing, thus generating a cumulative process of over-all industrial development.

The precise investment strategy that a developing country should adopt is not evident on a purely theoretical basis. Much depends upon the price elasticities and income elasticities of its traditional export industries. Moreover, a country can design a structure of tariffs and export duties that could prevent an inordinate amount of the benefits due to external economies from accruing to foreigners. And by earning more foreign exchange through more efficient operation of its export industries, a country may more effectively gain the resources to finance its internal capital investment programs; or resources may be freed from the export industries to be available for domestically oriented endeavors. Finally, careful attention should be given to the precise qualities of the economy's resources that may provide the basis for the proposed state-supported domestic—as contrasted with export-oriented—industries. At a minimum, it appears that a development program must be integrated with a foreign trade policy. [*For further discussion of the issues in this section, see* ECONOMIC GROWTH, *articles on* THEORY *and* MATHEMATICAL THEORY.]

Growth repercussions. Another variety of external economies may be designated as growth or investment repercussions. They were labeled "pecuniary external economies," however, by Scitovsky (1954). Consider the example where the steel industry enjoys high profits. It expands its capacity and consequently increases its output. The larger output reduces steel prices. The cost to steel-using industries thus falls, and they enjoy higher profits. Their enhanced profits, although external to the steel industry, may be attributed to additional investment in the steel industry.

From this sort of sequence, Scitovsky developed the following line of argument: The profit signal revealed to the steel industry alone is an inadequate measure of the profit that should guide investment in the steel industry. If the steel-using industries were integrated with the steel-producing industry, managers of the integrated industries would have a better guide for their decisions. However, the repercussions and interactions of investment in a major industry can extend throughout the entire economy, which would suggest that the entire economy be "integrated."

Thus it is asserted that the price system provides a poor guide for investment decisions. The policy implication is that central planning and decision making is a better way to allocate investment than is decentralized decision making, since the central authority can explicitly take into account such external economies. A milder policy prescription is that private investors be provided with better information about one another's intentions, which may be done through the French variant of economic planning [*see* PLANNING, ECONOMIC, *article on* WESTERN EUROPE].

The contention that private investors may be unable to exploit this class of pecuniary "external economies" recognizes that, in fact, a market mechanism and its system of price indicators do not provide "perfect" intelligence of what the future holds. But the price system is not the sole source of information in an economic system: businessmen communicate with one another in other ways; they communicate with engineers and scientists on technological possibilities, and they conduct consumer surveys. Conversely, central planners or government officials also operate under imperfect knowledge. The critical substantive issue here is therefore: can the aggregate of private investors—each highly knowledgeable about his own business and responding to prices he confronts in the market place—more efficiently use investable resources than can a central authority, which may have less detailed knowledge about consumer preference and technology but a broader view of the economy in its entirety? Both types of decision making will be "imperfect" because all decision makers have imperfect knowledge. In part, the question will turn upon how highly developed the price system and private communication systems are in a particular society. In a developing economy the information system may be poor. Hence, a case may be made for a high degree of central planning in such a setting.

However, even if an instance can be found of the price system being an inferior information system, the case for central planning and control of investment is not established. The price system combined with private investment decision making provides widely diffused control over investable resources. Centrally controlled investment decision making is subject only to constraints that affect the entire economy. The choice is therefore one between many small decision makers making many small mistakes because of a poor information system, as opposed to the central authority possibly making fewer mistakes but perhaps making monumental ones. Which system is the most efficient is not obvious.

External economies and diseconomies are a manifestation of the fact that, in complex systems, one man's decision or behavior can often have an undesigned impact upon others. The trick in system design is to establish arrangements by which the mutually interacting and dependent behavior of all decision makers harmonizes so that the larger system operates in an optimal or efficient way.

The kinds of problems and phenomena we have discussed are not unique to the operation of a private enterprise social economy, although they have been most extensively treated by economists in such a context. The large multiproduct corporation, the government agency, a military service, or a university—organizations that may be characterized as "closed" systems and may be "centrally managed" to a high degree—have identical problems. Decision making and authority are necessarily diffused (governments consist of departments and bureaus, armies consist of divisions and squads, etc.); the decisions of many must nevertheless result in some coordinated and mutually consistent behavior; decision makers must be constrained as well as motivated; finally, they must be able to obtain knowledge about their constraints and opportunities, which includes the impact of the behavior of others. In varying degrees, discussions of externalities focus on these fundamental aspects of system or organization design and management.

The problems are basically those of specifying over-all system objectives, measuring effectiveness criteria, identifying and measuring the relevant cost concept, determining the relative merits of alternative information systems (with particular reference to the cost and worth of obtaining and communicating information), and specifying the appropriate "decision rules" that should guide individual decision makers.

Much of the economic literature on "externalities" suggests that economists have often failed to meet these problems head-on. On the other hand, the discipline of economics and much of the literature on the general operation of the price system —the product of nearly two hundred years of effort to understand the workings of a complex social economy—provide worthwhile insights into the problems that confront all large organizations.

J. A. STOCKFISCH

[See also WELFARE ECONOMICS.]

BIBLIOGRAPHY

COASE, R. H. 1960 The Problem of Social Cost. *Journal of Law and Economics* 3:1–44.

ELLIS, HOWARD S.; and FELLNER, WILLIAM (1943) 1952 External Economies and Diseconomies. Pages 242–263 in American Economic Association, *Readings in Price Theory*. Homewood, Ill.: Irwin. → First published in Volume 33 of the *American Economic Review*.

FLEMING, MARCUS 1955 External Economies and the Doctrine of Balanced Growth. *Economic Journal* 65:241–256.

KNIGHT, F. H. (1924) 1952 Some Fallacies in the Interpretation of Social Cost. Pages 160–179 in American Economic Association, *Readings in Price Theory*. Homewood, Ill.: Irwin. → First published in Volume 38 of the *Quarterly Journal of Economics*.

MEADE, J. E. 1952 External Economies and Diseconomies in a Competitive Situation. *Economic Journal* 62:54–67.

PIGOU, ARTHUR C. (1920) 1960 *The Economics of Welfare*. 4th ed. London: Macmillan.

ROBERTSON, D. H. (1924) 1952 Those Empty Boxes. Pages 143–159 in American Economic Association, *Readings in Price Theory*. Homewood, Ill.: Irwin. → First published in Volume 34 of the *Economic Journal*.

ROSENSTEIN-RODAN, PAUL N. 1943 Problems of Industrialization of Eastern and Southeastern Europe. *Economic Journal* 53:202–211.

SCITOVSKY, TIBOR 1954 Two Concepts of External Economies. *Journal of Political Economy* 62:143–151.

STOCKFISCH, J. A. 1955 External Economies, Investment, and Foresight. *Journal of Political Economy* 63:446–449.

VINER, JACOB (1931) 1952 Cost Curves and Supply Curves. Pages 198–232 in American Economic Association, *Readings in Price Theory*. Homewood, Ill.: Irwin. → First published in Volume 3 of the *Zeitschrift für Nationalökonomie*.

YOUNG, ALLYN A. 1928 Increasing Returns and Economic Progress. *Economic Journal* 38:527–542.

EXTRASENSORY PERCEPTION (ESP)
See PARAPSYCHOLOGY.

EXTREME VALUES
See NONPARAMETRIC STATISTICS, *article on* ORDER STATISTICS.

EYE MOVEMENTS
See under VISION.

F

FACTOR ANALYSIS

I. STATISTICAL ASPECTS — A. E. Maxwell
II. PSYCHOLOGICAL APPLICATIONS — Lloyd G. Humphreys

I
STATISTICAL ASPECTS

In many fields of research—for example, agriculture (Banks 1954), psychology (Burt 1947), economics (Geary 1948), medicine (Hammond 1944; 1955), and the study of accidents (Herdan 1943), but notably in psychology and the other social sciences—an experimenter frequently has scores for each member of a sample of individuals, animals, or other experimental units on each of a number of variates, such as cognitive tests, personality inventories, sociometric and socioeconomic ratings, and physical or physiological measures. If the number of variates is large, or even moderately so, the experimenter may wish to seek some reduction or simplification of his data. One approach to this problem is to search for some hypothetical variates that are weighted sums of the observed variates and that, although fewer in number than the latter, can be used to replace them. The statistical techniques by which such a reduction of data is achieved are known collectively as *factor analysis*, although it is well to note here that the principal component method of analysis discussed below (see also Kendall & Lawley 1956) has certain special features. The derived variates are generally viewed merely as convenient descriptive summarizations of the observed data. But occasionally their composition is such that they appear to represent some general basic aspects of everyday life, performance or achievement, and in such

cases they are often suitably labeled and are referred to as *factors*. Typical examples from psychology are such factors as "numerical ability," "originality," "neuroticism," and "toughmindedness." This article describes the statistical procedures in general use for arriving at these hypothetical variates or factors.

Preliminary concepts. Suppose that for a random sample of size N from some population, scores exist on each of p jointly normally distributed variates x_i $(i = 1, 2, \cdots, p)$. If the scores on each variate are expressed as deviations from the sample mean of that variate, then an unbiased estimator of the variance of x_i is given by the expression

$$a_{ii} = (N - 1)^{-1} \sum x_i^2,$$

summation being over the sample of size N. Similarly, an unbiased estimator of the covariance between variates x_i and x_j is given by

$$a_{ij} = (N - 1)^{-1} \sum x_i x_j.$$

Note that this is conventional condensed notation. A fuller, but clumsier, notation would use $x_{i\nu}$ for the deviation $(\nu = 1, \cdots, N)$ so that $\sum x_i^2$ really means $\sum_{\nu=1}^{N} x_{i\nu}^2$.

In practice, factor analysis is often used even in cases in which its usual assumptions are known to be appreciably in error. Such uses make the tacit presumption that the effect of the erroneous assumptions will be small or negligible. Unfortunately, nearly nothing is known about the circumstances under which this robustness, or nonsensitivity to errors in assumptions, is justified. Of course, the formal manipulations may always be carried out; the assumptions enter crucially into distribution theory and optimality of the estimators.

275

The estimated variances and covariances between the p variates can conveniently be written in square matrix form as follows:

$$
\mathbf{A} = \begin{bmatrix}
a_{11} & a_{12} & \cdots & a_{1p} \\
a_{21} & a_{22} & \cdots & a_{2p} \\
\vdots & \vdots & & \vdots \\
a_{p1} & a_{p2} & \cdots & a_{pp}
\end{bmatrix}.
$$

Since $a_{ij} = a_{ji}$, the matrix $\mathbf{A}$ is symmetric about its main diagonal.

From the terms of $\mathbf{A}$, the sample correlations, r_{ij}, between the pairs of variates may be obtained from

$$
r_{ij} = \frac{a_{ij}}{(a_{ii}a_{jj})^{\frac{1}{2}}},
$$

with $r_{ii} = 1$. The corresponding matrix is the *correlation matrix*.

The partial correlation concept is helpful here. If, to take the simplest case, estimates of the correlations between three variates are available, then the estimated correlation between any two, say x_i and x_j, for a given constant value of the third, x_k, can be found from the expression

$$
\frac{r_{ij} - r_{ik}r_{jk}}{(1 - r_{ik}^2)^{\frac{1}{2}}(1 - r_{jk}^2)^{\frac{1}{2}}}
$$

and is denoted by $r_{ij \cdot k}$.

In terms of a correlation matrix, the aim of factor analysis can be simply stated in terms of partial correlations (see Howe 1955). The first question asked is whether a hypothetical random variate f_1 exists such that the partial correlations $r_{ij \cdot f_1}$, for all i and j, are zero, within the limits of sampling error, after the effect of f_1 has been removed. (If this is so, it is customary to say that the correlation matrix, apart from its diagonal cells, is of rank *one*, but details will not be given here.) If the partial correlations are not zero, then the question is asked whether *two* hypothetical random variates, f_1 and f_2, exist such that the partial correlations between the variates are zero after the effects of both f_1 and f_2 have been removed from the original matrix, and so on. (If f_1 and f_2 reduce the partial correlations to zero, then the matrix, apart from its diagonal cells, is said to be of rank *two*, and so on.) The aim of the procedure is to replace the observed variates with a set of derived variates that, although fewer in number than the former, are still adequate to account for the correlations between them. In other words, the derived variates, or factors, account for the variance common to the observed variates.

Historical note. Factor analysis is generally taken to date from 1904, when C. E. Spearman published an article entitled " 'General Intelligence' Objectively Determined and Measured." Spearman postulated that a single hypothetical variate would in general account for the intercorrelations of a set of cognitive tests, and this variate was his famous factor "g." For the sets of tests that Spearman was considering, this hypothesis seemed reasonable. As further matrices of correlations became available, however, it soon became obvious that Spearman's hypothesis was an oversimplification of the facts, and multiple factor concepts were developed. L. L. Thurstone, in America, and C. Burt and G. H. Thomson, in Britain, were the most active pioneers in this movement. Details of their contributions and references to early journal articles can be found in their textbooks (Thurstone 1935; 1947; Burt 1940; Thomson 1939). These writers were psychologists, and the statistical methods they developed for estimating factors were more or less approximate in nature. The first rigorous attempt by a mathematical statistician to treat the problem of factor estimation (as distinct from principal components) came with the publication in 1940 of a paper by D. N. Lawley entitled "The Estimation of Factor Loadings by the Method of Maximum Likelihood." Since 1940, Lawley has published other articles dealing with various factor problems, and further contributions have been made by Howe (1955), by Anderson and Rubin (1956), and by Rao (1955), to mention just a few. Modern textbooks on factor analysis are those of Harman (1960) and Lawley and Maxwell (1963).

While methods of factor analysis, based on the above model, were being developed, Hotelling in 1933 published his *principal components* model, which, although it bears certain formal resemblances to the factor model proper, has rather different aims. It is widely used today and is described below.

The basic factor equations. The factor model described in general correlational terms above can be expressed more explicitly by the equations

$$
(1) \qquad x_i = \sum_{s=1}^{k} l_{is}f_s + e_i, \qquad k < p.
$$

In these equations k (the number of factors) is specified; f_s stands for the factors (generally referred to as *common* factors, since they usually enter into the composition of more than one variate). The factors are taken to be normally distributed and, without loss of generality, to have zero means and unit variances; to begin with, they will be assumed to be independent. The term e_i refers to a residual random variate affecting only the variate x_i. There are p of these e_i, and they are assumed to be normally distributed with zero means and to be independent of each other and of the f_s. Their variances will be denoted by v_i; the diagonal matrix of the v_i is called $\mathbf{V}$. The l-values are called *loadings* (weights), l_{is} being the loading of the ith variate on the sth factor. The quantities l_{is} and v_i are taken to be unknown parameters that have to be estimated. If a subscript for individual were introduced, it would be added to x_i and f_s, but not to l_{is} or v_i.

If the population variance–covariance matrix corresponding to the sample matrix $\mathbf{A}$ is denoted by $\mathbf{C}$, with elements c_{ij}, then it follows from the model that

$$(2) \qquad c_{ii} = \sum_{s=1}^{k} l_{is}^2 + v_i \,,$$

and

$$(3) \qquad c_{ij} = \sum_{s=1}^{k} l_{is} l_{js}, \qquad (i \neq j).$$

If the loadings for p variates on k factors are denoted by the $p \times k$ matrix $\mathbf{L}$, with transpose $\mathbf{L}'$, eqs. (2) and (3) can be combined in the single matrix equation

$$(4) \qquad \mathbf{C} = \mathbf{LL}' + \mathbf{V}.$$

Estimating the parameters in the model. Since the introduction of multiple factor analysis, various approximate methods for estimating the parameters l_{is} and v_i have been proposed. Of these, the best known is the *centroid*, or *simple summation*, method. It is well described in the textbooks mentioned above, but since the arithmetic details are unwieldy, they will not be given here. The method works fairly well in practice, but there is an arbitrariness in its procedure that makes statistical treatment of it almost impossible (see Lawley & Maxwell 1963, chapter 3). For a rigorous approach to the estimation of the factor parameters, I turn to the method of maximum likelihood, although this decision requires some justification. The maximum likelihood method of factor estimation has not been widely used in the past for two reasons. First, it involves very onerous calculations which were well-nigh prohibitive before the development of electronic computers. Second, the arithmetic procedures available, which were iterative, frequently did not lead to convergent estimates of the loadings. But recently, largely because of the work of the Swedish statistician K. G. Jöreskog, quick and efficient estimation procedures have been

found. These methods are still being perfected, but a preliminary account of them is contained in a recent paper (Jöreskog 1966). When they become better known, it is likely that the maximum likelihood method of factor analysis will become the accepted method. An earlier monograph by Jöreskog (1963) is also of interest. In it he links up work by Guttman (1953) on *image theory* with classical factor analytic concepts (see also Kaiser, in Harris 1963). (The image of a variate is defined as that part of its variance which can be estimated from the other variates in a matrix.)

The first point to note about eqs. (1) is that since the p observed variates x_i are expressed in terms of $p + k$ other variates, namely, the k common factors and the p residual variates, which are not observable, these equations are not capable of direct verification. But eq. (4) implies a hypothesis, H_0, regarding the covariance matrix $\mathbf{C}$, which can be tested, that it can be expressed as the sum of a diagonal matrix with positive diagonal elements and a symmetric positive semidefinite matrix with at most k latent roots: these matrices are respectively $\mathbf{V}$ and $\mathbf{LL}'$. The value postulated for k must not be too large; otherwise, the hypothesis would be trivially true. If the v_i were known, it would only be necessary to require $k < p$, but in the more usual case, where they are unknown, the condition can be shown to be $(p + k) < (p - k)^2$. Since the x_i are assumed to be distributed in a multivariate normal way, the log-likelihood function, omitting a function of the observations, is given by

$$(5) \qquad L = -\tfrac{1}{2}n \ln |\mathbf{C}| - \tfrac{1}{2}n \sum_{i,j} a_{ij} c^{ij},$$

where $n = N - 1$, $|\mathbf{C}|$ is the determinant of the matrix $\mathbf{C}$, and c^{ij} is the element in the ith row and jth column of its inverse, $\mathbf{C}^{-1}$. To find maximum likelihood estimators of l_{is} and v_i, (5) is differentiated with respect to them and the results are equated to zero. A difficulty arises, however, when $k > 1$, for there are then too many parameters in the model for them to be specified uniquely. This can be seen by an examination of eq. (4), for if $\mathbf{L}$ is postmultiplied by an orthogonal matrix $\mathbf{M}$, the value of $\mathbf{LL}'$, which is now given by $\mathbf{LMM}'\mathbf{L}'$, is unaltered since $\mathbf{MM}' = \mathbf{I}$, the identity matrix. This means that the maximum likelihood method, although it provides a unique set of estimates of the c_{ij}, leads to equations for estimating the l_{is} which are satisfied by an infinity of solutions, all equally good from a statistical point of view.

In this situation all the statistician can do is to

select a particular solution, one that is convenient to find, and leave the experimenter to apply whatever rotation he thinks desirable. Thus the custom is to choose L in such a way that the $k \times k$ matrix $J = L'V^{-1}L$ is diagonal. It can be shown that the successive elements of J are the latent roots, in order of magnitude, of the matrix $V^{-\frac{1}{2}}(A-V)V^{-\frac{1}{2}}$, so that for a given value of V, the determination of the factors in the factor model resembles the determination of the principal components in the component model.

The maximization of eq. (5) with the above diagonalization side condition leads to the equations

$$\hat{c}_{ii} = a_{ii}$$

or

$$(6) \qquad \hat{v}_i = a_{ii} - \sum_{s=1}^{k} l_{is}^2,$$

and

$$(7) \qquad \hat{L}' = \hat{J}^{-1}\hat{L}'\hat{V}^{-1}(A - \hat{V}),$$

where circumflex accents denote estimates of the parameters in question. Eq. (7) can usually be solved by iterative methods and details of those in current use can be found in Lawley and Maxwell (1963), Howe (1955), and Jöreskog (1963; 1966). The calculations involved are onerous, and when p is fairly large, say 12 or more, an electronic computer is essential.

A satisfactory property of the above method of estimation, which does not hold for the centroid and principal component methods, is that it can be shown to be independent of the metric used. A change of scale of any variate x_i merely introduces proportional changes in its loadings.

Testing hypotheses on number of factors. In the factor analysis of a set of data the value of k is seldom known in advance and has to be estimated. To begin with, some value of it is assumed and a matrix of loadings L for this value is estimated. The effects of the factors concerned are now eliminated from the observed covariance (or correlation) matrix, and the residual matrix, $A - LL'$, is tested for significance. If it is found to be statistically significant, the value of k is increased by one and the estimation process is repeated. The test employed is of the large sample chi-square type, based on the likelihood ratio method of Neyman and Pearson, and is given by

$$(8) \qquad X^2 = n \ln(|\hat{C}|/|A|),$$

with $\frac{1}{2}\{(p-k)^2 - (p+k)\}$ degrees of freedom. A good approximation to expression (8), and one easier to calculate, is

$$(9) \qquad X^2 = n \sum_{i<j} (a_{ij} - \hat{c}_{ij})^2/(\hat{v}_i\hat{v}_j).$$

There is also some evidence to suggest that the test can be improved by replacing n by $n' = n - \frac{1}{6}(2p+5) - \frac{2}{3}k$.

Factor interpretation. As already mentioned, the matrix of loadings, L, given by a factor analysis is not unique and can be replaced by an equivalent set LM where M is an orthogonal matrix. This fact is frequently used by experimenters when interpreting their results, a matrix M being chosen that will in some way simplify the pattern of loadings or make it more intuitively meaningful. For example, M may be chosen so as to reduce to zero, or nearly zero, as many loadings as possible in order to reduce the number of parameters necessary for describing the data. Again, M may be chosen so as to concentrate the loadings of variates of similar content, say verbal tests, on a single factor so that this factor may be labeled appropriately. Occasionally, too, the factors are allowed to become correlated if this seems to lead to more meaningful results.

It is now clear that given a matrix of loadings from some analysis, different experimenters might choose different rotation matrices in their interpretation of the data. This subjective element in factor analysis has led to a great deal of controversy. To avoid subjectivity, various empirical methods of rotation have been proposed which, while tending to simplify the pattern of loadings, also lead to unique solutions. The best known of these are the *varimax* and the *promax* methods (for details see Kaiser 1958; Hendrickson & White 1964). But another approach to the problem, proposed independently by Howe (1955), Anderson and Rubin (1956), and Lawley (1958), seems promising. From prior knowledge the experimenter is asked to postulate in advance (*a*) how many factors he expects from his data and (*b*) which variates will have zero loadings on the several factors. In other words, he is asked to formulate a specific hypothesis about the factor composition of his variates. The statistician then estimates the nonzero loadings and makes a test of the "goodness of fit" of the factors structure. In this approach the factors may be correlated or uncorrelated, and in the former case estimates of the correlations between them are obtained. The equations of estimation and illustrative examples of their application can be found in Howe (1955) and in Lawley and Maxwell (1963; 1964); the latter gives a quick method of finding approximate estimates of the nonzero loadings.

Estimating factor scores. As the statistical theory of factor analysis now stands, estimation is a twofold process. First, the factor structure, as described above, of a set of data is determined. In practice, however, it is often desirable to find, in addition, equations for estimating the scores of individuals on the factors themselves. One method of doing this, developed by Thomson, is known as the "regression method." In it the l_{is} are taken to be the covariances between the f_s and the x_i, and then for uncorrelated factors the estimation equation is

$$(10) \qquad \hat{\boldsymbol{f}} = \boldsymbol{L}'\boldsymbol{C}^{-1}\boldsymbol{x},$$

or, more simply from the computational viewpoint,

$$(11) \qquad \hat{\boldsymbol{f}} = (\boldsymbol{I} + \boldsymbol{J})^{-1}\boldsymbol{L}'\boldsymbol{V}^{-1}\boldsymbol{x},$$

where $\hat{\boldsymbol{f}} = \{\hat{f}_1, \hat{f}_2, \cdots, \hat{f}_k\}'$, $\boldsymbol{x} = \{x_1, x_2, \cdots, x_p\}'$, and, as before, $\boldsymbol{J} = \boldsymbol{L}'\boldsymbol{V}^{-1}\boldsymbol{L}$, and $\boldsymbol{I}$ is the identity matrix. If sampling errors in $\boldsymbol{L}$ and $\boldsymbol{V}$ are neglected, the covariance matrix for the errors of estimates of the factor scores is given by $(\boldsymbol{I} + \boldsymbol{J})^{-1}$.

If the factors are correlated and their estimated correlation matrix is denoted by $\boldsymbol{P}$, then eqs. (10) and (11) become, respectively,

$$(12) \qquad \hat{\boldsymbol{f}} = \boldsymbol{P}\boldsymbol{L}'\boldsymbol{C}^{-1}\boldsymbol{x},$$

and

$$(13) \qquad \hat{\boldsymbol{f}} = (\boldsymbol{P}^{-1} + \boldsymbol{J})^{-1}\boldsymbol{L}'\boldsymbol{V}^{-1}\boldsymbol{x},$$

while the errors of estimates are given by $(\boldsymbol{P}^{-1} + \boldsymbol{J})^{-1}$.

An alternative method of estimating factor scores is that of Bartlett (1938). Here, the principle adopted is the minimization, for a given set of observations, of $\sum_i e_i^2/v_i$, which is the sum of squares of standardized residuals. The estimation equation now is

$$(14) \qquad \hat{\boldsymbol{f}}^* = \boldsymbol{J}^{-1}\boldsymbol{L}'\boldsymbol{V}^{-1}\boldsymbol{x}.$$

It is of interest to note that although the sets of estimates gotten by the two methods have been reached by entirely different approaches, a comparison shows that they are simply related. For uncorrelated factors the relationship is

$$\hat{\boldsymbol{f}}^* = (\boldsymbol{I} + \boldsymbol{J}^{-1})\hat{\boldsymbol{f}};$$

for correlated factors it is

$$\hat{\boldsymbol{f}}^* = (\boldsymbol{I} + \boldsymbol{J}^{-1}\boldsymbol{P}^{-1})\hat{\boldsymbol{f}}.$$

Comparing factors across populations. If factors can be viewed as representing "permanent" aspects of behavior or performance, ways of identifying them from one population to another are required. In the past, identification has generally been based on the comparison of matrices of loadings. In the case of two matrices, a common approach, developed by Ahmavaara (1954) and Cattell and Hurley (1962), is to rotate one into maximum conformity in the least square sense

with the other. For example, the matrix required for rotating $\boldsymbol{L}_1$ into maximum conformity with $\boldsymbol{L}_2$, when they both involve the same variates, is obtained by calculating the expression $(\boldsymbol{L}_1'\boldsymbol{L}_1)^{-1}\boldsymbol{L}_1'\boldsymbol{L}_2$ and normalizing it by columns. The factors represented by $\boldsymbol{L}_1$ in its transformed state are likely to be more or less correlated, but estimates of the correlations between them are given by $(\boldsymbol{M}_0'\boldsymbol{M}_0)^{-1}$, standardized so that its diagonal cells are unity, where $\boldsymbol{M}_0 = (\boldsymbol{L}_1'\boldsymbol{L}_1)^{-1}\boldsymbol{L}_1'\boldsymbol{L}_2$ and $\boldsymbol{M}_0'$ is its transpose. This procedure is fairly satisfactory when the sample *covariance* matrices involved do not differ significantly. When they do, the problem of identifying factors is more complicated.

A possible approach to it has been suggested by Lawley and Maxwell (1963, chapter 8), who make the assumption that although two covariance matrices, $\boldsymbol{C}_1$ and $\boldsymbol{C}_2$, involving the same variates may be different, they may still have the same $\boldsymbol{L}$-matrix. This could occur if the two $k \times k$ covariance matrices Γ_1 and Γ_2 between the factors themselves were different. To keep the model fairly simple, they assume that the residual variances in the populations are in each case $\boldsymbol{V}$ and then set up the equations

$$(15) \qquad \begin{aligned} \boldsymbol{C}_1 &= \boldsymbol{L}\,\Gamma_1\boldsymbol{L}' + \boldsymbol{V}, \\ \boldsymbol{C}_2 &= \boldsymbol{L}\,\Gamma_2\boldsymbol{L}' + \boldsymbol{V}. \end{aligned}$$

For this model Lawley and Maxwell show how estimates of $\boldsymbol{L}$, $\boldsymbol{V}$, Γ_1, and Γ_2 may be obtained from two sample covariance matrices $\boldsymbol{A}_1$ and $\boldsymbol{A}_2$. They also supply a test for assessing the significance of the difference between the estimates of Γ_1 and Γ_2, and also for testing the "goodness of fit" of the model.

The method of principal components

The principal component method of analyzing a matrix of covariances or correlations is also widely used in the social sciences. The components correspond to the latent roots of the matrix, and the weights defining them are proportional to the corresponding latent vectors.

The model can also be stated in terms of the observed variates and the derived components. An orthogonal transformation is applied to the x_i $(i = 1, 2, \cdots, p)$ to produce a new set of uncorrelated variates $y_1, y_2, \cdots, y_p$. These are chosen such that y_1 has maximum variance, y_2 has maximum variance subject to being uncorrelated with y_1, and so on. This is equivalent to a rotation of the coordinate system so that the new coordinate axes lie along the principal axes of an ellipsoid closely related to the covariance structure of the x_i. The transformed variates are then standardized to give a new set, which will be denoted z_s. When this method is used, no hypothesis need be made about the nature or distribution of the x_i. The model is by definition linear and additive, and the basic equations are

$$(16) \qquad x_i = \sum_{s=1}^{p} w_{is} z_s, \qquad i, s = 1, 2, \cdots, p,$$

where z_s stands for the sth component, and w_{is} is the weight of the sth component in the ith variate. In matrix notation eqs. (16) become

$$\mathbf{x} = \mathbf{W}\mathbf{z},$$

where $\mathbf{x} = \{x_1, x_2, \cdots, x_p\}'$, $\mathbf{z} = \{z_1, z_2, \cdots, z_p\}'$, and $\mathbf{W}$ is a square matrix of order p with elements w_{is}.

Comparison of eqs. (16) with eqs. (1) shows that in the principal component model residual variates do not appear, and that if all p components are obtained, the sample covariances can be reproduced exactly, that is, $\mathbf{A} = \mathbf{W}'\mathbf{W}$. Indeed, there is a simple reciprocal relationship between the observed variates and the derived components.

A straightforward iterative method for obtaining the weights w_{is} is given by Hotelling in his original papers; the details are also given in most textbooks on factor analysis. In practice, all p components are seldom found, for a small number generally accounts for a large percentage of the variance of the variates and can be used to summarize the data. There is also a criterion, developed by Bartlett (1950; 1954), for testing the equality of the remaining latent roots of a matrix after the first k have been extracted; this is sometimes used to help in deciding when to stop the analysis.

The principal component method is most useful when the variates x_i are all measured in the same units. Otherwise, it is more difficult to justify. A change in the scales of measurement of some or all of the variates results in the covariance matrix being multiplied on both sides by a diagonal matrix. The effect of this on the latent roots and vectors is very complicated, and unfortunately the components are not invariant under such changes of scale. Because of this, the principal component approach is at a disadvantage in comparison with the proper factor analysis approach.

A. E. Maxwell

[*See also* Clustering; Distributions, statistical, *article on* mixtures of distributions; Latent structure; Statistical identifiability.]

BIBLIOGRAPHY

Ahmavaara, Y. 1954 Transformational Analysis of Factorial Data. *Suomalainen Tiedeakatemia, Helsinki, Toimituksia: Annales* Series B 88, no. 2.

Anderson, T. W.; and Rubin, Herman 1956 Statistical Inference in Factor Analysis. Volume 5, pages 111– 150 in Berkeley Symposium on Mathematical Statistics and Probability, Third, *Proceedings.* Edited by Jerzy Neyman. Berkeley: Univ. of California Press.

Banks, Charlotte 1954 The Factorial Analysis of Crop Productivity: A Re-examination of Professor Kendall's Data. *Journal of the Royal Statistical Society* Series B 16:100–111.

Bartlett, M. S. 1938 Methods of Estimating Mental Factors. *Nature* 141:609–610.

Bartlett, M. S. 1950 Tests of Significance in Factor Analysis. *British Journal of Psychology* (Statistical Section) 3:77–85.

Bartlett, M. S. 1954 A Note on the Multiplying Factor for Various χ^2 Approximations. *Journal of the Royal Statistical Society* Series B 16:296–298.

Burt, Cyril 1940 *The Factors of the Mind: An Introduction to Factor-analysis in Psychology.* Univ. of London Press.

Burt, Cyril 1947 Factor Analysis and Physical Types. *Psychometrika* 12:171–188.

Cattell, Raymond B.; and Hurley, John R. 1962 The Procrustes Program: Producing Direct Rotation to Test a Hypothesized Factor Structure. *Behavioral Science* 7:258–262.

Geary, R. C. 1948 Studies in Relationships Between Economic Time Series. *Journal of the Royal Statistical Society* Series B 10:140–158.

Gibson, W. A. 1960 Nonlinear Factors in Two Dimensions. *Psychometrika* 25:381–392.

Hammond, W. H. 1944 Factor Analysis as an Aid to Nutritional Assessment. *Journal of Hygiene* 43:395–399.

Hammond, W. H. 1955 Measurement and Interpretation of Subcutaneous Fats, With Norms for Children and Young Adult Males. *British Journal of Preventive and Social Medicine* 9:201–211.

Harman, Harry H. 1960 *Modern Factor Analysis.* Univ. of Chicago Press. → A new edition was scheduled for publication in 1967.

Harris, Chester W. (editor) 1963 *Problems in Measuring Change: Proceedings of a Conference.* Madison: Univ. of Wisconsin Press. → See especially "Image Analysis" by Henry F. Kaiser.

Hendrickson, Alan E.; and White, Paul O. 1964 Promax: A Quick Method for Rotation to Oblique Simple Structure. *British Journal of Statistical Psychology* 17: 65–70.

Herdan, G. 1943 The Logical and Analytical Relationship Between the Theory of Accidents and Factor Analysis. *Journal of the Royal Statistical Society* Series A 106:125–142.

Horst, Paul 1965 *Factor Analysis of Data Matrices.* New York: Holt.

Hotelling, Harold 1933 Analysis of a Complex of Statistical Variables Into Principal Components. *Journal of Educational Psychology* 24:417–441, 498–520.

Howe, W. G. 1955 Some Contributions to Factor Analysis. Report No. ORNL-1919, U.S. National Laboratory, Oak Ridge, Tenn. Unpublished manuscript.

Jöreskog, K. G. 1963 *Statistical Estimation in Factor Analysis: A New Technique and Its Foundation.* Stockholm: Almqvist & Wiksell.

Jöreskog, K. G. 1966 Testing a Simple Hypothesis in Factor Analysis. *Psychometrika* 31:165–178.

Kaiser, Henry F. 1958 The Varimax Criterion for Analytic Rotation in Factor Analysis. *Psychometrika* 23: 187–200.

KENDALL, M. G.; and LAWLEY, D. N.   1956   The Principles of Factor Analysis. *Journal of the Royal Statistical Society* Series A 119:83–84.

LAWLEY, D. N.   1940   The Estimation of Factor Loadings by the Method of Maximum Likelihood. Royal Society of Edinburgh, *Proceedings* 60:64–82.

LAWLEY, D. N.   1953   A Modified Method of Estimation in Factor Analysis and Some Large Sample Results. Pages 35–42 in *Uppsala Symposium on Psychological Factor Analysis, March 17–19, 1953*. Nordisk Psykologi, Monograph Series, No. 3. Uppsala (Sweden): Almqvist & Wiksell.

LAWLEY, D. N.   1958   Estimation in Factor Analysis Under Various Initial Assumptions. *British Journal of Statistical Psychology* 11:1–12.

LAWLEY, D. N.; and MAXWELL, ALBERT E.   1963   *Factor Analysis as a Statistical Method*. London: Butterworth.

LAWLEY, D. N.; and MAXWELL, A. E.   1964   Factor Transformation Methods. *British Journal of Statistical Psychology* 17:97–103.

MAXWELL, A. E.   1964   Calculating Maximum-likelihood Factor Loadings. *Journal of the Royal Statistical Society* Series A 127:238–241.

RAO, C. R.   1955   Estimation and Tests of Significance in Factor Analysis. *Psychometrika* 20:93–111.

SPEARMAN, C. E.   1904   "General Intelligence" Objectively Determined and Measured. *American Journal of Psychology* 15:201–293.

THOMSON, GODFREY H.   (1939) 1951   *The Factorial Analysis of Human Ability*. 5th ed. Boston: Houghton Mifflin.

THURSTONE, LOUIS L.   1935   *The Vectors of Mind: Multiple-factor Analysis for the Isolation of Primary Traits*. Univ. of Chicago Press.

THURSTONE, LOUIS L.   1947   *Multiple-factor Analysis*. Univ. of Chicago Press. → A development and expansion of Thurstone's *The Vectors of Mind*, 1935.

II
PSYCHOLOGICAL APPLICATIONS

The essential statistical problem of factor analysis involves reduction or simplification of a large number of variates so that some hypothetical variates, fewer in number, which are weighted sums of the observed variates, can be used to replace them. If psychological experimenters were satisfied with this sole, statistical objective, there would be no problem of psychological interpretation and of meaning of factors. They would simply be convenient abstractions. However, psychologists and psychometricians, starting with Charles Spearman (1904), the pioneer factor analyst, have wanted to go beyond this objective and have thereby created the very large psychological literature in this field. The goal of factor analysts following in the Spearman tradition has been to find not only convenient statistical abstractions but the elements or the basic building blocks, the primary mental abilities and personality traits in human behavior. Such theorists have explicitly accepted chemical elements— sometimes even the periodic table—as their model

and factor analysis as the method of choice in reaching their goal.

Factor interpretation and methodology

Factor extraction methods. There are several variations of factor methods, certain of which are more amenable to psychological interpretation than others. For example, the experimenter can start his analysis from a variance–covariance matrix or from a correlational matrix with estimated communalities (discussed below) in the principal diagonal. If he is interested in psychological interpretations of factors, he almost uniformly selects the latter, since use of the variance–covariance procedure results in obtaining factors that contain unknown amounts of common-factor, nonerror-specific, and error components. For purposes of psychological interpretation, including generalizing to new samples of psychological measures, the inclusion of nonerror-specific and error variance in the factors is undesirable. The intercorrelations and communalities, on the other hand, are determined only by the common factors.

The experimenter also has a choice among several methods of factor extraction, including the centroid, principal components (sometimes called principal axes), and maximum likelihood methods. Choice among these is based largely on feasibility criteria. The first was used almost exclusively before the advent of high-speed digital computers. The third is generally acknowledged to be superior statistically to the second, but it is too expensive in time and computer to use. The second is at present the method most frequently used by psychologists, since it extracts a maximum amount of variance with each successive factor. The centroid method only approximates this criterion, although frequently it is a close approximation. There is thus no pressing need to redo all previous work involving the centroid method now that computational facilities are available. The maximum likelihood method can and should be used, as a check on conclusions reached with the more economical principal components, when size of matrix and computer availability make it feasible.

The communality problem. When the experimenter elects to analyze correlations and communalities, he must estimate the latter. These communalities represent the proportion of common factor variance in the total variance of a variable: the amount that a variable has in common with other variables in a particular study. Unfortunately, from the methodological viewpoint, there is no way to obtain an unbiased estimate of the communality. Several rule-of-thumb methods are available, and there are theoretically sound upper and lower bounds for the communality estimate.

An unbiased reliability estimate can be used as an upper bound for the estimated communality. Reliability and communality differ to the extent that reliability includes specific nonerror variance. A lower-bound estimate in the population of persons is the squared multiple correlation between each variable and all of the others (Guttman 1954). The reader should note, however, that while this procedure provides a lower-bound estimate for the population, a sample value can be seriously inflated. The multiple correlation coefficient capitalizes on chance very effectively. For example, when the number of variables equals the number of observations, the multiple correlation in the sample is necessarily unity, although the population value may in fact be zero. The investigator who wants a lower-bound estimate may still utilize the Guttman theorem if he estimates the population values from sample values that are corrected for their capitalization on chance.

Number of factors. If he is interested in the psychological meaning of his factors, the experimenter has a further choice among criteria for determining the number of factors to retain and interpret. When estimated communalities are employed, no one of the possible criteria is more than a rule of thumb. The various criteria lead to radically different decisions concerning the number of factors to be retained; and different investigators, in applying one, several, or all of these criteria, will reach different conclusions about the number of factors.

One class of criteria for determining the number of factors has been characterized as emphasizing psychological importance without regard to sampling stability. Some investigators use some absolute value of the factor loadings, e.g., .30, either rotated or unrotated or both, without regard to the number of observations on which the correlations are based. A more recent suggestion has been to retain factors whose principal roots were greater than unity (Kaiser & Caffrey 1965). Such criteria appear to make an assumption that the number of observations is very large, so that the factors and loadings that are large enough psychologically are at the same time not the result of sampling error.

A second class of criteria has been characterized as emphasizing the number of observations, even though there are no known sampling distributions for factors or factor loadings. In several related criteria, factor loadings and/or residuals are compared in one way or another with the standard error of correlation coefficients of zero magnitude for the sample size involved. Factoring of the intercorrelations of random normal deviates as a method of obtaining empirical sampling errors has also been used.

A third criterion involves the "psychological meaning" of the rotated factors: the investigator merely states in effect that he is satisfied with the results of his analysis. Since any behavioral scientist of any modest degree of ingenuity can rationalize the random grouping of any set of variables, this does not appear to be a useful criterion scientifically. Without agreement on an objective criterion, however, psychological meaning of the factors tends to be the principal criterion used in deciding upon the number of factors to interpret.

Even in situations where probabilities of alpha and beta errors can be estimated, different investigators, depending on their temperaments or on social consequences, may set quite different standards for such errors. In determining the number of factors, however, there are no objective methods of error estimation, and the range of probabilities of alpha and beta errors resulting from differences among investigators or differences in social consequences is increased several-fold. For example, for one matrix of personality variables two investigators differ by a ratio of four to one in their assessment of the proper number of factors to retain and interpret. The difference between 12 and 3 factors is far from trivial. Such discrepancies reduce factor analysis to a hypothesis formation technique. As a method of discovery of psychological principles, or of hypothesis testing generally, ambiguities of this magnitude cannot be tolerated. The lack of a suitable test for number of factors has opened the door for a great deal of poor research.

Factor rotations. After the factors are extracted, the experimenter has to decide whether to rotate or not. Rotation of axes to psychologically meaningful positions follows inevitably from an interest in finding the psychological elements.

The rotation problem is seen most clearly in the two-factor case. First, the two factors are conceptualized as orthogonal (perpendicular) dimensions extending from values of -1.00 to $+1.00$. Then the points representing the loadings of the tests on these factors are fixed in the space defined by these dimensions. Imagine now that a pin is inserted at the origin of the two dimensions and that these are now rotated about the pin. Wherever they stop, new coordinates can be determined for the test points. It must be noted that the test points are located as accurately by the new dimensions as by the original ones, and that the intercorrelations of the tests are described with equal accuracy. There are, in point of fact, an infinite number of positions of the coordinates and thus an infinite number of mathematical solutions to the factor problem. The investigator interested in psychological meaning rotates the dimensions into some psychologically unique position. It is important, where possible, that factor descriptions of measures remain stable from sample to sample of either persons or measures, or both. This can be achieved, apparently in the great majority of cases, with an adequate rotational solution.

Rotation is almost uniformly performed when factors obtained are from a correlation matrix having communality estimates in the diagonal. Factors obtained from the variance–covariance matrix, on the other hand, are generally not rotated and are preferred by the experimenter interested in description alone rather than in explanation. The experimenter also has a choice among several different rotational methods, based upon different criteria and leading to either orthogonal or oblique factors.

Orthogonal versus oblique rotation.   Orthogonal rotations offer the simplicity of uncorrelated dimensions in exchange for a poorer fit of the test points. Oblique rotations offer a better fit for the test points in exchange for a complexity of correlated dimensions. If oblique rotations are used, the investigator can also elect to factor in the second and perhaps higher orders; i.e., he can factor the intercorrelations among his first-order factors, among his second-order factors, and so on. After factoring in several orders, the investigator also has the option of presenting and interpreting his results in the several orders, or, by means of a simple transformation, he can convert the oblique factors in several orders to orthogonal, hierarchical factors in a single order.

Until the advent of high-speed digital computers, basically the only method for achieving a given rotational result was hand rotation. There are now several computer programs for rotation to either orthogonal or oblique structure.

If the investigator elects an orthogonal solution to his problem, he has a number of programs among which to choose. One of the earlier programs is the quartimax of Neuhaus and Wrigley (1954). This was followed by Kaiser's varimax program (1958). An important difference between the two is that quartimax typically produces a general factor in ability data which is a function of the sampling of test variables, i.e., the general factor may reflect verbal, perceptual, or other specific emphasis, depending upon the nature of the tests

sampled. Varimax provides results that are more stable from one test battery to another. This is achieved by a more even distribution of variance among the rotated factors. In the opinion of many investigators, varimax rotations have achieved a near-ultimate status for the orthogonal case, but Schonemann (1964) has now developed a program that he calls varisim, which spreads existing variance more evenly among the several factors than varimax does. Results from the two programs are not completely parallel even for well-defined factors. There is as much rationale for varisim as for varimax. In consequence, the ultimate status of varimax has been dislodged, and we are again faced with a somewhat arbitrary choice among orthogonal rotational methods.

Oblique rotational programs are now fairly numerous and exhibit variability in results comparable to that among orthogonal ones. There is one important difference: no oblique program has as yet achieved the status that varimax once had. Because of the various sources of dissatisfaction with existing programs, there is much more research activity in the area of oblique rotation than in orthogonal rotation. There is still frequent resort to visually guided rotations if the investigator is striving for an oblique structure.

Methodological summary.   The investigator who wishes to find psychological meaning in his data, the one who is trying to discover the basic building blocks or causal entities in human behavior, has a difficult task. Important decisions for which there are no sound foundations must be made at several steps in the procedure. Communalities must be estimated; the estimate of the number of factors to be extracted and retained for rotations must be based upon inadequate criteria; and although subjective bias possibly resulting from hand rotations has been eliminated by rotations obtained on high-speed computers, the choice of rotational program among either oblique or orthogonal solutions may lead to quite different results.

In the absence of sound estimation methods, the criterion of replicability is typically offered as a substitute. Replicability is a very important criterion in science generally. When applied to factor analysis, however, one must be aware that seemingly parallel results may have been forced on the data, typically without intention on the part of the experimentalist to do so. For example, considerable congruence of factor patterns can be obtained from the intercorrelations of two independent sets of random normal deviates by extracting as many factors as variables and by rotating to oblique simple structure. The result will be one-to-one correspondence of the factors. The intercorrelations of the factors will differ, but even these differences will not be large, since they are randomly distributed about zero.

Methods of assessing the congruence of factor patterns also leave something to be desired. The most common method by far is that of visual inspection and unaided judgment. The most precise, the correlation between two estimated factor scores in the same sample, is rarely seen. Claimed replication of a factor is frequently without adequate foundation.

Early general factor interpretations

Mental energy.   Spearman did not have available any of the above-described techniques for the factor analysis of relationships among variables. Neither did he have access to the multitude of tests now available. He hypothesized that one general factor was sufficient to account for the intercorrelations among his variables, and he developed relatively simple methods to test this hypothesis. (Present methods of multiple factor analysis include Spearman's single factor as a special case.) In psychological interpretation Spearman is of interest, however, because he interpreted his single factor as "mental energy." This was considered the sole basis or building block of mental ability or intelligence. [See SPEARMAN.]

Multiple bonds.   Spearman's interpretation was challenged by Godfrey Thomson (1919) and by Edward Thorndike (Thorndike et al. 1926). Thomson proved that correlational matrices having the form required to satisfy Spearman's one-factor interpretation could also be "explained" by the presence of many overlapping elements. Thorndike discussed connections (bonds) between stimuli and responses as an alternative to Spearman's mental energy concept. Considering that there are many thousands of stimuli to which a person will respond differentially, and that tests sample these, the extent to which there is overlap in the elements sampled by two measures determines the degree to which they are correlated. If the intercorrelations of several measures have the formal properties necessary for Spearman's unitary mental energy explanation (one factor), they also can be explained by multiple bonds or overlapping elements (multiplicity of factors). [See THORNDIKE.]

Unitary mental energy is a basic building block, a general influence or "cause"; multiple bonds are a complex of stimulus–response connections that are acquired in a dynamic, complex physical and social environment. Multiple bonds that underlie the behavior under observation cannot be said to cause that behavior in the same sense that mental energy is said to cause intellectual performance.

Recourse to parsimony in this instance is not an acceptable solution, since the two explanations are so different. It should come as no surprise, for example, to learn that Spearman and his followers have stressed genetic bases for intelligence, while the multiple bonds notion lends itself most readily to a stress on environmental forces and learning.

Multiple factors

Thurstone's primary mental abilities.   Although Thurstone (1938) is considered to have broken with Spearman, the break was related only to the number of factors required to account for intelligence. Thurstone considered that some seven to nine factors were sufficient to account for the intercorrelations of the more than fifty tests he used. However, Spearman himself had come to doubt the single-factor explanation; the break was more apparent than real. On the issue of what lies behind factors there was no break. Careful reading of Thurstone's writings makes it quite clear that to him factors were much more than descriptive devices. Factors were functional unities; their ubiquity strongly suggested genetic determiners; after all, they were called primary mental abilities. [See THURSTONE.]

Ferguson's learning emphasis.   However, just as a single factor can be replaced by multiple overlapping bonds, so also can multiple group factors be replaced by sets of overlapping bonds. One need only assume that environmental pressures and learning come in somewhat separate "chunks." Demographic differences, e.g., parental occupation, region of the country, rural–urban differences, etc., could account for some of the "chunking" required. Ferguson (1956) has produced a very satisfactory explanation along these lines in which learning and transfer are important variables. Various kinds of learning are facilitated or inhibited by the variety of environments in which children develop. Learning transfers, both positively and negatively, to novel situations. The amount and direction of the transfer are determined by stimulus and environmental similarities. Learning and transfer, along with environmental differences, produce the clustering of measures on which the factors depend. [See LEARNING, article on TRANSFER.]

Physical analogies.   Thurstone (1947), in order to convince himself and others that factors were "real," constructed a factor problem that has attracted a good deal of attention. He showed that if dimensions of boxes were factored, the result was a three-factor solution which could be rotated into a position such that the factors represented the dimensions of length, breadth, and depth, the three basic dimensions of Euclidean space. He also showed that these factors were correlated, i.e., an oblique solution gave a better fit to the data than did an orthogonal one. The obliquity reflects, of course, the fact that the dimensions of man-made boxes tend to be correlated, i.e., long boxes tend to be big boxes.

In a situation more relevant to behavior Cattell and Dickman (1962) have demonstrated that the intercorrelations of the performance of balls in several "tests" yield four factors that can be identified as size, weight, elasticity, and string length. It is clear from this and the preceding example that factor analysis can sometimes identify known physical factors in data.

One question about these examples is the certitude with which the factors can be identified after rotation, granting that the correct number of factors can be obtained by present methods. Thurstone suggested the criteria of simple structure for the adequacy of rotations. Generally speaking, simple structure is achieved when the number of zero loadings in a factor table has been maximized while increasing the magnitude of loadings on a small number of variables. The application of these criteria to the examples described resulted in clear-cut identification of the three and four factors. It has been shown by Overall (1964), however, that if Thurstone had started with a different set of measurements, the criteria of simple structure for rotations would have led to differently defined factors, i.e., they would not have been the "pure" physical dimensions but would have represented complex combinations of those dimensions.

A more basic question is whether psychological data are similar to physical data, i.e., whether psychological dimensions obtained by factoring are similar to physical dimensions. The demonstration that three or four physical factors, as the case may be, can be recovered from correlational data does not prove that factors in psychological data have a similar functional unity. Not only is Thomson's alternative explanation theoretically acceptable for multiple factors, but it makes good psychological sense as well. Psychological tests measure performance on each of a series of items. These performances make up the total score. Although Thomson would not have suggested a one-to-one correspondence between item and element or stimulus–response bond, one can conclude that there are at least as many elements represented in a test as there are items. Thus the multiple bonds approach fits the actual measurement situation so well that

the adherents of the other point of view must bear the burden of proof—and for psychological, not physical, data.

Guilford's structure of intellect. The work of J. P. Guilford has been most influential in the factor analysis of human abilities (e.g., 1956). It has increased by ten times the small number of primary mental abilities proposed by Thurstone, but the approach to their interpretation remains much the same. Guilford's thinking about the nature of factors is modeled very closely after the periodic table of the chemical elements; he has in fact proposed a structure which points out missing factors and has proceeded in his own empirical work to "discover" many of these.

In spite of similarities in thinking about the nature of factors, the discrepancy in numbers between Guilford and Thurstone is highly significant, and it illustrates a basic difficulty with psychological tests and the attempts to find causal entities from the analysis of their intercorrelations. Not only do psychological tests measure performance on a relatively large number of pass–fail items, but there is at present no necessary or sufficient methodological or theoretical basis for deciding which items should be added together to make up a single test score (Humphreys 1962). The number of factors has proliferated in Guilford's work because he has produced large numbers of homogeneous experimental tests. By additional test construction, making each test more and more homogeneous, the number of factors could be increased still further. As a matter of fact, there is no agreed-upon stopping place short of the individual test item, i.e., a single item represents the maximum amount of homogeneity. This logic results in the same number of primary mental abilities as there are ability test items.

The progression from Thurstone to Guilford can be interpreted as further evidence for the multiple bonds theoretical approach. On the other hand, positing a functional unity inside the organism for each item represents a scientific dead end.

Cattell's structure of personality. The work of R. B. Cattell has been most influential in the factor analysis of the domain of personality (e.g. 1957). Cattell's thinking about the character of factors does not differ materially from that of Spearman, Thurstone, and Guilford in that for Cattell, factors are real influences.

The number of identified personality factors has increased considerably under Cattell's direction. Although measurement problems differ, Cattell's work parallels that of Guilford with human abilities. Self-report questionnaires present the multiple items problem with yes–no scoring of items. Personality investigators also have the problem of deciding which items should be added together in any given score. A great deal of additional work, however, has been done with rating scales and with so-called objective tests of personality. "Density" of sampling of the test or rating domain, a concept introduced by Cattell, is still involved in the proliferation of factors, even though the mechanism is not that of item selection. Thus, in obtaining ratings, one must decide on the number and overlap in meaning of traits to be rated. One must decide whether to include both extroversion and sociability or, even closer, both ascendance and dominance. While there is no rigorous method to depend on in the sampling of measures, decisions about what will be tested still affect the number of factors and their importance.

Furthermore, it is also typical of many experimental designs that large numbers of variables relative to the number of observations are analyzed; that many of these variables have low reliability and thus low communality; that many factors are retained for rotational purposes; and that rotations are made to an oblique structure. All of these elements contribute to possible capitalization on chance.

It is of interest that Cattell uses as a primary rotational criterion a count of the number of variables in the hyperplane, i.e., the multidimensional plane defined by all factors other than the one in question. (More simply, a measure having a zero loading on a factor is located geometrically someplace in the factor's hyperplane.) This criterion places a premium on the extraction of a large number of factors relative to the number of measures, on the use of variables of low reliability, and on the use of variables unrelated to the major purpose of the analysis. In the opinion of many critics Cattell has increased the probability of making Type I errors beyond tolerable bounds, although neither he nor his critics can assign a value to alpha in this situation.

A dramatic example of the difficulties that may be involved in typical factor analytic research is given by some data described by Horn (1967). He obtained a good fit to an oblique factor pattern derived from an analysis of ability and personality variables by factoring the intercorrelations of the same number of random normal deviates, based upon the same number of observations, as the psychological variables. This finding highlights the principle that replication of findings may be of little import in factor analytic investigations.

It is also apparent that the essential reason for factor analyzing intercorrelations, to seek some reduction or simplification of data, has not been realized. The number of variables and the number of factors have grown astronomically, and the end is not yet in sight. It is highly possible that the search for psychological meaning, the search for the basic building blocks or elements, has been responsible. If psychological data are different from physical data in important respects, and if the multiple bonds are a more accurate representation of the data than the chemical elements point of view, researchers would profit from taking another look at the reasons why they factor analyze. An economical description of complex data is itself an important scientific goal.

LLOYD G. HUMPHREYS

[*Directly related are the entries* CLUSTERING; MULTIVARIATE ANALYSIS; TRAITS. *Other relevant material may be found in* INTELLIGENCE AND INTELLIGENCE TESTING; PSYCHOLOGY, *article on* CONSTITUTIONAL PSYCHOLOGY; *and in the biographies of* SPEARMAN *and* THORNDIKE.]

BIBLIOGRAPHY

CATTELL, RAYMOND B. 1957 *Personality and Motivation Structure and Measurement.* New York: World.

CATTELL, RAYMOND B.; and DICKMAN, KERN 1962 A Dynamic Model of Physical Influences Demonstrating the Necessity of Oblique Simple Structure. *Psychological Bulletin* 59:389–400.

FERGUSON, GEORGE A. 1956 On Transfer and the Abilities of Man. *Canadian Journal of Psychology* 10:121–131.

GUILFORD, J. P. 1956 The Structure of Intellect. *Psychological Bulletin* 53:267–293.

GUTTMAN, LOUIS 1954 Some Necessary Conditions for Common Factor Analysis. *Psychometrika* 19:149–161.

HORN, JOHN 1967 On Subjectivity in Factor Analysis. Unpublished manuscript.

HUMPHREYS, LLOYD G. 1962 The Organization of Human Abilities. *American Psychologist* 17:475–483.

KAISER, HENRY F. 1958 The Varimax Criterion for Analytic Rotation in Factor Analysis. *Psychometrika* 23:187–200.

KAISER, HENRY F.; and CAFFREY, JOHN 1965 Alpha Factor Analysis. *Psychometrika* 30:1–14.

NEUHAUS, JACK O.; and WRIGLEY, CHARLES 1954 The Quartimax Method: An Analytical Approach to Orthogonal Simple Structure. *British Journal of Statistical Psychology* 7:81–91.

OVERALL, JOHN E. 1964 Note on the Scientific Status of Factors. *Psychological Bulletin* 61:270–276.

SCHONEMANN, P. H. 1964 A Solution of the Orthogonal Procrustes Problem With Applications to Orthogonal and Oblique Rotation. Ph.D. dissertation, Univ. of Illinois.

SPEARMAN, CHARLES 1904 "General Intelligence" Objectively Determined and Measured. *American Journal of Psychology* 15:201–293.

THOMSON, GODFREY H. 1919 The Proof or Disproof of the Existence of General Ability. *British Journal of Psychology* 9:321–336.

THORNDIKE, EDWARD L. et al. 1926 *The Measurement of Intelligence.* New York: Columbia Univ., Teachers College.

THURSTONE, LOUIS L. 1938 *Primary Mental Abilities.* Univ. of Chicago Press.

THURSTONE, LOUIS L. 1947 *Multiple-factor Analysis.* Univ. of Chicago Press. → A development and expansion of Thurstone's *The Vectors of Mind,* 1935.

FACTORIAL DESIGNS

See EXPERIMENTAL DESIGN.

FADS

See COLLECTIVE BEHAVIOR; FASHION; MASS PHENOMENA.

FAHLBECK, PONTUS ERLAND

Pontus Fahlbeck (1850–1923) was one of the cultural leaders of Sweden around the turn of the century. Successful in a career which combined scientific, political, and business interests, he was, at first, professor of history and political science at the University of Lund and, later, professor of political science and statistics at that university. It was largely thanks to his efforts that a chair in statistics, the first in Sweden, was established at Uppsala in 1910. In addition, he endowed a widely known foundation at the University of Lund that supports research in political science.

His scientific and political books and articles reflect, on the one hand, his broad socioeconomic perspectives and, on the other, his keen interest in the political problems of the day. Some influence from German *Kathedersozialismus* and social-law theory can be traced in his treatment of social problems. He described himself as moderately right wing in political matters and radical in social matters.

Fahlbeck began his academic career in history, concentrating on problems of European medieval history, and then took up political science, dealing with the Swedish constitution and its development in relation to social organization. His involvement deepened as he gradually moved toward general social science, or sociology in a broad sense. His interest focused on human society as a system of classes, the socioeconomic functions of class differentiation, and the transition from feudal society, with its class privileges, to the free groupings of modern society. In modern society, as he saw it, the legal differences between the social strata have been erased.

Fahlbeck's magnum opus is *Sveriges adel* ("The Swedish Nobility"; 1897–1902). Volume 1 is a historical study tracing each family from its en-noblement through subsequent generations. Out of a total of 2,735 families, some 25 per cent were extinct by 1898. The statistical analysis focuses on the process of extinction and includes death rates and survival tables, calculated by family. The second part is a demographic–statistical study of the then contemporary nobility. This many-faceted analysis has been referred to as a pioneering work. Throughout, Fahlbeck developed his argument on two planes—careful statistical analysis and speculative discussion. Notable are his strong emphasis on the importance of social circulation and of the leadership of the upper classes, his resigned attitude toward the deadly dangers resulting from the excessive refinement of the upper classes, and his dissatisfaction with Malthus and, in particular, neo-Malthusianism.

In general, Fahlbeck will be remembered not so much for the concrete results he produced but for the way in which he understood and dealt with some of the key issues which then confronted scientists. Like other brilliant men of his epoch, Fahlbeck was in a frustrating situation. He was aware of rapid socioeconomic developments and their great challenge to the rising social sciences, and he was also vaguely aware that the available scientific methods were inadequate to meet the challenge. At times he seemed to be far ahead of his contemporaries, groping for something that he could not articulate and that has perhaps still not been reached.

Fahlbeck's attitude toward statistical methods was ambivalent. He set forth his views on statistics, as an independent branch of social science, in two programmatic articles (1897; 1918). In the first he enthusiastically supported the actual and potential use of statistics and the numerical method in the social sciences. By the time he wrote the second article, Fahlbeck's attitude had changed. During the interval between the appearance of the two articles, the flourishing period of German demographic and social statistics had been cut off by the emergence of a strong, antitheoretical position in official statistics (von Mayr, Zahn). In England, in the meantime, the use of statistics in the biological sciences had begun, leading to a rapid and epoch-making development of advanced statistical methods, especially in the experimental area. In the period between the writing of the two articles, Fahlbeck had himself successfully used statistical methods in his study of the nobility. Yet, in his 1918 article he dismissed the advanced methods of statistics as "higher mathematics" and argued that in the social application of statistics there is room only for simple methods.

Despite the loose arguments and clichés of the

1918 article, Fahlbeck's position is not without its merits. Although his argument that the study of human behavior and social phenomena is the crucial area for statistical work is extreme, he was right to stress the key importance of studying them statistically. And his untenable view that simple methods suffice for the social sciences may have been an outgrowth of his frustration with the methods then available. His primary goal was the development of appropriate methods, comparable with those of the natural sciences, for dealing with the highest order of phenomena in the scientific hierarchy, that is, with human phenomena.

HERMAN WOLD

[See also ELITES; STRATIFICATION, SOCIAL; and the biography of GALTON.]

WORKS BY FAHLBECK

1897   *Den statistika typen eller regelbundenheten uti de menskliga företeelserna: Ett bidrag till statistikens teori* (The Statistical Type, or the Regularity of Human Phenomena: A Contribution to the Theory of Statistics). Lund (Sweden): Malströms Boktryckeri.

1897–1902   *Sveriges adel* (The Swedish Nobility). 2 vols. Lund (Sweden): Gleerup.

1900   La régularité dans les choses humaines ou les types statistiques et leurs variations. *Journal de la Société de Statistique de Paris* 41:188–201.

1918   *Statistiken och den numeriska kunskapsmetoden: Ett bidrag till frågan om statistikens ställning som vetenskap* (Statistics and the Numerical Method of Knowledge: A Contribution to the Question of the Status of Statistics as a Science). Lunds universitets årsskrift, No. 14. Lund (Sweden): Gleerup.

SUPPLEMENTARY BIBLIOGRAPHY

Festskrift till Pontus Fahlbeck den 15 oktober 1915. 1915 Lund (Sweden): Gleerup.

LAGERROTH, FREDRIK 1924 Minnesord över Pontus Erland Fahlbeck. Humanistika Vetenskapssamfundet i Lund, *Årsberättelse* [1923/1924]:20–28. → An obituary.

WALLENGREN, SIGFRID 1923 Pontus Fahlbeck. *Statsvetenskaplig tidskrift för politik–statistik–ekonomi* 26: 211–228. → An obituary.

FAIR TRADE LAWS

See RESALE PRICE MAINTENANCE.

FALANGISM

Falangism is the Spanish variant of the fascist doctrines that gained vogue in Europe during the 1930s. Its origins are purely theoretical, for falangism existed as an ideology on paper for several years before it became a significant political movement. The originators of Falangist doctrine were Ramiro Ledesma Ramos (1905–1936), sometime postal clerk and unemployed intellectual, and José Antonio Primo de Rivera (1903–1936), a young aristocrat and son of the former dictator General Miguel Primo de Rivera. The ideological basis of Falangist doctrine was first expounded by Ledesma in 1931 under the label "national syndicalism." Intoxicated by the spectacle of German national socialism, Ledesma endeavored singlehandedly to fabricate a Spanish fascistic program that would combine the two main radical forces in early twentieth-century Europe—nationalism and socialism. Ledesma's notion of "national syndicalism" was that of a revolutionary movement that would carry out the socioeconomic program of Spanish anarchosyndicalism under the aegis of a dictatorial nationalist state.

Falangism took formal shape in 1933–1934, after the founding of a new political movement called Falange Española (Spanish Phalanx). This organization was largely the creation of José Antonio Primo de Rivera, a restless, romantic, and energetic young man who wanted to complete the work begun by his father. Amid the frustrating experiences of the first two years of the Second Spanish Republic, he groped for a formula that could unify all the Spanish people and promote national rejuvenation. Like Ledesma, he thought it could be supplied by some kind of "Spanish fascism," which would combine nationalistic dictatorship and sweeping socioeconomic reform. Certain conservatives helped him found the Falange on October 29, 1933, and it soon absorbed the tiny group of radicals who followed Ledesma.

The classic doctrine of falangism was defined at the end of 1934 in a program written principally by Ledesma and referred to as the "Twenty-seven Points" (see Primo de Rivera 1942). The major principles announced were:

(1) Political unity of Spain and elimination of regional separatism.

(2) Abolition of political parties.

(3) Establishment of a nationalist dictatorship led by the party.

(4) Use of violence in regenerating Spain.

(5) Development of Spanish imperial power.

(6) Expansion and strengthening of the armed forces.

(7) Recognition and support of Catholicism as the official religion of Spain but rejection of any clerical influence in government.

(8) A sweeping economic reform, referred to as "revolution," which emphasized the following:

(*a*) Establishment of a complete system of national syndicates, embracing employers and employees, to organize, coordinate, and represent all of Spain's economic activity.

(*b*) Sweeping agrarian reform, reclaiming waste-land, improving techniques, concentrating scattered holdings, and reorganizing the great latifundia.

(*c*) Stimulation of industrial expansion.

(*d*) Basic respect for private property, but nationalization of all credit facilities to eliminate capitalist usury.

Together with these specific goals, a general mystique of Spanish nationalism and an interpretation of Spanish history exalting certain peculiarities of Spanish life were expounded, and almost all of Spanish liberalism and the nation's experience with constitutional parliamentary government were denounced. The fanaticism in the Spanish past was interpreted as a triumph of the nation's spirit. The Inquisition and some of the nation's more absolutist rulers were exalted and used as evidence that Spaniards needed forceful, authoritarian rule.

At the time this program was drafted the Falange probably had the support of only one per cent of the Spanish people. Its economic program remained vague because almost none of the party's few intellectuals had concrete experience with economic matters. One of the more confusing of the Twenty-seven Points was the declaration "We have a will to empire," for the Falangist notion of "empire" was never made clear. One Falangist leader soon went out of his way to indicate that "empire" meant only cultural influence and diplomatic leadership and not political or territorial domination. Other Falangists spoke in more aggressive terms, proposing the annexation of Portugal.

In October 1934 José Antonio Primo de Rivera was made *jefe nacional* (national chief) of the movement. In his person the *jefe* summarized the contradictions of Falangist doctrine, for he was an intellectual liberal and manifestly uncomfortable with the fascist aggressiveness of Falangist ideology. Most Falangists had originally referred to their movement as "fascist," but Primo de Rivera and other party leaders soon became worried about close identification with Italian fascism and German Nazism. By 1935 they were emphasizing that falangism was not intended to be "fascist" at all, but merely a native development of Spanish nationalism.

Since falangism began as an intellectual abstraction and changed greatly when finally placed in practice, it can be adequately understood only through a study of its historical evolution. The Falange was a rabid foe of the Spanish Republic, driven underground by the police and rendered physically impotent when the rebellion against the republic broke out, on July 17, 1936. The revolt but it lacked popular support and had already been was organized entirely by the Spanish Army, and the Falange, which had no official standing, was forced to collaborate with the rebels on the army's terms. During the first months of the civil war the movement lost most of its original leaders, for José Antonio Primo de Rivera, Ramiro Ledesma, and others were shot by the Republicans.

Nonetheless, in this climate of civil war, the membership of the party swelled enormously, for falangism was the only radical new ideology with which the Spanish right could combat the militant left. The military dictatorship had few clear political ideas, and after Generalissimo Francisco Franco emerged as head of the new Nationalist government, he and his advisers searched for some kind of official political ideology and structure. Falangism seemed the answer, for it stressed the defense of traditional Spanish institutions, proposed a solution to class warfare, and was the ideology most congenial to Nazi Germany and fascist Italy, the two states on which the military dictatorship had to rely to win the war. On April 19, 1937, the Falange was therefore elevated to the role of the state party of Spain, and the Twenty-seven Points were adopted as a government program.

Falangism was thus taken over as a tool of the military dictatorship; the Falangists did not in any way take over the Franco state. Franco became head of the Falange, which was reorganized, watered down, and mixed with a variety of more conservative groups. Officially, the party was fused with the reactionary, monarchist Carlist militia and renamed "Falange Española Tradicionalista de las Juntas de Ofensiva Nacional Sindicalista." The 27th point of the Falangist program, which had prohibited any such fusion, was then dropped. Power rested securely in the hands of Franco and the military hierarchy, almost none of whom was truly "Falangist." Indeed, most Spanish officers tended to sneer at the orthodox Falangists, calling them "our Reds."

Falangism had two main tasks after the end of the civil war, in 1939. The first was the creation of a nationwide system of workers' and employers' syndicates. This soon blanketed all urban and industrial regions, although it was slow to include the rural areas. The syndicates were organized by state functionaries from the top downward. They did not represent the workers but controlled them in the interests of the state and of the employers. Such a situation contrasted sharply with the original Falangist theory, in which the syndicates were supposed to be dynamic revolutionary organisms, helping to carry out a national economic reformation.

The second major task of falangism was ideological: to provide an authoritarian nationalist political theory that would supply intellectual and emotional support for the dictatorship. Falangism furnished the substance of the state propaganda machine, its antiliberal, antiparliamentary ideology being used to discredit all elements not within the Franco government and to indoctrinate the new generation of Spanish youth with loyalty to the regime. Falangist demagogy was widely employed in an attempt to convince the workers and the rest of the population that the present conservative dictatorship, protecting propertied interests and the *status quo*, was somehow a dynamic national revolution.

At no time was the Falange party organization allowed a position of independent authority inside the state, but Falangists were given a near monopoly on bureaucratic positions and many jobs in the lower echelon of the government apparatus. At the same time, the Falange National Council was packed with conservatives and army men so that there would be no danger of the movement's original ideological radicalism becoming more than rhetoric. As a result of the great influx of wartime members, the majority of Falangists had little sense of revolutionary national-syndicalist doctrine. They were largely an amorphous collection of opportunists and timeservers, who supported the regime as a means of gaining employment.

Since the nationalistic authoritarianism of Falangist propaganda was extended, on the international plane, to intense enmity against Britain, the United States, and the other Western democracies, falangism was especially useful to the Franco regime during the years 1937–1942, when the Nazi–fascist star was rising and the Spanish regime hoped to find a place inside the fascist new order. During this period it was often found convenient to revert to the original definition of falangism and to call it "Spanish fascism."

After 1943, however, with fascism on the wane in Europe, this definition came to be as much a liability as an asset to the Franco regime. From that time on, great efforts were made to erase the overtly fascistic, imperialistic aspects of Falangist ideology. The official government spokesmen and even Falangist leaders began to place especially heavy emphasis on the "Catholic" nature of falangism, to play up the "religious" aspect of the regime's political orientation. Falangist ideologues now began to say that not everything done by liberal regimes was bad, that in fact the Falange

itself was rather "liberal," or at least broad-minded and forgiving. The amount of money provided the Falangist organization fell off rapidly by 1945, as the Spanish regime tried anxiously to provide itself with a new façade. No more was heard about the Spanish "empire" or the virtues of violence. There was even some speculation that the Falange would be dismantled altogether. However, there was never any danger of the Franco regime's going that far, for the vague Falangist ideology was the only political ideology the military dictatorship possessed. Rather, the Falangist "new line" was expanded. "National revolution" now meant merely the continuation of the existing syndical system to keep the workers in their place. "Nationalism" and "antiliberalism" were used mostly to provide propaganda support for the regime and not to defame the progressive nations of the Western world.

Franco had always stressed the fact that falangism had not achieved final form as a doctrine, that the program of the state would continue to change. Presumably, it would never cease to do so. After 1945 emphasis was placed on the wide variety of political and ideological forces in the original "movement" behind the Franco government. Conservatives, moderate liberals, constitutional monarchists, clericals, and reactionary Carlists, who had always resented the relative ideological monopoly of falangism, were now permitted more voice.

In 1947 Franco arranged a plebiscite to turn his regime into a sort of regency, with some member of the Spanish Bourbon dynasty slated to succeed him when he wearied of his role as dictator or died. Falangist doctrine had always been more or less antimonarchist. In fact, much of the rank and file of the Falangist organization was rabidly so, deeming monarchism incompatible with any kind of vigorous modern political movement. Therefore, Franco's official establishment of the monarchy as his successor seemed to reduce the function of falangism even further.

The true result of the transformation of the regime into a pseudo regency was nonetheless that it increased the significance of falangism for the dictatorship. Franco's own monarchism was largely fraudulent; he had primarily sought a way to pacify restlessness about the future. Publicly favoring monarchist interests, Franco actually sustained Falangist propaganda and the Falangist bureaucracy so that monarchist influence would not become too strong. The Spanish dictator could thus threaten the monarchists with a revival of extreme falangism whenever they tried to place any pressure on his regime.

Although he cared even less about ideology than

before, Franco probably felt more comfortable with falangism and the party bureaucracy than with most other elements of his regime. The Falangists were so completely dependent on his personal benevolence that they dared not seriously oppose him, and their ideology of nationalism and authoritarian rule was still the most comfortable political rationale for his heterogeneous, but increasingly light-handed, tyranny.

The immediate future of the regime was assured in 1951, when the United States began its policy of *rapprochement* with Franco. It became clear that the regime would no longer suffer international pressure because of its quasi-fascist texture, and Franco responded by placing a regular Falangist at the head of the bureaucracy and appointing four new Falangist ministers in the 1951 cabinet shake-up. Falangist propagandists felt freer to return to some of their old prejudices. Nonetheless, and despite the fact that the United States was still, in the classic Falangist definition, a decadent liberal parliamentary democracy, the new doctrine had to be one of friendship with America, for the latter had indirectly become a principal supporter of the Franco dictatorship.

The growing prosperity of Spain in the 1950s finally made it possible for the regime to attempt to realize a few peripheral aspects of the original Falangist program of economic reform. A program of state-operated industrialization, directed by the National Institute of Industry (INI), lavished vast amounts of money on a great variety of industrial projects between 1951 and 1958. At a much slower pace, a new beginning was made in state irrigation projects and agrarian reform. This, however, had little to do with falangism per se, being directed by separate bureaucracies and paying little heed to the incomplete plans of the creators of falangism.

The last effort to define falangism politically and to turn it into a living, controlling force was made in 1956–1957. The growth of political opposition had made a mild shake-up of the government necessary. A commission of old-guard Falangists was called together, and three separate *anteproyectos* (draft proposals) were drawn up to define the Falangist position. (The *anteproyectos* were not officially published, but copies of them were made available to this author by one of the Falangist leaders involved.) These made it clear that the Twenty-seven Points were quite dead. There was no mention of "empire" or "violence." Instead, the new catechism stressed the pre-eminence of Catholicism, national unity, and social justice and the viability of a moderated capitalism.

With regard to the structure of the state, the Falangists approved Franco's Cortes (parliament), a rubber-stamp assembly elected indirectly from a state-controlled list of nominees. However, they requested the elevation of the Falangist National Council to a sort of upper chamber or senate. Their project acknowledged a king as successor to Franco in the role of chief of state but requested the appointment of a prime minister, or chief of government, who would carry on ordinary executive functions. He was to be responsible primarily to the chief of state, although it was stipulated that three adverse votes by the Falangist National Council should bring his resignation. Continuation of the one-party system was projected, and the Franco system of establishing a series of "fundamental laws" in lieu of a constitution was approved.

Such a project contained a wholly original statement of Falangist notions of political structure, for at no time previously had the party's organic goals been made so clear. Nonetheless, the *anteproyectos* were irrelevant, for there was no chance that they would ever be realized. The most influential pressure groups in Franco Spain—the hierarchy of the army and the Roman Catholic church—reacted with extreme anger. The *anteproyectos* were quietly buried without ever having been made public, and in the 1957 cabinet change falangism was further downgraded.

By that time the major interest in Spain was economic development, not politics. The Franco regime preferred to give the appearance of liberalization and a more purely technical kind of government. The tendency was thus toward the transcendence of falangism by a more "prismatic" political doctrine, permitting expression of pluralistic tendencies, within a limited range, under one-man rule. Such an orientation was much more effective in an era of increasing integration with liberal western Europe.

It was perhaps impossible to expect that Falangism, as an ideology or as a movement, could survive and flourish in the postfascist epoch of western Europe. Having attained a position of pseudo responsibility without effective power, it had served as an effective scapegoat, to be blamed or downgraded whenever the regime felt a show of "liberalization" to be necessary. Nonetheless, it did leave a significant legacy, since it provided the principal rationale for authoritarian unity and government in Spain. At the same time, by its rhetorical emphasis on economic reform and social justice, it probably constituted the most liberal force within the regime.

STANLEY G. PAYNE

[See also DICTATORSHIP; FASCISM; SOCIAL MOVEMENTS.]

BIBLIOGRAPHY

The changing emphases of Falangist doctrine are best seen in the publications of its creators and leaders. For the pre-World War II *period these are* Aparicio 1939; Ledesma Ramos 1935; Primo de Rivera 1942 *and* 1956; Redondo 1939. *For the later period see* Fernández Cuesta 1951; Arrese 1943, 1947, *and* 1957; *and the official journal of the movement,* Revista de estudios políticos. *General historical accounts and critiques are* Payne 1961 *and* Nellessen 1963.

APARICIO, JUAN (editor) 1939 *Antología: La conquista del estado.* Barcelona (Spain): Ediciones FE. → A compilation of articles that originally appeared in the periodical *La conquista del estado* in 1931.

ARRESE, JOSÉ LUIS DE 1943 *Escritos y discursos.* Madrid: Vicesecretaría de Educación Popular.

ARRESE, JOSÉ LUIS DE 1947 *Capitalismo, comunismo, cristianismo.* Madrid: Ediciones Radar.

ARRESE, JOSÉ LUIS DE 1957 *Hacia una meta institucional.* Madrid: Ediciones del Movimiento.

FERNÁNDEZ CUESTA, RAIMUNDO 1951 *Intemperie, victoria y servicio: Discursos y escritos.* Madrid: Ediciones del Movimiento.

[LEDESMA RAMOS, RAMIRO] 1935 *¿Fascismo en España? (Sus orígenes, su desarrollo, sus hombres),* by Roberto Lanzas [pseud.]. Madrid: Ediciones "La Conquista del Estado."

NELLESSEN, BERND 1963 *Die verbotene Revolution: Aufstieg und Niedergang der Falange.* Hamburg (Germany): Leibniz.

PAYNE, STANLEY G. 1961 *Falange: A History of Spanish Fascism.* Stanford Studies in History, Economics and Political Science, No. 22. Stanford (Calif.) Univ. Press.

PRIMO DE RIVERA, JOSÉ ANTONIO 1942 *Norma programática de la Falange.* Pages 589–597 in José Antonio Primo de Rivera, *Obras completas.* Compiled and edited by Augustín del Río Cisneros and Enrique Conde Gargollo. Madrid: "Diana."

PRIMO DE RIVERA, JOSÉ ANTONIO 1956 *Textos inéditos y epistolario.* Madrid: Ediciones del Movimiento.

REDONDO, ONÉSIMO (1939) 1954–1955 *Obras completas.* 2 vols. Madrid: Publicaciones Españolas.

Revista de estudios políticos (Madrid). → Published bimonthly since 1941.

FALLACIES, STATISTICAL

This article will be mainly concerned with statistical fallacies, but it should be noted that most other fallacious types of reasoning can be carried over into statistics.

Most fallacies seem foolish when pinpointed, but they are not the prerogative of fools and statisticians. Great men make mistakes, and when they admit them remorsefully, they reveal a facet of their greatness. The reason for mentioning the mistakes of eminent people in this article is to make it more fun to read.

Many fallacies, statistical or otherwise, have their origin in wishful thinking, laziness, and busyness. These conditions lead to oversimplification, the desire to win an argument at all costs (even at the cost of over*complication*), failure to listen to the opposition, too-ready acceptance of authority, too-ready rejection of it, too-ready acceptance of the printed word (even in newspapers), too-great reliance on a machine or formal system or formula (*deus ex machina*), and too-ready rejection of them (*diabolus ex machina*). These emotionally determined weaknesses are not themselves fallacies, but they provoke them. For example, they provoke special pleading, the use of language in more than one sense without notice of the ambiguity (if the argument leads to a desirable conclusion), the insistence that a method used successfully in one field of research is the only appropriate one in another, the distortion of judgment, and the forgetting of the need for judgment.

A logical or syntactical fallacy. We begin with an example of a fallacious argument in which the conclusion is correct:

> "No cat has no tail. One cat has one more tail than no cat. Therefore one cat has one tail."

A good technique for exposing fallacious reasoning is to use the same form of argument in order to deduce an obviously false result:

> "No cat has eight tails. One cat has one more tail than no cat. Therefore one cat has nine tails."

The fallacy can be explained by careful attention to syntax, specifically by noting that the following two propositions have been confused: (1) It is false that any cat has eight tails, and (2) the object named "no cat" has eight tails. P. M. S. Blackett once said, exaggerating somewhat, that a physicist is satisfied with an argument if it leads to a result that he believes to be true.

Arguments from authority. The book *Popular Fallacies* by Alfred S. E. Ackermann is more concerned with fallacies of fact than of reasoning, and here many fallacies depend on the acceptance of authority. It is interesting to see that the author was himself misled by authority on at least two occasions.

First, he argues that it is a fallacy "that cigarette smoking is especially pernicious," appealing to the opinions of several authorities: for example, "Of the various forms of smoking, cigarette smoking is the most wholesome, preferably without a holder," according to Sir Robert Armstrong-Jones, F.R.C.P., in the *Daily Mail,* January 1, 1927 (Ackermann [1907] 1950, pp. 174–175). (The current medical opinion is that, of cigarettes, cigars, and pipes, cigarettes are the least wholesome, at any rate in regard to lung cancer. Of course, Armstrong-Jones *might* be right after all.)

Then Ackermann refers to the thesis "that there is a prospect of atomic energy being of practical use." Lord Rutherford is quoted, from the *Evening News*, September 11, 1933, as saying that "anyone who expects a source of power from the transformation of these atoms is talking moonshine" (*ibid.*, pp. 708–709).

It would be unfair to blame Ackermann for relying on these authorities, but it is useful to hold in mind that the highest authorities can be wrong, even when they are emphatic in their opinions. Their desire not to seem too academic should sometimes be allowed for, especially when they hold an administrative appointment.

What should the question really be? When Gertrude Stein was on her deathbed, one of her friends asked her, "What is the answer?" After a few seconds she whispered back, "What is the question?"

It is important for the statistician to satisfy himself that a *right* question is being asked, by inquiring into the purposes behind the question. Chambers (1965) states that when a member of Parliament asked for some inland revenue figures that were not available from the published statistics, his invariable rule was to find out the purpose for which the information was needed. More often than not he found that the figures sought were irrelevant, that other figures already published were more helpful, or that the M.P. was misguided over the whole business.

It is often reasonable to make exploratory investigations without a clear purpose in mind. The fallacy we have just pointed out is the assumption that the questioner necessarily asks for information that is very relevant to his purposes, whether those purposes are clear or vague. The fallacy of giving the "right answer to the wrong question" is further discussed by A. W. Kimball (1957).

Ignoring the "exposure base." Consider, for example, the reports on traffic deaths that are issued after public holidays. Many readers conclude from the increased number of deaths that it is more dangerous to drive on public holidays than on ordinary days. The conclusion may or may not be correct, but the reasoning is fallacious, since it ignores the fact that many more people drive automobiles on public holidays and thus more people are exposed to the possibility of an accident. If holidays and ordinary days are compared on the basis of deaths per passenger mile, it might turn out that the holiday death rate is lower, since the reduction of the average speed caused by the vol-

ume of traffic also may reduce the seriousness, if not the number, of accidents.

"Deus ex machina"—the precision fallacy. When we know a machine or formal system that can produce an exact answer to a question, we are tempted to provide an answer and inquire no further. But exact methods often produce exact answers to wrong questions.

One of the main aims of statistical technique is to fight the danger of wishful thinking and achieve a measure of objectivity in probability statements. But absolute objectivity and precision are seldom if ever attainable: there is always, or nearly always, a need for judgment in any application of statistical methods. (This point is especially emphasized in Good 1950.) Inexperienced statisticians often overestimate the degree of precision and objectivity that can be attained. An elementary form of the precision fallacy, which is less often committed by statisticians than by others, is the use of an average without reference to "spread." A related trap is to gauge closeness by some measure of spread but to ignore systematic errors (bias) [*see* ERRORS, *article on* NONSAMPLING ERRORS].

The use of an average without a measure of spread can be especially misleading, or even comic, when the sample is small and the spread is therefore large. But even if the mean and standard deviation of the *population* are given, they can be misleading if the population is very skew. For skew populations it is better to give some of the quantiles [*see* STATISTICS, DESCRIPTIVE, *article on* LOCATION AND DISPERSION].

Randomization. An example of the precision fallacy occurs in connection with the important technique of randomization. Let us consider the famous tea-tasting experiment (see Fisher 1935, chapter 1; Good 1956). A lady claims to be able to tell by tasting, with better than random chance, whether the milk is put into her tea first or last. We decide to test her by giving her twenty cups of tea to taste, in ten of which the milk is poured first, and in ten last. If the lady gets many more than ten of her assertions right and if we have not randomized the order of the twenty trials, we might suspect that whatever sequence we selected for some psychological reason, the lady might have tended to guess for similar psychological reasons. So we randomize the order and can then apparently make use of the hypergeometric tail-area probability as a precise, objective, and effectively complete summary of the statistical significance of the experiment [*see* EXPERIMENTAL DESIGN *and* RANDOM NUMBERS].

But suppose we now examine the random sequence and spot some pattern in it—for example, that cups 3, 6, 9, 12, 15, and 18 had the milk in first. This would at once undermine the precise validity of our result in relation to its relevance to the hypothesis under investigation. We can partly remove this difficulty by means of "restricted randomization," but we cannot completely remove it, because every finite sequence exhibits some special features, however recondite. Only by judgment, necessarily subjective, can we decide that any given feature is unimportant. The only way we can preserve the precision is to make use of a "statistician's stooge" to perform the experiment for us, including the randomization (Good 1960–1961). He must report the number of successes to us but must on no account tell us the randomized order. Precision in a randomized experiment can be obtained only at the price of suppressing some of the information. The point made here is not universally accepted by statisticians.

If the number of cups of tea is very large, then the importance of the above criticism of randomization will usually be negligible. But long experiments are expensive, and in the statistical design of experiments the expense can never be ignored.

Randomization in itself is by no means a fallacious technique; what is fallacious is the notion that without the suppression of information, it can lead to a precise tail-area probability relevant only to a null hypothesis.

The suppression of information.   In its crudest forms the suppression of information is often at least as wicked as an outright lie. We shall later refer to some of the cruder forms. But we have just seen that randomization loses its precision unless some information is suppressed, and we shall now argue more forcibly that it is a fallacy to suppose that the suppression of information is always culpable.

One way of seeing this is in terms of digital communication. When an electrical "pulse" of a given shape is liable to have been attenuated and distorted by noise, some circuitry is often incorporated for the purpose of re-forming ("regenerating") the pulse. This circuitry, as it were, accepts the hypothesis that the pulse is supposed to be present rather than absent. Since noise in the electronic system makes the probability less than one that the supposed pulse is present, the regeneration loses some information. But allowing for the nature of the *subsequent* communication channel, it can be proved that the loss is often more than compensated. (This will not be proved here, but it is not surprising to common sense.) In pedagogy the corresponding principle is that simplification is neces-

sary when teaching beginners. In statistics the corresponding device is known as the *reduction of the data*, that is, the reduction of a mass of data to a more easily assimilable form. If the statistics are "sufficient," then there is no loss of information, but we often have to be satisfied with "insufficient" statistics in order to make an effective reduction of the data. Thus it is fallacious to say that the suppression of information is always a statistical crime. (Note that apparently sufficient statistics might not really be so if the model is wrong. People sometimes publish, say, only a mean and variance of a sample, and this prevents readers from checking the validity of the model for which these statistics would be sufficient.) [See SUFFICIENCY.]

Terminological ambiguities.   Important examples of terminological ambiguities occur both in the philosophy of statistics and in its practical applications. Often they are as obvious as the "no cat" ambiguity, once they are pointed out. But before they are pointed out, they lead to a great deal of argument at cross purposes. Thus, many of the problems in the philosophy of probability clear themselves up as soon as we distinguish between various kinds of probability (see Good 1959a). (We shall not discuss here whether they can all be reduced to a single kind or whether they all "exist." But they are all talked about.) [See PROBABILITY, *article on* INTERPRETATIONS.]

There is tautological, or mathematical, probability, which occurs in mathematical theories and requires no operational definition. It occurs also in the definition of a "simple statistical hypothesis," which is a hypothesis for which some probabilities of the form $P(E|H)$ are assigned *by definition*. (Here E represents an event or a proposition asserting that an event obtains, and the vertical stroke stands for "given" or "assuming.") There are *physical*, or material, probabilities, or *chances*. These relate to tautological probabilities by means of the *linguistic axiom* that to say that H is true is to say that the physical probability of E is $P(E|H)$, for some class of events, E. There are *logical* probabilities, or credibilities. There are *subjective*, or personal, probabilities, which are the intensities of conviction that a man will use for betting purposes, after mature consideration. There are *multisubjective* probabilities, belonging to groups of people. And there are *psychological* probabilities, which are the probabilities that people behave as if they accept, even before applying any criterion to test their consistency. By confusing pairs of these six kinds of probability, *fifteen different kinds of fallacy can be generated*. For example, it is often said that there is no sense in talking about the probability that a population parameter has a certain value, for "it either has the value or it does not, and therefore the probability is either 0 or 1." It need hardly be mentioned, to those who are not choked with emotion, that the probability need not be 0 or 1 when it is interpreted not as a physical probability but as a logical or as a subjective probability.

Even physical probabilities can be confused with each other, since they can be mistakenly referred to the same event. For example, apparent variations in the incidence of some crime or disease from one place or time to another are very often found to be due to variations in the methods of classification. Adultery would appear to increase enormously if Christ's definition were suddenly to be accepted in the law—"Whosoever looketh on a woman to lust after her hath committed adultery with her already in his heart" (Matthew 5.28). Since partners to adultery do not often turn in official reports, perhaps a better example is that of crime records. An example with documentation, quoted by Wallis and Roberts (1956), is that of felonies in New York. It was alleged that there had been an increase of 34.8 per cent from 1949 to 1950, but later it appeared that this was at least largely due to a revised method of classification.

This class of practical statistical fallacies is extremely common in the social sciences, and one should be very much on guard against it. As a further example, two standard definitions of the number of unemployed in the United States differ by a factor of over 3, namely, the "average monthly rate" and the "total annual rate." Putting it roughly, one measure for any given year is the average monthly number of people unemployed; the other, larger measure is the number of people who were unemployed at any time during the year. [See EMPLOYMENT AND UNEMPLOYMENT.]

An example of a terminological fallacy is the confusion of "some" and "all." It is perpetrated by John Hughlings Jackson in the following excerpt: "To coin the word, verbalising, to include all ways in which words serve, I would assert that both halves of the brain are alike in that each serves in *verbalising*. That the left half does is evident, because damage of it makes a man speechless. That the right does is inferable, because the speechless man understands all I say to him in ordinary matters" (quoted in Penfield & Roberts 1959, p. 62). Some damage to the left hemisphere seems here to have been confused with destruction of all of it.

Another example of the "some and all" fallacy is to assume that since some poems are better than others in the opinion of any reasonable judge, then, given any set of poems, one of them must be the

best. More generally, the possibility of *partial* ordering is easily overlooked. But sometimes the assumption of partial ordering, although truer than complete ordering, is too complicated for a given application. In a beauty competition, for example, each girl might be the best of her kind, but it might be essential to award the prize to only one of them.

In some social surveys respondents are asked to rank several objects in order of merit. An alternate design, which will often be less watered down by the need to reach decisions in doubtful cases, is to ask for comparisons of pairs of objects but to permit "no comparison" as a response for any given pair.

Ignoring a relevant concomitant variable. "The death rate in the American Army in peacetime is lower than that in New York City. Therefore leave New York and join the army." The fallacy is that the methods of selection for the army are biased toward longevity, both by age and by health, and these clearly relevant variables have been ignored. The fallacy can also be categorized as failure to control for exposure, since many inhabitants of New York City are subject to the possibility of death from infant diseases, chronic diseases, and old age, whereas very few men in the army are so exposed. The example can also be regarded as one of "biased sampling," a category of fallacy to be considered later.

Ignoring half of a contingency table. It is commonly believed that government scientists in the United Kingdom earn more on the average than university teachers. But, as Rowe pointed out (1962), the average age of university teachers is less than that of government scientists, because a large proportion of lecturers leave the universities before their mid-thirties. Rowe showed that the median earning of university teachers above the age of 35 is greater than that of government scientists. But he did not estimate what these men *would* have earned in government service. Thus, although he refuted the original argument, he did not ask the really relevant question. This question is very difficult to answer. A possible approach, which would shed some light, would be to find out the distribution of salaries as a function of job, age, and intelligence quotient.

The perennial problem here is which covariates to choose and where to stop choosing them, since the list of possibilities is typically impracticably large. A related issue is that the greater the number of conditioning classificatory variables (dimensionality of the contingency table), the fewer the cases in the relevant cross-classification cell. This is one of the unsolved problems of actuarial science, where the problem of estimating probabilities in multidimensional contingency tables is philosophically basic (for some discussion of this problem, with references, see Good 1965).

It sometimes happens that a fact is almost universally ignored, although in retrospect it is clearly highly relevant. In the late 1950s people in the United States were arguing that the standard of college teaching staffs was deteriorating, since the proportion of newly employed teachers who held a doctorate was decreasing. What was overlooked was that the proportion of teachers who took their doctorates after becoming teachers was increasing. Cartter (1965) states that Bernard Berelson was almost alone in his correct interpretation of the situation.

Biased sample.   At one time, most known quasi-stellar radio sources lay approximately in a plane, and this seemed to one writer to have deep cosmological significance. But these radio sources could not be definitely identified with optical sources unless they were located with great accuracy, and for this purpose they had to be occluded by the moon. Also, as it happened, most of the observations had been made from the same observatory. Hence there was a very strong bias in the sampling of the sources (this was mentioned by D. W. Dewhurst in a lecture in Oxford on January 28, 1965). As Sir Arthur Eddington once pointed out, if you catch fish with a net having a 6-inch mesh, you are liable to formulate the hypothesis that all fish are more than 6 inches in length. [See ERRORS, *article on* NONSAMPLING ERRORS.]

It is sometimes overlooked that atrocity stories usually form a biased sample. Newspapers tend to report the atrocities of political opponents more than those of friends. An exception was the Nazi atrocities, which were so great that the evidence for them had to be overwhelming before they could be believed. (For example, there appears to be no reference to them in the 1951 edition of the *Encyclopaedia Britannica*.)

Sometimes inferences from a sample are biased because of seasonal variations. According to Starnes (1962), Democratic Secretary of Labor Willard Wirtz stated just before an election that over "four and a half million more Americans have jobs than when this Administration took office in January of 1961." Wirtz later admitted that the figure should have been 1.224 million, and he said, "It isn't proper to compare January figures with October figures without a seasonal adjustment." Similarly, the Republican governor of New York, Nelson D. Rockefeller, once referred to a "net increase of 450,000 jobs" since he had taken office. The figure is worthless because it again ignores the adjustment for seasonal variations.

Bias is difficult to avoid in social surveys, for example, in the use of questionnaires, where poor wording is frequent and where one sometimes (especially in political and commercial surveys) finds tendentious wording.

Even with an unbiased sample, it is possible to get a biased conclusion by computing the significance level of various tests of the null hypothesis and selecting the one most favorable to one's wishes. Although these tests are based on the same sample and are therefore statistically interdependent, there will be a reasonable probability that one out of twenty such tests will reach a 5 per cent significance level. A suggestion of how to combine such "parallel" tests is given by Good (1958a).

The suppression of the uninteresting.   Suppose we have done an experiment, and it reaches a significance level of 5 per cent. Should we reject the null hypothesis? Perhaps the experiment has been performed by others without significant results. If these other experiments were taken into account, the total significance of all the experiments combined might be negligible. Moreover, the other results might have been unpublished because they were nonsignificant and therefore uninteresting. This explains why some apparent medical advances do not fulfill their early promise. The published statistics are biased in favor of what is interesting. As one physician said, "Hasten to use the remedy before it is too late" (Good 1958b, p. 283; Sterling 1959).

Sample too small.   One of the most frequent and elementary statistical fallacies is the reliance on too small a sample. In 1933 Meduna, believing that schizophrenia and epilepsy were incompatible because of the rarity of their joint occurrence, started to induce convulsions in mental patients by chemical means. Consequently, the beneficial effect of convulsions on depressives was eventually accidentally discovered. Meduna's sample was too small, and in fact it has now been found that schizophrenia and epilepsy are *positively* correlated (Slater & Beard 1963). One moral of this story is that experiments can be worth trying without theoretical reason to believe that they might be successful.

Misleading use of graphs and pictures.   Graphs and pictures are often used in newspapers in the hope of misleading readers who are not experienced in interpreting them. Sometimes graphs are inadequately labeled; sometimes the scale is chosen so as to make a small slope appear large; sometimes the graph is drawn on a board and the board is pictured in perspective so as to accentuate the most recent slope; sometimes too little of a time series is shown, and the graph is started at a trough (a device that is useful for salesmen of stocks, when they wish the public to invest in a particular equity).

A useful method for misleading with pictures is to depict, say, salaries by means of objects such as cash boxes whose *linear* dimensions are proportional to the salaries. In this way an increase is made to appear much larger than it really is. Another useful method for misleading the public is attributed by Huff (1954) to the First National Bank of Boston. The bank represented governmental expenditure by means of a map of the United States in which states of low population densities were shaded to indicate that total government spending was equal to the combined income of the people of those states. The hope was that the reader would get the impression that federal spending, as a fraction of the total income of the United States, was equal to the total area of the shaded states divided by the whole area of the country. [*See* Graphic presentation.]

"Smaller" versus "smaller than necessary." The confusion of "smaller" with "smaller than necessary" will be illustrated in a hereditary context, and an oversimplification of the theory of natural selection will be pointed out. Let us suppose that it is true that intelligent people tend to have fewer children than less intelligent people and that the level of intelligence is hereditary. (We are not here concerned with whether and where this supposition is true, nor with the precise interpretation of "intelligent.") It then appears to follow that the average level of intelligence will necessarily decline. This fallacy will be perpetrated on most readers of Chapter 5 of the book by the eminent zoologist Peter B. Medawar (1960, p. 86), in spite of the words italicized by us in the following quotation: "If innately unintelligent people tend to have larger families, then, *with some qualifications*, we can infer that the average level of intelligence will decline." In order to show that the argument without the qualification is invalid it is sufficient to use a mathematical model that, for other purposes, would be much oversimplified (see Behrens 1963). Imagine a population in which 10 per cent of men are intelligent and 90 per cent are unintelligent and that, on the average, 100 intelligent fathers have 46 sons, of whom 28 are intelligent and 18 unintelligent, whereas 100 unintelligent fathers have 106

Table 1 — Hypothetical proportions of intelligent and unintelligent sons

		SONS	
		Intelligent	Unintelligent
FATHERS	100 intelligent	28	18
	900 unintelligent	72	882
	Total	100	900

sons, of whom 98 are unintelligent and 8 are intelligent. It will be seen from Table 1 that the proportion of intelligent males would remain steady in expectation.

But now it must be determined whether the right question is being asked. Suppose we were convinced that the general level of intelligence was decreasing, and we made suggestions accordingly for encouraging the more intelligent to have more children. Should we not put these suggestions forward even if the general level of intelligence were *increasing*? Would we not like to see the rate of increase also increase? Yes, of course. Looking from this point of view, we might not fully agree with Medawar's arguments, but we might well agree with some of his recommendations.

"Regression fallacy." If we select a short or tall person at random, the chances are that his relatives will be closer in average height than he is to the mean height of the population. Francis Galton described this phenomenon as "regression." If now we consider the heights of the sons of tall men and of short men, we might infer that the variability of heights is decreasing with time. This would be an example of the regression fallacy. One way of seeing that the argument must be fallacious is by considering the heights of the parents of short and tall people: we would then infer that the variability of heights is *increasing* with time!

Wallis and Roberts (1956) mention several other examples of the regression fallacy. One is the widespread belief that the second year in the major leagues is an unlucky one for new baseball players who have successfully finished their first year.

Invalid use of formulas or theorems. The use of formulas or theorems in situations where they are not valid is a special case of the *deus ex machina* class of fallacies and is very frequent. The following are a few examples.

Implicit assumption of independence. In an experiment consisting of n trials, each successful with probability p, is the variance (the square of the standard deviation) of the number of successes equal to $np(1 - p)$, as it would be if independence held? (An example would be the quality inspection of items on an assembly line.) The formula is so familiar that it is tempting to assume that it is always a good approximation. But familiarity breeds mistakes. For a Markov chain the variance can be quite different (see, for example, Good 1963), as it can also be when sampling features of children in families or fruit on trees.

Another example of a fallacious assumption of independence relates to the variability of physiological traits. Why, even if there were only eight traits, each trichotomized into equal thirds, only one person out of $3^8 = 6561$ would be in the middle (normal) group for all eight traits!

Assuming form determines distribution. Let n_{ij} be the frequency of the "dinome," that is, pair of adjacent digits (i,j), in a sequence of N random sampling digits $(i,j = 0,1,2, \cdots, 9)$. Clearly $\sum n_{ij} = N - 1$. Let

$$\psi^2 = \frac{10}{N-1} \sum_{i,j} \left(n_{ij} - \frac{N-1}{100} \right)^2.$$

It has been erroneously assumed at least four times in the statistical literature that ψ^2 has asymptotically (for large N) a tabular chi-squared distribution. In one case this led to the unfair rejection of a method of producing pseudo random numbers. Presumably the erroneous distribution arose from the typographical identity of the expression for ψ^2 with the familiar statistic of the chi-square test. (For references to three of these papers and to a paper that gives a correct method of using ψ^2, see Good 1963.) The misapplication of the above so-called serial test is particularly disastrous when working with binary digits (0 and 1), that is, with base 2.

Assuming the winner leads half the time. There is a fallacy in assuming that in a long sequence of statistically independent fair games of chance between two players the ultimate winner will be in the lead about half the time. This is a misapplication of the law of large numbers. That it *is* a fallacy depends on one of the most surprising theorems in the theory of probability, the so-called arc sine law. In fact, the probability that a specified player will be in the lead for less than a fraction x of the time is approximately $(2/\pi)$ arc sin $x^{\frac{1}{2}}$ (see, for example, Feller 1950–1966, vol. 1, p. 251). This implies that however long the game, it is much more likely that a specified player will be ahead most of the time or behind most of the time than that he will be about even; for example, the probability that a specific player will be ahead 90 per cent or more of the time, or behind 90 per cent or more of the time, is about .40, while the probability that the player will be ahead between 40 and 60 per cent

of the time is only about .13. As Feller says, the arc sine law "should serve as a warning to those who easily discover 'obvious' secular trends" in economic and social phenomena.

The "maturity of the chances." An elementary misapplication of the law of large numbers, or "law of averages," is known as the maturity of the chances. In World War I many soldiers took shelter in bomb craters on the grounds that two bombs seldom hit the same spot. For the same reason P. S. Milner-Barry, the British chess master, decided to retain his London flat after it was bombed in World War II. As a matter of fact it *was* bombed again. At roulette tables, it is said, the chips pile up on the color that has not occurred much in recent spins. Of course, in practice, if a coin came down heads fifty times running, it would be *more* likely than not, in logical probability, to come down heads on the next spin, not *less* likely. In fact, it would probably be double-headed. There are circumstances, of course, when an event is less likely to occur soon after it has just occurred: this would be true for some kinds of accidents and in many situations where one is sampling without replacement. Usually the question is basically empirical, but the expression "maturity of the chances," or "Monte Carlo fallacy," usually refers to sequences of events that are statistically independent, at least to a good approximation.

Law of large numbers misapplied to pairs. A mnemonic for the fallacy of misapplying the law of large numbers when considering pairs of objects selected from a set is the well-known "birthday problem." If 24 people are selected at random, then it is more likely than not that at least one pair of them will have the same birthday (that is, month and day). This is simple to prove, but a good intuitive "reason" for it is that the number of pairs of people in a group of 24 people is 276, and $\exp(-276/365) < \frac{1}{2}$. (The crude argument here is based on a Poisson approximation to the probability of no "successes" in 276 roughly independent trials with common success probability 1/365.) The result is true a fortiori if births are not distributed uniformly over days of the year.

C. R. Hewitt, in a "Science Survey" program of the British Broadcasting Corporation in February, 1951, stated that the probability is less than 1/64,000,000,000 that two fingerprints of different people will be indistinguishable. From this he inferred that no two people have indistinguishable fingerprints and thus committed the birthday fallacy. The argument is fallacious even if we ignore resemblances of fingerprints among relatives, since the number of *pairs* of people in the world exceeds

4,000,000,000,000,000,000. The conclusion might be correct.

A similar fallacy arises in connection with precognition. Suppose, entirely unrealistically, that there is just one remarkable and well-documented case of somebody in the world having an apparently precognitive dream. How small must the apparent probability be in order that the report, if true, should by itself convince us of precognition? Presumably its reciprocal should be at least of the order of the population of the world times the number of dream experiences of a man times the number of his waking experiences. This triple product might be as large as 1,000,000,000,000,000,000,-000,000,000 (or 10^{27}). This informal application of statistics should discourage a too ready assumption that the evidence from apparently precognitive dreams is overwhelming. A formal application of statistical methods to this problem is very difficult. This discussion is not intended to undermine a belief in the possibility of precognition, but it is a plea for a better evaluation of the evidence.

Failure to use precise notation. An example of the fallacy of failure to use sufficiently explicit notation is given by the "fiducial argument." The purpose of R. A. Fisher's fiducial argument (1956, pp. 52–54) was to produce a final (posterior) distribution for a parameter without assuming an initial (prior) distribution for it. This was ambitious, to say the least, since *de nihilo nihilum.*

The argument starts off from a parametric distribution for a random variable, X. Fisher selected an example of which the following is a special case. For each positive number x_0, suppose that

$$P(X > x_0 \mid \theta) = \exp(-x_0\theta),$$

where θ is a positive parameter in whose value and final distribution we are interested. Writing $x_0 = u/\theta$, we get $P(X\theta > u \mid \theta) = \exp(-u)$. From this it can be proved, using the usual axioms of probability theory (although Fisher omitted the proof), that $P(X\theta > u) = \exp(-u)$ for any positive number, u, provided that an initial distribution for θ is assumed to exist. (It is not necessary to assume that this distribution is in any sense known.) Hence $P(\theta > \theta_0) = \exp(-x\theta_0)$, where $\theta_0 = u/x$. Fisher infers from this that

$$P(\theta > \theta_0 \mid x) = \exp(-x\theta_0),$$

where θ_0 is any real positive number. But this last equation does not follow from the axioms of probability unless the initial probability density of θ is proportional to $1/\theta$. The fallacy in the fiducial argument was due to Fisher's failure to indicate what is "given" in his probability notation. So great

was Fisher's authority that there are still many statisticians who make use of the fiducial argument; thus the analysis given here is currently considered controversial [*see* FIDUCIAL INFERENCE].

Assuming order of operations reversible. An example of the fallacy of assuming that the order of two mathematical operations can be interchanged is the assumption that the expectation of a square is equal to the square of the expectation. This occurs in M. J. Moroney (1951, p. 250), where he says that evidently the expected value of chi-square for a multinomial distribution is zero.

Correlation and causation. *Positive correlation does not imply causation, either way round.* There is a positive correlation between the number of maiden aunts one has and the proportion of calcium in one's bones. But you cannot acquire more maiden aunts by eating calcium tablets. (Younger people tend to have more maiden aunts and more bone calcium.) In New Hebrides people in good health are lousier than people with fever. The advice to acquire lice cannot be rationally given, since lice avoid hot bodies [*see* Huff 1954, p. 99; *see also* CAUSATION].

Zero correlation does not imply statistical independence, although it does so for a bivariate normal distribution and for some other special families of distributions.

If there is a positive correlation between A and B and also between B and C, this does not imply that the correlation between A and C is positive, even for a trivariate normal distribution. But the implication *does* follow if the sum of the squares of the first two correlation coefficients exceeds unity.

If the time order is wrong, then causation is unlikely, to say the least. In one survey vaccination was found to be positively correlated with various infectious diseases, when one looked at different districts in India. This was used by antivaccinationists for propaganda. If they had not been emotionally involved, they would probably have noticed that in several districts increased vaccination had *followed* an increase in the incidence of disease (Chambers 1965).

Post hoc, ergo propter hoc ("after this, therefore because of this"). D. O. Moberg, in a lecture in Oxford on February 2, 1965, stated that premarital intercourse seemed to be positively correlated with divorce and inferred that the propensity to divorce was increased by premarital intercourse. The inference *might* be correct, but an equally good explanation is that premarital intercourse and divorce are both largely consequences of the same attitude toward the institution of matrimony. It is also possible that untruthful responses are associated with a propensity to divorce or with a propensity to avoid divorce.

Ecological correlation. Suppose we find that in American *cities* the illiteracy rate and the percentage of foreign-born are associated. This does not imply the same association for *individuals* (see Goodman 1959). It would even be possible that every foreign-born person was highly literate. Cities might attract foreign-born people and also attract or produce illiteracy.

Wrong criteria for suboptimization. Granted that in most decision problems it is not so much a matter of optimization as of "suboptimization," that is, of approximate optimization, there is still an acute problem in choosing *what* to suboptimize. Various fallacies arise through choosing a wrong criterion or through not using a criterion at all (see Koopman 1956; Good 1962). Often a criterion is selected from too narrow a point of view, ignoring questions of consistency with higher-level criteria. For example, when coeducation at New College, Oxford, was being discussed at another Oxford college, the question of the relative requirements for education of men and women was ignored, but the effect on the atmosphere of the senior common room was mentioned. Another fallacy is to ignore the "spillover," or side effects, of some project. Sometimes, when an urgent decision is required, the cost in delay of detailed theory is unjustifiably ignored. At other times the cost of the theory is said to be too heavy, and the fact is overlooked that the results of this theory might be valuable in similar circumstances in the future and that the training of the theoretician is important. Sometimes the criterion of profitability is given too little weight, sometimes too much (see also McKean 1958; Hitch & McKean 1954).

Statistics of statistical fallacies. There is some unpublished work by Christopher Scott on the statistics of statistical fallacies and errors for the specialized field of sample surveys conducted by mail. Scott read the 117 articles and research reports that had been written in English on this topic up to the end of 1960. He excluded 22 of the reports either because they were duplicates of others or because they gave almost no details of method. Of the remaining 95 articles, he found one or more definite errors in 54 and definite shortcomings in another 13. Among the definite errors there were 14 cases in which the experimental variable was not successfully isolated, that is, a change in technique was reported as causing a change in the result, whereas the latter change could reasonably be ascribed to variation in some concomitant variable.

There were 9 cases in which obviously relevant data, such as sample size or response rate, were not reported, and 7 cases in which a necessary significance test was not given. There is not space here for further details, and hopefully they will be published elsewhere.

For misuses of the chi-square test, see Lewis and Burke (1949).

Good fallacies. It is a fallacy to suppose that all fallacies are bad. A clearly self-contradictory epigram can be a neat way of conveying truth or advice, to everybody except quibblers. For example:

"Only a half-truth can be expressed in a nutshell."

"Everything in moderation."

"It would be a *non sequitur* if it were not a tautology."

"Races in which people were immortal became extinct by natural selection."

"There's nothing wrong with chess players that not being people wouldn't put right."

In this article it has been necessary to omit reference to many kinds of fallacies. A more complete listing is given in the categorization of logical and statistical fallacies by Good (1959*b*).

IRVING JOHN GOOD

[*See also* ERRORS, *article on* NONSAMPLING ERRORS.]

BIBLIOGRAPHY

Further literature on fallacies is mentioned in Good 1959b. *In particular,* Thouless 1932 *for fallacies in ordinary reasoning and chapter 3 of* Wallis & Roberts 1956 *for fallacies in statistics are both very useful.* Wagemann 1935 *also gives an interesting general treatment.*

ACKERMANN, ALFRED S. E. (1907) 1950 *Popular Fallacies: A Book of Common Errors, Explained and Corrected With Copious References to Authorities.* 4th ed. London: Old Westminster Press.

BEHRENS, D. J. 1963 High IQ, Low Fertility? Statistical "Non Sequitur." *Mensa Correspondence* (London) no. 50:6 only.

CARTTER, ALLAN M. 1965 A New Look at the Supply of College Teachers. *Educational Record* 46:267–277.

CHAMBERS, S. PAUL 1965 Statistics and Intellectual Integrity. *Journal of the Royal Statistical Society* Series A 128:1–15.

FELLER, WILLIAM 1950–1966 *An Introduction to Probability Theory and Its Applications.* 2 vols. New York: Wiley. → The second edition of Volume 1 was published in 1957.

FISHER, R. A. (1935) 1960 *The Design of Experiments.* 7th ed. New York: Hafner; London: Oliver & Boyd.

FISHER, R. A. (1956) 1959 *Statistical Methods and Scientific Inference.* 2d ed., rev. New York: Hafner; London: Oliver & Boyd.

GOOD, I. J. 1950 *Probability and the Weighing of Evidence.* London: Griffin.

GOOD, I. J. 1956 Which Comes First, Probability or Statistics? *Journal of the Institute of Actuaries* 82:249–255.

GOOD, I. J. 1958a Significance Tests in Parallel and in Series. *Journal of the American Statistical Association* 53:799–813.

GOOD, I. J. 1958b How Much Science Can You Have at Your Fingertips? *IBM Journal of Research and Development* 2:282–288.

GOOD, I. J. 1959a Kinds of Probability. *Science* New Series 129:443–447.

GOOD, I. J. (1959b) 1962 A Classification of Fallacious Arguments and Interpretations. *Technometrics* 4:125–132. → First published in Volume 11 of *Methodos*.

GOOD, I. J. 1960–1961 The Paradox of Confirmation. *British Journal for the Philosophy of Science* 11:145–149; 12:63–64.

GOOD, I. J. (1962) 1965 How Rational Should a Manager Be? Pages 88–98 in *Executive Readings in Management Science*. Edited by Martin K. Starr. New York: Macmillan. → First published in Volume 8 of *Management Science*.

GOOD, I. J. 1963 Quadratics in Markov-chain Frequencies, and the Binary Chain of Order 2. *Journal of the Royal Statistical Society* Series B 25:383–391.

GOOD, I. J. 1965 *The Estimation of Probabilities: An Essay in Modern Bayesian Methods.* Cambridge, Mass.: M.I.T. Press.

GOODMAN, LEO A. 1959 Some Alternatives to Ecological Correlation. *American Journal of Sociology* 64:610–625.

HITCH, CHARLES; and MCKEAN, RONALD 1954 Suboptimization in Operations Problems. Volume 1, pages 168–186 in *Operations Research for Management*. Edited by Joseph F. McCloskey and Florence N. Trefethen. Baltimore: Johns Hopkins Press.

HUFF, DARREL 1954 *How to Lie With Statistics.* New York: Norton. → Also published in paperback edition.

JACKSON, JOHN H. (1931) 1958 *Selected Writings of John Hughlings Jackson.* Vol. 2. Edited by James Taylor. New York: Basic Books.

KIMBALL, A. W. 1957 Errors of the Third Kind in Statistical Consulting. *Journal of the American Statistical Association* 52:133–142.

KOOPMAN, B. O. 1956 Fallacies in Operations Research. *Journal of the Operations Research Society of America* 4:422–426.

LEWIS, D.; and BURKE, C. J. 1949 The Use and Misuse of the Chi-square Test. *Psychological Bulletin* 46:433–489. → Discussions of the article may be found in subsequent issues of this bulletin: 47:331–337, 338–340, 341–346, 347–355; 48:81–82.

MCKEAN, RONALD N. 1958 The Criterion Problem. Pages 25–49 in Ronald N. McKean, *Efficiency in Government Through Systems Analysis.* New York: Wiley.

MEDAWAR, PETER B. 1960 *The Future of Man.* New York: Basic Books; London: Methuen.

MORONEY, M. J. (1951) 1958 *Facts From Figures.* 3d ed., rev. Harmondsworth (England): Penguin.

PENFIELD, WILDER; and ROBERTS, LAMAR 1959 *Speech and Brain-mechanisms.* Princeton Univ. Press.

ROWE, P. 1962 What the Dons Earn. *The Sunday Times* (London) October 21.

SLATER, ELIOT; and BEARD, A. W. 1963 The Schizophrenia-like Psychoses of Epilepsy: Psychiatric Aspects. *British Journal of Psychiatry* 109:95–112.

STARNES, RICHARD 1962 Age of Falsehood. *Trenton Evening Times* December 19.

STERLING, THEODORE D. 1959 Publication Decisions and Their Possible Effects on Inferences Drawn From Tests of Significance—Or Vice Versa. *Journal of the American Statistical Association* 54:30–34.

THOULESS, ROBERT H. (1932) 1947 *How to Think Straight.* New York: Simon & Schuster. → First published as *Straight and Crooked Thinking*.

WAGEMANN, ERNST F. (1935) 1950 *Narrenspiegel der Statistik; Die Umrisse eines statistischen Weltbildes.* 3d ed. Salzburg (Austria): Verlag "Das Bergland-Buch."

WALLIS, W. ALLEN; and ROBERTS, HARRY V. 1956 *Statistics: A New Approach.* Glencoe, Ill.: Free Press. → An abridged paperback edition was published in 1965 by the Free Press.

FAMILY

The articles under this heading discuss the central aspects of the family as a universal institution in society. Closely related are the entries KINSHIP; MARRIAGE. *The reproduction function of the family is discussed in* FERTILITY; FERTILITY CONTROL; *the socializing function of the family is reviewed in* SOCIALIZATION *as well as in* CULTURE AND PERSONALITY; DEVELOPMENTAL PSYCHOLOGY; INFANCY; PERSONALITY, *article on* PERSONALITY DEVELOPMENT; MORAL DEVELOPMENT. *Stages in family life are reviewed in* ADOLESCENCE; AGING; DEATH; LIFE CYCLE; *as well as in* FAMILY, *article on* DISORGANIZATION AND DISSOLUTION. *Specialized aspects of the family are reviewed in* ADOPTION; AFFECTION; INCEST; NUPTIALITY; PATERNALISM; SEXUAL BEHAVIOR. *Many anthropologists, psychologists, and sociologists have contributed to an understanding of the family; the following biographies are of particular relevance:* BACHOFEN; BURGESS; ENGELS; FRAZER; FREUD; GESELL; HALL; LE PLAY; MCLENNAN; MAINE; MALINOWSKI; MORGAN, LEWIS HENRY; RADCLIFFE-BROWN; TYLOR; WALLER; WESTERMARCK.

I. COMPARATIVE STRUCTURE   *Raymond T. Smith*
II. DISORGANIZATION
    AND DISSOLUTION   *Clifford Kirkpatrick*

I

COMPARATIVE STRUCTURE

One of the few widely accepted generalizations of social science asserts that "the family" is an institution found in all human societies. There is controversy over just what constitutes the family and what its functions might be, but the generalization itself is widely accepted. In modern Euro–American societies it is accepted that the normal family is a coresidential group which consists of a married couple and their own children and which lives apart from other kin. This has become the reference type for comparative study, and it is argued that in modern, highly differentiated societies such as those of North America and Europe the family has become a highly specialized agency exhibiting the *essential* and irreducible characteristics which are significant for cross-cultural comparison (Parsons & Bales 1955, p. 10).

In all human societies provision must be made for biological and social reproduction if the society is to continue, and it is generally assumed that the family performs at least these functions. Mating is never simply random, and children require a long period of care by a limited number of individuals with whom they develop relations of intimacy if they are to grow up as normal human beings capable of playing adult roles. This conclusion is based partly upon experimental evidence (Bowlby 1951) and partly upon inference from the fact that in all known societies children are raised in small kinship-based groups and there are customary modes of regulation between children and their socially recognized parents and between the parents themselves. Looked at in this way there is a very close relationship between the family and the domestic group, and both constitute systems of relationship which vary over time. The form of these systems is tied to the physical processes of individual birth, maturation, and death, so that families, like individuals, pass through developmental stages (Fortes 1958). The processes of individual maturation and death are social as well as physical, since individuals are participants in social systems as well as in biological processes. Societies live longer than either individuals or families, but societies exist only through the patterned interaction of individuals who share common understandings. Mating and procreation provide for the continuity of the biological species, while socialization relates it to the equally important continuity of social structure and cultural pattern. It has been argued on both theoretical and empirical grounds that the primary function of the family is socialization, so that an intimate relation is established between biological and social processes, a relation which is reflected in the dependence of demographic trends upon social custom.

The generalizations set out above seem to hold true in a large number of different societies, but it is not certain to what extent the observations and descriptions used have been influenced by the definitions adopted by field investigators. Some writers have expressed doubt that the family is a universal human institution, but both the assertion and its refutation depend upon some agreed identification of what is being discussed.

Definitions

Domestic groups. A domestic group may be defined as a group of people who habitually share a common dwelling and a common food supply. These minimal activities of domestic groups may be greatly extended, and domestic groups may vary in size and stability. The word "family" has its origin in a Latin word which could be roughly equated with "domestic group," but for sociological purposes the two must be sharply distinguished. Domestic groups may be made up of individuals between whom no kinship ties exist, and, conversely, members of one family may be distributed over two or more domestic groups. The term "household" may be used interchangeably with "domestic group."

Biological family. In Euro–American societies the basic model of kinship and family ties is that of biological relatedness and sexual intercourse, so that kin and familial relations are thought of in terms of physical descent or sexual relations. This is not so in all societies, even though it appears that family relations are almost invariably intimately associated with sexual regulation and reproduction. Social relations of family and kinship can develop independently of genetic links or sexual relations, so that adoption or other forms of fictive kinship are just as real as blood ties. Even where actual genetic links exist they do not constitute *social* relations; these must be learned and developed separately. Similarly, marriage is always more than sexual mating. Schneider (see *Aspects of the Analysis . . .* 1965) has expressed in a particularly pointed and convincing way the objections to confusing an analytical definition of kinship with definitions stressing biological relatedness.

The relation between mother and child appears to be in a rather special category, since the human infant is part of its mother's physical being before birth and continues to be dependent upon her or a substitute for a considerable period afterward. The development of artificial feeding has modified this close dependence, but experience in rearing motherless infants has shown that adverse effects result from deprivation of close continuous contact with a mother figure in early infancy. The "mother figure" can be any suitable person, and experiments with monkeys have shown that, for them, even contraptions of wire and cloth can serve as "mothers" in some sense. This raises the question of just what we mean when we use words such as "mother" and should lead to a careful distinction between the activities involved in mothering on the one hand and the biological relationship of the mother to the child on the other. In the case of the father–child relationship, the more frequent disjunction between biological and social paternity has led to a distinction between *pater* and *genitor*. The former term is used to refer to a child's legally recognized father and the latter to his supposed biological father. In some societies a child's father (*pater*) may be a woman or a dead man. Among the Nuer of east Africa, the kin of a man killed in war before he had married would sometimes marry a woman to "his name." After payment of the bride price the woman cohabited with a lover, but any children born to her were the legal offspring of the dead "husband," inheriting from him and sacrificing to him as their ancestor. Cases such as this make clear the differences between biological and social links, and although the family is frequently, or even usually, coincident with a particular constellation of biological links, it cannot be defined in terms of them.

Nuclear family. The term "nuclear family" (or "elementary," "simple," or "basic") is most frequently used to refer to a group consisting of a man, a woman, and their socially recognized children. This is a straightforward use of the term; it refers to concrete groups, and the qualification "nuclear" suggests that this is the unit out of which more extensive family groups are built or grow. The group need not be coresidential provided regular relationships are maintained among its members. It need not exist as a separate and isolated entity but may be contained within more extensive groups provided it is given some recognition. It has been suggested that the nuclear family is *the* universal form of family relations, always fulfilling "distinctive and vital functions—sexual, economic, reproductive, and educational . . ." (Murdock 1949, p. 3). "The nuclear family is a universal human social grouping. Either as the sole prevailing form of the family or as the basic unit from which more complex familial forms are compounded, it exists as a distinct and strongly functional group in every known society" (p. 2). The evidence for this statement is far from conclusive, and much of it that does seem to support the generalization may be biased simply because of the way in which the data have been collected and presented. Cases such as the Nayar and the Ashanti (see below) tend to disprove the assertion, and this has now been recognized by Murdock.

Parsons has argued that the nuclear family exhibits characteristics which seem to be necessary (on theoretical grounds) for the socialization of children and the stabilization of adult personalities (Parsons & Bales 1955). He has argued elsewhere that the incest taboo is also universal in human societies for similar reasons and that taboo results in the perpetual creation of new nuclear-family groups through marriage (Parsons 1954). Even if one accepts the ideas that sexual intercourse must be regulated and that children must be cared for and socialized within small groups with the characteristics exhibited by the nuclear family, this does not necessarily mean that the nuclear family, as defined by Murdock, is universal. Levy and Fallers (1959) have suggested that a distinction should be made between the nuclear family as a concrete group and the "nuclear-family relationship complex." The latter would consist of the relationships of husband–wife, mother–son, mother–daughter, father–son, father–daughter, brother–sister, brother–brother, and sister–sister considered as a system of interaction between roles. By looking at the nuclear family as a system of roles rather than as a concrete grouping of individuals, it is possible to see that role behavior appropriate to this complex might be distributed among a number of individuals, groups, or agencies that do not themselves constitute a single group. Malinowski showed that certain aspects of what he considered to be the normal "father" role are played by the mother's brother in some societies with matrilineal inheritance and descent. Similarly, in some societies the "mother" role is played in whole or in part by mother surrogates, such as mother's sisters, mother's mothers, paid nurses, or teachers. In order to make statements such as these it is necessary to assume that we know what the "real" or "normal" nuclear-family role complex is, and here it is evident that there is a tendency to take the Euro–American family pattern as the type case. Despite this drawback, the concentration of attention upon a role complex rather than concrete groups is a step toward freeing the concept of nuclear family from the rigidity imposed upon it by Murdock. If one asserts that the nuclear-family relationship complex is institutionalized in all human societies—instead of speaking of the universal occurrence of nuclear-family *groups*—then it is possible to account for the normal development of children brought up in groups that are not nuclear families in the restricted sense. Where one parent is missing or no siblings are present, children may still be affected by the institutionalized nuclear-family role complex, different elements of which are activated by other kinsmen, neighbors, teachers, or even more remote individuals. We may also relate the necessary biological and social functions to this role complex rather than to concrete nuclear families and leave it to empirical investigation to show just how the roles are embodied in a particular society. While this goes some way toward freeing investigation from the analytical restrictions imposed by the concept of the universality of the nuclear family, there are good grounds for going even further and asking just what is meant by the roles involved in the supposedly universal nuclear-family role complex.

Compound family. The term "compound family" is used to refer to a concrete group formed through the amalgamation of nuclear-family units or parts of them. A polygynous household consisting of one man, his three wives, and their respective children would constitute a compound family, as would a family group constituted by remarried widows or divorcees with children from a previous marriage. A compound family need not constitute a coresidential group.

Joint family. According to the handbook *Notes and Queries on Anthropology* (see British Association . . . 1874), a joint family exists when "two or more lineally related kinsfolk of the same sex, their spouses and offspring, occupy a single homestead and are jointly subject to the same authority or single head." An example would be a group consisting of a man and his wife with their married sons and their wives and children. It would be wrong to think of such a group as being a mere mechanical aggregate of nuclear families. Joint families generally arise, exist, and persist because they carry out activities more extensive than would be possible for a nuclear-family group. Joint families grow as younger members bring in spouses rather than setting up independent households. As the younger married couples beget children, it may be possible to detect the existence of a number of nuclear-family cells within the structure of the joint family. The younger married couples will often have their own living quarters and may establish their own cooking facilities. If they have their own budgetary arrangements, then the joint family has really split—even if the young couples do not actually move out of the house. On the other hand, the joint family may be such a cohesive unit that it is difficult to see nuclear families within it as separate groups in any meaningful sense. The men may form one solidary group and the women another; the children may regard all the women of the house as their "mothers." Eventually, as the original family grows too big,

the joint family will either split or some persons will leave to form separate groups.

Extended family. An extended family is a dispersed version of the joint family. That is, the members of the constituent groups of an extended family do not all live together in one dwelling. They usually live close together and engage in common activities.

The concept of extended family really exhausts the usefulness of the word "family" for this kind of empirical classification, since an extended family is already a short lineage and can be discussed in terms of lineage theory, or it is a kindred and may be analyzed as such. Since birth is the criterion of membership in lineages and kindreds, they tend to develop considerable interest in the birth, training, and ultimate loyalties of their recruits, so that there is a close fit between these formations and the "families" which provide and train the recruits.

Comparative family studies

Because they are a part of all human experience and such a powerful agency in the formation of adult attitudes, familial relations have always been a subject of interest and discussion. Their changing and varied forms have been studied by such diverse and ancient disciplines as theology, classics, law, and philosophy. This interest quickened during the period known in Europe as the Enlightenment, but it was the late nineteenth-century interest in evolution that stimulated extensive comparative studies of family forms. Fantastic theories were proposed in an attempt to reconstruct the history of mankind and to account for the existence of seemingly pointless customs and strange kinship terminologies among non-European peoples. Bachofen's postulated development of society from promiscuity through a great period of mother right and female dominance to father right and patriarchy was an attempt to account for the recognized importance of matrilineal descent systems and the universal importance of motherhood. Other writers of the period argued in much the same way, although disagreeing on developmental priorities. Such writers as Sir Henry Maine, Edward Tylor, J. F. McLennan, Lewis H. Morgan, Friedrich Engels, Sir James Frazer, E. Westermarck, and Robert Briffault carried forward the debate on origins, and, although their theories were highly speculative, they encompassed a wide range of cases and paid particular attention to historical sources. Despite the shortcomings of both theories and sources, these writers laid the foundations for modern studies by systematizing existing information on the family, and they are still worth reading for their insight into problems that have been neglected.

It is surprising that students of the family have not paid more attention to a series of basic sociological works which concern themselves with the classification of social relationships. Maine, Tönnies, and Durkheim, in particular, set up dichotomous categories which they believed to represent fundamentally different types of social relationship: relations of status as opposed to contract; relations of *Gemeinschaft* as opposed to *Gesellschaft;* mechanical versus organic solidarity. In all these systems one pole was most clearly represented by relations of a familial or kinship type. Since it was generally assumed that we know what familial relations are, this reference was intended to be illustrative, although Tönnies, in his *Gemeinschaft und Gesellschaft*, attempted to show how natural will develops within the complex of relations that go to make up the family. The crux of the matter is that what we term familial relations are relations exhibiting a particular kind of solidarity that involves persons in total and permanent social relations. This type of relationship is contrasted with the partial and specialized character of *Gesellschaft* or contractual relations. Just where the boundaries of familial relations are drawn varies from one society or subgroup to another and is, of course, affected by a large number of empirical factors.

Intensive field-work methods developed during the early twentieth century by Boas, Kroeber, Lowie, and others in the United States and by Malinowski and Radcliffe-Brown in Britain produced a new body of detailed information on kinship, marriage, and the family. Malinowski's work on the family in Australia and Melanesia was a study of primitive matriliny and was intended to show (in part at least) that the nuclear family emerges naturally even where there is ignorance of the male role in the physiological process of reproduction. The Trobriand Islanders studied by Malinowski asserted that children are conceived when a spirit enters the body of a woman and that sexual intercourse is simply a matter of mutual satisfaction to the persons involved. Malinowski was impressed by the fact that men developed important social relationships with their wives' children even though they did not consider that there was any biological connection involved. Furthermore, men did not exercise the kind of authority over their children that is often associated with "paternity"; the mother's brother was more important in that respect. He concluded from these observations that the nuclear family is a universal institution but does not al-

ways assume the emotional configuration suggested by Freud's theory of the Oedipus complex; it is rather a "functional formation dependent upon the structure and upon the culture of a society" (Malinowski [1927] 1953, pp. 142–143). The implication of this idea was that the nuclear-family complex could be activated by various persons and agencies—in the case of societies with matrilineal descent groups it may be that repressed hatred between uncle and nephew replaces that found between father and son in patriarchal societies.

Radcliffe-Brown's brilliant and lucid treatment of the jural significance of kinship ties enabled him to look at the family in terms of the formal duties, rights, and obligations between the members and between them and external groups. Whereas Malinowski regarded wider kinship ties as "mere extensions" of the nuclear-family complex and the sentiments generated within it, Radcliffe-Brown spoke of the varying modes of incorporation, for jural purposes, of the unit of mother and children. He saw the relationship between a mother and her children as being somehow "basic" because of the close emotional and nurturant ties involved, while other kinship ties could be stressed or neglected to varying degrees depending upon the structure of the whole social and kinship system. In other words, Radcliffe-Brown's concern was not with the family as a locus of emotional solidarity, or socialization functions, or sexual satisfactions; he was more concerned to explore the ways in which the empirical reference points of birth, sexual relations, and child rearing could be variously stressed for legal purposes. Apart from the apparent invariability of the mother–child relationship, he was prepared to accept the fact that all the other activities and functions could be distributed in widely varying ways.

In the generation since these pioneers of field investigation, detailed work has been carried out in many parts of the world, yielding new information and continuous refinement of theory. The development of the Yale cross-cultural survey is an attempt to organize material from a wide range of sources in order to make inductive generalizations about human societies or to test particular hypotheses. Other writers make similar generalizations based upon a more selective use of sources. In either case it is evident that the generalizations are no better than the observations on which they are based. This is well demonstrated by Murdock's generalizations based on the cross-cultural survey files. Observations reported in monographic studies depend to a considerable extent upon the investigator's preconceived ideas and categories or upon his interests. In the field of family studies all these may be severely limited.

Parallel to the development of a wide-ranging comparative study of kinship and family structure, there has been a continuing tradition of interest in the family life of Europe and America. In the nineteenth century, Le Play constructed a typology of European family structures ranging from the patriarchal systems of the semifeudal eastern European areas, which resulted in the development of extended families, through the *famille-souche*, or stem-family, of the semi-industrial areas to what he considered to be the unstable and disorganized systems of the urban industrial areas. Le Play's typology, or something very like it, seems to have regained favor as a universal system of classification (see Levy in *Aspects of the Analysis . . . 1965*). The stem-family type is of particular interest because it seems to combine an emphasis upon the ideal of family continuity with an actual situation where most of the domestic units are small and self-liquidating.

As a result of their work on the development of capitalism and its institutional structure, Marx and Engels became interested in the development of the family, an interest which was quickened by the publication of Lewis H. Morgan's *Ancient Society* (1877). Marx read this work and made extensive notes on it, but it was Engels who published an extensive commentary on it after Marx's death, under the title *The Origin of the Family, Private Property and the State.* In this work Marx's general theories of social and economic history are combined with Morgan's speculative history of kinship institutions. The most general conclusion of the book is that a stable monogamous family system, dominated by male authority and prescribed and supported by law, has really developed as a device for the perpetuation of the private ownership of property. This conclusion has been widely misinterpreted to mean that Engels was opposed to any sort of family relationships and that the family should be abolished in socialist societies. On the contrary, Engels went out of his way to point out that the emotional and sexual elements involved in family relations can only be paramount when considerations of property do not enter into the picture. Thus, he argued that the proletariat make and break marital unions only upon the basis of mutual attraction, whereas in bourgeois marriage the conjugal pair are indissolubly united even when they have no love for each other and perhaps engage in adultery with other available partners.

The influence of Freud's work upon comparative family studies can only be mentioned in passing. It has produced some of the most penetrating hypotheses concerning the content of family relationships, particularly in European and American societies where psychoanalysis has been most widely practiced as a therapeutic technique. Studies of the relation between culture and personality focus upon the familial milieu as the context of personality development, and students of this field have produced some of the most detailed and intimate documentation of family life in non-Western cultures. It is also evident that Freud's thought has influenced the formation of hypotheses about the nature and functions of family structure, at least since the work of Malinowski.

Theoretical and research problems

Despite the considerable time and effort devoted to family studies and despite the refinement of definitions and the improvement of concepts, our knowledge of the family remains rudimentary. We use the term "family" in the loosest possible way, perhaps because of the very nature of the data themselves. For comparative study it is necessary to exercise great care in the construction of theoretical models in order to avoid distortions in observation and description. The bulk of family theory is derived from the Euro–American cultural tradition and from the study of European and American societies. The development and extension of psychoanalysis has produced both a large collection of empirical data and a growing sophistication in its interpretation. But this has been accompanied by a tendency to attribute functional necessity to observed patterns, so that there is a danger of assuming that the functions performed by small family groups in Euro–American societies *must* be performed by similar groups, similarly defined and constituted, in all societies. Parsons (see Parsons & Bales 1955) has tried to show the systematic relation between nuclear-family structure on the one hand and socialization for participation in wider social systems on the other. This analysis is very convincing in its establishment of the general conditions which seem to be necessary for adequate human socialization, but those conditions can be expressed in very general terms and could be met by a wide variety of actual persons and groups. If the nuclear family is to be thought of as that group that carries out primary socialization, then it is necessary to investigate the empirical composition of such groups in a wide range of societies.

Should we continue to use the model of nuclear family or even of nuclear-family relationship complex as a measure for cross-cultural comparison?

Is this anything more than a device for making all observations fit our conception of what should exist? Or is it mainly a problem of language? Will more flexible terms that are not derived directly from a particular cultural tradition enable us to overcome these difficulties? Similar problems have arisen in debates over the question of whether all societies have "law" or "a political system." In spite of some recent defense of the idea of the universality of the nuclear family from linguistic analysts (Lounsbury 1965), it would seem to be desirable to keep an open mind on the question.

Much of the work already done in the study of comparative family structure has been based upon the collection of information about norms, that is, the ideal modes of behavior in different societies; and, as we have suggested above, these have usually been translated into terms of the norms of Euro–American society. Many anthropologists have supplemented interview data and informant's statements with case material, genealogical investigation, sample surveys, and statistical analyses. The aim has been either to try to determine what the system "really is" or to discover the manner in which norms work out in practice. Pioneering work in this regard was done by Audrey Richards, John Barnes, and Meyer Fortes. Fortes has always stressed the importance of regarding the family as a process in time and of looking at the cyclical development of family structure. As the individuals who compose family groups grow older and as new members are born and others die, the structure of the group changes as well as the relationships between the individuals concerned. New possibilities for this type of analysis are presented by the development of computers. With the aid of these machines it is possible to simulate the experience of a whole community of families over a long time period by constructing models of family structure or household composition and then applying to them such variable elements as birth and death rates, age at marriage, duration of unions, and fertility patterns. In this way it is possible to determine what varieties of family and household types would be produced under varying circumstances over varying time periods.

A major controversy that has developed within anthropology has considerable bearing on the whole subject of comparative family studies. This controversy starts with Lévi-Strauss' idea that the building block of kinship systems is not the biological or nuclear family but a constellation of roles which includes the siblings of a marrying couple as well as their children. In disagreeing with Radcliffe-Brown's contention that it is the relations between members of the "elementary family" that constitute the unit of structure from which all kinship systems are built, he says:

Of course, the biological family is ubiquitous in human society. But what confers upon kinship its socio-cultural character is not what it retains from nature, but, rather, the essential way in which it diverges from nature. A kinship system does not consist in the objective ties of descent or consanguinity between individuals. ... The essence of human kinship is to require the establishment of relations among what Radcliffe-Brown calls "elementary families." Thus, it is not the families (isolated terms) which are truly "elementary," but, rather, the relations between those terms.   (Lévi-Strauss [1958] 1963, pp. 50–51)

From this starting point Lévi-Strauss proceeds to a complex analysis of preferential and prescriptive marriage systems, but the perspective which he introduced leads to a new assessment of intrafamilial relations.

Briefly, the question is whether the relations of nuclear family and of filiation always constitute a basic "natural" system which tends to counterbalance particular kinship ties stressed for jural purposes, or whether we should regard nuclear-family relations as being nothing more than a fortuitous complex of highly variable relations some of which may be dispensed with altogether. For example, if filiation is always bilateral (because every child must have a "father" and a "mother"), then where patrilineal descent is stressed for jural purposes the strong jural tie between father and child will be balanced by the tie between mother and child and, by extension, between the child and its mother's kin—a tie of complementary filiation. Conversely, it could be argued that where matrilineal descent is stressed, a compensating bond will exist between father and children and between the child and the father's kin. The point to be noted in this argument is that the ties between parents and children may be accorded great legal significance or may be simply affective, but they derive ultimately from the bonds of filiation and descent which arise within the nuclear-family relationship complex. These relations are socially rather than biologically defined, but they focus upon activities which are familial.

The contrary view is that relationships between a child and its parents may derive from the fact that the parents are married to each other rather than from any bond of filiation. Thus, the Trobriand Islanders assert that there is no genetic link between fathers and their children. A man is a "father" because he is the husband of the child's mother. Of course this ideological view of the matter seems to be related to the political and legal sphere rather than to the field of domestic relations, where fatherhood may be rooted in a set of activities rather than a set of abstract principles.

It is not necessary to document the details of this controversy here; adequate references will be found in Leach (1961) and Schneider (see Association of Social Anthropologists . . . 1966). The point of interest here is Leach's contention that relations between children and parents may be as variable as any other social relations and that we should be prepared to find societies in which even the mother–child relationship is conceived of as one wholly derivative from the fact of the mother's marriage to the father, who is thought of as the person with whom the child has a real consanguineal relationship. In such a situation the mother is an affine; she is not "mother" necessarily at all, but "father's wife."

The controversy outlined here does not focus upon the internal relations or the structure of the family as such; it is concerned with an understanding of the structure of total social systems. But it does bring into quite sharp focus the need to abandon a dogmatic view of the universality of nuclear-family relations and the need to differentiate clearly between the activities involved in domestic relations, the facts of biological interconnectedness, and the interlocking of familial and wider kinship relations. It seems likely that future research will operate with a bigger collection of more differentiated concepts derived from a splitting up of such notions as descent, filiation, sibling bonds, alliance, and, of course, the general notion of nuclear family.

Throughout the discussion so far it has been assumed that comparative family studies refer to comparisons between different *societies* and that "structure" means societal norms. Some of the most interesting modern research is concerned with the study of differences in family structure *within* societies; studies which throw light upon the nature of society itself. It has long been recognized that the structure of family relations appears to vary with class, ethnic group, and other factors. This raises the question of whether the variation lies at the level of culture (that is, in the norms themselves) or whether the actual distribution of empirically ordered "types" of family is the result of constraints operating to prevent the full realization of cultural ideals. For example, it is generally accepted that Hindus value a joint family system in which marriages are contracted at an early age and are indissoluble and in which brides are brought to live in their husband's father's house, where they

come under the authority of the senior woman and the men form a corporate group. In fact, it would seem that such ideal patterns are met only by the wealthier families, where a common interest in property serves as a binding factor, while the poorer families tend to be small and to consist of only a couple with their own minor children. It has also been suggested that the size of households would be limited under preindustrial conditions everywhere by the early death of parents and high infant mortality rates. Such arguments ignore the fact that purely demographic constraints can be circumvented, since family and kinship relations are not biological relations and since adoption or other forms of culturally defined kinship ties can be used as the basis of household formation.

Important though adoption and the collapsing of relationships may be as a means of keeping functioning groups intact, it must be realized that the exigencies of birth-and-death rates and other demographic variables do have an effect upon household composition, just as the biological processes of maturation have an effect. Sociologically, a more important consideration is the extent to which norms vary from group to group and result in the precipitation of different configurations of family organization. In the United States there has been discussion of "the culture of poverty" in relation to the incidence of fatherless families among lower-status and lower-income groups. In such cases it is difficult to determine whether the pattern of family living among these lower-income groups is determined by a simple inability to command the means of achieving valued patterns of behavior or whether different values are operative. In such cases the study of family life becomes a very sensitive index to the whole mode of integration of the over-all social system. This question is discussed further below.

Although knowledge of the genesis of emotional disturbance and social deviance is much more extensive than it was 25 years ago, it is still inadequate. The complexity of the relationship system of family groups is understood in only the most general terms despite the considerable body of detailed information pertaining to Euro–American families. The profound hatreds and bitter rivalries which are the counterpart of the relations of familial solidarity are well known to anthropologists, both as the source of conflicts with political and economic significance and as the basis of witchcraft beliefs and magical and religious practices. These conflicts are the product of the interaction systems themselves within small "multibonded" groups and may have considerable significance for wider system organization. It has often been remarked that the family is the unit within which primary socialization takes place and within which the growing child is taught the ultimate value orientations of the whole society. This is not necessarily done formally, but the values may be implicit in the general structure of the familial relationship system itself. If this is so, then it is important to know how these relationships are structured in different societies and just how the values are internalized by the growing child.

The range of variability

In the large Ashanti villages of central Ghana one can often see children carrying pots of food from their mother's house to the house of their father. The children may eat with their father and then go home to sleep at the house where their mother lives, while the mother may visit the father for the night. This pattern of divided residence and visiting back and forth seems to exist because the Ashanti traditional social system stresses matrilineal descent for important social purposes, such as inheritance of land, succession to office, and political status. Women often value the tie to their brother as highly as, or higher than, the relationship to their husband, since it is from the brother that their children will inherit. Because the child's place in society is mainly determined through its relationship to its mother and her matrilineal kin, the breaking of a marital tie is of little legal consequence either for the spouses or for the children. It is true that fathers have always had responsibility for the upbringing of their own children, including the provision of food and the teaching of crafts and skills, but these duties could be carried out even when the child did not reside with the father and even after the parents had broken their conjugal tie. According to Fortes (1949) another factor inducing women to remain in their own homes even after marriage is the very close relationship between mother and children, and particularly between mothers and daughters. This case demonstrates the way in which interests and relationships can cut right across the solidarity of the nuclear family, and it would be very difficult to demonstrate that the nuclear family is either a normal or a necessary coresidential unit among the Ashanti. The Ashanti concept of family is quite different from the European concept; Fortes mentions that persons who speak English often say, "Your mother is your family, your father is not."

The most extreme and best known example of the effect of matrilineal descent upon familial relationships was to be found among the Nayar caste of southern India in the period before the full effects of British rule were felt. Among the Nayar, it appears that the marital relationship was reduced to a merely symbolic level, being contracted at around the time that the girl reached puberty and shortly thereafter being ritually broken. Afterward, the women were allowed to have informal love affairs with men who visited them at night. The households consisted of a group of brothers and their sisters and the sisters' children, and any children born to the woman of the household became members of the matrilineal joint family. The children were discouraged from developing any strong attachments to either their *pater* or *genitor*, and while it would be impossible to argue that the role of father was completely absent from this social system, it was obviously diminished in favor of the solidarity of the property-owning matrilineal group. It seems likely that many of the functions that are normally fulfilled by fathers in relation to socialization and personality development were carried out by male members of the matrilineage (Gough 1952).

Cases such as these have led some writers, including Radcliffe-Brown, to suggest that the basic structural unit of kinship systems is the unit of mother and children, in other words, to separate the nuclear family into a number of paired relationships, or dyads, and to see how, in differing societies, they fit in relation to each other and to other groups. This is certainly a step in the right direction toward loosening the categories involved in the nuclear-family complex and exploring more fully their independent connections. Even in societies with pronounced patriarchal authority we find that the mother–children unit often forms an important subgroup, given special recognition and marked by close emotional ties among its members.

Among the Swazi as described by Hilda Kuper (see Radcliffe-Brown & Forde 1950), descent, inheritance of economically valuable possessions, and succession to office is patrilineal, but women are given a position of great prominence in the organization of domestic life. Homesteads are built in the form of a semicircular group of huts surrounding a cattle pen, each hut being occupied by a mother and her children. In the center of the arc is the "great hut" occupied by the mother of the male head of the compound (or one of his senior wives if his mother is dead). When a young man or a group of full brothers sets up a new homestead, their mother is installed in the place of honor, for it was she who reared them, watched over their rights, guarded their inheritance, fed and nurtured them. The father is respected as the head of the group, revered, and eventually worshiped as an ancestor, but the mother is loved and cherished. This pattern is common in patriarchal societies where the father is an authoritarian figure and the holder of property that the heir requires in order to attain full maturity—thus introducing an underlying tension into the formally respectful relationship. Parsons has suggested that the father role is always an "instrumental" one as opposed to the more emotional or "expressive" quality of the mother role (Parsons & Bales 1955, pp. 157–158). In a penetrating study comparing two adjacent groups in west Africa which share a basically similar culture, Goody has shown that in one of them the matrilineal inheritance of certain types of property alters the interpersonal relationships between close kin and even alters the mode of ancestor worship (1962). Since intrafamilial relationship patterns seem to be so responsive to the effect of outside influences, it is premature to assert too many conclusions about the structure of the nuclear family as such. The specialization of males and females in instrumental and expressive roles may be an aspect of sex-role differentiation in this case rather than of role specialization within a small group structure. Certainly women take on instrumental roles in the absence of men, but they retain the predominantly expressive quality appropriate to females.

In tribal societies where kinship is the basis of recruitment to all or most important social roles, the family must articulate directly with descent groups and becomes a mechanism for the continuous generation of new kinship ties. As Fortes says, "the workshop, so to speak, of social reproduction, is the domestic group" (Goody 1958, p. 2). In more differentiated social systems with an increased division of labor, a literary tradition, and a well-developed class or caste system, it is still true that families may be large, multifunctional units. In China and India, for example, the whole weight of tradition, values, and religious sentiment favored the growth of large patrilineal joint families and patriarchal authority. The uneven distribution of wealth and status seems to affect the realization of these ideals, so that the majority of households are small and contain only parents and children. This is not simply a matter of demographic determinism; the absence of a sufficient property base leads to the early secession of mature sons, who try to make out for themselves. Large joint families are found mainly among landowning and merchant groups, where sons have a continuing material interest in the patrimony to reinforce and sustain filial piety. Such large "families" are really lineages or descent groups which constitute perpetual corporations managing a common enterprise.

Le Play thought of the *famille-souche*, or stem-family, as preserving familial continuity while adapting to the demands of industrialism. While many of the younger members of the family migrated or went off to work in industrial centers, the main family, or stem, continued and was usually located on its own land or in its own house. A regular mode of inheritance designed to prevent fragmentation was imposed to ensure both the continuity and the integrity of the familial estate. The existence of such a system in twentieth-century rural Ireland has been described by Arensberg and Kimball (1940), and its presence in parts of the United States has been depicted (Zimmerman & Frampton 1935). On the small farms of rural Ireland it is customary for one son to inherit the family farm, while the other children marry out or migrate to the towns. The heir usually postpones his marriage until his father is nearly ready to hand over control, thus ensuring that the farm will not have to support more persons than it can carry and ensuring the continuity of one male line on an undivided farm. The stem-family is not a product of industrial society. Recent work by Laslett indicates that the preindustrial family system in England did not encourage the growth of large extended families occupying single dwellings; on the contrary, the nuclear-family household seems to have been the normal type of dwelling group, and when large household groups are found, they appear to have been made up by servants or craft laborers rather than by kin. There was also a continuous process of downward mobility in which the children of wealthy or high-status families were sloughed off into lower positions, while the main heir took over an intact patrimony (Laslett 1965).

The urban family system of modern Europe and America developed out of the system found in agrarian society (or "the world we have lost," as Laslett terms it). It has been a constant preoccupation of writers on the modern family to think of it as being somehow stripped of functions and reduced to a pale shadow of its former ample self. The ideal is that of a nuclear-family group living in its own house independently of other kin and subsisting upon the wages or salary of the husband–father. Falling birth rates, an increase in the incidence of divorce, a decline in home food processing, clothes making, and so on—all these have been held to signify a decline in family living and a shift toward increasing individualism and material values. Parsons and others have argued that the family system of the urban United States is not a denuded form of a more "normal" or "natural" family system but is itself a highly specialized form that articulates most satisfactorily with a highly differentiated economic and political system and with institutionalized values that stress achievement rather than inheritance. It is argued that the smallness and relative isolation of the family from other kinship ties is an adaptation that makes possible the spatial and status mobility of its members. The unit of mother and children remains the basic affective group within which there is close emotional identification, and the husband–father is closely integrated with it both emotionally and in terms of his status-conferring and economic-support functions. It is upon his position in the occupational system that the status and the style of life of the whole family group depends. This functional interpretation of the importance of the nuclear family in industrial society may be considerably weakened by the work of Laslett, referred to above. If the nuclear family has been the major form of European family structure for many centuries, predating the industrial revolution, and if this family form was the product of social values rather than of demographic or other constraints, then the modern family forms may be simply the continuation of a culturally preferred form.

Studies of the structure of kinship and family relations in modern industrial societies are rare in spite of the considerable literature on special problems of family living. Recent work in Britain has shown that lower-class families often live in close proximity to near kin and maintain intimate contact with them despite the "isolation" of the nuclear family (Young & Willmott 1957). The cooperation between mother and married daughters is particularly noticeable, and most writers have remarked upon the great importance of women in their role as mothers of grown-up children. Fathers are important, of course, as wage earners and supporters of their families, but in the lower class the status of the family tends to be fixed less by the occupation of the husband–father than by birth into a particular neighborhood and class. The network of relations between female kin is reinforced by daily contact, mutual help, and support in times of economic hardship, and is balanced by a tendency for men to spend their leisure time together rather than with the members of their own nuclear family.

A more extreme form of matrifocal family structure occurs in low-status ethnic groups where there appears to be some correlation with insecurity in male employment. In the plantation areas of the southern United States, the West Indies, and Latin America and in the urban areas of developing societies in Africa and Asia, one often finds high illegitimacy rates and unstable mating patterns. An array of types of domestic group is produced, the most distinctive being those in which a mother is surrounded by adult children and some of her daughter's children. Money income flows into such a household from a variety of sources, such as children's earnings, payment to daughters for the support of illegitimate children, the older woman's own labor, and perhaps government relief funds. This income is reallocated around the essential tasks of child rearing and nurturance, and it appears that a household group of this kind is a useful adaptation to conditions of economic insecurity. This form of domestic group appears to be always regarded as a deviant form, partly because of the instability of male roles in relation to it. Unlike the matrilineal situation, men do not have important legal ties to their sisters; it is the mother who is the focus of the familial solidarity, and her position derives from affective rather than jural relations. It would be wrong to suggest that this is the *typical* household or familial form in the societies in which it occurs. Even at the class levels where it is most frequently found it constitutes only a small proportion of actual household groups, but its significance is as an expression of the strength of mother–child relations and the relative weakness of marital ties.

This brief sketch has outlined only some of the major features of family structure. Variations within single societies have hardly been touched upon, and nothing has been said about pathological forms. Nor has attention been directed toward the attempts which have been made from time to time to do away with family solidarity in favor of allegiance to other groups, although such attempts provide valuable experimental data. The Israeli cooperative communities are probably the best recent examples of this, although no definite conclusions about the necessity or otherwise of nuclear-family relationships can be drawn (Spiro 1958). What these cases do perhaps indicate, along with some of the matrilineal and matrifocal cases, is that marriage is not the only means of securing social "legitimacy" for children. Spiro shows that children brought up in central nurseries and schools are in a sense children of the whole community, in spite of the specific relationships they may develop with their "own" parents. This is possible because of the relatively small size of the communities.

However the family may be defined or structured, it always constitutes an area of diffuse and permanent solidarity between a limited number of individuals, and this is probably its most important distinguishing characteristic. This is a view at least suggested by W. H. Rivers in his *Social Organization* when he deliberately identifies the family of parents and children as the basic unit in European society but points out that in other societies the family may be much bigger, that biological connection is no guide to kinship, and that genealogies express kinship ties but may be fabricated to fit social reality. Rivers is very wary about drawing any precise line between family relationships and other kinship ties. Such lines can be drawn in particular cases but are very difficult to define a priori.

RAYMOND T. SMITH

[*Directly related are the entries* KINSHIP *and* MARRIAGE; *see also* CONFLICT, *article on* ANTHROPOLOGICAL ASPECTS.]

BIBLIOGRAPHY

ARENSBERG, CONRAD M.; and KIMBALL, SOLON T. (1940) 1961 *Family and Community in Ireland.* Gloucester, Mass.: Smith.

Aspects of the Analysis of Family Structure, by Ansley J. Coale et al. 1965 Princeton Univ. Press.

ASSOCIATION OF SOCIAL ANTHROPOLOGISTS OF THE COMMONWEALTH, CONFERENCE ON NEW APPROACHES IN SOCIAL ANTHROPOLOGY, CAMBRIDGE, *1963* 1966 *The Relevance of Models for Social Anthropology.* Edited by Michael Banton. London: Tavistock. → See especially "Some Muddles in the Models" by David M. Schneider.

BACHOFEN, JOHANN J. (1861) 1948 *Das Mutterrecht.* 2 vols. 3d ed. Edited by Karl Meuli. Basel: Schwabe.

BELL, NORMAN W.; and VOGEL, EZRA F. (editors) 1960 *A Modern Introduction to the Family.* London: Routledge; Glencoe, Ill.: Free Press.

BOTT, ELIZABETH 1957 *Family and Social Network: Roles, Norms, and External Relationships in Ordinary Urban Families.* London: Tavistock.

BOWLBY, JOHN 1951 *Maternal Care and Mental Health.* Geneva: World Health Organization.

BRITISH ASSOCIATION FOR THE ADVANCEMENT OF SCIENCE (1874) 1954 *Notes and Queries on Anthropology.* 6th ed., rev. London: Routledge.

EVANS-PRITCHARD, E. E. 1951 *Kinship and Marriage Among the Nuer.* Oxford Univ. Press.

FORTES, MEYER (1949) 1963 Time and Social Structure: An Ashanti Case Study; Radcliffe-Brown's Thesis. Pages 54–84 in Meyer Fortes (editor), *Social Structure: Studies Presented to A. R. Radcliffe-Brown.* New York: Russell.

FORTES, MEYER 1958 Introduction. Pages 1–14 in Jack R. Goody (editor), *The Developmental Cycle in Domestic Groups.* Cambridge Papers in Social Anthropology, No. 1. Cambridge Univ. Press.

FRAZIER, E. FRANKLIN (1939) 1957 *The Negro in the United States.* Rev. ed. New York: Macmillan. → First published as *The Negro Family in the United States.*

GOODY, JACK R. (editor) 1958 *The Developmental Cycle in Domestic Groups.* Cambridge Papers in Social Anthropology, No. 1. Cambridge Univ. Press.

GOODY, JACK R. 1962 *Death, Property and the Ancestors: A Study of the Mortuary Customs of the Lodagaa of West Africa.* Stanford Univ. Press.

GOUGH, KATHLEEN 1952 Changing Kinship Usages in the Setting of Political and Economic Change Among the Nayars of Malabar. *Journal of the Royal Anthropological Institute of Great Britain and Ireland* 82: 71–87.

HALPERN, JOEL MARTIN 1958 *A Serbian Village.* New York: Columbia Univ. Press.

LASLETT, PETER 1965 *The World We Have Lost.* London: Methuen.

LEACH, EDMUND R. 1961 *Rethinking Anthropology.* London School of Economics and Political Science Monographs on Social Anthropology, No. 22. London: Athlone.

LÉVI-STRAUSS, CLAUDE (1958) 1963 *Structural Anthropology.* New York: Basic Books. → First published in French.

LEVY, MARION J. 1949 *The Family Revolution in Modern China.* Cambridge, Mass.: Harvard Univ. Press.

LEVY, MARION J.; and FALLERS, L. A. 1959 The Family: Some Comparative Considerations. *American Anthropologist* New Series 61:647–651.

LOUNSBURY, FLOYD G. 1965 Another View of the Trobriand Kinship Categories. *American Anthropologist* New Series 67, part 2:142–185.

MALINOWSKI, BRONISLAW (1927) 1953 *Sex and Repression in Savage Society.* London: Routledge; New York: Harcourt. → A paperback edition was published in 1955 by Meridian.

MEAD, MARGARET 1949 *Male and Female: A Study of the Sexes in a Changing World.* London: Gollancz; New York: Morrow.

MORGAN, LEWIS HENRY 1871 *Systems of Consanguinity and Affinity of the Human Family.* Smithsonian Contributions to Knowledge, Vol. 17, Publication No. 218. Washington: Smithsonian Institution.

MORGAN, LEWIS HENRY (1877) 1964 *Ancient Society.* Edited by Leslie A. White. Cambridge, Mass.: Belknap.

MURDOCK, GEORGE P. 1949 *Social Structure.* New York: Macmillan.

PARSONS, TALCOTT (1949) 1959 The Social Structure of the Family. Pages 241–274 in Ruth N. Anshen (editor), *The Family: Its Function and Destiny.* Rev. ed. New York: Harper.

PARSONS, TALCOTT 1954 The Incest Taboo in Relation to Social Structure and the Socialization of the Child. *British Journal of Sociology* 5:101–117.

PARSONS, TALCOTT; and BALES, ROBERT F. 1955 *Family, Socialization and Interaction Process.* Glencoe, Ill.: Free Press.

RADCLIFFE-BROWN, A. R.; and FORDE, C. DARYLL (editors) 1950 *African Systems of Kinship and Marriage.* Published for the International African Institute. Oxford Univ. Press.

Schneider, David M.; and Gough, Kathleen (editors) 1961 *Matrilineal Kinship*. Berkeley: Univ. of California Press.

Spiro, Melford E. 1958 *Children of the Kibbutz*. Cambridge, Mass.: Harvard Univ. Press.

Thomas, William I.; and Znaniecki, Florian (1918–1920) 1958 *The Polish Peasant in Europe and America*. 2 vols., 2d ed. New York: Dover.

Young, Michael; and Willmott, Peter 1957 *Family and Kinship in East London*. Institute of Community Studies, Report No. 1. London: Routledge; Glencoe, Ill.: Free Press. → A paperback edition was published in 1963 by Penguin.

Zimmerman, Carle C. 1947 *Family and Civilization*. New York: Harper.

Zimmerman, Carle C.; and Frampton, Merle E. 1935 *Family and Society: A Study of the Sociology of Reconstruction*. London: Williams & Norgate; Princeton, N.J.: Van Nostrand.

II

DISORGANIZATION AND DISSOLUTION

Aside from some slight semantic disagreements, most social scientists agree that some form of a familial group is universal among human beings. Likewise in every society some of the familial groups are imperfect in their functioning and deserving of the label "disorganized." Generally there is some relationship between disorganization and a more climactic, terminal situation called "dissolution." Family groups are eventually dissolved by death or some form of separation, insofar as these groups are organized around the matings of men and women. Of course, a family process, in the sense of overlapping and interacting generations, is immortal, providing there is reproductive replacement before the familial group of a particular generation disintegrates (Kirkpatrick [1955] 1963, pp. 192–195).

Nature and significance

The significance of familial disorganization and dissolution depends upon the institutional arrangements for family life in a particular culture. If stress is laid on the nuclear family, then kinfolk are less available to aid members of the smaller familial group. Some families are vulnerable in the sense that their members expect permanence, have made deep emotional commitments, and do not readily redirect affection and loyalty. On the other hand, people may be less hurt by familial instability in cultures where instability is an established norm and where kinfolk are helpful and meaningful.

In most cultures, the familial group helps prepare children both for membership in a society and for effective functioning as parents. Disorganization and dissolution are significant in that they tend to interfere with this socialization process. Furthermore, disorganization and dissolution are often cumulative and recurrent in the family process. There is a convergence of evidence in the United States that people with happy marriages tend to come from happy homes. Divorce also runs in families; divorced persons are divorce-prone, and children suffering from bereavement or parental divorce may be involved with delinquency, illegitimacy, and unwise marriage. The consequences of disorganization and dissolution experienced by the parents are commonly visited upon the offspring, perhaps for several generations. Some children, however, are warned by the fate of their parents and in marriage make an effort to reverse a trend toward disorganization.

Terminology. It is impossible to make a useful analysis of the nature and significance of family disorganization and dissolution without precise terminology. In current usage "disorganization" seems to imply maladjustment, malfunctioning, psychological decay, and the existence of family problems. Goode defines family disorganization as "the breakup of a family unit, the dissolution or fracture of a structure of social roles when one or more members fail to perform adequately their role obligation." He lists five types of family disorganization, namely, illegitimacy, dissolution, whether as a result of divorce, annulment, separation, or desertion; "empty shell family"; unwilled absence of one spouse; and "unwilled" major role failures (Goode 1964, pp. 91–92).

Clearly, such taxonomy makes no distinction between disorganization and dissolution. It seems from the inclusion of illegitimacy that a family can be "disorganized" by role failure even before it is organized. Caplow defines an organization as "a social system that has an unequivocal collective identity, an exact roster of members, a program of activity, and procedures for replacing members" (1964, p. 1). Following this line of thought, it would seem more proper to regard the "illegitimate family" as unorganized rather than as a type of family disorganization.

Distinction between disorganization and dissolution. In the present discussion a distinction will be made between family disorganization and family dissolution, and marital disorganization will be regarded as a special case of family disorganization. Family *dissolution* means disintegration, disruption, or chronic instability; it is characterized by "dependence, agency intrusion, member extraction, premature atypical departure and family violence" (Kirkpatrick [1955] 1963, p. 565).

Marital dissolution, as a special form of family

dissolution, may take the form of suicide, murder of spouse, annulment, separation (ranging from psychological withdrawal to legal separation), and, finally, divorce. The withdrawal from spouse may be accompanied by substitution for wife of a co-wife, concubine, mistress, or prostitute. Sometimes dissolution is by stages, for example, in a sequence of avoidance, suit for separate maintenance, legal separation, an interlocutory divorce decree, and finally an absolute divorce with the right of remarriage.

Family dissolution is an imperfect index of family *disorganization*. Divorce is an imperfect index of marital disorganization because there may be disorganization without divorce. For example, divorce was very difficult to obtain in England prior to liberalization of the laws in 1857 and again in 1937. When the divorce door is closed, marital disorganization may be inconspicuously endured. On the other hand, a couple with high expectations of marital bliss but relatively little marital disorganization may seek divorce as an exit from marriage. That marital disorganization is often not extreme is shown by the frequency of reconciliation, dropping of divorce suits, and remarriage to the former spouse. Thus, Harvey J. Locke (1951, pp. 54–55) found that about a fourth of the divorced couples he studied were in the same marital adjustment category as the less happy fourth of the married couples.

Religious and moralistic viewpoints. Family disorganization and dissolution are viewed by many people in moralistic and religious terms. The family at one time performed functions so important that disharmony and disruption were viewed with alarm. One assumption of the patriarchal system in western European culture was that paternal authority could insure efficiency and stability in family life. It is probably still the assumption of middle-class people in the United States that "nice" people get on together and as spouses stay together.

The Roman Catholic viewpoint concerning family disorganization and dissolution has remained rather clear and constant since the Council of Trent, 1545–1563. The ideal is patriarchal harmony established by a marriage sacrament directed toward the goals of parenthood and marital love. The Catholic doctrine assumes various impediments, such as disparity of religion, lack of consent, or intention to seek a divorce. Given the impediment of disparity of religion, the marriage of a Catholic to a non-Catholic, especially one unbaptized, can be nullified, thus permitting the Catholic party to obtain a civil divorce and marry a Catholic partner "in favor of the Faith." Even a marriage between Catholics may be dissolved by papal dispensation if the marriage is unconsummated and grounds exist for the marital disruption. In addition to nullification and dissolution by dispensation, the church grants separation from bed and board, which does not include the right of remarriage. The consummated and valid marriage between two Catholics is indissoluble and permits no remarriage unless terminated by death. Certain Protestant denominations hold equally religious and moralistic views (Kirkpatrick [1955] 1963, pp. 573–575).

The legalistic viewpoint. The legalistic view, which is prevalent in the United States, had its origins in canon law and was influenced by the common law of England. It is complicated by the lack of uniformity among the various statutes and decisions of the 50 states; the practice of seeking divorce in states other than the state of residence has brought controversial cases to the U.S. Supreme Court (Harper & Skolnick [1952] 1962, pp. 451–458).

Basic to the legalistic doctrine of divorce in the United States is *adversary procedure*. It is assumed that a relatively innocent party may be granted a divorce because of the relative guilt of the other party with reference to "grounds" specified in the statutes of the various states. There are four legal doctrines associated with the basic adversary procedure. If spouses cooperate in providing evidence calculated to obtain a divorce on certain grounds, that is *collusion*, and the divorce should be denied. If one party forgives an offense such as adultery and continues to live with the spouse, *condonation* is assumed, and the derivative inference is made that the damage to the innocent party was not great enough to justify a divorce. If one party shows that the other party is equally guilty, *successful recrimination* is established and the divorce is not to be granted. If one party plots the guilty behavior of the other party, that is *connivance*, and the divorce would be denied to the allegedly innocent party. Thus the legal operation of divorce is withheld from marriages so sick as to menace the well-being of both adults and children in the familial group (Kirkpatrick [1955] 1963, p. 595).

Social pathology. Disorganization and dissolution are subject to a third viewpoint, that of social pathology. This viewpoint assumes that well-functioning, organized families are "normal"; maladjustment and disruptions are regarded as deviant behavior. The families with problems should be brought back into line by monetary aid, psychological manipulation, and a therapy designed to help people achieve conformity to the social norms. With little reflection upon alternative frames of reference, there is concern for the cure of pathological situations.

Sociological viewpoint. A fourth viewpoint is that of scientific sociology. In the choice of this label there is no intended implication that sociology is a distinct, mature, and sophisticated science. Perhaps at the present time it is merely an attempt at clear, honest, abstract thinking about social phenomena, increasingly aided by systematic observation and analysis. From such an intellectual orientation, which is relatively free from concealed value assumptions and distorting preconceptions, family dissolution is sometimes seen as a relief of family disorganization. For certain infections, amputation is the choice of a lesser evil as compared with further spread of infection. So it may be with divorce.

The sociological viewpoint is generally deterministic and assumes that social changes make inevitable certain reactions in terms of disorganization and reorganization. According to this view, familial institutions, groups, and relationships are part of a larger social structure in which every aspect of the total configuration is related to every other aspect. Family disorganization may be one facet of a larger social disorganization.

Methods and trends in research

Family crisis. Research concerning crises of the family has been extensive. The great depression in the United States brought forth books on unemployment as a crisis for the family, and World War II brought an interest in bereavement and other trials visited upon the family by wartime conditions. More recently scholars have speculated as to the devastating influence that an atomic war would have on the family.

The confusion of terminology in regard to disorganization and dissolution is compounded by the concept of *family crisis*. Death, like divorce, can cause the dissolution of family units, and often bereavement is placed in the category of family crisis. Hill writes of the event (A) which interacts with the ability of the family to meet a crisis (B); both (A) and (B) interact with the definition which the family makes of the event (C), and thus the situation is an (X)—the crisis for a particular family. One family may take in its stride an impact which would crush another family that is lacking in resources and prone to regard a trifle as a crisis (Waller [1938] 1951, p. 460).

Endogenous and exogenous disorganization. Kirkpatrick drew a distinction between endoge-

nous and exogenous disorganization, the former having an internal origin and the latter a relatively external origin. Distinctions were also made between the normal and atypical, the timely and the premature, and the objectively severe as compared with the objectively trivial. It was suggested that the term "crisis" be restricted to exogenous disorganization due to an objectively severe atypical or premature event (Kirkpatrick 1955, p. 503). Insofar as family dissolution results from exogenous disorganization, as defined above, it would seem proper to speak of exogenous family dissolution; an example would be the wiping out of a family by flood or fire.

Bereavement. The assassination of President Kennedy in 1963 was a conspicuous atypical, extreme experience which brought premature bereavement. The disorganization in the Kennedy family, in the sense of shock and sorrow, was exogenous disorganization; and the dissolution, in the sense of the loss of the head of the family, could be regarded as exogenous dissolution. Perhaps all bereavement, save that due to violence within the family group, could be regarded as exogenous, and if premature or atypical, it would be a family crisis. An expected death from natural causes of old age would be less clearly a crisis by the criteria which have been set forth, although some degree of disorganization and dissolution might result. There is no claim of exclusive categories in the suggested terminology, and the distinctions are relative.

It is important to make a distinction between father-deceased bereavement and mother-deceased bereavement in view of their differential implications for the family in terms of economic consequences and implications for the offspring in terms of sex typing, identification, and preparatory affectional relationships with parents of the opposite sex. Many aspects of bereavement experience have been probed by Howard Becker, Willard Waller, Thomas D. Eliot, David M. Fulcomer, and others. Perhaps more attention should be paid to the loss of common memories. If a beloved person is no longer available to confirm a happening, there may be doubt about the reality of prior experience and uncertainty about personal identity. If the identity of A is essentially the identity of A *in relation to* B, the loss of B drastically alters the subjective identity of A. Improved knowledge of familial disorganization and dissolution calls not only for greater precision of terminology but also for further exploration of bereavement as a family crisis that may lead to subtle forms of exogenous disorganization.

Demographic investigation. Investigators have explored the distribution of familial disorganization and dissolution over *space*, by *social categories*, and in *time*. For example, relief cases of a certain type may be more prevalent in certain urban areas and within social categories such as "nonwhites." Furthermore, there may be fluctuations in the case load of social welfare agencies by time periods. Unemployment associated with the business cycle has generally meant an increase in the number of families dependent upon external financial assistance.

The most extensive investigation has been that of divorce regarded as a measure of familial dissolution and, more specifically, of marital dissolution. Numerous studies have noted variations in divorce rates by geographical region, sometimes considered in combination with various social categories. Paul Glick has studied "marriage instability" as measured by separation ratios, divorce ratios, and proportion of children not living with both parents. His hypothesis that marital disruption in the United States tends to be more closely related to urbanization than to regions of residence was only partially supported (1963, pp. 47–54).

Various writers such as William J. Goode, Robert Winch, and Christine H. Hillman have stressed the higher divorce ratios among persons of lower socioeconomic status (Goode 1964, pp. 88–90; Winch [1952] 1963, pp. 706–708). However, this evidence contains some inconsistencies when men and women are considered separately. One finds a rather high incidence of divorce among college women as compared both with less educated women and with men at the same college level (Kirkpatrick [1955] 1963, p. 589). It should be stressed that the proportion divorced in a particular group or category of people is affected by remarriage and the rapidity of remarriage. If every person receiving a divorce decree remarried on the same day, there would be no residue of unmarried "divorced persons" in the population.

Desertion, another mode of marital dissolution, may not be accurately reflected in the census categories "separated," "spouse absent," and "divorced," because of remarriage. During 1955 a Philadelphia court recorded 4,224 desertions handled, in contrast to only 2,812 divorces (Kephart 1961, p. 548). Desertion may be a substitute for divorce or preliminary to the legal action of divorce.

The demographic approach stresses the changing prevalence of divorce in various countries. The trend of the divorce rate after World War II was upward in many European countries, such as France, England, and Sweden, as well as in the United States and Canada (Jacobson 1959, table 42, p. 90; table 47, p. 98; Kirkpatrick [1955] 1963, p. 586). For the United States, rates are available from 1920 through 1960, expressed as divorces per year per one thousand married females 15 years of age and over. A curve based on such rates shows a drop during the depression in the 1930s, a huge peak in 1946 following the war, a decline to a plateau, and a figure of 9.2 on that plateau in 1960 as compared with 8.0 in 1920 (Carter & Plateris 1963). From a sociological point of view, this increase is far from spectacular.

The clinical approach. For many decades investigators have utilized methods less objective but perhaps more penetrating than those of the demographers. The various theories of Freud concerning emotion-laden interaction in the family group were integrated by J. C. Flügel. Waller, in his brilliant pioneer study of divorced couples (1930), drew upon psychoanalytic concepts in his analysis of alienation and postdivorce adjustment. He expressed original intuitions concerning motivation, as, for example, the suspicion that some ex-wives seek alimony not out of greed but because of jealous disinclination to see an ex-husband financially capable of marrying another woman. Some psychiatrists probably go to an extreme in regarding the seeking of divorce as an expression of neuroticism.

Historical and comparative studies. The older and well-known accounts of the family, such as those by Edward Westermarck, George Elliott Howard, and Arthur W. Calhoun, contain much historical and comparative information concerning disorganization and dissolution. A book by Lichtenberger, published in 1931, gives a thoughtful and comprehensive analysis of divorce.

More recently, Murdock (1950) made a systematic survey of divorce practices in 40 nonindustrial societies. In many of these societies he found divorce to be more frequent than in the United States, but he also found more preventives and functional adaptations. From this anthropological perspective, the American family does not seem to be in a state of hopeless decay. Following Murdock's lead, various anthropologists have investigated determinants of divorce rates in various cultures. Ackerman (1963), from a study of 62 societies, found certain forms of homogamy to be associated with low divorce rates. Christensen (1963) has given an elegant demonstration of the fact that the association between premarital pregnancy and divorce varies with a culture's sexual permissiveness.

Measurement and prediction. Beginning in the 1930s, researchers attempted to measure and predict marital disorganization. The investigators often collected information concerning background factors at the same time that information was requested concerning marital adjustment. Some of the correlations between the so-called prediction scales (based upon various items, for the most part premarital) and the adjustment scales probably involved a "halo effect" (see Kirkpatrick [1955] 1963, chapters 15, 18, and appendix). Well-adjusted respondents tended to report favorably on both their marriages and their childhood backgrounds. The reverse was probably true for maladjusted couples.

In the longitudinal or forecasting studies of such authors as Ernest W. Burgess and Paul Wallin, Truman L. Kelley and Louis M. Terman, information was first obtained on a sample of individuals, and then after a period of years further information was gathered concerning their marital adjustment. [*See the biography of* BURGESS.] In general, correlations between scores on a prediction instrument and some categories of outcome tended to be lower when the halo effect was controlled by the passage of time.

In connection with this body of research, a great deal of information was collected concerning factors associated with "marital adjustment" or other criteria of success. The findings of many of these studies were brought together, with the revelation that there was rather a striking lack of convergence in evidence (Kirkpatrick 1947). Cautious verbal generalizations about the convergence of findings concerning factors related to marital adjustment and a guide to the sources from which these findings were derived are available (see Kirkpatrick [1955] 1963, chapter 15 and appendix A).

Improvement of scientific knowledge

More precise terminology, pertinent distinctions, and rigorous theory would all be helpful in furthering scientific knowledge in the area under discussion. Since disorganization and dissolution are aspects of family behavior, any advance in knowledge of family systems in general would indirectly contribute to knowledge in this specific area.

Theories of mating.   Winch has systematically carried over his functional theory of the family to the area of family disorganization and dissolution. If he is correct in his theory of complementary mating, a foundation would be laid for generalizations concerning the kind of matings which would avoid family disorganization and dissolution ([1952] 1963, pp. 567–655).

Kirkpatrick derived a theory of mating from a basic postulate concerning the influence of prior satisfactions and dissatisfactions in the course of family experience; this theory was called a theory of "selective needs" based on prior satisfactions and dissatisfactions. In some respects it is different from the Winch theory, and in other respects it is convergent and supplementary (Kirkpatrick [1955] 1963, pp. 300–307). According to the Kirkpatrick theory, an extreme of marital disorganization and perhaps consequent familial disorganization would exist when the spouse violates "minus–plus needs" by providing more of the particular kind of dissatisfaction which was distressing during a prior phase of family experience. For example, the wife who fails to compensate for the dissatisfactions experienced by her husband with his mother and aggravates these same dissatisfactions by behavior similar to that of the mother, risks marital disorganization and possibly divorce.

Criteria of scientific worth.   Improvement of scientific knowledge in this as in other areas depends upon meeting five different criteria of scientific worth (Kirkpatrick 1939; 1959). One criterion is that of *verifiability*. In one sense verifiability implies repeatability of procedure, as in the case of experiments in the natural science field. There is some assurance that research is verifiable by others when it is presented as already verified by the investigators in the sense of proper sampling, validity and reliability of instruments, and correctness of logical inference. It is striking that so many findings concerning factors favorable to success in marriage have been nonverifiable or unverified.

A second criterion is *transmissibility*. A marriage counselor may achieve striking success and yet be unable to transmit his art or technique to a pupil. Often a description of divorce rates in a certain country cannot be transmitted to another scholar because symbols lack identical meanings for each person.

A third criterion of scientific worth is *consistency*. The contribution having this quality is logically sound, and the terms are carefully defined and consistently used with reference to their assigned meanings. Theory, hypotheses, research design, findings, and conclusion are interrelated. Any convergence or discrepancy in evidence is systematically presented.

The fourth criterion is *scope*. Family disorganization and disruption may be analyzed in a single brief case study, or a massive three-volume work may describe this aspect of family systems with global coverage. For example, Goode made an admirable study of divorce as affecting a sample of women in Detroit (1956) and in another book analyzed the family patterns as affected by industrialism in varied countries of the world (1963).

A fifth and somewhat multiple criterion is that of *implication*. Research having the quality of implication has one or more of four characteristics —namely, prediction, practical application, methodological innovation, and creative integration. It would be useful to construct a questionnaire that would predict divorce with 100 per cent accuracy. A study would have implications when, if applied to family counseling, it prevented 90 per cent of the needless divorces. It would be a methodological contribution to integrate the various measures of marital dissolution into an improved index of marital disorganization. Finally, the subcriterion of creative integration would be illustrated by a new integration of existing theories concerning family disorganization into a generalized theory that generated hypotheses subject to definitive verification by empirical research.

Statistics and indices. The improvement of scientific knowledge concerning disorganization and dissolution depends upon improved statistics. In recent years some improvements have been made in marriage and divorce statistics in the United States, which are often inferior to those of less wealthy countries. In 1958 a reporting system known as the "divorce registration area" was established. For inclusion in the divorce registration area a state must have central files of divorce records; include on its record forms certain standard items; receive regularly reports from local areas such as counties; and cooperate with the National Vital Statistics Division in regard to testing data for completeness and accuracy (Carter 1960). Further support to the movement for improved statistics was given by a committee on marriage and divorce statistics of the American Sociological Association, which published a report in June 1958. As part of an action program initiated by the federal agencies concerned with marriage and divorce statistics, a national sample of marriage and divorce transcripts was collected for the year 1960, and the official improved statistics for 1960 are based on this new source, which extends coverage beyond the 18 states in the divorce registration area.

There are various ways in which scientific knowledge would be advanced by improvement of marriage and divorce statistics. Certain needs and research possibilities will be mentioned.

The duration of marriage prior to divorce is a very important item of information. While it is claimed that the duration of marriage to the time of the decree is known for 96.2 per cent of all divorces granted in the United States during 1960, this information has not been fully used to compute the probability of divorce for couples marrying at a particular time. Such true probabilities for earlier years have been computed by Monahan (1959) and Jacobson (1959), but there is a tendency to regard mistakenly the ratio of divorces to marriages of the same year as expressing the risk of divorce.

Improved divorce statistics would reveal on a national basis the details of prior experience with marriage and divorce prior to a particular divorce that is being recorded and tabulated.

It would also be helpful to have national statistics on the total number of persons of various types who have been affected by divorce. People pass out of categories which imply a record of divorce, but they may carry the subjective experience of divorce with them into a remarriage or a relationship with a stepparent.

Statistics concerning divorce should be more closely related to improved statistics concerning separation and desertion. It may be that concern about the divorce of a particular date is inappropriate in view of the fact that the granting of a decree is merely a legal event far removed in time from significant experiences of the individual concerned (Monahan 1962).

It is highly important to have national statistics which are cross tabulated, showing the characteristics of one divorced spouse as matched with those of the other spouse. For research purposes it would be useful to have such cross tabulations by previous marital experience, religion, age at divorce, education, occupation and social status, and children resulting from prior marriages of the divorced spouses.

An interrelation of divorce, marriage, and birth statistics on a national basis would be helpful. Christensen (1963) has already demonstrated that such comparisons are useful in showing the association of premarital pregnancy with divorce. It may be that computer storage and retrieval of data will make the method of "record linkage" increasingly applicable.

Statistics concerning family dissolution which permit valid international comparisons would be desirable. Obviously, a country which regards divorce as a private family matter and lacks a governmental agency concerned with divorce may seem to have a low divorce rate because of underreporting. A logical extension of trends in the United States would be an international divorce registration area, having as members countries with acceptable statistics. Other countries might seek then to improve their indices of family dissolution.

Given the process of changing marital status, which is conspicuous in the United States and in other industrialized countries, there is need for statistics that contribute to an index of what might be called the *velocity* of family dissolution. The speed of separation, divorce, remarriage and redivorce, could be known only with the aid of information concerning prior family experience, which would be reported at each transition. It is known from unusually good statistics in Iowa for 1953 that the duration of marriage prior to a divorce ranges from an average of 6.3 years for primary marriages, to 3.2 when both parties have been married before, to 1.8 for couples breaking up their third marriage (Monahan 1959). Kirkpatrick attempted a crude measure of velocity of family dissolution by dividing the number of divorces per year by the number of persons who in the year following were in the status of divorced (1955, p. 534). A good index of velocity of family dissolution would require improved statistics and would take into account the speed with which children lose natural parents to acquire a stepparent and perhaps a series of such stepparents.

Knowledge of causes and consequences. The distinction between disorganization and dissolution must again be stressed. As compared with couples equally disorganized but undivorced (either contemporary or living in a previous century), certain modern couples seek divorce for special reasons. Often the woman is able to get a job and hence can insist on a high standard of marital happiness. Thus, dissolution may be a *preventive* of disorganization. Some people are less tied to marriage than others; family functions, religious taboos, or life-long commitment to parental roles may simply have less meaning for them (Landis 1963). The door of divorce is more open to certain couples than to others because of lenient laws in their locality, relative freedom to migrate elsewhere for an easy divorce, encouragement of relatives, opportunities for remarriage, and in general, the prospect of freedom without the economic, religious, and psychological penalties which have threatened other couples in various times and places. It can even be argued that divorce itself is a cause of divorce, in that frequent divorce weakens the norm of marital stability. Divorce frees bad matrimonial risks for remarriage and subsequent divorce; offspring imitate divorced parents; and the divorce of numerous friends makes the choice of divorce more normal and respectable (Kirkpatrick [1955] 1963, pp. 577–582).

Persons facing divorce during the latter half of the twentieth century in the United States have varied problems. Variations in the divorce laws of the 50 states contribute to the possibility of legal tangles. The divorce procedure is neither consistently routinized nor consistently established as an individualized therapeutic procedure; certainly, as compared with the bereaved person, the divorced person lacks a clearly defined role to play. The more meaningful any marriage is, the more painful will be its dissolution. But the confusion involved in divorce as compared with bereavement is often almost as disturbing as the previous frustration and deprivation. Seriously maladjusted couples are confused and torn between the choices of continued sickness in their marriage and the amputation brought about by the choice of divorce. The grim challenge is to find the choice which brings the lesser evil.

Effect on children. It can be argued that research concerning the effect of disorganization and disintegration on children is important, even if it is imperfect by the criteria previously mentioned. Children are the helpless victims of the mistakes of their elders; they have little control over their destinies and usually cannot select the stepparent who comes to them in the course of the divorce–remarriage process.

Much of the research has failed to compare the children of disorganized but undissolved homes with those from disorganized and broken homes of specific types. Landis and Nye found that children from broken homes fared as well or better, according to certain criteria, than children from intact but unhappy homes (Nye 1957). Burchinal (1964) considered homes reintegrated by remarriage, as well as broken and unbroken homes, and found no differential effect on adolescents.

In regard to the convergence of valid findings, much depends on the methods used, the type of effect on children, and the age of offspring at which possible effects are investigated. Landis (1963) found rather impressive evidence that happy parental marriages were favorably related to the dating experience of offspring. Robert R. Bell and James DeBurger, both using the sibling-cooperator method (Kirkpatrick & Cotton 1951, p. 82), found that parental divorce showed greater influence than bereavement on the marital adjustment of grown offspring (see Kirkpatrick [1955] 1963, pp. 665–674).

Applications of knowledge

Effective application of improved knowledge of family disorganization and dissolution depends on the emerging pattern of interprofessional cooperation. Lawyers, doctors, psychologists, social workers, educators, home economists, clergymen, and demographers, as well as social scientists, draw upon the growing body of knowledge in this area. That thriving interdisciplinary organization in the United States—the National Council on Family Relations—draws members from all of the above-mentioned professions. Furthermore, the emerging international organizations concerned with the family tend to be interprofessional in character.

Legal changes. Legal changes, both actual and proposed, tend to reflect a sharper international perspective. Varied explanations of the divorce trends in England include the influence of changes in the divorce laws. However, Max Rheinstein (1960) found little influence of legal changes on divorce rates in Germany. In the United States, a tabulation of the divorce laws in the various states as of 1952 was cross tabulated by the crude divorce rates of 1950 and the percentages of respondents in the various states answering "No" to a question on a poll of 1936 which read, "Should divorces be easier to obtain in your state?" There was a striking lack of correspondence between severity of the laws, behavior as to obtaining divorces, and public opinion concerning legal restrictions (Kirkpatrick 1955, p. 538). Of course, extreme differences in divorce law among various countries or extreme changes within an area, for instance, in South Carolina, do correspond in some degree with divorce rates.

David and Vera Mace note a more "folksy" and less legalistic type of divorce procedure in Russia than in the United States (Mace & Mace 1963, pp. 203–226). Olson (1961) makes similar observations with regard to Japan. In view of the long and, thus far, futile campaign in the United States to achieve either a uniform divorce law in the various states or federal control by a change in the constitution, it is interesting to observe that Australia established such a uniform federal law in 1959. This may well have some effect on the pattern of Australian divorce rates.

Family counseling. Counseling and therapy offer one means of applying improved knowledge concerning family disorganization and dissolution. At times, legal reforms converge with provisions for family counseling. In Australia the Matrimonial Causes Act (mentioned above) restricts dissolution before three years of marriage and provides for marriage counseling and conciliation; it authorizes federal payment for such services to approved marriage guidance organizations (Harvey 1964). The provision for counseling in connection with the divorce procedure in Australia and Japan may give encouragement to persons in the United States who, like Judge Paul W. Alexander, plead for a therapeutic approach, abolition of adversary procedure, and family courts that provide for counseling prior to the granting of a divorce (Kirkpatrick [1955] 1963, pp. 631–632).

There is some agreement, furthered by experience with counseling and therapy, that prevention of family trouble should be sought by a focus on education and counseling at an early period in the life span. Since family dissolution results in no small measure from the coming together of the wrong combinations of people, there is an argument for premarital counseling and guidance in the process of selecting mates. Many issues, however, remain controversial. For example, the small number of trained counselors in relation to potential demand provides an incentive to sacrifice quality to quantity by approving the activity of many relatively untrained persons as counselors.

Perhaps the dilemma of quality versus quantity may be solved to some extent by group counseling and therapy instead of individual treatment. The mutual support found in such groups is impressive. Certain instruments constructed for measuring attitudinal agreement, marital adjustment, and empathy in dyadic relationships might be adapted for self-analysis on the part of individuals and couples with minimal outside aid from experts (Kirkpatrick & Hobart 1954, pp. 10–19).

International trends. The international outlook with regard to family disorganization and dissolution offers an intellectual challenge that goes beyond the parochial applications of existing knowledge. However, some promising beginnings have been made; Goode, for instance, has noted the influence of industrialization upon differential family instability among the different social classes of various countries. These classes may vary, of course, as to degree of urbanization, type of kinship system, and feministic orientation (de Visscher 1956). The most valid generalization seems to be that with the spread of Western technology there tends to be increasing similarity in the family systems of the world, including their provision for marital dissolution. The diffusion of feminism may temporarily increase family dissolution, as women demand equality in the privilege of divorce and become economically independent of both husbands and kinfolk (Sysiharju 1960).

Family systems tend to have a certain resiliency under the impact of drastic social change. The free divorce of the 1920s in communist Russia has been replaced by a conservative and restrictive procedure. Hitler attempted reactionary change of the

German family (Kirkpatrick 1938), but after the political and military crisis had passed, the general feministic and egalitarian trends characteristic of Western civilization reappeared (Schelsky 1953). As the dominance of the independent nuclear family is proclaimed, evidence appears of the survival of functional kinship systems. Carle C. Zimmerman, who expressed concern about the return of the unstable "atomistic family," found substantial evidence that "friend-families" tend to be supportive and homogeneous in regard to low incidence of divorce (Zimmerman & Cervantes 1956, pp. 91–117; see also Shanas & Streib 1965).

Improved facilities for communication are characteristic of the modern world, on the international, the national, and the familial level. Cultural interaction may increase both the similarity of familial institutions and agreement concerning human goals such as peace, freedom, and happiness—ends to which social institutions are means. If improved communication reduces repression, hollow ritual, and pretense at every level, the pursuit of happiness and freedom may lead to an increase in divorce rates or other indices of familial dissolution in conservative areas of society. Nevertheless, if dissolution be distinguished from disorganization, certain increases in dissolution may mean merely a spread of higher aspirations and a reluctance to endure familial disorganization with its associated misery.

CLIFFORD KIRKPATRICK

[*See also* MARRIAGE, *article on* FAMILY FORMATION; *and the biographies of* WALLER; WESTERMARCK.]

BIBLIOGRAPHY

ACKERMAN, CHARLES 1963 Affiliations: Structural Determinants of Differential Divorce Rates. *American Journal of Sociology* 69:13–20.

BURCHINAL, LEE G. 1964 Characteristics of Adolescents From Unbroken, Broken and Reconstituted Families. *Journal of Marriage and the Family* 26:44–51.

CAPLOW, THEODORE 1964 *Principles of Organization.* New York: Harcourt.

CARTER, HUGH 1960 Plans for Improved Statistics on Family Formation and Dissolution in the United States. *Social Forces* 39:163–169.

CARTER, HUGH; and PLATERIS, ALEXANDER 1963 Trends in Divorce and Family Disruption. U.S. Dept. of Health, Education, and Welfare, *Health, Education, and Welfare Indicators* [1963], September:5–14.

CHRISTENSEN, HAROLD T. 1963 Timing of First Pregnancy as a Factor in Divorce: A Cross-cultural Analysis. *Eugenics Quarterly* 10:119–130.

GLICK, PAUL C. 1963 Marriage Instability: Variations by Size of Place and Region. *Milbank Memorial Fund Quarterly* 41:43–55.

GOODE, WILLIAM J. 1956 *After Divorce.* Glencoe, Ill.: Free Press.

GOODE, WILLIAM J. 1963 *World Revolution and Family Patterns.* New York: Free Press.

GOODE, WILLIAM J. 1964 *The Family.* Englewood Cliffs, N.J.: Prentice-Hall.

HARPER, FOWLER V.; and SKOLNICK, JEROME H. (1952) 1962 *Problems of the Family.* Rev. ed. Indianapolis, Ind.: Bobbs-Merrill.

HARVEY, LESLIE V. 1964 Marriage Counseling and the Federal Divorce Law in Australia. *Journal of Marriage and the Family* 26:83–86.

JACOBSON, PAUL H. 1959 *American Marriage and Divorce.* New York: Holt.

KEPHART, WILLIAM M. 1961 *The Family, Society, and the Individual.* Boston: Houghton Mifflin.

KIRKPATRICK, CLIFFORD 1938 *Nazi Germany: Its Women and Family Life.* Indianapolis, Ind.: Bobbs-Merrill.

KIRKPATRICK, CLIFFORD 1939 A Methodological Analysis of Feminism in Relation to Marital Adjustment. *American Sociological Review* 4:325–334.

KIRKPATRICK, CLIFFORD 1947 *What Science Says About Happiness in Marriage.* Minneapolis, Minn.: Burgess.

KIRKPATRICK, CLIFFORD (1955) 1963 *The Family as Process and Institution.* 2d ed. New York: Ronald Press.

KIRKPATRICK, CLIFFORD 1959 Sociological Significance of This Research. Pages 289–295 in Winston Ehrmann, *Premarital Dating Behavior.* New York: Holt.

KIRKPATRICK, CLIFFORD 1965 The Family. Pages 298–305 in *Encyclopedia of Social Work.* Edited by Harry L. Lurie. New York: National Association of Social Workers.

KIRKPATRICK, CLIFFORD; and COTTON, JOHN 1951 Physical Attractiveness, Age and Marital Adjustment. *American Sociological Review* 16:81–86.

KIRKPATRICK, CLIFFORD; and HOBART, CHARLES 1954 Disagreement, Disagreement Estimate, and Nonempathetic Imputations for Intimacy Groups Varying From Favorite Date to Married. *American Sociological Review* 19:10–19.

LANDIS, JUDSON T. 1963 Social Correlates of Divorce or Non-divorce Among the Unhappily Married. *Marriage and Family Living* 25:178–180.

LICHTENBERGER, JAMES P. 1931 *Divorce: A Social Interpretation.* New York: McGraw-Hill.

LOCKE, HARVEY J. 1951 *Predicting Adjustment in Marriage: A Comparison of a Divorced and a Happily Married Group.* New York: Holt.

MACE, DAVID; and MACE, VERA 1963 *The Soviet Family.* Garden City, N.Y.: Doubleday.

MONAHAN, THOMAS P. 1959 The Duration of Marriage to Divorce: Second Marriages and Migratory Types. *Marriage and Family Living* 21:134–138.

MONAHAN, THOMAS P. 1962 When Married Couples Part: Statistical Trends and Relationships in Divorce. *American Sociological Review* 27:625–633.

MURDOCK, GEORGE P. 1950 Family Stability in Non-European Cultures. American Academy of Political and Social Science, *Annals* 272:195–201.

NYE, F. IVAN 1957 Child Adjustment in Broken and in Unhappy Unbroken Homes. *Marriage and Family Living* 19:356–361.

OLSON, LAWRENCE 1961 How the Japanese Divorce. American Universities Field Staff, *East Asia Series* 9, no. 8.

RHEINSTEIN, MAX 1960 Divorce and the Law in Germany: A Review. *American Journal of Sociology* 65:489–498.

Schelsky, Helmut (1953) 1955 *Wandlungen der deutschen Familie in der Gegenwart*. 3d ed., enl. Stuttgart (Germany): Enke.

Shanas, Ethel; and Streib, Gordon F. (editors) 1965 *Social Structure and the Family: Generational Relations*. Englewood Cliffs, N.J.: Prentice-Hall.

Sysiharju, Anna-Liisa 1960 *Equality, Home, and Work: A Socio-psychological Study on Finnish Student Women's Attitudes Towards the Woman's Role in Society*. Helsinki: Tekijä.

U.S. National Center for Health Statistics 1964 *Marriage and Divorce: A Selected Bibliography of Statistically Oriented Studies*. Washington: Government Printing Office.

Visscher, Pierre de 1956 *Attitudes antiféministes et milieux intellectuels*. Louvain (Belgium): Institut de Recherches Économiques et Sociales.

Waller, Willard W. 1930 *The Old Love and the New: Divorce and Readjustment*. New York: Liveright.

Waller, Willard W. (1938) 1951 *The Family: A Dynamic Interpretation*. Revised by Reuben Hill. New York: Dryden.

Winch, Robert F. (1952) 1963 *The Modern Family*. Rev. ed. New York: Holt.

Zimmerman, Carle C.; and Cervantes, Lucius F. 1956 *Marriage and the Family: A Text for Moderns*. Chicago: Regnery.

FAMINE

"Famine is like insanity, hard to define but glaring enough when recognized. . . . one country will define as food shortage what another country would call famine" (Taylor 1947, pp. 98, 102). In recent years, and particularly in the United States, where food surpluses have been embarrassing politically (perhaps also morally), journals have been prone to report from abroad as "famines" what subsequently appear as shortages or merely threats of shortage. Shortages are not infrequently relieved before they become famines.

True famine is shortage of total food so extreme and protracted as to result in widespread persisting hunger, notable emaciation in many of the affected population, and a considerable elevation of community death rate attributable at least in part to deaths from starvation. Criteria do not exist to measure the degree of hunger, emaciation, or elevation of death rate serving to differentiate famine from shortage. The archetypical famine extends over a wide area and affects a large population. Starvation deaths on a small scale, as among members of an isolated family, a small hamlet, a group of travelers in wild country, an icebound ship, would not commonly be characterized as famine. Acute shortage of food for a few weeks, such as preharvest hunger in some parts of the underdeveloped world, is not famine. Lack of a particular customary food, such as sugar or beef, is not famine if there is abundance of other items. Shortage of a particular vitamin or mineral in a population, evidenced perhaps by uncommonly heavy incidence of scurvy, beriberi, pellagra, rickets, or impaired vision, is not famine, although in recent decades the word has been applied to such shortages.

The members of a community beset by famine gradually become greatly emaciated and increasingly weak and listless—eventually to the point of lying in homes or along the streets and roads, utterly inactive, skeletonized, often with swollen bellies, waiting for death. In famine-stricken regions beggars are encountered in abnormal numbers. There are riots, aimless wanderings, purposeful migrations; men, women, and children comb fields, alleys, and dumps, hoping to find a scrap of edible material. Livestock owned by the poor are sold or eaten.

A house-to-house survey in north China during the famine of 1920–1921 revealed that people were eating, among other items not in their normal diets, "flour made of ground leaves, fuller's earth, flower seed, poplar buds, corncobs, . . . sawdust, . . . cotton seed, elm bark, . . . peanut hulls, sweet potato vines ground . . ." (Mallory 1926, p. 2). Kravchenko (1946, p. 113), who as an official of the government witnessed the famine of 1932–1933 in the Soviet Union, quotes a young peasant woman: "I will not tell you about the dead. . . . The half-dead, the nearly-dead are even worse. There are hundreds of people in Petrovo bloated with hunger. I don't know how many die every day. Many are so weak that they no longer come out of their houses. A wagon goes around now and then to pick up the corpses. We've eaten everything we could lay our hands on—cats, dogs, field mice, birds. When it's light tomorrow you will see the trees stripped of their bark. . . . And the horse manure has been eaten. . . . Sometimes there are whole grains in it." Upon such horrors in a famine-ridden area are superimposed an upsurge of burglary, robbery with violence, murder for gain. Cannibalism occurs but is a rare as well as secret event of which little can be known. Sorokin (1942, p. 81) holds the opinion that less than one-third of one per cent of a population in noncannibalistic societies would practice cannibalism under pressure of starvation. Disease flourishes abnormally as resistance is reduced by low food intake.

The calamity of famine falls most heavily upon the poor, unless the state is dispossessing and punishing a former aristocracy or bourgeoisie. Food prices begin to rise even before damages to crops or military or political interferences with food inflow become generally apparent. People with ample purchasing power begin to accumulate stocks of food, either for their own future use or for sale at higher prices in weeks to come. Markets are swept clear of foodstuffs. Employment shrinks, and wages, where there is employment, seem not to rise in proportion to food prices. Families with low incomes (if not dependents of the wealthy) feel the pinch of hunger first. They sell their possessions—their clothing, household furnishings, house timbers; even the means customarily used to provision themselves with food are sold. According to Woodham Smith, during the great Irish potato famine of the 1840s fishermen all over Ireland pawned or sold their gear to buy meals (1962, p. 291). During that and other famines many poor peasants have eaten the seed necessary to produce a new crop. Children have been sold in Chinese famines; and men have sold themselves into slavery. Prostitution burgeons. Buyers seem always to appear, for although famine may decimate a large population, it does not annihilate. Some members of a stricken community profit from the circumstances of famine. Some are protected by their position in, or by power of, the government.

Causes. Famine has many causes. Nearly a century ago Walford (1878–1879, p. 450) listed 12, classifying them into natural causes beyond human control and artificial causes within human control. This distinction remains valid in a general way, although it is certainly true that man has learned to modify some of the natural causes as well as to minimize their impact. Natural causes include drought, excessive rains and flood, unseasonably cold weather, typhoons and other high winds, tidal waves, depredations by vermin and such insects as locusts, and plant diseases. They tend chiefly to reduce production of food and to destroy stocks. Occasionally, though mostly for short periods, floods or frosts restrict the flow of foodstuffs from surplus to deficit areas. The artificial causes—commonly political—include warfare that involves siege or blockade, or destruction of food stocks or growing grain; and wartime strains on economies that diminish manpower, machines, or fertilizers, thus reducing cultivated acreage, yields, and production. Revolutions, particularly when they involve a struggle between peasantry and officialdom, may reduce food acreages and yields and thus contribute to famine; so may excessive taxation or collection from peasants of grain surpluses, which happened in Soviet Russia in 1932–1933. It is difficult to perceive in the vague history of famines a major one in which political causes alone were operative, although this may be said of a good many minor famines—typified in

sieges of cities. An age-old device of war is to impose famine on the enemy.

The great famines of the world have been due to natural forces, frequently intensified, however, by political factors. Sometimes economic or demographic situations—prevalence of poverty, including unemployment, peasant agriculture of the bare subsistence type, or many landless agricultural laborers in a population of high density—are regarded as causes of famines. They certainly make for vulnerability to famine, but unlike natural or political catastrophes are chronic rather than episodic in character.

The principal natural causes of major famines have been deficiency of rainfall (drought) or excess of rainfall (flood). Probably no major famines, but only localized and minor ones, have been due to excessively cold weather, high winds, or infestations of insects or vermin. Even a great swarm of locusts consuming every growing plant would rarely spread over an area more than a fraction as large as that covered by major drought or flood. Plant disease in the form of potato blight, however, did emerge on one occasion—in Ireland in 1845–1849—as the outstanding natural cause of a famine of great severity. Drought outranks flood as a major cause, except perhaps in north China, where in some summers the Yellow River may rise so high that it overflows its diked banks and renders unproductive the vast agricultural plains of its valley. Few flood famines of major proportions are recorded elsewhere, but one did occur, in the years 1315, 1316, and 1317, in the British Isles and on the Continent east and north of the Pyrenees and Alps at least through present-day Poland; mortality was high (Lucas 1930). Continuous rain greatly reduced the harvests of grain crops, and pestilence (murrain) killed many farm animals.

Famine follows upon extreme shortage, insufficiently relieved by inshipment, of the staple starchy food crop of the afflicted area. That crop is usually grain—usually wheat or rye in temperate zones; rice, a millet, or sorghum in warmer climates. Famine or general food shortage in northeastern Brazil, however, will chiefly represent deficiency of the manioc crop; in Ireland it was the potato crop. The grains and starchy roots provide the bulk of the energy-yielding food for most of the world's population. In the absence of shortage of grain crops or (rarely) of starchy roots, a major natural famine is unlikely to occur. Grain is relatively cheap per thousand calories of nutriment, readily storable, and easily transported and processed into meal or flour. It is the most serviceable foodstuff to be brought in to ward off or relieve famine.

Geographical incidence. Whether natural or artificial, famine is always regional or local, never world-wide or continent-wide—or even nationwide in such vast countries as India, China, Russia, and Brazil. Conceivably, some large areas of the world have escaped, if judgment can be based upon the two major chronicles of famine (see Walford 1878–1879; Minnesota . . . 1950). Therein no mention is made of famine in Australia, in the great islands of the East Indies, or in Africa south of the Sahara. In North America and Central America, the only listing is of a famine in Mexico in 1051 ("Famine which caused the Toltecs to migrate"), and this is perhaps not clearly authenticated. South America seems to have experienced major famine only in northeastern Brazil (the *sertão*), an area subject to recurrent severe droughts. Although the chroniclers of world famine make no mention of Japan, historians record three famines there in different regions, in 1732–1733, 1783–1787, and 1832–1836, severe enough to provoke violent riots (Sansom 1963, p. 222).

Europe west of Russia has witnessed no natural famine since the great Irish calamity of the 1840s, although artificial famines on a much smaller scale accompanied World War II, at least in Greece and in the western part of Holland. There were food shortages elsewhere both then and during and after World War I. Ancel Keys (see Minnesota . . . 1950, p. 1251) lists since 1850 one famine in Persia (1871), one in Asia Minor (1874–1875), one in Egypt (1897), one in Brazil (1877), and one or two in Morocco (1877–1878), indicating infrequent occurrence in those countries. In Russia over the same period no fewer than ten famines are noted, and in India 13, not counting the most recent one, the great Bengal famine of 1943. The number of famines in China since 1850 is uncertain, but a severe one occurred in 1877–1878; others in 1919–1920 and 1929–1930; and lesser ones in 1906, 1911, 1916, and 1924. Russia, India, and China over the past century have encompassed the outstanding famine areas of the world. Each contains regions adjacent to deserts, where rainfall is regularly low, highly variable, and of summer incidence; crops tend to fail in the exceptionally low-rainfall years. These regions also have a rather dense and impoverished agricultural population. In Russia the region most frequently drought-ridden centers in the Volga basin; in China, the valley of the Yellow River; in India, the northwest and the Deccan plateau. Each country also contains regions of abundant and dependable rainfall, where famine rarely occurs. But in all the great famines of the twentieth century natural and artificial causes worked simultaneously—drought and flood, war and revolution.

Relation to disease. Since famine stimulates human diseases, statistical differentiation between deaths from starvation and deaths from disease is practically impossible, as is close measurement of the degree to which famine elevates death (and morbidity) rates above normal levels. A dependable ranking of the famines of even the past century from most to least lethal is out of the question. Nevertheless, it can probably be said that there was mortality of a million persons or more above average at least in the Irish famine of 1845–1849; the Indian of 1877–1878, 1896–1897, 1899–1900, and 1943; the Russian of 1921–1922 and 1932–1933; and the Chinese of 1877–1878 and 1929–1930.

Famine reduces resistance to many diseases, including malaria, influenza, and tuberculosis; smallpox, cholera, typhus, or relapsing fever may plague the afflicted regions, especially if the population is crowded into unsanitary refugee camps, as on the fringes of cities. Acute deficiency diseases take a much larger toll than usual, for reduced food consumption is certain to bring intake of some of the essential vitamins and minerals below requirements. Acute and protracted diarrhea ("bloody flux"), induced by polluted water and the eating of improper materials, appears to be a lethal scourge, particularly among children. Famine not only increases death rates but also reduces birth rates, thus slowing growth of population. Advancing scientific knowledge of diseases and growth of both national and international health services in the twentieth century have greatly lessened the risk of high mortality as a result of famine.

Relation to migration. The circumstances of famine induce people to flee from it, not only to escape but also to seek work that will permit them to restore purchasing power in some form to family and friends left behind. Refugees from the countryside often flock to cities, especially centers of government. Of those who flee, many return upon the abatement of famine conditions, but others find new homes. The drought-ridden *sertão* of northeastern Brazil has witnessed both the flight and return and the permanent export of population— not abroad, but to other parts of the nation (James 1942, p. 425; Smith 1879, pp. 398–435). Scarcity-induced migration that crosses national frontiers has not been common. The conspicuous example in history is the great migration of more than a million people from Ireland during and after the famine of the 1840s, the bulk of whom came to the United States, remaining to participate in and influence that country's development. Internal migrations that may have occurred in Russia, China, and India have not been carefully recorded or studied. In general, demographers appear not to lay much stress on famine as a cause of the surging migrations of history or prehistory. The unrecorded breakup of families attributable to famine migration must have caused millions of individual catastrophes. The famine in Ireland led to the conviction in Great Britain that at all times basic food must be available as cheaply as possible to the poor, and the Corn Laws that had long held grain-prices high were repealed in 1846. Famines or shortages there and elsewhere have tended to force a lightening of the burden of taxes and rents upon peasant farmers and a wider acceptance by governments of responsibility for prevention and relief.

Remedial measures. Five centuries ago famine was regarded almost throughout the world as inevitable and was so accepted, often as a manifestation of divine wrath. Occasionally, however, there were rulers who sought to prevent or relieve it. The Biblical story of Joseph in Egypt, storing grain in "fat" years against the "lean" that might follow, exemplifies probably the most common method of famine prevention in antiquity and medieval times. The rulers of the Inca Empire guarded against famine by storage and by construction of irrigation canals. Irrigation, a safeguard against famine because it both elevates and stabilizes the acre-yields of crops, was practiced some 5,000 years ago in Sumer and is very ancient elsewhere in Asia and north Africa, but famine can hardly have been the sole stimulus for irrigation. Flood control by dikes and dams is also an ancient device which militates against famine but has other values. Destruction of stores of grain and of irrigation and flood-control works is obviously a method of creating artificial famine.

Natural famines having their origin mainly in drought or flood, sometimes in plant disease or insect pest, are not now regarded as inevitable. Within nations, a naturally induced or threatened food shortage is certain to be met by domestic efforts to ward off or relieve it. This was not true in the Soviet Union as late as 1932–1933 but occurred there in 1963–1964, following a very severe drought, when a huge quantity of grain was imported and paid for. So it was in China a year or two earlier. India and Pakistan have been able since war ended in 1945 to arrange, partly on the basis of international credits, for sporadic grain imports sufficient to preclude famine; so also have Brazil and Yugoslavia. The disposition of all governments by the 1960s was to prevent or relieve famine or shortages within their own borders; and of some governments to donate or loan funds or food surpluses to prevent or relieve famine beyond their own borders. The capacity of nations to pay or to loan or donate has increased. International cooperation in famine relief or prevention has increased in the past century, as evidenced by such organizations as the Red Cross, the China Relief commissions, the American Relief Administration of World War I, the United Nations Relief and Rehabilitation Administration following World War II, and the Food and Agriculture Organization of the United Nations. Supplies have been available despite the huge growth of world population; and with the advancement in agriculture everywhere, few localities stand in such risk of drought or pests or plant disease as prevailed even half a century ago. If, nevertheless, natural calamity strikes, the network of transport, by ship overseas, by barge on canal and river, by rail, by truck on roads, even by air, has so grown and is now so far-flung and efficient that stricken regions can be reached. Governments have learned how to ration food in short supply in a manner more equitable than was possible earlier.

Progress in coping with natural famine is thus apparent politically, economically, and socially. Until the end of the twentieth century there seems no reason why true famine of natural origin should be endured in any country, for over so short a time world population seems unlikely to outrun food supplies. What the more distant future holds is purely conjectural. But even in the shorter term, it cannot be said that artificial famine, induced by war or revolution, may not again appear.

M. K. BENNETT

[*See also* FOOD.]

BIBLIOGRAPHY

BHATIA, B. M. 1963 *Famines in India: A Study in Some Aspects of the Economic History of India, 1860–1945.* New York: Asia Publishing House.

FISHER, HAROLD H. 1927 *The Famine in Soviet Russia, 1919–1923: The Operations of the American Relief Administration.* New York: Macmillan.

GOLDER, FRANK A.; and HUTCHINSON, LINCOLN 1927 *On the Trail of the Russian Famine.* Stanford Univ. Press.

JAMES, PRESTON E. (1942) 1959 *Latin America.* 3d ed. New York: Odyssey.

JASNY, NAUM 1949 *The Socialized Agriculture of the USSR: Plans and Performance.* Stanford Univ. Press.

KNIGHT, HENRY 1954 *Food Administration in India: 1939–47.* Stanford Univ. Press.

KRAVCHENKO, VICTOR 1946 *I Chose Freedom: The Personal and Political Life of a Soviet Official.* New York: Scribner.

LOVEDAY, ALEXANDER 1914 *The History and Economics of Indian Famines.* London: Bell.

LUCAS, HENRY S. 1930 The Great European Famine of 1315, 1316, and 1317. *Speculum* 5:343–377.

MALLORY, WALTER H. 1926 *China: Land of Famine.* New York: American Geographical Society.

MINNESOTA, UNIVERSITY OF, LABORATORY OF PHYSIOLOGICAL HYGIENE 1950 *The Biology of Human Starvation.* 2 vols. Minneapolis: Univ. of Minnesota Press.

SALAMAN, REDCLIFFE 1949 *The History and Social Influence of the Potato.* Cambridge Univ. Press.

SANSOM, GEORGE B. 1963 *A History of Japan.* Volume 3: 1615–1867. Stanford Univ. Press.

SMITH, HERBERT H. 1879 *Brazil: The Amazons and the Coast.* New York: Scribner.

SOROKIN, PITIRIM A. 1942 *Man and Society in Calamity: The Effects of War, Revolution, Famine, Pestilence Upon Human Mind, Behavior, Social Organization and Cultural Life.* New York: Dutton.

TAYLOR, A. E. 1947 Famine. Unpublished manuscript, Stanford Univ., Food Research Institute.

WALFORD, CORNELIUS 1878–1879 The Famines of the World: Past and Present. *Journal of the Royal Statistical Society* 41:433–526; 42:79–265.

WOODHAM-SMITH, CECIL B. 1962 *The Great Hunger: Ireland 1845–1849.* New York: Harper. → A paperback edition was published in 1964 by New American Library.

FANON, FRANTZ

Frantz Fanon (1925–1961), political theorist, was born in Martinique. He studied medicine in France after World War II, became a psychiatrist, and served in a government hospital in Algeria. In 1956 he resigned from French government service and joined the Algerian National Liberation Front (FLN), becoming first an editor of the party's journal and then, under the Provisional Government of the Algerian Republic, an ambassador to Ghana and a special envoy to the Congo. When he died in Bethesda, Maryland, of leukemia, he had established a reputation as the leading ideologist of the Algerian revolution. Subsequently, he came to be regarded as a major theorist of anticolonialism. His last work, *The Wretched of the Earth* (1961), is the clearest extant statement of this ideology.

Fanon began as a psychiatrist. He argued that neuroses can be understood and treated only if they are related to the cultural situation that gives rise to them, what he called their "sociogenesis." For Fanon, the crucial aspect of a social structure is the extent to which it creates institutions that fulfill men's needs. He maintained that "a society which forces its members to desperate solutions is a nonviable society, which must be replaced" (*Pour la révolution africaine*, p. 61).

Fanon argued that in the eyes of most men the fundamental conflict of the contemporary world is the race conflict: Black men and white men constitute two hostile camps. He was very clear that the source of this conflict, as of all conflicts, is oppression—in this case, a racial oppression which masks the oppression of capitalism and colonialism. "It is the white man who creates the Negro. But it is the Negro who creates negritude" ([1959] 1965, p. 47). Rooted in a tradition of universalistic rationalism, Fanon nevertheless rejected the French idea and policy of assimilation which, he felt, could never transcend paternalism and which tended to justify continued oppression. He defended the wearing of the veil by Algerian women as a symbol of nationalist opposition but thought that the veil would disappear after the success of the fundamental revolution against the colonizers.

Fanon sought ways for the colonized to purge themselves of the degrading effects of colonialism. For an individual or a group, the primary symptom of the fact that it has not attained human status is that it asks—indeed, appeals—for magnanimity. Rights can only be had if they are taken by purgative acts of violence. In a situation of collective denial of rights, there must be "collective catharsis." Violence is the means to this catharsis.

Fanon believed that renewal is not easy. It requires violence, which frees the individual from the mental deformities imposed by colonialism and creates the possibility of renewal. Politicization can then follow; for to politicize is to awaken the mind to the world. Thus, self-consciousness will be the guarantee of cultural openness. The liberation of the oppressed individual from the apathy that has been encouraged in him—Fanon spoke of the "cultural mummification of colonialism"—is the only possible basis of true liberation.

Neither this individual liberation nor real decolonization can be achieved without violence. Violence is "in the atmosphere" and is constantly giving rise to spontaneous outbursts of violent protest. This spontaneity is a great source of strength, placing pressure on the inherently reluctant leadership of protest movements. But it is also dangerous, because it is neither disciplined nor farsighted. Successful revolution requires the proper balance of spontaneity and self-control.

Nationalist movements in the contemporary world have been the principal vehicle of decolonization. However, for Fanon they are an uncertain instrument because they tend to be led by the urban middle classes and because they ignore, insofar as they can, the peasantry. But only the peasantry in the underdeveloped world is really revolutionary, for only it has nothing to lose. The urban proletariat, by contrast, is a privileged group which tends to look down upon the peasants. The chief characteristic of the urban nationalist elite is that its anticolonialism goes hand in hand with its spirit of accommodation. Its propensity to compromise, combined with the peasants' often premature acceptance of concessions, constitutes the chief danger to the anticolonialist revolution.

Fanon saw the colonial powers and their agents as following a policy of making minimal concessions which are intended to undermine the unity of the oppressed classes. He analyzed the guided steps to independence in much of Asia and Africa in these terms. Under pressure, the colonial powers cede authority to each national bourgeoisie, thus effectively in most cases creating new allies. The single-party systems of the "third world"—the under-developed world—have been "dictatorships of the bourgeoisie."

The struggle for national liberation of colonial countries can, according to Fanon, be understood only in the context of the struggle of the "third world" for full equality and self-realization. Fanon drew on Hegel and Marx for his analysis of the underlying contradictions of the capitalist world. He followed Sorel and Lenin in their emphasis on the necessity of organized violence to polarize society. And he drew on a modified version of Freud's theories for his analysis of how changes in the social structure lead to shifts in the personality structure, which in turn determine the possibilities of political action.

Fanon sought to go beyond nationalism to the world revolution of the colonized against the colonizers. He considered the attainment of national sovereignty to be insufficient. Fundamental emancipation of the once-colonial peoples can come about, according to Fanon, through their participation in this world-wide revolution. He thought that a "new man" must be created and that only through the reawakened self-consciousness of the oppressed peoples can a true international consciousness be created and man's humanity be established.

IMMANUEL WALLERSTEIN

[See also COLONIALISM; IMPERIALISM. *Other relevant material may be found in* MODERNIZATION.]

BIBLIOGRAPHY

1952   *Peau noire, masques blancs.* Paris: Seuil.
(1959) 1965   *Studies in a Dying Colonialism.* New York: Monthly Review Press. → First published as *L'an V de la révolution africaine.*
(1961) 1965   *The Wretched of the Earth.* Preface by Jean-Paul Sartre. New York: Grove. → First published as *Les damnés de la terre.*
Pour la révolution africaine: Écrits politiques. Paris: Maspero, 1964.

SUPPLEMENTARY BIBLIOGRAPHY
ISAACS, HAROLD R. 1965   Portrait of a Revolutionary. *Commentary* 40, no. 1:67–71. → An insightful discussion of Fanon.

FANTASY

Fantasy, man's capacity to "give to airy nothing a local habitation and a name," has long intrigued poets, playwrights, and painters but has only during the twentieth century become a formal area of scientific inquiry in psychology. In current usage the term is almost synonymous with "daydream." Within the area of experimental or clinical study, however, the term "fantasy" has a broader significance since it deals not only with imaginary activity spontaneously produced as part of the ongoing stream of thought (daydreams) but also with products of thought elicited upon demand from a clinician or in response to inkblots or ambiguous pictures. In effect, whether as a privately occurring daydream or as a publicly elicited story or imaginative response, fantasy generally seems to involve a complex associative activity in which events from the past are integrated into some more or less elaborate ongoing image. This image, usually visual but often auditory or verbal, is generally an inner "event" in which a new situation, possibility, personal role, or sequence of behavior is formulated either on a "mental screen" or as a story told to an examiner. Deriving from the Greek *phantasia* and still often spelled in Greek style as "phantasy," fantasy refers to man's remarkable ability to create an "as if" world either spontaneously or upon demand. It is possible that at one time such a capacity was not so widely developed, and people were more prone to regard their own fleeting imagery or brief daydreams as actual visions, omens, or appearances of deities, much as they responded to nocturnal dreams. Prophetic visions, such Ezekiel's "wheel" or John's Apocalypse, probably represent literary expressions of elaborate daydreams or fantasies used for expository or hortatory purposes.

History

Within psychology the formal study of fantasy as a behavioral phenomenon is probably traceable to Francis Galton's classic studies of individual differences in imagery. Although imagery itself as a field of inquiry has a somewhat separate history, the fact that much fantasy behavior involves some form of imagery led Galton to touch on issues involving the differences between persons in their internal private constructions. By 1890 William James in his great work, *The Principles of Psychology*, devoted portions of several chapters, including the famous one on the "stream of thought," to issues closely related to fantasy processes. James was among the first great psychologists to sense a continuity between normal phenomena characteristic of the ongoing self-stimulating properties of the living brain and the bizarre delusions or hallucinations of the insane or the inspirational visions of religious mystics. James also called attention to what he termed the reproductive and memorial facets of imagery, or the degree to which the image is of an object recently perceived or one called forth from the distant past. The fantasy presumably may represent a response to a stimulus perceived momentarily which triggers off a complex associative process in the ongoing stream of thought. The taste of the *madeleine* crumb produced in Proust a vivid memory of his childhood in Combray, a strong memorial association, whereas the sound of the song of the nightingale touched off a more "fanciful" association in Keats, the song that

> oft-times hath
> Charm'd magic casements, opening on the foam
> Of perilous seas, in faery lands forlorn.

> "Ode to a Nightingale," stanza 7, ll. 8–10

Psychoanalytic contributions. Although the nineteenth and early twentieth centuries were times of considerable research and controversy within psychology with respect to imagery and the possible existence of "imageless" thought, little attention was paid to the daydream itself as a spontaneously produced image complex. Interest in fantasy processes and dreams was limited at that period (and particularly following the emergence of Watsonian behaviorism in America) to the clinical psychiatrist and especially to the psychoanalyst. Freud's elucidation of the structure and interpretative possibilities of the phenomena of nocturnal dreaming, based largely on remarkable self-observation and intensive clinical work, also led quite naturally to explorations of other dreamlike phenomena, such as daydreams. When Freud realized that patients' accounts of infantile seductions (which he believed to be the foundation of neurotic developments) could not possibly have occurred, he was compelled to pay more attention to the nature of childhood fantasy as the source of such material. The free-association process of psychoanalysis itself also led to frequent reports of fantasies or daydreams, the most important, from a technical

psychotherapeutic sense, being those involving the relationship between analyst and patient. Many psychoanalysts, therefore, paid careful attention to daydreams of patients and began in some instances to experiment with eliciting fantasies when patients were resistant to or incapable of recalling night dreams. Freud himself during the early part of the twentieth century speculated on the psychological significance of the daydream in his papers "The Relation of the Poet to Day-dreaming" (1908) and "Formulations on the Two Principles of Mental Functioning" (1911).

Throughout the early decades of the twentieth century psychoanalysts made regular use of reports of spontaneous fantasies and published many papers in which myths or popular stories and literature were interpreted as forms of fantasy.

Projective methods. Some attempts were made to study children's fantasies through stories elicited from them or through their drawings, but the most influential advances in the psychological study of fantasy came from the development of so-called projective techniques.

Rorschach technique. The first and most famous of the projective methods was the Rorschach Inkblot Technique, developed by Hermann Rorschach, a Swiss psychiatrist. Of particular interest to him was his finding that persons who reported numerous "human movement" responses to the inkblots, such as "two footmen bowing, two ladies dancing," were characterized on the one hand by considerable motor inhibition or awkward motility and on the other by a heightened capacity for "inner living," imagination, or fantasy production. In contrast, persons who produced numerous color-dominated responses were more likely to be outgoing, motorically affective, and emotionally labile. The juxtaposition of the human-movement and color responses provided an indication of what Rorschach called the "experience type," the relative degree to which capacity for fantasy behavior and inner living were balanced with tendencies toward emotionality and direct action.

Rorschach's method, somewhat modified, spread slowly through Europe and was introduced into the United States in the late 1920s and early 1930s by David Levy and Samuel Beck. In the United States by the time of World War II it had been adopted by clinical psychologists, who saw the method as a means of exploring the private fantasy world of patients without direct questioning and of eliciting behavioral data that could be quantified, thus meeting to some extent the objections of academic psychology to the purely qualitative approach of clinical psychoanalysis and psychiatry. With the introduction of more formal academic courses within the universities and private seminars on Rorschach technique, a great deal of systematic research was generated to check specific features of the technique or to compare cultures, psychopathological groups, or dimensions of individual difference through the use of the elicited fantasy response to the inkblots. A summary of much of the work in this field and of the methodological and theoretical issues involved in the use of the Rorschach method is available in *Rorschach Psychology*, edited by Rickers-Ovsiankina (1960) [*see* PROJECTIVE METHODS, *article on* THE RORSCHACH TEST].

Thematic Apperception Test.   Beginning in the early 1930s at Harvard University's Psychological Clinic, a group of psychologists under the leadership of Henry A. Murray undertook extensive studies of various techniques using elicited fantasies to study the nature of the normal personality. A specific technique that emerged was Murray's Thematic Apperception Test, a method for eliciting imaginative stories in response to somewhat ambiguous pictures, for example, of a boy staring at a violin set before him on a table. The stories elicited by each of a series of 20 pictures were then analyzed in terms of the motivational pattern presumably involved in the story content, in effect an application of psychoanalytic interpretative methods, perhaps more systematic, quantifiable, and suitable for rigorous research requirements. With various modifications in scoring categories and picture content, the basic method is in widespread use today for clinical, industrial, and research purposes. Such scoring of motivational patterns from elicited fantasy products has been especially instrumental in the careful study by David McClelland, John Atkinson, and their numerous students of achievement motivation through fantasy. Because of the relatively objective scoring techniques available and high reliability of trained judges scoring for such motives as *achievement* and *affiliation*, the Thematic Apperception Test or related methods for scoring story material as a fantasy expression of a need or motive are perhaps more widely used in systematic research than the more diffuse Rorschach method. [*For relevant summaries of literature, see* Atkinson 1958; *see also* ACHIEVEMENT MOTIVATION; PROJECTIVE METHODS, *article on* THE THEMATIC APPERCEPTION TEST.]

Other projective methods.   Within clinical practice and, to a lesser extent, in formal research, a large variety of fantasy-eliciting techniques are used. These include various drawing procedures or such studies of artistic activity as finger painting,

eliciting responses to incomplete sentences or to requests like "Name your three wishes," choices of various symbolic objects, organization of mosaic patterns, and puppet play. All make some general assumptions that a long-standing personality predisposition or style, as well as a motive pattern or aspects of bizarre thought and pathology, will be manifested by such elicited quasi-fantasy expressions. The proliferation in the use of these projective techniques has not, however, been the fruit of sufficient systematic prior experimentation with any one technique as a rule, nor have any really significant contributions to systematic psychological theory resulted from their widespread application. Individual clinical psychologists may be especially gifted at eliciting material using a particular technique with which they have much experience, but such personalized effectiveness does not usually add to the general body of psychological knowledge.

Experimental approaches.   More recently, as a result of particular theoretical developments within psychoanalytic theory and progress in research in psychology and neurophysiology, greater attention has been paid to experimental efforts to study the nature of ongoing imagery or fantasy and daydream experience. New techniques—some involving electrophysiological measurement or systematic inquiry of subjects during sensory isolation, under the influence of special drugs, or during monitoring or vigilance tasks—have led to some increased sophistication and rigor in the study of the "stream of thought" in the normal adult. Recent developments in this area are summarized in Holt (1964) and Singer (1966).

Current theories and relevant research

Surprisingly little as yet is known of the range and variation of fantasy in normal adults and children or of differences in the content, frequency, or structure of daydreams among various cultural groups (Singer 1966). There has emerged, however, chiefly from psychoanalysis, a preliminary theoretical formulation of the function of daydreaming in the economy of the personality. Research reflects efforts to examine and test the implications of the theory of fantasy, which derives chiefly from the specific formulations of Freud.

Defensive or cathartic models.   One of Freud's more fascinating insights was his observation that the capacity to delay gratification, a vitally significant step in man's adaptive development, was somehow linked to his imaginative capacity. Two general conceptions of the relation between thought or fantasy and control mechanisms can be discerned in Freud's work and in that of most psychoanalytically oriented investigators or learning theorists who have developed the implications of the notion of the relations of thought and delay. One conception stems from Freud's early paper on the poet and daydreaming (1908), in which he stated that "unsatisfied wishes are the driving power behind fantasies" and pointed out the degree of similarity between daydreams and night dreams in their wish-fulfilling function. The daydreams that the poet transforms into artistic productions are disguised representations of unfulfilled infantile desires, defenses against direct recognition of these desires. As Freud put it: "Happy people never daydream."

This view that the daydream is an outgrowth of an unsatisfied wish and is a defense against its direct manifestation pervades much psychoanalytic thinking. Closely related to the defensive function of fantasy but perhaps more precise in formulation is Freud's second conception that all processes of thought, including fantasy, by allowing partial satisfactions (expenditure of small quantities of energy), partially reduce the drive and thereby permits delay in gross motor discharge. This theory of the catharsis or drive reduction obtained through play and fantasy in children or daydreams in adults has many important implications (see Rapaport 1956).

In effect, it proposes that where there is a delay in the opportunity to discharge a certain amount of energy through satisfaction of a need or through movements associated with attaining such satisfaction, the fantasied reproduction "in the mind's eye" of the gratifying activity or associated movements will partially reduce the amount of energy at least enough, say, so that rash or fruitless action will not occur. From a psychoanalytic standpoint (where the emphasis is on the inner origin of stimulation) such partial discharges may effectively control maladaptive overt discharge of many antisocial or asocial tendencies. Thus, regular watching of wrestling or boxing on television may curb man's tendency to assault his neighbor upon minimal provocation, and the conscious acceptance of daydreams of sexual conquest may effectively prevent rape, whereas inability to experience such thoughts may lead to overt impulse-gratifying behavior that has unfortunate consequences.

Within academic psychology the learning-theory formulation of the catharsis model does not specify the amount of instinctual energy but does emphasize that fantasied behavior has, in effect, secondary-reinforcing qualities that may lead to a lowering of drive strength consequent to engaging in a daydream about the goal object. It is assumed that if a child is hungry he begins to make motor reactions associated with searching for food. To the extent that he can, at an ideational level, reproduce an image of the movements that would gratify his hunger or of his mother coming in with the food, and if just about that time his mother does indeed come in, then the ideational representation acquires secondary-reinforcing properties. Provided his mother comes regularly but perhaps not invariably (intermittent reinforcement being superior in preventing extinction), the fantasy activity will be learned as one means of response in a state of need.

A number of interesting lines of research have been developed in attempts to test the cathartic theory of fantasy and some of the implications of this drive-reduction model. The theory also has some important implications for the logic of projective testing where, for example, one faces the interpretative task of deciding whether the person who provides a certain frequent response pattern to inkblots or photographs is likely to show the same or opposite pattern in overt behavior. In the case of the Rorschach, for example, there is evidence for an inverse relationship between perception of movement on the blots and overt movement, impulsivity, and other ego functions (Rickers-Ovsiankina 1960). Most of the evidence supports Rorschach's notion that human-movement responses are linked with controlled motility, on the one hand, and imaginative development on the other. An experiment by Page (1957) has provided an important link in this chain by demonstrating that only this human-movement response of all Rorschach factors is significantly associated with reported frequency of daydreaming.

Criticism of the cathartic model. When the focus in the projective method is not on the *structural* aspect of fantasy and motor behavior but on the relation of specific content to projective fantasy, a different finding emerges. The controversy between the alternative channel and direct expression theories of Thematic Apperception Test interpretation seems to be resolved by the large majority of studies in favor of direct expression. The literature on fantasied aggression as summarized by Buss (1961) and the extensive work by McClelland (1961) and Atkinson (1958) has certainly supported the idea that persons who produce aggressive or achievement-oriented themes behave accordingly in daily life.

An important step in the effort to test the drive-reduction model of fantasy came in Feshbach's study (1955) in which it was demonstrated that when insulted Ss were given an opportunity to express aggression through storytelling they showed less aggression in subsequent ratings than did a group given no opportunity for fantasied aggressive expression. Feshbach also found that viewing a filmed prize fight after induction of anger would partially reduce later aggressive ratings. It should be noted, however, that the very writing of the stories is perhaps a more motorically involved expression than pure daydreaming, the daily life phenomenon associated with drive reduction.

Where experimental efforts have focused attention not upon experimentally aroused anger but upon the arousal of stress, anxiety, or fear, the cathartic significance of daydream or fantasy activity is less in evidence or unsupported (Singer 1966). These results suggest that when we turn to stress rather than anger as the drive or affect involved, the effects of daydreaming are more complex; engaging in fantasy may enhance anxiety when the future situation is unstructured but may reduce it when a short-term stress is imminent by distracting the person from continued thought.

Particularly telling evidence against a catharsis theory has come in the works of Berkowitz (1964) and Bandura, Ross, and Ross (1963). These studies, concentrating on aggressive expression, seem to offer a body blow to the cathartic theory and to point up the importance of considering the pattern of environmental stimulation more thoroughly in understanding the meaning of fantasy play in relation to direct motor expression. Berkowitz, for example, found that Ss who viewed a movie scene in which a prize fighter was taking a "justifiable" beating showed a heightened tendency to aggressive behavior toward a fellow student soon after the show, compared with Ss who had been told the beating was undeserved [see AGGRESSION, *article on* PSYCHOLOGICAL ASPECTS]. The studies by Bandura, Ross, and Ross of modeling behavior indicate, too, that young children aroused to anger by frustration are likely to imitate directly the aggressive behavior of a previously witnessed live or filmed model [see IMITATION].

The evidence for a catharsis theory of fantasy seems weak, at best, in view of recent research and a restudying of the problem. The data, of course, are chiefly from the study of aggressive behavior, and in general there has been little concern either with naturalistic daydreaming behavior and its consequences (as against filmed or thematically stimulated responses) or with affects other than anger and aggressive behavior.

Fantasy as a cognitive skill. An alternative approach may be proposed that at least conceptually reconciles the Rorschach data on movement perception and motor inhibition and the results of the direct expression or modeling theories of fantasy aggression. Heinz Hartmann, while developing his concept of the autonomous ego, noted that fantasy may serve to prepare the person for a greater mastery of the outside world through increased insight into his own psychic processes. It seems preferable to go further than Hartmann and begin again with a fresh look at the origin of fantasy and imagery without the burden of concepts of cathectic dynamics or neutralized versus libidinized energy. One may start, instead, by regarding the development of fantasy behavior or daydreaming as a cognitive skill, a capacity for gradual internalization of response and for attending to the ongoing "reverberatory" behavior of one's brain— responses available to most children. Conceivably, children may differ constitutionally in their capacity to form visual or auditory images, but these differences for the most part account for only a small amount of the variance in subsequent development of daydreaming skills or styles. Special handicaps do exist, and it has been found that congenitally blind children are less imaginative in their spontaneous play and storytelling than otherwise matched sighted children (Singer 1966).

Fantasy play is thus an important feature in the development of children, a part of the continuous assimilation–accommodation pattern, as Piaget put it (1945). There are, however, certain particular factors that increase the likelihood that fantasy play will become an integrated skill, rather than a sporadic response pattern, and, thus, a capacity to manipulate or to attend to an inner dimension, which may be one of man's greatest assets. Similarly, if we recognize more clearly the potential of man's inner skills, we may make possible a further advance in man's fullest use of his capacities.

Factors in development of fantasy. What, then, are some circumstances conducive to fantasy development?

Identification and imitation. The modeling theory suggests that imitation of parents is probably an important element in fantasy development. The child who perceives his parents as benign persons will strive for identification more readily and learn more of their behaviors, and there is some evidence that persons showing more imagination on the Rorschach (human-movement responses) also report that their parents were benign and loving (Singer 1960). Identification with a specific adult figure, usually the mother, who represents inhibition of impulse, socialization, and storytelling, may be an important feature in fostering internalization. Several studies on daydreaming have yielded evidence of more frequent daydreaming by male and female adults who were more closely identified with their mother than with their father or who perceived their father as further from their ideal (Singer 1966). A similar finding was reported by Sharef (1959) in a doctoral dissertation at Harvard: he noted that young men who had a history of being chosen as a mother's confidant showed greater imaginative or introceptive tendencies. Some degree of modeling and imitation caused in part by eagerness to please, by the availability of copying of certain types of responses, and by the parent's rewarding these responses may foster fantasy skill. A well-known quotation from Goethe serves to make this point:

> From father I have looks and build
> And the serious conduct of living.
> My mother gave me gaiety
> And zest for fantasizing.
>
> *Xenions*

Opportunity for play. Given the closeness to at least one adult who encourages verbal interchange or fantasy play, a child still requires some opportunity to practice such activities. There are indications that extensive contact with other children is likely to provide less opportunity for such fantasy play unless the children are older and play a quasi-parental role, for example, a much older sister who plays "house" or "school" with a younger child. By and large, the extensive kaleidoscopic ebb and flow of physical motion and varied external stimulation provided by a group of children is most likely to involve a child in external behaviors and afford him little chance to practice fantasy play. A study carried out with children aged six to nine (Singer 1966) produced evidence that indicated that children reporting more fantasy play had significantly fewer older siblings, that is, they tended to be either first-born or only children and not members of large families.

One might argue that daydreaming thus becomes a defense against loneliness. At the same time many children who take great pleasure in elaborate fantasy games and who are eager to share these with others are frustrated by the disorganization of the other children and return to solitary play or, if they have some influence on the group, develop a more organized fantasy game, for example, pirates or detectives. Chance factors of being alone, of being encouraged to read, of story-telling or fantasy making as part of the family tradition as well as cultural aspects that strongly emphasize imaginative exchange or intellectual exploration, achievement motivation, upward mobility in society—all increase the likelihood of extensive involvement in fantasy play by a given child (Singer 1966). In effect, the child who plays extensively by creating fantasy people, situations, imaginary worlds, or scientific make-believe is practicing a complex series of skills related to what Kurt Goldstein has called the "attitude toward the possible." These children have a more complex vocabulary, develop structural and organizational skills, see relationships that others may have to be taught in school, and, perhaps most important, carve out for themselves a dimension of experience—attentiveness to their own associational flow—which may be a realm they can enter or leave at will. This dimension can, of course, become the basis of an extensive defensive maneuver should the outside world become too stressful or should the child fail to develop positive social skills with his peers. The development of an extensive inner life by no means excludes the possibility of enjoyment and skill in social experience, group games, or sports. It merely provides an additional medium for play and satisfaction. There is as yet no evidence that psychotic patients show any excessive predisposition toward daydreaming. Indeed, chronic patients are often characterized more by an impoverishment of inner living and daydreaming than by the excessive involvement in "private worlds" so often attributed to them [see DEFENSE MECHANISMS].

Adaptive aspects of fantasy. It is obvious that enhanced vocabulary and abstract skills represent great evolutionary advances in man. But let us also consider the adaptive manifestations of the more "fantastic" aspects of thought, daydreams, and reverie. The Rorschach findings about the inverse relationship between imagination and motor impulsivity are better explained not by a relatively mechanical catharsis theory but by viewing the person who has imagination as having a whole set of alternative responses in addition to motor activity. In a waiting room he need not be so restless (as was found in several studies) if he can provide himself with an inner source of stimulation to engage his interest and provide positive affective experience. He may voluntarily set up an inner sequence (imagining a movie, replaying a base-ball game) or he may permit the ongoing stream of consciousness, the reverberatory activity of his brain, to hold his attention. In situations of reduced sensory cues, this capacity may be an asset, as was found in studies of sensory deprivation (Holt 1964). Similarly, it was found (Singer 1966, p. 108) that persons required to monitor a blinking light in a dark room with all external cues reduced were more likely to remain awake and comfortable if at the same time they could engage in free associative talk. When these same persons were limited to monotonous counting, they tended to fall asleep and became quite irritable. There is also evidence that persons who have a history of daydreaming, that is, for whom attention to inner experience is a well-established pattern, are less susceptible to hallucination.

The person who has developed a considerable ability to picture events or scenes concerning people through reading and imaginative play has available a tool for greatly increasing his own response repertory. The ability to imagine a variety of social responses or scenes concerning people may enhance a person's ability to deal with novel or difficult social demands. Obviously, practice in actual situations is also necessary, but it is possible that such learning will come more quickly to a person who has engaged in some preparatory fantasy. The fact that fantasy originates in play brings it closer to humor and wit and makes it possible for the person who employs fantasy when anxious or in conflict to see a humorous, bizarre, or unusual facet to his dilemma and to obtain at least some temporary positive affective experience or to alleviate the stress through a comical fantasy. The development of an inner cognitive style of differentiated attentiveness to ongoing thoughts, memories, or marginal associations, or of an ability to manipulate such material at will, thus can be seen as an important feature of the over-all ego strength of the personality, a skill, much as is motor ability, empathic capacity, or precision in communication [see HUMOR].

Recent research developments

In addition to the research centering on theoretical issues, other areas of significant ongoing experimental work in the field of fantasy may be cited briefly. The extensive work of McClelland interpreting the fantasy content of stories in third-grade readers as evidence of achievement motivation has been particularly fruitful. McClelland's work has shown, for example, that indications of the degee of achievement motivation expressed in the fantasy products of various countries around the world are highly related to the *actual* economic development of the country over a period of years (McClelland 1961). These striking results suggest either that the inclusion of such achievement-oriented materials in the stories used in teaching young children stimulates them to become more achievement oriented or, what is more likely, that an already ongoing national achievement-oriented pattern is then consciously or unconsciously reflected in the thematic materials provided children. Most of the work of Atkinson and McClelland has emphasized the nature of motivation rather than the study of the fantasy process for its own sake. McClelland, however, has attempted a formulation of the relationship between degree of deprivation and the occurrence of a fantasy expression of the deprived need.

The greater awareness that during periods of reduced sensory stimulation man becomes increasingly responsive to internally produced stimulation, as well as the methodological advances in the study of night dreaming by electroencephalographic patterns and oculoretinograms, have encouraged studies of man's waking pattern of ongoing thought. A series of investigations has suggested, for example, that adult Ss who are engaging in daydreaming show relatively little eye movement but that ocular motility increases when attempts at suppression of ongoing thought occur (Singer 1966). Similarly, experimental studies of the relative degree of external stimulation necessary to prevent subjects from actually engaging in passing fantasies also suggest that a remarkable degree of ongoing thought activity occurs, at least for college adults, despite great demands on attention from the outside (Singer 1966). It seems likely that man's relative willingness or ability to attend to what appears to be an almost continuous ongoing stream of internal reverberatory associative activity may be a significant dimension for personality study [see DREAMS].

As yet, however, relatively little is known of the physiological basis of this stream of thought or of the factors that lead to relative priorities in attention to such internal processes. We also know little in a systematic way of individual differences in daydreaming and the personality correlates of such differences, although some studies have opened the way for further work in these areas. Formal data on whether there are differences between cultural or national groups in frequency, content, and structure of daydreaming or resort to inner living are scant indeed. Singer and McCraven (Singer 1966, pp. 57–63) did find some evidence that American-born subcultural groups (Negro, Jewish, Italian, Irish, German, and Anglo-Saxon) did differ in reported daydream frequency, with the more upwardly mobile groups (or less socially secure ones) showing more fantasy activity. An earlier comparison of American-born Irish and Italian schizophrenic adults by Singer and Opler also yielded evidence of differences in degree of fantasy activity between persons of differing cultural background (Singer 1966, pp. 64–65).

JEROME L. SINGER

[*Directly related are the entries* CREATIVITY; STIMULATION DRIVES. *Other relevant material may be found in* AESTHETICS; FINE ARTS; LITERATURE; PSYCHOANALYSIS.]

BIBLIOGRAPHY

ATKINSON, JOHN W. (editor) 1958 *Motives in Fantasy, Action, and Society.* Princeton, N.J.: Van Nostrand.

BANDURA, ALBERT; ROSS, DOROTHEA; and ROSS, SHEILA A. 1963 Vicarious Reinforcement and Imitative Learning. *Journal of Abnormal and Social Psychology* 67: 601–607.

BERKOWITZ, LEONARD 1964 The Effects of Observing Violence. *Scientific American* 210:35–41.

BUSS, ARNOLD H. 1961 *The Psychology of Aggression.* New York: Wiley.

FESHBACH, SEYMOUR (1955) 1958 The Drive-reducing Function of Fantasy Behavior. Pages 160–175 in John W. Atkinson (editor), *Motives in Fantasy, Action, and Society.* Princeton, N.J.: Van Nostrand.

FREUD, SIGMUND (1908) 1925 The Relation of the Poet to Day-dreaming. Volume 4, pages 173–183 in Sigmund Freud, *Collected Papers.* London: Hogarth. → First published as "Der Dichter und das Phantasieren."

FREUD, SIGMUND (1911) 1959 Formulations on the Two Principles of Mental Functioning. Volume 12, pages 215–226 in Sigmund Freud, *The Standard Edition of the Complete Psychological Works.* London: Hogarth. → First published as *Formulierungen über die zwei Prinzipien des psychischen Geschehens.*

HOLT, ROBERT R. 1964 Imagery: The Return of the Ostracized. *American Psychologist* 19:254–264.

McCLELLAND, DAVID C. 1961 *The Achieving Society.* Princeton, N.J.: Van Nostrand.

McKELLAR, PETER 1957 *Imagination and Thinking: A Psychological Analysis.* London: Cohen & West.

PAGE, HORACE A. 1957 Studies in Fantasy: Daydreaming Frequency and Rorschach Scoring Categories. *Journal of Consulting Psychology* 21:111–114.

PIAGET, JEAN (1945) 1951 *Play, Dreams, and Imitation in Childhood.* New York: Norton; London: Heinemann. → First published in French as *La formation du symbole chez l'enfant.* A paperback edition was published in 1962 by Norton.

RAPAPORT, DAVID (editor and translator) 1956 *Organization and Pathology of Thought: Selected Sources.* Austen Riggs Foundation, Monograph No. 1. New York: Columbia Univ. Press.

RICKERS-OVSIANKINA, MARIA C. (editor) 1960 *Rorschach Psychology.* New York: Wiley.

SHAREF, M. R. 1959 An Approach to the Theory and Measurement of Introception. Ph.D. dissertation, Harvard Univ.

SINGER, JEROME L. 1960 The Experience Type: Some Behavioral Correlates and Theoretical Implications. Pages 223–259 in Maria C. Rickers-Ovsiankina (editor), *Rorschach Psychology.* New York: Wiley.

SINGER, JEROME L. 1966 *Daydreaming: An Introduction to the Experimental Study of Inner Experience.* New York: Random House.

FARMING

See AGRICULTURE; LAND; LAND TENURE; PLANTATIONS; RURAL SOCIETY.

FASCISM

"Fascism" is used primarily to identify the political system by which Italy was ruled from 1922 to 1945. It is also used to identify a prototype of totalitarianism and is applied to variations of political systems thought to parallel the Italian one.

Historical development

Historically, fascism has its origins in the crisis of Italian parliamentary institutions. This crisis was caused in large part by a failure in the process of adjustment of the traditional parliamentary parties to new mass parties. It occurred at a moment of intensified difficulties caused by World War I, as deep economic and social upheavals were complicated by an upsurge of nationalism and the aftermath of the Bolshevik Revolution of 1917. Thus, the combination of the weakness of the liberal ruling class, the revolutionary aspirations of the working classes, the extremism of patriotism, the dissatisfaction with the 1919 peace settlements, the psychological dislocation of war veterans, the fears of property-owning classes, and the political role played by the army and the crown produced, four years after the armistice of 1918, the episode known as the March on Rome and the beginnings of a 23-year dictatorship of the Fascist party under the leadership of Mussolini.

As fascism sought, not without difficulty but with final success, to organize itself for the seizure of power, the clash of different ideological trends and the contradictions that were to mark its entire life stood out clearly. In the beginning, fascism showed a strong socialist inspiration. Many of the leaders had come to fascism from socialist and syndicalist movements, but they had differentiated themselves from orthodox socialists by maintaining an aggressive nationalistic attitude that had caused them to favor Italy's intervention in World War I, to be against what they described as the "unjust" peace settlements, and to support the political adventure of D'Annunzio's seizure of Fiume. Mussolini backed the occupation of the factories by the workers as part of a revolutionary program intended to give to the industrial working classes the political role they did not have. But, by playing on the themes of national grandeur and power, he was also enlisting the support of nationalistic activists, who thought in terms of territorial expansion and colonialism.

By the end of 1920, however, nationalism rather than socialism was providing the main driving force of fascism. The government of the time, headed by the liberal leader Giovanni Giolitti, rightly thought that a specific revolutionary danger did not exist and that prudent handling of the situation would lead, as it did, to a peaceful resolution of that particular conflict. But Italy's middle classes, the landowners, the business world, the army, and the crown saw in fascism the militant movement that, properly led, could make Italy safe from the Marxist peril. In 1921/1922 the original, and small, fascist movement was swamped by hundreds of thousands of new members, most of them of middle-class provenance, while it received subsidies from industrial quarters and weapons from the military establishment.

Fascism reoriented itself along fresh lines, with policies that stressed, above all, the need to restore the authority of the state at home and abroad. The state was conceived as the defender of law and order and as the unyielding supporter of the national interest in foreign affairs. The younger party members were organized into blackshirted squads that proceeded to destroy the physical structure and to liquidate the leadership of socialism and communism, which by then had become the chief targets.

When, after the 1919 elections, Giolitti failed to reach agreement with either the Socialists or the Christian Democrats, he imagined that fascism would see Italy through the political impasse by taming these two mass parties and that in the end liberalism would return to power. Liberal Italy greeted October 28, 1922, the day of the fascist seizure of power, as the beginning of an interlude that would stabilize political life, restore the authority of the state, and prepare the return to tradition shortly afterward.

The second period in the history of fascism goes from 1922 to 1925. In the course of these three years the fascist regime sought to answer a number of questions about its own direction and purpose. After the bloody violence of the preceding two years, these years appeared mild enough on the surface, and some of the liberal leaders even thought that their forecasts would be realized. Laissez-faire was the prevailing economic policy. Parties and the press seemed to function almost normally. The word "totalitarian" had not yet been invented.

But the inherent logic of the system was already at work. First, the blackshirted army had not been dissolved, and the dualism typical of a totalitarian state was born, with two sets of institutions—one answerable to the government, the other to the Fascist party. Second, the use of violence accepted as normal since 1922 could not be given up. Force was still the foundation of the regime. One after the other, the voices of the opposition were stilled. The climax was the murder of Matteotti, the Socialist party leader. For the old ruling class, this proved to be the final test of its sense of responsibility and its understanding of the nature of the modern political process. In the summer of 1924 the crown might still have succeeded in obtaining Mussolini's resignation. The advice it received was that no change should be attempted. The Vatican joined in this appraisal when it drove Luigi Sturzo, the leader of the Christian democratic movement, into exile.

In 1925, exploiting this extraordinary vote of confidence, fascism built the totalitarian structure. The press was silenced or taken over. All parties were abolished except the Fascist party. Constitutional changes were begun that created the unique figure of the leader embodying in his person the sum total of power.

The next ten years, from 1925 to 1935, represented a period of both practical consolidation and theoretical doctrinal development. With power safely in his hands, Mussolini began to consider the problem of the place of fascism in history. Fascism had been criticized as being a naked, pragmatic movement. It was necessary to acquire ideas and to develop an overview on the nature of man and of nations that could promise the recognition of fascism as one of the important revolutionary movements of the twentieth century.

The enemies were identified with great precision. Marxism still was the foremost opponent. But liberalism became another enemy to be fought. Showing little regard for those who had put him in office, Mussolini began to cultivate the ideas that led by 1927 to the labor charter, by 1930/1931 to the beginnings of the corporate state, and by 1934 to the establishment of the corporations themselves.

Some of these economic ideas did provide a certain amount of lively discussion at the time among those whose aim was primarily to find some third way between Marxism and liberalism. The key notions were that (*a*) the community alone was to have the right to determine what the national interest required; (*b*) therefore, the conflicting interests of owners, workers, technicians, and the state were to be brought together in a single unit, the corporation, operating under public control; (c) strikes and lockouts were to be forbidden; and (d) the doctrine of the primacy of the politician over the expert was to be abandoned. The divisiveness of politics was to be eliminated by the unity of expertise.

The world-wide depression that had hit the Western world after 1929 facilitated Mussolini's task. By 1931 the industrial and banking systems of Italy were in serious trouble. The totalitarian regime made possible a quick salvage operation, which placed the key industrial and financial sectors of the country under direct government ownership or control. By 1935 fascism had realized, at least on paper, the goals of a state-controlled society. In its repression of the individual and of social groups, fascism was steadily strengthening and centralizing its power, which was exercised in the name of an ideology that had become a key operational tool in the hands of the new elite.

In its third period, 1935 to 1943, violence and war became the substance of fascism. The first important manifestation of this totalitarian characteristic took place in 1935 with the aggression against Ethiopia, which provided the regime with a testing ground for its military policies, challenged the League of Nations, and furnished German Nazism with evidence of the might of fascist Italy. The second act was played on the battlefields of Spain, where both Nazism and fascism joined hands against republican Spain. Historically, this armed clash was of great significance, for it gave the enemies of Mussolini some idea of their strength and of guerrilla-warfare techniques. The third act was played in 1940, when Mussolini entered World War II on the side of Hitler after the defeat of France. Italy's defeat came soon, and by 1943 the fascist regime collapsed, as it had begun, through an intervention of the crown.

From 1943 to 1945 the Fascist Social Republic came feebly and fleetingly to life under the control of the Germans. The only point worthy of note is that Mussolini, on the eve of the final collapse and of his own death, tried in a clumsy way to go back to his syndicalist origins and appear as a defender of the proletariat. Industrial plants were now to be turned over to the workers themselves. But it was 1945 and too late.

The fascist regime—ideal and reality

As a movement based on a pragmatic appraisal of the conditions necessary to retain power, fascism was never too preoccupied with the task of a theoretical definition of its own origins and goals. The philosopher Giovanni Gentile sought to link it to Hegelian idealism, the jurist Alfredo Rocco attempted to develop a heavy-handed theory of the state, while Mussolini himself sought to provide the ideology of totalitarianism.

Instruments of power. But the real drive of fascism was in the building of instruments of power and not in the building of theory. Between 1925 and 1939, four main tools of power were developed and refined: charismatic leadership, single-party rule, terror, and economic controls.

Leadership. Around the leader, Benito Mussolini, a series of institutional privileges were built, intended to make his position unchallenged. Constitutionally, he was chief of state and, as such, was placed in a position that was not subordinate to that of the king. Although the monarchy was kept, the Great Council of Fascism had been given certain rights on questions affecting the succession to the throne which placed the monarchy in a dependent position. Politically, the constant rotation in office of Mussolini's subordinates kept competitors out of the way. Psychologically, the unique position of the leader was carefully maintained by all the devices of communication and propaganda typical of totalitarian states. The identification of fascism with Mussolini was made compulsory in meetings of parliamentary assemblies, of the Fascist party, of economic bodies, of schoolchildren, of every form of group life.

Party rule. The party became a capillary instrument of power going from its highest body, the Great Council of Fascism, which met from time to time to decide major questions of policy, through the secretary of the party and the provincial federations to the thousands of party units, which at the communal level were the daily instruments of propaganda and contact with the country. The party reached out in all directions with its subsidiary organizations, affecting the activities of schoolchildren and the cultural and sport activities of the people. The party became the carrier of the ideology and slogans of the leader, and, more important, the channel through which most of the life of the country had to flow. Jobs, advancement, and preferment had to be cleared in most instances through the party. Membership in the party was, at first, a right belonging to the small elite group that in the pre-1922 days had supported the party's fight for power; in a second phase which lasted into the early 1930s, membership was made available to all who applied; in a third and final phase, one could become a member only by moving up through the youth organizations that by then had been created. Thus, membership in the Fascist party was reserved at first to the fighters, later to the opportunists, and finally to the perfect citizens of a fascist state nurtured on the ideals of fascism from their most tender age.

Terror.   Although between 1925 and 1943 the party was the chief vehicle for the consolidation of the regime, it was no longer the chief instrument of terror, as it had been between 1920 and 1925. "Legalized" repressive functions were carried out by the Special Tribunal for the Safety of the State and by the secret police under the Ministry of the Interior. But from 1943 to 1945, the years of renewed bloody civil war between fascist militias and the resistance groups, the party again undertook the task of meting out summary justice to the increasingly rebellious population and was guilty of massacres that exceeded in scope anything that had been witnessed between 1920 and 1925.

Economic controls.   As the pseudo liberalism of the initial years gave way to controls on economic life equaling those on political life, fascism developed two principal instruments of policy. The first was the Institute for Industrial Reconstruction (IRI), which, started in 1931 as an antidepression device, was soon changed into an agency to pursue the military goals that after 1935 became the heart of the dictatorship. Controlling all major financial institutions and nearly all heavy industry through the IRI, the regime transformed it into an ever-expanding industrial complex on which fascist war production plans were based. The second was the corporation, which imposed central controls over all forms of economic activity, including all remaining so-called private activities. Before becoming a "political" tool in 1939, with the establishment of the Chamber of Corporations, the corporation had helped the government control both labor unions and employers' associations by bringing them all under the rule of a central bureaucracy. The corporations were the best example of a basic tenet of fascist doctrine: the supremacy of the expert over the politician. They were the evidence of the triumph of economics over politics, as parliamentary institutions, made up of representatives of the general interests of the community, were superseded by experts talking the language of economics and technology, given to the hard-headed discussion of facts and not to the empty rhetoric of parliamentarism.

Fascism in operation.   All told, this structure represented something new. As Mussolini said, "A party holding 'totalitarian' rule over a nation, is a new departure in history. There are no points of reference nor of comparison" ([1932] 1935, p. 36). Later analysts were to agree in large part with this statement and to say that totalitarianism did, indeed, represent a twentieth-century departure in the political evolution of mankind. In addition, the essence of totalitarianism was to be found in a combination of leadership, an ideologically inspired mass party, and violence, and in so total a claim by the ruling group over the lives of the individuals that no separateness, no autonomous legal system, and no group life could survive.

The totalitarian pattern of fascism, however, falls short of this model, in part because Mussolini gave too much weight to the state: "For Fascism the State is absolute, individuals and groups relative. Individuals and groups are admissible insofar as they [cannot attack the state]. . . . The Fascist state . . . has a will of its own. For this reason it can be described as 'ethical' " ([1932] 1935, pp. 37–38). And in article 1 of the labor charter of 1927 the Italian nation was described as an "organism having ends, a life and means superior in power and duration to the single individuals or groups of individuals composing it" (National Fascist Party [1927] 1935, p. 53). These were Hegelian influences that reflected the early role of the idealism of Gentile, whose presence could not be fully reconciled with the nihilism of authentic totalitarianism.

The party itself was one additional field in which fascist totalitarianism did not ring true. The party efforts to maintain ideological coherence, discipline, and a sense of mission were thwarted by the Italian belief in relativism, the spirit of compromise, and the refusal to take ideology seriously. The history of other totalitarian parties has shown that the party purge is of the essence in a totalitarian system. A domesticated totalitarian party, not wracked by fear, not cowed by the brooding image of the leader, but rather reduced to a mere vehicle for the securing of jobs, is no longer a revolutionary movement. The events from 1943 to 1945 showed that the behavior of blackshirted killer squads, the trial and execution of a few high-placed fascist leaders, including Mussolini's own son-in-law, were evidence only of the extremes of panic to which the surviving fascists were driven under the twin pressures of partisans' attacks and of German controls. The ease with which the country shed its fascist trimmings showed that in 25 years an effective hard core of fascist militants had not developed.

Hence, terror on a large scale and for preventive or repressive purposes never quite materialized. Fascism suffers by comparison with the apocalyptic liquidations for which Hitler and Stalin will be known to history. Instead of millions, Mussolini had on his conscience only a few tens of thousands of dead, excluding casualties due to direct military action during World War II. The will was lacking. Mussolini's cynical boasting was nearly always accompanied by a most lively sense of his inadequacy. The assured appearance of the leader on the public square was not matched by equal confidence in his private political activities. He had been a member of a democratic socialist party for too long to forget entirely the habit of doubt and skepticism. Hidden admiration for certain traditional forms of Italian culture stopped him from exercising his powers to the fullest extent. His ignorance made him avoid direct confrontation with established forms of conducting public business, which could therefore continue as before.

Mussolini's most persistent feeling probably was that of the crisis of the modern capitalistic order. He kept asking certain questions over and over again, without necessarily providing the answers. In 1932 he had asked, "Is this crisis, which has held us in its grip for the past four years . . . a crisis 'within' the system or 'of' the system?" (1935, p. 10). He felt he could not give an answer then, but in November 1933 he was to say, "Today my answer is: the crisis has sunk so deep into the system that it has become a crisis 'of' the system. . . . We can now assert that the capitalistic mode of production has been superseded" (pp. 10–11). Why is this so? Because by its very size capitalism has turned "into a social phenomenon, and it is precisely at this moment that capitalistic enterprise . . . falls like a dead weight into the arms of the State" (p. 16).

This is a purely Marxian analysis of the problem (the dominant socialized characteristics of a highly developed capitalistic system, the sudden crisis) up to the point at which the heir of capitalism is not the armed proletariat sitting on the ruins of the institutions of the bourgeois state, but is the "ethical state itself."

Mussolini tried hard, with the labor charter and the laws on the corporations, to give some unity to the new system. He made large theoretical claims for the corporations, which were to unite workers, owners, experts, the state, and the party and to which powers had been given extending from wage fixing to the regulation of production, the settlement of disputes, the drafting of collective labor contracts, and the prevention of strikes and lockouts.

But in his vaguely socialist dream, he was limited, on the one hand, by his recognition of private property as necessary to the fulfillment of the human personality and, on the other, by the overwhelming bureaucratic complexities of the all-or-

nothing paper structure of the corporate state, and this made it necessary for him to appoint to the governing boards of the corporations representatives not only of wine but also of vinegar producers, not only of umbrella but also of button manufacturers. The resistance of the property owners who had put Mussolini in power was subtle and stubborn. They saw, in the immense Roman bureaucracy and in a party where the stout of heart and the believers were few, the chance to use the state capitalism of fascism in the same way in which public systems in other countries have been used by anxious capitalists in trouble, that is, as a prop to keep them going until better times.

The easy way out for everybody was military adventure. Again, the final flare-up of the Social Republic in the spring of 1945 is evidence of the decay of a system on the eve of its liquidation. Until then, the vast structure of the production system had been used only to prepare for war and to enable the regime to find overseas the outlets not found at home.

Interpretations

As a phenomenon that, having spread from Italy to other countries, affected the course of history between the two world wars, fascism has been subjected to a 40-year effort at interpretation. The variety of analyses has been correspondingly great, with sharp contrasts among the points of view depending on the time, the interests, and the approaches of those dealing with it.

The fascists themselves, those with a more speculative frame of mind and able to write with some detachment after the event, have tended to see in fascism one phase of the world-wide shifting of the political discourse from multiparty to one-party systems and of the transfer of power from the legislative to the executive, in which violence was discipline and military aggression was reaction to foreign hostility. They still believe that some of the trends and programs foreshadowed by the fascist era should be developed in the future as part of the needs of modern government. Fascism without ideology, war, and concentration camps could find expression in a depoliticized society that would turn its back on the rhetoric of the nineteenth century, but not on deeply felt national sentiments, and seek its way under the guidance of stable and efficient leadership.

The parties in power at the end of World War I, when the crisis began, saw the fascist movement in a different light. To them it was the unavoidable reaction of the "healthier" political forces in the country to the process of disintegration of the community and the constitutional system, caused by forces largely identified with Marxism. Marxism, in its twin embodiment of socialism and communism, loomed as a many-sided assault on the traditional institutions. The infrastructure agencies (cooperatives, peasants' leagues, trade unions) moved against the state with excessive economic claims and with a systematic onslaught on the processes of production. The authority of the state itself was being weakened by a series of strikes that affected vital public services. Fascism was a reaction of certain social groups, primarily the middle classes and the well-educated urban youth, intended to restore law and order.

But the undermining of the liberal constitutional order was not carried out at this level alone, for at the national political level Marxist parties were acting in alliance with another large and new political formation, the Christian Democratic party. Marxism and Christian democracy as mass parties joined hands here in their attempt to deprive the parliament and cabinet of their traditional roles by imposing rigid programs, which, the liberals thought, were not in keeping with the discussion and compromise typical of a constitutional democracy. Party bosses, who were constitutional "outsiders," sought to dominate political life. Fascism was to restore the constitutional system through the destruction of mass parties, those intruders which, since 1919, had upset the apple cart. Hence, a dual purpose was attached to fascism: the immediate restoration of normalcy against communist subversion and the long-range return to parliamentary government freed from the obnoxious influence of mass party rule. In brief, fascism was an interlude at the end of which the forward march of liberalism could be resumed.

This view did not survive the events of 1924/ 1925, when the institutions of totalitarianism were set up and a fuller view of fascism stood revealed. The realization by the liberals of the illiberal realities of single-party dictatorship took place by stages between 1923 and 1925. By then, from Giolitti to Croce, Italian liberalism presented a united antifascist front. But what stood out most clearly was the liberals' singular attachment to certain constitutional values that ruled out modern variations, chiefly the constitutional transfer of power to mass democratic parties. Liberal elitism was in the end confronted and defeated by brutal and stronger varieties of fascist elitism. The critics of the liberals' position have pointed out that this was a historical mistake of which they were the first victims.

Many of the spokesmen for the new mass parties, from Sturzo to Tasca, have pointed out that it was the refusal of the old ruling class to come to terms with the new elite emerging from the mass upheavals of postwar Italy that was at the root of the triumph of fascism. Socialists and Christian Democrats, far from seeing in themselves the agents for the destruction of the state, saw in their programs the only hope for a democratic renovation of Italian life and institutions. Their view was that the liberals were the accomplices of fascism in an attempt to stop the normal democratic evolution of a society in rapid transformation.

The Marxists follow orthodox lines. Fascism was the defender of capitalistic society, threatened by the steady widening of the power of the Russian Revolution and of the influence of Marxism in Italy. Fascism was a repressive movement developing along the lines Marx had anticipated for the final phase of bourgeois society.

This understanding of fascism as a class phenomenon, deprived of mystery and uncertainty, simplified the task of the Marxist opposition, which, after 1925, was to be essentially communist opposition. The socialists were no longer an effectively organized force, whereas other Marxist groups, aware of the evolution of Stalinism, had moved toward the center with reformulation of a modern liberal–socialist faith. Through their firm rejection of fascism, the communists were to derive great political benefits after 1945, for they could then identify themselves with one clear alternative in which they claimed to have believed all along. However, the communist interpretation of fascism did run into some difficulties. At the beginning the difficulty lay in the fact that the clear-cut class lines which would have had to be present as capitalism engaged in a supreme attempt at survival were not there at all. Fascism drew mass support from lower middle classes, intellectuals, peasants, and workers. Ten years later the noncapitalistic inclinations of fascism had become apparent, at least in theory, even though the fledgling corporate state was submerged by the requirements of fascist military policy. At this stage, however, the communists could point to war as the logical outcome of a capitalistically inspired tyranny. But at the end the lines were confused once more as fascism tried to revert to one of its ideological roots, socialism. These difficulties, however, did not substantially weaken the appeal of the communist interpretation, because its key element was the condemnation of the bourgeoisie, which it made responsible for fascism. And to this analysis many non-Marxists found it possible to accede. Moreover, the Marxist interpretation had the advantage of appearing to deal seriously with the phenomenon of fascism. Whatever it was, it was not to be taken lightly. It was a phase in the development of certain contemporary societies.

Such views stand a better chance of withstanding the test of history than predominantly literary interpretations, widely accepted at times, of fascism as a bad dream, as an inexplicable and certainly short-lived aberration that would fade away with a return to rational behavior. This caustically ironic attitude was justified perhaps by the frequency with which fascism appeared clothed in grotesque garments or supported policies that, because they were unacceptable on the basis of tradition, could not be sustained. But it suffered from an incomplete analysis of the crisis of Italian society and from a belief that Italian history since 1870 had shown nothing but favorable progress along the lines of modern democracy and that the anarchy prevailing deep in the hearts of so many Italians had been conquered by a growing sense of community.

Related to the bad-dream school was the historical one of fascism as a periodic phenomenon of Italian history. Mussolini was linked to the long series of tyrants, large and small, adventurers, and Machiavellian princes, who for many centuries had dotted the Italian landscape. Italy was the victim of one more manifestation of an endemic disease. A lack of discrimination, a tendency to vague generalizations, and a belief in cyclical recurrence afflicted an account that later could not explain the unprecedented catastrophic events marking the end of fascism and the difficulties that have continued to beset Italy since 1945.

Evaluation

No adequate review of the fascist era, from the point of view of the social scientist, has been undertaken since 1945. The literature has tended to be reminiscent, episodic, and introspective. At best we have detailed narratives of short critical periods in the history of fascism. Slowly, however, general reflections and lines of agreement appear to emerge and suggest some preliminary conclusions.

The first concerns the weakness of Italy's prefascist ruling class, a class whose credit ledger in the years from 1848 to 1922 was certainly not a mean one. But between 1912 and 1922 that class had been guilty of a series of decisions taken outside the liberal constitutional system and against the interests of the country. The Libyan war was a surrender to nationalistic and colonial interests. The parliamentary manipulations of the spring of 1915 had brought the country into World War I under unfavorable conditions and against the inclinations of the country at large. The acceptance of the dismal rhetoric of D'Annunzio as the official ideology of a country at war released the worst aspect of the sentimental patriotism and aggressive nationalism that formed such a large part of the post-1919 crisis. The failure of the machinery of the state and of the administration to maintain order and, worse still, the arming by the government of the Black Shirts were the final evidence of the liquidation of a ruling class that no longer ruled, had no views of what it should do, and was ready to step aside in the hope of recovering the past sometime in the future.

The second is the recognition of the depth of a phenomenon that today is playing a decisive role in the transformation and behavior of social groups, that of anomie. World War I had imposed an altogether excessive and cruel effort upon Italy. The idiocy of generals who sent hundreds of thousands of young men to a useless death, the social upheavals caused by war industries and profiteering, the opening up, under the strains of conflict, of regions that for centuries had been cut off from communication not only with the rest of the world but almost with their neighbors, and the lack of any recognition after 1918 of the seriousness of the problems which peacetime Italy would confront caused an unendurable strain on the weak texture of Italian society. This created large and vague expectations on the part of millions of unemployed and uprooted peasants, war veterans, frontline heroes, and dissatisfied students. Liberal Italy was not prepared to meet them or even to recognize them.

Under such anomic conditions, the appeal of mass movements—Marxism, Christian democracy, fascism—was bound to be great. That of Marxism was notable, even though the Socialist party dated back to the late nineteenth century. Although the theoretical weaknesses of the old warrior had been exposed, its half-hearted revolutionary enthusiasm could not be concealed. The mass appeal of Christian democracy was based on yet untested slogans and on new men, and it quickly gathered strength. But Italian liberalism had lumped Christian democracy together with Marxism. Both were forms of the revolt of upstart political elites against the majesty of the liberal state. The last of the three, fascism made its appearance as something new, promising shelter, food, stability, jobs, and a vigorous political system to those who were looking for such assurances. It had the advantage over Marxism and Christian democracy of being helped by the ruling class and by the weapons placed at its disposal.

Fascism can thus be seen as a mass movement to which an anomic society turned in a period of crisis for reassurance and the promise of satisfaction of essential community needs. But the promise was not kept. Behind the seemingly innovative façade, economic and social stagnation prevailed. Perhaps the most typical fascist law was the one that attempted to stop internal migrations. By freezing population movements, by keeping the peasant on the land, fascism strengthened the anarchism of individuals and acted directly contrary to the needs of the country, preventing the modernization of its ancient, quasi-feudal structures.

Thus, fascism did not resolve the anomic state of Italian society that had made its rise possible in the first place. The process of integration and modernization could start in earnest only after 1945. Among all the industrialized countries of western Europe, Italy is still the one most substantially removed from the conditions of a modern state. This, in part, is the result of the long frost of fascism.

At the same time, however, fascism functioned as if it had understood the new conditions of economic life. Bits of the largely unused machinery and ideas of the corporate state have been retained in post-1945 Italy in such fields as collective bargaining, where national and compulsory uniformities are now imposed. Labor agreements binding even on those who have not participated in their negotiation and massive state intervention in the settlement of labor disputes are part of the practice of republican Italy. Equally significant has been the resurfacing of fascist corporativism, the acceptance of its features in Gaullist France. The controlling factor everywhere is found in the deep malaise of European capitalism, which in its support of monopoly practices, sharp dealings with public authority, secrecy of managerial decisions, and drive for sheltered markets has deepened many of the accepted defects and realized few of the expected promises of the industrial revolution.

MARIO EINAUDI

[*See also* CAUDILLISMO; DICTATORSHIP; FALANGISM; NATIONAL SOCIALISM; SOCIALISM.]

BIBLIOGRAPHY

ALATRI, PAOLO 1956 *Le origini del fascismo.* Rome: Editori Riuniti.

DEAKIN, FREDERICK W. 1962 *The Brutal Friendship: Mussolini, Hitler and the Fall of Italian Fascism.* New York: Harper; London: Weidenfeld & Nicolson.

DELZELL, CHARLES F. 1961 *Mussolini's Enemies: The Italian Anti-Fascist Resistance.* Princeton Univ. Press.

DORSO, GUIDO 1949 *Mussolini alla conquista del potere.* Edited by C. Muscetta. Turin: Einaudi.

FELICE, RENZO DE 1965— *Mussolini.* Volume 1: Il rivoluzionario, 1883–1920. Turin: Einaudi.

FINER, HERMAN (1935) 1964 *Mussolini's Italy.* Hamden, Conn.: Shoe String Press.

GAROSCI, ALDO 1943 *La vita di Carlo Rosselli.* 2 vols. Rome: Edizioni "U."

GOBETTI, PIERO 1960 *Scritti politici.* Edited by Paolo Spriano. Turin: Einaudi.

GRAMSCI, ANTONIO 1947 *Opere.* Vol. 1— Turin: Einaudi. → Eleven volumes published up to 1966.

MEGARO, GAUDENS 1938 *Mussolini in the Making.* Boston: Houghton Mifflin.

MUSSOLINI, BENITO (1932) 1935 *The Doctrine of Fascism.* Florence: Vallecchi. → First published in the *Enciclopedia italiana.* Reprinted in 1942 in Michael Oakeshott (editor), *The Social and Economic Doctrines of Contemporary Europe,* published by Macmillan.

MUSSOLINI, BENITO 1935 *Four Speeches on the Corporate State.* Rome: "Laboremus."

NATIONAL FASCIST PARTY, GRAND COUNCIL OF FASCISM (1927) 1935 The Labour Charter. Pages 51–62 in Benito Mussolini, *Four Speeches on the Corporate State.* Rome: "Laboremus."

ROCCO, ALFREDO 1926 *The Political Doctrine of Fascism.* New York and Worcester, Mass.: Carnegie Endowment for International Peace.

ROSSELLI, CARLO (1930) 1945 *Socialismo liberale.* Rome: Edizioni "U."

SALVATORELLI, LUIGI; and MIRA, GIOVANNI (1956) 1962 *Storia d'Italia nel periodo fascista.* 4th ed. Turin: Einaudi.

SALVEMINI, GAETANO 1936 *Under the Axe of Fascism.* New York: Viking; London: Gollancz.

SALVEMINI, GAETANO 1961 *Scritti sul fascismo.* Edited by Roberto Vivarelli. Milan: Feltrinelli.

STURZO, LUIGI (1919–1926) 1956–1957 *Il Partito Popolare Italiano.* 3 vols. Bologna: Zanichelli.

STURZO, LUIGI (1926) 1927 *Italy and Fascismo.* New York: Harcourt; London: Faber & Gwyer. → First published in Italian.

[TASCA, ANGELO] 1938 *The Rise of Italian Fascism, 1918–1922,* by Angelo Rossi [pseud.]. London: Methuen. → First published in French in 1938. Translated into Italian in 1950 as *Nascita e avvento del fascismo.*

VALERI, NINO (1956) 1958 *Da Giolitti a Mussolini: Momenti della crisi del liberalismo.* 4th ed. Florence: Parenti.

FASHION

Fads and fashion are related yet fundamentally different social phenomena. Fashion is the more important of the two. Its general nature is suggested by the contrasting terms "in fashion" and "outmoded." These terms signify a continuing pattern of change in which certain social forms enjoy temporary acceptance and respectability only to be replaced by others more abreast of the times. This parade of social forms sets fashion apart from custom, which is to be seen as established and fixed. The social approbation with which fashion is invested does not come from any demonstration of utility or superior merit; instead, it is a response to the direction of sensitivities and taste.

Although conspicuous in the area of dress, fashion operates in a wide assortment of fields. Among them are painting, music, drama, architecture, household decoration, entertainment, literature, medical practice, business management, political doctrines, philosophy, psychological and social science, and even such redoubtable areas as the physical sciences and mathematics. Any area of social life that is caught in continuing change is open to the intrusion of fashion. In contrast, fashion is scarcely to be found in settled societies, such as primitive tribes, peasant societies, or caste societies, which cling to what is established and has been sanctioned through long usage.

The picture of fashion as a distinctive social process in which collective judgment of what is proper and correct shifts in response to the direction of sensitivity and taste sets three major questions: What is the nature of the situation in which the fashion process operates? What is responsible for its operation? What societal role or function does the fashion process perform?

Areas of fashion.   Areas amenable to fashion are those that have been pulled into an orbit of continuing social change. The structuring of social life in such areas tilts away from reliance on established social forms and toward a receptiveness to novel ones that reflect new concerns and interests; thus, these areas are open to the recurrent presentation of prospective models of new social forms that differ from each other and from prevailing social forms. These models compete for adoption, and opportunity must exist for effective choice among them. Most significant in this selective process are prestigeful personages who through their advocacy of a model give social endorsement or legitimacy to it. Means and resources must be available for the adoption of the favored models.

Explanations of fashion

Most theoretical analysis of fashion centers on the major question of what is responsible for the operation of fashion. We may dismiss trivial answers such as that fashion is a crazelike outburst of collective disturbance or that it is a hoax perpetrated by venal-minded sets of persons seeking financial or personal gain. The more serious analyses fall into two categories. One type seeks to account for fashion in terms of psychological motives, the other in terms of societal or structured processes.

Psychological theories.   Psychological explanations generally treat fashion as an expression of feelings of revolt against the confinement of prevailing social forms. Scholars identify different feelings. Some regard as most important the effort to escape from ennui, or boredom, especially in the leisure class. Some ascribe fashion to playful and whimsical impulses to embroider the routines of life. Some attribute major weight to the excitement that comes from venturing into novel forms of conduct. Others regard fashion as a symbolic expression of hidden sexual interests. Particularly important is the view, most clearly expressed by Edward Sapir (1931), that fashion is an effort to add to the attractiveness of the self, especially under conditions which impair the integrity of the ego; fashion is seen as a means of rediscovering the self through novel yet socially sanctioned departures from prevailing social forms. Finally, some scholars trace fashion to desires for personal prestige or notoriety.

These various psychological explanations are deficient in that they do not explain how or why the various feelings give rise to a fashion process. Such feelings are present and operate in societies and areas of life in which fashion does not occur. We are given no account of why the feelings should lead to the formation of fashion rather than taking other channels of expression available to them. Instead of accounting for fashion, the feelings presuppose its existence as a medium for their play.

Simmel's view of fashion.   Most sociological explanations center on the idea that fashion is basically an emulation of prestige groups. Georg Simmel (1904) has given the most sophisticated presentation of this view. He contends that in an open-class society the elite class seeks to set itself apart visibly by distinctive insignia, such as dress and modes of living. Members of subjacent classes seeking higher status adopt these insignia. It is then necessary for the elite class to introduce new differentiating insignia, which in turn leads to a new wave of emulation. Simmel's scheme characterizes fashion as a recurring process. It provides an explanation of how new fashions are introduced and acquire sanction, an account of their spread, and an explanation of their disappearance. It also supplies an explanation for the absence of fashion from folk and caste societies and from certain areas in modern society, such as the area of utility and that of the sacred, in which status considerations are irrelevant.

However, this scheme fails to see fashion as a process that transcends and embraces the elite. The elite, although in the vanguard of fashion, is itself required to follow fashion's direction. Its prestige does not assure that anything it introduces will become the fashion; instead, its introductions must coincide with the direction of what is acceptable. People adopt a new model to be "in fashion" rather than to emulate prestige groups. Any concern of the elite to set itself apart as a distinctive status group takes place within the ongoing process of fashion; such concern does not account for the process or set it in motion.

Processes of social change

Fashion should be seen as a process of reaching out for new congenial social forms in an area that is a part of a continually changing world. The movement of that world introduces new horizons, germinates new inclinations and interests, and shifts orientation away from the past to the proximate future. The fashion process meets this kind of developing world through two major stages—innovation and selection. In the *innovative stage* new models or proposals—such as new dress designs, styles of furniture, themes in entertainment, approaches in philosophy, or theoretical schemes in science—are presented. Such models are geared to the current state of their respective fields; each seeks to sketch out a prospective line of movement. The models appear as rival claimants for adoption and thus initiate a *selective process*, which results in a new fashion. Prestigeful individuals and groups occupy a key role in the selection; they make the initial choices, and they give a stamp of endorsement to the model they embrace. To influence others, however, they must be qualified to give an endorsement. Further, the model they endorse must be found congenial to current trends in order to gain general dissemination. The history of fashion shows dramatic instances of the failure of a model to become fashionable despite an effective marshaling of prestige groups on its behalf, for example, the failure of the highly organized effort to check the trend toward shorter skirts in 1922–1923. Fashion leaders are the unwitting surrogates of the larger body of people sharing in the movement of fashion. The vague tastes and proclivities aroused in such people by their moving world are the ultimate source and shaper of fashion.

Historical continuity. The underlying connection between fashion and emerging taste helps to explain two important features of fashion: its historical continuity and its modernity. The history of fashion shows that new fashions are related to and grow out of their immediate predecessors. The typical picture is that of fashion trends—a feature that enables us to identify fashion periods and to speak of fashion cycles. Changing tastes and proclivities, while moving toward something new, must also take into account what is currently defined as proper and correct. Correspondingly, in devising their new models, fashion innovators always have to consider the prevailing fashion. Although the intrinsic nature of the object of fashion may set a limit to a trend (as in the case of the lengthening or shortening of the skirt), and although a trend may reach a point of exhausting its possibilities, a reversal or abrupt redirection of fashion necessarily has temporal linkage with the preceding fashion form.

Modernity. The feature of modernity in fashion is particularly significant. Fashion is always modern; it always seeks to keep abreast of the times. Fashion is sensitive to the movement of current developments not only in its given field but also in adjacent fields and, indeed, to general movements in the larger social world. Thus, fashion in women's dress is responsive to its own trend, to developments in fabrics, ornamentation, and in the fine arts, to exciting events such as the discovery of the tomb of Tutankhamen, to political happenings, and to major social shifts such as the emancipation of women or the rise of the "cult of youth." In an indirect and attenuated way, fashion in every field responds to the general or over-all direction of modernity itself. This responsiveness seems to be the chief factor in the formation of a "spirit of the times" or *Zeitgeist*.

Social functions of fashion

The remaining major question—what is the social role or function of fashion—has not received satisfactory consideration. The conventional answers are that fashion allows for the harmless play of fancy and caprice, for a mild and legitimate escape from the tyranny of custom, for socially sanctioned adventure into an area of novelty, for the display and parading of the ego, for a cloaked expression of sexual interests, for the invidious demarcation of elite classes, and for an external and spurious identification by lower status people with a higher status group.

Control functions. Fashions at different points in their careers may serve varied purposes; yet, the function of the fashion process cannot be reduced to such purposes. The functions of fashion derive, instead, from the fact that it introduces controlling social forms into a moving area of divergent possibilities. As such, it performs three significant functions. First, it introduces uniformity by selecting from many models one which is to carry the stamp of propriety and thus compel adherence. If all proposed models were to be followed, social life in a given fashion area would become chaotic. In this respect, fashion performs in a moving society the control function that custom performs in a settled society.

Second, fashion provides for an orderly march from the immediate past to the proximate future. By presenting new models and subjecting them to the process of competition and collective selection, the fashion process offers a continuous means of adjusting to a changing and shifting world. The fashion mechanism detaches social forms from the grip of the past, as suggested by the derogatory connotation of such expressions as "old-fashioned" and "out of date"; yet, in growing out of the preceding mode fashion maintains continuity of development.

Third, the fashion process nurtures and shapes a common sensitivity and taste, as is suggested by the congeniality and naturalness of current fashion in contrast to the oddness and incongruity of past fashions. This common sensitivity and taste is analogous on the subjective side to a "universe of discourse." Like the latter, it provides a basis for a common approach to the world and for handling and digesting the experiences the world yields. The value of a pliable and re-forming body of common taste to meet a shifting and developing world is apparent.

Collective taste

The term "taste," which is central in the above discussion, deserves clarification. It represents an organic sensitivity to objects of social experience, as when we say, for example, that "vulgar comedy does not suit our taste" or that "they have a taste for orderly procedure." Taste has a trifold character: it is like an appetite in seeking positive satisfaction; it operates as a sensitive selector, giving a basis for acceptance or rejection; and it is a formative agent, guiding the development of lines of action and shaping objects to meet its demands. Thus, it appears as a subjective mechanism, giving orientation to individuals, structuring activity, and molding the world of experience.

Tastes are themselves a product of experience; they usually develop from an initial state of vagueness to a state of refinement and stability, but once formed they may decay and disintegrate. They are formed in the context of social interaction, responding to the definitions and affirmations given by others. People thrown into areas of common interaction and having similar runs of experience develop common tastes.

The fashion process involves both a formation and an expression of collective taste in the given area of fashion. The taste is initially a loose fusion of vague inclinations and dissatisfactions that are aroused by new experiences in the field of fashion and in the larger surrounding world. In this initial state, collective taste is amorphous, inarticulate, and awaiting specific direction. Through models and proposals, fashion innovators sketch possible lines along which the incipient taste may gain objective expression and take definite form. Collective taste is an active force in the ensuing process of selection, setting limits and providing guidance; yet, at the same time it undergoes refinement and organization through its attachment to, and embodiment in, specific social forms. The origin, formation, and career of collective taste constitute the huge problematic area in the study of fashion. Major advancement in our knowledge of the fashion mechanism depends on the charting of this area.

Fads

Fads, like fashion, may occur in widely different areas of group life, such as games, recreation, entertainment, dietary practice, health and medical practice, dress, ornamentation, language, and popular beliefs. Although superficially fads seem to be similar to fashion, they actually constitute a separate genre of collective behavior. The most noticeable difference is that fads have no line of historical continuity; each springs up independent of a predecessor and gives rise to no successor. This separate, detached, and free-floating character signifies that fads, unlike fashion, are not part of a regulating social process that gives shape and structure to group life. The derogatory connotation of the term "faddish" points to the alien and questionable status of fads. We may note other significant differences. Fads do not require endorsement by a qualified prestige group in order to gain acceptance; they may spread from any section of hierarchized society. Fads are ephemeral, leaving no residue except in the occasional remnants of a detached cult. Fads follow the pattern of a craze or boom, thriving on spectacular and excitatory appearance, suddenly riveting attention and inducing a quasi-impulsive adoption, only to exhaust their attractiveness and undergo a rapid demise.

Fads, unlike fashion, may occur in any type of society, traditional or modern. Their universality suggests that they have a natural root in human existence. But we know little about the generic conditions that bring them into being. Most of the psychological explanations advanced to explain fashion seem far more appropriate as explanations of fads.

HERBERT G. BLUMER

[See also COLLECTIVE BEHAVIOR; STYLE.]

BIBLIOGRAPHY

BARBER, BERNARD; and LOBEL, LYLE S. 1952 Fashion in Women's Clothes and the American Social System. *Social Forces* 31:124–131.

BELL, QUENTIN 1947 *On Human Finery.* London: Hogarth.

BERGLER, EDMUND 1953 *Fashion and the Unconscious.* New York: Brunner.

CLERGET, PIERRE 1914 The Economic and Social Role of Fashion. Pages 755–765 in Smithsonian Institution, *Annual Report: 1913.* Washington: The Institution.

FISHBEIN, MORRIS 1932 *Fads and Quackery in Healing.* New York: Covici.

FLÜGEL, JOHN C. (1930) 1950 *The Psychology of Clothes.* London: Hogarth.

GREGORY, PAUL M. 1947 An Economic Interpretation of Women's Fashions. *Southern Economic Journal* 14: 148–162.

HURLOCK, ELIZABETH B. 1929a Motivation in Fashion. *Archives of Psychology* 17, no. 111.

HURLOCK, ELIZABETH B. 1929b *The Psychology of Dress: An Analysis of Fashion and Its Motive.* New York: Ronald Press.

JACK, NANCY K.; and SCHIFFER, BETTY 1948 The Limits of Fashion Control. *American Sociological Review* 13: 730–738.

KELLETT, ERNEST E. 1931 *Fashion in Literature: A Study of Changing Taste.* London: Routledge.

KROEBER, ALFRED L. 1919 On the Principle of Order in Civilization as Exemplified by Changes of Fashion. *American Anthropologist* New Series 21:235–263.

LANG, KURT; and LANG, GLADYS 1961 *Collective Dynamics.* New York: Crowell. → See especially Chapter 15 on "Fashion: Identification and Differentiation in the Mass Society."

MEYERSOHN, ROLF; and KATZ, ELIHU 1957 Notes on a Natural History of Fads. *American Journal of Sociology* 62:594–601.

MOROWITZ, HAROLD J. 1953 Fashions in Science. *Science* 118:331–332.

NYSTROM, PAUL H. 1928 *Economics of Fashion.* New York: Ronald Press.

RICHARDSON, JANE; and KROEBER, ALFRED L. 1940 Three Centuries of Women's Dress Fashions: A Quantitative Analysis. California, University of, *Anthropological Records* 5, no. 2:111–153.

SAPIR, EDWARD 1931 Fashion. Volume 6, pages 139–144 in *Encyclopaedia of the Social Sciences.* New York: Macmillan.

SIMMEL, GEORG (1904) 1957 Fashion. *American Journal of Sociology* 62:541–558.

SMELSER, NEIL J. (1962) 1963 *Theory of Collective Behavior.* London: Routledge; New York: Free Press. → See especially Chapter 7.

SOMBART, WERNER 1902 *Wirtschaft und Mode.* Wiesbaden (Germany): Bergmann.

SUMNER, WILLIAM GRAHAM (1906) 1959 *Folkways: A Study of the Sociological Importance of Usages, Manners, Customs, Mores, and Morals.* New York: Dover.

VEBLEN, THORSTEIN (1899) 1953 *The Theory of the Leisure Class: An Economic Study of Institutions.* Rev. ed. New York: New American Library. → A paperback edition was published in 1959. See especially Chapter 7.

YOUNG, AGNES B. 1937 *Recurring Cycles of Fashion: 1760–1937.* New York: Harper.

FATIGUE

Fatigue is an experienced state of discomfort, aversion, and inability to perform, otherwise known as tiredness or weariness (Bartley 1943; Bartley & Chute 1947). The term applies to the total individual (the organism-as-a-person) and not properly to an organ or tissue. Fatigue is to be distinguished from impairment, which refers to the inability of cells or tissues to perform. Fatigue is sometimes confused with work decrement, for quite often the inquirer is actually interested in work output rather than in the state of the performer.

Fatigue is brought about in various ways, one common cause being discomfort in muscles induced by exertion, another being impairment. Very often, however, fatigue arises from some sort of disorganization within the individual. This is induced, in part, through confrontation with circumstances that are disliked or considered futile and useless. The disorganization referred to here can be described at various body-process levels. Disorganization can involve a disruption in the proper timing of various processes or a conflict between these processes with subsequent tension, awkwardness, and forgetfulness that result in discomfort and the realization of inadequacy.

Chronic fatigue often represents an unwholesome outlook on daily routine or life in general or arises from personality disorganization rather than some debilitating body processes at a lower level (Muncie 1941).

Critique of common conceptions. The common outlook that confuses fatigue with impairment is characterized by several points, some of which are acceptable and some not (Bartley 1951). First is the view that activity modifies the acting system, and that the modification is a chemical one. Fatigue is taken to be such a modification. However, this is really *impairment* and is a phenomenon that takes place at the tissue level, whereas fatigue is a phenomenon at the personality level— the experience, the self-awareness of condition. It is also assumed that fatigue can be either a general body condition or specifically localized. The slowing down of a process is taken to be the evidence of fatigue or, by some writers, to be fatigue itself. Here again, it seems to be impairment that is at issue.

Conventional assumptions shift from considering fatigue as tissue effects to considering it as the way the organism-as-a-person behaves. Even at this level compensation is generally overlooked in human performance. This is evidenced in the tacit assumption made by many that the subject has only one way of performing a given task. For example, it is not presumed that one muscle fiber group may be recovering while some other group is taking its place in carrying on over-all performance. But this type of compensation does occur, and it makes many of the simple, customarily performed "fatigue" experiments inappropriate and inadequate.

It is also false to assume that fatigue developed in one kind of performance may be measured by using an altogether different performance as a test.

The concern with fatigue as distinct from work output arises most directly and forcefully in medical practice and is even encountered in athletics. Physicians are being constantly confronted with patients who complain of tiredness, sometimes in connection with convalescence from debilitating disease or simply as a syndrome of its own (Alvarez 1941; Harms & Soniat 1952; Muncie 1941). On the other hand, work output is generally the main concern in industry (Dill et al. 1936; Edwards et al. 1935). Fatigue is often a term incorrectly *inferred* when an individual notices certain symptoms. In this case, what is called fatigue is self-diagnosis rather than something that arises as a directly felt inability to perform. Thus, a patient may tell an ophthalmologist that he has visual fatigue, inferring this (a self-diagnosis) from the fact that after reading awhile what he sees becomes blurred. This is different than his reporting how he feels. Such a usage of fatigue is to be avoided if the language on fatigue is to be consistent.

Finally, according to the conventional view, there are several kinds of fatigue. The more basic categorization distinguishes *objective* fatigue (work decrement); *subjective* fatigue (the experience of tiredness); and *physiological* fatigue (change or reduction in a specific body process).

Although there are various additionally specified kinds of fatigue, when fatigue exists it is essentially the same in all cases. The core of fatigue is the self-realization of relative inability to carry on. It is a negative orientation toward a task demand. Although the stance toward demand is always es-

sentially the same, various fringe details (various sensory and other components) may vary from case to case, but they are mere details in the unique over-all syndrome that is distinguishable as fatigue.

For example, fatigue arising in intellectual tasks should not be called mental fatigue, if by that one means a special kind of fatigue. Mental fatigue is only the fatigue that arises in intellectual (mental) tasks. Despite the fact that many kinds of tasks may lead to fatigue, no implication that there are many *kinds* of fatigue should be made.

So many loosely related phenomena have been called fatigue that it has been suggested that the word be done away with entirely (Muscio 1921). Bartley and colleagues (Bartley 1943; 1951; 1957; Bartley & Chute 1945; 1947) have chosen rather to retain the word in its original meaning (i.e., for the phenomena first labeled "tiredness") and rename other phenomena associated with it.

Problems in studying fatigue. Many studies that are meant to be studies of fatigue begin with questions about the experience of tiredness and inability to continue performance and end up by bypassing these questions and by providing information about other problems. For example, an investigator may note that workers in a plant feel sluggish and ineffective during mid-morning and mid-afternoon. He may suppose that this has something to do with blood sugar level. In his study he finds that at these times blood sugar level is lowest. He may then try a plan whereby the workers take in the same total amount of food per day but eat varying numbers of meals. Some eat two, some three, some four, and some even five meals per day. Blood sugar level is then tested periodically throughout the day. It is found that where many meals are eaten the blood sugar level never falls as low at any part of the work day as it does when few meals are eaten. At this point, the investigator assumes his study is completed. He should continue and determine whether the feeling of sluggishness is eliminated or greatly reduced by redistributing food intake into a greater number of meals, with the total intake held constant. It is only when he has performed this additional step that the original questions of sluggishness and inefficiency receive an answer. It is only then that the investigation becomes a fatigue investigation.

One of the persistent problems in dealing with fatigue is its measurement. It is always expected that if an entity exists it can be measured. The definition of fatigue as a relation to demand in which the individual *feels* his own inability to go on makes easy measurement unattainable. When work output is all that is to be measured, such measurement is easily made. However, the problem of measuring fatigue as defined here is no different from the problem of measuring anxiety, depression, boredom, hope, anger, or a virtually uncountable number of other states of the organism-as-a-person. Thus, the concept of fatigue should not be singled out for criticism because it refers to a phenomenon difficult to quantify. Nevertheless, such criticism has been leveled, at times, against what is conventionally called "subjective fatigue," for that reason.

The first point to be recognized is that the phenomenon in question must exist in order to be measured or dealt with in any way. The first step in studying it is to produce it. The second is to manipulate conditions under which it occurs. The next point to realize is that the person fatigued is the only one able to state when it exists. The observations made by all others have to do with overt performance, body process, or both, which are not fatigue although they may be closely related to it in some way. It is also to be recognized that the problem of quantitatively dealing with fatigue involves either developing a fatigue scale or choosing a fatigue point, such as the point at which the performer is no longer able to continue.

It will become quickly evident that in most cases the crucial conditions that lead to fatigue lie within the subject himself rather than the external conditions that produce the demand. Whatever is done to study fatigue, the organism-centered approach is necessary. In fact, it is necessary in trying to understand work output as well.

In certain ways, the phenomena that are personalistic rather than environmental can be studied more concretely than might be supposed. For example, it certainly is possible to manipulate goals (which are personalistic phenomena). In setting a task for a subject one can tell him something that will indicate the amount of time required to perform the task. One can then vary the amount of time so indicated to see what remoteness of goals has to do with the self-assessments of the subjects at various moments during performance and whether this variable has anything to do with the point at which "exhaustion" is reached. Other such dimensions and their body-process concomitants can also be chosen.

Another problem in studying fatigue has to do with how far various subjects will push themselves either in their use of energy resources or in experiencing bodily discomfort. This problem is related to motivation, and its solution may actually be a way of dealing with or measuring motivation. This problem is encountered not only in psycho-logical experimentation but also in the physiological treadmill experiments. Some subjects "reach their limits" in muscular exertion before oxygen debt occurs, while others do not. No physiologist would expect that a subject would be exhausted before oxygen debt appears. These results illustrate the difference in the amount that individuals will push themselves. Thus the problem of subjectivity is as inherent in many phases of physiology as in psychology. Hence it cannot be disposed of by assuming that it occurs only in nonbehavioristic types of research.

Relieving fatigue. Various drugs and other substances have been tried by investigators to relieve fatigue and improve performance in athletic activities (Karpovich 1959; Smith & Beecher 1959).

Fatigue may often be relieved by inducing a change of attitude or attention or by shifting from one task to another rather than by rest (inactivity). Supposedly the needed change involves reorganization within the individual rather than a replenishment of energy.

Fatigue and the syndrome called *stress* by Selye (1956) have a lot in common, particularly certain factors of origin. Selye's discoveries and concepts go a long way toward providing a bodily basis for human incapacity, and when this is coupled with a monistic psychology, which attempts to understand human behavior, considerable progress seems to be possible.

S. HOWARD BARTLEY

[*Other relevant material may be found in* ACHIEVEMENT MOTIVATION; INFANCY, *article on* THE EFFECTS OF EARLY EXPERIENCE; SLEEP; STRESS.]

BIBLIOGRAPHY

ALVAREZ, W. C. 1941 What Is the Matter With the Patient Who Is Chronically Tired? *Journal of the Missouri State Medical Association* 38:365–368.

BARTLEY, S. HOWARD 1943 Conflict, Frustration and Fatigue. *Psychosomatic Medicine* 5:160–163.

BARTLEY, S. HOWARD 1951 Fatigue and Efficiency. Pages 318–347 in Harry Helson (editor), *Theoretical Foundations of Psychology.* New York: Van Nostrand.

BARTLEY, S. HOWARD 1957 Fatigue and Inadequacy. *Physiological Reviews* 37:301–324.

BARTLEY, S. HOWARD; and CHUTE, ELOISE 1945 A Preliminary Clarification of the Concept of Fatigue. *Psychological Review* 52:169–174.

BARTLEY, S. HOWARD; and CHUTE, ELOISE 1947 *Fatigue and Impairment in Man.* New York: McGraw-Hill.

DILL, D. B. et al. 1936 Industrial Fatigue. *Journal of Industrial Hygiene and Toxicology* 18:417–431.

EDWARDS, H. T.; THORNDIKE, A.; and DILL, D. B. 1935 The Energy Requirement in Strenuous Muscular Exercise. *New England Journal of Medicine* 213:532–535.

HARMS, H. E.; and SONIAT, T. L. L. 1952 The Meaning of Fatigue. *Medical Clinics of North America* 36:311–317.

KARPOVICH, P. V. 1959 Effect of Amphetamine Sulfate on Athletic Performance. *Journal of the American Medical Association* 170:558–561.

MUNCIE, WENDELL 1941 Chronic Fatigue. *Psychosomatic Medicine* 3:277–285.

MUSCIO, B. 1921 Is a Fatigue Test Possible? *British Journal of Psychology* 12:31–46.

SELYE, HANS 1956 *The Stress of Life.* New York: McGraw-Hill.

SMITH, G. M.; and BEECHER, H. K. 1959 Amphetamine Sulfate and Athletic Performance. *Journal of the American Medical Association* 170:542–557.

WHITING, HELEN F.; and ENGLISH, HORACE B. 1925 Fatigue Tests and Incentives. *Journal of Experimental Psychology* 8:33–49.

FEARS

See PHOBIAS.

FEBVRE, LUCIEN

Lucien Febvre (1878–1956) was born in Nancy, the capital of Lorraine, where his father was, at that time, teaching at the university. Both his father and his mother, however, came from Franche-Comté, and it was to this province that Febvre was deeply attached. He spent all his vacations there; he taught at the lycée at Besançon from 1897 to 1911; he was always interested in the life, the scenery, and the people of Franche-Comté; and he died there and was buried at Saint-Amour, on the border of Bresse and the Jura. Just as Michelet, to whom Febvre liked to compare himself, was a child of Paris, so Febvre might well be called a "peasant" of Franche-Comté—this, indeed, is what his friend, the novelist Léon Werth, called him.

Febvre's studies took him from the lycée at Nancy to the faculty of letters there, then to the Lycée Louis-le-Grand in Paris, and finally, from 1899 to 1902, to the École Normale Supérieure, from which he was graduated as agrégé in history and geography. His closest and most influential friend during these formative years was Henri Wallon, philosopher, psychologist, and physician, who later became his colleague at the Collège de France.

Febvre attained full intellectual maturity very early, well before 1911 when he defended his thesis at the Sorbonne. This brilliant thesis, *Philippe II et la Franche-Comté* (1911*a*), is a broad historical and geographical, as well as economic and social, study of this province in the second half of the sixteenth century. The work may be compared to the volumes of the *Histoire de Belgique* that Henri Pirenne was then writing: while the Franche-Comté "route" was certainly not as important as the "crossroads" of the Low Countries, Febvre's study is more profound and more erudite than Pirenne's and, since it is in the mainstream of historiography, has not dated as much.

At the École Normale Febvre came into contact with Paul Vidal de la Blache, who had established geography as an autonomous discipline in France, and with Lucien Gallois, another geographer. From the beginning of his scholarly life Febvre, in effect, had two professions, history and geography. His enthusiasm for geography was great, as is shown by the geographical preface to his thesis, by his numerous reviews of geographical books, and by his masterly work, *A Geographical Introduction to History* (1922). This volume is a long, vigorous, and brilliant argument against narrow determinism and in favor of a subtle possibilism that encompasses human evolution and history.

Geography was his first love, but he soon gained familiarity with all the sciences of man by spending time in the office of the new *Revue de synthèse historique*, founded in 1900 by Henri Berr and edited by him. Berr's editing communicated his own outgoing spirit: he tried to bring together in a kind of continuous conversation all the different kinds of history—intellectual, cultural, social, economic, institutional, political, and so forth—and the new human sciences, especially sociology. During his stay in Paris at the Fondation Thiers, from 1903 to 1906, Febvre established close ties with Berr and his group, soon becoming a key contributor to the *Revue de synthèse* and later to the other undertakings that arose out of it: the *Semaines de synthèses* and the vast series, *L'évolution de l'humanité*. Thus, when Febvre wrote in 1911 on the Franche-Comté, he was already something of a historian, a geographer, a sociologist, an economist, a psychologist, and a linguist.

Given this background, there is nothing surprising either in the appearance in 1922 of his *Geographical Introduction to History*, a book which had a tremendous impact on the small world of French historians and geographers, or in the founding in 1929 of the *Annales d'histoire économique et sociale*, which marked a decisive turning point in French historiography. It may seem that these achievements came relatively late in Febvre's career, but for five solid years he had been involved in World War I, always in the front line, ending up as captain of a machine gun company. In 1912 he had been appointed professor in the faculty of letters at Dijon and in 1919 he moved to the University of Strasbourg. There he and Marc Bloch became close friends, and it was with Bloch that he was to found, edit, and, indeed, to a large extent write the *Annales*.

The effect of the *Annales* was to establish a kind of hegemony of history over the other human sciences: while in general barriers were eliminated between disciplines, these disciplines were not considered equal in importance, history being accorded a preferred position, especially vis-à-vis social psychology and sociology and even more so vis-à-vis economics. This intellectual position might be labeled "historicism" if this term did not have such pejorative connotations and particularly if it were not so easily confused with the *Historismus* of German thinkers. The essential point is to make clear the differences between the *Revue de synthèse*, whose theme was the colloquy of the human sciences, and the *Annales*, which constituted a sort of Common Market, with history as the preponderant power.

Yet great as is Febvre's contribution in the *Annales*, it does not represent the true scope of his intellectual role. The key to this scope is his generosity, his deep-felt need to share his knowledge. Just as Paul Langevin, 1872–1946, was the "banker" for the physicists of his generation—that is, the lender, the disseminator of ideas, what Diderot had been for many of the writers of his time, so also was Febvre a banker: he never became tired of having people come in to see him, of listening, of guiding. When conversation did not suffice he wrote what he called his "letters of guidance." It was in this way that he trained Marc Bloch, his junior by eight years, and the present author as well. Often his "guidance" consisted of simply surrendering his own projects to others, especially after 1929, when work on the *Annales* became his principal activity. Himself a "peasant" and a marvelous historian of the land, he turned over this subject to Bloch, who produced *Les caractères originaux de l'histoire rurale française* (1931); later, after 1946, he turned over to the present author the task of establishing relationships between historical and economic studies. His own relatively brief writings on the work of François Simiand, Earl J. Hamilton, Giuseppe Parenti, Frederic C. Lane, and others, show how receptive he was to new ideas in economics.

Although Febvre thus abandoned some of his favorite topics to others, he does seem to have found, outside his primary field of intellectual activity, even outside the *Annales*, a kind of subject that delighted him: the history of art, of religion, or even, in the broad sense, of culture. History was *one* for him and whatever his particular concern, he surveyed the entire landscape. In 1928 he published *Martin Luther: A Destiny*, a book that he clearly enjoyed writing and that is written beautifully. Luther was not for Febvre simply a problem in biographical research, nor even a difficult subject made attractive by its very difficulty; Luther represented the problem of the unique individual in history and of the unpredictable power of such an individual.

All his life, indeed, Febvre liked to consort with the great minds of "his" century, the sixteenth. He was wonderfully well acquainted with them; to hear him read Rabelais was a pleasure. His excellent humanist education (which he received from his father and from an uncle rather than in school) explains his delight in writing his charming little book, *Autour de l'Heptaméron* (1944), or that masterpiece of classical erudition, *Origène et Des Périers* (1942a).

Increasingly, he fought for one kind of history while writing rather a different kind himself. In 1942, with the publication of *Le problème de l'incroyance au XVIᵉ siècle: La religion de Rabelais* (1942b), he seems to have emerged victoriously from this conflict: this time he had all the reins in his hand, and the book is his best one. In the first two parts of the work he treated Rabelais in the traditional way, using evidence from his life and his works, but he devoted the third part to the "mental apparatus" of the period—the words, the feelings, the concepts that are the infrastructure of the thought of the century, the basis on which everything was constructed or could be constructed, and which may have prevented certain things from being constructed.

Although the book was much praised, its originality limited its appreciation by historians. Febvre's work was ahead of its time, and it is only recently that the structuralists of the new literary criticism (for example, Michel Foucault, in his *Les mots et les choses: Une archéologie des sciences humaines*, 1966) have done similar research into the culture of a society.

Yet Febvre did not pursue his ideas, and his work remained incomplete. As he worked in the area of psychological, social, and cultural history, he seems to have had difficulty in stating problems, fixing bench marks, and drafting a methodology. Thus he was always uncertain about the nature of civilization, to use that convenient term. Often he insisted that civilization must be located in a particular time, that its changeful nature must be pinned down, and he protested against the frequent assertion that "man is always the same." But at the same time his *Rabelais* presupposes the long continuation of what he aptly called the mental apparatus of men, something beyond the individual or the unique. He might have stressed this transcendence more had he not been excessively impressed, as laymen tend to be, by the implications of the concept of relativity as formulated by Einstein. He was tormented by the perennial problem of the objective status of the "observer"—the historian—and of the events being observed—history.

He did not doubt, however, that history provides an understanding of one's own time and that such an understanding is indispensable to the historian. This is why to the very end of his life Febvre never left the intellectual battleground. It is no accident that he entitled the first volume of his collected articles *Combats pour l'histoire* (1953).

In 1947 he created the section of economic and social sciences of the École Pratique des Hautes Études, serving as chairman of this section until his death. He also revived the *Annales*, whose publication had been hampered by the war; he even tried, without any real success, to revive the project of publishing the *Encyclopédie française*, begun in 1933 by Anatole de Monzie and himself. And once again he did whatever he could to help other scholars. Really to appreciate the intellectual force of Febvre one must read not only his books but also his many articles and reviews and his marvelous letters. Those who were privileged to enjoy his informal conversation are certain that he is among the greatest of modern French historians.

FERNAND BRAUDEL

[*See also* HISTORY; *and the biographies of* BLOCH; PIRENNE; VIDAL DE LA BLACHE.]

WORKS BY FEBVRE

1911a *Philippe II et la Franche-Comté: Étude d'histoire politique, religieuse et sociale.* Paris: Champion.
1911b *Notes et documents sur la Réforme et l'Inquisition en Franche-Comté: Extraits des archives du Parlement de Dole.* Paris: Champion.
(1912) 1922 *Histoire de Franche-Comté.* 7th ed. Paris: Boivin.
(1922) 1925 *A Geographical Introduction to History.* New York: Knopf. → First published as *La terre et l'évolution humaine.*
(1928) 1929 *Martin Luther: A Destiny.* New York: Dutton. → First published as *Un destin: Martin Luther.*
1930 FEBVRE, LUCIEN et al. *Civilisation.* Paris: Renaissance du Livre.
(1931) 1935 DEMANGEON, ALBERT; and FEBVRE, LUCIEN *Le Rhin: Problèmes d'histoire et d'économie.* Paris: Colin.
1932 *L'individualité en histoire: Le personnage en histoire.* Paris: Renaissance du Livre.
1942a *Origène et Des Périers: Ou, l'énigme du* Cymbalum mundi. Paris: Droz.
(1942b) 1962 *Le problème de l'incroyance au XVIe siècle: La religion de Rabelais.* 2d ed. Paris: Michel.
1944 *Autour de l'*Heptaméron: *Amour sacré, amour profane.* Paris: Gallimard.
1946 Introduction. In Jules Michelet, *Michelet.* Paris: Éditions des Trois Collines.
1953 *Combats pours l'histoire.* Paris: Colin. → A collection of previously published articles.
1957 *Au coeur religieux du XVIe siècle.* Paris: S.E.V.P.E.N. → A collection of previously published articles.
1962 *Pour une histoire à part entière.* Paris: S.E.V.P.E.N. → A collection of previously unpublished articles.

SUPPLEMENTARY BIBLIOGRAPHY

BLOCH, MARC (1931) 1952–1956 *Les caractères originaux de l'histoire rurale française.* New ed., 2 vols. Paris: Colin. → Volume 2, *Supplément établi d'après les travaux de l'auteur: (1931–1944),* was written by Robert Dauvergne.
FOUCAULT, MICHEL 1966 *Les mots et les choses: Une archéologie des sciences humaines.* Paris: Gallimard.

FECHNER, GUSTAV THEODOR

Gustav Theodor Fechner (1801–1878) is considered to be the founder of psychophysics and thus of experimental psychology as a whole. He was also the founder of experimental aesthetics. Fechner was born in Lower Lusatia, then part of German northern Silesia. His father and both of his grandfathers were clergymen. Fechner studied medicine first at the University of Dresden and then at the University of Leipzig, obtaining his degree in 1822. His interests turned more and more to physics, however, and he was appointed instructor of natural philosophy at Leipzig the following year. During his years as a student, the lectures of Lorenz Oken on natural philosophy and of E. H. Weber on physiology made the most lasting impressions on Fechner. Oken is now forgotten, but he was then a renowned romantic natural philosopher and cured Fechner of his "man, the machine" approach. Fechner hailed Weber, the discoverer of "Weber's law," as the real father of psychophysics. [*See* WEBER, ERNST HEINRICH.]

After his appointment to the university faculty, Fechner began experimental studies of physical and chemical problems and supported himself by translating, revising, and publishing reference works and textbooks on physics and chemistry. The sheer volume of the work he did during these years is extraordinary. In addition to 28 investigations of his own, published between 1827 and 1840, he annually turned out 1,500 to 2,000 printed pages of textbooks and reference works between 1822 and 1838. He even found time to write several literary pieces, which he published under the pseudonym of "Dr. Mises."

Fechner was married in 1833, and in 1834 he was appointed professor of physics at Leipzig. But he occupied the chair only until 1839; after repeated attacks of severe exhaustion he was, for three years, completely incapacitated by a mysterious illness. The major symptoms were disturbances of vision, with hypersensitivity to bright light, sporadic total failure of digestion, obsessions, and, finally, more and more terrifying hallucinations. He recovered quite suddenly. It seems most likely that the illness was an atypical form of schizophrenia.

The initial impetus for the work on which Fechner's fame is based doubtless came from Oken, who fascinated him so much that at first he was resolved to emulate Oken's unrestrained philosophizing. However, Fechner's empirical research in physics and physiology saved him, and in the guise of "Dr. Mises," he himself participated in mocking this kind of romantic inventing of concepts, which appears to prove everything, while actually it proves nothing. Oken continued to exert some influence on Fechner, however, and later he returned to this kind of thinking without surrendering to it completely.

Psychophysics

The problem that concerned Fechner most was the connection between body and mind. His *Elemente der Psychophysik* (1860) aims at utilizing experimental procedures, such as those employed by Weber previously, to explore this connection more precisely, arriving, if possible, at mathematically formulated laws. Earlier, Johann Friedrich Herbart had demanded that psychological laws be formulated in mathematical terms, but he despaired of the likelihood that psychology would ever obtain the necessary experimental data. Fechner saw in Weber's threshold experiments the possibility of securing such data. He assumed that the difference between two sensations may be defined by the number of "just noticeable differences" (jnd) between them, and that these jnd's can be represented mathematically. He used the number of jnd's above the lower absolute threshold as a measure of the intensity of sensation evoked by a stimulus. In order to be able to describe the relationship between psychic and physical quantities mathematically, Fechner sought to establish a general functional relationship between sensations and stimuli of whatever magnitude. In the range within which Weber's law is valid—Weber's law states that jnd's are proportional to the magnitude of the stimuli—integration yields a function that describes the intensity of a sensation in terms of the logarithm of the stimuli, measured from the absolute threshold.

Since the acuity of the sensory apparatus fluctuates from instant to instant and from person to person, thresholds can be defined only statistically. Fechner perfected the experimental strategies that had earlier been used by Weber and by Vierordt, as well as by such astronomers and physicists as Lambert, Steinheil, and Laugier, to determine the degree of uncertainty or the accuracy of measurement in comparisons of stimuli. According to the nature of variation of the stimulus in comparisons of successive sensations, he distinguished three kinds of psychophysical methods of data collection: (1) the method of jnd's, in which the difference between the stimuli compared is gradually increased until it is perceptible or diminished until it is no longer perceptible; this is also called the method of limits; (2) the method of right and wrong cases, in which a standard stimulus is compared with randomly varied comparison stimuli; this method is also called the constancy method; and (3) the method of average error, in which a comparison stimulus is adjusted by the subject to correspond to a standard; this is also referred to as the reproduction method.

In calculating threshold values, Fechner employed the law of errors formulated by Gauss and Laplace, and in his posthumous *Kollektivmasslehre* (1897) he set forth the applicability of the law of errors to many other problems in psychology. The *Kollektivmasslehre* also contains his contributions to correlation statistics. It is the first textbook of statistics to be designed especially for behavioral scientists. Using carefully planned experiments, whose layouts resemble those today used in the analysis of variance, he endeavored to exclude from the calculation of reaction variability, which defines the threshold difference, those constant errors that arise from the particular features of the experimental procedure.

Fechner realized that "psychophysics" (his coinage) was an innovation of great importance: he called it a science "in the initial state of becoming," and his own work for all its scope, merely "a modest beginning of a beginning." His work was soon taken up by some of the greatest scientists of his time. As far back as 1858, Ernst Mach and Hermann von Helmholtz had begun to experiment on their own, stimulated by Fechner's preliminary report. Wilhelm Wundt followed in 1862, A. W. Volkmann in 1864, H. Aubert and J. R. L. Delboeuf in 1865, and J. Bernstein and Vierordt in 1868. Of the outstanding specialists in the field of psychology only one remained a skeptic: William James, who as late as 1890 declared that despite all its acumen and all its care, the psychological yield of the *Elemente* was "just nothing," not important enough to merit mention in even a footnote.

The methods of measurement developed by Fechner are now generally adopted in quantitative experimental psychology, although some of the mathematical implications of his derivations are open to serious criticism (Luce & Galanter 1963). They are employed with equal success in all sorts of fields and for the most diverse problems. In recent years, the problem of psychological scaling, which Fechner was the first to appreciate and deal with, has again come to the forefront; it has been remarkably clarified and given new depth, especially in the work of S. S. Stevens and G. Ekman (for example, Stevens 1934).

Fechner is remembered almost exclusively as a methodologist. The fundamental theoretical postulates he presented in his psychophysics have gone unnoticed and are generally attributed to later authors. Most noteworthy is his working hypothesis of "concrete parallelism," which assumes an isomorphism between phenomena of consciousness and "psychophysical phenomena," that is, those processes occurring in the cerebrum that are directly associated with the phenomena of consciousness. This assumption and its elaboration is usually attributed to Ewald Hering, Georg Elias Müller, Max Wertheimer, and, above all, Wolfgang Köhler, although it was clearly formulated in Volume 2 of Fechner's *Elemente*.

Aesthetics

Following his work in psychophysics, Fechner ventured also to transform the field of aesthetics from speculation to exact factual research. He summarized the results of his efforts in his *Vorschule der Aesthetik* (1876). He tried to derive the conditions that determine what is pleasing and what is displeasing, not from a higher ideal of beauty but from below, by systematic empirical comparison of the beautiful with the less beautiful. This endeavor was not as successful as his work in psychophysics. Fechner was the victim of a then prevalent confusion: to him, as to his contemporaries, "from below" meant not only "from perception to concept," but also "from the simple to the more complex," and the properties of the complex, it was then believed, are those of its simple constituents. The study by Christian von Ehrenfels, who proved that this postulate is false—and thereby not only opened up a new era in psychology but also made possible a more relevant theory of beauty—did not appear until three years after Fechner's death.

Fechner did, however, conduct a study—in line with his attempt to establish an experimental science of aesthetics—which makes him one of the earliest forerunners of modern opinion research. Two nearly identical versions of a Madonna reputed to have been painted by Hans Holbein were then being exhibited in Dresden, and Fechner asked the visitors to the exhibition to note on a sheet of paper which of the two they thought was more beautiful. At that time the public was unfortunately not accustomed to such questionnaires, and only 116 of the 11,000 visitors took the trouble to write their comments. Of these 116, some were art critics who had previously formed judgments, while others failed to follow instructions, thus rendering the results useless. Nonetheless, the experiment made a contribution to methodology that might have become as influential as psychophysics, had its significance been understood.

Analysis of systems

Around 1850, Fechner tackled another fundamental problem, that of the apparent finality of particular processes in animate and inanimate nature. In contrast to the neovitalists, he insisted that this finality be explained within the framework of the principle of causality. He laid down the axiom that every system in nature that is delimited with respect to its environment and hence is more or less closed, as well as every relatively autonomous part of such a system, tends, after a longer or shorter period of dislocation, to return to its previous state, and he specifically speaks of a "tendency toward stability." From this there is a direct road, via Ernst Mach's observation that the stable states of comparatively closed structures are formally distinct, to the concepts of equilibrium of Wolfgang Köhler and Ludwig von Bertalanffy. As Fechner used the concept of "stability," it was broader than it is today; it included not only what he called "simple stability" but also "complex stability," examples of which he found primarily in organisms. These examples are identical with Köhler's "stationary states" and Bertalanffy's "steady states." Thus, Fechner's works contain a surprising number of stimulating ideas which are still influential, though they may sometimes appear under different names [see PERSONALITY: CONTEMPORARY VIEWPOINTS; SYSTEMS ANALYSIS, *article on* PSYCHOLOGICAL SYSTEMS].

WOLFGANG METZGER

[*For the historical context of Fechner's work, see the biographies of* GAUSS; LAPLACE; WEBER, E. H. *For discussion of the subsequent development of his ideas, see* AESTHETICS; PSYCHOPHYSICS; QUANTAL

RESPONSE; SCALING; *and the biographies of* HELM-
HOLTZ; THURSTONE; WUNDT.]

WORKS BY FECHNER

(1836) 1943 Life After Death. Pages 21–90 in Gustav
Theodor Fechner, *Life After Death.* New York: Pantheon. → First published as *Das Büchlein vom Leben
nach dem Tode.*

1848 Ueber das Lustprinzip des Handelns. *Zeitschrift für
Philosophie und philosophische Kritik* New Series 19:
1–30, 163–194.

(1860) 1907 *Elemente der Psychophysik.* 2 vols. 3d ed.
Leipzig: Breitkopf & Härtel.

1871 *Ueber die Aechtheitsfrage der holbein'schen Madonna: Discussion und Acten.* Leipzig: Breitkopf &
Härtel.

1873 *Einige Ideen zur Schöpfungs- und Entwickelungsge-
schichte der Organismen.* Leipzig: Breitkopf & Härtel.

1874 *Ueber den Ausgangswerth der kleinsten Abweich-
ungssumme, dessen Bestimmung, Verwendung und
Verallgemeinerung.* K. Sächsische Gesellschaft der
Wissenschaften, Mathematisch-physische Klasse, Abhandlungen, 11, no. 1. Leipzig: Hirzel.

(1876) 1897–1898 *Vorschule der Aesthetik.* 2d ed. 2 vols.
in 1. Leipzig: Breitkopf & Härtel.

1877 *In Sachen der Psychophysik.* Leipzig: Breitkopf &
Härtel.

1882 *Revision der Hauptpuncte der Psychophysik.* Leipzig: Breitkopf & Härtel.

1888 Ueber die psychischen Massprincipien und das
weber'sche Gesetz: Discussion mit Elsas und Köhler.
Philosophische Studien 4:161–230.

Kollektivmasslehre. Edited by G. F. Lipps. Leipzig: Engelmann, 1897.

SUPPLEMENTARY BIBLIOGRAPHY

BORING, EDWIN G. (1929) 1950 *A History of Experimental Psychology.* 2d ed. New York: Appleton. → See
especially pages 275–296.

BORING, EDWIN G. 1942 *Sensation and Perception in
the History of Experimental Psychology.* New York:
Appleton.

BRETT, GEORGE S. 1921 *A History of Psychology.* Volume 3: Modern Psychology. London: Allen & Unwin.
→ See especially pages 127–239.

BURT, C. 1960 Gustav Theodor Fechner: *Elemente der
Psychophysik,* 1860–1960. *British Journal of Statistical Psychology* 13:1–10.

HALL, G. STANLEY 1912 *Founders of Modern Psychology.* New York: Appleton. → See especially pages
123–177, "Gustav Theodor Fechner."

KÜLPE, O. 1901 Zu Gustav Theodor Fechners Gedächt-
nis. *Vierteljahrsschrift für wissenschaftliche Philosophie und Soziologie* 25:191–217.

LASSWITZ, KURD (1896) 1910 *Gustav Theodor Fechner.*
3d ed. Stuttgart (Germany): Frommann.

LUCE, R. DUNCAN; and GALANTER, EUGENE 1963 Psychophysical Scaling. Volume 1, pages 245–308 in
R. Duncan Luce, Robert R. Bush, and Eugene Galanter (editors), *Handbook of Mathematical Psychology.*
New York: Wiley.

MICHELS, WALTER C.; and HELSON, HARRY 1954 A
Reconciliation of the Veg Scale With Fechner's Law.
American Journal of Psychology 67:677–683.

STEVENS, S. S. 1934 The Volume and Intensity of Tones.
American Journal of Psychology 46:397–408.

THURSTONE, L. L. 1929 Fechner's Law and the Method
of Equal-appearing Intervals. *Journal of Experimental
Psychology* 12:214–224.

WIRTH, WILHELM 1912 *Psychophysik: Darstellung der
Methoden der experimentellen Psychologie.* Leipzig:
Hirzel.

WUNDT, WILHELM 1901 *Gustav Theodor Fechner: Rede
zur Feier seines hundertjährigen Geburtstages.* Leipzig: Engelmann.

FECUNDITY
See FERTILITY.

FEDERALISM

Federalism and its kindred terms—e.g., "federal"
—are used, most broadly, to describe the mode of
political organization which unites separate polities
within an overarching political system so as to
allow each to maintain its fundamental political
integrity. Federal systems do this by distributing
power among general and constituent governments
in a manner designed to protect the existence and
authority of all the governments. By requiring that
basic policies be made and implemented through
negotiation in some form, it enables all to share
in the system's decision-making and decision-
executing processes.

Different conceptions

No single definition of federalism has proved
satisfactory to all students, primarily because of
the difficulties in relating theoretical formulations
to the evidence gathered from observing the actual
operation of federal systems. Attempts at definition
have also foundered on the problems of distinguishing between (1) the federal principle as a broad
social concept and federalism as a narrower political device; (2) two classic but different conceptions
of federalism; (3) authentically federal *systems*
and political systems which utilize elements of the
federal *principle*; (4) mature and emergent federal
systems; and (5) federalism and "intergovernmental relations" as distinct political phenomena.

Social and political principle. Federalism, conceived in the broadest social sense, looks to the
linkage of people and institutions by mutual consent, without the sacrifice of their individual identities as the ideal form of social organization. First
formulated in the covenant theories of the Bible
(Kaufman 1937–1948), this conception of federalism was revived by the Bible-centered "federal"
theologians of seventeenth-century Britain and New
England (Miller 1939), who coined the term
"federal"—derived from the Latin *foedus* (covenant)—in 1645 to describe the system of holy and

enduring covenants between God and man which lay at the foundation of their world view. This conception of federalism was given new theoretical form by nineteenth-century French and German social theorists. Closely related to the various theories of social contract, it is characterized by the desire to build society on the basis of coordinative rather than subordinative relationships and by the emphasis on partnership among parties with equal claims to legitimacy who seek to cultivate their diverse integrities within a common social order (Boehm 1931). [See SOCIAL CONTRACT.]

As a political device, federalism can be viewed more narrowly as a kind of political order animated by political principles that emphasize the primacy of bargaining and negotiated coordination among several power centers as a prelude to the exercise of power within a single political system, and stress the value of dispersed power centers as a means for safeguarding individual and local liberties. This means, in effect, that political institutions common to different political systems, when combined within a federal system and animated by federal principles, are effectively endowed with a distinctive character. For example, while political parties are common in modern political systems, parties animated by the federal principle show unique characteristics of fragmentation and lack of central discipline that increase the power of local groups within the system as a whole (Grodzins 1960a).

Federation and confederation. Federal ideas have been systematically conceptualized in two different ways. On the one hand, federalism has been conceived as a means to unite a people already linked by bonds of nationality through distribution of political power among the nation's constituent units. In such cases, the polities that constitute the federal system are unalterably parts of the national whole, and federalism invariably leads to the development of a strong national government operating in direct contact with the people it serves, just as the constituent governments do. On the other hand, federalism has also been conceived as a means to unify diverse peoples for important but limited purposes, without disrupting their primary ties to the individual polities that constitute the federal system. In such cases the federal government is generally limited in its scope and powers, functioning through constituent governments which retain their plenary autonomy, and, to a substantial degree, is dependent upon them.

Both conceptions of federalism have evolved from early federal experiments. The principles of strong national federalism were first applied by the ancient Israelites, beginning in the thirteenth cen-

tury B.C., to maintain their national unity through linking their several tribes under a single national constitution and at least quasi-federal political institutions (Bright 1959). Several centuries later, the Greek city-states experimented with federal-style institutions as means for the promotion of intranational harmony and cooperation, primarily for defensive purposes, through associations (e.g., the Achaean League) that came close to what were later defined as confederations (Freeman 1863). A modified form of the Greek view was developed by the sixteenth-century theorists (Gierke 1913). They held that federalism meant a permanent league of states united through a perpetual covenant, binding under international law, in which the constituent states delegated enumerated powers to a general government while retaining full rights of internal sovereignty.

However, when the American system—the prototype of modern federal systems—emerged in the late eighteenth century, its architects developed a conception of federalism much like that of ancient Israel. From the first, American federalism functioned to serve a people with a single national identity and was constituted with a strong national government to serve that people on a national basis, though, as late as 1789, *The Federalist* could. describe the new American constitution as "partly national and partly federal" in deference to the then-accepted views. The successful efforts of the supporters of that constitution to appropriate the term "federalist" for their own use (Main 1961, pp. ix–xi) restored to common usage the older conception of federalism as a noncentralized national union bound by municipal law, with a general government superior to the governments of the constituent states (Diamond 1963).

Just as the American system became the prototype for other modern federal systems, so the American conception of federalism became the generally accepted one. The other conception was ultimately subsumed under the word "confederation" and its kindred terms. The two systems described by these different conceptions reflect, in part, the distinctions implied in the German *Staatenbund* (confederation) and *Bundesstaat* (federation), terms developed in the mid-nineteenth century (Mogi 1931). A certain degree of confusion remains because the terms invented to describe both systems were used indiscriminately for many years.

Though the American conception of federalism is today almost universally accepted as the most accurate usage, the confederal conception remains a living and legitimate aspect of the federal idea in its largest political sense. Today, the latter is most prominent among certain advocates of limited European union (the Common Market exemplifies a confederal form) and among many so-called world federalists. [See INTERNATIONAL INTEGRATION.]

Federalism and related systems. Federal systems are often confused with four other forms of political order which make use of specific federal principles. The use of some federal principles in multiple monarchies, legislative unions, empires, and decentralized unitary systems can have important consequences similar to those in authentically federal systems. But the fact that such principles do not permeate the four systems makes the distinctions between them and true federations extremely important.

Federal systems differ from *multiple* (or dual) *monarchies* in two essential ways. The central constitutional characteristic of the multiple monarchy is that union exists only in the person of the sovereign and is maintained only through the exercise of executive power in his name. No significant common institutions exist to unite the constituent polities—no common legislatures, no common legal system, and little in the way of a common political substructure. On the contrary, each constituent polity maintains its own political system, which the monarch guarantees to support under the terms of his compact with the realm. Multiple monarchies have historically been less than democratic regimes. Even where there have been tendencies toward democratization, the very fact that union exists only by virtue of the common sovereign has tended to elevate the position of the monarch to one of real power. Attempts to transfer sovereignty or the attributes of sovereignty elsewhere by their very nature stimulate the division of this kind of association of civil societies into separate polities. Thus, the Austro–Hungarian Empire was held together by the Hapsburg emperors and disintegrated when that family ceased to rule (Sharma 1953, chapter 7). The dual monarchy of Sweden and Norway ceased to function when democratic government was introduced, transferring the attributes of sovereignty from the monarch to the nation(s). In Spain, on the other hand, the inability of the Spaniards to transform a multiple monarchy into a federal system, in a locale which by nature demanded peninsular union of some sort, led to the consolidation of the constituent polities into something approximating a unitary state which remained highly unstable because of the local barriers to consolidation that could neither be accommodated nor eradicated (Elliott 1964). [See MONARCHY.]

Multiple monarchies have been transformed into stable and unified polities through *legislative union*. The United Kingdom is a case in point. The centrifugal tendencies of the seventeenth-century dual monarchy linking England and Scotland were finally eliminated through a legislative union of the two nations in 1707. Legislative union bears very close resemblance to federal union at several crucial points. Though designed to direct public allegiance to a single national authority, the terms of the union encourage the political system to retain certain noncentralizing elements. The government of the nation remains national rather than central in character, since it is created by a perpetual covenant which guarantees the constituent parties their boundaries, representation in the national legislature, and certain local autonomies, such as their own systems of municipal law. Legislative unions usually unite unequal polities. The centralizing tendencies induced by this are somewhat counterbalanced by the residual desire for local self-government in the constituent states. Thus, in the United Kingdom the cabinet has acquired a supremacy not foreseen in 1707, but within the framework of cabinet government Scotland has acquired a national ministry of its own with a separate administrative structure, based in Scotland, for most of its governmental programs (Milne 1957).

Federal systems also differ from *empires* allowing cultural home rule. Such empires have often been termed federal—in some cases because they claim to be. The Roman Empire was the classic example of this kind of political system in the ancient world, and the Soviet Union may well be its classic modern counterpart. In both cases, highly centralized political authorities possessing a virtual monopoly of power decide, for reasons of policy, to allow local populations with different ethnic or cultural backgrounds to maintain a degree of cultural home rule, provided that they remain politically subservient to the imperial regime. While this often appears to offer a substantial degree of local autonomy, its political effects are purposely kept minimal. Any local efforts to transform cultural home rule into political power are invariably met with suppressive force from the central government, even to the point of revoking cultural rights, as examples from the history of both empires reveal.

Federal systems are clearly different from *decentralized unitary states*, even though such states may allow local governments considerable autonomy in some ways. In such states local powers are invariably restricted to local matters, as determined by the central authorities, and are subject to national supervision, restriction, and even withdrawal, though tradition may mitigate against precipitous action by the central government in areas where local privileges have been established. Still, as the English experience has shown, even powerful traditions supporting local autonomy have not stood in the way of great reconcentration of power by democratically elected parliaments when such action has been deemed necessary by a national majority.

Mature and emergent federal systems. Several recent studies (Macmahon 1955; Wheare 1946) have attempted to draw distinctions between mature and emergent federal systems. The thrust of their argument is that federalism, when used to unify separate political systems to form a new nation, and federalism, as a form of decentralized government in an established nation, encourage markedly different kinds of political behavior. In the former case, federalism serves as a means to bring tenuous unity to nations composed of highly autonomous polities, with the locus of power remaining among the constituent units. As federal systems mature, so the argument goes, power is increasingly concentrated at the center, and federalism remains only to promote a certain amount of decentralization within an otherwise highly unified political system. Wheare goes so far as to argue that federalism is a transitional phenomenon useful in promoting progressively larger polities which are then gradually discarded (in fact, if not in form) as an unnecessary encumbrance. This argument may have some validity in describing the history of nonfederal political systems which have utilized federal principles to promote national unity. For example, it can be used to describe the evolution of the United Kingdom into its present constitutional state. It cannot be applied, however, to any of the three exemplary federal systems—Canada, Switzerland, and the United States. Their national ties existed from the first, and their national governments were granted broad powers at the outset. Nor has federalism declined in importance as those nations have matured.

There are undoubtedly differences between mature and emergent federal systems, but those differences are more likely to relate to the character of conflict and negotiation between the general and constituent governments than to their relative strengths.

Federalism and intergovernmental relations. Because the study of federalism at its most immediately empirical level heavily stresses the study of intergovernmental relations, the two are often considered to be synonymous. Federalism, however, is something much more than the relationships between governmental units, involving as it does principles which are designed to establish the proper character of those relationships and which must also affect the character of other political institutions within federal systems. As already indicated, federalism concerns the way in which federal principles influence party and electoral systems in federal polities just as much as it concerns the way in which local governments relate to their regional or national ones, or to each other. Moreover, the study of intergovernmental relations exists apart from the study of federalism, since such relationships are to be found in all political systems, federal or otherwise, where there is more than one government extant within a given polity.

Characteristics and operational principles

The most useful way to attempt to understand federalism as a political phenomenon is to undertake a survey of the basic characteristics of federal systems, principles, and processes in order to understand both the manner and the direction of their development.

As a first step it seems necessary to identify the various federal systems that exist today or have existed in the past; only then can we analyze them as operating political systems. However, identifying federal systems is no simple matter, as we have just seen. The difficulties are heightened by the wide functional differences easily observed in the various political systems which call themselves federal and by the often greater operational similarities between self-styled "federal" and "unitary" systems. Contrast, for example, the political systems of Australia and the Soviet Union, Canada and Mexico, Switzerland and Yugoslavia, or compare the United States and Great Britain.

Moreover, federal systems have historically been marked by great internal distinctions between theory and practice, perhaps more so than other political systems. In the United States, the measure of the maintenance of federalism was long considered to be the degree of separation of government activities by level, because it was generally believed that such separation actually existed. In fact, American federalism from the first had been characterized by extensive intergovernmental functional collaboration within the framework of separate governmental structures (Elazar 1962). Similarly, the Canadian federal system has always been described as one in which the federal government is clearly dominant—the repository of all powers not explicitly granted to the provinces. Yet since the brief period of federal supremacy in the years immediately following confederation, the provinces have consistently gained power at federal expense (Smiley 1965). The Russian federal constitution goes so far as to grant each Soviet republic the right of secession—a patent impossibility under the realities of the Russian political system.

Nevertheless, some basic characteristics and operational principles common to all truly federal systems can be identified, and help us to define such systems. These may be divided into three essential elements and a number of supplementary ones.

Written constitution. First, the federal relationship must be established or confirmed through a perpetual covenant of union, inevitably embodied in a written constitution that outlines, among other things, the terms by which power is divided or shared in the political system and which can be altered only by extraordinary procedures [*see* CONSTITUTIONS AND CONSTITUTIONALISM]. Every existing federal nation possesses a written constitution, as do most of the other nations incorporating elements of the federal principle. Juridically, federal constitutions are distinctive in that they are not simply compacts between the rulers and the ruled but involve the people, the general government, and the polities constituting the federal union. Moreover, the constituent polities retain local constitution-making rights of their own.

Noncentralization. The political system must reinforce the terms of the constitution through an actual diffusion of power among a number of substantially self-sustaining centers that are generally coincident with the constituent polities established by the federal compact. Such a diffusion of power may be termed *noncentralization*. It differs from decentralization—the conditional diffusion of specific powers to subordinate local governments by a central government, subject to recall by unilateral decision. It is also more than devolution—the special grant of powers to a subnational unit by a central government, not normally rescindable. Noncentralization ensures that no matter how certain powers may be shared by the general and constituent government at any point in time, the authority to participate in exercising them cannot be taken away from either without mutual consent. Constituent polities in federal systems are able to participate as partners in national governmental activities and to act unilaterally with a high degree of autonomy in areas constitutionally open to them —even on crucial questions and, to a degree, in opposition to national policies, because they possess effectively irrevocable powers.

Areal division of power. A third element that appears to be essential in any federal system is the internal division of authority and power on an areal basis (Maass 1959), what in the United States has been called territorial democracy. It is theoretically possible to create a federal system whose constituent units are fixed but not territorially based. There were premodern protofederations of nomadic tribes, and some observers have seen federal elements in nations constitutionally structured to accommodate social and political divisions along ethnic, religious, or even ideological lines. Nevertheless, no authentic federal system has existed without an areal basis for the federal division. Historically, when areal divisions of power have given way to divisions on the basis of functional interest, federalism has been replaced by pluralism. In modern democratic theory the argument between federalists and antifederalists has frequently revolved around the respective values of areal and functional diffusions of power. Theorists who have argued the obsolescence of federalism while endorsing the values used to justify its existence have generally based their case on the superior utility of pluralism (Mogi 1931, pp. 1059–1115). Proponents of the federal-areal division argue that the deficiencies of territorial democracy are greatly overshadowed by the neutrality of areal representation of functional interests, and they argue further that any other system devised for giving power to these interests has proved unable to cope with the complexities and changes of interest endemic in a dynamic age while certainly limiting the advantages for local differentiation inherent in the areal system.

Studies of federal systems indicate the existence of other elements that supplement the three basic ones. While all of them are not always present in every federal system, their near universality leads to the conclusion that they serve important functions in the maintenance of federalism in each. Similarly, while many of them are found individually in various kinds of political systems, it is their combination within a single system structured around the basic elements that is characteristic of federalism.

Maintaining union. Generally characteristic of modern federal systems are direct lines of communication between the public and both the general and the constituent governments, which allow the public to exert direct influence on both governments and permit them to exercise direct authority over a common citizenry. The people may (and usually do) elect representatives to all governments which serve them. All of the governments may (and usually do) administer programs so as to serve the individual citizen directly. The courts may serve both levels of government, applying the relevant laws directly.

The existence of those direct lines of communication—one of the major features distinguishing federations from leagues—is usually predicated on the existence of a sense of common nationality binding the constituent polities and peoples of federal nations together, another element requisite for the maintenance of a successful federal system. In some countries this sense has been inherited, but in most it has had to be invented. Federalism in Germany has been based on a common sense of an inherited German nationhood. In the United States, Argentina, and Australia a sense of nationhood had to be at least partly invented. National consciousness soon became second nature in those countries, since none of their constituent states ever had much more than a partially developed national consciousness of its own. Canada, Switzerland, and Yugoslavia have had to invent a sense of common nationality strong enough to embrace "nationality groups" whose intense national feelings are rooted in the constituent polities. In such newly formed federal systems as India, Malaysia, and Nigeria, the future of federalism is endangered by the absence of a common sense of nationality. Contrary to some theories, federalism has not proved to be a particularly good device for integrating diverse nationalities into a single political system unless it has been accompanied by other factors compelling integration.

Geographic necessity has been a major factor promoting the maintenance of union within federal systems, even in the face of strong pressures toward disunion. The Mississippi Valley in the United States, the Alps in Switzerland, the island character of the Australian continent, and the mountains and jungles surrounding Brazil have served as direct geographic influences promoting unity. More political than "natural," but no less compelling geographically, have been the pressures for Canadian union generated by that country's neighbor to the south or for the federation of the German states generated by their neighbors to the east and west.

Maintaining noncentralization.   It has been well demonstrated that the constituent polities in a federal system must be fairly equal in population and wealth or at least balanced geographically or numerically in their inequalities, if noncentralization is to be maintained. The United States has been able to overcome its internal inequities because each geographic section has included both great and small states. In Canada, the ethnic differences between the two largest provinces have served to inject balance into the system. The ex-

istence of groups of cantons in different size categories has helped maintain Swiss federalism. Similar distributions exist in every other system whose federal character is not in question.

The existence of a large polity dominating smaller states with which it is nominally federated on equal terms has often been one of the major reasons for the failure of federalism. In the German federal empire of the late nineteenth century, Prussia was so obviously dominant that the other states had little opportunity to provide national leadership or even a reasonably strong hedge against the desires of its king and government. Similarly, even without the problem of the Communist party, the existence of the Russian Soviet Federal Socialist Republic, which occupies three-fourths of the area and contains three-fifths of the population of the Soviet Union, would have severely crippled the possibilities of maintaining authentic federal relationships in that country.

Successful federal systems have also been characterized by the permanence of the boundaries of their constituent units. This does not mean that boundary changes cannot occur, but it does mean that as a matter of constitutional law such changes can be made only with the consent of the polities involved and that, as a matter of political policy, they are avoided except in the most extreme situations. Boundary changes have occurred in the "classic" federal systems—the United States divided Virginia during the Civil War, Canada has enlarged the boundaries of its provinces, and Switzerland has divided cantons—but they have been the exception rather than the rule, and in every case at least the formal consent of the constituent polities was given. Even in weaker federal systems, such as those of Latin America, state boundaries have tended to remain relatively secure. When boundary changes have been made, as in the postwar redrawing of *Länder* boundaries in West Germany to account for the diminished territory of the Federal Republic and the alteration of state lines to recognize linguistic unities in India, the essential heartlands of the polities involved have been preserved.

In a few very important cases, noncentralization is both reflected and supported through the constitutionally guaranteed existence of different systems of law in the constituent polities. Though the differences in those systems are likely to be somewhat eroded over time—the extent of their preservation varying from system to system—their continued existence as separate systems and the national mixture of laws which their existence promotes act as great bulwarks against centralization [see LEGAL SYSTEMS]. In the United States, each state's legal system stems directly and to a certain extent uniquely from English law, while federal law occupies only an interstitial position binding the systems of the fifty states together insofar as necessary. The resulting mixture of laws keeps the administration of justice, even in federal courts, substantially noncentralized (Macmahon 1955, chapter 11). In Canada, the existence of common law and civil law systems side by side is one constitutional guarantee of French-Canadian cultural survival. Noncentralized legal systems, a particularly Anglo-American device, are often used in legislative as well as federal unions. They are rare in other political cultures and have become less common in all federal systems established since 1900. More common is the provision for modification of national legal codes by the subnational governments to meet special local needs, as in Switzerland.

The point is generally well taken that unless the constituent polities have substantial influence over the formal or informal amending process the federal character of the system is open to question. Since many constitutional changes are made without recourse to formal constitutional amendment, the position of the constituent polities must be additionally protected by a constitution designed so that any serious changes in the political order can be made only by the decision of dispersed majorities which reflect the areal division of powers. This protection, which federal theorists have argued is important for popular government as well as for federalism (Diamond 1963), is a feature of the most truly federal systems.

Noncentralization is strengthened in all federal systems by giving the constituent polities guaranteed representation in the national legislature and, often, by giving them a guaranteed role in the national political process. In some federal systems, notably those of the United States and Switzerland, the latter is guaranteed in the written constitution. In others, such as Canada and those in Latin America, certain powers of participation have been acquired and have become part of the traditional constitution.

Recent studies have shown that the existence of a noncentralized party system is perhaps the most important single element in the maintenance of federal noncentralization (Macmahon 1955). Noncentralized parties initially develop because of the constitutional arrangements of the federal compact, but once they have come into existence, they tend to be self-perpetuating and to function as decentralizing forces in their own right.

The United States and Canada provide two examples of the different forms which can be assumed by a noncentralized party system. In the United States, where party responsibility is minimal and virtually nonexistent on the national level, a two-party system has developed, with the parties actually coalitions of the several state or, in some cases, local party organizations functioning as national units only for the quadrennial presidential elections or for purposes of organizing the national Congress. Party financing and decision making are functions which are dispersed either among the state organizations or among widely divergent factions operating nationwide. In Canada, on the other hand, the parliamentary form of government, with its concomitant requirement of party responsibility, means that at the national level considerably more party cohesiveness must be maintained simply in order to gain and hold power.

The noncentralized party system in Canada has developed through a fragmentation of the parties along regional or provincial lines. The parties with nationwide bases are still divided internally along provincial lines, with each provincial organization autonomous. Individual provinces are frequently dominated by regional parties that send only a few representatives to the national legislature, adding to the fragmentation of the system. Very often, the party victorious in national elections is the one which is briefly able to expand its base to most nearly national proportions.

European-style federal systems where parliamentary government is the norm follow the Canadian model. Australia and Switzerland come closest to paralleling it, and traces of it can be found in the German Federal Republic. A more centralized variation of the same pattern exists in countries like India, in which the national government is dominated by one very large and diffuse national party which is held together nationally by personal leadership but is quite factionalized in the states where it must share the governing power with other parties.

Federal nations with less developed party systems frequently gain some of the same decentralizing effects through what the Latins call *caudillismo*—noncentralized personal leadership systems which diffuse power through strong local leaders operating in the constituent polities. Caudillistic noncentralization is most characteristic of Latin American federal systems but apparently exists in such new federations as Nigeria and Malaysia as well [see CAUDILLISMO].

The importance to federalism of a noncentralized party system is well illustrated by contrast with those formally federal nations dominated by one highly centralized party, such as the Soviet Union, Yugoslavia, and Mexico. In all three cases, the dominant party has operated to limit the power of the constituent polities in direct proportion to the extent of its dominance.

Ultimately, however, noncentralization is maintained to the extent that there is respect for the federal principle within each federal system. Such respect is necessarily reflected in the immediate recognition by the decision-making publics that the preservation of the constituent polities is as important as the preservation of the nation as a whole. In the words of the American Chief Justice Salmon P. Chase, federalism looks to "an indestructible Union, composed of indestructible States" (*Texas v. White*, 7 Wallace [1869]). This recognition may be based on loyalty to particular constituent polities or on an understanding of the role played by federalism in animating the political system along certain unique lines. Thus, those who value government by conciliation and partnership, with emphasis on local control, are likely to have respect for the federal principle.

Citizens of a federal nation must show that respect in two ways, by showing self-restraint and by cultivating the political art of negotiation. Federalism can exist only where there is considerable tolerance of diversity and willingness to take political action through conciliation even when the power to act unilaterally is available. The usual prerequisite to action in federal systems is the ability to build consensus rather than the power to threaten coercion. Western federal nations can furnish many examples of the exercise of national self-restraint in dealing with difficult federal problems. Even in a federal system as centralized as that of India, the constitutional right of the national government to assume control of the state governments is exercised as little as possible— notably when the communists win local elections— and is then clearly a temporary action.

The historical record indicates that the dual purpose implied in Chase's dictum has been at least as responsible for the creation of federal systems as has the single interest in political unification. The Canadian confederation came into being not only to create a new nation out of the British North American colonies but also to give Ontario and Quebec autonomous political systems of their own. Similarly, every move toward greater union in the Swiss confederation has been made in order to preserve the independence of the cantons from both outside encroachment and revolutionary centralism (Sharma 1953, pp. 269–275). A good case can be made that similar motivations were important in the creation of Australia, Malaysia, Nigeria, and the United States.

Maintaining the federal principle. Several of the devices commonly found in federal systems serve to maintain the federal principle per se and are consequently supportive of both the national government and the constituent polities. Two of these are particularly common and important.

The maintenance of federalism requires that the nation and its constituent polities each have a substantially complete set of governing institutions of their own with the right—within limits set by the compact—to modify those institutions unilaterally. Separate legislative and administrative institutions are both necessary. This does not necessarily mean that all governmental activities must be carried out by separate institutions at each level. It is possible for the agencies of one government to serve as agents of the other by mutual agreement. But each government must have the needed institutions to function independently in the areas of its authority and the structural resources to cooperate freely with the other government's counterpart agencies.

In this regard, the contractual sharing of public responsibilities by all governments in the system appears to be a central characteristic of federalism. Sharing, broadly conceived, includes common involvement in policy making, financing, and administration of government activities. In contemporary federal systems, it is characterized by extensive intergovernmental collaboration. Sharing can be based on highly formal arrangements or informal agreements. In federal systems, it is usually contractual in nature. The contract—politically a limited expression of the compact principle—is used in formal arrangements as a legal device to enable governments responsible to separate polities to engage in joint action while remaining independent entities. Even where government agencies cooperate without formally contracting to do so, the spirit of federalism that pervades ongoing federal systems tends to infuse the participating parties with a sense of contractual obligation.

In any federal system, it is likely that there will be continued tension between the federal government and the constituent polities over the years and that different "balances" between them will develop at different times. The existence of this tension is an integral part of the federal relationship, and its character does much to determine the future of federalism in each system. The question of federal–state relations which it produces is perennially a matter of public concern because virtually all other political issues arising in a federal system are phrased in terms of their implications for federalism. In this way federalism imposes a way of looking at problems that stands apart from the substantive issues raised by the problems themselves. This is particularly true of those issues which affect the very fabric of society. In the United States, for example, the race question is a problem of federal–state as well as Negro–white relations, and the same is true of the cultural question in Canada and the linguistic question in India.

The end product. The very terminology of federalism is characterized by a revealing ambiguity that is indicative of the end product of federal systems. The word "federalize" is used to describe the unification of "sovereign" states into a federal polity and also the permanent devolution of authority and power within a nation to subnational governments. In this ambiguity lies the essence of the federal principle—the perpetuation of both union and noncentralization.

Viewed from the top, the combination of the elements discussed above results in a federal rather than a central government—i.e., a government composed of a nationwide coalition of political institutions, some with predominantly local power bases (such as the national legislature), others with predominantly national power bases (such as the national bureaucracy). This government, whose power is thus diffused vertically and laterally, functions in cooperation with the constituent polities which it must conciliate in order to act. Decision making is characterized by heavy reliance upon negotiation and bargaining and by minimal reliance upon the exercise of force. Operations are characterized by a measure of disorder, since noncentralization breeds multiple power centers located at or cutting across all levels of government. Each of these centers seeks to keep open routes of access to the others, usually succeeding because it is in the best interests of all to maintain this kind of disorder as part of the "rules of the game."

Viewed locally, a federal system consists of governmental inputs from different sources whose local connections normally serve to fragment local authority. However, because such a system rewards those who actively seek to reconcile the diffuse elements and bind them together for a larger purpose, local political leaders can control these inputs to a great extent. While this may not prevent the national government from exercising great power at any given time or from increasing its total power over time, it does mean that as long as the federal principle remains operative, the public can and almost invariably does limit certain kinds of national government actions or guides such actions

into particular channels (often directed toward strengthening the constituent governments) by invoking the terms of the compact.

Viewed theoretically, these patterns of behavior and the arguments advanced to justify them serve to reaffirm the fundamental principles that (1) the strength of a federal polity does not stem from the power of the national government but from the authority vested in the nation as a whole; (2) both the national government and the governments of the constituent polities are possessed of delegated powers only; and (3) all governments are limited by the common national constitution.

All this should make it apparent that federalism is a form of popular government embodying elements of both republicanism and democracy. The federal structures occasionally adopted by nondemocratic systems must generally be considered "window dressing" except insofar as the injection of the federal principle may serve as a democratizing force in itself. In Yugoslavia, for example, the existence of a federal superstructure has proved useful in fostering such decentralization as the Communist party leadership wished to allow and may even have played a role in stimulating decentralizing tendencies.

Empirical and theoretical development

Ancient protofederal systems. Long before the term "federal" was invented, there were political systems that embodied elements of the federal principle. The Israelite political system was probably the first example in recorded history of a union of constituent polities based on a sense of common nationality, with national and tribal political institutions and some division of functions between the two partly formalized by a written constitution. As a republic it was never able to overcome the problems of national executive leadership and succession and, after some two hundred years, revised its constitution to superimpose a limited monarchy on its federal institutions. Still, as many of the seventeenth-century federalists noted, it came closer to resembling a modern federal system than any comparable premodern nation. Its classic intellectual product, the Bible, was the first book to discuss the problems of a federal polity.

Permanent leagues of independent states united by a sense of common need but without any sense of common nationhood were found in various parts of the Greek world. They were entrusted with certain matters in the realm of foreign affairs and defense but were in every respect accountable to their member states. The classic example of this system was the Achaean League (251–146 B.C.), a protofederal system often erroneously considered to be the first federal polity (Freeman 1863). The Greeks left some descriptions of their leagues but no theoretical discussions of the league as a political system. Except for Aristotle's criticisms, the great Greek political theorists ignored federalism as a political principle because the very idea contradicted their conception of the small, unified polis as the only basis upon which to build the good regime.

Several of the great ancient empires, notably the Persian, Hellenic, and Roman, structured their political systems around the principle of cultural home rule. Since political life was virtually inseparable from the religious and cultural aspects of society in the ancient world, imperial recognition of local constitutions offered a measure of contractual devolution of political power; however, as in more recent examples of this form of imperialism, such home rule was not a matter of local right but represented a conditional grant subject to unilateral revocation by the imperial rulers.

Medieval experiments. Elements of the federal principle are foreshadowed in medieval feudalism through its emphasis on essentially immutable contractual relationships that permanently link the contracting parties while guaranteeing their rights. However, the hierarchical character of these relationships, coupled with the lack of practical mechanisms to maintain the terms of the contracts, led to the degeneration of those elements in most feudal societies. Another movement in the direction of federalism grew out of the development of medieval commercial towns in central Europe which formed leagues for mutual defense and assistance following the Greek model. The most important development in this period was the first confederation of Swiss cantons in 1291 for mutual aid in defense of their independence. The success of this effort was in no small measure due to its connection, from the beginning, with quasi-popular government. These embryonic federal experiments all proceeded pragmatically while federal theory was confined to juridical discussions of the corporate relationships between polities in the Holy Roman Empire.

Ultimately a fusion of contractual elements from feudalism with political mechanisms from the commercial confederacies gave rise to the immediate antecedents of modern federalism. The Christian states on the Iberian Peninsula created a political system which in its most advanced stages came very close to authentic federalism. During the years of the reconquest, most of the peninsula was reorganized under the *fuero* system, which established local governments with relatively liberal political institutions in order to encourage resettlement. New states were formed through feudal-style contractual relationships designed to protect local rights. Three of these states joined in a quasi-federal arrangement under the crown of Aragon, each of them (plus several in Italy added later) retaining its own constitution and governing institutions as well as acquiring representation in the over-all Aragonese government. Unification of Spain under a multiple monarchy in 1469 left most of these federal elements intact for the next two and a half centuries, but the demands of the monarchy ultimately subverted them, transforming Spain into a precariously centralized state.

In the sixteenth century, certain emergent civil societies, influenced by the Reformation to return to Scripture as a political source and by the Spanish system of political organization, as well as by local necessity, began to apply federal principles for state-building purposes. The Hapsburg heirs to the Spanish crown had applied Iberian principles to the organization of their other European possessions. Their governmental reforms in the Netherlands provided an organizational basis for the federation of the United Provinces in the late sixteenth century. When that country gained its independence, it established a political system which, while unable to solve the most crucial technical problems of federalism, maintained itself in federal style for two hundred years, until Napoleon put an end to its existence, leaving a residue of noncentralization that marks the Netherlands today.

The Swiss, in the meantime, were developing their own techniques for combining feudal and commercial elements to create a loose confederation of cantons, which was also influenced by Biblical ideas and, perhaps negatively, by contacts with Hapsburg Spain. Achieving full independence in 1648, the Swiss confederation remained loosely leagued for two centuries (except for the Napoleonic interlude), until it adopted a federal constitution in 1848.

First modern formulations. The protofederalism of the United Provinces and the Swiss cantons, coming at the outset of the age of nationalism, also stimulated the first serious efforts to formulate federal theories based on modern political ideas. Jean Bodin analyzed the possibilities of federation in light of the problem of sovereignty. Hugo Grotius and Samuel Pufendorf examined federal arrangements as aspects of international law. These theorists all treated federalism as an aspect of international law. Johannes Althusius (1603), analyzing the Dutch and Swiss constitutions, was the first to perceive that federalism was really concerned with problems of national unity. The real father of modern federal theory, he was also the first to connect federalism with popular sovereignty and to distinguish between leagues, multiple monarchies, and confederations. His retention of hierarchical principles and his emphasis on the corporate organization of society both flawed the federal character of his work and reflected the empirical roots of his analysis.

Thus the rise of the nation-state in the sixteenth and seventeenth centuries stimulated federal solutions to the problems of national unification. In all but a few countries on the periphery of western Europe, the application of federal principles foundered on three problems: (1) the conciliation of feudally rooted hierarchies with a system demanding fundamental social equality in order to facilitate the sharing of power; (2) the reconciliation of local autonomy with national energy in an era of political upheaval that required most nations to maintain a state of constant mobilization basically incompatible with the toleration of local differences; and (3) the problem of executive leadership and succession, which is particularly complex in federal systems and was not solved until the United States invented the elected presidency.

Modern federalism.   The rise of modern imperialism also contributed to the emergence of federalism, as indicated by the works of the important prerevolutionary political theorists of the eighteenth century, e.g., Montesquieu and Adam Smith. Here, too, the Spanish experience was influential, but it remained for the British to create the requisite popular institutions in their colonization of North America and for the Biblically influenced colonists to create the theoretical justification for these institutions. The theoretical ambiguity of those quasi-federal institutions led Americans to assume that their relationship to the British government was federal, while London entertained no such notion (Becker 1922). The Americans' response to their view of the imperial system helped them develop the federal ideas they were later to use so creatively.

The founders of the United States of America can be said to have transformed and organized the principles of federalism into a practical system of government. They were able to do so partly because their nation developed without the disadvantages that plagued earlier federal systems. As a postfeudal society, the United States had no serious problem of coping with hierarchies. As a relatively isolated nation, external pressures for centralization were not present for nearly 150 years. American political inventiveness took care of the internal

problems of applying the federal principle, though not without having to fight a major civil war to resolve some of them. Though the specific forms of American federalism were not widely imitated with success, its basic principles of organization were emulated by almost every other nation attempting the federal solution to the problems of popular government in a pluralistic civil society. The creation of the theoretical framework for those principles was part and parcel of the invention of federalism. Set forth in its basics in the debate over ratification of the constitution, that framework had at its core *The Federalist* (1787–1788), the classic formulation of the principles of modern federalism. Equally important to the evolution of federal systems, however, were the arguments of those who wished to preserve even greater state autonomy; many of these arguments were transformed into tools to promote extraconstitutional decentralization during the nineteenth century.

From the first, American contributions to federal theory—even those of the few theorists not actively involved in politics—have been rooted in the practical concerns of maintaining a federal system. Most of these contributions have, accordingly, been formulated as discussions of constitutional law. The courts, particularly the federal Supreme Court, have conducted continuing debate on the meaning and character of federalism through the medium of case law. Leading political figures, such as Gallatin, Calhoun, Lincoln, Wilson, and the Roosevelts, have made real contributions through their state papers. The pragmatic orientation of those contributions, however, has tended to obscure their more lasting theoretical importance (Anderson 1955).

The French Revolution, while stimulating the development of popular government, was essentially hostile to the spirit and institutions of federalism. Its immediate heirs tried to destroy federal institutions in western Europe in the name of democracy, and the subsequent bearers of its tradition have proved equally hostile to federal ideas—except insofar as some of them have equated federalism with decentralized government.

In the nineteenth century, several of the new Latin American nations, following the United States example and also influenced by the federal elements in the Hispanic imperial tradition, experimented with federalism, with distinctly mixed results. Even where federalism survived in theory, the instability of Latin American governments and the frequent recourse to dictatorial regimes hampered its effective operation. Even so, the three largest Latin American nations—Argentina, Brazil, and Mexico—retain federal systems of varying political significance; federal principles are also included in the political systems of Colombia and Venezuela.

In the mid-nineteenth century European politicians and political theorists, stimulated by necessity, the American example, and the very influential studies of Tocqueville (1835), turned to consider federalism as a form of democratic political organization. Though practical applications remained few, numerous works were produced, primarily in the German-speaking countries, where doctrinaire and metaphysical analyses of federalism in relation to the problems of nationalism, sovereignty, and popular consent were in vogue. The most important of these works were the theoretical formulations of Bluntschli (1849–1852), based on his observations of federal reorganization in Switzerland, and the historical studies of Gierke. In the end, federal principles were used in the unification of Germany, and Switzerland adopted a modern federal constitution. Fully federal solutions were rejected in other nations, but several adopted quasi-federal institutions to meet particular problems of unification and decentralization.

During the late nineteenth century, British interest in imperial federalism was manifested in several ways. Canada and Australia were given federal constitutions and dominion status in 1867 and 1901, respectively, and the foundations were laid for the federal unification of India. British political theorists interested in imperial unity and internal devolution explored contemporary (Bryce 1888) and historical (Freeman 1863) federal experiments and presented arguments of their own as to the utility and proper organization of federal systems (Labillière 1894).

Whereas in the nineteenth century federalism was used to abet ethnic nationalism, in the twentieth it has been used as a means to unify multiethnic nations. Several of the ethnically heterogeneous nations created or reconstructed after World War I, including the Soviet Union and Yugoslavia, formally embraced federalism as a nominal solution to their nationality problems. The United Kingdom added a federal dimension at the same time to accommodate the Irish. Extension of nation-building activities to Asia and Africa, where ethnic diversity is even greater than in Europe, has led to new efforts in the same vein. In nations outside of the totalitarian orbit, such as India and Malaysia, federalism has been used to secure political and cultural rights for the larger ethnolinguistic groups. In Africa, where the survival of separate ethnic groups has been called into question by the native nationalists, federalism has been applied in several nations, including Nigeria and Cameroon, as a device for sharing political power rather than a way to maintain cultural autonomy.

The contemporary study of federalism. The emergence of political science as a discipline in the late nineteenth century stimulated a shift from an explicitly normative to a predominantly empirical interest in federalism. Such noted British scholars as Bryce (1901) and Dicey (1885) were the first to study federalism as part of their general interest in political systems. American scholars began their work in the 1870s, as the Civil War generation was passing into history, but their first works still reflected the issues of the war. Thus Burgess (1886) concluded that the utility of the states was dissipated by modern technology, just as their power was destroyed by the war, while Wilson (1885) accepted the view that the war had wrought great changes but still saw federalism as alive and vital.

Though these men and their colleagues laid the foundations for the empirical study of federal systems with the tools of contemporary political science, federalism as a field of study was neglected for many years. The rise of other problems to attract the attention of scholars, the negation of earlier legalistic and metaphysical approaches, and the decline of normative interest in the federal principle combined to dissuade younger political scientists from examining questions of federal government, except incidentally, until the twentieth century was well advanced.

Renewed interest in the field first developed when American students of public administration found themselves confronted with problems of intergovernmental relations at nearly every turn. The study of intergovernmental relations in the administrative realm brought about significant gains in the understanding of the process of federal government, not the least of which was a growing recognition that the assumptions about federalism underlying their work, borrowed whole from nineteenth-century theorists, needed serious re-examination. Beginning in the 1930s and 1940s, American and British political scientists began to raise fundamental questions about the nature of federal systems and the interrelationships of their governmental components (Anderson 1946). In the 1950s these questions were expanded to include, among others, problems of political influence, the role of political parties, the historical development of federal systems, and the meaning of earlier federal theories (Bachelder & Shaw 1964). By the early 1960s, students of existing federal governments were rediscovering the need to clarify the principles of federalism in order to understand the operation of those governments. Students of comparative government were also becoming increasingly interested in problems of political integration, centralization, and decentralization—all of which stimulated new interest in the systematic study of federalism.

Evaluation

While many attempts to establish federal systems have ended in failure, such systems, once established, have proved to be most durable. No authentic federal system that has lasted for even 15 years has ever been abandoned except through revolutionary disruption (as in the case of Germany), and in every such case federalism—showing remarkable resilience—has ultimately been restored. Certain theories to the contrary, there is no evidence that federalism represents a transitional stage on the road to unitary government. No federal system in history has ever "evolved" into a unitary one, nor has any established system been structurally consolidated by internal decision. On the contrary, federal devices to conciliate minority populations have been used in place of force to maintain unity even in consolidated systems. Moreover, federal systems or systems strongly influenced by the federal principle have been among the most stable and long-lasting of polities.

At the same time, relatively few cultures have been able to utilize federal principles in government. Anglo–American civil societies have done so most successfully. Even those not fully committed to federalism have, without exception, included elements of the federal principle in whatever systems they have chosen, no doubt because both constitutionalism and noncentralization rate high on the scale of Anglo–American political values.

Of the 16 formally federal nations that exist in the world today, Australia, Cameroon, Canada, India, Malaysia, Nigeria, and the United States were created under British colonial tutelage. These seven include all the nations established since World War II that have been able to maintain federal systems, and they provide most of the successful examples of federalism in operation. Of the nine remaining federal nations, Argentina, Brazil, and Mexico fall directly within the Hispanic political tradition and Austria, Germany, and Switzerland, though they follow the Germanic political tradition, were also influenced by Hispanic ideas at some point in their development. Both political traditions have been influential in stimulating federal inclinations in many of the nonfederal nations, but they have been notably less successful in fostering lasting federal institutions; the Hispanic

tradition has failed to combine federalism and stability, while the Germanic has tended toward authoritarian centralization. (The three remaining nations, Libya, the Soviet Union, and Yugoslavia, are federal in name and formal structure but hardly in any meaningful sense of the term.)

The successful operation of federal systems requires a particular kind of political environment, one which is conducive to popular government and has the strong traditions of political cooperation and self-restraint that are needed to maintain a system which minimizes the use of coercion. Beyond the level of tradition, federal systems operate best in societies with sufficient homogeneity of fundamental interests—or consensus—to allow a great deal of latitude in political operations and to place primary reliance upon voluntary collaboration. The existence of severe strains on the body politic which lead to the use of force to maintain domestic order is even more inimical to the successful maintenance of federal patterns of government than of other forms of popular government. Moreover, federal systems are most successful in civil societies with the human resources to fill many public offices competently and with material resources plentiful enough to allow a measure of economic waste in payment for the luxury of liberty.

DANIEL J. ELAZAR

[See also CENTRALIZATION AND DECENTRALIZATION; CONSTITUTIONAL LAW, article on DISTRIBUTION OF POWERS; PRESIDENTIAL GOVERNMENT. Other relevant material may be found in GOVERNMENT; INTERNATIONAL INTEGRATION; NATION; STATE.]

BIBLIOGRAPHY

ALTHUSIUS, JOHANNES (1603) 1932 Politica methodice digesta. Edited by Carl J. Friedrich. Cambridge, Mass.: Harvard Univ. Press. → The first European book directed entirely to the discussion of federalism. Text in Latin with a comprehensive English introduction.

AMERICAN ACADEMY OF POLITICAL AND SOCIAL SCIENCE 1965 Intergovernmental Relations in the United States. Edited by Harry W. Reynolds, Jr. Annals, Vol. 359. Philadelphia: The Academy.

ANDERSON, WILLIAM 1946 Federalism and Intergovernmental Relations: A Budget of Suggestions for Research. Chicago: Public Administration Service.

ANDERSON, WILLIAM 1955 The Nation and the States: Rivals or Partners? Minneapolis: Univ. of Minnesota Press. → One of the best descriptions of the American federal system.

ASPATURIAN, VERNON V. 1950 The Theory and Practice of Soviet Federalism. Journal of Politics 12:20–51.

BACHELDER, GLEN L.; and SHAW, PAUL C. 1964 Federalism: A Selected Bibliography. Unpublished manuscript, Michigan State Univ., Institute for Community Development and Services.

BECKER, CARL L. (1922) 1958 *The Declaration of Independence: A Study in the History of Political Ideas.* New York: Vintage. → An important study of the origins of American federal ideas.

BIRCH, ANTHONY H. 1955 *Federalism, Finance and Social Legislation in Canada, Australia, and the United States.* Oxford: Clarendon.

BLUNTSCHLI, JOHANN K. 1849–1852 *Geschichte des schweizerischen Bundesrechtes.* 2 vols. Zurich: Meyer & Zeller. → A theory of federal organization based on the reconstruction of the Swiss Confederation in 1848.

BOEHM, MAX H. 1931 Federalism. Volume 6, pages 169–172 in *Encyclopaedia of the Social Sciences.* New York: Macmillan. → Devoted primarily to a discussion of federalism as a social theory.

BONDURANT, JOAN 1958 *Regionalism vs. Provincialism: A Study in Problems of Indian National Unity.* India Press Digests, Monograph Series, No. 4. Berkeley: Univ. of California Press.

BRETT, LIONEL (editor) 1961 *Constitutional Problems of Federalism in Nigeria.* Lagos (Nigeria): Times Press.

BRIGHT, JOHN 1959 *A History of Israel.* Philadelphia: Westminster Press. → The best description of federal institutions in ancient Israel.

BRYCE, JAMES (1888) 1909 *The American Commonwealth.* 3d ed., 2 vols. New York and London: Macmillan. → An abridged edition was published in 1959 by Putnam. A classic work whose descriptions of federal–state relations follow conventional American opinions of the period.

BRYCE, JAMES 1901 *Studies in History and Jurisprudence.* New York: Oxford Univ. Press. → Includes Bryce's theoretical considerations of federalism.

BURGESS, JOHN W. 1886 The American Commonwealth. *Political Science Quarterly* 1:9–35. → One of the earliest pronouncements on the "demise of the states" in the United States.

CANADA, ROYAL COMMISSION ON DOMINION–PROVINCIAL RELATIONS 1940 *Report.* 3 vols. Ottawa: Patenaud. → Volume 1: *Canada: 1867–1939.* Volume 2: *Recommendations.* Volume 3: *Documentation.* The most comprehensive survey of the Canadian federal system.

CLAREMONT MEN'S COLLEGE, CLAREMONT, CALIF., INSTITUTE FOR STUDIES IN FEDERALISM 1961 *Essays in Federalism,* by George C. S. Benson et al. Claremont, Calif.: The College.

CODDING, GEORGE A. 1961 *The Federal Government of Switzerland.* Boston: Houghton Mifflin.

COWEN, ZEHMAN 1959 *Federal Jurisdiction in Australia.* New York: Oxford Univ. Press.

DIAMOND, MARTIN 1963 The Federalist. Pages 573–593 in Leo Strauss and Joseph Cropsey (editors), *History of Political Philosophy.* Chicago: Rand McNally. → An important discussion of *The Federalist* as a major contribution to democratic political theory.

DICEY, ALBERT V. (1885) 1961 *Introduction to the Study of the Law of the Constitution.* 10th ed. With an introduction by E. C. S. Wade. London: Macmillan; New York: St. Martins. → First published as *Lectures Introductory to the Study of the Law of the Constitution.* The classic liberal work on the British constitution that considers the questions of federalism in comparison with legislative union.

ELAZAR, DANIEL J. 1962 *The American Partnership: Intergovernmental Co-operation in the Nineteenth-century United States.* Univ. of Chicago Press. → A study of the evolution of intergovernmental relations in the United States.

ELAZAR, DANIEL J. 1966 *American Federalism: A View From the States.* New York: Crowell.

ELLIOTT, JOHN H. 1964 *Imperial Spain: 1469–1716.* New York: St. Martins. → Historical description of Spanish protofederal systems and their decline.

Federalism and Economic Growth in Underdeveloped Countries: A Symposium, by Ursula K. Hicks et al. 1961 New York: Oxford Univ. Press.

FREEMAN, EDWARD A. (1863) 1893 *The History of Federal Government in Greece and Italy.* 2d ed. London and New York: Macmillan. → A classic attempt to trace the origins of federalism.

GIERKE, OTTO VON (1913) 1934 *Natural Law and the Theory of Society: 1500 to 1800.* Translated with an introduction by Ernst Barker. Cambridge Univ. Press. → A study of the early modern origins of federal ideas. A translation of five subsections of Volume 4 of *Das deutsche Genossenschaftsrecht.* A paperback edition was published in 1957 by Beacon.

GOLDWIN, ROBERT A. (editor) 1963 *A Nation of States: Essays on the American Federal System.* Chicago: Rand McNally.

GRAVES, W. BROOKE 1964 *American Intergovernmental Relations: Their Origins, Historical Development, and Current Status.* New York: Scribner.

GRODZINS, MORTON 1960a American Political Parties and the American System. *Western Political Quarterly* 13:974–998. → A very important descriptive analysis of the role of a noncentralized party system in the maintenance of federalism.

GRODZINS, MORTON 1960b The Federal System. Pages 265–282 in U.S. President's Commission on National Goals, *Goals for Americans.* Englewood Cliffs, N.J.: Prentice-Hall. → A comprehensive description of the American federal system.

GRODZINS, MORTON 1966 *The American System: A New View of Government in the United States.* Chicago: Rand McNally.

HAMILTON, ALEXANDER; MADISON, JAMES; and JAY, JOHN (1787–1788) 1961 *The Federalist.* Edited with introduction and notes by Jacob E. Cooke. Middletown, Conn.: Wesleyan Univ. Press. → The classic foundation of federal theory.

KAUFMANN, YEHEZKEL (1937–1948) 1960 *The Religion of Israel: From Its Beginnings to the Babylonian Exile.* Univ. of Chicago Press. → An abridgment and translation of *Toldot Hā-emūnāh Hā-yisrāelit.* An important discussion of the origins of covenant theory in the Bible.

LABILLIÈRE, FRANCIS P. DE 1894 *Federal Britain: Or, Unity and Federation of the Empire.* London: Low, Marston. → A compendium of studies relating to the idea of British imperial federalism.

LIVINGSTON, WILLIAM S. (editor) 1963 *Federalism in the Commonwealth: A Bibliographical Commentary.* London: Cassell.

MAASS, ARTHUR (editor) 1959 *Area and Power: A Theory of Local Government.* Glencoe, Ill.: Free Press. → Pioneering effort to formulate theories about the areal distribution of power and its consequences.

MACMAHON, ARTHUR W. (editor) (1955) 1962 *Federalism: Mature and Emergent.* New York: Russell. → An excellent collection of articles on federalism in theory and practice, with emphasis on the United States and Europe.

MAIN, JACKSON T. 1961 *The Anti-Federalists: Critics of the Constitution, 1781–1788.* Chapel Hill: Univ. of North Carolina Press. → A study of the movement opposed to the ratification of the American constitution.

MILLER, PERRY (1939) 1961 *The New England Mind: The Seventeenth Century.* Boston: Beacon. → An important discussion of seventeenth-century "federal theology" and its application in the New World.

MILNE, DAVID 1957 *The Scottish Office and Other Scottish Government Departments.* New York: Oxford Univ. Press. → A survey of the history and functions of the separate ministries for Scotland.

MOGI, SOBEI 1931 *The Problem of Federalism: A Study in the History of Political Theory.* 2 vols. London: Allen & Unwin. → Compendious historical survey of the various theories of federalism.

RIKER, WILLIAM A. 1964 *Federalism: Origin, Operation, Significance.* Boston: Little.

SCHMIDHAUSER, JOHN R. 1958 *The Supreme Court as Final Arbiter in Federal–State Relations: 1789–1957.* Chapel Hill: Univ. of North Carolina Press.

SHARMA, BRIJ M. 1953 *Federalism in Theory and Practice.* 2 vols. Chandausi (India): Bhargava. → One of the few comprehensive studies of federal systems throughout the world; gives special emphasis to the Indian situation.

SMILEY, DONALD V. 1962 The Rowell–Sirois Report, Provincial Autonomy, and Post-war Canadian Federalism. *Canadian Journal of Economics and Political Science* 28:54–69.

SMILEY, DONALD V. 1965 The Two Themes of Canadian Federalism. *Canadian Journal of Economics and Political Science* 31:80–97.

TOCQUEVILLE, ALEXIS DE (1835) 1945 *Democracy in America.* 2 vols. New York: Knopf. → First published in French. Paperback editions were published in 1961 by Vintage and by Schocken.

U.S. COMMISSION ON INTERGOVERNMENTAL RELATIONS 1955 *A Report to the President for Transmittal to the Congress.* Washington: Government Printing Office.

U.S. CONGRESS, HOUSE, COMMITTEE ON GOVERNMENT OPERATIONS (1955) 1956 *Intergovernmental Relations in the United States: A Selected Bibliography.* Washington: Government Printing Office.

WELLS, ROGER H. 1961 *The States in West German Federalism: A Study of Federal–State Relations, 1949–1960.* New York: Bookman.

WHEARE, KENNETH C. (1946) 1964 *Federal Government.* 4th ed. New York: Oxford Univ. Press.

WILSON, WOODROW (1885) 1961 *Congressional Government: A Study in American Politics.* New York: Meridian. → The classic study of a legislature-centered federal government.

FEEBLEMINDEDNESS
See MENTAL RETARDATION.

FEEDBACK
See CYBERNETICS; HOMEOSTASIS; MODELS, MATHEMATICAL; SIMULATION.

FERENCZI, SÁNDOR

Sándor Ferenczi, one of the earliest psychoanalysts, was born in Miskolc, Hungary, in 1873 and died in Budapest, in his house in the Buda hills, in 1933. He was for a time Sigmund Freud's closest friend and collaborator.

Early life. Ferenczi was one of 11 children. His parents, whose surname had originally been Fraenkel, were well-to-do, owning the largest bookstore in Miskolc. A biographer, Izette De Forest (1954), tells us that Ferenczi's parents were unusually enlightened in the freedom and companionship they gave to their children and that the life of the family was gay and spontaneous, devoted to the enjoyment of scholarship, music, drama, poetry, and languages. The famous psychoanalyst Ernest Jones (1953–1957)—who knew Ferenczi well—tells us, however, that Ferenczi was haunted throughout life by a quite inordinate and insatiable longing for his father's love. Ferenczi himself said in a letter to Freud that his feelings about Freud and other colleagues were bound up with his childhood difficulties with his father and brothers.

After graduating from the local Gymnasium, Ferenczi studied medicine in Vienna, receiving his degree in 1894. He had a year of compulsory service as a physician in the Austro-Hungarian army and then interned in various hospitals in Budapest, notably St. Rókus Korház. There he specialized in neurology and neuropathology, also developing his skill in hypnotism. In 1900 he opened an office in Budapest for the practice of neurology.

Development of interest in psychoanalysis. When Ferenczi first read Freud's *The Interpretation of Dreams* he was not able to assimilate its teachings. It was his rereading of Breuer and Freud's *Studies on Hysteria* that impressed him with the claims of psychoanalysis. He wrote to Freud in 1907 and, accompanied by Dr. F. Stein of Budapest, who introduced him, called on Freud in February 1908. The impression that he made brought an invitation to spend a fortnight in August with the Freud family at their summer place. He became a member of the Vienna Psychoanalytic Society, the small group that met on Wednesday evenings with Freud.

Later career. Ferenczi and Freud traveled together extensively, and between 1908 and 1933 they exchanged more than a thousand letters. In 1909 Ferenczi accompanied Freud on a trip to the United States, where Freud lectured at Clark University. In 1910, at Freud's suggestion, Ferenczi proposed the founding of the International Psychoanalytic Association; and in 1913 he founded the Hungarian Psychoanalytic Society. In 1916 he underwent a brief personal analysis with Freud; it lasted only three weeks, for two hours a day, since Ferenczi had to return to his military duties as a medical officer in Hungary. According to Freud, the analysis was continued later. In 1918 Ferenczi was elected president of the International Psycho-analytic Society; he relinquished the presidency in 1919. His failure to be invited again to be president of the society was a keen disappointment to him and may have been a consequence of his advocacy of lay analysis.

In 1919, after 18 years of indecision, Ferenczi married. The marriage was a very happy one, and although there were no children, Ferenczi delighted in his relationship with his wife's daughters by a former marriage.

Ferenczi came to New York City for eight months in 1926–1927 to give a course of lectures at the New School for Social Research. During his visit he gave analytic training to eight or nine people, mostly laymen.

As Ferenczi's views on psychoanalytic technique diverged more and more from Freud's in later years, he gradually withdrew from Freud. Although there was never a sharp break, a sense of estrangement developed between them.

Personality. Ernest Jones described Ferenczi as follows:

He [Ferenczi] had an altogether delightful personality which retained a good deal of the simplicity and a still greater amount of the imagination of the child; I have never known anyone better able to conjure up, in speech and gesture, the point of view of a young child. . . . He had a very keen and direct intuitive perception, one that went well with the highest possible measure of native honesty. . . . He had an exceptionally original and creative mind. . . . As is often the way, however, with people who throw out masses of ideas like sparks, their quality was very uneven, since judgment—objective and critical judgment—was the one gift denied to Ferenczi. . . . (1959, pp. 199–200)

At times, Jones says, Ferenczi could be somewhat masterful, and even dictatorial; and toward the end of his life, especially during his final illness, he "lost most of his old cheerfulness and vitality, became heavy, depressed, and ungracious, withdrew from his friends, and—most serious of all—allowed his scientific judgment to be gravely deflected" (Jones 1959, p. 200).

Early contributions to psychoanalysis. Freud always gave Ferenczi generous credit for ideas the two had worked out in common, and at times it is not possible to distinguish their respective shares. Among Ferenczi's important early papers are "Stages in the Development of the Sense of Reality" (1913); a paper on the relationship of homosexuality and paranoia (1912a); and a paper describing transitory symptom formation during psychoanalytic treatment (1912b). He worked out in detail the implications of Freud's explanation of

hypnosis as depending on the masochistic attitude of the person hypnotized; and he discriminated between the different forms of homosexuality.

In the paper on the development of the sense of reality—praised by Jones as "the best he [Ferenczi] ever wrote" (Jones 1933)—Ferenczi listed four stages through which the child passes in moving from domination by the pleasure principle to acceptance of the reality principle. These four periods are the period of unconditional omnipotence (intrauterine), the period of magical–hallucinatory omnipotence (earliest infancy), the period of omnipotence by the help of magic gestures, and the period of magic thoughts and magic words. He showed that the child at first has all his wishes gratified and believes himself omnipotent. Later, when the child finds that wishes are no longer immediately gratified and has to accept some limitations upon his power, he attempts to circumvent these frustrations by imagining the gratification of his wishes, or by making magical gestures, or by using magical thoughts and words. When at last the individual realizes that the environment does not conform to his wishes, that gratification is entirely conditional upon work, and that even work does not always lead to success, then the sense of reality may be said to be fully developed.

Theory of genital sexuality. Influenced by Darwin and Lamarck as well as by psychoanalytic thought, Ferenczi sought in *Thalassa: A Theory of Genitality* (1924) to explicate the relationship of sexuality to the evolution of the race. Ferenczi pointed out that pregenital sexual impulses can be expressed and gratified by genital activity. For instance, a man can express urethral or anal tendencies in the way he performs and experiences sexual intercourse. Such a mixture of partial sexual drives, and indirect expression of them, Ferenczi chose to call "amphimixis." Sexual intercourse can also express various fantasies, including the fantasy of reunion with the mother through return to the womb, a fantasy revealed in the course of psychoanalysis of patients. Since the penis goes into the birth canal during intercourse and the seminal fluid does go into the uterus, sexual intercourse is well suited to the acting out of this fantasy.

Assuming a phylogenetic origin for this fantasy, Ferenczi speculated that it derives from the marine background of the race; mankind's ancestors were fishes. Thus, in wishing to return to the womb, man is also expressing the wish to return to the sea, the origin of all life.

In general, psychoanalysts have ignored these

speculations. They believe that Ferenczi did not have a satisfactory way of testing his speculations by an appeal to evidence.

Contributions to technique.   Ferenczi is acknowledged to have been a gifted therapist. He proposed a number of innovations in technique: at first these centered on the so-called "active" technique; later they had to do with a greater participation by the therapist in the psychoanalytic interaction, a participation that included the granting of more— and more direct—gratifications to patients than most analysts believed advisable. These later experiments led Freud to write, "He was persuaded that we could accomplish far more with our patients if we gave them enough of the love they had longed for in childhood" (1933, pp. 297–299). Most analysts reject Ferenczi's belief that granting more gratification to patients is therapeutic. Ferenczi's strong interest in the reactions of disappointment and mistrust that the child suffers in his relationship with his parents has led a few of his pupils, notably Alice Balint (1949), to investigate early parent–child relationships.

Ferenczi's early contributions to psychoanalysis have been so fully assimilated that their origin is often forgotten, although his later writings, which were more speculative and deviated from Freudian orthodoxy, have been less widely accepted.

FRANK AULD, JR.

[*For the historical context of Ferenczi's work, see* PSYCHOANALYSIS *and the biography of* FREUD. *For discussion of the subsequent development of his ideas, see* SEXUAL BEHAVIOR, *articles on* SEXUAL DEVIATION: PSYCHOLOGICAL ASPECTS *and* SEXUAL DEVIATION: SOCIAL ASPECTS.]

WORKS BY FERENCZI

(1908–1914) 1952   *First Contributions to Psycho-analysis.* London: Hogarth. → Contains a selection of Ferenczi's essays that were originally published in German. First published in English as *Contributions to Psychoanalysis.* Later editions have the title *Sex in Psychoanalysis.*

(1908–1925) 1927   *Further Contributions to the Theory and Technique of Psycho-analysis.* New York: Liveright. → Contains a collection of some of Ferenczi's most important contributions to psychoanalysis. Translated from the German.

(1908–1933) 1955   *Final Contributions to the Problems and Methods of Psycho-analysis.* London: Hogarth. → A collection of papers written in or first published in German.

(1912a) 1950   On the Part Played by Homosexuality in the Pathogenesis of Paranoia. Pages 154–184 in Sándor Ferenczi, *Selected Papers.* Volume 1: Sex in Psychoanalysis. New York: Basic Books. → First published in German.

(1912b) 1950   Transitory Symptom Constructions During the Analysis. Pages 193–212 in Sándor Ferenczi, *Selected Papers.* Volume 1: Sex in Psychoanalysis. New York: Basic Books. → First published in German.

(1913) 1950   Stages in the Development of the Sense of Reality. Pages 213–239 in Sándor Ferenczi, *Selected Papers.* Volume 1: Sex in Psychoanalysis. New York: Basic Books. → First published in German.

(1924) 1949   *Thalassa: A Theory of Genitality.* New York: Psychoanalytic Quarterly. → First published as *Versuch einer Genital-theorie.*

(1924) 1925   FERENCZI, SÁNDOR; and RANK, OTTO   *The Development of Psychoanalysis.* New York: Nervous and Mental Disease Pub. → First published as *Entwicklungsziele der Psychoanalyse.*

Selected Papers. 3 vols. New York: Basic Books, 1950–1955. → Volume 1: *Sex in Psychoanalysis,* 1950. Volume 2: *Theory and Technique of Psychoanalysis,* 1952. Volume 3: *Problems and Methods of Psychoanalysis,* 1955.

SUPPLEMENTARY BIBLIOGRAPHY

BALINT, ALICE   1949   Love for the Mother and Mother-love. *International Journal of Psycho-Analysis* 30: 251–259.

BALINT, MICHAEL   1949   Sándor Ferenczi: Obiit 1933. *International Journal of Psycho-Analysis* 30:215–219.

DE FOREST, IZETTE   1954   *The Leaven of Love.* New York: Harper.

FREUD, SIGMUND   1933   Obituary: Sándor Ferenczi. *International Journal of Psycho-Analysis* 14:297–299.

JONES, ERNEST   1933   Obituary: Sándor Ferenczi, 1873–1933. *International Journal of Psycho-Analysis* 14: 463–466.

JONES, ERNEST   1953–1957   *The Life and Work of Sigmund Freud.* 3 vols. New York: Basic Books. → Volume 1: *Formative Years and the Great Discoveries,* 1953. Volume 2: *Years of Maturity,* 1955. Volume 3: *Last Phase,* 1957. See especially Volumes 2–3.

JONES, ERNEST   1959   *Free Associations: Memoirs of a Psycho-analyst.* New York: Basic Books.

FERGUSON, ADAM

"I hear he [Ferguson] is about to publish . . . a natural history of man: exhibiting a view of him in the savage state, and in the several successive states of pasturage, agriculture and commerce" (Reid [1764–1788] 1895, p. 42). Thus wrote Thomas Reid on December 20, 1765, to his friend Dr. David Skeene. Reid had just succeeded Adam Smith in the chair of moral philosophy at Glasgow. Nearly a century later, Karl Marx singled out Ferguson, although not with complete accuracy, as the first in modern times to develop the theory of the division of labor in economy and society. Still later, Gumplowicz, distinguished exponent of the conflict theory of society, saw in Ferguson's *History of Civil Society* "the first natural history of society" and in Ferguson himself "the first sociologist" (Gumplowicz 1892, p. 67). William Dunning found in him one who combined "the critical spirit of Hume and the historical spirit of Montesquieu" most attractively and "studied society and its institutions . . . to determine by the light of history whither society was moving, not by superhuman wisdom to fix its course" (Dunning [1920] 1936, p. 63).

These brief characterizations may serve to epitomize the thought, and the place in the history of social thought, of one of the outstanding "moral philosophers" of Scotland of the later eighteenth century.

Adam Ferguson was born in the manse of Logierait, Perthshire, in 1723, and was educated for the Christian ministry (like so many leaders of thought in the Scotland of his day) at St. Andrews and Edinburgh. At the age of 21, he was appointed deputy-chaplain—and later chaplain—of the famous Highland "Black Watch" regiment. In 1757, Ferguson succeeded Hume as keeper of the Advocates' Library in Edinburgh, and in 1759 he was appointed to the chair of natural philosophy in the university there; he was transferred five years later to the chair of pneumatics and moral philosophy. He filled this post with distinction until 1785, when for reasons of health he resigned it. He continued literary activities at a more leisurely pace in retirement.

In 1767, he published his *Essay on the History of Civil Society*, using "history" in the then current static–descriptive sense as well as in a "temporalizing" sense. This work strongly reflects, by Ferguson's own admission, the influence of Montesquieu. Two years later, Ferguson published the *Institutes of Moral Philosophy*, an outline of the course of lectures that he followed, with variations, throughout his teaching career. In 1783, he published *The History of the Progress and Termination of the Roman Republic*, a work that reached many editions. His two-volume *Principles of Moral and Political Science*, "being chiefly a Retrospect of Lectures delivered in the College of Edinburgh," was published in 1792. This was in reality only a greatly expanded and more finished version of the *Institutes*, with some variations. Most of these works appeared almost immediately in translation in Germany and France, and some also in Italy and Russia. He was also widely known and read in America.

Ferguson was a principal founder and charter member of the Royal Society of Edinburgh; on a visit to the Continent in 1793, he was made an honorary member of the Berlin Academy of Science. He was closely associated, through personal friendship, various literary clubs, and correspondence, with others from Edinburgh, such as Hume, Lord Kames, William Robertson, John Home, Adam Smith (with whom he had a temporary falling-out), and Edward Gibbon, all of whom had high regard for Ferguson. Abroad he received the acclaim of men like Baron d'Holbach in France and Schiller, Jacobi, Herder, and others in Germany. He spent his last years, with failing eyesight, at St. Andrews, where he died in 1816, at the age of 92. He was buried in the old cathedral churchyard, and the beautiful epitaph that Sir Walter Scott, boyhood playmate of the Ferguson children, wrote for him is still to be seen there.

Whereas Ferguson's fame at home and abroad rested chiefly on his *Civil Society*, this work is best understood in the broader setting of his entire social and moral philosophy, which is more adequately stated in his *Principles*. "Moral philosophy" covers comparative anthropology, individual and social psychology, and "natural religion" and is applied to jurisprudence, economics and politics, and ethics. The basic concern of moral philosophy is human nature itself. "Human nature," Ferguson once observed, "is my trade"—meaning, no doubt, the business of his chair. Man is viewed as a rationally intelligent, morally evaluating, active, and therefore progressive animal, always and everywhere living in society. He is to be studied, therefore, not only as an individual but also as a member of the community. The community is at once the source of his being, the field of his operations, the end of most of his actions, and the indispensable means— through the invention and use of language as his principal instrument of communication—to the realization of his essential humanity.

Key elements in Ferguson's social theory are a clear-cut distinction between "physical law," which he saw as a generalization of behavioral fact on every level, and "moral law," which he saw as a generalization of values and norms of conduct; a sharp differentiation of the cultural and traditional from the biological; a juxtaposition of the principles of "union" and of "rivalship" or conflict; the division of labor in economy and society; and a consistently evolutionistic viewpoint skeptical of planned progress—evolution, however, usually in an ontogenetic and cultural, rather than a biological, application.

Ferguson's moral philosophy in particular was essentially that of the ancient Stoics: Man is by his very nature an active being and a social being; all action involves choices, both of ends and of means to ends; choices are made between moral values and result in either happiness or misery, both for the actor and for his fellow men. If norms of conduct and systems of such norms are to be effective, they must be rationally based on empirical knowledge both of human nature and "of the situation in which [man] is placed." "Men of real fortitude, integrity and ability are well placed in every scene" ([1767] 1819, p. 506). "Everyone indeed is answerable only for himself; and, in preserving the integrity of one citizen, does what is required of him for the happiness of the whole" (1792, vol. 2, p. 512).

Like most of his Scottish contemporaries, Ferguson was averse to "metaphysics," or abstract philosophizing; yet he was not without philosophical acumen, a regard for system, a sense of "wholism," and a clear understanding of basic methodology. In this sense, he was an exponent of the "common-sense" philosophy and one of its founders.

WILLIAM C. LEHMANN

[*For the historical context of Ferguson's work, see the biography of* HUME.]

WORKS BY FERGUSON

(1767) 1819 *An Essay on the History of Civil Society.* 8th ed. Philadelphia: Finley.

(1769) 1800 *Institutes of Moral Philosophy.* New ed., enl. Basel: Decker.

(1783) 1841 *The History of the Progress and Termination of the Roman Republic.* 3 vols. Philadelphia: Wardle.

1792 *Principles of Moral and Political Science.* 2 vols. Edinburgh: Trahan.

SUPPLEMENTARY BIBLIOGRAPHY

DUNNING, WILLIAM A. (1920) 1936 *A History of Political Theories From Rousseau to Spencer.* New York: Macmillan.

GUMPLOWICZ, LUDWIG 1892 *Die soziologische Staatsidee.* Graz (Austria): Leuschner & Lubensky.

JOGLAND, HERTA H. 1959 *Ursprünge und Grundlagen der Soziologie bei Adam Ferguson.* Berlin: Duncker & Humblot.

KETTLER, DAVID 1965 *The Social and Political Thought of Adam Ferguson.* Columbus: Ohio State Univ. Press.

LEHMANN, WILLIAM C. 1930 *Adam Ferguson and the Beginnings of Modern Sociology.* New York: Columbia Univ. Press.

REID, THOMAS (1764–1788) 1895 *Works.* 2 vols. London: Longmans.

SMALL, JOHN 1864 Biographical Sketch of Adam Ferguson, LL.D.: Professor of Moral Philosophy in the University of Edinburgh. Royal Society of Edinburgh, *Transactions* 23:599–665.

FERTILITY

Demographers distinguish fertility (actual reproduction) from fecundity (the capacity for reproduction). The distinction is important, because in all societies actual reproduction is less, often much less, than the potential maximum. The rather wide variations in actual fertility among societies have no known general relation to differences in fecundity. In specific instances, low fertility may be explained by such biological factors as venereal disease. However, it is likely that group fertility levels vary generally in relation to social factors that affect either the social norms about the proper number of children or a limited number of means of fertility control. These means are *intermediate* between the social organization or social norms, on the one hand, and actual fertility, on the other hand.

Davis and Blake (1956) have provided the following useful classification of these "intermediate variables":

Factors affecting exposure to intercourse:
  (A) Those governing the formation and dissolution of unions in the reproductive period:
    (1) Age of entry into sexual unions.
    (2) Permanent celibacy: proportion of women never entering sexual unions.
    (3) Amount of reproductive period spent after or between unions.
      (a) When unions are broken by divorce, separation, or desertion.
      (b) When unions are broken by death of husband.
  (B) Those governing the exposure to intercourse within unions:
    (4) Voluntary abstinence.
    (5) Involuntary abstinence (from impotence, illness, unavoidable but temporary separations).
    (6) Coital frequency (excluding periods of abstinence).
Factors affecting exposure to conception:
    (7) Fecundity or infecundity, as affected by involuntary causes.
    (8) Use or non-use of contraception:
      (a) By mechanical and chemical means.
      (b) By other means.
    (9) Fecundity or infecundity, as affected by voluntary causes (sterilization, subincision, medical treatment, etc.).
Factors affecting gestation and successful parturition:
    (10) Foetal mortality from involuntary causes.
    (11) Foetal mortality from voluntary causes.

Most of the intermediate variables are regulated by a complex structure of normative prescriptions (Nag 1962; Freedman 1963). For example, how many children a couple should have is a problem so recurrent and with so many social ramifications in each society that it would be a sociological anomaly if appropriate social norms did not develop as a social solution to guide behavior. Moreover, different combinations of values for these variables may produce identical fertility levels, whereas societies or groups with very different fertility levels may have similar values on some of the intermediate variables. Of course, the connection between some of these intermediate cultural variables and a society's fertility level need not be apparent to members of the society.

Measurement of fertility

Fertility can be defined as the number of births occurring in a population unit during a specified time period. The unit may be the individual male or female, the male–female couple, the social stratum or other groupings of individuals or couples, or the whole society. For any of these levels, birth rates or frequency distributions may be computed separately or adjusted for a large variety of social, economic, or demographic characteristics. In most official statistics, the time period is short, giving a cross-section picture of what happens in a particular year or period. An important departure from cross-section rates is the measurement of fertility over the childbearing span of historical cohorts of women [see Cohort Analysis].

"Period" measures. The most common fertility measure is the *crude birth rate*, or number of births per thousand population per annum. It is usually computed for whole nations or for major demographic strata within nations, such as the urban population. More refined measures are important for some purposes, but the crude birth rate is still often used in evaluating the contribution of fertility to population growth in relation to mortality and migration. Table 1 shows the considerable variation in crude birth rates among major world regions.

Birth rates are called *age-specific* when they are computed for fairly narrow age groups (usually one or five years), usually with reference to the female population only. Since the crude birth rate is a function of both the age–sex distribution of the population and of the age-specific fertility rates, various methods are used to eliminate the effect of varying age–sex distributions in a comparison of different populations. This may be done either by standardization (in this case, the use of a common age–sex distribution to weight the different age-specific rates) or by the computation of one of the four remaining measures in common use by demographers:

(1) Births per annum per thousand women in the childbearing years (the *general fertility rate*).

(2) Births per annum per thousand women in specified age groups (*age-specific birth rates*).

Table 1 — Crude birth rates and gross reproduction rates for less and more economically developed regions of the world, 1963

	Crude birth[a] rate	Gross reproduction[a] rate
Less developed regions	41–42[b]	2.6–2.7[b]
Africa	48	3.0
North	46	2.9
West	54	3.4
South and east	45	2.7
Asia (excluding Soviet Union)	40–41[b]	2.5–2.6[b]
Southwest	45	3.0
South central	44	2.9
Southeast	49	2.9
East	35–37[b]	2.1–2.3[b]
America (excluding North America)	41	2.8
Middle	45	3.0
South	40	2.7
More developed regions	22	1.4
North America	24	1.8
Europe	19	1.3
Northern and western	18	1.3
Central	18	1.2
Southern	21	1.3
Oceania	24	1.8
Soviet Union	25	1.4
World total	35–36[b]	2.25–2.31[b]

a. Provisional weighted averages of most recent rates available in 1963 for countries within each region.

b. No absolute figure obtainable because of varying estimates for mainland China; figures given here correspond to range of best alternative estimates.

Source: Adapted from "Conditions and Trends . . ." 1965.

(3) The *gross reproduction rate* or "total fertility rate" (a simple summation of the age-specific birth rates for female babies or all babies).

(4) The *net reproduction rate* (an adjustment of the gross reproduction rate to take into account the effect of mortality on reproduction rates).

These are all "period" measures—that is, measures based on the births and deaths of a *particular* year or other time period considerably shorter than the reproductive span of the couples in the population. The rates do not take into account the earlier reproductive history of the units measured; they may therefore be misleading about long-run reproductive trends, especially for populations in which efficient family-planning methods are widely used. Short-run variations in conventional period rates may result from variations in the number of women marrying at each age and in child-spacing patterns, rather than from the number of children born over the childbearing span. For example, marriage rates and the birth of a first child are rather closely correlated with the business cycle in highly industrialized countries (Kirk & Nortman 1959).

Fertility measures of historical cohorts. A major methodological advance in recent years is the measurement of the cumulative fertility of historical *cohorts* of women, taking into account the family-building sequence of marriage and the spacing of successive children (France . . . 1953). Ideally the data needed for each historical birth cohort include the percentage of each cohort dying, the percentage of the single marrying, the percentage with one previous birth having another, and so on. From annual empirical probabilities of this type, it is possible to reconstruct, to date, the cumulative fertility of a particular cohort or of the whole population. But only a few countries are beginning to collect these data.

In cohort analysis, the stages of family building are related to specific historical dates, not just to abstract age categories. It is therefore possible to link variations in family-building patterns for particular cohorts to time series for economic or other social phenomena.

Data for fertility studies. The newer, more sophisticated measures cannot be used in most countries at present, because they lack even the elementary data required for the simpler conventional measures. However, special efforts are being made to improve fertility statistics in some of the developing countries in order to measure the success of programs to reduce the birth rate [see POPULATION, *article on* POPULATION POLICIES].

Sample surveys are used increasingly to estimate fertility and other related phenomena, especially where other statistical resources are lacking. For example, a series of sample surveys is the principal basis for our knowledge of African populations. The sample survey is also often used to collect information about social factors that may affect fertility, since some of the most important intermediate variables, such as age at marriage or use of contraception, do not appear at all in the official series.

Fertility in preindustrial societies

Despite the lack of statistical data, it can be asserted with some confidence that fertility rates have been moderately high to very high in almost all preindustrial societies throughout history. With the high mortality levels that have prevailed in such societies, fertility had to be moderately high for the society to survive.

An increasing volume of data for contemporary preindustrial societies indicates, without exception, that fertility is at least moderately high (see Table 2). With the exception of the Tikopia, the

Table 2 — Distribution of less and more economically developed countries by level of crude birth rate, 1963

Crude birth rate (per thousand population)[a]	Less developed regions[b]	More developed regions[b]
Under 15.0	—	3
15.0–19.9	1	17
20.0–24.9	4	10
25.0–29.9	1	3
30.0–34.9	3	—
35.0–39.9	11	—
40.0–44.9	21	1
45.0–49.9	28	1
50.0–54.9	12	—
55.0–59.9	5	—
60.0 and over	2	—
Total countries[c]	88	35

a. Wherever a crude birth rate had not yet been published for 1963, the most recent available rate was used.
b. See Table 1 for geographical composition of these regions.
c. Excluding countries having fewer than 250,000 inhabitants in 1960, countries having no satisfactory data, and a few countries for which examination of available data had not been completed in 1963.

Source: Adapted from "Conditions and Trends . . ." 1965.

only substantiated instances of relatively low fertility in preindustrial societies are those subject to extreme social disorganization (Lorimer 1954, chapter 3). From the point of view of a preindustrial society, of course, high fertility is a functional adjustment to high mortality; but from the point of view of the reproducing couple, high fertility is motivated by the central importance of familial and kinship ties in their lives. Motivations for larger numbers of children are increased when children enhance the ability of the familial unit to attain socially valued goals, and when such goals are attained through kinship and familial ties rather than through other social relationships.

Fertility and social values. Although a reasonably large number of children may be vitally important to parents in a preindustrial society, this does not necessarily mean that the normative value is for the highest possible fertility. But evidence on the existing norm in preindustrial societies is less than satisfactory. Ford (1945) has indicated that the normative pressures against childlessness and against very small families are great and probably universal in preindustrial societies. However, he has also concluded that mothers are ambivalent about childbirth in many circumstances and that considerable social pressure may be required to ensure adequate reproduction. Davis and Blake (1956) have pointed out that since to have some children is very important, a society with high and variable mortality is likely to have built into its structure very strong pressures for bearing children early in marriage, before the death of one or both parents, and also to have additional children as a safeguard against the catastrophic loss of the essential minimum number. On the other hand, if unfavorable conditions develop, this may result in "too many" children. Therefore, there may be a delicate balance between pressures that tend toward higher fertility, to ensure at least a certain minimum number of children, and contrary pressures that encourage abortion or infanticide in order to minimize or eliminate what, under difficult subsistence conditions, becomes an intolerable surplus. In any case, although there is general agreement that fertility is likely to be high in almost all preindustrial societies, there is also a body of evidence about the existence of control practices that keep fertility below a potential biological maximum, and about cultural and social factors that produce variations in fertility through these practices.

Cultural effects on intermediate variables. On the question of control, there is evidence that the "natural fertility" of man is probably higher than that reported for most preindustrial societies (Lorimer 1954, chapter 1; Henry 1961), but genetic differentials in fecundity cannot be ruled out. Health conditions reducing fecundity and increasing fetal mortality may constitute a functional, if unintended, adjustment to keep fertility below maximum levels.

Evidence has been assembled on the use of a wide variety of control measures—including contraception, abstinence, abortion, and infanticide—in many preindustrial societies (Himes 1936; Devereux 1955; Nag 1962). Unfortunately, the evidence usually demonstrates the existence of certain practices in a culture without specifying either the extent of use or the effect on fertility. Nevertheless, there is a basis for the tentative generalization that more or less effective methods of control potentially were available in many preindustrial societies, probably affected fertility levels in some, and, presumably, might have had a much wider use and effect were it not for the rewards derived from having children in such societies and the risk that these rewards would be lost because of unpredictably high mortality [see FERTILITY CONTROL].

There are no empirically validated general explanations for the variations in fertility from high to very high among preindustrial societies. It is often possible to point to particular intermediate variables as the immediate causes of less than maximum fertility, but even in these instances the *level* of the intermediate variables is a topic that

so far has given rise to explanations that are at best speculative.

Among the most important attempts at general explanation are those linking variations in kinship structure to variations in fertility (Lorimer 1954, chapter 2). A specific example of importance is the hypothesis that neolocal nuclear family systems and related economic arrangements led to late marriage or nonmarriage in preindustrial Europe, producing relatively low birth rates (Eversley 1963). If this is true, it runs counter to the most commonly held theories, which associate such birth rates with industrialization. It has also been suggested that some institutions may function to limit fertility, although this is not their deliberate purpose. For example, many religious systems prescribe periods of sexual abstinence, which usually (although not always) have the indirect effect of limiting fertility (Nag 1962).

Another unintended restraint on fertility is the possible reduction in fecundity resulting from poor nutrition and health conditions, whether these affect the whole society or only the lowest strata. This is one possible explanation for the fact that in some Indian studies the poorest rural workers have the lowest fertility. Another finding is that the period of amenorrhea and temporary sterility following a pregnancy apparently is lengthened if an infant lives and is breast-fed. This suggests that variations in infant mortality and in weaning practices may also affect fertility (Potter et al. 1966).

Lack of an adequate contraceptive technology has been suggested as an explanation for high fertility in preindustrial societies (Davis & Blake 1956, p. 223). An opposing point of view is that contraceptive practices are not developed or widely disseminated when available, because the structure of such a traditional society provides little motivation for small rather than large families. *Coitus interruptus*, probably the principal means for modern fertility decline in England and France, has been practiced for centuries by some couples within many preindustrial societies. If sufficient motivation for small families had been present, such a method might have been adopted more widely, in at least a few preindustrial societies.

These are only illustrations of theories and studies indicating that a variety of cultural factors in preindustrial societies affect the intermediate variables in such a way as to keep fertility below its maximum biological potential. Since many of the limits on fertility are based on cultural patterns without consciously recognized links to family size, changes in such practices initially may lead to higher fertility before modern family-planning practices take their place. For example, this might be the result of a further relaxation of traditional sanctions against the remarriage of widows in India.

Fertility in industrial countries

Transitional decline of fertility. The large decline in fertility in economically developed countries in the nineteenth and twentieth centuries is unprecedented. Most sociologists and demographers would probably agree that there have been two basic causes for the general decline. In the first place, there has been a major transfer of functions from the family to other specialized institutions, so that fewer children are required to achieve socially valued goals. Second, a sharp reduction in mortality has reduced the number of births necessary to have any desired number of living children.

The historical timing of fertility decline in most countries, rather long after the beginning of the modern process of economic development and social change, has been explained in terms of a descriptive model of the "demographic transition." This model assumes that fertility and mortality are both high in the preindustrial period. The rapid population growth associated with modern economic development is then attributed to a decline in mortality that occurred while fertility remained relatively stable at rather high levels. It is further assumed that after a considerable time lag, fertility begins to fall, reducing the rate of population growth as it approaches the level of mortality. The usual explanation of this time lag is that whereas low mortality is always positively valued, there are no low fertility norms to carry over from the preindustrial period; they must be developed gradually in a trial-and-error process, under the influence of lower mortality and the changing consequences of varying numbers of children.

This simple model of the demographic transition is under revision as the result of a number of important studies. Some have shown a considerable variability in the actual course of the demographic transition (Hatt et al. 1955; Ryder 1957). Especially significant has been the work of a number of economic historians (for instance, Eversley 1963) probing, in detail, European data for the medieval period and for the seventeenth and eighteenth centuries. These studies have tried to relate changes in economic organization and in family structure to changes in age at marriage, rate of marriage, and illegitimacy. An important, if controversial, hypothesis emerging from this work is that a rise in fertility rather than a fall in mortality may be responsible for the population growth during the early stages of industrialization.

Explanations for the decline in fertility that eventually occurred throughout the Western world sometimes concentrate on the intermediate variables and sometimes on the changes in social structure, which first produced the small family norms and then affected the intermediate variables.

The role of contraception. Most scholars probably would agree that the mass adoption of contraception is the most important change immediately responsible for the decline in fertility in modern industrial countries. Notable exceptions are Ireland, where men have tended to marry late or not at all, and Japan and the countries of eastern and central Europe, where abortion has been widely practiced since World War II.

It has generally been assumed that contraception was the most important factor in the development of the small family that gradually became the norm for western Europe. But this assumption must remain, at best, a plausible hypothesis, since there is an almost complete lack of systematic comparative data for many of the other intermediate variables affecting fertility. The only study providing a series of historical statistics on the use of contraception is that by Lewis-Faning for England (Great Britain . . . 1949). He demonstrated that as the use of contraception increased, fertility declined, and that contraception was adopted first in those social classes whose fertility fell first. The practice was found to have spread to other social classes in reasonably close correspondence to observed patterns of differential fertility. There is also illustrative evidence about the adoption of contraception—especially *coitus interruptus*—by significant elements in the French population in the late eighteenth and early nineteenth centuries; and it so happens that this was the period in which fertility in France began to fall (France . . . 1960).

Since the war several studies have provided statistical evidence of the mass use of contraception in a number of Western countries and have related the practice to fertility levels (e.g., Freedman 1961, pp. 116–118). These studies do indeed demonstrate that many populations with a history of marked secular decline in fertility now practice family planning on a massive scale; but another finding that they also have in common is that contraceptive practice is not necessarily highly rational and effective, even when the *average* number of children per family is limited to two or three. Even in the United States, where contraception is virtually universal for the fecund at some time in married life, many couples use ineffective means, many do not begin contraception early in marriage (although they do not want all their children immediately), some begin only after having more children than they want, and many conceive despite contraceptive efforts to postpone pregnancies (Freedman et al. 1959, chapters 3–6). In Japan and a number of east European countries, the failure of contraception as practiced to produce the small families desired has been followed by massive supplementary use of legal abortion.

Biological theories. Before World War II, it was not uncommon to attribute the decline in fertility to a decrease in biological fecundity. The main argument was that development of industrial–urban society brought about a decrease in fecundity. This was held to be a consequence either of genetic selection or of the stresses supposedly associated with urban life—especially for the higher status groups, whose fertility fell fastest. Although such explanations may be valid for special situations, the prevailing scholarly opinion does not assign it great importance in the over-all fertility decline in Western countries. Kiser and Whelpton, in the Indianapolis study, demonstrated both that a modern urban population can have a high fertility rate during periods when contraception is not used and that fecundity differences are not associated with socioeconomic status in the way that they should be if the biological argument about fecundity decline is true (see Whelpton 1943–1958, vol. 2, pp. 303–416). This argument has also been weakened by the difficulty of reconciling it with the temporal changes in fertility that have been observed to follow changes in economic conditions.

Whatever combination of intermediate variables was responsible, there is no question that fertility fell rapidly in all the developed Western countries, so that just before World War II small families averaging closer to two than three children were characteristic. In many countries, fertility was below the level required for replacement even with the very low prevalent mortality, and concern about a declining and aging population led to national investigations and official pronatalist policies.

Sociological theories. Many explanations were advanced for these unprecedented fertility declines. The dominant ideas before World War II, however, were all related to the changing functions of family and children in an urban–industrial society. To summarize the theories: Industrial urbanization was associated with a complex division of labor in all spheres of life; with the associated high rate of social and physical mobility, this inevitably led to a growth of secularism and rationalism, the declining influence of such traditional forces as religious faith, and the shattering of traditional family and other primary group associations. An essential element in this view of urban life was the idea that the family would lose its functions to other specialized institutions. On the one hand, children would cease to be productive assets in a familially based economy, and, on the other hand, they would be impediments to active participation in the larger organizations from which the rewards of an urban society would come. The dominant view was that as whole populations became involved in the urban market and society, family planning would become universal and the size of family planned would continue to decline.

It is plausible that a shift in functions from the family to other institutions is one basic explanation for the secular decline in fertility in the developed countries. But in retrospect there is little systematic evidence in prewar studies linking *specific* changes in the functions of the family to the decline of fertility at *specific* times and places. There are still no satisfactory answers to some important comparative historical questions, for example: Why did fertility begin to decline much earlier in France than in England, where urban–industrial development was earlier and more intense? Why has fertility remained higher in the Netherlands than elsewhere, despite that country's early involvement in the nexus of international trade?

One line of theory and research has stressed the joint role of social mobility and rising standards of living in motivating couples to restrict family size. This is one explanation offered for the early decline of fertility in France (Blacker 1957). Banks (1954) has linked the onset of the fertility decline in England with a change in economic conditions that made restriction of family size necessary for the maintenance and advance of living standards in the rising middle class. More recent statistical studies produce conflicting results, with some indicating no correlation between mobility and fertility in the United States (Westoff et al. 1961) and others finding a relationship in France (Bresard 1950), England (Berent 1952), and Brazil (Hutchinson 1961). Even in those cases in which a relationship is found, it is possible that the distinctive fertility of the mobile population is simply an averaging of the fertility levels of their positions of origin and destination, and not a distinctive consequence of social mobility itself.

Postwar fertility increase in the West. A decrease in childlessness is only one of the important postwar demographic trends that direct attention to the need for a re-evaluation of the role of family and children in society. In most of the developed countries in which fertility reached very low levels before the war, there has been an increase in the proportion of people marrying, a decrease in the age at marriage, and an increase or stabilization in the average family size of those who marry. There is, however, little evidence of a return to large families since the war; the shift is from having no children or one child to having from two to four. In a number of countries, an increase in the number of marriages, rather than in the number of children per marriage, accounts for a significant part of the postwar rise in fertility.

Since the war, urban sociologists have given increasing recognition to the persistence and even the resurgence of primary groups, including the family, as the means by which stable individual personality organization is maintained in impersonal specialized societies. Part of this revaluation of urban society involves more attention to the persistent influence of traditional ideologies in religious and other associations with ends that are not primarily economic or political. Such associations had been doomed to extinction by prewar sociologists, who were fond of stressing the growth of secular rationalism. By contrast, a community study by Lenski (1961) shows the persistence of Catholic ideology in many areas of life, including fertility, even after the consideration of the influence of rising education, socioeconomic status, and urbanization. These results are confirmed, with more demographic detail for fertility, in the Princeton study (Westoff et al. 1961).

Some sociologists and demographers have suggested that the leveling off in the long-run secular decline in fertility may mean that family size has reached a level appropriate to its functions under urban–industrial conditions. From this viewpoint, considerable experimentation may be required before a stable social norm is developed governing the size of such an important unit as the family. The very low fertility of the 1930s is seen as an experimental "overshooting" of an "equilibrium solution," with a readjustment following when the dysfunctional consequences were widely felt. The increasing convergence of family size in many countries to a small range of one to four children may be additional evidence that a family-size pattern appropriate to urban–industrial societies is developing (Universities–National Bureau Committee for Economic Research 1960, pp. 36–76).

Differential fertility

Differential fertility refers to variation in fertility among significant subgroups in a population. In principle, almost any classification of the population may be a basis for measuring fertility differences. Scholarly attention, however, has centered on groups of people whose differing positions in the society give them different resources, styles of life, and power. Such groups frequently are distinctive in social norms and culture traits affecting fertility.

General principles. Classifications used in studies of differential fertility include those based on education, occupation, income, wealth, landholding, caste, social class, labor-force status of the wife, religion, ethnic–racial groupings, regional divisions, bureaucratic positions, intelligence, and size of place of residence. Occupation and education have been the most frequently used bases for classification, both because they are readily available in censuses and in official vital statistics and because they are significant indicators of status and style of life in most modern societies.

Social groups or strata that differ in their fertility differ also on one or more of the intermediate variables affecting fertility. Differentials may result from *deliberate* controls, such as contraception, or from the *unintended consequences* of other variations. For example, in some places, the rate of spontaneous abortions is higher in lower-status than in higher-status groups, and this has an unintended effect on the status differentials.

For a number of contemporary societies, there is evidence that the low-fertility subgroups have used deliberate family-limitation practices—mainly contraception and abortion—more extensively and effectively than other groups. Substantiating data are available, for example, for the United States, England, Japan, Hungary, Czechoslovakia, Puerto Rico, Turkey, India, and Taiwan.

It is more difficult to establish unequivocally whether the higher fertility subgroups have larger families because they want them or because they do not have the knowledge or means to restrict family size. Low motivation toward a small-family goal may reduce interest in learning and practicing effective family-planning methods. In the United States, there is evidence that the practice of contraception for spacing births becomes more effective as the number of children born to a couple approaches the desired total. This suggests that ineffective family planning may reflect a desire for more children rather than inability to use the proper means. On the other hand, the important Indianapolis study by Kiser and Whelpton in 1940 found that low-status and high-status groups expressed similar attitudes about desired family size but that the low-status groups had more children because they practiced contraception less effectively (Whelpton 1943–1958).

At least in societies in which socially significant groups of people deliberately practice family limitation, differential fertility levels will be affected by distinctive subgroup attitudes about how many children a family should have. Presumably, fertility will be higher and family limitation practices less prevalent or effective in subgroups in which larger numbers of children are rewarding in various ways. The relatively high fertility of the agricultural sector of many populations, for example, can be linked to the utility of children, whether as laborers in the family enterprise, as an alternative to urban social-security programs to meet the risks of illness, disability, and old-age, or as the members of essential primary social groups. Similar functions have been ascribed to larger numbers of children among low-status urban groups during the period of transition to a modern economy.

Fertility differentials often do not correspond to the differentials in the *rate of reproduction*—a measure that also takes mortality into account. For example, in countries as different as India and England, the mortality rate is considerably higher in lower-status than in higher-status groups. Therefore, by the time a given cohort of women has reached the end of the childbearing period, differences between social strata in the number of living children per mother often vary considerably from differences in the average number of children ever born to each mother.

Fertility differentials by status measures. Such stratification measures as education, occupation, or income have been studied most extensively in relation to fertility, partly because data are available in standard demographic sources, but also because stratification is important in social and economic theory (United Nations . . . 1953, chapter 5). Socially patterned differences in life style and economic activity presumably may influence either the social norms about family size or the variables immediately determining fertility, such as fetal mortality and effective access to contraception. But there is no single, universally valid relation between status measures and fertility, because such particular indications of status as education or landownership vary in their significance in different societies and because the value attached to large families is greater in some societies than in others. Indeed, the resources that go with high status are

likely to be used to achieve large families in some societies and small families in others.

For preindustrial societies, there is evidence in some studies of a positive correlation between fertility and status, especially among agricultural populations (Stys 1957). The nature of the evidence varies. Fertility has been found to increase with size of landholding; agricultural tenants or workers have been found to have lower fertility than landholders; persons with low-status occupations have been reported to have lower-than-average fertility. The evidence for a positive correlation is reported in regional studies for England, Germany, Poland, China, the United States, India, and the Philippines for various periods between the seventeenth and twentieth centuries.

A plausible explanation of positive correlations between fertility and status in *pre*industrial societies is that dependence on relatives and children for a variety of social needs increases the social valuation of large families, so that those with higher status use their power to increase family size (for example, by early marriage). It is also plausible that in some instances poor health, poor nutrition, the absence of males seeking work, or high maternal mortality among fertile lower-status mothers may explain the lower fertility for lower-status groups. The thesis that higher fertility invariably goes with higher status in all preindustrial societies is certainly not supported by the evidence. For example, in some contemporary regional studies of peasant populations in India, there is no correlation between status measures and fertility (Chandrasekaran 1963).

A negative correlation between occupational status and fertility in Western urban populations appears with the earliest pertinent census data in the nineteenth century (United Nations 1953). In the period of transition to a mature industrial–urban society, negative correlations between broad status measures and fertility are found wherever systematic data are available. Although the evidence is mainly for Western countries, similar negative relationships have been reported for the advanced changing urban sectors in such diverse places as India, Taiwan, Chile, Puerto Rico, and Lebanon. Plausible explanations for these negative correlations center on the idea that high-status groups live first in the developing urban–industrial sectors in which they enjoy a number of advantages. These would include superior access to information about the means for fertility control, later marriage because of higher educational standards, and lower mortality rates (making fewer births necessary for any desired number of children). Such families, it is argued, would find the economic value of children relatively small in the course of acquiring higher living standards for themselves and their children. They would also be likely to participate in extrafamilial activities, which could occupy time that might otherwise have been given to additional children. Whatever the explanation, the existence of the negative relation between status and fertility is well documented for many places.

The lower fertility of high-status groups in the period of transition to advanced industrialization may be the result of both the smaller proportion marrying at important child-bearing ages and the use of contraception to limit family size within marriage. Historical data for status differentials in the use of contraception corresponding to differentials in fertility are available only for England, as already mentioned (Great Britain . . . 1949). However, similar differentials in use of contraception have appeared later in other countries, as data become available. More recently, there is evidence that the differential use of legal abortion is producing fertility status differentials in Japan and in some countries of eastern Europe.

At least in the United States, the higher fertility of low-status groups is partly a consequence of their rural origin rather than of their status in the urban community (Goldberg 1959). There is a high proportion of farm-reared persons in low-status groups, whether these are defined in terms of occupation, income, or education. When only couples living in cities for at least two generations are considered, either the status differentials become slightly positive or the negative correlation is reduced. This is consistent with the thesis that the negative correlation is part of the *transition* to a mature urban society rather than an intrinsic characteristic of such a society.

The negative relation of status to fertility is most pronounced in data for the period before World War II. However, even at that time there were many exceptions within broad occupational groups. For example, low fertility is reported among service workers, such as barbers and waiters, having frequent contact with higher-status groups. For the period between the world wars, the highest income groups sometimes had higher fertility rates than the next income group, especially when comparisons are made for persons of high educational or occupational status.

There was a sharp contraction in fertility differentials in many countries in the "baby boom" following World War II. Fertility generally increased most in those social strata which had the lowest fertility before the war. However, even in the United States, where this phenomenon was very pronounced, there continued to be significant negative correlations between various status measures and fertility (Grabill et al. 1958).

Postwar studies, mainly in the United States, indicate that there is now very little relationship between measures of social status and the number of children desired and expected. It is not yet known whether the expectations and desires of each stratum will be realized in action. Apart from possible changes in what is desired, the present evidence is that lower-status groups still are less effective in planning their fertility to attain desired family size.

Some scholars believe that in a mature urban–industrial society fertility eventually will be positively correlated with status—and especially with income (Universities–National Bureau . . . 1960, pp. 209–240). A basic assumption is that effective use of contraception, together with very low mortality rates, will diffuse throughout the society, so that the fertility of each stratum will directly reflect the value of varying numbers of children in that stratum. Children, it is argued, having lost their differential utility as laborers or as social security resources, will be valued by all social classes for direct satisfactions, such as those yielded by durable consumer goods. The higher-income groups will then be able to afford and will choose to have more children than low-income groups. There is some support for this argument in data showing that there is a small positive correlation of income and fertility among couples who plan family size effectively and that this correlation is highest for couples with an urban background (Whelpton 1943–1958, vol. 3, pp. 360–415).

This projection of a positive correlation in the mature urban society makes assumptions, still unverified, about the elasticity of demand for children. One could just as well argue that the higher educational status generally found with higher income may lead to a broadening of interests, which will compete for attention with the demands of larger families. The theory also assumes that in the modern welfare state even the lowest status groups can receive from nonfamilial institutions assistance formerly received from children in meeting the risks of illness, disability, unemployment, old age, and loneliness.

Differentials by city size and farm residence.   In industrialized countries, fertility is almost always highest in the farm sector and tends to decrease as the size of the community increases. The explanation generally offered is twofold: it is said that contraception diffused from larger to smaller cities, and from there to the farms, and that the functional advantages of larger families are greatest, and their costs least, in smaller communities and on farms.

With the postwar rise in birth rates, fertility differentials by city size probably decreased in many countries, since fertility increased most in the status groups concentrated in large cities. Nevertheless, the traditional differentials persist in most Western countries for which there are adequate data. It is not yet clear whether the remaining inverse relation of fertility to city size in developed countries is a permanent feature of their structure, or a transitional phenomenon.

In the United States, at any rate, urban–rural fertility differentials have existed from a very early time. Declines in fertility in the rural and urban sectors followed parallel courses until about 1940, but since then urban fertility rates have risen more than the rural rates, thus reducing the differential. In a number of preindustrial countries (India, for example) urban–rural fertility differentials either do not exist or are minimal (Robinson 1961). In such societies, cities are often administrative and political centers in which familial organization does not differ greatly from that in rural areas; the city lacks the specialized institutions that take over many family functions in industrial societies.

Religious differentials. Most research on religious fertility differentials deals with the specific influence of the Roman Catholic church in limiting the practice of family planning (except by periodic abstinence) and in supporting norms for larger families. The doctrines of the church do not require large families, but they do restrict the means that may be used to achieve smaller families. The fact that empirical findings differ with the country studied suggests that the influence of the church depends on other variables in the society. In the United States, close attachment to the church is associated with higher fertility and with lesser use of the most effective fertility-control practices, even among higher-status groups. Lenski (1961) explains this result by an emphasis in Catholicism on familial rather than economic mobility values. But studies in Puerto Rico and other Latin American areas find no relation between attachment to the church and fertility. Indeed, international comparisons of fertility do not show any significant correlation between fertility and the percentage of Catholics in the population, when the level of general social development is taken into account.

Most of the other major world religions do not have specific doctrines about family limitation. However, religious practices frequently have an indirect effect on fertility. For example, in both India and China major religious traditions support a strong preference for at least one and preferably two sons, thus increasing the pressures for additional children. A pervasive fatalism in a religious ideology may have a greater effect than a specific injunction against contraception in impeding rational planning of fertility.

Other differentials. In industrial societies, wives who work away from home are found to have fewer children than those who stay at home. Some women work because they cannot have children, but the lower fertility of working women persists even when only fecund women are considered. Where the wife's work is closely tied to the home, lower fertility may not result. In Japan and Puerto Rico, women who worked at home or in small family enterprises were found to have higher fertility than other working wives.

Fertility differentials between ethnic, racial, or regional populations are extensively studied, because of their practical economic or political significance. But the *meaning* of the differentials depends on their specific historical and cultural context. Sometimes it is possible to explain such differentials in terms of status or rural–urban differences; otherwise, no successful analytic generalization of these studies has been made.

Consequences of differential fertility. Much of the early interest in differential fertility was eugenic. It was feared that the genetic quality of the population would deteriorate if low-status groups had higher-than-average fertility. This assumes that lower-status groups are more poorly endowed genetically—for example, with respect to intelligence—but this has not been scientifically established. Certain types of mental abnormality have a known genetic basis, but they are not sufficiently numerous to affect broad status differentials. It is likely that high or low fecundity itself may have a genetic basis, but this also is not known to have any specific connection to broad socially significant strata. Whether there are important genetic differences between social strata is still an open question. Probably, there is greater consensus that differential fertility may produce a social problem, regardless of the genetic origin of the problem, if fertility is high in groups with limited personal or social resources for child-rearing. There is some evidence that intellectual development is greater for children reared in small families; but the apparent contraction of fertility differentials in the postwar period in industrial countries has reduced the earlier concern about the social and biological consequences of differential fertility.

Differential fertility may affect the rate and character of social mobility. Varying rates of reproduction of different social strata affect the relative number of opportunities available in each stratum, depending on the extent of social inheritance of position. More generally, the rate of recruitment of new members is one important determinant of the continuity, structure, and power of any subgroup in the population. Recruitment from other groups by adoption or invasion is an alternative to reproduction, but differential fertility is often the principal determinant of the relative growth of population subgroups from generation to generation. Where success of groups contesting for political power depends on their size, a lively concern about comparative reproduction rates often is evident.

RONALD FREEDMAN

[*Directly related are the entries* GENETICS, *article on* DEMOGRAPHY AND POPULATION GENETICS; POPULATION. *Other relevant material may be found in* MIGRATION; MORTALITY; NUPTIALITY.]

BIBLIOGRAPHY

BANKS, JOSEPH A. 1954 *Prosperity and Parenthood: A Study of Family Planning Among the Victorian Middle Classes.* London: Routledge.

BERENT, JERZY 1952 Fertility and Social Mobility. *Population Studies* 5:244–260.

BLACKER, J. G. C. 1957 Social Ambitions of the Bourgeoisie in 18th Century France, and Their Relation to Family Limitation. *Population Studies* 11:46–63.

BRESARD, MARCEL 1950 Mobilité sociale et dimension de la famille. *Population* 5:533–566.

CHANDRASEKARAN, C. 1963 Physiological Factors Affecting Fertility in India. Volume 2, pages 89–96 in International Population Conference, New York, 1961, *Proceedings.* London: International Union for the Scientific Study of Population.

Conditions and Trends of Fertility in the World. 1965 *Population Bulletin of the United Nations* No. 7.

DAVIS, KINGSLEY; and BLAKE, JUDITH 1956 Social Structure and Fertility: An Analytic Framework. *Economic Development and Cultural Change* 4:211–235.

DEVEREUX, GEORGE 1955 *A Study of Abortion in Primitive Societies: A Typological, Distributional, and Dynamic Analysis of the Prevention of Birth in 400 Preindustrial Societies.* New York: Julian.

DUNCAN, OTIS DUDLEY 1965 Farm Background and Differential Fertility. *Demography* 2:240–249.

EVERSLEY, D. E. C. 1963 Population in England in the Eighteenth Century: An Appraisal of Current Research. Volume 1, pages 573–582 in International Population Conference, New York, 1961, *Proceedings.* London: International Union for the Scientific Study of Population.

FORD, CLELLAN S. 1945 *A Comparative Study of Human Reproduction.* Yale University Publications in Anthropology, No. 32. New Haven: Yale Univ. Press.

FRANCE, INSTITUT NATIONAL D'ÉTUDES DÉMOGRAPHIQUES 1953 *Fécondité des mariages: Nouvelle méthode de mesure,* by L. Henry. Travaux et Documents, Cahier No. 16. Paris: Presses Universitaires de France.

FRANCE, INSTITUT NATIONAL D'ÉTUDES DÉMOGRAPHIQUES 1960 *La prévention des naissances dans la famille: Ses origines dans les temps modernes,* by H. Bergues et al. Travaux et Documents, Cahier No. 35. Paris: Presses Universitaires de France.

FREEDMAN, RONALD 1961 The Sociology of Human Fertility: A Trend Report and Bibliography. *Current Sociology* 10, no. 2:35–121. → A report on research since 1945 with an annotated bibliography of 636 items.

FREEDMAN, RONALD 1963 Norms for Family Size in Underdeveloped Areas. Royal Society of London, *Proceedings* Series B 159:220–245.

FREEDMAN, RONALD; WHELPTON, P. K.; and CAMPBELL, A. A. 1959 *Family Planning, Sterility, and Population Growth.* New York: McGraw-Hill.

GLASS, DAVID V.; and EVERSLEY, D. E. C. 1965 *Population in History.* London: Arnold.

GOLDBERG, DAVID 1959 The Fertility of Two-generation Urbanites. *Population Studies* 12:214–222.

GRABILL, WILSON H.; KISER, C. V.; and WHELPTON, P. K. 1958 *The Fertility of American Women.* Prepared for the Social Science Research Council in cooperation with the U.S. Department of Commerce, Bureau of the Census. New York: Wiley.

GREAT BRITAIN, ROYAL COMMISSION ON POPULATION 1949 *Papers.* Volume 1: Family Limitation and Its Influence on Human Fertility During the Past Fifty Years, by E. Lewis-Faning. London: H.M. Stationery Office.

HATT, PAUL K.; FARR, N. L.; and WEINSTEIN, E. 1955 Types of Population Balance. *American Sociological Review* 20:14–21.

HENRY, LOUIS 1961 La fécondité naturelle: Observation, théorie, résultats. *Population* 16:625–636.

HIMES, NORMAN E. (1936) 1963 *Medical History of Contraception.* New York: Gamut; London: Allen & Unwin.

HUTCHINSON, BERTRAM 1961 Fertility, Social Mobility and Urban Migration in Brazil. *Population Studies* 14:182–189.

KIRK, DUDLEY; and NORTMAN, DOROTHY L. 1959 Business and Babies: The Influence of the Business Cycle on Birth Rates. Pages 151–160 in American Statistical Association, Social Statistics Section, *Proceedings.* Washington: The Association.

LENSKI, GERHARD E. (1961) 1963 *The Religious Factor: A Sociological Study of Religion's Impact on Politics, Economics, and Family Life.* Rev. ed. Garden City, N.Y.: Doubleday.

LORIMER, FRANK 1954 *Culture and Human Fertility: A Study of the Relation of Cultural Conditions to Fertility in Non-industrial and Transitional Societies.* Paris: UNESCO.

NAG, MONI 1962 *Factors Affecting Human Fertility in Non Industrial Societies: A Cross-cultural Study.* Yale University Publications in Anthropology, No. 66. New Haven: Yale Univ. Press.

POTTER, R. G. et al. 1966 Application of Field Studies to Research on the Physiology of Human Reproduction. A chapter in M. Sheps (editor), *Public Health and Population Change.* Univ. of Pittsburgh Press.

ROBINSON, WARREN C. 1961 Urban–Rural Differences in Indian Fertility. *Population Studies* 14:218–234.

RYDER, NORMAN B. 1957 The Conceptualization of the Transition in Fertility. *Cold Spring Harbor Symposia on Quantitative Biology* 22:91–96.

RYDER, NORMAN B. 1960 The Structure and Tempo of Current Fertility. Pages 117–136 in Universities–National Bureau Committee for Economic Research, *Demographic and Economic Change in Developed Countries.* Princeton Univ. Press.

STYS, W. 1957 The Influence of Economic Conditions on the Fertility of Peasant Women. *Population Studies* 11:136–148.

UNITED NATIONS, DEPARTMENT OF SOCIAL AFFAIRS, POPULATION DIVISION 1953 *The Determinants and Consequences of Population Trends: A Summary of the Findings of Studies on the Relationship Between Population Changes and Economic and Social Conditions.* Population Studies, No. 17. New York: United Nations. → See especially Chapter 5.

UNIVERSITIES–NATIONAL BUREAU COMMITTEE FOR ECONOMIC RESEARCH 1960 *Demographic and Economic Change in Developed Countries.* National Bureau of Economic Research, Special Conference Series, No. 11. Princeton Univ. Press.

WESTOFF, CHARLES F. et al. 1961 *Family Growth in Metropolitan America.* Princeton Univ. Press.

WHELPTON, P. K. 1943–1958 *Social and Psychological Factors Affecting Fertility.* 5 vols. New York: Milbank Memorial Fund. → Volume 1: *The Household Survey in Indianapolis.* Volume 2: *The Intensive Study: Purpose, Scope, Methods and Partial Results.* Volume 3: *Further Reports on Hypothesis in the Indianapolis Study.* Volume 4: *Further Reports on Hypotheses and Other Data From the Indianapolis Study.* Volume 5: *Concluding Reports and Summary of Chief Findings From the Indianapolis Study.*

FERTILITY CONTROL

"Fertility control," as the term is used in this article, refers to patterns of human behavior that have as their primary objective the prevention of unwanted pregnancies and births. Individuals and couples adopt these patterns in accordance with their cultural values, reinforced by formal or informal social pressures.

The methods of fertility control are traditionally grouped into four categories: abstinence, contraception, sterilization, and induced abortion. The boundaries between these categories, however, are not clearly delineated and will become even less so in the future. The rhythm method, for example, is a method of contraception, but it also requires abstinence during a portion of the menstrual cycle. Oral contraception interferes with reproduction for periods of time and is sometimes referred to as temporary sterilization, while surgical sterilization has been called permanent contraception.

The term "birth control," coined by Margaret Sanger in 1914 (Lader 1955), is generally used as a synonym for contraception. From the beginning, the term was intended to exclude abortion, and, in general, sterilization and abstinence have also been excluded. A number of terms substituted for birth control, such as family limitation, child spacing, family planning, and planned parenthood, appear, for the most part, to be intended to promote social acceptance rather than to improve communication.

History. Under some circumstances pregnancy and/or childbearing have been considered undesirable or have actually been proscribed in human societies since the dawn of history. Anthropologists have noted the practice of abortion among many preliterate peoples throughout the world. It is also probable that abstinence and *coitus interruptus* became known as methods of fertility control at the same time as the connection of coitus with pregnancy. It would appear, however, that fertility control was practiced only sporadically throughout most of man's long history. Since levels of mortality were generally high in premodern societies, only those societies survived where the level of natality was also high.

The practice of fertility control on a scale sufficient to influence the trend of the birth rate began in France toward the end of the eighteenth century (France . . . 1960) and in other countries during the nineteenth century (Himes 1936). Generally, it spread from the well-to-do and educated classes to the underprivileged, and from the cities to the countryside. In some countries, however, farm owners were among the first to restrict the size of their families in order to avoid property division.

At present, fertility control is practiced in one form or another and with varying degrees of success by most couples in the industrialized countries of the world and by social minorities, mainly urban, in nonindustrialized countries. However, even in societies where fertility control is not widely practiced, many recent surveys have shown that the majority of couples approve the idea of family limitation (see, for example, Berelson 1966). The preferred size of family, as indicated by the respondents, tends to be substantially smaller than the average number of children per family in the community.

Methods of contraception

Contraception, according to the usage of most writers on the subject, includes all nonpermanent measures to prevent coitus from resulting in conception. In older demographic literature, it has been customary to distinguish between "appliance methods," that is, mechanical devices and spermicides, and "nonappliance methods," such as withdrawal or the rhythm method. More recently, the major distinction is between the "traditional methods" and the "modern methods," the latter referring to oral and intrauterine contraceptives. Still another classification is made by the Roman Catholic church, which distinguishes between "natural birth control," that is, the rhythm method (see below), and "artificial birth control," comprising all other methods.

Folk methods.   The principal folk methods of contraception are *coitus interruptus* and the douche. *Coitus interruptus* or withdrawal of the male prior to ejaculation is the oldest contraceptive procedure known to man. It appears in the Old Testament (Genesis 38) and has been noted by anthropologists in many parts of the world. In western and northern Europe, where relatively late marriage has long coexisted with close and frequent social contacts between unmarried adults and with a strong condemnation of pregnancy out of wedlock, withdrawal appears to have been the method by which premarital pregnancies were averted. At a later time, the practice was transferred into married life. There can be no doubt that *coitus interruptus* was the principal method by which the historical decline of the birth rate in the West was achieved. Statistical studies suggest a level of effectiveness similar to that of vaginal methods (see Table 3).

Postcoital douches with plain water, vinegar, and various products advertised under the name of "feminine hygiene," long used for purposes of family limitation, have lost popularity in recent decades. Since sperm has been found in the mucus of the cervical canal within 90 seconds after ejaculation, medical opinion considers the contraceptive effectiveness of douching as quite unsatisfactory.

Vaginal methods.   Vaginal contraceptive methods are designed to prevent the entry of sperm into the uterus by a mechanical barrier and/or to kill the sperm by chemical action. The condom or sheath, a cover for the penis during intercourse, made its first appearance in England in the eighteenth century. Since the latter part of the nineteenth century, the early "skin" condoms, made from the intestines of sheep and other animals, have gradually been replaced by the cheaper and more convenient rubber sheaths. A large proportion of the condoms sold in the United States prior to 1938 were inferior in quality. Since supervision over condoms has been assumed by the Food and Drug Administration, their quality has improved greatly.

The condom offers protection not only against unwanted pregnancy but also against venereal disease. It can be used without special instruction and elaborate preparation in any situation where coitus is possible.

The diaphragm, known in the United Kingdom as the Dutch Cap, was invented by a German physician, Wilhelm P. J. Mensinga, prior to 1882. Before the advent of oral contraceptives, it was the contraceptive device most often recommended by physicians in private practice and in birth control clinics throughout the United States and Europe. The diaphragm, inserted into the vagina and covering the cervical *os*, prevents the entry of sperm into the uterus. To fit a diaphragm, a pelvic examination by a physician or other trained health worker is necessary. Because of this requirement, the method is not suitable for general use in countries where medical personnel and medical facilities are scarce.

The contraceptive effectiveness of the condom and diaphragm is high and appears to be approximately equal for the two methods. Occasional failures occur, for example, if a condom tears or a diaphragm is displaced during coitus. A rate of 2 to 3 pregnancies per 100 women per year would seem to be a high estimate for consistent users. If motivation is weak, much higher pregnancy rates must be expected.

Chemical contraceptives consist of a spermicidal compound and a vehicle for its introduction and distribution within the vagina. Various creams and jellies and, more recently, foams with a highly spermicidal action, have been developed by the pharmaceutical industry. Insertion into the vagina is accomplished, prior to intercourse, by means of an applicator. The effectiveness of these methods seems to be lower than that of the diaphragm or the condom. Because vaginal tablets can be manufactured easily and cheaply and because no pelvic examination, fitting, or apparatus is needed, they have been considered eminently suitable for programs of population control in the economically underdeveloped regions of the world. However, the results of clinical and field trials have not been encouraging, and it does not appear likely that this method will prove sufficiently acceptable and effective to be of value in reducing the rate of population growth.

Rhythm method.   The rhythm or safe period method of contraception, also known as periodic continence, is based on the fact, recognized independently in the early 1930s by Ogino in Japan and Knaus in Austria, that conception is possible during only a small fraction of each menstrual cycle. The fertile days can be determined either by the application of a simple formula to the menstrual history of the woman or by the observation of changes in basal body temperature during the menstrual cycle, or by a combination of both.

Rhythm is at present (that is, in 1966) the only method of fertility control, other than complete abstinence, sanctioned by the Roman Catholic church. Its contraceptive effectiveness has been the subject of much controversy. The theoretical effectiveness of the method, correctly taught and understood, and consistently practiced according to the Ogino formula, is roughly comparable to that of vaginal methods. The use-effectiveness, on the other hand, which may be modified by errors of instruction or comprehension and by the couple's willingness to take chances, has been consistently less than that of vaginal methods in comparable situations.

Oral methods. The contraceptive "pill," long thought of as an attractive solution to the problem of fertility control, became a reality in the late 1950s. Since 1956 several oral contraceptives have been extensively tested in many countries. No permanent or serious side effects were noted in any of the clinical trials, but laboratory studies of various organ systems have in some instances revealed deviations from normal values. The significance of these changes cannot yet be evaluated. Women who discontinue the medication conceive promptly. Oral contraceptives have established themselves not only as virtually 100 per cent effective, if taken according to prescription, but also as highly acceptable to most users, including many women in the lower socioeconomic strata who had been unsuccessful with other contraceptive methods.

Intrauterine methods. Intrauterine contraceptive devices (IUDs) are small, variously shaped objects (rings, spirals, loops, etc.) which are inserted into the uterus by a physician. The procedure takes only a few minutes and requires no anesthesia. The devices are made of chemically inert materials, such as polyethylene or stainless steel, and may remain in the uterus for an indefinite period. The mechanism of action of the IUDs is not fully understood. The best available evidence suggests that the presence of a foreign body in the uterus reduces the time required for the movement of the ovum through the Fallopian tube from three to four days to one day or less and that the fertilized ovum, therefore, reaches the uterus at a time when neither it nor the endometrium is ready for implantation. There is some evidence, however, that the ovum may not be fertilized at all.

Since 1960 several types of IUDs have been carefully studied in the United States and elsewhere

(Tietze 1966; International Conference . . . 1964). In some cases the uterus expels the device, usually during a menstrual period and occasionally without the woman being aware of it, or the device must be removed because of side effects such as bleeding and/or pain. No evidence has been produced that the IUDs are carcinogenic, nor does their use interfere with fertility after they have been removed. During use, 2 to 3 accidental pregnancies per 100 women per year must be expected even with the more successful types of IUDs. These failures may occur after an unnoticed expulsion or, more frequently, with the device *in situ*. No case of fetal malformation attributable to an IUD has been reported.

The sociological importance of the IUDs lies in the fact that they offer the only fully reversible method of birth control now available which requires a single decision rather than sustained motivation on the part of the users. The insidious dissipation of user interest, which has played so frustrating a role in all other methods of contraception, is of little importance with the IUD. Regardless of apathy, fatigue, or sexual excitement, the contraceptive device is in place and no further action is required of either the man or the woman.

Extent of contraceptive practice

The first nationwide investigation of the extent of contraceptive practice in the United States was the Growth of American Families (GAF) Study, conducted in 1955 (Freedman et al. 1959). A second survey along similar lines was carried out in 1960 (Whelpton et al. 1965). According to these surveys, the proportions of white couples with wives 18–39 years of age who had taken up the practice of birth control prior to the interview were

Table 1 — Per cent of white couples ever using contraception: United States, 1955 and 1960

	1955	1960
Religion of wife:		
Catholic	57	70
Protestant	75	84
Jewish	86	95
Education of wife:		
Grade school	48	66
High school, 1–3	65	78
High school, 4	74	83
College	84	88
Income of husband:		
Under $3,000	58	70
$3,000–$3,999	69	77
$4,000–$5,999	74	80
$6,000 or more	79	85
Entire sample	70	81

Source: Adapted from Whelpton et al. 1965.

70 per cent in 1955 and 81 per cent in 1960. Among couples who had never tried to prevent conception, many were found to be sterile or subfecund. The extent and type of contraception varied with religious affiliation and with such indications of socioeconomic status as wife's education and husband's income (see Table 1).

Among nonwhite couples, included for the first time in the 1960 GAF Study, only 59 per cent reported use of contraception, a substantially lower proportion than among the lowest educational and income groups of white couples.

The great majority of couples using birth control relied on one or more of five methods (see Table 2). It should be noted that the 1960 survey was completed before oral contraceptives came into general use.

Close correlations were found in the GAF surveys between choice of contraceptive method and level of education, as well as other indicators of socioeconomic status. Use of the rhythm method by Catholics was strongly associated with advanced education. A similar association was found for the diaphragm among Protestants and among those Catholics who had experience with "artificial birth control." Conversely, use of the douche and especially of withdrawal were inversely associated with educational level, while the condom was a popular method at all socioeconomic levels. The findings of the GAF Study have been confirmed, to a large extent, by the Family Growth in Metropolitan America (FGMA) Study (Westoff et al. 1961). According to a nationwide survey taken in late 1965 (Ryder & Westoff 1966), about

Table 2 — Per cent distribution of users by last method used: United States, 1955 and 1960

| Last method used | Entire sample | RELIGION OF WIFE | | |
		Protestant	Catholic	Jewish
1955				
Condom	29	31	16	56
Diaphragm	25	29	12	37
Rhythm	24	14	56	2
Douche	9	11	6	—
Withdrawal	8	8	8	3
All other	5	7	2	2
	100	100	100	100
1960				
Condom	28	30	17	49
Diaphragm	22	26	7	35
Rhythm	23	14	55	5
Douche	9	11	5	2
Withdrawal	8	8	10	2
All other	10	11	6	7
	100	100	100	100

Source: Adapted from GAF Study, 1955 and 1960 (special unpublished tabulations, privately communicated).

Table 3 — Per cent of married women, under 45 years of age, ever using and currently using oral contraception: United States, 1965

	Ever using	Currently using
Age:		
Under 20	42	28
20–24	46	30
25–29	37	22
30–34	24	13
35–39	15	8
40–44	9	5
Education:		
Grade school	12	7
High school, 1–3	26	15
High school, 4	26	16
College, 1–3	32	19
College, 4	37	22
Race and religion:		
White	27	16
Catholic	21	11
Non-Catholic	29	18
Negro	19	12
Entire sample	26	15

Source: Adapted from Ryder & Westoff 1966.

6.4 million married women under 45 years of age (26 per cent) had used oral contraception, while 3.8 million were relying on the "pill" at the time of the interview. Use was found inversely associated with age and directly with education (see Table 3).

In the United Kingdom the first major investigation of the contraceptive habits of the population was conducted in 1946–1947 on behalf of the Royal Commission on Population. In 1959–1960 new data were obtained from the Population Investigation Committee's marriage survey (Rowntree & Pierce 1961). In terms of religious affiliation and socioeconomic status, the patterns of contraceptive practice were found to be similar to those reported in the United States. In regard to methods, there are important differences. While the condom is the most widely used method in both countries, British couples tend to rely far more often on *coitus interruptus* and far less often on the diaphragm than American couples. Catholic couples in the United Kingdom showed less preference for the rhythm method than Catholic couples in the United States.

In Japan ten surveys on birth control were conducted between 1950 and 1965 (Muramatsu 1966). During this period the proportion of couples who reported current use of contraception increased from 19 per cent to 52 per cent. The proportion of couples practicing contraception was higher in the six major cities of Japan than in the other urban areas and was lowest in the rural districts. The familiar socioeconomic gradient was also present. The condom, the most widely used method of contraception in Japan, was reported by a majority of users in each survey since 1952. Next in popularity was the rhythm method, an example of a prophet (Ogino) honored in his own country.

The extent of contraceptive practice and the methods used have also been studied in a number of other countries throughout the world. Generally speaking, the practice of contraception is inversely correlated with the level of the birth rate and rarely reaches 10 per cent of all couples in the rural areas of the developing countries. The proportion tends to be higher in towns and among the better educated. It has been suggested that the more widespread practice of contraception in industrialized societies is connected with the decline, in these societies, of the extended family and the correspondingly greater opportunities afforded to young, unmarried adults for training in contraceptive practices (Ryder 1959).

Effectiveness

Study of the effectiveness of contraception requires a distinction between "theoretical effectiveness" and "use-effectiveness." Theoretical effectiveness is the effectiveness of a method under ideal conditions, that is, used consistently and according to instructions, without any omissions or errors of technique. Use-effectiveness refers to the contraceptive practice of a particular population and reflects such variables as the socioeconomic and cultural characteristics and the degree of motivation of the couples concerned.

Theoretical effectiveness is not accessible to measurement and can only be inferred from the performance of the most successful group of users. Use-effectiveness is measured in terms of failure rates per 100 woman-years of use, according to the formula first proposed by Raymond Pearl (1932), or preferably by means of cumulative failure rates, according to the life table procedure described by R. G. Potter (1963).

Comprehensive information on the effectiveness of contraception, as practiced by young urban couples in the United States during the 1950s, was obtained during the course of the FGMA Study (Westoff et al. 1961, pp. 83–101). During the 28,607 months of exposure to the use of contraception reported by the couples included in the survey, 534 accidental pregnancies occurred, corresponding to a failure rate of 22.4 per 100 years of exposure. Failure rates for individual methods ranged from about 14 per 100 years of exposure for the condom and the diaphragm to about 40 for the rhythm method and the postcoital douche (*ibid.*, Table B-2). These rates reflect use-effectiveness—not theoretical effectiveness. Some of the couples admitted that they were "taking chances" in their contraceptive practice. Without such omissions, both admitted and unadmitted, it must be presumed that the failure rate for each method would have been much lower.

This conclusion is strongly supported by the results of reinterviews with the same couples about three years later. It was found that the couples who had used contraceptive measures since marriage and already had the number of children they desired experienced a failure rate of only 3.7 per 100 years of exposure for all contraceptive methods combined and a rate of 2.6 if they used the condom, the diaphragm, or withdrawal (Westoff et al. 1963, pp. 38–44). Couples who intended to have additional children and who, therefore, wanted to postpone pregnancy rather than prevent it altogether had much higher failure rates, similar to those experienced prior to the first interview.

Sterilization

Surgical sterilization was originally used to protect women whose life or health was threatened by pregnancy. Dr. James Blundell of London is credited with having first proposed the procedure in 1823. Effective techniques were developed in the latter part of the nineteenth century when aseptic surgery and anesthesia became available. At about the same time, sterilizing operations began to be widely used on males, mainly in connection with operations on the prostate. Growing confidence in the efficacy and safety of surgical sterilization led to its use for eugenic purposes, that is, to prevent persons suffering from hereditary disabilities, especially mental deficiency, various psychoses, and idiopathic epilepsy, from having offspring.

In the United States, 32 states adopted legislation between 1907 and 1937 regulating the practice of eugenic sterilization. Some of these laws have been declared unconstitutional, but the majority are still in force. However, few states have used their authority extensively, and the total number of persons sterilized under these eugenic laws from their inception up to the end of 1965 was 65,000. During the early 1960s the number of eugenic sterilizations averaged about 500 per year.

Outside the United States sterilization for eugenic reasons is legally regulated in a few countries, notably in Scandinavia and in Japan. In Germany eugenic sterilization, involving a minimum of 200,000 persons, was practiced under the Eugenic Law of July 14, 1933, until 1945. This estimate does not include inmates of concentration camps who were sterilized without legal authorization.

In recent years discussion has centered on the legality and/or propriety of voluntary sterilization as a method of family limitation and on the use of sterilization in countries where high birth rates and rapid population growth threaten to produce serious economic and social difficulties (Blacker 1962).

Permanent sterilization in women is ordinarily accomplished by salpingectomy, that is, by the cutting, ligation (tying), and partial removal of the Fallopian tubes. In the male, the sterilizing operation (vasectomy) consists of the cutting, ligation, and removal of a portion of the spermatic duct. Since sterilization does not involve removal of the sex glands, it does not produce loss or impairment of sexual desire or of capacity for sexual response. Restoration of fertility by a second operation is possible but not certain. This fact restricts sterilization to persons permanently ineligible for parenthood and to mature couples who have all the children they want or are likely to want in the future. According to a number of studies, the great majority of sterilized patients are satisfied with the result, feel relieved from the nagging fear of pregnancy, and have no complaints. Regrets and more serious psychological side effects have, however, been occasionally noted in sterilized persons of both sexes, who were poorly chosen and/or not suitably prepared for the operation. Such undesirable side effects are most likely to occur if the marriage is unhappy or on the brink of breaking up, or when the operation is accepted reluctantly, under pressure from a spouse or other persons.

The number of voluntary sterilizations in the United States during the late 1950s is estimated at 110,000 annually, including 65,000 operations on women and 45,000 vasectomies. Later estimates are not available. Sterilization of women has been popular in Puerto Rico since the 1940s and has also gained wide acceptance in Japan (Koya 1961). In India the government encourages voluntary sterilization as a method of population control. By mid-1965 about 900,000 operations had been reported, two-thirds on men and one-third on women. South Korea, too, has included vasectomy in its national family planning program, and 49,000 vasectomies were performed from 1962 to 1964.

Abortion

Induced abortion, that is, termination of unwanted pregnancy by destruction of the fetus, has been performed throughout man's history. Some cultures prescribe abortion under specific circumstances, others tolerate it, still others condemn it. In the United States most state laws stipulate prevention of the death of the pregnant woman as the sole ground on which pregnancy may be interrupted. In practice, many (but by no means all) reputable hospitals permit therapeutic abortion in cases where a serious threat to health is to be averted and for certain eugenic reasons, as when a pregnant woman catches a disease that is likely to cause malformations in the fetus. In New York City the number of therapeutic abortions equaled about one-fifth of one per cent of the number of live births in 1960–1962 (Gold et al. 1965). In a few countries, such as Denmark and Sweden, the interpretation of medical necessity for abortion is far more liberal, since it takes into account less serious threats to the woman's physical or mental health, as well as her economic situation. In 1963 legal abortions amounted to about 5 per cent of the number of live births in Denmark, and to about 3 per cent in Sweden (Tietze 1966).

In still other countries, abortion is legally available either at the request of the pregnant woman or on broadly interpreted social indications. In the Soviet Union abortion was legalized after World War I. In 1936 this policy was reversed, and for the next two decades abortion was permitted on medical grounds only. In 1955 another reversal took place, and abortion on request was once more legalized. The adoption of similar legislation in most countries of eastern Europe has been followed by very rapid increase in legal abortions. In Hungary legal abortions have outnumbered live births since 1959 (Mehlan 1966). In Japan the Eugenic Protection Law of 1948 authorized interruption of pregnancy for economic as well as medical reasons. The subsequent interpretation of this law has been tantamount to making abortion available unconditionally.

In several countries where the practice of abortion is restricted by law, estimates of its incidence have been obtained by the survey method (see, for example, Armijo & Monreal 1965; Hong 1966). This approach has not yet been used successfully in the United States. In 1959 a committee appointed by the Conference on Abortion at Arden House, New York, concluded that a "plausible estimate of the frequency of induced abortion . . . could be as low as 200,000 and as high as 1,200,000 per year . . ." (Planned Parenthood . . . 1958, p. 180). No new data which would permit a more precise evaluation are available.

Methods of the future

Continuing research in the field of human and animal reproduction promises new methods of fertility control, which may become available over the coming decade. Among the following procedures, some are now undergoing clinical evaluation, others are being studied in selected human volunteers, and still others are in various stages of development with laboratory animals: long-acting ovulation suppressants administered by injection; compounds suppressing spermatogenesis, for use as oral or injectable contraceptives in males; immunization of females against sperm; immunization of males against sperm, resulting in suppression of spermatogenesis; blocking of the spermatic duct by injections of plastic material which can be easily removed; compounds acting on the fertilized ovum prior to implantation; and compounds with destructive action on the young embryo.

CHRISTOPHER TIETZE

[See also FERTILITY; POPULATION, articles on POPULATION GROWTH and POPULATION POLICIES.]

BIBLIOGRAPHY

Publications in the field of fertility control, both medical and sociological, are extremely numerous, and the rate of publication will undoubtedly increase; accordingly, the works cited in this article constitute only a minute fraction of the available literature and may be rapidly superseded by new developments. A classified bibliography covering all aspects of the field (but with emphasis on the medical side) is Tietze 1965. Studies in Family Planning, an occasional publication of the Population Council, regularly summarizes much current research, especially that which deals with the social and demographic aspects of fertility control. The proceedings of the many international conferences on fertility control are published by the Excerpta Medica Foundation of Amsterdam.

ARMIJO, ROLANDO; and MONREAL, TEGUALDA 1965 Epidemiology of Provoked Abortion in Santiago, Chile. *Journal of Sex Research* 1:143–159.

BERELSON, BERNARD 1966 KAP Studies on Fertility. Pages 655–668 in International Conference on Family Planning Programs, Geneva, 1965, *Family Planning and Population Programs: A Review of World Developments.* Univ. of Chicago Press.

BLACKER, C. P. 1962 Voluntary Sterilization: The Last Sixty Years. *Eugenics Review* 54:9–23; 143–162.

CALDERONE, MARY S. (editor) 1964 *Manual of Contraceptive Practice.* Baltimore: Williams & Wilkins.

CONFERENCE ON RESEARCH IN FAMILY PLANNING, NEW YORK, *1960* 1962 *Research in Family Planning: Papers Presented at a Conference Sponsored Jointly by the Milbank Memorial Fund and the Population Council, Inc.* Princeton Univ. Press.

FRANCE, INSTITUT NATIONAL D'ÉTUDES DÉMOGRAPHIQUES 1960 *La prévention des naissances dans la famille: Ses origines dans les temps modernes,* by H. Berques et al. Travaux et Documents, Cahier No. 35. Paris: Presses Universitaires de France.

FREEDMAN, RONALD; WHELPTON, P. K.; and CAMPBELL, A. A. 1959 *Family Planning, Sterility, and Population Growth.* New York: McGraw-Hill.

GOLD, EDWIN M. et al. 1965 Therapeutic Abortions in New York City: A Twenty-year Review. *American Journal of Public Health* 55:964–972.

GREAT BRITAIN, ROYAL COMMISSION ON POPULATION 1949 *Papers.* Volume 1: Family Limitation and Its Influence on Human Fertility During the Past Fifty Years, by E. Lewis-Faning. London: H.M. Stationery Office.

HIMES, NORMAN E. (1936) 1963 *Medical History of Contraception.* New York: Gamut.

HONG, SUNG BONG 1966 *Induced Abortion in South Korea.* Seoul: Dong-A.

INTERNATIONAL CONFERENCE ON FAMILY PLANNING PROGRAMS, GENEVA, *1965* 1966 *Family Planning and Population Programs: A Review of World Developments.* Univ. of Chicago Press. → Edited by Bernard Berelson and others.

INTERNATIONAL CONFERENCE ON INTRA-UTERINE CONCEPTION, SECOND, NEW YORK, *1964* 1964 *Proceedings.* Excerpta Medica Foundation, International Congress Series, No. 86. Amsterdam: The Foundation.

JAFFE, FREDERICK S. 1964 Family Planning and Poverty. *Journal of Marriage and the Family* 26:467–470.

KOYA, YOSHIO 1961 Sterilization in Japan. *Eugenics Quarterly* 8, no. 3:135–141.

LADER, LAWRENCE 1955 *The Margaret Sanger Story and the Fight for Birth Control.* New York: Doubleday.

MEHLAN, K.-H. 1966 The Socialist Countries of Europe. Pages 207–226 in International Conference on Family Planning Programs, Geneva, 1965, *Family Planning and Population Programs: A Review of World Developments.* Univ. of Chicago Press.

MURAMATSU, MINORU 1966 Japan. Pages 7–19 in International Conference on Family Planning Programs, Geneva, 1965, *Family Planning and Population Programs: A Review of World Developments.* Univ. of Chicago Press.

PEARL, RAYMOND 1932 Contraception and Fertility in 2,000 Women. *Human Biology* 4:363–407.

PLANNED PARENTHOOD FEDERATION OF AMERICA 1958 *Abortion in the United States.* New York: Hoeber.

POTTER, R. G. JR. 1963 Additional Measures of Use-effectiveness of Contraception. *Milbank Memorial Fund Quarterly* 41:400–418.

ROWNTREE, GRISELDA; and PIERCE, RACHEL M. 1961 Birth Control in Britain. Part 1: Attitudes and Practices Among Persons Married Since the First World War. Part 2: Contraceptive Methods Used by Couples Married in the Last Thirty Years. *Population Studies* 15:3–31, 121–160.

RYDER, NORMAN B. 1959 Fertility. Pages 400–436 in P. M. Hauser and O. D. Duncan (editors), *The Study of Population.* Univ. of Chicago Press.

RYDER, NORMAN B.; and WESTOFF, CHARLES F. 1966 Use of Oral Contraception in the United States, 1965. *Science* 153:1199–1205.

TIETZE, CHRISTOPHER (editor) 1965 *Bibliography of Fertility Control: 1950–1965.* New York: National Committee on Maternal Health.

TIETZE, CHRISTOPHER 1966 Contraception With Intra-uterine Devices: 1959–1966. *American Journal of Obstetrics and Gynecology* 96:1043–1054.

TIETZE, CHRISTOPHER; and NEUMANN, LUSSIA (editors) 1962 *Surgical Sterilization of Men and Women: A Selected Bibliography.* New York: National Committee on Maternal Health.

WESTOFF, CHARLES F.; POTTER, ROBERT G.; and SAGI, PHILIP S. 1961 *Family Growth in Metropolitan America.* Princeton Univ. Press.

WESTOFF, CHARLES F.; POTTER, ROBERT G.; SAGI, PHILIP C.; and MISHLER, ELIOT G. 1963 *The Third Child: A Study in the Prediction of Fertility.* Princeton Univ. Press.

WHELPTON, PASCAL K.; CAMPBELL, ARTHUR A.; and PATTERSON, JOHN E. 1965 *Fertility and Family Planning in the United States.* Princeton Univ. Press.

FEUD

Feud has been defined by Lasswell as ". . . relations of mutual animosity among intimate groups in which a resort to violence is anticipated on both sides" (1931, p. 220). This definition includes two important concepts—"violence" and "intimate [or related] groups"—that require amplification.

Nature of violence.   Concerning the concept of violence, the question arises, Is any type of violence between intimate groups a feud, or are there specific characteristics that denote the violence of a feud? The concept is commonly refined in terms of intensity and duration. Thus, there appears to be general agreement that the violence typical of a feud may range from beating, which leaves only slight injuries, to killing several members of the opposite group. A feud involves prolonged and intermittent hostilities. As a logical consequence, a single fight or a single killing cannot be defined as a feud. Long intervals of relative peace sometimes elapse between the fights and slayings (Lowie [1920] 1947, p. 414). Bohannan says that "feud occurs when the principle of self-help gets out of hand" (1963, p. 290), implying that if an injury is redressed through violence and the self-redress is final and more or less accepted by the other party, such violence does not merit the term "feud." Lasswell states that feuds often continue so long after they begin that the precipitating episodes are even forgotten (1931, p. 221). Evans-Pritchard (1940, p. 293) agrees with the criterion of prolonged violence. However, he points out that a feud cannot go on indefinitely; otherwise the relationship of the fighting groups (among the Nuer, their membership in the same tribe) would be severed, and further hostilities, not occurring between related groups, could no longer by implication be called feud (1940, pp. 279, 283).

We may conclude, then, that feud involves prolonged, often intermittent violence which must end at some point short of the obliteration of the second criterion of feud—the intimate relationship of the feuding groups. Of course, concluding a feud does not necessarily mean that mutual hostility is transformed into indifference or friendship. A new feuding cycle most likely erupts between the old combatants any time that a new crime or injury is committed by an individual against a member of the other side.

The chain of violent acts that marks the feud is initiated in order "to secure revenge, reprisal, or glory for a particular individual or family within the group" (Wright 1942). Another common characteristic of the violence that may be classified as feud is the claim that the actual acts of hostility are regulated by customs shared by the two fighting groups (Radcliffe-Brown 1952, p. 215). In other words, the hostilities of the two groups are patterned upon, and subject to, rules which both sides observe. Furthermore, the initial act of violence is regarded as injury to the whole group to which the victim belongs (family, clan, or village), and the members consequently stand under an obligation to avenge the injustice (Radcliffe-Brown 1952, p. 215; 1940, p. xx; Nadel 1947, p. 151). Paraphrasing Durkheim, Radcliffe-Brown calls their duty an expression of "collective solidarity." However, this principle works also with regard to the opposite party, where it produces a group liability, with the effect that any member of the offender's group may be slain for the crime of his relative, his friend, or a coresident (Radcliffe-Brown 1952, p. 215; Nadel 1947, p. 151).

According to Radcliffe-Brown (1952, p. 215; 1940, p. xx), another aspect of the violence of feuds is that it is justified by "public sentiment." Unfortunately, he fails to specify whether this public sentiment pertains to the group of avengers, to both of the groups in conflict, or to the society at large. If we recall his statement that the acts of violence are regulated by custom, we may conclude that this public sentiment pertains to the larger society of which the two fighting groups are constituent segments. Not all acts of violence justify development of such a sentiment: in order that a violent revenge be considered a justifiable act, its magnitude should be valued as an equivalent to the injury suffered (Radcliffe-Brown 1952, p. 215; 1940, p. xx; Nadel 1947, p. 151). Who, however, determines the equivalent? Implied in the writings of Radcliffe-Brown and Nadel is the notion that the criteria for equivalence are sufficiently objective, i.e., part of a general custom known to all, so that it is often unnecessary for a specified authority to deliver an opinion on the balance between the injury and revenge. Among the Nuba, for example, "equivalence" is so specific that not only must a man be killed for a man and a woman for a woman, but the age of the person killed in revenge should approximate that of the original victim. For death in excess of requirement a compensation must be offered in the form of a person who is adopted into the offended clan (Nadel 1947, pp. 151–152). In most other primitive societies such compensation is usually tendered in terms of a payment known in the literature as "blood money." Bearing in mind Bohannan's important point that feud occurs when "self-help gets out of hand," Radcliffe-Brown's and Nadel's principle of equivalence of revenge applies to feud only when such equivalence is not achieved by the first retaliation of the injured party. There have to be more than two acts of violence to justify the application of the term "feud."

The characteristics of violence that form one of the two major criteria of feud may be summed up as follows: (1) the violence of a feud ranges in intensity from injury to killing; (2) it is initiated on behalf of a particular individual or family that is a member of the more inclusive "injured group"; and (3) it is of long duration, involving at least three instances of violence—injury, revenge, and counterrevenge. Hostile acts consisting of an injury and of an equivalent revenge that is accepted as final by both parties do not merit the term feud and should more properly be called self-redress. The nature of self-redress is, in most cases, basically different from the prolonged violence called feud.

Nature of feuding groups. The second major criterion of feud, which requires the committed violence to occur between two "intimate [or related] groups," is far more important and complex (Lasswell 1931). It is almost generally agreed that the two groups fighting each other must be related in order to qualify such hostilities as a feud. However, various authors differ in their explanation of the nature of this relationship. An imprecise position is assumed, for example, by Wright, who states that "most primitive groups observe different war practices toward a related group with which friendship normally exists and toward a wholly alien group. Hostilities of the first type, although group sanctioned, are usually of the nature of a feud to secure revenge, reprisal, or glory for a particular individual or family within the group" (1942). Others who have studied feuds—for example, Malinowski ([1941] 1964, p. 261)—go further, claiming that relationship between the two groups obtains from the fact that they both belong to "the same larger cultural unit." Similarly, those who use the phrase "members of the same society" do not necessarily identify the political unit involved. For example, Max Gluckman (1940, p. 41) speaks of a type of intertribal feud within a larger nation, while Hobhouse and his associates restrict the relationship of feuding groups to membership in the same tribe: "Feuds would thus also be the appropriate name for reprisals exercised by one branch of a community upon another, e.g., as between two clans or two local groups within a tribe" (Hobhouse et al. [1915] 1930, p. 228). Besides this type of an "internal self-redress" called feud, these authors recognize another type of redress which exists between two segments of otherwise unrelated communities and is labeled "external self-

redress." A similar limitation of the application of the concept of feud to the fighting done by groupings that belong to the same tribe is upheld quite explicitly by Evans-Pritchard. He contrasts these hostilities with the intertribally organized violence which he calls war: "Thus, if a man of one tribe kills a man of another tribe, retribution can only take the form of intertribal warfare" (1940, p. 278). "Between segments of the same tribe, opposition is expressed by the institution of the feud" (1940, p. 283).

Some authors theorize that marriage ties constitute the link between the two feuding groups. Accordingly, hostilities in a society with exogamous subgroups such as clans, lineages, or local communities are all regarded as feuds and not as wars (Schneider 1964, p. 282; also implied by Colson 1962, p. 120).

The relationship between the hostile groups is far less nebulous and more related to the feuding itself than the marriage-tie hypothesis would imply. Evans-Pritchard has the following to say about those Nuer who engage in intratribal fighting: "Then either the contradiction of feuds is felt and they are settled, the unity of the tribe being maintained thereby, or they remain so long unsettled that people give up all hope and intention of ever concluding them and finally cease to feel that they ought to be concluded, so that the tribe tends to split and two new tribes come into being" (1940, p. 279). This statement suggests that the nature of the relationship of two feuding groups lies in the fact that the more inclusive group of which the two are members is, at least to some degree, politically organized. The political organization may mean that there exists a formally designated authority with jurisdiction over both feuding groups; in other cases it may consist of only the most informal arbiters or go-betweens, who customarily settle internal political problems. Gluckman ([1956] 1959, p. 20) went so far as to claim that feuding, by creating a necessity for the existence of such go-betweens, tends to unite the members of the larger grouping. There are good examples of formal political authority terminating feuds between subgroups by the use of force, in the event that the customary exchange has failed. The present author would hesitate to designate as a feud fighting which occurs between politically unrelated groupings and would criticize Wagner (1940, p. 223) and Schneider (1964, p. 279) for holding that an overall political organization is not necessary to qualify a condition of strife as a feud. Wherever feuds do occur, there exists a politically influential authority (a formal chief, an informal headman, a council of important men, or an individual of very limited power, such as a go-between), who is usually too weak or disinterested in controlling his constituents, with the result that prolonged fighting is not prevented. The weaker the political control, the longer the feuds last and the harder it is to conclude them (see especially Evans-Pritchard 1940, pp. 278–279; and Gluckman [1956] 1959, p. 19).

Feud and war. The criterion of an over-all political organization that relates the two feuding groups may also be used to mark the boundary between feud and war. Whereas feuds can occur only within a politically organized whole, war occurs beyond such an organization and always involves two groups that are politically unrelated (Nadel 1947, p. 301). One should not, however, go to the extreme and claim that it would be "advisable to include all external, group-sanctioned violence against other human beings in the conception of primitive war" (Schneider 1964, p. 276). There seem to be two kinds of hostility external to politically organized groupings: hostility which is "exercised by a part of a community only upon members of another community" and which should properly be called "external self-redress," or retaliation; and hostility which means "an operation conducted in the name of the community as a whole," and which thus deserves to be regarded as war (Hobhouse et al. [1915] 1930, p. 228).

These structural criteria that distinguish feud, external redress, and war appear to be more politically relevant and suitable than the following, which are of only circumstantial nature. For example, the claim that only publicly initiated hostilities should be called war, while the privately initiated ones should be labeled feuds, constitutes a most impractical criterion. However, Schneider's criticism of anthropologists for misusing the term "war" is erroneous; it is based on his contention that hostilities within a society that is segmented into exogamous groups (such as clans, lineages, or communities) cannot be called war (Schneider 1964, pp. 279, 282). He disregards the fact that exogamy is a social-structural feature and war is a political phenomenon and that, therefore, presence or absence of exogamy is irrelevant to this problem. To make the term "war" cross-culturally applicable and meaningful, one should define it in terms of political-structural features. Data on the Kapauku Papuans of New Guinea bear out the fallacy of such an analysis (Pospisil 1958). These Papuans live in localized exogamous lineages. Several lineages, belonging to different sibs, unite for defense purposes into a political confederacy. Beyond this unit no political organization exists. Interconfed-

ational strife, which is true war, is marked by organization, by participation of whole confederacies as units in the fighting, and by ferocity involving slaughter, arson, rape, etc. On the contrary, fighting within a confederacy is done, as a rule, with sticks, not with bows and arrows, and does not result in death. No raping of women, burning of houses, killing of pigs, or destruction of gardens accompany these internal hostilities. To consider both types of fighting as feud would be to obscure rather than clarify the ethnological reality. Bearing the political-structural criteria of feud and war in mind, one can readily see how erroneous are the claims that war is uncommon or nonexistent in "the lowest stages" of social development (Hobhouse et al. [1915] 1930, p. 228) and that it requires for its existence a "certain development of social organization." Indeed, it is the feud that requires a complex social development—a large social entity with an over-all political organization that is segmented into subgroups.

Feud and law. The fact that feuds are fought between subgroups of a more inclusive grouping possessing an over-all network of political relations has led to the conclusion that feud is a primitive juridical mechanism and that it is an expression, or manifestation, of primitive law. Accordingly, Malinowski writes, "Fighting, collective and organized, is a juridical mechanism for the adjustment of differences between constituent groups of the same larger cultural unit" ([1941] 1961, p. 261). Spencer contends that after a north Alaskan Eskimo was killed, ". . . his own kin became embroiled and the legal mechanism of the feud was put into motion" (1959, p. 161). The notion that feuding is a manifestation of primitive law led Lasswell to the conclusion that there must be two types of feuds: "While the blood vengeance feud was itself the expression of primitive law, the modern feud is at least formally illegal and characteristically fills the interstices left in the functioning of the prevailing system of legal organization" (1931, p. 220). Many anthropologists have disagreed with the idea that feud is the expression of primitive law and have proposed or implied a unitary definition of feud. Hoebel (1949, p. 3) considers that feud lies outside the sphere of law. He bases this distinction on the fact that the counter-killings do not stop and that there is nothing one may regard as a mutually recognized coercive sanction against the killer and his group. Similarly, Bohannan (1963, p. 290) calls feud "a faulty jural mechanism" because it does not lead to a final settlement—to peace and rectitude. Radcliffe-Brown, on the other hand, refuses to regard feud as law, not because of its functional aspect, but because it lacks "the exercise of recognized authority in settling disputes" (1940, p. xx).

Pospisil (1956) defines law by means of four criteria, none of which is inherent in the phenomena of feuds: (1) law is manifested in a decision made by a political authority; (2) it contains a definition of the relation between the two parties to the dispute (*obligatio*); (3) it has a regularity of application (intention of universal application); (4) it is provided with a sanction. Law, which is characterized by these four criteria, is present in all societies—indeed, in every functioning group or subgroup of people—that he has investigated. In the primitive societies in which feud is endemic, law exists in those subgroups which have developed leadership, thus coexisting with feuds without incorporating them into the jural mechanism. Whereas law presupposes decisions passed by an authority holding jurisdiction over both litigants and a regular respect for, and compliance with, these decisions by the parties to the dispute, a feud represents an intergroup fight in which all the participants ignore and even defy the jurisdiction of the over-all political authority, which is usually weak or uninterested. Consequently, whereas law is a means of intragroup settlement of disputes, a feud—because of the feuding parties' defiance of the superordinated political structure—is basically an intergroup phenomenon, although it occurs within a more inclusive, politically organized unit. The difference between law and feud is again of political-structural nature, as are the differences between feud, war, and external redress. That law stands in opposition to feud and that the latter is actually the antithesis of the former rather than its manifestation, is well documented in those societies in which feuds are stopped by legal decisions of the over-all authority, who either has enough power to enforce his will or possesses the skill to persuade the quarreling parties to accept his solutions (see especially Nadel 1947, p. 154; Evans-Pritchard 1940, pp. 278–279).

Finally, it should be pointed out that not every case of "internal self-redress" constitutes a feud. When a counterkilling is accepted by the over-all political authority as a just punishment of the culprit or of his subgroup and the subgroup of the defender is induced or forced to accept such a verdict and to refrain from further counterkillings, the sanctioned reprisal constitutes a case of legal self-redress that is true law (Hoebel 1949, p. 3; Pospisil 1958, p. 256; Bohannan 1963, p. 290). Hoebel, for example, writes, "If the kin group of the original killer customarily accepts the action of the avengers as just, and stays its hands from further counterkilling, then we have legal law" (1949, p. 3).

In conclusion, we may summarize the salient features of feud and set it off from the related concepts of law, war, external self-redress, and legal self-redress. The essence of feud has been found to be a series (at least three instances) of acts of violence, usually involving killings, committed by members of two groups related to each other by superimposed political-structural features (often involving the existence of an over-all political authority) and acting on the basis of group solidarity (a common duty to avenge and a common liability). This definition sets feud apart from war and external self-redress because the last two terms refer to acts of violence committed by members of politically unrelated groups: in war both combat groups act as units in the organized fighting; in external self-redress members of two subgroups only, each belonging to a different, politically unrelated group, participate in the hostilities. This definition also distinguishes feud from law. Feud is an internal affair, conducted by members of the subgroups of an over-all political organization who ignore or even defy its political authority. In its conduct, then, feud refers to intergroup phenomena. Law, on the contrary, is an intragroup affair in the full sense of the term: a decision of the authority who holds jurisdiction over both parties to the dispute is passed, and both disputing parties are induced or forced to comply with its provisions.

LEOPOLD POSPISIL

[See also WAR. *Other relevant material may be found in* JUDICIAL PROCESS, *article on* COMPARATIVE ASPECTS; LAW, *article on* LAW AND LEGAL INSTITUTIONS; POLITICAL ANTHROPOLOGY, *article on* POLITICAL ORGANIZATION.]

BIBLIOGRAPHY

BOHANNAN, PAUL 1963 *Social Anthropology.* New York: Holt.

COLSON, ELIZABETH 1962 *The Plateau Tonga of Northern Rhodesia.* Manchester (England) Univ. Press.

EVANS-PRITCHARD, E. E. 1940 The Nuer of the Southern Sudan. Pages 272–296 in Meyer Fortes and E. E. Evans-Pritchard (editors), *African Political Systems.* Oxford Univ. Press.

GLUCKMAN, MAX 1940 The Kingdom of the Zulu of South Africa. Pages 25–55 in Meyer Fortes and E. E. Evans-Pritchard (editors), *African Political Systems.* Oxford Univ. Press.

GLUCKMAN, MAX (1956) 1959 *Custom and Conflict in Africa.* Glencoe, Ill.: Free Press.

HOBHOUSE, LEONARD T.; WHEELER, GERALD C.; and GINSBERG, MORRIS (1915) 1930 *The Material Culture and Social Institutions of the Simpler Peoples: An*

Essay in Correlation. London School of Economics and Political Science Monographs on Sociology, No. 3. London: Chapman.

HOEBEL, E. ADAMSON 1949 Introduction. Pages 1–5 in Roy F. Barton, *The Kalingas*. Publications in Anthropology, Social Anthropological Series. Univ. of Chicago Press.

HOEBEL, E. ADAMSON 1954 *The Law of Primitive Man: A Study in Comparative Legal Dynamics*. Cambridge, Mass.: Harvard Univ. Press.

HONIGMAN, JOHN J. 1960 [Review of] *The North Alaskan Eskimo*, by Robert F. Spencer. *American Anthropologist* New Series 62:340–341.

LASSWELL, HAROLD D. 1931 Feuds. Volume 6, pages 220–221 in *Encyclopaedia of the Social Sciences*. New York: Macmillan.

LOWIE, ROBERT H. (1920) 1947 *Primitive Society*. New York: Liveright. → A paperback edition was published in 1961 by Harper.

MALINOWSKI, BRONISLAW (1941) 1964 An Anthropological Analysis of War. Pages 245–268 in Leon Bramson and George W. Goethals (editors), *War: Studies From Psychology, Sociology, Anthropology*. New York: Basic Books.

NADEL, SIEGFRIED F. 1947 *The Nuba: An Anthropological Study of the Hill Tribes in Kordofan*. London and New York: Oxford Univ. Press.

POSPISIL, LEOPOLD 1956 The Nature of Law. New York Academy of Sciences, *Transactions* 18:746–755.

POSPISIL, LEOPOLD 1958 *Kapauku Papuans and Their Law*. Yale University Publications in Anthropology, No. 54. New Haven: Yale Univ. Press.

POSPISIL, LEOPOLD 1964 Law and Societal Structure Among the Nunamiut Eskimo. Pages 395–431 in Ward H. Goodenough (editor), *Explorations in Cultural Anthropology: Essays in Honor of George Peter Murdock*. New York: McGraw-Hill.

RADCLIFFE-BROWN, A. R. 1940 Preface. In Meyer Fortes and E. E. Evans-Pritchard (editors), *African Political Systems*. Oxford Univ. Press.

RADCLIFFE-BROWN, A. R. 1952 *Structure and Function in Primitive Society: Essays and Addresses*. London: Cohen & West; Glencoe, Ill.: Free Press.

SCHNEIDER, JOSEPH 1964 Primitive Warfare: A Methodological Note. Pages 275–283 in Leon Bramson and George W. Goethals (editors), *War: Studies From Psychology, Sociology, Anthropology*. New York: Basic Books.

SPENCER, ROBERT F. 1959 *The North Alaskan Eskimo*. U.S. Bureau of American Ethnology, Bulletin No. 171. Washington: Government Printing Office.

WAGNER, GUNTHER 1940 The Political Organization of the Bantu of Kavirondo. Pages 197–238 in Meyer Fortes and E. E. Evans-Pritchard (editors), *African Political Systems*. Oxford Univ. Press.

WEDGWOOD, CAMILLA H. 1930 Some Aspects of Warfare in Melanesia. *Oceania* 1:5–33.

WRIGHT, QUINCY (1942) 1965 *A Study of War*. 2d ed. Univ. of Chicago Press.

FEUDALISM

Feudalism conventionally denotes the type of society and the political system originating in western and central Europe and dominant there during the greater part of the Middle Ages. However, the term is also applied to other societies and systems of government with similar characteristics, in antiquity and in modern times; in the Marxist usage it refers to a type of society and economy characterized by serfdom, generally succeeding the economic systems based on slavery and preceding capitalism.

The word from the Germanic *fehu-od* (from which is derived the English and French *fief*)— that is, "property in cattle" and, later, "tenure" or "property in land"—stresses the importance, in the system, of land tenure and the rights and privileges attached to it. Since the seventeenth century, the complex of tenurial and personal relationships and economic, social, and political dependencies that centered on the fief have increasingly been regarded as a scaffold of social stratification and political organization. This view, often reflecting actual political and social problems in eighteenth-century England and France, created the notion of a period dominated by "feudal laws" (Montesquieu) that were comprehensive enough to denote a regime and to dominate and rule a society. The later meaning of the word, although basically rooted in eighteenth-century usage, came to denote, through abuse of language, such social realities as the political predominance of a landholding aristocracy and the exploitation of the small and weak by the powerful. It also came to denote any political system in which the power of the state was weakened or paralyzed by the privileges of the few and made inefficient by the fractioning of political power, or by the opposition of powerful political or economic aristocratic factions.

Historical scholarship since the nineteenth century has brought to light more and more of the variety of economic, social, and political forms to be found in feudal societies at any one time, as well as the changes inevitable in any social and political framework lasting over five hundred years. Nevertheless, some major features do recur, and a certain rhythm of evolution seems to have been common to rather large areas as they reacted to similar economic, social, and political changes. Hence, it is possible to speak about feudal institutions without implying that all aspects of economic, social, and political life predominant in the greater part of the European Middle Ages were always present. Such institutions can also be found in other societies; sometimes they evolve from similar conditions, but often they are isolated phenomena in different frameworks or without the interrelations deemed essential in the European system. (In these cases the term "feudal tendencies" might be a better description.)

Despite the great variety of definitions of feudalism, some minimal common characteristics of a fully developed feudal system would be accepted by most scholars. These include: (1) lord–vassal relationships; (2) a personalized government that is most effective on the local level and has relatively little separation of political functions; (3) a system of landholding consisting of the granting of fiefs in return for service and assurance of future services; (4) the existence of private armies and a code of honor in which military obligations are stressed; and (5) seignioral and manorial rights of the lord over the peasant (see Coulborn 1956; Hall 1962).

Perhaps the fullest definition of feudalism in the political sphere was given by Weber ([1922] 1957, pp. 375–376), who considered feudalism one type of "patriarchal authority." According to Weber: (1) The authority of the chief is reduced to the likelihood that the vassals will voluntarily remain faithful to their oaths of fealty. (2) The political corporate group is completely replaced by a system of relations of purely personal loyalty between the lord and his vassals and between these, in turn, and their own subvassals (subinfeudation). (3) Only in the case of a "felony" does the lord have a right to deprive his vassal of his fief. (4) There is a hierarchy of social rank, corresponding to the hierarchy of fiefs, but it is not a hierarchy of authority in the bureaucratic sense. (5) The elements in the population who do not hold fiefs with some political authority are "subjects"—that is, patrimonial dependents. (6) Powers over the individual budgetary unit (domains, slaves, and serfs), the fiscal rights of the political group to the receipt of taxes and contributions, and powers of jurisdiction and compulsion to military service are all objects of feudal grants.

In the social sector an important element of feudalism is the bearing of arms as a class-defining profession. Here feudalism is distinguished by a relative closing of the social status system in which (for the groups dependent primarily on the land) the distribution of goods and services is closely integrated with the hierarchy of social statuses. Within the economic sector feudal government and society appear uniformly to rest upon a landed, or locally self-sufficient, economic base as distinguished from a pastoral, commercial, or industrial one. The merchant community, although it may play a significant role in the economy, is essentially outside the feudal nexus. The appearance of certain technological features of government and economy, notably centralized communications and means of large-scale political organization, serve to undermine the feudal institutions (Hall 1962).

Whatever the variations within the economic, social, or political sphere, perhaps the most important problem in the analysis of feudal societies or systems is the extent to which in any given place we can find these feudal characteristics developing or coexisting in all the major institutional spheres. The classical age of feudalism is usually dated from the eleventh to the thirteenth centuries and located in northern France. Other societies in different historical periods, whether European or non-European, are compared to this northern French society to determine the extent to which feudal institutions and tendencies developed within them.

Feudalism in western Europe

The specific features of feudalism were the outcome of the encounter of two types of society, the Romanized and the Germanic. Their fusion into a new society, the Romano–Germanic, was accompanied by a merging and reshaping of their respective institutions. Neither the German nor the Roman traditions were homogeneous, and throughout central and western Europe they differed according to the strength of the local (often pre-Roman, Celtic) institutions and the effectiveness of Romanization, on the one hand, and the distance of the new Germanic societies from their earlier, preinvasion habitats, on the other.

At the time of their encounter, both societies were in a state of transition. The late Roman or Romanized West was passing through the profound crisis of a disintegrating empire, a weakening of central power, and a dislocation of the bureaucratic state machinery; the economic breakdown was seen in the diminishing importance of cities as centers of administration and of specialized economic activities, in the process of devaluation, and in the slowing down of the money economy. State and society were groping for new norms of existence. Public authority was delegated to the great landowners, who already exercised some authority over their immediate dependents; economic life was shifting from city to countryside and was concentrated on the larger estates, which tried to achieve autarchy in supplying their needs; insecurity was creating private warrior bands; freed slaves were being absorbed into the peasantry, who lost their status as free men to become the dependent semiservile "colonate." The Germanic tribes (*Sippen*), through migration and settlement, had loosened or lost their tribal ties. There remained the cohesion of families and of the newer and weaker village communities, which in time came to represent territorial units rather than strong kinship relations. The transition from tribal to state organization continued in the fifth and sixth centuries, but the lack of a competent administration combined with an extremely low level of literacy and restricted money circulation helped to weaken the traditional units; nowhere was a state structure able to take over and to fulfill its public duties.

The early medieval state, like that of the Frankish Merovingians (end of the fifth to beginning of the eighth century), presents, consequently, a juxtaposition of divergent elements of state and society (hardly ever integrated into a coherent whole). From this point of view, the features associated with feudalism are the direct outcome of a society striving for patterns of organization and cohesion in a period of declining state power and the disruption of traditional kinship security groups.

The most striking feature of the developing system is the new stratification of society. Roman social hierarchy was far more polarized than that of the Germanic tribes. The latter, although not egalitarian, as some nineteenth-century historians claimed, was basically a society of free men with a charismatic and hereditary chieftainship. The new administrative and military needs had already singled out the royal Merovingian entourage of warriors and officials and had sanctioned their standing by a higher *Wergeld*. At the beginning of the eighth century, however, the permanent need for professional, highly trained military men (mounted warriors) brought about a radical change in society. The former peasant–warrior lost his military value. Private bands of warriors, a phenomenon that had its antecedents as much in the imperial bodyguard and in the private armies of the Roman senatorial class as in the ancient Germanic followers (*Gefolgschaft*) of the chieftain, sprang up around the king and local magnates.

Vassalage.   The nexus between the chieftain and his free followers was taken over by the institution of *vassalage* (although the word itself points to a more humble origin, as "vassal" derives from the Celtic *gwas*, meaning "youngster" or "servant"). Beginning in the early Carolingian period (eighth century), the new institution was integrated into the framework of state and society until it became official, recognized and sanctioned in public law and put to the service of the state. With the tremendous expansion of the empire of Charles the Great and for two centuries thereafter, vassalage as a type of social cohesion became the normal way of assuring not only military service but also public authority. Although the ancient oath of fealty of subjects to the ruler remained, it was felt that it did not sufficiently assure either loyalty or political allegiance. Consequently, an oath of vassalage, more binding and directly linked with the ruler, was demanded from appointed officials. The

heads of military and administrative circumscriptions—dukes, marquis, and counts—became vassals of the king. This new type of relation, which abandoned the charismatic character of the earlier period, was based mainly on the notions of fealty and absolute loyalty, strengthened by the religious element inherent in the oath itself, and it bound the contracting parties in a contractual relation.

The principles of vassalic relations, first applied at the highest state level, spread rapidly to the lower rungs of the social ladder. Magnates and royal officials assured their own standing and the performance of the services of their office by contracting vassals, and the same process continued downward to the simple warrior and local administrative officer. Thus, a pyramidal structure of bonds and dependencies arose, a scaffold of state structure and state machinery, the apex of which, ideally, was the king.

Economic and social relations.   The economic premises of the new social order were rooted in early medieval economy and grew out of the same social changes that made vassalic relations possible. The weakening of the *Sippe* not only created insecurity but also changed the economic bases of existence. The village community, far weaker than the *Sippe* organization, could not offer adequate security, and social cohesion took the new form of individuals seeking the protection of the powerful man in their vicinity, drawing both on the patron–client pattern of the Roman tradition and on the Germanic notion of *Grundherr*, the rich and strong proprietor, whose influence transcended the boundaries of his property and his direct dependents. Such proprietors included ecclesiastical institutions as well as secular lords. The peasants—and often whole villages—commended themselves into the protection of the powerful, relinquishing their property and receiving it back as a "precarium" (from *preco*, "to beg for"), a possession (later, hereditary tenure) burdened by certain economic obligations. Conversely, they received the protection of the establishment or the lay lord. This protection against outside (fiscal, administrative, military, or juridical) pressures not only made the peasant economically dependent but also initiated the process through which he lost his standing as free man and citizen. His dealings with state authority were henceforth channeled through his overlord. In this sense, the king, who combined competences of state sovereignty (often theoretical in the ninth and tenth centuries) and vassalic suzerainty, lost his subjects, whom he could reach only through the mediation of their overlords.

The material basis of the vassalic contract was

the fief. This was usually an agricultural territory (but there existed also money fiefs) granted by the lord to the vassal at the "homage" (from *homo*, "man") ceremony when the vassal swore to serve the lord as his "man." At the highest level of the feudal echelon the fief was usually a seigniory—that is, an economic and political entity invested with public powers of administration, taxation, and jurisdiction. A seigniory might comprise anything from a single village to a large complex of villages. It was the degree of public authority and the degree of immunity from the interference of an overlord which differentiated it from a simple fief and fixed its place in the hierarchy of fiefs in the kingdom. The seigniory comprised, as a rule, a large territory where the exercise of public rights was shared, in different degrees, by the lord and the men who became his vassals ("subvassals" of the overlord) through enfeoffment and homage. Public power became an object of inheritance, since it accompanied the inheritance of the fiefs and seigniories.

At the bottom of the feudal ladder was the simple knight who owed to the overlord his own service and was supported by a fief just large enough to assure him a living in keeping with the standards of his class. Such a fief could coincide with a village or part of it, and its economic organization was usually described as a manorial economy. The lord of the manor also had noneconomic rights over the tenants on his manor, the most characteristic being the rights of jurisdiction deriving from land tenure.

The movement of commendation, common to all strata of society, brought about a complete transformation of its social stratification and cohesion and, finally, of the concepts of the state and its authority. Thousands of links of dependence ran from the apex to the lowest echelons of society. Their scope, meaning, and aim changed from step to step. Whereas in higher echelons commendation created a professional caste of warriors soon to become the nobility, in the lower echelons it created a class of people serving the lords in different capacities. As long as the service was basically military, the link of commendation created vassalage, which had come to be regarded as the only condition fitting a free man. Lower down, commendation created serfdom of varying degrees, but always connoting economic dependence, social degradation, and exclusion from the community of free men and subjects.

The hierarchic principle of cohesion and dependence was sustained economically by the legal hierarchy of land and by the fixed relation of men to land. Only where feudalization did not penetrate the depth of society were there free communities, direct subjects of royalty, and allodial (entirely independent) property. Ireland and Scotland preserved clannish cohesion; Frisia preserved independent communities; in Saxony and parts of Spain there were free men; and German nobility kept allodial property late into the twelfth century. In all other territories all land except the royal domain had the legal status of tenure or dependent possession.

The main economic feature of the fief was the holder's privilege not to work the land himself but to receive income in specie, money, and work from the peasant population. The peasants themselves held their land as servile tenures astricted as to payments and services, which varied widely according to the type of servile tenure. But it is a striking feature of the system that the obligations of the peasant were those deriving from his own legal status and that of the land he held. The theoretical symmetry between the status of a man and that of his holding was soon destroyed by marriage and inheritance. A serf might, for example, be the tenant of a "free mansus" (*mansus*, "a unit of family holding"), his duties deriving from his status as serf and the obligations inherent in the free mansus.

Stabilization of the system. Around 1100 the major features of feudalism began to stabilize and integrate into a coherent politico–economic system. Yet, complete integration was never achieved. Rights of possession, economic privileges, and public authority often remained undefined, consequently competing and overlapping. Starting in the second half of the twelfth century, political theoreticians with legal training tried to describe the institutions of government and society as forming a logical whole. One of the stabilizing factors was the general rule linking vassalage with fiefs and their regular, hereditary transmission. Occurring on all levels of the feudal hierarchy, it assured a solid scaffold of social structure. Not only were the simple knight, his immediate overlord, and every lord up to the apex of the feudal hierarchy henceforth concerned with fiefs and seigniories, as pure vassalage links would have postulated, but the family as a whole became a major factor in the feudal mechanism. On the upper level of the hierarchy, that of the great tenants-in-chief of the crown with quasi-state authority, it was the dynasty that counted. Below them, the traditional vassals of the dynasty were often regarded not only as members of the household (*maisnie*) but as a part of the noble lineage (*lignage*). The relations between lords and vassals were often conceived in terms of family relations, and the competences of the lord were not unlike the Germanic *mundeburdum* or the Roman *patria potestas*. The custom of sending the vassals' children to be raised at the court of the overlord strengthened this type of relation, as did the meetings of the vassals at the lord's court in times of festivity, which were held as much for business reasons as for socializing.

Rise of the nobility. In the twelfth century a two-hundred-year-old process of class formation came to an end, producing a class of nobility. The old warrior class of the eighth century was by then a class pursuing the profession of arms, which assured it a privileged place in society and a major share in political power; moreover, it was a class which could transmit its economic, social, and political standing to its descendants, becoming, consequently, a hereditary nobility. Despite the marked differences within the class itself, differences based primarily on the extent of political power and the control of economic resources, all fief holders regarded themselves, and were regarded by others, as the highest class in society.

The most characteristic feature of the military nobility was its new warrior ideal—the knight. "Knighthood" was a designation of rank and dignity; it was, by implication, the expression of the new ethos—chivalrousness. Fusing ancient Germanic ideals of the "heroic age" with newer concepts of ecclesiastical origin, chivalry (from *chevalier*, "a mounted warrior") expressed the worldly ideals of the fighting class and the new ethical teachings of the church. Fighting should not be an end in itself but should serve social and religious ideals in a basically other-world-oriented society. Biblical virtues—the protection of women, the weak, and the poor and the defense of religion— were the aims that enabled the church to sanction war and bloodshed. The ideal of the "Christian knight" (*miles Christianus*) which represented the ethos of the warrior caste, imprinted its character on the period. Its early, extreme theoretical formulation was by Bernard of Clairvaux, who regarded the knight as a permanent candidate for martyrdom, and its early institutionalization was in the military orders created at the time of the Crusades in the Holy Land and the Christian reconquest of Spain.

The ideals of monasticism and warriorship merged into the ideal of the Christian knight par excellence. Chivalry became institutionalized, adopting a military–ecclesiastical initiation rite ("dubbing") and elaborating a code of behavior and a set of virtues fitting a member of the class. Henceforth, membership in the nobility depended not only on origin but on the formal act of "knighting." The chivalrous virtues and rules of behavior and the image the class had of itself were perpetu-

ated by upbringing and education. The noble child passed a period of graded apprenticeship, living with a noble family (very often the vassal's overlord) before dubbing, which could be given only by someone who was himself a knight. The introduction of chivalric rites and what became in the later part of the thirteenth century a formal code of chivalrous behavior made the noble class more exclusive, thus affecting social mobility. The code became, especially after the fourteenth century, extremely formalized and served to exclude nonmembers who acquired economic position in nonnoble pursuits (commerce and banking) and who, by buying fiefs, tried to penetrate the ranks of nobility. It also excluded knights who engaged in commercial pursuits.

While the nobility was guarding its ranks against outsiders, its own internal differentiation proceeded swiftly. The baronial class, in many cases, split into magnates, "greater barons," or *grandes*; beneath them "smaller barons," or *hidalgos*; and below them simple knights. Although social mobility existed, it tended to be rather limited. Marriages and dowries were usually contracted in a closed class market, and marriage with a lower-born noble was regarded with disdain. Local variations always existed—for example, social mobility was greater in England than on the Continent, and German *ministeriales* (sometimes serfs but in any case not nobles) in royal military service were ennobled and could exercise the highest state functions, even at the end of the twelfth century (although Germany at this time was not yet entirely feudalized). The features and ideals of the nobility that are described above survived long after the class lost its political standing and parts of its economic position or even economic privileges.

Growth of political units. As the links of cohesion strengthened, the administrative framework, grouping fiefs and seigniories into larger political units, became clearer. Generally speaking, there were two main lines of development. One was the creation of strong local principalities (Anjou, Normandy, Flanders), which at the turn of the eleventh century succeeded in dominating the different seigniories in their territories, recapturing some of the public authority (control of castles and mints —in some places a monopoly of the princely dynasty), and often developing princely bureaucratic administrations. This process built up the strong centralized provinces, which during the next hundred years were taken over by the Capetians and became the foundations of the kingdom of France.

The second line was followed by Germany. In twelfth-century Germany, less feudalized than France, public authority was often still in the hands of local princely dynasties with allodial possessions, who exercised their competences not as the king's vassals but, theoretically, as his officials. Their power was strengthened at the beginning of the century when the "quarrel of investiture" weakened the standing of royalty. To create stronger cohesion and forge links of dependence, the crown tried to bring the highest nobility into direct vassalic dependence, in the process resigning to it public authority in the principalities. The principalities, by forging vassalic links with the local nobility, were supposed to become well-ordered administrative units directed by the crown. The principalities achieved, indeed, strong governments, but the crown never succeeded in bringing them into a rigid state framework. Germany, especially after the interregnum at the end of the Hohenstaufen dynasty (middle of thirteenth century), was made up of principalities and their rulers (*Länder* and *Landesherren*) within a loose framework of the empire. Legislation forced the emperor to enfeoff noble escheats, which could otherwise have enlarged the royal domain and thus strengthened his position at the expense of the princely class. Finally, the principle of election of the emperor by the imperial electors (*Kurfürsten*) assured their dominance. Consequently, Germany never reached any degree of state unity. On the contrary, the principalities became independent, strongly organized states, with princely power based on authority delegated by the emperor and on vassalic links obligatory within their territories. In England, after the Norman conquest, sovereignty and suzerainty assured a preponderant power to the crown. Feudal particularistic tendencies, brought to light in the middle of the twelfth century by rival claims to the throne, were quickly checked, leaving royalty in full possession of its powers. In Italy the development followed the lines of Germany, but the place of the principalities was taken by the emerging cities, the "communes," which created territorial units virtually independent of the central power.

The decline of feudalism. The decline of feudalism was a general phenomenon of European history that owed as much to the economic transformations of the twelfth and thirteenth centuries as it did to features inherent in the feudal system itself. The economic transformations were the result of the twelfth-century "urban revolution." The revival of money economy, the renewal of city life with its more complex division of labor, the rise of the new social stratum of burgesses—all proclaimed new needs and new possibilities. They enabled the state to perform and enlarge its functions without constant recourse to feudal services. The new market situation enabled the peasants to accumulate money from the sale of surplus production and initiated the commutation of manorial services into money payments. The final result was the disruption of the manorial economy and a profound change in the standing of the nobility.

Insecurity decreased in the far better policed states of the central Middle Ages, and the rural population did not depend for its survival or defense on the local magnate. The political power he wielded could be, and was, more efficiently used by state officials. Inherited political power consequently lost its practical and moral justification.

The change in the position of the feudal lord is even more marked when compared with the all-important lord–vassal relations of the earlier period. As already mentioned, the inheritance of fiefs greatly contributed to the solidity of the system. At the same time, it brought with it a notable change in the feudo–vassalic establishment. As heredity was the rule and the renewal of the vassalic oath usually only a formality, the economic element in the relationship overshadowed the personal and intimate elements. Previously undefined and unlimited duties of service were replaced by fixed and measured obligations. Thus, the military service was fixed for 40 days yearly; other aids and services were measured in stereotyped proportions according to the size of the fief. The fact that from the end of the tenth century a vassal could hold fiefs from different lords created a problem of multiple, often opposed, loyalties.

The weakening of the ties of dependence in the upper strata of society and the process of dissolution on the manorial level brought about a complete transformation in patterns of social cohesion and state organization. Different strata of society became crystallized in the pattern of "estates." The estate grouped people of the same social class, who had a similar economic standing and enjoyed the same privileged position in the state in relation to the crown and to other estates. Unlike the former feudal links of cohesion, which were vertical, the new links binding man to man were horizontal. Men joining others of their own class sought assurance and confirmation of their privileged position more than security and protection. A man's standing was no longer described in terms of dependence on a feudal overlord, but in terms of his belonging to a given "estate." The hierarchic pattern continued to exist but as a hierarchy of strata of society rather than a hierarchy of individuals. Moreover there were no formal links of dependence between the different estates. In a sense, all were in direct relation to the crown, and all claimed a share in political power, whether on the national or the local level.

Feudalism in other areas

Japan. Outside western Europe, the greatest convergence of feudal characteristics in the various institutional spheres probably occurred in Japan, where it developed at the end of the twelfth century and persisted in its "pure" form until the Tokugawa regime. Here we may follow Hall's analysis (1962).

The origin of feudalism in Japan seems to have coincided with the establishment of the Kamakura shogunate by Minamoto Yoritomo in 1192. Although vassalage and enfeoffment may have existed even before the twelfth century, only a small portion of Japanese society was organized around these practices by 1192. In Japan during the Kamakura period (1185–1333) the legal government was still centered on the emperor. It operated through the traditional civil administration (greatly weakened) and an expanding system of semipublic domains (*shōen*). Independent of these administrative and fiscal relationships, there were numerous more informal hierarchies based upon clan ties and military allegiances. Military hierarchies tended to form around the local magnates. It was primarily through the development of hierarchies of such allegiances as they came to center upon the office of shogun, or military dictator (or on certain other high military posts), that feudal institutions crystallized.

Yoritomo's importance to the development of feudalism in Japan lay in regularizing and extending the practice of pledges of military allegiance combined with protection of landholdings. Yoritomo's authority to appoint *shugo*, or "constables," and *jitō*, or "stewards," and to interfere in the *shōen* system was based on his assertion of supreme military command in a time of national crisis. Through such appointments and through the increase of legal powers, the feudal nexus in government and society steadily encroached upon the imperial–*shōen* complex, giving rise to a new type of institutional nexus.

At the apex of the state structure military authority gradually overshadowed civil authority, and during the thirteenth century the balance between civil and military power shifted steadily in the direction of the latter. Similarly, at the provincial level, military interests gained over civilian as the *shugo* increasingly took on the stature of military governors. Locally, the *shugo* were able to build up their economic support largely through the plural holding of *jitō* rights to numerous *shōen*. They used their superior status in the shogunal hierarchy to assert their influence among local *bushi*, or members of the military class. Before long the *shugo* had absorbed many civil administrative powers at the same time that they achieved personal leadership of province-wide military bands, which they organized increasingly on a lord–vassal basis. Below the *shugo* the step-by-step expansion of the *jitō*'s land rights among the *bushi* also served to extend the feudal element in Japanese society.

As local *bushi* became *ryōshu*, or landed proprietors, they began to divide these lands among family members or retainers, extending the practice of combining grants of land with ties of military loyalty. The new military bonds forged between *shugo* and proprietary *jitō* or between *jitō* and vassal families became the basis of this ever-widening feudal system of social and political organization.

The warfare that embroiled most of Japan during the middle of the fourteenth century hastened feudal trends in all parts of the country. Under the Ashikaga shogunate (1338–1573) the imperial center lost all of its effective power. The shogunate, now located at the very seat of the imperial court in Kyoto, absorbed most of the powers and functions of the civil government, although even now the emperor continued to play a crucial role as the ritual symbol of sovereignty and the source of the shogun's delegated authority.

In the provinces the key figures were the *shugo*, who by the end of the fourteenth century had developed into true regional overlords, having acquired the combined powers of the former civil and military governors. They held title, under the shogun, to territories the size of entire provinces, serving as the ultimate authority in both civil and military affairs.

By 1500, however, most of the jurisdictional territories of the *shugo* had been broken into fragments and a wave of new magnates of local origin had inherited the pieces. The *shugo* had disappeared and with them not only a generation of *bushi* leaders but also the last remnants of imperial law and civil land management based on the *shōen*.

The end of this relatively "pure" type of feudalism came in Japan with the more centralized Tokugawa regime (1603–1867). Although based on the feudal structures and to some extent perpetuating them, this regime, through its policy of centralization, in fact froze the feudal institutions, depriving them of vitality and autonomy.

Japanese feudalism differed from the European pattern in several important respects: (1) the continuous importance of the imperial center in spite of its loss of political function; (2) the weakness, perhaps even total absence, of contractual elements in the relations between lords and vassals; (3) the full, personal, familistic expression of these relations; and (4) the lack of any representative institutions. Nevertheless, like the European pattern, it is a major example of feudalism, since it clearly demonstrated a relatively high degree of convergence of feudal characteristics in the different institutional spheres.

Russia. In other societies the extent of such convergence was smaller. The regime of the feudal (patrimonial) principality in medieval Russia was accompanied by a certain immunity from political authority, conferred by private possession of land. The connection became firmly established because of the importance of military functions in local politics in pre-Muscovite central Russia and, later, its national importance in Muscovy. Whenever possession of land was hereditary, the authority connected with it was also hereditary. This was the normal pattern in pre-Muscovite times, and it again became general in the seventeenth century, the nonhereditary *pomest'e* ("benefice" or "military holding") being merely a historical interlude, even if a rather long one. In pre-Muscovite Russia the essential sociopolitical relation was not between lord and vassal but between the *votchinnik* ("patrimonial lord") and the population of his *votchina* ("landed possession" or "patrimony"), which came close to that of ruler and subject. There was no link between the prince's service and possession of land, and although there was hereditary landholding, the prince's service was not hereditary, and subjects were free to leave their principalities. Yet, even though the *pomest'e* was not hereditary, there was a connection between military function and possession of land. It was based not on a feudal contract involving mutual fealty between a suzerain and a vassal, but rather on the absolute sovereignty of the tsar, who, requiring service from any of his subjects, granted a *pomest'e* in return for such service (Szeftel 1956).

Three distinct types of sociopolitical structure are relevant to Russian feudalism: the *votchina* regime, the *pomest'e* regime, and Western feudalism.

The *votchina* regime was characterized by the growth of the manorial power of the lord of the estate over the population laboring on it or merely settled in its vicinity. Such power could be enforced by immunity privileges. The *votchina* estates were owned by political rulers (princes), by private persons, or by the church. Although it represented, to a certain extent, the social aspects of feudal tendencies the *votchina* system did not contain a counterpart to the political aspects. There was no formal

political connection between the vassal's service and the control of the land.

The *pomest'e* regime tended to make the control of the land depend on service rendered to the state by the landholder. There was no dispersion of political power in this regime as it grew up in the Muscovite state of the sixteenth and seventeenth centuries. The power was concentrated in the person of the supreme ruler, the tsar.

In the *standard type* of feudalism (Western feudalism) some characteristics of both the *votchina* and the *pomest'e* regimes are combined. However, for this type to develop, certain traits which were lacking in either or both of these regimes are essential. Like the *votchina* regime, the standard type of feudalism presupposes the expansion of the manor and the growth of the manorial rights of the lord. On the other hand, like the *pomest'e* regime, feudalism of the standard type is characterized by the conditionality of rights on the land. The control of the land by the lower-class landlord depends on the service he renders to the seignior.

The important point of difference between the *pomest'e* regime and feudalism of the standard type is that while in the former political power is concentrated in the hands of the supreme ruler, in the latter the political authority is usually dispersed. Thus, no lord–vassal relationship of the western European type could develop in pre-Muscovite Russia, no code of chivalry was based on it, and there could be no consistent heredity of functions.

The key to understanding the differences between the Russian and Western developments is the great migratory and resettlement movement in medieval central Russia. This mobility of the rural population was fundamentally caused by the rapid exhaustion of soil that was not too fertile to begin with and by extensive primitive agriculture. Although the movement produced some feudal traits in Russian life, it was also the source of instability in social relationships. In Russia the shifting local population did not provide the "free servant" with many bases to rely on, and there was no other protection for his liberty than the temporary character of his service and the right of free departure.

Byzantium. The constellation of feudal characteristics in the Byzantine Empire was rather different from that found in Russia, centering primarily on the system of the *pronoia* ("providence," "foresight," "care"). To give lands to a person in *pronoia* is to give lands into his care. In practice it meant that estates were given for administration to high officers of the state or army, to monasteries, and to private persons, as a reward for services.

The grants differed from simple donations in that the *pronoia* land was bound to the recipient, the *pronoiarios*; that he received it for a definite period only, usually for life; that he could not sell the *pronoia* estate; and that it was not hereditary.

The system developed under the eleventh-century Byzantine rulers who tried to reduce the power of the military class and to increase that of the civil bureaucracy by demilitarizing the administration. This policy clearly reflected the decay of the former organization of the military–peasant colonies (*themes*). The military commander (*strategos*), who usually served as governor of a province, was replaced by the *practor*, who had been the supreme justice on the staff of the *strategos*. The *practor*, of course, was a civilian, and thus, the primacy of the military command in the *themes* gave way to the primacy of a civilian administration based upon the new aristocracy of scholars and civilians in the capital.

But the preponderance of the civilian aristocracy in the capital did not lead to a strengthening of the central power in the rural districts. Generals and great landowners outweighed the civilians. The emperors of the Ducas dynasty had already been compelled to give great privileges both to their civilian adherents and to their military or landowning adversaries; with the accession of Alexius Comnenus, 1081–1118, the military aristocracy took over the state. It was under the Ducas that the *pronoia* system was first developed and that Byzantium approached quasi feudalization. The new class of the *pronoia* owners became liable for military service, replacing the former class of peasant soldiers of the decaying system. The owner of a *pronoia* estate, when summoned, had to appear with a certain number of horsemen, according to the size of the *pronoia*.

Since within the *pronoia* the formerly free peasants became more or less serfs, they came under the jurisdiction of the *pronoiarios*, although this jurisdiction was restricted. The central government, thus, gave up many of its prerogatives including that of direct taxation, and the *pronoiarios* became small rulers, whose estates appeared as little kingdoms within the empire. The crown became more and more dependent on them, which contributed to the weakening of the central government and to the decline and disintegration of the empire (Ostrogorski 1940; Kantorowicz 1956).

In sum, Byzantine feudalism was characterized by the relative predominance of economically independent small estates combined with a growing political decentralization—without, however, the concomitant development of an over-all system of vassalage, a feudal–chivalrous military class, or special feudal political institutions.

Parallel cases. The Byzantine type of feudalism is found in many other societies, especially in periods of the decline of great empires—to some extent at the end of the Roman Empire, in the later Sassanid period in Iran, and in the aftermath of Aśoka's kingdom in India. In many cases institutions of this type of feudalism developed when officials abused their rights to collect taxes and turned their offices into hereditary fiefs. In other cases the political traits of feudalism (usually many politically self-sufficient patrimonial units having some interrelations and an orientation toward one budding center) were more highly developed than feudal economic characteristics. Such cases can be found in China under the Shang and, even more clearly, under the Chou; in ancient Mesopotamia under the Kassites, in Mittani, in the Iran of the Parthian regime, in the *iqtâʻ* institution of medieval Islam, and possibly in ancient Egypt.

In none of these cases, however, was there a fully developed system of vassal–lord relations or a full-fledged social organization of a military–political class. At most, only rudiments of each existed.

Emergence and demise of feudal systems

In spite of all the differences in their origins and features, the feudal systems of the various societies analyzed above—and many more could be included—manifest some common characteristics. Perhaps most important is that they played a major role in the development of "high" cultures or civilizations. Feudal systems can be found, even if in varying degrees, in almost all of the great civilizations of the past, where they were central in keeping and developing great traditions under circumstances often inimical to their maintenance.

The importance of this characteristic can best be seen by examining the varying conditions under which feudal institutions develop. One such set of conditions is the *partial* dismemberment of relatively comprehensive, widespread sociopolitical systems (Hintze 1929; Coulborn 1956). The reasons for such dismemberment may vary greatly: the clash of cultures, the invasions of nomads, or the development of internal contradictions that cause the imperial system to lose its effectiveness and its essential resources. However, the dismemberment is not by itself crucial to the development of feudalism; rather, it is the combination of the dismemberment and the persistence or development of the ideals of a "great empire" and of orientations toward broader societal frameworks among some of the elite groups (such as the church or the new military class) who gain control over the governmental and economic functions and the contradictions between the idea of an empire and the lack of material and administrative positions to administer one. In some cases, such as that of Chinese feudalism, these orientations were developed by active groups that were unable to establish any viable broader system but, nevertheless, developed some vision of such a system. [See EMPIRES.]

Within most feudal systems, ideological orientations to such broader frameworks were of great importance, even if they were only partially institutionalized. Any feudal system is, thus, always characterized by some inherent imbalances in its structure, as it contains more and less differentiated centripetal and centrifugal structures and orientations. However, the exact location of such institutional imbalances in any feudal system—whether in the economic, political, or cultural sphere—varies greatly.

The demise of the feudal system is predicated on changes in those conditions—technological, political, and economic—that increase the effectiveness of the wider frameworks and that may enable the restoration or the establishment of unitary frameworks and of central powers within them. In less differentiated societies this can give rise to a restoration of patrimonial or imperial systems. In more differentiated societies—as in western Europe and in Japan—the feudal background made the later transition to modernity easier and more stable, and in some cases, it might have facilitated —after a period of the "estate" system or of absolutism—the development of a relatively pluralistic system.

JOSHUA PRAWER AND
SHMUEL N. EISENSTADT

[See also BUREACRACY; EMPIRES; MANORIAL ECONOMY; VILLAGE. Other relevant material may be found in EVOLUTION, article on SOCIAL EVOLUTION; KINSHIP; STATUS, SOCIAL; and in the biographies of BLOCH; BÜCHER; FUSTEL DE COULANGES; GIERKE.]

BIBLIOGRAPHY

BARRACLOUGH, GEOFFREY (editor) (1938) 1948 *Mediaeval Germany, 911–1250: Essays by German Historians.* 2 vols. Oxford: Blackwell.

BLOCH, MARC 1931 (1952–1956) *Les caractères originaux de l'histoire rurale française.* New ed. 2 vols. Paris: Colin.

BLOCH, MARC 1932 Feudalism, European. Volume 6, pages 203–210 in *Encyclopaedia of the Social Sciences.* New York: Macmillan.

BLOCH, MARC (1939–1940) 1961 *Feudal Society.* Univ. of Chicago Press. → First published in French.

BLOCH, MARC (1941) 1942 The Rise of Dependent Cultivation and Seigniorial Institutions. Volume 1, pages 224–277 in *The Cambridge Economic History of Europe From the Decline of the Roman Empire.* Cambridge Univ. Press.

BODDE, DERK 1956 Feudalism in China. Pages 49–92 in Rushton Coulborn (editor), *Feudalism in History.* Princeton Univ. Press.

BOUTRUCHE, ROBERT 1959 *Seigneurie et féodalité.* Volume 1: Le premier âge des liens d'homme à homme. Paris: Aubier.

BRUNDAGE, BURR C. 1956 Feudalism in Ancient Mesopotamia and Iran. Pages 93–119 in Rushton Coulborn (editor), *Feudalism in History.* Princeton Univ. Press.

CAHEN, CLAUDE 1940 *Le régime féodal de l'Italie normande.* Paris: Geuthner.

CAHEN, CLAUDE 1953 L'évolution de l'iqtâ' du IXᵉ au XIIIᵉ siècle: Contribution à une histoire comparée des sociétés médiévales. *Annales: Économies, sociétés, civilisations* 8:25–52.

CAHEN, CLAUDE 1960 Réflexion sur l'usage du mot "féodalité." *Journal of the Economic and Social History of the Orient* 3:2–20.

CALMETTE, JOSEPH (1923) 1947 *La société féodale.* 6th ed. Paris: Colin.

CAM, HELEN M. (1950) 1963 *England Before Elizabeth.* 2d ed., rev. London: Hutchinson's University Library.

CHARANIS, PETER 1944/1945 On the Social Structure of the Later Roman Empire. *Byzantion* 17:39–57.

CHARANIS, PETER 1948 The Monastic Properties of the State in the Byzantine Empire. *Dumbarton Oaks Papers* No. 4:51–118.

CHARANIS, PETER 1951 On the Social Structure and Economic Organization of the Byzantine Empire in the Thirteenth Century and Later. *Byzantinoslavica* 12:94–153.

COULBORN, RUSHTON (editor) 1956 *Feudalism in History.* Princeton Univ. Press.

CRONNE, H. A. 1939 The Origins of Feudalism. *History* New Series 24:251–259.

DUBY, GEORGES 1961 Une enquête à poursuivre: La noblesse dans la France médiévale. *Revue historique* 226:1–22.

EDGERTON, WILLIAM F. 1956 The Question of Feudal Institutions in Ancient Egypt. Pages 120–132 in Rushton Coulborn (editor), *Feudalism in History.* Princeton Univ. Press.

EHTÉCHAM, MORTÉZA 1946 *L'Iran sous les Achéménides. Contribution à l'étude de l'organisation sociale et politique au premier empire des Perses.* Fribourg (Switzerland): Imprimerie Saint Paul.

GANSHOF, FRANÇOIS L. (1944) 1961 *Feudalism.* With a foreword by F. M. Stenton. New York: Harper. → First published as *Qu'est-ce que la féodalité?*

GENICOT, L. 1962 La noblesse au moyen âge dans l'ancienne "Francie." *Annales: Économies, sociétés, civilisations* 17:1–22.

GRANET, MARCEL 1952 *La féodalité chinoise.* Instituttet for Sammenlignende Kulturforskning, Oslo, Serie A: Forelesninger, 22. Oslo: Aschehoug.

GUILHIERMOZ, PAUL 1902 *Essai sur l'origine de la noblesse en France au moyen âge.* Paris: Picard.

HALL, JOHN W. 1962 Feudalism in Japan: A Reassessment. *Comparative Studies in Society and History* 5:15–51.

HALPHEN, L.   1933   La place de la royauté dans le système féodal. *Anuario de historia del derecho español* 9:313–321.

HINTZE, OTTO   1929   Wesen und Verbreitung des Feudalismus. Akademie der Wissenchaften, Berlin, Philosophisch-historische Klasse, *Sitzungsberichte* [1929]: 321–347.

KANTOROWICZ, ERNST H.   1956   "Feudalism" in the Byzantine Empire. Pages 151–166 in Rushton Coulborn (editor), *Feudalism in History*. Princeton Univ. Press.

KEES, HERMAN   1932–1933   Beiträge zur altägyptischen Provinzialverwaltung, und der Geschichte des Feudalismus. Gesellschaft der Wissenschaften zu Göttingen, Philologisch-historische Klasse, *Nachrichten* [1932]: 85–119; [1933]: 579–598.

KOSMINSKII, E. A.   1955   *Osnovnye problemy zapadno-evropeiskogo feodalizma v sovetskoi istoricheskoi nauke* (Basic Problems of West European Feudalism as Reflected in Soviet Historical Science). Moscow: Akademiia Nauk SSSR. → Text in Russian and English.

MITTEIS, HEINRICH   1933   *Lehnrecht und Staatsgewalt: Untersuchungen zur mittelalterlichen Verfassungsgeschichte*. Weimar (Germany): Böhlaus.

MITTEIS, HEINRICH   (1940) 1959   *Der Staat des hohen Mittelalters: Grundlinien einer vergleichenden Verfassungsgeschichte des Lehnszeitalters*. Weimar (Germany): Böhlaus.

MOR, CARLO G.   1952   *L'età feudale*. 2 vols. Milan: Vallardi.

OSTROGORSKI, GEORGIJE   1929   Die wirtschaftlichen und sozialen Entwicklungsgrundlagen des byzantinischen Reiches. *Vierteljahrschrift für Sozial- und Wirtschaftsgeschichte* 22:129–143.

OSTROGORSKI, GEORGIJE   (1940) 1957   *History of the Byzantine State*. New Brunswick, N.J.: Rutgers Univ. Press. → First published in German.

OSTROGORSKI, GEORGIJE   1941   Agrarian Conditions in the Byzantine Empire in the Middle Ages. Pages 194–223 in *The Cambridge Economic History of Europe From the Decline of the Roman Empire*. Volume 1: The Agrarian Life of the Middle Ages. Cambridge Univ. Press.

OSTROGORSKI, GEORGIJE   (1948–1951) 1954   *Pour l'histoire de la féodalité byzantine*. Brussels: Institut de Philologie et d'Histoire Orientales et Slaves. → A translation of two separate works, first published in Russian and Serbian respectively.

Les peuples de l'orient méditerranéen. 4th ed. Volume 2: L'Égypte, by Étienne Drioton and Jacques Vandier. (1938) 1962   Paris: Presses Universitaires de France.

POLIAK, ABRAHAM N.   1939   *Feudalism in Egypt, Syria, Palestine and the Lebanon, 1250–1900*. London: Royal Asiatic Society.

PRAWER, JOSHUA   1959   La noblesse et le régime féodal du royaume latin de Jérusalem. *Moyen âge* 65:41–74.

PRAWER, JOSHUA   1966   Estates, Communities and the Constitution of the Latin Kingdom. Israel Academy of Sciences and Humanities, *Proceedings* 2:1–42.

PRESTAGE, EDGAR (editor)   1928   *Chivalry: A Series of Studies to Illustrate Its Historical Significance and Civilizing Influence*. New York: Knopf.

REISCHAUER, EDWIN O.   1956   Japanese Feudalism. Pages 26–48 in Rushton Coulborn (editor), *Feudalism in History*. Princeton Univ. Press.

SANCHEZ-ALBORNOZ Y MENDUIÑA, CLAUDIO   1942   *En torno a los orígenes del feudalismo*. 3 vols. Mendoza (Argentina): Univ. Nacional de Cuyo.

SEVČENKO, IHOR   1952   An Important Contribution to the Social History of Late Byzantium. Ukrainian Academy of Arts and Sciences in the United States, *Annals* 2: 448–459.

SOCIÉTÉ JEAN BODIN POUR L'HISTOIRE COMPARATIVE DES INSTITUTIONS   1936   Les liens de vassalité et les immunités. Brussels, Université Libre, Institut de Sociologie Solvay, *Revue* 16:7–118.

SOCIÉTÉ JEAN BODIN POUR L'HISTOIRE COMPARATIVE DES INSTITUTIONS   1938   *La tenure*. Recueil, Vol. 3. Brussels: Librairie Encyclopédique.

SOCIÉTÉ JEAN BODIN POUR L'HISTOIRE COMPARATIVE DES INSTITUTIONS   1949   *Le domaine*. Brussels: Librairie Encyclopédique. → See especially Georgije Ostrogorski's "Le grand domaine dans l'empire byzantin."

STEINDORFF, GEORG; and SEELE, KEITH C.   (1942) 1957   *When Egypt Ruled the East*. Univ. of Chicago Press. → A paperback edition was published in 1963.

STENTON, F. M.   (1932) 1961   *The First Century of English Feudalism, 1066–1160*. 2d ed. Oxford: Clarendon.

SZEFTEL, MARC   1956   Aspects of Feudalism in Russian History. Pages 167–182 in Rushton Coulborn (editor), *Feudalism in History*. Princeton Univ. Press.

THORNER, DANIEL   1956   Feudalism in India. Pages 133–150 in Rushton Coulborn (editor), *Feudalism in History*. Princeton Univ. Press.

VASILIEV, A. A.   1933   On the Question of Byzantine Feudalism. *Byzantion* 8:584–604.

VERNADSKY, GEORGE   1939   Feudalism in Russia. *Speculum* 14:300–323.

WEBER, MAX   (1922) 1957   *The Theory of Social and Economic Organization*. Edited by Talcott Parsons. Glencoe, Ill.: Free Press. → First published as Part 1 of *Wirtschaft und Gesellschaft*.

FIDUCIAL INFERENCE

R. A. Fisher (1930) proposed a statistical method for obtaining from observed data a probability distribution concerning a parameter value; he called the distribution a *fiducial probability distribution*. The theory of confidence intervals, as developed by J. Neyman, was initially presented in the literature as a clarification and development of fiducial probability [*see* ESTIMATION, *article on* CONFIDENCE INTERVALS AND REGIONS]. Fisher denied the equivalence and in his subsequent theoretical papers developed and extended fiducial probability.

As an example, consider a sample of independent measurements, $X_1, \cdots, X_n$, on a physical characteristic μ, and suppose that the measurement error is normally distributed with mean 0 and known variance σ_0^2. Fisher requires that fiducial inference be based on the simplest statistic containing all the information about the parameter, in this case, on the sample mean $\bar{X}$. [*The sample mean here is a minimal sufficient statistic; see* SUFFICIENCY.] The expression $W = \bar{X} - \mu$, involving the variable $\bar{X}$ and the characteristic μ, has a known distribution: normal with mean 0 and variance σ_0^2/n. In an application of the method, the value of $\bar{X}$ is obtained and substituted in the expression $W = \bar{X} - \mu$; the expression is solved for μ in terms of W, giving $\mu = \bar{X} - W$; the fiducial distribution of μ then derives from the known distribution of W: μ is normal with mean $\bar{X}$ and variance σ_0^2/n. A 95 per cent fiducial interval is $\bar{X} \pm 1.96\sigma_0/\sqrt{n}$.

Fisher claimed that a fiducial probability statement has the same meaning as an ordinary probability statement. In the example, suppose that the 95 per cent fiducial interval as calculated in a specific application is 163.9 ± 0.8. The fiducial statement is that there is 95 per cent probability that the unknown value of μ lies in this interval. The interval 163.9 ± 0.8 is also a 95 per cent confidence interval, but as a confidence interval its interpretation is different [see ESTIMATION, *article on* CONFIDENCE INTERVALS AND REGIONS]. Confidence methods and fiducial methods do not, however, always lead to the same numerical results.

The proponents of the confidence method claim that in this context probability statements concerning μ cannot be made; the value of μ is something that exists: either it *is* in the interval or it *is not*, and we don't know which.

The proponents of the fiducial method reply that probabilities concerning realized values are commonplace: in the play of card games, for example, a player may observe his own hand and perhaps other cards (say, those already played) and make a probability statement concerning the distribution of cards in the concealed hands.

The rejoinder is that μ did not arise from a random process such as the card shuffling and dealing. The relevance of this rejoinder is perhaps the key element to criticisms of the fiducial method.

In more complex problems the fiducial method may give a result different than the confidence method. In one prominent problem mentioned below, the Behrens–Fisher problem, the fiducial method gives an answer where confidence methods have not yet produced an entirely satisfactory result.

In his original paper on the fiducial method, Fisher (1930) considered a statistic, T, obtained by the maximum likelihood method for estimating a parameter, θ. Let $F(T, \theta)$ be the cumulative distribution function for the statistic T. The probability density function for T is obtained by differentiating with respect to T: $f(T, \theta) = \partial F(T, \theta)/\partial T$. Correspondingly, the fiducial density function for θ, given an observed value for T, is obtained by differentiating with respect to θ: $g(\theta, T) = \partial F(T, \theta)/\partial \theta$.

Fisher illustrated the method with the correlation coefficient r of a sample from a bivariate normal distribution with population correlation coefficient ρ.

For more complex problems, Fisher proposed the use of a *pivotal quantity*, $W = h(T, \theta)$, a function of the statistic T and the parameter θ that has a fixed known distribution regardless of the value of θ. For the first example, $W = \bar{X} - \mu$ is a pivotal quantity. In an application, the observed value of the statistic T is substituted in the expression $W = h(T, \theta)$; the parameter θ is expressed in terms of W; and the fiducial distribution of θ is obtained from the known distribution of W.

Fisher's original method for obtaining a fiducial distribution is a special case of the pivotal method. As a function of a continuous statistic, T, the cumulative distribution function $W = F(T, \theta)$ has a uniform distribution on the interval $(0, 1)$; this relationship is called that of the *probability integral transformation*. The fiducial density of θ for fixed T is obtained from the uniform distribution of W, in the same way as the density of T for fixed θ is obtained by differentiation.

As a second example, consider a random sample, $X_1, \cdots, X_n$, from a normal distribution with mean μ and variance σ^2, both unknown, and suppose that interest centers on the parameter μ. The quantity $t = \sqrt{n}(\bar{X} - \mu)/s_x$, using the sample mean $\bar{X}$ and sample standard deviation s_x, has a known distribution, the t-distribution on $n - 1$ degrees of freedom. In an application, the values of $\bar{X}$ and s_x are substituted and the parameter is solved for $\mu = \bar{X} - ts_x/\sqrt{n}$. This equation gives a fiducial distribution for μ that is of t-distribution form ($n - 1$ degrees of freedom), located at $\bar{X}$ and scaled by the factor $s_x/\sqrt{n}$.

The Behrens–Fisher problem is an extension of this example. Consider a first random sample, $X_1, \cdots, X_n$, from a normal distribution with mean μ_x and variance σ_X^2, and a second independent random sample, $Y_1, \cdots, Y_m$, from a normal distribution with mean μ_Y and variance σ_Y^2. The Behrens–Fisher problem concerns inference about the parameter difference, $\mu_x - \mu_Y$. The fiducial method gives a distribution described by $\bar{X} - t_1 s_X/\sqrt{n}$ for μ_X and a distribution described by $\bar{Y} - t_2 s_Y/\sqrt{m}$ for μ_Y. (Here t_1 and t_2 are independent t variables with $n - 1, m - 1$ degrees of freedom.) The fiducial distribution for $\mu_X - \mu_Y$ is the difference, that of $\bar{X} - \bar{Y} - (t_1 s_X/\sqrt{n} - t_2 s_Y/\sqrt{m})$; some percentage points are given in Fisher and Yates ([1938] 1949, p. 44).

For many problems involving normal and chi-square distributions, the fiducial distribution has the form of a Bayesian posterior distribution as based on a prior distribution with uniformity characteristics [*see* BAYESIAN INFERENCE].

Fisher (1956) considers a wide range of statistical problems and derives the corresponding fiducial distributions.

A central criticism of the fiducial method has been concerned with whether fiducial probabilities are in fact probabilities in an acceptable sense. Some recent analysis, mentioned later, has clarified this question.

Other criticism seems to fall under three headings. First, fiducial probabilities in some examples may not add or integrate to a total of 1. James (1954) and Stein (1959) produce examples that can yield fiducial distributions that do not integrate to 1. Second, in some examples more than one reasonable pivotal quantity may be present; these can lead to several inconsistent fiducial distributions (see Creasy 1954; Fieller 1954; Mauldon 1955). In other examples no reasonable pivotal quantity may be present. Third, if a fiducial distribution from a collection of data is used as a prior distribution for a Bayesian analysis on a second collection of data, the resulting distribution may be different from the fiducial distribution based on the combined collection of data [*see* Lindley 1958; *see also* BAYESIAN INFERENCE].

Fraser (1961) uses transformations to investigate fiducial probability. The transformation approach applies to a large proportion of Fisher's examples, and it introduces an additional range of problems for which fiducial distributions can be obtained.

In a later paper (Fraser 1966) the emphasis in the transformation approach is focused on error variables. Consider the example involving a sample of measurements, $X_1, \cdots, X_n$, on a physical quantity, μ. Let e be a variable describing the error introduced by the measuring instrument: in the example, e is normally distributed with mean 0 and variance σ_0^2. A measurement, X_i, can then be expressed in the form $X_i = \mu + e_i$. Correspondingly, the sample mean takes the form $\bar{X} = \mu + \bar{e}$, where $\bar{e}$ is normally distributed with mean 0 and variance σ_0^2/n. Now consider an application and suppose there is *no information* concerning μ. With no information concerning μ, there is no information concerning $\bar{e}$ other than that describing its distribution. Probability statements can then be made concerning the unknown $\bar{e}$ just as the card player makes statements concerning the realized but unrevealed cards in his opponents' hands.

Suppose the normal distribution of $\bar{e}$ with vari-

ance σ_0^2/n gives a 95 per cent probability for $\bar{e}$ lying in the interval 0.0 ± 0.8. Then, *with an observed* $\bar{x} = 163.9$, the probability statement concerning $\bar{e}$ is equivalent to the statement that μ is in the interval 163.9 ± 0.8 with probability 95 per cent.

This analysis involving error variables applies to many of Fisher's examples, and it extends to other problems. The name structural probability has been introduced (Fraser 1966) to distinguish it in cases where the method conflicts with the fiducial method. None of the criticisms mentioned concerning fiducial probability apply to structural probability.

D. A. Sprott (1964) uses a more general class of transformations to analyze a wider range of fiducial distributions.

Some alternative methods have been proposed for obtaining probability distributions concerning parameter values: Dempster (1963; 1966) proposes *direct probabilities*, and Verhagen (1966) proposes *induced probabilities*.

D. A. S. FRASER

[*See also* ESTIMATION, *article on* CONFIDENCE INTERVALS AND REGIONS.]

BIBLIOGRAPHY

A survey of fiducial methods and criticisms may be found in Fraser 1964.

CREASY, MONICA A. 1954 Limits for the Ratio of Means. *Journal of the Royal Statistical Society* Series B 16:186–194.

DEMPSTER, A. P. 1963 On Direct Probabilities. *Journal of the Royal Statistical Society* Series B 25:100–110.

DEMPSTER, A. P. 1966 New Methods for Reasoning Towards Posterior Distributions Based on Sample Data. *Annals of Mathematical Statistics* 37:355–374.

FIELLER, E. C. 1954 Some Problems in Interval Estimation. *Journal of the Royal Statistical Society* Series B 16:175–185.

FISHER, R. A. (1930) 1950 Inverse Probability. Pages 22.527a–22.535 in R. A. Fisher, *Contributions to Mathematical Statistics.* New York: Wiley. → First published in Volume 26 of the *Proceedings* of the Cambridge Philosophical Society.

FISHER, R. A. (1956) 1959 *Statistical Methods and Scientific Inference.* 2d ed., rev. New York: Hafner; London: Oliver & Boyd.

FISHER, R. A.; and YATES, F. (1938) 1949 *Statistical Tables for Biological, Agricultural, and Medical Research.* 3d ed., rev. & enl. New York: Hafner; London: Oliver & Boyd.

FRASER, D. A. S. 1961 The Fiducial Method and Invariance. *Biometrika* 48:261–280.

FRASER, D. A. S. 1964 On the Definition of Fiducial Probability. International Statistical Institute, *Bulletin* 40, part 2:842–856.

FRASER, D. A. S. 1966 Structural Probability and a Generalization. *Biometrika* 53:1–9.

James, G. S. 1954 Discussion on the Symposium on Interval Estimation. *Journal of the Royal Statistical Society* Series B 16:214–218.

Lindley, D. V. 1958 Fiducial Distributions and Bayes' Theorem. *Journal of the Royal Statistical Society* Series B 20:102–107.

Mauldon, J. G. 1955 Pivotal Quantities for Wishart's and Related Distributions, and a Paradox in Fiducial Theory. *Journal of the Royal Statistical Society* Series B 17:79–85.

Sprott, D. A. 1961 Similarities Between Likelihoods and Associated Distributions a Posteriori. *Journal of the Royal Statistical Society* Series B 23:460–468.

Sprott, D. A. 1964 A Transformation Model for the Investigation of Fiducial Distributions. International Statistical Institute, *Bulletin* 40, part 2:856–869.

Stein, Charles 1959 An Example of Wide Discrepancy Between Fiducial and Confidence Intervals. *Annals of Mathematical Statistics* 30:877–880.

Verhagen, A. M. W. 1966 The Notion of Induced Probability in Statistical Inference. Division of Mathematical Statistics, Technical Paper No. 21. Unpublished manuscript, Commonwealth Scientific and Industrial Research Organisation, Melbourne, Australia.

FIELD THEORY

In psychology, the term "field theory" is used primarily to designate the point of view of Kurt Lewin and his co-workers. Although the term has its origin in physics, where it is employed to refer to the conceptualization of electromagnetic phenomena in terms of fields of electromagnetic forces, field theory in psychology is not an attempt to explain psychological events in terms of physical processes. Rather, it refers to a "method of analyzing causal relations and of building scientific constructs" (Lewin 1943a), which Lewin felt could be applied as fruitfully in psychology as it had been in physics. [*See* Lewin.]

Lewin's early interests and writings—much influenced by the German philosopher Ernst Cassirer—were concerned with the nature of theory in science. Much of his own research orientation and of his great impact on psychology arose from his way of thinking about theorizing. His approach to theorizing in psychology was characterized by several major themes:

(1) *An emphasis on the psychological explanation of behavior* focuses on the purposes which underlie behavior and the goals toward or away from which behavior is directed; it stresses that one has to deal with what exists psychologically, what is real for the person being studied.

(2) *An emphasis on the total situation* stresses that the most fundamental construct is that of the psychological "field," or life space. All psychological events are conceived to be a function of the life space, which consists of the person and the environment viewed as *one* constellation of interdependent factors. Lewin made it evident that it is meaningless to explain behavior without reference to both the person and his environment and that psychological events are not determined by the characteristics of the individual—"instincts," "heredity," "needs," "habits"—acting independently of the situation.

(3) *An emphasis on systematic rather than historical causation* indicates that psychological events have to be explained in terms of the properties of the field which exist *at the time* when the events occur. Lewin rejected the notion of "action at a distance" and stressed that past events can have a position only in the historical causal chains whose interweaving creates the present situation.

(4) *The dynamic approach*, like that of the gestalt school, accepts the view that living systems tend to maintain a dynamic equilibrium in relation to their environments. Related to this view was Lewin's interest in the processes by which equilibrium is restored when it is disturbed and his interest in such motivational processes as the arousal of need tensions, the setting of goals, goal-directed action, and the release of tension.

Lewin was not only a metatheoretician but also a bold and original experimentalist. However, the themes underlying Lewin's approach to theorizing have played a central role in his empirical work on psychology. These themes are reflected in his research preoccupation with the psychological environment (the person's perception of the situation confronting him), his emphasis on social and group influences upon behavior, his stress on the contemporaneous rather than the historical determinants of behavior, and his focus on dynamics (motivation, conflict, and change). The range and impact of the work of Lewin and his associates is indicated by a list of some of the research areas in psychology which they opened up for experimental investigation: dynamic studies of memory, resumption of interrupted activities, substitute activity, satiation, level of aspiration, studies of different types of group leadership, group decision. Many of the terms associated with Lewin are now part of the common vocabulary of psychologists—e.g., "life space," "valence," "locomotion," "overlapping situation," "cognitive structure," "action research." In the space available here, it will be impossible to do more than sketch some of Lewin's central theoretical notions. This is done in five sections which deal with (1) dynamic concepts, (2) structural concepts, (3) socially induced change, (4) level of aspiration, and (5) group dynamics.

Dynamic concepts

After several years of work at the University of Berlin on the more traditional problems of perception and learning, Lewin turned to the study of motivation. In 1926 he published the first of a series of over twenty brilliant articles by himself and his students, "Untersuchungen zur Handlungs- und Affektpsychologie" ("Investigations Into the Psychology of Behavior and Emotion"), which appeared in *Psychologische Forschung*. Here most of the concepts which later became so famous first appeared. Among them are the concepts "tension," "valence," "force," and "locomotion," which play a key role in Lewin's theorizing about motivation.

A system in a state of *tension* is said to exist within the individual whenever a psychological need or an intention (sometimes referred to as a quasi need) exists. Tension is released when the need or intention is fulfilled. Tension has the following conceptual properties: (*a*) it is a state of a region in a given system which tries to change itself in such a way that it becomes equal to the state of surrounding regions, and (*b*) it involves forces at the boundary of the region in tension. A *positive valence* is conceived as a force field in which the forces are all pointing toward a given region of the field (the valent region which is the center of the force field); all the forces point away from a region of *negative valence*. The construct *force* characterizes the direction and strength of the tendency to change at a given point of the life space. Change may occur either by actual locomotion (i.e., change in position) of the person in his psychological environment or by a change in the structure of his perceived environment.

There exists a definite relation between tension systems of the person and certain properties of the psychological environment. In particular, a tension may be related to a positive valence for activity regions in the psychological environment which are perceived as tension reducing, and a negative valence for the region in which the behaving self is at present. However, the existence of a region of positive valence (a goal region) depends not only upon the existence of tension but also upon whether there are perceived possibilities for reducing the tension.

When a goal region which is relevant to a system in tension exists in the psychological environment, one can assert that there is a force acting upon the behaving self to locomote toward the goal. A tension for which there is a cognized goal leads not only to a tendency to actual locomotion toward the goal region but also to thinking about

this type of activity. This may be expressed by saying that the force on the person toward the goal exists not only on the level of doing (reality) but also on the level of thinking (irreality).

The Zeigarnik quotient. From the foregoing assumptions about systems in tension it is possible to make a number of derivations. Thus, it follows that the tendency to recall or resume interrupted activities should be greater than the tendency to recall or resume finished ones. Zeigarnik (1927) and many others have conducted experiments in which subjects are given a series of tasks to perform and are then prevented from completing half of them. Later, the subjects are asked to recall the tasks they had performed. The results are presented in the form of a quotient, commonly called the Zeigarnik quotient (ZQ):

$$\frac{\text{uncompleted tasks recalled } (RU)}{\text{completed tasks recalled } (RC)}.$$

Zeigarnik predicted a quotient of greater than 1. The obtained quotient was approximately 1.9, clearly supporting Lewin's assumptions. However, since many completed tasks were also recalled, it was obvious that additional factors were involved. Analyzing the situation of the subject at the moment of recall, Zeigarnik concluded that in addition to the force on the person to think about, and hence to recall, the uncompleted tasks, there was also present a force to recall both uncompleted and completed tasks exerted upon the person by the experimenter's instructions to "try to recall the tasks you worked on earlier." The Zeigarnik quotient could be viewed as a function of the relative strengths of the induced force to recall all tasks and of the force to recall the uncompleted tasks. As the strength of the force induced by the experimenter increases in relation to the force toward the task goals, the quotient should decrease toward 1; as it decreases in relative strength, the quotient should increase beyond 1. These additional predictions, which follow from an analysis of the situation at recall, were borne out in experiments by Zeigarnik and others. Thus, if the strength of motivation associated with the interrupted task is relatively high, or the strength of the experimenter's pressure to recall is low, or if the task is interrupted near its end, the Zeigarnik quotient will be high.

A number of more recent experiments have indicated that the situation of recall is frequently even more complex than indicated above. When not finishing a task is interpretable as a personal failure (e.g., in an experiment where the tasks are presented as measures of a socially esteemed ability) and when recall of failure threatens one's self-esteem, or when the recall of success raises a lowered self-esteem, the Zeigarnik quotient tends to be less than 1.

Substitute value. Käte Lissner initiated the study of the value which one activity has for reducing a tension originally connected with another activity by a technique involving resumption of the interrupted task; some of the other experimenters have employed the technique of recall. The substitute value is measured by the amount of decrease in resumption or recall of the interrupted original activity after a substitute activity has been completed. The results of the experiments on substitute value can be summarized as follows: (1) Substitute value increases with the perceived degree of similarity between the original and the substitute activity and with the degree of difficulty of the substitute activity (Lissner 1933). (2) Substitute value increases with increasing temporal contiguity between the original and the substitute activity and with the attractiveness of the substitute activity (Henle 1942). (3) The substitute value of an activity (e.g., thinking, talking, or doing) depends upon the nature of the goal of the original task. Tasks that are connected with the goal of demonstrating something to another person (e.g., the experimenter) require an observable substitute activity (not merely "thinking" without social communication); "realization tasks," in which the building of a material object is the goal, require "doing," not only telling how it can be done; for intellectual problems, talking (or telling how it can be done) can have a very high substitute value (Mahler 1933). (4) "Magic solutions," "make-believe solutions," or solutions which observably violate the requirements of the task have little substitute value for tasks at the reality level. However, if the situation is a make-believe or play situation, make-believe substitutions will have substitute value (Sliosberg 1934; Dembo 1931). (5) A substitute activity which is identical with the original activity will have little substitute value if it does not serve the same goal. Thus, building a clay house for Tony will have little substitute value for building a clay house for Nicky. If the emphasis is on building a clay house and not upon the "for somebody," then, of course, substitution will occur (Adler & Kounin 1939). (6) Having someone complete the subject's interrupted task tends to have little substitute value, particularly when completion of the task is related to self-esteem. However, when pairs of individuals work cooperatively on a task, the completion of the task by one's partner has considerable substitute value (e.g., Lewis & Franklin 1944).

The research findings with respect to substitute value have implications for a wide range of problems in psychology—from the relative gratification value of individual versus socially shared projective or fantasy systems to the development of specialized roles within a group. Let us briefly illustrate with the very important finding that the actions of another person can be a substitute for one's own actions if there is a cooperative relationship. The fact of substitutability enables individuals who are working cooperatively on a common task to subdivide the task and to perform specialized activities, since none of the individuals in a cooperative situation has to perform all the activities by himself. In contrast, the individual in a competitive situation is less likely to view the actions of others as substitutable for similarly intended actions of his own. Thus, when a competitive situation exists in a group, specialization of activities is less likely to develop (Deutsch 1949*a*; 1949*b*).

Satiation. The concept of tension systems has also been fruitfully employed in experimental studies of satiation. With regard to most needs, one can distinguish a state of deprivation, of satiation, and of oversatiation. These states correspond to a positive, a neutral, and a negative valence of the activity regions which are related to a particular need or tension system. Karsten (1928) has studied the effect of repeating over and over again such activities as reading a poem, writing letters, drawing, and turning a wheel. The main symptoms of oversatiation appear to be (1) the appearance of subunits in the activity that lead to the disintegration of the total activity and a loss of meaning of the activity; (2) increasingly poorer quality of work and greater frequency of errors in performing the task; (3) an increasing tendency to vary the nature of the task, accompanied by a tendency for each variation to be quickly satiated; (4) a tendency to make the satiated activity a peripheral activity by attempting to concentrate on something else while doing the task—this is usually not completely successful, and the mind wanders; (5) increasing dislike of the activity and of similar activities, accompanied by an increased valence for different tasks; (6) emotional outbursts; (7) development of "fatigue" and similar bodily symptoms which are quickly overcome when the individual is shifted to another activity.

Satiation occurs only if the activity has, psychologically, the character of marking time or of getting nowhere. If the activity can be viewed as making progress toward a goal, the usual symptoms of satiation will not appear. Embedding an activity in a different psychological whole, so that its meaning is changed, has practically the same effect on satiation as shifting to a different activity. The rapidity with which satiation occurs depends upon factors such as the nature of the activity—with increasing size of its units of action and with increasing complexity satiation occurs more slowly —and the state of the person—the more fluid the state of the person, the more quickly he is satiated. The rate of satiation and cosatiation of similar activities (i.e., the spread of satiation effects from one activity to similar activities) decreases with age and with lack of intelligence (Kounin 1941).

Structural concepts

Lewin attempted to develop a geometry, which he termed "hodological space," to represent a person's conception of the means–end structure of the environment, of what leads to what. Although Lewin's "hodological space" was never developed adequately from a mathematical viewpoint, it served to highlight the necessity of considering a person's conception of his environment in analyzing his behavior possibilities and in characterizing the direction of his behavior. For example, an individual who walks around a fence to get to a ball behind it is, psychologically, walking toward the ball as he physically walks away from it.

Cognitive structure. The view that direction in the life space is dependent upon cognitive structure has been applied to provide insights into some of the psychological properties of situations which are cognitively unstructured.

Most new situations are cognitively unstructured, since the individual is unlikely to know "what leads to what." As he strikes out in any direction, he does not know whether he is going toward or away from his goal. His behavior will be exploratory, trial-and-error, vacillating, and contradictory rather than efficient and economical. If reaching the goal has positive significance and not reaching it has negative significance for the individual concerned, then being in a region that has no clear cognitive structure results in psychological conflict, since the direction of the forces acting upon him is likely to be both toward and away from any given region. There will be evidences of emotionality as well as cautiousness in such situations. In addition, the very nature of an unstructured situation is that it is unstable; perception of the situation shifts rapidly and is readily influenced by minor cues and by suggestions from others.

Lewin has employed his characterization of cognitively unstructured situations to give insight into the psychological circumstances of the adolescent (1939–1947) as well as those of minority group members (1935), of people suffering from physical handicaps (Barker 1946), of the *nouveaux riches*, and of other persons crossing the margins of social classes. It may be applied to any situation in which the consequences of behavior are seemingly unpredictable or uncontrollable; in which benefits and harms occur in an apparently inconsistent, fortuitous, or arbitrary manner; or in which one is uncertain about the potential reactions of others.

Conflict. Lewin has brilliantly employed his structural concepts, in conjunction with his dynamic concepts, to give insight into the nature of *conflict situations*. He distinguishes three fundamental types of conflict:

(1) The individual stands midway between two positive valences of approximately equal strength. This type of conflict is unstable. As the individual, due to the play of chance factors, moves from the point of equilibrium toward one goal region rather than the other, the resultant force toward that region increases, and, hence, he will continue to move toward that region. This follows from the assumption that the strength of force toward a goal region decreases with increasing distance from the goal.

(2) The second fundamental type of conflict occurs when the individual finds himself between two approximately equal negative valences. The punishment situation is an example. This type of conflict is very much influenced by the structure of the situation. Let us illustrate three varieties of this type of conflict: (a) the individual is between two negative valences, but there are no restraints keeping him in the situation—e.g., a girl who will have to marry an unpleasant suitor or become an impoverished spinster if she remains in her village (there is nothing to prevent her from leaving her village); (b) the individual is between two negative valences, but he cannot leave the field—e.g., a group member who is faced with the prospect of losing social status or of performing an unpleasant task (he cannot leave the group); (c) the individual is in a region of negative valence and can leave it only by going through another region of negative valence—e.g., a man is cited for contempt of Congress for not testifying whether or not some of his acquaintances were members of the Communist party (to purge himself of contempt he must become an informer).

It is evident that the situation depicted in (a) will lead the person to go out of the field. Only if restraints prevent the individual from leaving the field will such a situation result in more than momentary conflict. Restraints as in (b) introduce a conflict between the driving forces related to the negative valence and the restraining forces related to the barrier. There is a tendency for a barrier to acquire a negative valence which increases with the number of unsucccessful attempts to cross it and which, finally, is sufficiently strong to prevent the individual from approaching it (Fajans 1933). Thus, the conflict between driving and restraining force is replaced by a conflict between driving forces, as in (c) above. This fact is particularly important for social psychology since, in many situations of life, the barriers are social. When a person turns against the barrier, he is in effect directing himself against the will and power of the person or social group to whom the erection of the barrier is due.

(3) The third fundamental type of conflict situation occurs when the individual is exposed to opposing forces deriving from a positive and a negative valence. One can distinguish at least three different forms of this conflict: (a) a single region has both positive and negative valence. (The Freudian concept of ambivalence is subsumable under this variety of conflict.) For example, a person wishes to join a social group but fears that being a member will be too expensive. (b) A person is encircled by (but not actually in) a negative or a barrier region and is attracted to a goal which is beyond it—e.g., a person who has to go through the unpleasant ordeal of leaving his home or his group in order to pursue some desired activity. In this situation, the region of the person's present activity tends to acquire negative valence as long as the region which encircles the person hinders locomotion toward desired outer goals. Thus, being a member of a minority group or being in a ghetto or in a prison often takes on negative valence, apart from the inherent characteristics of the situation, because one can get to desired goals from the region only by passing through an encircling region of negative valence. (c) A region of positive valence is encircled by or is accessible only through a region of negative valence. This type of situation differs from (b) in that the region of positive valence rather than the region in which the person is to be found is encircled by the negative valence. The "reward situation," in which the individual is granted a reward only if he performs an unpleasant task, is an example of this type of conflict.

Lewin ([1939–1947] 1963, p. 259), as well as Miller (1944), has pointed out that the forces corresponding to a negative valence tend to decrease more rapidly as a function of psychological distance than do the forces corresponding to a positive valence. The amount of decrease depends also upon the nature of the region which has a positive or negative valence. It is different in the case of a dangerous animal which can move about than it is in the case of an immovable unpleasant object. The difference in the gradients of decrease for forces deriving from positive and negative valences accounts for the apparent paradox that a strong fear or a strong tendency to withdraw may be taken as evidence of a strong desire for the goal. Only with a very attractive goal will the equilibrium point between approach and avoidance tendencies be close enough to the negatively valent region to produce a strong force away from the goal. On the other hand, strengthening the negative valence of a region may very well have the effect of weakening the forces in conflict, since the equilibrium point may be pushed a considerable distance away from the valent regions. [See CONFLICT, article on PSYCHOLOGICAL ASPECTS.]

Socially induced change

It should be noted that Lewin's motivational concepts do not presuppose that motivation is primarily induced by physiological deficits; his conceptualization suggests that tension and valences may be aroused socially (e.g., by an experimenter's instructions to perform a task); he also indicated that the forces acting upon an individual may be "imposed" or may directly reflect the individual's own needs.

The concept of powerfield is relevant in this connection. It is an inducing field; it can induce changes in the life space within its area of influence. The distinction between own and induced forces has been found to be useful in explaining some of the differences in behavior under autocratic and democratic leadership (Lippitt & White 1943). Thus, children in a club led by authoritarian leaders (who determined policy, dictated activities, and were arbitrary and personal in evaluation of activities) tended to develop little of their own motivation with respect to club activities. Although the children worked productively when the leader was present (i.e., when his powerfield was psychologically effective), the lack of personal motivation toward group goals clearly evidenced itself in (1) change of behavior when the leader left the club, (2) absence of motivation when the leader arrived late, (3) lack of carefulness in the work, (4) lack of initiative in offering spontaneous suggestions in regard to club projects, (5) lack of pride in the products of club effort. [See LEADERSHIP.]

The distinction between own and induced forces has also been employed to explain why workers are usually happier and more productive when they can participate in the decisions which affect their work. Participation in goal setting is more likely to create own forces toward the goal and thus reduce the necessity to exert continuous social influences toward the same end (Coch & French 1948).

Level of aspiration

Perhaps no other area of research that Lewin and his students have opened to experimental investigation has been the object of so many studies as that of level of aspiration. The level of aspiration may be defined as the degree of difficulty of the goal toward which the person is striving. The concept of level of aspiration is relevant only when there is a perceived range of difficulty in the attainment of possible goals and a variation in valence among the goals along the range of difficulty.

In discussing the level of aspiration, it may be helpful to consider a sequence of events which is typical for many of the experimental studies in this area: (1) A subject plays a game (or performs a task) in which he can obtain a score (e.g., throwing darts at a target); (2) after playing the game and obtaining a given score, he is asked to tell what score he will undertake to make the next time he plays; (3) he then plays the game again and achieves a different score; (4) he reacts to his second performance with feelings of success or failure, with a continuing or new level of aspiration, etc. In the foregoing sequence, point (4) (reaction to achievement) is particularly significant for the dynamics of the level of aspiration.

In outline form, the theory of the level of aspiration is rather simple (Lewin et al. 1944). It states that the resultant valence of any level of difficulty will be equal to the valence of achieving success times the subjective probability of success, minus the valence of failure times the subjective probability of failure. The level of aspiration (i.e., the goal an individual will undertake to achieve) will be the level of difficulty that has the highest resultant positive valence. The subjective experience of success or failure is determined by the relation of the individual's performance to his level of aspiration (providing, of course, that the performance is seen to be self-accomplished) and not simply by his absolute accomplishments.

Experimental work on the level of aspiration has brought out the variety of influences which affect the positive and negative valences of different levels of difficulty. It has indicated that cultural and group factors establish scales of reference which help to determine the relative attractiveness of different points along a difficulty continuum. Some of these influences are rather stable and permanent in their effects. It has been found, for example, that most people in Western cultures, under the pervasive cultural pressures toward "self-improvement," when first exposed to a level of aspiration situation initially give a level of aspiration which is above the previous performance score, and under most conditions they tend to keep their level of aspiration higher than their previous performance. In addition to broad cultural factors, the individual's level of aspiration in a task is likely to be very much influenced by the standards of the group to which he belongs. The nature of the scales of reference set up by different group standards may vary. Reference scales do not derive solely from membership in a definitely structured social group; they also may reflect the influence of one's self-image, of other individuals, or of groups that either establish certain standards for performance or that serve as models for evaluating self-performance. Thus, the level of aspiration of a college student with respect to an intellectual task will vary, depending upon whether he is told that a given score was obtained by the average high school student, the average college student, or the average graduate student.

Research has given some insight into the factors determining the values on the scale of subjective probability. A main factor which determines the subjective probability of future success and failure is the past experience of the individual in regard to his ability to reach certain objectives. If the individual has had considerable experience with a given activity, he will know pretty well what level he can expect to reach, and the gradient of values on the subjective probability scale will be steep. However, it is not only the average of past performances which determines an individual's subjective probability scale but also the trend—whether he is improving, getting worse, or remaining the same. Furthermore, there is experimental evidence to indicate that the last or most recent success or failure has a particularly great influence on the individual's expectation of his future achievement level. In addition, there is evidence that the subjective probability scales, as well as the performance of others, can influence the subject's own probability scale. Personality factors—for example, self-confidence—may also influence subjective probability.

The level of aspiration theory has widespread implications for many social phenomena. It gives insight into the reasons for social apathy in the face of pressing political and international problems. People are not likely to attempt to achieve even highly valued objectives when they see no way of attaining them. Similarly, it sheds some light upon why social revolution tends to occur only after there has been a slight improvement in the situation of the oppressed groups—the improvement raises their level of aspiration, making goals which were once viewed as unattainable now perceived as realistic possibilities.

Concepts of group dynamics

Apart from papers dealing with group decision and social change (Lewin 1935–1946; 1947a; 1947b) Lewin actually wrote very little on the theory of group dynamics. However, from the research investigations of his colleagues and students at the Research Center for Group Dynamics a formidable array of concepts has emerged. [See GROUPS.]

Let us begin our discussion of the concepts of group dynamics by briefly considering the concept of group. Lewin ([1935–1946] 1948, p. 48) wrote:

The essence of a group is not the similarity or dissimilarity of its members, but their interdependence. A group can be characterized as a "dynamic whole"; this means that a change in the state of any subpart changes the state of any other subpart. The degree of interdependence of the subparts of members of the group varies all the way from a loose "mass" to a compact unit.

French (1944) pointed out that in addition to interdependence, membership in a group presupposes identification with the group. Deutsch (1949a) indicated that the interdependence is promotive or cooperative rather than, for example, competitive. Thus, a group may be tentatively defined as being composed of a set of members who mutually perceive themselves to be cooperatively or promotively interdependent in some respect(s) and to some degree.

Cohesiveness. One of the key concepts, which has been the subject of much experimental investigation, is that of cohesiveness. Intuitively, cohesiveness refers to the forces which bind the parts of a group together and which, thus, resist disruptive influences. Hence, the study of conditions affecting group cohesiveness and of the effects upon group functioning of variations in group cohesiveness is at the heart of the study of group life. Festinger, Schachter, and Back (1950) have defined cohesiveness, in terms of the group member, as "the total field of forces which act on members to remain in the group." The nature and strength of the forces acting upon a member to remain in the group may vary from member to member.

Various measures of individuals' "cohesiveness" to their groups have been employed in experimental investigations: desire to remain in the group, the ratio of "we" remarks to "I" remarks during group discussion, ratings of friendliness, evaluations of the group and its sociometric choice versus outgroup sociometric choice, and others. Deutsch

(1949a), in a theoretical paper, provides a rationale for the use of a wide variety of measures by developing the hypotheses that members of more cohesive (cooperative) groups, as compared with members of less cohesive (competitive) groups, would, under conditions of success: (a) be more ready to accept the actions of other group members as substitutable for similarly intended actions of their own (and therefore would not have to perform them also); (b) be more ready to accept inductions (i.e., be influenced) by other members; and (c) be more likely to cathect positively the actions of other group members. From these core hypotheses, with the addition of more specific assumptions, it is possible to derive the influence of more or less cohesiveness upon many aspects of group functioning. Thus, from the substitutability hypothesis, it is possible to predict that more specialization of function, more subdivision of activity, and more diversity of membership behavior would occur in the more cohesive groups. The inductibility hypothesis leads to the prediction that members of more cohesive groups would be more attentive to one another, be more understood by one another, be more influenced by one another, and be more likely to change and have more internalization of group norms than members of less cohesive groups. The cathexis hypothesis leads to predictions of greater friendliness, greater ratio of in-group sociometric choices, etc., in the more cohesive groups. Data in a variety of experiments (e.g., Deutsch 1949b; Schachter 1951; Back 1951) support the foregoing predictions. [See COHESION, SOCIAL.]

Communication. In a well-integrated program of research, Festinger and his co-workers have developed a series of fertile hypotheses (Festinger 1950) and have conducted some ingenious experiments on the communication process within groups. In brief, these investigators have been concerned with three sources of pressures to communicate within groups: (a) communications arising from pressures toward uniformity in a group (Back 1951; Festinger & Thibaut 1951; Schachter 1951); (b) communications arising from forces to locomote in a social structure (Kelley 1951; Thibaut 1950); and (c) communications arising from the existence of emotional states (Thibaut 1950; Thibaut & Coules 1952). [See INTERACTION.]

Pressures toward uniformity. Festinger (1950; 1954) has indicated two major sources of pressures toward uniformity in a group: social reality and group locomotion. He indicates that when there is no single objective basis for determining the validity of one's beliefs, one is dependent upon social reality to establish confidence in one's beliefs. Thus, to evaluate the validity of his opinions or to evaluate his abilities or even the appropriateness of his emotions (Schachter 1959), he will compare them with those of others. Festinger (1954) posits that to facilitate accuracy of evaluation of their opinions or abilities, people will seek out others with similar opinions or abilities for comparison and will avoid dissimilarity or attempt to reduce it when it exists. Also, lack of agreement among members of a group provides an unstable basis for beliefs which depend upon social consensus for their support, and hence —in line with Heider's discussion of the tendency toward cognitive balance (1958) or Festinger's theory of cognitive dissonance (1957)—forces will arise to produce uniformity. [See CONFORMITY.]

Pressures toward uniformity among members of a group may also arise because such uniformity is desirable or necessary in order for the group to locomote toward some goal. Greater uniformity in opinion within a group can be achieved in either of the following ways: (*a*) by actions (i.e., communications) that are directed at changing the views of others or one's own views or (*b*) by actions to make others incomparable in the sense that they are no longer effective as a comparison for one's opinions —e.g., by rejecting or excluding people with deviating opinions from the group.

Experiments have shown that increasing the attraction to the group, and thus increasing the importance of the group as a comparison object, increases the amount of influence which is attempted and the amount of opinion change which occurs when there is opinion discrepancy within a group (Back 1951). It has also been demonstrated that the more relevant or important the opinion is for the functioning of the group, the more pressure there will be for uniformity in a group (Schachter 1951; Festinger & Thibaut 1951). Also, as may be expected from theoretical considerations, there is evidence that when pressures toward uniformity exist, the concern is mainly with those members of the group who have opinions most divergent from one's own. Thus, members exert influence mainly on those whose opinions are most divergent from their own.

Pressures toward change.   The experiments revealing the tendency to direct communication toward deviants in the group, and through communication to exert social pressure upon them, provide support for Lewin's theory of group decision and social change. Lewin (1947*b*) began his analysis of change by pointing out that the *status quo* in social life is not a static affair but a dynamic process that flows on while still keeping a recognizable form. He borrowed the term "quasi-stationary equi-

libria" from physics to apply to such ongoing processes, which are kept at their present level by fields of forces preventing a rise or fall. The field of forces in the neighborhood of the level of equilibrium presupposes that the forces against exceeding the equilibrium level increase with the amount of raising and that the forces against lowering increase (or remain constant) with the lowering. Thus, if we assume that a group standard is operating to determine the level of worker productivity in a factory, any attempt upon the part of the worker to deviate from the standard by higher productivity will only result in stronger forces being induced upon him by his co-workers in order to push him back into line. That is, as the Festinger experiments have demonstrated, the deviant will be exposed to stronger pressures toward uniformity the more he deviates. However, as Lewin points out, the gradient of forces may change at a distance from the equilibrium level, so that after an individual has gone a certain distance from the equilibrium level, the forces may push him away from rather than pull him toward the group standard.

Lewin's analysis of the *status quo* as a quasi-stationary equilibrium has two major implications. First, it points out that change from the *status quo* can be produced either by adding forces in the desired direction or by diminishing opposing forces. However, the two methods of producing change have different consequences: if forces are added, the process on the new level will be accompanied by a state of relatively high tension, since the strength of forces in opposition will be greater; if the opposing forces are decreased, the new level will be accompanied by lower tension. Second, it highlights the difficulties of attempting to change group-rooted individual conduct and attitudes through efforts directed at the individual and not his group. If one endeavors to change the prejudices of an individual without changing the prejudice of the group to which he belongs, an individual will either be estranged from his group or be under pressure from his group to revert to his initial attitudes. Isolated individuals may perhaps change their attitudes because of their individual experiences, but the person who is deeply enmeshed in the social life of his community is unlikely to be able to resist the pressures to conform on matters of community importance if he wishes to continue in good standing. [See ATTITUDES, *article on* ATTITUDE CHANGE.]

Considerations such as the foregoing have led to a series of experiments in various settings— in the school, with neighborhood groups, in industry, in an interracial workshop—on the relative efficacy of changing behavior by efforts directed at individuals or at a group (Lewin 1935–1946). A typical procedure has been to compare the results of a lecture or individual instruction in changing behavior regarding the use of certain foods with the results of a group decision favoring the use. Results have clearly indicated that the group decision method produces more change.

The present status of field theory

In previous sections of this article, work that was directly initiated or stimulated by Lewin or his immediate associates has been described. The large sweep of this work, the brilliant innovations, the experimental ingenuity cannot help but be impressive. Even though Lewin died in 1947, his impact on psychology continues to be felt in the extension and application of his ideas by others. We turn, briefly, to a discussion of some current work in psychology—a theory of achievement motivation, balance and dissonance theory, and T-group training (laboratory training groups) which extends Lewin's ideas.

A theory of achievement motivation. Atkinson (1957; 1964) has developed a theory of achievement motivation that is an extension and elaboration of ideas advanced in the theory of level of aspiration developed by Lewin, Festinger, and Sibylle Escalona. Atkinson's theory attempts to account for the determinants of the direction, magnitudes, and persistence of achievement-motivated performance. Achievement motivation is the resultant of two opposed tendencies: $T_s - T_f$ (the tendency to achieve success minus the tendency to avoid failure. In Atkinson's notation this is represented as T_{-f}.).

The tendency to achieve success is assumed to be a multiplicative function of the motive to achieve success (M_s) which the individual carries about with him from situation to situation, the subjective probability of success (P_s), and the incentive values of success at a particular activity (I_s): $T_s = M_s \times P_s \times I_s$. Similarly, the tendency to avoid failure is assumed to be a multiplicative function of the motive to avoid failure (M_{af}), the subjective probability of failure (P_f), and the negative incentive value of failure (I_f): $T_f = M_{af} \times P_f \times I_f$.

So far, Atkinson's analysis parallels the level of aspiration theory, if one assumes, quite properly, that the Lewinian concept of valence is equivalent to Atkinson's motive times incentive: namely, that the valence of success $= M_s \times I_s$ and that the valence of failure $= M_{af} \times I_f$. He, however, introduces the additional assumptions that $I_s = 1 - P_s = P_f$

and that $I_f = -P_s$. In other words, his theory details more unequivocally the relationship between the perceived level of difficulty and the incentive values of success and failure. It states, in effect, that the value of success increases with the perceived difficulty of the task, while the displeasure at failure increases with the perceived ease of the task. (Notice that in Atkinson's theory $P_s \times I_s$ must equal $-P_f \times I_f$ and, hence, that whatever differences in strength there are between T_s and T_f will be due solely to the differences between M_s and M_{af}.) In addition, he has specified methods of measuring M_s and M_{af}; M_s is measured by the methods developed by McClelland and his associates (1953) to measure need achievement and M_{af} is measured by the Mandler–Sarason Test of Anxiety (1952).

Atkinson (1964) summarizes a considerable amount of research that is consistent with his theory. The wide applicability of the theory is indicated by the range of content to which the theory has been applied: motivational effect of ability grouping in schools, strength of achievement motive and occupational mobility, fear of failure and unrealistic vocational aspiration, preferences for degrees of risk, and the effects of success and failure. [See ACHIEVEMENT MOTIVATION.]

Cognitive balance. One of the notions implicit in Lewin's view of the life space as cognitively structured, and generally in the gestalt view that organization tends to be as "good" as possible, is that when a structure of beliefs and attitudes is imbalanced or disharmonious, a tendency will arise to change one's beliefs and attitudes until they are balanced. Lewin's view is brought out most clearly in his discussion of cognitively unstructured situations and in his discussion of the cognitive structure of different types of conflict situations. Heider (1946; 1958), one of Lewin's most brilliant associates, has extended this notion in his theory of cognitive balance. [See THINKING, *article on* COGNITIVE ORGANIZATION AND PROCESSES.]

Heider points out that cognitive stability requires a congruence among causal expectations with respect to related objects. That is, for a state of complete cognitive harmony to exist, the various implications of a person's expectations or judgments of any aspect of the cognized environment cannot contradict the implications of his expectations or judgments of any other aspect of the cognized environment. Thus, if a person judges X to be of potential benefit to his welfare, he cannot at the same time judge that Y (which is also judged to be of benefit to his welfare) and X are antagonistic and still have a stable or balanced cognitive structure. (Let X and Y be things, people, the products of people, or the characteristics of people.) When the cognitive structure is in a state of imbalance or is threatened by imbalance, forces will arise to produce a tendency toward locomotion that will change the psychological environment or produce a tendency toward change in the cognition of the environment. Under conditions which do not permit locomotion, the tendency for cognitive change is enhanced.

Heider specifies further that (*a*) in regard to attitudes directed toward the same entity, a balanced state exists if positive (or negative) attitudes go together; a tendency exists to see a person as being positive or negative in all respects; (*b*) in regard to attitudes toward an entity combined with belongingness, a balanced state exists if a person is united with the entities he likes and if he likes the entities he is united with; the converse is true for negative attitudes; (*c*) if two entities are seen as parts of a unit, a balanced state will exist if the parts are seen to have the same dynamic character (positive or negative). If the two entities have different dynamic characters, a balanced state can exist if they are seen to be segregated (i.e., by breaking up the unit).

Heider's theory has had wide ramifications in social psychology. Cartwright and Harary (1956) extended balance theory to cover a greater range of phenomena and also removed some of its ambiguities by using the mathematical theory of linear groups. Newcomb (1953; 1961) has applied Heider's theory to the "balancing" of interpersonal relations, particularly in his analysis of communicative acts and the development of friendships. Rosenberg and Abelson (1960) have applied a modification of Heider's theory to the problems of attitude change.

Dissonance theory. Leon Festinger, one of Lewin's most renowned students, has developed a theory (1957) which is similar to balance theory in its stress on the need to avoid cognitive inconsistency (dissonance) but differs from it in emphasizing postdecisional processes. Lewin (1939–1947), in a discussion of the behavior of a housewife who buys food, had suggested that behavior before and after decisions about purchasing food differed: prior to the decision, the more expensive the food, the less likely it was to get to the family table; after the decision, the higher its cost, the more likely it was to be used. Festinger's theory generalizes the idea that the postdecision situation may differ from the predecision situation. It makes the original assumption that making a decision per se arouses dissonance and pressure to reduce the dissonance. [*See* Thinking, *article on* cognitive organization and processes.]

Postdecision dissonance results, according to Festinger, from the fact that the decision in favor of the chosen alternative is counter to the beliefs which favor the unchosen alternative(s). To stabilize or freeze the decision after it has been made, the individual will attempt to reduce dissonance by changing his cognitions so that the relative attractiveness of the chosen, as compared with the unchosen, alternative is increased, or by developing cognitions which permit the alternatives to be substitutable for one another, or by revoking the decision psychologically. In Festinger's view (1964), the crucial difference from the predecision state of dissonance is that the predecisional conflict is "impartial" and "objective"; it does not lead to any spreading apart of the attractiveness in favor of the to-be-chosen alternative. Festinger writes: "Once the decision is made, however, and dissonance–reduction processes begin, one should be able to observe that the differences in attractiveness between the alternatives change, increasing in favor of the chosen alternative" (1964, pp. 8–9).

A variety of interesting and ingenious experiments have been stimulated by Festinger's view of the postdecision process. (See Brehm & Cohen 1962, for a detailed review.) These experiments have often involved "nonobvious" predictions which appear to defy common sense. Many of these predictions derive from the notion that if a decision produces insufficient rewards, the person will change his beliefs so as to make the decision seem more rewarding. Festinger (1961, p. 11) writes: "Rats and people come to love the things for which they have suffered." Presumably they do this to reduce the dissonance induced by the suffering, and their method of dissonance-reduction is to enhance the attractiveness of the choice which led to their suffering in order to justify it.

The theory of dissonance has stimulated extensive research into many aspects of social psychology: attitude and behavioral change, perceptual distortion, selective exposure to information, work productivity, and so forth. Recently, dissonance theory has been the subject of methodological criticism (Chapanis & Chapanis 1964) and theoretical criticism (Deutsch et al. 1962; Rosenberg 1965) which pose some difficult but perhaps not unresolvable problems for the theory.

T-group training. T-group training (laboratory training in groups) utilizes the experiences and interpersonal relations which occur in a temporary, laboratory-created group to help the participants develop insights into group processes, insights into the way that they themselves function in groups, and skills of participation in groups. The National Training Laboratories, which has become one of the key institutions concerned with the application of behavioral science to social practice, was established in 1947 with the cosponsorship of Lewin's Research Center for Group Dynamics and has been very much influenced by Lewin's ideas. His articles "Conduct, Knowledge, and Acceptance of New Values" (Lewin & Grabbe 1945) and "Frontiers in Group Dynamics" (1947) present the intellectual base for the development of the conception of laboratory training groups. These articles highlight the importance of the group in the process of individual re-education and change. In recent years, a considerable literature has been developed in connection with the laboratory method of training individuals in groups (see Bradford et al. 1964). While some of this literature is evangelistic in tone, this, too, is consonant with Lewin's active and continuing concern that social science be used to make the world a better place in which to live.

Although it cannot be said that Lewin's specific theoretical construct—his structural and dynamic concepts—are central in current research in psychology, his impact on psychology has been a major one. His impact is reflected in the general orientations which, today, are more and more taken for granted. These are that psychological events have to be explained in psychological terms; that central processes in the life space (e.g., distal perception, cognition, motivation, goal-directed behavior) rather than the peripheral processes of sensory input or of muscular action should be the focus of investigation; that psychological events have to be studied in their interrelations with one another; that the individual has to be studied in his interrelations with the group to which he belongs; that the attempt to bring about change in a process is the most fruitful way to investigate it; that important social psychological phenomena can be studied experimentally; that the scientist should have a social conscience; and that a good theory is valuable for social action as well as for science.

MORTON DEUTSCH

[*Directly related are the entries* GESTALT THEORY; PERSONALITY; PHENOMENOLOGY; SOCIAL PSYCHOLOGY; THINKING, *article on* COGNITIVE ORGANIZATION AND PROCESSES; *and the biography of* LEWIN. *For comparison, other relevant approaches to psychological phenomena may be found in* PERSONALITY: CONTEMPORARY VIEWPOINTS; PSYCHOANALYSIS. *Relevant also are* ACHIEVEMENT MOTIVATION; ATTITUDES; COHESION, SOCIAL; CONFLICT; GROUPS; LEADERSHIP; SYSTEMS ANALYSIS, *article on* PSYCHOLOGICAL SYSTEMS; *and the biographies of* BRUNSWIK; CASSIRER; HULL; TOLMAN.]

BIBLIOGRAPHY

ADLER, DAN L.; and KOUNIN, JACOB S. 1939 Some Factors Operating at the Moment of Resumption of Interrupted Tasks. *Journal of Psychology* 7:255–267.

ATKINSON, JOHN W. (1957) 1958 Motivational Determinants of Risk-taking Behavior. Pages 322–339 in John W. Atkinson (editor), *Motives in Fantasy, Action, and Society: A Method of Assessment and Study.* Princeton, N.J.: Van Nostrand. → First published in Volume 64 of *Psychological Review.*

ATKINSON, JOHN W. 1964 *An Introduction to Motivation.* Princeton, N.J.: Van Nostrand.

BACK, KURT W. 1951 Influence Through Social Communication. *Journal of Abnormal and Social Psychology* 46:9–23.

BARKER, ROGER G. (1946) 1953 *Adjustment to Physical Handicap and Illness.* 2d ed. New York: Social Science Research Council.

BRADFORD, LELAND P.; GIBB, JACK R.; and BENNE, KENNETH D. (editors) 1964 *T-group Theory and Laboratory Method: Innovation in Re-education.* New York: Wiley.

BREHM, JACK W.; and COHEN, ARTHUR R. 1962 *Explorations in Cognitive Dissonance.* New York: Wiley.

CARTWRIGHT, DORWIN; and HARARY, FRANK 1956 Structural Balance: A Generalization of Heider's Theory. *Psychological Review* 63:277–293.

CHAPANIS, NATALIA P.; and CHAPANIS, ALPHONSE 1964 Cognitive Dissonance: Five Years Later. *Psychological Bulletin* 61:1–22.

COCH, LESTER; and FRENCH, JOHN R. P. 1948 Overcoming Resistance to Change. *Human Relations* 1:512–532.

DEMBO, TAMARA 1931 Der Ärger als dynamisches Problem. *Psychologische Forschung* 15:1–144.

DEUTSCH, MORTON 1949a A Theory of Cooperation and Competition. *Human Relations* 2:129:152.

DEUTSCH, MORTON 1949b An Experimental Study of the Effects of Co-operation and Competition Upon Group Process. *Human Relations* 2:199–231.

DEUTSCH, MORTON; KRAUSS, ROBERT M.; and ROSENAU, NORAH 1962 Dissonance or Defensiveness? *Journal of Personality* 30:16–28.

FAJANS, SARA 1933 Die Bedeutung der Entfernung für die Stärke eines Aufforderungscharakters beim Säugling und Kleinkind. Untersuchungen zur Handlungs- und Affektpsychologie, No. 12. *Psychologische Forschung* 17:215–267.

FESTINGER, LEON 1950 Informal Social Communication. *Psychological Review* 57:271–282.

FESTINGER, LEON 1954 A Theory of Social Comparison Processes. *Human Relations* 7:117–140.

FESTINGER, LEON 1957 *A Theory of Cognitive Dissonance.* Evanston, Ill.: Row, Peterson.

FESTINGER, LEON 1961 The Psychological Effects of Insufficient Reward. *American Psychologist* 16:1–11.

FESTINGER, LEON 1964 *Conflict, Decision, and Dissonance.* Stanford Studies in Psychology, No. 3. Stanford Univ. Press.

FESTINGER, LEON; SCHACHTER, STANLEY; and BACK, KURT (1950) 1963 *Social Pressures in Informal Groups: A Study of Human Factors in Housing.* Stanford Univ. Press.

FESTINGER, LEON; and THIBAUT, JOHN 1951 Interpersonal Communication in Small Groups. *Journal of Abnormal and Social Psychology* 46:92–99.

FRENCH, JOHN R. P. 1944 Organized and Unorganized Groups Under Fear and Frustration. Pages 229–308 in *Authority and Frustration*, by Kurt Lewin et al. Univ. of Iowa Press.

HEIDER, FRITZ 1946 Attitudes and Cognitive Organization. *Journal of Psychology* 21:107–112.

HEIDER, FRITZ 1958 *The Psychology of Interpersonal Relations*. New York: Wiley.

HENLE, MARY 1942 *An Experimental Investigation of Dynamic and Structural Determinants of Substitution*. Contributions to Psychological Theory, Vol. 2, No. 3, Serial No. 7. Durham, N.C.: Duke Univ. Press.

KARSTEN, ANITRA 1928 Psychische Sättigung. *Psychologische Forschung* 10:142–254.

KELLEY, HAROLD H. 1951 Communication in Experimentally Created Hierarchies. *Human Relations* 4:39–56.

KOUNIN, JACOB S. 1941 Experimental Studies of Rigidity. Parts 1–2. *Character and Personality* 9:251–282. → Part 1: The Measurement of Rigidity in Normal and Feeble-minded Persons. Part 2: The Explanatory Power of the Concept of Rigidity as Applied to Feeble-mindedness.

LEVY, S. 1953 Experimental Study of Group Norms: The Effects of Group Cohesiveness Upon Social Conformity. Ph.D. dissertation, New York Univ.

LEWIN, KURT (1935) 1948 Psycho–Sociological Problems of a Minority Group. Pages 145–158 in Kurt Lewin, *Resolving Social Conflicts: Selected Papers on Group Dynamics*. New York: Harper. → First published in Volume 3 of *Character and Personality*.

LEWIN, KURT (1935–1946) 1948 *Resolving Social Conflicts: Selected Papers on Group Dynamics*. New York: Harper.

LEWIN, KURT (1939–1947) 1963 *Field Theory in Social Science: Selected Theoretical Papers*. Edited by Dorwin Cartwright. London: Tavistock.

LEWIN, KURT (1943a) 1963 Defining the "Field at a Given Time." Pages 43–59 in Kurt Lewin, *Field Theory in Social Science: Selected Theoretical Papers*. London: Tavistock.

LEWIN, KURT (1943b) 1948 The Special Case of Germany. Pages 43–55 in Kurt Lewin, *Resolving Social Conflicts: Selected Papers on Group Dynamics*. New York: Harper. → First published in Volume 7 of *Public Opinion Quarterly*.

LEWIN, KURT (1946) 1948 Action Research and Minority Problems. Pages 201–218 in Kurt Lewin, *Resolving Social Conflicts: Selected Papers on Group Dynamics*. New York: Harper. → First published in Volume 2 of the *Journal of Social Issues*.

LEWIN, KURT (1947a) 1963 Frontiers in Group Dynamics. Pages 188–237 in Kurt Lewin, *Field Theory in Social Science: Selected Theoretical Papers*. Edited by Dorwin Cartwright. London: Tavistock. → First published in Volume 1 of *Human Relations*.

LEWIN, KURT (1947b) 1958 Group Decision and Social Change. Pages 197–211 in Society for the Psychological Study of Social Issues, *Readings in Social Psychology*. 3d ed. New York: Holt.

LEWIN, KURT; and GRABBE, PAUL (1945) 1948 Conduct, Knowledge, and Acceptance of New Values. Pages 56–68 in Kurt Lewin, *Resolving Social Conflicts: Selected Papers on Group Dynamics*. New York: Harper.

→ First published in Volume 1 of the *Journal of Social Issues*.

LEWIN, KURT et al. 1944 Level of Aspiration. Volume 1, pages 333–378 in J. McV. Hunt (editor), *Personality and the Behavior Disorders*. New York: Ronald Press.

LEWIS, HELEN B.; and FRANKLIN, MURIEL 1944 An Experimental Study of the Role of the Ego in Work. Part 2: The Significance of Task-orientation in Work. *Journal of Experimental Psychology* 34:195–215.

LIPPITT, RONALD; and WHITE, RALPH K. 1943 The "Social Climate" of Children's Groups. Pages 485–508 in Roger G. Barker, Jacob S. Kounin, and Herbert F. Wright (editors), *Child Behavior and Development*. New York: McGraw-Hill.

LISSNER, KÄTE 1933 Die Entspannung von Bedürfnissen durch Ersatzhandlungen. Untersuchungen zur Handlungs- und Affektspsychologie, No. 18. *Psychologische Forschung* 18:218–250.

McCLELLAND, DAVID C. et al. 1953 *The Achievement Motive*. New York: Appleton.

MAHLER, WERA 1933 Ersatzhandlungen verschiedenen Realitätsgrades. Untersuchungen zur Handlungs- und Affektspsychologie, No. 15. *Psychologische Forschung* 18:27–89.

MANDLER, GEORGE; and SARASON, SEYMOUR B. 1952 A Study of Anxiety and Learning. *Journal of Abnormal and Social Psychology* 47:166–173.

MILLER, NEAL E. 1944 Experimental Studies of Conflict. Volume 1, pages 431–465 in J. McV. Hunt (editor), *Personality and the Behavior Disorders*. New York: Ronald Press.

NEWCOMB, THEODORE M. 1953 An Approach to the Study of Communicative Acts. *Psychological Review* 60:393–404.

NEWCOMB, THEODORE M. 1961 *The Acquaintance Process*. New York: Holt.

ROSENBERG, MILTON J. 1965 When Dissonance Fails: On Eliminating Evaluation Apprehension From Attitude Measurement. *Journal of Personality and Social Psychology* 1:28–42.

ROSENBERG, MILTON J.; and ABELSON, R. P. 1960 An Analysis of Cognitive Balancing. Volume 3, pages 112–163 in *Attitude Organization and Change*, by Milton J. Rosenberg et al. New Haven: Yale Univ. Press.

SCHACHTER, STANLEY 1951 Deviation, Rejection and Communication. *Journal of Abnormal and Social Psychology* 46:190–207.

SCHACHTER, STANLEY 1959 *The Psychology of Affiliation: Experimental Studies of the Sources of Gregariousness*. Stanford Studies in Psychology, No. 1. Stanford Univ. Press.

SLIOSBERG, SARAH 1934 Zur Dynamik des Ersatzes in Spiel- und Ernstsituationen. *Psychologische Forschung* 19:122–181.

THIBAUT, JOHN 1950 An Experimental Study of the Cohesiveness of Underprivileged Groups. *Human Relations* 3:251–278.

THIBAUT, JOHN; and COULES, JOHN 1952 The Role of Communication in the Reduction of Interpersonal Hostility. *Journal of Abnormal and Social Psychology* 47:770–777.

ZEIGARNIK, BLUMA 1927 Das Behalten erledigter und unerledigter Handlungen. Untersuchungen zur Handlungs- und Affektspsychologie, No. 3. *Psychologische Forschung* 9:1–85.

FIELD WORK

Field work is the study of people and of their culture in their natural habitat. Anthropological field work has been characterized by the prolonged residence of the investigator, his participation in and observation of the society, and his attempt to understand the inside view of the native peoples and to achieve the holistic view of a social scientist. A society can be said to provide a ready-made laboratory for the social scientist in somewhat the same way that the human organism serves the biologist.

Field studies have long been the mark of cultural anthropologists and to a somewhat lesser degree of sociologists; they are increasingly being done by political scientists, social psychologists, and other social scientists. A difference exists between anthropology and sociology in the history, problems, and methods of field work. Today, however, the trend is toward similarity.

Anthropologists began to do field studies toward the end of the nineteenth century, although Morgan's study of the Iroquois appeared somewhat earlier. The major emphasis on anthropological field work has been primarily British and American, with such notable exceptions as the work of Thurnwald in Germany and of Lévi-Strauss in France. Among the first expeditions were those of Boas in British Columbia and of Haddon with his associates in the Torres Strait region of the Pacific. Their goal was to extend the boundaries of the knowledge of man by studying wide variations in his cultures.

The publication of Malinowski's *Argonauts of the Western Pacific* in 1922 revealed the great potentialities of field work. This study of Trobriand Islanders, among whom Malinowski had lived for almost three years, set new standards for field workers which continue to operate. Field work came to mean immersion in a tribal society—learning, as far as possible, to speak, think, see, feel, and act as a member of its culture and, at the same time, as a trained anthropologist from a different culture. It is significant that this method was forged in the study of small, homogeneous tribal societies in which it would have been difficult for the investigator to have avoided face-to-face relations. In recent years the range in type and size of societies studied by anthropologists has been much extended. With this extension, new problems and new methods have developed, but certain others have remained constant.

Beginning field work

The anthropologist chooses the geographical and cultural area for his field project, studies the literature, and, if the language has been recorded, learns as much of it as possible before going into the field. Today, he will most likely also be interested in a specific problem and in social or culture theory, and he will endeavor to be *au courant* with the literature.

He then has to consider whether he goes to the field alone, with his family, or as part of a team. In the past the norm was the lone field worker; today it is common for the investigator's spouse and children to travel into the field. The research team—a number of anthropologists or scientists representing different disciplines—is a new trend. Each method has its advantages and disadvantages. Being alone gives a greater intensity to the field experience and may provide more intimate data, since the field worker is thrown upon the native people for company. On the other hand, it has the disadvantages of loneliness and of being limited to what one person can accomplish. The family has an advantage in reducing loneliness, and a mate and children may be useful entering wedges into the community and in securing data from their own sex and age groups. A team obviously extends the range of data which can be collected. A disadvantage of a family or team is that relationships with native peoples may be more difficult if one is quickly accepted and the other (or others) disliked.

Whether the field worker goes alone or with his family or as a member of a team, approval for the project and, if possible, cooperation must be secured from those who have authority in the society. Authority may reside in a group of clan elders, a chief, a tribal king, officials of a colonial government or an independent nation, the general manager of an industrial company, or the leaders of any other dominant economic, social, or political group. The questions of those in power, whoever they be, are usually concerned with whether the investigator threatens the *status quo* and whether he can be trusted not to reveal any information which they would consider harmful to the individual or the community. The traditional position of the anthropological field worker is that he is there as scholar to learn rather than as an instrument of change and that he never betrays an informant. (In applied social science, anthropologists, sociologists, economists, and others sometimes both study and help to implement social change, but this is a quite different type of field work [*see, for example,* ANTHROPOLOGY, *article on* APPLIED ANTHROPOLOGY].)

The nod of approval from those in power is only the first step. The field worker must then gain the good will of the people he wishes to study. He has to explain his presence to them, as he did to those in authority, as simply and as honestly as possible. In general there is no substitute for honesty. In some societies, both tribal and modern, people may be flattered by someone being interested enough to travel a long way to find out about their customs and to learn their language. The anthropologist must from the beginning differentiate himself from other aliens of his race or culture, such as missionary, government official, trader, planter, or work supervisor, whom the indigenous people may have known. It is extremely important that they have opportunities to observe and to know the field worker. The nearer his house is to the hub of activities, the easier it is for reciprocal observations and for easy social relations. The location of the house may also symbolically establish an important difference between the field worker and other aliens.

Gradually the field worker's role evolves. It usually has many facets and will not be the same in all situations or for all field workers. He may begin by rendering certain services. In a tribal society he often brings material goods ranging from ornaments to useful spades and knives. He may dispense simple remedies, such as aspirin and antimalarial medicine, to those needing them. In modern societies he often accepts invitations to speak to meetings of teachers, to church congregations, a chamber of commerce, and any other significant group that invites him. He is not only being helpful; he is making it easy for people to see and to know him.

The first steps

During the first month or so the field worker proceeds very slowly, making use of all his sensory impressions and intuitions. He walks warily and attempts to learn as quickly as possible the most important forms of native etiquette and taboos. When in doubt he falls back on his own sense of politeness and sensitivity to the feelings of others. He likewise has to cope with his own emotional problems, for he often experiences anxieties in a strange situation. He may be overwhelmed by the difficulties of really getting "inside" an alien culture and of learning an unrecorded or other strange language. He may wonder whether he should intrude into the privacy of people's lives by asking them questions. Field workers vary in their degree of shyness, but most people of any sensitivity experience some feelings of this type when they first enter a new field situation.

Sooner or later, when the field worker has established rapport with the people and has learned how to handle his own anxieties, he establishes a routine of work. It is usually wise to begin with relatively impersonal tasks. If he has not already done so, learning the language is among the first essentials. Field workers naturally vary in their linguistic abilities, and languages differ in degrees of complexity. But learning any unrecorded language presents manifest difficulties for anyone. Margaret Mead (1939) has made the useful distinction between *using* and *learning* the native language. The field worker frequently learns to speak and understand a language without learning it as a linguist would. In parts of Oceania where pidgin English is common, a combination of it and the native language may be the method of communication. In Africa, the field worker may have to know the language of the former or present colonial power, a lingua franca such as Swahili, and as much as possible of a native language. Often he works through an interpreter, either all the time or on certain problems where his fluency in the appropriate language is not sufficient for understanding. The status, sex, and personality of the interpreter may present difficulties in certain situations, and it may be useful, therefore, to have several interpreters. No easy solution to the language problem exists. Ideally, the field worker should be an expert in the native language. Usually he simply does the best he can within the limitations of time and the inherent difficulties of the situation.

Making a census is another early task which has the value of being impersonal and essential. It is necessary to locate people in space and to know the composition of households. As the field worker goes from one household to another, he also gets acquainted with the occupants. (In modern large societies, a government census is usually available.)

Participation in the culture

Participating and observing become an ever more important part of the routine. The field worker somewhat resembles a natural historian: he observes and notes, as far as possible, whatever comes within his range, even though he may not always know the relevance of all his observations. He follows long and devious sequences, such as those involved in initiation, marriage, and death rituals, which may be six or more months in preparation, and, at the same time, he observes the minutiae of daily life in which they occur. He accompanies the people on their economic tasks—hunting, fishing, planting, cooking, and others. He listens to them converse and gossip when they are at ease and picks up new clues which he later follows up. A woman anthropologist alone in the field can usually participate more fully than a man alone, because a man is generally restricted to being with other males. But even where social segregation between the sexes is strict, a woman can work with men as well as with women. No one fears her.

The intensity of the field worker's participation varies from one situation to another and between investigators. Among the Nuer, Evans-Pritchard was given little choice. The Nuer were "persistent and tireless" visitors, in and around his camp all the time, and he suffered from a lack of privacy (Evans-Pritchard 1940). Some anthropologists participate in ritual dances, feasts, and similar social events; others limit themselves to taking notes. The field worker's sense of the social situation and his personal desires and limitations dictate how much and when he will participate.

Whatever the degree of the field worker's participation in the whole society, friendships with a few people develop, and they help him to find a niche in the community. It is these friends who often become his best informants. They may include servants or other employees, a chief, medicine man, and many others. Often, too, an informal adoption as a "son," "daughter," "sister," or "brother" helps the anthropologist find his place and extends or deepens his range of knowledge. *In the Company of Man* (Casagrande 1960) provides profile sketches of key informants who were close associates and important teachers for each of the contributing anthropologists.

When the field worker has become familiar with the social contours and feels more or less accepted, he begins to work systematically on such anthropological problems as kinship systems, forms of marriage and residence, economic and political organization, witchcraft and magical beliefs and practices, or any other aspect of life which is significant in the society and interesting to him. He asks questions in structured and unstructured interviews and notes the measure of agreement or disagreement between the patterns which emerge from the answers and the actual behavior he observes. Usually, a discrepancy exists between the ideal and the real. Another method, used effectively by Oscar Lewis (1961), is the tape recording of long interviews with different members of one family, resulting in a significant humanistic account. Hortense Powdermaker (1962) had inter-African conversations recorded by an African assistant, which revealed spontaneous tones of feeling and subtleties of African life.

Unexpected and chance events, such as a quarrel, often reveal facets of a culture which the field worker had not known existed or, perhaps, only dimly suspected. Then, too, lies may be as informative on certain levels as the truth. For instance, in a study in Mississippi, one of the major values of middle-class white people—the straining for an aristocratic family background—was revealed in their consistent lying about their backgrounds (Powdermaker 1939). Failures and newcomers, who reveal the pressures which they resist or try to conform to, may be another excellent source of data.

Whomever the anthropologist is interviewing or however he is participating, there must be a high degree of reciprocal communication between him and the people he studies. This need represents an important difference between the methods of the social and the natural sciences. The chemist and physicist do not communicate personally with molecules or atoms, but communication for the social scientist depends to a large degree on his psychological involvement. The field worker faces a special problem, however, for he must be both detached and involved. If this dual role is an inherent part of the anthropologist's personality or self image (strengthened by his training), he plays it spontaneously and easily. As Goffman (1961) puts the problem, the degree of tension felt by a field worker corresponds to the level of congruence between spontanous and unspontaneous (playing the rules of the game) roles.

The notion that involvement connotes a lack of scientific objectivity is mistaken. It is only when an anthropologist is aware of his involvements that he can then detach himself and observe. Hidden or unconscious involvements (positive or negative) are dangerous, for the obvious reason that the investigator cannot step outside of them. An obsessive identification with either the underdog or the top social levels limits the field worker's communication and his objectivity. In a highly stratified society it is important for him to move easily within its different segments.

In addition to a capacity for open involvements and for becoming detached from them, personal qualities such as kindness, patience, tact, endurance, and the ability to "take" both loneliness and ambiguity are helpful. Other idiosyncratic characteristics may be useful in one field situation and not in another.

Despite its reputation, the so-called culture shock is not often one of the problems of a trained anthropologist. First, he arrives with a general knowledge of the people and their culture through having immersed himself in the literature. Second, his penetration into the culture is so gradual that by the time he achieves any understanding of it, he is apt to take it for granted. In fact, he has to be on his guard against this tendency. Culture shock is more likely to be experienced when he returns to his own modern urban society after an extended period in a tribal one.

The theoretical orientation of the field worker is significant from the beginning. Historical reconstruction, functionalism, a structural or cultural approach, and psychological anthropology are among the major frames of reference. Each influences the field worker's choice of problems, the type of data he collects, the kind of clues he picks up, some of his techniques, his hypotheses, and his interpretations. The collecting of data and theorizing are not necessarily separate processes. As the field worker participates, observes, and interviews, much of the time he is also thinking of hypotheses, of comparative data, and of relevant theories; it is also true, of course, that problems and hypotheses frequently arise out of empirical data in the field. Because of the personal nature of field work, it is imperative that while in the field the anthropologist accurately record empirical data separately from hypotheses and interpretations and distinguish the impressions from the definitive data. Thus, he should tell us the number of informants he used; give details of their age, sex, and social status; and provide precise descriptions of the methods used in securing data. Scientific standards demand as complete honesty as possible and data that may be negative as well as positive in terms of hypotheses. It should be possible for a reader to make different interpretations from the data. One of the most rigorously honest presentations is Cora DuBois's study of the Alorese (1944).

New trends in field work

The above points are relatively constant in all anthropological field work. Among the new trends are an emphasis on specific problems rather than on holistic studies; working in larger and more complex societies; a greater concern with sampling; the use of sociological surveys along with the traditional participation, observation, and interviewing; and a frank recognition of the fact that the field worker is a human instrument and part of the situation studied.

A team has obvious advantages in working on complex problems and in large societies. One of the early cross-disciplinary teams in the field was that of the anthropologist Clyde Kluckhohn and the physician Dorothea Leighton, who studied the Navajo (1946). An experiment in regional research was made by a team of 12 social scientists, all anthropologists except one historian and one political scientist, who worked on political development in Uganda and Tanganyika under the direction of

Audrey Richards (1960), then the director of the East African Institute of Social Research. The members of this team worked independently. A comparative study of child rearing in six cultures by six research teams, each consisting of a man and a woman worker, under the direction of John and Beatrice Whiting (1963), represents still another kind of team. A more extensive cross-disciplinary approach was used in a study (Rogler & Hollingshead 1965) of schizophrenia in Puerto Rico conducted by a sociologist, psychiatrists, an anthropologist, and social workers. As yet there have been relatively few field teams initiated by anthropologists which cover a large number of disciplines.

Anthropologists in the past were not unaware of the problem of sampling. An adequate sample might be almost impossible in historical reconstruction. But in small functioning communities, the whole population of the village usually appeared in the field worker's genealogical charts, and it was relatively easy for him to establish the frequency of forms of behavior without any elaborate statistical methods. Today, working in larger societies, the anthropologist often employs assistants to make a random survey at the beginning of the field study to establish patterns, or toward the end to substantiate or negate qualitative aspects of the research. But getting a truly random sample may present difficulties if the investigator and his assistants have no access (or much less) to one group.

Another new problem arises in working in those complex contemporary societies which have dual power structures representing different ideologies. To work with both is decidedly not easy. There is also the problem of centricity: most anthropologists find it more difficult to overcome ideological centricity than ethnocentricity. Training enables an anthropologist to study cannibalism, witchcraft, and other tribal customs with relative objectivity. It is less easy to be objective on issues which threaten strong political or other social commitments. On the other hand, a person who has no commitments would not be able to understand those of others.

Field work in sociology

As they work on problems in complex modern societies, anthropologists come closer to sociology. Field work has long been the practice of sociology, although its history and methodology have differed from those of anthropology. In contrast with the early anthropologists, who traveled far for comparative materials, the first field workers in sociology were primarily interested in the reform of their own society, in which the industrial revolution and the rise of an urban proletariat had brought many urgent social problems. In England, Beatrice Potter (later Mrs. Sidney Webb) and Charles Booth and, in France, Le Play did field studies among the poor through involvement with them, direct observation, and interviewing.

American sociologists followed in the European tradition of being critics of modern society. Initial empirical research included the *Hull-House Maps and Papers* (1895) and W. E. B. DuBois's *The Philadelphia Negro* (1899). Field work among the urban poor was developed at the University of Chicago by such men as Louis Wirth, Robert E. Park, and their many able students. They studied conditions among ethnic and racial minorities and such groups as criminals, hoboes, and prostitutes. These people were foreign, perhaps with an exotic quality, to many of the middle-class American sociologists. They explored at home, while the anthropologists of the same period were studying exotic peoples in distant lands.

The traditional distinction in subject matter is weakening. Members of both disciplines and of other social sciences increasingly study "primitive" preliterate and modern literate societies. Problems, too, become interchangeable; studies such as those of social structure, communities, social change, and interpersonal relations (e.g., those involved in social mobility, social conditioning, role playing) are common to both disciplines.

A few sociologists, such as Robert and Helen Lynd and William Foote Whyte, in their respective eminent studies, *Middletown* (1929) and *Street Corner Society* (1943), have used anthropological methods and techniques as models. But in general, the trend in sociology has been to emulate the natural sciences as far as possible and to limit field problems to those on which quantifiable data can be secured, primarily through the use of surveys. In 1959 Nathan Glazer wrote, "The sociologist today—whether his field of interest is the community, criminology, marriage and the family, world politics, social classes, housing—is a man who asks people questions and then statistically analyzes the answers to them. If he does not ask the questions himself, he hires some one else to ask them; or, if not that, he analyzes the statistics gathered by those who *have* asked questions—census-takers, social workers, and others" ([1959] 1964, pp. 43–44). The beginning of sociology in England coincided with the development of statistics there, and the relationship between the two is, thus, no accident.

Many sociological field studies lack personal participation and detailed observation; formal questionnaires can be a barrier to establishing relations between the field worker and the people he studies. According to John Bennett and Kurt Wolff (1955), the typical sociologist attempts to have the detachment and objectivity of the natural scientist and to view the people he studies as objects or, at best, "subjects" rather than as fellow human beings with whom he enters into some kind of personal relations.

There seems to be a new trend in which anthropology and sociology change places methodologically, at least to some degree. Increasingly anthropologists try to eliminate or deny the humanism of their approach and to select those field problems which they think lend themselves to a rigorous scientific method. Some anthropologists try to emulate the methods of the natural scientists, but the imitation, unfortunately, is often of the mechanistic notions of causality common to nineteenth-century science. These have now been replaced by principles of indeterminacy and by probability curves. It was a sociologist, Melville Dalton, who pointed out this time lag. He wrote, "Influenced by the dogmatism of nineteenth century science, research methodology in the social and psychological sciences is now more cocksure than in the increasingly humbler physical sciences" (Dalton 1959, p. 273).

The field worker as an individual

A quite new development, not yet strong enough to be called a trend, is the recognition that the field worker is himself an inherent part of the situation studied and that his personal as well as his scientific reactions are an important part of the research process. Field workers, of course, have long known that they are *human* instruments of research, although some have tried to be, or to present an image of, faceless robots. But there has been a reluctance to recognize the scientific significance of the field worker's personality and his all-too-human characteristics. Relatively little space has been given in publications to his mistakes, to the trial-and-error nature of some of his procedures, to the role of chance, to the influence of his reactions on a strange people and on their culture, and other such important personal factors. With a few exceptions, anthropologists have included only a few paragraphs or pages on these points in the introductions to their monographs or have relegated them to private conversations. After a long period of emulating natural scientists, some sociologists now recognize the peculiarly human characteristics of their discipline. In *Sociologists at Work* (Hammond 1964) 13 eminent sociologists give candid personal accounts of how their field research projects evolved, of their frustrations as well as their achievements in the field, of what actually happened rather than of what should have happened. *Stranger and Friend: The Way of an Anthropologist* (Powdermaker 1966) gives probably the frankest and most detailed account of one anthropologist's field studies, of mistakes as well as successes, of relationships between the field worker and the peoples studied, and of how her personality and training related to the type of work done.

The field is a laboratory in which the role of the investigator is significant and relevant to the study of the people and their culture, and obviously the more candid and revealing the field worker is about his role, the more scientific is the report and the more helpful it is to other investigators. The recognition of the significance of the personal characteristics of the field worker to his research confirms the point that field work is an art as well as a science.

HORTENSE POWDERMAKER

[*See also* ETHNOGRAPHY; INTERVIEWING; OBSERVATION.]

BIBLIOGRAPHY

ADAMS, RICHARD N.; and PREISS, JACK J. (editors) 1960 *Human Organization Research: Field Relations and Techniques.* Homewood, Ill.: Dorsey.

ARENSBERG, CONRAD M.; and KIMBALL, SOLON T. 1965 *Culture and Community.* New York: Harcourt. → See especially pages 28–47, "The Community-study Method."

BENNETT, JOHN W.; and WOLFF, KURT H. 1955 Toward Communication Between Sociology and Anthropology. *Yearbook of Anthropology* 1:329–351.

BERREMAN, GERALD D. 1962 *Behind Many Masks: Ethnography and Impression Management in a Himalayan Village.* Society for Applied Anthropology, Monograph No. 4. Ithaca, N.Y.: The Society.

[BOHANNAN, LAURA] (1954) 1964 *Return to Laughter*, by Elenore Bowen [pseud.]. Garden City, N.Y.: Doubleday.

CASAGRANDE, JOSEPH B. (editor) 1960 *In the Company of Man: Twenty Portraits by Anthropologists.* New York: Harper.

DALTON, MELVILLE 1959 *Men Who Manage: Fusions of Feeling and Theory in Administration.* New York: Wiley.

DUBOIS, CORA A. (1944) 1960 *The People of Alor: A Social-psychological Study of an East Indian Island.* Cambridge, Mass.: Harvard Univ. Press.

DUBOIS, W. E. B. 1899 *The Philadelphia Negro: A Social Study, Together With a Special Report on Domestic Service by Isabel Eaton.* Series in Political Economy and Public Law, No. 14. Philadelphia: Univ. of Pennsylvania.

EVANS-PRITCHARD, E. E. (1940) 1963 *The Nuer: A Description of the Modes of Livelihood and Political Institutions of a Nilotic People.* Oxford: Clarendon.

FIRTH, RAYMOND W. (1936) 1957 *We, the Tikopia: A Sociological Study of Kinship in Primitive Polynesia.* 2d ed. London: Allen & Unwin. → A paperback edition was published in 1963 by Beacon.

GILLIN, JOHN 1949 Methodological Problems in the Anthropological Study of Modern Cultures. *American Anthropologist* New Series 51:392–399.

GLAZER, NATHAN (1959) 1964 The Rise of Social Research in Europe. Pages 43–72 in Daniel Lerner (editor), *The Human Meaning of the Social Sciences.* New York: Meridian.

GOFFMAN, ERVING (1956) 1959 *The Presentation of Self in Everyday Life.* Garden City, N.Y.: Doubleday.

GOFFMAN, ERVING 1961 *Encounters: Two Studies in the Sociology of Interaction.* Indianapolis, Ind.: Bobbs-Merrill.

HAMMOND, PHILLIP E. (editor) 1964 *Sociologists at Work: Essays on the Craft of Social Research.* New York: Basic Books.

HENRY, JULES; and SPIRO, MELFORD E. 1953 Psychological Techniques: Projective Tests in Field Work. Pages 417–429 in International Symposium on Anthropology, *Anthropology Today.* Edited by A. L. Kroeber. Univ. of Chicago Press.

Hull-House Maps and Papers: A Presentation of Nationalities and Wages in a Congested District of Chicago, Together With Comments and Essays on Problems Growing Out of the Social Conditions. 1895 New York: Crowell.

JUNKER, BUFORD H. (1960) 1962 *Field Work: An Introduction to the Social Sciences.* Univ. of Chicago Press.

KLUCKHOHN, CLYDE 1945 The Personal Document in Anthropological Science. Pages 79–173 in Louis R. Gottschalk, Clyde Kluckhohn, and Robert Angell, *The Use of Personal Documents in History, Anthropology and Sociology.* New York: Social Science Research Council.

KLUCKHOHN, CLYDE; and LEIGHTON, DOROTHEA (CROSS) (1946) 1951 *The Navaho.* Oxford Univ. Press.

KLUCKHOHN, FLORENCE R. 1940 The Participant–Observer Technique in Small Communities. *American Journal of Sociology* 46, no. 3:331–343.

LEWIS, OSCAR 1953 Controls and Experiments in Field Work. Pages 452–475 in International Symposium on Anthropology, *Anthropology Today.* Edited by A. L. Kroeber. Univ. of Chicago Press.

LEWIS, OSCAR 1961 *The Children of Sánchez: Autobiography of a Mexican Family.* New York: Random House. → A paperback edition was published in 1963 by Vintage.

LYND, ROBERT S.; and LYND, HELEN M. (1929) 1930 *Middletown: A Study in Contemporary American Culture.* New York: Harcourt. → A paperback edition was published in 1959.

MALINOWSKI, BRONISLAW (1922) 1960 *Argonauts of the Western Pacific: An Account of Native Enterprise and Adventure in the Archipelagoes of Melanesian New Guinea.* London School of Economics and Political Science, Studies, No. 65. London: Routledge; New York: Dutton. → A paperback edition was published in 1961 by Dutton.

MEAD, MARGARET 1939 Native Languages as Field-work Tools. *American Anthropologist* New Series 41:189–205.

NADEL, S. F. 1939 The Interview Technique in Social Anthropology. Pages 317–327 in F. C. Bartlett et al. (editors), *The Study of Society: Methods and Problems.* London: Routledge; New York: Macmillan.

NASH, DENNISON 1963 The Ethnologist as a Stranger: An Essay in the Sociology of Knowledge. *Southwest Journal of Anthropology* 19, no. 2:149–167.

OSGOOD, CORNELIUS 1953 *Winter.* New York: Norton.

PAUL, BENJAMIN D. 1953 Interviewing Techniques and Field Relationships. Pages 430–451 in International Symposium on Anthropology, *Anthropology Today.* Edited by A. L. Kroeber. Univ. of Chicago Press.

POWDERMAKER, HORTENSE 1939 *After Freedom: A Cultural Study in the Deep South.* New York: Viking.

POWDERMAKER, HORTENSE 1962 *Copper Town; Changing Africa: The Human Situation on the Rhodesian Copperbelt.* New York: Harper.

POWDERMAKER, HORTENSE 1966 *Stranger and Friend: The Way of an Anthropologist.* New York: Norton.

RICHARDS, AUDREY I. (editor) 1960 *East African Chiefs: A Study of Political Development in Some Uganda and Tanganyika Tribes.* London: Faber; New York: Praeger.

RIESMAN, DAVID; and BENNEY, MARK 1956a The Sociology of the Interview. *Midwest Sociologist* 18:3–15.

RIESMAN, DAVID; and BENNEY, MARK (editors) 1956b The Interview in Social Research. *American Journal of Sociology* 62, no. 2. → See especially pages 137–252.

ROGLER, LLOYD H.; and HOLLINGSHEAD, AUGUST B. 1965 *Trapped: Families and Schizophrenia.* New York: Wiley.

WAGLEY, CHARLES; and GALVÃO EDUARDO 1949 *The Tenetehara Indians of Brazil: A Culture in Transition.* Columbia University Contributions to Anthropology, No. 35. New York: Columbia Univ. Press. → See especially the preface.

WAX, ROSALIE H. 1952 Reciprocity as a Field Technique. *Human Organization* 11, no. 3:34–37.

[WITHERS, CARL] (1945) 1961 *Plainville, U.S.A.,* by James West [pseud.]. New York: Columbia Univ. Press.

WHITING, BEATRICE B. (editor) 1963 *Six Cultures: Studies of Child Rearing.* New York: Wiley.

WHYTE, WILLIAM F. (1943) 1961 *Street Corner Society: The Social Structure of an Italian Slum.* 2d ed., enl. Univ. of Chicago Press.

WHYTE, WILLIAM F. 1957 On Asking Indirect Questions. *Human Organization* 15, no. 4:21–23.

FIGGIS, JOHN NEVILLE

The work of John Neville Figgis (1866–1919) in political philosophy constitutes the fusing of two interests and two careers. Born in Brighton, England, and educated at Cambridge University, he developed and matured as a student of history and political thought under the influence of Maitland. Influenced also by another distinguished Cambridge teacher, Mandell Creighton, he recognized a call to the religious life, which led him to the Church of England and eventually to a monastic order of that church, the Community of the Resurrection. He continued writing and occasional lecturing on both religious and political–historical topics until his death.

In his historical works on political theory, Figgis laid greatest emphasis, in the tradition of Gierke and Maitland, on the importance of man's corporate life as the foundation of the state. His *Churches in the Modern State* (1913) is a popular exposition of the nature of corporate life and an application of his theory to the question of the nature of a church and its relation to the state. It exhibits a passionate concern for freedom in the face of the growing power and authority of the state.

From his scholarly studies of the history of political thought, especially that of the Middle Ages and the early modern period, Figgis concluded that there are two ways of understanding the corporation. He assumed that a corporation is "a society of men bound together for a permanent interest," and he recognized as corporations such bodies as the family, the club, the union, the college, and the church. Bodies other than the state must be understood *either* as creatures of the state *or* as real persons with lives of their own and an origin independent of the state. From Figgis' point of view, the former approach is wrong, and the latter is true to the facts of history and social life.

The monistic theory

Figgis traced the theory that the corporation is a creature of the state to the concept of absolute sovereignty, which in turn he traced to the abstract idea of unity. Modern monism (the theory of the unitary or all-embracing state) derives, he suggested, from the ancient conception of the city-state as an organic unity and from the view developed in Roman law of the position and authority of the emperor as sovereign. These notions were imported into the Roman Catholic church in the medieval period and developed (with only a slight setback—the conciliar movement in the fifteenth century) into the nineteenth-century doctrine of the absolute power and infallibility of the pope. In the course of this "*crescendo* of Papal claims," attempts were made by some popes—for example, Boniface VIII, 1294–1303, and John XXII, 1316–1334—to claim secular power as well as spiritual power and authority. With the rise of national states after the Renaissance, these attempts failed, but a political theory was developed by Machiavelli, Bodin, and Hobbes that claimed for the ruler in the secular realm the same authority that the popes had been able to establish for themselves in the church. According to this theory, as Figgis described it, the sovereign of the state, whether one man, a few men, or all men, is the sole source of social authority and social life; no other society (corporation) has a life of its own. Each society in the state exists, carries on its affairs, and exercises its authority over its members with the permission, tacit or express, of the sovereign. All such societies are merely creatures of the state; they have no innate life of their own and no original right or authority.

This theory of corporations is rejected by Figgis on two main grounds: first, that it does not square with the facts of history; and second, that the implications of this doctrine are inimical to the self-development and freedom of the individual. The evidence to support the first argument was developed by Gierke in his monumental *Das deutsche Genossenschaftsrecht*. Gierke had shown that there is another way to conceive of corporations and even a spirit of corporate life. Figgis accepted Gierke's approach and developed evidence of his own from his analysis of the situation in his own day of social groups vis-à-vis the state. He was especially concerned with the problem of the relation of churches to the state in a period of religious heterogeneity. Put simply, the question is, What authority does a modern state (for example, England in the late nineteenth or early twentieth century) have over the churches that have been organized within its borders? (The problem of England is especially complicated because it has both an established church and unestablished churches, which are both national and international.) The state clearly has the right to prevent or punish violations of law. But does not a church have the right to determine its membership conditions, its ritual, and even its purpose without state interference? The issue had been met in the courts where some members of a church sued to prevent church leadership supported by a majority of the membership from amalgamating with another church (1913, pp. 18–20). The results of these cases pointed sometimes to the monistic theory (when churches were prevented from changing) and sometimes to the other theory (when churches were left to themselves). Similar cases arose and continue to arise in connection with trade unions, and the issue has not really been settled.

The second argument against the monistic theory, namely, that its implications for individual freedom are repugnant, hinges on the demonstration that there is a growing trend, independent both of the development of one-man rule and of democratic rule, toward the destruction of smaller organizations either by their consolidation into larger ones or by their absorption into the state. Believers in freedom for the individual must condemn this development because it cuts off from more and more individuals their sources of social power and their support against the might of the state. It does not matter that the state is one which exhibits popular sovereignty. The life of man is a social life, and if ultimately there is no society other than the state, man becomes a creature of the state. Figgis did not live to see the rise of modern totalitarianism in the third and fourth decades

of the twentieth century, but he did foresee it. Much evidence could be found in the later period to confirm his fears.

The corporation as a real person

A more adequate theory of corporate life, Figgis held, sees any corporation (especially such a voluntary association as a church) as possessing an inherent life of its own, generated out of the spirit and will of its members. He recognized the affinities of his approach to that of Rousseau. A corporation is a living force with powers of self-development. It has a life greater than the mere sum of the individuals composing it and is not merely a matter of contract. Each such body has its own individuality, its own ethos. The existence of such bodies is a "social fact" that may or may not be recognized by the state. Failure to recognize it leads to a condition akin to that of individuals in slavery. Recognition of the real personality of corporations by the state leads to a conception of the state as a *communitas communitatum*.

Groups that arise in society out of the efforts of individuals to realize themselves do not develop without genuine authority over their members, and this authority manifests itself in a government that has legislative, executive, and judicial powers. The authority of the group comes from the consent of its members. The group carries on activities that are public for its members, but private in relation to the state. But Figgis realized that this distinction between public and private does not satisfactorily describe life in modern societies. Instead of seeing society as a collection of individuals confronting an entity called the "state" and being unified by it, he saw society as a complex of individuals, groups, and corporations presided over by a rather special sort of group called the "state." Figgis was part of that pluralistic movement that saw the state as one group in society having distinctive functions, but one which was not in all ways superior to every other group, either in its claims on the individual or in its benefits to him. The state is a strong power that is needed to prevent injustice between groups and to secure to each group its rights. It does not create the groups, but in pursuing its own goals it has to regulate them, limit their activities, and settle conflicts among them. However, the resolution of conflicts has tended to produce, Figgis believed, unwarranted interference in the internal life of groups. His doctrine, reminiscent of that of Mill, is that the state has the right to limit the activities of groups only insofar as they impinge on other groups or individuals and that the internal life of the group is inviolable. For Figgis, this is the meaning of the doctrine of the real personality of corporations, and it seems to stand or fall on the adequacy of the distinction between the internal (private) and the external (public) activities of groups.

Although Figgis never developed a systematic political theory in any detail, he offered hints as to the proper point of view of an adequate political theory, and from these hints his readers may gain some idea of the sort of theory he would defend. The recognition of the real personality of groups, the importance of "self-realization" for groups, and the characterization of the state as the *communitas communitatum* suggest that his theory would derive from Gierke and Maitland on the one hand and from the British Hegelians on the other. His concern for freedom speaks of the influence of Mill and Acton. Yet he never does come to grips with the question, What is a state? If corporations are real persons, it is self-contradictory to say that it is a *communitas communitatum,* for if the state is taken to be a real person, what happens to other groups which are internal to it? If, however, the other groups are seriously thought to be independent of the state, in what sense does it continue to be a *communitas?* The doctrine of the real personality of corporations seems to introduce rigidities of its own that inhibit the clear observation of the facts of social life. The subsequent development of pluralism (political, social, and economic) carried further the "discrediting" of the state and provoked, in turn, a reaction in the direction of statism that Figgis would have deplored.

HENRY M. MAGID

[*For the historical context of Figgis' work, see* PLURALISM *and the biographies of* ACTON; GIERKE; GREEN; MAITLAND; MILL. *For other relevant material see* SOVEREIGNTY; STATE; VOLUNTARY ASSOCIATIONS.]

WORKS BY FIGGIS

(1896) 1922 *The Divine Right of Kings.* 2d ed. Cambridge Univ. Press. → First published as *The Theory of the Divine Right of Kings.* A paperback edition was published in 1965 by Harper.
1907 *Studies of Political Thought: From Gerson to Grotius, 1414–1625.* Cambridge Univ. Press.
(1913) 1914 *Churches in the Modern State.* 2d ed. London and New York: Longmans.
1917 *The Will to Freedom, or the Gospel of Nietzsche and the Gospel of Christ.* New York: Scribner.
1921 *The Political Aspects of St. Augustine's* City of God. London: Longmans.

SUPPLEMENTARY BIBLIOGRAPHY

MAGID, HENRY M. 1941 *English Political Pluralism: The Problem of Freedom and Organization.* Columbia University Studies in Philosophy, No. 2. New York: Columbia Univ. Press. → See especially pages 10–30 on "Figgis: The Significance of the Real Personality of Groups."
TUCKER, MAURICE G. 1950 *John Neville Figgis: A Study.* London: Society for Promoting Christian Knowledge.

FILM

Cinema, which by now should mean both motion pictures for theaters and films for television, is simultaneously an art and an industry because its means of creation and its systems of distribution involve expensive technology. This has been true since the early nickelodeon days of the public viewing parlor, when five cents illuminated a 50-foot-long scene. Today's distribution of color television into living rooms at the rate of $105,000 for a 50-second commercial only inflates the problem in terms of the costs involved and the relative quality of the product.

What effect this artistic, social, and economic phenomenon has on the cultural values of both creators and viewers is an international problem of the first magnitude, since cinema is a world-wide language that can be grasped by the illiterate as well as by the educated. Nothing less than the control of men's minds and emotions is at stake. Since aesthetics, in this case, has become linked both with economics and with political action responsive to the uses of visual communication, cinema is the major cultural force in the second half of the twentieth century.

The relation between those who create the picture and those who pay its costs is a conflict between the front office and the sound stage as old as Michelangelo's quarrels with the papacy, or as complex as Shakespeare's efforts to gain the good graces of his patrons. What is unique to cinema is the degree of interdependence between artistry and finance.

The question cannot be dismissed as a matter of preference. What is art to one may indeed be an industry to another, and vice versa. The inseparability of the equation makes it difficult to evaluate. The union of film art and the picture industry is a marriage contracted in hell, lived on earth, and rewarded in heaven.

Problems of film production. A poet needs only paper and pen to be in business; a novelist has the option of adding typewriter and ribbons to these tools; a painter can start work once he has brushes, paints, and canvas; and a sculptor can fashion almost any durable material. A musician is not obliged to own or rent an orchestra to compose a symphony. But a motion picture director requires a fully equipped studio to compose a motion picture. An impoverished painter could steal hair from a cat to make a brush, but a film director will find that cameras, lenses, lights, developing tanks, and editing apparatus are relatively inexpensive compared with actors' salaries, set construction, or shooting on location.

Cinema is the only art form solely dependent on machinery. The electronic extension of motion pictures via television is more expensive and involves more machinery. Never before in man's artistic history has the artist been so subordinate to the means which shape his ends; and, conversely, never before has the patron or sponsor or producer been so dependent on talent for the utilization of his machinery for production, distribution, and exhibition. A camera collecting dust is not a money-making gadget, nor is a script collecting dust a motion picture that can be projected.

A writer–director in cinema is like an orchestral conductor; his script, or score, cannot be experienced without the collaboration of myriad different craftsmen employing different instruments. Ideally, they should be hired for their specific competence in dealing with a special challenge. This is a problem of correct casting of craftsmen, but under strict union regulations of seniority the writer–director is obliged to accept the run-of-the-mill worker, who is not generally inclined to support artistic adventures. Also, the number of employees allotted to an assignment has been prescribed by union rules. There are qualitative considerations aside from the quantity of workers, assistants, and collaborators. A studio may employ specialists as diverse as architects (to design sets) and experts in Zen Buddhism (to do "research").

Since the basic concepts of a motion picture must be filtered through so many individuals before the picture reaches its final version, and since these concepts are primarily visual, the relation of the number of individuals involved to the degree of aesthetic coherence in the picture's imagery is obviously crucial. A cinematic law might be postulated: The greater the number of collaborators in the creation of a picture, the less coherent its imagery will be.

Production problems begin with the "source," which is either a story or a body of factual material. The source may be a novel, a play, a short story, or an "original treatment"; it may even be a social essay, a political theme, or a report on actualities. The author of the source will usually have his ideas and emotions translated into script form by other writers; the final shooting script may be prepared by yet another batch of writers, including dialogue specialists. Such has been the prevailing pattern in Hollywood's film and television studios; the same is true of Italy, France, Yugoslavia, Hungary, Czechoslovakia, Poland, the Soviet Union, Japan, Nationalist China, and the Chinese People's Republic. In England and Sweden the tendency has been to use an individual writer, as is the preference in independent production in the United States. In fact, the writer–director personality as a single force explains the rising quality throughout the world of the feature film. Such figures as Ingmar Bergman, Federico Fellini, Michelangelo Antonioni, Jean-Luc Godard, François Truffaut, David Lean, Tony Richardson, Stanley Kubrick, and Sidney Lumet are directors who also serve as their own writers, in close cooperation with a scenarist.

Final decisions over script in terms of plot and story values, over casting of stars and other actors, and over the editing of the shots were made by producers or executive producers during the years of the mass production system. Thus a studio like Twentieth Century-Fox, Metro-Goldwyn-Mayer, or Warner Brothers used to program its merchandise, during the heyday of studio monopoly, by planning ten westerns, five musical comedies, a dozen social dramas (with love interest), half a dozen situation comedies, five war dramas, and a flock of Grade B thrillers. Depending on how these products sold in the market place, the program for the following year was adjusted. The producer system reigned. In the 1930s and 1940s the producer was like a lord commanding his manor, but he was also in competition with a neighboring producer under company management whose power also rose or fell according to the success of his product. Executive producers were like dukes ruling over a collection of lordly producers. Such duchy strongholds were set up at M-G-M, for example, under the supreme authority of the king, Louis B. Mayer. Industry ruled over art (Crowther 1957; Ross 1952).

For the creative talent there was no choice; Faust was compelled to sell his soul to the devil. Throughout the 1930s novelists and playwrights from the East (whose fate is perhaps epitomized by that of F. Scott Fitzgerald) accepted front office control; there was no other, since Samuel Goldwyn ran a one-man M-G-M.

Rise and fall of the independents. The celebrated case of *United States* v. *Paramount* ended the reign of the studio chiefs when the Supreme Court held that a producer cannot be an exhibitor. This bill of divorcement, known as the Anti-Block Booking Decision, separated the ownership of studios from ownership of movie theaters (Conant

1960). The principle behind the Supreme Court's decision was the Sherman Anti-Trust Act of some seven decades earlier, a principle never before applied to the distribution of an American art form. The 1907 Patents Trust case had already broken the production monopoly held by the Edison interests, so that dozens of new producing companies were founded at that time. These were consolidated or eliminated throughout the first two decades of the century, climaxing in the monolithic studios of the 1930s and 1940s. Following the Anti-Block Booking Decision, independent production boomed, mainly through stars and directors forming their own companies. It would naturally be assumed that the liberation of talented creators from the assembly line production system would permit more audacious pictures with fresh plots and deeply delineated characterizations. Such hopes have proven hallucinatory. Although the economic base shifted in the 1950s, the cultural superstructure remained solidly attached to box office values. Men of talent had been conditioned by formula, and upon risking their own money and reputations, they played the new game in the safe style of the old one.

In the 1960s no longer does the producer represent the banker; he may be the same person. Or the actor may be his own director, and the writer his own producer. But the Muse Unchained can inspire only those who are capable of appreciating freedom and adventure. On the whole, the product of a company dominated by an actor or director cannot be distinguished from the run-of-the-mill product of a major manufacturer. The suspicion grew that Faust couldn't deliver any more than the devil. To give the devil his due, it must be said that the banker began to suspect that the artist (actor, director, or writer–producer) was not interested so much in creating a new art as in accumulating new money.

Films and audiences in the 1960s. The artistic bankruptcy of Hollywood existed before the coming of television. There were, of course, a few good pictures made during the early 1950s, among which *High Noon, Shane, On the Waterfront*, and *Marty* were outstanding. But bad money makes more bad money—all, unfortunately, of an identical green. Major manufacturing companies took on serials for TV; the Saturday serial of silent days became nightly, national, and network. Artistic values have continued to suffer, while the major portion of many studios' income has come from the sale or rental of previous features to television, the production of serials and features for television, and the rental of studio space and facilities to television.

Hollywood in the mid-1960s continues at an artistic low level, with an accompanying hostility toward serious pictures. Artistic initiative has shifted from Hollywood to abroad. The American motion picture audience has been fragmented, thanks to television. The fragmentation is quite similar to the division in other entertainments, such as the theater, books, and magazines. The potential market for quality pictures is at an all-time high; for instance, there are over four thousand film societies at American universities, with an attendance of over 2.5 million. Nevertheless, the old answers to the problem of quality continue in force. The "blockbuster" produced by the major studio—one thinks of *Ben Hur, Spartacus, Guns of Navarone, Cleopatra*—has been an old answer. Independent production, which has given us such pictures as *The Bridge on the River Kwai, Anatomy of a Murder*, and *Lawrence of Arabia*, is still an old answer.

What is new is that the fragmented audience may be as small as that of art houses or film societies, or as large as that of national circuits. Moreover, producers realize that there is less financial risk in a good low-budget film than in a good high-budget film. *Lawrence of Arabia*, for example, did not make the profit, in proportion to its costs, that was made by *Tom Jones*. In Europe, where governments frequently underwrite a portion of production costs, financing is both less complex and more easily arranged; dual producerships involving partners from different European countries assure lower costs. Among the major film-producing countries, only the United States does not in some measure subsidize film production. Also, there is greater artistic freedom in Europe, where the film is recognized as a director's medium.

Ingmar Bergman, more than any foreign director, has demonstrated that artistic independence can collect, however modestly in his case, at box offices. Of American producer–directors, Stanley Kramer has been the most successful in proving that political subjects can also collect; his *The Defiant Ones, On the Beach, Judgment at Nuremberg*, and *Ship of Fools* all dealt with unmistakably political themes, and all made money. It is possible that successes like these may slowly be encouraging the major producers to abandon their reliance on time-worn formulas. For instance, a "sleeper" like *David and Lisa*—a small-budget picture with virtually unknown actors that dealt with the theme of mental illness with unusual realism—may have influenced one of the more progressive major studios to distribute *Love With a Proper Stranger*, in which a young girl's love affair was treated with an absence of conventional moralizing that was quite new to the American screen. In this way even a few examples of artistic boldness may have an impact on the entire industry. At any rate, by the late 1960s the foreign director, the native producer, and the major releaser were all influencing and in turn being influenced by a more enterprising production outlook.

What was hopefully different about this outlook was a greater reliance on the individual. Stanley Kubrick was able to make *Dr. Strangelove*, the most independently audacious American film since *Citizen Kane*, because the distributor who paid for the production (Columbia) did not have script-approval rights. The result was a uniquely stylized and satirical film that could not otherwise have been made and that in certain categories achieved box office records. Carl Foreman, who enjoyed script freedom for *The Victors*, did a controversial picture that was more successful financially than D. W. Griffith's masterpiece *Intolerance*, which had to wait several decades for its proper recognition. It is clear that the fragmented movie audience of the 1960s can be reached if the proper means are employed.

Of gods and bankers.   If a signature, as John Houseman terms it, is now more possible on a film than before, then the artistic prospects appear good. In Europe, films are advertised through the name of the director as well as the stars. This emphasis on basic creative talent is beginning to receive recognition in America, but only a few directors, such as George Stevens, John Huston, and Stanley Kramer, are widely known to the public. Stanley Kubrick, Sidney Lumet, and John Frankenheimer are relatively unfamiliar except to younger, serious audiences. The clearer the director's own contribution becomes, the more likely he is to be recognized as a factor in box office receipts and the greater the support he is likely to gain from the bankers who finance motion pictures. It is not so crucially important that the mass of people can't tell one Ford from another, except on wheels; the gentlemen who own and control the apparatus of manufacture and distribution know who is most likely to return profits on their loans. Ingmar Bergman has rejected offers from every major American owner of the apparatus. That he was wanted makes it easier for younger directors to enter doors. Fellini's financial success in Europe with *La Dolce Vita* gave him the opportunity to be his own boss in *8½* after years of hocking his soul to Roman financiers. The artistic and financial success of *8½* permitted Fellini to exercise his freedom with wider scope in *Giulietta degli Spiriti*, but not, unfortunately, with similar success. It is doubtful whether a single creative person is capable of having the

judgment to control objectively the writer as well as the director in him. Both Wall Street and the studios should take note that the single gifted individual is sufficient unto himself in any art except the film. Indeed, the varied talents of the writer–director–producer are inherently at odds with each other. Even so catholic a genius as Leonardo da Vinci would have found himself hard put to be the following (all in his own image): writer, director, producer, editor, promoter, manager of a seven-ring circus, handholder, advertiser, salesman, and psychoanalyst for actors. It is excessive to expect so much, even from a cinematic god.

The writer in him will tell the director how to shoot, but the director will prevent the editor in him from trimming shots before the saturation point. Conversely, the promoter in him will cast actors or actresses who have box office appeal but are not necessarily suitable for the characters they are to portray. When all these talents work well together in one body and one mind, we have the rarest of exceptions: a work of art that is a financial success. Who can deny how different the second half of *Lawrence of Arabia* might have been had David Lean, a truly gifted director, been able to maintain an artistic coherence? Or—conversely —how much more gratifying *Cleopatra* could have been for the mass audience had an administrative intelligence controlled excesses of writing and direction.

Casting of artistry by financial authority is as important for total achievement as the casting of financial acumen by the creator. Louis B. Mayer is as dead as Erich von Stroheim, the director he defeated in the cutting room when *Greed* was mutilated. History is always on the side of the creator, but this is of little consolation during periods of creative struggle. Stroheim, who never had the opportunity to cast bankers, would soon be a cinematic god if he were alive in today's market place.

Nevertheless, living gods are rare in cinema. Orson Welles was once such a demon, Federico Fellini is today in Italy, Ingmar Bergman in Sweden, and Akira Kurosawa in Japan. Perhaps the greatest of them all is Luis Buñuel, an enigmatic genius who has been making and breaking rules for forty years. No American director can be said to enjoy this stature. Those who are their own producers—John Ford, Elia Kazan, Stanley Kubrick, George Stevens, Billy Wilder, William Wyler, Fred Zinnemann—obviously produce the better American pictures. Should this trend expand through one fragmented audience into others, it could parallel the first golden age, the years of D. W. Griffith, Thomas H. Ince, Mack Sennett,

Charles Chaplin, Douglas Fairbanks—when directors did their own casting of bankers. The question of for whom a picture is intended is more important now than previously, primarily because art and industry are wedded as never before. It is a different kind of liaison, a marriage made in heaven, lived in hell, and rewarded on earth.

The television monopoly. In the nonfragmented audience of television viewers, the film writer–director lives in a serfdom unparalleled in the history of creativity in America. Since television has become the center of every home and the heart of the advertising world, the financial prizes are tempting beyond imagination. Not even in the decades when Hollywood's monetary rewards were reckoned as phenomenal has there been so much money paid out to so many people for so little talent.

Following the exposure of the rigged quiz shows, the TV networks assumed programming control in 1960. Between that year and 1966 network profits rose from about $21 million to more than $80 million. The prime time between 7:30 P.M. and 10:30 P.M. is controlled by the three networks, who produce the programs on film or tape, either directly or through affiliates or associates, and sell the time and costs to the sponsor. Thus the networks act as both producers and distributors, in violation of the Sherman Anti-Trust Act and in direct contravention of the *United States* v. *Paramount* Supreme Court ruling. Although the attorney general of the United States could go to court and win a decree that would separate television program production (90 per cent of which is on film or tape and comes out of Hollywood) from television program exhibition, no action is taken. The advertisers remain in show business and get more powerful every year, though they are, in turn, dependent on the networks for time slots and programs. The competition between advertisers for prime time strengthens the monopoly power of the networks.

Hollywood film producers of programs for sale to the networks claim, and rightly so, that they cannot get their shows on television unless they invite a network to participate in (1) a portion of the copyright ownership, meaning a share of present and future profits; (2) domestic syndication rights, which are the major profit source in booking films into local television stations; (3) foreign syndication rights, which are increasingly profitable and are cushions for future income during a producer's dry period or his old age. "Residuals"—the profit from replays—are highly lucrative in the

rebooking of such popular serials as *Gunsmoke, Bonanza, I Love Lucy*, and dozens more.

The box office standard of judgment for motion pictures has been replaced by the television rating systems, which estimate, with varying degrees of inaccuracy, the alleged millions viewing a given program at a given time. Although quality drama and public affairs documentaries may have audiences in the millions—larger than audiences in the past who viewed such programs in theaters or classrooms—these films are unceremoniously scuttled in favor of more shows with mass appeal. The lowest common denominator ensures the advertiser of the widest market for his sales pitch. Thus *Playhouse 90* and *Matinée*, which provided quality entertainment and a proving ground for fresh acting, writing, and directing talent, were replaced by soap operas and quiz shows. Protest letters went unheeded; economics wrote the ticket.

The four major sources of sponsorship—the automobile, cigarette, drug, and soap industries—are in competition among themselves for prime time, and so are the companies that make up each of these industries. The packager of filmed shows for television syndication knows in advance what kind of story his writers need write, what sort of flashy, attention-arresting direction his directors should deliver, and what name stars will attract ratings. What this attitude does to the quality of programs can be seen nightly. Newton Minow's "vast wasteland"—the term he used as chairman of the Federal Communications Commission (FCC) in describing their world to the National Association of Broadcasters—has become in a few years an expanding Sahara with an occasional oasis on a Sunday afternoon.

Proposals for federal regulation. The cultural future of film in America for the mass audience lies in the hands of the FCC, which, however, is disinclined to use the powers given it by Congress to police the abuses of both stations and networks in their violations of frequency and length of commercials and in their failure to provide the statutory proportion of public service programming. Since a third of the Congress is personally interested in commercial returns of local broadcasting stations and/or in stock ownership in broadcasting companies, there has been no effort to strengthen the spine of the FCC. The Johnson administration is known as the broadcaster's ally in Washington.

Nonetheless, the proposals of the FCC to control and foster competition in television program production and procurement of programs should be noted for the sake of their historical interest. The proposed rules would prohibit network corporations from (1) engaging in syndication in the United States or distributing independent programs for exhibition outside the United States; (2) acquiring syndication and foreign sales rights in programs produced by other persons and licensed directly to the network corporations for exhibition; (3) acquiring rights to share in the profits from syndication and foreign sales of such programs. They would also require network corporations to divest themselves of distribution and profit-sharing rights in domestic syndication and overseas sales of which they are presently possessed.

To achieve these ends the proposed FCC rules would set a limit on undue concentration and would stimulate competition. A network could not offer a weekly evening program schedule in which more than 50 per cent of the time, or a total of 14 hours per week, whichever is greater, is occupied by programs produced by the network or in which it has acquired the first-run license from an independent producer. This stricture is exclusive of newscasts and special news programs and sustaining programs. The net result of the rule—if ever passed and rigorously administered—would be to make prime time available every evening for the exhibition of some programs in which the network corporations have no financial or proprietary interests. The market would then be broadened for the independent program producer and competition among such producers would be encouraged. The films would then reflect the program judgments not only of the network corporations but also of a large number of competitive elements who wish to reach the American people through television.

What this ruling would do for the television audience is what the Anti-Block Booking Decision did for the motion picture audience, namely, encourage the tastes of the multiple public. This would make for a more democratic atmosphere in a pluralistic society.

The aesthetics of film. The closed market place for stories and ideas has limited experiments with program content while indulging technical maneuvers to hook and hold the attention of the majority. Cinema aesthetics, catering to Nielsen ratings tastes, have emphasized excessive movements of frame and camera, excessive pacing to shots, and unrelated camera angles or compositions—all superimposed on a superficial story line and on thin characterizations. On the other hand, in the open market place of international film production for theaters, the aesthetic advances are remarkable, as seen in the color utilizations, for example, of An-

tonioni in *Deserto Rosso* and Fellini's *Giulietta degli Spiriti*. Alain Resnais, Jean-Luc Godard, and François Truffaut fragment time and space in ways which enhance theme, plot, and characters.

Cinema aesthetics is being furthered through the works of such gifted artists rather than through the theories of critics, many of which are unrelated to contemporary cinema. For example, Kracauer (1960) has revealed the realistic nature of photography as a phenomenon affecting credibility; Lawson (1964) has emphasized the audio–visual nature of cinema that makes it a new art form. In contemporary cinema it is clear, as never before, to what degree movements and light affect meaning. This approach comes closer to the *sui generis* possibilities of cinema, which set it apart as a language, a craft, and an art. Knowledge of these possibilities is helpful in assisting the viewer to analyze the factors affecting his reactions and his judgment. With such a "grammar of cinema" at his fingertips, he is armed to withstand the hourly assault of TV programs and the clever techniques of popular film productions. This grammar, rooted in movements and light, finds that the frame, with its composition and inner action and frame movement; the shot, with its variety of frame movements in conjunction with edited movements between shots; and the edit, with its various jugglings of time through the juxtaposition of shots, comprise what might be called the "seven faces of time" (Gessner 1965).

Unless in the second half of the 1960s the federal government of the United States moves to protect its citizens in their free access to the best in cinema, the American people will continue to be denied full participation in the most dominant art of the twentieth century. In practical terms, such protection can be achieved through breaking the TV monopolies and by offering government subsidies for production, as is already the practice in Sweden, France, Italy, and the United Kingdom. The British Broadcasting Corporation (BBC), subsidized by government funds and a tax on receiving sets, is a particularly good example for study, since it is wholly free in making creative judgments. Some of the more interesting films produced anywhere emerge under BBC sponsorship. In the United States, only the National Educational Television approximates, on a smaller scale, the BBC approach, but not with the BBC's imaginative audacity. Sweden taxes every seat in its movie theaters to support a cinema training program for talented youth and to subsidize experimental productions not designed for box office success. These examples, it is to be hoped, might influence the eventual creation in America of a national film academy which would train and produce youthful talent, and of an audacious cinema in the tradition of the country where the art and industry were born.

ROBERT GESSNER

[*See also* COMMUNICATION, MASS; DRAMA.]

BIBLIOGRAPHY

AGEE, JAMES (1958) 1963 *Agee on Film: Reviews and Comments.* London: Owen.

ANDERSON, JOSEPH L.; and RICHIE, DONALD 1960 *The Japanese Film: Art and Industry.* New York: Grove.

ARNHEIM, RUDOLF (1957) 1960 *Film as Art.* Berkeley: Univ. of California Press.

BABITSKY, PAUL; and RIMBERG, JOHN 1955 *The Soviet Film Industry.* New York: Praeger.

BATZ, JEAN-CLAUDE 1963 *À propos de la crise de l'industrie du cinéma.* Brussels: Université Libre de Bruxelles, Institut de Sociologie.

COMMISSION ON FREEDOM OF THE PRESS 1947 *Freedom of the Movies: A Report on Self-regulation,* by Ruth A. Inglis. Univ. of Chicago Press.

CONANT, MICHAEL 1960 *Antitrust in the Motion Picture Industry: Economic and Legal Analysis.* Berkeley: Univ. of California Press.

CROWTHER, BOSLEY 1957 *Lion's Share: The Story of an Entertainment Empire.* New York: Dutton.

EMERY, F. E. 1959 Psychological Effects of the Western Film: A Study in Television Viewing. II. The Experimental Study. *Human Relations* 12:215–232.

FABREGAT CUNEO, ROBERTO 1957 El proceso del cine en el mundo y en la cultura y la deformación de los temas culturales al través del cine. *Revista mexicana de sociología* 19:387–404.

FARBER, MANNY 1963 The Fading Movie Star. *Commentary* 36:55–60.

GANS, HERBERT J. 1962 Hollywood Films on British Screens: An Analysis of American Popular Culture Abroad. *Social Problems* 9:324–328.

GESSNER, ROBERT 1963–1964 On Teaching Cinema in College: A Modest Proposal for an Ideal Academic Program. *Film Culture* No. 31:47–50.

GESSNER, ROBERT 1965 Seven Faces of Time: An Aesthetic for Cinema. Pages 158–167 in György Kepes (editor), *The Nature and Art of Motion.* New York: Braziller.

GOODMAN, EZRA 1961 *The Fifty Year Decline and Fall of Hollywood.* New York: Simon & Schuster.

HANDEL, LEO A. 1950 *Hollywood Looks at Its Audience: A Report of Film Audience Research.* Urbana: Univ. of Illinois Press.

HARRIS, THOMAS 1957 The Building of Popular Images: Grace Kelly and Marilyn Monroe. *Studies in Public Communication* 1:45–48.

HUACO, GEORGE A. 1965 *The Sociology of Film Art.* New York: Basic Books.

JACOBS, LEWIS 1960 *Introduction to the Art of the Movies: An Anthology of Ideas on the Nature of Movie Art.* New York: Noonday.

KAUFFMANN, STANLEY 1966 *A World on Film.* New York: Harper.

KRACAUER, SIEGFRIED 1960 *Theory of Film: The Redemption of Physical Reality.* New York: Oxford Univ. Press.

LAWSON, JOHN H. 1964 *Film, the Creative Process: The Search for an Audio–Visual Language and Structure.* New York: Hill & Wang.

LINDGREN, ERNEST (1948) 1963 *The Art of the Film.* 2d ed. New York: Macmillan.

MACCANN, RICHARD D. 1964 *Film and Society.* New York: Scribner.

POWDERMAKER, HORTENSE 1950 *Hollywood, the Dream Factory: An Anthropologist Looks at the Movie-makers.* Boston: Little.

ROSS, LILLIAN (1952) 1953 *Picture.* London: Gollancz. → A paperback edition was published in 1962 by Doubleday.

ROSTEN, LEO C. 1941 *Hollywood: The Movie Colony, the Movie Makers.* New York: Harcourt.

SCOTCH, NORMAN A. 1960 The Vanishing Villains of Television. *Phylon* 21:58–62.

STORK, LEOPOLD 1962 *Industrial and Business Films.* London: Phoenix House.

TALBOT, DANIEL (editor) 1959 *Film: An Anthology.* New York: Simon & Schuster.

TYLOR, PARKER 1960 *The Three Faces of the Film.* New York: Yoseloff.

WOLFENSTEIN, MARTHA; and LEITES, NATHAN 1950 *Movies: A Psychological Study.* Glencoe, Ill.: Free Press.

FINANCE, LOCAL

See LOCAL FINANCE.

FINANCIAL INTERMEDIARIES

Financial intermediaries issue (indirect) debt of their own to buy the (primary) debt of others. Their issues attract funds from alternative expenditures by nonfinancial spending units on consumption, tangible investment, or primary debt. Their lending directs the flow of funds to expenditure by borrowers on consumption, tangible investment, or primary debt. They intermediate between the sources of funds that flow to them and the ultimate users of these funds.

The intermediaries may be identified by their balance sheets, which show a high proportion of financial to tangible assets and of indirect debt to equity. Their income statements report high ratios of income from interest and dividends to total income and of expense for interest and dividends to total expense.

There are bank (monetary) intermediaries and nonbank (nonmonetary) intermediaries. The former are commercial banks and the central bank, together constituting the monetary system, which issues indirect debt, subject to unique regulations, in the form of money. The indirect debt which is issued by nonbank intermediaries is not used as a means of payment.

Both types of intermediary are to be distinguished from other institutions that transmit funds from ultimate lenders to ultimate borrowers. These other institutions do not issue their own indirect debt in soliciting funds. They include security dealers, brokers, and exchanges.

Types of intermediary. The principal nonbank financial intermediaries in the United States are the following:

Depositary intermediaries
  Credit unions
  Mutual savings banks
  Savings and loan associations
Insurance and pension intermediaries
  Casualty and miscellaneous insurance companies
  Fire and marine insurance companies
  Fraternal insurance organizations
  Government retirement, pension, insurance, and social security funds
  Group health insurance
  Private life insurance companies
  Private noninsured pension funds
  Savings bank life insurance departments
Finance companies
  Factors
  Mortgage companies
  Personal finance companies
  Sales finance companies
Investment companies
  Closed-end companies
  Face-amount certificate companies
  Industrial loan companies
  Open-end companies
Agricultural credit organizations
  Federal land banks
  Livestock loan companies
  National farm loan associations
  Production credit associations
Government lending institutions
  Banks for cooperatives
  Federal Home Loan Banks
  Federal intermediate credit banks
  Federal National Mortgage Association
  Federal Savings and Loan Insurance Corporation

This list is not complete; it omits such domestic intermediaries as the American Express Company, the Export–Import Bank, small business investment corporations, and pawnbrokers, as well as international intermediaries in which the United States participates, including the International Monetary Fund and the International Bank for Reconstruction and Development. (Detailed classifications of intermediaries in the United States may be found in the following sources: "A Quarterly Presentation of Flow of Funds . . ." 1959; Goldsmith 1958, pp. 50–55; Goldsmith & Lipsey 1963, vol. 1, pp. 27–36.)

Nonbank intermediaries may be classified in many ways. In terms of proprietorship, they may be governmental or private, and the private organizations may be stock, unincorporated, mutual, or cooperative. They may be primary, dealing with the general public, or secondary, dealing with other financial institutions. Grouped according to assets, they may be lenders principally on real estate, for example, or agricultural products or consumer durables. Grouped according to liabilities, they may borrow mainly at short term or at long term, and their obligations may or may not carry insurance benefits. They pay their creditors interest, dividends, capital gains, or indemnities. They vary in regional distribution, rate of growth, cyclical stability, degree of concentration, and tax status. Each of them reflects an opportunity for private enterprise to profit from transmission of funds between lenders and borrowers or a governmental desire to supplement private financial arrangements.

Growth in the financial system of the United States has consisted partly in proliferating types of intermediary. At the beginning of the nineteenth century, commercial banks and private insurance companies were available for the deposit and borrowing of funds. Savings banks and savings and loan associations were operating before mid-century, and by 1880 there were mortgage companies. The pace and quality of economic growth in the first two decades of the twentieth century were especially congenial to financial innovation: to this period one may credit the postal savings system, credit unions, finance companies, investment companies, and federal agencies for agricultural credit. Pension funds and various additional federal lending agencies, especially in the area of mortgage finance, were generated by the circumstances of the 1920s and 1930s. International intermediaries have been the notable innovations of the 1940s and 1950s (Goldsmith 1958, chapter 4; Kuznets 1961, pp. 304–305). It is one aspect of relative economic maturity that the pace of innovation in financial intermediaries has diminished. Existing intermediaries introduce adaptations in service which seem to provide a sufficient flow of funds at full employment and at an acceptable rate of growth in national income.

Dimensions of intermediation in the U.S. At the end of 1963, financial assets held by nonbank intermediaries amounted to one-fifth of all financial assets in the national balance sheet—to about $510,000 million in an aggregate of $2.42 billion. In terms of their portfolios, they were three-fifths larger than the monetary system. The bulk of their assets, approximately $360,000 million, was financed by indirect debt to consumer households and nonprofit organizations. This debt amounted to one-third of the financial assets in those sectors.

The distribution of financial assets among the types of nonbank intermediary is unequal. Intermediaries in the insurance and pension categories accounted for one-half of all intermediary assets at the end of 1963, savings and depositary institutions for one-third, and the remainder was widely dispersed among other categories.

Nonbank intermediaries do not grow at a uniform rate. The reason is that they sell indirect debt in specialized forms to different classes of savers, buy primary debt at different terms from different classes of investors, encounter dissimilar regulatory restraints and stimuli, and experience diverse changes in technical conditions of producing the service of intermediation. Each responds uniquely to the phases of short and long cycles in real economic development; to changes in life expectation and age distribution of the population; to variations in the price level, in the distribution of income between sectors, and in relative growth rates for various kinds of real capital. During a recent decade, 1948–1958, growth among intermediaries varied from 521 per cent for credit unions to 35 per cent for mutual savings banks (Goldsmith et al. 1963, vol. 2, pp. 114–115; see also Friend 1963, pp. 666–667; 1964, pp. 16–45).

Theory of financial intermediation. Nonbank financial intermediaries participate in four markets. They are net buyers on markets for primary securities; on markets for money balances—to be held as reserves of liquidity either voluntarily or by regulatory rule; and on markets for productive factors—labor in particular, but also capital goods and land. They are sellers on markets for their own issues of indirect debt—in such forms as savings and loan shares, savings bank deposits, and pension claims. (See Patinkin 1956.) This last market will be discussed first. (We neglect here operations by intermediaries on foreign exchange markets and the bearing of intermediation on international balances of payments.)

Markets for nonbank indirect financial assets (NIFA). Demand for NIFA, issued by nonbank intermediaries as their own indirect debt, comes mainly from consumer households. Consumers demand NIFA as a component of their personal wealth along with such other components as money balances, primary securities, business equity, housing, and durable goods. NIFA are relatively more important in the personal wealth of consumers at medium income levels than of consumers at extremes of the income distribution.

Consumers add to their portfolios of NIFA by saving, borrowing, and displacing funds from alternative assets. NIFA qualify as a superior, or luxury, good in the consumer budget.

Economists have experimented with many forms of demand function for NIFA (Brown & Friend 1964, pp. 125–128; Tobin & Brainard 1963). Demand rises with the real rate of interest paid by intermediaries relative to rates of return on other assets. It rises with permanent disposable income, and apparently it responds to intermediaries' advertising. It is depressed by risks involved in holding NIFA and increased by insurance against these risks. These are typical arguments in demand functions for NIFA, but others are relevant for particular assets. A stock market boom intensifies demand for shares in investment funds. Age distribution of consumers is significant to demand for insurance. Growth in union membership enhances demand for uninsured pension fund claims.

Demand for NIFA is confronted by conditions of supply—a supply function for individual intermediaries and for the industry. (Studies of the supply function include Hensley 1958; *Trade Association Monographs for the Commission on Money and Credit* 1962.) The supply of NIFA offered by intermediaries varies inversely with the rate of interest on NIFA. At each such rate of interest, supply tends to rise as rates of interest on the primary securities that intermediaries hold rise. It is the spread between primary (lending) rates and NIFA (borrowing) rates that creates opportunity for profit in intermediation. Since, in the long run, the primary rate tends to vary with the marginal productivity of tangible wealth, the supply of intermediation is responsive to opportunities for real investment.

Because intermediation incurs costs for wages and depreciation, its supply is depressed by increases in wage rates and in prices of capital goods and is increased by technological advance that economizes labor and capital. Increases in risk and uncertainty of investment in primary securities, which typically are at long term, and of the much more liquid NIFA debt, which is typically at short term, inhibit the supply of NIFA. Conditions of supply in intermediation are affected, perhaps more profoundly than in any other industry, by governmental intervention in the form of subsidy, special tax terms, and sundry regulatory devices. The net effect of governmental intervention in the United States has probably been to stimulate both supply and demand. The justification may be that there are external benefits of intermediation that wholly free markets would not realize.

There is a separate industry of firms supplying each variety of NIFA. These industries are imperfectly competitive, and some of them satisfy the specifications of oligopoly. Governmental restrictions on freedom of entry of new firms are accountable for some loss of competitive impulse. In addition, there is reason to suspect the existence of internal economies of scale for the intermediary firm that are not compatible with free competition. The evident imperfections of competition have led to numerous governmental restraints on the structure of the intermediary industry and its market behavior.

Taken in conjunction, the demand and supply functions for nonmonetary intermediation determine the volume of NIFA and their market rates of interest. These functions determine the spread between primary rates and NIFA rates and the gross profit to intermediation. The gross profit, adjusted principally for labor and capital costs, determines net profit, which, in relation to profit opportunities elsewhere, regulates the desired flow of equity funds into the industry. It is equity funds, in turn, which help to provide the factor of safety for NIFA that induces consumer households to invest in these assets at yields below primary rates of interest.

Markets for primary securities. Nonmonetary intermediaries are net buyers of primary securities: they acquire securities with funds that flow to them on the market for NIFA and, in much smaller volume, sell primary securities of their own, mainly equities, to finance increases in their net worth. The latter may be dropped from consideration here with the generalization that they increase in response to governmental capital requirements, to gains in intermediaries' net earnings, and to general advances in prices of common stocks.

Historically the development of intermediaries has been a necessary condition for broad and active markets in primary securities. Intermediation supports an infrastructure of security exchanges, dealers, and brokers. Reciprocally, efficient market facilities for primary securities reduce the operating costs, risks, and uncertainties of intermediaries' portfolios. (For illustrations see Basch 1964, chapter 6; Nevin 1961, chapter 4.)

By supplying attractive media for savings and by support of markets for investors' issues of primary securities, nonbank intermediation facilitates division of labor between saving and investment. One result is that primary securities accumulate in amounts that are relatively large in comparison with national income.

Aside from stimulating the organization of security markets and growth in primary securities, intermediaries influence the allocation of savings among investment opportunities and, hence, the quality of primary securities. Successful intermediation depends heavily on arbitrage between opportunities to finance investment and to acquire primary securities. From the standpoint of society, such arbitrage promotes allocative efficiency in the saving–investment process. On markets for primary securities, one manifestation of allocative efficiency is uniformity in interest rates and other terms of lending for similar securities. Intermediation works against fragmentation of security markets.

By encouraging saving, and so accelerating growth of capital, intermediation tends to reduce interest rates on primary securities. To the extent that intermediation allocates savings efficiently, it results in a capital stock of high productivity and so tends to raise interest rates on primary securities. The net effect of intermediation on interest rates, in the long run, is probably to raise them.

Efficient nonbank intermediation increases the short-run stability of rates of interest on primary securities. Each increase in primary rates first widens profit margins in intermediation and then induces increases in rates paid on NIFA. Insofar as more attractive yields on NIFA stimulate saving and divert the public's demand from money balances, the effect is to intensify the flow of funds through nonbank intermediaries toward purchase of primary securities. Conversely, short-period declines in primary rates may shrink the flow of funds toward purchase of primary securities. If intermediation does temper short-run fluctuations in primary rates, the result is a reduction in market-risk premia on primary securities. (For an alternative view see Minsky 1964.)

Markets for goods. Nonbank intermediation influences aggregate propensities to consume, the quality of consumption, and the stability of consumption. There is a dual effect on total consumption, since NIFA attract savings, while consumer credit, financed through intermediaries, facilitates consumption. Intermediation is important for the quality of consumption, partly because it changes relative costs to consumers of different classes of goods, partly also because it permits flexible adjustments in life-cycle patterns of consumption. Finally, intermediation is pertinent to temporal stability in consumption to the extent that changes in consumer stocks of NIFA and in consumer debt, as well as in yields and costs of NIFA and debt, lead to acceleration or deferral of consumer spending (Enthoven 1957–1964; [U.S.] Board of Governors . . . 1957).

Influences of intermediation can be traced through markets for goods other than consumption goods. As the savings outlet that provides the alternative to financing investment from internal sources, through direct issues of primary securities to savers, through the monetary system, and through government, nonbank intermediation participates in selecting investment opportunities and in shaping the structure of the capital stock. It is involved in allocating savings between private and governmental investment, between domestic and foreign uses. Furthermore, it is a factor in the short-run stability both of total investment and of components including housing and business inventory (Grebler & Maisel 1963).

Measurements of national income originating in nonbank intermediation are ambiguous. It may be estimated that saving by these institutions on their own account is less than 1.5 per cent of national saving in the United States, that their tangible investment is about 0.25 per cent of national investment, and that they employ about 1.5 per cent of the civilian labor force. Their impact on markets for goods and factors is mainly indirect, through the saving–investment decisions of other sectors.

Market for money. There has been intensive debate regarding the effect of growth and innovation in NIFA, and of changes in their yields, on the demand for and the supply of money. The central issue has been the degree of substitutability between NIFA and money balances in the asset portfolios of consumer households especially, but also of business firms.

If demand for money is negatively elastic to yields on NIFA, changes in these yields resulting from a monetary policy that raises (lowers) the rate of growth in the supply of money may raise (lower) growth in demand for money and so offset the intended effects of monetary policy on markets for goods, factors, and primary securities. Since substitutability of NIFA for money is not perfect, interference from NIFA with monetary policy may presumably be overcome by sufficiently large and timely adjustments in the money supply. Alternatively, interference of NIFA with monetary policy might be overcome by bringing within the orbit of monetary control those nonbank intermediaries which issue NIFA most closely resembling money.

If NIFA are near substitutes for money, tradi-

tional monetary controls can also be obstructed by responses of nonbank intermediaries. There are other implications. For example, if commercial banks must be restrained more tightly over long periods or subjected to more vigorous and volatile control for short periods because nonbank intermediaries weaken monetary discipline, there is discrimination against banks. The discrimination may be criticized on grounds of equity or because it undermines the capitalization and solvency of banks. If banks dispose of savings differently than do nonbank intermediaries, the discrimination may also be criticized for its allocative effects on the stock of capital. (The literature concerning effects of nonbank intermediation on monetary controls is very large. It includes Commission on Money and Credit 1961, pp. 78–81; Gurley & Shaw 1960, chapter 6; Johnson 1962; Great Britain, Committee on the Working of the Monetary System 1959, pp. 129–135.)

Equilibrium of the market for money, at a relatively stable price level, appears to be an important prerequisite for development of nonbank intermediation and of NIFA, even with price-escalator provisions. Inflation is a tax not only on money balances but also on the real value of NIFA as well, and correspondingly diminishes real demand for NIFA. Furthermore, inflation often concentrates savings in sectors of the community that prefer other dispositions of savings than NIFA. International data suggest that nonmonetary intermediation lags where inflation is habitual and erratic.

Integration between nations, in monetary and trade institutions and policies, has important implications for nonbank intermediation, with regard both to markets for NIFA and to intermediary portfolios of primary securities. For example, one can expect innovations in NIFA, such as Euro-currencies, and international arbitrage by intermediaries, such as investment funds, that will tend to unify markets for savings.

Regulation. Nonbank intermediation is typically subject to intensive governmental regulation and intervention. At the extreme, there is government ownership and management. Short of this limit, regulation and intervention include subsidy and other stimulants as well as various restraints on private enterprise in intermediation.

There are seven common objectives of regulation: to increase propensities to save, to guide the allocation of savings to investment, to limit short-period instability of growth, to strengthen the solvency of intermediaries, to improve intermediaries' operating efficiency, to correct the distribution of income and wealth, and to stabilize the balance of payments. (The last will not be discussed here.)

The basic technique of accelerating savings through nonbank intermediaries is to intensify demand for NIFA, relative to consumption, at given levels of national income. Rates of interest may be raised on NIFA, innovations introduced, savers' safety guaranteed. For these objectives, competition may be intensified among intermediaries, tax concessions granted to them, deposits insured, and portfolio limits relaxed.

Regulation of intermediaries is traditionally concerned with savings allocation. For the benefit of housing or, say, investment in agriculture and small business firms, regulation has provided incentives for intermediaries that guide savings to desired ends. Programs to overcome regional lags in development have included subsidized allocations of loanable funds through intermediaries. Measures against restraint of competition among intermediaries are partly concerned with allocative efficiency.

Nonbank intermediaries have contributed at times to short-period turbulence in the saving–investment process. Measures to correct their influence toward overinvestment include minimal requirements for liquidity and net worth. Measures to correct their influence toward underinvestment include guarantee of their portfolios and provision of rediscount facilities.

The solvency of intermediaries has been an objective of high priority in regulation. The costs of insolvency that have seemed to justify intensive regulation include inequity to savers, misallocation of savings, and contagious economic instability. Measures to protect solvency include net-worth requirements, supervision of operations, limits on portfolio selection, and loan insurance. There is basis for argument that regulatory preoccupation with solvency has imperiled some other objectives, such as allocative efficiency.

Operating efficiency is not often a primary objective of regulation. Its purpose is to liberate real resources for other uses, to reduce spreads between rates of interest on primary securities and rates on NIFA, and to strengthen solvency. Economic operation can be essential for the comparatively primitive forms of intermediation that are appropriate in early stages of national economic development. It has counted heavily in the growth of such intermediaries in the United States as credit unions.

Distributive considerations enter into some regulatory techniques. The purpose may be merely to prevent inequitable incidence on some social classes of gains and losses from intermediation, or it may be to change the distribution of income and wealth. The first purpose is illustrated by regulation of insurance companies' portfolios in the interest of beneficiaries, or of investment funds to limit conspiratorial gains of insiders. The second purpose is illustrated by various special credit arrangements for agriculture or war veterans or regions suffering a slow tempo of development.

These objectives of regulation have given rise, especially in the United States, to a complex apparatus of federal and state regulatory techniques administered by governmental departments, commissions, and institutions. Dissatisfaction with this apparatus has inspired intensive re-evaluation by both private and governmental bodies. The principal occasions in the United States were during the decade before World War I, during the 1930s, and in the early 1960s by the Commission on Money and Credit. There were other national investigations in the course of the 1960s: in Japan the Committee on Financial System Research; in the United Kingdom, Committee on the Working of the Monetary System; in Canada, Royal Commission on Banking and Finance.

These recent studies of regulations concerning both monetary and nonbank intermediaries had to do, in part, with irrationalities in regulatory agencies and techniques. They were also directed to goals of regulation and, for the first time, to possible benefits of applying a general theory and compatible techniques to regulation of various classes of intermediaries. There is no precedent for their attempts to define optimality in the financial superstructure of capitalism. They did not reach common conclusions on either principles or techniques of regulation.

International differences.   There is notable diversity of nonbank intermediation between countries. First, NIFA per capita vary widely (Kuznets 1955; Goldsmith 1955). This is explained partly by differences in real income and wealth per capita, since income and wealth elasticities of demand for NIFA are high. It is explained, too, by differences in centralization of decisions to save and invest: economic centralism is not a fertile environment for nonbank intermediation. Again, NIFA appear to be high, relative to income, where price inflation has been modest and low where inflation has been rapid, chronic, and erratic. Nonbank intermediaries are relatively strong where the monetary system does not practice broad diversification of portfolios and indirect debt, where public debt is not finely differentiated, and where social security is not financed mainly from current government revenues. The evidence is that non-bank intermediation has been retarded by social instability and defects of legal structure. There are also imponderables of social framework, social mobility, and personal motivation that affect the pace of intermediation. Governmental assistance and foreign aid figure prominently in growth of NIFA. Finally, development in intermediation varies between countries according to the accessibility and quality of complementary institutions. All of these and other factors relating to international differences can be classified according to their effects on conditions of demand and supply for NIFA.

The quality as well as the scale of nonbank intermediation varies internationally. There is variation in primary securities acquired by intermediaries, in NIFA, and in institutional structure. One observes rough correspondence of qualitative with quantitative development: such intermediaries as investment funds appear where real income per capita is high; small cooperatives for agricultural credit, where income is lower. Still, the quality of intermediation is not uniform between countries at comparable stages of economic development. Differences in composition of wealth and output are partly responsible, and the form of political organization is pertinent. The distribution of income by level of income is another factor, as is the distribution of population by age and degree of urbanization. Within the orbit of capitalism, the social choice between alternative methods of mobilizing and allocating savings deeply affects the environment of nonbank intermediation. One can trace in the quality of intermediation the unique historical experience of each society that has given momentum to some intermediaries rather than others; the mores and traditions that condition savers for or against lotteries, perhaps, and for or against concentrations of financial power; the mobility of ownership in enterprise; and the geographic extent of the economic system. From differences in savers' tastes to differences in technological conditions of intermediation and patterns of governmental intervention, there are numerous factors to explain the international diversity in intermediation. One may infer that optimal development of intermediation will have strikingly indigenous characteristics.

E. S. SHAW

[*See also* BANKING; BANKING, CENTRAL; MONEY.]

BIBLIOGRAPHY

ALHADEFF, DAVID A. 1960 Credit Controls and Financial Intermediaries. *American Economic Review* 50:655–671.

BASCH, ANTONIN 1964 *Financing Economic Development.* New York: Macmillan.

BIRNBAUM, EUGENE A. 1958 The Growth of Financial Intermediaries as a Factor in the Effectiveness of Monetary Policy. International Monetary Fund, *Staff Papers* 6:384–426.

BROWN, MURRAY; and FRIEND, IRWIN 1964 An Econometric Model of the United States With Special Reference to the Financial Sector. Pages 117–172 in Irwin Friend, Hyman P. Minsky, and Victor L. Andrews (editors), *Private Capital Markets.* Published for the Commission on Money and Credit. Englewood Cliffs, N.J.: Prentice-Hall.

BRUNNER, KARL; and MELTZER, ALLAN H. 1963 The Place of Financial Intermediaries in the Transmission of Monetary Policy. *American Economic Review* 53, no. 2:372–382.

CANADA, ROYAL COMMISSION ON BANKING AND FINANCE 1964 *Report.* Ottawa: Queen's Printer and Controller of Stationery.

COMMISSION ON MONEY AND CREDIT 1961 *Money and Credit: Their Influence on Jobs, Prices, and Growth.* Englewood Cliffs, N.J.: Prentice-Hall.

ENTHOVEN, ALAIN C. 1957–1964 The Growth of Instalment Credit and the Future of Prosperity. *American Economic Review* 47:913–929.

ETTIN, EDWARD C. 1963 The Development of American Financial Intermediaries. *Quarterly Review of Economics and Business* 3:51–69.

FEIGE, EDGAR L. 1964 *The Demand for Liquid Assets: A Temporal Cross-section Analysis.* Englewood Cliffs, N.J.: Prentice-Hall.

FRIEND, IRWIN (1963) 1964 Determinants of the Volume and Composition of Saving With Special Reference to the Influence of Monetary Policy. Pages 649–688 in Commission on Money and Credit, *Impacts of Monetary Policy.* Englewood Cliffs, N.J.: Prentice-Hall.

FRIEND, IRWIN 1964 The Effects of Monetary Policies on Nonmonetary Financial Institutions and Capital Markets. Pages 1–116 in Irwin Friend, Hyman P. Minsky, and Victor L. Andrews (editors), *Private Capital Markets.* Published for the Commission on Money and Credit. Englewood Cliffs, N.J.: Prentice-Hall.

GIES, THOMAS C.; MAYER, THOMAS; and ETTIN, EDWARD C. 1963 Portfolio Regulations and Policies of Financial Intermediaries. Pages 157–264 in *Private Financial Institutions.* Englewood Cliffs, N.J.: Prentice-Hall.

GOLDSMITH, RAYMOND W. 1955 Financial Structure and Economic Growth in Advanced Countries: An Experiment in Comparative Financial Morphology. Pages 113–167 in Universities–National Bureau Committee for Economic Research, *Capital Formation and Economic Growth.* Part 1: Sources and Channels of Finance in Capitalist Countries. Princeton Univ. Press. → Includes eight pages of comment by Edward S. Shaw and a reply by Raymond W. Goldsmith.

GOLDSMITH, RAYMOND W. 1955–1956 *A Study of Saving in the United States.* 3 vols. Princeton Univ. Press.

GOLDSMITH, RAYMOND W. 1958 *Financial Intermediaries in the American Economy Since 1900.* National Bureau of Economic Research, Studies in Capital Formation and Financing, No. 3. Princeton Univ. Press.

GOLDSMITH, RAYMOND W.; and LIPSEY, ROBERT E. 1963 *Studies in the National Balance Sheet of the United States.* 2 vols. National Bureau of Economic Research, Studies in Capital Formation and Financing, Vol. 11. Princeton Univ. Press. → The second volume was published under the joint authorship of Raymond W. Goldsmith, Robert E. Lipsey, and Morris Mendelson.

GREAT BRITAIN, COMMITTEE ON THE WORKING OF THE MONETARY SYSTEM 1959 *Report.* Papers by Command, Cmnd. 827. London: H.M. Stationery Office. → Commonly known as the Radcliffe Report.

GREAT BRITAIN, COMMITTEE ON THE WORKING OF THE MONETARY SYSTEM 1960 *Principal Memoranda of Evidence.* 3 vols. London: H.M. Stationery Office.

GREBLER, LEO; and MAISEL, SHERMAN J. (1963) 1964 Determinants of Residential Construction: A Review of Present Knowledge. Pages 475–620 in Commission on Money and Credit, *Impacts of Monetary Policy.* Englewood Cliffs, N.J.: Prentice-Hall.

GURLEY, JOHN G.; and SHAW, E. S. 1955 Financial Aspects of Economic Development. *American Economic Review* 45:515–538.

GURLEY, JOHN G.; and SHAW, E. S. 1956 Financial Intermediaries and the Saving–Investment Process. *Journal of Finance* 11:257–276.

GURLEY, JOHN G.; and SHAW, E. S. 1960 *Money in a Theory of Finance.* With a mathematical appendix by Alain C. Enthoven. Washington: Brookings Institution.

HARBRECHT, PAUL P. 1959 *Pension Funds and Economic Power.* New York: Twentieth Century Fund.

HENSLEY, R. J. 1958 Economies of Scale in Financial Enterprise. *Journal of Political Economy* 66:389–398.

JOHNSON, H. G. 1962 Monetary Theory and Policy. *American Economic Review* 52:335–384.

KHUSRO, A. M. 1957 Liquidity Preference in India. *Indian Economic Review* 3, no. 3:24–40.

KUZNETS, SIMON 1955 International Differences in Capital Formation and Financing. Pages 19–111 in Universities–National Bureau Committee for Economic Research, *Capital Formation and Economic Growth.* Part 1: Sources and Channels of Finance in Capitalist Countries. Princeton Univ. Press.

KUZNETS, SIMON 1961 *Capital in the American Economy: Its Formation and Financing.* National Bureau of Economic Research, Studies in Capital Formation and Financing, No. 9. Princeton Univ. Press.

MINSKY, HYMAN P. 1964 Financial Crisis, Financial Systems, and the Performance of the Economy. Pages 173–380 in Irwin Friend, Hyman P. Minsky, and Victor L. Andrews (editors), *Private Capital Markets.* Published for the Commission on Money and Credit. Englewood Cliffs, N.J.: Prentice-Hall.

NEVIN, EDWARD 1961 *Capital Funds in Underdeveloped Countries: The Role of Financial Institutions.* London: Macmillan; New York: St. Martins.

NIHON GINKŌ (BANK OF JAPAN) 1959 *Outline of the Financial System in Japan.* 3d rev. ed. Tokyo: The Bank.

OTT, DAVID J. 1961 The Financial Development of Japan. *Journal of Political Economy* 69:122–141.

PAAUW, DOUGLAS S. 1960 *Financing Economic Development: The Indonesian Case.* Glencoe, Ill.: Free Press.

PATINKIN, DON (1956) 1965 *Money, Interest, and Prices: An Integration of Monetary and Value Theory.* 2d ed. New York: Harper.

PATINKIN, DON 1961 Financial Intermediaries and the Logical Structure of Monetary Theory. *American Economic Review* 51:95–116.

A Quarterly Presentation of Flow of Funds, Savings, and Investment. 1959 *Federal Reserve Bulletin* 45:828–859.

SMITH, WARREN L. 1959 Financial Intermediaries and Monetary Controls. *Quarterly Journal of Economics* 73:533–553.

THORN, RICHARD S. 1958 Nonbank Financial Intermediaries, Credit Expansions, and Monetary Policy. International Monetary Fund, *Staff Papers* 6:369–383.

TOBIN, JAMES; and BRAINARD, WILLIAM C. 1963 Financial Intermediaries and the Effectiveness of Monetary Controls. *American Economic Review* 53, no. 2:383–400.

Trade Association Monographs for the Commission on Money and Credit. 1962 Englewood Cliffs, N.J.: Prentice-Hall. → Monographs include American Mutual Insurance Alliance, *Property and Casualty Insurance Companies: Their Role as Financial Intermediaries;* Miles L. Colean, *Mortgage Companies: Their Place in the Financial Structure;* Investment Company Institute, *Management Investment Companies;* Leon T. Kendall, *The Savings and Loan Business: Its Purposes, Functions, and Economic Justification;* Life Insurance Association of America, *Life Insurance Companies as Financial Institutions;* National Association of Mutual Savings Banks, *Mutual Savings Banking: Basic Characteristics and Role in the National Economy;* and National Consumer Finance Association, *The Consumer Finance Industry.*

[U.S.] BOARD OF GOVERNORS OF THE FEDERAL RESERVE SYSTEM 1957 *Consumer Installment Credit.* 4 parts in 3 vols. Washington: Government Printing Office. → See especially Part 2.

U.S. COMMITTEE ON FINANCIAL INSTITUTIONS 1963 *Report to the President of the United States.* Washington: Government Printing Office.

U.S. CONGRESS, HOUSE, COMMITTEE ON BANKING AND CURRENCY, SUBCOMMITTEE ON DOMESTIC FINANCE 1963 *Comparative Regulations of Financial Institutions.* Washington: Government Printing Office.

FINANCING, POLITICAL
See POLITICAL FINANCING.

FINE ARTS

I
ART AND SOCIETY

Societies of all kinds and of all periods have given birth to what can today be classified as art, but there exist no significant propositions as to the nature of the relationship between particular social systems and the kinds of art that develop under them. The problem was first seriously posed during the Enlightenment, when philosophers arguing in favor of differing political organizations suggested that desirable art would necessarily follow desirable government. But the view of Shaftesbury and others that freedom was a prerequisite of great art was hardly borne out either by the previous or subsequent history of England, where architecture, sculpture, and painting, although reaching a higher peak than they had for some centuries, were hardly superior to those engendered under despotic regimes in Italy, France, and central Europe.

In more recent years the problem has been raised in more sophisticated terms: quality, it is admitted, may be capricious in its incidence, but style will necessarily be governed by fundamental social laws. E. H. Gombrich has demonstrated the fallacies that usually underlie such reasoning [see STYLE], but it will in any case be impossible to make any authoritative large-scale statements about the relationship of art to society until the very few studies of particular societies and their arts have been greatly increased in number, scope, and depth. History remains our only source of guidance.

The artist in history

Research into the status of artists at different periods, while of interest in itself, does not seem to throw much light on the nature or quality of the art produced, nor does it even give an indication of the esteem in which art has been held. Moreover, for many societies and epochs the data are extremely scanty.

Greece. In Greece between the sixth and third centuries B.C. a flowering of the arts so spectacular that it influenced all subsequent history appears to have been almost totally neglected by the innumerable writers of genius who lived through it. However, outlines of the artists' lives and a few anecdotes of their personalities must have been recorded, because later historians such as Pliny evidently drew on lost sources of this kind. But nowhere in classical Greek literature is there anything to suggest that individual artists were held in serious consideration, and by inference we can assume that they were considered as being little superior to craftsmen. This, however, certainly does not imply that the Greeks were indifferent to the masterpieces that were produced: indeed, Plutarch points out in a much-quoted phrase (in *Pericles*) that "no generous youth, from seeing the Zeus at Olympia or the Hera at Argos, longs to be Phidias or Polyclitus, for it does not of necessity follow that if the work delights you with grace, the one who wrought it is worthy of your esteem."

It is noteworthy that in all the discussions that took place during the golden age on the nature of inspiration, examples were never chosen from among sculptors or painters, and it is clear that although artists in classical times could be either slave or free, the mere association of their work with manual labor was enough to prevent their being highly esteemed. For this reason, which was to recur later in the Middle Ages, an architect stood a greater chance of earning renown than a painter or sculptor, for, when successful, he would be considered more as an entrepreneur than a manual laborer. However, as frequently occurs in the social history of the arts, sufficient skill could on occasion enable its possessor to overcome this indifference to the individual artist and defy even the most rigid conventions. There are, for instance, records indicating that as early as the last quarter of the sixth century B.C., "several potters . . . were able to erect impressive dedications on the Acropolis" (Cook 1960, p. 272), and it is also well known that at much the same time we begin to find frequent examples of signed work.

During the Hellenistic period the social status of the artist certainly improved, and legends about the relations between Alexander the Great and Apelles, which are recorded by Pliny, indicate at the very least an ideal that was no longer held to be absurd—and incidentally set a highly important precedent for subsequent royal patronage. We are, however, still very largely ignorant not only about the status of the artist in antiquity but also about the nature of his training and mode of life generally, although we do find hints of exhibitions, dealers, and other features of the artistic scene that later became commonplace. If we are entitled to assume, as seems probable, that the artist in classical antiquity was considered to be little more than a craftsman, it remains the more surprising that the development of sculpture and painting was so extraordinarily striking. For it is often held that artistic change is encouraged by the notion of the artist's individuality, whereas, almost by definition, the craftsman is employed exclusively to satisfy public demand.

Rome. For Roman times, too, the evidence is scattered, fragmentary, and conflicting. It seems clear that to Cato and those who thought like him art was something essentially foreign—even degrading—and this view must clearly have been reflected in their opinion of the artists themselves. On the other hand, archeological research and literary references illustrate obviously enough the admiration felt for Greek sculpture, and Pliny's stories of the Greek artists must surely have suggested to many that the superior ones among them could achieve recognition far higher than that likely to have been granted to mere craftsmen. If, however, we risk the premise that some acknowledgment of the artist as an individual with a will of his own, who does not merely respond to the pressures of the market, is at least a likely prerequisite of adventurous art, then the highly derivative nature of Roman sculpture (and also the extremely conservative tendencies of the ancient Egyptians) might imply that the position of the artist was a very lowly one. But the dangers of such a circular argument are too great to make it worth pursuing. Certainly the Romans never included the visual arts among the *artes liberales*, and this, together with the physical destruction and chaos that followed the collapse of the Western Empire, proved to be of decisive importance for the Middle Ages.

Middle Ages. The state of our researches into the artist's position in medieval times must reinforce our skepticism about any broad-based conclusions to be drawn from antiquity. For here too the arts were almost completely ignored by serious writers. However, a considerable number of scattered documents—of the very kind which have not survived from ancient Greece or Rome—can still be traced, and these show us how complex the situation was. Their investigation has recently been undertaken by Andrew Martindale (1966). Since his researches constitute by far the most valuable contribution that has yet been made to the subject, they have been heavily drawn upon in the following discussion.

Enough documentation certainly survives to prove what was only conjecture in any discussion of earlier periods: until the fifteenth century most artists were generally considered superior craftsmen. In 1323, for instance, a Paris scholar listed among "those craftsmen working with their hands" not only "the most ingenious makers of all sorts of image, whether contrived in sculpture or in painting or in relief" but also "the most cunning constructors of instruments of war" and the "makers of bread." Moreover, from tax returns and other sources we can see that artists, like other craftsmen, tended to live together in communities in particular parishes and that they made no distinction between work that would now be considered mechanical, such as decorating saddles (in London the painters' guild was a branch of the saddlers'), and painting devotional images. The artist was incorporated into a guild, and his training followed the usual practice by which, as a youth of about 12, he would enter a master's shop as an apprentice. There he would help out and familiarize himself with technical processes, to emerge after some years as a journeyman, before finally becoming an independent master able to engage apprentices of his own. Thus Lorenzo

Ghiberti, after winning in 1403 the competition for the second set of bronze doors for the baptistery of San Giovanni in Florence (this was a means of attracting artists which was always to remain popular with committees), was in a position to employ as many as 21 apprentices a few years later. The guilds also served other purposes, some of which, such as the maintenance of a certain status and ritual dignity, have been carried on by the academies into our own day. In general, however, their concern was essentially with more practical matters, above all, to protect both the artist and his client from fraud.

But a too-uniform pattern must not be read into the Middle Ages, and many of the striking developments that occurred in Renaissance Italy were already present in embryo. Then, as later, the law of supply and demand operated powerfully in favor of change. It is true, as Martindale stresses, that a king might bring painters into his household for reasons that had little to do with their professional ability and treat them, once there, with scant respect or reward—he instances a "Jack of St. Albans," who was required to dance on a table, and Giotto, whose gift of repartee seems to have been at least as highly prized as his art; yet it is hard to believe as he does that such appointments did nothing to raise the status of painting as an occupation (all our experience of psychology surely suggests the contrary). Martindale himself implies that the occasional institution of the post of "town painter" (a practice adopted, above all, in Venice) may well have been inspired by imitation of such royal gestures. Competition between towns was also of the greatest importance. The terms of Giotto's nomination in 1334 as city architect of Florence ("architect"—though he had made his name as a painter) will serve as an example:

As in the whole world there is to be found none better qualified . . . than Master Giotto di Bondone, the painter of Florence, he shall therefore be named in his native city as Magnus Magister and publicly regarded as such, so that he may have occasion to abide here; for by his presence many can have the advantage of his wisdom and learning, and the city shall gain no small honour because of him.

These terms show what lip service burghers were prepared to pay to the arts—and artists—for enhancing their own reputations (and doing down a rival city).

It is true that Italy in general and Florence in particular were exceptional in paying such honors, but the wording of the appointment reminds us that the rivalry between secular and religious communities, towns and courts, and one city and another could play as significant a part in elevating the position of the artist as could the rivalries between individual patrons in later years. Certainly the artists often thought of themselves as much more than mere craftsmen, as can be seen from the very many self-laudatory inscriptions that they put on their own works: we find examples of these as early as 1100.

Renaissance. The Renaissance did, of course, bring great changes in the status of the artist—one could instance a fragment of a letter from Prince Frederico Gonzaga, who was trying to get hold of any example of Michelangelo's

never-sufficiently-to-be-praised work . . . sculpture or painting, as he chooses, we do not mind which it is as long as it is by him . . . at least a drawing, if it is well done in charcoal. . . . And you must tell him that his work will be placed in a most honourable position, and that we shall feel eternal gratitude towards him, and that we shall never forget such a special favour, and will always be ready to do anything we possibly can to give him pleasure. (quoted in Luzio 1913, pp. 246–247)

But it must always be remembered that Michelangelo's position was a wholly exceptional one and that many of the customs of the Middle Ages were carried on well after his death. However, the letter does point up the new role that had been assumed ever since the fifteenth century by secular patrons in Burgundy, Italy, and elsewhere.

The early humanists who did so much to raise the value of art seem themselves to have been more interested in the remains of antiquity than in contemporary painting or sculpture, but by the middle of the fifteenth century a number of rulers were aware of the possibilities of private patronage as distinguished from the traditional construction and decoration of public buildings. And toward the end of the century Lorenzo de' Medici, whose role as an art lover has been much exaggerated, did anticipate the modern practice of advertising abroad the supremacy of his country's artists in order to enhance its prestige. Other collectors all over Italy, and soon all over Europe, acquired contemporary works of art, which were then evidently kept accessible to other artists and connoisseurs. From these princely collections sprang most of the great national museums, following the example of Anna Maria Ludovica, the last of the Medici, who in 1743 left the accumulated family treasures to the city of Florence. Elsewhere, beheading or exile usually proved a more effective means of acquiring art treasures.

Nonetheless, appreciation of art, and even admiration for the artist, could go hand in hand with habits formed in earlier ages. Well into the seventeenth century, for example, we come across patrons insisting on the use of specified colors in the canvases painted for them, and the nature of commissions generally shows how little individuality was allowed to the artist and how much he was still treated as a craftsman. It was usual for a patron when ordering a picture to pay for the stretcher and the priming, and frequently also the canvas and some of the more expensive colors. He would then indicate the dimensions, insist on a specific time limit for its completion, and make arrangements about the subject matter. As these specifications must have usually taken the form of spoken agreements, it is difficult for us to gauge how strictly they were enforced; yet the survival of preliminary drawings and, later, of painted oil sketches can occasionally give us an idea of any changes required. Most significant of all in this context is the method of payment. The price of the picture was decided in advance—according to a seventeenth-century Italian author, this could be done by finding out how long the work would take and estimating what the painter's daily earnings should be "by comparison with the pay of a craftsman engaged in similar work." A proportion of this was paid at once, and further sums were paid at different stages in its progress, ending, on completion, with the final settlement, to which would be added a bonus. This bonus was the only allowance made for the vagaries of independence. Further indications of the artist's status (and perhaps of the very nature of artistic creativity) can be deduced from the fact that in certain cities, notably Venice, it was a custom until the end of the eighteenth century for artists to work together in families. All this should be borne in mind when the "individualism" of Renaissance artists is being assessed.

In Italy especially, artists were keenly preoccupied with their place in society throughout the fifteenth century, and innumerable arguments were produced to establish their claim to be considered wholly superior to craftsmen. Particular attention was concentrated on the "intellectual" as opposed to the "manual" aspects of their work. Leonardo, whose respect for antiquity led him to the erroneous conclusion that painting had then been one of the liberal arts, only to be "driven out" at a later date, stressed above all the painter's need to have a thorough knowledge of mathematics. It is through instances such as this that we can probably see most clearly how a study of social pressures on the artist can sometimes help us to understand the nature of his art. The Renaissance stressed imagination and science at the expense of the faithful portrayal of reality, and categories of subject matter were tentatively drawn up and later codified to put these ideas into effect, with "history painting" at the top of the list and "genre" at the bottom.

The social status of artists was largely determined by their choice of subject matter until well into the nineteenth century. At the same time, the guilds, which had once been of such service to the artist, were now considered degrading to him through their association with other crafts, and their dissolution was gradually achieved not so much by theoretical arguments as by the practice, adopted first by sovereigns and then by private citizens, of employing artists in defiance of all established traditions. But the process was a slow one, and into the seventeenth and even the eighteenth century the guilds continued to play a significant, if increasingly marginal, part in the life of artistic communities in Italy, France, and elsewhere; nor was the distinction between "arts" and "crafts" made final before the French Revolution.

The rise of the modern artist

The decay of the guilds has sometimes been held responsible not only for the "individualism" and enormous increase in the speed of artistic change that characterize the Renaissance but also for the emergence of the "neurotic" artist so much associated with the early and mid-sixteenth century— and indeed with later times. The force of this argument would be much increased were it possible to conduct any serious research into the state of mind of artists in earlier times. What is certain, however, is that as the guilds decayed, new associations arose that took their place and assumed some of the same functions (Pevsner 1940).

Academies. The Accademia dei Virtuosi al Pantheon, founded in Rome in 1543, was concerned with the same sort of charitable works that had been carried out by medieval guilds. The Accademia del Disegno, established in Florence in 1563, had the grand duke of Tuscany and Michelangelo as its first copresidents (the juxtaposition itself is revealing). While it was intended primarily to promote the newly won status of artists, one of its aims was teaching young men to maintain a high standard of art—but significantly, the instruction was more in the realm of general education than in the technical field, which had been the aim of the earlier guilds.

Dealers. Other features of the present situation first began to emerge during the sixteenth and seventeenth centuries. The enormous reputation of Italian art attracted the attention of collectors else-where in Europe who, as they were unable to travel themselves, either had to summon particular artists to their courts or mansions or, when this was impossible, to rely on dealers and international agents. Hitherto, such men, who had been operating ever since the Middle Ages, had included works of art among innumerable other commodities. But now they began to assume much greater importance, as can be seen by studying the career of Jacopo Strada (immortalized in a magnificent portrait by Titian), who supplied pictures and antiques to the German courts.

Venice was the most commercialized of Italian cities, and it is there that we find in the person of Aretino the prototype for so many dubious figures familiar since his day—the man who is at once artistic adviser to the great (he received a gold chain from François i), dealer, and collector (in the pursuit of which activity he tried to blackmail Michelangelo). In general, however, dealers in contemporary art played a relatively small role in Italy and confined their often extortionary attentions to young painters who had as yet had no chance of finding patrons directly or to those who suffered during the many financial crises that upset what was always a precarious economic situation. It was in the north, where both courtly patronage and contempt for trade were of much less importance than in Italy, that art dealing first assumed really significant proportions. In sixteenth-century Antwerp and, much more so, in seventeenth-century Amsterdam artists often dealt with middlemen who sometimes—as is the modern practice—paid them a regular allowance in return for their entire output. This breakup in the direct relationship between patron and artist and the consequent "rationalization" of the market obviously played its part in encouraging that specialization of subject matter—flowers, genre, portraiture, etc.—for which Dutch artists were particularly renowned.

Exhibitions. It is in the north too that we can find the origins of the modern picture exhibition. During the later Middle Ages these had been frequently associated with religious festivals at which artists and other craftsmen had shown their wares, but such occasions (which continued until a much later period) belong more to the history of commerce than to the history of art. By the mid-sixteenth century, however, exhibitions were organized by the artists' guilds in Antwerp, and some kinds of formal arrangements had come into being. Meanwhile, another tradition of almost equal importance was slowly beginning to develop in Italy, whereby churches and their cloisters were decorated with pictures on particular saints' days. At first these occasions had no commercial purpose whatsoever and were designed, for instance, by the Virtuosi al Pantheon, purely as an act of homage to a patron saint. By the early seventeenth century, however, artists had seen the possibilities for self-advancement that were inherent in the custom and were anxious to display their pictures on the various opportunities available each year—even though there was as yet still no question of selling them. Nor were there any catalogues or other regular promotional procedures.

The Paris salon. By far the most important step in the development of the modern exhibition was taken in Paris in 1667, when for the first time, what was intended to be an annual *salon* was organized for its members in the Louvre by the Académie Royale, the most authoritative of the early academies. Exhibitions took place thereafter at irregular intervals, although they were well established by the second quarter of the eighteenth century, and printed catalogues were sold. For the first time, the general public, as opposed to a highly restricted circle of the rich and powerful, had the opportunity to see current production without having to crane their necks in dark churches or wheedle their way into the palaces of the aristocracy. As an inevitable result the artist could appeal to a wider circle than ever before, the much-debated phenomenon of "bourgeois taste" began to make itself seriously felt, and criticism sprang into being.

Art criticism. Criticism had hitherto been confined to historians and theorists, usually arguing from basic principles, and to amateur poets, who were likely to write laudatory sonnets about works they particularly admired. It had been bedeviled by the problem of whether a person who was not a practicing artist was in a position to make any useful comments, and in any case, it had only rarely dealt with new works. Yet critics could prove to be very influential. Often the critic, who was never in any sense a professional, served as adviser to the more important patrons. Thus G. P. Bellori, the most prominent critic of the seventeenth century, whose idealizing theories profoundly affected his own and all future generations, worked for Queen Christina of Sweden and for the popes; and Winckelmann, his even more important successor in the eighteenth century, was employed by Cardinal Albani.

In any case, such great theorists, historians, and scholars belong to a wholly different class from the pamphleteers who in 1738 began—much to the justified indignation of the artists—to review the salons. Their tone was often low and scurrilous, but the popularity of their work can be gauged from the fact that there were 2 written criticisms in 1738, 10 in 1773, and 28 ten years later. While most of their articles are now forgotten, they are of importance for the historian of art because they anticipate later writers who reached the far larger and more ignorant publics of the nineteenth and twentieth centuries and because they include one genius, Diderot.

Connoisseurs. One other extremely important phenomenon occurred during the period under consideration: the arrival on the scene of the *connoisseur*, the "man of taste," often holding little political power and of relatively small means but deeply concerned with the arts. He was able to exert considerable influence, particularly on artists whose talents were not easily adaptable to official commissions likely to be offered by great princes or clerics. Such a man in seventeenth-century Rome was Cassiano dal Pozzo, who employed Poussin for many years, or Pierre Crozat (admittedly of infinitely greater wealth), who nourished the very unusual genius of Watteau. Indeed, many of the most beautiful houses, pictures, and statues of the eighteenth century were produced for such individuals, who, being far removed from the court or church, proved to be extremely rewarding patrons—and friends.

By the end of the eighteenth century many of the institutions associated with today's artistic scene were already in being: the private collector, the dealer, the exhibition, the critic, and even the museum of modern art (in the form of state purchases, in France especially, of promising new works). Huge fortunes could be earned—Sir Joshua Reynolds left £100,000 on his death in 1792—and huge reputations gained (Reitlinger 1961).

The ideology of genius. It cannot be denied that the artist's situation has changed radically since the late eighteenth century. Once again the main cause must be attributed to a new conception of the artist's status. The idea of wayward "genius" and "inspiration," which had been confined by the ancients to poets and thinkers, was extended during the Renaissance to artists—at first rather tentatively and then with growing assurance. The towering achievements of Michelangelo and his strange, austere character, notable for its *terribiltà*, were, more than any theoretical writing, responsible for the acceptance of this concept. In the sixteenth century Benvenuto Cellini implied that artists were entitled to live above the law, and in the seventeenth Salvator Rosa claimed to be unable to paint unless "carried away by the transports of enthusiasm." He refused to accept the traditional advance payment for commissioned pictures, claiming he could not know when a painting would be finished.

By the seventeenth century it was a commonplace that artists were likely to have difficult characters, at the very least, and that this might even be a prerequisite of their talent—this despite the strenuous efforts of nearly all the leading artists of the day to conform to established patterns of social behavior so as to raise their status.

In the eighteenth century William Blake was only one among many who denied that art could be taught—an assumption underlying the many new academies that had been founded all over Europe to improve standards of design—and soon afterward Goya claimed for the artist the right to look to his own fantasies rather than to the outer world for the subject matter of his art. It is, however, exceedingly important to stress that scarcely one, if any, of the serious artists of the nineteenth century ever put into practice the vast claims that had been made for the rights of genius by their predecessors and encouraged by the German *Sturm und Drang*.

Nonetheless, nearly all of them did maintain that where artist and public conflicted, it was the artist's moral duty to be true to himself rather than to his patrons. This was a stand that had hitherto been possible only for the very great, whose reputations were already assured and whose "difficult" works could therefore be taken on trust even when they were not fully understood. But this change of attitude occurred when, because of the increased birth rate and the urbanization that had been stimulated by the industrial revolution, a much bigger and presumably rather different public began to have the opportunities to see, and then to buy, modern art. Unfortunately, not even the minimum basic research into this change of patronage from a "cultivated aristocracy" to a *nouveau-riche, ignorant bourgeoisie*" has yet been undertaken. The general validity of this traditional view will merely have to be assumed.

Art and politics. Two other important new developments took place at this time, about which we can be much more certain. First, there was the great politicization of life that occurred as a result of the French Revolution. Artists had occasionally played a part in the important issues of their day —Tilman Riemenschneider had suffered torture for his support of the Peasants' Revolt of 1525, Lucas Cranach had strongly backed the Reformation, Michelangelo had helped to defend Florence against the Medici in 1527, and so on—but never before had their styles, as opposed to their occasional subject matter, been associated with political views. In the eighteenth century, it is true, some writers—notably Diderot—had tried to identify certain artists with certain social and political causes (again, as in the case of John Baptiste Greuze,

usually on the basis of subject matter), but their lack of success had been total. And those who see in the classicism of David some sort of bourgeois opposition to court circles are merely projecting into the past what would never have been suspected—by him or his patrons—before 1789. Nonetheless, David's career does mark a watershed. Actively engaged in politics himself (and always, until his last years in exile, on the winning side, whichever it was), he initiated a great stylistic revolution that was inevitably confused with political revolution. Thereafter, art and politics became inextricably confused, so that in 1825 we can find the writer Louis Vitet exclaiming, "Le goût en France attend son 14 Juillet" (quoted in Grate 1959, p. 17), although in fact he was calling for an end to Davidian classicism in the name of that painterly romanticism whose leading exponent was Delacroix, soon to become a convinced reactionary!

Public galleries. The other important innovation was the widespread inauguration of public art galleries, above all, the Louvre in 1793 and in 1824 the National Gallery in London. They kept on permanent view collections of old masters, often dimmed by yellowing varnish, as a sort of standing reproach to any artistic change—this danger had been anticipated by Constable, one of the first to suffer in this way, and countless innovators could have echoed his fear that "the manufacturers are made the criterions of perfection, instead of nature." This was particularly ironic because most public art galleries had been founded not only because of the general belief of the Enlightenment that art could improve the quality of civilization and help to "soften manners," but above all, because it was hoped that galleries, like the academies, would benefit living artists: the Louvre was at first opened only to artists on seven out of every ten days.

The artist and the bourgeoisie

A new conception of the artist, of "ignorant" public opinion, and of the politicization of all culture (so that every new step, previously welcomed, was now looked upon as potentially subversive by a public that dreaded above all else a new social upheaval)—all these factors played a vital and often tragic role in the history of nineteenth-century art, especially as the century drew to a close. In almost every country in Europe, but particularly in France, an "official art," sponsored by the principal dealers, the academies, and the richer collectors, confronted those painters, sculptors, and, later, architects whom today we look upon as the finest artists of their times. Controversy centered particularly (but not only) on the "lack of finish" characteristic of nearly all that vital art which was trying to break away from the formulas imposed by David and his school—formulas which were clung to with savage and paradoxical obstinacy by those very academies that he had wanted to abolish. There is ample evidence to show that lack of finish was equated with excessive ease and superficiality, and the now familiar charge, usually made in the presence of great and unfamiliar pictures, that "my little daughter aged ten can paint better than that" is first to be found early in the nineteenth century. More damaging to adventurous artists than public scorn was the hostility of their conservative colleagues, for no mechanism for showing their work had yet replaced the salon or academy exhibitions. In France the organization of such exhibitions was until 1880 under the direct control of the government.

In the earlier part of the century royal or other patrons were sometimes sufficiently powerful to ignore the pressures of the academy, and Delacroix received important public commissions long before he was grudgingly admitted to the Institut de France in 1857, after his eighth application. Later this dichotomy tended to disappear, and more and more artists found themselves excluded from the *salons* (and hence public attention) by restrictive juries. Unsuccessful efforts were made to organize independent exhibitions, and some artists, such as Courbet and Manet, followed an eighteenth-century precedent set by Greuze and others and showed their work privately. The Revolution of 1848 brought a "free" exhibition, Napoleon III organized the Salon des Refusés in 1863, and a group of artists (later to be called the impressionists) showed their works together in 1874 and thereafter at irregular intervals until 1886. Above all, the year 1884 saw the first Salon des Indépendants—a direct rival at last to the official exhibition—which did away with the jury system altogether.

Meanwhile the *salon* itself was beginning to break down, at first under the sheer weight of numbers (White & White 1965) and then, in 1890, because of a split due more to personal quarrels than to any conflict of principle. Gradually, independent dealers began to take over the function of sponsoring modern art, although how important official backing remained can be seen from the fact that in 1900, when he was already the most famous artist in France and possibly in the world, Auguste Rodin said that unless he was successful at the Great Exhibition of that year, he would have to enter the Institut, "parce que c'est à *eux* seuls que vont les grandes commandes."

Dealers as patrons.   The dealers who now came to the fore were very different from any that had

been seen hitherto. According to Durand-Ruel, the most conspicuous of them, a mature picture dealer should be at the same time an enlightened patron ready, if necessary, to sacrifice his immediate interests to his artistic convictions and a man who would rather fight against the speculators than associate with their interests (Venturi 1939, vol. 1, p. 17). He himself is of additional interest because, while supporting the impressionists at a time when they were looked upon as dangerous revolutionaries —the potential instigators of a new Commune—he remained a staunch reactionary, bitterly hostile to the republican regime; and there is some reason to believe that he relished this double assault on the values of the triumphant *tiers état*. The eventual rewards that came to Durand-Ruel when the impressionists achieved popularity may have played their part in encouraging other dealers, such as Vollard and Kahnweiler, who, like their Dutch predecessors in the seventeenth century, tended to monopolize the output of their favorite artists but whose role in the development of modern painting is analogous to that of Renaissance patrons— as can be seen from their portraits, like those of Pope Leo X or Philip II of Spain, painted by the greatest artists of their times.

Along with a new type of dealer went a new type of critic, concerned not only with reviewing the annual salons but also with interpreting the "misunderstood artist" and explaining him to the public: witness the writings of Baudelaire on Delacroix, Duranty and Duret on the impressionists, Fénéon on the neo-impressionists, and so on.

The avant-garde.   The concept of the avant-garde, that is, of an art that will by its very nature be in conflict with received opinion, had been aired in passing early in the nineteenth century, but only toward its end became the doctrine that has affected all subsequent thinking on the arts. Manifestoes and apologists began to accompany every new movement, culminating in those of the Italian futurists in 1910, in which for the first time, artists and writers went out of their way to court public hostility: there could be no better indication of how far the situation had changed since 1874, when Degas had asked his friend Giuseppe de Nittis to exhibit with the impressionists, explaining that "puisque vous exposez au Salon, les gens mal documentés ne pourront pas dire que nous sommes l'exposition des refusés" (Nittis 1895, p. 237).

Yet despite all this, the critics (and the public) of the end of the nineteenth century were already chastened by the ridicule that now covered those who had rejected first the romantics and then the realists. Opposition to new developments reached a final paroxysm of fury and then, in Western countries at least, tended to disappear following World War II, so that it is now not unusual for an art that appears to defy the traditional rules to be backed by conservative governments; for ever since the intensification of artistic rivalries induced by the international exhibitions of the nineteenth century, all governments have felt the need to encourage artistic output. Similarly, museum directors, warned by the sad experiences of their predecessors who lost so many vital opportunities of enriching their collections with modern works at accessible prices, now pay increasing attention to contemporary developments. Especially in the United States, such directors have often been indirectly assisted by a national policy of taxation that assists patrons intending to bequeath their collections to public museums—a policy often deplored not only on grounds of social morality but also because it has curtailed the role of the museum as an arbiter of taste.

All these developments, combined with the more cautious attitude of critics, have necessarily robbed the avant-garde of its original significance to the extent that works which are considered the most modern of their day are often rapidly acquired by the very people whom they were originally designed to challenge. Dissatisfaction with "academic art" and a recognition of past misunderstandings, as well as the actual nature of much twentieth-century painting and sculpture, have also led to an obsession with the act of creation itself (sometimes at the expense of the created work), so that universities and other educational bodies have been anxious not only to acquire contemporary art but also to observe the artist at work by incorporating him within their communities—often with no specific duties. The nature of artistic development is as yet too-little understood for it to be clear whether or not this new relationship with society is a beneficial one.

FRANCIS HASKELL

[See also CREATIVITY, article on SOCIAL ASPECTS; STYLE. A guide to other relevant material will be found under ART.]

BIBLIOGRAPHY

ANTAL, FREDERICK 1948 Florentine Painting and Its Social Background. London: Routledge.

COOK, R. M. 1960 Greek Painted Pottery. Chicago: Quadrangle Books.

CROZET, RENÉ 1954 La vie artistique au 17ème siècle. Paris: Presses Universitaires de France.

DIDEROT, DENIS (1759–1767) 1957–1963 Salons. Edited by Jean Seznec and Jean Adhémar. 3 vols. Oxford: Clarendon.

EASTON, MALCOLM 1964 Artists and Writers in Paris: The Bohemian Idea, 1803–1867. London: Arnold.

FRANCASTEL, PIERRE 1965 La réalité figurative: Éléments structurels de sociologie de l'art. Paris: Gonthier.

GOMBRICH, E. H. 1960 The Early Medici as Patrons of Art. Pages 279–311 in Italian Renaissance Studies. Edited by E. F. Jacob. London: Faber.

GOMBRICH, E. H. 1963 Meditations on a Hobby Horse, and Other Essays on the Theory of Art. London: Phaidon. → See especially pages 86–94, "The Social History of Art," for criticism of Arnold Hauser's Social History of Art. A number of research projects are implied by the criticism.

GRATE, PONTUS 1959 Deux critiques d'art de l'époque romantique: Gustave Planche et Théophile Thoré. Stockholm: Almqvist & Wiksell.

HASKELL, FRANCIS 1963 Patrons and Painters: A Study in the Relations Between Italian Art and Society in the Age of Baroque. New York: Knopf.

HAUSER, ARNOLD 1951 Social History of Art. 2 vols. London: Routledge.

LUZIO, ALESSANDRO (editor) 1913 La galleria dei Gonzaga; venduta all'Inghilterra nel 1627–1628: Documenti degli archivi di Mantova a Londra. Milano (Italy): Cogliati. → The translation of the extract in the text was provided by Francis Haskell.

MARTIN, ALFRED VON (1932) 1944 Sociology of the Renaissance. London: Routledge. → First published in German. A paperback edition was published in 1963 by Harper.

MARTIN, W. 1907 The Life of a Dutch Artist. Part 6: How the Painter Sold His Works. Burlington Magazine 9:357–369.

MARTINDALE, ANDREW 1966 The Rise of the Artist. Pages 281–314 in Joan Evans (editor), The Flowering of the Middle Ages. New York: McGraw-Hill.

NITTIS, GIUSEPPE DE 1895 Notes et souvenirs du peintre Joseph de Nittis. Paris: Librairies-imprimeries Réunies.

PELLES, GERALDINE 1963 Art, Artists and Society. Englewood Cliffs, N.J.: Prentice-Hall.

PEVSNER, NIKOLAUS 1940 Academies of Art: Past and Present. New York: Macmillan.

REITLINGER, GERALD 1961 The Economics of Taste: The Rise and Fall of Picture Prices, 1760–1960. London: Barrie & Rockliff.

SALMON, PIERRE 1958 De la collection au musée. Brussels: Office de Publicité.

SCHLOSSER, JULIUS VON 1965 L'arte di corte nel sècolo XIV. Milan (Italy): Edizioni di Comunità.

VENTURI, LIONELLO 1939 Les archives de l'impressionnisme. 2 vols. Paris and New York: Durand-Ruel. → The translation of the extract in the text was provided by Francis Haskell.

WACKERNAGEL, MARTIN 1938 Der Lebensraum des Künstlers in der florentinischen Renaissance. Leipzig: Seemann.

WHITE, HARRISON; and WHITE, CYNTHIA 1965 Canvases and Careers: Institutional Change in the French Painting World. New York: Wiley.

WITTKOWER, RUDOLF; and WITTKOWER, MARGOT 1963 Born Under Saturn; the Character and Conduct of Artists: A Documented History From Antiquity to the French Revolution. London: Weidenfeld & Nicolson.

II
THE RECRUITMENT AND SOCIALIZATION OF ARTISTS

"Recruitment" is a term used to refer to the underlying processes for bringing new members into a group. Sociologists are especially interested in understanding those social forces that encourage individuals to join, or repel them from joining, an occupational or professional group and to embark on a particular career within that group.

In many occupations the process of recruitment can be readily understood. For example, consider the military, from whom the word "recruitment" was originally borrowed. We know in clear terms the subjective and objective meaning of the professional soldier. We are aware of the symbols, such as money, glory, social advancement, travel, and adventure, which attract persons to become soldiers. We are equally aware of the symbols that distract, discourage, and repel the individual from this profession—fear, lack of sympathy with the cause, discipline, death, separation from loved ones and from one's community.

By contrast, there is a great vagueness concerning the recruitment of the artist. It is very difficult, first of all, to define the term "artist"; any attempt at an essential, or even an operational, definition of the artist—an attempt in which many generations of aesthetes have failed—is bound to founder (see Gabor 1963, p. 148, who makes the same point for the definition of "art"). The reasons for this become apparent as soon as several crucial questions are asked. For example, who is an artist, and why is he one? Does it depend on the amount of time spent working as an artist? Then how does one include individuals like Charles Ives, an American composer whose entire working career was spent in an insurance company?

Does working as an artist qualify one to be included in this category? Then we must exclude individuals of high artistic potential whose creative urge is latent or shows itself in activities other than art. Can we rely on contemporary recognition by institutions within the art world, such as galleries, museums, or private collectors? But to do this would exclude practically all the impressionist painters, not to mention Rembrandt at the time that he created some of his most important masterpieces. In view of these difficulties, we must rely on connotative and denotative examples in order to define our term "professional artist," while keeping in mind the shortcomings of this method.

When speaking of a professional artist, I think of Pablo Picasso, Marc Chagall, Alberto Giacometti, Ernest Hemingway, William Faulkner, Anton Webern, and Arnold Schönberg, to name a few outstanding figures from the first half of the twentieth century. Such men devote their time and psychic energy to creative endeavors or would do so if circumstances permitted. In other words, their primary work is or would be directed toward ex-ploring the "fundamental categories" of human existence, the attempt to exalt or denigrate authority, "to explore or explain the universe, to understand the meaning of events, to enter into contact with the sacred or to commit sacrilege, to affirm the principles of morality and justice and to deny them, to encounter the unknown, . . . to stir the senses by the control of and response to words, sounds, shapes, and colors" (Shils 1960a, p. 290).

Control of the arts. In some countries and during some eras there has been fairly tight control of the arts, both in the number of recruits and in the course of their careers. For example, during the guild era in Europe no disciple could change masters unless his first teacher agreed to break his contract, and all disciples had to remain with the master for three years (Tomasini 1953, pp. 135, 140). Furthermore, there was an attempt to establish mastership as a hereditary privilege (Dobb 1947, pp. 116–117). Willetts writes that during the existence of the Sung Academy in China (12th century) "its appointments seem to have been sine-cures with promotions through four ranks." The French Académie Royale de Peinture et de Sculpture had a similar elaborate hierarchy. In both academies "admission and promotion were by competitive examination. In both, the candidate was required to submit his personal version of a set theme, after gaining official approval of his proposed treatment by means of a preliminary sketch" (Willetts 1958, p. 518).

In twentieth-century Europe and the United States the arts are characterized by a relative absence of centralized occupational control, as compared, for example, with the academies mentioned above or with the medical profession in the United States, with its institutional self-awareness, its standards of competence and discipline, and its relatively stabilized recruitment. Moreover, in these countries the demand for the visual arts—and for other arts as well—is rapidly and vastly expanding. This combination of an expanding market and an absence of tight controls suggests that the world of art—fine and commercial—must recruit in a rather generous, if not excessive, fashion. Unlike certain occupations, the world of art need not underrecruit for the purpose of controlling a valuable skill, with its accompanying monetary rewards, prestige, and honor.

Much of the rather "open" recruitment in art is reflected in various gentle practices and policies of many art schools in the United States. Probably few applicants are refused admittance. Students occasionally drop out of school of their own voli-tion but are rarely expelled as from medical or engineering schools. There are few or no crucial tests or other hurdles that a student must pass to remain in school. Grades seem mainly to yield encouragement or prestige and seem not to be utilized to restrict enrollment or to force the repeating of courses. Anyone who has the time and money can go to any number of commercial and fine arts schools. (These data on art schools, as well as the following section on the students' family background and public school experience, are based on Strauss 1955*a*; see also Griff 1960; 1964*a*; 1964*b*.)

Early socialization of the artist

Because recruitment into the art world is neither tightly limited nor carefully controlled, we should not be led to assume that artists somehow drift into art. There exists a whole social paraphernalia for getting persons committed to their artistic identities; and the fact that the machinery is not usually visible to the person himself does not, of course, make it any less real.

The chief mechanism for pumping a flow of talent into art today is the public-school system—aided by the art schools and often abetted unknowingly and unwillingly by the student's family. This is true, among other reasons, because nowadays artists do not appear to come from very high or very low social classes. An artistic career is not generally initiated by an education at prep school or an elite college, nor do persons of low economic standing usually become artists by emulating models found in their communities (they are far more likely to emulate athletes). Parents in various strata introduce their offspring to art, stressing humanist, hobbyist, and other values; but not many parents consider the visual arts a propitious locale on which to fight the battle for class and occupational success. As a consequence, few parents directly influence their children to enter the field of art. Moreover, attendance at galleries and museums, with or without parents, plays no discernible part in recruitment; it is, in fact, a rare art student who reports having any art "in his background." Nor do students entering art school usually know artists of any kind except their public-school teachers; nor are they especially acquainted with art history or with the biographies of famous artists.

Public-school experiences. The public-school art teachers begin to exert their influence quite early in the career of the artist, generally in grammar school. Impoverished or misguided though their teaching may be, they may introduce the youngster to the satisfactions and delights of drawing and painting. These teachers serve to keep interest in art alive throughout the school years by bestowing

approval upon the child, singling him out for special honors, placing his work in public view, or assigning him honorific tasks, such as decorating the blackboards. Some students mention that as early as kindergarten, teachers singled them out for praise and isolated them from their classmates so that they could concentrate on their art.

In high school the child who has been recognized for his artistic virtuosity continues to take art courses and often has the opportunity to major in art. Art teachers may begin to suggest that he go on to art school—a step that otherwise might not occur to some—and may procure information and even scholarships for their protégés. The high-school milieu affords additional prestige, for the child may win a school prize, or even a national one, or receive acclaim for decorating a stage set, drawing for the school paper, and other such activities.

Saturday morning art classes. Complementing the role of the high school in the recruitment process are the typical Saturday morning classes sponsored by the community art museum. These special classes, which are to be found in Europe as well as in the United States, play a crucial role in encouraging an art career. For school children whose art instruction is limited (especially in the private or parochial schools, where art instruction may be absent), they provide the first exposure to advanced courses and qualified teachers. The Saturday classes provide students not only with material facilities, such as oils, brushes, and models, but also with professional instruction and the encouragement offered by the milieu of a museum. Also, for both children and adolescents, this may be their first (and perhaps only) opportunity to come into contact with peers having similar dispositions toward art.

Another important effect of the Saturday morning classes is that they single out the artistic person: that is, they signify to those in his social milieu, as well as to himself, that he has been socially recognized as having an unusual ability, absent in others, which has certain rewards. In addition, these classes stimulate the nascent attributes of independence and freedom from external restraint that are associated with artists, because they separate the individual from his social milieu perhaps for the first time in his life. This *may* accelerate for these children the normal personality development from unilateral to autonomous thinking, studied by Piaget (1923). Finally, the experience of the Saturday classes may reinforce a sense of security for some children; in the childhood and adolescent world of comparisons, they can brag about their painting ability, which may, indeed, be the only outstanding skill they have.

Parental attitudes

The portrait that emerges from a study of the childhood and adolescent social experiences of the individual who possesses artistic skills reveals the congruence of encouragement and reward, of aspiration and fulfillment. He learns that his contribution is socially meaningful and constructive, and at the same time he is encouraged to exercise freely that which he most basically feels is himself. Except for the normal tensions of childhood and adolescence all the factors favoring the retention and nourishment of an artist's career are present.

Discontinuities in this pattern become apparent when the person declares publicly that he wishes to prepare for a career in art. The parents of the would-be artist make two very strenuous objections to his desire. The first is that the painter cannot hope to support himself solely from the sale of his paintings and that this will make it impossible for him to attain many of the symbols of success that families cherish. The second objection is directed at the bohemian stereotype of the artist, which the family wishes to avoid because it violates the professed mores of our culture. (The fact that artists often seem to become bohemians is, of course, closely related to their financial problems.)

When the student's intention to become an artist is discovered, there is a reversal in the attitude of his parents toward him. Thus, a crisis is engendered, which becomes aggravated during the period beginning with the announcement of his intentions and ending with the termination of his formal education. The entire family makes a determined effort to dissuade him. They remove his paintings from the walls where they were prominently displayed. Artistic achievements and the large remunerations for paintings received by artists become topics to be avoided.

It is at this point that the germ of self-estrangement (commonly referred to as alienation) is first implanted. Going contrary to the wishes of one's parents causes one's conscience to suffer. It suffers because of the strong affective relationship between parents and child, because of intensive cultural imperatives emanating from the mores and reinforced by religious institutions—particularly the dogma concerning filial duties—and because of the acute sensitivity and imagination characteristic of the artist qua artist. While the exertion of the individual toward independence is normal during this period, this breaking away may have added significance for the career of the artist. Rank, for

example, in discussing the creation of individuality said:

> The gradual freeing of the individual from dependence by a self-creative development of personality replaces the one-sided . . . dependence on the mother. . . . The person in the third and highest level of development, the creative type, such as the artist or the philosopher, creates a world for himself which he can accept without wanting to force it on others; and he accepts himself. Such a person creates his own inner ideals, which he affirms as his own commandments. At the same time he can live in the world without falling into continual conflict with it. (1932; quoted in Mullahy 1948, pp. 177, 183–184)

There appears to be an inconsistency in parental attitudes toward the child who chooses the artistic career. It has been stated that the young artist is encouraged and rewarded and that his early success in art is a source of gratification for his parents as well as for him. However, the parents' later disapproval of his career choice becomes understandable if the difference between school success and occupational success is considered. School success is confined largely to the yardstick of the report card ("My daughter gets all A's in art"), and there is also recognition in the form of prizes, articles in the local newspaper, or acknowledgment on graduation programs. However, when a child graduates from high school new standards and criteria of judgment are applied, which are associated with symbols of financial success and social prestige. Art is not an avenue leading to the attainment of these symbols, and parents know this. Moreover, these reactions reflect some significant attitudes toward the fine artist and toward art in contemporary culture.

Cultural variations. Contemporary industrial culture stresses conformity, respectability, rationality, practicality, and security. These are a few of the essential values incorporated in the cultural complex that Max Weber called "rational bourgeois capitalism." Art and the life of the artist are antinomies of this. Fine art is nonutilitarian. Moreover, the artist tends to be nonconformist and to violate many of the behavioral patterns prescribed by society. His choice of career opposes the success theme so strongly emphasized and so pervasive in contemporary culture. The parents of artists may themselves have failed to achieve success, and they, with all good intentions of loving parents, want their children to avoid the disappointments that they have experienced. Also, to parents who value success for their children as an affirmation and confirmation of their worthiness as parents, there is little comfort in the notion that the young artist may achieve recognition posthumously. Yet, this is frequently all the young artist can offer as justification for the sacrifices he proposes.

Parental opposition to a career in art is neither recent nor geographically confined; nor, for that matter, is parental encouragement. The way in which a son is forced to struggle against his parents because he suffers from an internal ebullition of artistic desire, which they try to suppress, has become a classic ritual (Fry 1929, p. 6 in the 1958 edition). Yet, instances of the encouragement of artistic careers have also been notable (Haskell 1963, pp. 20–21; Tomasini 1953). The experience of the contemporary composer Gian-Carlo Menotti provides an example:

How well I remember as a child watching the profound sorrow of all Milan as the funeral of Puccini passed through the streets. It was a loss for each of us as well as for our country. No wonder that a young Italian boy's wanting to be a composer could only be a source of satisfaction and pride to his family and friends. But the family's regard for music was only a reflection of the general public's esteem in which the composer was held in Italy.   (1953, pp. 42–43)

The explanation for this variation in attitudes is open to debate and awaits further research. Two hypotheses, however, immediately come to mind. One is suggested by Menotti:

It is my contention that the average American has little or no respect for the creative artist and is apt to consider him as an almost useless member of the community. The average American father still views with dismay the fact that one of his sons may choose to become a composer, writer, or painter. He will consider any such pursuit a sign of "softness," an unmanly and, I venture to say, un-American choice.

I must add in all frankness that this hostility toward the arts is not uncommon in Europe within a certain class of society. But it exists only in a very small percentage of the population, mostly among the *nouveaux riches* and the very orthodox members of the aristocracy who still feel that it is more noble to patronize than to create. Moreover, even in this latter small moribund class, artistic activity is at least looked upon as an essential element of gracious living rather than the adornment of uneventful Sunday afternoons. (1953, pp. 39–40)

An alternative hypothesis is suggested by an artist turned popular writer: "Art needs a proper climate. The average Frenchman is no more artistic than the average American. . . . But the French climate is good for art, because in France an artist isn't expected to earn as much as a stockbroker. He is justified in his existence even if he is just a *little* artist. He doesn't have to be a Picasso. He counts as a necessary human factor although he hasn't reached the very top" (King 1958, p. 8).

Preparation for a career in art

After graduating from high school the neophyte artist enrolls in an art school or art institute, where he takes a basic course in the fundamentals of drawing, painting, and illustration. There he is thrown together with a large group of individuals having a variety of talents and backgrounds. For many, the first year is a joy. They work and learn (perhaps for the first time) in a milieu that is permeated with art. The school may be in a museum, or at least very near one, and the students are socially united by their common interest in art.

Specialization ensues during the subsequent years. In the second year, the students are divided into fine arts, commercial or applied arts, and art education sections. Further specialization takes place during the third and fourth years, but the most important specialty, in terms of the recruitment process, is fine arts.

The fine arts student searches for a teacher compatible to his temperament both as an artist and as an individual. Some seek and readily accept technical instruction; others expect to get instruction only upon request; still others are hostile to any instruction, asseverating that it is a violation of artistic mores for an instructor even to touch their canvases.

Competition for grades is discouraged because of the inherent difficulty in judging art; both talented and untalented students, as well as instructors, mention this. Usually, the only institutionally fostered competition that is meaningful is the rivalry for the traveling fellowships, which takes place during the senior year. Both students and instructors have suggested that some students deliberately alter their natural style during the fellowship competition in order to cater to the known tastes of the judges. However, in general, we can say that the art school does not constitute a disruptive force, in terms of the unity of the self, as other types of schools frequently do. In other words, the intensive competition that tempts or forces students to engage in subterfuge or parroting their mentors in order to receive passing or superior grades is not present in the art school. What emerges in the art school is a consistency between self and fulfillment. Thus, the self-estrangement that for the average person begins with formal schooling and continues indefinitely does not, for the most part, affect the art student.

Vocational choices. As the student nears the end of his academic training he becomes anxious over what he will do when he graduates. Some may succumb to the prodding of their parents (or fiancées or wives) and take a few commercial art courses before they graduate. For the same reasons, others may take courses in art education or may return for a year after they graduate to take courses in art education. Still others pass through four years of training and delay their decisions until they graduate. A very few will win traveling fellowships lasting for a year or two and thereby postpone their decisions temporarily. A few, both those who have completed their fellowships and those who did not win one, will find galleries that will give them small subsidies. Eventually, however, each must find a source of steady income. Some will find work in the post office or in stores and will paint in the evenings or on weekends. A prolonged siege of this work is disheartening, especially when the individual realizes that he may have to do this for many years—that is, until he is recognized— or that he may have to work at whatever he is doing for the rest of his life. In the end, most return to art in secondary ways—some as art educators and many as commercial artists.

Whichever alternative is chosen, it will be a secondary choice and one that implies taking a job which the person feels is not his basic calling. It is at this point in the recruitment process of the artist that the state commonly referred to as alienation begins to be seriously experienced. As mentioned above, the first signs of alienation appear in connection with the students' conflict with their parents, as they finish high school, but in art school this parental opposition is usually overcome or disregarded. However, there is this important difference between finishing formal art school and finishing high school. While parents will strenuously object to their child's going to art school, they will, in most cases, continue to support their child because the mores demand it. After graduation, however, there are no moral imperatives necessitating continued support and certainly none that would obligate the parents to support the child indefinitely. It must also be pointed out that it is at this point in the student's life that the philosophies to which he has been exposed in his intellectual quest as artist—no matter how ingenuous they may appear—begin to fructify.

These circumstances raise a number of important questions concerning the artist. One of the most important of these is, What happens to one's artistic identity when one enters various types of employment? Griff (1960; 1964b) has sought the answer to this question in a study of commercial (i.e., advertising) artists. Commercial artists were selected for study because it was believed that these people had chosen the extreme alternative among the possibilities available to the artist. It was felt that the role of the commercial artist differs in so many fundamental ways from that of the fine artist that a study of it could serve as a paradigm for what happens in the case of less extreme vocational choices.

Art and advertising

There are few institutions whose basic values are more opposed to one another in all fundamental respects than are those of art and advertising— their vocabularies, their traditions, their standards and rules, beliefs and symbols, criteria for the selection of subject matter and problems, modes of presentation, canons for the assessment of excellence—are all antithetical.

The traditions of art seem by their very nature to entail a measure of tension with the traditions of advertising and its close allies, commerce and industry. The very intensity and concentration of commitment to these value orientations reflect the distance that separates the two. Art, like genuine religion, continues to be vitally concerned with the sacred or the ultimate ground of thought and experience and the aspiration to enter into intimate contact with it. Thus, art involves the search for truth, for the principles embedded in events and actions, or for the establishment of a relationship between the self and the essential, whether the relationship be cognitive, appreciative, or expressive (Shils 1960b).

In contrast, the traditions of advertising emphasize the selection of the mundane as subject matter; its presentation in terms of immediate perception as well as by the use of standardization, classification, and clichés; the necessity for certainty of cognition and direction; the deliberate attempts to manipulate through the use of visual stimuli based upon emulation, fear, and sex; and the assessment of excellence in terms of attention value, consumption, and fidelity (called brand loyalty) to the product of one's client.

In addition, there are innumerable technical differences between advertising and the fine arts, based upon the problems of graphic reproduction. The commercial artist must consider the different qualities of papers and printing inks and the effect these will have on the final version of his work. He must consider that the painting as seen in the original and then on the printed page will be different, because the flat surface of the paper eliminates the third dimension together with the brush strokes and canvas pores. Since it is necessary to make the product and accompanying message stand out (known technically as highlighting), a sharp linear style is used; a firm principle of advertising art is recognition through a silhouette.

The differences in compositional techniques are also readily apparent. For example, in many automobile ads there appears to be an illusion of deep space, but upon careful analysis it can be seen that the eye does not move from the front plane to deep space; compare this to a painting by a Dutch master, where the eye moves into the interior from the front of the room and then into the distance through an open door or window. In the advertisement the automobile covers the horizon, extends along most of the composition, and blocks the eye from easy recession into the background. Even the space in the background is indeterminate and has the function of forcing the nearer objects toward the eye, thus forcing the viewer to concentrate on the advertised product (Parker 1937, pp. 119–122).

Role identification and artistic values. Commercial artists range in type from those who remain symbolically attached to the role of the fine artist to those who reject this role completely. Between these two extremes lies a third group that identifies with both roles (see Griff 1960, pp. 219–241, for an extended account of the three roles mentioned here).

The traditional role.   Some artists work as commercial artists, but subjectively identify themselves as fine artists "temporarily" engaged in the commercial field. In other words, they identify with what they regard as the artist's *traditional role*; their rationalization for working in the commercial field is that the normative standards of contemporary society preclude any economically feasible alternative. Underlying this assumption is the belief that society will give lip service to, but in reality will not support, the artist's primary identity—that of the fine artist as he emerged at the end of the nineteenth century. In supporting their premise they cite numerous examples, both past and present, of other individuals who have tried, without success, to live exclusively from their paintings. In addition, there is the actual attempt by many of them to live from the sale of their paintings. Finding this to be an impossibility, they may have turned to commercial art. Also, there is the further realization that other aspects of the reward system of society are absent (i.e., prestige, praise, or admiration of others for their dedication to their ideals). Instead, in many cases, negative sanctions have been applied against them in the form of derision and questions concerning the practicality of their labors, as well as their "sanity."

The commercial role.   Artists who assume the "commercial role" see art (both fine and commer-

cial) as a utilitarian product, and they conceive of themselves as instruments for the transformation of verbal symbols (dictated by a client) into visual ones. Consequently, their ideological orientation is directed toward pleasing and satisfying their clients. Conceiving their roles in this manner the commercial-role artists refrain from interjecting or altering in any way the intent of their clients unless specifically directed to do so. Thus, they accept a norm that is not only upheld by their occupational group but also sanctioned by the larger society: The customer is always right. In carrying out this belief, they define their roles as having been successfully fulfilled when the requirements of their clients have been met as parsimoniously as possible. This means the creation of illustrations in the quickest and cheapest fashion.

In contrast to the attitudes held by the traditional-role artists, the commercial-role artists reject the notion that they are artists working in the commercial field because of extenuating circumstances. On the contrary, they believe that the traditional role is a nineteenth-century anachronism and therefore should be discarded by the contemporary artist.

The compromise role.   The "compromise role" is a mixture of both the traditional and the commercial roles. Like the commercial-role artists, those who assume the compromise role believe that they are instruments of the clients; however, they conceive of themselves as active, rather than as passive, agents. In carrying out this conception of themselves, they translate the demands of the client but at the same time attempt to persuade him to accept innovations, specifically the interjection of fine arts symbols into their illustrations. Thus, many feel that they are involved in a crusade for better art. They believe that by raising the standards of their clients' art, they are at the same time raising the level of taste of the public.

The resemblance between the compromise role and the traditional role lies in the fact that both are concerned with fine arts. However, the artists who choose the compromise role do not consider the commercial field onerous or harmful to fine arts or believe that their status should be independent of the secular realm. They believe, as do the commercial-role artists, that their legitimate position in society lies in the commercial field. They reflect to a great extent the Bauhaus definition of the artist. This definition stresses the importance of the artist's working in a society rather than being isolated from it. The definition also stresses that the artist, while working in a society, should exert all his technical, moral, and aesthetic skills to influence the products of mass production (Moholy-Nagy 1929).

The study of the recruitment of the artist is part of a broader field called the sociology of art. This field is still in its infancy, and much fundamental work must be done before its outlines, contributions, and limitations will be known and understood. Griff's study (1964a) of art students in Chicago is a step in that direction; further research will confirm, invalidate, or suggest revisions of it. Meanwhile, what is needed now are similar data from the other fine arts and from those areas that are emerging as new fine arts, such as photography and the film. In this connection, important research could be accomplished by studying how an area emerges as a fine art. Other important questions and areas of needed research are: What are the career patterns of successful and unsuccessful artists? What are the social conditions responsible for the fame of an artist, the capriciousness of fame, and immortality; the social conditions hindering or encouraging creative endeavors; the relationship between contemporary patrons and styles of art; the social and psychological conditions impeding artists or aiding them to break with traditional and acceptable styles of art, thus innovating new styles; and the social roles of critics and patrons? Once research on these questions has been undertaken, it will be possible to clarify the more significant and elusive questions, such as whether the artist is a reflection of his society, or whether art is a reflection of the age.

MASON GRIFF

[*Directly related are the entries* CREATIVITY *and* PROFESSIONS. *Other relevant material may be found in* ARCHITECTURE; CRAFTS; FASHION; LITERATURE; STYLE; *and in the biographies of* LUKÁCS *and* RANK.]

BIBLIOGRAPHY

CLARK, KENNETH 1956 *The Nude: A Study in Ideal Form.* New York: Pantheon. → A paperback edition was published in 1959 by Doubleday.

COOMARASWAMY, ANANDA K. 1946 *The Religious Basis of the Forms of Indian Society.* New York: Orientalia. → A social-psychological analysis of Indian art.

COWAN, LOUISE 1959 *The Fugitive Group: A Literary History.* Baton Rouge: Louisiana State Univ. Press. → An excellent study of the effect that face-to-face interaction has upon the emergence of an original poetical style.

DOBB, MAURICE (1947) 1964 *Studies in the Development of Capitalism.* Rev. ed. New York: International Publishers.

DUDEK, LOUIS 1960 *Literature and the Press.* Toronto (Canada): Ryerson. → This study parallels in many important ways Griff's studies of painters; however it concentrates on the literary artist. Contains a wealth of material and a source of innumerable research pos-sibilities, as well as insights into the problem of contemporary literature being overwhelmed by mass society. It also explores the effects of mass society on the creative product of literary authors.

FRY, ROGER (1929) 1952 *Cézanne: A Study of His Development.* 2d ed. New York: Macmillan; London: Hogarth. → A paperback edition was published in 1958 by Noonday.

GABOR, DENNIS (1963) 1964 *Inventing the Future.* New York: Knopf. → A paperback edition was published in 1964 by Penguin.

GIMPEL, JEAN (1958) 1961 *The Cathedral Builders.* New York: Grove. → First published in French. A technical, historical, and sociological account of the building of cathedrals in Europe from 1050–1350.

GRIFF, MASON 1959 Alienation and the Artist. *Arts in Society* [1959], Fall: 43–54. → A social and historical study of the alienation of the artist during the nineteenth century.

GRIFF, MASON 1960 The Commercial Artist: A Study in Changing and Consistent Identities. Pages 219–241 in Maurice Stein, A. Vidich, and D. White (editors), *Identity and Anxiety.* Glencoe, Ill.: Free Press.

GRIFF, MASON 1961 Creativity and Syrenes. Unpublished manuscript. → Suggests the relationships between creativity and social factors; also contains a number of specific research suggestions.

GRIFF, MASON 1964a The Recruitment of the Artist. Pages 61–94 in Robert N. Wilson (editor), *The Arts in Society.* Englewood Cliffs, N.J.: Prentice-Hall. → A discussion of the problems of the neophyte artist; based on a study of students attending a large art school in Chicago.

GRIFF, MASON 1964b Conflicts of the Artist in Mass Society. *Diogenes* 46:54–68. → A report based on a social-psychological study of the artist who, unable to earn a living from his paintings, becomes a commercial (advertising) artist.

HARRISON, JANE E. (1913) 1927 *Ancient Art and Ritual.* London: Butterworth. → An important sociological study of dramatic art. See especially pages 119–169 on "The Transition From Ritual to Art."

HASKELL, FRANCIS 1963 *Patrons and Painters: A Study in the Relations Between Italian Art and Society in the Age of the Baroque.* New York: Knopf; London: Chatto & Windus. → Contains innumerable suggestions for further research in the sociology of art; also serves as an example of scholarship in this area.

KING, ALEXANDER 1958 *Mine Enemy Grows Older.* New York: Simon & Schuster.

MACK, GERSTLE 1935 *Paul Cézanne.* New York: Knopf. → A less technical and more sociological account of Cézanne than Fry 1929.

MENOTTI, GIAN-CARLO 1953 A Plea for the Creative Artist. Pages 37–45 in Fernando Puma (editor), *The 7 Arts.* Garden City, N.Y.: Doubleday.

MOHOLY-NAGY, LÁSZLÓ (1929) 1946 *The New Vision.* New York: Wittenborn. → First published in German.

MULLAHY, PATRICK 1948 *Oedipus: Myth and Complex.* New York: Hermitage. → See especially pages 162–207 for the section entitled "The Theories of Otto Rank."

MUMFORD, LEWIS (1952) 1960 *Art and Technics.* New York: Columbia Univ. Press.

PARKER, PAUL 1937 The Analysis of the Style of Advertising Art. Master's thesis, Univ. of Chicago, Department of Art. → A technical and social analysis of advertising art compared with fine art; written by a commercial artist.

PARKER, PAUL 1938 The Iconography of Advertising Art. *Harper's* 177:80–84.

PEVSNER, NIKOLAUS 1940 *Academies of Art: Past and Present.* Cambridge Univ. Press; New York: Macmillan.

PIAGET, JEAN (1923) 1959 *The Language and Thought of the Child.* 3d ed., rev. New York: Humanities Press. → First published as *Le langage et la pensée chez l'enfant.*

RANK, OTTO 1932 *Art and Artist: Creative Urge and Personality Development.* New York: Knopf.

SHILS, EDWARD 1958 Ideology and Civility: On the Politics of the Intellectual. *Sewanee Review* 66:450–480.

SHILS, EDWARD 1960a Mass Society and Its Culture. *Dædalus* 89:288–314.

SHILS, EDWARD 1960b The Traditions of Intellectuals. Pages 55–61 in George B. de Huszar (editor), *The Intellectuals.* Glencoe, Ill.: Free Press. → Discusses the tension between intellectuals and the business class.

STERN, L. 1958 George Lukács: An Intellectual Portrait. *Dissent* 5:162–173. → Includes discussion of Lukács' theories concerning art and mass society.

STRAUSS, ANSELM 1955a The Art School and Its Students: A Study and Interpretation. Unpublished manuscript. → A report based on the same research as that discussed in Griff 1964a.

STRAUSS, ANSELM 1955b Some Aspects of Recruitment Into the Visual Arts. Unpublished manuscript. → Derived from the same study as that described in Griff 1964a.

TOMASINI, WALLACE J. 1953 The Social and Economic Position of the Florentine Artist in the 15th Century. Ph.D. dissertation, Univ. of Michigan.

WILLETTS, WILLIAM 1958 *Chinese Art.* 2 vols in 1. New York: Braziller. → See especially pages 501–652 on "Painting and Calligraphy," and within that chapter, the section "Status of the Artist." A paperback edition was published in 1958 by Penguin.

FIRM, THEORY OF THE

The theory of the firm is that branch of economic theory which deals with the determination of the most important economic variables associated with the individual business unit, such as price, output, and growth. There are no readily defined boundaries for the theory, although it is usually distinguished from the theory of production, which deals with the selection of inputs and techniques of production by the firm; from programming, which explains how optimal techniques of production may be discovered; and from the study of business enterprise and the corporation, which have a more institutional focus [*see* CORPORATION; PRODUCTION; PROGRAMMING]. The theory of the firm is closely associated with the concept of the industry; the industry is composed, roughly, of those firms producing similar products. The relationship between the firm and the industry will be described in some detail later in this article.

The theory of the firm has a considerable his-

tory in economic thought, going back at least as far as Cournot (1838) and appearing implicitly a good deal earlier. The development of consumer theory and the basing of economics upon a theory of individual choice obviously called for an analogous development in the treatment of units of production, and after 1900 more and more attention was directed to the theory of the firm.

There are many possible approaches to the theory of the firm. These approaches may be categorized in various ways, the most fruitful of which seem to result from the division between: (*a*) static and dynamic approaches; (*b*) those theories that derive their results from the assumption of profit maximization and those that do not; and (*c*) deterministic and probabilistic theories.

Static and dynamic approaches. By a static theory of the firm we mean a theory that describes the characteristics of a firm in a position of equilibrium. We will deal first with the case in which this equilibrium arises when the firm is maximizing its profits.

The first part of the static theory to be well developed was the theory of the price and output policy of a profit-maximizing monopolist. A monopolist is defined as the only supplier of a particular "commodity." He is therefore confronted by a market demand curve giving a total revenue (R) that varies with output:

$$(1) \qquad R = f(x), \qquad f'(x) < 0,$$

where x is the quantity produced and sold. (Inventories are seldom allowed for in the simple theory.) Total costs (C), which include normal profits, are also affected by output. Normal profits are defined as those only just sufficient to keep the entrepreneur and his firm in the given industry:

$$(2) \qquad C = g(x).$$

Profit is maximized when $R - C$ is maximized, when

$$(3) \quad \frac{dR}{dx} - \frac{dC}{dx} = 0 \quad \text{and} \quad \frac{d^2R}{dx^2} - \frac{d^2C}{dx^2} < 0,$$

i.e., output is set at a profit maximizing level when marginal cost equals marginal revenue and marginal cost is rising faster (or falling less quickly) than marginal revenue.

Perhaps one of the most striking things about this solution is that it makes no assertion about the level of profits. In fact, it is often assumed that the monopolist must make in the normal way profits that are in some sense "supernormal."

It was the achievement of Pigou (1928) and others to see that some of the results obtained above are in fact of wider applicability and hold for the static theory of the firm in perfect competition as well as in monopoly. The chief differences between the two cases arise from the fact that in perfect competition price is treated as fixed, so that marginal revenue equals price. Thus

$$(4) \qquad \frac{dR}{dx} = P, \qquad \frac{d^2R}{dx^2} = P,$$

where P is the price of the product as seen by the firm. It follows that

$$(5) \qquad \frac{dC}{dx} = P, \quad \text{and} \quad \frac{d^2C}{dx^2} > 0.$$

This is to say that in perfect competition marginal cost equals price and that marginal cost is rising at the point of equilibrium output. Since in perfect competition entry is free and all factors of production are freely available at given prices, it is also deduced that average cost is equal to price in equilibrium and that average cost is at its lowest at the point of equilibrium output.

The above results are very important in welfare economics and form a part of the basis for asserting the optimality of perfectly competitive systems. [See WELFARE ECONOMICS.] But this fact has led to much confusion in the theory of the firm. It has led some writers to the paradoxical view that the theory of the firm is merely a part of welfare economics and that no evidence of the actual behavior of firms is relevant to the theory. Others have been unwilling to accept any evidence that tends to cast doubt on the universality of perfect competition in the real world. Both of these pitfalls should be carefully avoided.

It was pre-eminently Chamberlin's contribution (1933) to the static theory of the firm to notice that some degree of monopoly power is consistent with free entry and that the equality of average costs and prices is consistent with monopolistic equilibrium. (This point was noted also by Robinson [1933], but she was, on the whole, more concerned with considering certain special aspects of monopoly theory.) Chamberlin centered the bulk of his attention on achieving the marriage of monopoly and competition, and he proceeded in an elaborate diagrammatic exposition to show how it could be accomplished in certain hitherto unexplored situations.

The Chamberlinian relationship which is best known is summarized in Figure 1. Here all firms are assumed to have identical cost curves and identical demand curves. CC' is the average cost curve of any one of the firms. DD' is the demand curve confronting any one of the firms, after allowance is made for exit and entry of firms and for the assumption that all firms charge identical prices: dd' is the demand curve that would face the firm if it could alter its prices without action or reaction by its competitors. In equilibrium the number of firms must adjust until all firms make only normal profits, and each firm still remaining in the industry believes that it is making maximum profits. This will occur at point T in Figure 1 if each firm believes its rivals will ignore its price policy.

Chamberlin's argument for the universal applicability of his models seems, in retrospect, somewhat unconvincing. Even if the economic world is in the main some blend of monopolistic and competitive elements, there is no reason to think that it is the very simplified blend that Chamberlin has assumed. If the world is more complex than Chamberlin has surmised, it is at least possible that other models, and perhaps simpler models, may be more useful predictors of economic behavior. The merits of any consistent model are not to be determined so much by argument as by performance.

An alternative to Chamberlin's approach has emerged from the development of the theory of oligopoly. Indeed, some writers seem to claim that oligopoly is in fact the norm in nonperfectly competitive markets. Unfortunately there are many competing oligopoly theories; they are not always presented in testable form; those that are testable in principle would often be difficult to distinguish empirically; and little testing has so far been attempted.

The dynamic theory of the firm has, on the other hand, received only limited treatment. The out-

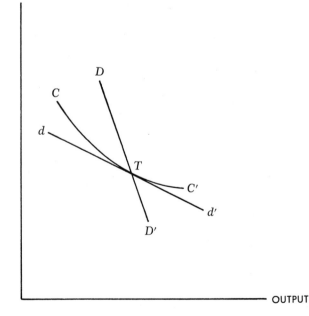

Figure 1 — *Equilibrium under monopolistic competition*

standing contribution to the subject is probably contained in Hicks (1939). Hicks's treatment is, however, confined to a discussion of intertemporal equilibrium. The question of the path of adjustment to a new equilibrium position, or the extent to which the costs of the firm depend upon the production experience of the firm, has been largely ignored until recent years (Clower 1959; Arrow 1962).

Profit maximization. Next we turn to the controversy over the role of profit maximization in the theory of the firm. The assumption of profit maximization has proved a very useful starting point for investigations in many areas closely connected with the theory of the firm, particularly in the theory of investment and replacement. But some economists have been suspicious of the profit maximization assumption and have preferred to substitute something else. This substitute has usually taken one of two forms: utility maximization or behavioral relations. The former is generally used in static equilibrium systems, the latter are usually not. An example of utility maximization is provided by the work of Scitovsky (1943). He shows in effect that if entrepreneurs maximize utility rather than profit, if utility is influenced by effort, and if effort is related to the size of output, then the traditional deductions of minimum average costs, in equilibrium, of perfect competition will be falsified.

An alternative utility maximization hypothesis asserts that utility is affected by the level of expected profits and by the variance of these profits. If variance decreases with output, the entrepreneur might, for example, decide to operate at outputs above minimum cost output, even under conditions of perfect competition.

One group of writers, of whom the best known is Papandreou (1952), has tended to argue that a large number of considerations will enter the utility function of the entrepreneur, so that propositions derived from profit maximizing assumptions are bound to be misleading. This approach is no doubt highly plausible, but the advantage of plausibility is purchased at the expense of any meaningful hypothesis. Putting it another way, while we increase the immediate acceptability of the theory of the firm by increasing the number of variables that the firm is said to consider in maximizing utility, we achieve this by reducing the number of testable results of the theory.

Some writers have felt that the deduction of the behavior of the firm from static equilibrium models is beyond the present powers of the economist and have instead directed their attention to the formu-lation of behavioral hypotheses about the firm. Such hypotheses may or may not be consistent with the profit maximization hypothesis. One of the leading species of this genus is the so-called "full-cost pricing principle." Roughly, this asserts that prices of manufactured products will be set at a level that will yield a "normal" profit to a firm operating with modern equipment at a high level of capacity utilization. A great deal of effort has been expended in trying to show that such behavior is consistent with profit maximization. However, the behavioral hypothesis itself, which was first suggested by interviews with businessmen, cannot be said to have been subjected to rigorous statistical testing.

Somewhat similar remarks can be made about many of the alternative behavior hypotheses that have been offered for consideration. It has, for example, been suggested that firms aim at maximizing their share of the market rather than their profits. It has also been suggested that firms "satisfice"—that is, that they only seek to increase profits if profits fall below a certain "acceptable" level. In both these cases it can be said that discussion has been aimed more at finding justifications for these hypotheses than at testing their validity by observation. A similar difficulty has plagued efforts to develop a behavioral theory of the growth of the firm.

The theories discussed above have been concerned with explaining only the main features of the behavior of firms. Recently, however, effort has been devoted to the development of models that could predict the detailed conduct of business units in particular aspects of their work. Thus the detailed pricing policy of a particular department of a department store may be studied and a formula found that will enable us to predict this behavior. Much of this work has been stimulated by the suggestions of H. A. Simon (1959), and it remains until now largely descriptive in character. Little effort has been directed toward rationalizing the observed behavior in terms of profit maximization or utility maximization. It may indeed be surmised that simple explanations of detailed behavior patterns would be difficult in models excluding uncertainty and decision costs.

Probabilistic theories. Another line of development in the theory of the firm involves a twofold departure from the neoclassical formulation. First, the notion of static equilibrium of the individual firm is abandoned. Second, the focus changes from deterministic theories of the behavior of a single firm to probabilistic rules about the behavior of large groups of firms. This approach is also behavioral in orientation. While there may be a recognition of the desire for profit maximization, its effect is in many individual cases swamped by a myriad of other forces. As a result, the impact of any change in parameters at best changes the probabilities that govern the conduct of the firm.

The originator of this approach to the theory of the firm appears to have been Alfred Marshall. In the second edition of his *Principles of Economics* (1890) Marshall introduced the notion of the "representative firm" to explain the determination of long run supply price. The representative firm is not any particular firm; rather it is a descriptive fiction by means of which Marshall attempted to amalgamate a dynamic probabilistic theory of the firm with an essentially static and deterministic theory of price determination for the industry.

Marshall's attempt to harness the static with the dynamic approaches was vigorously rejected by most of his successors. Foremost among the critics was Robbins (1928), who objected correctly but irrelevantly that Marshall's implied theory of the firm was inconsistent with static equilibrium assumptions.

Marshall's approach fell into disuse for nearly 25 years but was re-established by P. K. Newman and J. N. Wolfe (1961). They showed that the Marshallian doctrine could be interpreted in terms of the stationary state of a probabilistic (Markov) process. [*See* MARKOV CHAINS.] It was shown that if the probabilistic laws governing the rise and decline of firms were affected by the price of the product, then a particular size distribution of firms and consequently a particular output would emerge from each price. It will be seen that this formulation allows by means of a single process the simultaneous determination of price, output, and the size distribution of firms.

More concretely, we may imagine the probability that a firm will change its size in any period as being governed by a "transition matrix," or matrix of transition probabilities, **A**. This takes the following form:

$$\mathbf{A} = \begin{array}{c} \\ 1 \\ 2 \\ \vdots \\ n \end{array} \begin{array}{cccc} 1 & 2 & \cdots & n \\ \left[\begin{array}{cccc} a_{11} & a_{12} & \cdots & a_{1n} \\ a_{21} & a_{22} & \cdots & a_{2n} \\ \vdots & \vdots & & \vdots \\ a_{n1} & a_{n2} & \cdots & a_{nn} \end{array} \right] \end{array}$$

where a_{12}, for example, is the probability that a firm in the first size-class at a particular period will be in the second size-class one period later. (The figures on the left-hand margin and across the top of the matrix are of course the various size-classes.)

If the matrix **A** obeys certain so-called Markovian assumptions, its continued application to a large group of firms will ultimately produce a definite size distribution that is independent of their initial distribution. And if the entries in the transition matrix are not fixed but are different for each price prevailing, there will be a different size distribution of firms for each particular equilibrium price. [*See* MARKOV CHAINS.]

This sketch of the probabilistic theory of the firm is necessarily incomplete. It will, however, be seen that this theory has the merit of dealing with the firm more nearly in the context in which it appears in real life than does a static theory. Nevertheless, the theory remains highly abstract, and its practical usefulness has yet to be demonstrated.

It will be apparent that the theory of the firm is moving increasingly in the direction of empirical science—that is, toward the formulation and testing of hypotheses about how firms actually behave. This is true whether the hypothesis being put forward is cast in deterministic or probabilistic form. It is at the same time less tied to the assumption of profit maximization. But profit maximization has not lost its usefulness, however frequently it may seem to be contradicted as a descriptive hypothesis. Profit maximization will always be the aim of at least some firms during at least some portion of their history. And so we would expect that profit maximization would continue to play an important role in the *normative* aspect of the theory of the firm.

The firm and the industry. The notion of the industry goes far back in economic thought; it probably derived intact from the market place. By the time of Marshall's *Principles of Economics* (1890) it had come to occupy an important place in economic theory. The industry was there defined as a group of firms producing an identical product. This definition is highly ambiguous, but to some it seemed to imply a homogeneity of output that was most easily related to a state of perfect competition. Chamberlin's assumption of identical cost and demand curves for all firms enabled him to work with "groups" that behaved rather like Marshallian industries. But the abandonment of perfect competition created difficulties for the concept of the industry, once differences in cost and demand conditions between firms were admitted. In the first place, firms might be selling apparently identical products at different prices. Moreover, as Robinson (1933) pointed out, a shift of demand in a perfectly competitive industry would (in the absence of external economies at any rate) have an unambiguous effect upon price and output, while in an imperfectly competitive "industry" it might not. The latter seemed a particularly damaging point, since one of the main motives for the development of the theory of the firm seems to have been to obtain greater certainty about the shape of the industry supply curve. Finally, Triffin (1940) argued that general equilibrium under conditions of nonperfect competition admitted no clear conceptual division between industries. Perhaps partly as a result of these arguments there has been a tendency for theoretically oriented economists to avoid using the concept of the industry and to some extent to neglect the study of the determinants of supply.

From a pragmatic point of view these developments seem ill judged. Ever since Plato and Aristotle, philosophers have been vexed by the problems of finding useful categories under which the large numbers of slightly differing objects we see about us can be grouped. Any such grouping is almost always an abstraction, and the important question is not whether it is a truly homogeneous grouping but whether it is a useful grouping. On the basis of the experience of students of economic institutions, the concept of the industry appears a highly useful abstraction for many purposes, although not for all. The spread of quantitative techniques seems likely to reinforce that conclusion, since statistics are usually available only on an industry basis. Indeed, from the statistical point of view the problem of defining the industry appears to arise from asking the wrong questions. The question should be whether some characteristics of a group of firms (e.g., the mean output of the firms or the mean price charged by them for their products) change in a statistically significant way as the result of changes in some specified variable. It would be difficult in an uncontrolled situation to test for the effects of a very large number of variables. The preponderating influence of a small number of strategic variables is an assumption that must be satisfied if testing is to give useful results. These strategic variables may be those predicted by standard theory or they may not, but this question is one of fact and not of theory.

The conclusion seems to be that the concept of the industry may well remain of great practical use whatever theory of the firm is adopted. This was one of the essential messages of Marshall's "representative firm." In that construct the "industry" is preserved, although firms are neither in equilibrium nor perhaps even operating under conditions of perfect competition. In this respect at least, Marshallian notions appear to have had a more "modern" empirical flavor than most of the later work on the theory of firm and industry. [*See* MARKETS AND INDUSTRIES.]

External economies. A good deal of attention has been given to the effect of changes in the total output of the industry upon the costs of the individual firms in the industry. These effects are termed "external economies" when the costs of production of the firms in the industry are lowered by an increase in the output of the industry. Since it is commonly argued that all firms have identical minimum costs in the long run equilibrium of perfect competition, all firms will in this case be affected equally.

It is usual to distinguish between pecuniary external economies, which arise through reduced factor prices, and technological external economies, which arise through improved organization of industry. The latter are most significant from the welfare point of view, but much doubt has been expressed about the frequency of their occurrence in a perfectly competitive milieu. However, for political or other reasons it may be impossible to enforce perfect competition, and the external economies associated with monopoly may be of great practical importance in some lines.

Scitovsky (1954) has suggested that a further source of external economies would arise if different stages of production were expanded (or contracted) in an uncoordinated way. Such external economies are essentially temporary in character. However, where monopolistic conditions are present, this type of external economy may lead to the permanent neglect of otherwise profitable investment opportunities.

It would appear that the estimation of the actual size of external economies in particular industries would be extremely useful. The task is made difficult, however, by the absence of data, by the uneven pace of technical advance, and by the great variation among the production processes performed by firms that are perforce lumped together in the same "industries." [*See* EXTERNAL ECONOMIES AND DISECONOMIES.]

J. N. WOLFE

[*See also* COMPETITION; MONOPOLY; OLIGOPOLY. *Other relevant material may be found in* DECISION MAKING, *article on* ECONOMIC ASPECTS.]

BIBLIOGRAPHY

AMERICAN ECONOMIC ASSOCIATION 1952 *Readings in Price Theory.* Edited by Kenneth E. Boulding and George J. Stigler. Homewood, Ill.: Irwin.
ARROW, KENNETH J. 1962 The Economic Implications of Learning by Doing. *Review of Economic Studies* 29:155–173.

CHAMBERLIN, EDWARD H. (1933) 1956 *The Theory of Monopolistic Competition: A Re-orientation of the Theory of Value.* 7th ed. Harvard Economic Studies, Vol. 38. Cambridge, Mass.: Harvard Univ. Press.

CLOWER, ROBERT W. 1959 Some Theory of an Ignorant Monopolist. *Economic Journal* 69:705–716.

COURNOT, ANTOINE A. (1838) 1960 *Researches Into the Mathematical Principles of the Theory of Wealth.* New York: Kelley. → First published in French.

CYERT, RICHARD M.; and MARCH, JAMES G. 1963 *A Behavioral Theory of the Firm.* Englewood Cliffs, N.J.: Prentice-Hall.

DORFMAN, ROBERT 1951 *Application of Linear Programming to the Theory of the Firm, Including an Analysis of Monopolistic Firms by Non-linear Programming.* Berkeley: Univ. of California Press.

HICKS, JOHN R. (1939) 1946 *Value and Capital: An Inquiry Into Some Fundamental Principles of Economic Theory.* 2d ed. Oxford: Clarendon.

MARSHALL, ALFRED (1890) 1961 *Principles of Economics.* 9th ed., 2 vols. New York and London: Macmillan. → The second edition was published in 1891.

NEWMAN, PETER K.; and WOLFE, J. N. 1961 A Model for the Long-run Theory of Value. *Review of Economic Studies* 29:51–61.

PAPANDREOU, ANDREAS G. 1952 Some Basic Problems in the Theory of the Firm. Pages 183–219 in Bernard F. Haley (editor), *A Survey of Contemporary Economics.* Volume 2. Homewood, Ill.: Irwin.

PENROSE, EDITH T. 1959 *The Theory of the Growth of the Firm.* New York: Wiley.

PIGOU, ARTHUR C. 1928 An Analysis of Supply. *Economic Journal* 38:238–257.

ROBBINS, LIONEL 1928 The Representative Firm. *Economic Journal* 38:387–404.

ROBINSON, JOAN (1933) 1961 *The Economics of Imperfect Competition.* London: Macmillan; New York: St. Martins.

SCITOVSKY, TIBOR 1943 A Note on Profit Maximisation and Its Implications. *Review of Economic Studies* 11:57–60.

SCITOVSKY, TIBOR 1954 Two Concepts of External Economies. *Journal of Political Economy* 62:143–151.

SIMON, HERBERT A. 1959 Theories of Decision-making in Economics and Behavioral Science. *American Economic Review* 49:253–283.

STIGLER, GEORGE J. 1951 The Division of Labor is Limited by the Extent of the Market. *Journal of Political Economy* 59:185–193.

TRIFFIN, ROBERT 1940 *Monopolistic Competition and General Equilibrium Theory.* Harvard Economic Studies, Vol. 67. Cambridge, Mass.: Harvard Univ. Press.

WOLFE, J. N. 1961 Co-ordination Assumptions and Multiple Equilibria. *Quarterly Journal of Economics* 75:262–277.

FISCAL POLICY

I
OVERVIEW

Fiscal policy is an aspect of public finance, of making and financing government expenditures. It is distinguished from other aspects of public finance in being concerned with decisions about certain "over-all" variables—such as total expenditures, total revenues, and total surplus or deficit—in terms of their "over-all" effects—such as their effects on national income, total employment, and the general level of prices.

The management of their total revenues and expenditures and of the relation between them has become one of the principal instruments by which governments seek to achieve a high level of economic activity and general price stability. This effort encounters many problems—including the compatibility of these two objectives with each other and with other goals, the uncertainty of the size and timing of the necessary actions, and the difficulty of making and carrying out decisions in a large and political organization. Nevertheless, there is widespread confidence that the fiscal instrument is sufficiently powerful, and its use sufficiently understood, to make a substantial contribution to successful economic performance.

The distinction between fiscal policy and the other aspects of public finance that deal with particular expenditures and taxes and their particular consequences is an abstraction from the complexity of the real world. In fact, decisions about the "over-all" variables are made up of decisions about particulars. Also, any decision that has "over-all" effects will also have particular effects on particular individuals, industries, or sectors of the economy.

While the boundary between fiscal policy and other aspects of public finance is necessarily arbitrary, the concept of fiscal policy is useful for analysis and for policy making. Every particular expenditure, tax, and debt issue may have a different over-all effect from every other. Yet for certain purposes it may be both convenient and safe to regard some large categories of expenditures, taxes, and debt issues, or even their totals, as single variables. In fact, it may be impossible to do otherwise, since existing knowledge is too crude to permit distinction among all possible variables.

It is necessary to distinguish fiscal policy not only from other aspects of public finance but also from monetary policy, which also consists of over-all measures usually evaluated in terms of over-all effects—on national income, total employment, or the price level, for example. This distinction can be drawn in various ways, depending upon the definition given to monetary policy. The distinction and connection are clearest if monetary policy is defined as policy with respect to the quantity of money. Fiscal policy can then be defined as policy with respect to total government sources and uses of funds and their composition. Certain sets of actions are a mixture of both monetary and fiscal policy—such as an increase of government expenditures financed by an increase in government borrowing, which in turn causes or is permitted to cause an increase in the money supply. Even in the mixed cases it is possible to distinguish between the monetary and fiscal aspects and to consider what effects flow from each. Its relation to monetary policy is one of the central problems of fiscal policy; this will be discussed below.

Pre-Keynesian theory. Fiscal policy began to assume a leading role in economic thinking, economic controversy, and economic policy only in the 1930s. But as long as there have been governments there has been fiscal policy, and a substantial body of doctrine about it existed long before the 1930s. Although we shall be concerned here mainly with "modern," i.e., post-1930, fiscal policy, a few words should be said about earlier ideas and practice. Modern thinking about fiscal policy, after first abandoning much of prior doctrine, has since reincorporated a great deal of it.

Neither fiscal theory nor fiscal practice before the 1930s was primarily concerned with maintaining high employment and stabilizing the rate of growth of total national output. Economic thinking and policy in general were much less dominated by the high employment problem than they later came to be and were more focused on problems of long-run growth, efficiency in the use of employed resources, and equity in the distribution of income. It was believed that in the long run the economy would tend to produce at a rate determined by "real" factors—the supply of labor and capital and the state of technology. Prices and wage rates would tend to adjust to changes in total money expenditures for goods and services so as to leave real output unchanged.

This view still left the possibility that variations in the general level of prices would have unwanted distributional effects in the long run and would cause unemployment in the short run. This was commonly regarded as a monetary problem, which could be handled by appropriate management of the quantity of money. At the same time, certainly by the 1920s, the possible contribution of budget policy, particularly variation of public works expenditures, to short-run economic stabilization, was widely but not universally recognized. However, a well-developed theory of how budget policy worked was lacking. There was uncertainty and disagreement about whether budget policy was an independent instrument of economic stabilization or only a particular way of carrying out monetary policy which might nevertheless be helpful in special circumstances. Moreover, the small size of government budgets relative to national incomes severely limited the possibility of a major contribution of budget policy to economic stabilization.

Before the depression, attention in economic thinking about fiscal policy focused on its consequences for the distribution of the total output among uses, rather than on its consequences for the level of output in the short run. The main consequences of fiscal policy were considered to be its effects on (*a*) the division of output between consumption and investment and (*b*) the division of output between public and private use. Standards of good fiscal policy were largely derived from the desired objectives for these two divisions of the national output. (There was, of course, a vast literature on aspects of public finance other than "fiscal policy" which was concerned with other consequences.)

A major theme was the connection among budget balancing, saving, investment, and economic growth. If government expenditures were larger than tax receipts, the deficit would have to be financed by borrowing. The government's borrowing would absorb part of the nation's current private saving, which would therefore not be available to finance private investment. Investment would be lower than if the budget had been balanced, and consequently the rate of economic growth would also be lower.

This argument that total savings will be larger if there is a budget surplus than if there is a deficit is true only if the taxes used to achieve the surplus depress private savings by an amount less than the tax collections. Kinds of taxes are conceivable of which this would not be true. However, it is not necessary to adopt such taxes. Indeed, the same argument that calls for balancing the budget and running a surplus in order to promote economic growth also calls for avoiding kinds of taxation that depress private saving.

The conclusion that government budgets should be balanced was also reached by consideration of the proper division of the national product between private and public uses. The requirement that government expenditures should be financed by taxation was considered necessary to prevent a politically dangerous and economically wasteful excess of government spending. Ultimately the citizen might be thought of as buying services from the government and as obtaining the right amount when he acquires the amount whose cost he is willing to pay in taxes.

It is not demonstrable a priori that the total amount of government expenditures that would be made if they had to be paid for in taxes is the "best" amount, or even better than the amount that would be made if they could be financed by borrowing.

Government expenditures have a real cost in private expenditures that must be forgone, however they are financed. The "discipline" argument for budget balancing is that citizens will not accurately appraise this real cost if they can borrow to pay it. Once this possibility of error is admitted, it becomes a question of fact in what direction the errors run. If the citizens may underestimate costs which are financed by borrowing, so may they overestimate costs financed by taxation and either overestimate or underestimate the benefits of expenditures.

As has been noted, consideration of the desirable division of the national product between consumption and investment and between public and private uses led economists before the 1930s to budget balancing as a basic principle of fiscal policy. But the common popular support for the budget-balancing idea was probably not chiefly based on the economists' argument. The idea that government budgets should be balanced has a direct and intuitive appeal as a particular application of principles of conduct accepted as having moral and utilitarian validity in a much broader field. The "folk wisdom" basis of popular thinking about budgets probably explains the strong resistance of that thinking to the revolutionary change in economists' views of the matter that began in the 1930s.

Post-Keynesian theory. Earlier thinking about fiscal policy was challenged in the 1930s at its root—namely, the proposition that fiscal policy does not affect total national output. Successful challenge to this proposition brought the level of total output and total employment to the forefront of the objectives of fiscal policy. It also radically altered thinking about policy to achieve the traditional objectives.

The revolution in thinking about fiscal policy can be dated from the publication of John Maynard Keynes's *General Theory of Employment, Interest and Money* in 1936. This work had its precursors and was subsequently explained, extended, refined, and in part controverted by others. But the *General Theory* was the turning point. All serious argument about fiscal policy since it was published, even the argument that completely denied the Keynesian conclusions, has been influenced by it.

The first step in the new approach to fiscal policy was to loosen the link between the quantity of money and total money expenditures or total money income. If the ratio of total money income to the supply of money was fixed (or if not fixed, at least determined by factors that fiscal policy could not influence), fiscal policy that did not affect the supply of money would not affect total money income.

The new theory provided a way for fiscal policy to affect total money income, without a change in the supply of money. This, of course, implied a change in the ratio of money income to money supply. For example, suppose the government increases its expenditures without equally increasing taxes and without increasing the supply of money. The increase in government expenditures will initially increase the incomes of individuals and businesses. Since there has been no increase in the money supply, the ratio of their money holdings to their incomes has declined. Older theory would have emphasized reactions to a decline in this ratio which took the form of attempts of individuals and businesses to build up their money holdings by cutting their expenditures, which would in turn reduce total income. The newer theory emphasized two other possibilities. One was that money holdings were already "redundant," so that there would be no felt need to increase money holdings as incomes increased. The other possibility was that individuals and businesses would try to build up their money holdings by selling interest-bearing securities (rather than by cutting their expenditures). This would reduce the prices of such securities, and raise the interest rates they yielded, until a point was reached at which people would no longer consider it worthwhile to sell securities at low prices, or give up interest, in order to get more money.

In the early years of the "new fiscal theory" there was some disposition to carry the argument even further. That is, not only was the effectiveness of fiscal policy asserted, but the effectiveness of monetary policy was denied. If people were willing to absorb a change in their money holdings without any reaction, or if they reacted in a way that affected only interest rates, which did not in turn affect either private investment or saving, there would be no route by which a change in the money supply could affect total money income.

Controversy between the pre-Keynesian view and the extreme post-Keynesian view raged for some years in the late 1930s. But in time a consensus emerged on an intermediate position. The ratio of total money income to the money supply is not fixed, but can be affected by changes in interest rates, which can be changed by fiscal policy; but the ratio is not infinitely variable, and a change in the money supply will affect money income, either through an effect on interest rates and investment, or directly. Under this formulation the national money income may be affected by fiscal policy, or by monetary policy, or by various combinations of the two. Wide disagreement remains, however, about the probable magnitudes of the effects of each kind of action.

The foregoing discussion has run entirely in

terms of the effect of fiscal action upon total money income and money expenditures. It will be recalled that earlier thinking held that variations in money income and expenditures would not in any case affect real output and employment, except temporarily, but would affect only prices and wage rates. The Keynesian analysis assumed that as long as employment was below some level, considered the full employment level, wage rates would be stable and variations in money income would be directly reflected in employment and real output. Some of Keynes's early followers tended to argue as if this assumption, made for purposes of analysis, were also descriptive of the real world. However, there has since been a general recognition that the actual situation is more complicated. There is no single point of "full employment" below which variations in money income affect only employment and output without affecting prices and wage rates and above which only prices and wage rates, but not employment and output, would be affected. At least over a considerable range of employment levels, variations in money income will affect both prices and output, although the price effect will presumably be larger and the output effect smaller, the higher the initial level of employment. This makes the choice of the "desired" behavior of money income difficult, but it still leaves the behavior of money income an important objective of fiscal policy.

Sources and uses of funds. Discussion of the new fiscal policy initially concentrated on the effects of variations in government expenditures, taxes being given. Emphasis was placed on the stimulative effects of "deficit spending," that is, of government spending not offset by tax revenues. It was shown that on certain assumptions the increase in the national income resulting from an increase in deficit spending would be a multiple of the increase in deficit spending. The increase in government spending initially causes private incomes to rise by an equal amount. Recipients of the additional private income will be induced to spend more, which will generate more income for others, who in turn will spend more, and so on in a "multiplier" process whose limit depends on the proportion of their additional income that people spend.

It soon became clear that similar effects could be expected from variations in taxes, expenditures being given. A reduction in taxes would increase, and an increase in taxes would reduce, private spending, which would affect private incomes, and thereby affect private spending, and so on in the multiplier process.

If an increase of government expenditure would increase the national income by some multiple of

the increase, and an increase of taxes would reduce the national income by some multiple of the tax increase, an equal increase of expenditures and taxes would affect the national income in one direction or the other if the expenditure and tax multipliers were unequal. There is no a priori reason to think that the multipliers are equal. In the 1940s and 1950s there was a great deal of discussion of the implications of equal changes of expenditures and revenues. Most of it revolved about the "balanced-budget multiplier theorem," which showed that on certain assumptions the multiplier of an equal increase in expenditures and revenues will be 1; that is, the total increase in spending from an equal increase in government spending and taxes will equal the increase in government spending.

The balanced-budget multiplier theorem demonstrated that the budget deficit or surplus could not logically be regarded as the sole source and measure of the effects of the budget on total spending, and opened the way to a more general view of the possibilities of fiscal policy.

The government may be conceived of as obtaining funds from a variety of sources and using funds in a variety of ways. The total sources and total uses are equal, if borrowing and the use of existing balances are considered sources of funds. Each of the sources and uses of funds has some effect on total national spending, but the effects of different sources and uses need not be equal per dollar. If every dollar used has an equal positive effect on total spending, and if every dollar obtained, including dollars borrowed, has an equal negative effect, then fiscal policy can have no net effect.

The new fiscal policy first said that the effect of borrowing funds to finance a deficit was less per dollar than the effect of obtaining funds from taxes and also less, and of opposite sign, than the effect of spending funds. Therefore, an equal increase of government spending and borrowing, or an equal decrease of taxes and increase of borrowing, would have an effect on total spending.

The balanced-budget multiplier discussion said that the effect of obtaining funds by taxing was different, per dollar, and of opposite sign from the effect of spending funds. Therefore an equal increase of taxes and government expenditures would have a net effect on total expenditures—an expansive effect if the expenditure multiplier was larger than the tax multiplier.

Once we have gone this far, it is a logical next step to say that different government expenditures and different taxes have different effects per dollar. In this case a shift from one kind of government expenditure to another, or from one kind of tax to another, would have a net effect on total expenditure. This net effect could be achieved without a change in the size of the deficit or surplus or in the total size of the budget.

Formally the possibility exists of obtaining any desired effect on total spending through any one of a large number of combinations of sources and uses of government funds. Any differences in the effect per dollar of any two sources or uses of funds would constitute a lever that could be used to affect total spending. Whether in fact the number of such levers is large depends on whether the differences in the effects of various sources and uses of funds are significant, whether the differences are known with some certainty, and whether the various sources and uses of funds can in practice be manipulated to serve some objective with respect to total spending.

Little is reliably known about the differences in the effects of various fiscal actions upon total spending. There is fairly general agreement that an increase in spending or a decrease in taxes has a larger expansive effect, per dollar, than the contractive effect of an increase in government borrowing, although even this would be disputed with respect to some kinds of government borrowing. If this is true, then any combination of fiscal actions that includes expenditure increases and tax decreases, but no expenditure decreases or tax increases, will have an expansive effect. But if the combination includes tax and expenditure actions that separately have effects of different directions, the direction of the net effect would be uncertain.

Modern theory opens up the possibility of a large number of combinations of fiscal actions that could affect total spending, some but not all of which would affect the surplus or deficit. We do not know even the direction of the effect of many of these combinations, including some that affect the surplus or deficit. Where there is considerable confidence about the direction of the effect, the magnitude of the effect is still uncertain, to a degree that varies with the particular action.

Theories concerning implementation. The new theory held out the possibility of achieving any desired level or rate of change of money national income. It said that given any objective for the behavior of money national income, and given all the factors other than fiscal policy that affect its behavior, there is some combination of government expenditure programs and tax rates that will achieve the objective. However, this proposition stops far short of specifying what the proper fiscal policy is at any time.

The implementation of fiscal policy must contend with several difficulties:

(1) It is not certain what behavior of money national income should be the objective of fiscal policy. The money national income is an intermediate objective, important because of its influence on employment, production, prices, economic growth, and the balance of payments. What the effect of a particular level and rate of change of money national income will be on these aspects of the economy is always impossible to tell precisely. Even if it were known what the effects would be, what would be the "best" effects would still have to be determined.

(2) The fiscal policy necessary to achieve any given course of money national income will depend upon the other autonomous factors that affect the national income in the future period in which the fiscal decisions will operate. If these other factors —which may be summed up as private tendencies to invest and consume—are strong, a less expansive fiscal policy will be required than if they are weak. These other factors are variable, and prediction of them is subject to a wide margin of error.

(3) The effects of various fiscal actions upon the money national income are known only very roughly. Presumably, for example, a one-point reduction in the basic rate of the individual income tax will make the money national income higher than it would otherwise have been. But informed estimates of the magnitude and timing of the effects will vary widely, and this will also be true of other fiscal actions.

(4) Even if the target for behavior of money national income, the autonomous factors affecting the national income, and the effects of all fiscal actions are precisely known, the proper fiscal policy is not uniquely determined. There will almost certainly be more than one combination of tax and expenditure actions that would yield the target national income. A choice will have to be made among these combinations, and it will have to be made on criteria other than the effect on national income, since the combinations are alike in that respect.

(5) Since the behavior of money national income is affected to some, much-disputed, degree by monetary policy, the policy packages among which a choice must be made consist not only of various combinations of fiscal actions but also of various combinations of fiscal and monetary policy.

(6) For all the foregoing reasons, the range and variety of fiscal policies that might reasonably be thought at any time to give a good combination of effects on employment, production, prices, etc., will be large, and it will not be possible objectively and certainly to select one policy as best. The selection of a policy to follow will be made in the political process, by people who are sensitive to

the political consequences of the selection. This may introduce a bias into the selection, causing it to depart systematically from what is probably the best choice.

This list of difficulties does not constitute an argument against fiscal policy or even against using fiscal policy to achieve desired effects on employment, production, growth, prices, and the balance of payments. There will be a fiscal policy as long as there is government. This fiscal policy will have effects, and it is obviously desirable that it should have good rather than bad effects. But the difficulties listed here do suggest the problems that must be overcome to assure the choice of the fiscal policy that will have the best effects, or is most likely to have the best effects.

General strategies of implementation. Two main lines of thinking about the strategy of implementing fiscal policy have emerged in the postwar period, although each has variants and the two lines tend to meet when each is elaborated with regard to the conditions of the real world. One approach is direct and activist, the other indirect and passive.

The direct, activist approach might be called the "do your best" approach. It recognizes that the appropriate target for money national income, the future state of the economy upon which fiscal policy will operate, and the future effects of various fiscal actions cannot be known with certainty. Nevertheless, in this view, the responsible authorities in government must make, and act upon, their best estimates of these factors. While there will be departures from the ideal result, these departures, it is believed, will be smaller than would be yielded by any alternative system.

The indirect, passive approach would call for fiscal policy to adhere to some predetermined objective rule or standard which would not require forecasting short-run economic fluctuations. An effort was made to find such a rule which would, first, keep fiscal policy from being an independent destabilizing force and, second, insofar as consistent with the first objective, make fiscal policy a stabilizing force. This effort was more evident in the United States than elsewhere, perhaps because the American political process did not leave budget policy to "experts," and this generated more public interest in specifying guides to budget policy.

The rule commonly suggested set as a standard a fixed relation between expenditure programs and tax rates such that revenues would exceed expenditures by some constant amount X (which might be positive, zero, or negative) when the national income was at some standard level Y. Examples of proposed budget rules may be found in the articles by the Committee for Economic Development and by Milton Friedman included in American Economic Association, *Readings in Fiscal Policy* (1955). Thus the actual surplus would be constant when the actual national income was at the standard. To this degree the budget would be neutral. If this rule were followed, the actual surplus would be below X when the actual national income was below the standard Y, and the surplus would be above X when the actual national income was above the standard Y. The farther the national income was below the standard, the less the government would subtract from the private income stream in taxes, and the more it would add in expenditures, so that the larger the government's support for total spending and income would be. To this degree the budget would be stabilizing; it would resist variations in the actual national income relative to the standard. The standard level of national income would rise through time with the growth of potential national output. If actual national income did not rise as fast as potential, adherence to the rule would generate a rising deficit (or falling surplus), which would tend to accelerate the growth of actual national income.

The logic of the rule did not require that the standard national income should be equal to the potential or "full employment" national income, although it did require that the standard bear a certain constant relation to potential national income. However, in fact, the standard was usually prescribed as the full-employment national income, and the rule called for balancing the budget (or running some specified constant surplus or deficit) at full employment. Thus discussion of the rule focused attention on what the surplus or deficit would be at full employment, as distinguished from the actual surplus or deficit. The "full employment surplus" became a widely-used shorthand measure of the impact of fiscal policy. Whereas changes in the actual surplus or deficit result from changes in other economic conditions as well as from changes in budget policy, changes in the full employment surplus result almost entirely from changes in budget policy. Use of the full employment surplus for analysis or prescription did not necessarily imply that the full employment surplus should be constant, and the concept came to be used in the 1960s by many who did not accept the rule of constant full employment surplus.

Supporters of the indirect, passive approach recognized that in principle an active policy based on perfect foresight would yield superior stabilization results. However, perfect foresight was not possible, and actual decisions, if freed of all conventional rules, would not even be governed by the best possible economic forecasts. The political decisions might be random and destabilizing, or might be biased in an inflationary, expenditure-increasing direction. Therefore, a less ambitious and more restrained policy would lead to better results. In fact, a high degree of stability (meaning steadiness of growth) could be expected from a passive fiscal policy, especially if combined with a stabilizing monetary policy. In some variants this stabilizing monetary policy is also considered to be governed by a rule, such as a constant rate of growth of the money supply; in other variants the monetary policy is flexible and discretionary.

Probably the basic criticism of the indirect approach is that the establishment of a budget rule requires a forecast of what economic conditions will be on the average during the period when the rule is in force. A rule that might be highly inflationary in one set of conditions might be highly deflationary in another. Therefore the rule does not eliminate the need for forecasting but requires a more difficult, because longer-run, kind of forecast than a more active and flexible policy requires.

The choice between these two approaches reflects differences of opinion about the operation of the economic and political systems as well as some differences in evaluating the consequences of inflation and rising government expenditures. While these differences have not been resolved, experience and discussion have tended to narrow the difference between the two approaches. Advocates of what is called here the direct approach do not want or expect a continuous adjustment of fiscal policy to actual or forecast economic conditions, but only an adjustment at intervals. They would also recognize that it may not be desirable to change fiscal policy to deal with economic changes that are small or quite uncertainly forecast. And they have had, at least when in responsible positions, to accept as some restraint the popular sentiment favoring balanced budgets.

At the same time, at least many supporters of a "rule" of fiscal policy would recognize that it may be necessary or desirable to change the rule from time to time. They would also accept the possible necessity at some time to depart temporarily from the rule.

Once these points are reached, the differences between the two approaches come down to questions about the frequency of changes in fiscal policy and the strength of the evidence required to justify a change. These are matters of gradation, on which a continuous graduation of positions may be taken.

The fiscal–monetary "mix." If fiscal policy is not the only instrument by which the government can influence the money national income, it is not a sufficient guide to fiscal policy to say that it must be so managed as to bring about the desired national income. It can only be said that the available instruments should be used in combination to effect the desired result, but this leaves open the question of the combination in which the various instruments should be used. The main question of combining instruments concerns the combination of fiscal and monetary policy.

Even though fiscal and monetary policy may both be capable, in general, of affecting the national income, there may be special circumstances in which they are not alternative instruments. For example, it has been thought that at the bottom of a deep depression, profit prospects may appear so bleak that no expansion of the money supply would stimulate an increase in investment or other private spending. In this case monetary policy would not be an alternative to fiscal policy for promoting recovery. However, whether this is a realistic possibility has been disputed, and there is no suggestion that such circumstances have emerged in the postwar world.

Fiscal actions and monetary actions may differ in the speed with which they can be taken, have effect, and be modified or reversed if necessary. This may provide the basis for a division of labor between fiscal and monetary policy, the more flexible instrument being used in those circumstances in which a quick and possibly reversible effect is needed. In much of the earlier postwar writing it was assumed that monetary policy was the more flexible instrument and therefore should be relied upon for short-run adjustments of the impact of the combined fiscal–monetary package. However, later study suggested that the lag between monetary action and its effects might be long and variable. This raised the question whether monetary policy was in fact the more flexible and manageable element in the monetary–fiscal combination. Thus, the principle remains that in the division of labor between fiscal and monetary policy, the more flexible instrument should be used for the more rapid and frequent adjustments, but which is the more flexible instrument is uncertain.

If the desired money national income for any period can be achieved by one of several combinations of fiscal and monetary policy, the choice among these combinations requires the invocation of some additional objective. Two such objectives have seemed particularly relevant: economic growth and balance-of-payments equilibrium.

On certain assumptions, the economy will grow more rapidly with a large budget surplus than with a small budget surplus or deficit, if in each case there is the appropriate monetary policy to attain the desired current rate of money national income. Unless there are fully offsetting effects, the larger surplus will mean larger total savings and larger total investment. Some offsets may be expected. Getting the larger surplus will require some combination of higher taxes, which may reduce private saving or have other growth-restraining effects, and lower public expenditures, some of which might have had growth-promoting effects. Also, the more expansive monetary policy required to accompany the larger surplus may depress private saving. Therefore, a larger-surplus policy cannot be said to be a faster-growth policy without further specification, but it is probably possible to design a larger-surplus policy that will be a faster-growth policy. Even this would not, of course, by itself make the larger surplus preferable. A larger surplus leads to faster growth only at some cost, in the form of reduced current consumption and possibly also in other forms; whether it is legitimate or wise for government to decide to pay that cost is a question that would still have to be answered.

In the late 1950s and early 1960s attention was focused on the balance-of-payments implications of the combination of fiscal and monetary policy. This new interest was largely derived from concern with the position of the United States, which was running a persistent balance-of-payments deficit along with more unemployment and less inflation than most of the rest of the world. A country in such circumstances seeks both domestic expansion and contraction of its external deficit. It was suggested that these two objectives might be simultaneously approached by a more expansive fiscal policy combined with a less expansive monetary policy. More generally, it could be shown that if domestic income and the balance of payments depend upon monetary and fiscal policy and on no other, and if these two policies affect no other objectives, the two objectives determine the best combination of the two policies. While these conditions may never be fully met, they may be approximated for short periods.

Definition of the budget. Any fiscal policy which uses the budget position—the size of the deficit or surplus—as a guide to action requires a decision on what is to be included in the budget—how it is to be defined. As was indicated earlier, government fiscal operations can be described by a statement of the sources and uses of government funds, the sources and uses being necessarily equal. The creation of a budget that can have a surplus or a deficit requires the selection of some but not all of these sources and uses of funds for inclusion in the budget. Which items should be included depends on the policy purpose to be served by the over-all budget figures. Aside from this purpose, there is no "true" budget.

The appropriate definition of the budget depends on whether the main purpose of budget policy is (a) to affect the money national income, (b) to exercise "discipline" over government spending, by requiring that expenditure be matched by taxation, or (c) to affect national saving by controlling the relation between government revenues and the government expenditures that are not for investment. Different emphases on these three objectives lead to different answers to the questions that arise about the definition of the budget. These questions relate chiefly to four kinds of transactions:

(1) Trust account transactions in which the government accumulates a fund from a particular class of individuals, out of which payments are made, simultaneously or subsequently, for specified purposes. Social insurance funds are a leading example.

(2) Loan transactions in which the government at some times lends money to private borrowers or to other governments or purchases their debt, and at other times receives repayment or sells the debt.

(3) Capital expenditures for the acquisition by government of assets (including loans) that yield a subsequent return, whether in money or in nonmonetary benefits.

(4) Transactions in which there is a considerable lapse of time between the accrual of a liability to or from the government and the corresponding cash payment.

Different treatments of these kinds of transactions are illustrated by the three "budgets," or statements of government receipts and payments, commonly used in the United States:

The *administrative* budget, which excludes trust account transactions, is almost entirely on a cash basis, and makes no distinction between loan or capital transactions and current transactions;

The *cash-consolidated* budget, which includes trust account transactions and is entirely on a cash basis;

The government sector of the *national income accounts*, which also includes trust account transactions, but excludes loan transactions and reflects corporate-profits-tax liability accruals rather than cash payments.

None of these three financial accounts used in the United States distinguishes between capital and current transactions. However, many other governments use capital budgets which do make this distinction.

Since the main object sought in postwar thinking about fiscal policy has been a certain effect, presumably stabilizing, upon money national income, the search for definitions of the budget has focused on that which would be most revealing of the effects of fiscal policy on money national income. What is desired is the most comprehensive definition of the budget consistent with the requirement that all fiscal policies yielding an equal surplus in the budget so defined have, under similar general economic conditions, equal effects on money national income. This test can be literally met only if every expenditure has the same effect, per dollar, as every other expenditure and the same effect, with sign reversed, as every receipt. This is to say that the test cannot be literally met by any real budget. The test does suggest the desirability of excluding from the budget transactions that are markedly different in their effect per dollar from the transactions included and that vary substantially in magnitude relative to the transactions included. However, if important items are excluded in order to make the budget more homogeneous and thus to give the size of the surplus or deficit a more stable meaning, problems arise in establishing criteria and mechanisms for controlling the excluded items. In practice, some compromise beween homogeneity and comprehensiveness in defining the budget must be found.

It seems clear that if the budget is intended to reveal the effects of fiscal transactions on money national income, there is no good reason for excluding trust account transactions from the budget. Many, and probably most, of the receipts and expenditures made by trust accounts are quite similar in their aggregate economic effects to many of the receipts and expenditures included in the regular budget. A more difficult problem is the treatment of loan transactions. If the government makes a loan to a private business, a local government, or a foreign government, is this more like a government grant or purchase, in which case it should be treated as an expenditure, or more like government purchase (repayment) of its own securities, in which case it should not be treated as an expenditure? Probably the answer depends upon the terms and circumstances of particular kinds of loans.

If the main objective of budget policy is to stabilize, or otherwise influence, total money expenditures, there is no good reason to distinguish between the current and capital expenditures of government. Capital spending, at least when it is for purchase of real goods and services, is likely to have as great a direct and indirect effect on total spending in the economy as does current spending. The amount of taxation needed for economic stabilization does not depend on whether the government's expenditures are for current or capital purposes.

Emphasis on the "disciplinary" function of a budget rule may provide a rationale for excluding the trust accounts from the budget. The purpose of requiring that the budget be balanced may be to assure that government expenditures are not made unless taxpayers have demonstrated their willingness to pay taxes for them. However, this purpose does not require the inclusion in the budget of transactions that have their own disciplinary safeguards. If the government undertakes a particular expenditure program to which specific revenues are assigned, with a definite plan and commitment over some period, the disciplinary function of budget balancing does not require inclusion of these transactions in the budget. The cogency of this argument for excluding a trust fund from the budget depends upon whether the trust fund actually conforms to this description, which is sometimes, but not always, the case.

A similar case on "disciplinary" grounds can be made for excluding from the budget capital transactions where the productivity of government capital investments can be objectively measured and compared with the cost of capital. This would provide a test of the desirability of public investments that would be superior to the test of the willingness of the community to pay taxes for them. Where the investment yields a product that is sold in the market—as is the case with a government-owned railroad—this objective test of productivity may be available. But there are many kinds of government investment—education being one example—where the product is difficult to measure or even to define. To remove the requirement that such expenditures be financed by taxation may leave no adequate limits to their expansion.

One case for use of a capital budget may be found in the desire to separate the government decision about the total amount of saving in the economy from the decision about the total amount of government investment. The total saving of the economy is equal to private saving plus the excess of taxes over current, noninvestment expenditure of government. The government, or the community through the government, may decide to make this total larger or smaller by deciding on a larger or smaller excess of taxes over current expenditures. (This assumes that private savings do not increase or decrease by an amount equal to the change in the excess of taxes over current expenditures.) The government may decide to run a large current surplus in order to generate large total savings and thus permit large total investment and a high rate of growth. This decision by itself logically implies nothing about the proportions in which the investments would be private and government. On the other hand, the government may decide on a larger or smaller amount of public investment. This by itself implies nothing about what total saving should be. The decision to have a large amount of public investment may reflect a judgment that many public investments are more productive (or otherwise desirable) than private investments and should be made instead of them—not in addition to them. The existence of large opportunities for productive investment may be a reason for wanting high savings and a large excess of taxes over current expenditure. But this would be equally true whether the opportunities were for public or private investment.

If a capital budget is used, the government would decide, by deciding on the size of its current surplus, how much it should contribute to total saving. It would decide this in terms of the value the community places on economic growth and the supply of productive investment opportunities, public and private. The government would also decide on the desirability of particular public investments in terms of their productivity, taking into account the cost of capital. Proponents of the capital budget maintain that this would result in better decisions about both the government's contribution to saving and the government's investment than does a budget which lumps together current and capital expenditure.

A different kind of concern with the effect of budget policy on total saving may justify the exclusion of trust accounts from the budget. It may be desired to balance the budget so that all private savings will be available to finance private investment, either on the grounds that growth will be promoted thereby or that "consumers' sovereignty" requires that the amount of private investment should be determined by private saving. If individual citizens voluntarily make payments into a government-managed fund from which they will subsequently receive benefits, these savings should, on this principle, not be available to finance government expenditures, as would happen if they were lumped into the budget. The force of this argument depends upon the degree to which the trust account in fact has the character of a private voluntary savings institution.

The idea of the capital budget does not neces-sarily imply that the current budget should be balanced by taxation; the rule may be a surplus or deficit in the current budget. However, much discussion of the idea has assumed that the issue was between balancing the current budget and balancing the total budget. Since net government capital expenditures are likely to be positive, balancing the current budget will be more expansionary than balancing the total budget. This has won some support for the capital budget idea from those who believe there is need for an expansionary fiscal policy but who do not want to violate community sentiment in favor of balancing "some" budget.

Budget flexibility. Fiscal action taken at any time has its effects on some future time. The appropriateness of the action is its appropriateness to the future time at which its effects occur. Fiscal action therefore requires or implies a forecast. The reliability of the forecast will be greater the nearer the future period to which it relates. For this reason attention has been directed to increasing the flexibility of fiscal policy, so that it will have its effects more quickly and the time for which forecasts have to be made will be shortened. Increased flexibility has been sought along three main lines, sometimes called built-in flexibility, formula flexibility, and discretionary flexibility.

Built-in flexibility. The stabilizing effect of the variation in government tax receipts or liabilities and unemployment compensation payments that automatically accompanies variation in the national income has already been noted. Recognition of the value of this automatic response of the budget has naturally led to the question whether this response could be strengthened. However, a basic difficulty arises in considering possible ways to strengthen the built-in stabilizing response. The extent to which tax receipts vary with a change in the national income depends upon the tax rates applied to individual and corporate incomes at the margin —the proportion of an increase in an individual's or corporation's income that is taken in taxes. If these marginal rates are high, the proportion of a change in national income that is absorbed in a change in tax receipts will be large, and this will have a stabilizing effect on the economy. However, if these rates are high, taxes will take a large proportion of the additional income that an individual or corporation may earn by productive activity. At least beyond some point this will weaken the incentive to productive activity and will adversely affect economic efficiency and growth. Thus the stabilizing value of high marginal tax rates can be obtained only at the cost of other important economic objectives.

In general, the marginal rates of tax, and also the rates of unemployment compensation payments, have been so closely determined by a combination of other factors economically and politically more important as to leave no room for adjusting them to increase "built-in" stabilization.

To get around this difficulty there have been proposals intended to increase the automatic responsiveness of tax collections or unemployment compensation to changes in the over-all state of the economy without increasing their responsiveness to the condition or activity of any individual. The general principle may be illustrated by the following hypothetical scheme: Weekly withholding of income tax from each taxpayer will be reduced by $2.00 for every percentage point by which the latest published seasonally adjusted figure for the rate of unemployment exceeds 4 per cent (and annual liability will be correspondingly reduced). Such a scheme would greatly increase the variability of tax collections in response to variations in the rate of unemployment without increasing the amount of tax taken out of an additional dollar of income earned by any individual.

Formula flexibility. Consideration of proposals for formula flexibility has not proceeded beyond an elementary and formal stage. One difficulty is that while, once the formula is adopted, reliance on long-term forecasting is eliminated, the formula itself implies a long-run forecast of the way in which fiscal policy should respond to changes in the economy. Formula flexibility buys speed of response in exchange for discretion in deciding what the response should be. This may be a worthwhile exchange, but that has not been satisfactorily demonstrated. Possibly a more serious difficulty is political. Governments may be willing to take active fiscal measures when the need is clear and present but unwilling to commit themselves in advance to the automatic occurrence of such measures.

Discretionary flexibility. Efforts to increase the flexibility of the budget have been largely concentrated on discretionary measures. Preparations are sought which, while leaving the government in all cases free to act or not, will enable the government to decide more quickly and will speed up the effects of the decisions taken. The classic case of such preparations is the "shelf of public works." Ideally this is a reserve of government construction projects for which legislative authorizations and appropriations have been made, plans drawn, and sites obtained, so that work can be started quickly when the Executive decides to do so. Interest in the shelf of public works has diminished, at least in the United States, since the end of World War II. Federal nonmilitary public works activities have not been large, and the volume of projects that seem desirable enough to authorize but not urgent enough to begin immediately has been small relative to the size of the economy and its potential fluctuations. The volume of these that could quickly reach a high rate of operation and, if necessary, be stopped without great loss is even smaller. Also, it has appeared that the need for expansive action might arise when construction is running at a high rate, so that increasing public works would not be appropriate.

The revenue side of the budget seems to hold out greater possibility for quick and powerful fiscal action. Federal revenues in the United States are about 20 per cent of the gross national product. Changes in tax rates that are administratively feasible could increase or decrease the available after-tax incomes of individuals or businesses by large amounts in a short time. The period required for legislative enactment of a tax change may be long, however, and there have been a number of proposals for shortening this period. These involve advance legislative authorization to the president to make a specified tax cut, possibly subject to Congressional veto within a limited period, or an agreement by Congress to act upon a presidential recommendation within a limited period. In fact, even without such arrangements the legislative process would allow quick Congressional action on a tax change if a strong majority of Congress were agreed on the need for it.

Deliberate and systematic effort to use fiscal policy to keep the economy operating close to its potential while avoiding inflation and serving other objectives became standard practice in most Western industrial countries after World War II. The results of that experience were varied and interpretation of the results even more varied. But the experience did not contradict the idea that fiscal policy, at least when accompanied by appropriate monetary policy, is a powerful instrument for affecting economic performance in basically free economies. This instrument by itself may be unable to reconcile inconsistencies where they arise between some objectives, such as full employment and price stability or domestic stabilization and international equilibrium. Even aside from this, knowledge and institutions are inadequate for management of the fiscal instrument to achieve its ideal effectiveness. Yet there is little doubt that the results of freeing fiscal policy from older inhibitions have on the whole been beneficial and that further opportunities for improved use of the fiscal instrument, based on experience and study, remain.

HERBERT STEIN

[*See also* DEBT, PUBLIC; MONETARY POLICY; MONEY; PUBLIC EXPENDITURES; TAXATION.]

BIBLIOGRAPHY

AMERICAN ECONOMIC ASSOCIATION 1955 *Readings in Fiscal Policy*. Homewood, Ill.: Irwin. → Contains an extensive classified bibliography.

ANDO, ALBERT; and MODIGLIANI, FRANCO 1965 The Relative Stability of Monetary Velocity and the Investment Multiplier. *American Economic Review* 55:693–728.

COLM, GERHARD 1955 *Essays in Public Finance and Fiscal Policy*. Oxford Univ. Press.

DEPRANO, MICHAEL; and MAYER, THOMAS 1965 Tests of the Relative Importance of Autonomous Expenditures and Money. *American Economic Review* 55:729–752.

DOW, J. C. R. 1964 *The Management of the British Economy: 1945–1960*. Cambridge Univ. Press.

Economic Policy in Our Time, by Étienne S. Kirschen et al. 3 vols. 1964 Amsterdam: North-Holland Publishing. → Describes the experience of eight industrial countries.

FRIEDMAN, MILTON (1951) 1959 The Effects of a Full-employment Policy on Economic Stability: A Formal Analysis. Pages 117–132 in Milton Friedman, *Essays in Positive Economics*. Univ. of Chicago Press. → First published in French in Volume 4 of *Économie appliquée*.

FRIEDMAN, MILTON; and MEISELMAN, DAVID 1964 The Relative Stability of Monetary Velocity and the Investment Multiplier in the United States: 1897–1958. Pages 165–268 in *Stabilization Policies: A Series of Research Studies Prepared for the Commission on Money and Credit*. Englewood Cliffs, N.J.: Prentice-Hall.

FRIEDMAN, MILTON; and MEISELMAN, DAVID 1965 Reply to Ando and Modigliani and to DePrano and Mayer. *American Economic Review* 55:753–785. → Contains a rejoinder by Ando and Modigliani on pages 786–790 and by DePrano and Mayer on pages 791–792.

KEYNES, JOHN MAYNARD 1936 *The General Theory of Employment, Interest and Money*. London: Macmillan. → A paperback edition was published in 1965 by Harcourt.

KIMMEL, LEWIS H. 1959 *Federal Budget and Fiscal Policy: 1789–1958*. Washington: Brookings Institution. → Contains a description of and references to early writings of economists and others.

LEWIS, WILFRED 1962 *Federal Fiscal Policy in the Postwar Recessions*. National Committee on Government Finance, Studies in Government Finance. Washington: Brookings Institution.

MUNDELL, ROBERT A. 1962 The Appropriate Use of Monetary and Fiscal Policy for Internal and External Stability. International Monetary Fund, *Staff Papers* 9:70–77.

SAMUELSON, PAUL A. 1942 Fiscal Policy and Income Determination. *Quarterly Journal of Economics* 56:575–605.

SIMONS, HENRY C. (1942) 1948 Hansen on Fiscal Policy. Pages 184–219 in Henry C. Simons, *Economic Policy for a Free Society*. Univ. of Chicago Press. → First published in the *Journal of Political Economy*.

U.S. CONGRESS, JOINT COMMITTEE ON THE ECONOMIC REPORT 1947 *Economic Report of the President: Hearings Before the Joint Committee on the Economic Report*. Washington: Government Printing Office.

U.S. COUNCIL OF ECONOMIC ADVISERS 1947 *Annual Report to the President, Second*. Washington: Government Printing Office.

U.S. PRESIDENT 1947 *Economic Report of the President*. Washington: Government Printing Office. → Published annually since 1947.

II
WARTIME FISCAL POLICY

The objectives and methods of peacetime fiscal policy are not invalidated by the onset of a major war. However, the overriding goal of winning the war modifies both the relative emphasis placed on the various objectives and the mixture of procedures adopted to achieve them.

The experience of the United States in World War II will serve to illustrate the points involved. The magnitude of that war and its grave threat to the nation demanded the greatest feasible effort. The public, with minor exceptions, strongly supported the war. On balance there could be no recourse to the resources of other countries; instead, the United States supplied large amounts of matériel to its allies. However, the war was considered a temporary interlude in the national life, as is evidenced by the speed and completeness of demobilization at its conclusion.

The magnitude of the war required policies designed to achieve maximum engagement and utilization of human and material resources: a substantial proportion of the resources previously employed in producing civilian goods had to be shifted quickly to the military effort. Patriotic fervor was such that people were willing to sustain exactions, toil, inconvenience, and hardship not acceptable at other times, but only if they believed these burdens were being fairly shared by everyone. In the absence of both the opportunity and the reason to borrow abroad, all borrowing had to come from the same public that paid the taxes and bore the other burdens of the war, although not necessarily in the same proportions. Because of the expectation that the war would be a temporary condition, people were willing to postpone the purchase of many durable and semidurable goods, thus freeing resources for the war effort. The same expectation also strengthened public resistance to efforts by particular groups to use the wartime emergency as an occasion for permanently altering the social and economic structure of the economy.

These wartime conditions had several implications for fiscal policy. The use of a draft to select persons for military service was an obvious necessity, but its superior equity over "buying" recruits also gave it a superficial attractiveness as a method of recruiting industrial and other supporting efforts. It was not, however, a practical method for eliciting the intensive, tedious, continued efforts required in war production. Moreover, such use of the draft and concomitant military command system would have threatened the postwar economy with the perpetuation of a totalitarian economic system.

Accordingly, it was deemed imperative to rely as much as possible on governmental expenditures and fiscal incentives to stimulate maximum utilization of human and material resources, and on taxation and borrowing to support the resulting financial costs of the war. However, certain direct controls were required to reinforce and complement the fiscal measures. To have diverted resources from civilian to military use through fiscal measures alone would have been a slow, incomplete, and very costly process; priorities and direct allocations were an effective addition, which, although sometimes drastic, were justified in the public mind by the war emergency. Furthermore, it was clear that, despite heavy taxation, persons with large incomes and accumulated wealth could virtually monopolize the purchase of scarce, necessary consumer goods, while persons with small incomes suffered intense hardship. Rationing, although administratively difficult and sometimes arbitrary, could assure broad distribution of the supply. For reasons of economy and morale price and wage controls were needed to prevent spiraling inflation, gross inequities, and permanent shifts in the economic positions of different persons and groups.

While fiscal measures alone cannot be expected to achieve the objectives, or cope with the economic problems, of a major war, they should be made to do as much as possible, thereby reducing the need to employ measures disruptive of the market economy. The major objectives of an effective wartime fiscal program are fairness of burden distribution, stimulation of military and supporting production, avoidance of inflation, and salutary consequences for the postwar economy. In practice these goals must be pursued through political and administrative processes in which policy and action are determined by what people believe, whether or not it is in accord with reality.

Taxation versus borrowing.   The major alternatives for financing governmental expenditures are taxation, borrowing of private savings, and expansion of the money supply. The last usually takes the form of loans from commercial and central banks rather than direct money issue. Because of its inflationary effects, it is the least desirable alternative. No case has yet been noted of a major war financed by taxation alone. During World War II the U.S. federal government collected in taxes 45 per cent of its expenditures, a somewhat higher percentage than during World War I or the Civil War and a somewhat lower percentage than was collected by Great Britain and Canada in World War II.

The relative shares of war costs to be paid from taxation and from borrowing have been determined by various factors. A traditional belief that still seems to be influential is that through borrowing, a country can shift much of the cost of the war to "future generations" in the postwar years. This belief has no validity for a country relying on internal resources. While a relatively small part of the real economic burden of the war can in some sense be shifted to postwar years, the amount thus postponable cannot be increased by financing the war through borrowing instead of taxing. What can be changed by this means is the distribution of the cost among persons. Wartime borrowing places financial burdens during the war on lenders, who after the end of the war are repaid out of taxes, which in turn are paid by the lenders and nonlenders alike. [See DEBT, PUBLIC.]

The desirability of the redistribution resulting from wartime borrowing can be measured by applying the criteria listed above. With respect to fairness of burden distribution, there are conflicting considerations. Financing through taxation avoids the injustice of levying a double burden on members of the armed forces; once on the battlefield and again through taxation to reimburse wartime lenders. However, to pay the total cost of a major war through currently collected taxes would require imposing a heavier burden on low-income groups than would be necessary if part of the cost were met by accumulating debts to be serviced after the war out of collections from progressive taxes.

With respect to production incentives, lending to the government has a less adverse effect than paying taxes does, since the patriotic efforts of workers, farmers, and businessmen are strengthened by the assurance of a tangible reward in the form of current assets and postwar spending power.

Taxation is distinctly superior to wartime borrowing as a means of minimizing inflation both during and after the war. To the citizen's mind his tax payments are gone forever, while what he loans to the government creates for him an asset that psychologically encourages his continued expenditure. To minimize this effect, the government seeks through shortages, rationing, and patriotic appeals to maximize private savings and to tap them through the sale of war bonds and other securities. The inadequacy of voluntary savings commonly necessitates borrowing from banks as well, with consequent expansion of the money supply. If the economy moves into war from a low level of output, as was the case in the United States in 1940–1941, some growth in the money supply is needed to finance expanded production and any price increases that may be required to stimulate and transfer resource utilization. Also, the chances for a prosperous postwar economy are improved by sufficient wartime borrowing from the public and from banks to provide the reserves of liquid assets needed to support demand during the postwar transition period. However, such borrowing throughout the war greatly exceeded these needs and created an excessive volume of liquid assets. Although the resulting inflationary pressures were largely suppressed during the war, the liquid assets contributed importantly to the inflationary spending of the postwar period.

All these considerations may be variously evaluated and balanced in choosing between more taxes or more borrowing. The conclusion almost certainly will be that more should be paid through taxation than will be politically feasible, because the psychological limits to taxation are undoubtedly much below the economic limits set by adverse effects on production incentives. The psychological limits appear to be determined more by the rapidity and extent of rate increases than by the previous level of the rates. In the United States the political and psychological limits undoubtedly were closely approached by 1943, when Treasury Department efforts to secure substantial tax increases met with great political resistance and a minimum of public support.

Use of income taxes. The major sources of expanded revenue to finance World War II were taxes on net income, particularly the personal income tax but also the corporation income tax and excess profits tax. The characteristics of progressive income taxation are especially needed in time of war. The progressive income tax is highly flexible in that rates and exemptions can be readily changed, yields at given rates increase more than proportionately to the rise in national income, and with current collection, rate increases can be quickly reflected in government revenues. The income tax is the best adapted of all taxes for adjusting the tax load in accordance with the social consensus on what is equitable. Taxes on net income do not drive businesses into bankruptcy and are less likely than most other taxes to be shifted forward in higher prices with consequent wage and price escalation. However, despite its merits, the income tax can be overused; very high income tax rates may impair incentives to produce and unquestionably stimulate the search for ways to avoid or evade the tax. [*See* TAXATION.]

Use of sales taxes. An exception to the heavy use of the income tax by nations fighting World War II was in the Soviet Union, where sales taxation is part of the apparatus of socialist income distribution. In other countries the use made of sales taxes and other gross transactions taxes differed greatly, but the rates generally were not greatly increased during the war, perhaps because of the regressive incidence of the taxes and their tendency to upset wage stabilization programs. In the United States the pre-emption of the sales tax field by the states was a factor, as was a political reluctance to introduce a general sales tax that might well remain as a permanent element of the postwar system. In Great Britain a heavy "purchases tax" on sales at the wholesale level was imposed, at rates ranging up to 100 per cent. The objective was not only to raise revenue but also to discourage the purchase of scarce, less necessary goods. A very modest use of this principle was made in the United States in the form of moderate excise taxes on scarce durable goods, with the unintended sequel that they were treated as purely revenue taxes and their repeal was delayed long after the shortages had turned to surpluses.

Special taxation. A major question regarding the concept of fairness in war taxation is to what extent higher rates or special taxes should be imposed on increases of income realized because of the war. The corporate excess profits tax, which has become an expected element in wartime tax structures, is the principal illustration of taxation used for this purpose. It has the twofold objective of raising revenue where psychologically and economically it will presumably hurt the least and of preventing businesses from reaping unconscionable profits from the common emergency. In practice, the excess profits tax has proved to be extremely difficult to administer in harmony with its objectives; in a complex business society truly excessive profits are hard to define with precision and even harder to measure. Yet having in the tax system an "excess profits tax," even a weak or arbitrary one, seems to be essential to promote morale and make more acceptable the wartime controls that limit the incomes of workers and farmers.

The principle of special taxation on increases of income was not extended to individuals, despite considerable support for such action, no doubt because both the formulation and administration would have been even more difficult than for corporate business. The tax would also have damaged the war effort by impairing the incentives of war workers, whose new-found prosperity was indeed the target of the proposals.

Substantial resistance appeared to any tax changes that would permanently modify the relative economic positions of taxpaying groups and might therefore be considered reforms. Perhaps the clearest illustration is the estate tax, which was increased only moderately. The reasoning of the Congress seemed to be that if higher wartime rates continued into the postwar years, the result would be a major shift in the distribution of wealth and income; while strictly as wartime levies the rate increases would arbitrarily fall only on the estates of persons who died during the war.

New methods of raising revenue did not prove popular with the wartime congresses. An effort by the Treasury Department late in the 1942 session to secure a progressive tax on personal expenditures was summarily rejected. The idea of distinguishing part of the income tax as a refundable, compulsory loan, proposed by J. M. Keynes in 1940, was strongly supported by some economists in the United States administration, and it was incorporated to a small degree in the "victory tax" on income—a tax designed to hit lower incomes, with war workers again the main target. The compulsory loan feature was in effect repealed before collection. The compulsory loan was, however, used in Great Britain and, for a short time, in Canada. The experience can scarcely be considered a success (Heller 1951). Keynes's objective in proposing compulsory lending was to raise the psychological limits of wartime taxation, but apparently the taxpayers rarely distinguished between the loan part and the tax part of the payment.

External resources. Countries in a position to supplement their domestic resources with resources from other countries have used various methods to accomplish the transfer. For the most part, intergovernmental loans were used during World War I, but the repayment mechanism broke down after the war; the United States, which was the principal creditor, imposed such heavy protective tariffs as to make repayment in goods virtually impossible. In World War II the use of intergovernmental loans was minimized, and large use was made of the Lend-Lease program, which in effect was a method of common burden sharing with no postwar indebtedness liability. At the opening of World War II the British nationalized foreign securities held by citizens and, as the situation required, either sold them for foreign exchange or used them as collateral for loans. The British also incurred large foreign exchange debts in Commonwealth countries, some of which were not liquidated until long after the war. The Germans made substantial drafts on the resources of countries that they occupied during the war (Lindholm 1947).

"In-between" periods. Turning from major wars to periods marked by minor war or heavy cold war defense budgets, we find that some of the characteristics discussed above are absent. The economic and financial requirements during such periods impose burdens that large and growing economies may absorb with little difficulty—except for potentially greater inflationary pressures than would be present in time of real peace. There is little sense of national emergency or outpouring of patriotic fervor and willingness to sacrifice. There is gradual although reluctant recognition that the problem may continue indefinitely rather than be quickly ended. It may prove to be significant that thus far the experience of the United States with modern fiscal policy has not been during periods of substantially unimpaired peace but during periods of major war, reconversion from war, minor war, and the "gray area" between war and peace.

In a situation falling between peace and war the appropriate fiscal policies tend to be similar to those of a peacetime period, although of course much depends on the size and rate of growth of defense and military expenditures. At times, even the need for further fiscal stimulus may emerge. In an "in-between" period the use of control measures to supplement fiscal policy is usually resisted, and if they are imposed, their administration is less successful in achieving compliance than in a time of major war.

Fiscal measures must be carefully oriented. The policy toward borrowing should depend on current conditions, not on projections into a doubtful "postwar" period. The tax system should be developed for the long run, not for a short-run emergency. An excess profits tax, for example, would be less appropriate in an "in-between" period than in time of major war, as well as more difficult to design and administer, since there is no valid base period against which to measure the excessiveness of profits.

In short, a period between peace and major war is an unusually difficult one in which to operate fiscal policy. The economy may develop too much inflationary pressure for successful containment through fiscal and monetary policy alone, while the absence of patriotic fervor and sense of urgency prevents wartime controls from being either acceptable or readily administrable. It is a period in which quasi controls, "voluntary" restraints, and other halfway measures, unsatisfactory as they are for all concerned, may represent the only feasible supplement to fiscal and monetary policies.

ROY BLOUGH

BIBLIOGRAPHY

British White Paper on War Finance. 1946 [U.S.] Board of Governors of the Federal Reserve System, *Federal Reserve Bulletin* 32:723–748. → First published as *National Income and Expenditures in the United Kingdom: 1938–1945*. Great Britain, Parliament, Papers by Command, Cmd. 6784.

CHICAGO, UNIVERSITY OF, LAW SCHOOL 1952 *Defense, Controls, and Inflation: A Conference*. Edited by Aaron Director. Univ. of Chicago Press.

COLM, GERHARD 1935 War Finance. Volume 15, pages 347–352 in *Encyclopaedia of the Social Sciences*. New York: Macmillan.

CRUM, WILLIAM L.; FENNELLY, JOHN F.; and SELTZER, LAWRENCE H. 1942 *Fiscal Planning for Total War*. New York: National Bureau of Economic Research.

HARRIS, SEYMOUR E. 1951 *The Economics of Mobilization and Inflation*. New York: Norton.

HELLER, WALTER W. 1951 Compulsory Lending: The World War II Experience. *National Tax Journal* 4: 116–128.

KEYNES, JOHN MAYNARD 1940 *How to Pay for the War: A Radical Plan for the Chancellor of the Exchequer*. New York: Harcourt; London: Macmillan.

LINDHOLM, RICHARD W. 1947 German Finance in World War II. *American Economic Review* 37:121–134.

MURPHY, HENRY C. 1950 *The National Debt in War and Transition*. New York: McGraw-Hill.

PAUL, RANDOLPH E. 1954 *Taxation in the United States*. Boston: Little.

STUDENSKI, PAUL; and KROOS, HERMAN E. (1952) 1963 *Financial History of the United States: Fiscal, Monetary, Banking, and Tariff, Including Financial Administration and State and Local Finance*. 2d ed. New York: McGraw-Hill.

SUMBERG, THEODORE A. 1946 The Soviet Union's War Budgets. *American Economic Review* 36:113–126.

TAX INSTITUTE 1944 *Curbing Inflation Through Taxation*, by Marriner S. Eccles et al. New York: The Institute.

FISHER, IRVING

Irving Fisher (1867–1947), American economist, had originally intended to become a mathematician. He studied at Yale with the eminent mathematician J. Willard Gibbs but was drawn toward economics under the influence of William Graham Sumner. As Fisher himself reported, he was fascinated by Sumner. He was also deeply influenced by the astronomer Simon Newcomb, who had published a number of economic texts, including the remarkable *Principles of Political Economy*.

From 1892 to 1895 Fisher taught mathematics at Yale, with an interval in 1893 and 1894, when he visited Europe, spending time in Berlin and Paris. After 1895 he transferred from the mathematics to the economics department, remaining at Yale until his retirement in 1935.

A prolific writer, gifted in the most varied subjects, active as a mathematician, statistician, demographer, economist, businessman, reformer, and teacher, Fisher left behind him some thirty books and hundreds of papers and theoretical studies, as well as many popular articles dealing with a wide spectrum of subjects, ranging from economic theory to public health.

Fisher made a fortune from his invention of a visible card index file system, which he marketed in 1910. The corporation he founded merged with others in 1926 to form Remington Rand, Inc., of which he was a director until his death. He was also a founder and director of several agencies for economic analysis and forecasting, and a director of a considerable number of other companies. Part of Fisher's fortune was lost in the 1929 stock-market crash.

He was connected with a large number of associations and interested in many public causes. He was concerned with the problems of world peace and campaigned for six months throughout the United States in favor of U.S. participation in the League of Nations. He published two books (1923; 1924) and many articles on the subject. He was an ardent proponent of prohibition (see 1926; 1928a). His objectivity in selecting statistical data for these books has been questioned by some of his opponents.

Fisher also devoted a good deal of his time to campaigning for improved hygienic, sanitary, and eugenic practices. These crusades were an outcome of his own severe attack of tuberculosis in 1898, which interrupted his work for four years and gave him an interest in problems of health. In 1913, together with H. A. Ley and ex-President Taft, he founded the Life Extension Institute, with a view to generating public awareness of the contribution that sound living and periodic medical examinations can make to good health. He published *How to Live* (see Fisher et al. 1915), which has run into 90 editions and sold more than 400,000 copies in the

United States; it has also been translated into ten languages. None of Fisher's economic writings was as successful.

His deep concern with problems of eugenics arose from his belief that civilization could be saved only if the trends of physiological decadence of the superior elements and excessive reproduction of the inferior were reversed. Fisher served as president of the Eugenics Research Association, the American Eugenics Society, the Life Extension Institute, and the Vitality Records Office.

Like Walras, and like Pareto in the earlier part of his life, Fisher was always actively concerned with public policy, trying to modify the existing situation and to protect the organization of the economic system. He saw clearly that economic difficulties are very often monetary difficulties, and he constantly recommended active intervention by the public authorities in monetary affairs. He was an apostle of managed currency and of stabilization of the purchasing power of money. In his book on stable money he related that between 1912 and 1934 he prepared no less than 99 speeches, 37 letters to newspapers, 161 special articles, 9 submissions to appropriate governmental bodies, 12 circulars, and 13 books, a total of 331 documents intended to disseminate his ideas on monetary stabilization. Fisher was founder and president of the Stable Money League, a body whose aim was to make propaganda in favor of the "compensated" dollar.

Contributions to economics

The very lucidity of Fisher's thought may have led superficial minds to undervalue its true worth. Since no effort is necessary to comprehend his meaning, there is a tendency to underestimate the complexity and, in many instances, the originality of his thinking. In contrast to Marx and Keynes, he could develop his ideas fully, specify them, and so strip them of their obscurities and contradictions that the formulas which emerged were extraordinarily plain and clear. Whatever the difficulty of the subject, Fisher excelled at distinguishing the theoretical from the practical, at using only perfectly defined concepts, at identifying problems, treating each in a concise, clear paragraph, and at relegating to appendixes elements that were accessory to the main theme. His essential contribution lay, first, in his reduction of the copious accumulation of inconsistent notions in earlier writings to a contradiction-free synthesis that made full use of their valid elements and, second, in his lucid presentation of this synthesis.

The remarkable characteristic of Fisher's work is that it contains no *basic* error. Taken as a whole, and aside from a few minor errors of detail, it offers only valid ideas. His work is characterized by the ability to clarify, whether analytically or synthetically, rather than by the power of creative imagination. This is where Fisher's true originality is to be found.

Use of mathematics.   Fisher must be considered one of those who laid the foundations of modern economics, particularly of econometrics. He contributed more than any other scholar to the introduction into economics of scientific methodology and mathematical thinking, and he played an essential role in the development of specific concepts and theories which lie at the base of today's economics.

Even as a student, Fisher perceived the immense potential that a scientific approach offered in the field of economics, and he became one of the most brilliant pioneers in the cause of mathematical economics. He believed that sooner or later every science tends to become mathematical and that the social sciences are therefore only more backward than astronomy, physics, and mathematics. He was convinced that all those who, like Gibbs, systematically relied on mathematics as a working tool would find their reward in the form of important discoveries. But he was also aware of the need to limit the use of mathematics. He was an economist; while mathematics was one of his tools, he never fell into the trap of mere formalism, characteristic of so much of the work done today. His work, like that of Pareto, teems with judicious comments on the scope and nature of theories, on the power and limits of the application of mathematical techniques, and on scientific method in general.

In 1929 two young mathematical economists, Charles Roos and Ragnar Frisch, proposed to Fisher that he join them in founding a society aimed at disseminating mathematical thinking in economics. He welcomed the suggestion with enthusiasm. The international Econometric Society was founded the next year, with Fisher as its first president. By now this society has several thousand members, including many of the most distinguished economists. [See ECONOMETRICS.] This may serve to indicate how much the atmosphere has changed since the young Fisher noted, in 1891, that mathematical economics was still almost as much on the defensive as it was during the 1870s and 1880s, when Jevons and Walras were pleading for it so ardently, and so vainly.

Theory of value and prices.   In the *Mathematical Investigations in the Theory of Value and Prices* (1892), a work of his youth, Fisher's aim was to present a general mathematical model of the determination of value and prices. He claimed to have specified the equations of general economic equilibrium for the case of independent goods (chapter 4, sec. 10), although the only mathematical economist whose work he had consulted was Jevons. With commendable honesty he recognized the priority of Walras's *Éléments d'économie politique pure* (1874) as far as the equations of the general equilibrium are concerned and likewise the priority of Edgeworth's *Mathematical Psychics* (1881) as regards the concept of utility surfaces. It appears that, although only a student, Fisher had independently developed a theory of general economic equilibrium that was identical to part of Walras's and included the concept of the indifference surface, one of the fundamental bases of modern economic theory [*see the biography of* WALRAS].

Given the existence of these earlier formulations, the truly new elements in the *Investigations* were its clarity of presentation, its illustration of the general theory of equilibrium by a mechanical model in the case of independent goods, and its generalization of equilibrium theory to the case in which the utility of each good depends on the quantities of other goods consumed. A comparison of Fisher's text with Walras's will show how much more clear and concise Fisher's exposition is. Fisher, however, apparently did not perceive the distinction between ordinal and cardinal utility; it was Pareto who emphasized the concept of ordinal utility and used it systematically. Although the *Investigations* does have a valuable appendix on utility and the history of the mathematical method in economics, on balance, the assessment made by Ragnar Frisch (see Schumpeter 1948), that the *Investigations* is a work of monumental importance, seems exaggerated and unjustified.

Capital and income. Fisher's study of capital and income (1906) was intended to place the fundamental concepts in this field on a rational and rigorous basis and to develop the theorems flowing from these concepts. According to Fisher, his aim was to supply the long-missing link between the ideas and habits that govern business management and the theories of abstract economics.

This aim was satisfactorily realized. *The Nature of Capital and Income* contains the theoretical foundations of accounting science, both at the enterprise level and for the economy as a whole, as well as of actuarial science. Moreover, it presents these fundamentals in the framework of a general economic theory. Thus, Fisher prepared a rigorous foundation for the subsequent work on national income and wealth.

With this book Fisher apparently became the first economist to develop a theory of capital (including human capital) on an actuarial and accounting basis; both disciplines are essential parts of any economic calculus. His theoretical constructions issued from a concrete examination of accountancy and actuarial operations; this is the only valid approach, and many economists (even including Keynes, in the *Treatise on Money* as well as in the *General Theory*) have erred by postulating a priori relationships between economic aggregates.

Also in *The Nature of Capital and Income* Fisher presented a systematization of the two concepts of capital and income, both rigorously defined. He showed very clearly how these two concepts are linked through the rate of interest. Capital consists of a stock of goods; income is a flow of services. The value of capital is given by the present value of the future flow of income from it. The direction of the causal relation is not from capital to income but from income to capital; it is not from the present to the future but from the future to the present. In other words, the value of capital is the discounted value of expected income. [*See* CAPITAL.]

He saw with unprecedented clarity that the economic present is no more than the capitalization of the future and that therefore the economic present is only a synthetic projection of the anticipated future. Fisher demonstrated convincingly that in economics only the future counts, and that past costs have no direct relevance to value. In point of fact, his research resulted in a rigorous definition of the bases on which it is possible to ground a valid theory of interest.

The only notable omission in this work is Fisher's failure to give the mathematical relations between capital and income in continuous notation. Such a formulation, which could well have found a place in an appendix, would have shown even more clearly the link between capital and income (see Allais 1965*a*).

The analysis of capital and income in this book is so satisfactory that it is hardly possible to go beyond it, and it retains all its relevance today. Curiously enough, *The Nature of Capital and Income*—which is Fisher's masterpiece, in my opinion—was not duly appreciated, and Pareto and Schumpeter are among the few economists who have recognized its value.

Monetary theory. In *The Purchasing Power of Money* (1911) Fisher completely recast the theory of money, giving a full demonstration of the principles that determine the purchasing power of money in the formal framework of the equation of exchange

$$(1) \qquad MV + M'V' = PQ$$

and applying these principles to the study of historical changes in purchasing power.

It is impossible, without doing grave injustice to the author, to analyze or even summarize this book, which is powerfully original in its close association of theory and econometric analysis with factual data. For Fisher, the purchasing power of money (or its reciprocal, the general price level) depends wholly on five well-defined factors: (1) the stock of money in circulation, M; (2) its velocity of circulation, V; (3) the volume of deposits, M'; (4) their velocity of circulation, V'; and (5) the over-all volume of transactions.

In his preface Fisher stated that, fundamentally, his ambition was only to renovate and amplify the old "quantity theory" of money. He claimed that if the previously presented version is modified appropriately, it must be accepted as a basically correct theory.

Although Fisher is all too widely believed to have been an intransigent quantity theorist, he specified in many places the limiting conditions on the quantity theory's validity. A few quotations should dissipate any doubt as to his real position:

. . . the theory is correct in the sense that the level of prices varies directly with the quantity of money in circulation, provided the velocity of circulation of that money and the volume of trade which it is obliged to perform are not changed. . . .   ([1911] 1920, p. 14)

The strictly proportional effect on prices of an increase in M is only the *normal* or *ultimate* effect after transition periods are over. The proposition that prices vary with money holds true only in comparing two imaginary periods for each of which prices are stationary or are moving alike upward or downward and at the same rate. . . .   (*ibid.*, p. 159)

Therefore the "quantity theory" will not hold true strictly and absolutely during transition periods. . . . (*ibid.*, p. 161)

There is no doubt that the weak point in Fisher's theory is his inability to free himself from the trammels of the *ceteris paribus* assumption, which Bishop Berkeley had introduced in the eighteenth century. In his attempt to show the correctness of the quantity theory, Fisher shed fresh light on a significant number of questions, but in a sense he wanted to prove too much and was led into giving insufficient weight to short-term transitional phenomena.

Long before *The Purchasing Power of Money* first appeared in 1911, Walras had attempted to escape from this blind alley by defining the concept

of "real wanted cash balances." The Cambridge school, including Pigou and Keynes, did no more than take up Walras's idea, but nobody was able to develop an operational formulation of the theory of money, and the coefficients that were defined could not be rendered determinate. An operational formulation has only been developed in the recent past, for example, by the present author (Allais 1965b). The equation of exchange $MV = PQ$ had already been used by Newcomb in his *Principles of Political Economy*, and indeed it was to Newcomb that Fisher dedicated his book on money.

From a monetary viewpoint, the main contributions of Fisher's work seem to be a notable clarification of the significance of the formal framework of the equation of exchange; the definition of statistical methods for estimating the different parameters of this equation, in particular the velocities of circulation of notes and coin and of deposit money, and for estimating the over-all volume of transactions; the estimates themselves; and finally, a definitive clarification of the influence of demand deposits on prices and of the need to include them in the definition of the supply of money.

Although Fisher was responsible for remarkable progress in monetary theory, he was not exempt from errors of judgment. Thus, chapters 11 and 12 are devoted to the verification of the equations of exchange. But an equation of this kind, which is the definition of the velocity of circulation, cannot be verified; all that the statistics can demonstrate is the compatibility of the different estimates of the velocity of circulation.

Whatever its limitations, *The Purchasing Power of Money* clarified much that had been confused. Fisher did not use the fertile Walrasian concept of desired cash balance explicitly, nor did he attain the fruitful Keynesian concept of liquidity preference. And it is true that he did not reach a satisfactory synthesis of the theory of money with price theory (although taking his work as a whole, he came nearer to such a synthesis than did Keynes). Nevertheless, he produced analyses of monetary questions—in particular of the velocity of circulation and of the equation of exchange—that in many respects are definitive. [*See* MONEY, *articles on* QUANTITY THEORY *and* VELOCITY OF CIRCULATION.]

Theory of interest.   For Fisher, the rate of interest is governed by the balance between the supply of capital, as determined by the psychology of savers, and the demand for capital, as determined by the possibilities of, and the outlook for, investment.

As with some of his other works, the major contribution of *The Theory of Interest* (1930a) is not so much the presentation of major new ideas as the clarity and rigor of exposition of an extremely complex subject. The fundamental theses of the book had already been developed before Fisher by John Rae (1834) and, above all, by Böhm-Bawerk (1884–1912). Fisher, indeed, underlined his debt in the dedication of his book: "To the memory of John Rae and of Eugen Böhm-Bawerk, who laid the foundations upon which I have endeavored to build."

At the outset, Fisher made the distinction between nominal interest and real interest. The major part of the book (chapters 4–18) is devoted to the theory of the determination of the real rate of interest. Then follows a special chapter, 19, on the relation of interest to money and prices. Fisher's theory of the real rate of interest is a synthesis of psychological theories, such as the theory of abstinence, and physical theories, such as the theory of productivity. The objectivity with which he accomplished this synthesis enabled him to give due weight to the significance of each of the different aspects. While the central themes of the book are all to be found in greater or lesser measure in Böhm-Bawerk's work, the clarity of Fisher's presentation and the rigor of his analysis are incomparably greater.

Throughout his analysis, Fisher quite correctly distinguished two problems, namely, how the interest rate is determined and why it is always positive. He contended correctly, and in contrast to the approach taken by many earlier writers, that the determination problem should be the one studied first. He stressed, again quite correctly (chapter 8, secs. 4, 5), that from a psychological or technical viewpoint there is nothing in the nature of men or things that should lead one to expect that the rate of interest, expressed in terms of whatever good is chosen as unit, will be positive rather than negative. Long before Keynes, Fisher showed clearly that the rate of interest in terms of a given good cannot become negative if the good can be stocked without significant expense, a condition that is met by money (chapter 2, sec. 3, chapter 11, sec. 9). In his discussion of the case of the interest on unredeemable bonds (chapter 13, sec. 10), he also pointed out the impossibility of a zero or negative interest rate. But since he does not appear to have seen that land rents, like unredeemable bonds, are in practice a kind of perpetual income, he failed to realize that in a social organization based on private land ownership the rate of interest cannot be zero or negative (see Allais 1947, vol. 2, pp. 479–499).

Fisher's theory of interest, like that of Böhm-Bawerk, is a capitalistic theory springing from an examination of the nature of capital. In a sense, it is the opposite pole to a theory such as that of Keynes, which is essentially a monetary theory of the rate of interest. (The present author has discussed this point: Allais 1947, vol. 1, p. 27.) Neither Fisher nor Keynes succeeded in approaching the indispensable synthesis of the two points of view. In discussing the repercussions of the theory of interest on monetary problems, Fisher showed conclusively that when prices are at peak levels, interest rates are high, not because the price level is high but because it has risen; and that when prices are low, interest levels are low, not because the price level is low but because it has declined (chapter 19, sec. 10).

Fisher's *Theory of Interest* is not entirely free of error. For example, in the discussion of the optimum date for tree felling (chapter 7, sec. 6), Fisher stated that the date is given by the equality of the marginal growth rate of the forest and the rate of interest. This result is wrong and leads to an overestimation of the optimum length of the interval between two fellings—for no account is taken of the fact that the earlier the trees are felled, the earlier will it be possible to repeat the cycle. The quantity to be maximized is not the present value of a single felling, but the present value of all the income from successive fellings. Elsewhere, Fisher appears to have considered that the reason for the difference between long-term and short-term interest rates reflects the nearness or distance of the redemption date (chapter 13, sec. 11). He failed to observe what Keynes saw clearly, namely, that short-term loans have the advantage of being relatively more liquid and are therefore remunerated at a lower rate. Finally, Fisher stated that the productivity of nature is a factor tending to support the interest rate (chapter 8, sec. 6). Counterexamples showing that this point of view is untenable can be found (see, among others, Allais 1947, vol. 2, p. 721).

Nevertheless, in an over-all view allowing for these minor criticisms, Fisher's analysis of interest represents a successful attack on one of the most difficult problems of economic theory, one that such men as Walras, Pareto, and Marshall had not fully grasped and for whose first deep analysis the credit goes to Böhm-Bawerk.

While it is true that Fisher did not completely resolve the issues of the basis of interest and the relation between the physical productivity and the value productivity of capital, he was responsible for a remarkable growth of understanding in this field. His analyses, particularly of the propensities to save and invest and of the interdependence of the rate of interest with other components of the economic system, prepared the way for his followers. [*See* INTEREST.]

Monetary policy.   Three of Fisher's works are devoted to projects for monetary reform: *Stabilizing the Dollar* (1920), *Stamp Scrip* (1933*b*), and *100% Money* (1935). It is not unfair to say that throughout his life he was absorbed, even obsessed, by concern for the maintenance of a stable purchasing power of money—in other words, the avoidance of both inflation and deflation.

Stabilization of purchasing power.   Fisher's first book on monetary policy (1920) contains a plan for a reform of the gold standard, intended to stabilize purchasing power. Its principle, which was stated as early as 1911 in *The Purchasing Power of Money* (chapter 13, sec. 5), is very simple. If prices in terms of gold rise by one per cent, the official price of gold should be lowered by one per cent in order to maintain the purchasing power of the dollar; conversely, if prices in terms of gold decline by one per cent, the official price of gold should be raised by one per cent. In this system, the increase (or decrease) of the official price of gold must apply to all currencies if the principle of fixed exchange parities is to be respected. But a single country can also apply the system, as long as it is prepared to accept variations in its currency exchange rate in line with the price fixed for gold in terms of national currency. *Stabilizing the Dollar* also contains a systematic bibliography on the stabilization of the purchasing power of money, in which Fisher cited many authors (e.g., Rooke 1824; Newcomb 1879; Marshall 1887) whose ideas corresponded closely to his own.

Despite Fisher's assertions to the contrary (appendix 2, 1D) the cogency of his propositions is based on the quantity principle, which is valid only over the long term. Although his plan therefore applies only to long-term price movements, it would have been entirely viable and effective during the nineteenth century. Certainly, if the system had been in operation in that period, the long-run increases and declines in the price level, which actually occurred and whose drawbacks are evident, could have been avoided. It is also certain that it would have enabled full internal and external currency convertibility to be maintained after World War I. One might even claim that the introduction of this system would have been a necessary condition for the maintenance of convertibility. Indeed, as Fisher himself stressed, the link with gold is not strictly indispensable, and under a system of paper money, price stability can be underpinned by appropriate limitation of the volume of newly issued means of payment. He himself stated that the operation of his plan would be facilitated rather than hindered by the internal demonetization of gold, the sole essential feature of his scheme being the full convertibility of paper money into gold ingots (chapter 4, sec. 6). These ideas still have some potential value. In point of fact, they had been applied during the Middle Ages to prevent nominal prices from declining, and the fixed price of gold, introduced in the nineteenth century, was in a way a regression of practice.

Stamped money plan.   The objective of Fisher's stamped money plan of 1932 and 1933 was to furnish an efficient method of combating the hoarding of money, which has extremely injurious effects in a period of depression, the more so as the rate of hoarding tends to accelerate. Here again, the original idea was not Fisher's own but was first suggested by Silvio Gesell in his book *The Natural Economic Order* (1906–1911, part 2) as a means of lowering the rate of interest.

In the system advocated by Gesell, notes in circulation would retain their value only if validated each month by a stamp sold through the post office network. The price of the stamp could be fixed in the light of circumstances; Gesell proposed a figure equivalent to a depreciation of the order of 5 per cent per annum. Gesell's aim was not so much to combat depression as to lower the rate of interest toward zero in order to suppress all unearned income in a market economy.

In *Booms and Depressions* Fisher took up the idea with his customary clarity, pointing out that it constitutes a method of discouraging hoarding. He wrote:

Let one hundred of these dollars be given to each citizen. . . . This "gift" would be to all of us from all of us (and so no gift at all). . . . After all the 12 stamp spaces have been filled, the dollar could be redeemed either by another of the same kind or by an ordinary dollar, at the option of the government. If the stamped dollar, renewed, runs for nine years (108 months), the funds for this redemption will have already been provided to the government by the public. . . . This strange-appearing plan will not seem so strange if we think of it as a loan to the public from the government, to be repaid in monthly installments of one per cent.   (1932, pp. 227–229)

Gesell's suggestion was taken up by Keynes also, who pointed out that it would permit the level of interest rates to be lowered (1936, chapter 23, sec. 6).

There is no doubt that a scheme of this kind is a valid antidepression weapon, provided it is extended also to cover bank deposits—which is feasible. Fisher believed that in normal times there would be no need to have recourse to this system but that if the need for it became evident, it could be introduced with beneficial effect. It has been objected that anyone wishing to hoard would not be prevented from hoarding land, precious stones, or precious metals, but from a monetary viewpoint this is not a valid objection: what is at issue is how to avoid generalized overproduction by rendering it undesirable to hoard *money*.

The proposals for monetary reform by Gesell, Keynes, and Fisher have not been understood. The idea of stamped money has been derided as an economic absurdity. Yet the only objection that may validly be raised is that in normal circumstances, i.e., when monetary policy is implemented reasonably, hoarding is moderate and the stamping of money is unnecessary. So far as the monetary aspect is concerned, the policy of validation of money through stamps is recommended by Fisher only in case of need. As for Keynes's notion that lower interest rates would increase the real national income, it can be shown that losses are wholly negligible by comparison with the capitalistic optimum situation with an interest rate of a few per cent (see Allais 1962).

Today the danger is not deflation but inflation, and the current interest in the stamped money plan is quite limited, if it exists at all. But from a theoretical point of view, this system—as well as that of the stable dollar—has many features that merit reflection.

The aim of *Stamp Scrip*, which was published in 1933, a few months after *Booms and Depressions*, was to describe the stamped-money experiments made in the Austrian towns of Schwanenkirchen and Wörgl and in a score of American cities in 1932, to assess the merits of these experiments, and to reply to certain objections that had been put forward. In Fisher's own words, the book was prepared "in a few days of fast and furious work"; the speed with which it was written had, to say the least, unfortunate consequences for its quality.

Hundred per cent reserve. Fisher's aim in *100% Money* was to show that economic fluctuations can be largely eliminated if demand deposits are totally backed by a corresponding amount of cash, thus depriving the banking system of its right— more or less erratically exercised—to create money; and to show that a system of this kind "would actually stop the irresponsible creation and destruction of circulating medium by our thousands of commercial banks which now act like so many private mints" (1935, p. xi).

The fact is that the degree of potential instability of a banking system becomes greater as the coverage ratio departs farther from unity. Credit is generally the process in which a banker makes a loan of money he does not possess to a client who nevertheless considers the money as available. The system can continue to operate as long as depositors as a whole have sufficient confidence in its stability. But once confidence is shaken, the banks are unable to honor demands for withdrawals. In its basic conception this system is irrational, and its only justifications are its historical acceptance and the savings of gold that it permitted in the nineteenth century, when the price of gold was fixed—the possible consequence of this fixity under a gold standard being long-term decreases of the price level. Fisher's *100% Money* sets forth a valid plan to rationalize the monetary system. Some of the aims of the plan have been implemented since 1934, when the Federal Deposit Insurance Corporation was founded: since then a bank failure caused by depositors withdrawing funds from the banking system has become a practical impossibility. However, the present system has the drawback that the management of the over-all money supply is less easy than it would have been under a "100 per cent money" system.

Again, the original idea was not Fisher's, as he acknowledged in his preface. He himself gave the credit for the suggestion to a group of economists from the University of Chicago, including, among others, Henry C. Simons, Aaron Director, Frank H. Knight, Henry Schultz, Paul H. Douglas, and A. G. Hart. In November 1933 this group circulated an unsigned 26-page mimeographed paper entitled "Banking and Currency Reform" (see Walker 1935; Hart 1935). However, the credit for the original idea should not go to the Chicago school. Much earlier, in 1898, Walras was stressing the unstable nature of the system of issue of banknotes and was proposing a 100 per cent coverage ratio (1898, pp. 348, 365, 374, 375 of the 1936 French edition). Ludwig von Mises adopted much the same position in 1928 in his book *Geldwertstabilisierung und Konjunkturpolitik*.

A system of 100 per cent money is perfectly feasible providing that banking activity is split into two clearly separated branches, deposits and lending. Depositors would pay charges to cover the cost of managing their accounts, and banks would make loans with funds they had borrowed for that purpose. Introducing the system would involve certain transitional problems, but they could easily be overcome, and their resolution would give governments a much greater mastery of monetary policy than could be acquired in any other way. The idea of this reform has generally been abandoned today; its only proponents are a few economists such as Milton Friedman in the United States (1959) and Maurice Allais in France (1947).

Other works on monetary policy. Three other books written for the lay public should be mentioned among Fisher's published works on monetary reform. These are *The Money Illusion* (1928b), *Booms and Depressions* (1932), and *Inflation?* (1933a). The first and last of these are, by comparison with his other works on the subject, of limited interest.

Booms and Depressions is of more importance. It has three parts, dealing with theories, facts, and remedies, respectively. Nine main factors are considered: overindebtedness, volume of currency, price level, net worth, profit, production, psychological factors, currency turnover, and rates of interest. Most stress is placed on the factor of overindebtedness.

When the 1929 slump occurred, Fisher was over 60 years old; yet he tackled the very difficult theory of economic fluctuations. He finally reached the conclusion—which contains a large element of truth—that business cycles are due on the one hand to the existence in the banking system of uncovered demand deposits and on the other to the opportunities for hoarding offered by the circulating monetary media. These views led him to recommend regulation of the demand for and supply of money through steadily depreciating circulating money and 100 per cent coverage of demand deposits as a cure for business cycle ills (see 1933b; 1935).

Appraisal of monetary policy. Nowhere in his writings did Fisher really take up the central problem of variations in the demand for money with the level of economic activity, and despite the reservations he himself made, his approach was too narrowly oriented toward quantity theory. As Schumpeter aptly put it, "the scholar was misled by the crusader." His propaganda in favor of the compensated dollar resulted in his misinterpretation of the price stability that ruled up to 1929 and, correspondingly, his total unawareness of the gravity of the situation. He was one of the most optimistic supporters of the doctrine of the "new economic era." Although he had done quite well from his investments in the 1920s, he had to absorb large losses in the 1929 crisis. But as soon as he assessed its scope properly, he became an indefatigable proponent of the various plans for the restoration of prosperity that have been summarized above. To-

gether with George Frederick Warren, he persuaded President Roosevelt to devalue the dollar in order to stimulate a rise in the price level in the United States.

Contributions to statistics

Fisher's work on money and prices, in particular his propositions for stabilization of the dollar, led him to considerable advances in two branches of statistical science: price indices and distributed lags.

Index numbers. The aim of Fisher's book *The Making of Index Numbers* (1922) is to identify the characteristics of the best feasible index of prices for use in measuring changes in the purchasing power of money. This book, in which he tried to systematize and rationalize index number theory by defining a certain number of criteria, is in fact an extension of chapter 10 of his *Purchasing Power of Money* and of the appendix to that book. His research into the qualities of a satisfactory price index was a by-product of his general analysis of the equation of exchange.

Whereas Fisher's approach in *The Purchasing Power of Money* was deductive, in *The Making of Index Numbers* it was inductive and empirical: he compared the results of using different formulas on the same historical data. He used two principal criteria of evaluation, the "time reversal test" and the "factor reversal test," and recommended use of the "ideal" index, the geometric mean of the Paasche and Laspeyre indices.

There can be no doubt that Fisher's study, which was the most extensive at that time in the field of index numbers, was a fruitful springboard for much of the progress made subsequently [*see* INDEX NUMBERS].

Distributed lags. Fisher was the first to envisage a systematic dependence of the present on the past in economics, and thus he opened up a whole new area. The existence of systematic effects explains why it has been possible successfully to analyze economic and geophysical time series using autoregressive equations

$$(1) \qquad b_0 y_t + b_1 y_{t-1} + \cdots + b_h y_{t-h} + \cdots = \epsilon_t,$$

which when inverted can be written formally as

$$(2) \quad y_t = a_0 \epsilon_t + a_1 \epsilon_{t-1} + a_2 \epsilon_{t-2} + \cdots + a_p \epsilon_{t-p} + \cdots,$$

in which y_t is the cumulative effect of earlier actions, ϵ_{t-p}, weighted by coefficients a_p, which decline with distance in time. The accepted English term for this formulation, "distributed lags," was coined by Fisher. This term is intended to convey that each ϵ_{t-p} acts with a certain delay, so that lags of different length must be taken into account when studying the influence of the past.

In his study "Our Unstable Dollar and the So-called Business Cycle" (1925) Fisher proposed a formulation of the type

$$y(t) = y_0 + \int_0^\infty \alpha(\theta)p(t-\theta)\,d\theta,$$

in which the weights $\alpha(\theta)$ are distributed lognormally, for study of the interdependence of the level of economic activity $y(t)$ and past values $p(t-\theta)$ of the general level of prices.

Later, in his *Theory of Interest* (chapter 19, sec. 6), he used weights α, which declined linearly with time, to study the relationship between the rate of interest and earlier rates of increase of the price level.

The line of approach initiated by Fisher was later to prove particularly fertile in econometric thought. [*See* Distributed lags.]

Influence

Unlike Adam Smith, John Stuart Mill, and Alfred Marshall, Fisher wrote no systematic treatise. The reason for this is doubtless that Fisher was preoccupied above all with research and that his manifold practical activities took much time. In Schumpeter's well-chosen words, Fisher's works "are the pillars and arches of a temple that was never built. They belong to an imposing structure that the architect never presented as a tectonic unit" ([1948] 1960, p. 237). But these foundations are solid.

Fisher was not an eminent philosopher, like Cournot, and he did not have a universal mind, like Pareto; he did not share Walras's preoccupation with social problems or try to study the philosophy of the social and economic organization of the time, as did Keynes and Schumpeter. But the fact remains that he made major contributions to the fundamental problems of capital, interest, and money.

As Schumpeter observed in his remarkable biographical article, Fisher, unlike Marx, Marshall, and Keynes, did not found a school. He had many pupils, but few disciples. In his crusades he joined forces with many other groups and individuals, but he remained almost alone in his scientific work. Perhaps it was the derision aroused by his crusading activity that led to his isolation; one of his critics has written: "His career was marked by neglect at its inception and ridicule at its close" (Lekachman 1959, p. 293).

For many years, Fisher's influence was nonetheless considerable. He was president of the American Statistical Association, of the international Econometric Society, of the National Institute of the Social Sciences, and of the American Association for Labor Legislation. The appearance of a book by Fisher was invariably an event, and it would be reviewed widely, though the reception might be favorable or hostile. In the case of both *Stamp Scrip* and *100% Money*, the reaction among Fisher's fellow economists and in official circles was unfavorable. In fact, Fisher was often considered prone to draw too rapid conclusions from abstract conceptions and therefore inclined to suggest measures whose chances of success were correspondingly uncertain.

Although there has never been a Fisher school in the sense that there has been a Keynesian school, Fisher's influence on a great number of young economists was nevertheless profound (see Sasuly 1947). As a disciple of Fisher, the author of the present article is among those who have recently produced systematizations, generalizations, or extensions of Fisher's theoretical and econometric work on capital, income, interest, and money (see Allais 1943; 1947; 1954; 1965a; 1965b).

Assessment

The opinion of Fisher's work has not generally been as high as its merit warrants, especially in the United States, where its value has been grossly underestimated.

To a remarkable extent Fisher combined within himself the eminently Anglo-Saxon preoccupation with facts and practical action and the essentially Latin quality of clarity of conception and exposition. He was at one and the same time theorist and practitioner, having the characteristics, therefore, of a great engineer.

Fisher had, above all, an extraordinary feeling for things concrete, and the whole body of his work is permeated by an unceasing search for numerical applications. For him no theory was of use unless it led to applied work and the quantitative analysis of factual data. Fisher always maintained close contact with businessmen and tried to familiarize himself with their reactions and preoccupations, so as to analyze them and compare them with the theoretical models of economic science. He was deeply interested in practical action. Economic science, as he saw it, was not merely pure philosophical speculation; it should be used, as engineering is, to achieve practical ends.

Fisher's normative approach tended to lower the esteem in which he might otherwise have been held. This unfortunate fate he shares with Marx, whose remarkable sociological accomplishments have been partially discredited by his political attitude, and with Walras, whose normative propositions have been considered by many as unsophisticated or even downright infantile.

Men who are accepted as geniuses have been known to spout nonsense on certain issues. As Pareto wrote: "It is somewhat hard to believe, although it is no more than the truth, that the great Newton wrote a book which proved that the prophecies of the Apocalypse had come to pass." No one would conclude from this that Newton's *Mechanics* is not a first-level achievement of the human spirit.

Fisher marks a decisive stage in the history of economic science. He was the first economist to combine profound theory and authoritative observation. He contributed powerfully to the construction of theoretical mathematical models aimed at the explanation of reality, and at the same time, whether in working out his assumptions or interpreting his results, he never lost his extraordinary preoccupation with reality, which he observed and analyzed with a refined sense of the concrete.

Simultaneously a theorist and a practitioner, Fisher combined to the highest degree two supposedly incompatible characteristics: an *esprit de géometrie* and an *esprit de raffinement*; these are, despite Pascal's opinion, but two sides of one and the same medal—intelligence. Because of these qualities, Fisher ranks with the greatest contributors to economic science. Like physics, economics calls for the study of abstract constructions at the same time that it requires the observation and analysis of facts. When Fisher died in 1947, the present author wrote (Allais 1947) that it was because of the combination of these two qualities that Fisher had to be given a place in the hall of fame of modern economics. A year later Schumpeter described him as America's greatest scientific economist. The future will certainly confirm this judgment. Fisher opened up a new horizon. Others will go beyond the point he reached; they have done so already, for it is easier to progress when the way is posted with signs.

MAURICE ALLAIS

[*For the historical context of Fisher's work, see the biographies of* BÖHM-BAWERK; NEWCOMB; PARETO; RAE; SUMNER; *and* WALRAS.]

WORKS BY FISHER

(1892) 1961   *Mathematical Investigations in the Theory of Value and Prices.* New Haven: Yale Univ. Press.

(1896) 1925   *Elements of Geometry.* New York: American Book Co. → In collaboration with Andrew W. Phillips.

(1897a) 1960   A Bibliography of Mathematical Economics. Pages 173–209 in Antoine A. Cournot, *Researches Into the Mathematical Principles of the Theory of Wealth.* New York: Kelley.

(1897b) 1943   *A Brief Introduction to the Infinitesimal Calculus.* New York: Macmillan.

(1906) 1927   *The Nature of Capital and Income.* New York and London: Macmillan.

1907   *The Rate of Interest: Its Nature, Determination and Relation to Economic Phenomena.* New York: Macmillan.

(1910a) 1912   *Elementary Principles of Economics.* New York: Macmillan. → First published as *Introduction to Economic Science.*

1910b   *National Vitality: Its Wastes and Conservation.* U.S. 61st Congress, 2d Session, Senate Document No. 419. Washington: Government Printing Office.

(1911) 1920   *The Purchasing Power of Money: Its Determination and Relation to Credit, Interest and Crises.* New ed., rev. New York: Macmillan.

1914   *Why the Dollar Is Shrinking? A Study in the High Cost of Living.* New York: Macmillan.

(1915) 1946   FISHER, IRVING et al. *How to Live: Rules for Healthful Living Based on Modern Science.* 21st ed., rev. New York: Funk & Wagnalls.

1920   *Stabilizing the Dollar: A Plan to Stabilize the General Price Level Without Fixing Individual Prices.* New York: Macmillan.

(1922) 1927   *The Making of Index Numbers: A Study of Their Varieties, Tests, and Reliability.* 3d ed., rev. Boston: Houghton Mifflin.

1923   *League or War?* New York: Harper.

(1924) 1926   *America's Interest in World Peace.* Rev. ed. New York: Funk & Wagnalls. → A revised edition and condensation of *League or War?*

1925   Our Unstable Dollar and the So-called Business Cycle. *Journal of the American Statistical Association* 20:179–202.

(1926) 1927   *Prohibition at Its Worst.* 5th ed. New York: Alcohol Information Committee.

1928a   *Prohibition Still at Its Worst.* New York: Alcohol Information Committee.

1928b   *The Money Illusion.* New York: Adelphi. → Contains a systematic bibliography.

(1930a) 1961   *The Theory of Interest.* New York: Kelley. → Revision of *The Rate of Interest* 1907.

1930b   *The Stock Market Crash—and After.* New York: Macmillan.

1932   *Booms and Depressions: Some First Principles.* New York: Adelphi. → Contains a systematic bibliography.

1933a   *Inflation?* New York: Adelphi.

1933b   *Stamp Scrip.* New York: Adelphi.

1933c   *After Reflation, What?* New York: Adelphi.

1934   FISHER, IRVING; and COHRSSEN, HANS R. L. *Stable Money: A History of the Movement.* New York: Adelphi.

(1935) 1945   *100% Money: Designed to Keep Checking Banks 100% Liquid; to Prevent Inflation and Deflation; Largely to Cure or Prevent Depressions; and to Wipe Out Much of the National Debt.* 3d ed. New Haven: City Printing.

1937   Note on a Short-cut Method for Calculating Distributed Lags. International Statistical Institute, *Bulletin* 29, no. 3:323–328.

1942   *Constructive Income Taxation: A Proposal for Reform.* New York: Harper.

SUPPLEMENTARY BIBLIOGRAPHY

ALLAIS, MAURICE   (1943) 1952   *Traité d'économie pure.* 2d ed. Paris: Imprimerie Nationale. → First published in 1943 as *Économie pure.*

ALLAIS, MAURICE   1947   *Économie & intérêt: Présentation nouvelle des problèmes fondamentaux relatifs au rôle économique du taux de l'intérêt et de leurs solutions.* 2 vols. Paris: Librairie des Publications Officielles.

ALLAIS, MAURICE 1954 *Les fondements comptables de la macro-économique: Les équations comptables entre quantités globales et leurs applications.* Paris: Presses Universitaires de France.

ALLAIS, MAURICE 1962 The Influence of the Capital-output Ratio on Real National Income. *Econometrica* 30:700–728.

ALLAIS, MAURICE 1965a The Role of Capital in Economic Development. Pages 697–978 in Study Week on the Econometric Approach to Development Planning, Vatican City, 1963 [*Travaux scientifiques et discussions*]. Pontificia Accademia delle Scienze, Rome, Scripta Varia, Vol. 28. Chicago: Rand McNally; Amsterdam: North-Holland Publishing.

ALLAIS, MAURICE 1965b *Reformulation de la théorie quantitative de la monnaie: La formulation héréditaire, relativiste et logistique de la demande de monnaie.* Paris: SEDEIS. → An abridged version was published in the December 1966 issue of the *American Economic Review.*

BÖHM-BAWERK, EUGEN VON (1884–1912) 1959 *Capital and Interest.* 3 vols. South Holland, Ill.: Libertarian Press. → First published as *Kapital und Kapitalzins.* See especially Volume 1: *History and Critique of Interest Theories,* 1884; and Volume 2: *Positive Theory of Capital,* 1889.

CAGAN, PHILLIP 1956 The Monetary Dynamics of Hyperinflation. Pages 25–117 in Milton Friedman (editor), *Studies in the Quantity Theory of Money.* Univ. of Chicago Press.

DAVIS, HAROLD T. 1941 *The Analysis of Economic Time Series.* Bloomington, Ind.: Principia Press.

DOUGLAS, PAUL H. 1947 Irving Fisher. *American Economic Review* 37:661–663.

EDGEWORTH, FRANCIS Y. (1881) 1953 *Mathematical Psychics: An Essay on the Application of Mathematics to the Moral Sciences.* New York: Kelley.

FISHER, IRVING NORTON 1956 *My Father, Irving Fisher.* New York: Comet.

FISHER, IRVING NORTON 1961 *A Bibliography of the Writings of Irving Fisher.* New Haven: Yale Univ. Library.

FRIEDMAN, MILTON (1959) 1961 *A Program for Monetary Stability.* New York: Fordham Univ. Press.

GESELL, SILVIO (1906–1911) 1958 *The Natural Economic Order.* London: Owen. → First published in German as *Die Verwirklichung des Rechtes auf den vollen Arbeitsertrag* and *Die neue Lehre vom Geld und Zins.*

HART, ALBERT G. 1935 The "Chicago Plan" of Banking Reform. *Review of Economic Studies* 2:104–116.

KEYNES, JOHN MAYNARD 1936 *The General Theory of Employment, Interest and Money.* London: Macmillan. → A paperback edition was published in 1965 by Harcourt.

KOYCK, LEENDERT M. 1954 *Distributed Lags and Investment Analysis.* Amsterdam: North-Holland Publishing.

LEKACHMAN, ROBERT 1959 *A History of Economic Ideas.* New York: Harper. → Published in French in 1960.

MARGET, ARTHUR W. 1938 *The Theory of Prices: A Reexamination of the Central Problems of Monetary Theory.* Vol. 1. Englewood Cliffs, N.J.: Prentice-Hall.

MARSHALL, ALFRED 1887 Remedies for Fluctuations of General Prices. *Contemporary Review* 51:355–375.

MORET, JACQUES 1915 *L'emploi des mathématiques en économie politique.* Paris: Giard & Brière.

NERLOVE, MARC 1958 *Distributed Lags and Demand Analysis for Agricultural and Other Commodities.* U.S. Dept. of Agriculture, Handbook No. 141. Washington: Government Printing Office.

NEWCOMB, SIMON 1879 The Standard of Value. *North American Review* 129:223–237.

RAE, JOHN (1834) 1905 *The Sociological Theory of Capital.* New ed. annotated by C. W. Mixter. New York: Macmillan. → First published as *Statement of Some New Principles on the Subject of Political Economy Exposing the Fallacies of the System of Free Trade and of Some Other Doctrines Maintained in the Wealth of Nations.*

ROOKE, JOHN 1824 *An Inquiry Into the Principles of National Wealth, Illustrated by the Political Economy of the British Empire.* Edinburgh: Balfour.

SASULY, MAX 1947 Irving Fisher and Social Science. *Econometrica* 15:255–278.

SCHUMPETER, JOSEPH A. (1948) 1960 Irving Fisher: 1867–1947. Pages 222–238 in Joseph A. Schumpeter, *Ten Great Economists: From Marx to Keynes.* New York: Oxford Univ. Press. → First published in Volume 16 of *Econometrica* as "Irving Fisher's Econometrics."

SCHUMPETER, JOSEPH A. (1954) 1960 *History of Economic Analysis.* Edited by E. B. Schumpeter. New York: Oxford Univ. Press.

SELIGMAN, BEN B. 1962 *Main Currents in Modern Economics: Economic Thought Since 1870.* New York: Free Press.

SUDELA, AMELIA G. 1937 Biographical Sketch of Irving Fisher; Selected Bibliography of the Economic Writings of Irving Fisher. Pages 441–450 in *Lessons of Monetary Experience: Essays in Honor of Irving Fisher.* New York: Farrar & Rinehart.

VILLARD, HENRY H. (1948) 1957 Monetary Theory. Volume 1, pages 314–351 in Howard S. Ellis (editor), *A Survey of Contemporary Economics.* Homewood, Ill.: Irwin.

VON MISES, LUDWIG 1928 *Geldwertstabilisierung und Konjunkturpolitik.* Jena (Germany): Fischer.

WALKER, CHARLES H. 1935 The "Chicago Plan" of Banking Reform. II: The Application of the Proposals in England. *Review of Economic Studies* 2:117–121.

WALRAS, LÉON (1874–1877) 1954 *Elements of Pure Economics: Or, the Theory of Social Wealth.* Translated by William Jaffé. Homewood, Ill.: Irwin; London: Allen & Unwin. → First published as *Éléments d'économie politique pure.*

WALRAS, LÉON 1898 *Études d'économie politique appliquée: Théorie de la production de la richesse sociale.* Lausanne (Switzerland): Rouge.

WESTERFIELD, RAY B. 1947 Irving Fisher. *American Economic Review* 37:656–661.

FISHER, R. A.

Ronald Aylmer Fisher (1890–1962) achieved world-wide recognition during his lifetime as a statistician and geneticist. He continued the work begun in England by Karl Pearson at the beginning of the twentieth century, but he developed it in new directions. Others also contributed to the tremendous surge in the development of statistical techniques and their application in biology; but these two men, by their energetic research and example, in turn held the distinction of dominating the statistical scene for a generation.

Fisher was born in East Finchley, near London. Apart from a twin brother who did not live long, he was the youngest of seven children. His father, George Fisher, was an auctioneer; no particular scientific ability is evident in the achievements of his relatives, except perhaps those of an uncle who, like Ronald Fisher, was a wrangler in the mathematical tripos at Cambridge. Fisher attended school at Stanmore Park and then went to Harrow, where he was encouraged in his mathematical interests and won a scholarship to Gonville and Caius College, Cambridge. His leanings in mathematics followed the English tradition in natural philosophy, and his university student years, from 1909 to 1913, culminated in his receiving first a distinction in optics for his degree papers in 1912 and then a studentship in physics during his postgraduate year. He had, however, already noticed from studying Karl Pearson's *Mathematical Contributions to the Theory of Evolution* that natural philosophy need not stop with the physical sciences.

After leaving Cambridge, Fisher spent a short time with the Mercantile and General Investment Company. When World War I broke out in 1914, his very bad myopia prevented him from joining the army, and he taught mathematics and physics for four years at various English public schools. In 1917 he married Ruth Eileen Guinness, who was to bear him eight children.

Fisher did not really begin his full-time statistical and biological career until 1919, when he became statistician at Rothamsted Experimental Station, an agricultural research institute in Harpenden, Hertfordshire. His earlier years had, however, been a valuable gestation period. In a short paper published in 1912 while he was still at Cambridge, he had already proposed the method of maximum likelihood for fitting frequency curves. Two more solid papers established his permanent reputation for research. The first was his remarkable paper on the sampling distribution of the correlation coefficient, published in Karl Pearson's journal *Biometrika* in 1915, in which his geometrical powers of reasoning were first fully displayed. The second, published in 1918, examined the correlation between relatives on the basis of Mendelian inheritance and exhibited his ability to resolve crucial problems of statistical genetics. Fisher received from Karl Pearson an offer of a post at University College at the same time that he received the Rothamsted offer, but he wisely chose Rothamsted, largely because of the much greater scope and independence of this new statistical post but also, perhaps, because his

contacts with Pearson had not been particularly promising. Pearson was apt to bulldoze his way into research problems without worrying unduly about territorial rights. Having been previously stymied by the correlation distribution problem, he took over Fisher's solution with enthusiasm but without the further close consultation that professional etiquette would seem to require. Fisher was aggrieved by this treatment, and it may well have been the start of the long and bitter feud that developed over the years. Fisher had reason to criticize much of Karl Pearson's work, but the personal animosity that developed between them was something more than a substantive disagreement. As late as 1950, when a selection of Fisher's best statistical papers was published, the omission of the 1915 *Biometrika* paper was a silent reminder of Fisher's feelings.

The period at Rothamsted, from 1919 to 1933, was the most brilliant and productive of Fisher's career. The institute, with its teams of biologists and congenial research atmosphere, was precisely the environment Fisher needed. His own wide range of biological interests enabled him to understand his colleagues' problems and to discuss their statistical aspects constructively with them. His statistical activities were represented by the publication of his best-known book, *Statistical Methods for Research Workers* (1925a), which has been published in 13 English editions and also translated into several foreign languages. Fisher's varied accomplishments included doing much of his own computing and initiating many of his own genetical experiments on poultry, snails, and mice, although it is for his creative theoretical ability that he will be remembered. By 1929 he had been elected a fellow of the Royal Society of London. He published his classic on population genetics, *The Genetical Theory of Natural Selection* (1930a), in which he did much to reconcile Darwin's theory of evolution by natural selection with Mendel's genetical principles, which were unknown to Darwin. In the later chapters of this work he discussed the theory, first suggested by Francis Galton, of the evolution of a genetic association between infertility and ability. This could result from marriages between those successful because of high innate ability and those successful because of social advantages due to relatively infertile parents' having concentrated their material resources on one or two children. His energetic views included proposals for family allowances proportional both to size of family and to size of income, which would offset the penalty imposed on children by parental fertility.

Fisher's genetic and eugenic interests were soon

to be reflected in his move to London in 1933, when he was appointed Galton professor at University College as successor to Karl Pearson. This move, however, no doubt fanned the flames of their feud. When Pearson retired, the college isolated the teaching of statistics in a new department of statistics, under his son Egon; the Galton professor was left with eugenics and biometry. In spite of Egon Pearson's greater tolerance and appreciation of Fisher's new statistical techniques, which emphasized precise methods of analysis in small samples, Fisher felt frustrated, as he indicated at the time in a letter to W. S. Gosset. Moreover, Jerzy Neyman, who held a post in the statistics department from 1935 to 1938, incurred Fisher's wrath by publishing work that Fisher regarded as unnecessary or misguided; their proximity in the same building at University College exacerbated Fisher's sense of injury. The recurrence of feuds of this kind was by now beginning to be as much a manifestation of Fisher's own temperament as of his antagonists'. His wide interests and strong personality made him a charming and lively companion when he chose to be and a generous colleague to those who were in sympathy with his work, as many have testified. But his emotions as well as his intellect were too bound up in his work for him to tolerate criticism, to which he replied in vigorous and sometimes quite unfair terms. Apart from such lapses from objectivity, Fisher proceeded to consolidate his scientific reputation both by the development of the study of genetics (especially human genetics) in his department and by the continued publication of statistical works, such as *The Design of Experiments* (1935*a*), *Statistical Tables for Biological, Agricultural, and Medical Research* (with F. Yates, in 1938), and further original papers in his departmental journal (the *Annals of Eugenics*) and elsewhere.

The third main phase of Fisher's scientific career was his appointment to the Arthur Balfour chair of genetics at Cambridge, from 1943 until his retirement in 1957. During this time he wrote two more books—*The Theory of Inbreeding*, in 1949, and *Statistical Methods and Scientific Inference*, in 1956—and also edited the collection of his papers published in 1950 (see 1920–1945); but most of his important work was already under way. Honors continued to accumulate, including three medals from the Royal Society (a royal medal in 1938, a Darwin medal in 1948, and a Copley medal in 1955), a knighthood in 1952. Shortly before he retired, he became master of his Cambridge college. He was an honorary member of the American Academy of Arts and Sciences, a foreign associate of the National Academy of Sciences, a member of the Pon-

tifical Academy of Sciences, and a foreign member of the Royal Danish Academy of Sciences and Letters and of the Royal Swedish Academy of Sciences.

After retirement he visited the division of mathematical statistics of the Commonwealth Scientific and Industrial Research Organisation in Adelaide, Australia, where he was a research fellow at the time of his death.

Contributions to statistics and genetics

Statistics.   To turn in somewhat more detail to Fisher's original work, a formal listing of his contributions to statistics item by item might result in an underemphasis of the strength of their impact, which was due to their simultaneous variety and depth. Moreover, a formal listing is unsatisfactory since the intimate relation of Fisher's contributions to the practical problems arising from his professional environment sometimes meant that their academic presentation was incomplete or late, or both. Work of great value, such as the technique of analysis of variance, received inadequate discussion in *Statistical Methods for Research Workers* because it had hardly reached any degree of finality when this book was published in 1925, and it was still rather cluttered with ideas of intraclass correlation; apparently, Fisher never bothered to redraft the discussion for the later editions.

Excluding Fisher's mathematical work in genetics, it is nevertheless convenient to try to list his chief contributions to statistical theory under two main headings: (1) fundamental work in statistical inference, and (2) statistical methodology and technique. The first group would include his important work on statistical estimation, mainly represented by two papers, one published in the *Philosophical Transactions* of the Royal Society (1922), and the other published in the *Proceedings* of the Cambridge Philosophical Society (1925*b*). Before writing these papers, Fisher had already been much concerned with precise inference in small samples for familiar quantities, such as the correlation coefficient, chi-square, etc., and had produced a steady flow of papers on their sampling distributions, of which his 1915 paper on the correlation coefficient is the best known. He was very careful to distinguish between an unknown population parameter and its sample estimate. When the sampling distribution of the estimate was available in numerical form, a test of the significance of any hypothetical value of the parameter became possible. These precise tests of significance—for example, of an apparent correlation r in the sample on the "null hypothesis" of no real correlation $(\rho = 0)$—were particularly valuable at the time because of the tendency among biologists and other research workers not to bother with them. Fisher's own emphasis on them was, however, rather inconsistent with his subsequent attack on the Neyman–Pearson theory of testing hypotheses, especially since an unthinking use of these significance tests by some workers, as in the failure to recognize that a nonsignificant result does not imply the truth of the hypothesis tested (e.g., $\rho = 0$), caused some reaction against their use later on.

It is evident that Fisher had begun to think about his general theory of estimation before 1922; apart from his advocacy of maximum likelihood in 1912, the notion of sufficiency had also arisen in the special case of the root mean square deviation as an estimate of the true standard deviation σ in the case of a normal, or Gaussian, sample. Nevertheless, the general theory was first systematically developed in the two papers cited, and it included a discussion of the concept of consistency and a heuristic derivation of the asymptotic properties of maximum likelihood estimates in large samples [see ESTIMATION, *article on* POINT ESTIMATION]. It also included a crystallization of the concept of information on a parameter θ in the formula

$$ I = E \left\{ \left(\frac{\partial L}{\partial \theta} \right)^2 \right\}, $$

where $L = \log p(S|\theta)$ is the logarithm of the probability of the sample S when the parameter has true value θ. The importance of this work lay in (1) examining the actual sampling properties of maximum-likelihood estimates, particularly in large samples (the *method* of maximum likelihood goes back quite a long way, at least as it is analogous to maximum a posteriori probability by Bayes' inverse-probability theorem on the assumption of a uniform a priori distribution); and (2) emphasizing that a sample provides, in some appropriate statistical sense, a definite amount of information on a parameter. Fisher's concept of information, preceding Shannon's, which was introduced in quite a different context (see Shannon 1948), was especially appropriate for large samples because of the possible ordering of normally distributed estimates in terms of their variances (squared standard deviations). [See INFORMATION THEORY.] Fisher justified his concept more generally in the use of small samples by thinking in terms of many such samples; it is curious that he missed the exact inequality relating the information function and the variance of an unbiased estimate known as the Cramér–Rao inequality. In any case, however, the arbitrariness of the variance and unbiasedness remains; and in small samples Fisher introduced the general notion of a sufficient statistic, which, by

rendering conditional distributions of any other sample quantities independent of the unknown parameter, exhausted the "information" in the sample [see SUFFICIENCY].

The next remarkable contribution in this general area came with Fisher's brief paper entitled "Inverse Probability" (1930*b*). Fisher had always been derisory of the estimates and inferences resulting from the Bayes inverse-probability approach. He felt that a unique and more objective system of inferences should be possible in fields where statistical probabilities operate and noted that an exact sampling distribution involving a sample quantity or statistic T and an unknown parameter θ leads (under appropriate regularity and monotonicity properties) to the feasibility of assigning what he termed a "fiducial interval," with a known fiducial probability that the parameter θ is contained in the interval. The interpretation accepted at the time, and implied by Fisher's own wording in this paper, was that this interval, which is necessarily a function of the statistic T, is in consequence a random interval and that fiducial probability is a statistical probability with the usual frequency connotation. Referring to the case of a true correlation coefficient ρ, he said, "We know that if we take a number of samples of 4, from the same or different populations, and for each calculate the fiducial 5 per cent value for ρ, then in 5 per cent of cases, the true value of ρ will be less than the value we found" ([1930*b*] 1950, pp. 22, 535). With some restrictions (for example, to sufficient statistics) it was thus apparently identical with the theory of confidence intervals developed about the same time by Neyman (1937). [See ESTIMATION, *article on* CONFIDENCE INTERVALS AND REGIONS; FIDUCIAL INFERENCE.]

On inductive inference questions, Fisher often did not make it clear what he was claiming; but it should be stressed that regardless of what his interpretation was or of its relevance to the problem at hand, it still was formulated in terms of an assumed statistical framework. Nevertheless, its formal bypassing of Bayes' theorem was a masterly stroke which received attention outside statistical circles (cf. Eddington's remark, "We can never be sure of particular inferences; therefore we should aim at a system of inference that will give conclusions of which in the long run not more than a stated proportion, say $1/q$, will be wrong" [1935*a*] 1960, p. 126).

Later, Fisher attempted to extend fiducial theory to more than one parameter. His first paper (1935*b*) discussing this extension took as one example the problem of inferring the difference in population means of two samples coming from normal populations with different variances. The difficulty here (which Fisher may not have realized at the time, since he himself never examined in detail the logical relations of sufficient statistics in the case of more than one parameter) is that the effect of the unknown variance ratio cannot be segregated in the absence of a "sufficient" quantity for it that does not involve unwanted parameters, such as the individual population means. In rejecting a criticism along these lines by the present author (Bartlett 1936; for further details see, for example, Bartlett 1965), Fisher explicitly gave up the orthodox frequency interpretation for fiducial probability which he appeared to have assumed earlier. He and others attempted to formulate a theory for several parameters that would be both unique and self-consistent, but this has yet to be achieved in any generality, and to many this search is misguided in that it does not eliminate from fiducial theory the arbitrariness that Fisher had so strongly criticized in the Bayes approach.

A rather different and somewhat more technical estimation problem that Fisher solved in 1928 is the derivation of sample statistics that are unbiased estimates of the corresponding population quantities and of the sampling moments of these statistics. The population quantities are the cumulants or semi-invariants first introduced by Thiele (1903), and Fisher's combinatorial rules for obtaining the appropriate sample statistics and their own cumulants constituted a striking example of Fisher's intuitive mathematical powers. Another paper published in 1934 is worth noting as an original and independent contribution to the theory of games developed about the same time by von Neumann and Morgenstern. [*See* GAME THEORY, *article on* THEORETICAL ASPECTS.]

Fisher's work on the design of experiments is so important logically as well as practically that it may be regarded as one of his most fundamental contributions to the science of statistical inference. It is, however, convenient to consider it in the second general area of statistical methodology and technique, in conjunction with analysis of variance. Fisher perceived the simultaneous simplicity and efficiency of balanced and orthogonal experimental designs in agriculture. Replication of the same treatment in different plots is essential if any statistical assessment of error is to be made, and formally equal numbers of plots per treatment are desirable. However, simplification in the statistical analysis is illusory if the analysis is not valid. When observations are collected haphazardly, the most sensible assumptions about statistical variability have to be made. In controlled experiments there is the opportunity for deliberately introducing randomness into the design so that systematic variation can be separated from purely random error. This is the first vital point Fisher made; the second naturally accompanied it. With the analysis geared to the design, all variation not attributable to the treatments does not have to inflate the error. With equal numbers of plots per treatment, each complete replication can be contained in a separate block, and only variability among plots in the same block is a source of error; variability between different blocks can be automatically removed in the analysis as irrelevant. The third point arose from treatment combinations, such as different fertilizer ingredients. For example, if nitrogenous fertilizer (N) and phosphate (P) are to be tested, the recommended set of treatment combinations is

Control (no fertilizer), N, P, NP,

where NP denotes the treatment consisting of both the ingredients N and P (each in the same amount as when given alone). This design maintains simplicity and may improve efficiency, for if phosphate has no effect, or even if its effect is purely additive, the plots are balanced for nitrogen and doubled in number, and similarly for phosphate. Moreover, if both ingredients do not act additively, an interaction term can be defined that measures the difference in effect of N (or P) in the presence and absence of the other ingredient. Such a definition, although to some extent arbitrary, completes the specification of the treatment effects; and the whole technique of *factorial experimentation* typified by the above example is of the utmost importance both in principle and in practice. As Fisher put it:

The modifications possible to any complicated apparatus, machine, or industrial process must always be considered as potentially interacting with one another, and must be judged by the probable effects of such interactions. If they have to be treated one at a time this is not because to do so is an ideal scientific procedure, but because to test them simultaneously would sometimes be too troublesome, or too costly. In many instances . . . this impression is greatly exaggerated. (1935a, p. 97)

A further device that naturally arose in factorial designs was that of *confounding*, by which some of the higher-order interaction effects in designs with three or more factors are assumed to be unimportant and are deliberately arranged to coincide in the analysis with particular block contrasts. This enables the number of plots per block to be smaller and the accuracy of the remaining treatment effects thereby to be increased.

To a large extent the practical value of these experimental methods was not dependent on the statistical analysis, but the simplicity and clarity of the analysis greatly contributed to the worldwide popularity of these designs. This analysis was in principle classical least-squares theory, but the orthogonality of the design rendered the estimation problem trivial, and the concomitant assessment of error was systematized by the technique of "analysis of variance." Basically, this technique is a breakdown of the total sum of squares of the observations into relevant additive parts containing any systematic terms ascribable to treatments, blocks, and so on. Once the technique was established and the appropriate tests of significance were available (on the assumption of normality and of homogeneity of error variance) from Fisher's derivation and tabulation of the "variance-ratio" distribution, it could handle more complicated least-squares problems, such as more complex and even nonorthogonal experimental designs or linear and curvilinear regression problems. One useful extension was the adjustment of observed experimental quantities, such as final agricultural yield, by some observed quantity measured prior to the application of treatments. This technique was referred to as analysis of covariance, although this last term seems more appropriate for the simultaneous analysis of two or more variables—that is, the technique of multivariate analysis.

Fisher was active in the development of multivariate analysis. Earlier workers had of course encountered multivariate problems in various contexts, and Fisher had followed up his geometrical distribution of the correlation coefficient with a derivation of the distribution of the multiple correlation coefficient (1928b), again brilliantly using his geometrical approach. The problem exercising Harold Hotelling in the United States and P. C. Mahalanobis in India, as well as Fisher, was the efficient use of several correlated variables for discriminatory and regression problems. Fisher's name is particularly associated with the concept of the discriminant function, some function of the variables that will efficiently distinguish from the measurements of these variables for a single individual whether he came from one or another of two different populations.

Contributions to genetics. Fisher's work in genetics was comparable in importance to his purely statistical contributions and equally reflected his originality and independence of outlook. In the first decade of the twentieth century, Mendelian genetics was still a new subject, and its quantitative consequences were not yet properly appreciated. It was in dispute whether they were consistent with Dar-

win's theory of evolution by natural selection or even with the observed inheritance of metrical characters. Fisher took the second and lesser problem first, and in his 1918 paper he gave a penetrating theoretical analysis of correlation, breaking it down into nongenetic effects, additive gene action, and further complications, such as genic interaction and dominance. He was thus able to demonstrate the consistency of Mendelian principles with the observed correlations between sibs or between parents and offspring. Then, in his book on the genetic theory of natural selection, he tackled the larger problem. He pointed out that the atomistic character of gene segregation (in contrast to Darwin's hypothetical "blending" theory of heredity) is essential for maintaining variability, which in turn is the basis of the process of natural selection. He clarified the theoretical role of mutations, showing that mutations provide a reservoir from which eventually only favorable ones can survive. He emphasized the possibility of the selection of modifier genes, for example, in rendering the action of many mutant genes recessive by modifying the heterozygote phenotypically toward the natural wild type. The relative importance of this theory of the evolution of dominance was queried, for example, by Sewall Wright, among others, but this did not prevent it from being a relevant thesis that stimulated further research. The effect of modifier genes was also shown to be important in the phenomenon of mimicry.

At the Galton laboratory, Fisher's work in human genetics included linkage studies and the initiation of serology research on the human blood groups. An exciting moment in the work on serology came when G. L. Taylor and R. R. Race studied the Rhesus blood groups. Fisher was able to predict, from the experimental results to date, the effective triple structure of the gene, and hence two more anti-sera and one more allele, which were soon successfully traced. Such predictions may be compared with Fisher's earlier theoretical predictions in the theory of evolution, for example, on the evolution of dominance. They made possible the maintenance of a healthy link with experimental and observational work, which was often initiated or encouraged by Fisher himself. It was in this spirit that he collaborated for several years with E. B. Ford in sampling studies of natural populations.

In retrospect, Fisher's wholehearted immersion in his own research problems, fundamental and broad as these were, did cause him to ignore some important theoretical trends. His neglect of purely mathematical probability, which had been rigorously formulated by A. N. Kolmogorov (1933), seemed to extend to developments in the theory of random or stochastic processes, although these were very relevant to some of his own problems in evolutionary genetics. In England, A. G. McKendrick had published some brilliant papers on stochastic processes in medicine, and G. U. Yule on the analysis of time series, but Fisher never appeared to appreciate this work; in particular, his own papers on the statistical analysis of data recorded in time sometimes showed a rather over-rigid adherence to classical and unduly narrow assumptions. In appraising Fisher's work, one must consider, in addition to these general boundaries that demarcate it, his occasional specific errors and, more importantly, his temperamental bias in controversy. Fisher's scientific achievements are, however, so varied and so penetrating that such lapses cannot dim their luster or reduce his ranking as one of the great scientists of this century.

M. S. BARTLETT

[*For the historical context of Fisher's work, see* STATISTICS, *article on* THE HISTORY OF STATISTICAL METHOD; *and the biographies of* GALTON; GOSSET; PEARSON; YULE. *For discussion of the subsequent development of Fisher's ideas, see* ESTIMATION; EXPERIMENTAL DESIGN; FIDUCIAL INFERENCE; HYPOTHESIS TESTING; LINEAR HYPOTHESES, *article on* ANALYSIS OF VARIANCE; MULTIVARIATE ANALYSIS.]

WORKS BY FISHER

1912   On an Absolute Criterion for Fitting Frequency Curves. *Messenger of Mathematics* New Series 41: 155–160.

1915   Frequency Distribution of the Values of the Correlation Coefficient in Samples From an Indefinitely Large Population. *Biometrika* 10:507–521.

1918   The Correlation Between Relatives on the Supposition of Mendelian Inheritance. Royal Society of Edinburgh, *Transactions* 52:399–433.

(1920–1945) 1950   *Contributions to Mathematical Statistics.* New York: Wiley.

(1922) 1950   On the Mathematical Foundations of Theoretical Statistics. Pages 10.308a–10.368 in R. A. Fisher, *Contributions to Mathematical Statistics.* New York: Wiley. → First published in Volume 222 of the *Philosophical Transactions*, Series A, of the Royal Society of London.

(1925a) 1958   *Statistical Methods for Research Workers.* 13th ed., rev. New York: Hafner. → Previous editions were also published by Oliver & Boyd.

(1925b) 1950   Theory of Statistical Estimation. Pages 11.699a–11.725 in R. A. Fisher, *Contributions to Mathematical Statistics.* New York: Wiley. → First published in Volume 22 of the *Proceedings* of the Cambridge Philosophical Society.

(1928a) 1950   Moments and Product Moments of Sampling Distributions. Pages 20.198a–20.237 in R. A. Fisher, *Contributions to Mathematical Statistics.* New York: Wiley. → First published in Volume 30 of the *Proceedings* of the London Mathematical Society.

(1928b) 1950   The General Sampling Distribution of the Multiple Correlation Coefficient. Pages 14.653a–14.763 in R. A. Fisher, *Contributions to Mathematical Statistics.* New York: Wiley. → First published in Vol-

ume 121 of the *Proceedings* of the Royal Society of London.

(1930a) 1958   *The Genetical Theory of Natural Selection.* 2d ed., rev. New York: Dover.

(1930b) 1950   *Inverse Probability.* Pages 22.527a–22.535 in R. A. Fisher, *Contributions to Mathematical Statistics.* New York: Wiley. → First published in Volume 26 of the *Proceedings* of the Cambridge Philosophical Society.

1934   Randomization and an Old Enigma of Card Play. *Mathematical Gazette* 18:294–297.

(1935a) 1960   *The Design of Experiments.* 7th ed. New York: Hafner. → Previous editions were also published by Oliver & Boyd.

(1935b) 1950   The Fiducial Argument in Statistical Inference. Pages 25.390a–25.398 in R. A. Fisher, *Contributions to Mathematical Statistics.* New York: Wiley. → First published in Volume 6, part 4 of the *Annals of Eugenics.*

(1938) 1963   FISHER, R. A.; and YATES, FRANK *Statistical Tables for Biological, Agricultural, and Medical Research.* 6th ed., rev. & enl. New York: Hafner.

1949   *The Theory of Inbreeding.* Edinburgh: Oliver & Boyd; New York: Hafner.

(1956) 1959   *Statistical Methods and Scientific Inference.* 2d ed., rev. New York: Hafner. → Previous editions were also published by Oliver & Boyd.

SUPPLEMENTARY BIBLIOGRAPHY

BARTLETT, M. S. 1936   The Information Available in Small Samples. Cambridge Philosophical Society, *Proceedings* 32:560–566.

BARTLETT, M. S. 1965   R. A. Fisher and the Last Fifty Years of Statistical Methodology. *Journal of the American Statistical Association* 60:395–409.

EDDINGTON, ARTHUR STANLEY 1935   *New Pathways in Science.* New York: Macmillan.

KOLMOGOROV, ANDREI N. (1933) 1956   *Foundations of the Theory of Probability.* New York: Chelsea. → First published in German.

NEYMAN, JERZY 1937   Outline of a Theory of Statistical Estimation Based on the Classical Theory of Probability. Royal Society of London, *Philosophical Transactions* Series A 236:333–380.

NEYMAN, JERZY 1967   R. A. Fisher (1890–1962): An Appreciation. *Science* 156:1456–1462. → Includes a two-page "Footnote" by William G. Cochran.

SHANNON, C. E. 1948   Mathematical Theory of Communication. *Bell System Technical Journal* 27:379–423, 623–656.

THIELE, THORWALD N. 1903   *Theory of Observations.* London: Layton.

YATES, F.; and MATHER, K. 1963   Ronald Aylmer Fisher. Volume 9, pages 91–129 in Royal Society of London, *Biographical Memoirs of the Fellows of the Royal Society.* London: The Society. → Contains a bibliography on pages 120–129.

FLETCHER, ALICE CUNNINGHAM

Alice Cunningham Fletcher (1838–1923), American ethnologist, was born in Cuba during a temporary residence of her American parents on the island. She traveled widely in her early years and eventually settled in the Boston area, where she studied American archeology and ethnology at the Peabody Museum at Harvard University. It was out of intense concern for the welfare and rights of the American Indian that she began her scientific studies of them. Although she was eventually to gain great and well-merited recognition as a scholar, the recommendations in behalf of American Indians that she made in the name of anthropological authority suffered from an uncritical commitment to benevolent philosophies of the nineteenth century. The policy she advocated was based on the assumption that it was both inevitable and desirable for the Indians to be assimilated into white society and for their tribal culture to be rapidly destroyed.

In 1870 she held a post with the Women's National Indian Association as administrator of funds from which small loans were made to Indians so that they might buy their own lands and build homes. Then, in 1879, she met Thomas Henry Tibbles—frontiersman, minister, journalist, and ardent worker in the cause of Indian rights—and asked that she be allowed to take part in his work on the frontier. Tibbles found it difficult to take seriously the plans of the small, seemingly delicate woman, already 40 years old and a product of city life, but Alice Fletcher prevailed. On September 1, 1881, she arrived in Omaha, Nebraska, to begin work on field studies that were to become standard references in North American ethnology. But many anthropologists familiar with Fletcher's work are not aware of the fact that this field work permitted her to initiate the large-scale implementation of her well-intentioned but misguided notions and thus to affect the course of Indian affairs throughout the country up to the present day.

In Omaha, she was met by Tibbles and Bright Eyes La Flesche, an educated Omaha Indian woman associated with Tibbles' work and soon to become his wife. Tibbles' autobiography, *Buckskin and Blanket Days* (1957), reflects both his admiration for Alice Fletcher's determination and exasperation at her cheerful obliviousness to what wiser minds had heretofore recognized as realities in dealing with Indians and Indian agents. He never identified her by name but referred to her only as "High Flyer," the name bestowed on her by his Omaha helper, Wajapa. After introductions to members of the Omaha tribe, the two women, Tibbles, and Wajapa set off on a journey to the Winnebago reservation—the Ponca settlement north of the Niobrara River which was made up of removed and demoralized remnants of the tribe whose members had returned to their old haunts—and finally to the Rosebud Sioux reservation in South Dakota. Tibbles had not underestimated the hardships, bad weather, and inconveniences that

could be expected on the trip, but Alice Fletcher withstood them all equally.

She was impressed by Tibbles, Wajapa, and Bright Eyes and was grateful to them. Although they could converse in the several languages encountered on this first journey and could communicate with equal ease with her, a lady newly arrived from Boston, it apparently never occurred to her that the two Indians were highly atypical and that for all of Tibbles' vast knowledge of Indian life, his Indian policy derived entirely from the white Christian values he shared with her.

Alice Fletcher had long since decided that what was best for the Indians was a Congressional act whereby every adult Omaha would be allotted 80 acres, to remain tax-free and to be held in trust by the government for a period of 25 years. After that time those who were judged competent would be granted fee patents and control over their holdings. Reservation lands left over after the distribution of allotments were to be sold for the benefit of the tribe to finance development of their farms. It is doubtful that the Omaha understood the nature of Fletcher's solution for their problems; they only feared dispossession, as their neighbors the Ponca had experienced, and were in no position to question her narrow interpretation of their plea, "Make my home secure" (La Flesche 1923).

Alice Fletcher had influential friends in Washington, and the act was quickly pushed through legislative procedures and passed August 7, 1882. She was appointed special agent to oversee the surveying and allotment. In subsequent years she performed similar work among the Winnebago and Nez Percé, who, along with many other tribes, were allotted land under the Dawes Severalty Act of 1887, patterned after the Omaha Act.

In 1910, after an absence of many years, she returned to the Omaha for a brief visit. She observed, ". . . the act has not been altogether evil nor has it been wholly good for the people" (Fletcher & La Flesche 1911, p. 640). The Omaha were certainly far better off materially and were more cheerful than they had been when she first knew them, and it is small wonder that she viewed their future with optimism. She saw the tendency to lease rather than work the land as nothing more than an unfortunate phase of adjustment to land ownership, although it was really an indication of a major trend. The few well-run farms that she thought would be models proved to be short-lived exceptions. Finally, those items which she noted as "quaint survivals of old customs under a new guise" were really instances of adaptations, of cultural persistence, and of a desperate clinging to tribal identity that characterize Omaha life to the present day.

Margaret Mead spent the summer of 1930 with the Omaha (Mead 1932, *passim*). In keeping with her desire to conceal the identity of the group, which she called the "Antlers," Mead did not mention Fletcher by name but paid respectful tribute in her statement that the traditional life and history had been so completely recorded for the Antlers that she chose to work with this group because she would be able to devote her attention entirely to modern conditions. Mead did not disclose that the same scholar who had provided such excellent ethnographic data was also the "well-intentioned lady of missionary leanings" whose benevolent efforts resulted in the social and economic chaos Mead observed. But Mead thought that philanthropic Americans of that time could not have been expected to understand that individual landownership by Indians would not solve the economic problems that the loss of the buffaloes had created. In any case, the inadequacy of the Omaha plan was demonstrated wherever allotment took place. Between the time that fee patents were issued and the beginning of the administration of John Collier as commissioner of Indian affairs in 1938, twothirds of allotted Indian lands had passed into white ownership (Fey & McNickle 1959, p. 78). Fletcher's "strong paper" on individual allotments was far weaker than the tribal treaty relating to undivided lands.

In matters unrelated to economics her outlook was scientifically objective. Tibbles always disapproved strongly of her interest in Indian dancing and singing and of her desire to observe and record ceremonies: to him such matters were part of Indian "savagery" to be rigorously discouraged and repressed. Alice Fletcher, however, was impressed by the artistry, poetic sophistication, and scientific significance of these customs in contrast to the Indians' material life, and she made important pioneering studies of Indian music and ceremony. Her obviously sincere concern for Indian welfare and her untiring efforts to record ceremonial life accurately won the esteem of her informants. She collected highly secret data with relative ease and maintained generally excellent relations with both colleagues and informants by a combination of humor, patience, total unselfishness, and lack of vindictiveness when crossed. Her small stature and seeming frailness apparently disarmed people who did not appreciate her strength and determination. During one field trip she suffered a siege of "inflammatory rheumatism," which was to leave her crippled for the rest of her life.

As she lay in pain, her Indian friends gathered daily to cheer and console her with songs. As soon as she was able, and with an amazing display of musical aptitude and memory, she carefully transcribed a large number of the songs (Hough 1923, p. 255).

Fletcher's theoretical interests were influenced by nineteenth-century evolutionary concepts but went beyond mere collection of facts or broad ascription of traits to given stages of development. Her investigations of Omaha religion carried her into comparative work among other Siouan speakers of the Plains, and as she suspected the existence of yet older layers of cosmology and ritual from other sources, she turned to the Caddo as the likely carriers of more ancient forms. She had observed the Pawnee hako ceremony in the 1880s, and as her awareness of problems of diffusion increased, she returned as an experienced field worker to the Pawnee in the 1890s and recorded the ceremony (Fletcher 1904).

Her scientific endeavors won rapid recognition in the anthropological profession. From 1883 onward, her name appears often in the *Proceedings* of the American Association for the Advancement of Science (AAAS) in connection with papers dealing with aspects of Plains culture. In 1896 she was vice president of the AAAS. In 1884/1885 she was in charge of Indian exhibits at the New Orleans industrial exposition. It pained her that Indians were represented by crude artifacts, and she wrote a letter, which was published and circulated among Indian groups, stressing the importance of education if Indian people were to take their rightful place in creating technological wonders like those of the white man (Fletcher 1885, pp. 1–4).

The Chicago world's fair of 1893 included a special congress of anthropology, and she took an active part in the proceedings along with the major anthropologists of her day, such as Frederic Ward Putnam, Franz Boas, and Zelia Nuttall.

After 1890, when she made her home in Washington, D.C., Alice Fletcher was a member of the Women's Anthropological Society (WAS) and served as its president in 1895. The WAS was founded in 1885 by Matilda Stevenson, famous for her studies of Pueblo groups, and was disbanded in 1899, when the group was received as a whole into the heretofore all-male Anthropological Society of Washington. Alice Fletcher was elected president of that society in 1903 and of the American Folklore Society in 1906. She worked closely with Frederic Ward Putnam in his research on the Serpent Mound in Ohio, and in 1900 they engaged in a fund-raising campaign to buy the site as a historic landmark, turning the deed over to the Ohio Archeological and Historical Society.

By the time of her death, at the age of 85, Alice Fletcher had become sort of a living legend in anthropology, active to the end in promoting scholarly enterprises and good works.

NANCY OESTREICH LURIE

[*Other relevant material may be found in* INDIANS, NORTH AMERICAN.]

WORKS BY FLETCHER

1885   *A Letter From the World's Industrial Exposition at New Orleans to the Various Indian Tribes Who Are Interested in Education.* Carlisle, Pa.

1904   The Hako: A Pawnee Ceremony. U.S. Bureau of American Ethnology, *Twenty-second Annual Report, 1900–1901.* → The entire issue is devoted to Alice C. Fletcher's work.

1911   FLETCHER, ALICE C.; and LA FLESCHE, FRANCIS The Omaha Tribe. U.S. Bureau of American Ethnology, *Twenty-seventh Annual Report, 1905–1906.* → Much of the research on the volume as a whole antedated that done on the hako ceremony published earlier. The entire issue is devoted to Alice Fletcher's and Francis La Flesche's work.

SUPPLEMENTARY BIBLIOGRAPHY

Alice C. Fletcher Memorial Meeting. 1923 *El palacio* 15, no. 5:83–88. → Contains sentimental tributes by Alice C. Fletcher's friends.

FEY, HAROLD E.; and MCNICKLE, D'ARCY 1959 *Indians and Other Americans: Two Ways of Life Meet.* New York: Harper. → Although Alice Fletcher's role is not noted, this account reviews the devastating effects of the Dawes Act of 1887 and the amount of land loss up to 1933.

HOUGH, WALTER 1923 Alice Cunningham Fletcher. *American Anthropologist* New Series 25:254–258. → An obituary containing the most extensive biographical data in the form of a chronology of events and achievements and a bibliography of Alice C. Fletcher's writings.

LA FLESCHE, FRANCIS 1923 Alice C. Fletcher. *Science* New Series 58:115 only. → An obituary stressing the nature of Alice C. Fletcher's personality.

LAMB, DANIEL S. 1906 The Story of the Anthropological Society of Washington. *American Anthropologist* New Series 8:564–579.

LUMMIS, CHARLES F. 1923 In Memoriam: Alice C. Fletcher. *Art and Archeology* 16:75–76.

MEAD, MARGARET 1932 *The Changing Culture of an Indian Tribe.* Columbia University Contributions to Anthropology, Vol. 15. New York: Columbia Univ. Press.

TIBBLES, THOMAS H. 1957 *Buckskin and Blanket Days: Memoirs of a Friend of the Indians Written in 1905.* Edited by Theodora B. Cogswell. New York: Doubleday. → Thomas H. Tibbles' memoirs were written in 1905 but checked and expanded, with a biographical introduction by T. Cogswell, in 1957. Tibbles takes full credit for inspiring the Dawes Act of 1887, and although he often refers to Alice Fletcher as "High Flyer" and pays her grudging respect as a remarkable woman, it is clear that he resented her overshadowing him in the role of friend and benefactor to the Indians.

FLEURE, H. J.

Herbert John Fleure, British geographer and anthropologist, has done much to further the view that the study of man and his societies should not be divorced from the study of their environments and that an evolutionary approach to the condition of man and his cultures in the various regions of the world is essential to the discipline of human geography. He vigorously championed this subject at a time when it was not generally recognized as a university discipline in Britain.

Fleure grew up in Guernsey. In 1897, when he was 20, a scholarship to the University College of Wales, Aberystwyth, enabled him to take courses in the natural sciences; he specialized in marine zoology. He spent the year 1903–1904 studying at the University of Zurich, where Rudolf Martin stimulated his interest in anthropology. The following year he returned to Wales and received the degree of D.SC. He then began to teach courses in zoology, geology, and botany at Aberystwyth and in 1907 was elected to a newly established lectureship in geography. His intellectual development was influenced by Darwinism and by the works of such German earth scientists as Eduard Suess and Ferdinand von Richthofen.

Fleure became professor of zoology in 1910 but continued to teach geography, and in 1917 his persistent advocacy of this subject was rewarded by his appointment to the endowed (Gregynog) chair of geography and anthropology. In the same year he became honorary secretary of the Geographical Association and editor of its journal (now *Geography*), and through these agencies he worked strenuously to advance the cause of human geography in education. From 1930 until his retirement in 1944, Fleure was professor of geography in the University of Manchester. He has been president of three sections of the British Association for the Advancement of Science, and of many learned societies. In 1936 he was elected fellow of the Royal Society.

Fleure quickly established his reputation as an anthropologist with an anthropometric survey of Wales conducted in 1916 (Fleure & James 1916). He first outlined a scheme of world regions, defined by the quality of life within them, in an article published in 1917. Suspicious of the concept of "natural regions," he saw, long before prehistoric archeology and paleoecology had established the antiquity and extent of man's alteration of his surroundings, that human societies can fashion their own environments and that "environment" is a term of cultural appraisal. In his *Human Geography in Western Europe* (1918) he first presented his conception of that discipline. The first of the ten volumes of *The Corridors of Time,* written in collaboration with Harold Peake, appeared in 1927, and the last volume appeared in 1956. From the first volume (*Apes and Men*) to the last (*Times and Places*), this series presents Fleure's mature views on the development of human societies in the major regions of the world since prehistoric times. A balanced judgment on such issues as diffusion and independent development springs from a broad training in the sciences of man.

Fleure has stressed the significance of culture contacts in all periods of human history as leading to the questioning of routine, the cross-fertilization of ideas, objective thought, and the release of innovative effort. Always guarded in his conclusions, Fleure has been chary of general laws in human geography, where the likelihood prevails that different responses will arise in different regions at different times.

In addition to the works mentioned, Fleure has contributed extensively to encyclopedias and also to journals of geography, anthropology, sociology, folklore, and archeology.

E. ESTYN EVANS

[*See also* GEOGRAPHY; REGION.]

WORKS BY FLEURE

1916   FLEURE, H. J.; and JAMES, T. C. Geographical Distribution of Anthropological Types in Wales. *Journal of the Royal Anthropological Institute of Great Britain and Ireland* 46:35–153.

(1917) 1919   Human Regions. *Scottish Geographical Magazine* 35:94–105. → A revision of the paper "Régions humaines" published in May 1917 in *Annales de géographie.*

1918   *Human Geography in Western Europe: A Study in Appreciation.* London: Williams & Norgate.

1922   *The Peoples of Europe.* Oxford Univ. Press.

1923   *The Races of England and Wales: A Survey of Recent Research.* London: Benn.

(1927) 1929   *The Races of Mankind.* Garden City, N.Y.: Doubleday.

1927–1956   PEAKE, HAROLD; and FLEURE, H. J. *The Corridors of Time.* 10 vols. New Haven: Yale Univ. Press. → Volume 1: *Apes and Men,* 1927. Volume 2: *Hunters and Artists,* 1927. Volume 3: *Peasants and Potters,* 1927. Volume 4: *Priests and Kings,* 1927. Volume 5: *The Steppe and the Sown,* 1928. Volume 6: *The Way of the Sea,* 1929. Volume 7: *Merchant Venturers in Bronze,* 1931. Volume 8: *The Horse and the Sword,* 1933. Volume 9: *The Law and the Prophets,* 1936. Volume 10: *Times and Places,* 1956.

1951   *A Natural History of Man in Britain: Conceived as a Study of Changing Relations Between Men and Environments.* London: Collins.

FLOURENS, PIERRE

Pierre Flourens (1794–1867) was a French neurophysiologist who came from Languedoc. His intellectual aptitude became apparent to his family when he was still very young, and his education was accelerated. By the time he was 15 he was a student at the celebrated faculty of medicine at Montpellier; he received his medical degree before he was 20.

Flourens was drawn to Paris, where he became a protégé of Georges Cuvier, who introduced him to the intellectual elite of the city. In 1828 he became deputy professor to Cuvier at the Collège de France; in 1830, professor at the Musée d'Histoire Naturelle; and in 1855, professor at the Collège de France. He also became a member of the Académie des Sciences in 1828 and was made perpetual secretary of that institution in 1833. In 1840 Flourens was elected to the Académie Française.

While still a young experimenter, Pierre Flourens devised a rigorous technique for investigating the brain. Before him, researchers had plunged a trocar into the brain through a trephined aperture that permitted no precise localization and that concealed pressures and hemorrhages from the investigator. Flourens carefully uncovered the brain and its meninges, avoiding damage to the blood vessels, and precisely excised the area to be studied.

In 1822 Flourens began to study the effects of extirpation of successive layers of the cerebellum. He found that at an intermediate point of extirpation a loss of stability and motor skill appears, as if the animal, although still able to walk, run, fly, or swim, has lost its "balance wheel." This was the original discovery of the function of coordination.

Flourens also studied the effects of eliminating one of the semicircular canals of the ear. The result was "an impetuous movement of the head," which shifted violently in the spatial plane of the canal in question. This again was an original discovery, opening up the further study of the semicircular canals as distinct from the cochlear apparatus.

Flourens also experimented on the brain stem. In the lower portion, in the medulla oblongata, he precisely delimitated the small point that is the seat of the "vital node," which if punctured causes instantaneous death by suddenly terminating respiration. In the upper portion a selective extirpation, anterior to the corpora quadrigemina, gave the first experimental indication of a relay in the central nervous apparatus of sight.

Finally, he made experiments on the cerebral hemispheres. This work was particularly difficult and time consuming. The terrain had been little explored by anatomists, and little was known of the connections and relays. Flourens' work was divided into two series: in one he performed complete ablations of the cerebral hemispheres; in the other, limited ablations by regions, sometimes by progressive removal.

The series of total ablations produced the following results: loss of intelligence and judgment; loss of all voluntary initiative; and relative diminution of instinctive activities, with retention of automatic motility and locomotion.

The series of limited ablations produced losses of the same kind, greater or lesser according to the region and the individual case; but these losses were only partial and proved to be capable of attenuation or compensation.

Above all, Flourens reached the fundamental conclusion that the degree of disorder in any particular faculty seemed to depend *only* on the quantity of cerebral tissue removed, regardless of its location. Generalizing from this fact, Flourens became opposed in principle to all attempts to establish "cerebral localizations"; and his own doctrine of the "homogeneity" of the brain became the focus of a historic dispute.

There is, to be sure, a case against Flourens, but it should be reviewed with detachment. In the first place, Flourens, like others at that time, failed to recognize the significance of certain paralytic effects because he did not experiment on primates. Next, it should be noted that the first indisputable demonstration of cerebral localization did not occur until 1870, after Flourens had died. Last, Flourens' conclusions with regard to the "homogeneity" of the brain and the theory that effects are related to the magnitude of the ablation were again based on experiments limited to lower mammals. Indeed, even so great an investigator as Lashley was similarly misled to conclude from his famous experiments on rats that there are "mass-action" effects.

Lately, with the refinement of physiological conceptions, the problem of homogeneity has again been raised, and some researchers have concluded that in the neocortex the highest functions of nervous integration go beyond "analytical" regional localization. These researchers explicitly evoke the memory of Flourens.

AUGUSTE TOURNAY

[*See also* NERVOUS SYSTEM; *and the biographies of* BROCA *and* LASHLEY.]

WORKS BY FLOURENS

(1824) 1842 *Recherches expérimentales sur les propriétés et les fonctions du système nerveux dans les animaux vertébrés.* Paris: Baillière.
(1841) 1858 *Histoire des travaux de Georges Cuvier.* 3d ed. Paris: Garnier. → First published as *Analyse raisonnée des travaux de G. Cuvier.*
(1844) 1850 *Histoire des travaux et des idées de Buffon.* 2d ed. Paris: Hachette. → First published as *Buffon.*
1856–1862 *Recueil des éloges historiques lus dans les séances publiques de l'Académie des Sciences.* 3 vols. Paris: Garnier.

SUPPLEMENTARY BIBLIOGRAPHY

[A Bibliography of] Marie Jean Pierre Flourens. 1868 Volume 2, pages 642–646 in Royal Society of London, *Catalogue of Scientific Papers (1800–1863).* London: Clay.
VULPIAN, M. 1888 Éloge historique de M. Flourens. Académie des Sciences, Paris, *Mémoires* 2d series 44:cxlix–clxxxiv.

FLOW-OF-FUNDS ACCOUNTS

See NATIONAL INCOME AND PRODUCT ACCOUNTS.

FOLK MEDICINE

See MEDICAL CARE, *article on* ETHNOMEDICINE.

FOLK MUSIC

See MUSIC, *article on* ETHNOMUSICOLOGY.

FOLK SOCIETY

See COMMUNITY–SOCIETY CONTINUA; PEASANTRY; REGION; TRIBAL SOCIETY; VILLAGE; *and the biographies of* ODUM *and* REDFIELD.

FOLKLORE

Folklore means folk learning; it comprehends all knowledge that is transmitted by word of mouth and all crafts and techniques that are learned by imitation or example, as well as the products of these crafts. Objects which are mass produced and knowledge which is acquired through books or formal education are a part of culture, which includes the total body of learning, but they are not folklore. In nonliterate societies folklore is virtually identical with culture, but in literate industrialized societies it is only a fragment of culture. Anthropologists and humanists have defined folklore differently, but their definitions are in fundamental agreement in excluding all learning that is transmitted by writing.

Folklore includes folk art, folk crafts, folk tools, folk costume, folk custom, folk belief, folk medicine, folk recipes, folk music, folk dance, folk games, folk gestures, and folk speech, as well as those verbal forms of expression which have been called folk literature but which are better described as verbal art. Verbal art, which includes such forms as folktales, legends, myths, proverbs, riddles, and poetry, has been the primary concern of folklorists from both the humanities and the social sciences since the beginnings of folklore as a field of study, and it is with this principal segment of folklore that this article is concerned.

European interest in folklore goes back at least to the sixteenth century and the age of exploration, but the modern study of folklore is generally considered to date from the early years of the nineteenth century, when the Grimm brothers began collecting German folktales in the field. The term folklore was first introduced into English in 1846 by William John Toms, who urged that accounts of "the manners, customs, observances, superstitions, ballads, proverbs, &c., of the olden time" be recorded in Britain for future study and for comparison with the materials which were being recorded in Germany by the Grimm brothers and other scholars.

Forms of verbal art

A variety of forms or genres of verbal art have been distinguished by folklorists, but neither the categories nor the terminology has been standardized. The following categories have proved useful.

Prose narrative. Myths, legends, and folktales are three important kinds of prose narrative or "tale," which is one of the most widespread forms of verbal art. The differences between myths, legends, and folktales are hotly disputed, but distinctions similar to those made here are recognized in some nonliterate societies and have long been employed by students of European folklore.

Myths. In the society in which they are told, myths are considered to be truthful accounts of what happened in the past. They are taught to be believed, and they can be cited as authority in answer to ignorance, doubt, or disbelief. Myths are the embodiment of dogma; they are usually sacred, and they are often associated with theology and ritual. Their characters are usually not human beings, but they often have human attributes. Myths account for the origin of the world, of mankind, of death; for characteristics of birds and animals; or for features of the landscape. They may recount the activities of the deities, their victories and defeats, their friendships and enmities, their love affairs, and their family relationships. They may "explain" details of ceremonial paraphernalia or ritual, or why taboos must be observed.

Legends. Like myths, legends are regarded as true by the narrator and his audience, but they are usually secular rather than sacred. Their principal characters are human, and they concern a period less remote than that of myths. They tell of migrations, wars and victories, deeds of past chiefs and kings, and succession in ruling dynasties. They include local tales of buried treasure, ghosts, fairies, and saints. Legends correspond to *Sagen* in German and *traditions populaires* in French.

Folktales. Prose narratives that are regarded as fiction are called folktales. They usually recount the adventures of animals or humans, but ogres and even deities may appear in them. A variety of subtypes can be distinguished, including drolls or noodles, trickster tales, tall tales, dilemma tales, formulistic tales, and moral tales or fables. Folktales are known as *Märchen* in German and as *contes populaires* in French. They have been known as fairy tales in English, but this is inappropriate both because fairies seldom appear in folktales and because narratives about fairies are usually regarded as true. Some folklorists use the term *Märchen* in English while employing "folktale" to include all three categories, but this is unnecessary when "prose narrative" better serves this purpose.

The distinction here between truth and fiction refers only to the beliefs of those who tell and hear these tales, and not to our beliefs, to historical or scientific fact, or to any ultimate judgment of truth and falsehood. In diffusing from one society to another, a myth or legend may be accepted without being believed, thus becoming a folktale in the borrowing society. Occasionally the reverse may also happen. In a period of rapid cultural change an entire belief system and its mythology may be discredited. Even in cultural isolation there may be some skeptics who do not accept the traditional system of belief. Nevertheless, it is important to know what the majority in a society believes to be true at any given point of time, for people act upon what they believe to be true.

Aphorisms. Proverbs, maxims, and similar terse, sententious sayings can be grouped together. Again usage varies, but in this article proverbs are distinguished from "proverbial phrases" or metaphorical comparisons and from maxims or mottoes like "Honesty is the best policy," which can be applied only in the literal sense. Proverbs have a deeper meaning, one which can be understood only through the analysis of the social situations to which they are appropriate. While prose narratives are world-wide in their distribution, proverbs are primarily an Old World genre, important throughout Europe, Asia, and Africa. Proverbs have been reported from the Americas and from Oceania, but not in large numbers and not with sufficient documentation to determine whether they are in fact proverbs or some other form of aphorism.

Riddles. Riddles differ from proverbs in that they require an answer, but they may also be concisely stated. African riddles are usually phrased as short declarative sentences, rather than as questions, so that they resemble proverbs in form and so that initially it may be difficult for an outsider to recognize the implicit question to which he is expected to provide the correct answer. Riddles vary considerably in their form of statement; and many European riddles take the form of rhyming poems, as in the case of Humpty Dumpty. Riddles again are primarily an Old World genre, although some have been recorded in other parts of the world.

Poetry, tongue-twisters, and verbal formulas. Poetry is widespread, at least in the form of song texts, but has received far less attention than the forms of verbal art mentioned thus far. Tongue-twisters have been recorded in various parts of the world but have been little studied. Incantations, invocations, passwords, greetings, and other verbal formulas have also been neglected by folklorists, although they appear in linguistic studies and in ethnographic descriptions of ritual and etiquette. Like tongue-twisters and some song texts, verbal formulas are often obscure in meaning and both difficult and almost pointless to translate. Comprehension is often less important than correct recitation, and verbatim accuracy may be essential to their religious, magical, or social effectiveness. In view of this it is not surprising that these forms have received less attention than prose narratives, proverbs, and riddles, in all of which both comprehension and communication are involved.

These forms of verbal art are not watertight compartments, as the case of rhyming riddles suggests. Dilemma tales, which are widespread in Africa, leave the solution up to the audience. Often classified with riddles, they are clearly a borderline form; they seem usually to call for argumentation rather than a correct answer. Trickster tales may be either myths or folktales; and ballads are narratives in songs. Some tales incorporate songs in the development of the plot, and others end by quoting a proverb to summarize a moral. The social significance of verbal art is stressed in the following section, but its aesthetic attributes are also important. Their study provides a common meeting ground for the humanities and the social sciences that is rarely if ever equaled in other data on human behavior. Language imposes limitations on the artist in folklore as the medium of expression does in the graphic and plastic arts, music, or the dance. In the case of verbal art the medium of expression is the spoken word, and verbal art is subject to the limitations of the phonetics, grammar, and vocabulary of the language. For this reason linguists are best qualified to consider the question of style, which can be defined as what the artist is able to achieve within the limitations of his techniques and media. Linguists have, in fact, contributed several important discussions of this subject. More often they have recorded prose narratives as a convenient means of collecting texts for linguistic analysis, with the result that many of the most accurately recorded and carefully transcribed collections of verbal art are to be found in linguistic studies.

Some functions of verbal art

Amusement is an obvious function of folktales, riddles, and tongue-twisters, but verbal art has other, more important functions.

Education. In nonliterate societies verbal art plays a major and often explicitly recognized role in education. It is important to learn myths and legends because they contain information that is believed to be true. Proverbs are often characterized as the distilled wisdom of past generations. Learning the values of a culture as they are expressed in proverbs is similarly considered important in its own right; without some command of proverbs, individuals in many African societies cannot effectively fulfill their roles as adults. Whereas African proverbs are considered to be the province of adults, riddles are for children. Riddles teach the characteristics of plants, animals, and other things in nature, as well as some features of technology, material culture, and social structure. Even folktales that are regarded as fictitious are recognized by Africans as important in the education of children, because so many of them are moral tales. The importance of verbal art in education has been noted in nonliterate societies throughout the world. Verbal art provides a medium for the transmission of knowledge, values, and attitudes from one generation to another and thus contributes to the continuity of culture.

Social control. Verbal art helps to maintain conformity to cultural values and accepted patterns of behavior. It is widely used to express social approval and disapproval, to apply social pressure, and to exercise social control. Proverbs, songs of ridicule, and even riddles and folktales may be used to criticize those who deviate from the accepted norms and social conventions. On the other hand, proverbs, praise names, and praise songs give recognition and reward to those who conform. African proverbs are especially important in this respect. When action is contemplated that may lead to social friction, open hostilities, or direct punishment by society, proverbs can be used to express warning, defiance, or derision of a rival or enemy. They may also express advice, counsel, or warning to a friend.

Because of the high regard in which they are held, and because they are considered especially appropriate to adult life, African proverbs are highly effective instruments of social control. Because they express the morals and ethics of a society, they are convenient standards for appraising behavior in terms of the approved norms. And because they are pungently, sententiously, and wittily stated, they are ideally suited for commenting on the behavior of others.

Social authority. Verbal art serves to validate social institutions and religious rituals. Malinowski showed how, in the Trobriand Islands of the Pacific, myth provides a warrant and a charter for magic, ceremony, ritual, and social structure. Myths can be cited as authority on questions of religious belief and ritual procedure, and to justify rights to land, fishing grounds, social position, tribute, or political authority. This important function can be seen in many societies, but it is not confined to myth. When dissatisfaction with or skepticism of an accepted pattern is expressed, or when doubts about it arise, there is usually a myth or legend to validate it; however, a moral folktale or a proverb may serve the same purpose.

Sociopsychological function. Verbal art provides a psychological release from the restrictions imposed on the individual by society. Ever since Greek myths were recorded in writing, it has been recognized that characters in myths do things that are regarded as shocking, sinful, and even criminal in daily life. Myths and folktales provide an opportunity for people to talk about kinds of behavior that society prohibits them from indulging in, and about kinds of success that they can scarcely hope to achieve themselves.

This can be illustrated in our own society by "dirty jokes" and, formerly, mother-in-law jokes. In the case of the latter, their popularity has declined as fewer young couples live with their in-laws and the family is increasingly fragmented. In American Indian societies that practice mother-in-law avoidance, the trickster violates his own mother-in-law. Tales of polygynous marriages feature far more prominently among the monogamous Pueblo groups than in societies where polygyny is accepted. In West Africa the Ashanti and Dahomeans recognize the value of being able to criticize and laugh at authority and other matters, both secular and sacred, in a way they cannot do normally, through folktales and songs. Even rid-

dles and tongue-twisters, although considered the province of children, sometimes involve sexual references that are considered off-color by adults.

The familiar theme of rags to riches, the widespread tale of the magic flight or of the seven-league boots, and tales of resurrection after death are also meaningful in terms of psychological release. Viewed in this light, verbal art reveals man's attempt to escape in fantasy from the restrictions of his geographic environment, from his own biological limitations as a member of the human species, and from the repressions imposed upon him by society, whether these result from social and economic inequalities, from sexual taboos, or from the Ashanti taboo against laughing at a person afflicted with yaws.

Cultural continuity. When the functions of education, control, authority, and release are viewed together, it can be seen that verbal art has the broader function of maintaining the continuity and stability of culture. It is used to inculcate customs and ethical standards in the young, to reward the adult with praise when he conforms or to punish him with criticism or ridicule when he deviates, to provide him with rationalizations when he questions the institutions and conventions of his society, and at the same time to provide him with a compensatory escape from the hardships and injustices of everyday life. It operates to ensure cultural continuity from generation to generation through its role in education, by emphasizing conformity to the accepted cultural norms, and through the validation of social and religious institutions. By providing a psychological escape from the institutions and norms which it sanctions and enforces and by providing discontented individuals an opportunity to talk about forbidden forms of behavior, rather than practicing them, verbal art preserves the established customs and institutions from direct attack and change.

Political uses of verbal arts. Despite the fact that verbal art serves to continue and stabilize culture, it has also been used for the purposes of political propaganda and social change. During the emergence of the independent nations of Africa, myths, legends, and song texts have been used to promote ethnic unity, regionalism, nationalism, anticolonialism, and pan-Africanism.

The Yoruba creation myth provided the basis for the Society of the Children of Oduduwa (Egbe Omo Oduduwa), established for the purpose of uniting the people of the Western Region of Nigeria, and Bakongo mythology has been used for political purposes by Joseph Kasavubu's Abako party in the Congo. In Katanga a common myth has been cited by politicians to show why the

Lunda, Luena, and Chokwe should unite in support of Tshombe and his Conakat party, or, conversely, why the Luena and Chokwe should join in opposition to the Lunda. African praise songs have been adapted to honor new political leaders; songs of allusion have been used to criticize colonial officials and rival politicians; and the hymn "God Bless Africa," first sung publicly in 1899, has been adopted as a closing anthem by the African National Congress and as the unofficial national anthem of several African countries, and it was sung at the 1958 Conference of Independent African States in Accra, Ghana.

In the Soviet Union in 1936, the Communist party "discovered" the effectiveness of folklore as a political weapon. Scholars reversed earlier theories that regarded folklore as a product of the upper classes filtering down to the lower classes, and claimed that the working people were the creators of folklore.

Folktales and songs have been used to advance the theme of the class struggle in the Soviet Union, in China, in Cuba, and elsewhere. The Nazis used Teutonic mythology to promote their idea of a master race. In earlier times Krylov used fables to needle the Russian aristocracy, and the first Chinese edition of *Aesop's Fables* was suppressed by officials who recognized their satire and suspected that they had been invented locally. Further study of the political uses of verbal art, which have only recently been recognized by folklorists, will undoubtedly reveal other instances of this kind.

The recording of verbal art is a well-recognized field technique in linguistic and anthropological research, and it can be helpful in studying political attitudes. Verbal art provides useful materials for school curricula and important data for the study of law, values, psychology, and history in nonliterate societies. Writing and industrialization have undermined its social significance far more in urban United States than in most literate societies, but they have never destroyed verbal art or the other segments of folklore.

WILLIAM BASCOM

[*Directly related are the entries* COMMUNICATION; DRAMA; HISTORY, *article on* ETHNOHISTORY; MUSIC, *article on* ETHNOMUSICOLOGY. *Other relevant material may be found in* CRAFTS; HISTORIOGRAPHY; MYTH AND SYMBOL; PRIMITIVE ART.]

BIBLIOGRAPHY

BASCOM, WILLIAM (1954) 1965 Four Functions of Folklore. Pages 279–298 in Alan Dundes (editor), *The Study of Folklore*. Englewood Cliffs, N.J.: Prentice-Hall. → First published in Volume 67 of the *Journal of American Folklore*.

BASCOM, WILLIAM 1955 Verbal Art. *Journal of American Folklore* 68:245–252.

BASCOM, WILLIAM 1965a Folklore and Literature. Pages 469–490 in Robert A. Lystad (editor), *The African World: A Survey of Social Research*. New York: Praeger. → A bibliography appears on pages 558–560.

BASCOM, WILLIAM 1965b The Forms of Folklore: Prose Narratives. *Journal of American Folklore* 78:3–20.

BENEDICT, RUTH 1935 *Zuni Mythology*. 2 vols. Columbia University Contributions to Anthropology, Vol. 21. New York: Columbia Univ. Press.

DORSON, RICHARD M. 1959 *American Folklore*. Univ. of Chicago Press.

FISCHER, JOHN L. 1963 The Socio-psychological Analysis of Folktales. *Current Anthropology* 4:235–295.

Funk & Wagnalls Standard Dictionary of Folklore, Mythology and Legend. Edited by Maria Leach. 2 vols. 1949 New York: Funk & Wagnalls.

GRIMM, JAKOB; and GRIMM, WILHELM (1812–1815) 1948 *Grimm's Fairy Tales*. Complete ed., rev. Translated by Margaret Hunt; revised by James Stern. London: Routledge. → First published in German.

HERSKOVITS, MELVILLE J.; and HERSKOVITS, FRANCES S. 1958 *Dahomean Narrative: A Cross-cultural Analysis*. Northwestern University African Studies, No. 1. Evanston, Ill.: Northwestern Univ. Press.

JACOBS, MELVILLE 1959 *The Content and Style of Oral Literature: Clackamas Chinook Myths and Tales*. Wenner-Gren Foundation for Anthropological Research Publications in Anthropology, No. 26. Univ. of Chicago Press.

MALINOWSKI, BRONISLAW (1926) 1948 Myth in Primitive Psychology. Pages 72–124 in Bronislaw Malinowski, *Magic, Science and Religion and Other Essays*. Glencoe, Ill.: Free Press; Boston: Beacon. → A paperback edition was published in 1954 by Doubleday.

OPLER, MORRIS E. 1940 *Myths and Legends of the Lipan Apache Indians*. Memoirs of the American Folk-Lore Society, Vol. 36. Philadelphia: The Society.

RATTRAY, R. S. 1930 *Akan-Ashanti Folk-tales*. Oxford: Clarendon.

RAUM, O. F. 1940 *Chaga Childhood: A Description of Indigenous Education in an East African Tribe*. Oxford Univ. Press.

THOMPSON, STITH 1946 *The Folktale*. New York: Dryden.

THOMPSON, STITH 1953 Advances in Folklore Studies. Pages 587–596 in International Symposium on Anthropology, New York, 1952, *Anthropology Today: An Encyclopedic Inventory*. Univ. of Chicago Press.

FOLKWAYS

See the biography of SUMNER.

FOLLETT, MARY PARKER

Mary Parker Follett (1868–1933) was a social philosopher who attempted to apply the principles she deduced to practical problems in business, politics, and social work. She was born a member of an old Quincy, Massachusetts, family and was educated at Thayer Academy, Radcliffe College, and the Sorbonne. While still a student at Radcliffe she spent the year 1890–1891 at Newnham College, Cambridge, England, where she formed many lifelong friendships. Her intellectual contribution to the social sciences is contained in two books, *The New State* (1918) and *Creative Experience* (1924), and a posthumous collection of papers, *Dynamic Administration*, published in 1942 (see 1926–1930). She died in London.

Among the earliest to see the importance of the group in understanding an individual and his thoughts, she rejected schemes which postulate a dualism between the individual and society, as well as most other forms of causal interaction between these two entities, in favor of the notion of integration.

The New State is a plea for a political order based on an interlocking hierarchy of membership groups, beginning at the neighborhood level. The unit of the community is the socialized individual, that is to say, the individual who, through associational membership, has become a fully participating member of society. This is the new individualism of the new state. In the ideal democracy, therefore, integration of the individual personality and the society is so complete that no conflict, either psychological or social, is conceivable. "Democracy does not register various opinions; it is an attempt to create unity" (1918, p. 209).

In *Creative Experience* Follett discussed the prevention and elimination of the failure of integration, that is, of social conflict. She was particularly interested in problems of social change and conflict in small-scale social systems, such as factories, wage boards, regulating commissions, community centers, and neighborhoods.

The concept of circular response, developed in *Creative Experience* and in later essays and lectures, is her principal contribution to the analysis of failures of integration. Circular response rests upon the theory that the unit of social analysis is the pattern of relations between actors, conceived as a single situation produced by a union of their interests (1924, p. 188). No response by an actor is wholly predictable for he must continually modify his behavior to adjust to the expected responses of others, who constitute his environment. This modulation of both the activity and the sentiments of the actors in an environment constitutes circular response. As Follett put it: "The most fundamental thought about all this is that reaction is always reaction to a relating. . . . I never react to you but to you-plus-me; or to be more accurate, it is I-plus-you reacting to You-plus-me" (1924, p. 62). Somewhat similar theories have been used by Foote and

Cottrell (1955), but their chosen unit of analysis is the episode or event rather than the single social act.

Thus, the only good solution to social conflict is not compromise, not conquest, but integration. Integration in this context means the creation of a novel solution that penalizes no one and that becomes the only sure base for progress toward an ideal democracy. If integration is to be achieved, various forms of coordination must be introduced as fundamental principles of organization: (1) *direct contact* between the responsible people who have to carry out policies, rather than hierarchical control; (2) *early contact* between these responsible people, so that policy may be created by them, rather than later meetings that can only try to resolve differences between policies already evolved by isolated groups; (3) the reciprocal relating of all factors in a situation, that is, equal attention to all the variables in the social system.

Coordination in these various forms is a continuing process, since in any complex social environment there exist many points of creativity, and established policies can never be executed as designed but must constantly be reformed in consonance with basic goals.

The sources of Follett's ideas are to be found in the thinking of her own time: she borrowed much from Cooley's concept of the primary group, which became her ideal social setting, and from G. H. Mead's analysis of the "I" and the "me." Her work also reflects the psychological approach to politics of such English political philosophers as Graham Wallas as well as the emphasis on purpose or will or thought in contemporary idealist political thinking. Follett did not appreciate the role of institutional structures, bureaucracy, or force. She firmly rejected Durkheim's proposition that social facts may be conceived of as "things," and her approach to the concept of the state was unsophisticated. She never mentioned the existence of legitimate power or the prevalence of legitimized and idealized peace that has its source in bloody conquest.

Her early papers were in political analysis, but she later found that she could more conveniently study the operation of political influences in industrial systems. Her positions in the Department of Vocational Guidance of the Boston school system and on the Massachusetts Minimum Wage Board gave her access to basic data with which to test her generalizations. She never presented her data in the form of tables, preferring to communicate by generalization and illustrative story.

Professional sociologists have tended to ignore Follett's writings, although they contain many interesting and sensible statements on the subjects of primary group analysis and the creative process in society. Nor are there many references to her work in writings on industrial relations or political science. Curiously, the pluralistic concept of the state is occasionally attributed to her by political scientists (for example, de Grazia 1952), although she had been highly critical of that concept in *The New State:* her emphasis on integrative behavior is not compatible with the concept of the state as an amalgam of discrete political groups.

JOHN MOGEY

[*See also* CONFLICT, *article on* POLITICAL ASPECTS; GENERAL WILL; POLITICAL PROCESS; REPRESENTATION, *article on* THEORY; *and the biographies of* COOLEY; MEAD; WALLAS.]

WORKS BY FOLLETT

1892   Henry Clay as Speaker of the United States House of Representatives. *American Historical Association, Annual Report* [1891]:255–265.

(1896) 1909   *The Speaker of the House of Representatives.* New York: Longmans.

1918   *The New State: Group Organization, the Solution of Popular Government.* New York: Longmans.

(1924) 1951   *Creative Experience.* Gloucester, Mass.: Smith.

(1926–1930) 1942   *Dynamic Administration: The Collected Papers of Mary Parker Follett.* New York: Harper. → Contains a bibliography.

SUPPLEMENTARY BIBLIOGRAPHY

DE GRAZIA, ALFRED (1952) 1962   *Politics and Government: The Elements of Political Science.* 2 vols. New ed., rev. New York: Collier. → First published as *The Elements of Political Science.*

FOOTE, NELSON N.; and COTTRELL, LEONARD S.   1955   *Identity and Interpersonal Competence: A New Direction in Family Research.* Univ. of Chicago Press.

WOOD, ARTHUR E.   1926   The Social Philosophy of Mary P. Follett. *Social Forces* 4:759–769.

FOOD

I. WORLD PROBLEMS   *Nevin S. Scrimshaw*
II. CONSUMPTION PATTERNS   *Yehudi A. Cohen*

I
WORLD PROBLEMS

Low per capita food production and high rates of population growth in underdeveloped areas cause food shortages in many less developed countries, particularly in tropical and semitropical regions. Even though 60 to 80 per cent of the people in these countries are engaged in farming, their productivity is so low that it does not meet the needs of the population. By contrast, in some industrialized countries less than 8 per cent of the population is engaged in an agricultural industry that produces vast surpluses. Although these surpluses help to meet the needs of many other parts of the world, malnutrition is widespread and persistent in the underdeveloped areas and is responsible for much of the high mortality in these areas, whether by itself or in combination with infections of various types.

Factors limiting adequate food production are primarily social and economic rather than physical. The lack of knowledge and the illiteracy of the rural population complicate attempts to increase food production as well as to control population in underdeveloped countries. Long-standing customs, limited agricultural training activities, and inadequate storage and distribution facilities help to perpetuate low agricultural production in these areas. Lack of the tools of scientific agriculture and scarcity of money or credit for their purchase are major additional factors. Moreover, this inadequacy of the food supply is part of a vicious circle that keeps productivity low: malnourished populations are more vulnerable to disease and less capable of sustained work than are well-nourished populations.

Continued increases in food production can be anticipated in most of the less developed countries although in many areas they will not be large enough to maintain adequate per capita food supplies. The additional food necessary to give at least a subsistence ration to most persons is likely to continue to come from the food surpluses of the industrialized countries and to be augmented by the exploitation of new protein sources.

The over-all world food supply is failing to keep pace with population growth but is not yet limiting the world's explosive population increase (Food and Agriculture Organization . . . 1966).

Food and history.   The replacement of exclusive dependence upon hunting, fishing, and gathering by the beginnings of agriculture was the first great step in human development. The rate and scope of social evolution have depended to a major extent on the development of more effective means of obtaining food. In primitive cultures, man's struggle for food consumes most of his time, thought, and energy. The creation of a surplus of food over and above what is needed to live leads to successive refinements in the subdivision of labor, which in turn make possible social and technical advances and thus the production of even greater quantities of food.

For millennia the food supply was a major factor limiting the growth of human populations and determining their density in any particular area. It is only in the last century that improvements in agricultural production have become sufficiently widespread to remove food as the limiting factor in most population growth. In combination with improved control and prevention of infectious and other diseases, an exponential increase in numbers of people has been the result.

Pressure for good agricultural land for the production of food has been a major factor in the turbulent warfare of the historical record. Crop failures have resulted in population losses through death and emigration, which have impoverished and impeded the social and economic development of populations and even whole countries. For example, Ireland has never recovered from the high losses from starvation and emigration as a direct consequence of the potato famine of the 1840s; the political history of the United States and Canada has perhaps been equally changed by hundreds of thousands of Irish immigrants. Another example of the importance of food problems is found in the major political and economic consequences of the failure of agricultural production in the communist countries.

Contemporary problems

Paradoxically, the principal nutrition problem of the industrialized countries today is one of overeating, with a consequent increase in obesity, cardiovascular disease, diabetes, and hypertension. [See OBESITY.]

In contrast, nutritional difficulties in underdeveloped countries are similar to those experienced in the industrialized countries 50 to 100 years ago. Children under five years of age and, to a lesser extent, pregnant and nursing mothers are most affected.

Common deficiencies. The most common severe nutritional deficiencies are those of protein and vitamin A. The best indicator of the prevalence of protein deficiency ("kwashiorkor") is the mortality rate for children one to five years of age, which is commonly 20 to 50 times higher in underdeveloped countries than in areas like western Europe, the United States, Australia, New Zealand, and Japan. Infant mortality rates (deaths of children under one year of age) are two to four times higher in most less developed countries than in those that are industrialized. Early weaning with improper substitutes and inadequate supplementation of breast milk are important factors in high mortality rates for infants who survive the dangerous first months of life.

Vitamin A deficiency is also most common among preschool children; it causes severe eye lesions which often result in blindness. In Indonesia and other countries of southeast Asia, deaths from secondary infection are particularly common in children with vitamin A deficiency. This deficiency could be readily prevented by the green and yellow vegetables that are, or could be, widely available in most countries.

Another common problem—marasmus, or partial starvation—is seen most often among infants who have been prematurely weaned and fed watery gruels that are deficient in both calories and protein. A form of acute thiamine deficiency (infantile beriberi) is a cause of death among nursing infants in some southeast Asian countries, where a polished rice diet results in thiamine (vitamin B_1) deficiency in mothers. Beriberi also still occurs among many adults in these areas. Pellagra, caused by inadequate niacin and tryptophan intake, is seen in those populations of Africa that subsist on maize as the principal staple, but it is seldom seen in the maize-eating populations of Latin America, where additional niacin is provided by both beans and coffee.

Women experiencing repeated cycles of pregnancy and lactation are likely to develop iron deficiency anemia, loss of bone calcium, and reduced lean body mass. Malnutrition in other adults is less common, except in times of famine, although individuals unable to obtain work, or too old or sick to work, may be seriously undernourished because they cannot afford to buy adequate food. Alcoholism is a common cause of malnutrition in both underdeveloped and industrialized countries because money is spent on alcohol rather than on proper food.

The cost of malnutrition. The cost of malnutrition to less developed areas is exceedingly high; it includes the waste of resources in rearing infants who die before they can become useful citizens and the reduced working capacity of malnourished adults. From a quarter to a third or more of the children die before they reach school age, largely from infections that would not be fatal to a well-nourished child or from clinical malnutrition precipitated by a prior episode of acute infectious disease (Scrimshaw 1966). Nearly all children among the less privileged populations of underdeveloped countries show retarded growth and development at the time they reach school age; and although they are rarely seriously malnourished during school years, they do not make up for the deficit acquired during preschool years. Recent evidence suggests that the retardation in physical development in infancy is paralleled by impaired mental development, which is probably permanent. This means that the future development of a country is compromised by serious malnutrition in young children. Moreover, attempts to provide adequate medical care are complicated and made more costly by both the greater amount and the longer duration of illness of both malnourished children and adults.

An unfortunate aspect of malnutrition in adults is that the workers so adapt themselves to malnutrition by reduced vitality and activity that they scarcely realize they are underfed. The final result is lethargy, lack of drive, and loss of initiative. For both industrial and farm workers it leads to absenteeism because of sickness and to higher accident rates because of early fatigue. In general, the countries of the world with the lowest per capita consumption of food are also those where the efficiency of the workers is lowest.

Reasons for malnutrition

Although for the world as a whole the long-term trend of per capita food production has been upward, there has been a decline in per capita food production in communist Asia and in India, as well as in many parts of Latin America and southeast Asia (Food and Agriculture Organization of the United Nations 1963). If the high population growth rates in the less developed countries increase as projected, still more of these countries will soon be unable to maintain present levels of per capita food production. It is important to recognize that increased food needs will continue to arise not only from a growing population but also from greater per capita income. As people in the less developed countries improve their financial status, much of the increase is spent for food. In some countries where food production has not kept pace, this situation has led to a substantial rise in imports of food, and in others the effect of growth in income has been balanced by rising food prices. Either result has serious economic and political consequences.

Using food shipments from regions of high per capita productivity to meet part of the food needs of the increased numbers of people in the less developed countries is not a satisfactory solution, because it involves considerable problems of transporting and financing, which are further complicated by political issues. Ideally, adequate food production should be achieved in each area, unless foreign exchange is available for food purchases from cash crop or industrial exports.

Physical waste. Unfortunately, the largest loss of food to insects and rodents occurs in those countries with the greatest food shortages. For example, in some of the grain storage bins of India, the loss to rodents alone is over 30 per cent. Conservative official estimates of total such *preventable* food losses in India indicate that they are greater than the present large annual food deficit and constitute at least 25 per cent of the total grain production; if such losses were prevented, India would have food for export.

In tropical regions of the food-short countries, mold causes additional spoilage. In the case of peanuts, an important source of protein in Africa and India, one type of mold (*Aspergillus flavus*) produces a substance called "aflatoxin," which even in trace amounts is highly carcinogenic for experimental animals. This mold also grows freely on cereal grains, sweet potatoes, and legumes, and even slightly moldy food is likely to be unfit for human consumption. Lack of refrigeration also results in spoilage of fruits and vegetables, which are a glut on the market when in season and unavailable or prohibitively expensive the rest of the time.

The great majority of the malnourished populations of the world depends on either a cereal staple such as rice, wheat, or corn, or starchy roots such as manioc or potatoes. The former are more nutritious, but the latter produce more calories per acre, require less labor, and are somewhat easier to store without serious loss.

Cultural waste. It is a mistake to conclude that the malnutrition of less developed areas is solely due to inadequate food production, lack of storage facilities, or even lack of purchasing power. Ignorance of the nutritional needs of young children and lack of understanding of the relationship between food and health are of equal or greater importance. The failure to give any food supplement to breast-fed infants before 9 to 12 months of age in many countries; the use of rice-water, barley-water, cornstarch or even sugar-water as a weaning food; and the variety of taboos surrounding the giving of eggs to young children are examples of common practices which lead to malnutrition and death of children under five years of age, even among families whose older children and adults do not suffer from malnutrition. In underdeveloped countries, one often sees a critically malnourished child with a woman who is wearing new clothes and jewelry and who is totally unaware of the true reason her child is dying.

The various erroneous beliefs surrounding the proper feeding of children with infections are often the most important factors in the chain of multiple causation leading to acute nutritional disease. For example, in both south India and Central America children with measles are given water in which a small amount of cereal and various local herbs has been cooked—a diet grossly deficient in protein and calories. Such beliefs also cause the family to spend money for charms, ceremonies, and useless proprietary medicines.

In underdeveloped areas the seemingly irrational beliefs regarding food may be quite elaborate. Particularly common is the practice of classifying foods and prohibiting certain combinations. In Peru, for instance, foods are "hot, cold, heavy, or light." A complex of beliefs indicates when and to whom a given class of foods can be fed. Certain classes of food are considered appropriate or inappropriate, without relation to their nutritive value, at times such as pregnancy or during one or another illness. Few societies recognize the true relationship of foods to health.

Improving production and conservation

The yield increases of the industrialized countries are due to chemicals, mechanization, good seeds and animal breeds, and their effective use. Chemicals and machinery could achieve miracles in the less developed areas, but they require greater capital investment and know-how than are presently available. Selective breeding of plants and animals could also be extremely effective: types of both have been developed which are much more productive and sometimes also more resistant to disease. For example, virus-resisting potatoes, rust-resistant wheat, hybrid corn and, most recently, high lysine corn and gossypol-free cottonseed are part of the "miracle" of food production in the industrialized countries, along with greatly improved breeds of poultry, cattle, sheep, and swine.

Some of these superior varieties can be introduced directly into less developed countries, but most require additional research for their adaptation to different environmental conditions. Agricultural research and its application through agricultural extension have been a major factor in high yields in the developed countries. Production of most improved varieties requires considerable knowledge of scientific agriculture as well as much initial capital investment, and the education of government officials is also an important factor. Poorly informed administrative and policy officials often block the efforts of extension workers and farmers by ill-considered taxes or import controls, unwise emphasis on cash crops, neglect of agricultural research, indifference or hostility to producer cooperatives, and failure to provide for rural credit.

Limiting physical waste. Solution of the food problems of less developed areas will require extensive improvements in the conservation and handling of food as well as in its production. Of first importance is reducing preventable food losses through the use of insecticides and rodenticides, construction of rat-proof and dry storage facilities, fumigation of grain, and improved distribution by using protective packaging materials and more rapid transportation. Controlled atmosphere and cold storage facilities are useful for some seasonal and highly perishable crops, and refrigeration is essential for the proper conservation of meat, poultry, and fish.

Smoking and salting are simple and effective means of preserving meat and fish for adult consumption, but in general they do not provide food that is suitable as major protein sources for infants and young children. Sun-drying is widely used for many foods, but this has serious limitations in a hot, moist climate, especially when proper storage conditions are unavailable. Using artificial heat is more costly and involves the same problems of storage and packaging. Thermal processing or canning represents a big economic step because it requires sealable containers as well as higher temperatures. In industrialized countries spray-drying has been extensively employed for milk and a variety of other products that are fluid before processing. Obviously, the handling of frozen foods in tropical underdeveloped countries in the early stages of industrial development poses problems that preclude the widespread application of freezing as a method of food storage. Freeze-drying seems too expensive to apply to food staples, but the shelf life of certain types of food may be extended by low doses of ionizing radiation. Chemical preservatives and other additives that have been important in the efficient utilization of the food supply in modern nations are also needed in underdeveloped countries. Examples are antioxidants to slow down the process by which fats become rancid and propionates to inhibit molds.

New food sources. Nutritional requirements can be satisfied by an adequate source of calories and sufficient quantities of each of the essential amino acids, fatty acids, vitamins, and minerals in any utilizable form, whether natural or synthetic. There are many compelling reasons why most nutrients will continue to be supplied largely from plants and animals for a long time to come, but new and exotic sources of food are being explored.

Oilseed meals, such as cottonseed flour, can serve as valuable new sources of proteins provided that they are carefully processed. Furthermore, much nutritional benefit can be derived from the enrichment of certain foods. For example, the quality of most protein-containing foods of vegetable origin can be improved by combining them with foods of complementary essential amino acid content or by adding the missing amino acids in synthetic form. Other examples include the enrichment of salt with potassium iodide for the prevention of goiter, a measure which has proved as practical and effective in Guatemala and Colombia as in the United States and Switzerland; the prevention of beriberi and pellagra by the addition of B-complex vitamins to cereal products; the enrichment of margarine and skim milk with vitamins A and D so that they are nutritionally acceptable substitutes for butter and whole milk, respectively, and the addition of the amino acid lysine to wheat and wheat flour.

In a number of underdeveloped areas where milk cannot be depended upon to furnish needed protein, vegetable mixtures that were developed to serve this purpose are proving to be commercially successful and are bringing about important nutritional improvements. Furthermore, the world catch of marine fish has increased enormously in recent years, and processes have been developed for the production of a low-cost fish protein concentrate. In the meantime, fresh, canned, and smoked fish are compensating for the protein inadequacy of the diet in Japan and a number of other countries. Attempts to use algae, green leaves, and even grass as sources of protein have met with little success because of poor palatability and excessive costs, but this could be changed by technological developments. Other possible protein sources are food yeast, which can be grown with several inexpensive carbohydrates, such as molasses and sulfite liquor of the paper industry. Other microorganisms can be produced by using petroleum by-products or natural gas as their source of energy.

Synthetic foods. Palatable synthetic foods simulating bacon, hamburger, ham, chicken, fish, and scallops have already been developed from soy protein isolate. Protein fibers are spun like nylon and reconstituted into textured foods that can be flavored in any desired manner. At present these are as expensive as the foods they simulate, but as the number of mouths to feed increases and costs of the process are brought down they are likely to prove useful. The nutritional needs of the body can already be reduced to chemically known substances that can be synthesized or extracted from natural products. To meet the demands of an enormously increased world population, the eventual use of wholly synthetic foods seems likely. Ironically, most of the efforts to achieve this are being stimulated by the nutritional requirements of man in space rather than by terrestrial food problems.

Social science research. Much of the malnutrition in the world today, particularly among young children, can be prevented by changes in feeding practices. Increased production and purchasing power will not alone automatically eliminate malnutrition; too often the additional money is spent on soft drinks, alcohol, or other consumer items that will not improve inadequate diets. Nutritional education must be a major part of efforts to eliminate malnutrition.

There is much that the social scientist can contribute to solving world food problems. Persons responsible for nutrition and health education need to understand the reasons for food practices and beliefs, yet these have too often been neglected by social scientists even when studying a culture in detail. Even less research has been done on the most appropriate and effective means of inculcating food habits in various cultures (See Mead 1943; 1964).

An exception was the introduction in Guatemala of the low-cost protein-rich vegetable mixture, Incaparina, which benefited from preliminary field studies by anthropologists. The success of this product is attributable in large part to its introduction as a variant on the traditional *atole* rather than as a new food product. It will not always be possible to use this technique, for new foods often will have no local counterpart. The guidance of social scientists who have made advance studies will be particularly needed for the introduction of products that have never before been used for human feeding, such as fish protein concentrate or bacterial protein.

There is also need to study changes in food habits or attempts to impose new foods, for their impact on other aspects of culture. Gifts of unfamiliar surplus foods may simply be unused or they can upset patterns of life that are oriented about indigenous staples. Authoritarian methods of forcing nutritional standards on a child or a community may endanger cooperation in other important matters.

A major obstacle to introducing agricultural techniques is the lack of local technological knowledge and competence. Agricultural extension agents and teachers often attempt to induce change blindly without understanding the existing beliefs and traditions that they are trying to alter. Similarly, although technology is making rapid progress in devising practical techniques for family planning, motivating people to make use of them remains a problem. In order to make such programs more effective, there is an urgent need for studies of the ways in which the desired changes can be achieved.

The agricultural revolution

The world is now in the midst of a revolution in food production, conservation, and distribution that is as far-reaching in its effects on societies as the original development of agriculture; it is comparable in significance to the industrial revolution, with which it is closely allied. Farm production in the industrialized countries has risen spectacularly within a few decades, simultaneously with a sharp reduction in the numbers of persons engaged in farming and the actual amount of land under cultivation. This has meant food for greatly increased numbers of people. Equally important, the workers no longer needed in agriculture are freed for the production of consumer goods and services to an extent beyond any previously seen in history. It is this freedom which has made possible modern economic and social development.

With the need for farm labor decreasing, the cities of the industrialized countries have received the increase in population. Nevertheless, food production in these countries is rising despite the diminishing farm population, thus providing enough food for the growing urban markets. In many of the less developed countries, population is outgrowing available land, and people from the rural areas are migrating to the cities in ever larger numbers. However, in most such countries farming remains largely at subsistence levels, and transportation and storage facilities are inadequate to meet the demands of the cities for food distribution.

An efficient agriculture thus becomes a prime requisite of economic and social development. Subsistence agriculture adds nothing to the national economy; and until enough farm families contribute to meeting the food needs of urban families, the manpower and capital required for industrialization will not be available. Once food production rises sufficiently to provide a firm basis for economic and social development, the process tends to accelerate. Research results accumulate and are applied; capital is amassed and invested; machines are constructed and put to work. As the process continues, more and more people are available, educated, and trained for the complex tasks of a technically advanced society. Unless the health and intelligence of the people are such that they can make good use of modern knowledge and technology, no amount of investment in material things can ensure satisfactory social and economic development. A good food supply is needed to prevent excessive morbidity and mortality from disease as well as the poor learning and working capacity that result from malnutrition. At present, the growing per capita shortage of food in many countries will continue to thwart the ambitions and make a mockery of the goals of economic planners.

NEVIN S. SCRIMSHAW

[*Other relevant material may be found in* AGRICULTURE; MORTALITY; POPULATION, *article on* POPULATION GROWTH; TECHNICAL ASSISTANCE; *and in the biography of* SAUER.]

BIBLIOGRAPHY

ALTSCHUL, AARON M. 1965 *Proteins: Their Chemistry and Politics.* New York: Basic Books.

BROWN, LESTER R. 1963 *Man, Land and Food: Looking Ahead at World Needs.* U.S. Department of Agriculture, Foreign Agricultural Economic Report No. 11. Washington: Government Printing Office.

BROWN, LESTER R. 1965 *Increasing World Food Output.* U.S. Department of Agriculture, Foreign Agricultural Economic Report No. 25. Washington: Government Printing Office.

BURGESS, ANNE; and DEAN, REGINALD F. A. (editors) 1962 *Malnutrition and Food Habits: Report of an International and Interprofessional Conference.* New York: Macmillan.

CONFERENCE ON MEETING PROTEIN NEEDS OF INFANTS AND PRESCHOOL CHILDREN, WASHINGTON, D.C., *1960* 1961 *Progress in Meeting Protein Needs of Infants and Preschool Children: Proceedings.* . . . National Research Council Publication No. 843. Washington: National Academy of Sciences–National Research Council.

FOOD AND AGRICULTURE ORGANIZATION OF THE UNITED NATIONS *The State of Food and Agriculture.* → Published since 1947. The authoritative annual review of developments in the world food and agricultural situation. See especially the 1966 volume.

FOOD AND AGRICULTURE ORGANIZATION OF THE UNITED NATIONS 1963 *Third World Food Survey.* Freedom From Hunger Campaign Basic Study No. 11. Rome: FAO.

JELLIFFE, D. B. 1955 *Infant Nutrition in the Subtropics and Tropics.* Monograph Series, No. 29. Geneva: World Health Organization.

MEAD, MARGARET 1943 The Problem of Changing Food Habits. Pages 20-31 in National Research Council, Committee on Food Habits, *The Problem of Changing Food Habits: Report of the Committee on Food Habits; 1941–1943.* National Research Council Bulletin No. 108. Washington: National Academy of Sciences–National Research Council.

MEAD, MARGARET 1964 *Food Habits Research: Problems of the 1960's.* National Research Council Publication No. 1225. Washington: National Academy of Sciences–National Research Council.

RITCHIE, JEAN A. S. 1950 *Teaching Better Nutrition: A Study of Approaches and Techniques.* Food and Agriculture Organization of the United Nations, Nutritional Studies, No. 6. Washington: Government Printing Office.

SCRIMSHAW, NEVIN S. 1966 The Effect of the Interaction of Nutrition and Infection on the Pre-school Child. In International Conference on Prevention of Malnutrition in the Pre-school Child, Washington, D.C., 1964, *Pre-school Child Malnutrition: Primary Deterrent to Human Progress*. National Research Council Publication No. 1282. Washington: National Academy of Sciences–National Research Council.

II
CONSUMPTION PATTERNS

The consumption of food, like other biologically supportive activities, is an aspect of cultural behavior. In no society are people permitted to eat everything, everywhere, with everyone, and in all situations. Instead, the consumption of food is governed by rules and usages which cut across each other at different levels of symbolization. These symbolizations define the social contexts and groupings within which food—or a particular kind of food—is consumed, and prohibit or taboo the consumption of particular foods. An important dimension of the social contexts regulating the consumption of food is the principle that patterns of consumption and distribution must be examined as one. For example, there are some societies in which it is believed that a person will die if he eats food which he has grown himself, while in others it is felt that a person may eat only food which he himself has grown or acquired by purchase or other exchange. Between these two extremes are several other patterns.

In all societies the distribution and consumption of food is an expression of a variety of social relationships: those of social proximity and distance, religious-ritual fraternity and status, political superordination and subordination, bonds within and between families, and the like. The definition of food, its distribution, and its consumption always take place with reference to individuals as occupants of statuses and categories within institutionalized groupings.

In other words, food is used symbolically to represent only some social forms and personal feelings in a society, and these are usually among the important forms and personal feelings in the group's life. Thus, by noting the specific and bounded social contexts—clan, village, in-law relationships, friendship, and the like—within which food is employed symbolically, it is often possible to infer which are the important groupings and relationships within the society. For example, a taboo on eating the totemic animals associated with one's clan is indicative of the significance of clans in the organization of the society's institutions; it is not the taboo per se which suggests the importance of clan relationships but the fact that some rule governing the consumption of food—in this case, forbidding it—is associated with the clan. Why clans usually prohibit their members from eating the animals associated with these groups is a separate question, and one about which there is still considerable uncertainty.

Among some Melanesian people the rule that a man must give part of the harvest of a crop to his sister, while his wife receives a similar prestation from her brother, provides a clue to the importance of certain matrilineal ties; in societies that have a caste system the rule that the members of different castes may not eat together indicates the importance of formal distance between castes as well as the caste organization itself. Correlatively, when food ceases to be employed as a vehicle for the expression of social sentiments within a grouping, e.g., in a clan, or when proscriptions concerning the consumption of food are attacked, it can be assumed that significant changes are taking place in the socioeconomic structure of that society.

The rules governing the distribution of food within a society reflect and reinforce prevailing ethical and moral orientations in that society. For example, when the government of the United States willingly distributes food supplies to poor people in other societies but not within American society itself, it appears that its dominant values implicitly tend to define poverty as an indication of moral failure, if not as sinful. Hence, the assumption often appears to be that if there were gratuitous distributions of food to poor Americans, such action would be construed as reward or even approval of such moral failure. But since it is characteristic that the criteria pertaining to the distribution of food within a social system differ entirely from those relating to other groupings or societies, American society can make prestations of food to people in other societies while refusing (or being unable) to do so within its own social boundaries.

Almost every society defines a few foods as acceptable for consumption under some circumstances but wholly unacceptable in others. For example, foods which are associated with amusement and relaxation are usually considered inappropriate to ritual or ceremonial occasions. In pluralistic and stratified societies, most foods which are grown indigenously are eaten by people in all groups; however, in almost all such societies, there are a few foods and drinks which are not universal or which will be consumed by members of different groups in different contexts or situations. Thus, for example, the same alcoholic beverages in a pluralistic society will be drunk under different conditions and in entirely different places by members of different groups. Such definitions both symbolize and reinforce the consciousness of separateness and distance existing between bounded groups in pluralistic and stratified societies.

For reasons which are not yet completely clear, the major transitional crises of the life cycle—the *rites de passage*—are marked in almost all societies by ritual or ceremonial distribution and consumption of food. One possible hypothesis to explain these nearly universal customs is that each of the three transitional crises (birth, marriage, death) initiates a significant alteration in socioeconomic relationships and reciprocities and that these are symbolically noted in displays, distributions, prestations, token exchanges, and consumption of food. An individual's birth automatically establishes reciprocal rights and duties between him and others to whom he is related in a series of interlocking social networks; marriage in all societies is a transitional ceremony which establishes bonds and reciprocities between the kin groups of the marrying couple; an individual's death terminates, and requires readjustments in, reciprocal economic relationships.

In addition to these ritual celebrations through distribution and consumption of food, as well as other forms of wealth (e.g., bride wealth), a great many societies celebrate historical or ceremonial events according to calendrical systems. These recurrent and fixed celebrations are usually governed by ritual consumptions of food, as in the American Thanksgiving feast or in the custom of many Americans to celebrate their Independence Day with family picnics. Calendrically regulated religious events are similarly celebrated.

One of the fundamental principles governing the organization of social relationships in all societies is the division of labor by sex; most societies also stipulate divisions of labor according to the additional criteria of age, status or ranking, group membership, and the like. Although the division of labor is most apparent in the production of food, it also plays a major role in the consumption of food. There is probably considerable, even systematic, overlap between rules governing the division of productive labor and those governing food consumption, of which kinship is undoubtedly of prime importance; thus far, little work has been done on this problem. A possible model for such an analysis would be a horticultural society in which the wife does most of the productive work, raising food which her husband then gives to his sister.

The distribution and consumption of food within the nuclear family also symbolize institutionalized relationships. For example, among the Tallensi of west Africa there are many expressions of the separateness of father and son and of the father's absolute authority. One of these symbolizations is the rule that a son may not look into his father's granary during the father's lifetime. After the father's death, his eldest surviving son is conducted ritually by his father's brothers to peer into the deceased's granary. This son thus acquires control over the distribution of the food stored in the granary, and this prerogative, among others, symbolizes and supports his control over the patrilocal extended family.

To cite another illustration, where it is the assigned task of the woman of a household to distribute the food within the nuclear family, e.g., by serving meals to members of the household, the manner in which she distributes the food may symbolize relationships to her husband and children at different stages of the family cycle (and to other members of the household, if present). Thus, status relationships within the family are sharply delineated by such rules as whether a woman eats with her husband or separately, when and whether a man eats with his children, etc. Among the Manus of the Admiralty Islands, near New Guinea, the estrangement between husband and wife during the first few years of marriage, and the competitive relationship in which each stands in relation to the kin of the other, is symbolized in part by the shame they feel in eating together. The most competitive relationships among the Manus are between brothers-in-law and between sisters-in-law: these people may not eat together.

The special significance of food in the symbolization of kinship relationships generally can be seen in the fact that behavior with respect to food in the nuclear family often varies with the degree of segregation or division of role relationships; the latter is in turn dependent on the degree to which the nuclear family is connected to a wider nexus of kinship networks. Thus, one of the symbolizations of the greatly reduced segregation of role relationships between husband and wife in modern complex societies—attendant on the weakening of wider kinship matrices—has been the tendency to minimize and blur the division of labor with respect to the distribution of food within the family. In the lower social strata of Western societies, for example, men do not cook or otherwise participate in the distribution of food within the family; in these strata there is usually a strong connection between the nuclear family and wider kinship groupings and a marked degree of segregation in role relationships between husband and wife. In higher social strata in some Western societies, on the other hand, there are situations in which men do cook and participate in the distribution of food within the nuclear family; these situations tend to arise as segregation in role relationships between spouses becomes weakened as part of the attenuation of wider kinship relationships.

Most societies provide for separateness between nuclear families. One of the symbolizations of this separateness is in the confinement of the preparation and consumption of food to the social boundaries of the nuclear family. In most polygynous organizations, each wife has her own hearth or kitchen; she and her children eat separately, the husband either eating with each nuclear family serially or eating with his senior wife. While such arrangements are usually interpreted by anthropologists as being designed to maintain peace among co-wives, these patterns of consumption must also be understood as representations of the social-structural differentiations which most societies make between nuclear families. Among some Mexican Tarascan groups who possess a stem-family organization, in which a son continues to live with his father after marrying, the son's wife and her mother-in-law share a common kitchen, and the two nuclear families eat jointly. When dissension occurs, or in anticipation of the son's plans to found an independent household, his wife will sometimes establish her own kitchen, and the two families will eat separately. Among the Cheyenne Indians of North America, where men were forbidden to speak directly to their mothers-in-law, the men were required to provide all the meat by hunting; this was cooked in the mother-in-law's lodge, but then her daughters carried the food to their respective tepees for eating. The hunting and gathering Tiwi of Northern Australia are one people who do not separate the component nuclear families of polygynous households into consumption units. Instead, each polygynous household cooks and eats as a unit. This is probably because each household head has many more wives, especially elderly ones, than he has children; hence, there are few component nuclear families in each household.

There are four patterns which govern the distribution of food, and hence the consumption of food; three of these are patterns of sharing. Although they have a tendency to shade off into one another, they are easily identifiable and clearly illustrate the basic principle that it is a characteristic of social systems to symbolize social relationships by means of different patterns of distributing and consuming food. These four patterns are (1) recurrent exchange and sharing of food; (2) mutual assistance and sharing in times of need; (3) narrowed and reluctant sharing; and (4) nonsharing.

(1) *Recurrent exchange and sharing.* There are several variations on this pattern of sharing; all, however, are associated with and symbolize a combination of factors which tend to give rise to maximal solidarity within the community: social affiliation based on consanguineal kinship; physical proximity between households; the prescription or careful control of residence by, among other factors, rules of residence; the conduct of interpersonal communication in stable and consistently functioning primary or face-to-face groupings. In brief, the combination of highly integrated kin groups, physical proximity, and sedentary life appear to yield strong feelings of social proximity. Recurrent exchange and sharing of food is one of the symbolic representations of this solidary state.

Among most peoples characterized by this kind of social organization, there is a constant flow of gifts of food from household to household within the solidary grouping. Among other societies, whose cultures are suffused with religious ceremonial (e.g., the Hopi and Tallensi), the recurrent distribution of food, too, takes place in a religious ceremonial context. Among still others (e.g., the Kurtatchi and the Papago), there are unelaborated but repeated donations, prestations, and exchanges of small token amounts of food among kinsmen.

Regardless of the variations on the theme, these recurrent and repetitive exchanges of food almost always take place within the sociological boundaries of the solidary community. Also, such recurrent exchanges of food are in addition to ceremonialized or ritualized feasts.

(2) *Mutual assistance and sharing in times of need.* The primary difference between type (1) and the social organization with which mutual assistance in times of need is associated is that in the latter the ties and alignments of kinship are not solidified into corporate kin groups. The bonds of kinship, qualitatively speaking, are equally strong in both social organizations, but in the present instance these ties are not elevated to the level of exclusive and solidary groupings.

A degree of social and emotional solidarity arises in such a community from the strong and marked tendency to affiliate primarily with kinsmen, real or fictive. Usually the members of such a community are mostly kinsmen, and sometimes entirely kinsmen. An element of fissility, and a corresponding degree of social distance, is introduced into such a social organization by a variety of factors. First, physical mobility and change in community membership are usually permitted, thus resulting in the simultaneous presence of kinsmen and non-kinsmen within the group. Where nonkinsmen join the community, they are sometimes addressed and treated as kinsmen; preference for consanguineal ties is the mainspring of such relationships. But of equal, if not greater, significance is the fact that kinsmen have the right to sever relationships with their group and either establish or join an entirely independent one. While extreme personalization of relationships is the rule in this social organization, social cohesiveness and proximity are proportionately weakened by movement away from kinsmen and by the intrusion of nonkinsmen into the community. Among many peoples (e.g., the Andamanese, Arunta, South African Bushmen, Plains Indian tribes) the exigencies of the food-producing environment, rather than tensions and quarrels, appear to have necessitated such adjustments on the social-structural level. In either event, the consequences, in terms of fission and social distance, are similar.

It is possible to observe a process of compromise in this social organization between forces which give rise to social proximity and those resulting in social distance. Any of these, when taken alone, is productive of either solidarity or fissility. For example, clanship among the Navajo or the peasants of Shantung province in pre-Republican China would, when taken separately, produce a high degree of social solidarity. Obversely, the isolation of the family—geographically, and hence emotionally, among the Navajo and almost entirely emotionally among Shantung peasants—gave rise to the emotional inbreeding of the family vis-à-vis the community. The simultaneity of factors making both for solidarity and for fissility produces a compromise between the two and places such peoples at this point along the continuum of social cohesiveness and solidarity rather than at the point of maximal or minimal solidarity. Mutual assistance in times of need is characteristic of such societies.

In nomadic hunting and gathering societies having this type of social organization, mutual assistance and sharing in times of need often take the form of the immediate dispensation of meat to almost all the households of the community as soon as an animal is captured or slain, especially to those who do not have meat. In sedentary societies, mutual assistance in times of need takes the form of aid rendered to kinsmen, real or fictive, when economic help is objectively required. There is, of course, mutual assistance in time of need in societies which practice recurrent exchange and sharing; however, as the present instance indicates, there are many societies in which there is mutual assistance without the elaboration of recurrent exchange.

This is not meant to imply that there are no feasts and exchanges whatever in this social organization; these are present, but they occur only on specific occasions, e.g., religious events and the life crises marked by *rites de passage*. Nor is the idea or concept of recurrent prestation unknown in such societies, but such exchange is almost always confined to gifts of goods, not food.

(3) *Narrowed and reluctant sharing.* By this is meant that whatever assistance is rendered to people is given very reluctantly and grudgingly. This pattern of food distribution is ordinarily associated with fragmented social systems in which the isolated nuclear family unit is the significant unit of association; socially, geographically, and emotionally isolated from all other family units, it constitutes neither a society nor a community. Nor do the several family units constitute a society, structurally or functionally, when they come together.

The primary characteristic of this social system is the presence of relatively great geographic distances between households and families and, concomitantly, clearly demarcated social boundaries. Physical space or distance in this social organization serves as a boundary-maintaining force only indirectly and incidentally; this is an important consideration, because even when the family units in such a social system unite for temporary amalgamations, they continue to maintain their great social distance from each other. Although the ties of kinship in this social organization may be highly formalized, there are rarely any functioning kin groups outside the family, and kinship ties become increasingly diffuse as the physical distance between kinsmen increases.

One of the material symbolizations of this social atomism or fission is the pattern of narrowed and reluctant sharing, as among the Kaska and Ojibwa Indians. Even when individuals in these societies are willing to extend aid, they are willing to do so only to a very limited number of people. The cultures of such peoples generally contain the ideal prescription of generosity and mutual assistance in times of need, but this ideal is rarely, if ever, achieved; in actual behavior, generosity and assistance are extremely restricted—qualitatively and in the number of persons toward whom such behavior is manifest. Another way of stating this is that behavior with respect to food in such societies approaches parsimoniousness but never quite achieves it, reflecting the atomization of social relationships beyond the nuclear family.

(4) *Nonsharing*. This is a general category; it has thus far not been possible to determine different types of nonsharing behavior with respect to food, as has been done in connection with patterns of sharing, because there are too few societies in the category of nonsharing from among which discrete types of nonsharing could be elicited.

Here "nonsharing" means the absence in a culture of enforceable prescriptions to share food with others, no matter how great their need; where nonsharing is found as the dominant pattern, the individuated accumulation of wealth is an end in itself, rather than a means to cooperative or competitive generosity. That is, people in many societies, as in the first two categories described above, amass food or other forms of wealth in order to be able to distribute it in socially prescribed forms of generosity, and there is often competition to be the most generous.

In societies characterized by nonsharing, there are rarely, if ever, any closed groups within the community in which membership, feeling of belonging, and reciprocity are fixed and inalienable. Few, if any, institutionally significant statuses are ascribed; authority, group cohesiveness, interfamilial support, and mutual assistance are almost always absent. Similarly, allegiances are expedient and frequently contractual. While considerations of kinship appear to play occasional roles in interpersonal associations, such considerations are decidedly secondary; instead, kinsmen and nonkinsmen alike enter into the economically competitive struggle, and personal profit and success emerge as predominant values. Power resides among those who are monetarily powerful rather than among those persons whose social dominance derives from ascribed high status or who have succeeded in other spheres of competitive activity.

Societies characterized by this system superficially resemble societies in which narrowed and reluctant sharing is found, in that the effective socioeconomic unit appears to be the independent nuclear family. The resemblance, however, is superficial. In societies in which nonsharing is the dominant pattern, the social isolation of the family does not derive from physical distance between family units. Instead, the principal isolating factor appears to be the search for individually accumulated wealth. Examples of societies characterized by nonsharing of food are the Alorese, the Marquesans,

highland peasants in Jamaica, the Yakut of Siberia, and the Yurok Indians.

The comparative ethnographic data reveal with marked clarity that no matter how highly elaborated a pattern of recurrent exchange and sharing might be, to say nothing of other patterns, in no society is an individual expected to give up everything he possesses. In no society is true "selflessness" an expected or imposed value to which the individual must adhere. For example, among the Arapesh of New Guinea, who have elaborated recurrent exchange to an extreme and among whom a man does not eat food which he himself has grown, personal ownership and rights in property are clearly delineated with definite notions of "mine" and "yours." The Kwoma, too, who believe that a man would die if he ate his own harvest, also specify individual ownership of the yield of the land, each person's crop being put in a separate bin in a storehouse. The Copper Eskimo prescribe that even if only one seal is caught, it must be distributed equally throughout the community. However, it has been observed among them that during the winter, when each woman cooks indoors, she can hide the choicer portions of meat for her husband and herself until after visitors have left; in the summer, on the other hand, when most of the cooking is done out-of-doors and everyone can see what is in the pot, no concealment is possible. It can be suggested that the provision in all cultures for personal ownership and retention—no matter how great the pressures to share—is due, at least in part, to the need for material representations of individuation and personal separateness, i.e., self-awareness. As Hallowell noted in his paper "The Self and Its Behavioral Environment," "It seems necessary to assume self-awareness as one of the prerequisite psychological conditions for the functioning of any human social order, no matter what linguistic and culture patterns prevail" ([1937–1954] 1955, p. 75).

At the same time that the social forces which make for extreme degrees of social proximity maximize predispositions to share food, factors making for social distance within a maximally solidary community will mitigate the predisposition to share. That is, it can be assumed that every society contains some forces, however few and small, which help to make for social distance. In a society in which extreme social proximity helps to produce a pattern of recurrent food sharing, those factors making for social distance in the same society will help to produce a proportionate reluctance to share.

For example, high social status, such as chieftainship, is determined in a variety of ways. It can be postulated that social distance is greater between persons of high and low ascribed statuses than between persons of high and low achieved statuses. Assuming some degree of reluctance in most people to share food with others, even in societies in which people appear strongly predisposed to share, it follows logically that reluctance to share would covary with ascribed high status even in societies in which there is strong social cohesiveness and solidarity. In other words, it can be assumed that persons with ascribed high status in solidary communities will employ their social distance from the "masses" or "commoners" as a mechanism which enables them to amass and retain more for themselves; this is not necessarily conscious on their part. For example, among the Manuans of Samoa, who have an elaborate hierarchy of chieftainship, a high income is one of the few feudal privileges. Although chiefly wealth is kept in circulation by the requirement that chiefs be generous to commoners, the chiefs nevertheless generally have more food than anyone else. Among the Dahomeans, the economic organization was usually characterized by a surplus which eventually brought about the concentration of wealth in the hands of the hereditary leisure classes.

The evidence is conclusive that patterns in the consumption of food are almost always governed by cultural symbols and that the ways in which food is distributed and consumed reflect a society's dominant modes of social relationships and groupings, especially those pertaining to kinship ties.

                                        YEHUDI A. COHEN

[*See also* DRINKING AND ALCOHOLISM; EXCHANGE AND DISPLAY; *and the biography of* MAUSS.]

BIBLIOGRAPHY

COHEN, YEHUDI A. 1961 Food and Its Vicissitudes: A Cross-cultural Study of Sharing and Nonsharing. Pages 312–350 in Yehudi A. Cohen, *Social Structure and Personality: A Casebook.* New York: Holt.

COHEN, YEHUDI A. 1964a The Establishment of Identity in a Social Nexus: The Special Case of Initiation Ceremonies and Their Relation to Value and Legal Systems. *American Anthropologist* New Series 66:529–552.

COHEN, YEHUDI A. 1964b *The Transition From Childhood to Adolescence: Cross-cultural Studies of Initiation Ceremonies, Legal Systems, and Incest Taboos.* Chicago: Aldine.

DURKHEIM, ÉMILE (1893) 1960 *The Division of Labor in Society.* Glencoe, Ill.: Free Press. → First published as *De la division du travail social.*

FIRTH, RAYMOND W. (1939) 1965 *Primitive Polynesian Economy.* 2d ed. Hamden, Conn.: Shoe String Press.

HALLOWELL, A. IRVING (1937–1954) 1955 *Culture and Experience.* Philadelphia Anthropological Society, Publications, Vol. 4. Philadelphia: Univ. of Pennsylvania Press. → A collection of essays by one of the most influential thinkers in American anthropology; in the classical anthropological tradition but with a strong orientation toward psychological conceptualizations of cultural processes. Included are many papers on the Ojibwa Indians.

MAUSS, MARCEL (1925) 1954 *The Gift: Forms and Functions of Exchange in Archaic Societies.* Glencoe, Ill.: Free Press. → First published as *Essai sur le don: Forme et raison de l'échange dans les sociétés archaïques.*

MEAD, MARGARET (editor) 1937 *Cooperation and Competition Among Primitive Peoples.* New York: McGraw-Hill. → A paperback edition was published in 1961 by Beacon. Descriptions of social and economic life in thirteen primitive societies, and interpretive chapters by the editor. One of the milestones in comparative studies in anthropology.

RICHARDS, AUDREY I. (1932) 1948 *Hunger and Work in a Savage Tribe: A Functional Study of Nutrition Among the Southern Bantu.* Glencoe, Ill.: Free Press. → A paperback edition was published in 1964 by World Publishing. A classic study of patterns of food consumption in one culture area, but with generalizations of wide applicability.

SAHLINS, MARSHALL D. 1965 On the Sociology of Primitive Exchange. Pages 139–236 in Conference on New Approaches in Social Anthropology, Jesus College, Cambridge, 1963, *The Relevance of Models for Social Anthropology.* New York: Praeger.

FORCED LABOR

See INTERNMENT AND CUSTODY; SLAVERY.

FORECASTING

See POPULATION, *especially the article on* POPULATION GROWTH; PREDICTION; PREDICTION AND FORECASTING, ECONOMIC. *Related material may be found under* TIME SERIES.

FOREIGN AID

I. POLITICAL ASPECTS   *George Liska*
II. ECONOMIC ASPECTS   *Gerald M. Meier*

I
POLITICAL ASPECTS

Pecuniary grants and other material donations by one government to another are among the recurrent features of interstate relations. The two basic types of grants are *tribute* and *subsidy*. Tribute is typically a donation from a state that is somehow more vulnerable to a less vulnerable state in exchange for protection or immunity; subsidy originates typically with a state that is at least financially stronger, and the donor expects in return a performance that serves his security strategy.

Contemporary foreign aid may comprise elements of tribute, when it secures immunity from verbal hostility and feelings of guilt, for instance. But its direct line of descent is from subsidies. The elementary political economy of subsidies is unchanging: the subsidy is an inducement for the recipient to behave in a way that would supplement the donor's exertions or substitute for them, and do it at a cost that is less than the cost of alternative courses of action, including war and greater national exertions in war. The basic assumption is clearest in aid for military effort. It holds that there is a definable unit of fighting power or defense power that can be had more cheaply from outside the donor's military establishment. The assumption is vindicated whenever domestic armaments have reached one or more of the limits set by internal supply of material resources, conditions of social stability within a political order, and countervailing responses by third states. The same basic principle of diminishing returns of strictly internal efforts can be applied to economic welfare and other nonmilitary components of national security and international stability, and serves as the rationale of foreign aid.

Objectives

The ultimate objective of the donor is to convert superior economic power into a pattern of political alignments that would improve his regional or global position. The recipient expects foreign aid to generate new resources of power, welfare, and prestige. His principal aim may be to consolidate the regime's authority with respect to opposition forces, to keep abreast of growing popular needs or of growth in other states, or to equip himself for effective or even offensive action with regard to other countries. Calculation of political advantage to be derived from aid is at its most pragmatic when diplomacy of maneuver and alignment predominates in a relatively flexible and relaxed multipolar situation; it may be temporarily subordinated to ideological determinants, or to the compulsions of force or the general interest when the global or regional balance of power is exposed to a hegemonial drive and polarized in consequence. Subsidies then become an emergency expedient to confirm lesser states in their readiness to resist the onslaught or to convert to resistance those states reluctant to subordinate their immediate concerns to the maintenance of the existing international system.

The expanded foreign aid activities following World War II conformed, on the whole, to the fundamental principles of the statecraft of subsidies. Foreign aid was part of a policy of coalition building by the United States, the preponderant

yet defensive power in the system; it became part of a coalition-frustrating policy in the hands of the Soviet Union in a later phase of the cold war. The peculiar character of the contest enlarged the meaning of the coalition to be built or frustrated and drew into the compass of foreign aid not only active, military allies; economic and military aid were used to attract the uncommitted, floating allegiance of "independents" as well as to consolidate established commitments. The need to win the apparently decisive uncommitted states made both contestants edge away from damaging antecedents and associations. The more conservative United States repudiated the paternalistic and colonial elements in its past and among its allies; the revolutionary Soviet Union disclaimed its militant tradition as an export commodity and disowned its overly expansionist Chinese ally whenever expedient for reassuring alarmed neutrals. Yet the need to retain the allegiance of the inner core of committed partisans has imposed a limit on profitable opportunism also in the international contest; it is a dubious electoral and diplomatic strategy to woo untested new friends in such a way as to alienate old comrades-in-arms.

Difficulties in implementing the objectives. Three special circumstances have warped the implementation of the political economy of subsidies beyond the unavoidable measure of distortion introduced by hegemonial conflict.

One was an *overemphasis on the role of economic changes and processes in assuring political stability and on the role of domestic politics in unstabilizing foreign policy activities.* In this respect, the effect of liberal predispositions was comparable with the affirmations of Marxist ideology and was reinforced by the need of meeting the Soviet practice of internal political subversion and manipulation of economic malcontents. Growing demands for external assistance consequently acquired great authority, but the recipients all too often lacked the will and ability to use this assistance responsibly and effectively.

Another deforming influence has been the *association of foreign aid with decolonization;* it added psychological and propagandistic biases to those imparted by a deterministic ideology and an opportunistic political strategy. Foreign aid came to be widely regarded as a duty for the advanced states and as a reparation for the uncritically asserted grievances of recipients.

The consequent moral advantage of recipient countries was enhanced by a political advantage owing to the third distorting circumstance, the *sharp increase in military–technological inhibitions on warlike settlements of conflicts between major powers.* A demonstrable capacity to wage a major nuclear war has remained a fundamental condition of the efficacy of all political action by the principal powers, including dispensation of foreign aid; at the same time, however, the economic power and activities of the donor states have been largely deprived of their essential support in usable conventional military force. Thermonuclear stalemate and severance of economic power from the ultimate military sanction behind political control have combined to increase the ability of the more ambitious among the lesser states to act with impunity. Competitive economic growth has become the prime functional substitute for war as a test of superiority for the two competing superpowers and politico-economic systems. Consequently, foreign aid activities, the principal device for extending the economic competition to third and lesser states, were temporarily overstrained.

The distorting ideological, psychological, and military circumstances produced a disparity between power and control or influence that was unfavorable to the donors. This disparity at first intensified the donors' competition over the Afro–Asian nations; only progressively and uncertainly has the disparity begun to foster a tacit understanding between the superpowers, regarding the rules and limits of foreign aid competition, that may eventually match comparable understandings in the domain of the arms race.

American and Soviet approaches. Undeniable differences of style and spirit have separated the so-called capitalist and the so-called socialist major donors. But both have been confounded by comparable uncertainties regarding the objectives of foreign aid and the means or strategies for attaining the objectives. The immediate, short-term objective of both the United States and the Soviet Union has been negative: to prevent forces favorable to the competitor from becoming established or consolidated to the detriment of one's allies and sympathizers in embattled lesser countries. The long-term, positive objective has been to promote a structure of world order that would reflect the internal organization, or the domestic ideal, of the superpowers: the supremacy of one class or elite in one case, pluralism of competing forces within the limits of consensus on essentials in the other. The uneasy coexistence of short-term preventive objectives and long-term constructive objectives compelled both major donors repeatedly to decide between often uncongenial, immediate beneficiaries of foreign aid and ultimate, actually favored beneficiaries. In practice, this often meant that the

Soviet Union aided or appeared to aid bourgeois-nationalists against local communists and that the United States helped dictatorial oligarchs, at least temporarily, against local liberals or democrats.

The ambiguity of objectives has been reflected in uncertainties over strategies. The unresolved issue has been whether to choose a strategy keyed to individual countries or a strategy keyed to the international system as a whole. A one-country strategy of foreign aid as implemented by the United States would promote the capacity for political independence of individual recipients, on the assumption that the exercise of such independence would be consistent with American interests. As implemented by the Soviet Union, this strategy would aim at subverting the identity of a noncommunist regime, on the assumption that formal political independence no less than formal political democracy is only a disguise for rule by elements hostile to the Soviet Union. In both cases, the stress is on the peculiar needs, conditions, and opportunities in the target country, while the repercussions of aid to that country in comparable or related countries are downgraded.

The one-system strategy would reverse the priorities, assigning high priority to the foreign policy behavior of recipients and its international repercussions. An American one-system strategy of longer range would promote behavior conducive to an elementary world order and, secondarily, to the progressive breakup of the Sino–Soviet bloc. The corresponding strategy of the Soviet Union would promote the progressive erosion of Western positions in the less developed countries as a group, producing an irretrievable breakdown of the Western system rather than piecemeal subversion in one country after another.

No clear choice between the two principal kinds of strategy has been made by either superpower, in part because of the untoward relationships between domestic and external political behavior of many recipient regimes. The United States has had to cope with the problem of regimes that are internationally pro-Western but internally antireform; the Soviet Union has had the problem of countries that are internationally neutralist and outwardly anti-West but domestically anticommunist. On the whole, doctrinaire supporters of foreign aid as a panacea in the West and of communism and local Communist parties as paramount concerns in the Sino–Soviet bloc have tended to favor the one-country approach, concentrating on immediate and locally promising conditions. Those primarily concerned with foreign policy have stressed the immediate needs of a coherent foreign aid policy and the long-range requirements of a propitiously evolving international system, in view of the unlimited stakes of the global conflict and the limited efficacy of foreign aid in any one country, if administered in separation from over-all political and military strategies.

Types of aid

However used, foreign aid has differed from its antecedents in the modern European state system. Chief among them are the more or less overt dynastic subsidies for military manpower, chiefly in the seventeenth and eighteenth centuries, and the more or less officially sponsored but privately subscribed loans in the nineteenth and early twentieth centuries. Throughout, the principles and practices of "foreign aid" were adjusted to the type of control over individuals, whether authoritarian or constitutional, and to the prevailing scope of governmental functions, whether they were mercantilist, laissez-faire, or welfare-statist. They were also adapted to the predominant ways of managing international political alignments and military conflicts—as relatively temporary or hopefully indefinite commitments, implemented by levies of manpower or by advance building of infrastructures such as railroads and air bases.

However, political and technological changes have, on the whole, fostered a growing temporal and qualitative gap between grant and anticipated performance. The difference between economic grant and expected political performance was always there; but even in the field of military aid and security the typical performance of the recipient came to differ radically from the donor's whenever concession of facilities replaced supplementary manpower as the principal return for the aid given. The balance between specific and immediate acts and slowly evolving general conditions, as the purposes of foreign aid, has tended to shift in favor of the conditions expected to generate policies congenial to the donor even after the termination of the aid relationship.

The growing gap between grant and performance has become increasingly hard to span for two interacting sets of reasons. One has had to do with the instability of governing elites and their frequent replacement by competing elites. Revolutionary break and repudiation of indebtedness, anticipated in the lot of French loans to the tsarist regime in Russia, has become the rule, albeit with exceptions. The other set of reasons has had to do with the diffusion of aid relationships as an apparently stable and permanent feature of international relations. Aid from a richer or well-established state has come to constitute a well-nigh automatic counterpart to diplomatic recognition and practically its most valuable by-product. However, this recognition in kind has nòt been governed by norms comparable with those of recognition in law, regarding effective internal political control, responsible international conduct, and nonidentification of material aid with moral approval.

Acquisitive and creative aid. The distance between grant and anticipated performance, whatever may be its long-range effect on foreign aid, helps distinguish between two types of aid in the post-World War II era through the maze of administrative and propagandistic nomenclature. One kind of aid may be described as acquisitive; it is closest to traditional subsidies in that it is extended in the anticipation of a relatively specific, tangible, or immediate advantage for the donor. The acquisition may range from a facility such as a military base or a base for political operations, through an alliance commitment (or repudiation of alliance commitment to the donor's adversary), to the control over large segments of a country that would otherwise be economically and politically nonviable. Alternatively, the donor can give aid in anticipation of a long-range economic and political development in a favored direction. Such aid may be called creative or developmental. Acquisitive aid generally has large military components for internal or external security; creative aid typically is economic, even though it may release indigenous resources for military outlays. Although a few aid relationships may be wholly acquisitive or creative in motive and purpose, most are primarily one or the other. The volume of aid determines whether aid is merely token aid, designed to manifest the donor's interest in the country as an encouragement to friendly groups, or whether more important aid constitutes a down-payment, committing the donor to long-term contributions as long as the recipient goes on displaying willingness and capacity to administer a politically and economically promising development process.

The two main types of aid, acquisitive and creative, have a different bearing upon two classes of problems that are raised by foreign aid: the distribution of aid and the control over aid and related policies. The problem of distribution has so far concerned chiefly the choice between military and economic aid and choice among alternative recipients.

Distribution of aid

Military versus economic. In the United States, allocation of resources between economic and military forms of assistance has been a major, if sometimes distracting, issue. The faith in economic means, in the guise of liberalized trade and private investments, was marked in American foreign policy before, during, and after the period of planning for peace during World War II. It received a confirmation from the successful economic reconstruction of western Europe under the European Recovery Program, which became the doubtfully valid model for subsequent programs of economic assistance elsewhere, following the disappointment of exaggerated expectations from technical-assistance programs short of large-scale aid for development. The military–political crises of the cold war produced countervailing stresses in favor of military assistance to countries and regimes threatened from within or without. The resulting debate over the proper ratio between economic and military aid was confused by ambiguous official categories of aid, such as "defense support." The outcome of this debate was marked by the contrast between nominal victories for advocates of economic aid and the less spectacular shifts in the actual ratio, due in large part to the continuing demand by many recipients for substantial military aid.

The issue between economic and military aid has been largely a false one. As long as economic aid promotes development, it also fosters social mobilization and, thereby, some political instability. Not all governmental elites that administer outside assistance are anxious to be self-liquidating. To neutralize their increased vulnerability, they found that military aid for internal security was both necessary and legitimate. Moreover, military assistance can be a means to the goal of economic assistance by providing a developing country with forces not only for local defense but also for internal development that a nationwide, properly controlled and used military establishment can generate. The United States has, therefore, been justified in granting military assistance not only for the immediate purposes of its containment and alliance policy. On its part, the Soviet Union has been led to disseminate military assistance to willing takers by the desire to break open the containment ring and secure immediate political gains in crucially important or vulnerable noncommitted countries.

Alternative recipients—allies or neutrals? With regard to the distribution of aid among alternative recipients, both major donors have faced a related problem: whether to give preferential or exclusive assistance to their allies or to distribute aid widely among noncommitted countries as well. Only a minority power willing to remain so or prepared to rely on military conquest could probably afford the

purism of aid only to allies. There is no other ready criterion. Different flaws vitiate such criteria as that of the need of potential recipients, their capacity to effect and absorb changes with outside assistance, or their ability and willingness to make their internal conduct or external policies conform to the interests and policies of the donor.

A distribution following any one criterion or coherent set of criteria becomes well-nigh impossible once there is an aid race between major donors. Such competition occurred between the United States and the Soviet Union and reached its peak in the late 1950s. The competition was aggravated by failures of perception. For one thing, the competing powers long ignored the similarity or identity of many of their problems and frustrations in the domain of foreign aid. For another, both insiders and outsiders tended to judge and compare the performance of the superpowers in not really comparable situations. The temporary beneficiary of the political and intellectual misapprehension was the Soviet Union, which gained easy, and apparently lasting, initial successes in the conflict-ridden Western orbit, displaying largesse toward noncommunist countries and reserving strict aid policies for communist countries.

Multilateral versus bilateral aid. Multilateral administration and distribution of foreign aid through international agencies has been widely advocated as a way out of the frustrations of bilateral methods. A change-over on a major scale has been inhibited, however, by the growing structural disequilibrium in the United Nations. The disequilibrium has favored numbers over the intrinsic weight of states and their contributions, and has been inimical to progressive expansion of the organization's functional scope in regard to the dispensing of aid and similar long-range activities. Moreover, most recipient countries have actually been reluctant to rely primarily on multilateral modes of allocation and control of economic assistance.

A more practical way of dispersing donor–recipient relations, and distributing aid in a quasi-multilateral manner, may occur by means of the multiplication of both Western and communist donors. A deliberately planned division of labor among ex-colonial powers has been preached in the West and practiced by the Soviet-bloc countries (excepting Communist China) in the late 1950s and early 1960s. The alternative way of dividing labor is a less concerted and even superficially competitive one, whenever one power acts in the place of and over the protests of another in an alienated country or part of the world. In the postwar period, the United States acted in countries bent upon repudiating both the presence and the presents of former colonial masters. As psychological decolonization in the former European empires advanced, as experience with powers other than the former metropoles grew, and as the colonial revolt spread to Latin America, the process has tended to be reversed. West Germany has been developing her economic activities abroad; France and Britain have been recovering their positions of the preferred donors in parts of Asia and Africa and have even moved to act by means of trade or aid on behalf or in lieu of the United States in disaffected countries of Latin America. It is unclear at the time of writing whether the competitive trade-and-aid activities of Communist China and the Soviet Union in Africa and Asia will ultimately prove to have been instruments of a break or of a more or less reluctant division of labor. In any event, the over-all result has been a larger total bulk of aid and its wider diffusion, if not a more rational distribution.

Control of aid

The other major problem is that of control. It concerns such issues as those of "strings" and "intervention," and it has remained unresolved in either theory or practice, although regularization of foreign aid depends on a general acceptance of a few principles or propositions. Some form of control over each other's behavior is the precondition of any cooperation between self-willed sovereign actors, not least in the sphere of foreign aid. Control becomes reciprocal whenever lesser states extract a greater leeway from stalemate among greater powers. Some strings are inevitably attached to grants by one state to another but are likely to be effective as well as legitimate only if they are adapted to suit particular types of aid and the corresponding kinds of anticipated performance. And no effort can do away with at least indirect or unintended intervention by the donor once a government accepts aid and thus admits its inability to cope with its tasks in a strictly internal manner. The donor's right to intervention generally stops short of forcible or dictatorial interference, but there are two exceptions. First, the assistance may be so massive that it creates responsibility for the recipient's existence, and circumstances could be so critical that they endanger the vital interests of both recipient and donor. Alternately, an invitation to intervene may be extended by the recipient, induced by past or anticipated assistance from the interventionist power and directed against a force other than clear majority will of the people concerned.

The occasions for intervention would be reduced by a policy that may be described as one of remote control. Under such a policy, the donor seeks to act on policies of sensitive governing elites by way of precedent-creating action in comparable situations accessible to a more direct exercise of influence. Alternatives to remote control are direct control, over the internal or external activities of a pliant or trustful government, and indirect control, obtained by promoting congenial political groups likely to sway politics in the direction favored by the donor without his constant interference. The previously noted one-country strategy overtaxes the capacity for relatively direct forms of controls, notably if the donor is unable to act upon reliable theoretical knowledge of relationships between economic aid and economic development and between economic development and political stability. The one-system strategy by contrast heightens the bearing of remote control by consistent policies in comparable situations, creating a body of rules by way of discernible authoritative precedents; flexibility is subordinated to the rule-making function of policy and reserved for diplomatic instruments with an immediate, predictable, and easily manipulable impact on men and events.

Critique and prospects

The problems besetting foreign aid indicate its shortcomings. The political future of foreign aid depends on its qualities as an instrument of current policies and as a foundation of a new system of international politics and of a new world order. There is a possible conflict between the two tests insofar as the traits that constitute the standing of foreign aid as an instrument of national policy tend to endear assistance to proponents of new forms of relations among nations. Foreign aid as an economic weapon too frequently tends to be separated from a complementary exercise of political influence and military power. Furthermore, aid is often rendered in the anticipation of counterperformance, the maturity of which is commonly all the more delayed and uncertain the more voluminous is the assistance. Consequently, results are not forthcoming, cannot be convincingly related to the grant, or are reversible by contrary developments before they are consolidated. The paucity of demonstrable positive returns encourages negative appraisals of foreign aid: as a waste or an expedient without which things would be still worse. The difficulty in consolidating provisional results is frustrating to the donor, even though it may be stabilizing internationally if it besets all the rival donors.

The shortcomings of foreign aid as an instrument of foreign policy become critical when changes in the international system reduce the donors' needs that commonly motivate aid. Among such changes are technological developments that lessen the dependence of the major powers on alliances and military facilities on foreign soil, and political events that dampen the intensity of competition over intermediate unaligned states. The task of controlling aid relationships from a position of exploitable political weakness becomes less impossible for major donors, but also less pressing. Military–political competition that has polarized the state system is apt to give way either to an outright military clash or to international politics of increasing diplomatic flexibility, marked by a shift of the focus of sought gains and feared losses from small, uncommitted states to relations and combinations among middle and great powers. Insofar as trends of this kind prevail, international agencies might get a chance to supersede bilateral foreign aid activities and routinize the allocation and administration of aid for economic development through application of objective criteria of need and capacity; the agencies themselves might, however, first have to undergo a change in their structure or spirit, and conform more realistically to the balance of material needs and contributions of the aid-giving and the aid-receiving countries. Conversely, if foreign aid were made multilateral, it might be hampered in a multipolar world by the diffusion of the tendency for each major economic power center to claim and obtain a preferential right to foreign aid activities in its regional orbit.

As long as the rendering of foreign aid and its results remain in large part the function of more pressing and compelling political, military, and diplomatic strategies, foreign aid activities in themselves are unlikely to constitute a basis of a new system of international politics. Such a system would implement a scientific theory of economic and political development, so far largely lacking, and would rest on the willingness of both donors and recipients to implement common interests in the expansion of individual and group welfare, of political choices, and of exchanges of all kinds. A sustained program of foreign aid free from subservience to political contests would provisionally take the place of free trade as the chief integrating element in a system of international relations governed by the distribution of developmental functions among unevenly endowed states. So conceived, the new system of international politics would supplement the older ideal of dividing the production and consumption of security among more or less favored states in a system of collective security; and it would supplant the diametrically opposed view of foreign aid as a perpetuation of subsidies by partly altered means in a still essentially mercantilist statecraft marked by contest over insufficiently expanding and expandable assets.

Barring unpredictable upheavals, the ultimate test of foreign aid as a positive and enduring factor in but slowly evolving international politics is a long-range one. It concerns the fitness of foreign aid to contribute to a stable world order. To a limited but real extent, international order and stability rest on domestic orders. Foreign aid makes a contribution in this area when it promotes coalitions of political and functional elites, meaning especially the modernizers and the guardians of the modernization process in developing countries. To be both stable and stabilizing, the coalitions must be able to agree on the scope and rate of manageable change, to be implemented by the elites and absorbed by the masses, in a process of growth that is largely independent of intercessions, restraints on modernizers, and compensations to dispossessed groups from the outside. Only very few underdeveloped countries, not necessarily representative of the fundamental problem, have managed to initiate and perpetuate such a process that would be largely self-sustaining politically as well as economically. The liberal explanation that failure to overcome underdevelopment in backward countries is a source of instability and war has been gaining ground over its Leninist counterpart, that the source is found in maladjustments due to economic overdevelopment in industrialized, capitalist–imperialist countries. To the extent that these hypotheses are valid and foreign aid helps relieve critical economic maladjustments, not least by reducing the gap between unequally developed countries, foreign aid can promote international stability.

In the international arena, foreign aid activities tend to promote stability when they provide rival powers with outlets for moderately competitive behavior, reducing the incentive to violent forms of rivalry. Foreign aid activities can relieve international tensions when they are informed by a realistic appraisal of possible gains for either side, and they may stabilize the international system both in the short and the long run insofar as contemporary major powers accept the fact that they are building up new economic and military powers that may eventually recast alignments to their disadvantage. The generation of reserve power may reduce the pressures on governments to avert by force unfavorable developments that may be foreshadowed by trends in the arms race or by rates of competitive economic growth. Such an anticipation may have been partly responsible for some major wars in the past, including both world wars of the twentieth century.

Two decades after the end of World War II, there has been a widespread desire to evaluate the intervening experience with different forms of large-scale governmental aid. A continuing retreat of foreign aid from the forefront of direct great-power competition would favor a new balance between acquisitive and creative aid. This might entail depoliticization of foreign aid in one respect, that of allowing considerable autonomy to objective needs of development, and its politicization in another respect, that of a progressive definition and acceptance of reciprocal rights and obligations on the part of recipients as well as donors. The new balance would reflect the growing need for the so-called revolution or rising expectations to come to terms with the less spectacular but no less significant decline of expectations attached to foreign aid. Any new compromise between the demands of the revolution in the less developed countries and the consequences of the evolution in the industrial donor countries could not but alter the manifestation of a technique that can be shown to be a recurrent, but not continuous, and a useful, but not indispensable, feature of international statecraft.

GEORGE LISKA

[See also ALLIANCES; COLONIALISM; IMPERIALISM; MODERNIZATION; TECHNICAL ASSISTANCE. A guide to other relevant material will be found under INTERNATIONAL RELATIONS.]

BIBLIOGRAPHY

The writings on foreign aid in the West, and in the United States in particular, can be grouped into categories of official and scholarly publications.

Among the official sources, the most important are records of the annual hearings before the foreign relations committees of the two houses of Congress and the special reports occasionally ordered by both branches of the government. Major examples are U.S. Congress 1957, prepared for a special committee of the 85th Congress; U.S. President's Committee 1959; U.S. Committee . . . 1963.

Among the scholarly sources, the executive–legislative process in relation to foreign aid is analyzed in Haviland 1958. The school of thought stressing the long-range economic development of foreign aid is represented by Millikan & Rostow 1957 and 1958. The school of thought stressing short-range political control and objectives is represented by Liska 1960 and Morgenthau 1962. The background writings for the two contrasting approaches are Rostow 1960 and Staley 1954, respectively. A successful attempt to present a balanced approach is Millikan & Blackmer 1961.

A larger body of scholarly literature is concerned with the description, analysis, and evaluation of particular forms and programs of economic and military aid, with reference to particular countries or regions. Outstanding among these are Brown & Opie 1953; Price 1955; Montgomery 1962; Jordan 1962. While also regionally focused, Wolf 1960 is valuable mainly as an attempt to evolve theoretical criteria for the allocation of aid.

The foreign aid activities of the communist-bloc countries have been described in U.S. Department of State 1958; Berliner 1958; Allen 1960. Important information regarding assistance through the United Nations can be found in Asher et al. 1957 and Sharp 1952 and in such periodicals as Foreign Affairs, International Organization, and International Conciliation.

Sources on the antecedents of foreign aid are uneven. A classic source on the liberal period is Feis 1930, which can be supplemented with Michon 1927. No single source deals exhaustively with dynastic subsidies. However, see Braubach 1923 and less systematic references in Horn 1930 and Pinkham 1954. Relevant for the understanding of the broader contemporary context of foreign aid activities are Calvocoressi 1962; Emerson 1960; Ehrhard 1957; Martin 1962.

ALLEN, ROBERT L. 1960 Soviet Economic Warfare. Washington: Public Affairs Press.

ASHER, ROBERT E. et al. 1957 The United Nations and Promotion of General Welfare. Washington: Brookings Institution.

BERLINER, JOSEPH S. 1958 Soviet Economic Aid: The New Aid and Trade Policy in Underdeveloped Countries. Published for the Council on Foreign Relations. New York: Praeger.

BRAUBACH, MAX 1923 Die Bedeutung der Subsidien für die Politik im spanischen Erbfolgekriege. Bonn and Leipzig: Schroeder.

BROWN, WILLIAM ADAMS; and OPIE, REDVERS 1953 American Foreign Assistance. Washington: Brookings Institution.

CALVOCORESSI, PETER 1962 World Order and New States. London: Chatto & Windus.

EHRHARD, JEAN (1957) 1958 Le destin du colonialisme. 3d ed. Paris: Éditions Eyrolles.

EMERSON, RUPERT 1960 From Empire to Nation: The Rise to Self-assertion of Asian and African Peoples. Cambridge, Mass.: Harvard Univ. Press. → A paperback edition was published in 1962 by Beacon.

FEIS, HERBERT (1930) 1961 Europe, The World's Banker, 1870–1914: An Account of European Foreign Investment and the Connection of World Finance With Diplomacy Before the War. New York: Kelley.

HAVILAND, H. FIELD 1958 Foreign Aid and the Policy Process: 1957. American Political Science Review 52:689–724.

HORN, DAVID B. 1930 Sir Charles Hanbury Williams and European Diplomacy (1747–1758). London: Harrap.

JORDAN, AMOS A. 1962 Foreign Aid and the Defense of Southeast Asia. New York: Praeger.

LISKA, GEORGE 1960 The New Statecraft: Foreign Aid in American Foreign Policy. Univ. of Chicago Press.

MARTIN, LAURENCE W. (editor) 1962 Neutralism and Nonalignment: The New States in World Affairs. New York: Praeger.

MICHON, GEORGES (1927) 1929 The Franco–Russian Alliance, 1891–1917. London: Allen & Unwin. → First published in French.

MILLIKAN, MAX F.; and BLACKMER, DONALD L. M. (editors) 1961 The Emerging Nations: Their Growth and United States Policy. A study from the Center for International Studies, Massachusetts Institute of Technology. Boston: Little.

MILLIKAN, MAX F.; and ROSTOW, W. W. 1957 A Proposal: Key to an Effective Foreign Policy. A study from the Center for International Studies, Massachusetts Institute of Technology. New York: Harper.

MILLIKAN, MAX F.; and ROSTOW, W. W. 1958 Foreign Aid: Next Phase. *Foreign Affairs* 36:418–436.

MONTGOMERY, JOHN D. 1962 *The Politics of Foreign Aid: American Experience in Southeast Asia.* Published for the Council on Foreign Relations. New York: Praeger.

MORGENTHAU, HANS J. 1962 A Political Theory of Foreign Aid. *American Political Science Review* 56:301–309.

PINKHAM, LUCILE 1954 *William III and the Respectable Revolution: The Part Played by William of Orange in the Revolution of 1688.* Cambridge, Mass.: Harvard Univ. Press.

PRICE, HARRY B. 1955 *The Marshall Plan and Its Meaning.* Ithaca, N.Y.: Cornell Univ. Press.

ROSTOW, W. W. (1960) 1963 *The Stages of Economic Growth: A Non-Communist Manifesto.* Cambridge Univ. Press.

SHARP, WALTER R. 1952 *International Technical Assistance: Programs and Organization.* Chicago: Public Administration Service.

STALEY, EUGENE (1954) 1961 *The Future of Underdeveloped Countries: Political Implications of Economic Development.* Rev. ed. Published for the Council on Foreign Relations. New York: Harper.

U.S. COMMITTEE TO STRENGTHEN THE SECURITY OF THE FREE WORLD 1963 *The Scope and Distribution of United States Military and Economic Assistance Programs: Report to the President of the United States.* Washington: Government Printing Office. → Known as the Clay Committee report.

U.S. CONGRESS, SENATE, SPECIAL COMMITTEE TO STUDY THE FOREIGN AID PROGRAM 1957 *Foreign Aid Program: Compilation of Studies and Surveys.* 85th Congress, 1st Session, Senate Document No. 52. Washington: Government Printing Office.

U.S. DEPARTMENT OF STATE 1958 *The Sino–Soviet Economic Offensive in the Less Developed Countries.* Department of State Publication No. 6632; European and British Commonwealth Series, No. 51. Washington: Government Printing Office.

U.S. PRESIDENT'S COMMITTEE TO STUDY THE UNITED STATES MILITARY ASSISTANCE PROGRAM 1959 *Composite Report.* 2 vols. Washington: Government Printing Office. → Known as the Draper Committee report.

WOLF, CHARLES JR. 1960 *Foreign Aid: Theory and Practice in Southern Asia.* Princeton Univ. Press.

II

ECONOMIC ASPECTS

The international transfer of economic resources is the essence of foreign economic aid. The flow of public assistance consists of grants and loans in cash and kind, including technical assistance, from a donor government or international organization to other governments or enterprises in recipient countries. The sources, forms, and purposes of financial and technical assistance are extremely varied [see TECHNICAL ASSISTANCE]. Of primary importance, however, is the flow of resources to poor countries in order to accelerate their development. The purely economic function of this aid should be distinguished from that of direct military assistance, which may also be received by a developing country; moreover, aid should properly be considered as only that part of the foreign capital inflow that normal market incentives do not provide. [*See* INTERNATIONAL MONETARY ECONOMICS, *article on* PRIVATE INTERNATIONAL CAPITAL MOVEMENTS.]

Several aspects of foreign economic aid require particular emphasis: the historical evolution of aid programs; the determination of the objectives and magnitude of aid; the appraisal of the relative merits and demerits of different types of aid; the criteria of effective use of aid; and the burden of aid.

Evolution of aid programs. Foreign assistance programs have evolved through a series of legislative measures and administrative procedures required at different times for various purposes. Before World War II economic aid came mainly from metropolitan countries in support of overseas colonies and dependencies, was on a purely bilateral basis, and involved relatively small amounts of financial grants. [*See* COLONIALISM, *article on* ECONOMIC ASPECTS.]

The United States, however, early supported a large-scale assistance program through loans from the Export–Import Bank of Washington; since 1954 this bank has concentrated increasingly on capital assistance to less-developed countries. Aside from the lend–lease arrangements, which provided economic support to wartime allies, the first general foreign aid program supported by the United States came with the Economic Cooperation Act of 1948. This initiated the European Recovery Program (Marshall Aid Program), which during 1948–1952 furnished loans and grants to 17 western European countries that confronted problems of reconstruction and balance of payments pressures. Although aid under this program was not directly related to the problems of newly developing countries, it demonstrated the potential of international aid and was a prototype for subsequent aid programs.

In 1950 the U.S. Congress passed the Act for International Development, which incorporated a technical assistance program ("Point Four"). This was the first of a series of Foreign Assistance Acts. A variety of agencies have administered U.S. aid in the course of these successive programs. The United States has also provided, under Public Law 480 and "Food for Peace" programs, for the sale of surplus agricultural commodities for local currencies. In 1957 the Development Loan Fund was

Table 1 — United States government foreign aid by program: fiscal years 1941–1960[a]
(converted to millions of U.S. dollars)

	1941–1948	1949–1952	1953–1956	1957	1958	1959	1960	Total
Gross total—all programs[b]	70,318	21,529	23,893	5,472	5,429	6,690	5,077	138,408
Investment in international financial institutions	3,385	—	—	35	—	1,375	80	4,875
Gross grants	57,167	18,959	20,924	4,142	3,963	3,860	3,654	112,669
Lend–lease	48,672	—	—	—	—	—	—	48,672
UNRRA and related aid[c]	3,473	53	—	—	—	—	—	3,526
Aid to occupied areas	3,591	2,791	270	1	1	2	2	6,658
ERP, MSA, and other economic aid[d]	514	11,778	6,622	1,502	1,244	1,369	1,314	24,343
Farm surplus disposal[e]	—	49	653	281	365	312	314	1,974
MDAP and MSA military aid[f]	—	3,073	13,377	2,358	2,353	2,177	2,023	25,361
Other grants[g]	914	1,214	2	—	—	—	—	2,130
Gross credits[b]	9,766	2,570	2,969	1,295	1,466	1,455	1,343	20,864
Lend–lease settlement	2,957	56	—	6	—	—	—	3,019
Export–Import Bank	2,570	880	1,547	237	760	708	399	7,101
British loan	3,750	—	—	—	—	—	—	3,750
ERP and MSA economic aid	—	1,532	512	106	232	240	315	2,937
Farm surplus[h]	—	—	860	937	474	506	629	3,406
Other credits	487	102	49	9	i	i	i	647

a. Fiscal years ending June 30; details may not add to totals because of rounding.
b. Includes net accumulation of foreign currency claims deriving from farm surplus disposal.
c. Includes post-UNRRA and Interim Aid.
d. ERP—European Recovery Program; MSA—Mutual Security Act; other aid includes contributions to UN agencies, technical assistance to Latin America, Inter-American and related highways, Trust Territory development, Libyan Special Purpose Fund, etc.
e. Donations of agricultural products plus dollar equivalent of foreign currency grants derived from farm surplus disposal.
f. MDAP—Mutual Defense Assistance Program.
g. Greek–Turkish, Chinese stabilization, and military aid; Philippine, Korean, and other Far East aid grants.
h. Dollar equivalent of loans made in foreign currencies derived from the farm surplus disposal programs, plus the net accumulation of such currencies.
i. Less than $500,000.

Sources: Foreign Grants and Credits by the United States Government, 1952, p. 81, appendix B; U.S. National Advisory Council on International Monetary and Financial Problems; Higgins 1962, table 3-1.

created to administer long-term, low-interest loans from the United States. The magnitude of American foreign aid from 1941 to 1960 is summarized by program in Table 1.

Although the United States has been the largest donor, many other countries have also participated in international economic assistance. Since 1954 the Soviet Union has entered into assistance agreements with developing countries and has also extended technical assistance on an increasing scale. While a considerable part of aid from noncommunist Western countries has consisted of grants, the Soviet system has concentrated on long-term "bulk" credits, under which agreements for deliveries of goods on credit are negotiated. Although there has not been much difference in the length of loans and terms of repayment between Soviet and Western agreements, a larger proportion of Soviet aid has allowed for repayment in local currency or local products, and Soviet loans have had lower interest rates.

Soviet technical assistance has usually been supplied as part of a larger, integrated program

Table 2 — Commitments by the centrally planned economies of bilateral economic aid to underdeveloped countries, 1954–1960 (millions of U.S. dollars)

	Before 1958	1958	1959	1960	Total
Donor:					
China (mainland)	82	26	—	21	129
Czechoslovakia	21	68	76	50	215
East Germany	7	—	22	—	29
Poland	—	—	6	30	36
Rumania	—	11	—	—	11
U.S.S.R.	712	345	782	804	2,643
Yugoslavia	—	10	67	58	135
Total, donor countries	822	460	953	963	3,198
of which:					
Credits	769	460	945	939	3,113
Grants	53	—	8	24	85
Recipient:					
Africa	—	—	181	60	241
Latin America	4	102	6	120	232
Middle East	203	282	272	270	1,027
Southeast Asia	615	76	494	513	1,698
Total, recipient countries	822	460	953	963	3,198

Source: UN, Department of Economic and Social Affairs 1961, table 16, p. 34.

consisting of loans, development goods, and bilateral trade; in contrast, technical aid from Western countries has usually been connected to individual projects or to specific training objectives. Communist-bloc technical experts have also concentrated on relatively few conspicuous projects that entail complex technology, while American technical assistance has emphasized the broader and more basic needs of agriculture, health, and education.

As may be noted in Table 2, commitments (which were not in all instances implemented) made by the centrally planned economies to the underdeveloped countries amounted, by the end of 1960, to approximately $3,200 million. Table 3 compares the magnitude of aid from the Sino–Soviet bloc with that of the United States.

Other countries have also sponsored bilateral aid programs—notably the United Kingdom, France, West Germany, Canada, and Japan. Table 4 summarizes the magnitude of bilateral aid during 1958–1960.

Regional organizations have also been significant contributors to aid: the Colombo Plan for Cooperative Economic Development in South and Southeast Asia, inaugurated in 1950; the Organization for American States, formed in 1951 and strengthened by the Inter-American Development Bank in 1959, the Act of Bogotá of 1960, and the Charter of Punta del Este, which launched the "Alliance for Progress"; and the Organization for Economic Cooperation and Development (OECD), which in 1961 succeeded the Organization for European Economic Cooperation (OEEC).

Finally, the United Nations and a number of its specialized agencies play a prominent role in foreign aid: the International Bank for Reconstruction and Development (IBRD), International Finance Corporation (IFC), United Nations Special Fund (UNSF), International Development Association (IDA), Technical Assistance Board (TAB), World Health Organization (WHO), Food and Agriculture Organization (FAO), and regional economic commissions.

Utilizing the capital subscribed by member nations, the loans raised in the markets of member countries, and the return on its own operations, the IBRD has been the principal development-financing institution of the United Nations. The IDA has provided loans at very long term and with no or low interest, and it has had great latitude in its selection of projects for financing. This has enabled the IDA to meet the special needs of developing countries that, for balance of payments reasons, were nearing the limit of their capacity

Table 3 — Comparison of economic credits and grants extended to less-developed countries by the Sino–Soviet bloc and the United States (millions of U.S. dollars)

| | SINO–SOVIET BLOC | UNITED STATES* | |
	Mid-1955–December 1961	Mid-1955–December 1961	Mid-1948–December 1961
Total	4,371	9,449	12,727
Latin America	465	1,341	2,080
Argentina	104	360	524
Brazil	4	961	1,515
Cuba	357	20	41
Middle East	1,077	1,896	2,723
Cyprus	1	10	10
Egypt	615	394	479
Iran	6	411	672
Iraq	216	13	21
Syria	178	69	70
Turkey	17	980	1,452
Yemen	44	19	19
Africa	601	502	512
Ethiopia	114	115	125
Ghana	182	35	35
Guinea	110	4	4
Mali	65	2	2
Somalia	62	15	15
Sudan	22	64	64
Tunisia	46	267	267
Asia	2,112	4,881	5,973
Afghanistan	204	138	184
Burma	93	68	90
Cambodia	65	195	232
Ceylon	58	77	77
India	963	2,726	3,221
Indonesia	641	308	541
Nepal	55	40	44
Pakistan	33	1,329	1,584
Europe	116	829	1,439
Iceland	5	35	70
Yugoslavia	111	794	1,369

* U.S. figures include credits and grants from ICA obligations; DLF loans approved; Export–Import Bank long-term loans authorized; and Public Law 480 funds earmarked for country use under Title I, authorizations under Title II, and shipments under Title III.

Source: U.S. Congress, Committee on Appropriations, p. 207.

to borrow abroad for development projects on conventional terms. The IFC has been instrumental in assisting private industrial development by investing without government guarantee in productive private enterprises. During the year 1961/1962, the IBRD and its two affiliates, the IFC and IDA, made new commitments of more than $1,000 million. Although not itself a lending agency, the UNSF has made greater investment feasible and more effective by granting assistance for preinvestment work in the form of surveys, training, and applied research. Contributions to the United Na-

Table 4 — Bilateral aid to underdeveloped countries, 1958–1960
(millions of U.S. dollars)[a]

Contributing country	CALENDAR YEAR 1958			CALENDAR YEAR 1959			CALENDAR YEAR 1960		
	Grants	Loans	Repayments	Grants	Loans	Repayments	Grants	Loans	Repayments
Australia[b]	37.0	1.2	—	34.4	0.6	—	39.2	1.7	—
Belgium[c]	4.0	—	—	30.0	—	—	86.0	—	—
Canada	47.3	9.5	—	60.3	1.3	—	48.1	—	—
Denmark	—	—	—	—	—	—	0.7	—	—
France	524.5	227.6	41.2	665.2	176.2	42.4	687.0	87.0	19.0
Germany (FRG)	5.2	74.4	16.0	6.6	46.1	17.5	6.2	77.5	16.9
Italy	10.2	—	1.7	9.0	30.5	8.9	8.9	16.8	10.0
Japan	177.4	—	—	4.0	—	—	2.5	78.6	—
Netherlands	20.8	1.7	—	21.7	2.3	—	28.2	3.6	—
New Zealand[d]	4.2	0.2	—	5.0	0.3	—	6.3	—	—
Norway	1.2	—	—	1.0	—	—	0.9	—	—
Sweden	0.8	—	—	0.9	—	—	1.0	—	—
Switzerland	0.1	—	—	0.1	—	—	—	—	—
United Kingdom	143.0	67.0	20.0	151.0	137.0	25.0	165.0	176.0	22.0
United States	1,132.0	796.0	167.0	1,157.0	733.0	205.0	1,320.0	723.0	220.0
Yugoslavia	—	—	—	—	—	—	0.3	26.0	—

a. Omits aid from Sino–Soviet bloc.
b. Fiscal years ending 30 June of years stated.
c. Advances to Ruanda–Urundi with no specific schedule of repayment are treated as grants.
d. Fiscal years ending 31 March of years stated.

Source: UN, Statistical Office 1961, table 157, p. 467.

tions Expanded Program of Technical Assistance amounted to over $41.5 million in 1961, compared with less than $20 million a decade earlier.

The amount of capital assistance from the United Nations has been small in comparison with bilateral programs, but it has particular importance because of its multilateral character. The same is true for the technical assistance programs provided by the United Nations itself and by several of its specialized agencies. Table 5 indicates the magnitude of multilateral aid, 1958–1960, while Table 6 shows the magnitude of public aid by source and type, 1953/1954–1958/1959. In recent years the relative share of the flow of capital to underdeveloped countries has been approximately 90 per cent on a bilateral basis and only 10 per cent on a multilateral basis, with the IBRD, IFC, and IDA accounting for slightly over one-half of the multilateral aid.

Objectives and magnitude of aid. Foreign aid is usually a component of a nation's foreign policy; for this reason its objectives are diverse. The underlying objectives may be mixed even for a particular act of assistance by a single government

Table 5 — Multilateral aid to underdeveloped countries, 1958–1960
(millions of U.S. dollars)

Source*	CALENDAR YEAR 1958			CALENDAR YEAR 1959			CALENDAR YEAR 1960		
	Grants	Loans	Repayments	Grants	Loans	Repayments	Grants	Loans	Repayments
EDF	—	—	—	0.1	—	—	3.4	—	—
IBRD	—	345.7	47.0	—	310.3	68.5	—	340.1	91.5
IFC	—	4.9	—	—	7.8	—	—	13.6	—
UNICEF	18.3	—	—	20.4	—	—	18.3	—	—
UNRWA	31.8	—	—	34.1	—	—	34.7	—	—
UNSF	—	—	—	0.3	—	—	2.0	—	—
UNEPTA	25.9	—	—	24.7	—	—	24.1	—	—
Other UNTA	10.8	—	—	11.3	—	—	13.5	—	—

* The following abbreviations have been introduced in the table: EDF, Development Fund of the European Economic Community; IBRD, International Bank for Reconstruction and Development; IFC, International Finance Corporation; UNICEF, United Nations Children's Fund; UNRWA, United Nations Relief and Works Agency for Palestine Refugees in the Near East; UNSF, United Nations Special Fund; UNEPTA, United Nations Expanded Programme of Technical Assistance; and other UNTA, all programs of technical assistance administered by the United Nations, the specialized agencies, and the International Atomic Energy Agency, other than EPTA.

Source: UN, Statistical Office 1961, table 157, p. 467.

Table 6 — Total governmental aid, multilateral and bilateral, by type, 1953/1954–1958/1959

	1953/1954–1955/1956 ANNUAL AVERAGE			1957/1958–1958/1959 ANNUAL AVERAGE		
	Grants	Loans (net)	Total	Grants	Loans (net)	Total
Total aid in billions of U.S. dollars	1.5	0.5	2.0	2.2	1.1	3.3
Bilateral aid	1.4	0.4	1.8	2.1	0.8	2.9
Multilateral aid	0.1	0.1	0.2	0.1	0.3	0.4
Total aid as percentage distribution by type	74.4	25.6	100	66.0	34.0	100
Bilateral aid	77.0	23.0	100	70.9	29.1	100
Multilateral aid	48.3	51.7	100	27.2	72.8	100

Source: UN, Secretary-General 1961, p. 48.

to another—since humanitarian motives, military interests, and political purposes tend to fuse with the purely economic objective.

Solely in terms of the direct economic goal, foreign aid is intended to augment the resources of the recipient country so that its rate of development may be raised. The largest proportion of the flow of public funds has been devoted to investment projects in industry, agriculture, mining, and basic "overhead" facilities, such as power and transportation [see CAPITAL, SOCIAL OVERHEAD]. To achieve a higher rate of economic development, however, a country must also experience social development through investment in human resources, introduction of new techniques of production, and institution building. Technical assistance programs fulfill some of these requirements by improving health and education and supporting rural community development. Even though social projects are difficult to evaluate in terms of economic criteria alone and hence are a questionable objective of economic aid, financial and technical assistance may nonetheless be necessary to initiate social programs that will contribute to higher productivity. An even more controversial objective of foreign aid is stabilization assistance in the form of balance of payments, or general purpose, loans to a country that has current external liabilities in excess of its international reserves or to a country that cannot meet its current liabilities out of current foreign exchange earnings without restricting essential imports.

Clarity on the objectives of foreign aid is the necessary first step in determining how much aid is needed by a recipient country. But even when the objectives are clearly defined, it is still extremely difficult to calculate the magnitude and duration of external assistance required to attain these objectives. Nonetheless, such calculations are commonly attempted, especially in relation to the recipient country's development plan. Although the statistical exactitude of this type of calculation

is illusory, its logic is of interest, and improvement of the concepts and methodology underlying these quantitative estimates may result from more intensive consideration of the problems involved.

The usual type of calculation proceeds as follows: A target is set for the desired increase in per capita real income over a given time period. On the basis of estimated annual population growth and the economy's marginal capital–output ratio (the ratio between the value of additional capital and the value of additional annual output produced), it is concluded that a certain percentage of national income must be saved and invested to attain the per capita income target. If domestic saving is less than this amount and cannot be immediately raised by domestic policy measures, the balance must be sought from external sources. To the extent that private foreign investment does not fill the gap, public funds from abroad are required.

This exercise is, however, a highly oversimplified way to calculate aid requirements. Capital–output ratios have not yet been measured accurately enough to justify their use in deriving quantitative conclusions. Moreover, exclusive concentration merely on the relationships between a capital–output ratio, a savings ratio, and population growth is a much too mechanical and narrow interpretation, for it misses the inner complexity and subtleties of the development process. Other factors besides investment are strategic in accelerating development, and the full implications of external aid cannot be appreciated without a more comprehensive analysis of the role of foreign capital. In the broadest context the analysis should consider how the foreign aid relates to a greater national effort to increase the rate of development, and it should examine the differential impact of various forms of capital assistance in terms of their costs and benefits.

Although the calculation of foreign aid requirements is difficult, the underlying rationale for such aid is clear. It is not possible to relate any one source of funds to a specific type of use, but the net capital imports can offset, or "finance," the difference between the value of products used and the value of products produced domestically; or the difference between net investment and net domestic savings; or the value of imports and factor payments abroad *minus* the value of exports and factor receipts. All these differences constitute a shortfall in real resources that results when the claims of the development plan exceed the available domestic resources. This gap in real resources is in turn reflected in a foreign exchange gap. To the extent that the use of foreign exchange reserves or an inflow of private capital does not fill the gap, public capital assistance from abroad will be necessary to give command over the additional resources. The size of a development plan is therefore constrained by the amount of foreign economic aid that is forthcoming.

While the dependence on external aid may have to be large at the outset of the development program, most plans aim for a progressive reduction in aid and the eventual realization of a self-financing plan. To achieve this the plan relies on a high marginal rate of domestic saving. It is expected that the proportion that can be saved out of an increase in output will be much higher than the average savings ratio at the plan's beginning. The proportion of national income invested and financed by domestic savings would then increase, and the ratio of net foreign capital imports to additional investment would decline. The reliance on foreign aid will also diminish if, as development proceeds, the composition of investment alters toward projects with a lower import content, the production of import-substitutes increases, export revenue expands, and total domestic output grows without inflationary financing.

Forms of aid. The significance of foreign aid depends not only on its magnitude but also on the terms on which it is made available. The various forms of financial assistance can be differentiated by their terms—whether "hard" loans, "soft" loans, or grants; by the parties they involve—whether government-to-government or government-to-enterprise and whether furnished by national or multilateral agencies; and by their conditions—whether for specific projects or for a general development program.

Hard loans carry a commercial rate of interest, have a relatively short amortization period, and require repayment in foreign currency. Various types of soft loans are possible: very long-term loans repayable in foreign currency at a low rate of interest or without interest; loans repayable in local currency; long-term loans at low interest with a long grace period for payment of principal and interest.

Since they require neither servicing nor repayment, grants rather than loans are sometimes proposed for projects involving "social" development. It is thought that loans are appropriate for self-liquidating "economic" projects, where the criterion can be ability to service the loan, but that grants should be made for such nonself-liquidating projects as education, health, and community development, where the criterion is simply "need." International grants do have the merit of adding no burden of interest and amortization charges upon the recipient country, and they are a clear manifestation of the donor's willingness to offer a unilateral income transfer.

There is, however, little justification in differentiating between "social" and "economic" capital, insofar as both can contribute to an expansion of total output, which is the basic consideration in determining the recipient country's capacity to service foreign obligations. If in the interest of assuring effective use of grants, the granters attempt to exercise more control over the recipient country than would be the case for loans, then grants may, of course, be resented. And while it may be politically inexpedient for a donor nation to offer grants, there may be less political opposition to loans—even with generous low-interest and long-term provisions.

Although the greater part of all economic aid has been on a bilateral basis, several arguments are advanced in favor of providing more aid through multilateral channels: better coordination of assistance activities can be achieved; the aid is more acceptable to recipient nations; the practice of discrimination among recipients is more difficult, and the aid program is less susceptible to political influences; tied loans (requiring expenditure in the lending country) are avoided; and more appropriate technical assistance may be obtained by drawing upon the experience of all nations.

In some areas and for some activities international auspices may not be feasible. And few would insist that all types of aid be administered by international agencies. Short of complete multilateralism, however, there is still considerable scope and need for the multilateral coordination of bilateral programs—multilateral supervision of the technical, financial, and commodity aid supplied by individual countries.

Another major issue is whether aid should be given only for a specific project or extended for general purposes too. Advocates of the project approach claim that only by financing soundly conceived projects will foreign aid contribute to an increase in productive capital. The IBRD, for instance, has tended to give prime consideration to the foreign exchange requirements of specific projects, emphasizing the economic soundness of the projects and their direct contribution to the productivity of the borrowing country. Moreover, it is claimed that the review of specific projects has some educational value and allows the donor to act more readily as a critic of the details of the recipient's development plan.

It has become increasingly clear that the effectiveness of aid depends not merely on the productivity of specific projects but more generally on the complementarity of different projects and the appropriateness of the developing country's allocation of total investment expenditures from both domestic and foreign sources. Similarly, the narrow view that aid should be confined to the foreign exchange component of specific projects misses the fundamental principle that the receipt of aid allows the country to acquire command over resources in general, not simply to increase command of foreign resources in particular. Insofar as changes occur in the general program of development, it is impossible to identify exactly the inflow of capital with a specific project; the inflow contributes to the whole program. The effectiveness of aid depends upon the country's allocation of its general resources. The same consideration is relevant for determining the country's capacity to service foreign debt, as noted below.

Use of aid.   Even if aid is provided in substantial amounts and on favorable terms, there remains the ultimate problem of achieving its most effective use. External assistance should add to—not substitute for—the country's own developmental efforts. If capital assistance is to result in a higher rate of investment, it must be prevented from simply substituting for domestic sources of financing investment, and it should not be dissipated in supporting higher personal consumption or an increase in nondevelopment current expenditure by the government.

If external assistance were to be used for bolstering current consumption, the scope for the use of foreign capital would obviously be practically boundless. When this use is excluded, the economically warranted demand for capital is limited by the country's ability to use capital productively—that is, by the country's "capital absorptive capacity." In the short run, even if not in the long run, there may be a limit to how much capital assistance can be effectively used when the investment must not only cover its costs but also yield a reasonable increase in income. It should also be recognized

that the effective use of capital assistance may depend in large part upon the effectiveness of technical assistance. For the purpose of contributing technical aid is essentially to raise absorptive capacity. Once the pace of development gains momentum, the absorptive capacity will be higher, and foreign capital can then be utilized more effectively.

When capital assistance is not confined to specific investment projects but is available on a general-purpose basis, the allocation of the foreign capital is decisive in determining whether it contributes as much as possible to raising the growth potential of the recipient economy. An efficient allocation of investment resources then depends upon the application of investment criteria based on the country's entire development program and the adoption of appropriate domestic policy measures to supplement the use of foreign aid. Since the formation of capital depends, in the last resort, on domestic action, there can be no simple equivalence between the amount of aid received and the subsequent rate of development. The effectiveness of the use made of foreign aid in the country's entire development program will be more decisive in determining whether development is to be sustained than is the initial amount of aid received.

It is therefore proper to emphasize the necessity of self-help measures, as American aid programs have increasingly done. Unless recipient governments adopt measures to mobilize fully their own resources and to implement their plans, the maximum potential from aid will not be realized. It has become increasingly evident that to realize this objective in many poor countries it is necessary to undertake basic reforms in land tenure systems, the tax structure, education, and governmental administration. Additional attention must therefore be given to the sociocultural and political aspects of aid.

Burden of aid.   Significant as the benefits from aid may be, they are not without their costs. For the donor there is a burden in mobilizing aid; for the recipient, a burden of debt servicing and repayment.

Although the mobilization of aid is not limited by a physical incapacity on the part of donor countries to provide the needed resources, there is a problem of paying for the transference of the resources. Unless inflation is to be endured, it is necessary to withdraw—by taxation or government borrowing—the money equivalent of the resources to be transferred.

Moreover, the donor nation may be intensifying the difficulty of maintaining equilibrium in its balance of payments, unless it requires that its loans and grants be expended in the country of origin. If such "tied" aid is necessary out of balance of payments considerations, and the alternative to tied funds would be no aid at all, then the larger amount of tied aid is to be preferred, even though the condition that the aid be expended in the donor country may diminish the value of the aid to the recipient country as compared with freedom to import from a third country.

The willingness of an individual country to bear the burden of providing resources out of public funds may depend on the willingness of other countries to share in the burden. An increase in the total flow of aid becomes politically more feasible if there is a belief that the burden is being shared equitably. But there is no unambiguous formula for determining what constitutes an equitable distribution among the contributors of aid. A refined proposal would have the developed countries contribute according to a progressive tax schedule applied to the country's per capita real gross national product. Perhaps the most practicable solution is to accept the commonly advocated proposal of a flat-rate levy on national income—say, one per cent of the national income of the donor nations.

For the recipient country the burden of foreign aid depends upon the country's capacity to service its external obligations. When the return flow of interest and of amortization payments exceeds the inflow of new capital assistance, the country confronts a transfer problem in servicing the debt. It will have to generate an export surplus to cover the net outward transfer of amortization on capital account and of interest payments on current account. This entails a transformation of the economy such that resources can be reallocated to the sector producing exports or import-substitutes. To accomplish this the country may have to endure internal and external controls or experience exchange depreciation. The adverse effects of these measures of balance of payments adjustment might be interpreted as the indirect costs of foreign aid, to be added to the direct costs.

The direct cost of servicing capital assistance, however, is not a burden in itself. Even though part of the increased production from the use of foreign capital has to be paid abroad in interest—and this is a deduction that would not be necessary if the savings were provided at home—nonetheless the country has benefited from additional investment. What does matter in mitigating the burden of the debt is the country's ability to avoid the necessity of adopting restrictive measures in order to find sufficient foreign exchange for the remittance of the external service payments. To minimize these indirect costs the country's development program must give due consideration to the debt-servicing capacity of the country.

This becomes part of the problem of selecting appropriate investment criteria. To provide for adequate servicing of the foreign debt the capital should increase productivity sufficiently to yield an increase in real income greater than the interest and amortization charges. If this is done, the economy will have the capacity to raise the necessary funds—either through a direct commercial return or greater taxable capacity. Moreover, to provide a sufficient surplus of foreign exchange to avoid a transfer problem, the capital should be utilized in such a way as to generate a surplus in the other items of the balance of payments equal to the transfer payments abroad. If it is realized that the ability to create a sufficiently large export surplus depends on the operation of all industries together, not simply on the use made of foreign investment, it is then apparent that a project financed by foreign aid need not itself make a direct contribution to the balance of payments. Instead of such a narrow balance of payments criterion, the basic test for the allocation of capital aid is simply that it should be invested in the form that yields the highest social marginal product. As long as capital is distributed according to its most productive use and the excess spending associated with inflation is avoided, the necessary export surplus can be created indirectly. The essential point is that the allocation of foreign aid according to the criterion of productivity will also be the most favorable for debt servicing, since it maximizes the increase in income from a given amount of capital and thereby contributes to the growth of foreign exchange availabilities.

The problem of debt servicing will also be eased for the aid-receiving country when capital assistance is offered at lower interest, for longer terms, and with more stability and when the creditor country follows a more expansionary domestic policy and a more liberal trade policy.

Need for further research. Foreign aid has been extended mainly in an *ad hoc* fashion in response to immediate policy situations and without the opportunity for a substantial amount of prior research. Its practice, however, has suggested several areas of basic research that merit considerably more investigation. Of fundamental importance is the need for clear criteria in determining aid requirements, its optimal allocation among recipients, and its most effective use.

Since foreign economic aid is only a single component of the total flow of resources from rich to poor countries, it is important to investigate more thoroughly the relationships between capital assistance, private foreign investment, and international trade. Under what conditions can loans and grants stimulate private foreign investment? And under what conditions are they competitive? To what extent are the benefits of foreign aid being offset by adverse foreign trade policies? Might not more be gained from policies that stabilize the poor countries' foreign exchange earnings than from additional capital assistance?

Insofar as the effective use of foreign aid may depend on social and political reforms, it would be instructive to examine more systematically the sociocultural and political aspects of foreign aid. This should serve to correct the tendency to overemphasize capital productivity and technical productivity at the expense of noneconomic variables that are strategic in the development process. [See ECONOMIC GROWTH, article on NONECONOMIC ASPECTS.]

The impact of technical assistance might also be greater if additional research were undertaken on the special problems of adapting techniques of production to the special circumstances of the poor countries. Not only should research be directed toward new scientific advances of particular utility to underdeveloped economies, but the problems of diffusing the new technology and gaining its acceptance in the recipient society must also be solved.

Further, attention should be given to the possible means of coordinating the many different actual and potential sources of foreign assistance and to feasible arrangements for giving greater continuity to the flow of aid.

Finally, on the basis of accumulated experience in a variety of countries it would be useful to have a number of case studies of foreign aid as a basis for a comparative study of the conditions under which different types of aid have proved effective.

GERALD M. MEIER

[See also COMMUNITY, article on COMMUNITY DEVELOPMENT; ECONOMIC GROWTH; PLANNING, ECONOMIC, article on DEVELOPMENT PLANNING; TECHNICAL ASSISTANCE.]

BIBLIOGRAPHY

ALTER, G. M. 1961 The Servicing of Foreign Capital Inflows by Underdeveloped Countries. Pages 139–162 in International Economic Association, Economic Development for Latin America. Edited by Howard S. Ellis. New York: St. Martins.

ASHER, ROBERT E. 1961 Grants, Loans, and Local Currencies: Their Role in Foreign Aid. Washington: Brookings Institution.

BENHAM, FREDERIC C. 1961 Economic Aid to Underdeveloped Countries. Oxford Univ. Press.

BERLINER, JOSEPH S. 1958 Soviet Economic Aid: The New Aid and Trade Policy in Underdeveloped Countries. New York: Praeger.

BROWN, WILLIAM A.; and OPIE, REDVERS 1953 American Foreign Assistance. Washington: Brookings Institution.

CHENERY, HOLLIS B.; and STROUT, ALAN M. 1966 Foreign Assistance and Economic Development. American Economic Review 56:679–733.

FEI, J. C. H.; and PAAUW, D. S. 1965 Foreign Assistance and Self-help: A Reappraisal of Development Finance. Review of Economics and Statistics 47:251–267.

Foreign Grants and Credits by the United States Government. → Issued since 1948, under various titles, by the U.S. Department of Commerce, Office of Business Economics. Reports prior to No. 15 (1948) are classified restricted and are available only to authorized officials of the U.S. Government. See especially the issue for 1952, page 81, Appendix B.

HIGGINS, BENJAMIN 1962 United Nations and U.S. Foreign Economic Policy. Homewood, Ill.: Irwin.

LITTLE, I. M. D.; and CLIFFORD, J. M. (1965) 1966 International Aid: A Discussion of the Flow of Public Resources From Rich to Poor Countries, With Particular Reference to British Policy. London: Allen & Unwin; Chicago: Aldine.

NEALE, ALAN D. 1961 The Flow of Resources From Rich to Poor. Cambridge, Mass.: Harvard Univ., Center for International Affairs.

OHLIN, GORAN 1966 Foreign Aid Policies Reconsidered. Paris: Organization for Economic Cooperation and Development, Development Center.

PINCUS, JOHN A. 1965 Economic Aid and International Cost Sharing. Baltimore: Johns Hopkins Press.

ROSENSTEIN-RODAN, P. N. 1961 International Aid for Underdeveloped Countries. Review of Economics and Statistics 43:107–138.

SINGER, H. W. 1965 External Aid: For Plans or Projects? Economic Journal 75:539–545.

UN, DEPARTMENT OF ECONOMIC AND SOCIAL AFFAIRS 1961 International Flow of Long-term Capital and Official Donations: 1951–1959. New York: United Nations. → See especially page 34, Table 16.

UN, SECRETARY-GENERAL 1961 International Economic Assistance to the Less-developed Countries: Report to the Economic and Social Council. New York: United Nations. → See especially page 48.

UN, SECRETARY-GENERAL 1962 The United Nations Development Decade; Proposals for Action: Report. New York: United Nations.

UN, STATISTICAL OFFICE 1961 Statistical Yearbook, 1960. New York: United Nations. → See especially Table 157, page 467. Copyright United Nations 1961. Data reproduced by permission.

U.S. CONGRESS, HOUSE, COMMITTEE ON APPROPRIATION Foreign Operations Appropriations: Hearings. → See especially the hearings for 1963.

U.S. CONGRESS, JOINT ECONOMIC COMMITTEE 1961 Economic Policies Toward Less Developed Countries. 87th Congress, 1st Session. Washington: Government Printing Office.

U.S. NATIONAL ADVISORY COUNCIL ON INTERNATIONAL MONETARY AND FINANCIAL PROBLEMS Report of Activities. → Published since 1945.

WOLF, CHARLES JR. 1960 Foreign Aid: Theory and Practice in Southern Asia. Princeton Univ. Press.

FOREIGN POLICY

For half a century the making of foreign policy has been studied in Western democratic countries as a field of specialization separate from the making of public policy in general. This intellectual differentiation rests upon implicit and explicit assumptions about the way the foreign policy field differs from other areas of public policy. The leading assumption is that foreign policy is "more important" than other policy areas because it concerns national interests, rather than special interests, and more fundamental values. A second assumption builds upon the first: since foreign policy questions evoke a different political response, it is assumed that political institutions function differently when they confront foreign policy issues. In addition, of course, different institutions are also involved, in that some governmental agencies are concerned exclusively or substantially with foreign policy. There is growing uncertainty among political scientists, in the United States at least, as to the validity of these assumptions. There is also considerable skepticism concerning the theoretical value of treating foreign policy processes as analytically distinctive—a skepticism that will undoubtedly draw all the different public policy research fields closer together in the future. Nevertheless, the present state of our knowledge reflects, for better or worse, a set of beliefs about the uniqueness of foreign policy processes within the political order.

This orientation toward foreign policy making can be traced to World War I and the events leading up to it—although it might have developed in the United States in any case, since these were America's first years of great-power status and a period in which increasing attention was given to foreign relations. In the United States the war experience convinced some people that isolationism was no longer an appropriate response to international problems and that the United States must remain actively involved in the affairs of the world. Foreign policy became, for these people, the most important area of public policy, and responsible international participation the only viable political stance. And in both England and the United States the war gave rise to movements to end the traditional secretive practices of the world's statesmen and diplomats, movements that found concrete expression in Wilson's plea for "open covenants of peace, openly arrived at" and in the conference diplomacy of the League of Nations. Points One and Fourteen, and Wilsonian philosophy generally, were major building blocks in the progressive "democratization" of foreign policy.

Logically, this struggle for greater public participation in, and control over, foreign relations could have resulted in the assimilation of foreign policy to the working principles and practices of everyday politics in democratic countries. That it has not may be attributed to the prior claim for the "primacy of foreign policy," to the ineluctable requirements of secrecy imposed by the demands of national political and military strategies, and to the small amount of interest in foreign policy on the part of the general public.

Nevertheless, the study of foreign policy making was permanently affected by the liberal, rationalist, democratic ideology, with its twin convictions that the people, once they were educated, would make liberal and wise decisions in foreign policy and that man could improve his political institutions and their policy outputs if he would only think about them intelligently. These convictions explain the focus of attention, down to the present day, on the search for "better" ways to handle foreign policy, both organizationally and politically, so that public values and common sense might be more freely admitted into policy-making circles, and "better" policies (that is, responsible international participation) might eventuate.

The bulk of scholarly enterprise in the field of foreign policy making lies along one or the other of these two lines of concern, which I shall summarize here as "rationality" and "ideology." By "rationality" I mean a concern for the organization and structure of policy making which generally (but by no means exclusively) reflects a belief that certain policy-making relationships or arrangements can be found that are for one reason or another more "rational" than any others—that is to say, better designed to implement the values and decisions of intelligent and responsible foreign policy makers. By "ideology" I mean a concern for democratic control of foreign policy making which generally (although, again, not exclusively) reflects a belief that foreign policy decisions should be made by politically responsive or responsible individuals or groups and that the foreign policy of a democratic society can be wise and strong only to the extent that it commands the understanding and support of the public. Cutting across these two major approaches to the subject of foreign policy making are three different levels of analysis: the individual, the institutional, and the systemic. There are thus six major classifications, or clusters, into which the political scientist's study of foreign policy making may be conveniently divided for explanatory purposes. We shall look at each of these in turn, largely in the American context, since by its intellectual antecedents and history this subject has been of interest predominantly to American scholars. Having done this, we will be in a better position to identify and discuss research on foreign policy making in other countries and research through cross-national comparisons.

The rational approaches

Rational–institutional approach. The central focus of the study of foreign policy making has long been on the institutions of government that are chiefly responsible for the formulation and administration of foreign policy. And in the present period, as in the past, the motivating force seems to be the uncovering of more efficient, effective ways of organizing the policy-making machinery so that it rationally serves the interests or purposes of the analyst, whether these purposes are economy, speed of decision, singularity of authority, or coherence in execution. The executive departments and agencies—the Executive Office of the President, the Department of State, the Foreign Service, the Department of Defense, the Central Intelligence Agency, the U.S. Information Agency, the Peace Corps—have been studied and, in many cases, restudied from different perspectives in the various historical periods that mark America's development as a major power in world affairs. And certain of the functions of these institutions have come in for some scrutiny—diplomacy, for one, because the work of the diplomat is involved in so many of the processes of foreign policy making and execution, and intelligence, for another, because of the steady enlargement in the scope of covert political operations. Some examples of studies in this area are the works by Ransom (1958), Ilchman (1961), and McCamy (1964) on the executive side and Carroll (1958) on the congressional side.

In recent years, also, growing attention has been paid to the planning function in foreign affairs; this has been in response to the fear that without the assignment of adequate institutional responsibilities for thinking about the future, no one will have the time to give advance thought to emerging problems and to their avoidance or solution. (Current concern with foreign policy planning represents, perhaps better than anything else, the faith that political problems, like scientific or engineering problems, can be solved by the timely application of rational thought and organization.)

Because of the complexity of the institutional framework for making foreign policy and the frequency with which the institutions are altered either formally or through usage, the rational–institutional outlook has also focused on interagency coordination as a technique for rationalizing the continuously unwieldy processes of foreign policy

formulation and agreement within the government. Actually, the phrase "administration of foreign affairs" refers as much to the coordination of powerful and nearly autonomous foreign policy agencies both at home and "in the field" as it does to the processes of policy making and execution within these agencies (Brookings Institution 1960). The development of high-level coordinating mechanisms like the National Security Council has drawn the interest of scholars, government officials, and members of Congress (see Hammond 1961) who have feared that the coordinating institutions may take over important policy-making functions.

Rational–individual approach. The development of the social sciences, especially of psychology, under the impetus of the political and social crises of World War II resulted in a new orientation toward the individual as the organizing point for political research. In opposition to what was felt to be the empty formalism of traditional institutional and administrative analyses, some students of foreign policy making shifted their focus to individuals and the ways in which they perceived the internal and external factors that came to bear on their institutional settings. The major products of this new line of inquiry have been decision-making studies (e.g., Snyder et al. 1962) that attempt to understand both the factors in human choice and the logic of administrative structure in the foreign policy field by examining the processes of individual and group decision making in institutional settings.

Recent developments in organization theory, although based on research in other types of institutions (e.g., Cyert & March 1963), have considerable relevance to the study of behavior in foreign policy agencies and should be an important influence on future research. The behavior of individuals when they occupy policy-making roles is central to the analysis of decision making, in game models as in the real world, and it explains the continuing interest in biographies and memoirs of policy officials. Students of foreign policy look to political biography, both conventional and psychoanalytic (see George & George 1956), for life experiences that help to illuminate the relations between individuals possessing particular personality types, backgrounds, and the like and the operating norms of particular policy-making offices.

Rational–systemic approach. At still another level, the search for more rational arrangements of organization and structure in the foreign policy field has led scholars to study the patterned interactions of individuals and institutions that constitute the universe of foreign policy making. These studies of interactions or systems cover dyadic relationships between political actors as well as more inclusive studies of how men and institutions handle problems or produce policies. And if the focus, on the individual level, is on reality as perceived by persons in policy-making roles, here the focus may be said to be on the objective reality created by the interactions of two or more political institutions.

The interactions of individuals and institutions involve accommodations of power and interest that we customarily associate with politics rather than administration. This is the case whether the individuals or institutions stand in some hierarchical relationship to one another or are relatively autonomous, deriving their power independently from other sources. Yet much of the scholarly work at the systemic level overlooks these sources of conflicts of power and interest, approaching the subject instead as if there were some arrangements of the foreign-policy-making institutions of government that were rationally or optimally designed to achieve a superior kind of foreign policy. Some commonly studied partial systems of foreign policy making, described in the phrases "executive–legislative relations" and "bipartisanship," are often treated in this way. The three-cornered relationship of the president, his party in Congress, and the opposition party in Congress has often been examined (e.g., Woodrow Wilson Foundation 1952) to see if a way could be discovered to remove the friction in the system that is presumed to interfere with the smooth functioning of a unified, national-interest-oriented policy machinery. [See BIPARTISANSHIP.]

Recent scholarship, however, has begun to change this emphasis on the structural aspects of foreign policy interactions. Instead of attempting to eliminate or bypass the political features of foreign-policy-making systems by emphasizing administrative arrangements, contemporary scholars have been concentrating precisely on these features (Huntington 1961; Robinson 1962; Schilling et al. 1962). They have begun to study the interactions of individuals within and between foreign policy agencies as sets of bargaining relationships, which are similar to the bargaining processes that take place in other areas of public and political life where competitions of power and of interest are more overt and accepted. This bargaining orientation is thus less committed to the "rational" aspect of foreign policy making; its normative implications tend rather to be those of science in general —that is, one needs to understand how a system operates before one can calculate the consequences of attempting to make any given change in it.

Another body of literature that might appropriately be described in this category consists of "case studies" that reconstruct the way specific issues, policies, or events were handled by the governmental participants in the foreign-policy-making process. These are more likely to be historical–descriptive (e.g., Jones 1955) than analytical in nature, and they find their rationale in the assumption that the mysteries of the governmental process will yield to the accumulated weight of information on how the system has actually worked in specific instances in the past.

The ideological approaches

The second major approach to the study of foreign policy making I have called "ideological," because in one form or another it is concerned with the democratization of foreign policy—with the possibilities and procedures for introducing a substantial measure of public values into every stage in the formulation of foreign policy. This approach starts from the general premise that the foreign policy area has different roots and different requirements of interest and support in the political system than do other policy areas. It then branches out in two directions. One line of inquiry, based explicitly on the primacy of the foreign policy area over other policy areas, seeks to alter the bases of interest and support in order to optimize public knowledge of, participation in, and control over, foreign policy decision making. A second line of inquiry seeks to discover what the different roots and requirements of interest and support are, in order to understand the operative political processes, sometimes for the purpose of facilitating democratic control and sometimes for more general social science purposes. In both of these lines of inquiry, the central objects of study are most often either nongovernmental groups or the interactions between the nongovernmental and the official elements.

Ideological–institutional approach. Just as the foreign policy institutions of government have been the central focus of study for those seeking better modes of organizing the foreign policy machinery, so the institutions of nongovernmental foreign policy activity have come in for a large share of the attention of those interested in a greater democratic perspective for foreign policy. In this context, foreign policy has benefited from an inclination in political science generally to explore the group basis of politics; thus, the role of organized interest groups in foreign policy making has become an important area of study (Cohen 1959). Much of this research has been limited to the positions, interests, and demands of particular organizations, and thus it has shared in the empty formalism of some of the rational–institutional studies. But increasingly, interest-group activities are being examined at the points where they intersect the domains of other participants in the process of foreign policy making: that is, they are more and more being treated as parts of a political system. And attention is also being turned to skill groups of a comparatively unorganized nature, such as scientists and "academic strategists," which are playing a larger role in the technical complexities of foreign policy making in a nuclear environment (Gilpin & Wright 1964).

The widespread conviction that a sound and stable foreign policy requires an interested, informed, intelligent public opinion has led to extensive, although far from satisfactory, investigations of the major channels through which foreign policy attitudes and information are transmitted to public audiences. The role of the universities as factors in the development of interest in, and knowledge about, foreign affairs has been a subject of study for some years, although precise measures of the impact of educational institutions at all levels on the foreign policy thinking of students are still lacking. The media of mass communication have been intensively scrutinized for many years (see Hero 1959), although their impact on foreign policy attitudes and information is still largely a matter of intelligent speculation (guided by deep concern) rather than of demonstrable fact.

It was noted above that most of the ideologically oriented studies of foreign policy making were nongovernmental in nature. An important exception concerns the treatment of the U.S. Congress. Part of the study of Congress as a foreign-policy-making institution is approached from the point of view of clarifying its internal organization and procedures and of understanding its interactions as part of the governmental process; hence, it was discussed under the rational–institutional heading. But important parts of this study of Congress are approached from the point of view of understanding and improving its representative role in the foreign policy field, and so they merit inclusion here also. This ideological perspective on the Congress is concerned with that body as a major object of public representation on foreign policy matters and as a channel through which public preferences and aspirations are made a constituent ingredient of foreign policy (Dahl 1950).

Ideological–individual approach. One of the most important and durable approaches to the subject of popular participation in foreign policy making has been through public opinion studies—through sampling and aggregating the attitudes of ordinary citizens. These studies find their rationale in the belief that if foreign policy were to be formulated both democratically and wisely, the average man would have to be interested, well-informed, and enlightened. And in order to discover the conditions of public interest, information, and attitudes at any point in time, as well as possible changes in these conditions over time, it has been necessary to explore the many dimensions of public opinion on foreign policy. In fact, the phrase "public opinion and foreign policy" generally refers to the foreign policy outlook of ordinary citizens rather than of those groups or publics that might be politically more effective in presenting their views.

After thirty years of public opinion research, the data on public attitudes toward foreign policy questions have reached mountainous proportions and have formed the bases for many studies of the public opinion process, both in its political and its psychological dimensions (see especially Almond 1950; Scott & Withey 1958; Deutsch & Edinger 1959). Normatively, these data, which continually show the large majority of the population to be uninterested and uninformed on foreign policy, have been used to justify and guide governmental and private efforts to capture public attention and to enlighten the public on foreign policy matters.

A growing feeling that data drawn from samples of the general population have already yielded whatever significance they contain is leading to new directions in research on public opinion. Scholars are beginning to use opinion data more imaginatively, seeking to relate the foreign policy opinions of attentive and interested individuals to more formal steps in governmental foreign policy making. Similarly, students of public opinion are focusing their attention more narrowly on the leadership elements among nongovernmental groups—on those persons who, by virtue of their special positions or qualifications, have an especially powerful role in shaping the views and the policies of public groups. [See PUBLIC OPINION; see also Rosenau 1963.]

Ideological–systemic approach. Careful study of the processes of public participation and control in foreign policy making has led rather directly to the systemic level, since it has been readily observed that any effort to explore the influence of public factors on governmental decision makers almost automatically compels the investigator to study the patterns of interaction between public and governmental actors. The broadest studies of a systemic variety are, once again, case studies of the interactions of the governmental and the non-governmental spheres as they have actually taken shape in a particular policy-making circumstance (e.g., Cohen 1957; Bauer et al. 1963) or as they may be traced out through a detailed analysis of how a single nongovernmental group or institution confronts the governmental process (Cohen 1963). Still lacking in this effort to understand how the public influences foreign policy making, however, are studies at the decision-making points to establish with some accuracy the constraints and opportunities that foreign policy officials read into the public mood: too often the subject is approached as if "the public" were always a source—if not *the* source—of constraints on wise governmental initiative and decision making in foreign policy.

A more circumscribed but still striking pattern of interactions that has been studied from the perspective of "who is to control" is the civil–military relationship. For many years the main concerns of these studies were the devices and techniques for maintaining civilian—hence, ultimately, public—control over military personnel and institutions, which were generally presumed to pose a threat to democratic government by their very existence, if not by their hidden aspirations to power. This simplistic viewpoint has given way in recent years to more complex approaches to the question of civil versus military contributions to public policy, since the military have perforce been accorded a larger role even while civilian authority has been substantially strengthened (Stein 1963).

Research needs

The persistent and increasingly imaginative exploitation of the approaches to the study of foreign policy making discussed above has taught us a great deal about the subject, but in a rather segmented way. This review points up how little there is in the way of explicit general models of the foreign-policy-making process—or, more precisely, processes, since there is no single combination of forces that is always operative and no single path that is followed in every instance. While much necessary work remains to be done in each of the above classifications before we can lay claim to confident understanding of how the parts of the foreign-policy-making system operate, such work would be helped immeasurably by more elaborate theories governing the whole system of foreign policy making.

In addition to a dearth of general theories, and perhaps as a contributing factor to that dearth, there has been very little comparative analysis in

the study of foreign policy making. Rather, our analyses of institutions, individuals, and even systems have been singular and for that reason not always cumulative. At the present time we cannot have very great confidence in the generality of our hypotheses and insights. Comparisons are possible between similar institutions or similar policy-making functions in different countries or different political settings, or with respect to the same institutions or functions operating in different historical periods. It is also possible to compare the behavior and interactions of participants across a representative range of policy issues arising in any one political system. Such comparative analyses seem to be a very promising means of formulating a generally applicable model of foreign policy making.

We noted at the beginning of this article that the subject of foreign policy making has been most extensively pursued in the United States. Much less work—and much less sophisticated work—has been done on foreign policy making elsewhere in the world. How does one account for this situation?

In the first place, the historical circumstances and the political setting that have inspired this research in the United States have not been present to any important extent in other countries. Even in Great Britain, where the movement for open diplomacy had some force during World War I, the stronger political traditions of executive discretion in foreign affairs have discouraged an open exploration of foreign policy making, especially where one could detect in that exploration some aspirations for greater public participation. In countries that did not undergo political experiences comparable to those of the United States, the political culture has directed the attention of scholars to other kinds of problems.

Second, interest in modern methods of social science research has developed more slowly elsewhere in the world than in the United States. Apart from public opinion research, which has had an extensive development, research on foreign policy making that has been done in other countries has usually been historical–descriptive in nature and can be characterized as rational–institutional. With few exceptions (e.g., Frankel 1963), the major works on foreign policy making in countries other than the United States have dealt with the formal administrative apparatus for the conduct of foreign relations.

Third, the lack of a tradition of comparative analysis in this field has meant that even American scholars have been slow to turn their attention to aspects of foreign policy making in other countries. Quality studies dealing with individual countries have only recently started to appear (e.g., Speier & Davison 1957; Bishop 1961; Mendel 1961); genuinely comparative studies have still to be made.

There is no reason to believe that our growing knowledge of foreign-policy-making processes in the United States will help us to understand what these processes are like in other countries: we have long since learned that propositions drawn from the American political system are of limited relevance to other political contexts. The comparative study of political systems is now expanding rapidly; the comparative study of foreign-policy-making processes could be made an important part of that endeavor.

BERNARD C. COHEN

[See also CIVIL–MILITARY RELATIONS; INTERNATIONAL RELATIONS; MILITARY POLICY; NATIONAL INTEREST; NATIONAL SECURITY; PUBLIC POLICY; SCIENCE, article on SCIENCE–GOVERNMENT RELATIONS.]

BIBLIOGRAPHY

ALMOND, GABRIEL A. (1950) 1960 *The American People and Foreign Policy.* New York: Praeger.

BAUER, RAYMOND A.; POOL, ITHIEL DE SOLA; and DEXTER, L. A. 1963 *American Business and Public Policy: The Politics of Foreign Trade.* New York: Atherton.

BISHOP, DONALD G. 1961 *The Administration of British Foreign Relations.* Syracuse Univ. Press.

BROOKINGS INSTITUTION, WASHINGTON, D.C. 1960 *United States Foreign Policy: The Formulation and Administration of United States Foreign Policy.* Washington: Government Printing Office.

CARROLL, HOLBERT N. 1958 *The House of Representatives and Foreign Affairs.* Univ. of Pittsburgh Press. → A paperback edition was published in 1966 by Little.

COHEN, BERNARD C. 1957 *The Political Process and Foreign Policy: The Making of the Japanese Peace Settlement.* Princeton Univ. Press.

COHEN, BERNARD C. 1959 *The Influence of Non-governmental Groups on Foreign Policy-making.* Boston: World Peace Foundation.

COHEN, BERNARD C. 1963 *The Press and Foreign Policy.* Princeton Univ. Press.

CYERT, RICHARD M.; and MARCH, JAMES G. 1963 *A Behavioral Theory of the Firm.* Englewood Cliffs, N.J.: Prentice-Hall.

DAHL, ROBERT A. 1950 *Congress and Foreign Policy.* New York: Harcourt.

DEUTSCH, KARL W.; and EDINGER, LOUIS J. 1959 *Germany Rejoins the Powers: Mass Opinion, Interest Groups, and Elites in Contemporary German Foreign Policy.* Stanford Univ. Press.

FRANKEL, JOSEPH 1963 *The Making of Foreign Policy: An Analysis of Decision-making.* Oxford Univ. Press.

GEORGE, ALEXANDER L.; and GEORGE, JULIETTE 1956 *Woodrow Wilson and Colonel House.* New York: Day.

GILPIN, ROBERT; and WRIGHT, CHRISTOPHER (editors) 1964 *Scientists and National Policy-making.* New York: Columbia Univ. Press.

HAMMOND, PAUL Y. 1961 *Organizing for Defense: The American Military Establishment in the Twentieth Century.* Princeton Univ. Press.

HERO, ALFRED O. 1959 *Mass Media and World Affairs.* Boston: World Peace Foundation.

HILSMAN, ROGER 1956 *Strategic Intelligence and National Decisions.* Glencoe, Ill.: Free Press.

HUNTINGTON, SAMUEL P. 1961 *The Common Defense: Strategic Programs in National Politics.* New York: Columbia Univ. Press.

ILCHMAN, WARREN F. 1961 *Professional Diplomacy in the United States, 1779–1939: A Study in Administrative History.* Univ. of Chicago Press.

JONES, JOSEPH M. 1955 *The Fifteen Weeks: February 21–June 5, 1947.* New York: Viking.

KOGAN, NORMAN 1963 *The Politics of Italian Foreign Policy.* New York: Praeger.

MCCAMY, JAMES L. 1964 *Conduct of the New Diplomacy.* New York: Harper.

MENDEL, DOUGLAS H. 1961 *The Japanese People and Foreign Policy: A Study of Public Opinion in Posttreaty Japan.* Berkeley: Univ. of California Press.

PHILLIPS, CLAUDE S. JR. 1964 *The Development of Nigerian Foreign Policy.* Evanston, Ill.: Northwestern Univ. Press.

RANSOM, HARRY H. 1958 *Central Intelligence and National Security.* Cambridge, Mass.: Harvard Univ. Press.

ROBINSON, JAMES A. 1962 *Congress and Foreign Policy-making: A Study in Legislative Influence and Initiative.* Homewood, Ill.: Dorsey.

ROSENAU, JAMES N. 1963 *National Leadership and Foreign Policy: A Case Study in the Mobilization of Public Support.* Princeton Univ. Press.

SCHILLING, WARNER R.; HAMMOND, P. Y.; and SNYDER, G. H. 1962 *Strategy, Politics and Defense Budgets.* New York: Columbia Univ. Press.

SCOTT, WILLIAM A.; and WITHEY, STEPHEN B. 1958 *The United States and the United Nations: The Public View, 1945–1955.* New York: Manhattan.

SNYDER, RICHARD C.; BRUCK, H. W.; and SAPIN, B. (editors) 1962 *Foreign Policy Decision Making: An Approach to the Study of International Politics.* New York: Free Press.

SPEIER, HANS; and DAVISON, W. PHILLIPS (editors) 1957 *West German Leadership and Foreign Policy.* Evanston, Ill.: Row, Peterson.

STEIN, HAROLD (editor) 1963 *American Civil–Military Decisions: A Book of Case Studies.* Birmingham: Univ. of Alabama Press.

U.S. CONGRESS, SENATE, COMMITTEE ON GOVERNMENT OPERATIONS 1961 *Organizing for National Security.* Inquiry of the Subcommittee on National Policy Machinery. Washington: Government Printing Office.

WOODROW WILSON FOUNDATION 1952 *United States Foreign Policy: Its Organization and Control.* A report by William Y. Elliott. New York: Columbia Univ. Press.

FOREIGN TRADE

See INTERNATIONAL TRADE.

FORENSIC PSYCHIATRY

See under PSYCHIATRY.

FORGETTING

It seems quite unnecessary to be concerned with a definition of "forgetting." Each of us has had innumerable experiences, often painful, with this phenomenon, and we know that, in general, the longer the period between the point at which we learn something and the point at which we try to remember it, the less likely we are to remember correctly. The growth of living organisms is always accompanied by deterioration processes. Forgetting is the behavioral deterioration process that may be likened to organic deterioration and is in opposition to the growth process called "learning." We do not, in fact, know much about the organic or physiological correlates of forgetting, and it is not easy to understand why, in the evolutionary process, forgetting should remain so powerful a process in man when, from almost any point of view, it is unadaptive. It is almost as if we have "room" for only so much learning, and when more learning is to be added than the room will hold, some of the old learning must go. Indeed, in a manner of speaking, the theories of forgetting are based on this notion.

Learning must occur before forgetting can occur. This fact, seemingly trivial, is the key to an understanding of the processes causing forgetting and must also be the foundation of any applied program aimed at retarding forgetting.

Sources of evidence

A review of the experimental studies of forgetting can but lead to the impression that the evidence on which we base our knowledge of forgetting comes from quite a restricted set of materials and procedures, and thus our generalizations about forgetting may be severely restricted. It is a fact that most of our data come from what is classically known as rote-learning tasks, and the subjects for experimentation have been preponderantly college students. The study of the forgetting of motor skills has lagged; the memory for ideas, concepts, and principles has never been systematically investigated. Yet, when probes into these areas have been made, the results have given us no reason to believe that the basic laws are different from those derived from rote-learning tasks. The extensive use of college students—whose use has not been dictated by theoretical concern but has been largely a matter of convenience—may make us wary of generalizing these conclusions to all ages and ability levels. But again, the evidence available does not indicate that any serious distortions in the laws of forgetting are attend-

ant upon the particular subjects that have been used in experimental work.

Nonsense syllables and nonwords. We must look to the tasks and materials from which most of our contemporary knowledge of forgetting is derived. The materials are simple verbal units. These may be words, or they may be a sequence of letters not found in English dictionaries. Calling these latter units "nonsense syllables," or "nonsense material," has produced considerable misunderstanding. It has often been assumed that a nonsense syllable (for example, RUH) is an artificial unit which removes the study employing such units from contact with real-life situations. It might be argued that experimentation is always, in fact, artificial (a vacuum does not exist in nature) and that it is only by such procedures that fundamental laws are obtained, because these procedures allow for the control of variables. In fact, the original use of nonsense syllables by Ebbinghaus in his pioneering studies on memory was, to a large extent, based on this premise. But there are three other facts that must be set forth and that may be more critical than an argument based on a philosophy of science.

To say that a nonsense syllable is not related to real life is simply erroneous. A word common to an adult must be, in essence, a nonsense syllable to a child before its meaning is acquired. The use of verbal units not in dictionaries may be tapping the same or similar processes that are involved when the child changes from a nonverbal organism to an organism with a verbal repertoire that can be correctly applied. Or a nonsense syllable may be likened to a word in a foreign language, and thus to the college student it is anything but removed from real life.

The second point is that a derogation of the use of nonsense syllables assumes a dichotomy between what is meaningful and what is nonsense. But measurements of meaning, by any of many techniques, do not support such a schism. There is a continuum between words and nonwords. Many so-called nonsense syllables have greater meaning than some words. Nonsense words, like "real" words, have varying affective connotations. Indeed, it could probably be demonstrated that affective reactions to such nonsense syllables as WOR are much more intense than those to such common words as THE. A nonsense unit, therefore, should mean only a word that does not appear as an entry in a dictionary, but this distinction per se between words and nonwords appears to have little psychological relevance.

The third reason for not viewing nonwords as

something significantly apart from words is probably the most critical when reference is made to the use of these materials only in the study of forgetting. This reason is simply that the evidence indicates that words and nonwords "behave" the same as far as forgetting is concerned. This point will be given elaboration at a later point in the discussion.

Manner of presenting verbal units.   In the bulk of the studies on forgetting, verbal units are formed into lists, so that in a single task the subject learns several items. The items might be formed into a *serial* list in which the subject must learn to reproduce not only the items but also a particular order of the items. A second widely used type of list is the paired-associate list. The subject is presented a series of pairs and is required to learn to reproduce the second member of each pair when the first member is shown alone. Acquiring the order of the pairs is not a part of the task; indeed, the investigator usually prevents his subject from learning the order by presenting the pairs in a different order from time to time. The paired-associate task is a counterpart of the task of learning a vocabulary of a foreign language, in which the first member of the pair is a word in the learner's native language and the second member is its foreign equivalent.

Other tasks that have also been used include prose passages, sentences, and lists of words to be recalled in any order. But for reasons that need not be detailed here, at the present stage in the development of psychological research, the paired-associate task possesses properties that make it a superior vehicle for studying forgetting, and much of the discussion will be cast around this task. This does not imply that there is evidence that forgetting varies as a function of the task. Such comparisons are difficult to make, although insofar as they have been made there is no convincing evidence that the type of task is a critical variable in the study of forgetting.

Rapid single-unit technique.   Most of the research on forgetting has been with multiple-unit tasks (for example, several pairs of items in a paired-associate task). What must be considered a most amazing technical breakthrough was made in 1959 by Lloyd R. Peterson and Margaret J. Peterson. These investigators were able to devise a situation in which a *single* verbal unit was presented for learning and the subsequent course of forgetting could be measured over a period of time. A syllable, such as RZL, was presented for study for two seconds. Then, in order to prevent the subject from rehearsing the syllable, he was given a neutral task (for example, counting) for a few seconds. Finally, he was asked to recall the syllable originally shown to him. The startling fact is that lawful and reliable forgetting curves were obtained in which forgetting was essentially complete (the subject could not reproduce the unit) after 20 *seconds*. The exploitation of this technique has been, and is being, pursued by many investigators. The classical studies have used forgetting intervals of hours or days, and thus the sheer labor and mechanical problems in the performance of these studies were great. Although it is perhaps too early to say with assurance that the laws of forgetting observed under the Peterson–Peterson technique are the same as those for classical studies, the evidence thus far points strongly to this conclusion. If this is true, the study of forgetting may proceed at a pace hitherto impossible with classical procedures. In the Peterson–Peterson technique, seconds are comparable to hours or even days with the classical list method.

Single-task studies of forgetting

We may turn next to an examination of the reliable experimental facts in single-task studies of forgetting. A distinction must be drawn between single-task and multiple-task studies if we are to focus on the processes believed critical for an understanding of forgetting.

The laboratory situation can be described as follows. A subject who has not previously served in a laboratory experiment involving verbal learning is given a single list of verbal units to learn. These are normally presented over and over, each unit being exposed for a short interval of time (for example, two seconds), until the subject is just able to reproduce the list perfectly. Assume, further, that the subject returns 24 hours later and is asked to recall all of the units he can. We ask now about the general quantitative aspects of forgetting in such a situation and, in particular, what variables cause the amount of forgetting to vary.

Amount forgotten.   Over the 24-hour period, the subject will forget from 15 to 20 per cent of the units. Thus, if the list contained ten paired associates, we will expect about eight of these to be recalled correctly. Under the conditions specified above, this amount of forgetting remains fairly constant across a wide range of materials and tasks. Some gross measures may indicate a degree of forgetting as great as 30 per cent, but when refined techniques of measurement are used, the 15 to 20 per cent loss will usually be found. With intervals longer than 24 hours, more forgetting will, of course, occur, but we do not know with any precision the rate of fall for many longer intervals with various materials. Because of the relatively large amount of data available on forgetting after 24 hours, we will use this interval as a basic reference interval.

Significance of the degree of learning.   We may now ask about variables that influence the amount of forgetting during the 24-hour period. The facts, as viewed at the present time, provide a conclusion that seems not only to be opposite to that expected as research in an area proceeds but also opposite to that often expected according to "common sense." For we can name only one variable that substantially influences the rate of forgetting in the single-task situation. Obviously, considerable clarification and elaboration are needed.

Characteristics of the verbal units will produce enormous differences in the rate at which the list is learned. As might be expected, a list of common words is learned much more rapidly than a list of difficult nonwords. The differences are so large that even the casual reader will be convinced that this is true. Thus, it is clear that a list of five 3-letter words, such as CAT, PEN, BUS, FAR, and ELK, would be learned more rapidly than a list of five nonwords, such as RZL, DBQ, HFG, BJX, and PCR. Technically, we say the words have a higher level of meaningfulness than do the nonwords. But if both sets are learned to an equal degree, they will be equally remembered 24 hours later. The critical point is the "equal degree of learning," because degree of learning is the one variable that does influence the amount of forgetting. This can be demonstrated in two ways. First, when the number of practice trials is varied within a given task, it will be found that the greater the number of practice trials, the less the forgetting. Second, when units within the task are examined, one may note that those units which have been given correctly many times during learning will prove to be remembered better after 24 hours than those given correctly only a few times. So we say that if the degree of learning is equal for materials of widely different meaningfulness, they will be forgotten at the same rate.

Meaning related to degree of learning.   The foregoing conclusion might seem contradictory to the experience of many, because most of us have long believed that retention of more meaningful material is better than that of less meaningful material. But this belief may have arisen as follows. If we spend an equal amount of time in learning the two kinds of material, retention of the list of words would assuredly be better after 24 hours than the retention of the list of nonwords. Even if a subject spent twice as much time studying the nonword list, retention of the words might still be better. This is because differences in rate of learning such lists vary so markedly that even after a longer study period on the nonwords the degree of learning will still be less than the degree of learning for words. But under such circumstances, the differences in amount remembered after 24 hours must be ascribed to the degree of learning achieved and not to the differences in the material. Differences in the material produce differences in learning, but if the level of learning achieved for materials of different difficulty prior to the introduction of the retention interval is equivalent, we may expect essentially equal amounts of forgetting, which, as noted earlier, will be about 15 to 20 per cent over 24 hours.

Similarity related to degree of learning.   Let us consider another variable that produces wide differences in learning. If the number of duplicated letters among nonwords is varied within a list of paired associates, the greater the number of duplicated letters, the more difficult it is to learn the task. Technically, this is called "variation in intralist formal similarity." But again, if the level of learning achieved for a list with high similarity is equivalent to that for a list with low similarity, the amount of forgetting will not differ measurably over a 24-hour period. The same situation will prevail if we use a list of synonyms and a list of words with very little similarity of meaning. The former will be more difficult to learn, but differences in forgetting cannot be demonstrated if the levels of learning attained are equivalent.

Individual differences in rate of learning.   The general principle that degree of learning is the only critical variable in the single-task situation can be pursued one step further. There is evidence leading to the conclusion that there are no individual differences in forgetting. One proposition that has been ubiquitous in psychological research is that any set of measurements will produce a distribution of reliable individual differences. Some individuals are slow learners; others are fast learners. Some have excellent depth perception; others have poor depth perception. Measurements on living organisms of all levels have supported the proposition that there is a consistent range of individual differences. To suggest that this proposition does not hold true for forgetting requires a careful exposition of the extent of the data available for its support.

For one characteristic of individuals, the data are quite clear. The rate at which a person learns a given task is not related to rate of forgetting. A subject who learns a list very slowly will show no more forgetting than a subject learning the same task very rapidly, if the level of learning attained is equivalent. Such a fact is not without some support in incidental observations. It is not unusual for students in the author's classes to observe (when discussing their performance in the course) that they do not learn rapidly, but once they have learned something well, they remember it well. A slow-learning student, therefore, may take much longer to achieve a level of learning attained by a rapid-learning student, but given the equivalent degree of learning, forgetting does not differ.

Rate of learning is, of course, only one of hundreds of characteristics on which people differ reliably. Some people are more emotional than others; some are more conservative than others. Do none of these many possible characteristics produce differences in rate of forgetting? Here the evidence is less convincing, but it is pointing toward the conclusion that if these characteristics are related to rate of forgetting, the magnitude of their effect is small.

Consider, for example, the following situation. Subjects of widely different learning abilities are given the same period of time to study a given task, and immediately following this study period they are tested. The test scores will show a wide range, indicating that rate of learning differed markedly among the subjects. After 24 hours, a recall test is given. The recall scores are then correlated with the scores taken immediately after learning. Such a procedure will produce very high correlations across a wide variety of materials. The high correlations can be taken to indicate again the strong relationship between degree of learning and retention. If there were wide individual differences in rate of forgetting that vitiate the relationship between learning and retention, such high correlations would not be found. This is to say that a given person's retention score can be predicted with a high degree of accuracy if only his learning score is known. Under such circumstances, it does not seem possible to attribute to individual differences a role of consequence in forgetting. That such a conclusion runs contrary to the conclusions concerning the role of individual differences in many other situations is indeed a puzzle, and perhaps future research will change the conclusion. But the available data allow at least a tentative conclusion that individual differences in forgetting are, at best, of very small magnitude.

Multiple tasks and forgetting theory

The reason for making the distinction between single-task forgetting and multiple-task situations may now be examined. Very early in the period in which the study of learning and memory was brought into the laboratory, it was discovered that if two tasks were learned in immediate succession and the subject's retention of the first task was then tested, severe forgetting was observed. That the second task was in some way responsible for this forgetting was shown by control conditions in which only the single task was learned and tested for retention.

Retroactive and proactive inhibition. The amount of forgetting produced by the learning of a second task, interpolated between the learning and recall of a first task, is called "retroactive inhibition." The amount of retroactive inhibition that can be produced in the laboratory is very great; under appropriate conditions recall of the first task can be reduced to zero.

The discovery of retroactive inhibition had two important consequences. First, it became an object of study per se, and hundreds of experiments have been performed in which such variables as the similarity between tasks, the degree of learning of the interpolated task, and various time relationships have been studied.

The second consequence of the work on retroactive inhibition is that it has largely set the theoretical thinking of investigators. This thinking has preponderantly tended toward the use of *interference* as a fundamental cause not only of forgetting observed in the retroactive situation but of all forgetting. Certainly the role of interference in retroactive inhibition cannot be disputed: the higher the similarity between the two tasks, the greater the amount of retroactive inhibition. Furthermore, subjects are regularly observed to give items from the interpolated task when they are asked to recall the first task. A theory built around an interference notion seemed quite appropriate.

In more recent years, a second source of interference was discovered that has only served to refine and reinforce the notion that interference must be a major cause of forgetting. This second source of interference is identified as "proactive inhibition." Again, a subject learns two tasks, but this time he is asked to recall the task subsequently learned. Of course, some time must elapse between the learning of the second task and the request for its recall to expect forgetting to occur, but given this situation, there will be greater forgetting than would occur for a single list. It is as if the originally learned task interferes with the recall or retention of the subsequently learned task. The magnitude of proactive inhibition increases with time between the learning of the second task and its recall. After 24 hours, we may expect the amount of forgetting produced by proaction to be as great as that produced by retroaction. The combined effects of both retroaction and proaction may be studied by having the subject learn three lists and then subsequently requesting the recall of the second.

Interference theory. The refinements in the interference theory have consisted of increased specification of the mechanisms involved. In order to study these mechanisms, certain fairly standard interference paradigms have been devised. The most widely used is known as the "A–B, A–C paradigm." This may be visualized as representing a paired-associate arrangement in two successive lists in which the left-hand unit (stimulus term) is identical in both lists and the right-hand unit (response term) differs. With the first list the subject learns to give a response to a specific stimulus, but with the second list he must learn a new response to the same stimulus. When the several items in the two lists have this relationship, interference or negative effects are observed in learning the second list.

Extinction and spontaneous recovery. It is an easy step to assume that the negative effect in learning the second list must somehow be related to the forgetting observed in the retention tests for either list at some later point in time. The evidence points to the fact that something akin to an extinction process occurs in learning the second list. More particularly, the associations developed in learning the first list are extinguished or unlearned in the process of learning the second list. Therefore, if immediately after learning the second list, recall of the first list is requested, serious retroactive inhibition should occur. It does; it is as if the response terms of the first list are not available to the subject. But now, assume that 24 hours elapse before recall of the first list is requested. Retroactive inhibition will occur, but it will be less in magnitude than the amount measured immediately after second-list learning. Independent evidence suggests that following extinction a form of spontaneous recovery occurs, just as in the case of an extinguished conditioned response. Such spontaneous recovery would account for the decreased retroactive inhibition observed after the 24-hour retention interval.

Next, let us examine the role of extinction and spontaneous recovery in proactive inhibition. If following learning of the second list there is a recovery over time of the associations in the first list, these recovered associations should interfere with the recall of the second list. The greater the recovery, the greater the interference; hence, such a mechanism would account for the fact that proactive inhibition increases with time.

The use of extinction and recovery mechanisms in an interference theory of forgetting has further implications. Suppose the second list is learned by distributed practice; that is, we carry out a trial or two, let an interval elapse, give another trial or two, another interval, and so on. These intervals, inserted in learning, should allow some spontaneous recovery of the first-list associations. But the next learning trials should produce some extinction of the first-list associations. Thus, over a series of such learning and rest cycles, we would have successive recovery and extinction cycles. Again, generalizing from work in other areas of learning, we find that such extinction–recovery cycles may lead to more permanent extinction of the first-list associations. Distributed practice on the second list, therefore, should decrease the amount of proactive inhibition. Tests of this proposition are positive. Indeed, when the distribution intervals are long (such as 24 hours), enormous reduction in proactive inhibition will occur. In general, it is fair to say that the use of extinction–recovery notions, as subprocesses under a general interference theory of forgetting, have proved very useful.

Rapid single-unit technique. Earlier we discussed the technique of studying retention of single items over very short intervals and, in addition, noted that near-complete forgetting had been observed in as short a period as 20 seconds. Experimental evaluations of this phenomenon have now made it fairly reasonable to assume that this rapid forgetting is produced by proactive interference. It is common to use a single subject many times in the single-item studies. The subject is given different units at different times, and retention is tested at various intervals following presentation. Thus, in effect, the subject builds up a repertoire of units as the experiment proceeds. If it is assumed that the previously presented units interfered proactively, the rapid forgetting of the item of the moment may be accounted for. The interpretation seems to hold. Given the appropriate arrangement of conditions, it can be shown that the greater the number of previous items presented, the greater the rate of forgetting the item at hand. The first item presented to the subject shows little, if any, forgetting over time. It seems reasonable to conclude, therefore, that we are not confronted with new principles of forgetting when studying retention of singly presented items over short intervals of time.

Pre-experimental associations. We now come to the final step in the analysis of the interference theory of forgetting. As previously discussed, when the subject learns a single list, forgetting will be approximately 15 to 20 per cent over 24 hours. The facts of retroactive and proactive inhibition produced in the laboratory made it reasonable to suspect that interference also accounted for this 15 per cent to 20 per cent loss. More particularly, it would appear that the interference must arise proactively from sources outside the laboratory. The reasoning is as follows. Assume that the subject is 20 years old at the time he learns this single list. If forgetting the list is to be attributed to interference, it is much more probable that he would have learned "something" that would interfere during these previous 20 years than during the 24-hour retention interval. The latter, of course, would be a source of retroactive interference. The longer the retention interval, the more important would interference from retroactive sources become.

What could be the source of interference from outside the laboratory? The subject has a large verbal repertoire that he has built up during the years. This includes not only a great many verbal units but also associations among those units. It is known, furthermore, that there are varying strengths of associations among letters, and a major reason for the difficulty of learning nonwords is that the required associations are contrary to the existing stronger habits or associations. In effect, then, when a subject is required to learn a nonword, he must extinguish, or at least suppress, the associations he brings to the laboratory session. If one were to apply the extinction–recovery theory, it would be expected that during the retention interval the older associations would recover and interfere with those built up in the laboratory, thus producing the forgetting observed at recall. Or, if the materials involved words, pre-experimental associations among those words and with other words would have to be extinguished if the task of the laboratory required new associations. But again, the old habits should recover with time and interfere with recall. Thus the interference theory, as refined and shaped by the facts derived from the studies of retroactive and proactive inhibition in the formal laboratory setting, was given a direct counterpart in the single-list situation, with the interference stemming from habits the subject had learned outside the laboratory. This translation seemed quite appropriate, and the magnitude of the interference to be expected from outside sources could surely account for the 15 per cent to 20 per cent forgetting observed.

To test the application of the theory to the single-list situation requires the construction of learning tasks that will be differentially interfered with by associative habits that the subject brings to the laboratory. This, in turn, requires a knowledge of the associative habits that the subject has, in fact, developed over the years. From various word-association tables and letter-association tables, something *is* known of the associative network of the average college student. For example, it is known that words occurring with great frequency in our language have more and stronger associations than do words occurring with low frequency. It might be expected, therefore, that if a verbal task were constructed of frequently used words in such a way that the already established habits were inappropriate or contrary to the habits that must be acquired to master the task, an effective proactive situation would be devised. Furthermore, proactive inhibition should be greater than for a task constructed of infrequently used words, since the pre-experimental associations among the infrequently used words are minimal. Clearly, it would be predicted that more of the task constructed of frequently used words would be forgotten; forgetting should be greater because proactive interference after a day, a week, or a month should be greater.

Tests of such expectations have been disappointing. Little, if any, difference in the forgetting of the various tasks has been observed. The same has been true when associations among letters have been used to construct nonwords that should be differentially susceptible to previous habits.

We can see that although the interference theory has been quite successful in accounting for observed facts in the formal retroactive-inhibition and proactive-inhibition paradigms, the translation of this theory to account for the forgetting observed for a single list has not. In study after study we find that 15 to 20 per cent of the task is forgotten over a 24-hour period; we cannot get differential forgetting of any appreciable amount for different materials. The success of the interference theory in other contexts will not allow it to be given up easily. Rather, it would appear that the more fruitful approach would be to continue to devise tasks in which the amount of interference from already established habits would be different. This, in turn, may require further extensive assessment of the habit repertoires of the subjects.

Implications of interference theory. There are further untested implications of the interference theory as outlined above. If proactive inhibition from outside sources is responsible for the forgetting of a single list, we would expect more forgetting for a given task for older people than for younger people. For example, a college student should show more forgetting of a verbal task than should a first-grader. This should follow because the number of potential interfering associations should be greater for the college student. We might also predict that a genius would show more forgetting than an imbecile. The genius has, in his lifetime, learned infinitely more than the imbecile; hence, the sources of potential interference should be greater. Other similar propositions can be deduced from the interference theory. It will probably not be abandoned despite its inadequacy in the single-list situation until a variety of tests of the theory have been negative.

BENTON J. UNDERWOOD

[*See also* LEARNING. *Other relevant material may be found in the biography of* EBBINGHAUS.]

BIBLIOGRAPHY

McGEOCH, JOHN A. 1932 Forgetting and the Law of Disuse. *Psychological Review* 39:352–370.

MELTON, ARTHUR W. 1963 Implications of Short-term Memory for a General Theory of Memory. *Journal of Verbal Learning and Verbal Behavior* 2:1–21.

PETERSON, LLOYD R.; and PETERSON, MARGARET J. 1959 Short-term Retention of Individual Verbal Items. *Journal of Experimental Psychology* 58:193–198.

POSTMAN, LEO 1961 The Present Status of Interference Theory. Pages 152–179 in Conference on Verbal Learning and Verbal Behavior, New York University, 1959, *Verbal Learning and Verbal Behavior: Proceedings.* New York: McGraw-Hill.

UNDERWOOD, BENTON J. 1957 Interference and Forgetting. *Psychological Review* 64:49–60.

UNDERWOOD, BENTON J.; and POSTMAN, LEO 1960 Extraexperimental Sources of Interference in Forgetting. *Psychological Review* 67:73–95.

FOUNDATIONS

The foundation may be defined as an instrument for the contribution of private wealth to public purpose. In this broad sense, foundations existed in antiquity and include perpetuities set up by the pharaohs for religious purposes, Greek and Roman endowments, and the ecclesiastical and charitable trusts made in Tudor England and later.

Early charitable trusts. For example, Plato established his famous Academy on land that Cimon the Athenian had given for public use. Before his death in 347 B.C., Plato directed that the income of his own adjacent fields should be used for the perpetual support of the school. This foundation survived nearly nine hundred years, until it was finally suppressed by the Christian Emperor Justinian in A.D. 529 for teaching pagan doctrines.

The corporate personality, able to receive and hold property in perpetuity, was primarily a Roman legal concept. In the Roman Empire during the first two centuries of the Christian era, foundations to aid the needy—usually associated with municipalities but sometimes private associations—became common. Under Constantine special laws were passed extending this principle to the churches.

The foundation in perpetuity (*vaqf, vakif*) has been common in Islamic countries. Examples of deeds of trust appeared in the early Hittite civilization (c. 1200 B.C.), but after the foundation principle was given specific approval by Muhammad it spread widely. A *vaqf* has been defined as the appropriation of a particular article in such manner that it becomes subject to the rules of divine property: the appropriator's right in such objects is extinguished and they become the property of God, who returns the derivative benefits to his people. Three broad categories of obligation are recognized: first and foremost, a man's duty to his own family; second, the maintenance of God's worship according to the tenets of Islam; and, finally, charity in the everyday sense, including works of public utility. No world estimates of either the number or accumulated wealth of *vakiflar* are available, but they are reported to exist in considerable numbers in Turkey, Saudi Arabia, India, Iran, and other countries with substantial Muslim populations. In 1964 the Turkish administrator of *vakiflar* reported more than seventeen thousand properties under his supervision.

In England, after Henry VIII dissolved the monasteries, the secular charities grew to such numbers that in 1601, under Elizabeth I, a special act was passed. Commonly called the Statute of Charitable Uses, it became the legislative cornerstone for the creation, control, and protection of such funds. The registry of charitable trusts compiled in the 1960s in England may record as many as 200,000, many of them surviving from Tudor and Stuart times.

As early examples of foundations in the United States, consider the two funds established in Boston and Philadelphia in 1791, under the will of Benjamin Franklin, to assist "young married artificers of good character." Portions of these funds were to accumulate for two hundred years and are still accumulating. But the first substantial fund that corresponds to the more modern concept of a foundation was the Peabody Education Fund, set up in 1867 by George Peabody, with a principal sum of over $2 million to "aid the stricken South."

Development of the foundation concept. About the beginning of the twentieth century the foundation idea began to take deeper root in American soil, and with a significant difference from the old concept of the fixed charitable trust. Large endowments were set up, often in perpetuity, but with wide latitude in their use. The new doctrine asserted that the funds of foundations are largely the venture capital of philanthropy, best invested in activities requiring risk and foresight that are not likely to be supported either by government or private individuals. The usual purpose is not relief or even cure; it is prevention, research, and discovery "to promote the well-being of mankind." Characteristically, the larger foundations have great freedom of action, with their trustees devoting less time to conserving money than to exploring new and enterprising ways of spending it.

Andrew Carnegie was a chief architect of these ideas, first through his essay *The Gospel of Wealth* (first published as *Wealth* in 1889; see Carnegie 1886–1899) and then through the foundations he himself established. In 1902 he set up his first important foundation, the Carnegie Institution of Washington, ". . . to encourage, in the broadest and most liberal manner, investigation, research, and discovery, and the application of knowledge to the improvement of mankind" ("Articles of Incorporation" [1902] 1965, p. 577). In the same year John D. Rockefeller's General Education Board was established with Mr. Carnegie as an active trustee.

Others that are now well known—like the Milbank Memorial Fund and the Russell Sage Foundation—followed rapidly. In 1911 various Carnegie benefactions culminated in the Carnegie Corporation of New York, the largest and most general of the Carnegie group. The Rockefeller Foundation, giant of the early foundations and still the world's second largest, was initiated in 1913; in 1914 appeared the Cleveland Foundation, the first of the community foundations inviting multiple trust funds.

The first three decades of the twentieth century constituted a period of increasing but gradual growth. Of the 5,050 foundations with known dates of origin included in the latest *Foundation Directory*, some 285, or less than 6 per cent of the group, had been established by the end of the lush 1920s. The fourth decade, the depression 1930s, seemed scarcely conducive to accumulations of surplus wealth; and some foundations did disappear or find their assets severely impaired. However, the *Foundation Directory* tabulates 288 new foundations originating in that decade, including the incorporation in 1936—with an initial endowment of $25,000—of the now gigantic Ford Foundation.

Postwar growth. By the middle 1940s a new group of foundations had sprung up in various sections of the United States, induced in part by high postwar levels of taxation resulting from World War II. Many of these were family foundations, set up by a living individual, with contributions and direction closely held within the family group. Another large segment was composed of company-sponsored foundations set up by business corporations to receive substantial contributions in years of good profits—or especially high taxes—and to disburse these funds, through good years and bad, in customary patterns of corporation giving. Both of these types of foundations differ in one significant respect from the older, traditional type: they usually have no large initial corpus but carry on their often substantial programs with moneys received currently. They may eventually accumulate substantial assets, but presently they are conduit foundations rather than the fixed-endowment type.

By 1964, date of publication of the second edition of the *Foundation Directory*, it was estimated that there were somewhat more than fifteen thousand foundations in the United States; but nine thousand were too small to meet the *Directory*'s size qualifications. Assets totaled $14,500 million, and grants were in the neighborhood of $800 million annually. These, however, are not large sums in the total American economy or even in its philanthropic segment. All foundations together are able to spend only about 8 cents of the annual dollar of private philanthropy. The significance of the foundation contribution lies in its special qualities and directions rather than in its gross total.

Moreover, although foundations are numerous and have been increasing at a rate of about 1,200 a year, most assets are in the hands of a relatively small number of large foundations. The 176 large foundations, each possessing $10 million or more, accounted for $11,000 million in assets, or 76 per cent of the total for the whole group. Among this group were 10 foundations with assets exceeding $150 million, headed by the gigantic Ford Foundation which, at market values of its stock holdings in late 1964, had assets of over $4,000 million.

The foundation as it exists in America has not spread extensively in other countries. England has less than a dozen foundations of substantial size which have freedom in programming. Canada has a growing number of foundations. A few examples exist in continental Europe, South America, Australia, India, and the Far East. In 1964 New Zealand issued its first directory (*A Directory of Philanthropic Trusts* 1964), including 63 trusts. Evidence increases of lively interest in other countries, and as surplus wealth becomes available and changes are made in tax structures, this typically American development may be extensively copied.

Types of foundations. Foundations differ so widely that description is difficult without some effort at classification. One such division is into grant-making and operating foundations. The former carry out their objectives by making gifts to independent agencies or persons and usually have small staffs merely to evaluate (or, in some cases, stimulate) requests for support. The latter themselves conduct operations in the fields of their choice and may have professional staffs of considerable size.

General foundations. Nearly all the larger, well-known foundations such as Ford, Rockefeller, Carnegie, Kellogg, and Sloan are general foundations. Operating under broad charters, they support the research projects in education, health, and welfare that characterize foundation work in the public mind. Usually they have large endowments, but some smaller foundations also support programs of national significance and properly fall within this category. Foundations of this type have a board of trustees (directors, managers) with broad interests, and a trained professional staff to serve as the "eyes" of the foundation, seeking out promising new ventures, evaluating projects offered, handling details of grants—or actual operations, if the foundation is of the operating type—and following through on results, so that future programs may be guided by past experience.

Special purpose foundations. Special purpose foundations are created—many of them by will or trust instrument rather than by incorporation—to serve a charitable purpose closely detailed, usually in the charter or perhaps in a letter of gift. The purpose may be as narrow as that of the Prairie Chicken Foundation of Illinois, devoted to preserving remnants of prairie chicken flocks, or as broad as advancement of education. Criticism of such foundations is not directed against program concentration on particular needs or projects, as some of these foundations efficiently serve useful ends, but against rigid restrictions freezing concentration for a long period or perpetually.

Community foundations. Community foundations are composite foundations, usually set up as trusts rather than as corporations, and functioning under community control in a way seldom found in other philanthropic endowments. Capital gifts are received, and the principal is administered by the trust departments of local banks. Income is distributed, together with such portions of the principal as may be authorized in any trust, under the supervision and control of a distribution committee. The foundation reserves the power to transfer to other similar purposes any funds which can no longer be effectively used for the ends originally designated. The donors may be numerous; each donor may specify how his gift is to be used or leave it to the discretion of the distribution committee, but usually the use of the donation is limited to the city or county within which the community foundation is situated.

Company-sponsored foundations. Typically, the company-sponsored foundation is a tax-exempt, nonprofit legal entity separate from the parent company but with a trustee board consisting wholly or principally of corporation officers and directors. Except in the case of foundations associated with large national companies, their programs are likely to be confined to the communities within which the parent company has offices and to center on philanthropies that benefit the corporation, its employees, its stockholders, or its business relationships. They are conduit foundations in that they not only disburse their investment income, as do nearly all foundations, but typically receive substantial new funds every year, or at least every year of good corporate profits.

Family foundations. Family (or personal) foundations are usually established by a living person or persons rather than by bequest. Generally they are initially small and may have no administrative organization or headquarters other than the office of the donor or a law firm. The trustees are apt to be the donor or donors, his immediate family, and perhaps his lawyer, banker, or business associate. At the outset, programs may differ little from the personal giving of wealthy men and women who have not incorporated their charity and probably include gifts to the local community fund, hospital, the donor's college or church, etc. Assets are no adequate measure of potential; such foundations may make substantial grants out of new annual gifts. Many of these initially small foundations may become recipients of large bequests upon the deaths of donors; and as experience accumulates, programs may change. Nearly all the large general foundations of today began as family foundations with limited funds oriented toward personal charities.

The relative numbers, assets, and grant activities of these five types of foundations are indicated by Table 1, taken from the *Foundation Directory* and including all American foundations of substantial size at the time of its publication.

Table 1 — Assets and grants of 6,007 foundations by type of foundation, 1964

CLASS	NUMBER	ASSETS		GRANTS	
		Amount (in millions)	Per cent	Amount (in millions)	Per cent
General	190	$ 9,289	64	$384	49
Special purpose	479	1,277	9	62	8
Community	102	425	3	18	2
Company-sponsored	1,716	1,177	8	143	19
Family and miscellaneous	3,520	2,343	16	173	22
Total	6,007	$14,511	100	$779*	100

* Entries do not add to this total because of rounding.

Source: Foundation Directory 1964, p. 22.

Fields of foundation activity. Table 2 shows education to be the most favored field of foundation activity, although before large governmental expenditures were channeled into medical research, grants made in the field of health were equally important. Similarly, expansion of social security, private insurance and retirement plans, and increased governmental involvement in relief and similar fields formerly supported largely by voluntary contributions have resulted in declining foundation support in social welfare areas. The great recent expansion of research within educational institutions makes them logical channels for an ever-broadening stream of foundation activities in the sciences and international affairs.

The rise of international activities into second place is the most notable recent change, and later data indicate continuing growth in this area. Not all of these sums go abroad; many of these grants are made to American universities for area studies and like projects. It needs to be added that the Ford Foundation is the major factor in this increase in internationally oriented dollars, although other foundations have been entering the field or expanding their programs within it.

Welfare and health receive only modest founda-

Table 2 — Grants of 6,007 foundations, by major fields, 1964

Field	Amount (in millions)	Per cent
Education	$315	40
International activities	106	14
Welfare	96	12
Health	90	12
Sciences	86	11
Religion	46	6
Humanities	40	5
Total	$779	100

Source: Foundation Directory 1964, p. 44.

tion support. Closer analysis of the data reveals that this pattern is characteristic of the larger rather than the small foundations. Some five thousand small foundations, for example, gave 34 per cent of their grants in the field of welfare, as compared with a mere 6 per cent for foundations with assets above $10 million.

The sciences have been an expanding research interest. In the *Directory* tabulation, support for the physical sciences mounted to 40 per cent of the total science expenditure, with the life sciences—formerly the unchallenged leader—at 32 per cent. The social sciences received 28 per cent of the total.

Religion receives only 6 per cent of foundation grants, although as a category it receives an estimated half of all private philanthropic gifts in the United States. But most of this giving is done personally, rather than through a foundation, even where an individual could choose either channel.

The humanities come last in the *Directory* tabulation, at 5 per cent of the total. However, still more recent figures indicate a substantial rise in this area, stimulated through such special projects as Lincoln Center in New York.

Foundations in American society.   Because foundations are numerous and some of them bear the names of wealthy families, a popular misconception exists that they have tremendous assets and are able to make almost unlimited expenditures. Relatively, the resources of foundations are not large in the American economy and may be shrinking. In 1913 the federal government's total expenditures for education came to $5 million. The Carnegie Corporation of New York in that year spent a total of $5.6 million, so that if it had devoted all its funds to education, it could have more than equaled the federal government total. The Rockefeller Foundation is known around the world for its extensive fellowship program, on which it has spent $61 million in the past fifty years; but this total is less than the amount the American government spends in a single year today for its fellowship program alone.

Although in relative terms foundations constitute a minor segment of the American economy, their still considerable growth in numbers and in wealth has at times occasioned concern. As early as 1915 the Walsh Committee of the U.S. Senate charged that foundations were dominated by big business and were exerting strong conservative and reactionary influences. In the late 1940s it became evident that business enterprises in some numbers were seeking tax shelter under the foundation umbrella. To correct this and other abuses, the Revenue Act of 1950 set up "prohibited transactions" involving dealings between foundations and their donors or related persons. It taxes at ordinary corporation rates foundation profits from business enterprises not substantially related to the foundation's tax-exempt purposes, and it makes unreasonable accumulations of income a basis for loss of exempt status.

In the House of Representatives in 1952 the Cox Committee, and again in 1954 the Reece Committee, held special hearings on foundations, concentrating on program; but the charge then was the opposite of the Walsh charges. The Reece Committee attempted to demonstrate that foundations and certain educational institutions were engaged in a "diabolical conspiracy" to weaken and discredit the capitalistic system in the United States and to promote Marxist socialism. Neither the Walsh nor the Reece thesis was supported by substantial evidence, and no legislation followed.

In the 1960s the spotlight turned back to financial aspects, with allegations that certain foundations were serving primarily as tax shelters and business conveniences for their donors.

Some present tendencies. A few foundations now have more than a half century behind them, and a substantial record of experience is available for all foundations. The administration of foundations is becoming professionalized. While there are no institutions of special training for this field, national and regional conferences, informal luncheon groups, and other similar devices increasingly offer opportunities for exchange of experience. Foundations have resisted the formation of any closely knit national association, perhaps because of the high degree of individualism that characterizes the field and perhaps partially to avoid charges of collusion and wealth concentration.

Literature in the field, once sparse, is rapidly increasing. About two hundred foundations issue printed reports, usually annually; and histories of a number of the older foundations have recently been published. A few critical studies have appeared, and more are in progress.

Foundations are in some respects unique among American social institutions. They are the only important agencies in America free from the political controls of legislative appropriations and pressure groups, and free from the lay controls of having to temper programs with the judgments and prejudices of current contributors. Because of this position of unusual freedom, the foundations have an opportunity—and perhaps a special responsibility —to attack the longer range, more difficult, and often controversial questions which face the nation and the world; and many of them do spend a substantial part of their funds in pioneering ventures that would have difficulty in obtaining support from other private sources or from government.

F. EMERSON ANDREWS

[See also PHILANTHROPY.]

BIBLIOGRAPHY

ANDREWS, F. EMERSON 1956 *Philanthropic Foundations.* New York: Russell Sage Foundation.

ANDREWS, F. EMERSON 1958 *Legal Instruments of Foundations.* New York: Russell Sage Foundation.

ANDREWS, FRANK M. 1960 *A Study of Company-sponsored Foundations.* New York: Russell Sage Foundation.

Articles of Incorporation. (1902) 1965 Carnegie Institution of Washington, *Yearbook* 64:577–579.

CARNEGIE, ANDREW (1886–1899) 1962 *The Gospel of Wealth, and Other Timely Essays.* Cambridge, Mass.: Belknap Press. → Contains articles first published in various periodicals.

Community Foundations in the United States and Canada: 1964 Status. 1965 New York: Council on Foundations.

A Directory of Philanthropic Trusts. 1964 Wellington (New Zealand): Whitcombe & Tombs.

EMBREE, EDWIN R.; and WAXMAN, JULIA 1949 *Investment in People: The Story of the Julius Rosenwald Fund.* New York: Harper.

FORD FOUNDATION 1949 *Report of the Study for the Ford Foundation on Policy and Program.* Detroit: The Foundation.

FOSDICK, RAYMOND B. 1952 *The Story of the Rockefeller Foundation.* New York: Harper.

FOSDICK, RAYMOND B. 1962 *Adventure in Giving: The Story of the General Education Board, a Foundation Established by John D. Rockefeller.* New York: Harper.

Foundation Directory. 2d ed. Edited by Ann D. Walton and Marianna O. Lewis. 1964 New York: Russell Sage Foundation.

Foundation News. → Bulletin of the Foundation Library Center. Published since 1960.

GLENN, JOHN M.; BRANDT, LILIAN; and ANDREWS, F. EMERSON 1947 *Russell Sage Foundation: 1907–1946.* 2 vols. New York: Russell Sage Foundation.

GREAT BRITAIN, COMMITTEE ON THE LAW AND PRACTICE RELATING TO CHARITABLE TRUSTS 1952 *Report.* Papers by Command, Cmd. 8710. London: H.M. Stationery Office.

HOWARD, NATHANIEL R. 1963 *Trust for All Time: The Story of the Cleveland Foundation and the Community Trust Movement.* The Cleveland Foundation.

KEELING, GUY W. (editor) 1953 *Trusts and Foundations: A Select Guide.* Cambridge: Bowes & Bowes.

KELLOGG (W. K.) FOUNDATION 1956 *The First Twenty-five Years: The Story of a Foundation.* Battle Creek: The Foundation.

KEPPEL, FREDERICK P. 1930 *The Foundation: Its Place in American Life.* New York: Macmillan.

KIGER, JOSEPH C. 1954 *Operating Principles of the Larger Foundations.* New York: Russell Sage Foundation.

LINDEMAN, EDUARD C. 1936 *Wealth and Culture: A Study of One Hundred Foundations and Community*

Trusts and Their Operations During the Decade 1921–1930. New York: Harcourt.

LOMASK, MILTON 1964 *Seed Money: The Guggenheim Story.* New York: Farrar.

MACDONALD, DWIGHT 1956 *The Ford Foundation: The Men and the Millions.* New York: Reynal.

NATIONAL INDUSTRIAL CONFERENCE BOARD 1955 *Company-sponsored Foundations.* Studies in Business Policy, No. 73. New York: The Board.

NEW YORK UNIVERSITY 1963 *Proceedings of the Sixth Biennial Conference on Charitable Foundations.* Edited by Henry Sellin. New York: Bender.

RUSK, DEAN 1961 *The Role of the Foundation in American Life.* Claremont (Calif.) Colleges.

SHAPLEN, ROBERT 1964 *Toward the Well-being of Mankind: Fifty Years of the Rockefeller Foundation.* Garden City, N.Y.: Doubleday.

U.S. CONGRESS, HOUSE, SELECT COMMITTEE ON SMALL BUSINESS 1962 *Tax-exempt Foundations and Charitable Trusts: Their Impact on Our Economy.* Chairman's Report, 87th Congress. Washington: Government Printing Office.

FOURIER, CHARLES

Charles Fourier, French socialist thinker, was born at Besançon in 1772 and died in Paris in 1837. The sources of his thought remain obscure. To a great extent he was an autodidact, who owed much to his reading and still more to his reflections on what he read. Fourier's inclination was to become a military engineer, but his family—wealthy merchants—made him a tradesman in Marseilles. A setback in business in 1799, combined with his lack of business ability, reduced Fourier to the role of civil servant at Lyons. After 1816, when he inherited an income from his mother, he was finally able to devote himself entirely to his writing. In 1823 he settled permanently in Paris. Although he left a large body of published writings as well as many unpublished manuscripts, he never did write the "Grand Traité" that was to lay out his whole system in detail.

To use the language of the time, Fourier was a capitalist whose personal experience made him sensitive to the social plagues and the vices of a civilization based on commercial lies. The sole thought of his life was to find a "way out" that he might propose to his contemporaries. His first major book (1808) painted a cosmic fresco, showing blind humanity the path toward happiness and abundance. All his life he waited for the benefactor (king, minister, or financier) who would enable him to make even a partial test of his social "invention," or scheme.

This scheme assumes a correspondence between the cosmic order and the social order. It applies to the latter order the law of gravity established for the former by Newton and then applies to both orders a law of evolution, with eight ascending periods followed by the same number of descending periods. The peak is the reign of "harmony," in which "association" will be fully triumphant; however, humanity is still immersed in the fifth period, called "civilization" to distinguish it from the barbarism from which humanity has only recently emerged. The goal is the free governance of things by individuals who are at once completely free, fully mature, and highly organized. This goal explains the importance that Fourier attached to education, his criticism of the family and of the relations between the sexes, and finally his theory that the "passions" should be put to use instead of being repressed. The means of achieving this goal is the "phalanstery," a basic social unit whose organization rests on the mathematical rationality of social phenomena (the dimensions of groups, the balance of age groups, the alternation of activities) and which encompasses all aspects of the life of its members.

Fourier, an antirevolutionary and a strong opponent of Saint-Simon and Owen, believed his social system to be consistent with any form of government, including the monarchical one. Had not the French monarchy already shown great adaptability, having been feudal in the Middle Ages, absolute under Louis XIV, and bourgeois under Louis Philippe? There seemed to Fourier no reason why it could not also adapt to the new industrialism. This strange man thus combined traits that in others are generally mutually exclusive—political conservatism, social reformism, moral anarchism (at least in his conception of free love), and anti-Christian religiousness. Fourier believed in the goodness of human nature and rejected the dogma of original sin. He saw harmony as the law of the cosmos and held that what is true for nature must be true for society. This is why he gave to Newton's work the same importance that Marx was to see in that of Darwin; however, Marx abstracted from Darwinism a process of struggle, while Fourier found in Newton's theory a mechanism of attraction.

Fourier had only a limited influence on the development of society: his realm was that of thought, not of action. Yet the only thinkers who acknowledged a direct debt to Fourier were the Russian revolutionaries Herzen, Petrachevsky, and Tchernichevsky. While he was in some ways far ahead of his time, in many other respects he was a man of the past: his views apply much more to an agricultural and trading society than to one that is industrial and technological. Marx, of course, scorned him as a "utopian socialist." Nevertheless, Fourierism did not remain an abstract utopia. For thirty to forty years Fourierist ideas were realized in a series of community experiments, both in France and in a number of other countries, especially in the United States. For the most part, these experiments were attempts at the collective operation of a large rural estate, and they foreshadowed more modern forms of social organization. One of these enterprises took on an urban and industrial aspect—the *familistère* at Guise (in northern France). Today there remains not only a factory (like any other factory) but also a set of dwellings that is a unique example of Fourierist architecture. Some of Fourier's disciples put little trust in the success of these partial realizations of his scheme and held that a total transformation of society was called for. Rallying around Victor Considérant, 1808–1893, they entered into political life and became a real force for some years, but with the advent of Napoleon III they could do no better than merge into the bourgeois opposition to the Second Empire. As Charles Gide pointed out some time ago (1924), there is a direct relationship between Fourierism and the cooperative movement which played an important role before 1914 and of which there are now new developments, for example, in Yugoslavia, Israel, and the countries of the Third World.

ÉMILE POULAT

[*For the historical context of Fourier's work, see* SOCIALISM; UTOPIANISM; *and the biographies of* MARX; OWEN; SAINT-SIMON.]

WORKS BY FOURIER

(1808) 1857 *The Social Destiny of Man: Or, Theory of the Four Movements.* New York: Dewitt. → First published as *Théorie des quatre mouvements et des destinées générales: Prospectus et annonce de la découverte.*

1822 *Traité de l'association domestique agricole.* 2 vols. Paris: Bossange.

1829–1830 *Le nouveau monde industriel et sociétaire: Ou invention du procédé d'industrie attrayante et naturelle distribuée en séries passionnées.* Paris: Bossange.

1835–1836 *La fausse industrie morcelée, répugnante, mensongère, et l'antidote: L'industrie naturelle, combinée, attrayante, véridique donnant quadruple produit.* 2 vols. Paris: Bossange.

1841–1845 *Oeuvres complètes de Ch. Fourier.* 6 vols. Paris: Librairie Sociétaire.

1851–1858 *Publication des manuscrits de Charles Fourier.* 4 vols. Paris: Librairie Phalanstérienne.

SUPPLEMENTARY BIBLIOGRAPHY

BESTOR, ARTHUR E. 1950 *Backwoods Utopias: The Sectarian and Owenist Phases of Communitarian Socialism in America, 1663–1829.* Philadelphia: Univ. of Pennsylvania Press.

Bibliothèque internationale de sociologie de la coopération. → A monographic series published since 1955; each volume has a separate author and publisher.

BO, GIUSEPPE DEL 1957 *Charles Fourier e la scuola societaria: 1801–1922.* Milan (Italy): Feltrinelli. → A very valuable catalogue of the Fourierist collection assembled by the Giangiacomo Feltrinelli Institute.

BOURGIN, HUBERT 1905 *Fourier: Contribution à l'étude du socialisme français.* Paris: Société Nouvelle de Librairie et d'Édition. → Still the basic work on Fourier, in part outdated but not replaced.

DESROCHE, HENRI CH. 1962 *Fouriérisme ambigu: Socialisme ou religion? Revue internationale de philosophie* 16:200–220.

DESROCHE, HENRI CH. 1964 *Coopération et développement: Mouvements coopératifs et stratégie du développement.* Paris: Presses Universitaires de France.

GAUMONT, JEAN 1924 *Histoire générale de la coopération en France: Les idées et les faits, les hommes et les oeuvres.* 2 vols. Paris: Fédération Nationale des Coopérateurs de Consommation.

GIDE, CHARLES 1924 *Fourier: Précurseur de la coopération.* Paris: Association pour l'Enseignement de la Coopération.

HÉMARDLINQUER, J. J. 1964 *La "découverte du mouvement social": Notes critiques sur le jeune Fourier. Mouvement social* 3, no. 48:49–70.

Phalange: Revue de la science sociale. → Published from 1832–1849 under varying titles by the Bureau de Phalange. Fourier was a frequent contributor from 1832–1840.

POULAT, ÉMILE 1957 *Les cahiers manuscrits de Fourier: Étude historique et inventaire raisonné.* Paris: Entente Communautaire. → Contains an important chapter by Henri Desroche.

POULAT, ÉMILE 1962 *Écritures et tradition fouriéristes. Revue internationale de philosophie* 16:221–233.

ZIL'BERFARB, JOGANSON J. 1964 *Sotsial'naia filosofia Sharlia Fur'e i ee mesto v istorii sotsialisticheskoi mysli pervoi poloviny XIX veka* (The Social Philosophy of Charles Fourier and Its Place in the History of Socialist Thought in the First Half of the Nineteenth Century). Moscow: Nauka.

FRANK, JEROME

Jerome N. Frank (1889–1957) was an American lawyer, public official, judge, law teacher, and writer on law and social philosophy. As an active participant in public affairs, first as a middle-ranking figure in the New Deal and later as a United States circuit court judge, Frank was respected as an effective, if sometimes turbulent, influence for change. He had opponents but few enemies. He was a generous person, kind, unpretentious, enthusiastic in behalf of his friends, and a witty companion as well. His passion was writing, and even in the most demanding periods of his service in Washington, he produced books and articles on a wide variety of subjects. They remain the chief source of his influence.

Frank was born in New York but grew up in Chicago; he attended the University of Chicago, taking his law degree in 1912. The university left in Frank's mind strong traces of attitudes that were typical of the institution's early outlook: a sense of identification with the liberal and progressive theme in the spirit of the nation; a wide-ranging enthusiasm for ideas, particularly new ideas; and a preference for innovations, especially if they could be called "reforms." After leaving the university, Frank practiced law for 17 years in Chicago, where he was a conspicuous and successful counselor and attorney, mainly in the field of commercial and financial transactions. He and his wife, a well-known poet, also belonged to the literary world of Chicago.

Intellectual interest and a sense of immediate need led Frank to undergo psychoanalysis, an event in his personal history that had a far-reaching impact on his thinking. In 1930 Frank published his most famous book, *Law and the Modern Mind*, which views the law in a Freudian perspective and interprets the methods and processes of law as social magic. Thus, judges are shown as father figures of mystical authority, dressed in robes and required to sit on high benches so that they evoke irrational deference. This kind of magic, according to Frank, helps maintain social order. The book came at a moment when Freudian insights were just beginning to touch the literature of political science, anthropology, literary criticism, sociology, and law; and it created a storm. Its sparkle and force made it a conspicuous factor in the acceptance of psychoanalysis as an important element in American views of man as a social being.

Frank had moved to New York in 1929; there he continued to practice law and joined a number of intellectual circles. He lectured at the New School for Social Research and in 1930 began an intermittent association with the Yale Law School, which lasted until his death.

The Yale Law School of the early 1930s was a lively place, well suited to Frank's personality and interests. The staff included William O. Douglas, Walton H. Hamilton, Thurman Arnold, Abe Fortas, Underhill Moore, and a number of psychologists, economists, and statisticians, as well as more orthodox law professors. The school imbued Frank with the sense that the world was about to be remade, if not reborn. It was one of the centers of American "legal realism," a controversial philosophical movement, which was concerned with directing attention from the "law in the books," the doctrinal law of the appellate courts, to "the law in action," the patterns of usage and practice that actually prevail in daily life, in the lower courts, and in business. Frank fought zestfully for the latter view of the law, a view which was strongly resisted.

After this stimulating experience he joined several members of the Yale faculty in the adventurous first wave of President Roosevelt's New Deal and was appointed general counsel of the Agricultural Adjustment Administration. This radical experiment in direct controls was headed by George Peek, a rural conservative and, like most of his agrarian staff, suspicious of urban, volatile, intellectual types like Frank himself and the extraordinary group he assembled, a group which included Arnold and Fortas from Yale, Adlai Stevenson, and Alger Hiss, among many others. The conflict between this group, led by Frank, and the older breed of agricultural experts lasted nearly two years; it ended in one of the spectacular explosions of the New Deal, with Frank and a considerable number of his allies in the Department of Agriculture being dismissed. Frank was soon reappointed, first to the staff of the Reconstruction Finance Commission and then as a member—from 1937 to 1939—and as the chairman—from 1939 to 1941—of the Securities and Exchange Commission, where he played an active part in the development of policy, particularly under the Public Utility Holding Company Act of 1935.

During this period he published *Save America First* (1938), a far-ranging comment on the economic element in social experience, which included an argument against American participation in the European war. It was written in the spirit of senators Borah and Norris and the older tradition of agrarian Populism; before June 1940 Frank took part as an isolationist in the national debate over America's interest in the war.

In 1941 he was appointed judge of the United States Court of Appeals for the Second Circuit, sitting in New York; he later moved to New Haven when he began to teach regularly at the Yale Law School. Frank found stimulus in the company of his judicial colleagues, especially judges Learned Hand, Augustus Hand, and Charles E. Clark, as well as at the law school, where he maintained an active office and saw students and faculty members regularly. His opinions were colorful and often unorthodox in form, reflecting the range of his reading and the mannerisms of a style that had become unusually free and personal in tone. He did important judicial work in several fields of law, including procedure, finance, criminal law, and civil liberties. He was widely quoted on obscenity, immigration, the rights of the accused in criminal trials, and other subjects; and his views were much discussed in the law reviews.

The books and articles of the final period in Frank's life embody the unresolved contradictions of his view of law and of the social process. Quick, agile, and known for his brilliant *aperçus*, Frank did not have the discipline of a systematic scholar and permitted himself the luxury of inconsistent positions. In his teaching at Yale and in his writing, especially in *Courts on Trial* (1949), he stressed the importance, as well as the uncontrollable irrationality, of fact-finding in the processes of law, arguing that fact-finding constitutes a step in the trial of cases that dominates the apparently superior legal rules laid down by appellate judges. He deplored and ridiculed man's yearning for strict and predictable legal rules, but in the end his proposals for law reform aimed to bring trials under the more effective control of those rules and to make the rules clearer, more uniform, and more predictable. He argued that legal education should be brought closer to trial practice and also that legal practice should correspond more closely to the law taught in law schools. For many years he saw "natural law" as a dangerously vague and misleading slogan, but he never ceased to contend that the administration of law should give a larger place to ideas of ethics and individual justice.

In his work Frank revealed the strengths and shortcomings of the legal and social philosophy of which he was a militant partisan. He spoke persuasively for sensible reform, for simplicity, and for humane values in the law and in the social order generally. By preaching the need to relate theories to facts he helped men to build the law anew on the foundation of social need. If he never realized the equal need of relating facts to theories, he shared his faith in the autonomy of fact with many pragmatists.

EUGENE V. ROSTOW

[*See also* JUDICIARY; JURISPRUDENCE; *the detailed guide to related articles under* LAW; *and the biographies of* HAMILTON, WALTON H.; LLEWELLYN; POUND.]

WORKS BY FRANK

(1930) 1949 *Law and the Modern Mind.* New York: Coward.

1938 *Save America First: How to Make Our Democracy Work.* New York: Harper.

1942 *If Men Were Angels: Some Aspects of Government in a Democracy.* New York: Harper.

(1945) 1953 *Fate and Freedom: A Philosophy for Free Americans.* Rev. ed. Boston: Beacon.

1949 *Courts on Trial: Myth and Reality in American Justice.* Princeton Univ. Press. → A paperback edition was published in 1963 by Atheneum.

1957 FRANK, JEROME; and FRANK, BARBARA *Not Guilty.* Garden City, N.Y.: Doubleday.

1965 *A Man's Reach: The Philosophy of Judge Jerome Frank.* Edited by Barbara Frank Kristein. New York: Macmillan. → A selection of Frank's writings.

SUPPLEMENTARY BIBLIOGRAPHY

In Memoriam; Judge Jerome N. Frank: 1889–1957. 1957 *University of Chicago Law Review* 24:625–708. → See especially pages 706–708 for a bibliography of the non-judicial writings of Frank.

PAUL, JULIUS 1957 *The Legal Realism of Jerome N. Frank: A Study of Fact-skepticism and the Judicial Process.* The Hague: Nijhoff. → See especially pages 157–162 for a bibliography of the writings of Frank.

SCHLESINGER, ARTHUR M. JR. 1959 *The Age of Roosevelt.* Volume 2: The Coming of the New Deal. Boston: Houghton Mifflin.

FRAZER, JAMES GEORGE

Sir James George Frazer (1854–1941), British social anthropologist, folklorist, and classical scholar, was born in Glasgow. He attended the University of Glasgow from 1869 to 1874 and then went to Trinity College, Cambridge. He became a fellow of the college in 1879 and remained at Cambridge for the rest of his life. For one year, 1907/1908, he visited Liverpool University as professor of social anthropology, being the first to hold a chair with that name. Throughout his career he made little or no direct contact with the remote peoples who figure so extensively in his writings, and much of his simplification of their ideas (which explains some of his popular success) may be attributed to this absence of personal experience.

It is difficult now to appreciate Frazer's theories of magic and religion, since they have either been thoroughly assimilated or else outdated by extensive field research, yet in the intellectual life of his time, and particularly in the field of social anthropology, his work was of great importance. He himself appears to have anticipated the obsolescence of his work when he stressed that first-hand observation of foreign societies would furnish the science of man with a solid foundation which could never be shaken, and which would endure when many of the theories of his time, his own included, were forgotten or remembered only as curiosities. And with a characteristic skepticism that may now appear sententious he wrote that magic, science, and religion are nothing but theories of thought. . . . And as science has supplanted its predecessors, so it may hereafter be itself superseded by some more perfect hypothesis, perhaps by some totally different way of looking at the phenomena—of registering the shadows on the screen—of which we in this generation can form no idea. The advance of knowledge is an infinite progression towards a goal that for ever recedes.   (1890, pp. 712–713 in the abridged edition)

Although Frazer was directly in that current of opposition to established clerical orthodoxy that swept so many thinkers of his time (notoriously his friend William Robertson Smith) into socially painful controversy, he himself was consistently held in respect amounting to veneration. He treated Christianity as comparable with pagan religions and thus, at least by implication, deprived Christianity of its uniqueness, but he did so too tactfully to give real offense. He undermined rather than attacked the doctrinal convictions of his contemporaries. He was rewarded in his lifetime with public and academic honors, among them a civil list pension granted in 1905 for services to literature and anthropology. (It is interesting to note that he received his honorary D.C.L. at Oxford in the company of Lord Kitchener and Cecil Rhodes.) His wife was single-mindedly devoted to his reputation; indeed, R. R. Marett likened her to the guardian–wife of a priest of ancient Rome.

To his admirers Frazer appeared as a modern seer, a role that he accepted. He was revered by colonial administrators and missionaries as few anthropologists have been, and his extensive correspondence with them, together with his published questionnaire (1907), produced firsthand information about many peoples of the world. Men of letters (Kipling, Tennyson, T. S. Eliot, Ezra Pound, and D. H. Lawrence, to mention only a few) also took account of Frazer's writings, which have probably influenced the poetry of this century as much as they have the anthropology. A. E. Housman identified some of the characteristics that account for the popular appeal of Frazer's work when he described it as ". . . a museum of dark and uncouth superstitions invested with the charm of a truly sympathetic magic" and said it illuminated "the forgotten milestones of the road which man has travelled" (Dawson 1932, p. xi). Frazer's success in popularizing his subject and consolidating its practical relevance must be seen as one of his great claims to fame in the social sciences.

The development of the psyche. *The Golden Bough*, a reconstruction of the whole history of modes of human thought, orders a vast range of exotic beliefs and customs in terms of man's search for true knowledge and effective control of his environment and his condition. Frazer posited three elements in the development of the human psyche, and in the spirit of the evolutionary thinking of his time, he saw these as characterizing three stages in human mental advance: magical, religious, and scientific thought.

Magical thought assumed that the universe is regulated by impersonal and unchanging laws (in this respect, Frazer believed, magic is like science). These laws were known to the magician through his art and applied by him in a quasi-technical way to control events. But magical beliefs and procedures (unlike scientific ones) were derived from faulty reasoning by analogy and from superficial associations: the qualities of one object were supposed to induce similar qualities in another. (One of the many examples given by Frazer is the ancient Greek custom of eating ravens' eggs to produce black hair.) This homeopathic magic assumed a "law of sympathy," which operates in such a way that like produces like. In addition, there was "contagious magic," which assumed that things once in intimate contact would subsequently act upon one another: a man's hair or nail clippings, for example, were used to work evil upon him. Although Frazer oversimplified the problems of symbolic thought that such beliefs now present to anthropologists, his distinctions continue to have some elementary taxonomic value.

Magical thought, which was gradually discredited, in Frazer's opinion, because its failures became apparent, gave way to religious thought. In this phase superhuman beings were thought to control the world. The uniformity of nature ceased to be taken for granted, since the occurrence of natural events was assumed to depend upon the will of conscious personal agents. Man sought to gain the help of these agents by acts of supplication and propitiation.

Finally, recognizing more clearly the limits of his own powers of control and applying logico-experimental methods, man achieved the scientific stage.

Assessment of "The Golden Bough."   The main value of *The Golden Bough* for many of Frazer's contemporaries lay in its wide range of reference, its bold ordering of complex and varied information, and its perception of similarities in beliefs and customs that to them might have appeared quite distinct from one another. Frazer greatly overstressed the part played by deliberate reasoning in religious and magic belief and created a primitive man whose intellectual ambitions and processes of thought were those of a scholar like himself. (Even his evolutionary sequence reflects, psychologically, the process of growing up as many people with a pious upbringing like Frazer's experienced it: magical fantasies of power in early childhood, followed by adolescent religious belief, yielding in maturity to "scientific" agnosticism.)

Often Frazer preached the dangers of misinterpretation that he himself had failed to avoid. What he said of Robertson Smith's *Religion of the Semites* may be said of his own explanations of primitive thought: namely, that what now seems to be their inherent plausibility is in fact a presumption against them. Similarly Rousseau's views on the origin of society commended themselves to the most reasonable people of the previous century just because, if *they* had to reconstruct society from its foundations, they would have proceeded much as Rousseau supposed primitive men did. Thus Frazer and many of his contemporaries explained magical and religious thought by imputing a "natural" form of their own reasoning to very different peoples. Moreover, lacking knowledge of local languages and cultures, they were satisfied to take reports of isolated customs and beliefs quite out of their social context, and in this process they sometimes distorted even such evidence as they had.

An early critique of Frazer's work is that of W. Ridgeway (1924), who discussed divine kingship, one of Frazer's central themes in *The Golden Bough*. The divine king, according to Frazer, has a vitality that is believed to be the source of vitality in society and nature, and therefore, when his powers fail, he must be put to death so that a vigorous successor may continue to ensure prosperity. Ridgeway admitted that Frazer's exposition of the sacredness of kingship and the symbolism surrounding it did draw attention to these subjects and stimulate further investigation, but he charged that for many years Frazer's mode of analysis also distracted attention from the practical politics of ancient tribal monarchies. A more recent examination of Frazer's interpretation is Evans-Pritchard's *Divine Kingship of the Shilluk of the Nilotic Sudan* (1948). This shows in a particularly interesting way the hold Frazer's imagination had even on professional field observation: thus C. G. Seligman's investigations among the Shilluk, which used Frazer's concept of divine kingship, revealed just the set of beliefs and practices that fitted the Frazer argument. As Evans-Pritchard points out, there is very slight evidence for the actual ritual killing of the kings of Shilluk, while there is considerable evidence for the important role played by political conflicts within the ruling house. Many anthropologists thus became "enslaved," as Seligman was and as Malinowski once claimed to have been, by Frazerian anthropology (see also Leach 1965).

Influence of Frazer's ideas. Frazer's detailed contributions to anthropological thinking—his studies of the soul, of death, and of totemism and taboo, for example—belong to a framework of discussion that has now largely been abandoned, although it should be granted to him that in his time his was a more modern view than many others. He recognized, for example, that the notion of taboo has something to do with the Roman concept of *sacer*, with its dual connotation of "sacred" and "accursed," and though his general theory of totemism was crudely mechanistic, he did go some way toward identifying the bond of a common life that frequently links men and their totemic species.

But the significance of Frazer does not depend finally upon his anthropological theories. What he did was to introduce a comparative approach to the study of human social institutions. Here the very ambivalences and contradictions in his attitudes toward "the savage" may have served a purpose. While he had a certain ethnocentric contempt for the "dark and uncouth superstitions" he recorded, he also constantly implied that primitive thought is part of a single body of human tradition, linking his contemporaries (and himself) with much they despised. His self-deceived magicians and priests were also agents of human progress, the ablest and most intelligent of their time. In keeping with his own political philosophy, he also commended them for establishing intellectual despotism—and any statesman of his time who agreed with Frazer in principle was thereby accepting comparison with savages.

Frazer denied that all savages have an equal propensity to accept mystical explanations, asserting that in "savage as in civilized society there are sceptics as well as mystics" ([1923] 1931, p. 416); indeed, he believed that the "primitive mentality" that Lévy-Bruhl attributed exclusively to savages also characterizes such modern thinkers with mystical proclivities as Pascal, Newton, and Hegel. And on various occasions he stressed not only the common qualities of the thought of savage and civilized men but the positive contributions the former have made to the latter. Thus, in *Psyche's Task* (1909) he made a plea for the value of "superstitions": he saw their function in the maintaining of such institutions as civil order, private property, marriage, and the sanctity of human life. In a sense he anticipated the interest in "function" of Malinowski and Radcliffe-Brown. And in *The Golden Bough* he wrote that

of [all] the benefactors whom we are bound thankfully to commemorate, many, perhaps most, were savages. For when all is said and done, our resemblances to the savage are still far more numerous than our differences from him; and what we have in common with him, and deliberately retain as true and useful, we owe to our savage forefathers who slowly acquired by experience and transmitted to us by inheritance those seemingly fundamental ideas which we are apt to regard as original and intuitive. (1890, p. 264 in the abridged edition)

It is, then, as a powerful solvent of contemporary prejudices that Frazer's work stands out. Without him, the struggle to introduce anthropological knowledge and anthropological viewpoints to authorities in academic and public life would have been longer and harder. In an essential way, he made modern anthropology possible.

R. G. LIENHARDT

[*For discussion of the subsequent development of Frazer's ideas, see* ANTHROPOLOGY, *article on* THE COMPARATIVE METHOD IN ANTHROPOLOGY; CULTURE; MYTH AND SYMBOL; RELIGION; RITUAL; *and the biographies of* LÉVY-BRUHL; MALINOWSKI; SELIGMAN, C. G.; SMITH, WILLIAM ROBERTSON.]

WORKS BY FRAZER

(1887) 1910 *Totemism and Exogamy.* 4 vols. London: Macmillan.

(1890) 1955 *The Golden Bough: A Study in Magic and Religion,* 3d ed., rev. & enl. 13 vols. New York: St. Martins; London: Macmillan. → A one-volume abridged edition was published in 1922, and reprinted in 1955.

(1907) 1910 *Questions on the Customs, Beliefs and Languages of Savages.* Cambridge Univ. Press.

(1909) 1920 *Psyche's Task: A Discourse Concerning the Influence of Superstition on the Growth of Institutions.* 2d ed., rev. & enl. London: Macmillan.

(1923) 1931 *Garnered Sheaves: Essays, Addresses, and Reviews.* London: Macmillan.

SUPPLEMENTARY BIBLIOGRAPHY

BESTERMAN, THEODORE 1934 *A Bibliography of Sir James George Frazer, O.M.* London: Macmillan.

DAWSON, WARREN R. (editor) 1932 *The Frazer Lectures: 1922–1932.* London: Macmillan.

EVANS-PRITCHARD, E. E. 1948 *The Divine Kingship of the Shilluk of the Nilotic Sudan.* Cambridge Univ. Press.

LEACH, EDMUND R. 1965 Frazer and Malinowski. *Encounter* 25, no. 5:24–36.

RIDGEWAY, W. 1924 The Methods of Manhardt and Frazer, as Illustrated by the Writings of the Mistress of Girton (Miss Phillpotts, O.B.E.), Miss Jessie Weston, and Dr. B. Malinowski. Cambridge Philological Society, *Proceedings* Nos. 124–126:6–19.

FRAZIER, E. FRANKLIN

The most significant contributions of E. Franklin Frazier (1894–1962) to the literature of sociology are embodied in his writings in the fields of family behavior and race and culture contacts. Although these fields are commonly demarcated as separate areas of study, they were not always so conceived by Frazier.

Frazier's major contribution to the literature of the family is *The Negro Family in the United States* (1939). Building on earlier research (1932a; 1932b), the book analyzes the impact first of slavery and then of emancipation and urbanization upon the Negro family. These experiences produced in the Negro family variations from the dominant American family pattern—to wit, a more important role for the female; attachment of great significance to variations in skin color; and a higher incidence of illegitimacy, of common law relationships, and of other forms of family disorganization. Frazier's viewpoint that the structure and values of the Negro family in the United States are to be understood, except in the most isolated instances, as products of the Negro's American experiences involved him in a lively controversy with the anthropological scholar and Africanist, Melville Herskovits, whose studies led him to the conclusion that the major institutions of Negro life, including the family, incorporate African survivals to a significant extent.

Frazier's sociological conceptions were shaped mainly by his graduate training at the University of Chicago, from which he received the doctoral degree in 1931. There he studied with Ellsworth Faris, Robert E. Park, William F. Ogburn, and Ernest Burgess. He became associated with the program of research on the urban community and on race relations, directed by Park and conducted by a group of brilliant graduate students and young instructors that included Louis Wirth, Everett C. Hughes, and Herbert Blumer. Although critics labeled this group the "Chicago ecological school," its basic conception of sociology was in fact much broader than the study of ecological phenomena. The group believed that any social phenomenon may be understood within the context of the larger social system and that the larger social system may be coterminous with society itself.

The influence of this approach is reflected in Frazier's work on culture contacts (1949a; 1957). In his *Race and Culture Contacts in the Modern World* (1957), he analyzed the ecological and demographic relationships that result from contacts between people of diverse racial and cultural backgrounds and the effects of these relationships on economic, political, and social organization.

Perhaps the most interesting result of Frazier's work on culture contacts is his *Black Bourgeoisie* (1955), an analysis of the evolution, composition, and style of life of the Negro middle class in the United States. The Negro middle class, according to Frazier, differs from middle classes in general not only in composition but also in values. Frazier pointed out that the Negro middle class lacks the strong entrepreneurial tradition that has been the backbone of the middle classes in general. Negro business is small business, mainly of the service variety—restaurants, beauty parlors, food stores, undertaking establishments. Negro insurance companies and the Negro press may be exceptions, but even these are small compared to white organizations of the same type. Similarly, Negro banks are few and possess limited capital.

The black bourgeoisie, therefore, "is constituted of those Negroes who derive their principal income from services they render as white-collar workers." This class of white-collar workers, mainly professionals and clerical and sales personnel, has acquired a dominant position among Negroes. Although their incomes are limited, they have lost much of the old virtues identified with the middle class—industry, thrift, belief in the substantive values of education—and have, instead, emphasized conspicuous consumption and attractive social life, values more commonly associated with a leisure class. This emphasis upon society and social life represents "status without substance." This theme, that Negro values are distorted, recurs in many of Frazier's articles on Negro life in the United States: he saw the racial system as forcing the Negro to live in isolation and as endowing him with a sense of dependency and inferiority.

Frazier was born in Baltimore, Maryland. An apt and intellectually curious student, he received a B.A. degree with honors from Howard University in 1916. His first serious, formal encounter with sociology was as a graduate student at Clark University, from which he received an M.A. degree in 1920. There he studied with Frank Hankins, whom he credited with opening up to him the possibilities of sociology as a systematic study. In addition to graduate study at Chicago, his formal education included a year of study at the New York School of Social Work, 1920–1921, and a year in Denmark as a fellow of the Scandinavian–American Foundation, 1921–1922. His major academic affiliation was with Howard University, where he was professor of sociology from 1934 until he died.

Frazier was president of the American Sociological Society in 1948 and was awarded honorary degrees by Morgan College, Baltimore, in 1955 and by the University of Edinburgh in 1960.

G. FRANKLIN EDWARDS

[For the historical context of Frazier's work, see the biographies of BURGESS; HANKINS; HERSKOVITS;

OGBURN; PARK; for discussion of the subsequent development of his ideas, see RACE RELATIONS.]

WORKS BY FRAZIER

1932a The Negro Family in Chicago. Univ. of Chicago Press.

1932b The Free Negro Family: A Study of Family Origins Before the Civil War. Nashville, Tenn.: Fisk Univ. Press.

1939 The Negro Family in the United States. Univ. of Chicago Press. → A revised and abridged edition was published in 1948 by Dryden Press.

1949a Race Contacts and the Social Structure. American Sociological Review 14:1–11.

(1949b) 1963 The Negro in the United States. Rev. ed. New York: Macmillan.

(1955) 1957 Black Bourgeoisie. Glencoe, Ill.: Free Press. → First published in French. A paperback edition was published in 1962 by Collier.

(1957) 1965 Race and Culture Contacts in the Modern World. Boston: Beacon.

1964 The Negro Church in America. Liverpool University Studies in Sociology, No. 1. New York: Schocken; Liverpool (England) Univ. Press. → Published posthumously.

SUPPLEMENTARY BIBLIOGRAPHY

DAVIS, A. P. 1962 E. Franklin Frazier 1894–1962: A Profile. Journal of Negro Education 31:429–435.

EDWARDS, G. FRANKLIN 1962 Edward Franklin Frazier: 1894–1962. American Sociological Review 27:890–892.

ODUM, HOWARD W. 1951 American Sociology: The Story of Sociology in the United States Through 1950. New York: Longmans. → See especially pages 233–239 on "Franklin Frazier: 1894—."

FREE TRADE

See INTERNATIONAL TRADE and INTERNATIONAL TRADE CONTROLS.

FREEDOM

The word "freedom," with its synonym "liberty," has a strong laudatory connotation. It has therefore been applied to whatever actions, policies, or institutions may be deemed valuable, from obeying the law to attaining economic affluence. Political writings seldom provide explicit definitions of "freedom" in descriptive terms, but it is often possible to infer descriptive definitions from the context. If this is done, it will be seen that the concept of freedom refers most frequently to social freedom, which must be distinguished from other descriptive and valuational usages. Descriptive definitions of "freedom" designate empirically specifiable states of affairs and can therefore be accepted by anyone, regardless of his normative views on liberty. "Freedom" in a valuational sense is used to commend rather than to describe; it therefore means different things to writers committed to different ethical standards.

Social freedom

The concept of interpersonal or social freedom refers to relationships of interaction between persons or groups, namely, that one actor leaves another actor free to act in certain ways. This concept is best defined by reference to another interaction relation, that of interpersonal or social unfreedom.

Social unfreedom defined.   With respect to actor B, actor A is unfree to perform action x if and only if B makes it either impossible or punishable for A to do x. "B makes it impossible for A to do x" means that B performs some action y such that were A to attempt x, his attempt would fail. By denying a citizen a passport, the government makes him practically unable to travel abroad and, hence, unfree to do so. With respect to the United States, Communist China is unfree to conquer Formosa, and vice versa, since U.S. forces would presumably prevent either power from invading the other. If the Ku Klux Klan forcibly prevents Negroes from entering a public school, the Negroes are unfree to do so with respect to the Klan, but not with respect to the government. "B makes it punishable for A to do x" means that were A to carry out x, B would perform some action y that would deprive A. Governmental sanctions against illegal acts are only one example of punishability as an instance of social unfreedom. With respect to a union, a company would be unfree to withhold certain benefits if the union were to picket the company. Residents in a typical block of modern suburbia are unfree to deviate from certain tacit norms with respect to the "neighborhood," which tends to penalize nonconformists.

Social freedom defined.   Social freedom is not the contradictory of social unfreedom. I am not officially unfree to pay incomes taxes, yet, I am not free to pay them either; rather, I am unfree to withhold payment. A relationship of freedom refers to a set of at least two alternative actions or types of actions. I am unfree to do this; I am free to do this *or* that. An actor is free to act in any one of several ways, provided there is no other actor who makes him unfree to perform any of these actions. Thus, with respect to B, A is free to do either x or z if and only if B makes it neither impossible nor punishable for A to do either x or z. "Freedom to vote" means freedom either to vote or to abstain; but "freedom to propagate the truth" really means unfreedom to spread "erroneous" views. Furthermore, I may be free to act in one way or another with respect to one person or group, whereas another actor makes me unfree to engage in one of these activities. Officially, Americans are free to adopt any religion or to adhere to none, but many Americans are unfree to be agnostics with respect to certain nonofficial groups who subject "atheists" to all kinds of informal sanctions.

Testing statements about social freedom. Whether an actor *was un*free to do what he actually did can be determined with certainty, but only ex post facto. If A's attempt to do x was frustrated by B, or if A succeeded in doing x but was penalized by B for having done so, it follows by definition that A was, with respect to B, unfree to do x. That A is *un*free to do x, or that A was or is or will be *free* to do x or z, are empirical hypotheses that can be asserted only with a certain degree of probability, depending on the answers to such questions as: were A to carry out x, would B penalize him? If 60 per cent of all speeders in France are convicted, every French driver is to that extent unfree to speed, regardless of how many comply. A person's social freedom does not depend on his actual behavior. We often perform actions that we are unfree to do (for example, speeding) and refrain from actions that we are free to perform (for example, driving at any speed lower than the speed limit).

Social freedom and political freedom.   Relationships of interpersonal or social freedom and unfreedom may hold between any two persons or groups, for example, members of a family, buyers and sellers, legislature and executive, pope and emperor, members of the Common Market. A government's freedom may or may not be limited by an international organization, another government, a church, its own citizens, some interest group within or outside of its jurisdiction, etc. Political freedoms are a subclass of social freedoms and usually refer to the freedom of citizens or associations with respect to the government. Interest in political liberty has in various periods of history centered on freedom of religion, of speech and writing, of association (religious, political, economic), and of participation in the political process (suffrage). The idea of political freedom has been extended to cover demands for economic liberty, "freedom from want," national self-determination, etc.

Social freedom and control.   Social *un*freedom and control are overlapping categories. By *preventing* A from doing x, B makes A unfree to do x and controls his behavior. If B *punishes* A for having done x, one may infer that A was, with respect to B, unfree to do x; but B did not control A's behavior, since his threat of punishment failed to deter A from doing x. *Influence* is another form of control; however, if B succeeds, for example, in persuading A to vote Democratic, B does not thereby restrict A's freedom to vote Republican (or Democratic). Here, both control and freedom relationships hold between B and A.

Social freedom and power. Although there may be unfreedom without control and control without unfreedom, the concept of power had best be taken as comprising both control and unfreedom relationships. If B either has influence over A's not doing x, or prevents A from doing x, or makes it punishable for him to do so, B may be said to have power over A in this respect. The example of B persuading A to vote Democratic illustrates that power and freedom relationships may hold between the same pair of actors. The same is true in the following situations: B has power over A with respect to a limited range of alternatives; A is free within that range. Government, for example, has the power to compel citizens to serve in the armed forces but may leave them free either to submit to the draft or to volunteer. A may be, with respect to B, free to do x, either because B has no power to limit A's freedom or because he permits A to do x. The United States Congress is free to legislate as it pleases as far as the president is concerned, to the extent that he chooses not to exercise his veto power. To affirm that freedom of speech prevails in a given society is to refer to the following relationships of both freedom and unfreedom (and power) between any two of its members, A and B: A and B each leave the other free to say what he wants; with respect to B, A is unfree to prevent him from expressing his views, and vice versa; A and B are unfree to do so, not only with respect to each other but also with respect to the government, which protects everybody's *right* to free speech.

Social freedom and legal rights. It is true both that liberty depends "on the silence of the law" (Hobbes) and that "where there is no law there is no freedom" (Locke). I am socially free to act in a certain way only if (1) there is no effectively enforced law prohibiting or ordering me to do so and if (2) I have an effectively protected legal right to that effect, that is, if all others are unfree to hinder me from doing so. We must distinguish between freedom in the behavioral sense and in the legal sense. All drivers have the legal duty not to speed, but they are socially unfree to speed only to the extent that speeders are actually fined. Thus, driver A, who sped on a particular occasion without being detected, was socially free to do so on that occasion, even though he had no legal right to that effect. If 40 per cent of all speeders in France escape conviction, French drivers are to that extent socially free to speed.

Other descriptive meanings

Freedom of choice. Whereas social freedom refers to two actors and their respective actions, freedom of choice signifies a relationship between one actor and a series of alternative potential actions. "A has freedom of choice as to x or z" means that it is possible for A to do either x or z, or that both x and z are open as well as avoidable to A, or that A will bring about x provided he chooses to do x. Conversely, if it is either impossible or necessary for A to do x, A has no freedom of choice as to x. It is in this sense that Hume defines liberty as "the power of acting or not acting, according to the determinations of the will." Freedom of choice is neither a necessary nor a sufficient condition for social freedom. If A cannot do x, he is unfree to do so only if his inability has been caused by some other actor B. Otherwise, A remains free to do x, even though he has no freedom of choice as to x. Most men are incapable, yet at liberty, to become millionaires or to run for high political office. Unemployment during a recession diminishes freedom of choice, not social freedom, unless the recession itself can be causally linked, for example, to specific governmental policies. The high cost of television time renders this medium inaccessible to most; this restricts freedom of choice for prospective broadcasters, not their freedom of speech. Everybody is socially "free to sleep under bridges" or at home, including the homeless, who have no choice in the matter. (In all such cases, the illusion of paradox arises because the actor is likely to value the opportunity he lacks, not the freedom he has.) Conversely, we do have freedom of choice with respect to most punishable actions; we can be made unfree to do them precisely because they are open to us.

Free will. Indeterminists often hold that human beings have "free will," that is, that their actual choices and resulting behavior are not causally determined but constitute chance events. Determinists can with perfect consistency deny this doctrine and yet affirm that men often have freedom of choice. They argue that the fact that A *has* the choice of doing either x or z does not preclude the possibility of explaining and predicting A's *actual* choice by virtue of causal (for example, psychological or sociological) laws.

Free actions. Of an action itself, it can be said that it was either a free or an unfree one, as when we say: "this murder was a free action," or "he paid his taxes, but not freely." Involuntary behavior is unfree, and so are nondeliberate actions, for example, those that the actor has been conditioned to perform. Voluntary actions are free, unless they are motivated by fear of punishment. A's handing over his money to B, who points a gun at him, is an unfree action (yet it is a voluntary action, determined partly by B's threat and partly by A's desire to save his life). But if A refuses to comply with B, then A acts freely. One may do freely what one is unfree to do. Again, if B persuades A to do *x* without threats of punishment, A's action *x* is a free one. Sometimes, however, "free" is used more broadly to refer to actions that are autonomous, that is, determined exclusively by the actor's own decisions and not by the influence of others, as when John Stuart Mill said: "The only freedom which deserves the name is that of pursuing our own good *in our own way*."

Free persons.   "Free" often refers to a characteristic, not of actions but of persons. A person may be said to be free to the extent that he has the disposition to act freely, or to act autonomously, or to develop his capacities to the fullest. Marx, for example, prophesied a society "in which the free development of each is the condition for the free development of all." "Freedom" becomes a synonym for "self-realization." Laski uses the term almost exclusively in this sense in his article on liberty (1933).

Feeling free.   Liberty is often said to consist in doing what one desires. It would be more accurate to say that an actor *feels* free to the extent that he does what he wants. Freedom as a state of mind must be distinguished from freedom as a state of affairs. Among the things I want to avoid doing, there may be some I am free to do and others I am unfree to do. Some persons derive a feeling of freedom from the fact that they are left free to act out any one of several alternatives. Others feel free when they "escape from freedom" into submission to some authority that conditions them to want to do its will. Dostoevski's grand inquisitor plays on these two meanings of the word: "Today, people are more persuaded than ever that they have perfect freedom; yet they have brought their freedom to us and laid it humbly at our feet."

A free society.   Is it legitimate to use "free" as a characteristic of a group, such as when democracy is held to be a free society? There is no such thing as freedom in general; every organized society consists of an intricate network of specific relations of both freedom and unfreedom. Citizens in a democracy have the political freedom to partici-

pate in the governmental process through "free" elections. Voters, parties, and pressure groups are thereby empowered to *limit* the freedom of their elected officials. Democracy also requires that "civil liberties" be protected by legal rights and duties, and these duties again imply limitations of freedom. In a perfect dictatorship, the ruler has unlimited freedom with respect to his subjects, whereas they are totally unfree with respect to him. In a democracy, both liberties and restrictions of freedom are distributed more evenly, for example, among the various branches of government, between government and governed, majority and minority. *Equal* freedom, not *more* freedom, is the essence of democracy. (Strictly speaking, it is not meaningful to say that there is "more" freedom in one *society* than in another; but it is possible to define degrees of social freedom in the sense that one *actor* has greater freedom in a certain respect than another.) A society in which liberties are evenly distributed may be called a free society. However, here we come close to using "freedom" in a valuational sense: a society is free in which those and only those freedom relations hold that are *desirable*.

Valuational meanings

Because of the laudatory connotation of the word "freedom," writers have been inclined to define it to cover those and only those relationships of *both* social freedom and unfreedom that they happen to value and wish to commend to others. Such persuasive definitions of freedom are useful not as tools of the empirical social sciences but as rhetorical devices; they enable the writer to express his normative views in assertive form. For example, by stating that "to obey the laws laid down by society is to be free," Rousseau in effect exhorts citizens to obey such laws; he is not trying to explicate the meaning of freedom. Persuasive definitions of freedom have been used to propound almost every political ideology, as is illustrated by the following examples.

Freedom as protection of basic rights.   Classical liberalism from Locke to Spencer and his followers advocated that government ought to restrict a person's freedom when and only when necessary to protect another person's basic rights (often held to correspond to natural rights). Accordingly, *"no society in which these liberties are not, on the whole, respected, is free"* (Mill). Conversely, a society *is free*, provided it is based on these laissez-faire principles. And a person who enjoys these legal rights and is subject to the corresponding legal duties is free, however unfree he may be in other regards and with respect to actors other than the government, for example, because of economic exploitation or social pressure. Thus, the United States Supreme Court once held that minimum-wage and maximum-hour laws violate the constitutional principle of liberty, because such regulations are not necessary to the protection of basic rights but constitute "arbitrary" limitations of "freedom of contract" of both employer and employee.

Freedom as satisfaction of basic needs. Neo-liberals point out that the right to acquire the necessities of life is of little value to those who lack the opportunity to acquire them, that government ought to make them available to all, and that this may require governmental restriction of individual freedom through regulations concerning public health, education, and welfare. Social welfare, not social freedom, is their ultimate goal; but they still use the word "freedom" to designate this end. "Personal freedom means, in fact, the power of the individual to buy sufficient food, shelter, and clothing" (Sidney and Beatrice Webb). And so, "the distinction between welfare and liberty breaks down altogether" (Ralph Barton Perry). Conversely, those who are unable to bring about what society ought to enable them to achieve, but who are free with respect to the government to make the attempt, are said to lack "true freedom." "Freedom from want," unlike freedom of speech, does not refer directly to social freedom, but to absence of want and presence of a satisfactory living standard for all. It is only in an indirect sense that "necessitous men are not free men" (Franklin D. Roosevelt). They have little freedom of choice and are socially unfree with respect to the economically powerful. "Freedom" is applied not only to the welfare goal itself but also to whatever restrictions of social freedom are deemed necessary to achieve it. The Supreme Court now interprets liberty to be compatible with minimum-wage laws and other "reasonable regulations and prohibitions imposed in the interest of the community." "Freedom" includes desirable social unfreedom and excludes undesirable social freedom.

Freedom as government by consent. This persuasive definition of freedom is used to express the norm that government ought to be based on consent of the governed, and this usually means representative government and majority rule. For example, "the liberty of man in society is to be under no other legislative power but that established by consent in the commonwealth" (Locke). Under such a system, men are free because their freedom is limited only by measures in the enact-ment of which they were free to participate. With a slight shift in emphasis, "freedom" stands no longer for the government's duty to be responsive to the will of the citizens but for the citizen's duty to obey governmental enactments reflecting the will of the majority or the "general will." According to Rousseau, the citizen is free whether he fulfills this obligation freely or whether he has been "compelled to be free." And so "freedom" comes to refer no longer to having the choice of acting in one way or another, but to acting in no other way than that prescribed by authority.

Freedom as moral constraint. The definitions of freedom taken up so far, including even the persuasive ones, are made up entirely of descriptive terms. However, definitions of freedom often include ethical words, such as "right," "ought," or "virtue." In such cases, not only the term to be defined (freedom) but also the defining expression has valuational meaning. For example, "Liberty can consist only in the power of doing what we ought to will" (Montesquieu). Similarly, a person is often said to be free, not if he acts freely or develops his capacities, but if he realizes his "best" or "essential" self. For example, "Liberty may be defined as the affirmation by an individual or group of his or its own essence" (Laski 1933, p. 444). Some have held that a person is most likely to realize his essence if he is left free to choose for himself.

According to another tradition, which extends from Plato via the Stoics and Christian thought to Neo-Hegelianism, man reaches the highest form of self-realization by submitting to some moral norm imposed by his own "higher self," which is usually identified with faith, reason, or moral conscience. "I call him free who is led solely by reason" (Spinoza). "Obedience to a law which we prescribe to ourselves is liberty" (Rousseau). Freedom no longer signifies the absence of unwelcome, but the presence of welcome restraints. "For freedom is not acquired by satisfying yourself with what you desire, but by destroying your desire" (Epictetus). In short, freedom is unfreedom to do wrong, whereas freedom to deviate from the prescribed path is license. "If unbridled license of speech and of writing be granted to all, nothing will remain sacred and inviolate. . . . Thus, license will gain what liberty loses" (*Encyclical libertas* 1888).

If "freedom" becomes a label for anybody's moral or political ends, then everybody's value commitment to freedom will be vacuous. All will agree that liberty is the supreme good, but they will agree on nothing else. Meaningful disagreement about the *value* of freedom presupposes agreement about the *meaning* of freedom in nonvaluational terms. The concept of social freedom provides an adequate basis for a fruitful discussion of the normative, as well as the empirical, aspects of liberty. In this discourse, the divergent views about which social freedoms ought to be extended or limited will depend on the value one assigns to such other social goals as equality, justice, or welfare, which may compete with the goal of freedom.

FELIX E. OPPENHEIM

[*See also* DEMOCRACY; EQUALITY; JUSTICE; NORMS; POLITICAL THEORY; VALUES.]

BIBLIOGRAPHY

ADLER, MORTIMER J. 1958–1961 *The Idea of Freedom.* 2 vols. Garden City, N.Y.: Doubleday. → Contains significant quotations about freedom selected from all major writings from the Greeks to the present. Bibliography covers anthologies and periodical literature.

AMERICAN SOCIETY FOR POLITICAL AND LEGAL PHILOSOPHY 1962 *Liberty.* Edited by Carl J. Friedrich. Nomos 4. New York: Atherton. → A collection of essays.

ARON, RAYMOND 1965 *Essai sur les libertés.* Paris: Calmann-Lévy.

BAY, CHRISTIAN 1958 *The Structure of Freedom.* Stanford (Calif.) Univ. Press.

BERLIN, ISAIAH 1958 *Two Concepts of Liberty.* Oxford Univ. Press.

CRANSTON, MAURICE (1953) 1955 *Freedom: A New Analysis.* 2d ed. London: Longmans.

HAYEK, FRIEDRICH A. VON 1960 *The Constitution of Liberty.* Univ. of Chicago Press; London: Routledge.

LASKI, HAROLD 1933 Liberty. Volume 9, pages 442–446 in *Encyclopaedia of the Social Sciences.* New York: Macmillan.

MULLER, HERBERT J. 1960 *Issues of Freedom: Paradoxes and Promises.* New York: Harper.

OPPENHEIM, FELIX E. 1961 *Dimensions of Freedom: An Analysis.* New York: St. Martins; London: Macmillan.

FRENKEL-BRUNSWIK, ELSE

Else Frenkel-Brunswik (1908–1958) was born of Polish-Jewish parents in the town of Lemberg, then part of the Austro–Hungarian Empire, and received her doctorate in psychology in 1930 at the University of Vienna. She continued at the university, as lecturer and research associate, until shortly after the Nazi *Anschluss* in 1938. With her husband, Egon Brunswik, she then moved to the University of California at Berkeley, where she remained until her death.

The professional life of Else Frenkel-Brunswik covers a period that was not one of great new theories or startling discoveries in psychology. It was, rather, a time of expansion and ferment. The boundaries of academic psychology were being extended from the study of segmental psychological processes in the experimental laboratory to a more profound conception of human personality in its development over time and its engagement with a complex sociocultural environment. Psychologists sought to grasp the implications of the revolutionary changes stemming from psychoanalysis, from the physical sciences, and from cataclysmic societal developments. To an unusual degree, Frenkel-Brunswik's career reflected these major intellectual and social developments and at the same time influenced the course of psychology.

Her doctoral thesis (1931) under Karl Bühler attempted a *rapprochement* between traditional associationism and the newer concepts of gestalt psychology. Subsequently, on the staff of the Psychological Institute, headed by Charlotte Bühler, she collaborated in a series of developmental studies (see, for example, Frenkel & Weisskopf 1937) derived from the biographies of 400 persons selected from various historical periods and walks of life. This research, although theoretically limited, exemplifies enduring features of her approach: the developmental view of personality; the combined use of phenomenological and behavioral data and of multiple assessment methods; and the functional view of behavioral striving in terms of adaptation and goal achievement.

The situation in Vienna provided three additional formative influences. First, there was the philosophical influence of the logical positivism of the "Vienna circle," which included such men as Neurath, Schlick, and Carnap. This produced an enduring concern with problems of theory development, conceptual and operational definition of terms, and the role of inference in personality measurement.

Second, there was the influence of psychoanalysis, which was of fundamental importance in shaping her future work. She had a personal analysis in Vienna. Although she did not become a practicing psychoanalyst, a clinical mode of thought continually informed her research, her teaching, and her experience of life. One of her initial studies drawing upon psychoanalytic theory was "Mechanisms of Self-deception" (1939).

A third influence derived from the sociopolitical situation during the 1930s. Frenkel-Brunswik was deeply affected by the tragic events of that period. However, it was only after she came to the United States that these concerns were explicitly reflected in her intellectual work.

Although the emigration from Austria in 1938 was in many respects painful, her situation in the United States offered tremendous opportunity and stimulation. She flourished there. Her first position in California was at the Institute of Child Welfare, and she maintained this association for the rest of her career.

Personality theory

One of her first publications in the United States was the paper "Psychoanalysis and Personality Research" (1940), which was read at the now-historic Symposium on Psychoanalysis by Analyzed Experimental Psychologists. In this paper, she wrote, not as an "analyzed experimental psychologist," but as a personality theorist in the broadest sense. She recognized that there was complementarity as well as conflict between the psychoanalytic, phenomenological, and behaviorist schools. Rather than starting with one of these theoretical positions, she sought to identify, in terms meaningful to all of them, the basic theoretical domains in the study of personality. She posited four such domains: the *central* and the *peripheral* levels of personality (following and enlarging upon Henry A. Murray's formulation); and the *proximal* and *distal* effects of behavior upon the environment (a perspective on behavior utilizing the distinction made by gestalt theorists and by Egon Brunswik). A truly comprehensive personality theory, she maintained, must encompass relationships between all four domains rather than being encapsulated within one or two. She argued also for the combined use of clinical and experimental modes of investigation. Although many of her then-radical proposals are now widely accepted, this paper stands as a fresh statement of the theoretical and methodological tasks of dynamic personality research.

In her monograph "Motivation and Behavior" (1942) Frenkel-Brunswik applied and developed further the theoretical position outlined in her 1940 article. This empirical study of adolescents made use of concepts and measures in several theoretical domains. There were self-reports obtained through questionnaires, observers' ratings of behavior in specific social situations, projective test material, and clinical ratings of underlying (central) motives based upon inferences from a wide variety of observational and test data. The concept of *alternative manifestation* was developed and operationalized, to help account for the relationships of underlying motives to overt behavior and conscious self-report, and theoretically sophisticated use was made of partial and multiple correlation techniques. In this study Frenkel-Brunswik provided one of the earliest models of systematic personality research. She dealt with various levels of personality, seen as dynamically interdependent, and she contributed to the methodology of inferential clinical ratings, relating

them to more-directly behavioral measures and giving them a legitimate place within the academic psychological investigation of personality. Her work on the clinical ratings was innovative in at least two respects. On the one hand, she developed techniques to increase the explicitness and reliability of clinical inferences. On the other, she anticipated the later research on social perception in her study of the influence of the rater's personality on his judgments of subjects' motivation and behavior.

Her sociopsychological interests took form in the early 1940s. In 1942 she had a Social Science Research Council fellowship for work in sociology and anthropology at the University of Chicago, Harvard, the Langley Porter Institute, and with Kroeber and others at the University of California. In 1943 she joined Sanford and Levinson in a study of personality and prejudice, and Adorno became their collaborator soon after. The study expanded over the next few years and was published under the title *The Authoritarian Personality* (1950). During this period she was also engaged in a related study of prejudice in children and families (see Frenkel-Brunswik & Havel 1953).

"The Authoritarian Personality"

Frenkel-Brunswik made certain distinctive and specifiable contributions to *The Authoritarian Personality;* these will be noted below. She also contributed in significant but less identifiable ways to the character of that work as a whole. The basic theoretical conception and methodology of the research were an emergent product of intimately collaborative effort by the four coauthors and reflected their common intellectual concerns. Without attempting to allocate specific credit to individual authors, I shall simply indicate the major features of this comprehensive project. It will be evident that they express Frenkel-Brunswik's earlier interests and are of importance in her subsequent work.

Theoretically, *The Authoritarian Personality* represented a convergence of previously disparate viewpoints: attitude theory in academic psychology; the sociological analysis of ideology; and psychoanalysis and related personality theories, notably that of Murray. Consciously held attitudes, values, and ideologies were regarded as aspects of personality. They were related to contemporaneous character traits, cognitive–emotional styles, ego defenses, and less conscious wishes and fantasies. The formation of ideology was seen in developmental perspective and was related to more general processes of ego and superego development. In retrospect, the approach may be seen as a form of psychoanalytic ego theory; that is to say, it drew upon traditional psychoanalytic concepts and at the same time emphasized and conceptualized ego processes that link the person more directly with his social environment. This approach, now widely held in various forms, was at the time a major innovation in social psychology.

Methodologically, the research on authoritarianism involved the conjoint use of previously disparate techniques: scales and other questionnaire devices, projective techniques, and semistructured clinical interviews. Intensive case studies were used to develop hypotheses and to guide the explicit formulation of variables that were then measured by means of questionnaires administered to groups. The continuing interplay of clinical and statistical analysis was an essential feature of the methodology. The Authoritarianism (F) Scale, perhaps the most widely used and most poorly understood product of the study, was one result of this interplay.

The most clearly identifiable contributions by Frenkel-Brunswik are in the chapters bearing her name. These deal with the construction and analysis of the intensive, semistructured interviews. The interviews were standardized in the sense that they covered a predefined set of topical areas and theoretical issues, and they required considerable advance training of the interviewers. At the same time they had a clinically "open" quality in that the interviewer tried to follow the threads of the subject's thought and feeling; within the loose structure of the topical areas and issues, the content and sequence of the interview were largely determined by the interviewee. This was, in short, a qualitatively distinct hybrid—a cross between the survey and the therapy interview—and an important contribution to personality–social research.

In the analysis of the interviews Frenkel-Brunswik developed an extensive series of categories that distinguish "high-authoritarian" from "low-authoritarian" subjects. The rating of each category required clinical inference on the part of the rater. To help control for the subjectivity in this process, the categories were defined in some detail and were scored by two independent raters, so that reliability could be determined. Categories were developed in three broad domains: parents and childhood; sex, people, and self; and dynamic and cognitive personality organization. The interpretive integration of findings in these domains led to the formulation of a smaller number of major themes and patterns.

One of the concepts developed here (and given greater prominence in her subsequent research) is *intolerance of ambiguity* (1949). This concept has a complex, many-faceted character. Its referents include a tendency toward oversimplification in per-

ceptions and conceptions of the external world; a deep uneasiness about ambiguity and lack of order in personal relationships and social structures; a proclivity to engage in moralistic, all-good or all-bad value judgments, without recognition of moral ambiguities; an inability to acknowledge ambivalence (emotional ambiguity) in one's experience of parents and significant others. This concept thus has motivational, emotional, cognitive, and moral aspects, and it refers to the person's experience of both self and external world. Although subsequent evidence has not fully supported Frenkel-Brunswik's initial formulation of intolerance of ambiguity as a relatively unified, pervasive *trait*, it does indicate the usefulness of this kind of multiple-component concept as a *genotype* underlying diverse overt behaviors.

Later career

The period from 1950 to 1955 was a lively and productive one for Frenkel-Brunswik. She visited Europe for the Rockefeller Foundation and reported on the condition of European psychology. She wrote a number of papers that reflected the growing breadth of her theoretical interests: on the interaction of sociological and psychological variables (1952; 1954b); on perceptual–cognitive functioning as an aspect of personality (1951); on psychoanalysis and the unity of science (1954a; 1957). In 1953 she began a study of aging; this work was completed and published by colleagues (Reichard et al. 1962) after her death. In 1954/1955, she was a fellow at the Center for Advanced Study in the Behavioral Sciences.

This period of great vitality was cut short by the tragic death of her husband, Egon, in 1955—a blow from which she never fully recovered. Her final dream had been a major treatise on values, a book that would bring together her lifelong interests in psychoanalysis, sociology, and philosophy. This hope was ended by her own premature death in 1958.

Frenkel-Brunswik's intellectual commitment, warmth, and intensity were reflected in her relationships with students. Although she did not do much formal teaching, she developed unusually close relationships through seminars, research collaboration, and informal contacts. She had a charismatic femininity. The number of present-day psychologists who feel a special gratitude to her and who regard her as a major formative influence in their personal and professional development is large indeed.

The contributions of Frenkel-Brunswik can perhaps best be grasped within the context of the radical new developments in American psychology during the period of roughly 1935 to 1950. She was a founding figure in the establishment of the new fields of personality psychology and social and clinical psychology. She forged important links between psychoanalysis and academic personality research. She contributed to the development of a conception of man that takes account of both reason and passion, of the most primitive and the most mature, of the autistic and the socially embedded aspects of his nature. Finally, she was multidisciplinary in the best sense of the word. She was ready to engage in disciplined search for the relevant, no matter how far it led from her disciplinary origins.

DANIEL J. LEVINSON

[*For the historical context of Frenkel-Brunswik's work, see* GESTALT THEORY; PERSONALITY: CONTEMPORARY VIEWPOINTS, *article on* COMPONENTS OF AN EVOLVING PERSONOLOGICAL SYSTEM; *and the biographies of* BRUNSWIK; BÜHLER; SCHLICK. *For discussion of the subsequent development of Frenkel-Brunswik's ideas, see* ATTITUDES; PERSONALITY, POLITICAL, *article on* CONSERVATISM AND RADICALISM.]

BIBLIOGRAPHY

The author was given access to an unpublished manuscript dealing with the life and work of Else Frenkel-Brunswik by Joan Havel Grant and Nanette Heiman. The manuscript is scheduled for publication in Psychological Issues *in 1968. It should be noted that Frenkel-Brunswik's works are sometimes listed in bibliographies and in library catalogues under Brunswik.*

WORKS BY FRENKEL-BRUNSWIK

1931   Atomismus und Mechanismus in der Assoziationspsychologie. *Zeitschrift für Psychologie* 123:193–258.

1937   FRENKEL, ELSE; and WEISSKOPF, EDITH Wunsch und Pflicht im Aufbau des menschlichen Lebens. Volume 1 in *Psychologische Forschungen über den Lebenslauf.* Edited by Charlotte Bühler and Else Frenkel. Vienna: Gerold.

1939   Mechanisms of Self-deception. *Journal of Social Psychology* 10:409–420.

1940   Psychoanalysis and Personality Research. *Journal of Abnormal and Social Psychology* 35:176–197.

1942   Motivation and Behavior. *Genetic Psychology Monographs* 26:121–265.

1949   Intolerance of Ambiguity as an Emotional and Perceptual Personality Variable. *Journal of Personality* 18:108–143.

1950   *The Authoritarian Personality*, by T. W. Adorno et al. New York: Harper. → Else Frenkel-Brunswik was a coauthor.

1951   Personality Theory and Perception. Pages 356–419 in Robert R. Blake and Glenn V. Ramsey (editors), *Perception: An Approach to Personality.* New York: Ronald.

1952   Interaction of Psychological and Sociological Factors in Political Behavior. *American Political Science Review* 46:44–65.

1953   FRENKEL-BRUNSWIK, ELSE; and HAVEL, JOAN Prejudice in the Interviews of Children. Part 1: Attitudes Toward Minority Groups. *Journal of Genetic Psychology* 82:91–136.

1954a   Psychoanalysis and the Unity of Science. *Dædalus* 80:271–350.

1954b   Environmental Controls and the Impoverishment of Thought. Pages 171–202 in American Academy of Arts and Sciences, *Totalitarianism: Proceedings of a Conference.* Cambridge, Mass.: Harvard Univ. Press.

1957   Perspectives in Psychoanalytic Theory. Pages 150–182 in Henry P. David and Helmut von Bracken (editors), *Perspectives in Personality.* New York: Basic Books.

SUPPLEMENTARY BIBLIOGRAPHY

REICHARD, SUZANNE K.; PETERSON, PAUL C.; and LIVSON, FLORINE 1962 *Aging and Personality: A Study of Eighty-seven Older Men.* New York: Wiley. → A report on a study directed by Else Frenkel-Brunswik.

FREQUENCY CURVES

See DISTRIBUTIONS, STATISTICAL; STATISTICS, DESCRIPTIVE.